CONTENTS

RECORDINGS

PENGUIN BOOKS

The Penguin Jazz Guide

Richard Cook was born in Kew and spent virtually all of his life in or around that part of London. An early passion for record collecting helped push him towards jazz and both interests endured. He got paid for a piece of music writing in 1979 and was so impressed that he kept going. He edited the *Wire* for seven years and was founding editor of *Jazz Review*; he also wrote for the *Sunday Times*, the *New Statesman* and *Punch* at different times and, in addition to the first eight editions of this book, was the author of a 'biography' of the Blue Note label, a study of Miles Davis and *Richard Cook's Jazz Encyclopedia*, published by Penguin. He also presented a well-liked and thoroughly idiosyncratic jazz programme on London local radio, and made some documentaries for BBC Radio 3; didn't like cameras much, though. Horse racing and malt whisky were his other passions and the only subjects on which he and his co-author ever disagreed. Sadly, Richard Cook succumbed to cancer in the late summer of 2007. He is greatly missed.

Brian Morton was born in Paisley. He was first published at the age of sixteen and has never stopped, though he has also worked as an academic, a newspaper journalist and a broadcaster on BBC Radios 3 and 4, and on BBC Radio Scotland, where he presented a daily arts programme for eight years. Jazz and improvisation gradually won out over other musical enthusiasms. Writing gradually won out over playing, and his improvising ensembles The Golden Horde, Phlogiston and People Without Government are now a distant memory. He lives with his wife, the landscape photographer Sarah MacDonald, and son John on a small farm in the west of Scotland. His older girls Fiona and Alice are there much of the time, too. Unlike Mr Cook, who was a devoted Islay malted man, Morton favours the great Speysides. With a good few drops of gypsy blood in his veins, he reckons he was a better judge of horseflesh, too. He misses the arguments.

Brian Morton and **Richard Cook**

The Penguin Jazz Guide

THE HISTORY OF THE MUSIC IN THE 1,001 BEST ALBUMS

PENGUIN BOOKS

PENGUIN BOOKS

Published by the Penguin Group
Penguin Books Ltd, 80 Strand, London WC2R oRL, England
Penguin Group (USA) Inc., 375 Hudson Street, New York, New York 10014, USA
Penguin Group (Canada), 90 Eglinton Avenue East, Suite 700, Toronto, Ontario,
Canada M4P 2Y3 (a division of Pearson Penguin Canada Inc.)
Penguin Ireland, 25 St Stephen's Green, Dublin 2, Ireland
(a division of Penguin Books Ltd)
Penguin Group (Australia), 250 Camberwell Road, Camberwell,
Victoria 3124, Australia (a division of Pearson Australia Group Pty Ltd)
Penguin Books India Pvt Ltd, 11 Community Centre, Panchsheel Park,
New Delhi – 110 017, India
Penguin Group (NZ), 67 Apollo Drive, Rosedale, North Shore 0632, New Zealand
(a division of Pearson New Zealand Ltd)
Penguin Books (South Africa) (Pty) Ltd, 24 Sturdee Avenue,
Rosebank, Johannesburg 2196, South Africa
Penguin Books Ltd, Registered Offices: 80 Strand, London WC2R oRL, England

www.penguin.com

First published 2010
004

Set in Fresco and FrescoSans
Typeset by dataformat.com
Printed in Great Britain by Clays Ltd, St Ives plc

ISBN 978-0-141-04831-4

www.greenpenguin.co.uk

THE '40s 83

THE '50s: 1951–1955   123

THE '50s: 1956-1960   169

THE '60s 266

Part 1: **1961-1965** 267

Part 2: **1966-1970** 332

THE '70s   381

Part 1: 1971-1976   382

Part 2: **1976-1980**   430

THE '80s 462

Part 1: 1981-1985 463

Part 2: **1986–1990**   498

THE '90s 547

Part 1: **1991-1995** 548

Part 2: **1996–2000**   597

THE RECENT SCENE: 2001–2010 659

INTRODUCTION

For a major art form, jazz is still disarmingly young. It is possible, even now, to speak to a man who once listened to men who had been present at the birth of the music. This means that nothing in jazz is impossibly remote, and yet it too has its event horizon, for we can know nothing – or nothing beyond hearsay – of jazz before it was taken down and preserved on record. To that degree, the history of jazz *is* the history of jazz recording.

Not until Stravinsky was a classical career significantly shaped by recordings, but jazz came along at a remarkable moment of cultural and technological change. The means to preserve and reproduce it were there from the beginning, and this played some part in the music's unprecedentedly rapid spread. If we take the Original Dixieland Jazz Band's pioneering jazz recordings of January and February 1917 as the moment the music's history begins, then by the end of the decade the music was not just known by a popular craze across Europe, and by the middle of the next decade it thrived on every continent.

Jazz was the first cultural phenomenon to justify the term 'viral'. Three different contagions stalked the world in 1918 and 1919. The most obvious was so-called 'Spanish 'flu', which actually had its origins in Midwest army camps and was carried to Europe when American soldiers began to be sent in support of the war against the Kaiser. By 1920, the pandemic had claimed what is now estimated to be between 50 million and 100 million lives across the globe. There might seem little connection between the H1N1 virus and a new form of popular music, but the parallels are striking. Jazz spread along the very same vectors, brought out of America to Europe, Asia, South America and Australasia by representatives of a country which had suddenly turned its back on its isolationism and was anxious to bring the American message to the world. As if to confirm the connection, whenever the jazz bug bit, moral guardians were quick to characterize the music itself as febrile and convulsive, and instinctively likened it to an infection: jazz was 'hot'; those who danced to it appeared to be in the grip of dangerous rigours; it exhausted the body and depleted the spirit. And it was unstoppable, carrying off the young and the fit, much as the 'flu did.

There was a third contagion. In 1917, the Tsarist government of Russia was overthrown by the Bolsheviks, a party whose avowed aim was the world spread of Communism. Almost as soon as it was born – and with scant regard to the ironies of presenting a music born in the aftermath of slavery as a banner for American freedoms – jazz was being presented as the music of individuality and self-reliance, a freethinking rhythm to set against the fixed march of Marxism. Needless to say, as Frederick Starr and others have shown, Russians were just as susceptible to jazz as everyone else.

It would be convenient to collapse the history of the two world wars of the 20th century and suggest that jazz was carried across the world by the sudden availability of jazz records. In fact, the main vectors remained for the moment human. The Original Dixieland Jazz Band (who lost one member to the 'flu) were in England a year after the war. James Reese Europe's orchestra toured the following year. It would be some time before jazz records became the main vehicle, and only after the original association of jazz and social dance was severed.

It is another of the ironies of the music that at the time and in the place where jazz was at its most creative and fresh, jazz recording was most scant. There are almost no jazz records from New Orleans in the 1920s, though jazz was certainly born there. To complicate matters, it is clear that some musicians at least were suspicious of the music – Freddie Keppard feared that his ideas would be stolen – or misunderstood what was required of them and changed styles when they entered a recording studio, playing music that was far more formal than any they would have played at a dance or rent party. A music that famously flourished in the whorehouses and shebeens of Storyville was curiously eager to clean up its own act when the world listened.

Quality and quantity always exist in a series of curious inverse relationships. When the very best and newest jazz was being made, there was no one taking it down. Arguably – though we argue against it – when the music reached the end of its creative evolution, jazz recording became unstoppable, making use of new technology again to flood a very small market with an impossibly large amount of 'product'.

When we began writing the *Penguin Guide to Jazz* (then quaintly subtitled *on CD, LP and Cassette*) twenty years ago, it was just about possible to claim that our first edition covered every jazz recording that was commercially available at time of writing. Two decades later, with LP and cassette consigned to the dustbin of history, that is no longer even remotely conceivable. The advent of CD and, very quickly thereafter, a vast proliferation of artist-owned labels – so much for the doomsday scenario of 1990 that one day soon everything would be run by two or three giant corporations – meant that there were soon many times too many CDs around even for two gluttonous listeners to listen to, let alone listen to often enough to form a proper judgement. What began as a comprehensive survey of available jazz recording has perforce evolved into a more selective account, though one that in its last edition still managed to cover more than 14,000 discs.

However, another issue intrudes, and a paradox. When we first published, a far larger proportion of what was available and reviewed was relatively recent material and much of it at least notionally modernist in style. Large tracts of music from the 1930s and 1940s had slipped out of the picture. By 2000 that picture was changing. By 2010, it has changed utterly. As well as encouraging creative initiative, the CD revolution has led to an enormous return of the repressed. Jazz recording now is unmistakably dominated by the back catalogue. Inevitably, the pressures are economic. Major labels find it easier to mine their own archives for reissues than to pay for new and innovative recordings: the first enjoys a sure market, the latter only an uncertain one. In addition, with copyright set at 50 years from the recording date, more and more recorded jazz enters the public domain each year. By 2000, copyright began to expire on the LP era, and the floodgates opened. In 2010, jazz finds itself in the extraordinary situation of commanding only 3 per cent of the total music market – 'That's wildly optimistic!' one record company executive recently told us – but with an array of commercial product that is wildly disproportionate to that. The rock era is only now slipping out of copyright. Check how many more early Elvis Presley compilations there suddenly seem to be.

It may seem perverse in the face of such an embarrassment of riches to scale down our operations so drastically, but when it becomes impossible to offer comprehensive coverage of jazz recordings, the only sensible recourse is to wipe the slate almost clean and start with a highly selective approach. The 10th edition of the *Penguin Guide to Jazz Recordings* is very much smaller than its predecessors. It makes no attempt to cover every star in the jazz firmament, or to review every work by the stars of greatest magnitude. Instead, it offers a simplified guide to the brightest constellations and, since we have also abandoned for the moment our alphabetical organization, a way of negotiating the history of the music from its earliest moments to the present.

A great deal of those earliest moments are now once again available to us, thanks to digital remastering and to the patient work of labels like Classics (perhaps over-represented in the early pages that follow), Hep, American Music and others. Many of the names of those years are among the great names of the music, familiar to all. The challenge, though, is to balance those unquestioned masters with the musicians who are still making the music today and still carrying forward its power to innovate and refresh. While we have a certain academic sympathy with the 'death of jazz' rhetoric that flourished for a time a decade or so ago, it is now clear that while jazz and improvised music have pushed harmony and rhythm, noise and silence as far as any of these is prepared to go, there is still a great deal of unclaimed land behind those frontiers where the music can still develop. Consequently, we have included a substantial number of very recent recordings in this edition.

It will be protested that it is impossible to judge whether a record made in 2004 or 2007 is 'important', let alone of classic status, because it simply has not been around long enough. We regard such an attitude as bad critical faith and take courage from the poet Robert Frost, who said it was laziness to leave posterity to do the work of judgement. A masterpiece is a masterpiece from the moment it is coined. The passage of time will either confirm that or, eventually and inevitably, turn it into a stepping stone for lesser talents or an Aunt Sally for 'revisionist' critics. Not only do we have confidence in our choices, but we are not inclined to think that jazz – however defined – came to an end in 1955 (death of Charlie Parker) or 1969 (*Bitches Brew*) or any other arbitrary date. This music is, as Richard Cook passionately argued, a long game. If it were not still thriving in 2010, that would cast negative light on what was made in 1930 and 1960 and give comfort to those who have always argued that jazz is 'merely' a fad.

Newcomers to the book will not by definition be troubled by changes in format. Our account proceeds chronologically from and around 1917, when the first recordings were made, to not quite the present, which always runs away from us. A total of 1001 recordings have been selected, not for any arcane musical or historical reason but because that seems enough to offer a generous spread of periods, styles and personalities, yet is a small enough sample to suggest not a canon or a 'core collection' (such as we proposed in previous editions) but a reasonable survey of the field in all its complexity.

Needless to say, we are not suggesting that only these 1001 recordings are worth bothering about, though that view will confidently be attributed to us (as F. R. Leavis used to say); nor that these are the only recordings by a particular artist that might be listened to. In many cases, it will be clear that a recording has been selected from many similar ones rather than as an outstanding achievement. In the case of very important musicians, or crucially musicians who have evolved over years and decades, more than one recording has been selected. This is perhaps the most perilous aspect of this edition, for we have no wish to become embroiled in a relativist discussion as to whether Duke Ellington is 1.7 times more important than Miles Davis, or Mary Lou Williams only two thirds as important as Thelonious Monk. Some artists live long lives and change endlessly; some celebrate their longevity by staying with a reliable style for decades. Some artists flash very briefly across the sky, with just a single noteworthy work; others pack an astonishing amount of change and enterprise into a tragically short span. Our selection attempts to recognize these differences.

Readers puzzled by what might seem eccentricities of chronology in this edition of the *Guide* should be aware that we favour the old-fashioned insistence that decades end on a zero and begin on a one; hence our late celebration of the millennium. Some of the records selected may seem to fall in the wrong position in the *Guide*, especially in the early part of the book, which deals with contemporary reissues of classic material. By definition everything before the early '50s was originally released as a pair of single 'sides' and was only brought together with other material later. Overlapping compilations – 1937-42, 1938-9, 1935-44 – are difficult to organize in strict date order. We have tried to use common sense and to locate these recordings where they seem to make most sense, usually when an artist's most compelling work was being done, or otherwise to illustrate a cusp in the progress of recorded jazz. Sometimes, though, the positioning is just plain quirky.

For those who have encountered previous editions of our *Guide*, the most obvious and visible difference will be the abandonment of the 'star system' for rating CDs. Nothing caused us more agony and irritation in the past, as we finessed the difference between a *** Louis Armstrong record and a ***(*) CD by a rising star of today. Suffice it to say that while many of the records included here were accorded high marks in previous editions, and some 'core collection' status or the ultimate accolade of a crown, some have been upgraded and others (quite a few) have not been previously covered or not for some time. It was striking how often the need to select one record by an artist repositioned judgement and priorities, and how often we simply *changed our minds*, as we always have.

The editorial 'we' is not *pro forma*. Though Richard Cook passed away in 2007, his hand is still strongly evident here and very many of the reviews included are initially from his hand, even if they have been repositioned and in some cases revised. It has been Brian Morton's intention to reflect Richard's enthusiasms and misgivings as fully and as honestly as his own. The 10th edition remains a work of joint authorship.

Its present format was decided without consultation with Richard, but as a distinguished encyclopaedist of jazz he would have welcomed many new aspects. First and foremost, the abandonment of that invidious grading system. Then, a greater measure of biographical detail, which now includes full dates and place of birth and death. Our motivation here has been to rid the reference record of many lazily reproduced errors. We found that one distinguished contemporary had been consistently presented as a full decade younger than his actual age. We encountered many other inaccuracies and were reminded many times of the fascinating habit among African-American musicians of simply ignoring the year or years they spent in unwilling military service as if those years had never happened. More than one senior birthday celebration (see entry on Mal Waldron) seemed to come too soon for that reason.

Otherwise the main entry for each artist is much as before, with title, most recent release number (though these are subject to change) and full collective personnel for that record with instruments shown in the familiar abbreviations. Each entry aims to offer a brief biographical note and contextual comments as well as a review which might include track-by-track detail or a more general overview, depending on the particular instance. While further records by the same artist are cross-referenced, using the symbol *&*, further referencing has been kept to a minimum; we do not indulge the common practice of suggesting 'if you like this ... you'll like these', which almost invariably fails to deliver.

Richard's passing robs the book not only of a razor-sharp critical mind and a fine writer – and its most poignant aspect is that segment of new recording that has appeared since his death – but also the possibility of an internal dialogue between two authors who shared out the 'database' of new and reissued recordings on the basis of who felt more warmly disposed to an artist or record. Previous editions were not divided between the authors stylistically or chronologically. Those who claimed to know who had written what were almost always – and entertainingly – wrong. To mitigate the lack of a second voice in the 10th edition, we have asked musicians to offer some reminiscence, anecdote or comment (up to, but not including, self-review) or in the cases of artists no longer living or otherwise unresponsive, to comment on their work as well. These are not drawn from published sources but from an archive of interview notes and tapes made by Brian Morton for print or broadcast purposes over a period that spans, alarmingly, 1975 to the present, with a peak in the 1980s and 1990s. These comments, which are presented at the head of each review, are intended to offer personal grace notes rather than a privileged view. We have not altered our critical position as a result of any of them, though only a few might be thought to conflict, most charmingly that of saxophonist Odean Pope, who said we had picked his least favourite among his own records!

As before, we regard 'opinionated' as a description, not a criticism, and defend our choices and our rationales for them with a certain detachment. We by definition do regard these records as the 'best' jazz has to offer, which does not mean that there may not be better ones lurking out there, perhaps in plain sight; nor does it mean that we mightn't change our minds on a small proportion of them tomorrow, and then again the day after. Are they the most 'important'? We have no particular urge to stipulate a canon, but it would be less than honest to say that without Armstrong, Morton, Ellington, Parker *et al.*, you would have only a truncated and impoverished understanding of jazz. Last of all, to sneer at a word that often pops up in these contexts, are they 'essential'? Nobody died from not listening to jazz and in a world of urgent imperatives, it doesn't seem the most vital, and yet our lives would be substantially less worth living without the music contained herein. So, 'necessary', maybe not, but 'essential', in some unwilling way, yes. Our aim here, more than ever, has been to steer listeners towards a remarkable body of music, still small in comparison to the vast sweep of 'classical' music, quiet in comparison to the hectic pump-priming that is part of pop culture, still subject to all manner of prejudice and 'I don't like it because I've never tried it' resistance. If you find that your opinion of a record bought on recommendation here fails to square with ours, don't sue and don't give up on us. We include these records because we love and admire them, not to appear arcanely knowledgeable; so keep experimenting.

This edition comes with a longer than usual list of acknowledgements. Thanks are due first and foremost to the many, many musicians who sent in personal statements for publication. To those who wrote: 'We had a great time, the boys played well', we say thanks, but not quite what we were after. To those who shared a studio moment that otherwise would have been closed to us: you can scarcely know how much these have humanized and illuminated the music and the book.

As ever, we owe a great debt to those in the business who work without much reward to get the word out on jazz. They are too many to name individually, but for assistance above and beyond the call, big thanks to Ann Braithwaite of Braithwaite & Katz, to Scott Menhinick of Improvised Communications, Kerstan Mackness of Riot Squad, Mark Gilbert of *Jazz Journal* (incorporating *Jazz Review*, founder Richard Cook) and to all the management companies, distributors and labels who passed on information, sent out new CDs and 'maybe you missed this one' copies of previously overlooked records. We were and are grateful to and for them all.

Very special thanks to Richard's widow Lee Ellen Newman for graciously allowing this edition to proceed, like the last, in Richard's absence. It must be bittersweet for her to see it published over Richard's name and we hope that pride in the continuation of his work outweighs any misgivings about the content.

More personally, this edition would not have been possible without the patience, tolerance and love of Sarah Morton, who is married to the job but can find no mention of jazz on the marriage licence, and the cheerful good nature of Fiona, Alice and John Morton, the youngest of whom found it hard to credit that while he could knock off an Oxford Reading Tree book in a morning it took his father so many months and so much stress to finish his.

This edition is respectfully dedicated to the memory of Sir John Dankworth, who passed away as the final pages were being written, sparking memories of some happy hours spent learning about bebop, and to that of two on-off jazz lovers I was proud to call friends, Michael Dibdin and Norman Mailer.

Brian Morton

ABBREVIATIONS

acc	*accordion*	g	*guitar*
acl	*alto clarinet*	gfs	*goofus*
af	*alto flute*	g-syn	*guitar synthesizer*
ahn	*alto horn*	hca	*harmonica*
arr	*arranger*	hp	*harp*
as	*alto saxophone*	hpd	*harpsichord*
b	*bass*	ky	*keyboards*
bari tb	*baritone trombone*	kz	*kazoo*
bass h	*bass horn*	mand	*mandolin*
bb	*brass bass*	mar	*marimba*
bcl	*bass clarinet*	mca	*melodica*
bf	*bass flute*	mel	*mellophone*
bhn	*baritone horn*	ob	*oboe*
bj	*banjo*	org	*organ*
b mar	*bass marimba*	p	*piano*
bs	*baritone saxophone*	perc	*percussion*
bsn	*bassoon*	picc	*piccolo*
bsx	*bass saxophone*	picc t	*piccolo trumpet*
b-t	*bass trumpet*	pkt-t	*pocket trumpet*
c	*cornet*	sax	*saxophone*
cbcl	*contrabass clarinet*	sno	*sopranino saxophone*
cbsx	*contrabass saxophone*	sou	*sousaphone*
cel	*celeste*	ss	*soprano saxophone*
cl	*clarinet*	syn	*synthesizer*
clav	*clavinet*	t	*trumpet*
clo	*cello*	tb	*trombone*
Cmel	*C-melody saxophone*	tba	*tuba*
cond	*conductor*	thn	*tenor horn*
cor	*cor anglais*	ts	*tenor saxophone*
d	*drums*	uke	*ukulele*
dulc	*dulcimer*	v	*voice*
elec	*electronics*	vib	*vibraphone*
eng hn	*English horn*	vla	*viola*
euph	*euphonium*	vn	*violin*
f	*flute*	vtb	*valve trombone*
flhn	*flugelhorn*	wbd	*washboard*
frhn	*French horn*	xy	*xylophone*

BEGINNINGS

Igor Stravinsky said that the Recording Angel he cared about wasn't CBS but the one with the Big Book. In the same way, many early jazz artists were either indifferent to or plain suspicious of recording. It was a view initially shared by the otherwise expanding recording companies. Music had not been originally thought an important use of the new sound technology, whose chief applications were believed to be in business – particularly stenography – and factual communications. However, the expiry of several important patents in 1914 sent a pulse of innovation through the young industry, and along with the effort to develop new recording and reproduction equipment (which was far from standardized at this era) came a fresh consideration of what other consumer functions recording might serve.

Ragtime was already being recorded, but because ragtime was essentially a piano music and because the piano was the instrument that presented most difficulties for early recording, it was increasingly being created on small ensembles using struck idiophones like the xylophone and accordion instead, or sometimes saxophones. Ragtime could, of course, also be replicated on punched paper rolls for player pianos, but the difficulty in assessing early jazz performance here is that it was not uncommon for additional notes to be added (by creating more holes) in such a way as to suggest a virtuosity the player did not possess.

Musicians were largely justified in fearing that records would only poorly represent their art. Dame Nellie Melba famously distrusted recording on the grounds that playbacks of her peerless voice robbed it of its subtleties. Until 1925, only acoustic recording was possible, which meant that sound vibrations were physically transferred from a large gathering horn to a disc or cylinder by means of a cutting stylus, leaving a so-called 'hill and dale' trace which could be transferred to a hard master copy and thence to a finite number of commercial copies from which sound could be reproduced by a reverse process. The results were highly inconsistent and often unsatisfactory. They inevitably involved compromise in performance, so that any contemporary recording of early jazz can only be regarded as a partial or incomplete representation of the music as played.

However, both the Victor and Columbia companies began to explore the potential of popular music recording in the year before the US entered the First World War. Columbia famously missed the boat, recording the Original Dixieland Jazz Band at the end of January 1917 but failing to release 'Darktown Strutters Ball' and 'Indiana' until they were overtaken by Victor, who recorded the group on 26 February and released the legendary recording number '18255', which sold more than a million copies at 75 cents each.

It was apparently assumed that this success was a singleton, a chance novelty, and with America also embroiled in a European conflict for the next two years and business redirected towards a war economy – and a certain sentimental patriotism in music – jazz recording was sporadic until 1920, when the Okeh label began to do what Victor and Columbia had considered insufficiently commercial and target a predominantly black audience with what were described (with undeserved notoriety) as 'race records'. Perhaps astonishingly, but with a certain market logic, the segregation of musical charts in the US continued for decades and to a degree still persists today. OKeh was essentially a blues label, basing its early success on Mamie Smith's singing of Perry Bradford material, and for a time jazz musicians recorded mainly as accompanists to blues artists.

However, other labels began to show an interest in jazz. At Paramount, music recordings were created largely as a means of illustrating the company's own phonograph equipment. More specialized, but also much cruder, was the Gennett company, which took recording into the American hinterland (Indiana, in this instance, an accident of geography which explains why Bix Beiderbecke, and not one of the New Orleans players, stands tall in the early history of jazz. It wasn't until the middle of the '20s that jazz artists began to be recorded in the music's city of birth.

The irony remains that in order to gain an authentic sense of what early jazz performance sounded like, one also has to listen to the music of the great revival that followed the Second World War. For all their shortcomings, though, the earliest recordings are precious survivals ...

EUBIE BLAKE

Born James Hubert Blake, 7 February 1883, Baltimore, Maryland; died 12 February 1983, New York City
Piano

Memories Of You
Shout! Factory 30146
Blake (p rolls); Steve Williams (p); Gertrude Baum (p rolls); Noble Sissle (v). 1915–1973.

Eubie Blake said (1978): **'I used to sneak out of bed at night, get me some long pants and go play for this woman who ran a house. Ragtime was considered lowdown music, not for the music itself, but reason of the places it was played, bawdy houses and joints. I learned how to play and I've played the same way ever since.'**

If he'd known he was going to live so long, Blake famously said, he'd have taken better care of himself. As it was, he was a part of American music from the very birth of jazz till his death just days after his 100th birthday.

For all his longevity, little remains in print, but his importance is undiminished by the thinness of the documentation. The material here might more strictly be considered *Ur-jazz*, since it comes, some of it, from even before the Original Dixieland Jazz Band made the 'first' jazz records, and does so by virtue of being taken from mechanical piano rolls made by Blake. In a stylistic regress backwards into the obscure origins of the music, these are intriguing artefacts. The relationship between jazz and ragtime isn't securely understood by most listeners and much like the relationship between jazz and blues it is often asserted rather than explained. It's hardly the place to do that here, but listening to Blake down the years makes one realize what an elusive and transient concept 'swing' is. It has often been said that modern ragtime revivals take the music too fast, elevating dexterity over beauty of phrasing and stateliness. Blake was something of a show-off but even his survivals suggest that our understanding of this great music has been too much affected by *The Sting* and the ragtime craze that followed. *Memories Of You* comes up to date with a 1973 performance of 'I'm Just Wild About Harry' but reaches back to 'The Charleston Rag' and this is probably the only Blake disc anyone needs: wonderfully fleet performances and good guest spots. Untarnishable music.

ORIGINAL DIXIELAND JAZZ BAND
Formed 1916
Group

The Original Dixieland Jazz Band 1917-1921
Timeless CBC 1-009
Nick LaRocca (c); Emil Christian, Eddie Edwards (tb); Larry Shields, Artie Seaberg (cl); Bennie Krueger, Don Parker (as); J. Russel Robinson, Billy Jones, Henry Ragas, Henry Vanicelli (p); Tony Sbarbaro (d). 17 February–November 1920.

George Melly said (1998): **'It's strange music. It seems very far away in time, but also absolutely present, as if it had been badly recorded yesterday. It's a disappointment to many jazz fans who hear it for the first time, clunky and muffled, but it contains everything they love about jazz. Rhythm (even if it's a bit sticky), wild melody, weird sounds.'**

A group of young white players from New Orleans. Under Nick LaRocca's leadership they began working in Chicago in 1916, then went to New York and created a sensation at Resenweber's restaurant. Arrived in London in 1919 and played in Hammersmith for nine months. LaRocca's illness blocked further progress but there was a brief comeback a decade later in 1936. LaRocca then retired to become a builder.

The ODJB, for all their anomalous position, remain the place to start in dealing with the history of jazz on record. Whatever effects time has had on this music, its historical importance is undeniable: the first jazz band to make records *may* have been less exciting than, say, the group that King Oliver was leading in the same year, but since no such records by Oliver or any comparable bandleader were made until much later, the ODJB assume a primal role. Harsh, full of tension, rattling with excitement, the best records by the band have weathered the years surprisingly well. Although the novelty effects of 'Barnyard Blues' may seem excessively quaint today, the ensemble patterns which the group created – traceable to any number of ragtime or march strains – have remained amazingly stable in determining the identity of 'traditional' jazz groups ever since. The blazing runs executed by Shields, the crashing, urgent rhythms of Sbarbaro and LaRocca's thin but commanding lead cornet cut through the ancient recordings. Although the band were at the mercy of their material, which subsequently declined into sentimental pap as their early excitement subsided, a high proportion of their legacy is of more than historical interest.

Fifty-four of their recordings between 1917 and 1923 have survived, but there is no comprehensive edition currently available. Their 1917 sessions for Aeolian Vocalion, very rare records, are now available on a Retrieval early-jazz compilation. An ASV CD includes 18 tracks and offers a good cross-section of their work, although a couple of undistinguished later pieces might have been dropped in favour of the absent and excellent 'Mournin' Blues' or 'Skeleton Jangle'. One can hear the band grow in stature as performers as time goes on, but the excitement of their earliest dates remains crucial to the spread of the music.

Retrieval have gathered in the 17 sides which the group made for Columbia in London. These are tough records to find in good shape, and even the usually immaculate Retrieval have had to use one or two less than pristine originals, but sound is mostly fine. One problem with these tracks is that Shields is overpoweringly forward in the acoustic mix, leaving LaRocca almost in the shadows. The earlier performances, though, are up to the ODJB's best, including 'Satanic Blues' (recorded but never issued on Victor) and the first 'Tiger Rag' to be recorded in Britain. The 1920 sessions have poorer material, but there's a bonus in the four sides the group made for OKeh in 1922–3, with a different personnel.

The Timeless CD sweeps the board, since it covers all of their Victor sessions up to the end of 1921, in lively and enjoyable sound, which gives the best idea of the sensation this remarkable group must have caused.

JAMES P. JOHNSON

Born 1 February 1894, New Brunswick, New Jersey; died 17 November 1955, New York City
Piano

Carolina Shout

Biograph BCD 105
Johnson (p rolls). May 1917–June 1925.

Composer Conlon Nancarrow said (1983): **'Johnson is arguably the first completely American composer to emerge in the United States. And you notice I don't say "jazz" composer. His work was beyond category and beyond price.'**

A versatile and subtle jazz player and classical composer, Johnson is the inventor of stride piano. He came to New York as a youngster and was exposed to a huge range of music at rent parties and shebeens in the ghetto 'Jungles'. His interest shifted to formal composition during the '30s and '40s, but his influence on jazz piano is inestimable. Too little is known now about Johnson's orchestral music (of which much has been lost) to make any settled judgement about his significance as a 'straight' composer. Ironically, though, his enormous importance as a synthesizer of many strands of black music – ragtime, blues, popular and sacred song – with his own stride style has been rather eclipsed by the tendency to see him first and only as Fats Waller's teacher. Johnson was in almost every respect a better musician than Waller, and perhaps the main reason for his relative invisibility has been the dearth of reliable recorded material. This early Biograph brings together some staccato and lumpy piano rolls, hard listening but of unmistakable significance for the history and development of jazz in the period. 'Charleston' is a rarity, and 'Carolina Shout' had a profound impact on Duke Ellington. So much comes from these sketchy survivals that it is difficult to assess them aesthetically. All the elements of what would become hot jazz are there in embryo, but twinned with Johnson's other concerns. He valued them so equally that the distinction between his vernacular and classical work seems forced and ideological. He still awaits full and comprehensive analytical study. Anyone who takes up that challenge has to start with these early rolls.

EUREKA BRASS BAND

Formed 1920
Group

New Orleans Funeral And Parade

American Music AMCD-70
Percy Humphrey, Willie Pajeaud, Edie Richardson (t); Albert Warner, Sunny Henry (tb); George Lewis (cl); Ruben Roddy (as); Emmanuel Paul (ts); Joseph 'Red' Clark (sou); Arthur Ogle, Robert 'Son' Lewis (d).
August 1951.

Trumpeter Wynton Marsalis said (1990): **'Wherever you say it first emerged, in cat-houses, bars or out on the street, what came to be called jazz was music that had a social function. It bound African-American people together and confirmed their sense of community.'**

This sits here out of strict chronological sequence as a representative of a music that in its heyday went unrecorded. The group was formed in 1920 by clarinettist Willie Parker, so its provenance is not anachronistic and neither is the music. This is the most authentic available example of old New Orleans music in its original environment, even if this recording of traditional funeral and parade music was recorded in a French Quarter alleyway rather than actually on the job. The regulars of the Brass Band, as it was then, were augmented by Lewis for the day, although he plays flat, and the brass are similarly wayward in intonation. The recording is musty, the tempos ragged, the extra takes of four of the numbers an anti-climax, while some of the dirges threaten to dissolve altogether. But seldom has the old music sounded so affecting, the workmanlike attitude of the players lending it something like nobility. The remastering has been done very well, considering the source material, and the superb documentation – by Alden Ashforth, the teenage enthusiast who recorded the session – adds to the undeniable mystique.

Samuel Charters managed to record the Eureka again in 1956, for Moe Asch's Folkways label, and some 80 minutes of rehearsal music has also survived, now rather extravagantly spread across two CDs, worth chasing up by anyone interested in this period. Given that some of this is chatter, tune-ups and breakdowns, it's scarcely an essential way into this kind of music. But Charters's vivid notes bring the occasion back to life, and since it presents the Eureka players at their most typical (this time without Lewis), it may even be more valuable as a document.

JELLY ROLL MORTON &

Born Ferdinand Joseph Lemott (or La Mott, or La Menthe), 20 October 1890, New Orleans, Louisiana; died 10 July 1941, Los Angeles, California
Piano, voice

The Complete Library Of Congress Recordings
Rounder ROUCD 1888 8CD
Morton (p, v); Alan Lomax (v). May–June 1938.

Mary Lou Williams said (1976): **'I was afraid of him. He had this big mouthful of diamonds and he stuttered when he talked fast, which made him seem more frightening rather than ridiculous. He pushed me on to a stool in his office uptown and told me to play. I played "The Pearls" for him, hoping I wouldn't get dumped on my butt on the floor. He was supposed to hit out for almost no reason, especially girls.'**

Oral history is either the curse of jazz studies or its greatest resource, and probably both. In the summer of 1938, broke and almost finished, Morton was recorded – almost by chance at first – by Alan Lomax at the Library of Congress, and when Lomax realized the opportunity he had on his hands he got Morton to deliver a virtual history of the birth pangs of jazz as it happened in the New Orleans of the turn of the century. His memory was unimpaired, although he chose to tell things as he preferred to remember them, perhaps; and his hands were still in complete command of the keyboard. The results have the quality of a long, drifting dream, as if Morton were talking to himself. He demonstrates every kind of music which he heard or played in the city, re-creates all his greatest compositions in long versions unhindered by 78 playing time, remembers other pianists who were never recorded, spins yarns, and generally sets down the most distinctive (if not necessarily the most truthful) document we have on the origins of the music.

The sessions were made on an acetate recorder and, while the sound may be uncomfortably one-dimensional to modern ears, everything he says comes through clearly enough, and the best of the piano solos sound as invigorating as they have to be. Yet another edition of these priceless recordings has been issued by Rounder, amounting to eight CDs and what is surely the most comprehensive coverage of the speech and music to date. The overall sound quality has become something of a *cause célèbre* among jazz scholars – at times it does seem inferior to the previous four-disc edition on the same label – but for the general listener this should be accorded a warm welcome, expensive though it is. It is a wonderfully illustrated lecture on Morton's music by the man who created it. Indispensable records for anyone interested in jazz history.

& *See also* **The Piano Rolls** (1920, 1997; p. 9), **Jelly Roll Morton 1926–1928** (1926–1928; p. 25)

BABY DODDS
Born Warren Dodds, 24 December 1898, New Orleans, Louisiana; died 14 February 1959, Chicago, Illinois
Drums

Baby Dodds
American Music AMCD-17
Dodds; Bunk Johnson, Louis 'Kid Shots' Madison, Wooden Joe Nicholas (t); Jim Robinson, Joe Petit (tb); George Lewis, Albert Burbank (cl); Adolphe Alexander Jr (bhn); Isidore Barbarin (ahn); Lawrence Marrero (bj); Red Clark, Sidney Brown (tba); Alcide 'Slow Drag' Pavageau (b). 1944–1945.

Drummer Max Roach said (1981): '**Baby Dodds *played* behind the soloist. He could conjure up a whole range of tonal colours from his kit, and he varied the spectrum depending on who he was with, and how he was feeling about the music.**'

Clarinettist Johnny Dodds's brother was playing drums at 16 and developing great show-manship. He was with King Oliver in 1922, then in Chicago for 20 years, before playing in New York with Bunk Johnson during the revival. Exemplifying the New Orleans style while remaining at a tangent from it, he was the first drummer to be documented who embellished his playing rather than simply ticking out the time, and his inventiveness comes across even on primitive early recordings. A slice of living history, *Baby Dodds* features the leading drummer of New Orleans jazz talking at some length about his traps, his cymbals, his style and how it all comes together – for jazz bands, marching bands, funeral parades and whatever else a drummer had to play for. Most of the music is actually lifted from other records, notably Bunk Johnson's American Music CDs. Some of it is horse sense that still holds good – 'Tiger Rag is played too fast', he grumbles, and then we hear the tempo he liked to play for it – and when he talks us through a lesson in technique, the good-natured generosity of the man comes alive again, five decades after his death. Remastering of all the speech/drum tracks is excellent, and though the music comes in mainly for illustration the compilers have chosen well. Dodds finally slowed down in the '50s when he suffered a series of strokes, but he lived long enough to stand as a role model and example to the younger generation, and the first beboppers.

GEORGE 'POPS' FOSTER
Born 18 May 1892, McCall Plantation, Louisiana; died 30 October 1969, San Francisco, California
Double bass

George 'Pops' Foster
American Music ASMCD-105
Foster; Art Hodes (p). 1968.

Art Hodes said (1981): '**He knew Louis Armstrong before Louis Armstrong was Louis Armstrong, so who are you to doubt a word he says? George Foster *was* jazz, and don't forget it.**'

'Pops' worked on riverboats, including the *Belle of the Bend* with Fate Marable and with all the major New Orleans bandleaders, before moving to St Louis and eventually New York. A celebrated figure in the '40s revival, he carried on till the end, always rock-solid, his snapping tones a familiar aspect of many, many early recordings, including key Sidney Bechet sides. On this valuable recording, a little under 40 minutes in length, Pops and Art chat about the bassman's long career, and intersperse the dialogue with whichever tunes come up in this eavesdropped conversation, privately recorded by Hodes. Inevitably, some of the anecdotal detail in George's ghost-written autobiography is suspect, but the inconsistencies aren't as damaging as has sometimes been made out, and like the conversation with Hodes it remains a valuable memoir of the early days of jazz, and the spirit of a great survivor shines through the factitious stuff. Pops plays in his elemental style, grumbling away with the bow on 'Closer Walk With Thee', slapping on the others; they open and close with 'Mahogany Hall Stomp', which he always said was his favourite piece of music.

THE '20s

Two wonderful things happened for jazz in the 1920s. Electrical recording happened, and Louis Armstrong happened. The music's greatest master emerged in the middle of the decade with a series of recordings that some consider unmatched to this day, the pinnacle of jazz art. After 1925, despite the resistance of some companies, most studios switched to electrical recording, in which sound vibrations were encoded as an electrical signal and then decoded by the playback machine, giving a far higher level of audio fidelity. Curiously, perhaps, the greatest advantage of electrical recording fell to the other members of the ensemble, particularly pianists and bass players, though percussionists, too, who henceforward could be captured with a degree of fidelity. The jazz combo was always a flexible format, by no means fixed to one or two horns plus a 'rhythm section' of piano (or guitar), bass and drums. This became the convention for small-group jazz during the swing, bebop and hard-bop era, only to dissolve again in more recent years, where drummerless groups, or ensembles with stringed instruments, or with no harmony instrument, again became common.

After a slow start, jazz recording became a substantial and geographically widespread business, with a large number of subsidiary and specialist labels emerging, and in 1924 the first African-American recording company, Black Swan. Perhaps most important of all, though, was the beginning of jazz recording in New Orleans, recording some of the early masters of the music in their own unique cultural environment. Even at a time when many musicians were leaving the city to move north to Chicago and New York or West to California, it remained the cradle of jazz and its most important single centre, though again one has to wait until the revival to hear some aspects of New Orleans music in 'authentic' form. The 1920s was a paradoxical period in jazz history. The so-called 'Jazz Age' established a white, middle-class jazz audience (the novels and stories of Scott Fitzgerald capture some of its values) and reinforced a certain gap between the production and consumption of jazz music, and between the kinds of black music enjoyed by white and black audiences, with the latter somewhat favouring blues over sophisticated instrumental jazz.

Production and consumption of another sort became a major social issue in the 1930s. The Eighteenth Amendment to the Constitution was ratified on 16 January 1919 and enforced via the Volstead Act (which President Woodrow Wilson unsuccessfully attempted to veto) exactly a year later, prohibiting the manufacture, sale and consumption of alcohol. 'The Noble Experiment' wrought significant changes in American leisure, forcing alcohol underground, warping drinking habits and creating an ideal environment for organized crime. The ironic outcome was that jazz, which had developed in the brothel houses and shebeens of Storyville, was increasingly associated with Mob-run 'speakeasies' or 'blind pigs' in the northern cities. Among wealthier socio-economic groups, illicit drinking was largely confined to cocktail parties – the familiar backdrop of Fitzgerald's tales of the 'beautiful and damned' – and this in turn had the effect of sharpening class and ethnic differences, even above the Mason–Dixon line.

The 1920s was also the period of the 'Harlem Renaissance', a vivid outpouring of black poetry and art, whose interaction with jazz was only uncertain, intermittent and to some degree ambiguous. The complex racial demarcations of American culture – this at a time when Ku Klux Klan activity and violence in the South was at a higher pitch than any since Reconstruction – were never more evident. Jazz recording does not necessarily reflect those ambiguities very well, but they remain as a subtext to the decade's great music …

JELLY ROLL MORTON &

Born Ferdinand Joseph Lemott (or La Mott, or La Menthe), 20 October 1890, New Orleans, Louisiana; died 10 July 1941, Los Angeles, California
Piano, voice

The Piano Rolls
Nonesuch 79363-2
Morton (p rolls). 1920, February 1997.

In his own immortal words: **'Jazz is to be played sweet, soft, plenty rhythm'**, and with a **'Spanish tinge'**.

The first great composer in jazz – its inventor, he claimed – led a picaresque life in New Orleans as a pianist, pimp, billiards player, tailor, minstrel-show entertainer, hustler and more. Though these piano rolls date from earlier, he began recording in Chicago in 1923, then bandleading with his Red Hot Peppers, making some of the classic early jazz recordings. He scuffled over unpaid royalties during the '30s, then began recording his life story (and his history of jazz) for the Library of Congress in 1938. This sparked a series of attempted comebacks at the end of the decade but Morton died in California, bitter and unrewarded.

The Nonesuch disc is one of the most fascinating retrievals of recent years. Morton's 12 original piano rolls have been analysed in the light of his other recordings by Artis Wodehouse, who has subsequently converted the information to computer data and edited a previously missing interpretative element into the way the rolls are reproduced. The subsequently annotated rolls were then played back on a nine-foot Disklavier piano, in a concert hall, and recorded. The remarkable outcome may be the closest we can ever get to hearing what Morton might truly have sounded like at this early peak of his career. Or they may not. Sceptics will point to the issue that, however meticulous the homework, this is still only somebody's idea of how the rolls should sound. Yet the results are exhilarating enough to suggest that Jelly's ghost is indeed seated at the keyboard. If there is an inevitable sense of something mechanical in the delivery, it's offset by the rocking syncopations, rips and general brio which always seem to be among the hallmarks of a Morton performance. The odd combination of ferocity and gentility in 'Grandpa's Spells', the dizzying double-time break in 'Midnight Mama' and the unbridled virtuosity of 'Shreveport Stomps' have certainly never sounded more convincing. It is altogether a memorable event and essential for anyone intrigued by the early steps of the master.

& *See also* **Jelly Roll Morton 1926–1928** (1926–1928, p. 25), **The Complete Library Of Congress Recordings** (1938, but in 'Beginnings' section, p. 5)

LADD'S BLACK ACES / ORIGINAL MEMPHIS FIVE
Formed c.1917–19
Group

The Complete Ladd's Black Aces 1921–1924
Timeless TCD 77
Phil Napoleon, Benny Bloom, Harry Gluck (c); Moe Gappell, Vincent Grande, Sammy Lewis, Miff Mole, Charles Panelli (tb); Doc Behrendson, Jimmy Lytell (cl); Ken 'Goof' Moyer (cl, as); Loring McMurray (as); Cliff Edwards (k2); Rube Bloom, Jimmy Durante, Frank Signorelli (p); John Cali, Ray Kitchingham (bj); Joe Tarto (bb); Jack Roth (d); Vernon Dalhart, Arthur Fields, Mandy Lee, Billy de Rex (v): collective personnel. August 1921–August 1924.

Original Memphis Five: Columbias 1923–1931

Retrieval RTR 79026

Phil Napoleon (t); Tommy Dorsey, Miff Mole, Charles Panelli (tb); Jimmy Lytell (cl); Jimmy Dorsey (cl, as); Frank Signorelli (p); Ray Kitchingham (bj); Jack Roth, Ted Napoleon (d); Billy Jones, Joseph A. Griffith (v): collective personnel. May 1923–November 1931.

Trombonist Paul Rutherford said (1985): **'Here's where the trombone starts to become a really strong voice in jazz groups, with an equal status to the cornet and the clarinet or saxophone. It changes the nature of the sound quite a bit and it challenges the other front-line soloists.'**

Ladd's Black Aces and the Original Memphis Five were actually one and the same, one of the first white bands to follow up the success of the Original Dixieland Jazz Band. Phil Napoleon, a Bostonian born in 1901, originally Filippo Napoli and uncle to pianists Teddy and Marty Napoleon, formed a group as far back as 1917, but the band-name, first used by Napoleon in 1920, was generic rather than very specific and was later used by several other leaders, including Red Nichols and Miff Mole. Remarkably, Napoleon lived on – and continued using the OMF name – until 1990.

The Ladd's Black Aces identity was used for three years and all of their work under that flag is included on the Timeless CD. The Aces were a leaner, more streamlined outfit than the ODJB. Roth's drumming was simpler than Tony Sbarbaro's and the rhythms less relentless but no less driving. There's a relatively early use of saxophone which gives a solidity, if not much individual detail, to some numbers. Though Lytell was the outstanding improviser, actual solos were still few in number and breaks based around stop-time routines were more the norm. Napoleon's little arpeggiated rip, which he uses to start a phrase, is how he decided to swing, and while he played a firm lead, he sounds pedestrian alongside Miff Mole, who was the most advanced musician by far to play with the group. When he's present, which is on fewer than half of the 26 sessions, the front line swings as it never does elsewhere.

Yet the Aces were a remarkably consistent band. The feel got looser and more daring as time went on, but even the earliest sides have their own giddy momentum: the very first track, W. C. Handy's 'Aunt Hagar's Children's Blues', already sounds like a group that knew what had to be done. Jimmy Durante, in his first and, alas, last real jazz records, can just be heard stomping away on the piano on the first eight tracks. There's a curious, addictive quality to this music and the recordings, made acoustically (in other words, not yet electronically) for the Gennett company, stand the test of time very well indeed.

For the time being, there's only one available disc dedicated to the earliest work of the Original Memphis Five, although even this one goes as far forward as 1931. It's still very much an ensemble music, without the solos that modern ears expect in jazz, but it would still be good to see this huge body of music – more than 400 78rpm masters – given proper reissue. Napoleon plays his useful steadfast lead, and Lytell delivers some very decent work, though he showed no capacity for progress as a stylist and is comprehensively shown up by Jimmy Dorsey, who is on the 1931 'reunion'; Tommy is there as well.

Rough as they may be, these are key documents in the early years of jazz recording. Newcomers often react to them with surprise: any initial impression of crudity tends to give way to lasting fascination.

NEW ORLEANS RHYTHM KINGS
Formed 1922
Group

New Orleans Rhythm Kings 1922–1925: The Complete Set
Retrieval RTR 79031 2CD
Paul Mares (c); George Brunies, Santo Pecora (tb); Leon Roppolo, Omer Simeon (cl); Don Murray (cl, as); Boyce Brown (as); Charlie Cordella (cl, ts); Jack Pettis (Cmel, ts); Elmer Schoebel, Mel Stitzel, Jelly Roll Morton, Kyle Pierce, Red Log, Jess Stacy (p); Lou Black, Bob Gillett, Bill Eastwood (bj); Marvin Saxbe (g); Arnold 'Deacon' Loyacano, Chink Martin, Pat Pattison (b); Frank Snyder, Ben Pollack, Leo Adde, George Wettling (d). February 1922–1925, January 1935.

Clarinettist Kenny Davern said (1992): **'I did grow through a phase of grabbing people by the throat in New York and saying this was the only kind of jazz worth troubling about, that the New Orleans Rhythm Kings had it all taped. I got over that, but there are days now when I wonder if I was right.'**

One of the major groups of jazz records, from the first stirrings of the music in recording studios, and the New Orleans Rhythm Kings' sessions still sound astonishingly lively and vital some 80 years later. The band recorded in Chicago but had come from New Orleans: Mares was already a disciple of King Oliver (who hadn't yet recorded at the time of the first session here), Roppolo played fluent, blue clarinet, and even Brunies made more of the trombone – at that time an irresponsibly comical instrument in jazz terms – than most players of the day. The rhythms tend towards the chunky, exacerbated by the acoustic recording, but the band's almost visionary drive is brought home to stunning effect on the likes of 'Bugle Call Blues' (from their very first session, in August 1922), the relentlessly swinging 'Tiger Rag' and the knockabout 'That's A Plenty'. On two later sessions they took the opportunity to have Jelly Roll Morton sit in, and his partnership with Roppolo on 'Clarinet Marmalade' and 'Mr Jelly Lord' – something of a sketch for Morton's own later version – invigorates the whole band. 'London Blues' and 'Milenberg Joys' find Morton more or less taking over the band in terms of conception. The final session they made, early in 1925, is slightly less impressive because of Brunies's absence, and there are moments of weakness elsewhere in the original records: the use of saxes sometimes swamps the initiative, Mares isn't always sure of himself, and the beats are occasionally unhelpfully overdriven. But this is still extraordinarily far-sighted and powerful music for its time, with a band of young white players building on black precepts the way that, say, Nick LaRocca of the ODJB refused to acknowledge.

This superb Retrieval edition collects all of the original masters, 12 alternative takes and the reunion session of 1935, where Mares convened a gang of contemporary Chicagoans to play alongside himself and Pecora, the results of which are surprisingly strong. In excellent sound from top-quality originals, this is the NORK as they should be heard.

KID ORY
Born Edward Ory, 25 December 1886, LaPlace, Louisiana; died 23 January 1973, Honolulu, Hawaii
Trombone, voice

Ory's Creole Trombone
ASV CD AJA 5148
Ory; Thomas 'Mutt' Carey, George Mitchell, Joe 'King' Oliver, Bob Shoffner (c); Louis Armstrong (c, v); Johnny Dodds, Dink Johnson, Omer Simeon (cl); Stump Evans, Albert Nicholas, Billy Paige (cl, as, ss); Darnell Howard

(cl, as); Barney Bigard (cl, ts, ss); Joe Clarke (as); Lil Hardin Armstrong, Jelly Roll Morton, Luis Russell, Fred Washington (p); Bud Scott, Johnny St Cyr (bj); Ed Garland, John Lindsey (b); Bert Cobb (bb); Paul Barbarin, Ben Borders, Andrew Hilaire (d). June 1922–June 1944.

George E. Lewis, listening to Kid Ory in a 'blindfold test' (2008): **'There's someone who's deliberately playing in an archaic style, but doing so very subtly and very well, as if he's trying to recover some primitive essence, or perhaps because he's aware that he's expected to sound "New Orleans".'**

Composer of 'Muskrat Ramble' and an innovative player who made much use of mutes, slurs and other devices, Kid Ory invented the 'tailgate' style. Ironically, he spent much of his life away from Louisiana, going to California for his health just after the First World War, where he recorded the first-ever sides by an all-black group, 'Ory's Creole Trombone' and 'Society Blues', in 1922 (or possibly they recorded before that) and going under the charming name of Spike's Seven Pods Of Pepper Orchestra. For some purists, these – collected on this ASV compilation – and not the Original Dixieland Jazz Band's earlier discs mark the real start of jazz recording.

   Leadership of the group switched to Mutt Carey in 1925, which is why the strict-constructionists at the Classics label do not include subsequent tracks in their documenta-tion of Ory's work. The later things are equally valid representations, though. Ory perhaps does less special pleading later on, letting that vivid tailgating style speak for itself. Never-theless, he was always conscious of his place in the history of the music, and he acted up to it shamelessly. Ory's '40s albums had Creole cooking tips printed on the sleeves. On his comeback, after nearly a decade out of music fattening up chickens, the trombonist's rhyth-mic tailgating was still as salty as blackened kingfish and as spicy as good gumbo.

THE GEORGIANS
Formed 1922
Group

The Georgians 1922–23 / 1923–24
Retrieval RTR 79003 / 79036
Frank Guarente (t); Ray Stilwell, Russ Morgan, Archie Jones (tb); Johnny O'Donnell, Frank Smith, Dick Johnson, Harold 'Red' Sailiers (reeds); Arthur Schutt (p); Russell Deppe (bj); Joe Tarto (tba); Chauncey Morehouse (d): plus Elwood Boyer (t); Charlie Butterfield (tb); Henry Wade, Al Monquin (reeds); Roy Smeck (bj); Billy Jones, Eddie Cantor, Dolly Kay, Blossom Seeley (v). November 1922–November 1923, June 1922–May 1924.

Broadcaster Steve Race said (1991): **'I think it's almost more interesting to think of all those hot bands that either didn't record, or the recordings haven't survived. Some of them are rough and ready, but almost every time, you find some little gem or nugget buried away among the dross.'**

It became familiar later for small 'hot' groups to be hived out of large dance orchestras. The Georgians were originally a contingent from Paul Specht's more straitlaced dance orchestra, working at New York's Hotel Alamac. Led by the excellent Guarente, a King Oliver student, it stood at a point somewhere between the simple ensemble style of the Original Memphis Five and the looser, more inventive methods of the early black Chicago bands. Guarente, an Italian-American, even took some lessons from Joe Oliver in New Orleans. He was the only improviser of any special merit in the band, but Arthur Schutt, hitherto largely ignored by jazz history, contributed an increasingly sophisticated book of arrangements. The later tracks on the first CD, especially the likes of 'Land Of Cotton Blues' and 'Old Fashioned Love', show real finesse coupled with a proper sense of swing. Most of the tunes have something to commend them, and even novelty pieces like 'Barney Google' are sustained by Guarente's work, although here and there (as in the plodding treatment of 'Farewell Blues') the group fails to make much out of the music.

The second disc takes the story up to Guarente's departure in May 1924. The best of The Georgians' music is here, in such sides as 'Big Boy' (with a great vocal by Dolly Kay) and the pair of titles which turned out to be Guarente's swansong, 'Savannah' and 'Doodle Doo Doo'. Eddie Cantor turns up to sing at one session and the disc is padded with four titles by the full Specht orchestra.

PERRY BRADFORD

Born John Henry Perry Bradford, also known as 'Mule', 14 February 1893 (some sources cite 1895), Montgomery, Alabama; died 20 April 1970, New York City
Piano, voice

And The Blues Singers In Chronological Order

Document 5353
Bradford; Gus Aiken, Louis Armstrong, Johnny Dunn, Bubber Miley (c); Bud Aiken, William Dover, Herb Fleming, Charlie Green, Calvin 'Fuzz' Jones (tb); Harry Hull (btb, b, bhn); Buster Bailey (cl); Hersal Brassfield (cl, as, ts); Garvin Bushell (as, cl); Don Redman (as); James P. Johnson, Charles Edward Smith, Leroy Tibbs (p); Gus Horsley, Stanley Wilson (bj); Walter Wright (b, bhn); Ed Jackson, Kaiser Marshall (d); Julia Jones, Louise Vant (v, acc); Ethel Ridley, Mamie Smith (v). May 1923–February 1927.

Singer George Melly said (1993): **'The sound of Mamie Smith singing Bradford's "Crazy Blues" is about as close as you can get, I think, to what those early minstrel shows and the vaudeville circuit must have been like. It's where it all started.'**

Raised in Atlanta, Bradford had made his way to Chicago before the First World War, and was already a veteran on the circuit – as half of a song-and-dance act known as Bradford & Jeanette – before his own songwriting started to become known. He is not much more than a footnote in most jazz histories, but his association with some of the great names and his ability to create vivid blues settings and novelty songs of real musical worth – 'I Ain't Gonna Play No Second Fiddle' (with Louis Armstrong), 'Liza Johnson Got Better Bread Than Sally Lee' – make him a musician of real interest and charm. His vocals are workmanlike and it's really as a blues composer (he and Mamie Smith effectively kicked off the blues craze) that he is worth remembering. This Document set doesn't entirely exhaust the legacy and the chronological organization can be tiring, but it's probably the best resource and there are few better ways to drive away the black dog than to put on 'Fade Away Blues' and then sit back for the rest.

ARMAND PIRON

Born 16 August 1888, New Orleans, Louisiana; died 17 February 1943, New Orleans, Louisiana
Violin, voice, bandleader

Piron's New Orleans Orchestra

Retrieval RTR 79041
Piron; Peter Bocage (t); John Lindsay (tb); Lorenzo Tio Jr (cl, ts); Louis Warnecke (as); Steve Lewis (p); Charles Bocage (bj, v); Bob Ysaguirre (tba); Louis Cottrell (d); Esther Bigeou, Ida G. Brown, Lela Bolden, Willie Lewis (v). December 1923–March 1925.

Bruce Raeburn, author of *New Orleans Style and the Writing of American Jazz History*, says: **'Piron's orchestra is often described as a society band, but there is strong evidence that he was also playing blues to black audiences. So what you're dealing with is a group who kept their low-down music for when they were playing in Tremé [New Orleans neighbourhood] and played something sweeter and more genteel on record.'**

For the most part they were recorded in New York, but Piron's band was a New Orleans outfit and as such was one of the few to be documented in the '20s. This splendid reissue is a model of its kind: the sleeve-notes sum up years of research into the performers' activities, and this latest remastering of a set of terrifically rare originals is excellent. The music, however, comes with a gentle warning for anyone expecting raw, 'authentic' New Orleans jazz. Piron's group was a more genteel, proper orchestra than some New Orleans bands of the time, pitching itself somewhere between ragtime, society music and the glimmers of early jazz: though 1923 is early in jazz recording history, they still sound a much less modern band next to Oliver or Fletcher Henderson from the same year (one should compare their treatment of 'Doo Doodle Oom' with Henderson's 1923 Vocalion version). A few tracks, including the very first, 'Bouncing Around', brew up a potent mix of syncopation, with Tio's wriggling clarinet breaks and Bocage's urbane lead making their mark over an ensemble rhythm that is almost swinging. No one will claim these as classic jazz performances, but they mark a very important reference point in the evolution of the music, in New Orleans and beyond.

ORIGINAL INDIANA FIVE

Formed 1922; disbanded 1929
Group

The Original Indiana Five: Volume 1

Jazz Oracle BDW 8019

Johnny Sylvester (t); Vincent Grande, Charlie Panelli (tb); Nick Vitalo (cl, as); Johnny Costello (cl); Newman Fier, Harry Ford (p); Tony Colucci (bj); Tom Morton (d, v). May 1923–May 1925.

Trombonist Turk Murphy said (1981): **'The key is to listen to the trombone and where it sits in the harmony. Not so high up that it's fighting with the clarinet, and not clashing with the piano, or where later the bass would be.'**

The group hadn't much to do with Indiana, actually formed in Pennsylvania under the leadership of drummer Tom Morton, who remained a constant through various changes of personnel for the remainder of the jazz decade. This, the succeeding volume and a couple of other OI5 reissues were pioneering, as hardly anything of the group had been revived in recent times; this despite an evident popularity, for they made more than 100 titles during the '20s. The music is a closely argued example of the small-group jazz which several New York groups of the day pursued: perhaps not quite the equal of the Original Memphis Five, given that there were no soloists in the band the equal of Phil Napoleon and Miff Mole, but this is really ensemble music which picks up from the cues of the Original Dixieland Jazz Band.

A Frog reissue offers a decent sampler of some of their sessions, but it was trumped by the comprehensive three-disc Jazz Oracle edition, of which this fine first volume will suffice for all but specialist listeners. Not only are the transfers excellent, but the documentation is superb, offering formidable research into the lives of all the leading players in the group, and there are a few ancillary sessions which are not strictly the work of the OI5 but which are closely related. Even though little of this has a pressing claim on the general listener, enthusiasts will be impressed by the standard of these issues, and may be surprised at the heat which some sides generate.

JOE 'KING' OLIVER

Born 11 May 1885, New Orleans, Louisiana; died 8 April 1938, Savannah, Georgia
Trumpet, cornet, voice

King Oliver's Creole Jazz Band: The Complete Set
Retrieval RTR 79007 2CD
Oliver; Louis Armstrong (c); Honoré Dutrey, Ed Atkins (tb); Johnny Dodds, Jimmie Noone (cl); Stump Evans (ss, as); Charlie Jackson (bsx); Lil Hardin, Clarence Williams (p); Johnny St Cyr (bj, v); Bud Scott, Bill Johnson (bj); Baby Dodds (d); Jodie Edwards, Susie Edwards (v). April 1923–December 1924.

Poet and jazz critic Philip Larkin said (1976): **'If Armstrong was jazz's Gabriel, then I suppose Oliver was its Lucifer, a proud man who risked everything and owned to no one and nothing superior to himself.'**

The third King of New Orleans, after Buddy Bolden and Freddie Keppard, remains among the most stately and distinguished of jazz musicians, although newer listeners may wonder whether Oliver's records aren't entirely eclipsed by those of his protégé Louis Armstrong. Joe Oliver was in at the inception of jazz and it's our misfortune that his group wasn't recorded until 1923, when its greatest years may have been behind it: accounts of the band in live performance paint spectacular images of creativity which the constricted records barely sustain. Yet they remain magnificent examples of black music at an early peak: the interplay between Oliver and Armstrong, the beautifully balanced ensembles, the development of polyphony. Oliver's tight-knit sound, fluid yet rigorously controlled, projects the feel of his New Orleans origins, vivified by the electricity of his Chicagoan success. There is the brightness of the young Armstrong, content to follow his master but already bursting with talent, and the magisterial work of both of the Dodds brothers (only the recording stops us from hearing Baby's work in its full intensity). Ragtime and brass band music still guide much of what Oliver did, but the unsettled ambitions of jazz keep poking through too. If the music is caught somewhere between eras, its absolute assurance is riveting and presents a leader who knew exactly what he wanted.

There are 37 surviving sides by the Oliver (Creole) Jazz Band, including a handful of alternative takes. This two-disc set is the first to include all of them in one place (one disc, the Gennett coupling of 'Zulu's Ball' and 'Working Man Blues', is so rare that only a single copy of the original 78 is known to exist) and, while Robert Parker's stunning remastering in his first Jazz Classics volume, now deleted, doubtless sounded better to some ears, we have happily transferred our number one choice to Retrieval, for whom John R. T. Davies has done his usual outstanding job. The set also includes a pair of 1924 titles by the vaudevillians Butterbeans And Susie, with accompaniment by Oliver and Clarence Williams, and the famous pair of duets by Oliver and Jelly Roll Morton. Modern ears are still going to find this primitive in audio terms, but surely the excitement, panache and inventiveness of this incredible band will speak to anyone with even the slightest sympathy.

The Creole Jazz Band sides were the first genuinely important recordings by black musicians. Nothing that followed was half as successful. The Dixie Syncopators failed to reach anything like the same standard and Oliver made a grievous mistake (too proud?) in not accepting a situation at the Cotton Club. But for a shining moment, his group expressed everything that jazz was about, and that music comes down to us untarnished.

FREDDIE KEPPARD

Born 27 February 1890, New Orleans, Louisiana; died 15 July 1933, Chicago, Illinois
Trumpet

The Complete Set 1923–1926

Retrieval RTR 79017
Keppard; Elwood Graham, James Tate (c); Fred Garland, Eddie Vincent, Fayette Williams, Eddie Ellis (tb); Jimmie Noone (cl, as, v); Clifford King (cl, as); Johnny Dodds, Angelo Fernandez (cl); Joe Poston (as); Jerome Pasquall, Norval Morton (ts); Arthur Campbell, Antonia Spaulding, Adrian Robinson, Jimmy Blythe (p); Jimmy Bell (vn); Stan Wilson, Erskine Tate (bj); Bill Newton (tba); Bert Greene, Jasper Taylor, Jimmy Bertrand (d); Papa Charlie Jackson (v). June 1923–January 1927.

Trumpeter Ian Carr said (1990): **'What did Winston Churchill say about Russia? "A riddle, wrapped in a mystery, inside an enigma." That goes for Freddie Keppard, too, I think.'**

One of the great unanswered questions in jazz is how good Keppard really was. A bandleader in New Orleans at 16, he was touring by 1910, his massive sound shaking up the pre-jazz scene. Secretive about his own playing and alcoholic, he missed the chance to record early and was overtaken by Armstrong. The second 'King' of New Orleans cornet, after Buddy Bolden and before Joe Oliver, his handful of records offer ambiguous evidence and suggest a musician who cottoned on to ragtime but never quite got a grip on where jazz was going. He has a big, jabbing sound, when you can hear him, and, cut loose from his surroundings, he can work up genuine excitement. That happens only a few times on the 24 tracks which are his entire legacy, and even then his presence on a few of them is doubtful. The bigger-band sides with Doc Cook and Erskine Tate are often a disappointing lot, and one has to turn to the small-group performances with Jimmy Blythe, Jasper Taylor and Keppard's own Jazz Cardinals to hear him working at something like optimum level, in the rough-and-ready Chicago jazz of the day.

This Retrieval edition is so well remastered that it made us reconsider our verdict on Keppard. The Doc Cook band numbers have never sounded finer, and even the Erskine Tate tracks from 1923 stand up much better than before. One still needs ears sympathetic to the music of that day, but more than any other previous issue this brings Keppard back to life.

JIMMY BLYTHE

Born January 1901, Louisville, Kentucky; died 21 June 1931, Chicago, Illinois
Piano

Messin' Around Blues

Delmark DE 792
Blythe (pianola rolls). Early '20s.

Oscar Peterson, listening to Blythe on record, with tears in his eyes (1982): **'It's almost like seeing a Bible scene acted out in front of you, or one of the old myths. Very moving and part of where we all came from.'**

Born on the cusp of the new century, Blythe became an integral part of South Side music in the '20s. His extensive work for Paramount, Gennett and Vocalion mixes a strong blues piano approach with flakes of stride and boogie-woogie, revealing a determined and creative thinker. Not much is known about Blythe's life, a reversal of those cases where the musician is legendary but the recorded legacy is exiguous. Blythe turned up in Chicago at the end of the war, studied for a time with Clarence Jones and began making piano rolls a few years later. 'Chicago Stomp' from 1924 is reckoned to be the first boogie-woogie record-ing. He also recorded with Johnny Dodds and a good number of those recordings survive as well. The pianola rolls remastered on *Messin' Around Blues* come in immaculate sound that must be as close as anyone will now come to Jimmy in the all too frail flesh. Some rinky-dink moments on these pop-blues tunes for the nickelodeon market, but for the most part thoughtfully conceived and executed. A slice of living history.

GEORGIA MELODIANS
Formed 1923
Group

Georgia Melodians 1924–1926
Timeless Historical CBC 1-031
Probably: Ernie Intlehouse, Red Nichols (c); Herb Winfield, Abe Lincoln (tb); Merrit Kenworthy (cl, as, bsx); Clarence Hutchins (cl, ts, bs); Oscar Young (p); Elmer Merry (bj, g); Carl Gerrold (d); Vernon Dlahart (v). July 1924–April 1926.

BM says: '**I once spent a rather nervous week holed up in a house in Sana'a. It belonged to a Yemeni doctor who every afternoon at around five cranked his wind-up gramophone and played an ancient disc of the Georgia Melodians, "Everybody Loves My Baby". It seemed to be the only record he had, or liked. I've no idea how it came to be there.**'

A 'territory band', formed by Clarence Hill Hutchins, the Georgia Melodians came from Savannah to New York City, where the Edison Company recorded them. Though Joe Moore's notes reveal that the band broke up at the end of 1924, they continued to record until 1926. Players like Intlehouse, Kenworthy and Hutchins are about as obscure as any in recorded jazz, and listening to the music reveals why. This is hot dance music with a generous ration of solos (Edison's vertical-cut discs allowed for much longer playing time than normal 78s) and an honourable intention to swing, but it's poker-stiff at times. The very earliest tracks, once available on a Retrieval LP, are missing from this otherwise complete edition. Staple numbers such as 'Spanish Shawl' and 'Everybody Loves My Baby' can be heard better else-where, although they do a respectable job on 'San'. The group broke up in 1929, and nobody thought much about the music until these were reissued in the '90s. Beautifully clean trans-fers bring it all back strongly.

FIVE BIRMINGHAM BABIES
Formed 1924
Group

Heart Breakin' Baby
Frog 58
Red Nichols (c); Frank Cush, Chelsea Quealey (t); Abe Lincoln (tb); Sam Ruby (cl, Cmel); Bobby Davis (cl, as); Adrian Rollini (bsx, gfs); Irving Brodsky, Jack Russin (p); Tommy Fellini, Ray Kitchingman (bj); Herb Weil (d); Stan King (d, kz); Arthur Hull, Ed Kirkeby (v). July 1924–July 1927.

Gerry Mulligan said (1992): '**I knew Adrian Rollini had played bass saxophone long before I consciously heard him, but it was a shock eventually to hear those records and think: "Damn, I thought I invented that."**'

A little slice of jazz history, the Babies – who had no connection with Birmingham, Ala-bama – were closely related to the Goofus Five, set up by Ed Kirkeby, who was manager of the California Ramblers, as a way of playing hot music. Rollini was a kingpin on his big horn and on the melodica-like goofus (he also dabbled in 'hot fountain pen', a clarinet with a sax mouthpiece) and his unique sound figures here. It's a period piece, musically, but there are good breaks on Adrian's 'I Know What It Means' and on 'Heart Breakin' Baby', on which he had to split the royalty with Kirkeby, and how could you fail to love a band where the MC announces 'and on trombone ... Abe Lincoln!'?

LOVIE AUSTIN

Originally Cora Calhoun; born 19 September 1887, Chattanooga, Tennessee; died 10 July 1972, Chicago, Illinois
Piano, arranger

Lovie Austin 1924–1926

Classics 756
Austin; Shirley Clay, Natty Dominique, Tommy Ladnier, Bob Shoffner (c); Jimmy Cobb (c, tb); Kid Ory (tb); Johnny Dodds, Jimmy O'Bryant (cl); Eustern Woodfork (bj); W. E. Burton (d); Ford & Ford, Edmonia Henderson, Priscilla Stewart, Henry 'Rubberlegs' Williams (v). September 1924–August 1926.

Mary Lou Williams said (1975): **'She was a great example of a woman making it in a tough world. I looked her up one time in Chicago and just seeing her helped me, seeing how she handled herself.'**

Austin was an extraordinary figure whose status as one of the first women to make a contribution to jazz remains undervalued. She had a formal classical training, which stood her in good stead for the job of house pianist at Paramount in the early '20s. She started out in vaudeville but formed her own recording band in 1924, called the Blues Serenaders. All of their surviving work was once available on a fine Fountain LP, but this Classics CD has the bonus of sides made with vaudeville figures like Ford & Ford ('Skeeg-a-Lee Blues') and other vocalists of the period.

Though it will sound primitive to modern ears, Austin's music was a sophisticated variation on the barrelhouse style of the period. Many of the 'originals' betray their origins in earlier vernacular tunes – 'Peepin' Blues' is strangely familiar – but there was nothing generic or formulaic about Austin's approach, and it comfortably brought in elements of ragtime ('Frog Tongue Stomp') or island rhythms ('Rampart Street Blues'). The other great virtue of the collection is the presence of some of the great names of early jazz. Two of the earliest sides are by the trio of Austin, Tommy Ladnier and the short-lived Jimmy O'Bryant, performing a densely plaited counterpoint that seems amazingly advanced for its time. The quartet and quintet sides are harsher, with Burton's clumping beat on what sounds like a military side-drum little more than a distraction, but the simple metres and stop-time passages have a rough poetry about them that is good enough for the music to transcend the typically poor Paramount recording. Austin was not an improviser herself but her piano parts are a driving and integral part of music that consistently betrays her skills as an arranger and composer. Her songs were covered by Ma Rainey, Bessie Smith and Alberta Hunter, with whom she recorded late in life and to whom she voluntarily gave co-credit, a gesture Hunter never forgot.

Along with Lil Hardin Armstrong and Mary Lou Williams (who acknowledged her as an important influence), Austin was a key figure of her time and an unmissable presence. She sat cross-legged at the piano, with a cigarette perpetually burning between her lips. Her Stutz Bearcat sedan was fitted with *faux*-leopardskin upholstery. At the end of the decade she settled in Chicago and scarcely recorded again until 1961, when she was persuaded to accompany Hunter with a latter-day Blues Serenaders: a moment of living jazz history.

RED NICHOLS

Born Ernest Loring Nichols, 8 May 1905, Ogden, Utah; died 28 June 1965, Las Vegas, Nevada
Cornet, trumpet

The Red Heads Complete 1925-1927

Classics 1267

Nichols; Brad Gowans, Wingy Manone, Leo McConville (t); Miff Mole (tb); Bobby Davis, Fred Morrow, Jimmy Dorsey (cl, as); Arthur Schutt, Bill Haid (p); Eddie Lang, Dick McDonough (g); Vic Berton (d). November 1925–September 1927.

Cornetist Alex Welsh said (1982): **'Apparently, he always gave his father credit for instilling the discipline to stick at everything on his own terms. He gets a funny press, but Red was a major star and his playing is phenomenal, so bright and alert. I think it's a model career, in some ways.'**

Nichols's posterity labours under the burden of Danny Kaye's big screen portrayal of the trumpeter as a loveable eccentric and relaxed, overindulgent parent. The hokum of 'The Music Goes Round And Around' didn't do him any favours, either. Red's own training was in his father's brass band, and it seemed to stand him in good stead through his life. Unlike the sentimental portrait of the film, Nichols was a tough-skinned professional who insisted on a minimum of musical integrity and moved on briskly, as he did from the Casa Loma Orchestra, when his own musical needs were not observed. His precise, lightly dancing work on either cornet or trumpet might seem to glance off the best of Beiderbecke's playing, and the scrupulous ensembles and pallid timbre of The Five Pennies or whatever he chose to call a group on its day in the studios now seem less appealing. But it is unique jazz and, in its truce between cool expression and hot dance music, surprisingly enjoyable when taken a few tracks at a time.

Nichols went out under a whole range of names – The (Six) Hottentots, The Original Memphis Five, The Arkansas Travelers, The Five Pennies most famously – and recorded prolifically. Of the compilations, there is a good survey on Retrieval of the work with Miff Mole but, even if it is a more specialist choice, this Red Heads disc is probably the best track for track. It collects all of Nichols's sessions under this name for Pathé, and on titles such as 'Get A Load Of This', 'Plenty Off Center' and 'Trumpet Sobs' the line-up is down to three or four players – chamber-jazz of an unusually sparse sort, giving the young leader clear space to lead and improvise in. Pathé's thin recording wasn't helpful, but the music – lean, dancing and strikingly different from what was going on under either Armstrong or Beiderbecke in a similar period – exerts its own pale fascination. It's also as well to remember that, when he made the earliest sides here, Nichols hadn't even turned 21.

WILLIE 'THE LION' SMITH

Born William Henry Joseph Bonaparte Betholoff Smith, 25 November 1897, Goshen, New York; died 18 April 1973, New York City
Piano

Willie 'The Lion' Smith 1925-1937

Classics 662

Smith; Dave Nelson, Frankie Newton (t); June Clark, Jabbo Smith, Ed Allen (c); Jimmy Harrison (tb); Buster Bailey (cl, ss, as); Cecil Scott, Herschel Brassfield (cl); Prince Robinson, Robert Carroll (ts); Edgar Sampson (as, vn); Pete Brown (as); Buddy Christian, Gus Horsley (bj); Jimmy McLin (g); Bill Benford, Harry Hull (tba); Ellsworth Reynolds, John Kirby (b); O'Neil Spencer (d, v); Eric Henry (d); Willie Williams (wbd); Perry Bradford (v). November 1925–September 1937.

Humphrey Lyttelton said (1993): **'He came on *Jazz 625* [television programme] in around 1966. Here was this man who had been present at the beginnings of stride piano, working in New York before the First World War, sat at the piano with his "doiby" on his head and a cigar jutting up from his jaw, cheerfully belligerent, full of stories.'**

A founder-member of the New York stride pianists, Smith served in the First World War, then haunted the toughest New York clubs. He led occasional bands, toured, and became a self-appointed living historian and raconteur in his old age. He wrote 'Echoes Of Spring'. An unrivalled raconteur, Willie Smith came into his own when an old man, reminiscing from the keyboard, but these more youthful sessions stand up very well and are surprisingly little-known.

The disc opens with two of his few appearances on record in the '20s; each of the pair of sessions is by a pick-up group, both with Jimmy Harrison and one with Jabbo Smith in the front line. Typical small-group Harlem jazz of the period, with Perry Bradford shouting the odds on two titles. The remainder is devoted to sessions by Smith's Cubs, an excellent outfit: with Ed Allen, Cecil Scott and Willie Williams on washboard on the first eight titles, they can't help but sound like a Clarence Williams group, but the next three sessions include Dave Nelson (sounding better than he ever did on the King Oliver Victor records), Buster Bailey, Pete Brown and Frankie Newton, effecting a bridge between older hot music and the sharper small-band swing of the late '30s. Smith plays a lot of dextrous piano – he also has a 1934 solo, 'Finger Buster', a typical parlour show-off piece of the day – and the music has a wonderful lilt and sprightliness.

FLETCHER HENDERSON

Born 18 December 1897, Cuthbert, Georgia; died 29 December 1952, New York City
Arranger, bandleader

The Harmony & Vocalion Sessions: Volumes 1 & 2

Timeless CBC 1-064 / 1-069

Henderson; Bobby Stark, Louis Armstrong, Elmer Chambers, Howard Scott, Joe Smith, Tommy Ladnier, Russell Smith, Rex Stewart, Cootie Williams (t, c); Jimmy Harrison (tb, v); Charlie Green, Claude Jones, Benny Morton (tb); Jerome Pasquall, Buster Bailey, Benny Carter, Harvey Boone (cl, as); Don Redman (cl, as, gfs); Coleman Hawkins (cl, Cmel, ts, bsx); Fats Waller (p, org); Charlie Dixon, Clarence Holiday (bj, g); Ralph Escuderp, John Kirby, June Cole (bb, b); Kaiser Marshall, Walter Thompson (d); Lois Deppe, Billy Jones, Andy Razaf, Evelyn Thompson (v). 1925–September 1928.

Sun Ra said (1986): **'I pursue the sound of Fletcher Henderson. Not just his arrangements of notes on paper – anyone can do that – but the sound of that orchestra, which transcends anything that can be written down. He was a millionaire and beyond everyday concerns; that voice is the voice of a man who is able to consider another realm.'**

Henderson arrived in New York in 1920, seeking scientific work but ending up as an A&R man in the fledgling black record industry. He accompanied blues singers and began leading an orchestra at the Roseland Ballroom, recruiting Louis Armstrong and Coleman Hawkins. A car crash in 1928 dissipated his energy, but he continued to write and arrange and run occasional bands. His influence was immense, not just for his writing, which only now is being properly appreciated again (partly through the stewardship and advocacy of Sun Ra during his earthly life), but as a fosterer of talent. Henderson drifted into bandleading after casually working for the Black Swan record label, and his first records as a leader are routine dance music. The arrival of Louis Armstrong – whom Henderson first heard in New Orleans at the turn of the decade – galvanized the band and, eventually, every musician in New York, but he already had Don Redman and Coleman Hawkins working for him prior to Armstrong's arrival, and there are many good records before Louis's first session of October 1924.

By the mid-'20s Henderson was leading the most consistently interesting big band around. That doesn't mean all the records are of equal calibre; the title of a famous retrospective – 'A Study In Frustration' – gives some idea of the inconsistencies and problems of a band that apparently never sounded as good on record as in person. Even so, Redman was coming into his own, and his scores assumed a quality which no other orchestral arranger was matching in 1926–7. 'The Stampede', 'The Chant', 'Henderson Stomp', the remarkable 'Tozo' and, above all, the truly astonishing 'Whiteman Stomp' find him using the colours of reeds and brass to complex yet swinging ends. Luckily Henderson had the players who could make the scores happen. Though Armstrong had departed, Hawkins, Ladnier, Joe Smith, Jimmy Harrison and Buster Bailey all had the stature of major soloists as well as good section-players. The brass sections were the best any band in New York could boast – the softer focus of Smith contrasting with the bluesy attack of Ladnier, the rasp of Rex Stewart, the lithe lines of Harrison – and the group had Hawkins (loyal enough to stay for ten years), the man who created jazz saxophone. Henderson's own playing was capable rather than outstanding, and the rhythm section lumbered a bit, though string bass and guitar lightened up the feel from 1928 onwards. It took Henderson time to attain consistency; in 1925 he was still making sides like 'Pensacola' (for Columbia), which starts with a duet between Hawkins and Redman on bass sax and goofus! But there weren't many vocals, and this let the band drive through their three-minute allocation without interruption. If Henderson never figured out the best use of that time-span (unlike Ellington, his most serious rival among New York's black bands), his players made sure that something interesting happened on almost every record.

Some tracks made under the name The Dixie Stompers were made for Harmony, which continued to use acoustic recording even after most other companies had switched over to the electric process in 1925, and some may find these a little archaic in timbre.

LOUIS ARMSTRONG &

Born 4 August 1901, New Orleans, Louisiana; died 6 July 1971, New York City
Trumpet, cornet

Complete Hot Five And Hot Seven Recordings: Volumes 1–3
Columbia CK 86999 / 87010 / 87011
Armstrong; Bill Wilson (c); Homer Hobson (t); Kid Ory, Honoré Dutrey, John Thomas, Fred Robinson, Jack Teagarden (tb); Johnny Dodds, Don Redman (cl, as); Bert Curry, Crawford Wetherington (as); Jimmy Strong (cl, ts); Boyd Atkins (cl, ss, as); Happy Caldwell, Albert Washington (ts); Lil Hardin Armstrong, Earl Hines, Joe Sullivan (p); Johnny St Cyr (bj); Mancy Cara (bj, v); Lonnie Johnson, Eddie Lang (g); Rip Bassett, Dave Wilborn (bj, g); Carroll Dickerson (vn); Pete Briggs (bb); Baby Dodds, Tubby Hall, Kaiser Marshall, Zutty Singleton (d); Butterbeans & Susie, May Alix (v). November 1926–December 1928.

Trumpeter Digby Fairweather says: **'Louis Armstrong has been rightly called "The Shakespeare of Jazz". And even if – to less tempered ears – his musical surroundings on the Hot Five and Seven recordings may sound archaic, the ecstatic outpourings of his horn are arguably the most spontaneously creative and profound jazz improvisation on record.'**

For some, the story goes no further than this, and has no need to. Louis Armstrong – universally revered as 'Pops', never 'Satchmo' – was the first great soloist in jazz and had by 1930 laid down a body of music, albeit crudely documented by modern standards, which has not been surpassed to this day for precision, urgency and emotional freight. He learned to play cornet as a young teenager in a waifs' home. Buddy Bolden was still alive – and would be until 1931 – but he was also in an institution, the State Insane Asylum at Jackson, where he had been committed for alcohol-induced psychosis and dementia. By 1919, young Armstrong was a formidable player and he began recording with King Oliver in 1923 before going to New York to join the Fletcher Henderson Orchestra. He began recording under his own name in Chicago, 1925, with the Hot Five and Hot Seven for OKeh Records. By the end of the '20s, he was a great soloist, influencing everyone in jazz, shifting the emphasis from group playing to solo improvising and creating a new vocal style that is almost as influential as his trumpet-playing.

Armstrong's music is one of the cornerstones of jazz and these, his most famous records, remain a marvel. While we are envious of any who are discovering the likes of 'Wild Man Blues' or 'Tight Like This' for the first time, we acknowledge that the sound of the records – particularly the earliest, acoustic Hot Five dates – can seem 'difficult' to ears raised on digital sound. Considering he was playing with his peers – Ory and Dodds were two of the most respected performers in the field – the group's basic sound seems unexpectedly rough and unsophisticated. Yet when one focuses on Armstrong himself, that all falls away in the presence of his youthful mastery. Not yet 25 and playing cornet, he is still trying out for greatness, even if his spell with Henderson a year earlier had alerted the jazz community to his incipient brilliance. Earlier pieces like 'Jazz Lips' or 'Cornet Chop Suey' have a rough-and-ready quality which Armstrong's burgeoning power either barges past or transcends. There is a degree of vaudeville in the music already – 'Heebie Jeebies' – but much of the time he elevates his surroundings by sheer charisma.

By the time of the Hot Sevens, in 1927, with Dodds assuming a second-voice role that has even Armstrong compelled to play his best, the music seems mystical in its poetry and majesty. 'Potato Head Blues', with its incredible stop-time solo, the astounding improvisation on 'Wild Man Blues' and the glittering blues playing on 'Willie The Weeper' are but three examples. By the time of the second Hot Five, with Hines arriving on piano, Armstrong was approaching the stature of a concerto soloist, which makes these final small-group sessions something like a farewell to jazz's first golden age. Hines is also magnificent on these discs, and notably on the duet showstopper 'Weather Bird' the results seem like eavesdropping on great men speaking among themselves. There is nothing in jazz finer than 'West End Blues', 'Beau Koo Jack' or 'Muggles'. It goes without saying that these are indispensable.

All of this music has been reissued many times. In other editions of the *Guide* we have tried to pick our way through a swamp of good, less good and some plain bad packages, but here we would prefer to concentrate on this peerless music. Columbia do score heavily with a magnificent book and add a few rare takes and even offer 'Cornet Chop Suey' at two different speeds (therefore in different keys). With this music, more is definitely more.

& See also **Louis Armstrong 1947** (1947; p. 112), **Complete New York Town Hall And Boston Symphony Hall Concerts** (1947; p. 112), **California Concerts** (1951–1955; p. 130)

OSCAR 'PAPA' CELESTIN

Sometimes given as 'Celestine'; born 1 January 1884, Napoleonville, Louisiana; died 15 December 1954, New Orleans, Louisiana
Trumpet, voice

SAM MORGAN
Born 18 December 1887, Bertrandville, Louisiana; died 25 February 1936, New Orleans, Louisiana
Cornet

Papa Celestin & Sam Morgan
Azure AZ-CD-12
Celestin; Louis 'Kid Shots' Madison, Ricard Alexis, George McCullum, Guy Kelly (c); William Ridgley, August Rousseau, William Matthews, Ernest Kelly (tb); Willard Thoumy, Paul 'Polo' Barnes, Earl Pierson, Sid Carriere, Clarence Hall, Oliver Alcorn (reeds); Manual Manetta, Jeanette Salvant (p); John Marrero, Narvin Kimball (bj); Simon Marrero (b, bb); Abby Foster, Josiah Frazier (d); Charles Gills, Ferdinand Joseph (v). January 1925–December 1928.

Morgan; Ike Morgan (c); Jim Robinson (tb); Earl Fouche (as); Andrew Morgan (cl, ts); Tink Baptiste, O. C. Blancher (p); Johnny Davis (bj); Sidney Brown (b); Nolan Williams, Roy Evans (d). April–October 1927.

Retired Washington journalist Mac McCurdy remembered (1982): **'Celestin played in the Eisenhower White House. It was the year before he died, I think. It was a pretty strange moment, hoo-doo in the Executive Mansion. You didn't have to be Ralphe Bunche to see the ironies.'**

Little enough music was recorded in New Orleans in the '20s to make any survivals valuable, but the sessions led by Celestin and Morgan would be remarkable anyway. 'Papa' is probably now better known for his later 'voodoo' classic 'Marie Laveau', recorded just before he died. Despite devices imported from dance band trends, particularly in the later tracks, these early tracks sound like no other jazz of the period. Celestin has a fixer on the New Orleans scene, running bands simultaneously in different halls. The first three tracks are by the Original Tuxedo Jazz Orchestra, which Celestin was leading in the 1910s, with Madison and Celestin in the front line, and the deliriously exciting 'Original Tuxedo Rag' is a blazing fusion of ragtime, jazz and dance music that makes one ache to have seen this band in the flesh. The 13 subsequent titles from 1926 to 1928 are less frantic and are occasionally troubled by the mannerisms of the day, weak vocals in particular. But the reed sections manage their curious blend of sentimentality and shrewd, hot playing with surprising finesse; the ensembles are consistently driving; and the two-cornet leads are frequently as subtle and as well-ordered as those of Oliver's band. An undervalued soloist, Celestin is fine on 'My Josephine' and the superb slow piece 'It's Jam Up'. Outstanding clear and powerful remastering.

The eight titles by Morgan's band are among the classics of '20s jazz. They are a very rare example of a New Orleans group recorded in the city during this period, and it's been claimed that these are the most truthful recordings of how such a band sounded in its prime. Morgan's music is ensemble-based, solos and breaks threaded into the overall fabric, the playing driven by the gutsy slap-bass of Sidney Brown. Fouche might be the outstanding player, with his mile-wide vibrato, but it's as a band that these players have endured. There are few more exhilarating records from the period than 'Steppin' On The Gas' or 'Mobile Stomp'. Together with the Celestin tracks, this makes up one of the most essential reissues of early jazz, in outstandingly fine sound.

EDDIE LANG
Born Edward Langlois, 25 October 1902, New Orleans, Louisiana; died 26 March 1933, New Orleans, Louisiana
Guitar

The Quintessential Eddie Lang 1925–1932

Timeless CBC 1-043

Lang; Bix Beiderbecke, Joe 'King' Oliver (c); Tommy Gott, Fuzzy Farrar, Ray Lodwig, Manny Klein, Bill Moore, Louis Armstrong, Harry Goldfield, Leo McConville, Andy Secrest, Bill Margulis (t); Boyce Cullen, Miff Mole, Wilbur Hall, Loyd Turner, Tommy Dorsey, Bill Rank (tb); Arnold Brilhart, Alfie Evans, Harold Sturr, Don Murray, Doc Ryker, Frankie Trumbauer, Andy Sannella, Tony Parenti, Happy Caldwell, Chester Hazlett, Red Mayer, Jimmy Dorsey, Charles Strickfaden, Bernard Daly, Issy Friedman (reeds); Otto Landau, Matty Malnec, Henry Whiteman (vn); Roy Bargy, Clarence Williams, Itzy Riskin, Joe Sullivan, Irving Brodsky, J. C. Johnson, Frank Signorelli, Arthur Schutt, Rube Bloom (p); Hoagy Carmichael (p, cel); Cliff Edwards (uke, v); Harry Reser, Tony Colucci, Mike Pingitore (bj); Lonnie Johnson, Carl Kress (g); Red McKenzie (comb); Dick Slevin (kz); Arthur Campbell, Min Leibrook (tba); Steve Brown, Ward Lay, Joe Tarto, Mike Trafficante (b); Neil Marshall, Vic Berton, Kaiser Marshal, George Marsh, Stan King (d); Justin Ring (perc); Bessie Smith, Ukulele Ike, Noel Taylor, The Rhythm Boys, Bing Crosby (v). January 1925–February 1932.

Martin Taylor says: **'Eddie Lang is the grandfather of jazz guitar. We owe so much to him and the recordings are still to be marvelled at.'**

Eddie Lang was the first guitarist to make a major impact on jazz away from the blues, and even there he took a hand by recording many duets with 'authentic' bluesman Lonnie Johnson. Lang's polished, civilized but swinging art was worked out in dance bands and as an accompanist; Crosby hired him until Eddie succumbed to complications following a tonsillectomy. He was an important member of the white New York school of the period and can be found on records by Beiderbecke, Joe Venuti and the Dorseys; but the sides made under his own name were plentiful and, for all his restraint and good taste, he was a jazzman through and through. His most characteristic playing is as rhythmically driving as it is harmonically deft and inventive.

There are, inevitably a number of compilations available and much to recommend each of them. As a cross-section, the Timeless disc sweeps the board, quite beautifully remastered by John R. T. Davies, and with a shrewd selection of material. Lang's bell-like tone is immediately identifiable on the early piece by the Mound City Blue Blowers, from 1925, and he turns up elsewhere in dance bands led by Fred Rich, Jean Goldkette, Roger Wolf Kahn and Paul Whiteman, backing Ukulele Ike and Bessie Smith, partnering Lonnie Johnson, sitting in with Armstrong and Oliver, and taking a solo turn on Rachmaninov's Opus 3 *Prelude*. Could any other musician of the era claim such a CV?

JOHNNY DODDS

Born 12 April 1892, Waveland, Mississippi; died 8 August 1940, Chicago, Illinois
Clarinet, alto saxophone

Johnny Dodds 1926

Classics 589

Dodds; Freddie Keppard, George Mitchell (c); Kid Ory, Eddie Vincent (tb); Junie Cobb (cl); Joe Clark (as); Lockwood Lewis (as, v); Lil Hardin Armstrong, Jimmy Blythe, Arthur Campbell, Tiny Parham (p); Curtis Hayes, Cal Smith, Freddy Smith (bj); Eustern Woodfork, Johnny St Cyr (bj, v); Clifford Hayes (vn); W. E. Burton (wbd, v); Earl McDonald (jug, v); Jimmy Bertrand, Jasper Taylor (d, perc); Papa Charlie Jackson, Trixie Smith (v). May–December 1926.

Jimmy Giuffre said (1987): **'I liked that low, warm, thoughtful sound he got. He spoke through the clarinet rather than making it scream. It's much more idiomatic than some of the jazz guys on the instrument.'**

Johnny Dodds was the model professional musician. He rehearsed his men, frowned on alcohol and drugs, and watched the cents. In 1922, he was a member of King Oliver's Creole Jazz Band at Lincoln's Garden in Chicago, the band that included Louis Armstrong, Lil Hardin Armstrong, trombonist Honoré Dutrey, and Dodds's younger brother, 'Baby'. The clarinettist left in 1924, after a quarrel about money, and set out on a highly successful recording career of his own that faltered only with the beginnings of the swing boom.

His tone was intense and sometimes fierce, rather removed from the soft introspections of Jimmie Noone or George Lewis's folksy wobble. He favoured the lower – chalumeau – register of the instrument over the piercing *coloratura*. He doubles briefly on alto saxophone on the July 1926 cuts with Jimmy Blythe, perhaps to get some change out of Paramount's insensitive microphones; unlike Sidney Bechet, Dodds never seriously considered a full turn to the saxophones.

Though much of his most renowned work was with Louis Armstrong's Hot Five and Seven, the series of Classics compilations are the essential Dodds documents, though needless to say this out-of-copyright material is available in a number of forms. The Classics discs contain work for Brunswick, Columbia, Gennet, the ropey Paramount, Victor and Vocalion. The real classics are the cuts made for Columbia with the New Orleans Wanderers/Bootblacks, a line-up that included George Mitchell, Kid Ory, Joe Clark, Johnny St Cyr and Lil Hardin Armstrong. There are fine clarinet duets with Junie Cobb (and without brass) from 26 August 1926 which have been rather overlooked in the rush of enthusiasm for the Wanderers/Bootblacks performances of the previous month. Inevitably, very little matches up to these classics, but Dodds's reconciliation with King Oliver in September for a single track ('Someday Sweetheart') underlines the great might-have-been of their interrupted association. Dodds by this time was making too much regular money at Burt Kelly's Stables on the South Side to consider a longer recruitment. A pity, because there's a definite falling-off after 1926.

JELLY ROLL MORTON &

Born Ferdinand Joseph Lemott (or La Mott, or La Menthe), 20 October 1890, New Orleans, Louisiana; died 10 July 1941, Los Angeles, California
Piano, voice

Jelly Roll Morton 1926–1928
Classics 612

Morton; Ward Pinkett (t); George Mitchell (c); Kid Ory, Gerald Reeves, Geechie Fields (tb); Omer Simeon, Johnny Dodds (cl); Stump Evans (as); Bud Scott, Johnny St-Cyr (g); Lee Blair (bj); Bill Benford, Quinn Wilson (tba); John Lindsay (b); Andrew Hilaire, Tommy Benford, Baby Dodds (d). December 1926–June 1928.

Pianist Dave Burrell, who recorded *The Jelly Roll Joys* in 1991, says: '**It is an amazing body of work. Almost every song has something individual about it, even sometimes a little freakish, but there are no places in the whole work book where the music seems to be formulaic or routine.**'

The 1926-7 dates here were a summary of what jazz had achieved up to that time: as a development out of the New Orleans tradition, it eschewed the soloistic grandeur that Armstrong was establishing and preferred an almost classical poise and shapeliness. If a few other voices (Ellington, Redman) were already looking towards a more modern kind of group jazz, Morton was distilling what he considered to be the heart of hot music, 'sweet, soft, plenty rhythm', as he later put it.

The previous volume in the Classics series which this is part of ended with a 1926 date that allegedly featured King Oliver. The series then goes into the Victor sequence, which continues into the following 1928–1929 volume.

Morton's recordings for Victor are a magnificent body of work which has been done splendid but frustratingly mixed justice by various reissues stretching back to the start of the LP era. His Red Hot Peppers band sides, particularly those cut at the three incredible sessions of 1926, are masterpieces which have endured as well as anything by Armstrong, Parker or any comparable figure at the top end of the jazz pantheon. Morton seemed to know exactly what he wanted: as he had honed and orchestrated compositions like 'Grandpa's Spells' at the piano for many years, his realization of the music for a band was flawless and brimful of jubilation at his getting the music down on record. Mitchell, Simeon and the others all took crackling solos, but it was the way they were contextualized by the leader that makes the music so close to perfection.

& *See also* **The Piano Rolls** (1920, 1997; p. 9), **The Complete Library Of Congress Recordings** (1938, but in 'Beginnings' section, p. 5)

TINY PARHAM

Born Hartzell Strathdene Parham, 25 February 1900, Winnipeg, Manitoba, Canada; died 4 April 1943, Milwaukee, Wisconsin
Piano, bandleader

Tiny Parham 1926–1929
Classics 661
Parham; B. T. Wingfield, Punch Miller, Roy Hobson (c); Charles Lawson (tb); Junie Cobb (ss, as, cl); Charles Johnson (cl, as); Leroy Pickett, Elliott Washington (vn); Charlie Jackson (bj, v); Mike McKendrick (bj); Quinn Wilson (bb); Jimmy Bertrand, Ernie Marrero (d). December 1926–July 1929.

Fellow Canadian Oscar Peterson said (1995): **'It's strange music, and you wonder what he listened to in childhood that would make him go in this direction, but it swings in its awkward way!'**

Born in Canada, the huge pianist kept busy on the Chicago scene of the '20s, arranging for contemporaries such as King Oliver and leading his own groups. By the time of his death, though, he was working hotels and movie houses. Parham's jazz was an idiosyncratic, almost eccentric brand of Chicago music: his queer, off-centre arrangements tread a line between hot music, novelty strains and schmaltz. The latter is supplied by the violinists and the occasional (and mercifully infrequent) singing – but not by the tuba, which is used with surprising shrewdness by the leader. Some of his arrangements on this Classics disc are among the more striking things to come out of the city at that time – 'Cathedral Blues', 'Voodoo' and 'Pigs Feet And Slaw' don't sound like anybody else's group, except perhaps Morton's Red Hot Peppers, although Parham preferred a less flamboyant music to Jelly's. The 'exotic' elements, which led to titles such as 'The Head Hunter's Dream' or 'Jungle Crawl', always seem to be used for a purpose rather than merely for novelty effect and, with soloists like Miller, Hobson and the erratic Cobb, Parham had players who could play inside and out of his arrangements. The two-beat rhythms he leans on create a sort of continuous vamping effect that's oddly appropriate, and Tiny's own piano shows he was no slouch himself. There is a lot of surprising music on these discs, even when it doesn't work out for the best.

BIX BEIDERBECKE
Born Leon Beiderbecke, 10 March 1903, Davenport, Iowa; died 6 August 1931, New York City
Cornet

At The Jazz Band Ball
Columbia CK 46175
Beiderbecke; Charlie Margulis (t); Bill Rank (tb); Pee Wee Russell (cl); Jimmy Dorsey, Issy Friedman, Charles Strickfaden (cl, as); Don Murray (cl, bs); Frankie Trumbauer (Cmel); Adrian Rollini, Min Leibrook (bsx); Frank Signorelli, Arthur Schutt (p); Tom Satterfield (p, cel); Joe Venuti, Matty Malneck (vn); Carl Kress, Eddie Lang (g); Chauncey Morehouse, Harold McDonald (d); Bing Crosby, Jimmy Miller, Charlie Farrell (v). October 1927–April 1928.

Trumpeter Randy Sandke says: '**If Louis Armstrong is the Sophocles of jazz, Bix is its Aeschylus, another classic master who set the standard by which all who follow must be judged. As with all great classicists, no gesture is wasted and spontaneity and logic are intimately intertwined.**'

Seventy-five years after his alcohol-hastened death, Beiderbecke remains the most lionized and romanticized of jazz figures. His understated mastery, his cool eloquence and precise improvising were long cherished as the major alternative to Louis Armstrong's clarion leadership in the original jazz age, and his records have endured remarkably well, even though few of them were in an uncompromised jazz vein. He was mostly self-taught on piano and cornet, and never really learned to read accurately. His first extended exposure to jazz came when his well-intentioned parents sent him off to the military school within reach of Chicago: right time, right place. He joined the Wolverine Orchestra and made his first record in 1923, but it was his periods with Jean Goldkette in St Louis, 1926–7, and Paul Whiteman in New York, 1928–30, which brought him to wider attention. Whether fame or frustration fuelled his drinking scarcely matters; Beiderbecke was a clinical alcoholic, but a functioning one. There is nothing uncontrolled or wild about his playing, and his classically tinged 'In A Mist' suggests a musician literate at all levels.

It's a difficult discography and necessarily a rather small one, leading to fantasies of 'Beiderbecke tapes' turning up all over the place. This survey of Bix's OKeh recordings has the advantage of eliminating the commercial Whiteman material (though there is no convincing evidence that Bix bucked against the aesthetics of that band; he liked being a star) and concentrating on his most jazz-directed music; this disc includes some of the best of the Bix And His Gang sides, including the title-piece, 'Jazz Me Blues' and 'Sorry', plus further dates with Trumbauer. As a leader, Bix wasn't exactly a progressive – some of the material harks back to the arrangements used by the Original Dixieland Jazz Band – but his own playing is always remarkable: lean, bruised, a romantic's sound, but one that feels quite at home in what were still rough and elementary days for jazz.

FRANKIE TRUMBAUER &
Born 30 May 1901, Carbondale, Illinois; died 11 June 1956, Kansas City, Missouri
Alto and C-melody saxophones

Frankie Trumbauer 1927–1928
Classics 1186
Trumbauer; Bix Beiderbecke (c); Charlie Margulis (t); Bill Rank (tb); Pee Wee Russell (cl); Jimmy Dorsey (cl, as); Don Murray (cl, bs); Doc Ryker, Charlie Strickfaden (as); Adrian Rollini, Min Leibrook (bsx); Paul Mertz, Itzy Riskin, Frank Signorelli, Tom Satterfield (p); Matt Malneck (vn); Eddie Lang, Carl Kress (g); Chauncey

Morehouse, Harold McDonald (d); Seger Ellis, Irving Kaufman, Jerry Macy, John Ryan, Les Reis, Bing Crosby (v). February 1927–January 1928.

Instrument collector Guy Colline says: '**The C-melody saxophone is not excessively rare, but it doesn't turn up too often nowadays. Anthony Braxton plays one and I believe Scott Robinson does too. It has quite a narrow bore and the sound is consequently quite thin and unforceful. But it has its place in small-group jazz.**'

'Tram' was one of the master saxophonists of his era, coming to prominence with the Benson Orchestra of Chicago in the early '20s and striking up a famous partnership with Bix Beiderbecke. He spent his later years working in aviation and playing only rarely. The leading saxophonist of his day, he sometimes favoured the thin light sound of the C-melody instrument over the more orthodox alto. It gave him a certain distinctiveness of timbre, but it's often forgotten that Trumbauer was just as proficient on the other horn and one suspects a novelty interest in the C instrument.

An influence on Benny Carter (who felt he was never Trumbauer's equal) and Lester Young, he still sounds remarkable on his best records: a cool, almost neutral tone, and a way of slipping through the most contorted phrases in such a fashion as to make them graceful and as natural as breathing. It's a moot point as to whether it's his solo or Bix's which makes 'Singing The Blues' (1927) the classic it is. The disc here and the following *1928–1929* volume include all his sessions with Beiderbecke, and even though many of the sides get bogged down in poor vocals, effects and even blackface hokum (as in 'Dusky Stevedore' and the like), the best music is as good as white jazz got in the '20s: they often save the best for the ride-out chorus, which usually goes with a real swing, and besides Bix and Tram there's Bill Rank, Min Leibrook and Eddie Lang to listen to. These sides are easily available elsewhere in Beiderbecke editions, but this isn't a bad way to get them or to listen to them. Such is the cult of Bix, it's sometimes quite hard to hear his great partner for what he was.

& *See also* **BIX BEIDERBECKE, At The Jazz Band Ball** (1927–1928; p. 27)

DUKE ELLINGTON &
Born Edward Kennedy Ellington, 29 April 1899, Washington DC; died 24 May 1974, New York City
Piano

Duke Ellington 1927–1929
Classics 542 / 550 / 559
Ellington; Bubber Miley, Jabbo Smith, Louis Metcalf, Arthur Whetsol (t); Joe 'Tricky Sam' Nanton (tb); Otto Hardwick (ss, as, bs, bsx); Johnny Hodges (cl, ss, as); Rudy Jackson, Barney Bigard (cl, ts); Harry Carney (bs, as, ss, cl); Fred Guy (bj); Lonnie Johnson (g); Wellman Braud (b); Sonny Greer (d); Baby Cox, Adelaide Hall, Irving Mills, Ozie Ware (v). October 1927–March 1929.

Trumpeter Humphrey Lyttelton said (1993): '**To take a measure of Ellington, you have to look at a composer like Haydn or Geminiani, in terms of sheer amount of work produced, but with the qualification that Ellington wasn't just making music, he was also making the forms of the music as he did so.**'

Ellington bestrides the history of jazz on record, an impossibly rich legacy of sound that continues to energize the music. Arguably, without its existence and its example to fall back on, jazz might have been quicker to metamorphose into 'post-jazz' after Miles Davis's abstract experiments of the late '60s, early '70s, Duke's last years. As it is, they stand as a replenishing source, to which musicians and fans cyclically return. At some level, Ellington is the encyclopaedist of jazz, or its lexicographer. There are few aspects of the music which are not laid out, or adumbrated, in his half-century of activity.

He was born to a middle-class family, learned piano as a child, and became interested in ragtime, leading his own groups from around 1918. Duke Ellington & His Washingtonians worked in New York from 1924, and a residency at the Cotton Club from 1927 sealed its breakthrough. Long tours followed, with trips to Europe in the '30s, and an almost continuous presence in the studios. In the '40s, he played a series of annual Carnegie Hall concerts, wrote for the stage and briefly dispersed the big band, but reassembled it in 1949. Although the '50s saw a decline in his fortunes, his Newport appearance in 1956 reasserted his eminence. He also wrote for film and TV, and in the '60s continued to tour relentlessly. Illness slowed him down, but he was working up until his hospitalization for cancer early in 1974. Besides his major works, his individual compositions – with and without his frequent collaborator, Billy Strayhorn – number in the thousands.

These recordings come exactly a decade after the Original Dixieland Jazz Band sides start the clock on recorded jazz. By 1924, he was set to become that hitherto unknown phenomenon, a recording star. With 'East St Louis Toodle-oo', from the first important Ellington session, the music demands the attention. Any comprehensive edition will include much duplication, since Ellington spread himself around many different record labels: he recorded for Broadway, Vocalion, Gennett, Columbia, Harmony, Pathé, Brunswick, OKeh and Victor in the space of a little over three years. They also include the debut versions of 'Black And Tan Fantasy', Ellington's first masterpiece, and Adelaide Hall's vocal on 'Creole Love Call'. But the music rapidly became more subtly inflected. Ellington progressed quickly from routine hot-dance records to sophisticated and complex three-minute works which showed a rare grasp of the possibilities of the 78rpm disc. Yet during these years both Ellington and his band were still seeking an identifying style. Having set down one or two individual pieces such as 'Black And Tan Fantasy' didn't mean that Duke was fully on his way. The 1926-8 records are still dominated by the playing of Bubber Miley, and on a track such as 'Flaming Youth', which was made as late as 1929, it is only Miley's superb work that makes the record of much interest. Arthur Whetsol made an intriguing contrast to Miley, his style being far more wistful and fragile; his version of 'The Mooche' on the 1928 Victor version is in striking contrast to Miley's, and his treatment of the theme to 'Black Beauty' is similarly poignant. Joe Nanton was a shouting trombonist with a limited stock of phrases, but he was starting to work on the muted technique which would make him one of Duke's most indispensable players. The reed team was weaker, with Carney taking a low-key role (not always literally: he played as much alto and clarinet as baritone in this era), and until Bigard's arrival in 1928 it lacked a distinctive soloist. Hodges also didn't arrive until October 1928.

When the Ellington band went into the Cotton Club at the end of 1927, the theatricality which had begun asserting itself with 'Black And Tan Fantasy' became a more important asset, and though most of the 'Jungle' scores were to emerge on record around 1929-30, 'The Mooche' and 'East St Louis Toodle-oo' show how set-piece effects were becoming important to Ellington. The best and most Ellingtonian records of the period would include 'Blue Bubbles', 'Take It Easy' and 'Jubilee Stomp' (the 1928 versions), and 'Misty Mornin'' and 'Doin' The Voom Voom'. But even on the lesser tunes or those tracks where Ellington seems to be doing little more than copying Fletcher Henderson, there are usually fine moments from Miley or one of the others. These Classics CDs offer admirable coverage, with a fairly consistent standard of remastering, and though they ignore alternative takes Ellington's promiscuous attitude towards the various record companies means that there are often several versions of a single theme on one disc (Classics 542, for instance, has three versions of 'Take It Easy').

& See also **Duke Ellington 1937–1938** (1937–1938; p. 64), **The Duke At Fargo** (1940; p. 81), **Never No Lament** (1940–1942; p. 81), **Black, Brown And Beige** (1944–1946; p. 91), **Ellington At Newport** (1956; p. 189), **The Far East Suite** (1966; p. 336)

MIFF MOLE
Born Irving Mildred Mole, 11 March 1898, Roosevelt, New York; died 29 April 1961, New York City
Trombone

Slippin' Around
Frog DGF 19
Mole; Red Nichols (c, t); Leo McConville, Phil Napoleon (t); Dudley Fosdick (mel); Jimmy Dorsey (cl, as); Fud Livingston, Pee Wee Russell (cl, ts); Frank Teschemacher (cl); Babe Russin (ts); Adrian Rollini (bsx); Arthur Schutt, Lennie Hayton, Ted Shapiro, Joe Sullivan (p); Eddie Lang, Carl Kress (g); Dick McDonough (bj, g); Eddie Condon (bj); Joe Tarto, Jack Hansen (tba); Vic Berton, Ray Bauduc, Chauncey Morehouse, Gene Krupa, Stan King (d). January 1927–February 1930.

Trombonist Paul Rutherford said (1985): **'Mole's probably the first of those guys who's playing modern jazz trombone. You listen hard enough you can hear him doing things that guys like me are supposed to have invented. To some extent, we just went back to what the classics were doing.'**

Miff Mole was one of the master jazz musicians of the '20s. Though subsequently eclipsed by Teagarden, Dorsey and others, he was the first trombonist to make any significant impression as a soloist, sounding fluent and imaginative as far back as the early recordings of the Original Memphis Five and Ladd's Black Aces at the beginning of the decade. His partnership with Red Nichols was as interesting in its way as that of Armstrong and Hines or Beiderbecke and Trumbauer. Though sometimes seen as a kind of jazz chamber music, or at worst a white New York imitation of the real thing, their records were a smart, hard-bitten development out of their hot-dance environment and, with no vocals, little hokum and plenty of space for improvisation, the music has an uncompromising stance which may surprise those who've heard about it secondhand. This compilation brings together most of the sessions by Miff's Molers for OKeh, along with four Victor titles by Red And Miff's Stompers and a further pair of tunes credited to the Red Nichols Orchestra. The earlier dates have no more than five or six musicians on them, and titles like 'Hurricane' and 'Delirium' are intense little set-pieces. The later sessions have more players and feel more orchestrated, less private, though no less intriguing: two versions of Fud Livingston's 'Feeling No Pain' are remarkable, and so is the furious charge through 'Original Dixieland One Step'. Nichols, Russell, Rollini and others all have their moments, but Mole himself, alert and quick-witted and always able to find a fruitful line, has no peers here. The final two sessions, with the much-praised 'Shim-Me-Sha-Wabble' among them, seem rowdier and less personal.

EDDIE CONDON
Born 16 November 1905, Goodland, Indiana; died 4 August 1973, New York City
Guitar

Eddie Condon 1927–1938
Classics 742
Condon; Jimmy McPartland, Bobby Hackett (c); Max Kaminsky, Leonard Davis (t); George Brunies, Floyd O'Brien, Jack Teagarden (tb); Mezz Mezzrow, Frank Teschemacher, Pee Wee Russell (cl); Bud Freeman, Happy Caldwell (ts); Alex Hill, Jess Stacy, Joe Sullivan (p); Jim Lannigan, Artie Bernstein, Artie Shapiro, Art Miller (b); George Wettling, Gene Krupa, Johnny Powell, George Stafford, Big Sid Catlett (d). December 1927–April 1938.

It's a well-worn gag, but…: **'I envy Eddie Condon. He has achieved perfect equilibrium: half man, half alcohol.'**

Condon was the focus of Chicago jazz from the '20s to the '40s, garnering a personal reputation that far exceeds his actual musical significance. He is now best seen as a catalyst, a man who made things happen and in the process significantly heightened the profile of Dixieland jazz in America. He was rarely anything other than a straightforward rhythm guitarist, generally avoiding solos, but he had a clear sense of role and frequently laid out to give the piano-player more room. His chords have a melancholy ring but are always played dead centre.

After rolling in from Indiana, he became the quintessential Chicago jazzman despite spending little time there and being virtually inaudible on many of his own records. Ringleader of a gang of young white players in the '20s, he arrived in NY in 1928 and hustled his way to prominence, forming famous associations with the Commodore label, Nick's club and eventually his own place on West Third Street.

The Classics series offers an overview of a career that didn't get seriously under way on record until the '40s. The five '20s dates here are key staging-posts in the evolution of Chicago jazz, starting with the four classic titles cut by the McKenzie-Condon Chicagoans in 1927, in which McPartland and the ill-fated Teschemacher made up a superbly vibrant front line. Two 1928 sessions feature top-notch early Teagarden, and the 1933 band date includes the original versions of Freeman's famous turn on 'The Eel'. It then goes quiet until the first sessions for Commodore in 1938, the start of another classic Condon era. It's arguable that Condon would have been equally important if he hadn't played a note and simply cleared a path for others, but that does injustice to his musicianship, which was as steady and sure as his matutinal hand was shaky.

MEADE 'LUX' LEWIS
Born 4 September 1905, Chicago, Illinois; died 7 June 1964, Minneapolis, Minnesota
Piano

Meade Lux Lewis 1927–1939
Classics 722
Lewis; Albert Ammons, Pete Johnson (p). December 1927–January 1939.

Blue Note founder Alfred Lion said (1980): **'Just before Christmas in 1938, I saw and heard Meade "Lux" Lewis and Albert Ammons at the "Spirituals To Swing" concert at Carnegie Hall. Two weeks later, I brought them into the studio. That is where Blue Note was born.'**

Lewis encapsulated his contribution to jazz in his first three minutes as a soloist with his 1927 Paramount record of 'Honky Tonk Train Blues'. He recorded it again at his second session, and again at his fourth. All three are on this CD, along with 15 other variations on the blues and boogie-woogie. His signature-piece remains a marvellous evocation of a locomotive rhythm, perfectly balanced through all its variations, and if he became tired of it his listeners never did, though they overlooked equally good music. His 1936 session for Decca includes two extraordinary pieces on celeste, 'I'm In The Mood For Love' and 'Celeste Blues', and his 1939 session for Blue Note – which supplied the first Blue Note issue, 'Melancholy' and 'Solitude' – opens with a five-part investigation of 'The Blues', all rejected at the time but a remarkable sequence, at least as personal and imaginative as his train pieces. The sound on the CD is poor, but the music is marvellous.

DICKY WELLS
Born Williams Wells, 10 June 1907, Centerville, Tennessee; died 12 November 1985, New York City
Trombone

Dicky Wells 1927-1943
Classics 937
Wells; Bill Coleman, Shad Collins, Bill Dillard, Kenneth Roane, Gus McLung (t); Frankie Newton (t, v); John Williams, Fletcher Allen (cl, as); Cecil Scott (cl, ts, bs); Howard Johnson (as); Lester Young (ts); Don Frye, Ellis Larkins (p); Django Reinhardt, Roger Chaput, Freddie Green (g); Hubert Mann, Rudolph Williams (bj); Chester Campbell, Mack Walker (tba); Richard Fulbright, Al Hall (b); Lloyd Scott, Bill Beason, Jo Jones (d). January 1927-December 1943.

Dicky Wells said (1979): **'I made myself a nice pepperpot mute, punched with holes and some wire and paper. You're going to express yourself on the horn, you need to have something that gives you your very own sound.'**

Wells worked with various New York bands in the early '30s before spending eight years with Count Basie from 1938. Alcohol made him inconsistent but he was a gifted writer and was still playing in the '80s.

The important tracks here are the dozen Wells headed up in Paris on two memorable July days in 1937. The first two groups feature the trombonist with Bill Coleman and Django Reinhardt, with Dillard and Collins making up a three-man trumpet section on three titles. With no piano and Reinhardt driving all before him, the ensembles have a sound at once mercurial and light and limber, with quite magnificent playing from Coleman and Wells. There isn't a note out of place on 'Between The Devil And The Deep Blue Sea', 'Sweet Sue', the blues 'Hangin' Around Boudon' and 'Japanese Sandman'. The next session is comparatively lightweight, but it ended on what were effectively two trombone solos with rhythm accompaniment, and Wells's seven choruses on 'Dicky Wells Blues' make up one of the great pieces of trombone improvisation on record. His sound introduces a sober gaiety into the instrument's lugubrious temperament, and his vibrato and sudden shouting notes make every chorus fresh and surprising.

The disc opens with seven tracks with which Wells made his debut, with Lloyd Scott and Cecil Scott: lively if unexceptional New York jazz of the '20s. It ends on a septet date for Signature, from 1943, with Coleman, Young and Larkins (playing the Basie role). They take 'I Got Rhythm' far too fast, but there's compensation in the next three titles, with Dicky playing a beautiful slow introduction to 'I'm Fer It Too'.

JOHNNY HODGES *&*
Known as 'Rabbit'; born John Cornelius Hodge, 25 July 1907, Cambridge, Massachusetts; died 11 May 1970, New York City
Alto and soprano saxophones

Classic Solos 1928-1942
Topaz TPZ 1008
Hodges; Bunny Berigan, Freddy Jenkins, Bubber Miley, Ray Nance, Arthur Whetsol, Cootie Williams (t); Rex Stewart (c); Lawrence Brown, Joe 'Tricky Sam' Nanton, Juan Tizol (tb); Barney Bigard (cl, ts); Harry Carney (bs, as, cl); Otto Hardwick (as, bsx); Ben Webster (ts); Duke Ellington, Teddy Wilson (p); Fred Guy (bj); Lawrence Lucie, Allan Reuss (g); Hayes Alvis, Jimmy Blanton, Wellman Braud, John Kirby, Grachan Moncur, Billy Taylor (b); Cozy Cole, Sonny Greer (d); Mildred Bailey (v). October 1928-July 1941.

Saxophonist John Dankworth said (1993): **'There has never been a saxophone sound like it, but I think too much emphasis on the beauty of Hodges' playing has taken away from the logic and intelligence of his solos. They don't just sound good, they're perfectly formed.'**

There is probably no other voice in jazz more purely sensuous. Subtract Hodges' solos from Duke Ellington's recorded output and it shrinks disproportionately. He was a stalwart presence right from the Cotton Club Orchestra through the Webster–Blanton years and beyond. Sadly, perhaps, for all his pricklish dislike of sideman status in the Ellington orchestra, Hodges was a rather unassertive leader, and his own recordings under-represent his extraordinary qualities, which began to dim only with the onset of the '60s, and were often cast in jump styles which sit strangely with the lyrical role he took on in the Ellington band.

He studied with Sidney Bechet and took his place in Willie 'The Lion' Smith's group. In 1928, he joined Duke and remained for the next four decades. Influenced by Bechet, he played a good deal on soprano saxophone in the early days. It's a rougher sound in some respects than he got later on the larger horn, but it has a plain-spoken directness that goes to the heart.

This Topaz disc – and a similar ASV package – does a fairly good job of compiling a representative profile of Hodges at this period. Oddly perhaps, they don't overlap very much, which suggests that there is an alternative image of the younger man to the one painted here, which has him in plainer and more musicianly form. Topaz ignores things like the 1940 'Good Queen Bess' and the slightly earlier 'Warm Valley', but material from the 1929 Cotton Club Orchestra *is* included, filling in an important gap in the transition from blues and jump to the lyrical majesty of later years. Still combining alto and soprano, he stands out strongly wherever featured and 'Rent Party Blues' is a key early showing.

& *See also* **Everybody Knows Johnny Hodges** (1964–1965; p. 301)

MCKINNEY'S COTTON PICKERS
Formed 1926; disbanded 1934
Group

Put It There / Cotton Picker's Scat
Frog DGF 25 / 26
John Nesbitt, Langston Curl, Joe Smith, Leonard Davis, Sidney De Paris, George 'Buddy' Lee (t); Rex Stewart (c); Claude Jones, Ed Cuffee (tb); Don Redman, George Thomas (reeds, v); Milton Senior, Prince Robinson, Jimmy Dudley, Benny Carter, Coleman Hawkins, Ted McCord (reeds); Todd Rhodes, LeRoy Tibbs, Fats Waller (p); Dave Wilborn (bj, g, v); Ralph Escudero, Billy Taylor (tba); Cuba Austin, Kaiser Marshall (d); Jean Napier (v). July 1928–December 1930.

Mary Lou Williams said (1976): **'When McKinney's Cotton Pickers came to town, that was the best band most of us had ever heard. Todd Rhodes became a kind of mentor to me. He'd get me to play on jams and even once let me sit in with the band. Prince Robinson was a good player, too.'**

Originally led by drummer Bill McKinney, the Cotton Pickers were hired by Jean Goldkette for a residency at his Detroit Graystone Ballroom in 1927. Hugely popular, they eventually recorded several sessions in New York, but the band declined when several key players left in the early '30s, It was primarily John Nesbitt who built McKinney's Cotton Pickers (although Goldkette gave them their name). Redman's arrival in 1928 brought his distinctive touch as arranger to the band's book, but Nesbitt's driving and almost seamless charts were as impressive, and they remain so, more than 60 years later. McKinney's Cotton Pickers were among the most forward-looking of the large bands of their era: while the section-work retains all the timbral qualities of the '20s, and the rhythm section still depends on brass bass and banjo, the drive and measure of the arrangements and the gleaming momentum of their best records both suggest the direction that big bands would take in the next decade.

EARL HINES &

Known as 'Fatha'; born 28 December 1903, Duquesne, Pennsylvania; died 22 April 1983, Oakland, California
Piano

Earl Hines Collection: Piano Solos 1928–1940

Collectors Classics COCD 11
Hines (p solo). December 1928–February 1940.

Earl Hines said (1977): **'First off, I tried to play trumpet, but it hurt my ears. Then I found Louis Armstrong was playing exact things I wanted to play. So I think that's where my "trumpet style" on piano, if you want to call it that, comes from.'**

Earl Hines had already played on some of the greatest of all jazz records – with Louis Armstrong's Hot Five – before he made any sessions under his own name. The piano solos he made in Long Island and Chicago, one day apart in December 1928, are collected on this Classics CD – a youthful display of brilliance that has seldom been surpassed. His ambidexterity, enabling him to finger runs and break up and supplant rhythms at will, is still breathtaking, and his range of pianistic devices is equalled only by Tatum and Taylor. But these dozen pieces were a preamble to a career which, in the '30s, was concerned primarily with bandleading. The intuitive brilliance one heard on the 'Weather Bird' duet with Armstrong carried forward into his bandleading as well, where every component has its proper place in the mix, but one can readily hear Hines playing keyboard almost orchestrally, even at this early date.

& See also **Earl Hines Plays Duke Ellington** (1971–1975; p. 390)

JIMMIE NOONE

Born 23 April 1895, Stanton Plantation, Cut Off (Algiers), Louisiana; died 19 April 1944, Los Angeles, California
Clarinet

Jimmie Noone 1928–1929

Classics 611
Noone; George Mitchell (c); Fayette Williams (tb); Lawson Buford, Bill Newton (tba); Joe Poston (cl, as); Eddie Pollack (as, bs); Zinky Cohn, Alex Hill, Earl Hines (p); Junie Cobb, Wilbur Gorham, Bud Scott (bj, g); Johnny Wells (d). 1928–1929.

Jimmy Giuffre said (1987): **'Of the older fellows on clarinet, I'm drawn to Noone rather than Dodds. He had that soft-edged sound that seemed to flow over the rhythm rather than bounce off it.'**

Noone studied with his contemporary Sidney Bechet before joining King Oliver in 1918. He was a Chicago star during the '20s, but never made much impact in New York. A fondness for eating shortened his life and nowadays he's largely forgotten. What's needed is a good sampler of Noone's earlier material. There are examples of the great musician he could be, but they're scattered. The ballad playing on 'Sweet Lorraine' and 'Blues My Naughty Sweetie Gives To Me' is of a very high order and investigates a rare, cool vein in the Chicago jazz of the period. 'Oh, Sister! Ain't That Hot?', 'El Rado Scuffle', 'It's Tight Like That' and 'Chicago Rhythm' are further isolated successes, but the rest is rather discouraging.

Much of Noone's output was spoiled by weak material, unsuitable arrangements, poor sidemen or a sentimental streak which eventually came to dominate the playing.

These are all familiar characteristics of the period, but Noone seemed oblivious to the excessive sweetness which overpowered so many of the records with his Apex Club band, named after his resident gig in Chicago. It was an interesting line-up with Noone out front and Joe Poston playing melody behind him. Jimmie had a mellifluous, rather sad-sounding tone and preferred his solos to be insinuating rather than fierce. Where Johnny Dodds, the other great New Orleans player of the day, was comparatively harsh, Noone sought to caress melodies. But the plunking rhythm sections, still dominated by banjos even in 1928-9, and the unsuitable front-line partners failed to give Noone the kind of sympathetic settings which would have made his romantic approach more feasible. Poston tarnishes many of the tunes, and his replacement, Pollack, is even worse; even Earl Hines, who plays on 18 tracks, can provide only flashes of inspiration.

All the same, it's honest music and Noone points forward, albeit distantly, to some of the quieter jazz of a later age.

JABBO SMITH

Born Cladys Smith, 24 December 1908, Pembroke, Georgia; died 16 January 1991, New York City
Trumpet

Jabbo Smith 1929-1938

Classics 669
Smith; Omer Simeon, Willard Brown (cl, as); Leslie Johnakins, Ben Smith (as); Sam Simmons (ts); Millard Robins (bsx); Cassino Simpson, Kenneth Anderson, Alex Hill, William Barbee, James Reynolds (p); Ikey Robinson (bj); Connie Wainwright (g); Hayes Alvis, Lawson Buford (tba); Elmer James (b); Alfred Taylor (d). January 1929-February 1938.

Trumpeter Freddie Hubbard said (1982): **'You keep hearing about what's new in jazz, what's "revolutionary" and so on. A while back I heard a cat out of Milwaukee: old recordings from the 1920s but, I swear, he sounded like Fats Navarro, and bebop wasn't meant to begin for another fifteen-some years. So either he was ahead of it all or there really is nothing new.'**

Smith may have cut a dashing figure in late-'20s Chicago but he was cut down to size by drink and a poor attendance record and pretty much retired to Milwaukee. By 1940, he was barely visible, subsequently taking jobs outside music. He came back in the '60s and '70s and was in *One Mo' Time* on Broadway in New York in the '80s, reformed and intact, though understandably not the player he had been.

Until his rediscovery he was legendary as Armstrong's most significant rival – that was the basis on which Brunswick signed him – in the '20s, a dashing reputation that was won and lost before he reached his mid-20s. Like Pops, he'd learned to play in an orphanage. He had already made a name for himself with Charlie Johnson's orchestra, but it was the 20 sides he cut with his Rhythm Aces that have endured as Smith's contribution to jazz.

This Classics CD includes all of them, together with four tracks from a single 1938 session by Smith's then eight-strong group. Smith's style is like a thinner, wilder variation on Armstrong's. He takes even more risks in his solos – or, at least, makes it seem that way, since he's less assured at pulling them off than Louis was. Some passages he seems to play entirely in his highest register; others are composed of handfuls of notes, phrased in such a scattershot way that he seems to have snatched them out of the air. If it makes the music something of a mess, it's a consistently exciting one. Organized round Smith's own stop-time solos and dialogue with the rhythm, with the occasional vocal – a quizzical mix of Armstrong and Don Redman – thrown in too, the records seem like a conscious attempt at duplicating the Hot Five sessions, although in the event they sold poorly. Simeon is curiously reticent, much as Dodds was on the Hot Fives, and alto-players Brown and Smith do no more than behave themselves. The livewire foil is, instead, the extraordinary Robinson, whose tireless strumming and rare, knockout solo (as on 'Michigander Blues') keep everything simmering. Shrill and half-focused, these are still lively and brilliant reminders of a poorly documented talent.

BENNIE MOTEN
Born 13 November 1894, Kansas City, Missouri; died 2 April 1935, Kansas City, Missouri
Piano, bandleader

Band Box Shuffle 1929–1932
Hep 1070/2 2CD
Moten; Ed Lewis, Hot Lips Page, Joe Keyes, Dee Stewart, Paul Webster, Booker Washington (c); Thamon Haye, Dan Minor (tb, v); Eddie Durham (tb, g); Woody Walder, Eddie Barefield, Ben Webster (reeds); Harlan Leonard (cl, ss, as); Woody Walder (cl, ts); Jack Washington (cl, as, bs); LaForest Dent (as, bs, bj); Buster Moten (p, acc); Count Basie (p); Leroy Berry (bj, g); Vernon Page (tba); Willie McWashington (d); James Taylor, Bob Clemmons, Jimmy Rushing (v). 1929–1932.

Pianist Mary Lou Williams said (1976): **'Kansas City in those days, *everyone* played music and with everyone else. You'd see guys who didn't have a ride walking over from the Kansas side with a double bass on their back, just to play in a jam, and then walk back home again, and do it all over again the next night.'**

Moten was bandleading in Kansas City by 1920 and he built the most powerful outfit in the region for a decade. Moten's band progressed rather slowly, handicapped by an absence of both truly outstanding soloists and an arranger of real talent. The surprisingly static personnel did the best they could with the material, but most of the tunes work from a heavy off-beat. Walder has barely improved, and the arrival of Bennie's brother, Buster, with his dreaded piano-accordion, was enough to root the band in novelty status. There are some excellent moments – in such as 'The New Tulsa Blues' or 'Kansas City Breakdown' – but sugary saxes and pedestrian charts spoil many promising moments. Matters take an immediate upward turn with the joint arrival of Basie and Durham in 1929. 'Jones Law Blues', 'Band Box Shuffle' and 'Small Black' all show the band with fresh ideas under Basie's inspirational leadership (and soloing – here with his Earl Hines influence still intact). 'Sweetheart Of Yesterday' even softens the two-beat rhythm.

Under Basie's effective leadership, the Moten orchestra finally took wing, and its final sessions were memorable. There were still problems, such as the presence of Buster Moten, the reliance on a tuba prior to the arrival of Page, and a general feeling of transition between old and new; but, by the magnificent session of December 1932, when the band created at least four masterpieces in 'Toby', 'Prince Of Wails', 'Milenberg Joys' and 'Moten Swing', it was a unit that could have taken on the best of American bands. Page, Rushing, Webster,

Durham and especially Basie himself all have key solo and ensemble roles, and the sound of the band on 'Prince Of Wails' and 'Toby' is pile-driving. Ironically, this modernism cost Moten much of his local audience, which he was only recovering at the time of his death in 1935.

LUIS RUSSELL

Born 6 August 1902, Careening Clay, Panama; died 11 December 1963, New York City
Bandleader, piano

The Luis Russell Story

Retrieval RTR 79023 2CD

Russell; Louis Metcalf, Henry 'Red' Allen, Bill Coleman, Otis Johnson, George Mitchell, Leonard Davis, Gus Aiken (t); Bob Shoffner (c); Kid Ory, J. C. Higginbotham, Vic Dickenson, Preston Jackson, Dicky Wells, Nathaniel Story, Jimmy Archey (tb); Albert Nicholas (cl, ss, as); Charlie Holmes (ss, as); Darnell Howard, Henry Jones (cl, as); Bingie Madison (cl, ts); Barney Bigard, Teddy Hill, Greely Walton (ts); Will Johnson (g, bj); Lee Blair (g); Johnny St Cyr (bj); Bass Moore (tba); George 'Pops' Foster (b); Paul Barbarin (d); Walter Pichon, Sonny Woods, Chick Bullock, Palmer Brothers (v). January 1929–August 1934.

Drummer Roy Haynes worked with Russell from 1945. He said (2005): **'Russell was a great piano-player and a great leader. He ran things, but he let you express yourself and they said after I left to go with Lester Young that I changed the sound of that band. We used to play the Savoy Ballroom, the "Home of Happy Feet". The place just jumped.'**

Russell worked in New Orleans in the early '20s, but the break came as resident bandleader at the Saratoga Club in New York in 1928. Between 1935 and 1940, when it was sacked, the group was with Louis Armstrong full-time. At the time of his death he was driving cars and teaching piano.

He led one of the great orchestras of its period, having originally put it together in New Orleans in 1927, with such young local stars as Allen, Nicholas and Barbarin in attendance. Their 18 essential sides from seven remarkable sessions in New York are available on this Retrieval CD, and are also to be found, along with some useful small-group sessions – with a Mortonesque sound – from 1926 on Classics. By the time of the first recordings, the band had secured a prime Harlem residency at the Saratoga Club. This was a sophisticated outfit, first because of its soloists – with Higginbotham dominating the earlier sides and Allen, Nicholas and Holmes adding their own variations to the later ones – and second because of its increasing stature as an ensemble. 'Louisiana Swing', 'High Tension', 'Panama' and 'Case On Dawn' all show the orchestra swinging through the more advanced new ideas of counterpoint and unison variation while still offering chances for Allen and the others to shine as soloists.

HENRY 'RED' ALLEN

Born 7 January 1908, New Orleans, Louisiana; died 17 April 1967, New York City
Trumpet, voice

Henry 'Red' Allen & His Orchestra 1929–1933

Classics 540

Allen; Otis Johnson (t); J. C. Higginbotham, Jimmy Archey, Dicky Wells, Benny Morton (tb); Charlie Holmes (cl, ss, as); Russell Procope, Edward Inge, Albert Nicholas, William Blue (cl, as); Hilton Jefferson (as); Teddy Hill (cl, ts); Coleman Hawkins, Greely Walton (ts); Luis Russell (p, cel); Don Kirkpatrick, Horace Henderson (p); Will Johnson (bj, g, v); Bernard Addison (g); Bob Ysaguirre, George 'Pops' Foster (bb, b); Ernest 'Bass' Hill (bb); Walter Johnson, Manzie Johnson, Paul Barbarin (d); Victoria Spivey, The Four Wanderers (v). July 1929–November 1933.

Trumpeter Digby Fairweather says: **'His early recordings might once have been (mistakenly) dismissed as a good working alternative to Louis Armstrong, but his unique style – full of smears, whispers, aggravated grumbles and shouting declamations – remains one of the miracles of jazz trumpet.'**

Once described as 'the last great trumpet soloist to come out of New Orleans', but that, of course, was before Wynton Marsalis came along, 'Red' Allen – so called because he flushed while playing high-note solos – was certainly the last Crescent City native to make a mark in the '20s, recording his astonishing debut sessions for Victor in the summer of 1929. 'It Should Be You', 'Biff'ly Blues', 'Feeling Drowsy' and 'Swing Out' are magnificently conceived and executed, with the whole band (by day the Luis Russell Orchestra) playing with outstanding power and finesse, while Allen's own improvisations outplay anyone aside from Armstrong.

Though sometimes unfocused, the ideas run together with few seams showing and the controlled strength of his solo on 'Feeling Drowsy' is as impressive as the more daring flights on 'Swing Out'. The beautifully sustained solo on 'Make A Country Bird Fly Wild' works through a tricky stop-time passage with some of Pops's rhythmic risk and nobility of tone but with less predictability and less reliance on telegraphed high notes. Higginbotham is wonderfully characterful, agile but snarlingly expressive, and the vastly underrated Holmes matches the young Johnny Hodges for hard-hitting lyricism. An outstanding band. The CD carries on through the first sessions by the Allen-Hawkins Orchestra. Both were working with Fletcher Henderson and this could have been an explosive combination, but the records were comparatively tame, with pop material and vocals taking up too much space. Classics' sound is never very exciting, but hardly needs modern hi-fi or 20-bit remastering to appreciate the quality of these timeless recordings.

COLEMAN HAWKINS &

Known as 'Bean'; born 21 November 1904, St Joseph, Missouri; died 19 May 1969, New York City
Tenor saxophone

Coleman Hawkins 1929–1934

Classics 587
Hawkins; Henry 'Red' Allen, Jack Purvis (t, v); Russell Smith, Bobby Stark (t); Muggsy Spanier (c); Glenn Miller, J. C. Higginbotham, Claude Jones, Dicky Wells (tb); Russell Procope, Hilton Jefferson, Jimmy Dorsey (cl, as); Pee Wee Russell (cl); Adrian Rollini (bsx); Red McKenzie (comb, v); Frank Froeba, Jack Russin, Horace Henderson, Buck Washington (p); Bernard Addison, Jack Bland, Will Johnson (g); George 'Pops' Foster, Al Morgan, John Kirby (b); Gene Krupa, Charles Kegley, Josh Billings, Walter Johnson (d). November 1929–March 1934.

Jazz biographer John Chilton said (1989): **'Hawkins turned jazz, or more accurately, he turned jazz improvisation into art. He had a deep learning in the popular repertoire, but it was meeting Louis Armstrong in the [Fletcher] Henderson orchestra that allowed him to turn that knowledge into beautifully shaped improvisation.'**

Magnificent, monolithic, saturnine, essentially unrepeatable, Hawkins was the Olivier of the tenor saxophone, its most distinguished tragedian who nevertheless didn't baulk at 'stooping' to commercialism or even comedy when the occasion demanded. The working life of 'Bean' – the nickname came from the shape of his head – spanned four decades and it's worth noting that Hawkins outlived Lester Young, Charlie Parker, Eric Dolphy and John Coltrane, all of whom in some way learned and moved on from his example. His classic solo on 'Body And Soul' remains to this day the template for standards improvisation; his unaccompanied 'Picasso' an early cue for the explorations of younger players (Anthony Braxton, David Murray, Charles Gayle ...).

The first great role-model for all saxophonists began recording in 1922, but compilations of his earlier work usually start with his European sojourn in 1934. This valuable cross-section of the preceding five years shows Hawkins reaching a sudden maturity. He was taking solos with Fletcher Henderson in 1923 and was already recognizably Hawkins, but the big sound and freewheeling rhythmic command weren't really evident until later. By 1929, he was one of the star soloists in the Henderson band – which he remained faithful to for over ten years – and the blazing improvisation on the first track here, 'Hello Lola' by Red McKenzie's Mound City Blue Blowers, indicates the extent of his confidence. But he still sounds tied to the underlying beat, and it isn't until the octet session of September 1933 that Hawkins establishes the gliding but muscular manner of his '30s music. The ensuing Horace Henderson date of October 1933 has a feast of great Hawkins, culminating in the astonishing extended solo on 'I've Got To Sing A Torch Song', with its baleful low honks and daring manipulation of the time. Three final duets with Buck Washington round out the disc, but an earlier session under the leadership of the trumpeter Jack Purvis must also be mentioned: in a curious line-up including Adrian Rollini and J. C. Higginbotham, Hawkins plays a dark, serious role.

& *See also* **Coleman Hawkins 1939–1940** (1939–1940; p. 74), **The Stanley Dance Sessions** (1955–1958; p. 172)

THE '30s

The Wall Street Crash of 1929 had an immediate and deep effect on all aspects of American culture, but arguably not as great an impact as that of a further wave of new technology. The combined result was to shift the emphasis in jazz somewhat – and at this stage only somewhat – away from live performance and towards recording as a key activity. It cannot be over-emphasized enough that for the moment jazz – and swing, which derived from it – were still essentially musics for social dance, but the growing importance of sound film and radio, the latter particularly, meant that there were new outlets for studio-based music. In addition, many clubs and bars replaced a live band with an electric jukebox, creating a market for new recordings.

For the moment, though, the Depression exerted a negative pressure on record sales in America. Those who had confidently predicted that recorded music was a passing fad were comforted by a net market drop of something like 80 per cent in record buying between the Crash and the beginnings of the Roosevelt New Deal, a decline that must at the time have seemed irreversible and terminal.

As ever, though, there were countervailing forces that pointed strongly to a vigorous future revival. The spread of radio through the '30s and the steady amalgamation of the broadcasting and recording companies into large – one would now say corporate – bodies created an industry of considerable power and authority. Though again primarily targeted for speech use, radio proved to be a potent vehicle for new music and one of the innovations of the decade was the use of what are misleadingly called 'transcription' recordings, non-commercial discs manufactured specifically for broadcast purposes and not available to the general public. Creating 'transcriptions' provided concentrated studio work for band musicians who were otherwise squeezed out of work by economic slump and the rise of the jukebox.

There were other associated factors. The outsize transcription disc, many of which functioned in a different way to commercial records, favouring the otherwise abandoned inside-outward reading of the spiral groove, were capable of holding up to a quarter of an hour of recorded music. In addition to practical convenience, this also offered new creative opportunities, that were not for the moment taken up: most obviously the ability to create and document music that exceeded in duration the familiar two- to three-minute span of the usual 78rpm recording. Some artists – most notably Duke Ellington – experimented with longer pieces, but these had to be performed across two sides of a 78 record, with a break in the middle, and this restriction discouraged innovation.

The record companies experimented with new speeds, including 33$\frac{1}{3}$ which later became the norm for long-playing records. (Turntable speeds had varied according to company and system for much of the early history of recording.) Also in the early '30s were the first experiments in stereophonic recording, though for the moment this remained of largely scientific interest, with no direct application to commercial recording.

In stylistic terms, and in keeping with the still definite separation of recorded music into 'race' and mainstream categories, there was a steady eclipse of 'hot' small-group jazz by a smoother sound that reincorporated elements of 'sweet' music, together with a more accessible dance beat. By the end of the decade, and certainly by the time of the famous Benny Goodman Carnegie Hall concert in 1938, the swing style that Jimmie Lunceford's orchestra had pioneered and popularized had become a mass-market phenomenon. For perhaps the only time in the music's history, a jazz form *was* the popular music of its day ...

JIMMIE LUNCEFORD

Born 6 June 1902, Fulton, Mississippi; died 12 July 1947, Seaside, Oregon
Alto saxophone, bandleader

Jimmie Lunceford 1930–1934

Classics 501

Lunceford; Sy Oliver, Eddie Tompkins, Tommy Stevenson, William 'Sleepy' Tomlin (t); Henry Wells (tb, v); Russell Bowles (tb); Willie Smith, Earl Carruthers (cl, as, bs); LaForet Dent (as); Joe Thomas (cl, ts); Edwin Wilcox (p, cel); Al Norris (g); Moses Allen (bb, b); Jimmy Crawford (d, vib). June 1930–November 1934.

Drummer Chico Hamilton said (1993): **'I heard some young guy recently described as a "mega-star". Well, sixty years ago, when it wasn't so easy to get around, Jimmie Lunceford swept this country from coast to coast. He was a professor, a master, and he was known everywhere, with a style that was all its own, this two-beat thing, *ba-boom ba*, with that kick on the bass drum, so it looped right round. He set the whole country dancing ...'**

Lunceford studied music in Denver and at Fisk University and then taught in Manassas. His band scuffled for four years before playing at the Cotton Club and making a big name for a showy, almost vaudeville act, which toured relentlessly. Disillusion set in and the leader, who'd also taken up flying, died of a heart attack in questionable circumstances, possibly poisoned according to one recent biographer. The very fact he passed away in Oregon, though, was a measure of the Lunceford band's continent-spanning celebrity.

Lunceford's orchestra is the great also-ran band of its day. There were no special idiosyncrasies which lifted the Lunceford orchestra away from the consistent excellence to which it aspired. Its principal arrangers – Sy Oliver in particular, but also Edwin Wilcox (in the earlier days) and Willie Smith – created superbly polished, interlocking sections which gave their records a professional élan. Soloists stepped naturally out of and back into this precision machine, and there was never much danger of a Rex Stewart or a Lester Young breaking any rule. Lunceford's virtues were entirely different from those of the rough-and-ready (early) Basie band, or from Ellington's unique cast of characters.

This first set in a comprehensive Classics documentation shows the band coming together; there is a single 1930 session, followed by a jump to 1934. The important hit coupling of 'Jazznocracy' and 'White Heat' is here, as well as the remarkably nonconformist versions of 'Mood Indigo' and 'Sophisticated Lady'; once under way in earnest, Lunceford turned out some fine records. Until a formulaic staleness set in – almost inevitable given the band's relentless touring in less than ideal circumstances: there was a Depression, after all, and America was still a racist country – there was nothing quite to beat the orchestra for sheer excitement. Sitting on top of Lunceford's trademark precision, Smith was a rival to Hodges and Carter as one of the great alto stylists of the day, while Joe Thomas and Eddie Tompkins were excellent half-chorus players (contemporary players wouldn't understand why that was important and would regard it as an insult rather than a term of praise) who compressed enormous experience into just a few bars.

Lunceford's death isn't on most people's list of great American paranoid mysteries, but as a parable of the African-American musical experience, it's worth pondering.

CAB CALLOWAY

Born 25 December 1907, Rochester, New York; died 18 November 1994, Hockessin, Delaware
Voice

The Early Years 1930–1934
JSP CD 908 4CD
Calloway; R. Q. Dickerson, Lamar Wright, Ruben Reeves, Wendell Culley, Edwin Swayzee, Doc Cheatham (t);
De Priest Wheeler, Harry White (tb); Thornton Blue, Arville Harris (cl, as); Eddie Barefield (cl, as, bs); Andrew
Brown (bcl, ts); Walter Thomas (as, ts, bs, f); Earres Prince, Benny Payne (p); Morris White (bj); Roy Smeck (g);
Al Morgan (b); Jimmy Smith (bb, b); Leroy Maxey (d); Chick Bullock (v). July 1930–September 1934.

Cab Calloway said (1976): **'Louis Armstrong enthralled me but he didn't influence me. With
Louis, you listened to the man, not the band. I wanted to make the band swing for me.
That was the main thing, not what I was doing.'**

Cab was the younger brother of Blanche Calloway, who made some excellent recordings
of her own but lacked the kid's staying power. He was a peerless entertainer, who stuck
around long enough to win over a younger, pop-reared generation who liked his surreal
personality, and even made a cameo appearance in *The Blues Brothers*. Some of his routines
are now YouTube hits. He started out training for the law in Baltimore – prompting a surreal
fantasy of a white-suited Cab dancing his summing-up to the jury – but showbiz won out.
He was with the Alabamian And Missourians before he branched out on his own and had a
big hit in 1931 with 'Minnie The Moocher', which in turn sparked off a series of 'Hi-De-Hi,
Hi-De-Ho' routines.

At Calloway's very first session, in July 1930 with an astonishingly virtuosic vocal on 'St
Louis Blues', he served notice that a major jazz singer was ready to challenge Armstrong
with an entirely different style. It didn't take Calloway long to sharpen up the band, even
though he did it with comparatively few changes in personnel. Unlike the already tested
format of a vocal feature within an instrumental record, Calloway's arrangers varied detail
from record to record, Cab appearing throughout some discs, briefly on others, and usually finding space for a fine team of soloists. Some records are eventful to an extraordinary
extent: listen, for instance, to the dazzling 1930 'Some Of These Days'. The lexicon of reef-
ers, Minnie the Moocher and Smokey Joe, kicking gongs around, and the whole fabulous
language of hi-de-ho would soon have become tiresome if it hadn't been for the leader's
boundless energy and ingenious invention: his vast range, from a convincing bass to a
shrieking falsetto, has remained unsurpassed by any male singer and he transforms the
emptiest material.

Long residency at the Cotton Club, and good pay and conditions, meant that the personnel remained fixed, and the band made a colossal number of records. There are dead spots,
but most of them are still listenable today, and Calloway's status as a proto-rock-and-roller,
a generation earlier than Louis Jordan, remains unchallenged.

JOE VENUTI
*Born Giuseppe Venuti, 16 September 1903, Philadelphia, Pennsylvania; died 14 August 1978, Seattle,
Washington*
Violin

Joe Venuti 1930–1933
Classics 1276
Venuti; Charlie Teagarden, Manny Klein, Ray Lodwig (t); Jack Teagarden (tb, v); Tommy Dorsey (tb); Pete
Pumiglio (cl, bs); Jimmy Dorsey (cl, as, bs, t); Arnold Brilhart (as); Bud Freeman (ts); Adrian Rollini (bsx, gfs,
p, vib); Frank Signorelli, Lennie Hayton, Irving Brodsky, Phil Wall (p); Eddie Lang, Dick McDonough (g); Joe
Tarto, Ward Lay (b); Paul Graselli, Neil Marshall (d); Harold Arlen, Hoagy Carmichael, Smith Ballew (v). October
1930–May 1933.

All bass-players know this story: **'A New York musician got a call one day that a bassist
was needed for a gig downtown. He turned up at the appointed time, early on a freezing**

morning. Five minutes later, another bassist arrived, and then another, until there were thirty of them. The men shuffled about for a time, smoked and stamped to keep warm. Then the penny dropped. "Hang on", said one of them, "did Joe Venuti call you as well?"'

A legendary practical joker, Joe claimed to have been born on an emigrant ship in mid-Atlantic. He befriended Eddie Lang as a boy and they worked together on the New York dance band and small-group jazz recording scene. Joe formed his own band in the '30s, then returned from war service to feature regularly on radio. He made a comeback in the later '60s, but he was essentially a pre-war man.

Venuti wasn't the only violinist to play jazz in the '20s, but he established the style for the instrument as surely as Coleman Hawkins did for the saxophone. He was a key figure on the New York session scene of the era and appears on many dance band records alongside Beiderbecke, Trumbauer and the Dorseys; but his most important association was with Eddie Lang, and although their partnership was curtailed by Lang's death in 1933, it was a pairing which has endured like few other jazz double-acts. Their best work was packed into a relatively short period and it includes some of the most entertaining jazz of its day, quirky and wry. This 1930–1933 Classics volume covers sessions for Victor, OKeh, Columbia and Vocalion. Besides the strange feat of having two of the greatest American songwriters as featured vocalists, there's a greater emphasis on small groups here, and there are at least two classic dates: the magnificent tracks by the Lang-Venuti All Stars from October 1931, and the February 1933 session where Jimmy Dorsey played trumpet – and where Lang and Venuti played together for the last time.

& *See also* **EDDIE LANG, The Quintessential Eddie Lang 1925–1932** (1925–1932; p. 23)

CASA LOMA ORCHESTRA
Formed 1927, as Casa Loma 1929
Ensemble

Casa Loma Stomp / Maniac's Ball
Hep 1010 / 1051
Bobby Jones, Dub Shoffner, Joe Hostetter, Frankie Martinez, Grady Watts, Sonny Dunham, Frank Zullo (t); Pee Wee Hunt (tb, v); Fritz Hummel, Billy Rausch (tb); Glen Gray (as); Clarence Hutchenrider (cl, as); Pat Davis (as, ts); Art Ralston (as, ob, bsn); Les Arquette (cl, ts); Ray Eberle (as, cl); Kenny Sargent (as, v); Howard Hall (p); Mel Jenssen (vn); Jack Blanchette (g); Gene Gifford (g, bj); Stanley Dennis (b, tba); Tony Briglia (d); Jack Richmond (v). October 1929–December 1930, March 1931–February 1937.

Saxophonist Benny Carter said (1992): **'Casa Loma survived by giving the people what they wanted. It was a careful band, everything carefully rehearsed, nothing left to chance.'**

Formed by Glen Gray out of the Orange Blossoms – themselves an offshoot of the Jean Gold-kette orchestra – when that touring group was stranded at the Casa Loma Hotel in Toronto in the year of the Wall Street Crash, Casa Loma have a strange place in the music's history. The early stuff is competent dance band fare, although something peculiar happens halfway through a very stodgy 'Happy Days Are Here Again' (on the first disc, which is here really for reference rather than musical quality), when it suddenly bursts into a hot performance fired by Hunt's trombone. Similarly, 'San Sue Strut' seems to be twice as fast as anything else here and the title-track is a fair display of early white swing. It's the second CD which has all the famous Casa Loma music: Gifford's charts for 'White Jazz', 'Black Jazz' and 'Maniac's Ball' have the orchestra as a precision-driven locomotive, riffs piling on one another, tempos mercurial if uncomfortably stiff. Aside from Hunt, a genuine personality, the soloists lacked much individuality and the reed-players seem especially unremarkable, but Rausch's 'Smoke Rings' became a signature piece, and Hutchenrider was capable of some interesting statements. The assault on 'Put On Your Old Grey Bonnet' is exhilarating, but by the second version of 'Royal Garden Blues' the band sounds anonymous. Larry Clinton took over from Gifford and his 'A Study In Brown' is the farewell track here: it led nowhere. Scholars will welcome these handsome compilations.

DON REDMAN

Born 29 July 1900, Piedmont, West Virginia; died 30 November 1964, New York City
Alto and soprano saxophones, piano, celeste, vibes

Shakin' The Africann

Hep CD 1001
Redman; Henry 'Red' Allen, Shirley Clay, Bill Coleman, Langston Curl, Reunald Jones, Sidney De Paris (t); Claude Jones, Benny Morton, Fred Robinson, Gene Simon (tb); Jerry Blake (cl, as, bs); Robert Cole, Edward Inge (cl, as); Harvey Boone (as, bs); Robert Carroll (ts); Horace Henderson, Don Kirkpatrick (p); Talcott Reeves (bj, g); Bob Ysaguirre (bb, b); Manzie Johnson (d, vib); Chick Bullock, Cab Calloway, Harlan Lattimore, The Mills Brothers (v); Bill Robinson (tap-dancing). September 1931–December 1932.

Saxophonist Dewey Redman said (1999): **'I can't prove it, but I think he was my cousin, distant cousin. Little guy, played alto saxophone and conducted with his left hand – that tickled me.'**

Redman remains one of the essential figures of the pre-war jazz period and his band's strange theme tune, 'Chant Of The Weed', one of the age's most memorable. He started out as lead saxophonist and staff arranger with Fletcher Henderson's band (though he often didn't receive credit), infusing the charts with a breathtaking simplicity and confidence, eventually leaving in 1928 to front the highly successful McKinney's Cotton Pickers. This was his most celebrated music, but some of the music under his own leadership in the '30s surpassed his earlier charts, even if the recordings are inconsistent. *Shakin' The Africann* (sic) is a good sampling of Redman's activities just after leaving McKinney's Cotton Pickers. There are fine versions of the bizarre 'Chant Of The Weed', which deserves to be considered on its considerable musical daring as well as for its celebration of the jazzman's favourite relaxant, together with originals like 'Hot And Anxious' and 'Trouble, Why Pick On Me'. The set ends with two versions of 'Doin' The New Low Down' with tap-dancing from Bojangles Robinson and on the other version a slightly crazed vocal from Cab Calloway, as if there were any other kind. There are good Redman compilations around, in decent sound, but this is the set of choice: a fine band at its zenith, playing intelligent charts with improvisatory flair. Even before the 'Swing Era' was officially born, Redman's bands held the seeds of bebop.

ART TATUM &

Born 13 October 1909, Toledo, Ohio; died 5 November 1956, Los Angeles, California
Piano

Art Tatum 1932–1934

Classics 507
Tatum (p solo). 1932, March 1933–October 1934.

Buddy DeFranco said (1991): **'Art Tatum is the first modern jazz performer ... on any instrument.'**

Almost blind from birth, Tatum travelled widely in the '30s, recording as a soloist and accompanist until he formed a trio in 1943. A master of every kind of jazz piano style, he nevertheless was not interested in composing himself and preferred to work infinitesimal variations on standard material. He fell victim to uraemia, at just 45. The scale of Tatum's achievements makes approaching him a daunting proposition even now. His very first session, cut in New York in 1933, must have astonished every piano-player who heard any of the four tracks. 'Tiger Rag', for instance, becomes transformed from a rather old-fashioned hot novelty tune into a furious series of variations, thrown off with abandon but as closely argued and formally precise as any rag or stomp at one-quarter of the tempo. If Tatum had only recorded these and nothing more, he would be assured of immortality; yet, like Morton's early solos, they are both achievements in their own right and sketchbooks for the great works of his later years.

& See also **Complete Pablo Solo/Group Masterpieces** (1953–1955; p. 147)

NAT GONELLA
Born 7 March 1908, London; died 8 August 1998, Gosport, Hampshire, England
Trumpet

Nat Gonella And His Georgians
Flapper PAST CD 9750
Gonella; Bruts Gonella, Johnny Morrison, Chas Oughton, Jack Wallace (t); Miff King (tb); Jack Bonser, Jock Middleton, Joe Moore, Ernest Morris, Mickey Seidman, Albert Torrance (cl, as, bs); Pat Smuts, Don Barigo (ts); Harold Hood, Monia Liter, Norman Stenfalt (p); Roy Dexter, Jimmy Mesene (g); Will Hemmings (b); Bob Dryden, Johnny Roland (d). January 1935–October 1940.

Humphrey Lyttelton said (1990): **'Nat was one of my heroes, perhaps because he was English, one of us, and if one Englishman could play like Louis Armstrong, well ... Funny thing is, I didn't meet him until he was nearly 90 and near the end.'**

Nat's Georgians – in which brother Bruts played Joe Oliver to his Pops – was one of the most successful British hot bands of the pre-war years. There have been various 'Georgian' revivals (the title was taken from his big hit, 'Georgia On My Mind') since that time and in the '80s Nat was still singing, though no longer playing his horn. The Armstrong influence is so overt as to be unarguable, and yet Gonella brought something of his own as well, a wry, philosophical shrug as he threw off neat aphoristic solos with the biting tone and earthy humour his fans loved. This Flapper disc is a very good selection of early material. Nat spent a little time in America at the end of the decade, and its influence can be heard in the bluesier and more relaxedly rhythmic swing of the later cuts. The New Georgians stuff from 1940 is – heretical though it may be – superior to the original band's output. There's a novelty edge to many of the tracks, but Nat's vocal on 'The Flat Foot Floogie' and even 'Ol' Man River' is never less than musical and in the latter case quite moving. A bit of an institution, who will be fondly remembered by anyone over the age of 60 and who may prove mystifying to anyone under.

CHICK WEBB
Born William Henry Webb, 10 February 1909, Baltimore, Maryland; died 16 June 1939, Baltimore, Maryland
Drums

Rhythm Man / Strictly Jive

Hep CD 1023 / 1063

Webb; Ward Pinkett, Louis Bacon, Taft Jordan (t, v); Edwin Swayzee, Mario Bauza, Reunald Jones, Bobby Stark, Shelton Hemphill, Louis Hunt, Nat Story, George Matthews, Irving Randolph (t); Robert Horton, Jimmy Harrison, Sandy Williams, Ferdinand Arbello, Claude Jones, George Mathews (tb); Garvin Bushell, Hilton Jefferson, Benny Carter, Chauncey Houghton (cl, as); Louis Jordan (cl, as, v); Eddie Barefield, Pete Clark, Edgar Sampson (as); Elmer Williams (cl, ts); Wayman Carver (ts, f); Ted McRae, Sam Simmons, Elmer Williams (ts); Tommy Fulford, Don Kirkpatrick, Joe Steele (p); John Trueheart (bj, g); Bobby Johnson (g); Elmer James (bb, b); John Kirby, Beverley Peer, Bill Thomas (b); Bill Beason (d); Ella Fitzgerald, Chuck Richards, Charles Linton (v); collective personnel. March 1931–November 1934; June 1935–March 1940.

Mick Carlon is the author of *Riding on Duke's Train*: **'Step aside, Baby and Zutty: Here comes the future. With his pain-wracked spine and billion-watt smile, Chick Webb showed the thirties how to swing. Courage never sounded so danceable.'**

No recording does justice to the artistry of Chick Webb, who has some claim on the title of founder of the Swing Era. This tiny man was already an experienced bandleader when he took over the Savoy Ballroom in 1933, hiring Ella Fitzgerald two years later. He'd come to New York from his native Baltimore as a teenager and quickly made a reputation as a highly intelligent musician (though he never learned to read a score) and as a showman. Webb radically simplified some earlier elements of jazz drumming, minimizing the use of double-time passages and restricting his solo breaks to short but immaculately constructed fills. But he also knew the value of spectacle, playing a large kit that had been adapted to suit his physical infirmities – Webb suffered from congenital tuberculosis of the spine, and it killed him before he was 40 – and placed on a large riser in the middle of the band.

A Classics compilation goes back rather earlier than this nicely mastered set, and the two tracks included there by the 1929 Jungle Band are useful points of comparison for any-one not persuaded by Webb's later sophistication; they're crude and backward-looking. By 1931, Webb was running a great band. A fine session from that year includes a memorable arrangement by Benny Carter of his own 'Blues In My Heart' and a valedictory appearance by Jimmy Harrison, who died not long afterwards. Edgar Sampson handled the best of the earlier arrangements, and though the band didn't harbour a great future soloist of the magnitude of a Webster or Young (Ella tends to be the one alumna cited), Webb could boast fine soloists in Taft Jordan (later to join Ellington), Sandy Williams, Bobby Stark, Wayman Carver (who made a little history by getting his flute out) and Elmer Williams, as well as a rhythm section that was almost unrivalled for attack and swing. Webb's mastery of his enormous kit (a challenge for recording engineers of the day) allowed him to pack a whole range of percussive effects into breaks and solos which never upset the momentum of the band. His distance from the showmanship of Gene Krupa, who would far surpass him in acclaim, was complete. Buddy Rich, by contrast, was a devotee of Webb's and learned a lot of stagecraft listening to his music.

Listening to these two fine compilations in order gives a strong sense of a band steadily coming into its creative own. So headlong is the chronology and the procession of great swing numbers that the second set spills past the point of Chick's painfully early death. The best material on the first disc includes the fine 'Blue Minor', a feature for Sampson, while the second hits a peak with the terrific drive of 'Go Harlem' and the breaks in 'Clap Hands! Here Comes Charley'. Once Fitzgerald started singing with the band and began to secure a wider fame, though, some of the zip went out of their playing. In its heyday, though, there wasn't much to touch it.

JACK TEAGARDEN

Born Weldon Leo Teagarden, 20 August 1905, Vernon, Texas; died 15 January 1964, New Orleans, Louisiana
Trombone, voice

I Gotta Right To Sing The Blues
ASV AJA 5059

Teagarden; Leonard Davis, Red Nichols, Ray Lodwig, Manny Klein, Charlie Teagarden, Ruby Weinstein, Sterling Bose, Dave Klein, Harry Goldfield, Nat Natoli, Frank Guarente, Leo McConville, Charlie Spivak (t); Jack Fulton, Glenn Miller, Ralph Copsey, Bill Rank (tb); Benny Goodman (cl); Mezz Mezzrow, Arthur Rollini, Charles Strickfadden, Benny Bonaccio, John Cordaro, Chester Hazlett, Jimmy Dorsey, Art Karle, Eddie Miller, Matty Matlock, Joe Catalyne, Pee Wee Russell, Max Farley, Happy Caldwell, Arnold Brilhart, Bernie Day, Sid Stoneburn, Babe Russin, Larry Binyon, Gil Rodin, Irving Friedman, Adrian Rollini, Min Leibrook (reeds); Red McKenzie (kz, v); Fats Waller (p, v); Joe Sullivan, Jack Russin, Lennie Hayton, Arthur Schutt, Gil Bowers, Joe Moresco, Roy Bargy, Vincent Pirro, Howard Smith (p); Joe Venuti, Matty Malneck, Mischa Russell, Harry Struble, Walt Edelstein, Alex Beller, Ray Cohen (vn); Carl Kress, Jack Bland, Nappy Lamare, Eddie Lang, Dick McDonough, Perry Botkin, Mike Pingitore, George Van Eps (g); Treg Brown (bj, v); Eddie Condon (bj); Artie Bernstein, Art Miller, Jerry Johnson, Harry Goodman, Al Morgan (b); Norman McPherson (tba); Ray Bauduc, George Stafford, Herb Quigley, Stan King, Gene Krupa, Josh Billings, Larry Gomar (d). February 1929–October 1934.

Trombonist and singer Eric Felten says: **'When I hear Big T, I hear my grandfather playing: that gorgeous, rich trombone sound and those wonderful fillips and embellishments. Those beautiful swing era ornamentations would be banished by the Bauhaus austerity of bebop, but they graced the unpretentious, aching and honest way Teagarden sang and played the blues. Growing up in thrall to the modernists, I didn't listen to enough Teagarden, but I was lucky to have in my grandfather a teacher who was steeped in that Texas Tea. Like my grandfather, Teagarden was a farm boy who had a natural dignity as a man, and who wouldn't think of going out without a tie.'**

'Tea' took the trombone to new levels, with his impeccable technique, fluency and gorgeous sound, allied to a feel for blues playing which eluded many of his white contemporaries. He was also a fine, idiosyncratic singer. He was with Ben Pollack for five years from 1928 and with Paul Whiteman in the '30s, and finally led his own swing orchestra, though it left him broke in the end. He joined the Armstrong All Stars in 1946, stayed till 1951, then toured for the rest of a life increasingly wedded to alcohol.

Teagarden's star is somehow in decline, since all his greatest work predates the LP era and at this distance it's difficult to hear how completely he changed the role of the trombone. In Tea's hands, this awkward barnyard instrument became majestic, sonorous and handsome. By the time he began recording in 1926 he was already a mature and easeful player whose feel for blues and nonchalant rhythmic drive made him stand out on the dance band records he was making.

This compilation features 12 different bands and 18 tracks, which points up how easily Teagarden could make himself at home in bands of the period. One celebrated example is the treatment meted out to a waltz called 'Dancing With Tears In My Eyes', under Joe Venuti's leadership: Teagarden contravenes everything to do with the material and charges through his solo. Two early sessions under his own name have him trading retorts with Fats Waller on 'You Rascal You' and delivering his original reading of what became a greatest hit, 'A Hundred Years From Today'. Stricter jazz material such as two tracks by The Charleston Chasers is fine, but no less enjoyable are such as Ben Pollack's 'Two Tickets To Georgia', where Teagarden's swinging outburst suggests that he treated every setting as a chance to blow.

MILLS BLUE RHYTHM BAND

Formed 1930; disbanded 1938
Big band

Blue Rhythm

Hep CD 1008
Wardell Jones, Shelton Hemphill, Ed Anderson (t); Harry White, Henry Hicks (tb); Crawford Wethington (cl, as, bs); Charlie Holmes (cl, as); Ted McCord, Castor McCord (cl, ts); Edgar Hayes (p); Benny James (bj, g); Hayes Alvis (bb, b); Willie Lynch (d); Dick Robertson, Chick Bullock, George Morton (v). January–June 1931.

Jazz historian Bob Turner says: **'The family trees and lineages of these early bands are a lifetime's study. It's wonderful to see future stars in their early years, but it's almost more satisfying to find a group whose members have mostly just disappeared back into the anonymous mass of working stiffs.'**

Although it lacked any solo stars in its early years, the Mills Blue Rhythm Band was a very hot outfit when this record was made, even though it was originally used by its boss, Irving Mills, as a substitute band for either Ellington or Calloway. The lack of a regular front-man and a rag-tag sequence of arrangers prevented the band from ever establishing a very clear identity, but it still mustered a kind of fighting collectivism which comes through clearly on its best records. Cover versions of Ellington ('Black And Tan Fantasy') and Calloway ('Minnie The Moocher') reveal what the band's purpose was to start with, and the most interesting thing about the earlier tracks is usually the soloists' role, particularly the impassioned and badly undervalued trumpeter, Ed Anderson. John R. T. Davies remasters with his usual care and attentiveness.

BENNY CARTER&

Born 8 August 1907, New York City; died 12 July 2003, Los Angeles, California
Alto saxophone, trumpet, clarinet, voice

Benny Carter 1933–1936

Classics 530
Carter; Henry 'Red' Allen (t, v); Dick Clark, Leonard Davis, Bill Dillard, Max Goldberg, Otis Johnson, Max Kaminsky, Eddie Mallory, Tommy McQuater, Irving Randolph, Howard Scott, Russell Smith, Duncan Whyte (t); Ted Heath, Keg Johnson, Benny Morton, Bill Mulraney, Floyd O'Brien, Wilbur De Paris, Fred Robinson, George Washington, Dicky Wells (tb); Howard Johnson, Andy McDevitt (cl, as); Wayman Carver (cl, as, f); Glyn Pacque, E. O. Pogson, Russell Procope, Ben Smith (as); Coleman Hawkins (cl, ts); Chu Berry, Buddy Featherstonehaugh, Johnny Russell, Ben Webster (ts); Pat Dodd, Red Rodriguez, Teddy Wilson (p); George Elliott, Clarence Holiday, Lawrence Lucie (g); Al Burke, Ernest 'Bass' Hill, Elmer James (b); Big Sid Catlett, Ronnie Gubertini, Walter Johnson (d); Charles Holland (v). May 1933–April 1936.

Scottish trumpeter Tommy McQuater, who worked with Carter in London, said (1991): **'He was a gent, but he was also a taskmaster, who knew exactly what he wanted and wouldn't let you go till he got it. His charts were always immaculate, and being a trumpet-player who also played saxophone, he knew his way around the sections.'**

The distinguished gentleman of jazz, a dapper saxophonist, excellent trumpeter (which he kept playing surprisingly late) and an arranger with few peers, Carter was a last link to a jazz age now gone. He kept playing at the highest level until his last few years. By 1928, barely out of his teens, Benny was already arranging for various New York bands, and leading his own groups. In 1936, he was staff arranger for the BBC Dance Orchestra in London.

Back in the USA, he led his own big band, 1939–41, but cut back to a sextet before moving to Hollywood in 1945, where he wrote for film and TV, while continuing to make jazz records.

Carter's charts, like his playing, are characteristically open-textured and softly bouncing, but seldom lightweight; though he had a particular feel for the saxophone section, and he pioneered a more modern approach to big-band reeds, his gifts extend throughout the orchestra. As a soloist, he developed in a direction rather different from that of Johnny Hodges. In the early '30s his band was known as a proving ground for young talent, and the number of subsequently eminent names appearing in Carter sections increases as the decade advances. The London period under Henry Hall at the BBC saw some excellent recording with the local talent. There is little tension in a Carter solo, which is presented bright and fresh like a polished apple, and his seemingly effortless approach is rather hard to square with the values inherent in bebop.

& See also **Further Definitions** (1961–1966; p. 280)

THE SPIRITS OF RHYTHM
Formed late '20s
Group

The Spirits Of Rhythm 1933–1945
Classics 1028
Leonard Feather (p); Teddy Bunn, Ulysses Livingston (g); Leo Watson, Wilbur Daniels, Douglas Daniels (tiple, v); Wilson Myers, Wellman Braud, Red Callender (b); Virgil Scoggins, Georgie Vann (d, v); Red McKenzie, Ella Logan (v). October 1933–January 1945.

Avant-garde guitarist Derek Bailey rarely commented on his influences, but: **'I had an uncle who really liked Teddy Bunn, so I think he was quite important, early on.'**

Nonsense singing, rhythmic chases, a unique group sound defined by the Daniels brothers' use of the tiple (a kind of small Latin American guitar with variable tuning): there's not much to dislike about the Spirits Of Rhythm. Originally the Sepia Nephews and subsequently Ben Bernie's Nephews and the Five Cousins, the group was expanded in 1932 by the arrival of Teddy Bunn (who gives the Spirits the group's largest claim on jazz cachet) and later by Virgil Scoggins. It also acted as a support group to novelty vocalist Red McKenzie, so to some extent the Spirits was a concept rather than a distinct act, a throwback to the old pre-jazz string bands but also a foretaste of the sharp hipster groups that came up around bebop. Along with the very different Eddie Lang, Bunn was one of the undoubted giants of jazz guitar before Charlie Christian and Wes Montgomery revolutionized the instrument, ironically often smoothing out the very features which made it different from the horns and piano.

The Spirits were essentially a singing group. Watson and the two Daniels boys sang jovial scat lines, accompanying themselves on tiples, while Bunn kept up a solid but everchanging background. The sound is light and delicate, an almost harp-like backing for voices. Like Freddy Guy, for whom he once depped in the Ellington band, and Freddie Green, who did a similar job for Basie, Bunn understood the workings of a group instinctively and, despite being wholly self-taught, had the uncanny ability to anticipate even non-standard changes.

This Classics set contains the group's entire output. There are two versions of 'I Got Rhythm', both of them featuring Bunn quite strongly; but the outstanding track is 'I'll Be Ready', on which he plays crisp melodic breaks without a single excess gesture. Watson's full-on madness was better displayed elsewhere, but he has his moments here (one bizarre piece from 1934, 'Dr Watson And Mr Holmes'). There are three titles with the 'Swingin' Scots Lassie' Ella Logan (Annie Ross's aunt!) and a final date from 1945, where Bunn is the only survivor from the original line-up. It's not profound music, but if it doesn't make you smile, check for a pulse.

WINGY MANONE

Born Joseph Matthews Manone,13 February 1900, New Orleans, Louisiana; died 9 July 1982, Las Vegas, Nevada
Trumpet

Wingy Manone 1934–1935

Classics 798
Manone; George Brunies, Santo Pecora, Dicky Wells (tb); Matty Matlock, Sidney Arodin (cl); Eddie Miller, Bud Freeman (ts); Gil Bowers, Jelly Roll Morton, Teddy Wilson, Terry Shand (p); Nappy Lamare (g, v); Frank Victor (g); Harry Goodman, John Kirby, Benny Pottle (b); Ray Bauduc, Bob White, Kaiser Marshall (d). May 1934–May 1935.

Trumpeter Yank Lawson said (1985): **'Wingy was a buddy of Bing Crosby's and Bing used to send him a single cufflink every Christmas.'**
  Another version of the story was that the joker was violinist Joe Venuti, a notorious prankster: **'Wingy was a wild fellow; I remember him standing at a street corner blowing marijuana smoke in a policeman's face.'**

Wingy was much in thrall to Louis Armstrong as both trumpeter and vocalist, but he brought something of himself to the music as well, and his playing has a playful, dangerous edge. He lost his arm in a streetcar accident, but made do with a prosthetic arm; besides, trumpet is the only instrument that can be played, quite naturally, one-handed. He established himself in Chicago around 1930 and started leading his own bands a few years later.
  The first small groups, on the *1927–1934* volume of the Classics series, offer glimpses of precocious youngsters such as Freeman, Goodman and Krupa, yet stumble on the scrappy recording quality, off-the-peg arrangements and other, second-rate sidemen. Non-specialists should start with the superior Classics 798. Manone's derivative playing has grown in stature, his singing has a hip, fast-talking swagger about it, and the bands – with Miller, Matlock, Brunies and the excellent Arodin extensively featured – set a useful standard of small-group playing in the immediate pre-swing era. By 1935, the run of material was shifting away from jazz and into novelty pop, and it's ironic that Manone's 'Isle Of Capri' vocal sent up the genre, only to secure a hit. Even so, the group often mustered a surprisingly hard-bitten treatment on a tune such as 'March Winds And April Showers'.
  We don't hear him as a mere Armstrong copyist. There was a genuinely original talent there, too. He lived to a ripe age and wrote a hilarious memoir, *Trumpet on the Wing* (some of the stories may be what Huckleberry Finn called 'stretchers'), but retired to Las Vegas and made no more records after the end of the '50s.

TINY BRADSHAW

Born Myron C. Bradshaw, 23 September 1905, Youngstown, Ohio; died 26 November 1958, Youngstown, Ohio
Voice, piano, drums

Breakin' Up The House
Proper Pairs 23 2CD

Bradshaw; Shad Collins, Talib Dawud, Billy Ford, Henry Glover, Lincoln Mills, Sammy Yates (t); Leslie Ayres
(t, p); Leon Comegys, Eugene Green, George Matthews, Andrew Penn, Alfonso Young (tb); Don Hill, Bobby
Holmes, Russell Procope, Sonny Stitt (as); Ornington Hall (as, bs); Pritchard Chessman, Rufus Gore, George
Nicholas, Red Prysock (ts); Happy Caldwell (ts, cl); Charlie Fowlkes (bs); Duke Anderson, Wild Bill Davis (p);
Jimmy Robinson (p, org); Les Erskine, Willy Gaddy, Leroy Harris, Bob Lessey (g); Clarence Mack, Curley Russell,
Eddie Smith, Leonard Heavy Swain (b); Arnold Boling, Earl Fox Walker (d); Dorena Deane, Jack Wolf Fine (v).
September 1934–July 1951.

Pianist Billy Taylor said (1999): **'We'd see Tiny Bradshaw at the Howard in Washington,
when he came through town. Always an exciting show, and right there you have the real
start of the rock and roll style, though those guys could *really* play.'**

'He wrote and played them all,' it says on the cover of *The Great Composer*, a compilation of
Bradshaw's R&B material for King, and while that's a bit overdone, he was a fantastic enter-
tainer whose energy impressed Johnny Hodges. His was also a band in which jazz masters
of the future cut their teeth, Russell Procope in the early, swing-oriented group, Sonny
Stitt a decade later after Tiny had moved over to more commercial recording. A master of
blues and jump, born in Youngstown, Ohio, he graduated in psychology from Wilberforce
University but decided to stay with music instead, working with Luis Russell and the Mills
Blue Rhythm Band. This Proper set covers the waterfront from the early material, on which
Bradshaw scats like he's standing on the third rail, all the way through the years of struggle
to his return to recording in his final decade. It's not subtle music, and on record it pre-
sumably misses the key dimension of Tiny's Cab Calloway-inspired dancing and cavorting.
'Well, Oh Well' and 'The Train Kept A'Rollin'' were jukebox hits and the latter was even
picked up by the rock and roll crowd: The Yardbirds played it, and so more recently have
Aerosmith. The later jump sides are fairly generic, but Bradshaw never fails to entertain.

DJANGO REINHARDT&
*Born Jean-Baptiste Reinhardt, 23 January 1910, Lieberchies, Belgium; died 16 May 1953, Fontainebleau,
France*
Guitar

Django Reinhardt 1935–1936
Classics 739

Reinhardt; Bill Coleman, Alex Renard (t); George Johnson (cl); Maurice Cizeron (as, f); Alix Combelle (ts);
Garnet Clark, Emil Stern (p); Stéphane Grappelli, Michel Warlop (vn); Pierre Ferret, Joseph Reinhardt (g); June
Cole, Lucien Simoëns, Louis Vola (b); Freddy Taylor (v). September 1935–October 1936.

Guitarist Martin Taylor says: **'Whenever I meet guitarists who tell me they'd love to play
like Django I tell them to listen to Louis Armstrong. That's what Django did, that's why
Django phrased everything the way he did. Louis was Django's hero. Just listen to Louis
Armstrong play and you'll understand what Django was really about.'**

One of the Christian-name-only mythical figures of jazz, Django reinforces the dangerous
notion that damage is a spur to great art. Django's technical compass, apparently unham-
pered by loss of movement in two fingers of his left hand (the burn ended his apprenticeship as a violinist), was colossal, ranging from dazzling high-speed runs to ballad playing
of aching intensity. The personal myth almost outstrips the music. Django's survival as a
gypsy in occupied Europe famously depended on a jazz-loving Luftwaffe officer who saved

him from the camps and inevitable liquidation. Ironic, perhaps, given the guitarist's self-destructive personality.

Pity the poor discographer who has to approach this material. The Reinhardt discography is now as mountainous as his native Belgium is flat. The principle seems to be that anything with 'Paris' or 'swing', either in conjunction or separately, will sell records; and there is the additional problem that Django's name has become so iconic that it alone is often deemed enough. There are huge numbers of compilations on the market, some of them of questionable authority and quality, often inaccurately dated and provenanced and with only notional stabs at accurate personnels. However, only a plain fool could put out a compilation of Django's music that wasn't listenable, so the final choice will bear on the pocket, patience and hi-fi obsessions of the buyer/listener.

Classics are not known for their audio quality, but they document the music closely and painstakingly and, for reference, these performances include the finest of Django's pre-war work. The riches here may not seem like the most obvious ones – 'Nuages' most obviously of all – but they include 'Djangology', 'The Object Of My Affection', 'Georgia On My Mind', 'Shine', 'After You've Gone', tracks that find the Hot Club at its first peak, recording for HMV. There are also some excellent numbers with Django and Grappelli recorded with pianist Garnet Clark and the band of Michel Warlop.

There's little point analysing this music track by track. Its ease and grace shine through the 'audio rubble' virtuoso engineer Ted Kendall managed to clear away for the splendid JSP box, which is our pick for a more complete survey of the music, in handsome sound.

& See also **Pêche À La Mouche** (1947–1953; p. 111); **STÉPHANE GRAPPELLI, Jazz In Paris** (1956; p. 182); **MARTIN TAYLOR, Spirit Of Django** (1984; p. 486)

BENNY GOODMAN &

Born 30 May 1909, Chicago, Illinois; died 13 June 1986, New York City
Clarinet

The Complete Small Group Sessions
RCA Victor 68764 3CD
Goodman; Lionel Hampton (vib); Teddy Wilson, Jess Stacy (p); John Kirby (b); Buddy Schutz, Dave Tough, Gene Krupa (d). July 1935–April 1939.

Lionel Hampton said (1990): **'Kids nowadays probably don't appreciate this, but in the 1930s, to see a black man playing alongside a white man on a stage was still a shocking sight. I have always respected Benny Goodman for doing that.'**

Goodman studied clarinet from the age of 11, began working two years later, and joined the Ben Pollack band in Chicago. Studio work in New York followed until he began bandleading in 1934, becoming one of the most popular in America, and with the famous Carnegie Hall concert in 1938 made swing a national pastime. Unlike others, Goodman survived the big-band decline and toyed with bebop, as well as occasionally playing the classical repertoire. He continued to tour with small groups and occasional big bands in the '70s and '80s. Despite a martinet reputation, he was a hugely successful leader. The early hot style matured into a calmer manner, marked by unflinching dedication to his instrument.

Goodman's small groups set a new standard for 'chamber-jazz', the kind of thing Red Nichols had tried in the '20s, but informed with a more disciplined – and blacker – sensibility. That said, Goodman's own playing, for all its fineness of line and tonal elegance, could be blisteringly hot, and he is by far the strongest personality on all their records, even with Hampton and Krupa present. These tracks have been out many times over the years, but this is a notably handsome and comprehensive presentation. Perhaps the trio sessions, made before Hampton's arrival, are the most satisfying, since the brilliant empathy between Goodman and Wilson is allowed its clearest expression. Certainly the likes of 'After You've Gone' and 'Body And Soul' express a smooth yet spontaneously refined kind of improvisation. Hampton made the music swing a little more obtrusively, yet he often performs a rather contained ensemble role, the vibes shimmering alongside Wilson's piano, and it created a fascinating platform for Goodman's lithest playing. Soon to be formulaic, but it was a very good formula.

& *See also* **At Carnegie Hall 1938** (1938; p. 65); **B.G. In Hi-Fi** (1954; p. 157)

FATS WALLER
Born Thomas Wright Waller, 21 May 1904, New York City; died 15 December 1943, Kansas City, Missouri
Piano, organ

Fats Waller 1934–1935
Classics 732 / 746 / 760
Waller; Herman Autrey, Bill Coleman (t); Floyd O'Brien (tb); Rudy Powell (cl, as); Gene Sedric (cl, ts); Mezz Mezzrow (cl, as); Al Casey, James Smith (g); Billy Taylor, Charles Turner (b); Arnold Bolling, Harry Dial (d, vib). September 1934–August 1935.

Pianist Dr Billy Taylor said (1991): **'I saw Fats at the Lincoln Theater [in Washington, DC]. He was playing organ right in the middle of the hall where I could see his feet on the pedals. He walked right by me later, a huge guy with his entourage all round him, but I was struck dumb. I couldn't say anything. This was a kind of God, right?'**

The son of a clergyman, Fats worked in vaudeville until the mid-'20s and began composing with lyricist Andy Razaf. His fame came with the 'Fats Waller And His Rhythm' sessions for Victor, which began in 1934 and yielded hundreds of titles. A nonpareil humorist and lampooner of trite pop whose own best songs have remained in repertory, and 'Jitterbug Waltz' even appealed to modernists like Eric Dolphy. His piano style, which emerged from stride, was percussive and swinging, delicate and whimsical. He died of pneumonia on an overnight train.

Waller worked hard in the studios, and though his material has been traditionally looked down upon, he did usually make the most of it, even if the relentless clowning, yelled asides, importuning of soloists and general mayhem obscured much of what his hands were doing at the keyboard. This is often knockabout music, but whenever he gets to a good melody or does one of his own better tunes – such as the 12-inch master of 'Blue Turning Grey Over You' – its underlying seriousness rises to the surface. Autry and Sedric, the most ubiquitous yet least recognized of horn-players, are always ready to heat things up. Bill Coleman's presence on a few early sessions introduces some of his elegant horn, and the almost forgotten Rudy Powell replaced Sedric on several of the 1935 dates.

There's now a good comprehensive run of Waller's Rhythm recordings and his various solos, easy to follow in this format and respectably remastered. The first of these three volumes includes four piano solos as well as the session which produced 'Serenade For A Wealthy Widow'; 'Baby Brown' is another good one. The middle one has 'Rosetta', 'I'm Gonna Sit Right Down And Write Myself A Letter', the outstanding 'Dinah' and 'Sweet And Slow'. The follow-up 1935 volume includes several more of the best Rhythm tracks, with one of the best ever versions of 'Somebody Stole My Gal'.

JESS STACY

Born Alexandria Stacy, 11 August 1904, Bird's Point, Missouri; died 5 January 1994, Los Angeles, California
Piano

Ec-Stacy
ASV AJA 5172
Stacy; Bobby Hackett, Muggsy Spanier (c); Charlie Teagarden, Harry James, Ziggy Elman, Chris Griffin, Yank Lawson, Lyman Vunk, Max Herman, Billy Butterfield, Pee Wee Erwin, Anthony Natoli, Nate Kazebier, Bunny Berigan, Ralph Muzillo (t); Floyd O'Brien, Red Ballard, Joe Harris, Murray McEachern, Elmer Smithers, Buddy Morrow, Will Bradley, Jack Satterfield (tb); Benny Goodman, Johnny Hodges, Pee Wee Russell, Danny Polo, Hymie Schertzer, Bill De Pew, Dick Clark, Arthur Rollini, George Koenig, Vido Musso, Bud Freeman, Dave Mathews, Noni Bernardi, Matty Matlock, Art Mendelsohn, Eddie Miller, Gil Rodin, Sal Franzella, Henry Ross, Larry Binyon, Julius Bradley, Arthur Rando (reeds); Nappy Lamare, Allan Reuss, Frank Worrell, Ben Heller (g); Israel Crosby, Sid Wess, Artie Shapiro, Harry Goodman, Bob Haggart (b); Specs Powell, Gene Krupa, George Wettling, Ray Bauduc, Mario Toscarelli, Buddy Schutz (d); Lee Wiley (v). November 1935–June 1945.

Concord Records president Carl Jefferson said (1987): **'I talked to a lot of piano-players while we were planning the [Maybeck Recital Hall] series, and I was surprised how many mentioned Jess Stacy. I'd never heard him quoted as an influence, but everyone seemed to respect him, and I was surprised to find he was still alive.'**

Jess Stacy's solo on 'Sing, Sing, Sing' at the famous 1938 Benny Goodman Carnegie Hall concert is a high point of the swing era, but Stacy remains surprisingly little known apart from that and has only been taken up by a few enthusiasts. Stacy freelanced in Chicago until he joined Benny Goodman in 1935, and stayed – apart from a spell with Bob Crosby – for a decade. He later became a Condonite but left music to sell cosmetics in 1961, returning to the festival circuit in the next decade.

After a period of neglect, the great man was suddenly well represented on record. Classics' patient documentation of Commodore and Varsity material from 1938 and 1939 has its advantages but this ASV volume (which duplicates a good deal of stuff) usefully covers sideman work with Benny Goodman, Bob Crosby, Lionel Hampton, Bud Freeman and Pee Wee Russell for an exceptionally well-rounded portrait of a man who appeared in many interesting situations. His unassuming virtuosity went with a deceptively romantic streak – 'the intensity of Hines with the logic of Bix', as Vic Bellerby puts it – and his impeccable touch and undercurrent of blues feeling, even if tempered by a rather civilized irony, give him a rare position among the piano-players of the era. Anyone seriously interested in Stacy should certainly also get the Classics set for the two splendid blues-based fantasies in 'Ramblin'' and 'Complainin'' and an excellent solo session from 1939, but the ASV offers several rarities, including an aircheck version of Beiderbecke's 'In A Mist', three 1944 duets with Specs Powell and the beautiful 'Down To Steamboat Tennessee' with Muggsy Spanier and Lee Wiley.

TOMMY DORSEY

Born 19 November 1905, Shenandoah, Pennsylvania; died 26 November 1956, Greenwich, Connecticut
Trombone

The Best Of Tommy Dorsey And His Clambake Seven 1936–1938
Retrieval RTR 79012
Dorsey; Max Kaminsky, Pee Wee Erwin (t); Joe Dixon, Johnny Mince (cl); Bud Freeman (ts); Dick Jones (p); Bill Schaffer, Carmen Mastren (g); Gene Traxler (b); Dave Tough, Maurice Purtill, (d); Edythe Wright (v). December 1935–February 1938.

Dorsey alumnus Frank Sinatra said: **'Penguin guide?** *Penguin Guide?* **Hey, Sal, there's some crazy kid here, selling guides for penguins. Get rid of him, will ya?'** (We made this up.)

A ubiquitous figure on the New York dance band circuit of the '20s, Dorsey went on to lead one of the most successful swing-era big bands, although the jazz content of the records was often in doubt. The 'Sentimental Gentleman' of swing was a martinet, but he kept his band going in the post-swing era, eventually reuniting with his brother Jimmy. His perfect legato trombone style and singing high tone strongly influenced his band singer, Frank Sinatra. In 1956, he choked to death in his sleep.

Like all the great swing orchestras, Dorsey's band was as much about dance music as it was about jazz. Relatively few of the songs survive the era; the arrangements are more functional than challenging, solos are usually kept to a minimum, and the music looks back in time rather than ahead. All that said, the trombonist could claim several virtues. While he was the principal soloist, he could call on several fine jazzmen: above all Bunny Berigan, whose tantalizing first stint with the band (a mere five sessions) resulted in 'Song Of India', 'Marie', 'Mr Ghost Goes To Town' and 'The Goona Goo', to cite four memorable solos. Dorsey also had one of the best band singers of the era, Edythe Wright (and would later recruit Frank Sinatra), as well as his Clambake Seven small group.

Dorsey's small group was an initiative he began almost as soon as the bigger band became successful, and he ran it on and off alongside the main orchestra for the rest of his career. As with the big band, though, the group's material is often thin and prone to novelty material. Retrieval's 21-track selection mystifyingly leaves out some very good Sevens (including our favourite, 'Rhythm Saved The World', which is available on the relevant Classics volume), but otherwise offers a vivid portrait of some of Dorsey's best playing and excellent spots for Freeman, Erwin and Dixon.

JOE MARSALA
Born 4 January 1907, Chicago, Illinois; died 3 March 1978, Santa Barbara, California
Clarinet

Joe Marsala 1936–1942
Classics 763

Marsala; Pee Wee Erwin, Max Kaminsky, Marty Marsala (t); Bill Coleman (t, v); George Brunies (tb); Pete Brown, Ben Glassman (as); John Smith (ts); Dave Bowman, Joe Bushkin, Dick Cary, Frank Signorelli (p); Ray Biondi (vn); Adele Girard (hp); Eddie Condon, Carmen Mastren (g); Jack LeMaire (g, v); Jack Kelleher, Artie Shapiro, Haig Stephens, Gene Traxler (b); Danny Alvin, Stan King, Shelly Manne, Buddy Rich, Zutty Singleton (d); Dell St John (v). January 1936–July 1942.

Shelly Manne said (1979): **'Apparently, Joe's mother-in-law didn't trust Italians, thought they were all gangsters. Joe went to every length to persuade her this wasn't so. Then one day he was standing on a street corner, eating a snack, when a sedan pulled up opposite and the guys in it started firing a machine gun, killing the man standing next to Joe on the sidewalk. He ran, and he says he could never stomach the smell of peanut butter after that!'**

Armed with matinee idol looks and a dark, winey tone, Marsala also claims an honourable place in jazz history for his efforts to break down the race divide. It was an endeavour that won the respect of Leonard Feather, who composed all the material on the April 1940 session. Though Marsala had the projection and the sense of structure to perform effectively in big bands – he already had ten years in clubs and circus bands – he functioned best in small groups, notably the band which maintained a residency at the Hickory House on 52nd Street. A couple of early tracks were made for Decca under the name The Six Blue Chips;

Pee Wee Erwin was the main attraction. In 1937 Marsala married harpist Adele Girard, who had brought an attractive balance and sense of space to a front line of clarinet, trumpet and violin. In later years, and particularly on the sessions of May and November 1945, she was given more prominence, and on the late pair made for Musicraft ('East Of The Sun' and 'Slightly Dizzy') she is pushed well forward.

Neither Joe nor Adele felt comfortable with bebop and both of them went back into the studios. He effectively retired in 1948, and went into publishing, but still played occasionally, when it pleased him.

ANDY KIRK

Born 28 May 1898, Newport, Kentucky; died 11 December 1992, New York City
Bandleader, alto, baritone and bass saxophones, tuba

Andy Kirk 1936–1937

Classics 573

Kirk; Paul King, Harry Lawson, Earl Thomson, Clarence Trice (t); Ted Donnelly, Henry Wells (tb); John Harrington (cl, as, bs); John Williams (as, bs); Earl Miller (as); Dick Wilson (ts); Claude Williams (vn); Mary Lou Williams (p); Ted Brinson, Ted Robinson (g); Booker Collins (b); Ben Thigpen (d); O'Neil Spencer, Pha Terrell (v). March–December 1936.

Mary Lou Williams said (1976): **'Andy Kirk liked what I was doing, but I got frustrated that I couldn't put them down on paper myself. We'd sit for hours while he took them down. He was a sweet man, who knew something about music, not like Terrence Holder, who was a gambler, a fast-living type, though he could run a band.'**

Though he was often out front for photo opportunities, Andy Kirk ran the Clouds Of Joy strictly from the back row. The limelight was usually left to singer June Richmond or vocalist/conductor Pha Terrell; the best of the arrangements were done by Mary Lou Williams, who left the band in 1942; as a bass saxophonist, Kirk wasn't called on to take a solo. All the same, he turned the Clouds Of Joy into one of the most inventive swing bands. He took over Terrence Holder's Dark Clouds Of Joy in 1929 and with the writing and arranging skills of Mary Lou Williams turned the band into a successful touring and recording unit. His biggest success was with 'Until The Real Thing Comes Along' in 1936. His disposition was sunny and practical and he was a competent organizer (who in later life ran a Harlem hotel, the legendary Theresa, and organized a Musicians' Union local in New York City).

Inevitably, given Kirk's low musical profile, critical attention is more usually directed to other members of the band. The classic Clouds Of Joy cuts are those that feature Mary Lou Williams's arrangements and performances. The earlier material is still the best, with 'Moten Swing', 'Until The Real Thing Comes Along' and the hit 'Froggy Bottom' prominent. The band, surprisingly enough, has a quite distinctive sound, heavy but mobile, and with some of Williams's signature devices, which already suggest gospel or sacred music, already evident. It's difficult to imagine the lifestyle now but this was an orchestra that criss-crossed the country, often working under difficult conditions, but always playing, it's said, with the kind of professionalism that comes across on these fascinating sides.

ROY ELDRIDGE

Born David Roy Eldridge, 30 January 1911, Pittsburgh, Pennsylvania; died 26 February 1989, Valley Stream, New York
Trumpet

The Big Sound Of Little Jazz

Topaz TPZ 1021

Eldridge; Al Beck, Bill Coleman, Torg Halten, Mickey Mangano, Norman Murphy, Joe Thomas, Dick Vance, Graham Young (t); Fernando Arbello, Joe Conigliaro, Ed Cuffee, John Grassi, Jay Kelliher, Babe Wagner, Dicky Wells (tb); Buster Bailey, Benny Goodman, Cecil Scott (cl); Omer Simeon (cl, as, bs); Russell Procope (cl, as); Sam Musiker (cl, ts); Scoops Carey, Benny Carter, Joe Eldridge, Ben Feman, Andrew Gardner, Hilton Jefferson, Howard Johnson, Rex Kittig, Jimmy Migliore, Clint Neagley, Mascagni Ruffo (as); Tom Archia, Walter Bates, Chu Berry, Don Brassfield, Coleman Hawkins, Teddy Hill, Ike Quebec, Ben Webster, Elmer Williams, Dave Young (ts); Sam Allen, Teddy Cole, Rozelle Gayle, Clyde Hart, Horace Henderson, Bob Kitsis, Joe Springer, Jess Stacy, Teddy Wilson (p); Bernard Addison, Danny Barker, Ray Biondi, John Collins, Bob Lessey, Lawrence Lucie, Allan Reuss, John Smith (g); Biddy Bastien, Israel Crosby, Richard Fulbright, John Kirby, Ed Mihelich, Truck Parham, Artie Shapiro, Ted Sturgis (b); Bill Beason, Big Sid Catlett, Cozy Cole, Gene Krupa, Zutty Singleton, Harold 'Doc' West (d); Mildred Bailey, Billie Holiday (v). February 1935–November 1943.

Impresario Norman Granz said (1982): **'I think Roy might be the hungriest one of all. He has a real will to succeed, to be better than anyone else and to be able to do the old thing and the new thing with equal confidence. He walks a tightrope.'**

Eldridge was the marker between swing trumpet and the bebop revolution. The archetypal high-note artist, 'Little Jazz' became an all too enthusiastic participant in cutting contests, sometimes neglecting expression in favour of excitement and competition. And yet he remains perhaps the greatest brass-player of the generation after Louis Armstrong, though interestingly his first great influence was Jabbo Smith rather than Pops.

Eldridge moved to New York in 1934 and was quickly recognized as a new star. The introductory bars of '(Lookie, Lookie, Lookie) Here Comes Cookie' from the following year (and the first track on this fine Topaz gathering) offer a glimpse of the excitement the youngster must have caused. His ability to displace accents and play questionable intervals with perfect confidence and logic is immediately evident. More than just a high-note man, Eldridge combined rhythmic intuition with an ability to play intensely exciting music in the middle and lower register. His solo on 'Blue Lou' – recorded with the Fletcher Henderson band in March 1936 – is a perfect case in point. He does the same kind of thing with the Teddy Wilson band on 'Blues In C Sharp Minor', fitting his improvisation perfectly to the moody key; Chu Berry's follow-up and Israel Crosby's tensely throbbing bass complete a masterful performance. At the other end of the emotional spectrum, there are the starburst top Cs (and beyond) of 'Heckler's Hop', anchored on Zutty Singleton's tight drumming. The vocal tracks with Mildred Bailey are often quite appealing and show how responsive an accompanist Eldridge was, again able to play quietly and in contralto range when called upon. A solitary Billie Holiday track – 'Falling In Love Again' – gives only a flavour of that association. There's terrific richness here, everything from the Chocolate Dandies to the Little Jazz Ensemble with Chu, which sounds like a genuinely affectionate association, but the key linking factor is Eldridge's pin-sharp trumpet-playing. He does pathos when it's called for, but it's the way he bridges an old swing sound with the sharper attack and harmonic derring-do of the boppers who were just around the corner that stands out.

BILLIE HOLIDAY&

Born Eleanora Fagan Gough, 7 April 1915, Baltimore, Maryland; died 17 July 1959, New York City
Voice

The Billie Holiday Collection: Volume 2

Columbia 510722-2 (part of ten-CD sequence; *Best Of* compilation also available)
Holiday; Jonah Jones, Henry 'Red' Allen, Buck Clayton, Cootie Williams, Eddie Tompkins (t); Benny Goodman, Edmond Hall, Buster Bailey (cl); Cecil Scott (cl, as, ts); Johnny Hodges (as); Lester Young, Prince Robinson, Joe Thomas, Ben Webster (ts); Harry Carney (bs, cl); Teddy Wilson, James Sherman, Claude Thornhill (p); Allan Reuss, Freddie Green, Jimmy McLin, Carmen Mastren (g); Walter Page, John Kirby, Artie Bernstein (b); Cozy Cole, Jo Jones, Alphonse Steele (d). November 1936–September 1937.

Singer Karin Krog skipped school to hear Billie Holiday in Oslo: **'People still don't realize how much she was influenced by Louis Armstrong's singing – you can hear it in her phrasing and in her timing. She has an amazing sense of time – and seems able to float the songs out over the rhythm section, making it feel as if they are swinging harder than ever. Although she's recognized as a ballad singer, I think she was equally superb on up-tempo numbers.'**

Billie Holiday remains among the most difficult of jazz artists to understand or study. Surrounded as she is by a disturbing legend, it is very difficult to hear her clearly. The legendary suffering and mythopoeic pain which countless admirers have actively sought out in her work make it difficult for the merely curious to warm to a singer who was a sometimes baffling performer. The later records place the listener in an almost voyeuristic role. Nevertheless, Holiday was a singular and unrepeatable talent whose finest hours are remarkably revealing and often surprisingly joyful.

She had a wretched childhood, but did later adopt her errant father Clarence Holiday's surname. She was singing early and made her first records in 1933. Her pre-war sessions with Teddy Wilson established a reputation, followed by stints with Basie and Artie Shaw. Drink and narcotics problems, which attended the rest of her life, held back her solo and film career, but she worked through the '40s, despite a spell in prison, began recording for Decca in 1944, and signed with Norman Granz in 1952. Though her still little understood musicianship stayed intact, her voice declined to a croak, and it's hard to find a reason to prefer the later, death-rattle stuff to the energy and mischief of the younger Billie. Those who do presumably prefer the myth to the music.

Columbia's massive *Lady Day* edition offers the entire catalogue, 230 tracks including alternatives, airshots and a few V-Discs. The basic sequence starts with six and a half discs of the studio sessions in chronological order, then meanders through numerous alternative takes and a small amount of broadcast material for the remainder. There are also numerous essays and photos, as well as track-by-track analysis: all the familiar paraphernalia of the boxed-set age. The standard of these records – particularly considering how many tracks were made – is finally very high, and the best of them are as poised and finely crafted as any small-group jazz of the period. One of Holiday's innovations was to suggest a role for the singer which blended in with the rest of the musicians, improvising a line and taking a 'solo' which was as integrated as anything else on the record. On her earlier sides with Wilson as leader, she was still credited as responsible for the 'vocal refrain', but the later titles feature 'Billie Holiday And Her Orchestra'. She starts some records and slips into the middle of others, but always there's a feeling of a musician at ease with the rest of the band and aware of the importance of fitting into the performance as a whole.

Her tone, on the earliest sides, is still a little raw and unformed, and the trademark rasp at the edge of her voice – which she uses to canny effect on the later titles – is used less pointedly; but the unaffected styling is already present, and there are indications of her mastery of time even at the very beginning. While the most obvious characteristic of her singing is the lagging behind the beat, she seldom sounds tired or slow to respond, and the deeper impression is of a vocalist who knows exactly how much time she can take. She never scats, rarely drifts far from the melody, and respects structure and lyrical nuance, even where the material is less than blue-chip. But her best singing invests the words with shades of meaning which vocalists until that point had barely looked at: she creates an ambiguity between what the words say and what she might be thinking which is very hard to distil. And that is the core of Holiday's mystique. Coupled with the foggy, baleful, sombre quality of her tone, it creates a vocal jazz which is as absorbing as it is enduring.

Whatever one may think about the later albums, these sessions surrender nothing in gravitas and communicate a good humour which is all their own. The session producers – John Hammond or Bernie Hanighen – encouraged an atmosphere of mutual creativity which the singer seldom fails to respond to, and even on the less than immortal songs Holiday makes something of the situation: there is no sense of her fighting against the material, as there often is with Armstrong or Waller in the same period. On the many upbeat songs, she's irresistible. The informality starts to fade, though, and she becomes more like a singer with accompanists, but the blitheness of her youthful voice persists.

& *See also* **Lady In Autumn** (1926–1959; p. 134)

JIMMY DORSEY

Born 29 February 1904, Shenandoah, Pennsylvania; died 12 June 1957, New York City
Alto and baritone saxophones, clarinet, trumpet

Amapola
ASV AJA 5287
Dorsey; W. C. Clark, Shorty Sherock, Ralph Muzillo, Nate Kazebier, Johnny Napton, Shorty Solomon, Jimmy Campbell, Ray Anthony, Paul McCoy, Bob Alexy, Ray Linn, Marky Markowitz, Phil Napoleon, George Thow, Toots Camarata, Joe Meyer (t); Sonny Lee, Jerry Rosa, Al Jordan, Phil Washburne, Andy Russo, Nick Di Mai, Bobby Byrne, Joe Yukl, Bruce Squires (tb); Don Mattison (tb, v); Noni Bernard, Dave Matthews, Sam Rubinowich, Milt Yaner, Frank Langone, Bill Covey, Jack Stacey, Lem Whitney (as); Fud Livingston (as, ts); Leonard Whitner, Herbie Haymer, Don Hammond, Babe Russin, Skeets Hurfurt, Charles Frazier (ts); Chuck Gentry, Bob Lawson (bs); Freddy Slack, Joe Lippman, Johnny Guarnieri, Dave Mann, Bobby Van Eps, Freddy Slack (p), Guy Smith, Allan Reuss, Tommy Kay (g); Roc Hillman (g, v); Jack Ryan, Bill Mille, Slim Taft, Jack Ryan (b); Buddy Schutz (d); Ray McKinley (d, v); Bing Crosby, The Andrews Sisters, Frances Langford, Helen O'Connell, Kitty Kallen (v). July 1936–October 1943.

Dorsey brothers collector Dr Ray Stevens says: **'It was on May 30th, 1935. Jimmy and Tommy were rehearsing "Never Say Never Again Again" and they got into a fight over the tempo, as only brothers can. Tommy walked out, saying he'd form an even better band. More successful, certainly, but not better!'**

The elder, reed-playing Dorsey brother worked with his sibling on the NY session scene of the '20s before co-leading a band which he eventually took over after a quarrel with Tommy. A superb technician, admired by Charlie Parker, and his music matched his mild-mannered demeanour. He was reconciled with his brother, and their final venture as co-leaders ended with Tommy's death, followed by Jimmy's passing only months later.

Amapola collects 24 of the biggest hits by Dorsey's band over a seven-year period. The emphasis here is on the ballad and vocal feature side of Dorsey's discography, and if this is what you want, it's an ideal record – from the title-track, Helen O'Connell's signature rendition of 'Green Eyes' and Kitty Kallen's 'Besame Mucho' to the somewhat more swinging 'I Fall In Love With You Every Day' and the novelty 'Six Lessons From Madame La Zonga', these are the memories which Dorsey's amen corner will probably remember best. The odd soloist pops up here and there to remind us that it was basically a good band but the emphasis is on formation playing rather than improvisations, which both the Dorseys distrusted.

TEDDY WILSON

Born 24 November 1912, Austin, Texas; died 31 July 1986, New Britain, Connecticut
Piano

Teddy Wilson: Volume 1 – Too Hot For Words

Hep 1012
Wilson; Roy Eldridge, Dick Clark (t); Benny Morton (tb); Tom Macey, Benny Goodman, Cecil Scott (cl); Hilton Jefferson, Johnny Hodges (as); Chu Berry, Ben Webster (ts); John Trueheart, Lawrence Lucie, Dave Barbour (g); John Kirby, Grachan Moncur (b); Cozy Cole (d); Billie Holiday (v). January–October 1935.

Teddy Wilson said (1979): **'I'm sometimes asked if I plan to retire, but that would be like admitting I never wanted to play in the first place. All I ever wanted to do was play. You could have put a keyboard on the back of a railroad train and I would have played it.'**

Few jazz records have endured quite as well as Teddy Wilson's '30s music. He visited Chicago in 1928, fell in love with jazz there, and formed a duo with Art Tatum in 1931. After that, he was in New York with Benny Carter. His studio small-group work included classic sessions with Billie Holiday and Lester Young, and he then joined Benny Goodman. A brief spell with his own big band in 1939 preceded more small-group work, along with a staff job at CBS and teaching at Juilliard. He remained to the last the most gracious and poised of performers.

Wilson arrived in New York as an enthusiastic young stride pianist, already under the spell of Earl Hines and of Art Tatum, with whom he worked as a two-man piano team. But even here there are the signs of an individual whose meticulous, dapper delivery and subtle reading of harmony would be hugely influential. Amazingly, everything is in place by the time of the first band session in July 1935: the initial line-up includes Eldridge, Goodman and Webster, and the singer is Billie Holiday, who would feature as vocalist on most of Wilson's pre-war records. Two classics were made immediately – 'What A Little Moonlight Can Do' and 'Miss Brown To You' – and the style was set: a band chorus, a vocal, and another chorus for the band, with solos and obbligatos in perfect accord with every other note and accent. All the others seem to take their cue from the leader's own poise, and even potentially unruly spirits such as Eldridge and Webster behave.

The reissue of this series has been complicated by Holiday's presence, for all her tracks with Wilson are now also available on discs under her own name. Collectors will have to follow their own tastes, but we would opine that, of all the various transfers of this material, the Hep discs have the most truthful sound.

EDMOND HALL

Born 15 May 1901, Reserve, Louisiana; died 11 February 1967, Boston, Massachusetts
Clarinet

Edmond Hall 1936–1944

Classics 830
Hall; Billy Hicks (t, v); Sidney De Paris, Emmett Berry (t); Vic Dickenson, Fernando Arbello (tb); Meade 'Lux' Lewis (cel); Cyril Haynes, Teddy Wilson, Eddie Heywood, James P. Johnson (p); Red Norvo (vib); Leroy Jones, Jimmy Shirley, Al Casey, Carl Kress (g); Al Hall, Israel Crosby, Billy Taylor, Johnny Williams (b); Arnold Boling, Big Sid Catlett (d); Henry Nemo (v). June 1937–January 1944.

Wild Bill Davison said (1983): **'Edmond played and lived … generously. He wasn't one of those perfectionists who fuss over a single detail all day, but if he wasn't happy or you weren't happy, he'd just give more and more and more until you both were.'**

A New Orleans man, often unfairly eclipsed by lesser players. His three brothers all played clarinet too, but Ed spent several years with Claude Hopkins in the '30s and then freelanced for the rest of his life. Manfred Selchow's biographical researches are a model of their kind, as exhaustive and perfectionist as their subject.

Hall was one of the most popular musicians in the Eddie Condon circle, but his experience – with big bands in the '20s and '30s and with Louis Armstrong's All Stars – was much wider than that. He played in a driving manner that married the character of his New Orleans background with the more fleet methods of the swing clarinettists. This compilation starts off with an obscure session by Billy Hicks and his Sizzlin' Six, with Hall as a sideman (hence the oddity of dates), but the meat of it is in Hall's first three sessions for Blue Note (also available in a set as *Profoundly Blue* but in oddly poor sound) and a stray Commodore date. This is outstandingly fine midstream swing, with superb contributions from De Paris, Berry, the incomparably refined Wilson, Lewis, James P. Johnson and, above all, the magnificent Dickenson, whose solos on the blues are masterful statements of jazz trombone. And there is Hall himself. Though the final Blue Note date is a bit scruffy, sound is mainly excellent.

COUNT BASIE &

Born 21 August 1904, Red Bank, New Jersey; died 26 April 1984, Hollywood, Florida
Piano, bandleader

The Original American Decca Recordings
MCA GRP 36112
Basie; Buck Clayton, Joe Keyes, Carl Smith, Ed Lewis, Bobby Moore, Karl George, Harry 'Sweets' Edison, Shad Collins (t); Eddie Durham (tb, g); George Hunt, Dan Minor, Benny Morton, Dicky Wells (tb); Jack Washington (as, bs); Caughey Roberts, Earl Warren (as); Lester Young, Herschel Evans (cl, ts); Chu Berry (ts); Claude Williams, Freddie Green (g); Walter Page (b); Jo Jones (d); Jimmy Rushing, Helen Humes (v). January 1937–February 1939.

Saxophonist Gerry Mulligan said (1990): **'What strikes me about those pre-war Basie sides is how *light* it sounds. That rhythm section just dances around like they're carrying nothing heavier than feathers, but there's this great weight of horns coming in behind. There's never been anything quite like that band.'**

'Count Basic' still turns up as a misprint now and again, and it makes a wry point, because few great jazz musicians have ever attained such high status by playing so few notes or by writing out less material. And yet, the sound of the Basie band is absolutely distinctive: functional, coach-built jazz that relied on solos in a different way to the Ellington orchestra – where Duke's men created rich efflorescences, Basie's tended to highlight one aspect of the machine for a moment before slipping back into place, a cutaway approach that is equally exciting and equally creative.

Basie grew up in a musical family and took his first lessons from his mother. After experience in clubs and vaudeville he settled in Kansas City, joined the Bennie Moten band in 1929 and took over its leadership in 1935, moving to New York the following year. The orchestra became the most eminent of its day, with many important soloists and a uniquely swinging rhythm section characterized by Basie's own minimalist piano style. He also ran small groups within the band and cut back to an octet (1950–51) when the big band proved too expensive to run. European tours in the '50s and '60s restored his popularity, even after he had to lead the band from a wheelchair.

The arrival of the Basie band – on an East Coast scene dominated by Ellington, Lunceford and Henderson – set up a new force in the swing era and these records are still enthralling.

Basie's Kansas City band was a rough-and-ready outfit compared with Lunceford's immaculate drive or Ellington's urbane mastery, but rhythmically it may have been the most swinging band of its time, based not only on the perfectly interlocking team of Basie, Green, Page and Jones, but also on the freedom of soloists such as Lester Young, Buck Clayton and Herschel Evans, on the intuitive momentum created within the sections (famously, Basie had relatively few arrangements written out) and on the best singing team of all the big bands. There are paradoxical elements – the minimalism of the leader's piano solos that is as invigorating as any chunk of fast stride piano, Green's invisible yet indispensable chording, the deceptive drift of the band – but all go to make up an orchestra unique in jazz.

& See also **The Jubilee Alternatives** (1943–1944; p. 90), **The Complete Atomic Mr Basie** (1957; p. 216)

EDDIE SOUTH
Born 27 November 1904, Louisiana, Missouri; died 25 April 1962, Chicago, Illinois
Violin

Eddie South 1937–1941
Classics 737
South; Charlie Shavers (t); Buster Bailey (cl); Russell Procope (as); David Martin, Stanley Facey (p); Stéphane Grappelli (vn); Django Reinhardt, Isadore Langlois, Eddie Gibbs, Eugene Fields (g); Paul Cordonnier, Doles Dickens, Ernest 'Bass' Hill (b); Specs Powell, Tommy Benford (d); Ginny Sims (v). November 1937–March 1941.

Violinist Stéphane Grappelli said (1981): **'There is no doubt that Eddie South could have been a great classical player, if it were not for the colour of his skin. His technique was amazing and he could play anything.'**

South wasn't simply one of the most accomplished of jazz violinists; he might have been one of the best-schooled of all jazz musicians of his time, given a thorough classical grounding that, unusually, blossomed into a hot rather than a cool improviser's stance. If his reputation rests on his Paris recordings of 1937, there are some interesting footnotes to an unfulfilled career in the other tracks listed here.

South's slightly later Chicago and New York sessions are well played if comparatively lightweight – on songs such as 'Nagasaki' or 'Marcheta' he sounds almost like a vaudevillian – but the three sessions with Grappelli and Reinhardt are fascinating, the guitarist driven into his best form, the violinist playing his finest solos on 'Sweet Georgia Brown' and 'Eddie's Blues', and the date culminating in the extraordinary improvisation on Bach's D Minor Concerto for two violins by South, Grappelli and Reinhardt together. A further 1938 session in Hilversum has some more strong playing by South's regular quintet, but his final titles from 1940–41 belabour the material, which seems designed to cast South as a romantic black gypsy and sends him back to vaudeville. He seldom recorded again, despite a fair amount of broadcasting, and must be accounted as a talent out of his time.

LIONEL HAMPTON *&*
Born 20 April 1909, Louisville, Kentucky; died 31 August 2002, New York City
Vibraphone, drums

Lionel Hampton 1937–1938
Classics 524
Hampton; Ziggy Elman, Cootie Williams, Jonah Jones (t); Lawrence Brown (tb); Vido Musso (cl, ts); Mezz Mezzrow, Eddie Barefield (cl); Johnny Hodges, Hymie Schertzer, George Koenig (as); Arthur Rollini (ts); Edgar

Sampson (bs); Jess Stacy, Clyde Hart (p); Bobby Bennett, Allan Reuss (g); Harry Goodman, John Kirby, Mack Walker, Johnny Miller, Billy Taylor (b); Gene Krupa, Cozy Cole, Sonny Greer (d). February 1937–January 1938.

Lionel Hampton said (1990): **'Louis [Armstrong] asked me if I'd tried out on a vibraphone. I picked up the mallets and picked out his solo on "Cornet Chop Suey". That was how we came to do "Memories Of You".'**

Hampton was the first player to use vibes as a jazz instrument as opposed to a novelty. He learned drums in a Chicago boys' band, and went on to work with Les Hit and backing Louis Armstrong before switching to vibes and leading his own group in LA, where Benny Goodman recruited him and put him in his controversial mixed-race group. Hamp recorded for RCA Victor in New York in the later '30s, and ran his own big band from 1941, dominated by a show-stopping style that anticipated R&B and let the band survive the lean rock'n'roll years. In the '80s and '90s he was also a major figure in education, publishing and housing programmes.

'Memories Of You' was a success and Hampton quickly evolved a fleet, two-mallet style for the vibes that emphasized their percussive character, but also the possibility of rich, ringing harmony. He had the advantage of being a naturally outgoing and dramatic character, which helped his presentation. His Victor sessions of the '30s offer a glimpse of many of the finest big-band players of the day away from usual chores: Hampton cherrypicked whichever band was in town at the time of the session, and although most of the tracks were hastily organized, the music is consistently entertaining. If one has a reservation, it's that if you don't enjoy what Hampton himself does, these discs won't live up to their reputation, since he dominates. Hampton cut a total of 23 sessions between 1936 and 1941. The personnel varies substantially from date to date: some are like small-band sessions drawn from the Ellington or Goodman or Basie orchestras; others – such as the extraordinary 1939 date with Gillespie, Carter, Berry, Webster and Hawkins – are genuine all-star jams. Carter wrote the charts for one session, but mostly Hampton used head arrangements or sketchy frameworks. The bonding agent is his own enthusiasm: whether playing vibes – and incidentally establishing the dominant style on the instrument with his abrasive accents, percussive intensity and quickfire alternation of long and short lines – or piano or drums, or taking an amusing, Armstrong-influenced vocal, Hamp makes everything swing.

& See also **Salle Pleyel 1971** (1971; p. 384)

CLAUDE HOPKINS
Born 24 August 1903, Alexandria, Virginia; died 19 February 1984, New York City
Piano

Claude Hopkins 1932–1934
Classics 699
Hopkins; Ovie Alston (t, v); Albert Snaer, Sylvester Lewis (t); Fred Norman (tb, v); Fernando Arbello, Henry Wells (tb); Edmond Hall (cl, as, bs); Gene Johnson (as); Bobby Sands (ts); Walter Jones (bj, g); Henry Turner (b); Pete Jacobs (d); Orlando Roberson (v). May 1932–December 1934.

Claude Hopkins said (1977): **'It was my band, so I always figured I should get as much playing time out of it as I could, instead of just standing there shaking a baton.'**

Hopkins was a skilful pianist and liked to get a lot of solos with his band; the demands of arranging around him may have told against the ambitions of the group. It certainly never worked as well as the Earl Hines orchestra, and though Hopkins had fewer imposing soloists – brief stays by Smith and Dickenson in 1937 were wasted – the group's ensemble sound lacked character and the arrangements were often second rate. Classics tell the story in decent if unexceptional transfers. Some of the music on this disc promises more than it delivers: 'Mad Moments', 'Shake Your Ashes', 'Hopkins Scream' and especially Jimmy Mundy's arrangement of 'Mush Mouth' are exciting and surprising pieces, and 'I Would Do Most Anything For You' became the band's signature theme. Because of Hopkins's stride-tinged solos, there's less emphasis on tight ensemble playing than with some comparable bands, but the sections sound well-drilled and though there are no other striking soloists – Ed Hall was too self-effacing to demand a spot – the impression is of good musicianship. Hopkins later took a staff arranging job for CBS and ran small groups, but his main impact was as short as it was striking.

DUKE ELLINGTON *&*

Born Edward Kennedy Ellington, 29 April 1899, Washington DC; died 24 May 1974, New York City
Piano

Duke Ellington 1937–1938
Classics 675 / 687 / 700 / 717 / 726
Ellington; Charlie Allen, Freddy Jenkins, Harold 'Shorty' Baker, Wallace Jones, Cootie Williams (t); Rex Stewart (c); Joe 'Tricky Sam' Nanton, Lawrence Brow, Sandy Williams (tb); Juan Tizol (vtb); Johnny Hodges (cl, ss, as); Harry Carney (cl, as, bs); Pete Clarke, Otto Hardwick (as); Barney Bigard (cl, ts); Ben Webster (ts); Bernard Addison, Fred Guy, Brick Fleagle (g); Hayes Alvis, Billy Taylor (b); Fred Avendorf, Sonny Greer, Chick Webb, Jack Maisel (d); Ivie Anderson, Scat Powell, Mary McHugh, Jerry Kruger (v). March 1937–December 1938.

Composer and music historian Gunther Schuller said (1981): **'At this period, only Picasso had the same ability to produce not just good music (or painting), but great art on an almost industrial scale.'**

Ellington's mid- and late-'30s output is a subtle blend of commerce and art and even the most trifling pieces usually have something to commend them. Slightly before the period covered here, there was the four-part original recording of 'Reminiscing In Tempo', a dedication to Ellington's mother that was one of the first of his extended works; but it also has the joyful 'Truckin'' and two early 'concerto' pieces in 'Clarinet Lament' for Bigard and 'Echoes Of Harlem' for Cootie Williams.

In contrast to what had gone before, 1937 began a little thinly as far as full-band tracks are concerned, though two versions of 'Azure' shouldn't be missed. The stronger material came later in the year, which peaks on the still remarkable first recording of 'Diminuendo And Crescendo In Blue' but also has the tremendous 'Harmony In Harlem', 'Chatterbox' and 'Jubilesta', as well as several of the small-group sessions. The 1938 output includes a lot of distinctive Ellingtonia that has been obscured by some of his obvious hits: 'Braggin' In Brass', 'The Gal From Joe's', the new version of 'Black And Tan Fantasy', superbly played by the band which transforms itself from dance orchestra to complex jazz ensemble – and back again. Though seldom commented on, the rhythm section of Guy, Taylor or Alvis and Greer is unobtrusively fine. There are more neglected winners on the second volume devoted to that year, including 'I'm Slappin' Seventh Avenue' (which Cecil Taylor admired), 'Dinah's In A Jam', the lovely treatment of 'Rose Of The Rio Grande' and the very fine 'The Stevedore's Serenade'. At this stage, even minor slippages in quality are noticeable, but it's clear that even when coasting the Ellington band was creatively ahead of almost everyone else on the scene.

& See also **Duke Ellington 1926–1929** (1926–1929; p. 28), **The Duke At Fargo** (1940; p. 81), **Never No Lament** (1940–1942; p. 81), **Black, Brown And Beige** (1944–1946; p. 91), **Ellington At Newport** (1956; p. 189), **The Far East Suite** (1966; p. 336)

BENNY GOODMAN &

Born 30 May 1909, Chicago, Illinois; died 13 June 1986, New York City
Clarinet

At Carnegie Hall 1938: Complete

Columbia C2K 65143 2CD
Goodman; Ziggy Elman, Buck Clayton, Harry James, Gordon Griffin (t); Bobby Hackett (c); Red Ballard, Vernon
Brown (tb); Hymie Schertzer, George Koenig, Johnny Hodges (as); Arthur Rollini, Lester Young, Babe Russin
(ts); Harry Carney (bs); Jess Stacy, Teddy Wilson, Count Basie (p); Lionel Hampton (vib); Allan Reuss, Freddie
Green (g); Harry Goodman, Walter Page (b); Gene Krupa (d). January 1938.

Lionel Hampton said (1990): **'Benny didn't leave anything to chance, ever, and that concert
was planned right down to the posters and how we'd walk on stage. I sometimes say it
was just another day at work, but it was more than that.'**

A famous occasion, and the music still stands up extraordinarily well. This was one of those
events – like Ellington at Newport 1956 – when jazz history is spontaneously changed, even
if Goodman had clearly planned the whole thing as a crowning manoeuvre. Unmissable
points: Krupa's fantastically energetic drumming throughout, leading to the roof coming
off on 'Sing, Sing, Sing'; an Ellington tribute and a jam on 'Honeysuckle Rose' with various guests from other bands (George Simon called it 'ineffectual', but it's very exciting);
Ziggy Elman powering through 'Swingtime In The Rockies'; and the original quartet going
through its best paces. But the whole affair is atmospheric with the sense of a man and a
band taking hold of their moment. Columbia's new edition is a model effort, masterminded
by Phil Schapp, whose indomitable detective work finally tracked down the original acetates and gave us the music in the best sound we'll ever get; with powerful, even thrilling,
ambience.

& *See also* **The Complete Small Group Sessions** (1935–1939; p. 52), **B.G. In Hi-Fi** (1954; p. 157)

CHU BERRY

Born Leon Berry, 13 September 1910, Wheeling, West Virginia; died 30 October 1941, Conneaut, Ohio
Tenor saxophone

Chu Berry 1937–1941

Classics 784
Berry; Roy Eldridge, Hot Lips Page, Irving Randolph (t); Keg Johnson, George Mathews (tb); Buster Bailey
(cl); Charlie Ventura (ts); Clyde Hart, Horace Henderson, Benny Payne (p); Danny Barker, Al Casey (g); Israel
Crosby, Milt Hinton, Al Morgan, Artie Shapiro (b); Big Sid Catlett, Cozy Cole, Leroy Maxey, Harry Yeager (d).
March 1937–September 1941.

Saxophonist Frank Lowe said (1989): **'I never was convinced by all the screaming that was
supposed to be part of "avant-garde" music. I was more interested in what Chu Berry did
down in the middle and lower end of his instrument, a quieter approach, like someone
speaking to you, not shouting.'**

When Chu Berry died, fatally injured in a car wreck while on tour, they left his chair in the
Calloway band sitting empty as a mark of tribute. He had had a spell with Fletcher Henderson before signing up with Cab, and his tenor language was much influenced by Coleman Hawkins, though it had deceptive similarities to Lester Young, who evolved in parallel
rather than exerting an influence. Berry's reputation is still in eclipse. He died a little too

soon for the extraordinary revolution in saxophone-playing that followed the end of the war. He had a big sound, not unlike Coleman Hawkins, who considered him an equal, with a curiously fey inflexion that was entirely his own.

For someone who recorded a good deal, the catalogue has always been sparse. A self-effacing character, Berry found himself in the shadow of more celebrated figures such as Basie's ill-fated right-hand man, Herschel Evans. Berry was only ever a dep in the Basie orchestra, but he turned in one classic, 'Lady Be Good'. He had more prominence in the Calloway outfit, with whom he was employed at the time of his death. Too often under other leaders he was restricted to brief excursions from the woodwind bench, and Chu was a player who needed time and space to have his say.

The partnership with Eldridge was a happy, matey affair, and the 'Little Jazz' ensembles of November 1938 are among his best small-group performances. The version of 'Body And Soul' sits well alongside the great ones. 'Sittin' In' is introduced conversationally by the two principals. Talking or playing, they're both in rumbustious form and the warmth of the partnership was equalled only in the late sessions with Hot Lips Page, made within weeks of the road accident that ended Berry's life.

AVERY 'KID' HOWARD

Born 22 April 1908, New Orleans, Louisiana; died 28 March 1966, New Orleans, Louisiana
Trumpet

Prelude To The Revival: Volume 1

American Music AMCD-40
Howard; Andrew Anderson, Punch Miller (t, v); Duke Derbigny (t); Joe 'Brother Cornbread' Thomas (cl, v); Martin Cole (ts); ? Harris (p, v); Joe Robertson (p); Leonard Mitchell (g, bj, v); Frank Murray (g); Chester Zardis (b); Charles Sylvester, Junious Wilson, Clifford 'Snag' Jones (d); Matie Murray (v). 1937–1941.

Humphrey Lyttelton said (1997): **'Revivalist jazz is a bit like reproduction furniture, often much better made than the original.'**

So little jazz was recorded in New Orleans during the '30s that any archive material from the period is valuable. Sam Charters, perhaps not the most reliable judge, reckoned that Kid Howard would have been the next King of New Orleans trumpet after Joe Oliver. It was the spread of modern recording, rather than any shrewd anticipation of the great revival of interest in traditional jazz, that allowed men like Howard, who'd enjoyed only local fame in his youth, to be heard more widely. He is only on the first four tracks here, in barely pass-able sound, but they show a mature, hard-hitting musician displaying the inevitable debt to Armstrong but resolutely going his own way. He'd started out as a drummer and still liked to hit his notes on the head rather than whisper them. Anderson and Derbigny are less individual but they bridge the older and younger New Orleans traditions unselfconsciously enough. The sleeve-notes detail the detective work that went into finding and restoring the original acetates; ears unused to prehistoric sound, beware. There's also material on the record with Punch Miller as leader.

EDGAR HAYES

Born 23 May 1904, Lexington, Kentucky; died 28 June 1979, San Bernardino, California
Piano

Edgar Hayes 1937–1938
Classics 730

Hayes; Bernie Flood (t, v); Henry Goodwin, Shelton Hemphill, Leonard Davis (t); Robert Horton, Clyde Bernhardt, John 'Shorty' Haughton, David 'Jelly' James, Joe Britton (tb); Rudy Powell (cl, as); Roger Boyd, Stanley Palmer, Alfred Skerritt (as); Joe Garland (ts, bs); Crawford Wethington, William Mitchner (ts); Andy Jackson, Eddie Gibbs (g); Elmer James, Frank 'Coco' Darling (b); Kenny Clarke (d, vib); Orlando Roberson, Earlene Howell, Bill Darnell, Ruth Ellington (v). March 1937–January 1938.

Drummer Kenny Clarke said (1978): **'Forty years ago, coming over to Europe with Edgar Hayes. That was an education, and I guess that was my apprenticeship – a lot of freedom.'**

Hayes led a very good orchestra, which evolved out of the quaintly named Eight Black Pirates and the Symphonic Harmonists. He also did a stint with the Mills Brothers Blues Band, before setting up his own outfit. They had a big hit in 1937 with 'Star Dust', not one of their best records. There were good soloists: trombonist Horton was exemplary on both muted and open horn, Garland could play tenor, baritone and bass sax and arrange with equal facility, and Goodwin's trumpet shines; the rhythm section could boast the young Kenny Clarke, already trying to swing his way out of conventional big-band drumming. There are too many indifferent vocals, and some of the material is glum, but much of the first volume stands up to a close listen. A second disc picks up the story with a final Decca, but that was more or less the end of the Hayes story as far as big-band records were concerned.

BUNNY BERIGAN
Born Rowland Bernart Berigan, 2 November 1908, Hilbert, Wisconsin; died 2 June 1942, New York City
Trumpet, voice

Bunny Berigan 1937
Classics 766

Berigan; Irving Goodman, Steve Lipkins (t); Morey Samuel, Sonny Lee, Al George (tb); Mike Doty, Sid Pearlmutter, Joe Dixon (cl, as); Clyde Rounds, Georgie Auld (ts); Joe Lippman (p); Tom Morgan (g); Arnold Fishkind, Hank Wayland (b); George Wettling (d); Ruth Bradley, Gail Reese (v). June–December 1937.

Trumpeter Humphrey Lyttelton said (1995): **'Bunny Berigan's "I Can't Get Started" is one of the half-dozen greatest performances in jazz. It has everything: great technique, solid changes, a story in music, and the knowledge that his life was slipping away early.'**

Bunny Berigan's only flaw, in Louis Armstrong's opinion, was that he didn't live long enough. At the height of his career as an independent bandleader, he was making impossible demands on an uncertain constitution and his intake of alcohol was excessive. As a soloist, he could be wildly exciting or meltingly lyrical, cutting solos like those on the concerto-like 'I Can't Get Started' (two versions but the 1937 one is the classic). He was always one of the boys in the band, utterly inept as an organizer, and even stints with disciplinarians like Goodman and Dorsey didn't mend his ways.

Though he died prematurely burnt out, Berigan left a legacy of wonderful music. His tone was huge and 'fat', a far cry from the tinny squawk with which he started out. Typical devices are his use of 'ghost' notes and rapid chromatic runs that inject tension into music that without him sounds ready to fall asleep. Even such a short career can be divided into 'early' and 'late'. He matured quickly and declined faster, but for a time he was the most exciting player in jazz.

HARRY JAMES
Born 15 March 1916, Albany, Georgia; died 5 July 1983, Las Vegas, Nevada
Trumpet

Harry James 1937–1939
Classics 903
James; Jack Palmer (t, v); Tom Gonsoulin, Claude Bowen, Buck Clayton (t); Eddie Durham, Vernon Brown, Russell Brown, Truett Jones (tb); Earl Warren, Dave Matthews, Claude Lakey (as); Jack Washington (as, bs); Herschel Evans, Arthur Rollini, Drew Page, Bill Luther (ts); Harry Carney (bs); Jess Stacy, Pete Johnson, Albert Ammons, Jack Gardner (p); Bryan Kent (g); Walter Page, Thurman Teague, Johnny Williams (b); Jo Jones, Dave Tough, Eddie Dougherty, Ralph Hawkins (d); Helen Humes, Bernice Byers (v). December 1937–March 1939.

Creed Taylor said (1983): **'He had no small opinion of himself, an ego the size of Plymouth Rock, but then he was moored to Betty Grable and that can't have helped. I didn't care much for that vibrato, either. It just seemed to be saying: "Look at me!"'**

Born into a family of circus musicians, James joined Ben Pollack in 1935, switching to Benny Goodman as star soloist in 1937, then leading his own band from 1939, with Sinatra as vocalist. His taste for show-off virtuosity brought him million-selling records but the derision of many jazz followers. Marriage to Betty Grable ensured he was rarely far from the headlines. He was marked down for stardom very early and in late 1937 started to make recordings under his own name for the Brunswick label.

The sequence starts with three terrific sessions, two in which he fronts a small group drawn from the Basie band, one where he repeats the trick using Goodman sidemen (plus Harry Carney!). Unabashed by the heavy company, James often blows the roof off. Four tracks with Albert Ammons and Pete Johnson spotlight his tersest, hottest playing before the sessions with his proper big band close the disc, opening on his theme-tune, 'Ciri-biribin', which exemplifies what James was about: no better trumpet technician, a great capacity to swing, but with a penchant for schmaltz mixed with bravado. James considered singers a 'necessary evil', and presumably resented the young Sinatra's rise to fame. He himself was to be the focus of every performance. Some of this music resembles the Bunny Berigan orchestra, with all the technique but little of the judgement. Nevertheless, James could play a horn with the best of them and he took jazz to places it hadn't hitherto been.

DIZZY GILLESPIE &
Born John Birks Gillespie, 21 October 1917, Cheraw, South Carolina; died 6 January 1993, Englewood, New Jersey
Trumpet

The Complete RCA Victor Recordings
Bluebird 66528-2 2CD
Gillespie; Bill Dillard, Shad Collins, Lamar Wright, Willie Cook, Benny Harris, Miles Davis, Fats Navarro, Howard McGhee, Karl George, Snooky Young (t); Dicky Wells, Ted Kelly, J. J. Johnson, Kai Winding, Vic Dickenson, George Washington, Ralph Bledsoe, Henry Coker (tb); Trummy Young (tb, v); Buddy DeFranco, Tony Scott (cl); Charlie Parker, Johnny Bothwell, Marvin Johnson, Willie Smith, Benny Carter, Russell Procope, Ernie Henry (as); Dexter Gordon, Don Byas, Fred Simon, Lucky Thompson, Yusef Lateef, Coleman Hawkins, Ben Webster, Charlie Ventura, Robert Carroll, Teddy Hill (ts); Ernie Caceres, Gene Porter (bs); Al Haig, George Handy, Wilbert Baranco, Clyde Hart, Jimmy Jones, Frank Paparelli, Lennie Tristano, Sam Allen, James Foreman (p); Lionel Hampton (vib); Bill De Arongo, Buddy Harper, Mike Bryan, Remo Palmieri, Charlie Christian, Billy Bauer (g); Oscar Pettiford, Gene Ramey, Slam Stewart, Al Hall, Murray Shipinski, Milt Hinton, Richard Fulbright, Al McKibbon, Curley Russell, Charles Mingus, Ray Brown, Eddie Safranski (b); Specs Powell, Ed

Nicholson, Cozy Cole, Irv Kluger, Shelly Manne, Bill Beason, Big Sid Catlett, Earl Watkins, Stan Levey, J. C. Heard, Roy Haynes, Teddy Stewart (d); Vince Guerra, Sabu Martinez, Chano Pozo (perc); Johnny Hartman, Rubberlegs Williams, The Three Angels, Sarah Vaughan (v). May 1937–January 1949.

Dizzy Gillespie said (1984): **'There wasn't much else in South Carolina when I was coming up. Music was a purpose and a way to make sense of life, and I believe that is universally true. I'm a teacher, not a preacher, but I believe music can save you. Nobody was killed by it, whatever you might hear; they were killed by something else.'**

One of the unquestionable major figures of modern jazz, Dizzy was bebop's premier theoretician and became the music's durable ambassador, as significant in his way to the perception of jazz within and beyond America as Louis Armstrong had been a generation earlier, though Armstrong, of course, was still around, still playing and still statesmanlike when Gillespie made his name. Inevitably, some of his best work was released under Charlie Parker's leadership, but, away from Bird, Gillespie was able to develop his own conception of bop, whose highwire excitements sometimes camouflaged a high level of thought.

Dizzy began recording at the end of the '30s. In the Cab Calloway and Teddy Hill bands he cut the outline of a promising Roy Eldridge disciple. His associations with Thelonious Monk and Charlie Parker, though, took him into hitherto uncharted realms. While he continued to credit Parker as the real inspirational force behind bebop, Gillespie was the movement's scholar, straw boss, sartorial figurehead and organizer: his love of big-band sound led him into attempts to orchestrate the new music that resulted in some of the most towering jazz records, particularly (among those here) 'Things To Come' and 'Cubana Be'/'Cubana Bop'. But his own playing is at least as powerful a reason to listen to these tracks. Gillespie brought a new virtuosity to jazz trumpet just as Parker created a matchless vocabulary for the alto sax. It scarcely seems possible that the music could have moved on from Louis Armstrong's 'Cornet Chop Suey' to Gillespie's astonishing flight on 'Dizzy Atmosphere' in only 20 years. A dazzling tone, solo construction that was as logical as it was unremittingly daring, and a harmonic grasp which was built out of countless nights of study and experimentation: Gillespie showed the way for every trumpeter in post-war jazz.

The RCA set sweeps the board as the cream of Gillespie's studio work in the period. The big-band tracks are complete and in good sound, all the Victor small-group sessions are here, and there are prehistory tracks with Teddy Hill and Lionel Hampton as a taster of things to come, and four tracks with the Metronome All-Star bebop group, where Dizzy lines up with Miles, Bird, Fats and JJ.

& See also **Birks Works** (1956–1957; p. 187)

GEORGE CHISHOLM
Born 29 March 1915, Glasgow, Scotland; died 6 December 1997, Milton Keynes, Buckinghamshire, England
Trombone

Early Days 1935–1944
Timeless CBC 1-044
Chisholm; Tommy McQuater, Johnny Claes, Dave Wilkins, Kenny Baker, Stan Roderick, Alfie Noakes (t); Eric Breeze, Bruce Campbell, Dave Walters (tb); Jimmy Durant (ss, bs); Dougie Robinson, Harry Hayes (as); Benny Winestone (cl, ts); Danny Polo, Jimmy Williams, Andy McDevitt (cl); Reg Dare, Aubrey Franks, Jimmy Skidmore (ts); Eddie Macauley, Leonard Feather, Jack Penn, Billy Munn (p); Norman Brown, Ivor Mairants, Alan Ferguson, Dick Ball, Jock Reid, Tiny Winters, Charlie Short (b); Dudley Barber, Ben Edwards, Jock Cummings (d). (1935 and) January 1938–May 1944.

Guitarist Martin Taylor says: **'I once asked Stéphane [Grappelli] who was Django's** favourite jazz musician after Louis Armstrong and he said: "The Scottish trombonist George Chisholm. Django loved his playing."'

The irrepressible 'Chis' was a part of British jazz for decades and the slightness of his recorded legacy is to be regretted. Like most ambitious Scots of his generation, he went South to be recognized, arriving in London in 1935 to work the dance band/jazz scene. He played with Fats Waller and wrote arrangements for the Squadronaires. He subsequently became a radio and television personality, his dry Glaswegian wit unimpaired, but often a Lord of Misrule on otherwise tame variety shows. The exposure left his trad-to-mainstream credentials unimpaired and his Gentlemen Of Jazz were a guaranteed club turn.

This Timeless compilation brings together several dates in which Chisholm featured as a member of various London groups. Four titles by Polo's Swing Stars are fine, and there are a couple of good things under the name of Gerry Moore's Chicago Brethren, but the pick is probably the famous Jive Five session of October 1938, with all known takes included. Besides George proving that he had few peers on the slide horn outside the US at this period, there are glimpses of the admirable McQuater, as well as an acetate made in Leonard Feather's office in 1935, featuring a jam on 'Pardon Me, Pretty Baby' by the 20-year-old trombonist. Aside from its rough sound, transfers are very good. Some of the jokes were rough, too, but they don't transfer quite as well, and only really worked in the great man's own voice.

BOBBY HACKETT

Born 31 January 1915, Providence, Rhode Island; died 7 June 1976, Chatham, Maine
Trumpet, cornet

Bobby Hackett 1938-1940
Classics 890
Hackett; Sterling Bose, Harry Genders, Joe Lucas, Bernie Mattison, Jack Thompson, Stan Wilson (t); Jerry Borshard, George Brunies, Cappy Crouse, John Grassi, George Troup (tb); Brad Gowans (vtb, as); Bob Riedel (cl); Pee Wee Russell (cl, ts); Jerry Caplan, Louis Colombo (as); Bernie Billings, George Dessinger, Hank Kusen, Hammond Rusen (ts); Jim Beitus, Ernie Caceres (bs); Dave Bowman, Frankie Carle (p); Eddie Condon, Bob Julian, Bob Knight (g); Sid Jacobs, Eddie McKinney, Clyde Newcombe (b); Johnny Blowers, Don Carter, Andy Picard (d); Lola Bard, Linda Keene, Claire Martin, The Tempo Twisters (v). February 1938–February 1940.

Warren Vaché says: **'I would meet his plane at Newark just so I could carry his horn case and drive him around. When I played at the Robin Hood Dell in Philadelphia with Benny Goodman, Bobby was also on the bill. He'd just returned from the Benge factory in California, and had two new cornets and a slew of new mouthpieces. He'd play a chorus, then change horn *and* mouthpiece, return to the stage, play another chorus ... No matter what equipment he played he still sounded like Bobby Hackett.'**

Louis Armstrong liked to keep the opposition under close observation and so, for much of the '40s, Hackett played second trumpet under the wing of the man who had influenced his style so much. He was probably too modest for leadership, but in 1938 made the first recordings under his own name for the Vocalion label, with whom he stayed for the next two years, even though there were more lucrative possibilities elsewhere.

Hackett had worked in a trio with Pee Wee Russell, and, though temperamentally they were very different, to put it mildly, the clarinettist and guitarist Eddie Condon were first-call recruitments to the Hackett orchestra which recorded four sides in February 1938. Of these the best is the pairing of 'At The Jazz Band Ball' and 'If Dreams Come True', the latter a vehicle for Lola Bard. A different band but the same formula for the November session that same year, with 'Poor Butterfly' the best showing for Hackett's sweetly melancholy cornet.

One can hear why he was billed as the second Bix – and appeared in that guise at Benny Goodman's 1938 Carnegie Hall concert – but the intonation is different and the phrasing much more relaxed.

Thereafter he tended to use slightly larger bands with augmented saxophones. The sound is closer to the easy swing of the Miller orchestra, and the romantic tension seems to have deserted the leader. Here and there, there are flashes of brilliance, as on 'Bugle Call Rag' and 'I Surrender, Dear' from July 1939, the latter with a vocal by (the first) Claire Martin, but the latter half of the disc feels like a dying fall. Hackett continued to play with grace for the rest of his career, but the essential stuff is all here.

SAVOY SULTANS
Formed 1937
Group

Al Cooper's Savoy Sultans 1938–1941
Classics 728
Cooper; Pat Jenkins (t, v); Sam Massenberg (t); Rudy Williams (as); Ed McNeil, Sam Simmons, Irving 'Skinny' Brown, George Kelley (ts); Oliver Richardson, Cyril Haynes (p); Paul Chapman (g, v); Grachan Moncur (b); Alex 'Razz' Mitchell (d); Helen Procter, Evelyn White (v). July 1938–February 1941.

Drummer Panama Francis said (1976): **'I revived the band and the name to make a connection with the kind of group that used to play for dancers and for popular entertainment. We forget sometimes that's where this music came from.'**

Al Cooper was a modest saxophonist, but he led the very popular Savoy Sultans for many years, including a residency at New York's Savoy Ballroom from 1937 to 1946. The Sultans usually played opposite the Chick Webb band at the Harlem dancehall, and visiting bands were wary of competing with them, since they were so popular with the dancers. The records are another matter: simple head arrangements, average solos and merely capable playing make one wonder why they were held in such high regard. However, playing through these 24 tracks, one can hear some of the simple appeal of what wasn't really a big band but a small, mobile, flexible unit which covered whatever base the customers wanted. There's also ample evidence that groups of the time and earlier quite deliberately tamed and gentrified their playing for trips to the studios, which were still regarded as an exception and rarity by most musicians. Pat Jenkins is the best soloist but there are clear pitching problems in the ensemble, more intriguing than irritating. After the war, drummer Panama Francis assembled a new Savoy Sultans, a rare example of a small swing group being so convened at the time.

ZIGGY ELMAN
Born Harry Aaron Finkelman, 26 May 1914, Philadelphia, Pennsylvania; died 26 June 1968, Los Angeles, California
Trumpet

Ziggy Elman 1938–1939
Classics 900
Elman; Noni Bernardi, Toots Mondello, Hymie Schertzer (as); Jerry Jerome, Arthur Rollini, Babe Russin (ts); Milt Raskin, Jess Stacy (p); Ben Heller (g); Artie Bernstein, Harry Goodman, Joe Schwartzman (b); Nick Fatool, Al Kendis (d). December 1938–December 1939.

Trumpeter Jimmy Deuchar said of the notorious Elman embouchure: '**Nothing mysterious about it. When you have chops like that, you could probably play trumpet with your ****.**'

Though he played trumpet with enormous power, Elman has been dismissed in recent years as a *Schmaltzmeister*. Ziggy's image was set in stone by his appearance as himself in *The Benny Goodman Story*, though by then he was too ill to play his own solos, and his parts had to be dubbed in by Mannie Klein. Goodman had hired him in 1936, impressed by his adaptability and tone (and not put off by the weird embouchure; Ziggy played, literally, out of the side of his mouth). The postwar material is better-known, but it is never much more than routine. Hayes is a similarly underrated player, but he was to do more interesting things elsewhere, and DeVito always had fascinating ideas to share. What made the pre-war band interesting was the unusual front line of single trumpet and saxophone section. 'Fralich In Swing' is a Jewish wedding dance tune which Goodman had turned into a hit song, 'And The Angels Sing'. It loses none of its freshness with Elman blaring away in front. The remaining material for Bluebird sticks to the basic formula and relies on essentially the same pool of Goodman-trained players, which may account for the tightness of the section work. Benny's absence may account for the joyous, just-let-out-of-jail quality of some of the playing. Bernardi is exceptional, immediately distinguishable from his fellow altoists, and Stacy and Milt Raskin hold down the chords with calm precision. The sound quality on the whole is good, though there is some distortion on the December 1938 session.

PETE JOHNSON
Born 25 March 1904, Kansas City, Missouri; died 23 March 1967, Buffalo, New York
Piano

Pete Johnson 1938–1939
Classics 656
Johnson; Harry James, Hot Lips Page (t); Buster Smith (as); Albert Ammons, Meade 'Lux' Lewis (p); Lawrence Lucie, Ulysses Livingston (g); Abe Bolar, Johnny Williams (b); Eddie Dougherty (d); Joe Turner (v). December 1938–December 1939.

Musicologist Edward Tellman remembers: '**In his later years, Pete lived in upstate New York. When I first saw him, he was playing in a little club in Niagara Falls. He used to have to climb this big ladder to get to the space above the bar where the piano was. A rather ironic elevation for a jazz master, I subsequently thought.**'

Just two months from his death, Pete Johnson played his own 'Roll 'Em Pete' at one of John Hammond's 'Spirituals To Swing' concerts. Johnson had been present at the 1938 concert as well, but now he was reduced to playing the right-hand part only, having suffered a stroke and lost part of a finger while changing a flat tyre. Along with Meade 'Lux' Lewis and Albert Ammons, Johnson was part of a great triumvirate of boogie-woogie piano players who developed and popularized the style.

  Johnson's mastery of boogie-woogie and blues piano is evident from the first. Classics' survey begins with the Kansas City pianist accompanying Joe Turner on the singer's first studio date, before two quartet tracks with Harry James: 'Boo-Woo' is an outright classic. All this in the year of the Hammond concert. His complete 1939 date for Solo Art is another memorable occasion, nine solos that go from the Tatum-like elaborations on Leroy Carr's 'How Long, How Long Blues' to the furious 'Climbin' And Screamin'' and 'Shuffle Boogie'. The sound is thin, but Johnson's energy and invention shine through. There are four more tracks with a small band, including Page and Turner, a solo 'Boogie Woogie', two trio pieces and the first trio with Albert Ammons and Meade 'Lux' Lewis on 'Café Society Rag'.

  His 1939 session for Blue Note (the label's founder, Alfred Lion, had attended the 'Spirituals To Swing' concert and been inspired by it) is, unfortunately, split across two Classics volumes. The sequel opens on the stunning 'Holler Stomp', the most audacious of boogie showcases. 'You Don't Know My Mind', from the same date, is contrastingly dreamy and may remind blues aficionados of pianists such as Walter Davis and Lane Smith.

GENE KRUPA
Born 15 January 1909, Chicago, Illinois; died 16 October 1973, New York City
Drums

Gene Krupa 1939–1940
Classics 834
Krupa; Johnny Martel, Corky Cornelius, Torg Halten, Nate Kazebier, Johnny Napton, Shorty Sherock (t); Al Sherman, Floyd O'Brien, Red Ogle, Al Jordan, Sid Brantley (tb); Bob Snyder, Clint Neagley (as); Sam Donahue (ts); Sam Musiker (cl, ts); Tony D'Amore, Milt Raskin (p); Ray Biondi (g); Biddy Bastien (b); Irene Daye, Howard DuLany (v). July 1939–February 1940.

Drummer Buddy Rich said (1976): **'The funny papers liked to make out that we're big rivals – which we were – but that we probably hated each other like two boxers before a prizefight. So let me say, Gene was the tops; he was the President of the Drums. Always was, hands down.'**

There is a memorable photograph of the young Gene Krupa at the kit, hair slick, collar and lapels soaked with sweat, mouth and eyes wide and hungry, his brushes blurred to smoke with the pace of his playing. Received wisdom has Krupa down as a showman who traded in subtlety for histrionic power, but even in comparative neglect Krupa's impact on the jazz rhythm section is incalculable. He himself said: 'I made the drummer a high-priced guy.'

Krupa joined the Benny Goodman band in 1934 and stayed till 1938, when his boss finally decided there was room for only one of them on stage. The drummer recorded under his own name only twice during the Goodman years.

In the spring of 1938 Krupa moved to New York and started to manage his own career. Despite some good work for Brunswick, the extra work put a strain on his invention for a while but he was getting good at balancing both sides of the job. The following year saw a step-up in output and quality and there is a strong sense of consolidation in the band, which begins to sound like a more solidly integrated unit. Krupa's leadership is tight and very musical. Kazebier returns to the fold and O'Brien signs up to stiffen the brasses. Apart from a couple of novelty instrumentals made for dancing ('Dracula' and 'Foo For Two') the standard is very high and Krupa can increasingly be heard to experiment with rhythmic embellishments, off-accent notes, single beats on the edge of his cymbals, and with the dynamics. Even with such a powerful group, he was always prepared on occasion to play quietly and to contrast *fff* and *pp* passages within a single song, relatively unusual at that time when up was up and a ballad was a ballad. Into 1940, it's pretty much a question of steady as she goes, even with the inevitable personnel changes. By this point Krupa can be heard to be shaping the band to his new requirements, which were much less histrionic. The Benny Carter piece 'Symphony In Riffs', recorded for Columbia in September 1939, and the majestic two-part 'Blue Rhythm Fantasy' (nearly seven minutes in total) stand out as representative masterpieces.

MUGGSY SPANIER
Born Francis Joseph Spanier, 9 November 1906, Chicago, Illinois; died 12 February 1967, Sausalito, California
Cornet

Muggsy Spanier 1939-1942

Classics 709

Spanier; Ruby Weinstein, Elmer O'Brien (t); Ford Leary, George Brunies (tb, v); Rod Kless (cl); Karl Kates, Joe Forchetti, Ed Caine (as); Ray McKinstrey, Bernie Billings, Nick Caizza (ts); George Zack, Charlie Queener, Joe Bushkin (p); Bob Casey (g, b); Pat Pattison (b); Marty Greenberg, Al Hammer, Don Carter, Al Sidell (d), Dottie Reid (v). July 1939-June 1942.

Humphrey Lyttelton said (1991): **'He wasn't the greatest technician. Some of the solos play around with just four or five notes, but he gets something across every time. It's almost miraculous how he does that, like Picasso creating a recognizable likeness with just two strokes of his brush.'**

Recording as a teenager, Muggsy was off to a quick start in his native Chicago. He worked with Ted Lewis and Ben Pollack in the '20s and '30s, before forming his Ragtime Band in 1939. The records are classics but the band was a commercial failure. He stuck with Dixieland through the '40s and '50s, before moving west to join Earl Hines in 1957 and leading modest small groups up until his death.

Spanier's 1939 Ragtime Band recordings are among the classic statements in the traditional-jazz idiom. Bob Crosby's Bob Cats had helped to initiate a modest vogue for small Dixieland bands in what was already a kind of revivalism at the height of the big-band era, and Spanier's group had audiences flocking to Chicago clubs, although by December, with a move to New York, they were forced to break up for lack of work. Their recordings have been dubbed 'The Great Sixteen' ever since. While there are many fine solos scattered through the sides – mostly by Spanier and the little-remembered Rod Kless – it's as an ensemble that the band impresses: allied to a boisterous rhythm section, the informal counterpoint among the four horns (the tenor sax perfectly integrated, just as Eddie Miller was in the Bob Cats) swings through every performance. The repertoire re-established the norm for Dixieland bands, and even though the material goes back to Oliver and the ODJB, there's no hint of fustiness, even in the rollicking effects of 'Barnyard Blues'. 'Someday Sweetheart', with its sequence of elegant solos, is a masterpiece of cumulative tension, and Spanier himself secures two finest hours in the storming finish to 'Big Butter And Egg Man' and the wah-wah blues-playing on 'Relaxin' At The Touro', a poetic tribute to convalescence (he had been ill the previous year) the way Parker's 'Relaxin' At Camarillo' would subsequently be. His own playing is masterful throughout – the hot Chicago cornet sound refined and seared away to sometimes the simplest but most telling of phrases. This Classics CD adds eight tracks to the definitive 16 by Muggsy's big band, none of them outstanding but all grist to the Spanier collector's mill.

COLEMAN HAWKINS &

Known as 'Bean'; born 21 November 1904, St Joseph, Missouri; died 19 May 1969, New York City
Tenor saxophone

Coleman Hawkins 1939-1940

Classics 634

Hawkins; Tommy Lindsay, Joe Guy, Tommy Stevenson, Nelson Bryant (t); Benny Carter (t, as); Earl Hardy, J. C. Higginbotham, William Cato, Sandy Williams, Claude Jones (tb); Danny Polo (cl); Eustis Moore, Jackie Fields, Ernie Powell (as); Kermit Scott (ts); Gene Rodgers, Joe Sullivan (p); Ulysses Livingston (g, v); Lawrence Lucie, Bernard Addison, Gene Fields (g); William Oscar Smith, Artie Shapiro, Johnny Williams, Billy Taylor (b); Arthur Herbert, George Wettling, Walter Johnson, Big Sid Catlett, J. C. Heard (d); Thelma Carpenter, Jeanne Burns, Joe Turner, Gladys Madden (v). October 1939-August 1940.

Stan Getz said (1983): **'I guarantee you that everyone who has ever picked up a tenor saxophone has tried to reduplicate that performance, and every one of us wishes that one day we could do something like ["Body And Soul"]. Maybe that's the motivation.'**

The 11th of October 1939 marks an epoch in modern jazz. On that day, Coleman Hawkins recorded the version of 'Body And Soul' that became the template for a thousand thousand saxophone solos since. It sits, along with cuts by Louis Armstrong, Charlie Parker and Art Tatum, as among the very finest performances in the whole history of jazz.

Hawkins had been recording in Europe. He didn't exactly return to the USA in triumph, but his eminence was almost immediately re-established with the astounding 'Body And Soul', which still sounds like the most spontaneously perfect of all jazz records. Fitted into the session as an afterthought (they had already cut 12 previous takes of 'Fine Dinner' and eight of 'Meet Doctor Foo'), this one-take, two-chorus improvisation is so completely realized, every note meaningful, the tempo ideal, the rhapsodic swing irresistible, and the sense of rising drama sustained to the final coda, that it still has the capacity to amaze new listeners, just like Armstrong's 'West End Blues' or Parker's 'Bird Gets The Worm'. A later track on this Classics CD, the little-known 'Dedication', revisits the same setting; although masterful in its way, it points up how genuinely immediate the greatest jazz is: it can't finally compare to the original. If the same holds good for the many later versions of the tune which Hawkins set down, his enduring variations on the structure (and it's intriguing to note that he only refers to the original melody in the opening bars of the 1939 reading – which didn't stop it from becoming a huge hit) say something about his own powers of renewal.

The CD is let down by dubbing from some very surfacey originals, even though it includes some strong material – two Varsity Seven sessions with Carter and Polo, the aforementioned 'Dedication' and a 1940 date for OKeh which features some excellent tenor on 'Rocky Comfort' and 'Passin' It Around'.

& *See also* **Coleman Hawkins 1929–1934** (1929–1934; p. 38), **The Stanley Dance Sessions** (1955–1958; p. 172)

BUD FREEMAN
Born Lawrence Freeman, 13 April 1906, Chicago, Illinois; died 15 March 1991, Chicago, Illinois
Tenor saxophone

Bud Freeman 1939–1940
Classics 811
Freeman; Max Kaminsky (t); Jack Teagarden (tb, v); Brad Gowans (vtb); Pee Wee Russell (cl); Dave Bowman (p); Eddie Condon (g); Clyde Newcomb, Pete Peterson, Mort Stuhlmaker (b); Danny Alvin, Morey Feld, Al Sidell, Dave Tough (d). July 1939–July 1940.

Bud Freeman said (1982): **'I had ambitions to be a Shakespearean actor when I was a young man, but I've been strutting this stage ever since … You don't have to learn swordplay to be a jazz musician, though it might help with promoters!'**

Freeman was perhaps the first truly significant white tenor-player. If he looked, and chose to behave, like the secretary of some golf club in the Home Counties – episode one of his autobiography was called *You Don't Look Like a Musician* – his saxophone walked all over the carpets in spikes, a rawer sound than Lester Young's (to which it is often likened) and with a tougher articulation; it was for a time the only viable alternative to Coleman Hawkins's sound.

He was a member of the famous Austin High School Gang and perhaps its most polished alumnus. He made records in the 1930s with other leaders – Tommy Dorsey, Muggsy Spanier, Eddie Condon – but became a star in his own right with 'The Eel', a sinuous tenor melody that became a signature hit. The first pieces on the 1939 Classics volume features Freeman's Summa Cum Laude Orchestra, an octet with a starry line-up that swung with bullish ease, like a glee club at a gentlemen's club. The material from later in the year and next features a slightly different band with Teagarden (effusively vocal on 'Jack Hits the Road') in place of Gowans and a body of material that suggests the ODJB and Bix Beiderbecke. Freeman was most comfortable with his repertoire and there are a few moments when his tenor resembles Trumbauer's C-melody; Bud had started out on that horn and something of its quiet presence carried over into Bud's tenor work.

He enjoyed a long life and was still playing in his 70s, always with the reluctant grace of a man who really didn't want the spotlight but wouldn't want to let anyone down.

ARTIE SHAW

Born Arthur Jacob Arshawsky, 23 May 1910, New Haven, Connecticut; died 30 December 2004, Newbury Park, California
Clarinet

Artie Shaw 1939

Classics 1007
Shaw; Chuck Peterson, John Best, Bernie Privin (t); George Arus, Harry Rodgers, Les Jenkins (tb); Les Robinson, Hank Freeman (as); Tony Pastor (ts, v); Ronnie Perry, Georgie Auld (ts); Bob Kitsis (p); Al Avola (g); Sid Weiss (b); Buddy Rich (d); Helen Forrest (v). January–March 1939.

Visiting London as a conductor (1984), Artie Shaw said: **'Of course I still have a clarinet. I had it turned into a table lamp.'**

Shaw's amazing life makes his records seem tame. They form a unique part of the jazz literature, although his real successes were comparatively few and his ambitions always outran his achievements. He successively turned his back on each fresh phase in his life – much as he walked away from marriages to Lana Turner and Ava Gardner, just two of his eight wives – and eventually, after 1949, gave up playing clarinet altogether, though he did occasionally come out of retirement to conduct, mostly classical arrangements.

Shaw started out in dance bands before forming his own ensemble in 1936. Though his orchestra became one of the major swing-era big bands, he resisted commercialism and disbanded several orchestras during the period, during the late '30s and war years. As a clarinettist, he was as accomplished as Benny Goodman and the major soloist in his own band. Shaw was perhaps too rounded and curious a character to be bounded by the life of a jazz musician. As well as successive trips to City Hall and Reno, tying or untying various knots, he became a gifted writer of fiction and had a more than amateur interest in psychoanalysis.

Although 'Begin The Beguine' made him a success – Shaw switched the original beguine beat to a modified 4/4, and its lilting pulse was irresistible – euphoria turned to loathing when it dawned on him what it meant in terms of fawning fans and general notoriety. He never seemed satisfied with his bands, and most compilations paper across multiple break-ups and disbandments.

This, the second disc in the Classics series, picks up Shaw's story at the zenith. It's the gusto of the band and Shaw's piercing solos one remembers, a quite astonishing advance on the music of only a little over a year earlier. This sounds like a swing master close to full command and presented in good-sounding transfers. One is impressed with how often

Shaw got a musical result of one sort or another. Listen to the way the band makes the melody-line of 'The Man I Love' sing, or how Shaw makes the most of even a bit of hokum like 'The Donkey Serenade'. Only ten of the 22 tracks sport a vocal – a very low strike-rate compared to most other white bands of the day – and even then Shaw could boast the admirable Helen Forrest as his singer. It's sometimes disappointing that there weren't more interesting soloists, but Shaw by himself is always worth listening to. Track for track, this is a marvellous portrait of a swing band.

CHARLIE CHRISTIAN
Born 19 July 1916, Dallas, Texas; died 2 March 1942, New York City
Guitar

The Genius Of The Electric Guitar
Columbia CK 65564 4CD
Christian; Alec Fila, Irving Goodman, Cootie Williams (t); Cutty Cutshall, Lou McGarity (tb); Gus Bivona, Skippy Martin (as); Georgie Auld, Pete Mandello (ts); Bob Snyder (bs); Lionel Hampton (vib); Count Basie, Dudley Brooks, Johnny Guarnieri, Fletcher Henderson (p); Artie Bernstein (b); Nick Fatool, Harry Jaeger, Jo Jones, Dave Tough (d). 1939–1941.

Guitarist Jim Hall said (1992): **'Whenever I hear Charlie Christian, I react the way I did when I heard him for the very first time: How did he do that? How ... did ... he ... do ... that? It was almost a spiritual awakening. Makes me realize I know next to nothing about the guitar.'**

Who invented bebop? Parker and Gillespie seemed to arrive at near-identical solutions. Monk was never an orthodox bopper, but he had his two cents' worth. Kenny Clarke made significant changes in the rhythm department. And then there was Charlie Christian, who in some accounts was the first to develop the long legato lines and ambitious harmonic progressions that defined bop. His appetite for booze and girls was only ever overtaken by his thirst for music. He once improvised 'Rose Room' for nearly an hour and a half, a feat which prompted Benny Goodman to hire him. Though his greatest contributions, in terms of musical history, were at Minton's, his roles in the Goodman and Hampton bands represent the bulk of what is left to us from a strikingly foreshortened career. His first commercial outings were the September 1939 sides with Hampton. A single track from this time ('One Sweet Letter From You') and one from a month later ('Haven't Named It Yet') give a sense of the excitement the bandleader obviously felt at this freshly discovered young voice.

Christian was the first to make completely convincing use of the electric instrument, and though his style blended Texas blues riffing with Lester Young's long-limbed strolls, he was able to steer a path away from the usual saxophone-dominated idiom and towards something that established guitar as an improvising instrument in its own right. Goodman gave him considerable solo space in the sextet; amplification meant that the guitar could be heard clearly and Christian's solos on 'Rose Room' and 'Star Dust' remain models for the instrument.

There is now ample choice for collectors and just about any option will evidence Charlie's speed of thought and devotion to a sound which is both electric in its embrace of amplification and organic as well. Though we have tried to avoid box sets, some are more insistent than others. This Columbia set offers 98 tracks, including 70 master takes. If that's too much, there is a shorter compilation which will do for most. The sound quality is exquisite, a model for all reissue programmes. A devil's advocate question lurks, though. How important in the history of the music was Charlie Christian? Is there anything here that really merits such extravagant packaging, or was he just another of those artists re-created by a posthumous mythology, the kind of thing that inevitably attaches to a young genius who dies of TB at just 26? We've returned to these recordings umpteen times down the years. They have never failed to excite and satisfy.

WOODY HERMAN &

Born 16 May 1913, Milwaukee, Wisconsin; died 29 October 1987, Los Angeles, California
Clarinet, alto and soprano saxophones, voice

Woody Herman 1939

Classics 1128
Herman; Clarence Willard, Jerry Neary, Steady Nelson, Mac MacQuordale, Bob Price (t); Neal Reid, Toby Tyler (tb); Joe Bishop (flhn); Joe Estrin, Ray Hopfner, Joe Denton (as); Saxie Mansfield, Pete Johns (ts); Tommy Linehan (p); Hy White (g); Walter Yoder (b); Frank Carlson (d); Mary Martin, Mary Ann McCall, The Andrews Sisters (v). January–August 1939.

Woody Herman said (1977): **'["At the Woodchopper's Ball"] was a triumph of persistence. The record company just kept putting it out until the public gave in and made it a hit. Nothing more to it than that. It's not Beethoven.'**

Herman began playing as a child in vaudeville, took over the Isham Jones band in 1936 and kept it afloat until the mid-'40s. His Second (1947–9) and Third (1952–4) Herds were star-studded big bands, led with indomitable showmanship. He constantly updated his repertoire while never neglecting his library of swing-era hits and was still leading small groups and larger bands into his 70s, although his last years were troubled by tax problems.

On 4 April 1939, the band cut five titles, including 'At The Woodchoppers' Ball', 'Big Wig In The Wigwam', 'Blues Upstairs' and 'Blues Downstairs'. Although the immortal 'Woodchoppers' Ball' was no more than Joe Bishop's head arrangement on the blues, it eventually became a huge hit, selling in the millions. Some of the later sessions on this disc feature music of similar quality, including 'Casbah Blues' and 'Midnight Echoes'; but Herman still lacked a major arranging presence, and subsequent volumes in this series see the band return to the sweeter material of before, with novelties like 'Peace, Brother!' and 'The Rhumba Jumps' taking up too much studio time.

& *See also* **Blowin' Up A Storm!** (1945–1947; p. 102), **Woody's Winners / Jazz Hoot** (1965, 1967; p. 321)

JOHN KIRBY

Born 31 December 1908, Baltimore, Maryland; died 14 June 1952, Hollywood, California
Double bass

John Kirby 1939–1941

Classics 770
Kirby; Charlie Shavers (t); Buster Bailey (cl); Russell Procope (as); Billy Kyle (p); O'Neil Spencer (d, v). October 1939–January 1941.

Kirby's ex-wife Maxine Sullivan said (1980): **'Our CBS radio show was called *Flow Gently, Sweet Rhythm*. Some people like to think jazz has to be dirty and wild. No reason why it can't be elegant as well, and that's what John Kirby was.'**

They played in white ties and tails – and they often sounded that way – but the Kirby Sextet has exerted a small and subtle influence on recent jazz. The original septet, led by Buster

Bailey, shed a member and Kirby (a better organizer and front-man, despite his instrument) was appointed leader. Many of the early arrangements are, surprisingly, credited to Charlie Shavers, and it's fascinating to hear him sound so well-mannered, both with horn and with pencil. Titles like 'Opus 5', 'Impromptu' and 'Nocturne' on an earlier Classics volume and borrowings from Schubert, Chopin ('The Minute Waltz', inevitably) and Dvořák don't point to a burning desire to swing the classics the way Kirby's wife Maxine Sullivan was swinging Scottish folk material. It was more pragmatic than that. An ASCAP ban meant that groups could only perform out-of-copyright material. Kirby's music might seem a by-way, but play him alongside one of Dave Douglas's classical settings or some other similarly inclined recent leader and the lineage becomes more obvious.

HARLAN LEONARD

Born 2 July 1905, Kansas City, Missouri; died 1983, Los Angeles, California
Bandleader

Harlan Leonard And His Rockets 1940

Classics 670

Leonard; James Ross (t); Edward Johnson, William H. Smith (t); Fred Beckett, Walter Monroe, Richmond Henderson (tb); Darwin Jones (as, v); Henry Bridges (cl, ts); Jimmy Keith (ts); William Smith (p); Efferge Ware, Stan Morgan (g); Winston Williams, Billy Hadnott (b); Jesse Price (d); Myra Taylor, Ernie Williams (v). January–November 1940.

Poet Kenneth Rexroth said (1977): **'I asked him if it was true that he'd once fired Charlie Parker, and if so, in what circumstances, but he just smiled enigmatically, like a cat that had just eaten a canary.'**

The forgotten man of Kansas City jazz. Leonard worked with Bennie Moten from 1923 to 1931, then joined the Kansas City Sky Rockets and took over three years later, keeping the group going in the city until 1945, when he left the music business. When Basie left for New York, Leonard's orchestra took over many of the Count's local engagements. But he didn't make many records; all 23 surviving tracks are here. No one will claim it as a great band in the usual sense of innovative and packed with fine soloists, but it is a very good band indeed at what it does. At some level it lacked individuality and some of the tracks are built round the kind of devices which Basie was personalizing to a much greater degree, the section work is occasionally suspect, and the KC rocking rhythm is something they fall back on time and again. But something good is to be found in nearly all these tracks, and some fine soloists, too – Bridges is an outstanding tenorman and Beckett (admired by J. J. Johnson) a surprisingly agile trombonist, and the trumpets hit the spot whenever they have to. Scholars will prize six early arrangements by the young Tadd Dameron, and one shouldn't miss the blues-inflected vocals of Ernie Williams, a lighter Jimmy Rushing.

SIDNEY BECHET&

Born 14 May 1897, New Orleans, Louisiana; died 14 May 1959, Paris, France
Soprano saxophone, clarinet

Sidney Bechet 1940–1941

Classics 638

Bechet; Gus Aiken, Henry 'Red' Allen, Henry Goodwin, Henry Levine, Charlie Shavers (t); Rex Stewart (c); Jack Epstein, Vic Dickenson, J. C. Higginbotham, Sandy Williams (tb); Alfie Evans (cl); Rudolph Adler, Lem Johnson (ts); Don Donaldson, Earl Hines, Cliff Jackson, Mario Janarro, Willie 'The Lion' Smith, James Tolliver (p); Everett Barksdale, Tony Colucci (g); Wellman Braud, John Lindsay, Wilson Myers, Harry Patent, Ernest Williamson (b); Baby Dodds, J. C. Heard, Arthur Herbert, Manzie Johnson, Nat Levine (d); Herb Jeffries (v). September 1940–October 1941.

Soprano saxophonist Steve Lacy said (1983): **'The sound of Bechet playing "The Mooche" did it for me. That sound was so hard but also so lyrical, I was immediately hooked.'**

Bechet was the first great saxophone soloist in jazz, and perhaps the first musician to play extended solos in the music, as opposed to short breaks. Even before Louis Armstrong came along, he was playing vertical improvisations on the chords of a tune. Like Pops, Bechet grew up in New Orleans, transported his style north and then became the American star in Europe. A pioneer of the soprano saxophone, Sidney managed to combine its intense, sometimes treacherous tonality with the warm, woody sound of the clarinet.

Bechet himself contributed to the heav'n-taught image confected in a notorious Ernest Ansermet essay. Sidney's autobiography, *Treat It Gentle*, is a masterpiece of contrived ingenuousness; John Chilton's superb biography gets closer to the truth. Bechet was an exceptionally gifted and formally aware musician whose compositional skills greatly outshine those of Louis Armstrong, his rival for canonization as the first great jazz improviser. Armstrong's enormous popularity – abetted by his sky-writing top Cs and vocal performance – tended to eclipse Bechet everywhere except in France. Sidney's melodic sense and ability to structure a solo round the harmonic sequence of the original theme (or with no theme whatsoever) have been of immense significance in the development of modern jazz. Bechet made a pioneering switch to the stronger-voiced soprano saxophone in the same year as Ansermet's essay, having found a secondhand horn in a London shop. Within a few years, his biting tone and dramatic tremolo were among the most distinctive sounds in jazz.

After a relatively slow start to his recording career as leader, Bechet soon got into a groove, feeding an increasingly hungry audience with top-flight discs. In April 1941, Bechet fulfilled the logic of his increasingly self-reliant musical conception by recording two unprecedented 'one-man-band' tracks, overdubbing up to six instruments. 'Sheik Of Araby' is for the full 'band' of soprano and tenor saxophones, clarinet, piano, bass and drums; so time-consuming was the process that a second item, 'Blues For Bechet', had to be completed without bass or drums, leaving a fascinating fragment for RCA to release.

In September of the same year, Bechet made another classic trio recording, this time with Willie 'The Lion' Smith and Everett Barksdale, on electric guitar. Though the two sidemen provide no more than incidental distractions, the trio sessions were more compelling than the full band assembled on that day (Charlie Shavers plays monster lines on 'I'm Coming Virginia', as on the October 'Mood Indigo', but is otherwise ill-suited); 'Strange Fruit' is one of Bechet's most calmly magisterial performances, and the two takes of 'You're The Limit' seem too good to have been dumped in the 'unreleased' bin, though perhaps the absence on either of a commanding solo from Bechet put the label off. A month later, in the same session that realized 'Mood Indigo', Bechet cut the utterly awful 'Laughin' In Rhythm', a New Orleans version of 'The Laughing Policeman' that, despite a taut soprano solo, hardly merits revival. Dickenson also plays beautifully on 'Blue In The Air', one of the finest of Bechet's recorded solos.

& See also **King Jazz: Volume 1** (1945; p. 99), **The Fabulous Sidney Bechet** (1951–1953; p. 132)

CLAUDE THORNHILL

Born 10 August 1909, Terre Haute, Indiana; died 1 July 1965, New York City
Arranger

Snowfall
Hep CD 1058
Thornhill; large orchestra. September 1940–July 1941.

Singer and pianist Diana Krall said (2002): **'I grew up listening to Claude Thornhill records. They were considered to be very cool, and I guess they were.'**

Formally trained, Thornhill began working for New York bands in the mid-'30s – he arranged 'Loch Lomond' for Maxine Sullivan – before touring with his orchestra from 1940. After war service, he re-formed the orchestra in 1946 and hired Gil Evans and Gerry Mulligan to write many of the band's arrangements. Their work was the forerunner of the *Birth Of The Cool* school.

With the revival of interest in mood-music mandarins like Martin Denny and Arthur Lyman, it's not inconceivable that Thornhill's work could catch the ear of those seeking something in the classic easy-listening style. His band was never a striking commercial success, though Thornhill's interest in a meticulousness of sound – subtle section-work, carefully filtered reed textures, the static bass harmony provided by Bill Barber's tuba parts – resulted in little classics like his theme, 'Snowfall'. But his relationship to jazz is rather hazy, given the formalized tone of the band, and though there were major cool-school players in the orchestra and it features much of the early work of Gil Evans and Mulligan as arrangers, many of the recordings are exotically ephemeral.

The earliest studio recordings have been restored to print by Hep's excellent compilation, and from the first tracks it's clear why Thornhill was so popular with audiences seeking sweet music. There seem to be the scent of freesias and the feel of lace-work around such scores as 'Alt Wein' and 'Love Tales', dappled by the leader's piano. He stacks up clarinets, quietly, or threads the reed section around simple brass comments which can't even be called riffs. A piece such as 'Portrait Of A Guinea Farm' is as exotic as society music would ever get. 'Snowfall' itself is a flawless miniature. But there are also numerous vocal features, such as 'Mandy Is Two', which may bring on impatience in the listener. The sleeve-note suggests that Thornhill's band was 'too musical' to secure wider success, but that was not a problem which bothered such musical orchestras as Ellington's or Goodman's.

The sequel is *Buster's Last Stand*, also on Hep, and in fact the label has done more for Thornhill's reputation than anyone, with a nice list of compilation reissues that include some valuable transcriptions taken between 1947 and 1953.

DUKE ELLINGTON &
Born Edward Kennedy Ellington, 29 April 1899, Washington DC; died 24 May 1974, New York City
Piano

Never No Lament
RCA Bluebird 82876-50857-2 3CD
Ellington; Wallace Jones, Cootie Williams, Ray Nance (t); Rex Stewart (c); Joe 'Tricky Sam' Nanton, Lawrence Brown (tb); Juan Tizol (vtb); Barney Bigard, Chauncey Haughton (cl); Johnny Hodges (ss, as, cl); Harry Carney (bs, cl, as); Otto Hardwick (as, bsx); Ben Webster (ts); Billy Strayhorn (p); Fred Guy (g); Jimmy Blanton, Junior Raglin (b); Sonny Greer (d); Ivie Anderson, Herb Jeffries (v). March 1940–July 1942.

The Duke At Fargo
Storyville STCD 8316/8317 2CD
Largely as above. November 1940.

Gerry Mulligan said (1992): **'The arrival of Jimmy Blanton was the birth of the modern rhythm section. It was like putting a new engine into a Rolls-Royce, except this was an engine you wanted to just listen to, and not just drive around with!'**

Once all the late-'30s Ellington was back in print it became easier to see that he had been working towards this exceptional period for the band for a long time. Ellington had been building a matchless team of soloists, his own composing was taking on a finer degree of personal creativity and sophistication, and with the arrival of bassist Jimmy Blanton, who gave the rhythm section an unparalleled eloquence in the way it swung, the final piece fell into place. The 6 May 1940 session, which opens *Never No Lament*, is one of the great occasions in jazz history, when Ellington recorded both 'Jack The Bear' (a feature for Blanton) and the unqualified masterpiece 'Ko-Ko'. From there, literally dozens of classics tumbled out of the band, from originals such as 'Harlem Air Shaft' and 'Main Stem' and 'Take The "A" Train' to brilliant Ellingtonizations of standard material such as 'The Sidewalks Of New York' and 'Clementine'. The arrival of Billy Strayhorn, who stayed until he died in 1967, is another important element in the music's success.

Of the many surviving location recordings of the Ellington band, *The Duke At Fargo* is surely the very best, catching over two hours of material from a single dance date in North Dakota, part of it broadcast but most of it simply taken down by amateur enthusiasts. Storyville released a 60th-anniversary edition of the music in 2000, handsomely presented. The sound is probably as fine as it will ever be. Here is one of the greatest Ellington orchestras on a typical night, with many of the best numbers in the band's book and the most rousing version of 'St Louis Blues' to climax the evening. The sound is inevitably well below the quality of the studio sessions, but it's a fine supplement to them, and a definitive glimpse into a working day in the life of one of the great swing orchestras.

& *See also* **Duke Ellington 1927-1929** (1927-1929; p. 28), **Duke Ellington 1937-1938** (1937-1938; p. 64), **Black, Brown And Beige** (1944-1946; p. 91), **Ellington At Newport** (1956; p. 189), **The Far East Suite** (1966; p. 336)

THE '40s

Somewhere in the '40s, a new style of jazz emerged, called bebop, an onomatopoeic term that has never been any more helpful than any of the other labels applied to the music, but which, oddly, has rarely been questioned by musicians themselves, perhaps because it emerged among them rather than in the reviewing media. Needless to say, bebop (or rebop or bop) was not new at all but an inevitable evolution from what had been happening in swing throughout the previous decade. One might unpretentiously liken it to the 'inevitability' of Richard Wagner's new suspended harmony at a certain point in late Romanticism.

Part of the mystery of bebop is self-perpetuating. It is often claimed as a creative declaration of independence by African-American musicians, an attempt to raise jazz above the level of entertainment and to the status of a self-determining art form. To some degree this is the case, and the spasmodic virtuosity of bebop was in some measure a deliberate attempt to rid jazz of (mostly white) amateurs who had colonized black music and were making a substantial commercial and critical profit from it. Caliban had found his voice and his own book of spells.

However, the reality is more complex. The shift from big-band swing to small-band bop was as much about economic necessity as it was about artistic innovation. From the late autumn of 1941, the United States switched again to a war economy. Military conscription became an issue that was to have a lasting impact – largely negative, sometimes positive, often neutrally between the two, but ever-present – for the next 30 years and more. The ranks of big bands were thinned. At the market end of the equation, a new and stringent 'cabaret tax' meant that mounting live music became prohibitively expensive, encouraging small-group work in more unconventional places – music clubs rather than dance halls – while restrictions on the use of fuel – needed for the war effort – meant that driving across state lines, or even across a large metropolitan region, to see a favourite band was no longer possible. Having reached a peak of popularity around 1939, jazz became a minority enthusiasm again.

There were, of course, other implications arising out of the international situation, not least an influx of immigrants from fascist Europe, many of them musically educated, and in the opposite direction a fresh consideration of what American cultural values might mean abroad, both to the wartime allies and to the citizenry of the totalitarian regimes in Germany, Italy, Spain and the Soviet Union. If the Cold War began in 1918, as seems obvious, then the presentation of jazz as a kind of 20th-century Americanism acquired a new importance during the actual hostilities, and with increasing vigour thereafter.

One of the reasons why bebop's origins are somewhat shrouded is that the music emerged during a period when there were very few recordings being made. In its earliest incarnation, bop was a coterie music, played by a small avant-garde and enjoyed by a relatively exclusive and geographically delimited audience. Economic pressure was less significant here than a union ban on commercial recording, which lasted for much of the war. The American Federation of Musicians was alarmed that radio broadcasting was increasing pressure on music professionals by providing free-at-source entertainment that, in combination with wartime restrictions, prevented the majority of Americans from seeking out live entertainment in clubs and dance halls. There was a mutually reinforcing relationship between the rise of popular broadcasting, the availability of (relatively) cheap reproduction equipment and a new philosophy of domesticity in the US, often identified with the '50s, but as is usual with such broad-brush cultural phenomena somewhat older. Americans did not go out as much as they had a decade earlier, even during the oddity of Prohibition.

The AFM wanted to levy a royalty from the recording companies to guarantee some kind of kickback to union members whose earnings had been curtailed by radio. Negotiations were blankly hostile and on 1 August 1942 (as American forces gathered in the Pacific for the attack on Guadalcanal) the union called a strike and ban on instrumental recording. Needless to say, the dispute did not mean an end to jazz recording. On the contrary, it nationalized production to some extent, with a War Department initiative on behalf of the Armed Forces Radio Service to provide recordings for the entertainment of troops in the field. Between early 1943 and the eve of the Korean War, more than seven million so called V-Discs ('Victory' Discs) were manufactured and distributed. The terms of the agreement with AFM stipulated that musicians would not be considered to be strike-breaking provided that all masters and surplus discs be destroyed at the end of the war. It will readily be judged from what follows how rarely that happened in practice.

The dispute was only finally settled – or temporarily settled, since there was a further strike between October 1947 and January 1948 – in November 1944, when the major labels, still Columbia and Victor, agreed to pay a small percentage royalty into a union fund. However, one or two labels had already settled. Among them was Blue Note, a new imprint founded in 1939 by German immigrant Alfred Lion and the Communist writer Max Margulis, who underwrote the project. Blue Note, which had originally been inspired by John Hammond's 'From Spirituals To Swing' concert in 1938, was one of a number of new and independent jazz labels to emerge in the period. Jazz recording has historically flip-flopped between centrifugal and centripetal forces, the greater activity accumulating round major labels and corporations for a period, then devolving to a much larger number of small, specialist, sometimes niche imprints during periods when corporate investment in creative jazz becomes less generous and sympathetic.

Among the many new labels to appear in the '40s were impresario Norman Granz's Clef (later to hive off Norgran and Verve imprints and to become a large-scale operation), also Ross Russell's Dial and Herman Lubinsky's Savoy (who between them put out Charlie Parker's greatest work), and record store owner Milt Gabler's Commodore. Two of the most influential of all, Nesuhi Ertegun's Atlantic and Bob Weinstock's Prestige, only emerged at the end of the decade, but by then a creative infrastructure was complete ...

HOT LIPS PAGE
Born Oran Thaddeus Page, 27 January 1908, Dallas, Texas; died 5 November 1954, New York City
Trumpet

Hot Lips Page 1940–1944
Classics 809
Page; Jesse Brown, Joe Keyes (t); Vic Dickenson, Benny Morton (tb); Earl Bostic, Benjamin Hammond, George Johnson, Floyd 'Horsecollar' Williams (as); Don Byas, Ike Quebec, Ben Webster, Lem Johnson, Lucky Thompson (ts); Ace Harris, Leonard Feather, Clyde Hart, Hank Jones (p); Sam Christopher Allen (g); Teddy Bunn (g, v); Al Lucas, John Simmons, Carl 'Flat Top' Wilson (b); Ernest 'Bass' Hill (b, bb); Big Sid Catlett, Jack 'The Bear' Parker, Jesse Price (d). December 1940, November 1944.

Nat Adderley said (1985): '**Lips used to squeeze out notes so slow and thick they sounded like taffy; hot and sweet like taffy, too. All the guys used to listen to those records and I still hear the younger men trying to copy him.**'

An Armstrong imitator who never quite made it out of that constricting sack, Page has always hovered just below the horizon. The negative viewpoint dismisses him as an accomplished player who wasted much of his considerable talent on pointless jamming and dismal but lucrative rhythm and blues. More than 50 years after his death, though, Page still sounds fresh and vital, and more modern in his way than many more celebrated figures. His life story, as researched by Todd Bryant Weeks in *Luck's in My Corner*, is fascinating. Page started out with Ma Rainey, then worked with Walter Page (not a relative) in the Blue Devils, and was with Basie in 1936, just before the band broke big. Page, though, was scouted by Joe Glaser and went solo. The material recorded for Bluebird in April 1938 features a band that might have gone places had Page not been forced to disband.

The title of this Classics volume is slightly misleading. There is, to be sure, material from 1940 and from 1944, but nothing in between. Some of the interim period is covered in various bootlegged jam sessions which may be available. The drummerless 1940 group with Feather, Bunn and Hill is very good indeed, with Hill a considerable surprise for a bass-player of his day. Page also shows off his touch on the now seldom used mellophone. The real treat on this volume, though, is the later material featuring Byas. As Anatol Schenker's informative liner-notes suggest, 'These Foolish Things' made for Commodore is one of the high-points of '40s saxophone jazz. There is some Savoy material from June 1944, a bigger group in which Byas has to give ground to the great Ben Webster; but it is the two dates for Milt Gabler's label which stand out. Even the quasi-novelty items like 'The Blues Jumped A Rabbit' are excellent. It wouldn't be a Classics volume without an early appearance from a star of the future. On the last session, from November 1944, Hank Jones makes his recording debut backing Page, Dickenson and the very fine Thompson on 'The Lady In Bed' and 'Gee, Baby, Ain't I Good For You?'.

REX STEWART

Born 22 February 1907, Philadelphia, Pennsylvania; died 7 September 1967, Los Angeles, California
Trumpet

Rex Stewart And The Ellingtonians

Original Jazz Classics OJC 1710
Stewart; Lawrence Brown (tb); Barney Bigard (cl); Billy Kyle (p); Brick Fleagle (g); Wellman Braud, John Levy (b); Cozy Cole, Dave Tough (d). July 1940–1946.

Bassist John Levy said (1984): **'You know, some of the Ellington guys thought they were a cut above, because they were in the Duke's orchestra. I never got a sense of that from Rex. He was just happy to be playing jazz and he didn't mind who with. He did like it when he went to Paris and they shouted out his name, though.'**

For trumpeters of the '20s, Louis Armstrong was a model and a challenge. His achievement was so primal and so pre-eminent that it was extraordinarily difficult to see a way round or over it. Rex Stewart, a self-confessed Armstrong slave (though he also loved Bix), experienced the problem more directly than most when he took over Armstrong's chair in the Fletcher Henderson orchestra.

In reaction to the inevitable but invidious comparisons, Stewart developed his distinctive 'half-valving' technique. By depressing the trumpet keys to mid-positions, he was able to generate an astonishing and sometimes surreal chromaticism which, though much imitated, has only really resurfaced with the avant-garde of the '60s. As a maverick, Stewart was ideal for the Ellington orchestra of the mid-'30s, though some of his later sessions, despite the august company, step back a generation to the sound of the Hot Sevens. Stewart was never to lose that loyalty. He can even be heard singing in imitation of Pops here and there.

The *Ellingtonians* CD valuably brings together material from a few different dates. The

1946 material with Kyle, Levy and Cole is absolutely representative, though oddly the set ends with a couple of later 1946 sides that don't feature Rex at all. The best stuff comes from earlier, in 1940, with Brown and Bigard; 'Bugle Call Rag' perfectly illustrates the points above. Rex's originals 'Blues Kicked The Bucket', 'Flim-Flam' and 'Madeleine' are affable enough, but he was a player first and he had found his idiom early, so there's not much deviation in quality even when the song is second-rate. Stewart was revered in Europe and after the war went back to France to record for a number of labels, but the best of his small-group work is probably here.

LESTER YOUNG &

Born 27 August 1909, Woodville, Mississippi; died 15 March 1959, New York City
Tenor saxophone

The Complete Aladdin Sessions

Blue Note 32787 2CD
Young; Shorty McConnell, Howard McGhee (t); Vic Dickenson (tb); Willie Smith (as); Maxwell Davis (ts); Joe Albany, Jimmy Bunn, Nat Cole, Gene DiNovi, Wesley Jones, Dodo Marmarosa, Argonne Thornton (p); Irving Ashby, Nasir Barakaat, Dave Barbour, Fred Lacey, Chuck Wayne (g); Ted Briscoe, Red Callender, Curtis Counce, Rodney Richardson, Junior Rudd, Curley Russell (b); Chico Hamilton, Roy Haynes, Tiny Kahn, Lyndell Marshall, Johnny Otis, Henry Tucker (d). July 1942–October 1947.

Trumpeter Harry Edison said (1994): **'You have to remember that Lester came from the south. All that strange jive talk and the eccentric behaviour, those were mechanisms for survival. No one's going to beat on you if you're simple-minded, so act simple-minded. Some white man is always listening to you in case you're hatching something, so talk in a way no white man can understand. That's the key to Lester, those first years in Mississippi. Not anything that happened since or went into his body.'**

One of the most influential saxophonists ever, Lester Young marks a transition from swing to bebop. Borrowing from Frankie Trumbauer, he developed a dry, cool style, quite different from the Coleman Hawkins sound. He grew up near New Orleans and played in a family setting, but left home to start a professional career with Art Bronson and then with Walter Page's Blue Devils. Count Basie recruited the 25-year-old but Young soon left and joined Fletcher Henderson's band, where he replaced Herschel Evans but was initially ostracized for his unorthodox approach. He was soon back with Basie and started to record under his own name and as an accompanist for Billie Holiday. His improvisations grew ever more elegantly structured, built up from short, slightly staccato phrases. He grew increasingly dependent on drink and narcotics; his tone coarsened and his solos became more and more formulaic.

The truth is that Young's best work was nearly all done for others. The Aladdin sessions do, however, cover some of his best work as a leader, though even some of these are for another singer, Helen Humes. Young's cool, wry approach still seems slightly out of synch with prevailing expectations, though he is absolutely *simpatico* with Willie Smith, another figure now routinely overlooked in accounts of how jazz developed into its modern phase. The big pluses on this generously proportioned compilation are a rare glimpse of the 1942 Los Angeles session with Nat Cole and an instrumental 'Riffin' Without Helen', recorded as part of the Humes session, presumably while she was off powdering her nose.

& *See also* **The President Plays** (1952; p. 138)

LUCKY MILLINDER&

Born 8 August 1900, Aniston, Alabama; died 28 September 1966, New York City
Voice, bandleader

Lucky Millinder 1943–1947
Classics 1026
Millinder; Joe Guy, Frank Humphries, Joe Jordan, Chiefie Scott, Curtis Murphy, Leroy Elton Hill, Lamar Wright, Henry Glover, Thomas 'Sleepy' Grider, Archie Johnson, John Bello, Leon Meriam (t); Harold 'Money' Johnson (t, tb); Joe Britton, Gene Simon, George Stevenson, Alfred Cobbs, Frank Mazzoli (tb); Billy Bowen, Tab Smith, Preston Love, Bill Swindell, Burnie Peacock, John Harrington, Sam Hopkins, Big Nick Nicholas (as); Eddie 'Lockjaw' Davis, Michael Hadley, Sam 'The Man' Taylor, Bull Moose Jackson, Elmer Williams (ts); Ernest Purce (bs); Ray Tunia, Ellis Larkins, Bill Doggett, Sir Charles Thompson (p); Trevor Bacon (g, v); Lawrence Lucie, Bernard McKey (g); George Duvivier, Beverly Peer, Al McKibbon, Jerry Cox (b); Panama Francis (d); Sister Rosetta Tharpe, Wynonie Harris, Judy Carol, Leon Ketchum, The Lucky Seven, The Lucky Four, Annisteen Allen, Paul Breckenridge (v). August 1943–April 1947.

Jazz historian Bob Turner says: **'Millinder's band was an urban survival of the kind of outfit that was plying the Midwest. He hovers close to bop more often than he's given credit for, but Lucky knew his market and wasn't going to risk a change of style while things were going well.'**

The word 'irrepressible' jumps to mind. Millinder grew up in Chicago and had all kinds of showbiz jobs – including fortune-telling – before fronting bands. He ran the Mills Blue Rhythm outfit for a time. Lucky, who'd had a short dance career as Lucious Venable, recorded on his own account from the middle of the war onward to 1952, but later got out of music and worked in the alcoholic drinks business. Either way, he always had something to sell. Millinder's sessions for Decca (there are a scant four titles for V-Disc on this volume) are energetic but middleweight titles brought to life by some bright and alert solos. Much of it yearns to be slimmed down to R&B small-band size, and Millinder's use of vocalists such as Rosetta Tharpe and Wynonie Harris – as well as instrumentalists like Sam 'The Man' Taylor, Bull Moose Jackson and Bill Doggett – tells its own story about the direction of the music. A solitary date right at the end of the previous compilation (1941–1942) hints at a different direction: Dizzy Gillespie is in the band, and there's a spirited version of 'Little John Special' (alias 'Salt Peanuts'). But that was a moment of madness in the Millinder story. He sings here and there, but otherwise his great contribution – an almost maniacal energy in directing the band onstage – has been lost to posterity. These discs pall over the long haul, but in small doses they're a worthwhile and entertaining reminder of a staple part of black music in the early '40s.

& *See also* **MILLS BLUE RHYTHM BAND, Blue Rhythm** (1931; p. 48)

GEORGE LEWIS&

Born George Joseph François Louis Zeno, 13 July 1900, New Orleans, Louisiana; died 31 December 1968, New Orleans, Louisiana
Clarinet

George Lewis & His New Orleans Stompers: Volumes 1 & 2
American Music AMCD 100 / 101
Lewis; Avery 'Kid' Howard (t); Jim Robinson (tb); Lawrence Marrero (bj); Sidney Brown (bb on Vol. 1 only); Chester Zardis (b); Edgar Moseley (d). May 1943.

George Melly said (1998): **'They all raved about Lewis because he was thought to be the "real thing", and the stupid thing was that the worse he played, the more "authentic" they all thought it was. A complex man, I think, and I'd give a fiver to know what was going through his head.'**

One of the great primitives of early and classic jazz, Lewis had a raw and untutored tone and an impassioned, technically unembellished approach to soloing. Keystone of the post-war revival in traditional jazz, he toured indefatigably. Rarely has a traditional jazz musician been documented on record in so concentrated a way as was Lewis. American Music's patient documentation even gives street numbers and times of day for the earliest material here. Having been coaxed out of a 'retirement' working as a dockhand at the start of the war, Lewis was by the mid-'50s the surviving pillar of 'serious' revivalism, which he'd helped kick off with Bunk Johnson, working what looked like a politician's itinerary across the US.

The early material comes across with remarkable freshness. The first tracks on *Volume 1* of the 1943 material were recorded in the drummer's house and, though they're more raggedy than the later sessions at the Gypsy Tea Room (high-point: two takes each of 'Climax Rag' and 'Careless Love'), they provide an excellent starting-point for serious examination of this remarkable musician. Lewis's solo breaks are oddly pitched (possibly owing to tape yaw), but the pitching remains consistent relative to other players so it has to be considered an idiosyncrasy rather than poor articulation.

& *See also* **Jazz Funeral In New Orleans** (1953; p. 143)

STUFF SMITH

Born Hezekiah Leroy Gordon Smith, 14 August 1909, Portsmouth, Ohio; died 25 September 1967, Munich, Germany
Violin

The Stuff Smith Trio 1943
Progressive PCD 7053
Smith; Jimmy Jones (p); John Levy (b). November 1943.

Bassist John Levy said (1984): **'Stuff was managed by Joe Glaser – same manager as Louis Armstrong – who was supposed to be hand in hand with the Mob. He was even banned from working in Chicago because of that. But he got us booked into the Onyx Club in New York. Joe pretty much ran booking for black acts then.'**

Stuff played with Alphonso Trent in the '20s, then in a successful 52nd Street band with Jonah Jones. His career petered out in the '40s, and from the '50s he based himself in California and Europe. A capricious temper and a liking for alcohol did him few favours. What would have been Smith's 90th birthday prompted a certain reassessment of his work. Those who remember his final performances in Scandinavia are fewer on the ground these days, and emphasis has fallen on the earlier and better work. Initially influenced by Joe Venuti, Smith devised a style based on heavy bow-weight, with sharply percussive semiquaver runs up towards the top end of his range.

Like many '20s players, Smith found himself overtaken by the swing era and re-emerged as a recording and concert artist only after the war, when his upfront style and comic stage persona attracted renewed attention. Even so, he had a thriving club career in the meantime, most famously at the Onyx Club on 52nd Street, and managed to hold his ground while the bebop revolution went on around him.

The 1943 trio is typical of his pre-war and wartime work, an exhaustive documentation of the session of 17 November. Three full versions of 'Minuet In Swing' suggest that Smith went at a solo in a fairly deliberate way, attempting to maintain an energy level rather than rethinking his approach every time. On the other hand, an unissued 'Bugle Call Rag' shows that he could be thoughtful even on lighter material. It opens with the notorious 'Humoresque', which must have had violin teachers climbing out of windows all over town and there are multiple takes of 'Ghost Of A Chance' and 'The Red Jumps' (a Henry 'Red' Allen line) as well. It's a terrific set and a nice period example of a drummerless combo.

MILDRED BAILEY

Born Mildred Rinker, also known as 'Mrs Swing', 27 February 1907, Tekoa, Washington; died 12 December 1951, Poughkeepsie, New York
Voice

Mildred Bailey 1943–1945

Classics 1316

Bailey; Louis Armstrong, Roy Eldridge, Charlie Shavers, Dick Vance (t); Jack Teagarden, Henderson Chambers (tb); Barney Bigard, Hank D'Amico (cl); Aaron Sachs (cl, as); Coleman Hawkins, Emmett Carls (ts); Teddy Wilson, Vernon Duke, Ellis Larkins, Danny Negri (p); Red Norvo (vib); Al Casey, Tommy Kay, Chuck Wayne, Remo Palmieri (g); Oscar Pettiford, Clyde Lombardi, Billy Taylor, Al Hall (b); Sid Catlett, Eddie Dell, Specs Powell, J. C. Heard (d); Paul Baron Orchestra. November 1943–December 1945.

Former husband Red Norvo said (1983): **'Did we mind being called Mr and Mrs Swing? Well, it stuck better to her than to me! And, boy, could she swing. I don't think there was another singer of that time who swung harder.'**

Mildred Rinker sent a demo record to Paul Whiteman, who hired her in 1929. After four years, and a hit with 'Rockin' Chair', she went solo and sang with husband Red Norvo's group. A tempestuous personality and health problems saw her star decline in the '40s, though there was a brief comeback near the end. She had claims to be feted on a par with Holiday and Fitzgerald – and started recording before either of them, with her first version of 'Rockin' Chair' dating back to 1931 – but Bailey was more of a transitional figure. Her early records suggest a singer struggling, gently, with the old style of Broadway belting (difficult enough for someone with a small voice), while some of the later ones are almost too placid and formal; yet she never quite lost the vaudevillian tang which helped her put across risqué numbers like 'Jenny' or the wartime novelty 'Scrap Your Fat'. Lacking either Holiday's modern pathos or Fitzgerald's monumental swing, her art is modest, stylized and innately graceful.

During the war years, she was a reassuring and consolatory voice at a time of national need and sadness and more than a few serving soldiers mention the impact of her voice on a phonograph recording or on radio during furloughs as a connection to home. This volume of Classics' documentation is nearly all V-Disc material and starts with four titles with Teddy Wilson as sole accompanist; her delightful fluff on the intro to 'Rockin' Chair' was fortunately preserved. Even on 'Scrap Your Fat' she turns in a sterling effort. Bailey sustains interest over long periods on modern reissues. There is a consistency and a certain mildness that never seems dull or routine. Perhaps, alongside more dramatic divas, she simply spoke of familiar things in tones that suggested someone closer at hand and more approachable.

COUNT BASIE &

Born 21 August 1904, Red Bank, New Jersey; died 26 April 1984, Hollywood, Florida
Piano, bandleader

The Jubilee Alternatives
Hep CD 38
Basie; Harry 'Sweets' Edison, Al Killian, Ed Lewis, Snooky Young (t); Eli Robinson, Robert Scott, Louis Taylor, Dicky Wells (tb); Jimmy Powell, Earl Warren (as); Buddy Tate, Lester Young, Illinois Jacquet (ts); Rudy Rutherford (bs, cl); Freddie Green (g); Rodney Richardson (b); Jo Jones, Buddy Rich (d); Thelma Carpenter, Jimmy Rushing (v). December 1943–October 1944.

Former Staff Sergeant Joe McGann remembers: **'That was the sound of the war for me, "Jumpin' At The Woodside", and Jimmy Rushing singing. I know there was a recording ban on, but Basie was above all that. He was like the Manhattan Project, our secret weapon. I hummed that stuff crossing the Rhine.'**

During the Musicians' Union recording ban, few groups were able to record and those mostly for broadcast on the American Forces Radio Service. Splendidly remastered, the studio 'alternatives' to AFRS Jubilee show broadcasts give a useful impression of a band in transition. Rich and Jacquet are in on some tracks and the brass section is largely different from previous recordings. There's a new quality to the playing, perhaps a younger and more urgent sound, which might be put down to the wartime atmosphere, but might just as likely be a new, pre-bop generation asserting itself in jazz. Some good charts include Andy Gibson's 'Andy's Blues', Clayton's excellent 'Avenue C' and Smith's 'Harvard Blues', one of the best of the later Columbias. There's a great early version of Harry Edison's 'Beaver Junction' and two of 'Jumpin' At The Woodside', a signature Basie performance. Though their provenance is somewhat unusual, and there are some signs of a group not quite yet settled to its task, these are definitive Basie recordings.

& *See also* **The Original American Decca Recordings** (1937–1939; p. 61), **The Complete Atomic Mr Basie** (1957; p. 216)

ART HODES &

Born 14 November 1904, Nikoliev, Ukraine, Russia; died 4 March 1993, Harvey, Illinois
Piano

The Jazz Record Story
Jazzology JCD 82
Hodes; Duke DuVal (t); George Brunies (tb); Rod Cless, Cecil Scott (cl); George 'Pops' Foster (b); Joe Grauso, Baby Dodds (d). 1943–1946.

Art Hodes said (1981): **'You have to admit it's ironic. Your family emigrates and you end up in Chicago, the one place on the planet that's colder than Russia.'**

Hodes arrived in Chicago from his native Ukraine when he was only a few months old. As player, writer and broadcaster, he was a lifelong devotee and exponent of classic jazz, blues, stride and ragtime, but though better known in later years as a solo performer, he began his career in groups run by Wingy Manone, Joe Marsala and Sidney Bechet.

Until a decade or so ago it was believed that, apart from a couple of cuts with Wingy Manone, Art didn't record on his own account before the summer of 1939, though it was known that he had used a Victor Home Recording machine to make half a dozen discs at a gig in Racine, Wisconsin. These were thought to be unplayable and incapable of being dubbed, but Barry Martyn has managed to reconstruct four of them, and they stretch Art's recording career backward in time.

By the start of the war, he was an established artist. The *Jazz Record* material restores to circulation many of the sides Art cut and released with his own label. The very first tracks, '103rd Street Boogie' and 'Royal Garden Blues', appeared at the end of 1943, credited to the Columbia Quintet, which had played a residency at Childs' Restaurant in New Haven. The wonderful trio with Pops Foster and Baby Dodds is a little later, and there are further group recordings made by the band co-led by Art and three horns, including big Cecil Scott (who had 13 children, eating in shifts and sleeping in tiers); peppy and joyous, an unalloyed delight for anyone who loves traditional jazz.

& See also **Keepin' Out Of Mischief Now** (1988; p. 525)

DUKE ELLINGTON *&*

Born Edward Kennedy Ellington, 29 April 1899, Washington, DC; died 24 May 1974, New York City
Piano

Black, Brown And Beige
RCA Bluebird 86641 3CD

Ellington; Taft Jordan, Cat Anderson, Shelton Hemphill, Ray Nance, Rex Stewart, Francis Williams, Harold 'Shorty' Baker (t); Claude Jones, Lawrence Brown, Joe 'Tricky Sam' Nanton, Tommy Dorsey, Wilbur De Paris (tb); Jimmy Hamilton, Russell Procope (cl, ts); Otto Hardwick (as); Johnny Hodges (as); Al Sears (ts); Harry Carney (bs); Fred Guy (g); Junior Raglin, Sid Weiss, Oscar Pettiford, Al Lucas, Bob Haggart (b); Sonny Greer, Big Sid Catlett (d); Al Hibbler, Joya Sherrill, Kay Davis, Marie Ellington, Marian Cox (v). December 1944–September 1946.

Broadcaster Charles Fox said (1982): **'There was a huge fuss when Duke Ellington was made "Composer of the Week" on the BBC, letters from hither and yon complaining and demanding heads. And yet when you listen to this music, from the band's greatest period, it seems self-evident that, whatever else, a truly great composer – doesn't matter in what form – is at work.'**

This was a band in its pomp, sweeping all before it. Ellington had begun giving annual Carnegie Hall concerts in 1943 and they became an institution, stiffening wartime morale on the home front and bringing a new stratum of cultural confidence to African-American music in the US. Ellington was an impossible figure to ignore in the culture of the time, but not one who was easy to bend to the PR needs of wartime bi-partisanship. He remained loftily, sardonically aloof from a culture that seemed, for the moment (and Duke always understood the fickleness of fame), eager to embrace him.

While this stands a notch below the music on *Never No Lament*, it is still an essential Ellington collection. Besides numerous further examples of the composer's mastery of the three-minute form, there are the first of his suites to make it to the studios, including most of 'Black, Brown And Beige' – never recorded in its entirety in the studio – and 'The Perfume Suite'. New Ellingtonians include two brilliant individualists, Anderson and Jordan, as well as the lyrical Baker, Sears and Procope. Ellington's confidence may have been sagging a little from the loss of major soloists – Webster, Williams – and the indifference to some of his higher ambitions as a composer, but the orchestra itself is still inimitable.

& See also **Duke Ellington 1927-1929** (1927–1929; p. 28), **Duke Ellington 1937-1938** (1937–1938; p. 64), **Never No Lament** (1940–1942; p. 81), **The Duke At Fargo** (1940; p. 81), **Ellington At Newport** (1956; p. 189), **The Far East Suite** (1966; p. 336)

NAT COLE &

Born Nathaniel Adams Coles, 17 March 1919, Montgomery, Alabama; died 15 February 1965, Santa Monica, California
Piano, voice

Nat King Cole 1943–1944
Classics 804
Cole; Shad Collins (t); Illinois Jacquet (ts); Oscar Moore (g); Johnny Miller, Gene Englund (b); J. C. Heard (d). November 1943–March 1944.

According to a much-repeated story, drummer J. C. Heard said: **'When Nat Cole gave up playing piano, everyone got sick!'**

Nat didn't play much jazz after 1950, after his voice made him famous. It was to be a relatively short spell in the sunshine, for chain-smoking ended his life early. He began leading what became a hugely successful trio in 1939 and his piano style, influenced by Hines and Wilson, suggested a transition from swing to bop.

He began with a deceptively lightweight, jiving music ('Scotchin' With The Soda', 'Ode To A Wild Clam') which masked the intensity of his piano style. Smooth, glittering, skating over melodies, Cole's right-hand lines were breaking free of his original Earl Hines influence and looking towards an improvisational freedom which other players – Haig, Marmarosa, Powell – would turn into the language of bebop. Cole was less inclined towards that jagged-edge approach and preferred the hip constrictions of songs. With pulsing interjections from Moore and bassist Wesley Prince (subsequently Miller), this was a surprisingly compelling music.

Mosaic's comprehensive survey of the trios (out of print, now) ran to 18 CDs but Classics offers a way of collecting these tracks, albeit without much finessing of the material. The early ones throw up some interesting associations, including appearances by drummer Lee Young, Pres's brother, but for a one-volume sampling, the best is this *1943–1944* volume, with 'Straighten Up And Fly Right' and some deft standards interpretations. Nat's luxuriant swing, dextrous touch and intelligent arrangements all seem inexhaustible and Moore is almost his equal in their dazzling parallel runs.

& *See also* **After Midnight** (1956; p. 190)

JAZZ AT THE PHILHARMONIC
Established 1944
'Supergroup'

Best Of The 1940s Concerts
Verve 314534
Buck Clayton, Roy Eldridge, Joe Guy, Howard McGhee, Shorty Sherock (t); Bill Harris, J. J. Johnson, Tommy McTurk, Trummy Young (tb); Charlie Parker, Willie Smith (as); Coleman Hawkins, Illinois Jacquet, Jack McVea, Flip Phillips, Lester Young (ts); Nat Cole, Meade 'Lux' Lewis (p); Les Paul (g); Red Callender (b); Gene Krupa, Lee Young (d); Ella Fitzgerald, Billie Holiday (v); and others. July 1944–18 September 1949.

Norman Granz said (1982): **'I had to borrow $300 to put on the first Jazz At The Philharmonic concert. How much would it cost me now? I don't know ... Do you have an abacus?'**

Norman Granz was the jazz-loving son of Russian immigrants. Born in 1918, he came of age at the end of the swing era, organizing desegregated jam sessions in his home town of

Los Angeles. On 2 July 1944, his ambition extended to an all-star event at the Los Angeles Philharmonic Auditorium featuring Meade 'Lux' Lewis and other younger names. Around the same time, Granz and film maker Gjon Mili were involved with making a jazz movie called *Jammin' the Blues*, which went on to secure an Oscar nomination. So successful was the first Jazz Concert At The Philharmonic Auditorium (as the event was originally billed) that Granz planned further events and then tours, bringing together swing and bop stars and singers like Billie Holiday and Ella Fitzgerald (whom he later managed) under the JATP umbrella. Much of the music from these was released on Granz's Norgran imprint – he also ran Clef and Verve and consolidated his record interests under the latter name from 1956. After he sold out the main label to Metro-Goldwyn-Mayer and emigrated to Switzerland, he founded Pablo records in 1973, largely to release jam material from Jazz At The Philharmonic events. In turn, Pablo was also sold, to Fantasy.

At a time when mainstream jazz's public profile was at its lowest, Pablo was a valued source of good mainstream playing by big stars. Granz was shrewd enough to recognize that more very definitely meant more. There is often a sense of 'never mind the quality, check the personnel' on a JATP record, and finesse and expressive sophistication were sometimes lost in polite cutting sessions which put high-note playing and amicably fiery exchanges at a premium. Granz was criticized for favouring a relatively fixed roster of established reputations (Basie, Ella, Oscar Peterson, Joe Pass among them) and an older style of music over more innovative jazz, but audiences lapped up the records, either as gig souvenirs or as vicarious snapshots of high-price events in California or Montreux. Any further criticism of Granz stumbled on his dogged commitment to securing proper recognition and equal status for black artists. Few who worked for him had a negative word to say.

The very first Jazz At The Philharmonic concert, available as *The Beginning* and *The First Concert* on Charly and Jasmine, makes for surprisingly dull listening, and the ten-CD box set with which Universal eventually rationalized the shambolic JATP catalogue was too much and too expensive for most tastes. This single CD sampler brings together the best of the early years, including Flip Phillips's celebrated solo on 'Perdido', Billie and Ella on 'Flying Home', Bird on an astonishing 'Oh, Lady Be Good' and many others.

Granz lived on until 2001, an admired elder statesman whose cheerful vulgarization of jazz as a concert phenomenon nevertheless helped keep the music – and some of its great exponents – alive during the cold years.

TINY GRIMES

Born Lloyd Grimes, 7 July 1916, Newport News, Virginia; died 4 March 1989, New York City
Guitar

Tiny Grimes 1944–1949
Classics 5048
Grimes; James Young (tb); Charlie Parker, Red Prysock (as); John Hardee (ts); George Kelly (p, cel); Clyde Hart, Marlowe Morris, Joe Springer (p); Lucille Dixon, Charles Isaacs (b); Clyde Butts (b, v); Ed Nicholson, Sonny Payne, Jerry Potter, Harold 'Doc' West (d). September 1944–1949.

Courtney (Mc)Pyne said, after appearing in Grimes-ish garb: **'Well, he looks better in a kilt than I did!'**

A four-string guitar-player, Grimes was a sensation in the Tatum trio and then elsewhere in New York clubs of the '40s. Fame with Tatum spurred him into a solo career, first of all with a group featuring Charlie Parker, later with a full-regalia outfit called the Rocking Highlanders which featured another altoist, Red Prysock. This unvarnished compilation brings together all the material he recorded under his own name over the period, including a date for Blue Note, still very much in its R&B phase. The tracks with Bird are obviously of interest, but 'Red Cross' is exceptional and some of the later cuts, including versions of 'See See Rider' and the notorious 'Annie Laurie', are worth having as well. One of the best of the early vocals is 'Romance Without Finance'. A novelty act he may have been – certainly no great instrumentalist – but Grimes was part of the same style-switch that yielded up bebop, and it would be misleading to ignore him.

ERROLL GARNER &

Born 15 June 1921, Pittsburgh, Pennsylvania; died 7 January 1977, Los Angeles, California
Piano

Erroll Garner 1944–1945
Classics 873
Garner; Charlie Shavers (t); Vic Dickenson (tb); Hank D'Amico (cl); Lem Davis (as); Slam Stewart, Eddie Brown (b); Cliff Leeman, Harold 'Doc' West (d). December 1944–March 1945.

Pianist Dudley Moore said (1979): **'He was one of the most important pianists ever, and he's instantly recognizable with that slow, slow drag in the right hand, while chop-chop-chopping away with the left.'**

Erroll Garner was one of a kind. He was as *outré* as the great beboppers, yet bop was alien to him, even though he recorded with Charlie Parker. He swung mightily, yet he stood outside the swing tradition; he played orchestrally, and his style was swooningly romantic, yet he could be as merciless on a tune as Fats Waller. He never read music, and often pianists would be hired to teach him songs, but he could play a piece in any key, and delighted in deceiving his rhythm sections from night to night. His tumbling, percussive, humorous style was entirely his own. Garner's earliest recordings were done semi-privately, and though issued on Blue Note in the '50s they're in often atrocious sound. Most of his style is in place, and one can hear a debt to Tatum. The earlier Classics in this series include what there is of these survivals, and it's a difficult listen, but *1944–1945* puts together a session which has been a collectors' piece for many years: a jam with Shavers, Dickenson, D'Amico and Davis which includes extended versions of 'Gaslight' and some impromptu blues. Lovely stuff, with the principals all in good fettle, and a very rare glimpse of Garner with horns. A trio date with Brown and West (for Black And White) and a solo session for Signature fill up the disc. Garner gives an impression of being able to play anything you might throw at him, but not caring that much. 'Effortless' is overused as an honorific, but it sort of works here, and not always to the benefit of the music.

& *See also* **Concert By The Sea** (1955; p. 163)

DON BYAS

Born Carlos Wesley Byas, 21 October 1912, Muskogee, Oklahoma; died 24 August 1972, Amsterdam, Netherlands
Tenor saxophone

Don Byas 1944–1945
Classics 882
Byas; Charlie Shavers, Joe Thomas (t); Rudy Williams (as); Johnny Guarnieri, Kenny Watts (p); Clyde Hart (p, cel); John Levy, Slam Stewart, Billy Taylor (b); Cozy Cole, Slick Jones, Jack 'The Bear' Parker (d); Big Bill Broonzy (v). July 1944–March 1945.

Saxophonist Peter Brötzmann said (1992): **'He sounds like the most modern of the swing guys, like Coleman Hawkins in his sound, but his solos are something else: quite strange in some ways, quite weird at times, but very interesting.'**

Don Byas dominates the strip of turf between Coleman Hawkins and Charlie Parker, combining the old man's vibrato and grouchy tone with Bird's limber solo style and fresh, open diction. Hard these days to recognize just how highly regarded Byas once was, until one actually hears him. Byas was a complex player, whose development of a theme often seemed to step outside the source material altogether, drifting in and out of remote keys, mixing up the rhythm, but always managing to keep in place and never sounding rushed or temporized when he finishes. Byas left the Basie band in 1943 and became one of the unsung heroes of early bebop, matched only by Lucky Thompson, but he moved permanently to Europe in 1946, which may partly be why his reputation is not as high as it should be. Before he left, he made a number of fine recordings and left behind a stone classic in his rapid run-through of the 'I Got Rhythm' changes at Town Hall in June 1945 with bassist Slam Stewart, a remarkable performance that so closely prefigures the emergence of bebop it has to be considered an *Ur*-text of the new jazz.

It can be found here and there, but this Classics volume and those that follow in the series do the usual sturdy job of assembling a chronological picture. They reveal Byas as a kind of instant composer, credited with a steady flow of lines – 'Don's Idea', 'Double Talk', 'Free and Easy' – which work such rapid variations on orthodox changes that the whole harmonic trajectory seems to alter. Byas was always hugely flattered by the microphones of the time. The early material for Savoy captures a polished and vibrant stylist with a coherent solo approach. Shavers is abrupt and pugnacious. The July tracks are better than the later session, largely because they are simpler and concentrate on straight major-key exchanges between the two horns. In January 1945, Byas cut four sides for Jamboree, disappointing because they seem to slip back half a generation to the old jump and swing styles. 'Jamboree Jump' is also known as 'Byas-A-Drink', a neat feature for saxophone and Joe Thomas's Eldridge-like trumpet. Later material for Hub is dominated by Broonzy vocals and officially credited to Little Sam And Orchestra. There were other good things through 1945, and the companion volumes are worth sampling, but Europe beckoned and with his passage Byas's chances of going down as one of the major saxophone voices faded. A pity. He's a revelation every time one listens to him.

SID CATLETT

Born 17 January 1910, Evansville, Indiana; died 25 March 1951, Chicago, Illinois
Drums

Sid Catlett 1944–1946

Classics 974

Catlett; Charlie Shavers, Joe Guy, Gerald Wilson (t); Barney Bigard, Edmond Hall (cl); Bull Moose Jackson, Willie Smith (as); Eddie 'Lockjaw' Davis, Illinois Jacquet, Frank Socolow, Ben Webster (ts); Art Tatum, Marlowe Morris, Eddie Heywood, Horace Henderson, Pete Johnson (p); Bill Gooden (org); Al Casey, Jimmy Shirley (g); Oscar Pettiford, John Simmons, Gene Ramey (b). January 1944–1946.

Drummer Albert 'Tootie' Heath said (1999): **'I played a drum solo one time and "Sweets" [Harry Edison] said: "You thought that was something! Shit, that was just a bunch of old Sid Catlett riffs." I don't think anyone else there knew who he was talking about.'**

No one bridges the eras of Louis Armstrong and Charlie Parker so completely. 'Big Sid' collapsed at a concert in Chicago, at the end of the first flowering of bebop. Dead at 41, he left a comparatively small legacy, but he was a complete master of drums and cymbals whose virtuoso technique was unflashy and seldom drew attention to itself, though he could dominate most group settings. This hotchpotch of small-group dates – for Commodore, Session, Delta, Regis, Capitol, Manor and V-Disc – is fascinating. The extraordinary opening 'Rose Room' is virtually a duet with Bigard. Six quarter-tracks with Webster and Morris are similarly electric, and five more with horns include some splendid moments, though indifferently recorded. The next five sessions have less of interest but for its first half the CD is close to indispensable. Sid's mercurial style, with glistening cymbal work, unexpected rimshot fusillades and detailed snare rhythms, was among the very few swing-based methods that didn't sound passé in the bop era.

CHARLIE PARKER &

Born 29 August 1920, Kansas City, Missouri; died 12 March 1955, New York City
Alto and tenor saxophones

The Complete Savoy And Dial Studio Recordings / Newly Discovered Sides
Savoy 92911-2 8CD / 17188
Parker; Miles Davis, Dizzy Gillespie, Howard McGhee (t); J. J. Johnson (tb); Flip Phillips, Lucky Thompson, Wardell Gray, Jack McVea (ts); Tiny Brown (bs); Slim Gaillard (p, g, v); Clyde Hart, Jimmy Bunn, Duke Jordan, Russ Freeman, Erroll Garner, George Handy, John Lewis, Sadik Hakim, Bud Powell, Dodo Marmarosa (p); Red Norvo (vib); Arvin Garrison, Barney Kessel, Tiny Grimes (g); Nelson Boyd, Ray Brown, Red Callender, Arnold Fishkind, Bob Kesterson, Vic McMillan, Jimmy Butts, Tommy Potter, Slam Stewart, Curley Russell (b); Max Roach, Harold 'Doc' West, Zutty Singleton, Don Lamond, Specs Powell, Jimmy Pratt, Stan Levey, Roy Porter (d); Earl Coleman (v). September 1944–December 1948.

Trombonist George E. Lewis said (2008): '**It has become customary to say that Charlie Parker's solos are "only" collages of found materials, bits and pieces of music from all over, classical music, songs, things off the radio, put together on the spot, but not original to him. The really interesting point, of course, is not that the solos are assembled like that, but where those materials come from and how they came to be in Parker's possession. That has implications for all of jazz.**'

For good or ill, the iconic jazz life. That Parker had genius is beyond doubt, but it was based on long, effortful study; similarly with drugs, which played a part, but are not the only story. Though he had periods of disturbance, his career, which began in local blues groups in Kansas City before he joined Jay McShann's orchestra, was one of steady and concentrated work and a delivery that only seldom wavered, and only then *in extremis*. His role in the invention of bebop was critical, though he was certainly not the only begetter.

Parker's innovation – improvising a new melody-line off the top, rather than from the middle, of the informing chord – was a logical extension of everything that had been happening in jazz over the previous decade. However, even though the simultaneous inscription of bebop by different hands – Dizzy Gillespie, Charlie Christian and Thelonious Monk all have their propagandists – suggests that it was an evolutionary inevitability, any artistic innovation requires quite specific and usually conscious interventions. With its emphasis on extreme harmonic virtuosity, bop has become the dominant idiom of modern jazz and Parker's genetic fingerprint is the clearest.

Even at his most dazzlingly virtuosic, Parker always sounds logical, making light of asymmetrical phrases, idiosyncratically translated bar-lines, surefooted alternation of whole-note passages and flurries of semiquavers, tampering with almost every other para-meter of the music – dynamic, attack, timbre – with joyous arrogance. Dying at 35, he was spared the indignity of a middle age given over to formulaic repetition. The sides Parker cut on 26 November 1945 were billed by Savoy on the later microgroove release as 'The greatest recording session made in modern jazz'. There's some merit in that. The kitchen sink reproduction of fluffs, false starts and breakdowns gives a rather chaotic impression. Miles Davis, who never entirely came to terms with Parker's harmonic or rhythmic requirements, doesn't play particularly well (there is even a theory that some of the trumpet choruses – notably one on a third take of 'Billie's Bounce' – were played by Dizzy Gillespie in imitation of Miles's rather uncertain style), and some of the pianist's intros and solos are positively bizarre; pianist Argonne Thornton remembers being at the sessions. Despite all that, and Parker's continuing problems with a recalcitrant reed, the session includes 'Billie's Bounce', 'Now's The Time' and 'Ko-Ko'. The last of these is perhaps the high-water mark of Parker's improvisational genius.

Though this is undoubtedly the zenith of Parker's compositional skill as well, it is noticeable that virtually all of the material on these sessions draws either on a basic 12-bar blues or on the chord sequence of 'I Got Rhythm', the *Ur*-text of bebop. 'Ko-Ko' is based on the chords of 'Cherokee', as is the generic 'Warming Up A Riff', which was intended only as a run-through after Parker had carried out running repairs on his squeaking horn. The remainder of Parker's material was drawn from show tunes; 'Meandering', a one-off ballad performance on the November 1945 session, unaccountably elided after superb solos from Parker and Powell, bears some relationship to 'Embraceable You'. What is striking about Parker's playing, here and subsequently, is the emphasis on rhythmic invention, often at the expense of harmonic creativity (in that department, as he shows in miniature on 'Ko-Ko', Dizzy Gillespie was certainly his superior).

Availability on programmable CD means that listeners who find the staccato progression of incomplete takes disconcerting are able to ignore all but the final, released versions. Unfortunately, though these are usually the best band performances, they do not always reflect Bird's best solo playing. A good example comes on 'Now's The Time', which might have been an old KC blowing theme or a remembered solo by tenor saxophonist Rocky Boyd. There is no doubt that Parker's solo on the third take is superior in its slashing self-confidence to that on the fourth, which is slightly duller; Miles Davis plays without conviction on both.

None of the other constituent sessions match up to the erratic brilliance of 26 November 1945. There are nine other dates represented, notably intermittent in quality. The sessions with Slim Gaillard, creator of 'Vout', an irritating hipster argot, are pretty corny and timebound; a bare month after 'Ko-Ko', Parker seems to have come down to earth. An early session with guitarist Tiny Grimes and an unusual August 1947 date (under Miles Davis's control) on which Bird played tenor saxophone, excluded from previous Savoy CD reissues, have been restored. Of the remaining dates, that of 8 May 1947, a rather uneasy affair, nevertheless yielded 'Donna Lee' and 'Chasing The Bird'; by contrast, on 21 December 1947, Parker seems utterly confident and lays down the ferocious 'Bird Gets The Worm' and 'Klaunstance'; the sessions of 18 and 24 September 1948 yielded the classic 'Parker's Mood' (original take 3 is suffused with incomparable blues feeling) and 'Marmaduke' respectively.

The other key figures on these recordings are Max Roach, barely out of his teens but already playing in the kind of advanced rhythmic count that Parker required, and Dizzy Gillespie. Miles Davis was demonstrably unhappy with some of the faster themes and lacked Parker's ability to think afresh take after take; by the time of the 'Parker's Mood' date, though, he had matured significantly (he was, after all, only 19 when 'Ko-Ko' and 'Now's The Time' were recorded). A word, too, for Curley Russell and Tommy Potter, whose contribution to this music was until CD transfer often inaudible.

A point of frustration for many in the past has been the scattered nature of these sessions, spread across numerous LP and CD editions. But with Tony Williams's agreement, the Savoys and the Dials were finally brought within a single set for the first time in this ring-bound eight-disc collection. The master tracks for each date are programmed first, followed by the various alternative takes. There is full documentation in a handsome booklet, and the harsh sound of the Savoys and Dials has been made as hi-fi as the originals will probably ever allow.

The 'newly discovered sides' include an interesting enough 'Out Of Nowhere', 'Oop-Bop-Sh'bam', 'Jumpin' With Symphony Sid'/'Bebop' and a more unexpected 'East Of The Sun (And West Of The Moon)', which is not a number one associates with Parker. The rest of the tracks are familiar Savoys.

& *See also* **Charlie Parker With Strings** (1947–1952; p. 106), **The Quintet** (1953; p. 141)

TRUMMY YOUNG

Born James Osborne Young, 12 January 1912, Savannah, Georgia; died 10 September 1984, San Jose, California
Trombone

Trummy Young 1944–1946
Classics 1037

Young; Buck Clayton, Roy Eldridge (t); Harry Curtis, Bill Stegmeyer, Willie Smith, Ray Eckstrand (as); Nick Caiazza, Stan Webb, Herbie Fields, Ike Quebec, Leo Williams, Don Byas (ts); John Malachi, Kenny Kersey, Billy Rowland, Jimmy Jones (p); Mike Bryan, Allan Hanlon, Bill DeArango (g); Slam Stewart, Tommy Potter, Bob Haggart, Trigger Alpert, John Levy (b); Eddie Byrd, Jimmy Crawford, Specs Powell, Cozy Cole (d); Martha Tilton, Jack Leonard, The Holidays (v). February 1944–July 1946.

Trombonist J. J. Johnson said (1985): **'It wasn't the speed or the slide positions that made him distinctive. You just knew it was him from the very first note. He had that *thing* where he stood out, as himself, in any situation.'**

Young's major affiliation was with Louis Armstrong's All Stars, with whom he remained for 12 years, extending a career that might otherwise have stalled. He always deferred to Louis in those situations and it takes some understanding of what he was capable of when there were no such constraints to appreciate just how generously reticent some of those foreshortened spots were. Young had also played for Lunceford and Benny Goodman, but he was also active on the fringes of the bebop scene, where his terrific technique meant he could tackle some elements of the new music without strain.

Young is scarcely remembered as a leader, but he did manage to get his name on a few record labels in the '40s, and this disc neatly rounds up six such dates, variously released by Session, Duke, V-Disc, GI and HRS. The pick of them are probably the four titles made for Duke, which feature a crackling seven-piece band starring the elegant Buck Clayton and the huge-sounding Ike Quebec, whose tenor booms out of the speakers. Young is a bit of a bystander here, but he does get to take a vocal on 'I'm Living For Today'. Clayton is also on the first of the V-Disc titles and Eldridge takes over from him on the next date, which offers a storming 'Tea For Two'. Mostly, though, these are features for Tilton and Leonard. The GI session is rather ordinary but the final four titles, cut for HRS by Trummy's Big Seven, have some decent late-swing music, with Clayton and Buster Bailey and Young's own vociferous solo style in evidence.

SIDNEY BECHET&

Born 14 May 1897, New Orleans, Louisiana; died 14 May 1959, Paris, France
Soprano saxophone, clarinet

King Jazz: Volume 1

GHB BCD 501/502 2CD

Bechet; Hot Lips Page (t); Mezz Mezzrow (cl); Sammy Price, Fritz Weston (p); Danny Barker (g); George 'Pops' Foster (b); Big Sid Catlett, Kaiser Marshall (d); Douglas Daniels, Pleasant Joseph (v). March–August 1945.

Steve Lacy said (1983): **'The great strength of Sidney Bechet's saxophone-playing was that it was an old sound put in a modern context. He wasn't a revolutionary in saxophone terms, but what he did was like what Bach did: he took something that had been around for a long time, and he made it perfect.'**

The Bechet centenary came and went in 1997 with little more than a mild flurry of interest. Perhaps because there is no 'problematic' about Bechet, no need to rescue him from obscurity or debunk his undentable popularity, there was no real leverage for a reassessment. The one big event of the year, record-wise, was the appearance of the legendary King Jazz catalogue on CD. By rights, the label was the brainchild of Mezz Mezzrow, an extraordinary booster and self-promoter who managed to raise enough cash from a man who had made his pile in the war selling radar equipment to get the label under way. But Mezzrow was no better as a businessman than he was as a clarinettist, and he quickly got distracted into writing his (fictionalized) autobiography, *Really the Blues*, with the help of journalist Bernard Wolfe. However, the label's policy of recording much more than could be issued pays dividends now. The first sessions on the disc are of pianist Sammy Price with and without vocalist Pleasant Joseph. There follow, though, sessions from July and August with the Bechet–Mezzrow group. Some of these tracks – 'Revolutionary Blues', 'Perdido Street Stomp', 'The Sheik Of Araby' and 'Minor Swoon' – are classics of postwar Dixieland and, though Mezzrow's technical insufficiencies are in no way glossed over in the transfer, the brightness and unselfconscious ease of these performances warm the heart. For once Pops Foster and Danny Barker can be heard clearly, and the balance of the sound is as good as it is likely to get. Sammy Price plays on all the *Volume 1* sides except those from the August sessions. He's a decent player, slightly florid and overcooked as a soloist, but he comes into his own as a group accompanist, bettered only by Art Hodes. Fritz Weston comes in for the later dates and isn't remotely as idiomatic or as good.

& *See also* **Sidney Bechet 1940–1941** (1940–1941; p. 79), **The Fabulous Sidney Bechet** (1951–1953; p. 132)

BUNK JOHNSON

Born William Geary (or Gary) Johnson, 27 December 1889, New Orleans, Louisiana; died 7 July 1949, New Orleans, Louisiana
Trumpet

Bunk's Brass Band And Dance Band 1945

American Music AMCD-6

Johnson; Louis 'Kid Shots' Madison (t); Jim Robinson (tb); George Lewis (cl); Isidore Barbarin (ahn); Adolphe Alexander (bhn); Joe Clark (bass hn); Lawrence Marrero (bj, d); Alcide 'Slow Drag' Pavageau (b); Baby Dodds (d). May 1945.

Trombonist and broadcaster Campbell Burnap said (1985): **'Bunk's like a figure out of a western or some mafia novel. He had to skip town because he let down one of the marching band, and the krewe came after him in New Iberia and relieved him of his front teeth. So it goes. But then he claimed to be a decade older than he was. I guess he was pitching for "inventor of jazz" status.'**

A difficult and contentious man, Bunk Johnson remains mysterious and fascinating, still the figurehead of 'revivalist' jazz even though his records remain relatively difficult to find, and even marginalized where those by, say, George Lewis have kept their reputation. Deceitful about his age – he claimed to have been born in 1879, older even than Buddy Bolden, with whom he'd played – Johnson was rediscovered in 1942 and fitted out with new teeth. He had never recorded before, but many records came out of the next five years. They are, inevitably, of variable quality and one frequently wonders listening to them how much Bunk relied on his almost legendary status: it was somehow assumed that anything he cared to do was 'authentic'. However, when one listens to him, it's clear that he is a more sophisticated and lyrical player than the raw-boned curmudgeon of reputation.

This is a fine introduction to Johnson's music, since it features what would have been a regular parade band line-up on 11 tracks and a further nine by a typical Johnson dance group (recorded at George Lewis's home). Lewis sounds a little shrill on the *Brass Band* tracks, which makes one wonder about the credit for 'pitch rectification' on the CD. It is a pioneering record nevertheless, as the first authentic, New Orleans brass band session. The 'dance' tracks are very sprightly and feature some fine Lewis, as well as some of Johnson's firmest lead and even some respectable solos. The sound is quite clean as these sessions go, though some of the *Brass Band* acetates are in less than perfect shape.

Johnson's farewell, *Last Testament*, was reportedly the only session in which he really got his own way, choosing both sidemen and material; and New Orleans purists must have been surprised on both counts: he lined up a team of players quite different from the American Music cronies, and he chose rags and pop tunes to perform: 'The Entertainer', 'Kinklets' and 'The Minstrel Man'. He was for a time a living connection to the past, but one suspects that his past was made for him, and it's one of the paradoxes of the revival that the obvious cues were overlooked.

MARY LOU WILLIAMS &

Born Mary Elfrieda Scruggs (later Burley), 8 May 1910, Atlanta, Georgia; died 28 May 1981, Durham, North Carolina
Piano

The Zodiac Suite

Smithsonian Folkways SF CD 40810
Williams; unidentified big band, featuring Ben Webster (ts); New York Philharmonic Orchestra. December 1945.

Mary Lou Williams said (1975): **'I couldn't get the money I wanted and thought I deserved from Norman Granz, so eventually took scale [payment] just in order to get some of the *Zodiac* things played by legitimate musicians from the New York Philharmonic.'**

Duke Ellington described her as 'perpetually contemporary'. After she grew up in Pittsburgh, Mary Lou Williams's career encompassed weary days of travel with Andy Kirk's Clouds Of Joy band (she began as a part-time arranger and only grudgingly won recognition as a piano-player), staff arranging for Ellington, and bandleading. Along with her husband,

John Williams, she joined Terrence Holder's Clouds Of Joy orchestra, shortly to be taken over by Kirk. After divorcing Williams, she married trumpeter Harold Baker and co-led a group with him. Her later style shows a deep understanding of jazz history and a profound spiritual dimension.

The early work is best sampled from her work with the Clouds Of Joy, though there are a number of Classics volumes covering her own output from 1927 to the end of the war, when she was completing work on the ambitious *Zodiac Suite*.

On New Year's Eve 1945/6, Williams gave a remarkable performance of her *Zodiac Suite* with the New York Philharmonic at Town Hall. It's a sequence of dedications to fellow musicians (identified by their astrological characteristics) and combines straight orchestral writing of a slightly bland, film soundtrack sort with jazz interpolations and occasional sections ('Taurus' and 'Gemini', significantly) where the two seem to coincide. Williams had been profoundly dissatisfied with a partial reading of the music, recorded in 1957 for Norman Granz's Verve label, and the rediscovery of the 'lost' tapes from the Town Hall concert is a significant addition to the discography. The sound isn't always very reliable, with occasional crackles and some loss of resolution in the string parts, but Williams is caught in close-up and the piece remains a key moment in the recognition of jazz as an important 20th-century music, not 'classical', but with its own history and logic.

& *See also* **Free Spirits** (1975; p. 426)

BOYD RAEBURN
Born 27 October 1913, Faith, South Dakota; died 2 August 1966, Lafayette, Louisiana
Bass saxophone, leader

Jubilee Performances 1946
Hep CD 1
Raeburn; Gordon Boswell, Pete Candoli, Norman Faye, Conrad Gozzo, Wes Hensel (t); Eddie Bert, Dick Noel, Hal Smith, Britt Woodman, Ollie Wilson, Freddie Zito (tb); Lloyd Oto, Al Richman, Evan Vail (frhn); Harvey Estrin, Allen Fields (as); Harvey Klee (as, f); Wilbur Schwartz (as, cl); Frank Socolow (as, ts); Ralph Lee, Lucky Thompson, Shirley Thompson (ts); Hy Mandel (bs); Harry Babasin, Clyde Lombardi (bsx); Gus McReynolds (sax); Jules Jacob (eng hn, ob, ts); Dodo Marmarosa, Dale Pierce (p); Sam Herman, Tony Rizzi (g); Gail Laughton (hp); Tiny Kahn, Irv Kluger, Jackie Mills (d); Doug Jones (perc); David Allyn (v). 1945–1946.

Hep boss Alastair Robertson says: **'Raeburn broke the mould. George Handy's arrangements took the band away from the dance floor and into a concert jazz format. Young America was not ready for such innovation and within a year the band folded, but many years later I talked to Raeburn soloists Harry Klee and Britt Woodman, who spoke warmly of the experience.'**

In 1944, an unexplained fire at the Palisades Pleasure Park in New Jersey destroyed the instruments and music of one of the most challenging big bands of the period. Typically of Boyd Raeburn, his re-formed band and new book were even more adventurous than what had gone before, absorbing elements of Ellington, current swing and modern classicism. He was a leader at 20, and by 30 in charge of a challenging modernist group. The records weren't hits and he reverted to sweeter fare, retiring in 1957. Raeburn's was a musicians' band, held in the highest esteem by his peers, regarded with some suspicion by those who believed that bands were for dancing. Raeburn had an intelligent awareness of classical and 20th-century forms and was as comfortable with Bartók and Debussy as he was with Ellington and Basie. The bands were clangorous, neither 'sweet' nor 'hot', but a curious

admixture of the two, and arrangements were full of awkward time-signatures and tonalities. Tunes such as 'Tonsillectomy', 'Rip Van Winkle' and 'Yerxa', from earlier and (as yet)
not reissued sessions, are among the most remarkable of modern-band pieces. The Raeburn
bands of the time (like Kirk's or McShann's) are well worth scouring for the early work of
prominent modernists: Dizzy Gillespie, Serge Chaloff, Shelly Manne. It may be that simple
market forces pushed Raeburn back in the direction of the swing mainstream.

Hep have put out several good-quality Raeburn sets, including transcriptions that cast
George Handy's outlandish arrangements in excellent sound. The Jubilee airshots include
some scarifying arrangements of things like 'Body And Soul', but also include Finckel's
'Boyd Meets Stravinsky'. Hard to know how these were received at the time, so acute an
angle on bop harmony they take. In sum, this is an inconsistent body of work, but Raeburn
deserves a better shake than jazz history has so far given him.

WOODY HERMAN &

Born 16 May 1930, Milwaukee, Wisconsin; died 29 October 1987, Los Angeles, California
Clarinet, alto and soprano saxophones, voice

Blowin' Up A Storm!

Columbia 503280-2 2CD

Herman; Sonny Berman, Shorty Rogers, Cappy Lewis, Billy Rogers, Pete Candoli, Conte Candoli, Chuck
Frankhauser, Carl Warwick, Ray Wetzel, Neal Hefti, Irv Lewis, Ray Linn, Marky Markowitz (t); Bill Harris, Ed
Kiefer, Ralph Pfeffner, Neal Reid, Bob Swift, Rodney Ogle, Tommy Pederson (tb); Sam Marowitz, John LaPorta,
Les Robinson, Jimmy Horvath (as); Mickey Folus, Flip Phillips, Pete Mondello, Vido Musso, Ben Webster (ts);
Sam Rubinowich, Skippy DeSair (bs); Ralph Burns, Fred Otis, Tony Aless (p); Margie Hyams, Red Norvo (vib);
Chuck Wayne, Billy Bauer (g); Joe Mondragon, Chubby Jackson, Walt Yoder (b); Dave Tough, Don Lamond,
Johnny Blowers (d); Martha Raye, Frances Wayne, Carolyn Grey (v). February 1945–December 1947.

Woody Herman said (1977): **'If you're not moving forward, you're going backwards. Even
with the war on, I didn't want to make excuses for gaps in the band and the band book. I
wanted us to get better and better.'**

A brilliant rhythm section, a brass team that could top any big-band section on either coast
and arrangements that crackled with spontaneity and wit: Herman's 1945 band was both a
commercial and an artistic triumph. With Burns, Bauer, Tough and Jackson (who incidentally became the first bassist to amplify his instrument) spurring the horns on, the band
handled head arrangements and slicker charts such as Neal Hefti's 'Wild Root' with the
same mixture of innate enthusiasm and craft. There was a modern edge to the group that
suggested something of the transition from swing to bop, even though it was the Second
Herd that threw in its lot with bop spirit if not letter. Columbia have done their Herman
recordings some justice in a full CD reissue of their best music from the period. Besides
all the familiar material, there's the studio version of Stravinsky's 'Ebony Concerto' and a
series of alternative takes of some of the best-known numbers – though even Ralph Burns,
in his entertaining sleeve-note, says that most of these are clearly inferior to the masters.
The remastering has been scrupulously done and, with 40 tracks at mid-price, this should
rank as one of the great bargains in the area of big-band music on CD, with the likes of
'Northwest Passage', 'Your Father's Mustache', 'The Good Earth', 'Apple Honey' and 'Bijou'
all sounding terrific.

& See also **Woody Herman 1939** (1939; p. 78), **Woody's Winners / Jazz Hoot** (1965–1967; p. 321)

MUTT CAREY

Born Thomas Carey, known as 'Papa Mutt', 25 December 1886 (other sources give 1891), Hahnville,
Louisiana; died 3 September 1948, Elsinore, California
Trumpet

Mutt Carey And Lee Collins

American Music AMCD-72
Carey; Lee Collins (t); Hociel Thomas (p, v); Lovie Austin, J. H. Shayne (p); Johnny Lindsay (b); Baby Dodds (d); Bertha 'Chippie' Hill (v). February–August 1946.

Cornetist Alex Welsh said (1978): **'Mutt Carey was at the beginning of things, but he wasn't a front-man, really. He even sounds shy and a bit awkward and I suppose he was happiest when there were other horns around him. But that's how it was at the start of jazz: the group was more important than the soloist.'**

Carey played with his brother Jack's orchestra before the First World War and was in contact with most of the leading early figures in the music, including Buddy Bolden and Joe 'King' Oliver, but like so many of this generation he had to bide his time for the revival before he received much recognition. A player who sounded best in the confines of a group rather than a stellar soloist, he was none the less on hand when Kid Ory's group made the first jazz sides ever by a black group, so his place in the histories is relatively secure, even if his body of recorded work is vestigial.

Inevitably, much of Carey's early work went undocumented, but he was still around for the revival and there's a reasonable representation of his sound on record. An Upbeat compilation includes some fine players – Ory, Jimmy Archey, Minor Hall, Joe Darensbourg, Albert Nicholas – but much of the material is accompaniments to classic blues singer Hociel Thomas, another who had been recently plucked from obscurity. Their duets are also included on this American Music compilation, and she comes across in surprisingly good voice, though Carey, unfortunately, sometimes sounds uncomfortable and hesitant. That's typical of a musician who clearly didn't like to be exposed. He was a player for the collective. There's nice interplay on 'Go Down Sunshine', but it's the unsung Collins who often sounds better on his eight tracks. Good, rough music.

WOODEN JOE NICHOLAS

Born 23 September 1883, New Orleans, Louisiana; died 17 November 1957, New Orleans, Louisiana
Trumpet

Wooden Joe Nicholas

American Music AMCD-5
Nicholas; Jim Robinson, Louis Nelson, Joe Petit (tb); Albert Burbank (cl); Johnny St Cyr (g); Lawrence Marrero (bj); Austin Young, Alcide 'Slow Drag' Pavageau (b); Josiah Frazier, Baby Dodds, Albert Jiles (d); Ann Cook (v). May 1945–July 1949.

Clarinettist Kenny Davern said (1992): **'When I was coming up in New York, there was this very smooth "Dixieland" style around, shiny but dull, if you know what I mean. With the confidence of the very young, I started to speak up for the old New Orleans players, and particularly people like Wooden Joe Nicholas. If you want to hear the roots of jazz, that's where you have to go, and we're kind of blessed that he made any records at all. Buddy Bolden didn't.'**

A legend calls down the years. He himself was Albert Nicholas's uncle, but Wooden Joe's own main idol was Buddy Bolden, and hearing him play may offer us the best idea of what

Bolden himself might have sounded like. Nicholas blew a very powerful open horn, and was famous for dominating a dance hall sound. There was very little recording in New Orleans during the first jazz generations, but Wooden Joe was still around for the revival. These were his only recordings, and they are clustered together from a session at the Artesian Hall and two later dates. A lot of New Orleans history is tied up here: the fearsome blues singer Ann Cook is on one track, the legendary trombonist Joe Petit on another. Nicholas and Burbank are the main voices on all the tracks (Wooden Joe also played clarinet, and does so on two numbers): compared with the clarinettist's weaving lines, Nicholas is reserved in his phrasing and takes only a few breaks and solos. But much of his power and stately delivery was intact.

KENNY CLARKE

Known as 'Klook', and formally as Liaqat Ali Salaam; born 9 January 1914, Pittsburgh, Pennsylvania; died 26 January 1985, Paris, France
Drums

Klook's The Man

Properbox 120 4CD
Clarke; Benny Bailey, Donald Byrd, Dick Collins, Kenny Dorham, Claude Dunson, Henry Goodwin, Roger Guerin, Fats Navarro (t); Nat Adderley (c); Eddie Bert, Billy Byers, Henry Coker, Nat Peck (tb); Rudy Powell (cl, as); Cannonball Adderley, John Brown, Hubert Fol, John LaPorta, Frank Morgan, Hubert Rostaing, Sonny Stitt, Michel De Villers (as); Ernie Wilkins (as, ts, arr); Ray Abrams, Walter Benton, Jean-Claude Fohrenbach (ts); James Moody (ts, arr); Jerome Richardson, Frank Wess (ts, f); George Barrow (ts, bs); Charlie Fowlkes, Armand Migiani, Cecil Payne, Eddie De Verteuil (bs); Ronnie Ball, Jacques Denjean, Tommy Flanagan, Edgar Hayes, Hank Jones, Bernard Peiffer, Bud Powell, Ralph Schecroun, Horace Silver, Martial Solal, René Urtreger, Gerald Wiggins (p); Milt Jackson (vib); Kenny Burrell, John Collins, Eddie Gibbs, Al McKibbon, Charles Montaggioni (g); André Hodeir (vn, arr); Jean Bouchety, Paul Chambers, Frank 'Coco' Darling, Al Hall, Percy Heath, Eddie Jones, Wendell Marshall, Alf Messelier, Pierre Michelot, Jean Warland, James Anderson (v); Walter Fuller (arr). March 1938–November 1956.

Kenny Clarke said (1978): **'Michel Legrand fixed me up with his uncle's jazz band in Paris. I saw Michel on TV, on a Maurice Chevalier special, and phoned him up. In the fall I got sent a first-class liner ticket and I took everything I had with me and I'm still over here. J'aime bien Paris!'**

If there were a ballot on who actually invented bebop, Kenny Clarke would be a good outside candidate. 'Klook', so called because of the distinctive 'klook-mop' sound of his favourite cadence, is one of the most influential drummers of all time. He made his recording debut at 24 in Sweden with the dire James Anderson on vocals (it's all here on this Properbox), but while working with Dizzy Gillespie in the early '40s Clarke began to depart from normal practice by marking the count on his top cymbal and using his bass drum only for accents. It became the distinctive sound of bebop, imitated and adapted by Blakey and Roach, and it remains essential background work for drummers even today. Clarke had a strong but also quite delicate sound and he remained swing-oriented all through his career, even after bebop became the norm. His big band with Francy Boland kept the music alive during lean times.

The Properbox picks up the story after military service in 1946 with Klook and his 52nd Street Boys (including Navarro, Dorham, Stitt and Powell) recording 'Epistrophy' (which he co-wrote with Monk) and some other tunes. The rest of disc one was taped in Paris. There's then another big jump to the mid-'50s in Hollywood and New York following Clarke's short tenure with the Modern Jazz Quartet. The best stuff comes at the start of the third disc, and the June 1955 septet date with Byrd, both Adderleys, Richardson, Silver and Chambers, with cracking reads of 'Willow, Weep For Me', 'Bohemia After Dark' and 'Hear Me Talkin' To Ya'. The fourth begins strongly with the Pittsburgher meeting up with Detroit's finest at Rudy Van Gelder's. Thereafter, though, the selection tails away. Compilation boxes aren't ideal (though some of these volumes might be separately available, in which case the early two are best) but *Klook's The Man* provides a perfect introduction to one of the prime movers of the modern scene.

BILLY ECKSTINE

Born William Clarence Eckstein, 8 July 1914, Pittsburgh, Pennsylvania; died 8 March 1993, Pittsburgh, Pennsylvania
Voice, trumpet, valve trombone

Billy Eckstine 1944–1946

Classics 914

Eckstine; Dizzy Gillespie, Freddy Webster, Shorty McConnell, Al Killian, Gail Brockman, Boonie Hazel, Fats Navarro, Raymond Orr (t); Trummy Young, Howard Scott, Claude Jones, Jerry Valentine, Taswell Baird, Alfred 'Chippie' Outcalt, Walter Knox (tb); Budd Johnson, Jimmy Powell, John Jackson, Bill Frazier, Sonny Stitt, John Cobbs (as); Gene Ammons, Dexter Gordon, Wardell Gray, Thomas Crump, Arthur Sammons (ts); Rudy Rutherford, Leo Parker, Teddy Cypron (bs); John Malachi, Clyde Hart, Richard Ellington (p); Connie Wainwright (g); Oscar Pettiford, Tommy Potter (b); Shadow Wilson, Art Blakey (d); Sarah Vaughan (v). April 1944–October 1945.

Saxophonist Gerry Mulligan said (1992): **'In the '40s if you mentioned "the Band", it was universally understood who you meant, and it wasn't Duke or Basie. It was Eckstine. That was the place to be.'**

He changed the spelling of his name because a promoter thought 'Eckstein' was 'too Jewish'. Though he was a competent brass-player, it was Mr B's voice that was his fortune, a rich bass-baritone that caressed, but could also deliver a slap. He arrived in Chicago in 1938, found success as a vocalist with the Earl Hines band, and subsequently ran his own big band. He turned to small-group work in 1947 and enjoyed MOR success, though usually with a jazz flavour.

Eckstine's orchestra was a legendary incubator for young bebop talent, as a glance at the personnel shows, and it's a pity that the band's surviving performances are mostly of ballads and features for the leader. Not that one should decry anything that Eckstine himself does. His massive, smooth, sumptuous voice has its own virtues, and on the rare occasion when he handles an up-tempo piece – 'I Love The Rhythm In A Riff' – he is just as adept. There are glimmers of Gordon, Ammons, Gillespie and Navarro here, as well as Vaughan's debut on 'I'll Wait And Pray', but it's the power of the band as a whole, the lift given by the young Art Blakey and the rapt power of Eckstine's balladeering which are the merits of these tracks.

Miles Davis, Wardell Gray, Dizzy Gillespie, Sonny Stitt, Sonny Criss, Hobart Dotson, Gene Ammons, Cecil Payne, Leo Parker, Art Blakey and Sarah Vaughan all passed through the ranks, but by the immediate postwar years the 'legendary Billy Eckstine' was in danger of starving – as he melodramatically put it – from lack of work, and he had to move in a new MOR direction with smaller groups. They had their moments, but the big bands of the 1940s were where the action was. His impact was comparable to Lunceford's a decade earlier, but with incomparably more finesse.

CHARLIE PARKER &

Born 29 August 1920, Kansas City, Missouri; died 12 March 1955, New York City
Alto and tenor saxophones

Charlie Parker With Strings: The Master Takes

Verve 523984-2
Parker; Tony Aless, Al Haig, Bernie Leighton (p); Art Ryerson (g); Ray Brown, Bob Haggart, Tommy Potter, Curley Russell (b); Roy Haynes, Don Lamond, Shelly Manne, Buddy Rich (d); strings. December 1947–January 1952.

Ray Brown said (1991): **'Bird wanted nothing more than to play with strings. That, as far as he was concerned, was the pinnacle in recording terms, and Norman Granz granted it to him. Everyone argues about the results, but it's still Bird.'**

What to do with Parker's body of recording for Norman Granz's labels? Does it represent a creative falling-away after the mighty Savoy and Dial sessions, which seem to reinvent modern jazz with every successive take? The short and negative answer is yes; there is nothing here of quite that quality or force. The most positive answer is that in these sessions Parker achieved a maturity and grace of performance that was matched by high-quality recording and that the Verve years represent a kind of plateau across which he sailed, erratically and with inevitable diversions, but with ineffable grace throughout.

There are many, many fine small-group performances among the Verve sides, and the parent company has lost no time in putting out multiple repackagings of Parker's music, most of them derived from the grand ten-CD box that still turns up now and again for sale. We have opted this time to bite the bullet and present without further comment or justification the with-strings recordings – endlessly and pointlessly argued over – as a representation of this period. That Bird himself aspired to these like no other recordings in his career should be some reassurance that they are no sidebars or digressions, but absolutely of the essence. The music speaks handsomely for itself.

& *See also* **The Complete Savoy And Dial Studio Recordings** (1945–1948; p. 96), **The Quintet** (1953; p. 141)

DAVE BRUBECK &

Born 6 December 1920, Concord, California
Piano

The Dave Brubeck Octet

Original Jazz Classics OJC 101
Brubeck; Dick Collins (t); Bob Collins (tb); Paul Desmond (as); Dave Van Kriedt (ts); Bill Smith (cl, bs); Ron Crotty (b); Cal Tjader (d). 1946–July 1950.

Dave Brubeck said (1991): **'We were in Darius Milhaud's class at Mills [College, Oakland]. He asked how many of us played jazz, and eight of us put our hands up. That's how it started!'**

Though often derided as a buttoned-down formalist with an unhealthy addiction to classical music and complex time-signatures, Brubeck is one of the most significant composer-leaders in modern jazz. Tunes like 'Blue Rondo A La Turk', 'Kathy's Waltz' and Paul Desmond's 'Take Five' (which Brubeck made an enormous hit) insinuated their way into the unconscious of a whole generation of American college students. Though 'In Your Own Sweet Way' is probably the only Brubeck original that is regularly covered by others, he has created a remarkable body of jazz and formal music, including orchestral pieces, orato-rios and ballet scores. The Brubecks constitute something of a musical dynasty. His elder brother, Howard, is a 'straight' composer in a rather old-fashioned Francophile vein, while his sons, bassist and trombonist Chris, drummer Danny and keyboard-player Darius, have all played with Dave.

It used to be conventional wisdom that the only Brubeck records which mattered were those that featured the liquid alto of Paul Desmond. Such was the proprietary closeness of the relationship that it was stated in Desmond's contract that his own recordings had to be pianoless. What no one seemed to notice was that Desmond's best playing was almost always with the Brubeck group. Brubeck himself is not a particularly accomplished soloist, with a rather heavy touch and an unfailing attachment to block chords; it's fair to say that his instrument was the quartet as a whole.

The early *Octet* catches Brubeck at the height of his interest in an advanced harmonic language (which he would have learned from Darius Milhaud, his teacher at Mills College); there are also rhythmic transpositions of a sort that popped up in classic jazz and were subsequently taken as read by the '60s avant-garde, but which in the '50s had been explored thoroughly only by Max Roach. Brubeck has not been widely regarded as a writer-arranger for larger groups, but the better material on this recorded set underlines how confidently he approached the synthesis of jazz with other forms. Even the standards – 'What Is This Thing Called Love?', 'I Hear A Rhapsody', 'Laura' – are approached with inventiveness and it's clear that Brubeck, though the leading personality, was, much like Miles Davis on *The Birth Of The Cool*, surrounded by talented and like-minded musicians, who brought their own ideas to the table. Dave van Kriedt's 'Fugue On Bop Themes' and 'Serenade Suite' are just two of the more prominent examples. Tracks like 'Schizophrenic Scherzo' are a great deal more swinging than most products of the Third Stream, a movement one doesn't auto-matically associate with Brubeck's name.

& *See also* **Time Out** (1959; p. 240), **London Sharp, London Flat** (2004; p. 690)

ILLINOIS JACQUET
Born Jean Baptiste Illinois Jacquet, 31 October 1922, Broussard, Louisiana; died 22 July 2004, Queens, New York
Tenor saxophone, bassoon, voice

Illinois Jacquet 1945–1946
Classics 948
Jacquet; Emmett Berry, Russell Jacquet (t); Henry Coker (tb); John Brown (as); Tom Archia (ts); Arthur Dennis (bs); Bill Doggett, Sir Charles Thompson (p); Freddie Green, Ulysses Livingston (g); Billy Hadnott, Charles Mingus, John Simmons (b); Johnny Otis, Shadow Wilson (d). July 1945–January 1946.

Illinois Jacquet said (1983): **'My name comes from "Illiniwek", which is an Indian word for "superior man". I don't know how I came to deserve that!'**

Born in Broussard, Louisiana, and raised in Houston, Texas – you somehow know how Illinois Jacquet is going to sound. It's a big, blues tone, tinged with loneliness that some-how underlines Jacquet's status as a permanent guest star. He learned his showmanship in the Hampton band of the early '40s, trading on his remarkable facility in the 'false' upper register and on sheer energy.

Jacquet seems permanently saddled with the 'Texas tenor' tag. In fact, his playing can show remarkable sensitivity and he was one of the fastest thinkers in the business. His ability to take care of his own business was obvious from the shrewd self-management that kept him in the forefront of Norman Granz's Jazz At The Philharmonic. Just a few days after his triumphant debut with JATP, Jacquet cut the first of the sides included on this Classics compilation. Inevitably, he includes another version of 'Flying Home', accompanied this time by brother Russell (who takes the vocal on 'Throw It Out Of Your Mind, Baby'), trombonist Henry Coker and Sir Charles Thompson. The four July sides for Philo are pretty forgettable, and there isn't a chance to hear what Jacquet is really made of until he starts recording for Apollo in August. 'Jacquet Mood' and 'Bottoms Up' are both impressive uptempo numbers, and there is an early sighting of Jacquet the balladeer, an exquisite performance of 'Ghost Of A Chance'. He's back in the same mood early the following year, recording for Savoy in a band with Emmett Berry, who was credited as leader on half the releases. This time, it's 'Don't Blame Me' that reveals the romantic in him. The only other items are a couple of obscurities recorded in August 1945 for ARA. The sharp-eyed will have noted a credit for the 23-year-old Charles Mingus, playing bass on the Apollo sessions.

DODO MARMAROSA

Born Michael Marmarosa, 12 December 1925, Pittsburgh, Pennsylvania; died 17 September 2002, Pittsburgh, Pennsylvania (but see below!)
Piano

On Dial: The Complete Sessions
Spotlite SPJ-128
Marmarosa; Howard McGhee, Miles Davis (t); Charlie Parker (as); Teddy Edwards, Lucky Thompson (ts); Arvin Garrison (g); Harry Babasin (clo); Bob Kesterson (b); Roy Porter, Jackie Mills (d). 1946–December 1947.

Jazz writer Steve Voce says: '**I was sad to hear, in the spring of 1992, that Dodo Marmarosa had died. I set to work on his obituary and it was published in the *Independent* on 27 April. One also appeared in the *Guardian*. A few days later Marmarosa's sister phoned the *Independent* from Pittsburgh and pointed out that Dodo was standing by her side as she made the call. In the early '90s a British fan in the Pittsburgh area began calling Marmarosa's home to ask for an interview. By then reclusive, he wanted none of it. The fan persisted and it was Marmarosa himself who answered when the fan called yet again. "I'm sorry to tell you," said an exasperated Marmarosa, "that Mr Marmarosa passed away yesterday." The fan immediately called a record producer in England with news of the "death" and the producer called me. For his last few years Dodo moved into a local medical centre where he occasionally played piano and organ for the other residents. He had done this on the day of his death, before returning to his room complaining of feeling unwell.**'

A bebop enigma. Marmarosa played an important minor role in bop's hothouse days, recording with Parker in LA; but less than two years later he was back in his native Pittsburgh and heading for obscurity and silence. He had a foot in swing as well as the modern camp, and his precise articulation and sweeping lines make one think of Tatum as much as any of his immediate contemporaries: a pair of solos from 1946, 'Deep Purple' and 'Tea For Two', are strikingly akin to the older man's conception. But he had a gentle, even rhapsodic side, which colours the trio tracks here, and while he flirts with an even more audacious conception – hinted at on the two 'Tone Paintings' solos from 1947 – one feels he never satisfactorily resolved the different strands of his playing. Much of his best playing is to be found on Parker's Dials (a solitary example, 'Bird Lore', is on the Spotlite CD), but the solo, trio and sextet (with McGhee) tracks on *On Dial* include much absorbing piano jazz.

Many important figures drop out of the historical narrative, either through critical and commercial neglect or in some cases simply out of choice. Marmarosa's premature obituary surely has its ironic side, for the music he made and then turned his back on now seems more relevant than ever.

LENNIE TRISTANO &

Born 19 March 1919, Chicago, Illinois; died 18 November 1978, New York City
Piano

The Complete Lennie Tristano

Mercury 830921-2
Tristano; Billy Bauer (g); Clyde Lombardi, Bob Leininger (b). October 1946–May 1947.

Warne Marsh said (1980): **'Don't mythologize Lennie Tristano, or make some kind of monster out of him. He was, quite simply, the best educated and most knowledgeable musician around. Everyone benefited from that. No mystery.'**

If Charlie Parker is the Schoenberg of modern jazz, then Tristano is its Webern; he represents its 'difficult' phase. Few modern jazz musicians have been more and more misleadingly mythologized. References to a Tristano 'school' may well have some literal force, but they tend to imply that the musician designated a member is somehow considered unable to speak for him/herself, a kind of musical Stalinist. The truth is more complex.

Whereas most horn-led post-bop delved into uncomfortable psychic regions and cultivated a scouring intensity, Tristano ruthlessly purged his music of uncontrolled emotion. Perhaps because his basic instruction to his horn-players – most obviously Lee Konitz and Warne Marsh – was that they should use a deliberately uninflected and neutral tone, concentrating instead on the structure of a solo, Tristano has remained a minority taste, and a rather intellectual one. This is a pity, because Tristano's music is always vital and usually exciting. Though he abandoned the rhythmic eccentricities of bop in favour of an even background count, his playing is far from conventional, deploying long sequences of even semiquavers in subtly shifting time-signatures, adding sophisticated dissonances to quite basic chordal progressions. There is also a problem for the newcomers in the nature of the Tristano discography, much of which involves indifferent live recordings and posthumously released private tapes.

The early material for Mercury – some of it later released on a compilation which referred to the 'advance guard' of new jazz – catches Tristano just before bebop – specifically, Powell and Parker – had had a significant impact on his playing, so his style, refracted through Tatum and Hines, is like a mysterious, charged yet inscrutable distillation of swing piano's most elaborate settings. One is sometimes reminded of Tatum's (or Nat Cole's) trio recordings, yet Tristano's ideas, while harmonically dense, adapt bop's irresistible spontaneity better than either of those peers. Eleven of the 19 tracks are previously unreleased alternative takes, and the five versions of 'Interlude' (alias 'A Night In Tunisia') are as varied as Parker's Dials. In Bauer he had one of his most sympathetic partners: often lost to jazz history, the guitarist's lines are unfailingly apt yet fresh. Comparison between each take shows how insistent Tristano already was on making his music new from moment to moment. Some of the surviving masters were in imperfect shape, with occasional high-note distortions, but it won't trouble anyone used to music from this period.

& See also **Lennie Tristano / The New Tristano** (1954–1962; p. 151)

LOUIS JORDAN

Born 8 July 1908, Brinkley, Arkansas; died 4 February 1975, Los Angeles, California
Alto saxophone, voice

Louis Jordan 1946–1947

Classics 1010
Jordan; Aaron Izenhall (t); James Wright, Eddie Johnson (ts); Wild Bill Davis (p); Carl Hogan (g); Jesse Simpkins, Dallas Bartley (b); Joe Morris (d); The Calypso Boys (perc). October 1946–December 1947.

Chuck Berry said (1978): **'Louis Jordan pretty much invented rock and roll. I don't mean the music – though everyone stole his riffs – but the crowd. Louis Jordan invented the rock crowd.'**

Jordan came from a vaudeville family and never quite lost that ethos. He quit big bands in the early '40s to form his Tympany Five, one of the most successful small bands in jazz history, which helped to father R&B. Jordan was an incomparable funster as well as being a distinctive altoman and smart vocalist. His hit records, 'Five Guys Named Moe', 'Choo Choo Ch'Boogie', 'Caldonia' and many more, established the idea of the jump band as a jiving, irrepressible outfit. Rightly so: Jordan was a pro's pro, tirelessly seeking out fresh songs and constantly touring. But, surprisingly, the music seldom suffered, which is why his best sides still sound fresh. There are plenty of good compilations around, which gather up the hits, but it's more interesting in our context to dive into the narrative at a specific point and observe just how hard the group worked at looking as if they were merely at play.

We've picked one representative moment. The previous year or two's volumes have 'Choo Choo Ch'Boogie' and 'That Chick's Too Young To Fry' plus a couple of duets with Ella Fitzgerald, then eight tracks made for V-Disc, a radio ad for Oldsmobile and the sublime duet with Bing Crosby on 'Your Socks Don't Match'. Our favourite, though, has a sublime put-down in 'You're Much Too Fat And That's That', as well as Jordan's first two versions of 'Open The Door Richard!'. These and a few other, less celebrated songs, like 'Boogie Woogie Blue Plate' and the straight blues 'Roamin' Blues' and 'Inflation Blues', make it the first choice. If you find yourself not enjoying Jordan's music, check your pulse.

JOHN HARDEE
Born 20 December 1918, Corsicana, Texas; died 18 May 1984, Dallas, Texas
Tenor saxophone

John Hardee 1946–1948
Classics 1136
Hardee; Harold Baker (t); Trummy Young (tb); Russell Procope (as, cl); Ted Brannon, Billy Kyle, Billy Taylor (p); Tiny Grimes (g); Sid Catlett, Buddy Rich (d); and others. 1946–1948.

Johnny Griffin heard 'Hardee's Partee' in a 'blindfold' test (1992): **'Sounds like Hawkins with a cold! Just who *is* that? I'd guess he's from Texas. There was nobody playing like that in New York.'**

The album title *Forgotten Texas Tenor* says it all. He had a sound reminiscent of Coleman Hawkins, but after an early stint of recording, including some excellent, big-voiced work for Blue Note, he wasn't heard outside his home state. We believe we glimpsed him in France in 1975, at a festival in Nice, but no detail remains. He had a big, heavy tone but a deft touch with a tune. Not the most exciting or barnstorming of the Texas tenors, he had a quality that is hard to describe and hard to forget. His own material is good, in a functional sort of way, and while the better-known things, 'Hardee's Partee' and 'Boppin' In B flat', are hardly classics, the rest are individual enough to spark curiosity.

TYREE GLENN
Born Evan Tyree Glenn, 11 April 1912, Corsicana, Texas; died 18 May 1974, Englewood, New Jersey
Trombone, vibraphone

Tyree Glenn 1947–1952
Classics 1420

Glenn; Peanuts Holland (t); Nat Peck (tb); Johnny Hodges, Hubert Rostaing (as); Don Byas (ts); Harry Carney (bs); Åke Hasselgård, Jimmy Hamilton (cl); Hank Jones, Charles Norman, Billy Strayhorn, Thore Swanerud, Billy Taylor (p); Bill Doggett (org); Sten Carlberg, Jerome Darr, Jean-Jacques Tilché (g); Jean Bouchety, Simon Brehm, Milt Hinton, Wendell Marshall (b); Anders Burman, Sonny Greer, Jo Jones (d). January 1947–1952.

Louis Armstrong researcher Kjell Watkins says: **'Tyree Glenn was a replacement for Jack Teagarden in Armstrong's group. It takes big feet and a big heart to fill those shoes. When Louis and [manager] Joe Glaser were both in hospital, it was Tyree who volunteered to give a blood transfusion. I think that's a measure of him.'**

Glenn is, to our knowledge, the only vibes-player ever to work with Duke Ellington, but is better known as a trombone-player. He served time with Eddie Barefield, Benny Carter, Cab Calloway and Don Redman, but made his name with the Louis Armstrong All Stars. Influenced by Tricky Sam Nanton, he made a specialism of wah-wah solos. He's a warm-toned, rootsy player who nevertheless had some modernist touches that always seemed comfortably assimilated to his basic sound, so he never stood out (negatively) in Armstrong's company and helped keep the sound up to date.

Glenn started recording on his own account for Blue Star in Paris, easy bop discs with a warm and enveloping sound and with Byas in excellent heart. Glenn and the saxophonist recorded further sides in the Netherlands the following year, another four-horn front line, though with Peck in for the alto saxophonist. Glenn shows his facility on the vibes with 'My Melancholy Baby', but it's the interpretation of Dvořák's 'Humoresque' that takes the prizes. Subsequently, he recorded in Sweden with the Brehm Kvintett, then back in America in the spring of 1949 with Strayhorn and a group of Ellingtonians. Finally here, at the start of the new decade, some sides with organist Doggett and a piano-led small group with Jones. It doesn't add up to a paradigm-shifting body of work, but one wonders why these sides aren't better. Glenn's a fluid technician and has more to say than what's to be read off a section-chart. Plaudits to Classics for making him better known.

DJANGO REINHARDT&
Born Jean-Baptiste Reinhardt, 23 January 1910, Lieberchies, Belgium; died 16 May 1953, Fontainebleau, France
Guitar

Pêche À La Mouche
Verve 835419-2

Reinhardt; Vincent Casino, Jo Boyer, Louis Menardi, Rex Stewart (t); André Lafosse, Guy Paquinet (tb); Michel De Villers (as, cl); Hubert Rostaing (cl); Jean-Claude Forenbach (ts); Eddie Bernard, Maurice Vander (p); Joseph Reinhardt, Eugène Vées (g); Will Lockwood, Ladislas Czabancyk, Pierre Michelot, Emmanuel Soudieux (b); Al Craig, Ted Curry, André Jourdan, Jean-Louis Viale (d). April 1947–March 1953.

Stéphane Grappelli said (1981): **'What did I mean by Django's "monkey business"? I mean all the things the Americans admired him for! For me, it was too much; for them, it was, I think, part of his charm!'**

The war years obviously brought a certain non-musical poignancy, and the remarkable story of how Django was protected by a jazz-loving Luftwaffe officer, but the coldest and most detached audition still reveals a shift in Django's playing towards something altogether more inward, secretive, less joyous, and even when there are no obvious shadows gathering there is a hint of darkness and doubt, in keeping with a personality that was becoming ever more erratic and dissociated.

After the Liberation, Django became an international hero, travelling to America to work with Duke Ellington. His attitude to the Americans was a studied detachment. He would turn up and play, but show no sign of engagement with what was going on around him. Django and Grappelli, who'd spent the war years in London, were reunited after hostilities ceased, but much of the old magic had gone. Prefaced by a track each – 'Pêche À La Mouche' and 'Minor Blues' – from Django's quintet and orchestra, the 1947 sessions for Blue Star with the re-formed Hot Club are not classics like the great sides of the previous decade, but they have a spontaneity and ease that are both attractive and aesthetically satisfying. Producer Eddie Barclay gave Django a free hand to play what he wanted, and the music that emerged was bright, flowing and often thoughtful, with a rough edge that is only partially explained by the technical limitations of the recording.

There is one further session from 1947, under the leadership of Rex Stewart, which again might have served to remind Django of the huge cultural distance between him and the Americans. He plays with immense elegance on 'Night And Day' but never sounds as though he's on top of what Stewart is doing harmonically.

The later recording, which was issued as a 10-inch LP, not as 78s, saw the shadows move a little closer round the guitarist, but Django's solo on 'Brazil' is, as noted by Pierre Michelot, quite astonishing in its fiery grace, and he seems to have overcome some of the amplification problems he had been having since the war. He tackles 'Night And Day' again, on his own terms this time, and there are beautiful versions of 'Nuages' and 'Manoir De Mes Rêves'. He isn't a musician whose work divides easily into 'early' and 'late', but it's clear that the period between these two recordings was one of personal and artistic change and, in some respects, retrenchment. Django had made a great many miscalculations and had to spend too much time compensating for them. He seemed foredoomed to a short career, and he died near Paris, aged just 43.

& *See also* **Django Reinhardt 1935–1936** (1935–1936; p. 51); **MARTIN TAYLOR, Spirit Of Django** (1984; p. 486)

LOUIS ARMSTRONG &
Born 4 August 1901, New Orleans, Louisiana; died 6 July 1971, New York City
Trumpet, cornet

Louis Armstrong 1947
Classics 1072
Armstrong; Bobby Hackett (c); Jack Teagarden, Tommy Dorsey (tb); Benny Goodman, Peanuts Hucko, Barney Bigard (cl); Ernie Caceres (cl, bs); Charlie Barnet (as); Lionel Hampton (vib); Dick Cary, Mel Powell (p); Al Casey, Al Hendrickson (g); Bob Haggart, Harry Babasin, Arvell Shaw, Al Hall (b); Big Sid Catlett, George Wettling, Cozy Cole, Louie Bellson (d); Jeri Sullivan, Golden Gate Quartet (v). May–November 1947.

Complete New York Town Hall And Boston Symphony Hall Concerts
Fresh Sound DRCD 11291 3CD
Armstrong; Jack Teagarden (tb, v); Barney Bigard, Peanuts Hucko (cl); Dick Cary (p); Bob Haggart, Arvell Shaw (b); George Wettling, Big Sid Catlett (d); Velma Middleton (v). May & November 1947.

Trumpeter Randy Sandke says: **'Armstrong's laser-like, warm-as-the-sun sound reflects his boundless zest for life, love for the full spectrum of humanity, and his heroic triumph over nearly insurmountable odds.'**

After the final Hot Five records, Armstrong recorded almost exclusively as a soloist in front of big bands until the formation of the All Stars in 1947. He toured in the previous decade with the remnants of Luis Russell's orchestra, but not even Armstrong could resist the postwar slump, despite his Hollywood appearances. *Only* Armstrong could have come back quite so grandly, and intact: an invincible personality.

Although the records become more formal in shape – most of them are contemporary pop tunes, opened by an Armstrong vocal and climaxing in a stratospheric solo – the best of them showcase him as grandly as anything he'd done previously. Since his vocal stylings were becoming as important as his trumpet-playing, it was critical that he got some of the best tunes of the day.

After some years of comparative neglect, Armstrong bounced back via the film *New Orleans*, made during the period covered by the earliest tracks here, and the formation of the All Stars, following the celebrated 1947 Town Hall concert. This was a gloriously unrehearsed and spontaneous affair: onstage, at least, for the planning and promotion had been thorough.

Throughout, Armstrong sounds ready to resume his eminence, playing with riveting intensity. There is a moment after a couple of warm-up numbers, when pianist Dick Cary plays the wrong intro for 'Big Butter And Egg Man' and Pops has to cover for him, to no avail. There were rawly beautiful versions of 'Royal Garden Blues' and 'Muskrat Ramble' and a deliciously over-the-top 'Rockin' Chair' with Teagarden. This was the moment when revivalism or neo-traditionalism in jazz took off. It may have represented a prison to Armstrong in some regards. Ever afterward, this complex, brilliant musician was required to come out on stage and in some way pretend that he was a simple soul from the deep South who just happened to be there with trumpet and tux and a few ancient songs. It was formula and an audience situation – quickly repeated at Symphony Hall in Boston – that was instantly and unmistakably problematic but Armstrong had announced his return and resumed his eminence.

& *See also* **Complete Hot Five And Hot Seven Recordings** (1926–1928; p. 21), **California Concerts** (1951–1955; p. 130)

DEXTER GORDON &
Born 27 February 1923, Los Angeles, California; died 25 April 1990, Philadelphia, Pennsylvania
Tenor saxophone

Dexter Gordon On Dial: The Complete Sessions
Spotlite SPJ CD 130
Gordon; Melba Liston (tb); Teddy Edwards, Wardell Gray (ts); Jimmy Bunn, Charles Fox, Jimmy Rowles (p); Red Callender (b); Roy Porter, Chuck Thompson (d). June 1947.

Teddy Edwards said (1991): **'Dexter and I were each supposed to play solo. His took so long I only had five minutes left to record mine, and no time to prepare, so I had to figure out a plain blues. He moved slow, Dexter, and didn't make time for anyone else, but I got a hit ["Blues In Teddy's Flat"] out of it!'**

Gordon attained mythical proportions when he appeared as 'Dale Turner' in Bernard Tavernier's *Round Midnight*, playing a hybrid of himself and Bud Powell. Originally influenced by Lester Young, Long Tall Dexter favoured easy, behind-the-beat phrasing which could be turned to more confrontational use when required. In 1962, after drug-related problems, he moved to Europe and stayed for the next decade and a half.

Gordon's on-off partnership with fellow tenorist Wardell Gray was consistently productive, pairing him for much of the late '40s with another Lester Young disciple who had taken on board most of the modernist idiom without abandoning Young's mellifluously extended solo style. The Dial sessions – with Gray and, at Christmas 1947, Teddy Edwards – are definitive of West Coast idiom of the time. Spotlite brings together all the material, including a track with just Edwards up front. 'The Chase' was a studio version of the saxophone contests that Dexter and Gray had been conducting night after night in LA's Little Harlem. The earliest session features Melba Liston, who was presumably recruited for her arranging. The charts to 'Mischievous Lady' and 'Lullaby In Rhythm' sound tight and well-organized, more coherent than the tiresome 'Chase'. On the same day, Gordon also laid down three tracks with just rhythm, of which 'Chromatic Aberration' is perhaps the most interesting vis-à-vis the development of bebop, but 'It's The Talk Of The Town' is the occasion for one of his most expressive ballad solos of these years. The final Dial session, with Rowles at the piano, was made just before the AFM recording ban.

& *See also* **Doin' Alright** (1961; p. 275), **More Than You Know** (1975; p. 423)

FATS NAVARRO

Born Theodore Navarro, 24 September 1923, Key West, Florida; died 7 July 1950, New York City
Trumpet

The Complete Fats Navarro On Blue Note And Capitol

Blue Note 33373 2CD
Navarro; Howard McGhee (t); Ernie Henry (as); Allen Eager, Wardell Gray, Sonny Rollins, Charlie Rouse (ts); Tadd Dameron, Bud Powell (p); Milt Jackson (p, vib); Nelson Boyd, Tommy Potter, Curley Russell (b); Kenny Clarke, Roy Haynes, Shadow Wilson (d); Chano Pozo (perc). September 1947–August 1949.

Cornetist Nat Adderley said (1985): **'There's maybe something in the water in Florida that produces good trumpet-players. There's Blue Mitchell, Idrees Sulieman, and there's Fats Navarro, of course. He was one of the greatest of all on the instrument, but called back in a hurry, so we'll never really know ...'**

Brilliant, but unfortunate, 'Fat Girl' worked with Andy Kirk and in Billy Eckstine's legendary band, where he replaced Dizzy Gillespie. Fats was a more lyrical player and sounded easier in the middle register. His career was foreshortened by narcotics and tuberculosis, but he recorded some of the finest brass solos of the bebop era, many with bandleader Tadd Dameron.

These sessions are one of the peaks of the bebop movement and one of the essential modern-jazz records. Navarro's tone and solo approach were honed in big-band settings and he has the remarkable ability to maintain a graceful poise even when playing loudly and at speed. The contrast with McGhee (it seems extraordinary that some of their performances together have been misattributed) is very striking. Their duelling choruses on 'Double Talk' from a marvellous October 1948 session are some of the high-points of the record; there is, as with several other tracks, an alternative take which shows how thoughtful and self-critical an improviser the young trumpeter was, constantly refining, occasionally wholly rethinking his approach to a chord progression, but more frequently taking over whole segments of his solo and reordering them into a more satisfying outline. Navarro is rhythmically quite conservative, but he plays with great containment and manages to create an illusion, most obvious on 'Boperation', from the same session, that he is floating just above the beat; by contrast, McGhee sounds hasty and anxious. One hears the same effect rather more subtly on both takes of 'Symphonette' and on an alternative take of 'The Squirrel'.

THELONIOUS MONK &

Born 10 October 1917, Rocky Mount, North Carolina; died 17 February 1982, Weehawken, New Jersey
Piano

Genius Of Modern Music: Volumes 1 & 2

Blue Note 32137 / 32138
Monk; Kenny Dorham, Idrees Sulieman, George Taitt (t); Lou Donaldson, Sahib Shihab, Danny Quebec West (as); Billy Smith, Lucky Thompson, John Coltrane (ts); Milt Jackson (vib); Nelson Boyd, Al McKibbon, Bob Paige, Gene Ramey, John Simmons (b); Art Blakey, Max Roach, Shadow Wilson (d). October 1947–July 1948.

Saxophonist Steve Lacy said (1979): **'With Monk, everything fitted together. A song he'd written ten years ago and only played once or twice was somehow connected to something he was doing today. There was a system. It had structure.'**

Monk is one of the giants of modern American music whose output ranks with that of Morton and Ellington, as composition of the highest order. Though no one questions his skills as a pianist (they were compounded of stride, blues and a more romantic strain derived from Teddy Wilson and filtered through Monk's wonderfully lateral intelligence), it is as a composer that he has made the greatest impact on subsequent jazz music. Even so, it is vital to recognize that the music and the playing style are necessary to each other and precisely complementary. Though he has attracted more dedicated interpreters since his death than almost any musician, the originals are unsurpassed. Frequently misunderstood by critics and even some less-discerning musicians, he received due public recognition only quite late in his career, by which time younger pianists originally encouraged by him and his example (Bud Powell is the foremost) had recorded and died and been canonized. Far from being unrecognized in his lifetime, he was a major star who retired early, recording nothing in the last few years of his life. Present at the birth of bebop at Minton's Playhouse, he always roots his angular, asymmetrical themes in the blues and they have been a key element of modern jazz repertoire ever since, an object of almost obsessive attention by some musicians.

Though some of his work, like 'In Walked Bud' on *Genius Of Modern Music*, utilized a straightforward chord sequence, and though 'Eronel', one of the additional tracks from the critical July 1951 session with Milt Jackson, is relatively orthodox bop, Monk's interest in tough, pianistic melody, displaced rhythm and often extreme harmonic distortion (as in his treatment of 'Carolina Moon') sets him apart from the bop mainstream.

Monk recorded only intermittently in the years after the Minton's sessions. Thwarted first by an American Federation Of Musicians recording ban and later by a prison sentence and a blacklisting, Monk took time to regain the highs of these remarkable sides. The earliest of the sessions, with Sulieman, Danny Quebec West and Billy Smith, is not particularly inspired, though the pianist's contribution is instantly identifiable; his solo on 'Thelonious', built up out of minimal thematic potential, is emotionally powerful and restlessly allusive. A month later he was working with a more enterprising group (the difference in Blakey between the two sessions is remarkable) and producing his first classic recordings – of 'In Walked Bud' and 'Round About Midnight'.

The addition of Milt Jackson exactly a year later for the session that yielded 'Epistrophy' and 'Misterioso' was a turning-point in Monk's music, enormously extending its rhythmic potential and harmonic complexity. Jackson makes an incalculable contribution to the music, here and on the session of July 1951 which yielded the classic 'Straight, No Chaser'. The later recordings are more conventionally arranged and lack the excitement and sheer imaginative power of the earlier cuts, but they do help overturn the received image of Monk as a man who wrote one beautiful ballad and then dedicated the rest of his career to intractable dissonance. Between 1952 and 1955, when he contracted to Riverside Records, Monk's career was relatively in the doldrums. However, he had already recorded enough material to guarantee him a place in any significant canon.

& *See also* **Brilliant Corners** (1956; p. 198), **Underground** (1967–1968; p. 347)

TONY PARENTI
Born 6 August 1900, New Orleans, Louisiana; died 17 April 1972, New York City
Clarinet

Tony Parenti & His New Orleanians
Jazzology JCD-1
Parenti; Wild Bill Davison (c); Jimmy Archey (tb); Art Hodes (p); George 'Pops' Foster (b); Arthur Trappier (d). August 1949.

Wild Bill Davison said (1983): **'Nowadays, any kid who can actually play gets called a prodigy or a genius. Tony Parenti really was a genius, though, and he should have been the most famous guy in the music.'**

A prodigy in his native New Orleans, Parenti was offered a job by the Original Dixieland Jazz Band – he was too young to go, and he regretted it. He went to New York and played non-jazz sessions for CBS. From the mid-'40s onwards he worked in a sort of merger of Dixieland with more faithful New Orleans music, and he remained fascinated with the possibilities of ragtime. A New Orleans man who left the city in 1927, Parenti made many records but has frequently been overlooked. Never an original, he could still play with a ferocious intensity; though he approached the gaspipe manner at times, there was no little sophistication in an approach that seldom strayed far from Dixieland ideology. Jazzology JCD-1 was the one that started the Jazzology operation in 1949, and it still sounds hard-nosed and terrific: Davison was at his most vituperative-sounding, Parenti weaves his way round the front line with much invention, Hodes stomps through everything, and Foster slaps his strings harder than ever. Rough old recording, though that doesn't matter, and rather unnecessarily padded out with extra takes.

CHARLIE BARNET
Born 26 October 1913, New York City; died 4 September 1991, San Diego, California
Tenor, alto and soprano saxophones

The Capitol Big Band Sessions
Capitol 21258
Barnet; Jack Hansen, Irv Lewis, Dave Nichols, Lamar Wright Jr, Dave Burns, Tony DiNardi, John Howell, Doc Severinsen, Rolf Ericson, Ray Wetzel, Maynard Ferguson, John Coppola, Carlton McBeath, Al Del Simone, Marvin Rosen (t); Karle De Karske, Herbie Harper, Phil Washburne, Dick Kenney, Obie Massingill, Kenny Martlock, Bob Burgess, Harry Betts, Dave Wells (tb); Frank Pappalardo, Walt Weidler, Vinnie Dean, Art Raboy, Ruben Leon, Dick Meldonian (as); Al Curtis, Bud Shank, Kurt Bloom, Dave Matthews, Dick Hafer, Bill Holman, Jack Laird (ts); Bob Dawes, Danny Bank, Manny Albam (bs); Claude Williamson, Don Trenner (p); Iggy Shevak, Eddie Safranski, Ed Mihelich (b); Dick Shanahan, Cliff Leeman, Tiny Kahn, John Markham (d); Carlos Vidal (perc, v); Francisco Alvarez, Diego Ibarra, Ivar Jaminez (perc); Trudy Richards (v); strings. August 1948–December 1950.

Trumpeter Maynard Ferguson said (1992): **'Charlie had a temper, a drinking man's temper, I guess. He'd have a bottle beside him in the car, even driving through the city. When** he got riled, he got this bright red blotch, pyramid-shaped, right in the centre of his forehead. We used to see it and whisper, "It's *The Mark*!"'

Barnet was born into a wealthy New York family and with characteristic self-confidence broke the colour bar playing in Harlem in the mid-'30s. He struggled until 1939, when a Bluebird contract broke the band in a big way. He carried on against the current until 1949, when he quit to run hotels and play when he pleased. A bit of a playboy in his way, he enjoyed a good life and was married more often than Artie Shaw and Dinah Washington. Though Barnet's 'Cherokee' and 'Skyliner' are staples of the big-band era, he's never been highly regarded by the critics. His own playing, influenced by Johnny Hodges, is usually restricted to a few telling bars, but he was an enthusiastic advocate of other, greater players and he was one of the few bandleaders of the time to have virtually ignored racial distinctions, which may have cost him dear, though he doesn't seem to have cared much.

This was Barnet's 'bebop' band. He knew he couldn't play the new jazz but he was shrewd enough to hire players who were adept enough to handle a really tough score like 'Cu-Ba', the sort of thing that was coming out of Dizzy Gillespie's book. Arrangers such as Manny Albam and Pete Rugolo posed plenty of challenges for the band, and here and there are pieces which pointed the Barnet men in the direction of Stan Kenton, which was the last thing the leader wanted. After he famously broke up the band in 1949, there came a new version, which recorded the last four 1950 tracks with strings.

CHARLIE VENTURA

Born Charles Venturo, 2 December 1916, Philadelphia, Pennsylvania; died 17 January 1992, Pleasantville, New Jersey
Tenor saxophone

Complete 1949 Pasadena Concert
Fresh Sound FSRCD 314
Ventura; Conte Candoli (t); Bennie Green (tb); Boots Mussulli (as, bs); Roy Kral (p); Kenny O'Brien (b); Ed Shaughnessy (d); Jackie Cain (v). May 1949.

Jackie Cain said (1981): **'Charlie was the star and resented anyone else getting the spotlight, which is a difficult situation when you are a singer. I think he also disliked the whole thing with [my husband] Roy [Kral], for the same reason. But he was a fantastic musician and it's sad that he's been forgotten.'**

Ventura worked a day job in a navy yard but jammed after hours with local players. He worked with Gene Krupa during the war years, then ran his own big band and small group, as well as making Jazz At The Philharmonic appearances. His own 'Bop For The People' projects ran from the late '40s. Ventura was very popular in his day, but has since been entirely marginalized in jazz's history. Unfairly so, on the evidence of the early sessions, since his playing had chutzpah and skill, even if he was entirely derivative of Coleman Hawkins and took on the bop vernacular as only a sideline to his main swing language.

There is plenty of Ventura around to choose from, thanks to Classics' documentation and a fine Properbox, *Bop For The People*, but the famous Pasadena concert is a good place to start, not least because it features rising stars Roy Kral and Jackie Cain, who would achieve stardom on their own account subsequent to this, somewhat to Ventura's chagrin. It was a famous occasion at the Civic Auditorium. Ventura's introduction of the musicians (to 'The Peanut Vendor') gives some indication of this group's crowd-pulling quality. All the obvious stuff is featured, including 'High On An Open Mike', 'How High The Moon', 'Body And Soul', 'Lullaby In Rhythm' and 'Birdland', standard Bop For The People fare delivered by the septet with carefully drilled swing. A nicely preserved moment.

LEE KONITZ&

Born 12 October 1927, Chicago, Illinois
Alto and soprano saxophones

Subconscious-Lee

Original Jazz Classics OJC 186
Konitz; Warne Marsh (ts); Sal Mosca, Lennie Tristano (p); Billy Bauer (g); Arnold Fishkind (b); Denzil Best, Shelly Manne, Jeff Morton (d). January 1949–April 1950.

Lee Konitz said (1987): **'Everyone thinks that what I learned from Lennie [Tristano] was harmony and order, control! discipline!! What I got from Lennie was permission to be free.'**

The redoubtable Chicagoan came under the influence of Lennie Tristano early and along with Warne Marsh shaped the definitive cool saxophone sound (he was a part of the *Birth Of The Cool* project and won Miles's always begrudged admiration), but later he assimilated bebop and free playing as well. Konitz is one of the most extensively documented of contemporary musicians and his published conversations with British critic Andy Hamilton are required reading.

Astonishingly, Konitz spent what should have been his most productive years in limbo: teaching, unrecognized by critics; unrecorded by all but small European labels. Perhaps because of his isolation, Konitz has routinely exposed himself in the most ruthlessly unpredictable musical settings. *Subconscious-Lee* brings together material made under Lennie Tristano's leadership in January 1949, with quartet and quintet tracks made a few months later, featuring Marsh on 'Tautology' and four other numbers. The alto sound is light, slightly dry and completely unlike the dominant Charlie Parker model of the time. The remaining group material with Mosca and Bauer is less compelling, but there is a fine duo with the guitarist on 'Rebecca' which anticipates later intimacies.

& *See also* **Motion** (1961; p. 278), **Star Eyes** (1983; p. 483)

MILT JACKSON&

Born 1 January 1923, Detroit, Michigan; died 9 October 1999, New York City
Vibraphone

Wizard Of The Vibes

Blue Note 32140-2
Jackson; Lou Donaldson (as); Thelonious Monk, John Lewis (p); Percy Heath, John Simmons, Al McKibbon (b); Shadow Wilson, Kenny Clarke (d); Kenny Hagood (v). July 1948–April 1952.

Milt Jackson said (1982): **'I usually like a slow vibrato, the kind you could get before single-speed instruments started coming out. I think that's the key thing for me, getting the vibrato just right.'**

'Bags' moved to New York after his studies and joined Dizzy Gillespie at the start of recorded bebop in 1945. He was with various leaders before rejoining Gillespie in 1950, after which he formed his own quartet with members of the Gillespie rhythm section; it was this group that became the Modern Jazz Quartet in 1954 and occupied much of Jackson's energy for the rest of his life.

Playing with two mallets – most contemporary players have followed Gary Burton in playing with four – he created rapid bop lines with a ringing tonality that seemed to sweep overtones across everything in the line, creating a one-man-band effect that was all too rarely exploited solo.

Eight of the Blue Note tracks can also be found on records under Monk's name, while a quintet date with Donaldson and what was to become the MJQ was first issued as a 10-inch LP. The tracks with Monk are classics, rising to their greatest height with the riveting version of 'I Mean You'. The other date, though at a less exalted level, finds Jackson quite at home with Donaldson's uncomplicated, bluesy bop, and 'Lillie' is a handsome ballad feature for the vibesman. 'Bags' Groove', which became a kind of signature tune, receives a fairly definitive reading. Donaldson's presence keeps up the blues quotient, something that was always central to Jackson's art. Few players remained so close to that spirit, even if they weren't playing a strict blues sequence. The Rudy Van Gelder edition of this material adds five alternative takes, not one of them mere padding.

& *See also* **Bags Meets Wes** (1961; p. 281), **At The Kosei Nenkin** (1976; p. 432); **MODERN JAZZ QUARTET, Dedicated To Connie** (1960; p. 254), **The Complete Last Concert** (1974; p. 417)

TURK MURPHY
Born Melvin Edward Alton Murphy, 16 December 1915, Palermo, California
Trombone

Turk Murphy's Jazz Band Favourites
Good Time Jazz 60-011
Murphy; Don Kinch, Bob Scobey (t); Bill Napier, Skippy Anderson, Bob Helm (cl); Burt Bales, Wally Rose (p); Bill Newman (g, bj); Pat Patton, Dick Lammi, Harry Mordecai (bj); Squire Gersback, George Bruns (b, tba); Stan Ward, Johnny Brent (d). 1949–1951.

Turk Murphy said (1981): **'The modern way is to consider ensemble playing as a kind of necessary evil, something that needs to be endured until it's time for your own solo. Few even professional musicians understand the very precise harmonic co-ordination that you need in the front line, and the instrument that takes the brunt of demand is always the trombone.'**

Murphy's music might have been more credible if he hadn't gone on making it for so long. At the time of his earliest recordings, when he was a member of the Lu Watters circle, the Californian traditional jazz movement had some nous as revivalists of music which had lain, unjustly neglected, for many years. In that light, this Good Time Jazz compilation – there's another, similar one too – is both interesting and enjoyable, hammy though much of the playing is, and often painfully (as opposed to authentically) untutored, though the intention doubtless was to reproduce a group sound that reflected the values of the early bands. At this early stage, with the traditional jazz revival standing at an opposite tack to modernism, Murphy's work made a good deal of polemical sense, if nothing else. But after more than 20 years of this kind of thing, Murphy's one-track traditionalism began to sound tiresome and soulless.

FLIP PHILLIPS
Born Joseph Edward Fillipelli, 26 February 1915, Brooklyn, New York; died 17 August 2001, Fort Lauderdale, Florida
Tenor saxophone

Flippin' The Blues

Ocium 0011

Phillips; Harry Edison (t); Bill Harris (tb); Hank Jones, Dick Hyman, Lou Levy (p); Billy Bauer (g); Ray Brown, Gene Ramey, Jimmy Woode (b); Buddy Rich, Jo Jones, Joe McDonald (d). December 1949–August 1951.

Flip Phillips said (1990): **'Who is it who describes themselves as "the best of the best"? Is it the Marines? Jazz At The Philharmonic was like that: the best ... the ... best players in the world. I used to be asked if I felt I'd had enough coverage on my own account. Working in that company was career enough for me.'**

Phillips had a rather uneventful time in big bands, before joining Woody Herman in 1944. He then became closely identified with Jazz At The Philharmonic, jousting in an old-fashioned style far removed from the Lester Young consensus. His famous solo on 'Perdido' was one of JATP's defining moments. From 1960 he was living and working outside music in Florida, although he still played gigs and there have been a few albums since 1981, when he broke his studio fast.

Much of his work for Norman Granz's Clef label has been gathered together by the Ocium imprint, who always add a video or enhanced element to their packages. Not many listeners will want all that stuff, but the originals are long gone, so we have to recommend a compilation. While he was best known for his Jazz At The Phil blowouts, Flip displays a much more amenable and classic manner on most of the Ocium tracks. He was perfectly at ease in hardcore bebop company like Howard McGhee and Sonny Criss, but he also cruises along in the company of such players as Billy Butterfield, Harry Edison and Charlie Shavers and plays ballads in the lustiest Hawkins manner.

Of the Ocium releases, we slightly prefer *Flippin' The Blues* as the most musicianly. It pairs Flip with Bill Harris on ten bop-influenced titles, some with Sweets and Billy Bauer as part of a septet, other later cuts from August 1951 with Dick Hyman comping. Anyone unfamiliar with Phillips's work will be surprised how much it stands apart from anything else happening at the time. He's not so much a forgotten man as one who's never been readily pigeonholed and is therefore frequently ignored.

BUD POWELL &

Born Earl Rudolph Powell, 27 September 1924, Harlem, New York; died 31 July 1966, New York City
Piano

The Amazing Bud Powell: Volumes 1 & 2

Blue Note 781503 / 781504

Powell; Fats Navarro (t); Sonny Rollins (ts); Tommy Potter, George Duvivier, Curley Russell (b); Roy Haynes, Max Roach, Art Taylor (d). August 1949, May 1951, August 1953.

Kenny Drew said (1979): **'As years go by, Bud Powell seems greater and greater. I know he's admired, and some people revere him, but I don't think he gets his due in the history of this music.'**

From the age of 16, sponsored by Thelonious Monk, Powell was jamming at Minton's Playhouse. Though he adopted certain devices of the older piano-players Art Tatum and Teddy Wilson, Monk was his main influence, using unfamiliar intervals and adapting saxophone-lines. For much of his life, he suffered mental disturbance, possibly innate, but exacerbated by a racially motivated beating in 1945, from which he never recovered.

The chronology of Bud Powell's issued records is slightly complex. It was an intermittent career and Bud had bad performing nerves, so it's sometimes difficult to follow any 'development'. The sheer erratic brilliance of the Blue Note recordings has tended to cloud the outstanding work that Powell did for Norman Granz, but in the final balance the Blue Notes are remarkable. Despite the linking name and numbered format and the existence of a magnificent boxed set, the Blue Note CD transfers can quite comfortably be bought separately; indeed *Volume 1* – with its multiple takes of 'Bouncing With Bud' (one of which was previously on *The Fabulous Fats Navarro: Volume 1*), the bebop classic 'Ornithology' and Powell's own barometric 'Un Poco Loco' – was out of print for some time, and the fourth volume was issued only in 1987. *Volume 3* and *Volume 4* have to some extent been superseded by the magnificent *Complete*, which is a must for every Powell enthusiast, though perhaps too dark and troublous (as well as expensive) for the more casual listener. The multiple takes of 'Un Poco Loco' are the best place for more detailed study of Powell's restless pursuit of an increasingly fugitive musical epiphany. 'Parisian Thoroughfare' contrasts sharply with an earlier unaccompanied version, on Verve, and is much tighter; Powell had a more than adequate left hand; however, since he conceived of his music in a complex, multilinear way, bass and drums were usually required – not for support, but to help proliferate lines of attack. The quintet tracks are harshly tempered, but with hints of both joy and melancholy from all three front-men; Navarro's almost hysterical edge is at its most effective, and Powell plays as if possessed. *Volume 2*, which includes solo material, contains one of the most famous Powell performances: the bizarre, self-penned 'Glass Enclosure', a brief but almost schizophrenically changeable piece. There are also alternative takes of 'A Night In Tunisia', 'It Could Happen To You', 'Reets And I' and 'Collard Greens And Black Eyed Peas' (better known as 'Blues In The Closet').

& *See also* **The Amazing Bud Powell: Volume 5 – The Scene Changes** (1958; p. 225)

MILES DAVIS &
Born 26 May 1926, Alton, Illinois; died 28 September 1991, Santa Monica, California
Trumpet, flugelhorn, organ

The Complete Birth Of The Cool
Blue Note 94550
Davis; Kai Winding, J. J. Johnson, Mike Zwerin (tb); Junior Collins, Gunther Schuller, Sandy Siegelstein (frhn); John Barber (tba); Lee Konitz, Sahib Shihab (as); Benjamin Lundy (ts); Gerry Mulligan, Cecil Payne (bs); Al Haig, John Lewis, Tadd Dameron (p); John Collins (g); Nelson Boyd, Al McKibbon, Joe Shulman (b); Kenny Clarke, Max Roach (d); Carlos Vidal (perc); Kenny Hagood (v). September 1948–March 1950.

Saxophonist Gerry Mulligan said (1992): **'There's a little revisionism called for here. Miles booked the studio and called up the musicians, but he can't really claim responsibility for the music. Does it leave a bad taste? Perhaps a little, but I don't blame him. A few others might have spoken up before now.'**

The history of jazz could just about be told in the life-stories and work of Louis Armstrong, Duke Ellington, Charlie Parker and Miles Davis. In some regards, Miles is the most complex and problematic of the four: attracting adulation and disdain in equal measure; endlessly changing yet never sounding like anyone other than himself; endlessly experimenting yet innately hostile to the self-conscious experimentalism of the avant-garde; an enigma wrapped up in a conundrum, expressed in music of dark anger, joyous abandon and fragile purity. Even after he had scoured his speaking voice down to its famous husky growl, his trumpet-playing was pristine.

Miles was not a virtuoso trumpeter. Even so, early bebop sets suggest that he knew his way round the complex harmonics and rapid metres of the time and could hold his own in demanding company. Definitive's reattribution of this early material to Miles, on the

Complete Savoy And Dial Studio Recordings, might seem sharp practice, but some of the dates were nominally his.

The same applies, in trumps, to *The Birth Of The Cool*, a collaborative project which has always been treated as a Miles Davis record, to the eventual irritation of some of the other participants. After Miles's death, Gerry Mulligan went on record, without rancour but with unmistakable emphasis, to claim at least joint authorship of these astonishing performances. Whoever was the main creative force, Miles was the enabler, bringing together like-minded players in New York City, and, though the results (recorded at three sessions over the span of a year) were a commercial failure, these pioneering efforts by arrangers Mulligan, Gil Evans and John Carisi are allusive, magical scores that channelled the irresistible energy of bebop into surprising textures and piquant settings for improvisation.

Davis and Konitz play as if in sight of some new musical world. One can almost share in their delight and surprise as unexpected harmonic fragrances waft off the landscape in front of them. Airshot material by a different line-up has been available as *The Real Birth Of The Cool* on Bandstand. This was taped before the now classic studio sessions and shows the same music – 'Jeru', 'Budo', 'Godchild' – in evolution rather than finished and definitive. Nine of the same tracks appear on *Cool Boppin'*, which is valuable for some great early solos by the leader. The sound, recorded at the Royal Roost club, is no better than average, but there is sufficient of interest in the performances to make it a worthwhile buy, and there is some fine material under Tadd Dameron's leadership on the same disc, including some glorious moments when Davis lifts Dameron's wonky lyricism to new heights. The *Complete* brings together all the available material from this historic experiment, beautifully remastered and nicely packaged.

& *See also* **Miles Ahead** (1957; p. 208), **Kind Of Blue** (1959; p. 232), **The Complete Live At The Plugged Nickel** (1965; p. 331), **In A Silent Way** (1969; p. 361), **Agharta** (1975; p. 420)

LU WATTERS

Born 19 December 1911, Santa Cruz, California; died 5 November 1989, Santa Rosa, California
Trumpet

Doing The Hambone At Kelly's: Volumes 1 & 2

Jasmine JASMCD 2571 / 2590

Watters; Yerba Buena Jazz Band: Don Noakes, Warren Smith (tb); Wally Rose (p); Pat Patton (bj); Clancy Hayes (bj, v); Dick Lammi (tba); Bill Dart (d, wbd); Clancy Hayes's Washboard Five (on Volume 2 only). December 1949–June 1950.

Actor/director and jazz fanatic Clint Eastwood said (1995): **'My jazz education was getting into Hambone Kelly's – lying about my age, of course – and listening to Lu Watters doing that revival stuff. It was huge at that time in North California.'**

Lucious Watters was a true believer and his West Coast revivalists (Yerba Buena was the old Spanish name for San Francisco) purveyed an enthusiastic brand of Dixieland that achieved a remarkable level of authenticity as well as an enthusiastic following. Watters retired from music to work as a geologist and subsequently as a chef, but for a time he was the closest thing most Californians would have heard to a genuine New Orleans jazz group, and his historical importance outweighs the actual musical quality of these sides. A generous introduction to Yerba Buena (and to Hayes's spin-off Washboard Five).

THE '50s:
1951–1955

The '40s were a Janus-faced decade, looking both back and forwards stylistically. With the coming of bebop, and then with the sophistication of the cool school, jazz laid claim to the status of an art form, instead of merely that of a vernacular entertainment. The intelligentsia embraced bop, and erected around it an existentialist mythology that established the image of the jazz musician as a tortured individual shaping a new kind of identity in his solos. For the first time, jazz musicians and the jazz public were asked to consider the history of the music so far. The great revival brought to light a generation of New Orleans and other players who had not previously been documented, and while revivalism made exaggerated and sometimes absurd claims to authenticity and created a certain rift in the jazz audience between traditionalists and modernists, it also kept alive the collective values of early jazz, with its emphasis on ensemble playing rather than solos. It was clear, though, that the future belonged to bop and its more straightforward descendant 'hard bop', which straightened out and simplified the rhythm and put ever greater emphasis on a theme-and-solos approach.

The geographical diffusion of jazz is a complex matter, but by the turn of the '50s Chicago and particularly New York were established as the main centres of jazz activity. However, the war years and the early years of the new decade saw a rapid flowering of jazz in California. It already had deep roots there, but with the establishment of Lester Koenig's Contemporary and Richard Bock's Pacific labels, both in Los Angeles, in 1951 and 1952 respectively, there was at least some basis for talking about 'West Coast jazz' and for the elaboration of a mostly spurious rivalry – which often had more to do with styling and competition for media space than with music – between the two coasts.

These paired rivalries, if such they were, often extended no further than the pages of specialist music magazines, of which there were a growing number. The most influential was perhaps *Down Beat*, which had begun as a monthly in Chicago in 1934 and moved to fortnightly publication after the war, There was also a growing musicological interest in jazz, both its personal folklore and more technical study. The often repeated claim that present-day jazz musicians are the first to have come to the music by an academic route is justified only up to a point. In the '50s, partly as a result of a rapidly expanding student population, largely as a result of ongoing research into the sources of American vernacular music, and more specifically through the efforts of a musician like Dave Brubeck to take jazz to college campuses, jazz was considered with high seriousness, and also as an expression of what would later be called the counter-culture, but for now representing the embattled vestige of the oppositional culture of the '30s.

The '50s are much misrepresented as a period of bland conformity and quietism in American culture, when consumer values replaced political commitment among the middle class. Postwar prosperity reinforced a trend away from collective entertainment and towards the private consumption of music and art. Though many middle-class homes still had upright pianos and other instruments, record players and television sets became the prestige items. Developments in recording technology also made a significant impact.

The advent of magnetic tape around 1947 ended what has always, confusingly, been called the 'electrical' era in music recording. Tape was far more reliable, far more flexible and easily manipulated than previous means. It ultimately provided for multi-tracking and editing of performances – particularly valuable when complex music was being recorded – as well as enhanced clarity of sound, but given the emphasis on spontaneity and on individual expression (rather than the faithful translation of a written score), editing was slow to find a place in jazz recording and was still controversial when Miles Davis and Teo Macero constructed whole albums out of studio edits in the '60s. Both Thelonious Monk and Charles Mingus had utilized this capacity of the modern studio earlier but their editing and/or overdubbing was a technical adjunct and to some extent a restorative tool rather than part of the aesthetic.

Rapidly following the introduction of magnetic tape was the first appearance of the microgroove record, the modern LP, which eventually settled on the familiar 12-inch disc after some attempts to introduce the 10-inch disc as the industry norm. The favoured size was largely a matter of happenstance, but the capacity to include twenty minutes of music per side, either in a number of cuts or else, more radically, in a single continuous perform-ance (again but only for the moment less valuable to jazz players and producers than their colleagues in classical music) set a standard that was to remain in place until the triumph of CD over other fresh rivals in the '80s. The LP era is unmistakably the golden age of jazz recording, and the '50s offer limitless riches to the collector. The period from 1951 to 1955 was marked by political unease, continuing overseas conflict in Asia and the ossification of the Cold War. It was also the last period in which jazz had no dominant market rival, as was to be the case after 1954, when Sun Records issued the first recordings by a young man called Elvis Presley ...

GEORGE SHEARING
Born 13 August 1919, London; knighted 2007
Piano

Verve Jazz Masters: George Shearing
Verve 529900-2
Shearing; Marjorie Hyams, Cal Tjader, Joe Roland, Don Elliott (vib); Chuck Wayne, Dick Garcia (g); John Levy, Al McKibbon (b); Denzil Best, Marquis Foster, Bill Clark (d); Armando Peraza (perc). 1949–1954.

George Shearing said (1982): **'Music is a form of communication, and jazz is one of the highest forms of communication. Because you improvise, you put more of yourself into the music than a classical player would, so you communicate more of yourself in jazz.'**

The man Jack Kerouac's Dean Moriarty and Sal Paradise hail as 'God' in *On the Road* was a blind Englishman who had taken his piano style not from Bud Powell or Thelonious Monk but from Milt Buckner, locked hands on the chords, melody laid over the top without too much integration between the two. It's a highly effective style and it stood George Shearing, who was blind from birth, in very good stead. From a poor London family, he trained as a classical pianist but turned to jazz. He played dance band gigs before settling in the USA in 1946. His quintet won a huge following in a light-music smooth-jazz mould.

These are the MGM recordings which established the Shearing quintet as a commercial force. Clever rather than profound, appealing rather than attention-grabbing or radical, the front line of piano, vibes and guitar was a refreshing sound which, when allied to memo-rable themes such as 'Lullaby Of Birdland', proved immensely popular. Shearing had been listening closely to bebop and synthesized what he needed from it to make a cool, mod-ern sound. At this distance, away from any controversy about its standing, the results are smoothly enjoyable on any level. This compilation brings together the expected hits and the slightly more challenging material such as 'Conception', which was once covered by Miles Davis (although Shearing did complain that Miles got the bridge wrong!).

HUMPHREY LYTTELTON

Born 23 May 1921, Eton, Berkshire, England; died 25 April 2008, London
Trumpet, clarinet

The Parlophones: Volumes One–Four

Calligraph CLG CD 035-1 / 2 / 3 / 4
Lyttelton; Keith Christie, John Picard (tb); Wally Fawkes, Ian Christie (cl); Bruce Turner (ss, as, cl); Tony Coe
(as, cl); Ade Monsborough (as); Jimmy Skidmore, Kathy Stobart (ts); Joe Temperley (bs); George Webb, Johnny
Parker, Ian Armit (p); Freddy Legon (g, bj); Buddy Vallis (bj); Mickey Ashman, Brian Brocklehurst, Jim Bray (b);
Bernard Saward, Stan Greig, Eddie Taylor, George Hopkinson (d); Iris Grimes, Neva Raphaello (v). November
1949–August 1959.

Humphrey Lyttelton said (1993): **'The first of those things was recorded around the time
John Lennon and Paul McCartney were going to primary school and released on the label
that put out their hits later. So there, right in front of you, is part of the continuity of
British popular music in this period.'**

The doyen of postwar British jazz, Lyttelton was active for 60 years as a performer, broadcaster, writer, wit and general man-about-jazz, a tireless force whose early links with trad
jazz soon blossomed into a shrewd pan-stylistic outlook.

   The Parlophones are a must. One hundred titles are neatly spread across the four discs
(available only separately), and although in absolutist terms the set isn't complete – there
are no alternative takes, and titles by the collaborative bands with Graeme Bell and Freddy
Grant are being saved for a possible follow-up – what remains is a comprehensive picture
of ten years of work by arguably the most influential jazzman Britain has ever produced.
Even the earliest tracks show how Lyttelton wasn't content to regard jazz as any kind of
routine, and although the 1949–50 sessions are relatively formulaic, the playing is consistently creative and supple, with the rhythm sections never resorting to the trudge of
regulation trad. Lyttelton's own playing is wasteless and controlled, without losing the terminal vibrato which was a feature of the '20s stylists he admired. Fawkes and Christie were
important elements in this band, and so was Bruce Turner, a notorious recruit when he
arrived in 1953 but a crucial aide in Lyttelton's move from trad to mainstream. The progress through the '50s is marked by milestones such as 'The Onions' and the great hit, 'Bad
Penny Blues', before concluding with the 1957–9 sessions, which suggest how far Lyttelton
had progressed, from the sparky trad of 'Memphis Blues' to the sophisticated mainstream
inflexions of the likes of 'Hand Me Down Love'. There are also glimpses of young tykes such
as Tony Coe, Kathy Stobart, Jimmy Skidmore and Joe Temperley. Throughout the four discs
there are surprises, such as the extraordinary, haunting 'Jail Break' or Lyttelton's blues
playing behind Neva Raphaello on 'Young Woman Blues'. As a record of a crucial chapter in
British jazz, it's peerless stuff.

ELLA FITZGERALD &

Born 25 April 1917, Newport News, Virginia; died 15 June 1996, Beverly Hills, California
Voice

The Enchanting Ella Fitzgerald: Live At Birdland 1950–1952

Baldwin Street Music VBJH 309
Fitzgerald; Don Elliott (mel); Hank Jones, Raymond Tunia, Don Abney (p); Terry Gibbs (vib); Ray Brown (b);
Charlie Smith, Jimmy Crawford, Roy Haynes (d). December 1950–August 1955.

Ella's former husband Ray Brown said (1985): **'She was very, very private. She'd be telling a story about herself and leave such huge gaps in it that with anyone else, you'd have jumped in and said: "Hang on, what happened then?", but with Ella you left her to tell it her way.'**

The greatest jazz singer of them all. Fitzgerald was not what is called a 'libretto' singer. The words, in a sense, scarcely mattered to her, and she wasn't one of those, like Billie Holiday, who could invest a song with scouring drama. Instead, she sang note-perfect improvisations with a sense of time almost unequalled by any comparable instrumentalist. Fitzgerald's fabled break came when she won an Apollo Theater talent contest in 1934, aged only 17, and by the following year she was singing for Chick Webb's band. When Webb died in 1939, the singer inherited leadership of his band; by this time she was its undoubted star. But her recordings of the period are often hard to take because the material is sometimes insufferably trite. After Ella had a major hit with the nursery-rhyme tune 'A-Tisket, A-Tasket', she was doomed – at least, until the break-up of the band – to seek out similar songs. The calibre of her singing is consistent enough – the voice at its freshest, her phrasing straightforward but sincerely dedicated to making the most of the melody – but the tracks seem to spell the decline of what was, in the mid-'30s, one of the most swinging of big bands. The arrangements are often blandly supportive of the singer rather than creating any kind of partnership, and when the material is of the standard of 'Swinging On The Reservation' it's difficult to summon up much enthusiasm.

She'd been recording for 15 years before one could say there was material in which quality of singing was matched by consistency of material and sound. *The Enchanting* brings together four Birdland broadcasts, plus 'I Can't Get Started' from the Apollo, where it all started, plus a couple of tracks from a Basin Street show in 1955 by way of makeweight. Besides all the usual period charm – and it's a pretty good airshot sound, for its time – these are rare examples of the improvising Fitzgerald in her prime. She scats her way through such set-pieces as 'Air Mail Special', 'Lemon Drop' and 'Preview', and when she's on song she's breathtaking. Plus the expected mix of ballads and whatever her new release on Decca was at the time ('We hope you'll buy it'). Discussion of Ella's intelligence or lack of it are meaningless and largely insulting, but something of her personality comes down the years to us on these tapes. It's engaging enough, but strangely remote, a shy, self-conscious woman who is momentarily transformed by the act and art of song.

& *See also* **Sings The Cole Porter Songbook** (1956; p. 180), **Ella In London** (1974; p. 410)

JOE BUSHKIN
Born 7 November 1916, New York City; died 3 November 2004, Santa Barbara, California
Piano, trumpet

Piano Moods / After Hours
Collectables COL 7402
Bushkin; Buck Clayton (t); Eddie Safranski, Sid Weiss (b); Jo Jones (d). July 1950, 1952.

Joe Bushkin said (1985): **'Those songs served me well, but I got tired of writing all that late-night bar-room stuff. All those lonely guys telling me we were best friends, putting wet ring-marks on my piano and looking like they were about to barf.'**

Bushkin got a good classical grounding and later brought a bouncing, almost delicate sound to Tommy Dorsey's band. The wise-cracking New Yorker also served time with Bunny Berigan, Eddie Condon, the Armstrong All Stars and, in later years, a new generation of young swing players. He scored the stage play *The Rat Race* and wrote songs for Sinatra, and his

1955 'Midnight Rhapsody' became a hit. For a whole generation of swing fogies, his novelty number 'Ain't Been The Same Since The Beatles' was a rallying cry.

The keyboard touch is reminiscent in places of Nat Cole, light, springy, effortlessly melodic. Bushkin also learned trumpet after an accident almost put paid to his piano-playing. He made some good sides during the '40s, but came to the fore as a solo artist with one of the very first releases on Atlantic. The Collectables twofer brings together a pleasing pair of old dates for Capitol. It's not revolutionary stuff, but Bushkin had some effective harmonic ideas and listening to his work in some quantity one becomes aware of a distinct performing personality, wry, clever, but also gently debunking. There's nothing 'novelty' about his work, even when the intent is comic. Clayton makes an agreeable intervention and the rhythm guys seem to enjoy working within Bushkin's untroubled bounce.

STAN GETZ &

Born 2 February 1927, Philadelphia, Pennsylvania; died 6 June 1991, Malibu, California
Tenor saxophone

The Complete Roost Recordings
Roost 859622-2 3CD
Getz; Sanford Gold, Duke Jordan, Horace Silver, Al Haig (p); Jimmy Raney, Johnny Smith (g); Eddie Safranski, Teddy Kotick, Bill Crow, Leonard Gaskin, Bob Carter (b); Frank Isola, Tiny Kahn, Roy Haynes, Don Lamond, Morey Feld (d); Count Basie Orchestra. May 1950–December 1954.

Stan Getz said (1983): **'I tried to get the reediness out of my sound. I found I could project better that way and I like to stand well away from the microphone. I don't think it comes from anyone, in particular, but listening to Lester Young maybe influenced it, unconsciously – you tend to sound like music you love – and before that maybe Benny Goodman and Tea [Jack Teagarden].'**

After starring as one of Herman's 'Four Brothers', and delivering a luminous ballad solo on the 1948 'Early Autumn', Getz went out on his own and at first seemed much like the rest of the Lester Young-influenced tenormen: a fast, cool stylist with a sleek tone and a delivery that soothed nerves jangled by bebop. The 'Brothers' idea was pursued off and on for years, but Getz was destined to find himself as a sole horn, and with the dispersion of the bands it became irrelevant anyway. His phrasing was almost unbelievably fluent and legato, and his dark, rich sound, which always had a lot of breath in it, became one of the signature jazz sounds of the '50s and '60s and beyond.

So much attention has fallen on Getz's later work that these magnificent sessions are often overlooked. The earliest tracks, from a session in May 1950, catch a young man with his head full of bebop and his heart heavy with swing-era romanticism. Those contrary strains come together on the headily beautiful 'Yesterdays', a marriage of intellect and emotion that is rare not only in Getz's work but in jazz itself. These two early dates, one with Al Haig, one with Horace Silver, are electrifying. By 1951, he already sounds like the more settled, invincible Getz, but the short track-lengths (a relic of the 78 era) give the music considerable point and direction. The live session from Boston's Storyville Club with Jimmy Raney has long been prized, both musicians unreeling one great solo after another. Two studio dates with a similar band are at lower voltage but scarcely less impressive. Eight tracks with Johnny Smith, including the achingly lovely 'Moonlight In Vermont', offer Getz the lyricist in fullest flow, while the three with Basie at Birdland are a bonus. There is so much top-flight jazz in this set that it's quite indispensable; remastered to a consistent standard, it's breathtaking.

& *See also* **Focus** (1961; p. 277), **Nobody Else But Me** (1964; p. 304)

WARDELL GRAY

Born 13 February 1921, Oklahoma City, Oklahoma; died 25 May 1955, Las Vegas, Nevada
Tenor saxophone

Memorial: Volumes 1 & 2

Original Jazz Classics OJCCD 050 / 051
Gray; Art Farmer, Clark Terry (t); Sonny Criss, Frank Morgan (as); Dexter Gordon (ts); Jimmy Bunn, Sonny Clark, Al Haig, Hampton Hawes, Phil Hill (p); Teddy Charles (vib); Harper Crosby, Billy Hadnott, Dick Nivison, Tommy Potter, Johnny Richardson (b); Roy Haynes, Lawrence Marable, Art Mardigan, Chuck Thompson (d); Robert Collier (perc). November 1949, April and August 1950, January 1952, February 1953.

Clark Terry said: **'I get the feeling the young musicians don't even know who he was. Wardell was one of the very best, and it's shameful that he's so little appreciated now.'**

Like his friend and collaborator Dexter Gordon, with whom he recorded 'The Chase', Wardell Gray often had to look to Europe for recognition. His first postwar recordings were not released in the United States. There were not to be very many more, for Gray died in 1955, perhaps killed by drug-dealers, perhaps not. The shadow cast by Bird's passing, three months before, largely shrouded Gray's untimely departure. Unlike Gordon, Gray was less than wholly convinced by orthodox bebop, and he continued to explore the late-swing style of Lester Young. He started out with Earl Hines, and never quite abandoned that style, which may explain a certain later resistance to his work, for all its shining qualities.

The two-volume *Memorial* remains (ironically) the best representation of his gifts. The earliest of the sessions is a quartet consisting of Haig, Potter and Haynes, and it includes 'Twisted', a wry blues later vocalized by Annie Ross, whose version has tended to over-shadow the original. It's a perfect place to gauge Gray's Prez-influenced style and his softly angular approach to the changes. The CDs include some irrelevant alternative takes, but given how little there is, even pot-scrapings have some value. Too often Gray tries to dupli-cate what he feels are successful ideas rather than wiping the slate clean and trying again from scratch. The best of the rest is a 1952 session with Hawes and Farmer, who do inter-esting things with 'Farmer's Market' and that Parker shibboleth, 'Lover Man'. The sessions are also notable for the first recorded performances by Frank Morgan, who copied not just Bird's articulation but also some of his offstage habits and found himself in San Quentin for his pains.

STAN KENTON

Born 15 December 1911, Wichita, Kansas; died 25 August 1979, Los Angeles, California
Bandleader

City Of Glass

Capitol 832084-2
Kenton; various large personnels. December 1947–May 1953.

The Innovations Orchestra

Capitol 59965-2 2CD
Kenton; Buddy Childers, Maynard Ferguson, Shorty Rogers, Chico Alvarez, Don Paladino, Al Porcino, John Howell, Conte Candoli, Stu Williamson, John Coppola (t); Milt Bernhart, Harry Betts, Bob Fitzpatrick, Bill Russo, Eddie Bert, Dick Kenney (tb); Bart Varsalona, Clyde Brown, George Roberts (btb); John Graas, Lloyd Otto, George Price (frhn); Gene Englund (tba); Bud Shank, Art Pepper, Bob Cooper, Bart Caldarell, Bob Gioga, Bud Shank (reeds); Laurindo Almeida, Ralph Blaze (g); Don Bagley, Abe Luboff (b); Shelly Manne (d); Carlos Vidal, Ivan Lopez, Stenio Orozo, Jose Oliveira, Jack Costanzo (perc); strings. February 1950–October 1951.

Saxophonist/arranger Gerry Mulligan said (1990): **'Kenton always said: "Creativity is very closely linked to the cash register." I know lots of musicians – Ellington especially – have said something similar, and most of us have thought it, but Kenton meant it in a different way. He understood that side of things.'**

Often dismissed as pretentious, the Kenton orchestra with its vast body of recordings – still growing year on year, as more material is dusted off – has an enormous following. Kenton was raised in California, learned piano and toured with bands as a teenager. He formed his own band in 1940 and, with a yen to experiment, he tried to create a 'progressive jazz'. It was an instinct that never left him. He ran the 40-strong Innovations Orchestra in the early '50s, with strings, but gradually reverted to more conventional big-band music, with a couple of exceptions. Another of his experiments was the use of mellophoniums in the brass, and it makes an interesting noise. He did also bring forward singer June Christy, which is a star in his crown, whether you're pro or anti the rest.

There ought to be a Dantean warning at the threshold to the Kenton discography. Anyone venturing within should abandon all hope of getting out again knowing more than a fraction of it. Two recordings should suffice for most casual listeners. Sceptics will be satisfied and then back off. Enthusiasts will spiral down into the quite literally scores of currently available Kenton discs.

Kenton had been impressed by Bob Graettinger's writing. The 16 pieces arranged by Bob Graettinger which make up the first of these CDs number among the most exacting works Kenton was ever responsible for. Graettinger's two major pieces, 'City Of Glass' and 'This Modern World', are extraordinary works – Ellingtonian in their concentration on individuals within the band, yet using the bigger resources of the orchestra to create its own sound-world. All of his 14 originals create their own kind of jazz, atonal, dense and dark, and its suitability to Kenton's orchestra might almost be likened to Strayhorn's music for Ellington – except Graettinger was a more original thinker. Max Harrison's typically elegant sleeve-note supplies the fine context.

These recordings overlap in so many ways as well as showing Kenton's evolution over time that it makes sense to lump them together. The second disc is all of the LPs *Innovations In Modern Music* and *Stan Kenton Presents*, along with 14 extra tracks, offering a detailed look at Kenton's fine 1950–51 orchestra. With the swing era gone, and bebop acclimatizing jazz to more oblique areas of expression, there was no need for Kenton to be shy about the kind of scores he offered here; sifted with strings, 'Mirage', 'Conflict', 'Solitaire' and 'Soliloquy' are intriguing little tone-poems which, for all their occasionally arch details and overreaching style, work well enough to survive the years. There are one of Christy's finest vocals in 'Lonesome Road'; smart scores by Shorty Rogers like 'Jolly Rogers' and 'Round Robin'; Bob Graettinger's eerie 'House Of Strings'; skilful features for Manne, Pepper, Rogers and Ferguson; Bill Russo's lovely 'Ennui', one of four live tracks used to round off the second disc; and the feel of a very considerable orchestra entering its most challenging period, with soloists befitting an important band. Along with *City Of Glass*, this is surely Kenton's most valuable CD entry.

CHICO O'FARRILL
Born Arturo O'Farrill, 28 October 1921, Havana, Cuba; died 27 June 2001, New York City
Bandleader, arranger

Cuban Blues: The Chico O'Farrill Sessions
Verve 533256-2 2CD
O'Farrill; Mario Bauza, Paquito Davilla, Harry 'Sweets' Edison, Roy Eldridge, Bernie Glow, Carlton McBeath, Doug Mettome, Jimmy Nottingham, Al Porcino, Dick Sherman, Al Stewart, Nick Travis, Bobby Woodlan (t);

Eddie Bert, Carl Elmer, Vern Friley, Bill Harris, Bart Varsalona, Ollie Wilson, Fred Zito (tb); Vince De Rosa (frhn); Danny Bank, George Berg, Lenny Hambro, Ben Harrod, Leslie Johnakins, Gene Johnson, Charlie Kennedy, Jose Madera, Pete Mondello, Charlie Parker, Flip Phillips, Sol Rabinowitz, Wilbur Schwartz, Fred Skerritt, Howard Terry, Eddie Wasserman, Warren Webb, James Williamson (reeds); Ralph Burns, Gene DiNovi, Rene Hernandez, Fred Otis (p); Billy Bauer (g); Irma Clow (hp); Don Bagley, Ray Brown, Clyde Lombardi, Roberto Rodriguez (b); Jo Jones, Don Lamond, Buddy Rich (d); Candido Camero, Machito, José Mangual, Modesto Martinez, Luis Miranda, Ubaldo Nieto, Chano Pozo, Carlos Vidal (perc); Bobby Escoto (v). December 1950–April 1954.

Arturo O'Farrill Jr remembered (2002): **'I remember being very impressed with how seriously my father took listening to music. Same time every day, he'd mix a drink and really concentrate. It could be jazz or classical music, anything from Brahms or Chopin to Messiaen. He'd no interest in categories, just music.'**

The ideal background source for this attractive compilation is the atmospheric novel *The Mambo Kings Play Songs Of Love*, whose author, Oscar Hijuelos, provides the liner-note. O'Farrill studied composition in Havana before going to the USA in his later 20s, where he had considerable success writing charts for Benny Goodman, Stan Kenton, Charlie Parker and Dizzy Gillespie. On the strength of a powerful vogue for African-Cuban music, he built an orchestra of his own round Machito's rhythm section and recorded a series of 10-inch LPs for Norman Granz's Verve and Norgran labels. Technically the material stands up better than it does artistically. The recordings are wonderfully present and alive, and the remastering offers extra breadth without distorting the syrupy warmth of the originals. At more than 150 minutes, these two discs are a treat for the Latin-jazz enthusiast. All but the very committed, though, might find the diet a tad unrelieved and the pace a little relentless. The two *Afro-Cuban Jazz Suites*, one recorded under Machito's leadership in December 1950, the other under O'Farrill's own name two years later, are relatively ambitious in scope and content, but O'Farrill was not a man to overlook a successful formula, and the harmonic spectrum is otherwise kept comfortably narrow, with a substantial emphasis on danceable rhythms. One can readily imagine the brothers in *The Mambo Kings* moping through charts like 'Flamingo' while keeping an eye on the girls at the bar. This is music that requires some other sensory attraction.

LOUIS ARMSTRONG &

Born 4 August 1901, New Orleans, Louisiana; died 6 July 1971, New York City
Trumpet, cornet

California Concerts
GRP 050613 4CD
Armstrong; Jack Teagarden, Trummy Young (tb, v); Barney Bigard (cl, v); Earl Hines, Billy Kyle (p); Arvell Shaw (b); Barrett Deems, Cozy Cole (d); Velma Middleton (v). January 1951–January 1955.

Trumpeter Digby Fairweather says: **'Bereft of his dutiful big band, and now surrounded by sextets of worthy and gifted contemporaries, Armstrong's essential "California Concerts" were recorded at the formidable heights of his mature powers; his musical sculptures honed to perfection yet presented with undiminished verve and joy.'**

The All Stars period has often been treated unfairly. While there are many indifferent, lo-fi concert recordings of dubious provenance and quality, Pops is in almost invariable good form, and though the vaudevillian aspects of the group often come to the fore, there is always some piece of magic from the leader, either with the trumpet or vocally. One becomes conscious over time of more and more set phrases and a lot of material played for effect rather than for the music, but Armstrong alchemizes even the most hackneyed idea, and while nothing on these sets has any of the high-wire magic of the Hot Fives and Sevens, there is an unstaunchable invention in the solos. Fairweather is absolutely correct. Instead of starbursts, these are sculptures, solos of such robust construction that they seem like three-dimensional objects. Armstrong never really had peers, but these men around him were alert to his needs and they never let him down.

& *See also* **Complete Hot Five And Hot Seven Recordings** (1926–1928; p. 21), **Louis Armstrong 1947** (1947; p. 112) **Complete New York Town Hall And Boston Symphony Hall Concerts** (1947; p. 112)

CHARLES MINGUS&

Born 22 April 1922, Nogales, Arizona; died 5 January 1979, Cuernavaca, Mexico
Double bass, piano

The Complete Debut Recordings
Debut 12DCD 4402 12CD
Mingus; Miles Davis, Dizzy Gillespie, Louis Mucci, Thad Jones, Clarence Shaw (t); Eddie Bert, Willie Dennis, Bennie Green, J. J. Johnson, Jimmy Knepper, Kai Winding, Britt Woodman (tb); Julius Watkins (frhn); Charlie Parker, Lee Konitz, Joe Maini (as); Paige Brook, Eddie Caine (as, f); George Barrow, Phil Urso (ts); Frank Wess, Shafi Hadi, Teo Macero (ts, f); Danny Bank, Pepper Adams (bs); John LaPorta, Julius Baker (woodwinds); Spaulding Givens, Hank Jones, Wynton Kelly, Wade Legge, John Lewis, John Mehegan, Phyllis Pinkerton, Bill Triglia, Mal Waldron, Hazel Scott (p); Teddy Charles (vib); George Koutzen, Jackson Wiley (clo); Fred Zimmerman (b); Elvin Jones, Kenny Clarke, Al Levitt, Joe Morello, Dannie Richmond, Max Roach, Art Taylor (d); Phineas Newborn Jr, Horace Parlan (perc); Bob Benton, George Gordon, George Gordon Jr, Honey Gordon, Richard Gordon, Jackie Paris (v). April 1951–September 1957.

Max Roach said (1991): **'There was nothing in Charles's music that America couldn't forgive. This is a country that can absorb anything and take the sting out of it. What they couldn't forgive was that a black man should want to take control of the means of production, even of his own production.'**

With a complex ethnic mix in his veins – with African, Hispanic and Native American components; Mingus may be a corruption of the Scots 'Menzies' – this modern jazz giant grew up in the Watts district of Los Angeles. After learning cello and trombone, he took to double bass and started to write a workbook of compositions and develop a workshop approach that would continue through his life. He established a playing career, working with vibist Red Norvo, and then became involved in bebop, ultimately as part of Charlie Parker's most remarkable quintet, which performed at Massey Hall in 1953. A turbulent and difficult man, he none the less proselytized tirelessly for 'jazz' (he disliked the term) and for his own large-scale work, founding Debut Records and the Jazz Artists Guild in opposition to commercialization. In addition to pioneering modern bass-playing, Mingus is responsible for some of the greatest large-scale compositions in modern jazz. Mingus also transformed the conception of collective improvisation, restoring the energies and occasionally the sound of early jazz to an identifiably modern idiom. He pioneered overdubbing and editing, thereby paving the way for Miles Davis and Teo Macero.

This weighty box can really only be mined for pointers to more impressive work later. It and four subsequent volumes of 'Rarities' show the kind of musical environment in which Mingus moved and operated. The personnel list is probably as informative as any comment on the music inside could hope to be. Needless to say, Debut was not so very long for this world, though the lessons Mingus drew from running his own label were to last him for the remainder of his career, colouring his relationship with corporate labels ever after. These, if you will, are the grand pre-texts to the career of a great American composer.

& *See also* **Pithecanthropus Erectus** (1956; p. 175), **Mingus Dynasty** (1959; p. 247), **Charles Mingus Presents Charles Mingus** (1960; p. 259), **The Black Saint And The Sinner Lady** (1963; p. 291)

KID THOMAS (VALENTINE)

Born Thomas Valentine, 3 February 1896, Reserve, Louisiana; died 16 June 1987, New Orleans, Louisiana
Trumpet

Kid Thomas And His Algiers Stompers
American Music AMCD-10
Valentine; Bob Thomas, Harrison Barnes (tb); Emil Barnes (cl); George Guesnon (g, bj); Joseph Phillips (b); George Henderson (d). September 1951.

Trumpeter Ken Colyer said (1982): **'Kid Thomas must be the closest we can still get to the primitive jazz players who were working in New Orleans before the war. And he wasn't even there then. He didn't come into town until later, which is significant, I think.'**

Although originally from elsewhere in Louisiana, and arrived in the city rather late, in 1922, Valentine became one of New Orleans's most characteristic trumpeters, leading his Algiers Stompers from 1926, working extensively with George Lewis, then playing at home and on tour for the rest of a very long and busy life.

By the time he made his first records, almost 30 years later, he had led bands all over Louisiana but remained based in the city, where he continued to play for a further 35 years. He approached this awesome career with a Zen-like simplicity, reducing the New Orleans sound to its essentials and creating a lifetime's work from them. A fascinating lead-trumpeter, whose methods – including a severe observance of the melody, a blunt, jabbing attack and a vibrato that sounds like an angry trill – manage to create high drama and lyrical depth alike, and though he seldom took solos he was such a strong lead voice that he tended to dominate every band he played in.

He made a lot of records during his long life. The first (1951) sessions have survived in excellent sound and find Valentine and Barnes in their first prime. There are two trombonists, since Bob Thomas had to leave after three numbers, and the changed balance of the front line tells much about the sensitivity of the New Orleans ensemble. There isn't much to say specifically about Valentine's playing, beyond what's said more generally above, but it's effective and deeply affecting traditional jazz. Alden Ashforth's excellent notes chronicle the whole session in detail.

SIDNEY BECHET&

Born 14 May 1897, New Orleans, Louisiana; died 14 May 1959, Paris, France
Soprano saxophone, clarinet

The Fabulous Sidney Bechet
Blue Note 30607
Bechet; Jonah Jones, Sidney De Paris (t); Jimmy Archey, Wilbur De Paris (tb); Don Kirkpatrick, Buddy Weed (p); George 'Pops' Foster, Walter Page (b); Johnny Blowers, Manzie Johnson (d). November 1951–August 1953.

Richard Cook said (2003): **'In 1951, Alfred Lion and Francis Wolff were just moving into what now seems the golden age of hard bop and the beginnings of a jazz avant-garde. In that context, recording Sidney Bechet should have been perverse, except these men were more conservative than we tend to think and more business-minded. Think where they started.'**

This music must have seemed almost antediluvian at the height of bebop, and Bechet was off the American scene. Even so, there was a special chemistry to these sessions for Alfred Lion, originally released on 10-inch LPs and later amalgamated when the larger format became established. The soprano sound is still the same, with a broad vibrato and a cutting force. The two dates have a somewhat different sound and more than one commentator has understandably attributed that to the contrast between Pops Foster's slapped bass and Walter Page's pioneering walking style. However, there is a contrast in Sidney's own playing as well. He may sound more relaxed and precise on the earlier date, but there is an urgency about the 1953 sessions which is immediately arresting. There are some alternate takes on the reissue ('Ballin' The Jack', 'Blues My Naughty Sweetie Gives To Me' and 'There'll Be Some Changes Made', and 'Rose Of The Rio Grande' and 'Black And Blue' from the later session) which make this a very happy monument to an artist whose 'decline' was largely a matter of fashion rather than fact.

& *See also* **Sidney Bechet 1940–1941** (1940–1941; p. 79), **King Jazz: Volume 1** (1945; p. 99)

JIMMY FORREST
Born 24 January 1920, St Louis, Missouri; died 26 August 1980, Grand Rapids, Michigan
Tenor saxophone

Night Train
Delmark 435
Forrest; Chauncey Locke (t); Bart Dabney (tb); Charles Fox, Bunky Parker (p); Herschel Harris, John Mixon (b); Oscar Oldham (d); Percy James, Bob Reagan (perc). November 1951–September 1953.

Middleweight boxer Jimmy Frizzell says: **'I read somewhere that "Night Train" was my hero Sonny Liston's favourite song, so I listen to it over and over when I'm doing roadwork and on the train home after training. It's got a sound that makes you feel lonely and part of something at the same time, as if you've been away for a long time and are just getting back home.'**

Forrest had an almost iconic apprenticeship, working first with Fate Marable and then, alongside Charlie Parker, in the Jay McShann band. He also had stints with Andy Kirk and Duke Ellington before establishing himself as a leader. Early R&B experience invested his work with a strong, funky sound, which evolved into something richer and more complex, but always straight down the line rhythmically. Forrest had few bar-walking mannerisms and was a surprisingly restrained soloist for this idiom. After leaving the Ellington orchestra, he scored a big hit with the mournful swinger 'Night Train', an R&B classic based on Duke's 'Happy Go Lucky Local' and later made popular again by Oscar Peterson. It's the leading item on this eponymous Delmark, an album packed with short, funky jukebox themes which confirm that even in his pop days Jimmy was never merely a honker and wailer. It's a relatively anonymous band but this is hinterland music, about big open spaces and overlooked towns and people. A New York state of mind doesn't work.

BILLIE HOLIDAY&

Born Eleanora Fagan Gough, 7 April 1915, Baltimore, Maryland; died 17 July 1959, New York City
Voice

Lady In Autumn
Verve 849434-2 2CD
Holiday; Buck Clayton, Roy Eldridge, Harry 'Sweets' Edison, Joe Guy, Joe Newman, Charlie Shavers (t); Tommy
Turk (tb); Tony Scott (cl, p); Gene Quill, Benny Carter, Willie Smith (as); Romeo Penque (as, bcl); Al Cohn,
Lester Young, Budd Johnson, Flip Phillips, Paul Quinichette, Ben Webster, Coleman Hawkins (ts); Bobby
Tucker, Wynton Kelly, Billy Taylor, Carl Drinkard, Hank Jones, Jimmy Rowles, Milt Raskin, Mal Waldron (p);
Oscar Peterson (p, org); Barry Galbraith, Barney Kessel, Herb Ellis, Billy Bauer, Kenny Burrell, Freddie Green
(g); Janet Putnam (hp); Ray Brown, Red Callender, Aaron Bell, Leonard Gaskin, Red Mitchell, Carson Smith,
Milt Hinton, Joe Mondragon, John Simmons (b); Larry Bunker, Chico Hamilton, J. C. Heard, Gus Johnson,
Osie Johnson, Ed Shaughnessy, Alvin Stoller, Cozy Cole, Lennie McBrowne, Don Lamond (d); strings. July
1952–March 1959.

Billie Holiday's last accompanist, Mal Waldron, often expressed impatience at being asked
about her, but never failed to answer warmly: '**I never knew her do an unkind or cruel thing.
She was like a queen, even when things were bad, a very special person.**'

Holiday's last significant period in the studios was with Verve in the '50s, and this is the
best-known and most problematical music she made. Her voice has already lost most of its
youthful shine and ebullience: on 'What A Little Moonlight Can Do', Oscar Peterson does
his best to rouse the singer, but she only has the energy to glide. Whether this makes her
music more revealing or affecting or profound is something listeners will have to decide for
themselves. Sometimes the voice is funereal; then it takes on a persuasive inner lilt which
insists that her greatness has endured. And the best of the interpretations, scattered as
they are through all these records, show how compelling Holiday could still be.

    Although there is a complete edition available, Verve have now released Holiday's output
in seven separate sets, under various names. Preference among the discs depends mainly
on song selection and accompanists: Granz always made sure there were top-flight bands
behind her. *Solitude* has some lovely things: a classic 'These Foolish Things', a marvellous
'Moonglow'. *Recital* has some happy work, including 'What A Little Moonlight Can Do'
and 'Too Marvelous For Words', but there are some sloppy pieces too. *Lady Sings The Blues*
(replacing a previous disc under that title) has three or four of her best-known heartache
songs and includes the rehearsal tape with Tony Scott where they work up 'God Bless The
Child' – intriguing, but probably for scholars only. *Music For Torching* is small-hours music
of a high, troubling calibre. *All Or Nothing At All* rounds up seven long sessions across
two discs and includes some magnificent work from Edison and Webster (there is even a
warm-up instrumental cut while they were waiting for her to arrive at the studio), as well as
what is probably Holiday's most regal, instinctual late work. It all seems to come to a peak
on the very last track on disc two, the definitive version of 'Gee Baby, Ain't I Good To You?'.
Body And Soul is another edition of some of the same material.

    Songs For Distingué Lovers has been made available by Verve in their Master Edition
series and, with the original programme expanded to 12 tracks, putting the entire session
in one place, this is another front-rank recommendation, the music in its latest remastering
sounding particularly handsome. In comparison, the various spin-off compilations might
seem superfluous, except for those who prefer just the odd Holiday record in their collection, but the *First Issue* two-disc set is a beautifully chosen retrospective which eschews
Holiday's tortured epics and lines up the choicest examples of Tin Pan Alley instead, restoring something of the playful brilliance of the early years, and it is these cuts, rather than the
shadow-songs, that we return to most often.

    & See also **The Billie Holiday Collection: Volume 2** (1936–1937; p. 58)

SHARKEY BONANO

Born Joseph Gustaf Bonano, 9 April 1902, New Orleans, Louisiana; died 27 March 1972, New Orleans, Louisiana
Trumpet

At Lenfant's Lounge

Storyville STCD 6015
Bonano; Jack Delaney (tb); Bujie Centobie (cl); Stanley Mendelson (p); Arnold 'Deacon' Loyacano (b); Abbie Brunies, Monk Hazel (d); Lizzie Miles (v). August–September 1952.

There are several versions of this story: **'It's said that the maestro Arturo Toscanini once invited Sharkey to play in front of the brass section of the New York Phil, berating his men because they could not hit those pure top notes.'**

Although he was a New Orleans native, Bonano's early career points elsewhere. He tried out as a replacement for Bix with both the Wolverines and Jean Goldkette, for instance. After the war, he was much associated with New Orleans revivalism. This, though, followed a period when he drifted around several musical jobs across America, touring his own Melody Masters, waiting for renewed interest in the classic Louisiana style. When it came round, Bonano jumped the bandwagon with impatience. His showmanship finally found an outlet and it's this aspect of his performing style, wisecracking, handclapping, whistling, that sometimes puts off modern listeners.

Bonano returned to New Orleans and spent the rest of his life there, recording frequently in the aftermath of the great revival. Location recordings catch his able band in lively form. The leader's own playing suggests that he was more convincing as a front-man than as a soloist: if he pushes too hard, his tone thins out and his phrases buckle. But Delaney and Centobie are perfectly assured soloists and Bonano sensibly gives them the lion's share of the attention. Bonano's 'North Rampart Street Parade' and 'She's Crying For Me' sit quite comfortably alongside the more traditional stuff, like 'High Society' and 'Tin Roof Blues'. Lizzie Miles sings a couple of songs on her first recording, and shouts encouragement, too. The recordings are clear enough, though they don't have much sparkle.

GEORGE WALLINGTON

Born Giacinto Figlia, 27 October 1924, Palermo, Italy; died 15 February 1993, Cape Coral, Miami, Florida
Piano

George Wallington Trios

Original Jazz Classics OJCCD 1754
Wallington; Chuck Wayne (mandola); Charles Mingus, Oscar Pettiford, Curley Russell (b); Max Roach (d). September 1952–May 1953.

Alto saxophonist Jackie McLean said (1985): **'He was Italian ... no, he was *Sicilian*! And he had that Mediterranean fire about him. I think George Wallington was one of the best of the bebop piano players. Musicians liked working with him.'**

Wallington's departure from the music business was a great shame because he was a musician of considerable stature, who seemed to take his own talent lightly. The composer of 'Godchild' and 'Lemon Drop', he left his small mark on the music, even if his records aren't much heard nowadays, and musicians always respond to the name positively. More so even than Joe Albany or Dodo Marmarosa, George Wallington is the underrated master of bebop piano. His speed is breathtaking, his melodies unspooling in long, unbroken lines, and he writes tunes which are rather more than the customary convoluted riffs on familiar chord-changes. This OJC *Trios* disc is all piano, bass and drums, and there are marvellous, flashing virtuoso pieces like the ultrafast 'Cuckoo Around The Clock', although the elegance of 'I Married An Angel' is a harbinger of Wallington's later work. Chuck Wayne's mandola is a small reminder of home.

HOWARD RUMSEY

Born 7 November 1917, Brawley, California
Double bass

Sunday Jazz A La Lighthouse: Volumes 1–3

Original Jazz Classics OJCCD 151 / 972 / 266
Rumsey; Rolf Ericson, Chet Baker, Shorty Rogers (t); Milt Bernhart, Frank Rosolino (tb); Bud Shank (as, f); Herb Geller (as); Jimmy Giuffre, Bob Cooper (ts); Hampton Hawes, Frank Patchen, Lorraine Geller, Claude Williamson, Russ Freeman (p); Max Roach, Stan Levey, Shelly Manne (d). July 1952–February 1953; July 1952–August 1956; March–September 1953.

Howard Rumsey said (1982): **'The Lighthouse had been bought after the war by a guy called John Levine who owned about a dozen bars round town and didn't really know what to do with them, or the guys – longshoremen, mainly – who hung out there and got pasted. I just walked in one day and suggested I put on music on a Sunday afternoon – music for listening rather than dancing, which was pretty new – and because he wasn't there much, I ended up kind of taking over.'**

Not so much a distinctive instrumentalist or composer as a catalyst and fixer in West Coast jazz, but a figure of genuine importance, none the less. Rumsey studied in LA, then formed a small group with Stan Kenton and subsequently joined the Kenton orchestra. After the war, he formed the Lighthouse All-Stars, who performed regularly at the Hermosa Beach Lighthouse Club, which Rumsey effectively took over from an absentee landlord. From there, he became a skilled promoter of Californian concerts.

Their All-Stars Sunday afternoon concerts are still talked about by veterans of the Hermosa Beach scene, effectively 12-hour jam sessions that started in the afternoon and went on into the small hours. As such, they don't always translate well to records, but the three volumes of selected highlights from the salad days of the early '50s capture the spirit of the place perfectly: cool jazz delivered with a piquancy that often belies the laid-back ethos everyone assumes applied on the 'Coast'. There are passages here which are every bit as daring and every bit as confrontational as anything of the time in New York, but with a super-added awareness of modern classical music and an engaging determination to sound nonchalant rather than passionately engaged. It will either endear or frustrate, but it's all worth exploring, not least for the wealth of writing and arranging talent on show.

Which one to pick? To catch the excitement of these sessions, the best is *Volume 2*: a buzzing crowd, bandstands full of the hottest players; with 25 minutes of previously unreleased material, this one's a best buy. Sound is at times more atmospheric than accurate, but it's a terrific document of those sessions. The first volume is also excellent, with some fine work by Hawes. Watch out, too, for *Lighthouse At Laguna*, an off-territory appearance, and the good *Music For Lighthousekeeping*. Of Rumsey himself, it's fair to say that neither Charles Mingus nor Paul Chambers lived in fear of his technique, but he made things happen like Eddie Condon in another place and earlier era and he's a heroic figure for that alone.

GERRY MULLIGAN &

Born 6 April 1927, New York City; died 20 January 1996, Darien, Connecticut
Baritone and soprano saxophones, clarinet

The Original Quartet
Blue Note 94407-2 2CD
Mulligan; Chet Baker (t); Bob Whitlock, Carson Smith, Joe Mondragon (b); Chico Hamilton, Larry Bunker (d).
August 1952–June 1953.

Gerry Mulligan said (1992): **'It's said that that group came about because there was no piano in the club we were about to play. That's not the case: there was a piano there, but I decided not to use it.'**

Mulligan coaxed pure poetry out of an apparently cumbersome horn, though he himself said he had always felt the baritone was perfectly balanced and easily manoeuvred. He made a precocious start, writing and arranging 'Disc Jockey Jump' for Gene Krupa, and his influence as a composer/arranger continued to be felt on the *Birth Of The Cool* project, nominally led by Miles Davis. The story behind Mulligan's famous pianoless quartet with Chet Baker has been told so many times and in so many ways the details no longer matter. It was an influential group with a unique sound.

Everyone has his own version of how the quartet came to be – Chico Hamilton gives his own convincing, if self-serving account – but the audible reality is that Mulligan understood clearly that his baritone sound occupied sufficient of that middle-to-low register to be able to fill in that part of the sound, and touch in some implied harmonies as well. It became one of the epochal jazz groups, even if it had no such aspirations, formed for nothing more than a regular gig at The Haig (where some of the tracks were recorded) and even though many of its sessions were recorded quickly and with little preparation. In retrospect, it's the simplest pleasures which have made the music endure: the uncomplicated swing of the varying rhythm sections, the piquant contrast of amiably gruff baritone and shyly melodious trumpet, the coolly effective originals like 'Nights At The Turntable' and the irresistible 'Walkin' Shoes', and the subtle and feelingful treatments of standards such as 'Lullaby Of The Leaves'. Cool but hot, slick but never too clever, these are some of the most pleasurable records of their time. The two-disc set includes the basic library of 42 tracks and is an indispensable part of Mulligan's legacy.

& *See also* **What Is There To Say?** (1958–1959; p. 228), **The Age Of Steam** (1971; p. 383)

WILBUR DE PARIS

Born 11 January 1900, Crawfordsville, Indiana; died 3 January 1973, New York City
Trombone

Uproarious Twenties In Dixieland / Rampart Street Ramblers / New New Orleans Jazz
Collectables COL-CD-6614 2CD
De Paris; Sidney De Paris (c, v); Doc Cheatham (t); Omer Simeon (cl); Don Kirkpatrick, Sonny White (p); Eddie Gibbs, Lee Blair (bj); Bennie Moten, Harold Jackson (b); Wilbert Kirk (d, hca); George Foster, Freddie Moore (d).
September 1952–April 1955.

Doc Cheatham said (1985): **'Sidney could play, but Wilbur took care of business, and he took care of it real good.'**

De Paris ran a revival band with a difference. Since he and brother Sidney had been in the music first time around, and were not beholden to so-called New Orleans 'purism', he took an unusually free-spirited approach to what was basically revivalist repertoire. He was never more than a functional player, but he's the centre of gravity on these dates and they shine out in their period.

The music on these discs includes such ancient steeds as 'Hindustan', 'Colonel Bogey', 'In A Persian Market' and 'Twelfth Street Rag', but De Paris and his men took care to play them their way. There are numerous interesting touches and unexpected twists in the delivery. The front line is outstanding: Wilbur himself was no great shakes on either the slide or the valve trombone, but Sidney and Cheatham made up an impeccable brass one-two, Simeon was still in fine fettle, and they were later joined by Garvin Bushell, who replaced Omer and brought in bassoon and piccolo. The band was at Jimmy Ryan's in New York throughout the time they were making these records, so it was a tough and professional outfit. Atlantic gave them a clean studio mix, and although the rhythm playing is sometimes ordinary, they're never tired.

LESTER YOUNG &

Born 27 August 1909, Woodville, Mississippi; died 15 March 1959, New York City
Tenor saxophone

The President Plays
Verve 521451-2
Young; Oscar Peterson (p); Barney Kessel (g); Ray Brown (b); J. C. Heard (d). November 1952.

Ray Brown said (1992): **'He was falling apart, but he was also Lester Young. It was like listening to a wise man having a delirium, coming in and out of it and sometimes speaking very wisely, but in amongst all this rubbish. It was sad, but it was also grand.'**

Young's Verve story is a lot more complex than mere inexorable decline. The first seven sessions for the label were all tenor-plus-rhythm with, in succession, Nat Cole, Hank Jones, John Lewis and Oscar Peterson. The material was blues, a few workouts on familiar chords and standards, some of them rather surprising choices. None of the performances are bad, and Young contributes something fine to each of them – an unpredictable curlicue, a pale flurry of melody, a bashful beeping on a single note. Yet, at the same time, there is something wrong with all of them. Sometimes a solo will seem ready to fold up and die, and he will have to pull it round at the last moment. Other passages find him strong and hale, only to tamely crack a note or suddenly stumble, a beach jogger tripping over driftwood. It wouldn't matter so much if it happened only here and there – but it happens on every tune, to some degree.

It's a sad business and there are moments when it makes for extremely uncomfortable listening. But it would, again, be wrong to suggest that all is loss. Immediately after the war there was evidence of some of the less desirable traits that crept into his '50s work (a formulaic repetition and a self-conscious and histrionic distortion of tone and phrasing akin to his friend Billie Holiday's around the same time); it's clear that he is trying to rethink harmonic progression. A new device, much noted, is his use of an arpeggiated tonic triad in first inversion (i.e. with the third rather than the root in lowest position), which, whatever its technical niceties, smoothed out chordal progression from ever-shorter phrases. Some of that is evident in 1946 trios with Rich and Cole, and on other augmented line-ups from that time, which illustrate Pres's ability to reshape a theme and send it off in a new direction, while still using the same basic roster of melodic devices.

This 1952 session for Norman Granz (previously believed to have been made in August, not in November) includes the slightly bizarre sound of Young lewdly singing the lyric to 'It Takes Two To Tango': 'Drop your drawers, take them off ...' It's a curiosity, but the rest of the session is very good indeed.

There is a complete box of Young's Verve sessions. The exceptionally handsome booklet quotes a remark made by Coleman Hawkins, the earth to Lester's air sign: 'That Lester Young, how does he get away with it? He's stoned half the time, he's always late, and he can't play.' It was and it wasn't true.

& *See also* **The Complete Aladdin Sessions** (1942–1947; p. 86)

RED RODNEY

Born Robert Rodney (or Ronald) Chudnick, 27 September 1927, Philadelphia, Pennsylvania; died 27 May 1994, Boynton Beach, Florida
Trumpet

Red Rodney Quintets
Fantasy 24758
Rodney; Jimmy Ford (as); Ira Sullivan (ts); Phil Raphael, Norman Simmons (p); Phil Leshin, Victor Sproles (b); Phil Brown, Roy Haynes (d). 1952, 1955.

Red Rodney said (1982): **'I learned some good lessons from Bird and some very bad ones. I wish I could say it all comes out in the music. Some of it comes out in the wash. Bird never had that. I was lucky, and did.'**

Rodney was the red-haired Jewish boy in Charlie Parker's happiest band. Though diffident about his own talents, the young Philadelphian had done his learning up on the stand, playing with the likes of Jimmy Dorsey while still a teenager. Rodney was perhaps the first white trumpeter to take up the challenge of bebop, which he played with a crackling, slightly nervy quality. It sat well with Parker, and Rodney was an integral part of Bird's quintet in 1950 and 1951, having first worked with him slightly earlier than that. Rodney was not a prolific recording artist, and his career succumbed from time to time to one of the more common jeopardies of life on the road – there was a bankruptcy later on, and a stretch in jail – but there is some excellent stuff on disc.

Rodney's best work, the 1955 *Modern Music From Chicago*, now forms half of this valuable set, along with a slightly less compelling release, *Broadway*. The trumpeter is in great form on the first set, blowing intricate and deeply felt solos, especially on his own 'Red Is Blue'. Roy Haynes helped invent bebop rhythm, and he sounds totally in command of the idiom here, with Ira Sullivan and Norman Simmons filling out the harmony richly.

The earlier group has a much less distinguished line-up (most of them called Phil), and though there are some good things – 'Red Wig' and 'Coogan's Bluff' – there is nothing to match the delightful muted solo on 'Laura', which remains the outstanding moment on *Chicago*.

SHORTY ROGERS

Born Milton Rajonsky, 14 April 1924, Great Barringon, Massachusetts; died 7 November 1994, Van Nuys, California
Trumpet

The Sweetheart Of Sigmund Freud

Giant Steps GIST 009 2CD
Rogers; Conrad Gozzo, Maynard Ferguson, Pete Candoli, John Howell, Ray Linn (t); Harry Betts, Bob
Enevoldsen, Jimmy Knepper, Milt Bernhart (tb); John Graas (frhn); Art Pepper, Bud Shank, Jimmy Giuffre, Bob
Cooper, Bill Holman, Bill Perkins (reeds); Marty Paich, Russ Freeman, Hampton Hawes (p); Gene Englund
(tba); Curtis Counce, Don Bagley, Joe Mondragon (b); Shelly Manne (d); also orchestras led by Woody Herman,
Red Norvo, Stan Kenton, Maynard Ferguson, Louie Bellson and Howard Rumsey. May 1946–July 1953.

Reed-player and arranger Jimmy Giuffre said (1987): **'I don't think playing ever meant so
much to Shorty. I think he regards himself as one brushstroke among many and he'd
be quite happy if someone else was making it, as long as the music was working as he
imagined it.'**

Rogers grew up on the opposite seaboard, but he is forever seen as a kingpin figure in the
West Coast jazz of the '50s and after, scoring several of the classic big-band dates of the
period and subsequently writing a lot of music for TV and Hollywood. His own playing
was lithe if unremarkable, but it did the job and in context was exactly the right one for the
occasion.

Much influenced by the Davis–Mulligan–Lewis *Birth Of The Cool*, and even claiming a
revisionist role in the creation of that movement, Shorty Rogers turned its basic instrumentation and lapidary arranging into a vehicle for relaxedly swinging jazz of a high order. His
arrangements are among the best of the time. If they lack the gelid precision that Lewis and
Mulligan brought to *Birth Of The Cool*, Rogers's charts combine the same intricate texture
with an altogether looser jazz feel. While never an especially memorable soloist himself,
he could call on the top players of the day on a regular basis. Rogers seemed to be in the
studios all the time in the '50s and early '60s, and although his Atlantic albums are currently out of circulation, several of his RCA sets have made a comeback. The classic *Cool
And Crazy* sessions (alias *The Big Shorty Rogers Express*) have now been gathered in on this
set, along with another disc of early Rogers charts for Herman, Norvo and Kenton, plus
a few later dates with Ferguson and Rumsey. It is a quite irresistible package, excellently
remastered and with a fine sleeve-note. The tracks which made up the original 10-inch *Cool
And Crazy* still act as a benchmark in the appreciation of West Coast jazz, and their energy
and ingenuity seem completely undimmed a half-century on.

FREDDY RANDALL

Born 6 May 1921, London; died 18 May 1999, Teignmouth, Devon, England
Trumpet, cornet

Freddy Randall And His Band

Lake LACD123
Randall; Roy Crimmins, Norman Cave, Dave Keir (tb); Archie Semple, Dave Shepherd, Al Gay (cl); Betty Smith
(ts); Dave Fraser, Harry Smith (p); Ron Stone, Ken Ingerfield, Jack Peberdy (b); Lennie Hastings, Stan Bourne
(d). March 1953–July 1955.

Freddy Randall said (1984): **'I was out of the business for a while in the late '50s, early '60s,
bad chest. I don't quite know what happened in jazz around that time. You can blame
pop, I suppose, but even the jazz musicians went a bit funny.'**

Randall started out with a comedy group but worked with John Dankworth and formed
his own traditional band in the late '40s, recording extensively for Parlophone. Faded from
the scene after a spell of illness, but returned to active duty in the '70s, while running an
old people's home. (This detail has been sufficiently mined for jokes already; Freddy had
heard them all.) This disc, one of a pair of reissues on Lake, should be enough to con-

vert unbelievers to the energy and vitality of the best British trad. Randall's groups weren't rough-and-ready outfits. He led by example, his trumpet-playing crackling with conviction and imagination alike, and his groups were hard-bitten but swinging in their doughty way. Randall liked the sound of the Chicagoan brassmen rather than the New Orleans strain beloved by Ken Colyer, and his jazz has an incendiary quality to it which eluded many of his contemporaries. Not that there isn't a sense of fun in the tracks on the second CD, chosen by Paul Lake from the 70-odd sides he made for Parlophone between 1953 and 1955. 'Professor Jazz' still raises a smile, and anyone who calls one of his originals 'My Tiny Band Is Chosen' has a reserve of wit as well as commitment. A model reissue, in excellent sound, and it is a pity that Randall himself did not live to see it happen.

CHARLIE PARKER &

Born 29 August 1920, Kansas City, Missouri; died 12 March 1955, New York City
Alto and tenor saxophones

The Quintet: Jazz At Massey Hall
Original Jazz Classics OJC 044
Parker; Dizzy Gillespie (t); Bud Powell (p); Charles Mingus (b); Max Roach (d). May 1953.

Max Roach said (1985): **'The atmosphere was pretty difficult, but when you look at the people in that dressing room and the issues and problems they all had, it would need a whole conference of psychologists to work it all out. People should just be grateful that [the] music was made and recorded at all.'**

Perhaps the most hyped jazz concert ever, to an extent that the actuality is almost inevitably something of a disappointment. Originally released on Debut (a musician-run label started by Mingus and Roach), the sound, taken from Mingus's own tape-recording, is rather poor and the bassist subsequently had to overdub his part. However, Parker (playing a plastic saxophone and billed on the Debut release as 'Charlie Chan' to avoid contractual problems with Mercury, Norman Granz's parent company) and Gillespie are both at the peak of their powers. They may even have fed off the conflict that had developed between them, for their interchanges on the opening 'Perdido' crackle with controlled aggression, like two middle-weights checking each other out in the first round. There is a story that they didn't want to go on stage, preferring to sulk in front of a televised big game in the dressing room. Parker's solo on 'Hot House', three quarters of the way through the set, is a masterpiece of contain-ment and release, like his work on 'A Night In Tunisia' (introduced by the saxophonist in rather weird French, in deference to the Canadian – but the wrong city, surely? – audience). Perhaps because the game was showing, or perhaps just because Toronto wasn't hip to bebop, the house was by no means full, but it's clear that those who were there sensed something exceptional was happening. Powell and Roach are the star turns on 'Wee'. The pianist builds a marvellous solo out of Dameron's chords and Roach holds the whole thing together with a performance that almost matches the melodic and rhythmic enterprise of the front-men. The Massey Hall concert is a remarkable experience, not to be missed.

& *See also* **The Complete Savoy And Dial Studio Recordings** (1945–1948; p. 96), **Charlie Parker With Strings** (1947–1952; p. 106)

BEN WEBSTER

Born 27 March 1909, Kansas City, Missouri; died 20 September 1973, Amsterdam, Netherlands
Tenor saxophone

King Of The Tenors
Verve 519806-2
Webster; Harry 'Sweets' Edison (t); Benny Carter (as); Oscar Peterson (p); Barney Kessel, Herb Ellis (g); Ray Brown (b); Alvin Stoller, J. C. Heard (d). May–December 1953.

Oscar Peterson said (1991): **'I remember one time a bunch of guys waiting round the studio, impatient, wanting to get going. Ben was late and they were displeased. No one saw him arrive but suddenly we heard this saxophone along the corridor, just warming up gently. And everyone just stopped and listened. It was like oil on troubled waters.'**

Webster's unique timbre on the tenor – breathy, swooningly romantic – is high on most lists of favourite sounds in jazz. He played violin, then piano, before taking up sax at Budd Johnson's suggestion. Webster joined Bennie Moten in 1931 and worked with many bands before gaining his greatest eminence with Duke Ellington from 1940. He left in 1944, rejoined four years later for a short spell, then freelanced through the '50s. In 1964, he settled in Europe and eventually died in Amsterdam, unpredictable but beloved.

Approaching four decades after his death, his sound still haunts every tenor saxophonist who tackles a ballad. Ben Webster, often identifiable by a single, signature note, played jazz like few other musicians ever have. As he got older and less partial to any tempo above a very slow lope, he pared his manner back to essentials which still, no matter how often one hears them, remain uniquely affecting. Sometimes, all he does is play the notes of a melody, in a time that is entirely of his own choosing, and still he makes it uniquely absorbing. The best of his early work is with Duke Ellington – he remained, along with Paul Gonsalves, one of only two tenormen to make a genuine impression on Ducal history – but his records as a solo player, from the early '50s onwards, are a formidable legacy.

By 1953, Webster was ready to make his mark on the LP era – 78rpm duration was too short for such a patient improviser – and Norman Granz began recording him for his labels. *King Of The Tenors* blends a date with Oscar Peterson plus rhythm section with another where Edison and Carter sit in too, though the spotlight is always on Webster. 'Tenderly' has never been more tender, 'That's All' is sheer heaven, but 'Jive At Six' is a good piece of studio knockabout. Peterson may seem an unlikely partner, but just as Webster played superbly next to Art Tatum, so he mastered the potentially open floodgates of Peterson's playing. This and two other Verve discs, *Soulville* and *Meets Oscar Peterson*, are between them, in modern sound, indispensable mainstream jazz albums of their time.

CLIFFORD BROWN &
Born 30 October 1930, Wilmington, Delaware; died 26 October 1956, Pennsylvania Turnpike, west of Bedford
Trumpet

Memorial Album
Blue Note 32141-2
Brown; Gigi Gryce (as, f); Lou Donaldson (as); Charlie Rouse (ts); Elmo Hope, John Lewis (p); Percy Heath (b); Philly Joe Jones, Art Blakey (d). June–August 1953.

Freddie Hubbard said (1991): **'There's a lot of dead men's shoes in this business. I promise you, if Clifford Brown had lived, you wouldn't ever have heard of me or a lot of other trumpet guys.'**

Relative to the length of his career, Clifford Brown had a greater impact on the music than any comparable instrumentalist. In the days after he died – Richie Powell with him – and as the news filtered through to clubs and studios up and down the country, hardened jazz musicians put away their horns and quietly went home to grieve. Only 26, Brown was almost universally liked and admired. Free of the self-destructive 'personal problems' that haunted jazz at the time, he had seemed destined for ever greater things when his car skidded off the turnpike.

To this day, his influence on trumpeters is immense, less audibly than Miles Davis's, perhaps, because more pervasive. Though most of his technical devices – long, burnished phrases, enormous melodic and harmonic compression within a chorus, internal divisions of the metre – were introduced by Dizzy Gillespie and Fats Navarro, his two most significant models, it was Brownie who melded them into a distinctive and coherent personal style of great expressive power. Almost every trumpeter who followed, including present-day figures like Wynton Marsalis, has drawn heavily on his example; few though have managed to reproduce the powerful singing grace he took from the ill-starred Navarro.

After a first, near fatal car accident, Brown gigged in R&B bands and then worked briefly with Tadd Dameron, before touring Europe with Lionel Hampton towards the end of 1953, where he enjoyed a good-natured and stage-managed rivalry with Art Farmer, and recorded the excellent quartet, sextet and big-band sides now reissued on OJC and sampled on *Blue And Brown*. By this time, he had already recorded the sessions on the confusingly titled *Memorial* (OJC) and the Blue Note *Memorial Album*. The former combined European and American sessions and isn't the most compelling of his recordings, though Dameron's arrangements are as challenging as always, and there are some fine moments from the Scandinavians it features.

In their new RVG editions, both *Memorial Album* and the 1954 *Jazz Immortal* are tempting buys, even if you have the complete Blue Note edition, since once again the Van Gelder magic has been worked on the sound, which beats any previous issue (even if Mr VG didn't do the original engineering in both cases). The former has been extended to include all alternative takes and would make a fine introduction to Brown for a newcomer. The latter sets Clifford up with a gang of West Coasters in a series of Jack Montrose charts, and while the set might seem 'slick' in comparison with some of Clifford's playing situations, it does bring out the excellence of Brownie originals such as 'Daahoud' and 'Joy Spring' and the playing is handsome.

& *See also* **Alone Together** (1954–1956; p. 168)

GEORGE LEWIS &
Born George Joseph François Louis Zeno, 13 July 1900, New Orleans, Louisiana; died 31 December 1968, New Orleans, Louisiana
Clarinet

Jazz Funeral In New Orleans
Tradition 1049
Lewis; Avery 'Kid' Howard (t, v); Jim Robinson (tb); Alton Purnell (p, v); Lawrence Marrero (bj); Alcide 'Slow Drag' Pavageau (b); Joe Watkins (d, v); Monette Moore (v). October 1953.

Trad fan and collector Russell Sykes said (1999): **'When I heard this, I said: "That's what I want at *my* funeral. Just play the CD and then everyone go off for a drink.'** (Duly done: 24 March 2000. RIP Russell.)

A classic New Orleans record and one of the best albums in Lewis's enormous catalogue, *Jazz Funeral* should be a building block in any decent jazz library. It's not entirely clear why the record bears this rather mournful title, since most of the music is decidedly upbeat and only the slow version of 'Just A Closer Walk With Thee' would be associated with a burial procession, on the way to the cemetery, at any rate. What's exceptional about this album is that everyone seems to be in top form, with sparkling solos right through the band and tight, well-marshalled ensembles. The opening 'Ice Cream' sets things off in great style. 'Doctor Jazz' and 'When The Saints Go Marching In' are exemplary. George's clarinet is clearly pitched and in tune with everyone else, which isn't always the case at this vintage.

& *See also* **George Lewis & His New Orleans Stompers** (1943; p. 87)

ELMO HOPE

Born St Elmo Sylvester (or Sylvestor) Hope, 27 June 1923, New York City; died 19 May 1967, New York City
Piano

Trio And Quintet
Blue Note 784438 2
Hope; Freeman Lee, Stu Williamson (t); Frank Foster, Harold Land (ts); Percy Heath, Leroy Vinnegar (b); Frank Butler, Philly Joe Jones (d). June 1953–October 1957.

Saxophonist Johnny Griffin said (1989): **'I used to hang out with Elmo and Monk at their houses, and I can tell you they both could play in any style: Tatum, Basie, Duke, Fats Waller, Hines. Elmo** *chose* **to play the way he did, like Monk** *chose* **to play the way he did. It wasn't that he couldn't do it any other way.'**

A troubled man, burdened by a kind of genius, Hope was fortunate in having wife Bertha (also a formidable piano-player) to watch out for him, but he seemed fated to a short life. Elmo managed to sound sufficiently different from both his main influences, Bud Powell (with whom he went to school) and Thelonious Monk, to retain a highly individual sound. His reputation as a composer is now surprisingly slight, but he had a strong gift for melody, enunciating themes very clearly, and was comfortable enough with classical and modern concert music to introduce elements of fugue and canon, though always with a firm blues underpinning. Like a good many pianists of his generation, he seems to have been uneasy about solo performance (though he duetted regularly with his wife Bertha) and is heard to greatest effect in trio settings.

These Blue Note sessions are taut and well disciplined, though the trio tracks are better than the quintets, where the sequence of solos becomes mechanical and Hope progressively loses interest in varying his accompaniments. It's quite dismaying to hear this, a palpable diminution of attention. Originals like 'Freffie' and 'Hot Sauce' come across well, and the sound stands up down the years. Like many of his piano generation, the work is only now being properly studied and appreciated.

J. J. JOHNSON &

Born James Louis Johnson, 22 January 1924, Indianapolis, Indiana; died 4 February 2001, Indianapolis, Indiana
Trombone

The Eminent Jay Jay Johnson: Volumes 1 & 2
Blue Note 32143-2 / 32144-2
Johnson; Clifford Brown (t); Hank Mobley (ts); Jimmy Heath (ts, bs); Wynton Kelly, John Lewis, Horace Silver (p); Paul Chambers, Percy Heath, Charles Mingus (b); Kenny Clarke (d); Sabu Martinez (perc). June 1953–June 1955.

Trombonist and composer Michael Gibbs says: **'J.J. was always my idol – especially when I still harboured a desire to become a jazz trombonist. While I was at the Lenox School in**

1960 (its last year), J.J. and group came through town to play a concert and John Lewis asked him to stay on for the remaining two weeks and teach, or just hang. I got to have a few lessons with him. We played the Jay & Kai two-trombone arrangements to get me to phrase and swing. Damn! I couldn't have it any better!'

Trombonists found it hard to keep up in bebop, but J.J. developed an agile and pure-toned bop voice for the horn that was influenced by saxophone phrasing. He frequently hung an old beret over the bell of his horn to soften his tone and bring it into line with the sound of the reeds around him. He emerged in Benny Carter's orchestra, for a short time with Basie, and as part of Jazz At The Philharmonic, but will always be remembered for being one half of Jay & Kai, with fellow trombonist Kai Winding. After a spell working in film music (just one of several periods away from full-time music), he left California and returned to Indianapolis, with his adored wife Vivian, whose death left him broken-hearted.

The first volume of the Blue Note set is one of the central documents of postwar jazz. Johnson – who was working as a blueprint checker at the time of the earliest sessions – sounds fleet and confident, and he has a marvellous band round him, including a young Clifford Brown. 'Turnpike' and 'Capri' exist in two versions each and show Johnson's ability to rethink his phraseology, adjusting his attack on the original-release versions to accommodate Clarke's powerful but unemphatic swing (swamped on the September 1954 sessions by Mingus's chiming bass and the slap-happy Martinez); even on the slow-tempo 'Turnpike', Clarke provides an irresistible moving force underneath the melody. 'Get Happy' is appropriately upbeat and joyous, with notes picked off like clay pipes at a shooting gallery. In contrast, 'Lover Man' is given a mournful, drawn-out statement that squeezes out every drop of emotion the melody has to offer. The 1954 session yields some fine exchanges between Johnson and Kelly, notably on 'It's You Or No One' and 'Too Marvellous For Words', where the leader's tone and attack are almost as perfect as on 'Turnpike'. *Volume 2* is filled out with a less than inspiring 1955 date featuring Hank Mobley and Horace Silver, neither of whom seems attuned to Johnson's taxing idiom. In modern sound, these records come up fresh as paint.

& See also **Quintergy: Live At The Village Vanguard** (1988; p. 521)

VIC DICKENSON
Born 6 August 1906, Xenia, Ohio; died 16 November 1984, New York City
Trombone

The Essential Vic Dickenson
Vanguard VCD 79610
Dickenson; Ruby Braff, Shad Collins (t); Edmond Hall (cl); Sir Charles Thompson (p); Steve Jordan (g); Walter Page (b); Les Erskine, Jo Jones (d). December 1953, November 1954.

J. J. Johnson said (1985): **'He had a beautiful, lyrical sound. Part of that came from the fact he pressed the mouthpiece to his lip, not the skin above. His chops wore out easily, so he got used to playing in the middle register, and sometimes more slowly and with less pressure.'**

Dickenson had an attractively remote sound, as if playing behind a screen, but it was packed with wit and invention and his solos always leave a satisfied feeling. His early-'50s sessions for Vanguard are classics of the mainstream idiom. It's terrific stuff, mostly nice long versions of relatively unfamiliar material (including originals by Vic and Sir Charles) but centred on stretched-out versions of 'Jeepers Creepers', 'Old Fashioned Love' and 'Everybody Loves My Baby'. It's great that he's working in such distinctive company. Braff is crisp and buoyant, Hall pootles along in his own sweet way and Thompson keeps it all very tight;

check his own 'Sir Charles At Home' for his quick wit and invention. This is happy music, with very few shadows. Its appeal is undentable.

BENGT HALLBERG
Born 13 September 1932, Gothenburg, Sweden
Piano

All-Star Sessions 1953–1954
Dragon DRCD 402
Hallberg; Ernie Englund (t); Åke Persson (tb); Åke Björkman (frhn); Arne Domnérus (cl, as); Carl-Henrik Norin (ts); Lars Gullin (bs); Putte Wickman (cl); Simon Brehm, Red Mitchell (b); Robert Edman, William Schiøpffe, Bobby White (d). November 1953, January & March 1954.

Saxophonist Mats Gustafsson says: **'Together with Åke Persson, Jan Johansson and Lars Gullin, Hallberg was the epicentre of creative cool jazz in Sweden in the '50s and onwards. And he's still kicking ass ... Check his early trio recordings out! Together with the trio of Johansson, the most influential pre-free stuff in Sweden. Detail and clarity!'**

Hallberg played swing as a teenager, before adapting to bop and working with Stan Getz and other Americans. He has some reputation abroad, but his local status endures as one of the major figures in Swedish jazz. For overseas fans, it has always been a frustrating business tracking down his records, but the reissue of these early dates transformed the picture and delivered some of his best work in a single package.

At first glance, it may look padded, with multiple takes of some numbers (three of 'Blues In Fourths' with Gullin, Mitchell and White, two cuts each of 'Red Wails In The Sunset' and 'Doe Eyes') and brought up to respectable length with a number of cuts from March 1954, taken from a session organized by Leonard Feather on which Hallberg was merely a member of the band. However, his leadership and crisp arrangements are a strong feature on the rest of the set and the musicianship is of such high calibre that no one will protest at the attribution. With soloists of the quality of Wickman, Gullin and the pianist himself, it's unalloyed pleasure and the perfect introduction to a musician who deserves to be more than a coterie taste.

LARS GULLIN
Born 4 May 1928, Visby, Sweden; died 17 May 1976, Vissefjärda, Sweden
Baritone saxophone

Danny's Dream
Dragon DRCD 396
Gullin; Carl-Henrik Norin (ts); Rolf Berg (g); Georg Riedel (b); Alan Dawson, Robert Edman, Bosse Stoor (d). November 1953–January 1955.

Saxophonist Mats Gustafsson says: **'The *single* voice, the *single* melody-line, the *single* smoothness. Simplicity and magic, pure *beauty*, not just "Scandinavian". His compositions just kill me: "Danny´s Dream", "Silhouette", "Fedja"; these are DNA-changing themes. Listen to what was found in Lars's typewriter after his death: "My heart is the seat of my musical ideas, and my brain their rhythmic laboratory." Poetry.'**

A major figure in Scandinavian modernism, Gullin is eminent in Europe but still shockingly little known beyond. His career tailed off somewhat in the '70s and early death denied him the inevitable revival. A posthumous programme of reissue has, however, put his recordings back into circulation. He worked for a time on the Swedish swing band scene but then joined Arne Domnérus's group and started playing bebop. The postwar years saw a steady influx of American visitors and Gullin's cool, stylish sound, reminiscent of Gerry Mulligan but with an almost folkish quality all his own, sat well with the sophisticated idiom of the time. Gullin played with Chet Baker and others and held his own. Sadly, he also emulated the Americans in drug use, and it shortened his career.

Some hear the saxophone tone as dry and the delivery as plain to the point of dullness, but in reality Gullin liked to articulate straightforwardly and while his harmonic sense was second to none, he often preferred to stay close to the main melody, often creating an alternative line rather than simply working the changes. He swung effortlessly. His peak of productivity came in the early to mid-50s, and it seemed that the more he played, the better he played. Almost none of the Dragons from this period will disappoint, but this one, as well as including the definitive version of 'Danny's Dream' (his best-known composition) also includes all the quartet sessions for Metronome in which Gullin was supported only by Berg, Riedel, and either Edman or Stoor. As well as the title-track, there are fine performances of 'Manchester Fog', 'Lars Meets Jeff' (with Lars moving to piano) and 'Igloo', haunting masterpieces where Gullin's even dynamics and controlled expression do little to mask the intense beauty of his improvising and the poignancy and yearning which characterize the best of his writing. Four tracks with Norin sharing the front line vary the sound nicely, but it doesn't in any way mask Gullin's pre-eminence.

ART TATUM &

Born 13 October 1909, Toledo, Ohio; died 5 November 1956, Los Angeles, California
Piano

The Complete Pablo Solo Masterpieces
Pablo 4404 7CD
Tatum (p solo). December 1953–January 1955.

The Tatum Group Masterpieces: Volume 1
Pablo 2405-424
Tatum; Benny Carter (as); Louie Bellson (d). June 1954.

Norman Granz said (1982): **'Coming as close as they did to the end of his life, these are very special. I have a bias, but I don't think there has ever been anything finer done on the piano in the name of jazz.'**

Tatum's extraordinary achievement was set down in no more than four separate sessions over the course of a little over a year. Twenty years after his first solo records, this abundance of music does in some ways show comparatively little in the way of 'progression': he had established a pattern for playing many of the tunes in his repertoire, and changes of inflection, nuance and touch may be the only telling differences between these and earlier variations on the theme. But there are countless small revisions of this kind, enough to make each solo a fresh experience, and mostly he is more expansive (freed from playing-time restrictions, he is still comparatively brief, but there can be a major difference between a 2½-minute and a four-minute solo) and more able to provide dynamic contrast and rhythmic variation. He still chooses Broadway tunes over any kind of jazz material and seems to care little for formal emotional commitments: a ballad is just as likely to be dismantled as it is to be made to evoke tenderness, while a feeble tune such as 'Taboo' (*Volume 7*) may be transformed into something that communicates with great power and urgency. Tatum's genius (these records were originally known as *The Genius Of Art Tatum*) was a peculiar combination of carelessness – even at his most daring and virtuosic he can sometimes suggest a throwaway manner – and searching commitment to his art, and those contradictory qualities (which in some ways exemplify something of the jazz artist's lot) heighten the power of these superb solos.

It is tantalizing to conjecture what Tatum might have done in contemporary studios, for his whole discography is marred by inadequate recording – even these later solos are comparatively unrefined by the studio – but the CD versions are probably the best to date. Still, surely this is a moment to go back to the best original sources and give us a new overview of this profound body of work.

Having set down the astonishing solo sessions, Granz then embarked on a project to record Tatum in a variety of group situations. The overall quality isn't so consistently intense, which is why this time we have picked just one volume and not the entire eight-volume set. On the other discs, Tatum's partners are sometimes either relatively incompatible or simply looking another way: the cheery Lionel Hampton and Buddy Rich, for instance, work well enough in their trio record, but it seems to lighten the music to an inappropriate degree. Yet some of this music is undervalued, particularly the trio session with Callender and Douglass, the group working in beautiful accord. The sextet date with Edison, Hampton and Kessel is comparatively slight, and the meeting with Eldridge, while it has moments of excitement, again sounds like two virtuosos of somewhat contrary methods in the same room.

The meetings with Benny Carter, Buddy DeFranco and Ben Webster, though, are unqualified masterpieces. The Carter session that we have chosen is worth having just for the astonishing 'Blues In C', and elsewhere Carter's aristocratic elegance chimes perfectly with Tatum's grand manner, their differing attitudes to jazz eloquence a rare match. As music to study, live with and simply enjoy, this is the most approachable of all of Tatum's series of recordings: he finds the company stimulating and manages to vary his approach on each occasion without surrendering anything of himself.

& *See also* **Art Tatum 1933–1934** (1933–1934; p. 44)

MEL POWELL

Born Melvin Epstein, 12 February 1923, New York City; died 24 April 1998, Los Angeles, California
Piano

Borderline-Thigamagig
Vanguard VRS 8051
Powell; Ruby Braff (t); Paul Quinichette (ts); Bobby Donaldson (d). August 1954.

Ruby Braff recalled: **'Man, Mel played so smoothly that the music flowed like cat piss on velvet.'**

In 1990, already suffering the effects of muscular dystrophy, Mel Powell received the Pulitzer Prize for his *Duplicates*, a meaty concerto for two pianos and orchestra. Since the '70s, he had been recognized primarily as a straight composer. However, Powell has an almost legendary standing in the jazz world. He started out with George Brunis, Zutty Singleton and Bobby Hackett, and did duty as the intermission piano-player at Nick's club. Later, as an arranger for his friend Benny Goodman, he worked on such peerless charts as 'Clarinade' and 'The Earl'. Powell also worked for Glenn Miller and under Raymond Scott in the CBS orchestra. In 1952, though his jazz activities continued for a time, he began to study formal composition under Paul Hindemith at Yale.

A highly personal amalgam of Tatum (the virtuosity) and Teddy Wilson (the effortlessly driving swing), Powell's piano technique is spoken of with awe, but his records of the late '40s and '50s, once greatly prized, are scarcely known now. Perhaps the best general survey of his early career is *Piano Prodigy*, a compilation on the Spanish label Ocium, an imprint that always offers an interesting CD-Rom component. But that fine disc stops in 1948. Powell had recorded six years earlier for Commodore, a wartime swing classic with a part for Goodman, but already he was showing signs of a technique and ideas disconcertingly prescient of his illustrious namesake; but where Bud Powell's technique was often wayward, Mel floated through awkward cross-handed passages with a fleet intelligence. There was, to be sure, something slightly superficial about it, especially if you take the norm in jazz to be the sometimes neurotic inscapes of bebop, but there was no mistaking the sheer quality of 'Blue Skies (Trumpets No End)' or 'The World Is Waiting For The Sunrise'.

For us, though, the best of Powell's records are the bassless trios made as part of a run of LPs for John Hammond Sr. Powell was heard with Ruby Braff and Bobby Donaldson on *Borderline*, Paul Quinichette less successfully on *Thigamagig*. These were brought together as a Vanguard CD which has now been superseded by a pair of compilations which bring together the best of the Hammond material, not just the trios but also material from *Out On A Limb, Bandstand* and *Septet*. These are called *The Best Things In Life* and *It's Been So Long* and they make a good substitute for our favoured listing.

There are surprisingly few Powell originals among the trios, just the two title-tracks, the languidly ironic 'Bouquet' and the astringent 'Quin And Sonic', but it is in his approach to standard material like 'California, Here I Come' and 'Makin' Whoopee' that his qualities as an arranger and performer come across most clearly. The absence of a bass obviously throws some further weight on the piano left hand, and Powell's ability to state a clear and mobile bass-line while improvising with both hands is one of his most remarkable skills. If there is such a thing as 'progressive jazz', then this, rather than the bland referencing of Stravinsky fashionable at the same period, has to be it. Powell's perhaps not the warmest, or the most emotionally involving, player, but his work has qualities often overlooked in jazz: wit, irony and a fine analytic intelligence.

JAMES MOODY
Born 26 May 1925, Savannah, Georgia
Tenor, alto and soprano saxophones, flute

Moody's Mood For Blues
Original Jazz Classics OJCCD 1837
Moody; Dave Burns (t); William Shepherd (tb); Pee Wee Moore (bs); Sadik Hakim, Jimmy Boyd (p); John Latham (b); Joe Harris, Clarence Johnson (d); Eddie Jefferson, Iona Wade (v). January, April & September 1954, January 1955.

James Moody said (1992): **'I maybe sound the way I do because I'm a little deaf and don't hear high sounds so well. Low sounds, I'm OK with, but I think you hear the difference on flute, where I don't play way up there because I can't hear it.'**

Initially influenced by Lester Young, 'Moody' – which is how he prefers to be addressed – devised a harder and more abrasive tone, but then also majored on flute. His solo on 'I'm In The Mood For Love' became the basis of the vocalese fad. After a spell with Dizzy Gillespie's orchestra, he spent some time in Europe (France and Sweden) at the end of the '40s, but came back at the height of the bebop explosion.

Moody's Moods For Blues usefully puts together two short LPs from the period. They are performed in a style that draws somewhat on R&B but with a boppish fire, too. 'It Might As Well Be Spring' is included in both alto and tenor versions, quite an interesting comparison. He's joined on the extra 'I Got The Blues' by Eddie Jefferson, who reworked a vocal version of the hit, thereby (allegedly) giving King Pleasure the idea for adding his own lyrics to bebop tunes. Moody has a strongly vocalized tone and frequently appears to shape a solo to the lyric of a tune rather than simply to the chords or the written melody, and that vocalized sound is perhaps more evident on his alto-playing, though he even adapts it later in his career to flute, using a 'legitimate' version of Roland Kirk's vocalization. The saxophonist was off the scene for much of the '70s, certainly as far as significant recording was concerned, and his reputation went into something of a decline. Nevertheless, he proved to be a great survivor and still goes strong, still making compelling music in which playfulness and a certain dark sensibility vie for the foreground.

ART BLAKEY&

Also known as Abdullah ibn Buhaina; born 11 October 1919, Pittsburgh, Pennsylvania; died 16 October 1990, New York City
Drums

A Night At Birdland: Volumes 1 & 2

Blue Note 32146 / 32147
Blakey; Clifford Brown (t); Lou Donaldson (as); Horace Silver (p); Curley Russell (b). February 1954.

Blue Note owner Alfred Lion said (1980): **'At first, we didn't want to make club recordings. They seemed the opposite of what we did at Blue Note, making records in good sound and with time for rehearsal of the music. But I guess it turned out pretty good!'**

Self-taught as a pianist, Blakey led his own band at 15 and switched to drums when Erroll Garner came in. In NY he joined the Eckstine band and stayed till 1947, then freelanced until the Blue Note sessions that led to the formation of the Jazz Messengers. A master percussionist who investigated African and other styles, he was peerless in support of soloists and kept up standards unswervingly till the end.

It was still called the Art Blakey Quintet, when Alfred Lion decided to record the group at Birdland, but this was the founding nexus of the Messengers, even if the name was first used on a Horace Silver cover. Blakey wasn't as widely acknowledged as Max Roach or Kenny Clarke as one of the leaders in bop drumming and in the end he was credited with working out the rhythms for what came after original bebop, first heard to significant effect on these records. Much of it is based on sheer muscle. Blakey played very loud and very hard, accenting the off-beat with a hi-hat snap that had a thunderous abruptness and developing a highly dramatic snare roll. As much as he dominates the music, though, he always plays for the band and inspirational leadership is as evident on these early records as it is on his final ones. Both horn-players benefit: Donaldson makes his Parkerisms sound pointed and vivacious, while Brown is marvellously mercurial, as well as sensitive on his ballad feature 'Once In A While' from *Volume 1* (Donaldson's comes on 'If I Had You' on the second record). Silver lays down some of the tenets of hard bop with his poundingly funky solos and hints of gospel melody. The latest RVG editions restore the original 10-inch cover art and for once a new mastering really does bounce the sound up an extra level.

& *See also* **Art Blakey's Jazz Messengers With Thelonious Monk** (1957; p. 203)

BLUE MITCHELL

Born Richard Alan Mitchell, 13 March 1930, Miami, Florida; died 21 May 1979, Los Angeles, California
Trumpet

The Thing To Do

Blue Note 5943202
Mitchell; Junior Cook (ts); Chick Corea (p); Gene Taylor (b); Al Foster (d). July 1954.

Cornetist Nat Adderley said (1991): **'I don't hear anyone talking about the "Florida school" of trumpet-players, but you got to admit, there's something there. Fats Navarro, Idrees Suliemann, me, Blue Mitchell, and I think Blue's underrated: a really strong player, very secure in what he did. He didn't follow any trends or fashions.'**

Rather charmingly described by one British radio broadcaster as 'Red Mitchell's brother' – a glance at a photograph would show why the suggestion is absurd; Red's sibling was nick-named Whitey, and for a reason – Blue had a soulful delivery that was an asset whether it was deployed in an R&B situation or in straight jazz. That may sound like faint praise, for Mitchell was more than a utility player. His unadorned tone didn't jump out of the speakers, but he created coach-built solos that are never less than satisfying. Mitchell took over the Silver band in 1964, replacing the former leader with the young Chick Corea. By then, he was already a well-documented leader, with a bunch of nice Riverside dates to his name. *Big Six* from 1958 is particularly good, with Curtis Fuller and Johnny Griffin in the front line, Wynton Kelly, Wilbur Ware and Philly Joe Jones rounding out the group. Better was to come, though.

A Blue Note contract allowed Blue to play the kind of hard bop he and the label ate up, and 1964's *The Thing To Do* is his masterpiece. It kicks off with 'Fungii Mama', which is delivered with an energy and finesse that ought to have lifted this record into the premier league of Blue Note dates, and yet who ever mentions it now? Joe Henderson's 'Step Lightly' almost steals the show and rising star Chick Corea chips in at the end with 'Chick's Tune'. These were men set to make their own careers but Mitchell doesn't let anyone steal his thunder. His solos are briskly organized, and on the two Jimmy Heath tunes (all quality merchandise, this set-list) he smokes along nicely. Never just a journeyman player, Blue deserves reassessment, as does his regular playing partner Junior Cook. It's quite a hard record to date, this one, which suggests that it isn't just a routine blow but a carefully conceived modern jazz album.

LENNIE TRISTANO&

Born 19 March 1919, Chicago, Illinois; died 18 November 1978, New York City
Piano

Lennie Tristano / The New Tristano

Rhino/Atlantic R2 71595
Tristano; Lee Konitz (as); Gene Ramey, Peter Ind (b); Jeff Morton, Art Taylor (d). 1954 or 1955–1960 or 1962.

Lee Konitz said (1984): **'He was an overwhelming influence. I swear that ten years later I could identify someone who had worked with Lennie by the way they drank a glass of water.'**

Far from being the cerebral purist of legend, a kind of Glenn Gould figure, the blind Tristano was fascinated by every possibility of music-making and was a pioneer in studio overdubbing and in speeding up half-speed recordings to give them a cool, almost synthesized timbre. The key track in this regard was 'Requiem', perhaps the most striking item on the

1955 Atlantic sessions, reissued on this indispensable Rhino CD. His overdubbing and multitracking would influence Bill Evans. But the latter part of the album offers a rare club
date with Lee Konitz: the saxophonist sounds dry and slightly prosaic on 'If I Had You' and
much more like his normal self on a beautiful 'Ghost Of A Chance'. Tristano's own solos
are derived, as usual, from the refined and twice-distilled code of standards material. The
original Atlantic LP has also been reissued separately as *Lennie Tristano*.

The New Tristano is an essential record. The vagueness of the provenance underlines
just how precarious an existence some of these home recordings have. The multiple time-
patterns secured on most of the tracks suggest a vertiginous, almost mathematical piano
music that moves beyond its scientific sheen to a point where the ingenuities acquire their
own beauty: 'I can never think and play at the same time. It's emotionally impossible.' How-
soever the conjoining of technique, interpretation and feeling may work for the listener, this
is remarkable piano jazz, and the contrasting ballads of 'You Don't Know What Love Is' and
'Love Lines' suggest a world of expression which jazz has seldom looked at since.

& *See also* **The Complete Lennie Tristano** (1946–1947; p. 109)

JUNE CHRISTY

Born Shirley Luster, 20 November 1935, Springfield, Illinois; died 21 June 1990, Los Angeles, California
Voice

Something Cool: The Complete Mono And Stereo Versions
Capitol 34069
Christy; Pete Rugolo orchestra. 1953–1955.

June Christy said (1981): **'I believed in *Something Cool* when no one else did. None of us
thought it would ever sell. It was just something I wanted to do, for myself and maybe to
look back on. But it took off, and here I am.'**

June Christy's wholesome but peculiarly sensuous voice is both creative and emotive. Her
long controlled lines and the shading of a fine vibrato suggest a professional's attention to
detail and a tender, solicitous feel for the heart of a song. Her greatest moments are as close
to creating definitive interpretations as any singer can come.

She sounds amazingly confident just out of her teens on early recordings with Kenton,
already a swing-era canary with a feel for the cooler, more knowing pulse of the years ahead.
But her best work was done with Rugolo (although husband Bob Cooper's charts shouldn't be
forgotten). The masterpieces are *Something Cool* and *The Misty Miss Christy*, both perfectly
programmed and meticulously tailored to June's persona. 'Something Cool' itself is a story
that bears endless retelling, but 'Midnight Sun', 'I Should Care' and several others seem like
definitive interpretations, a marvel for Christy's perfect breath control and vibrato as well as
her emotional colouring. Rugolo's inventiveness is unstinting, often using the orchestra in
surprising ways but nothing that unsettles or diverts attention from the singer.

AL HAIG

Born 22 July 1922, Newark, New Jersey; died 16 November 1982, New York City
Piano

Esoteric
Fresh Sound FSRCD 38
Haig; Bill Crow (b); Lee Abrams (d). March 1954.

Mal Waldron said (1983): **'Al Haig was a genius, but he was also a very strange man. I don't think you'd ever have known what was going on in that head. The good stuff came out on the piano.'**

In 1969, Haig was charged with strangling his third wife, but acquitted at trial. After his death, research suggested that he had been persistently violent in the marriage; there was even some suggestion that Haig had confessed the murder to a friend. In his musical incarnation, he seems the perfect example of creative sublimation, any violence channelled into beauty.

If Haig denied himself the high passion of Bud Powell's music, he was still a force of eloquence and intensity, and his refined touch lent him a striking individuality within his milieu. The early sextet material, now on OJC, was made for Dawn and Seeco, though Al was also recording under Getz's leadership for larger imprints. The first trio album, originally released on Esoteric, is a masterpiece – one of the finest records of its era, we'd propose – that can stand with any of the work of Powell or Monk. Haig's elegance of touch and line, his virtually perfect delivery, links him with a pianist such as Teddy Wilson rather than with any of his immediate contemporaries, and certainly his delivery of an unlikely tune such as 'Mighty Like A Rose' has a kinship with the language of Wilson's generation. Yet his complexity of tone and the occasionally cryptic delivery are unequivocally modern, absolutely of the bop lineage. Voicings and touch have a symmetry and refinement that other boppers, from Powell and Duke Jordan to Joe Albany and Dodo Marmarosa, seldom approached.

PERCY HUMPHREY
Born 13 January 1905, New Orleans, Louisiana; died 22 July 1995, New Orleans, Louisiana
Trumpet

Percy Humphrey's Sympathy Five
American Music AMCD-88
Humphrey; Waldron Joseph, Jack Delany (tb); Willie Humphrey, Raymond Burke (cl); Stanley Mendelson, Lester Santiago (p); Johnny St Cyr (g, bj, v); Blind Gilbert (g, v); Richard McLean, Sherwood Mangiapane (b); Paul Barbarin (d). January 1951–June 1954.

Photographer Jean-Luc Magnan says: **'I think tourists went to Preservation Hall thinking it was going to be this swanky nightclub, with hostesses and cocktails and gourmet food. It's *plain*, man, and so's the music they make there.'**

The youngest Humphrey brother – Willie played clarinet, Earl trombone – started out as a drummer, worked with George Lewis in the '50s, and led the Eureka Brass Band and others, including his own Joymakers outfit. He seldom played outside the city in earlier years and had a day job selling insurance, but the formation of the Preservation Hall touring band made him something of an international star. The Sympathy Five (the name derives solely from the handwritten title on a discovered reel of tape) offer six 1954 titles on this American Music CD. Humphrey sounds in good spirits and his solos have a lean, almost wiry quality, played in the slightly breathless style of the New Orleans brass men. There's some danger of him seeming outshone by Burke and the splendid Delany, but Humphrey's ability to sound as if he might be doing his accounts while playing, nonchalant to the point of detachment, is what makes him attractive. There's a coiled-spring impression to some of the music, as if he might leap into action if anything worthwhile crops up.

JIMMY RANEY&

Born 20 August 1927, Louisville, Kentucky; died 10 May 1995, Louisville, Kentucky
Guitar

A
Original Jazz Classics OJC 1706
Raney; John Wilson (t); Hall Overton (p); Teddy Kotick (b); Art Mardigan, Nick Stabulas (d). May 1954–March 1955.

Jimmy Raney said (1984): **'There really weren't many bop guitarists around in the early days, which I guess made it easier. But there were those who thought the instrument wasn't suitable for bop, so in terms of visibility it was robbing Peter to pay Paul!'**

Of the bop-inspired guitarists Raney perhaps best combined lyricism with great underlying strength. His style approximately synthesizes Charlie Christian and Lester Young. Essentially a group player, he sounds good at almost any tempo but is most immediately appealing on ballads. *A*, which contains some of his loveliest performances, remains an overlooked classic. Overton anticipates some of the harmonic devices employed by Hank Jones, and bebop bassist Kotick plays with a firm authority that synchronizes nicely with Raney's rather spacious and elided lower-string work. On the first date, he overdubs a second guitar part over the intros and coda, an interesting device so smoothly done many listeners aren't even aware of it. 'Minor' (which has a familiar chord structure) clips along at an impressive pace, but never drops a stitch. 'Some Other Spring' is a perfect study-piece for improvising guitarists, intricate but completely logical. Wilson adds a dimension to the lovely 'One More For The Mode' (which uses fragments of Bach) and to four more romantic numbers, including 'A Foggy Day' and 'Someone To Watch Over Me'.

& *See also* **Wisteria** (1985; p. 498)

BUD SHANK&

Born Clifford Everett Shank Jr, 27 May 1926, Dayton, Ohio; died 2 April 2009, Tucson, Arizona
Alto saxophone

Jazz In Hollywood
Original Jazz Classics OJC 1890
Shank; Shorty Rogers (flhn); Jimmy Rowles, Lou Levy (p); Harry Babasin (b); Roy Harte, Larry Bunker (d). March–September 1954.

Bud Shank said (1985): **'With Kenton, Art [Pepper] played the alto solos. It was my job to lead the saxophone section. I think I learned more doing that, never felt particularly frustrated. I got my chance to play at the Haig, Monday nights, when Gerry [Mulligan] and Chet [Baker] were there. It started to fall into place.'**

Bud Shank has been the quintessential West Coast altoman for more than 40 years. He has appeared on numberless sessions but his playing has remained sharp, piercingly thoughtful and swinging in a lean, persuasive way. Originally a tenor-player, he switched and added flute while working with Charlie Barnet and Stan Kenton. The Ohioan's light, tender touch – and brilliantly individual flute-playing – was a significant component of the Lighthouse All Stars, and the L.A.4. He was once considered cool to the point of frigidity, but he eventually embraced bebop and his later work has grown fiercer and more inclined to collar the listener; but the early albums have a kind of snake-eyed ingenuity.

Jazz In Hollywood is an interesting find, two rather rare albums for the Nocturne label combined on one disc. One was Shank's debut, with a quintet including frequent partner Rogers; the other features a trio date for Lou Levy. The air-conditioned tone and slightly remote delivery perhaps sounds just right for someone who'd been through the Kenton machine, but there is Kentonian power as well. Even at this juncture, Shank is a musician who buttonholes attention, without seeming to. His lines are neat and crisp without being excessively original, but it's the delivery that makes them arresting. *Live At The Haig* is the obvious companion piece from the time, but it has flaws and is less individual than this early compilation.

& *See also* **Lost In The Stars** (1990; p. 546)

CHRIS BARBER
Born 17 April 1930, Welwyn Garden City, Hertfordshire, England
Trombone

The Complete Decca Sessions 1954/55
Lake LACD 141/2 2CD
Barber; Pat Halcox (c); Monty Sunshine (cl); Bertie King (as); Lonnie Donegan (bj); Jim Bray (b, bb); Ron Bowden (d); Beryl Bryden (wbd); Ottilie Patterson (v). July 1954, January 1955.

Chris Barber says: **'That first Festival Hall concert in 1954 was very important for us. We'd only played in jazz clubs before that. There was a rumour that Princess Margaret was going to attend, so the press were all there. Ottilie sang very well and got good write-ups, as she should have done, but it was Princess Margaret they were really there to see. She didn't turn up!'**

The godfather of British jazz and blues, Barber has an extraordinary following at home and in Europe, selling records mostly through his concerts and fan club in a way that antici-pated internet and other non-retail sources. Barber had been leading bands in his teens, but his first serious attempt was a cooperative group pulled together in 1953 during Colyer's extended 'vacation' in New Orleans. Though they subsequently worked together, the band split over their ultimate direction, and while Colyer (who felt the Armstrong Hot Fives were too modern!) went back to elemental New Orleans playing, Barber assumed not only leader-ship but the mantle of the entire trad movement, with Humphrey Lyttelton already moving towards swing mainstream. While the ensemble's the thing, Barber thinks more creatively about arrangements, the place of solos, counterpoint and rhythm, and it's surprising to hear how strongly this music survives the years. It sounds youthful and energetic, and it reminds us that it was still being played by men in their early 20s. The very first track, the highly improbable 'Bobby Shaftoe', works up a terrific head of steam, yet it's clearly all under control. Some of the shibboleths of the trad movement – such as the plink of the banjo – are there to be sure, but Barber's men were too good to let them seem like anything but a necessary part of the music. Halcox is still a bit green, but Sunshine is already master-ful, and the leader's own playing has a terrific bark. Donegan contributed his 'Skiffle Group' session, which yielded the hit 'Rock Island Line' and paved the way for British beat music. Barber likes to joke that he earned more money playing bass on Donegan's record than he ever did playing jazz trombone. The live tracks on disc two are just as impressive and are greeted with applause the like of which hasn't been heard again at a jazz concert in Britain (until the Jamie Cullum era). And with guest spots for Bertie King and material as diverse as 'Skokiaan' and 'Salutation March', Barber was serving notice that his musical remit was going to be as wide as he wanted.

JOHN DANKWORTH

Later Sir John Dankworth, born 20 September 1927, London; died 5 February 2010, Wavendon, Milton Keynes, Buckinghamshire, England
Alto and soprano saxophones, clarinet

The Vintage Years
Sepia RSCD2014
Dankworth: Derrick Abbott, Dickie Hawdon, Bill Metcalf, Eddie Blair, George Boocock, Charlie Evans, Tommy McQuater, Stan Palmer, Colin Wright, Dougie Roberts (t); Maurice Pratt, Keith Christie, Eddie Harvey, Bill Geldard, Laurie Monk, Gary Brown, Harry Puckles, Danny Elwood, Tony Russell, Gib Wallis (tb); Geoff Cole, Maurice Owen, Rex Rutley, Lew Smith (as); Tommy Whittle, Rex Morris, Pete Warner, John Xerri, Freddie Courteney (ts); Alex Leslie (bs); Dave Lee, Derek Smith, Bill Le Sage (p); Jack Seymour, Bill Sutcliffe, Eric Dawson (b); Allan Ganley, Kenny Clare (d). 1953–1959.

John Dankworth says: **'You know, the British boys all learned to play by listening to records, not hearing those bands in a club. We'd copy what we heard on Mel Powell and Glenn Miller recordings and they were very quiet. What a shock when the bands came over or we went there and saw them and it was *loud*! But it taught me that you can be quiet and still swing. You just maybe have to wait for a club audience to get the idea and calm down a bit!'**

One of the bop pioneers at Club Eleven in the later '40s, his Dankworth Seven and big bands were important in the '50s and '60s and the orchestra played Newport in 1959, with a short season on the same bill as the Ellington band. In later years, Dankworth worked more extensively in film and also became a force in music education from his and wife Cleo Laine's base at Wavendon. It's easy enough to argue that Dankworth was more important as a catalyst than as a musician. That, however, is belied by the early records. Unfortunately, the discography is in a poor state and only rather recently with the establishment of a 'home' label has it seemed at all likely that the big-band records will return to the light. In the meantime, there are a few good recent small-group discs to enjoy and it's worth searching out this excellent compilation of early singles and album material by the orchestra he formed after disbanding the Johnny Dankworth Seven in 1953. One obvious conclusion is how much Dankworth's musical ambitions were compromised by British jazz surroundings at the time. However, there are some very worthy names dotted through these personnels and the compilation as a whole does reflect his core values: rigorous harmony, subtler than usual dynamics (though one senses the sections resisting that), idiomatic voicings and part-writing, all qualities that stood him in good stead as a film composer.

Much of the earlier material here is akin to dance band music with a jazz leaning, but the later sides, such as a vivid reworking of 'How High The Moon' and 'Jive At Five', achieve the more purposeful jazz feel of the Seven recordings. None of the soloists betters Dankworth's own creamy contributions and it's a point of mild regret that he doesn't feature himself more. Except that wasn't the point and Dankworth, who died while this book was in production, has always been engagingly modest as a man and a player, letting the band appear to set the agenda.

JOHNNY ST CYR

Born 17 April 1890, New Orleans, Louisiana; died 17 June 1966, Los Angeles, California
Guitar, banjo

Johnny St Cyr
American Music AMCD-78

St Cyr; Thomas Jefferson (t, v); Percy Humphrey (t); Jim Robinson, Joe Avery (tb); George Lewis (cl); Jeanette Kimball (p, v); Leo Thompson (p); Ernest McLean (g); Richard McLean, Fran Fields (b); Paul Barbarin, Sidney Montague (d); Jack Delany, Sister Elizabeth Eustis (v). July 1954–May 1955.

Lonnie Donegan said (1983): **'The funny thing is that on some of those terrible old recordings Johnny St Cyr is the loudest thing you can hear and you realize that it's him who's stoking the engines.'**

The self-taught doyen of New Orleans rhythm guitarists – who worked with both Armstrong and Morton – was seldom noted as a group leader (and in fact doubled his music career with a day job as a plasterer), but American Music have pieced together a CD's worth of material. The first two tracks are rather dowdy treatments of 'Someday You'll Be Sorry' by a band with Percy Humphrey, Lewis and Robinson; but more interesting are the five previously unheard pieces by a quintet in which protégé Ernest McLean is featured rather more generously than Johnny himself, both men playing electric. The rest of the disc is jovial New Orleans music, fronted by the hearty Jefferson and the imperturbable Percy Humphrey. St Cyr, as always, is no more inclined to take any limelight than Freddie Green ever was, so it's nice to have a disc under his name.

BENNY GOODMAN&
Born 30 May 1909, Chicago, Illinois; died 13 June 1986, New York City
Clarinet

B.G. In Hi-Fi
Capitol 92684-2
Goodman; Ruby Braff, Charlie Shavers, Chris Griffin, Carl Poole, Bernie Privin (t); Will Bradley, Vernon Brown, Cutty Cutshall (tb); Al Klink, Paul Ricci, Boomie Richman, Hymie Schertzer, Sol Schlinger (saxes); Mel Powell (p); Steve Jordan (g); George Duvivier (b); Bobby Donaldson, Jo Jones (d). November 1954.

Mel Powell said (1989): **'Benny may have got hives when he heard bebop – or any of his players doing bebop – but you have to listen to that band [1954] and hear how much classical music, conservatory music, "art music" there is there. He'd listened to Bartók and Stravinsky, and it showed. Plus, I was there.'**

Goodman left the big-band era with his finances and his technique intact, and although this was a more or less anachronistic programme of trio, quintet and big-band sides in 1954, the playing is so good that it's a resounding success. Benny was interested in the new music, but he never felt very comfortable with it, and by the mid-'50s the bop accents are relatively few and confidently assimilated to his natural idiom. He had, by this stage, built an audience who wanted him for himself, not for his attentiveness to fashion. A few Goodman staples are mixed with Basie material such as 'Jumpin' At The Woodside', and Benny's readings match the originals. Shavers, Braff, Richman and Powell have fine moments; Goodman is peerless. The sound is dry but excellent, and the CD reissue adds four tracks, including a beautiful trio version of 'Rose Room'.

& *See also* **The Complete Small Group Sessions** (1935–1939; p. 52), **At Carnegie Hall 1938** (1938; p. 65)

OSCAR PETTIFORD
Born 30 September 1922, Okmulgee, Oklahoma; died 8 September 1960, Copenhagen, Denmark
Double bass, cello

Nonet & Octet 1954-55
Fresh Sound FSRCD 453
Pettiford; Donald Byrd, Ernie Royal, Clark Terry, Joe Wilder (t); Jimmy Cleveland, Bob Brookmeyer (tb); Gigi
Gryce, Dave Schildkraut (as); Jimmy Hamilton (cl, ts); Jerome Richardson (ts, f); Danny Bank (bs); Don Abney,
Joe Earl Knight (p); Osie Johnson (d). 1954–August 1955.

Art Ensemble Of Chicago bassist Malachi Favours said (1982): **'Pettiford was the most
melodic bass-player I ever heard, and his solos were on a different level to anyone else.
I heard him when I was starting out, and it almost discouraged me, but he showed what
was possible.'**

Pettiford's playing career began in a family orchestra, under the tutelage of his father. His
wonderfully propulsive bass-playing marks a middle point between Blanton and Mingus,
whose visionary genius and volcanic temperament he shared. He spent his last years in
European exile. Pettiford's facility on the cello is unparalleled in jazz, even by such gifted
doublers as Ron Carter, and the freedom and fluency of his solo line on the early 'Pendulum
At Falcon's Lair' are genuinely exhilarating. Oscar's placing of notes, his unfailing harmonic
awareness and his sheer musicality will win over all but the hardest-hearted sceptics.
    The octet and nonet performances and the big-band ABC recordings offer the best evi-
dence for the suggestion that Pettiford's experiments might even have eclipsed Mingus's,
had he lived long enough to see them through. The smaller groups are elegance itself, coolly
turbulent, if such a thing is possible, and packed with subtle musical ideas. The tracks that
made up *Another One* mark a high-point in jazz writing and ensemble playing at the period.
Pettiford helms with a brooding authority, his personal sound always evident, his compositional ideas ever more logical when heard in bulk. 'Bohemia After Dark' and the little-
known 'Kamman's A-Comin'' are classic modern performances, and should be in every
collection, as should the slightly later big-band material.

CHARLES THOMPSON
Born 21 March 1918, Springfield, Ohio
Piano

For The Ears
Vanguard 79604
Thompson; Emmett Berry, Joe Newman (t); Benny Morton, Benny Powell (tb); Pete Brown, Earle Warren
(as); Coleman Hawkins (as, ts); Skeeter Best, Steve Jordan (g); Aaron Bell, Gene Ramey (b); Osie Johnson (d).
1954–1956.

Drummer Ed Thigpen said (2000): **'Sir Charles is like one of those sequel trios, what do you
call them?** *Sequoia* **trees. Thousands of years old but still standing! And still playing like a
dream.'**

Sir Roland Hanna was knighted by the President of Liberia; Charles Thompson was 'knighted'
by Lester Young; which is the more impressive depends on your standpoint. Something of a
journeyman, Thompson nevertheless helped to define the new 'mainstream' in jazz during
the '50s and was relatively quiet after that, though he has enjoyed an Indian summer in his
late 80s and beyond, which means that he has been playing professionally for a staggering
80 years. Thompson made his debut aged ten and played privately with Bennie Moten until
he was picked up by Basie.
    The interesting thing about Thompson's style is that even in the swing era he sounded
boppish. Perversely, he sounds old-fashioned to most ears now, but that's relative. For a
player who has never left the lists, he's not often listed among the modern greats and that

has had a self-reinforcing impact on his availability. Thompson's vintage sessions for Vanguard – harbingers of the entire mainstream style – have never been satisfactorily around for long enough so that a new generation might pick up on him, and he shares the now-you-see-them fate which seems to attend everything cut for that label. This, then, is a valuable bulletin from Thompson's highly personal journey through the frontier land of swing and bop. There's some interesting material from 1956 with just Best and Bell (no drums) that includes a terrifically individual 'Stompin' At The Savoy', but the main interest is bound to be the tracks with Hawkins, who's in imperious form. He gets second billing on the date, though. It's emphatically Thompson's music, original, individual and sharply flowing, with hardly a phrase wasted.

RICHARD TWARDZIK

Born 30 April 1931, Danvers, Massachusetts; died 21 October 1955, Paris, France
Piano

Complete Recordings
Lone Hill Jazz LHJR 10120
Twardzik; Carson Smith (b); Peter Littman (d). December 1953–June 1954.

Chet Baker said (1981): **'I don't really like to talk about him ...'** Then, after fully a minute of silence: **'He was rather special, a special musician, with a great gift.'**

Twardzik was something of a one-off, a pupil of Margaret Chaloff, celebrated for his composition 'Yellow Waltz/Tango', but otherwise only known as one of jazz's many drug casualties. Twardzik worked with Charlie Mariano, Serge Chaloff and Chet Baker, and it was while on tour with Chet, shortly after recording the fine record *Rondette*, that he succumbed to an overdose. Plaudits to Lone Hill for scratching together the few things, solo and trio, that this singular talent recorded for Pacific, along with a few rehearsal extracts and concert tapes.

Twardzik never got the chance to spread his wings as a composer, but his revoicing of 'Round Midnight' (it features twice here) and a lovely version of 'I'll Remember April' are sufficient to suggest he might well have developed in a fascinating new direction that parallels some of the less orthodox boppers: Elmo Hope, Herbie Nichols. He also had a strong sense of the narrative underpinning of a song: 'Bess, You Is My Woman Now' seems to fit right back into an operatic context, moody and ambiguous. The quality of recording is inevitably variable, but as a snapshot of a lost figure who might well have been a significant presence, it's hard to beat.

DINAH WASHINGTON

Born Ruth Lee Jones, 29 August 1924, Tuscaloosa, Alabama; died 14 December 1963, Detroit, Michigan
Voice

Dinah Jams
Emarcy 814639-2
Washington; Clifford Brown, Clark Terry, Maynard Ferguson (t); Herb Geller (as); Harold Land (ts); Junior Mance, Richie Powell (p); Keter Betts, George Morrow (b); Max Roach (d). August 1954.

Drummer Jimmy Cobb said (1986): **'Dinah could be cruel, but I don't remember her being crazy. She was raised in the church and could read music pretty well, so she always knew what she was doing with the band.'**

Dinah joined Lionel Hampton in 1943, then went solo, in the end aspiring to a grand torch singer role in the '50s. She finally referred to herself as 'The Queen', and her gospel-and-blues methodology undeniably influenced the next generation of soul singers. She was married seven, eight or nine times. Even she seemed to lose count. Increasingly erratic, she died from an accidental pill overdose. Whether or not she counts as a 'jazz singer', Washington frequently appeared in the company of the finest jazz musicians and, while she was no improviser and stood slightly apart from such contemporaries as Fitzgerald or Vaughan, she could drill through blues and ballads with a huge, sometimes slightly terrifying delivery.

Washington's major 'jazz' record is fine, but not as fine as the closely contemporary Sarah Vaughan record with a similar backing group, and therein lies a tale about Washington's abilities. She claimed she could sing anything – which was probably true – but her big, bluesy voice is no more comfortable in this stratum of Tin Pan Alley than was Joe Turner's. Still, the long and luxuriant jams on 'You Go To My Head' and 'Lover Come Back To Me' are rather wonderful in their way, and there is always Clifford Brown to listen to.

LENNIE NIEHAUS
Born 11 June 1929, St Louis, Missouri
Alto saxophone

The Quintets & Strings
Original Jazz Classics OJCCD 1858
Niehaus; Stu Williamson (t); Bill Perkins (ts); Bobby Gordon (bs); Hampton Hawes (p); Monty Budwig (b); Shelly Manne (d); Thomas Hall, Christopher Kuzell, Barbara Simons (vla); Charlotte Harrison (clo). March–April 1955.

Lennie Niehaus said (1993): **'I wanted the strings to be part of the linear approach, not just an accompaniment, so I had to get them to play eighth notes in a particular way, so that it swung and the saxophone could play over the top of a "section".'**

Niehaus is certainly best known now for his soundtrack work for close friend Clint Eastwood. He provided music for *Play Misty for Me* and for *Bird* and has remained a close collaborator of the actor/director. The association doesn't seem to have made Niehaus any more visible as a recording leader and the body of recording that goes back to the '50s. The smooth West Coast veneer – a sound some consider reminiscent of Lee Konitz – belies a substantial portfolio of imaginative compositions and standards arrangements. He worked with Kenton before and after a period in the services, and though much of his recorded work is in the rather anonymous context of Stan's reed sections, his own most distinctive work has tended to be for mid-size bands. He made innovative use of voicings in such a way as to make three saxophones sound like a larger section but without the weight that would involve. His quintets and octets were full of innovative ideas, many of them the result of study with the émigré composer Ernst Krenek, who brought Second Viennese ideas to the US and was perhaps more directly influential in America even than Schoenberg.

The strings album for Contemporary was a logical follow-up and it is one of his best recordings of any period. Miraculously, the string-players – just three viola-players and a cellist, no violins – follow their parts without any hint of the stiffness classical players sometimes evince. Nor does Niehaus use them for slower material only. They are asked to negotiate some fairly difficult terrain. The only slight reservation is that so much of the material is generic, with not enough of Niehaus's own writing. Seven of the 12 tracks are standards, but a fine opening 'All The Things You Are' does at least establish the methodology of the group. 'Crosswalk' and 'Full House' are both outstanding ideas and the horns move dexterously over the charts and the other three winds all solo effectively. It's the strings' day, however. This isn't the kind of music one can readily imagine Dirty Harry listening to, but it's smart, cool, effective jazz.

SARAH VAUGHAN &
Born 27 March 1924, Newark, New Jersey; died 3 April 1990, Los Angeles, California
Voice

Sarah Vaughan
Verve 543305-2
Vaughan; Clifford Brown (t); Paul Quinichette (ts); Herbie Mann (f); Jimmy Jones (p); Joe Benjamin (b); Roy Haynes (d). December 1954.

Sarah Vaughan said (1980): **'I never planned to be in show business. I went in for the amateur hour at the Apollo because I wanted the $10, and I forgot that a week at the theatre went with the first prize. So it was kind of landed on me, this career!'**

One of the very great jazz voices, and one who managed to combine emotion and musicality in a balance denied to other of the great divas. Vaughan studied piano as a child, then joined the Earl Hines band in 1943 as vocalist. She left with Billy Eckstine to sing in his new band and went solo in the late '40s. Had many crossover hits during that decade but was always seen as a jazz vocalist, one of the most gifted, with a big range and variety of tone, a bop-per's way with scat – though she rarely used it – and the stage presence of a forbidding diva. Unaccountably, though, she never was as popular as Holiday or Fitzgerald.

Her vocal on the 1946 Dizzy Gillespie Sextet record of 'Lover Man' was Sarah Vaughan's banner arrival. Yet she'd already cut several fine sides – four with a Dizzy Gillespie small group, including a fine vocal version of 'Night In Tunisia' – and there were several other scattered appearances, but it wasn't until she hooked up with Norman Granz's label that she began to make quality records with any consistency. The session with Clifford Brown was a glorious occasion, and the kind of date that occurred far too infrequently during the rest of Sarah's career. A blue-chip band (even Mann doesn't disgrace himself) on a slow-burning set of standards that Vaughan lingers over and details with all the finesse of her early-mature voice: 'Lullaby Of Birdland' (the master take is a composite, and there is a 'partial alternative' take here too) is taken at a pace that suspends time or lets it drift, and the very slow pace for 'Embraceable You' and 'Jim' doesn't falter into a trudge. In the past we have wondered if the many slow tempos were perhaps too many, but in this superb new remastering it is very difficult to find any flaw in what should be recognized as one of the great jazz vocal records.

& *See also* **Crazy And Mixed Up** (1982; p. 468)

BARNEY KESSEL
Born 17 October 1923, Muskogee, Oklahoma; died 6 May 2004, San Diego, California
Guitar

To Swing Or Not To Swing
Original Jazz Classics OJC 317
Kessel; Harry 'Sweets' Edison (t); Georgie Auld, Bill Perkins (ts); Jimmy Rowles (p); Al Hendrickson (g); Red Mitchell (b); Irv Cottler (d). June 1955.

Barney Kessel said (1990): **'Back where I come from, they used to call guitars "starvation boxes". We'd have these hobos and itinerant preachers, playing old songs and hymns on them. I don't think that ever left me, and it maybe explains why I had trouble at first playing bebop lines. "Play like a horn", they'd say, but I was drawn back to that old sound.'**

'The blues he heard as a boy in Oklahoma, the swing he learned on his first band job and the modern sounds of the West Coast school': Nesuhi Ertegun's summary of Kessel, written in 1954, still holds good. Kessel has often been undervalued as a soloist: the smoothness and accuracy of his playing tend to disguise the underlying weight of the blues which informs his improvising, and his albums from the '50s endure with surprising consistency. This one for Contemporary is the most durable of all. The music suggests a firm truce between Basie-like small-band swing and the classic West Coast appraisal of bop. The inclusion of such ancient themes as 'Louisiana', 'Twelfth Street Rag' and 'Indiana' suggests the breadth of Kessel's interests, and although most of the tracks are short, nothing seems particularly rushed and the guitarist's features are often movingly personal, as if he really is stepping forward into the firelight for a turn. Lester Koenig's superb production has been faithfully maintained for the reissue and the sound flatters everyone. Interesting to hear the rest of the band adjust their delivery to suit what would have been an unfamiliar approach at the time. One craves to hear Kessel and Mitchell in duo for a couple of spots, but it's good enough as is.

HAMPTON HAWES

Born 13 November 1928, Los Angeles, California; died 22 May 1977, Los Angeles, California
Piano

The Trios: Volumes 1 & 2
Original Jazz Classics OJCCD 316
Hawes; Red Mitchell (b); Chuck Thompson (d). June & December 1955, January 1956.

Teddy Edwards said (1991): **'Some people play the blues and talk about the "jazz life". He lived them both. I never knew what he was going to do behind me, but I always knew he'd be waiting for me when I got to the end.'**

Hawes is still something of a coterie taste. Given the sheer exhilaration and lyrical intensity of his music, even given the remarkable story told in his classic autobiography, *Raise Up Off Me*, it is surprising that he is not better known. Hawes worked with Charlie Parker and learned from him, not always to his advantage. His approach to bop always seemed to imply something beyond, and while he was never any kind of avant-gardist, he knew that anything new in jazz was always rooted in something older, so even his most straightforward blues playing always implied a step away into the unknown. His performances are mostly sunlit, remarkably so in view of the life he led, but with thunderclouds on the horizon.

These were Hawes's first serious statements as leader and they are still hugely impressive, combining long, demanding passages of locked chording and fast, unpredictable melody-lines. The bebop idiom is still firmly in place, but already Hawes is demonstrating an ability to construct elaborate out-of-tempo solo statements which seem detached from the theme while still drawn entirely from its chord structure. Mitchell is a wonderful accompanist, already experimenting with his trademark tuning and getting a huge sound out of the bass. Thompson is a resolute and often sophisticated partner. Most of the pieces are familiar bop staples, but Hawes's blues lines on the first volume are by far the most interesting pieces, skeletal in structure but elaborated with a sure hand. The material on *Volume 2* is more varied in tonality and the dynamics are more dramatic, but it's Hawes's reading of

'Easy Living' that most completely confirms his originality. He easily becomes a collector's obsession, and anyone who enjoys this will also be drawn to *Four!*, *All Night Session* and *Everybody Likes Hampton Hawes*.

CHICO HAMILTON &

Born Foreststorn Hamilton, 21 September 1921, Los Angeles, California
Drums

Live At The Strollers
Fresh Sound FSRCD 2245
Hamilton; Buddy Collette (cl, as, ts, f); Jim Hall (g); Fred Katz (clo); Carson Smith (b). August & November 1955.

Chico Hamilton said (1982): **'I play a pretty small kit. Even my bass drum is a floor tom flipped over on its side. And I like to have everything low down. It's less tiring and I can get a softer, more exact sound. I don't want to be waving my arms in the air.'**

A less celebrated drum-led academy than Art Blakey's, and yet Hamilton has always surrounded himself with gifted young musicians of the quality of Eric Dolphy, Gerry Mulligan, Larry Coryell, Charles Lloyd and later Eric Person, and not forgetting Paul Horn. A perfectly convincing version of the origin of Gerry Mulligan's pianoless quartet was that it began in Hamilton's apartment, where there was no piano. Hamilton has unfailingly taken an inventive and even idiosyncratic approach to the constitution of his groups, and often the only identifying mark is his own rolling lyricism and unceasing swing. Anyone who has seen the classic festival movie *Jazz On A Summer's Day* will remember the almost hypnotic concentration of his mallet solo.

Recent years have seen early work slip out of copyright and, with predictable perversity, back into circulation. Mild as the early trios sound now, this was fairly unusual work at the time, with the drummer so foregrounded. A broadcast Strollers date from Long Beach helped bring the subsequent quintet to notice. An over-emphasis on later discs is explained by the presence of Dolphy, just emerging as a soloist and composer, but the earlier group with Collette (and the undervalued Hall) is just as good and Collette's multi-instrumentalism brings a polish and variety to the tracks that even Eric couldn't manage at this stage. The distinctive use of cello (later it was Nate Gershman) helps organize the sound round a warm middle register, and there is very little stratospheric playing. It's a mixed disc of standards – including a lovely 'Tea For Two' – a few Collette originals, including 'Fast Flute', which is co-credited to the leader, and a free improvisation, which opens up the group language in ways that would become more important later. Others will favour *Gongs East/ Three Faces of Chico* or some other record from this period, but this decently recorded live date is the most accurate glimpse of the band at its most spontaneously creative, steered but not overmastered by Chico.

& *See also* **Arroyo** (1990; p. 544)

ERROLL GARNER &

Born 15 June 1921, Pittsburgh, Pennsylvania; died 7 January 1977, Los Angeles, California
Piano

Concert By The Sea
Columbia CK 40589
Garner; Eddie Calhoun (b); Denzil Best (d). September 1955.

Pianist and Garner scholar Dudley Moore said: **'Poor old Eddie Calhoun got white hair and worry-lines from all that time staring at Erroll's left hand wondering what the **** he was going to do next!'**

Garner's most famous album is one of the biggest-selling jazz records ever made. *Concert By The Sea* doesn't advertise anything particularly special. It's just a characteristic set by the trio in an amenable setting. It is full of typical Garner moments like the teasing introduction to 'I'll Remember April' – Garner liked to keep audiences in suspense while he toyed with when to announce the melody – or the flippant blues of 'Red Top' and the pell-mell 'Where Or When'. These find Garner at his most buoyant; but rather more interesting is his well-shaped treatment of 'How Could You Do A Thing Like That To Me'. The recording was never outstanding, though the reissue serves it well enough, and its celebrity is still somewhat surprising, though Garner's isn't a body of work, any of it, that is distinguished by pristine hi-fi.

& *See also* **Erroll Garner 1944–1945** (1944–1945; p. 94)

JOE NEWMAN

Born 7 September 1922, New Orleans, Louisiana; died 4 July 1992, New York City
Trumpet

The Count's Men

Fresh Sound FSRCD 135
Newman; Benny Powell (tb); Frank Foster (ts); Frank Wess (f, ts); Sir Charles Thompson (p); Eddie Jones (b); Shadow Wilson (d). September 1955.

Joe Newman said (1983): **'My dad played piano in New Orleans during the Depression, so I kind of associated music with work and need, even though he worked as a driver, too. I wanted to play tenor saxophone and even made myself an instrument out of a piece of gas pipe. Got a tune from it it, too!'**

A deep-thinking musician with a reflective sound and a passion for jazz education. Newman was the Johnny Hodges of the Basie band. He also had stints with Illinois Jacquet and with Benny Goodman and continued to record under his own name until quite late in life. Newman was never a whole-hearted modernist. His sharp attack and bright sound were derived almost entirely from Louis Armstrong and, though he was chief among the cadre of the 'Basie Moderns' in the '50s, he maintained allegiance to the Count's music over any other. His preference for the middle register meant he was never an excessively dramatic soloist.

The Basie-derived group on *The Count's Men* share his values entirely and clearly relish the opportunity to record away from the Boss. 'A.M. Romp' reappeared later on *Good'n'Groovy*, and as always with Newman it's interesting to compare his different versions of a song. It's the tighter version with Sir Charles Thompson that really impresses, and newcomers to Newman's entertaining sound would do well to begin with the mid-'50s stuff. He was eminently responsive to context, even softening his trumpet tone markedly when the surroundings seemed to call for it. Perhaps his most ambitious work is on the octet *I'm Still Swinging*, but any glimpse of Joe in a small-group setting is worthwhile and rewarding.

RUBY BRAFF&

Born 16 March 1927, Boston, Massachusetts; died 9 February 2003, Chatham, Massachusetts
Cornet

2 × 2: Ruby Braff And Ellis Larkins Play Rodgers And Hart
Vanguard 8507
Braff; Ellis Larkins (p). October 1955.

Ruby Braff had interviewers with his morning beigel: **'Well, Ruby ...'** 'That's *Mr Braff* to
you ...'

Arguably ... no, in fact definitely ... one of the great cornet soloists ever, Reuben – hence
Ruby – Braff left Boston at the start of the '50s and began to record with Vic Dickenson and
Urbie Green, among others. A powerful, distinctive player with an outsize and often abrasive personality – some referred unkindly to his Mr Hyde-and-Mr Hyde temperament – he
was as capable of aching lyricism and a strangely elegiac quality as he was of the faster,
pungent stuff that came out of Dixieland. In fact, Braff is very difficult to position stylistically. There are moments of pure Armstrong or Red Allen, but there are also hints early on
of unorthodox harmony and an off-centre phrasing that anticipates the modern movement.
Even so, he was considered old-fashioned for many years and suffered a long mid-career
eclipse.

Braff's early material is scattered over a variety of reissue compilations, many of which,
like Black Lion's *Hustlin' And Bustlin'*, offer a nice impression of him in company with Dickenson and with a regular quintet co-fronted by Samuel Margolis (over whom posterity has
drawn a veil) and Ken Kersey. This one, though, is a masterpiece, played by a dream ticket of
such durability that Braff and Larkins got together in 1972 and 1994 to do it again, switching attention to another American great on *Calling Berlin* (meaning the composer not the
city!).

This is the Armstrong–Hines instrumentation, just about, and it immediately brings
into focus Ruby's Janus-faced approach. At some formal level, this is orthodox mainstream
swing, impeccably played, but listen to the playing on 'Mountain Greenery' (it's from *The
Garrick Gaieties*, 1926!) and it's clear that even this early Braff is leaning towards a more
modern conception in which the orthodox changes are subordinated to something more
impressionistic where specific note choices answer the needs of the solo rather than the
harmony. Larkins was the consummate accompanist and knew more about these songs
than almost anyone living. Ruby is in full voice, pungent and lyrical on 'My Funny Valentine', 'I Could Write A Book' (compare with Miles Davis's floating filigree), and the less well-
known 'Where Or When' and 'I Married An Angel'. The sound is up close and very faithful
to both instruments. Flawless jazz.

& *See also* **Being With You** (1996; p. 600)

RED CALLENDER

Born George Sylvester, 6 March 1916, Haynesville, Virginia; died 8 March 1992, Saugus, California
Double bass, tuba

Swingin' Suite
Fresh Sound FSRCD 458
Callender; Harry 'Parr' Jones, Gerald Wilson (t); John Ewing (tb); William Green, Hymie Gunkler (as); Buddy
Collette (f, ts); Clyde Dunn, Marty Berman (bs); Eddie Beal, Gerald Wiggins (p); Bill Pitman, Billy Bean (g); Bill
Douglass (d); Frank Bodde (perc). November 1955, April & May 1958.

Red Callender said (1987): **'You know that feeling where you wake up from a dream and can remember something of it but not how it ends? That's what the jazz life is like: remembering some, but trying to provide a happy end to the dream.'**

A first-call player on the West Coast scene, with an experimental streak underneath the reliability, Callender was one of the first modern players to use tuba as well as string bass, and to create meaningful solos on both of them. He had a busy career, featuring on scores of West Coast sessions, but was determined enough to pursue his own musical language as well.

Callender's octets were palpably influenced by Duke Ellington's ensemble writing and distribution of solo space. Apart from Collette, who is excellent throughout these sides, the groups are largely anonymous, but these were professional players who were able to deliver Collette's ideas with a modicum of swing. The 12 cuts from November 1955 are all Callender originals, mostly quite dry ideas, though 'Dancers' and 'Sleigh Ride' are more bracing (the latter managing to avoid most clichés associated with sleigh-ride music). There follow three further octets, with Gerald Wilson on trumpet and Collette on tenor only; he's back on flute for the sextet and quartet tracks (the former again with Wilson) from April and May 1958. It's scarcely sparkling music, but one senses bands that are fit-for-purpose and quietly adventurous. Red wrote a fine autobiography, called *Unfinished Dream*, that adds context and detail to his prolific but inevitably quite anonymous career.

LAMBERT, HENDRICKS & ROSS &
Formed 1957
Group

Sing A Song Of Basie
Verve 543827-2
Lambert, Hendricks, Ross; Nat Pierce (p); Freddie Green (g); Eddie Jones (b); Sonny Payne (d). 1955.

Yolande Bavan replaced Annie Ross in the group in 1962: **'When I say they were generous, they were musically generous as well as humanly kind. That music was so intricate it might have been cold, but Jon and Dave invested difficult music, for singers anyway, with real warmth.'**

Vocalese – the art of putting words to jazz instrumental solos – enjoyed a brief vogue in the '50s. It may have begun with the Mills Brothers and their clever vocal mimicry of horns but it developed along very different lines when Eddie Jefferson and then King Pleasure and Annie Ross began to fit words to famous jazz solos. Ross's virtuoso interpretation of Wardell Gray's 'Twisted' was a huge hit. Perhaps the finest exponent, though, was Jon Hendricks, who had an unfailing facility for glib rhymes and for words to fit instrumental effects.

The Basie record is in a sense atypical. For a start, one associates the group with bebop rather than the swing masters, but it was a smart place to begin. Their intention had been to re-create the Basie band with a large vocal ensemble but, when the studio singers proved inadequate, the trio ended up singing all the lines themselves via overdubbing, and the set became a kind of novelty hit. Hendricks's lyrics are often a hoot, and the record set a precedent for a style which many have followed, few bettered. It doesn't have 'Twisted', but that can be picked up on a compilation. This is a dazzling artefact, novelty or no, and it stands the test of time.

& *See also* **JON HENDRICKS, A Good Git-Together** (1959; p. 246)

FRANK MORGAN &

Born 23 December 1933, Minneapolis, Minnesota; died 14 December 2007, Minneapolis, Minnesota
Alto saxophone

Gene Norman Presents Frank Morgan
Fresh Sound FSR CD 71
Morgan; Conte Candoli (t); Wardell Gray (ts); Carl Perkins (p); Wild Bill Davis (org); Howard Roberts (g); Bobby Rodriguez, Leroy Vinnegar (b); José Mangual, Lawrence Marable (d); Ralph Miranda, Uba Nieto (perc). 1955.

Frank Morgan said (1990): **'Musicians became addicted because it was a badge proclaiming you as hip. There wasn't one user didn't know it was unhealthy, but your health was less important than your reputation on the scene.'**

Frank Morgan's story is not just about paid dues. Shortly after this record was made he was sentenced to a term in San Quentin for drugs offences. He maintained his involvement in music while in jail, jamming with the likes of Art Pepper. Though he had worked locally following his release, he reappeared on a wider stage in the mid-'80s, purveying a brand of chastened bop, his initially bright and Bird-feathered style only slightly dulled by a spell in the cage.

The son of Ink Spots guitarist Stanley Morgan, he began his career on the West Coast bebop scene, one of a group of saxophonists who hung on Charlie Parker's coat-tails, in both stylistic and personal terms. Morgan was a highly organized soloist, each statement having a songlike consistency of tone and direction but he was also an addict. The Savoy *Bird Calls* isn't the best place to pick up on what Morgan was doing at the time, partly because the material is relatively unfamiliar and partly because the dominant figure on the session is Milt Jackson, who is already thinking in new directions.

The GNP material on this Fresh Sound CD is a much better place to begin, though the septet tracks with Wild Bill Davis and three Latin percussionists are a touch crude; 'I'll Remember April' succumbs almost completely. Wardell Gray, on his last recordings before his violent death, lends an easy swing to 'My Old Flame', 'The Nearness Of You' and four other tracks, and Carl Perkins's bouncy clatter at the piano keeps the textures attractively ruffled. Morgan would be away from the music business for a long time. What might have been is all too obvious in these early dates.

& *See also* **Reflections** (1988; p. 514)

CARL PERKINS

Born 16 August 1928, Indianapolis, Indiana; died 17 March 1958, Los Angeles, California
Piano

Introducing
Boplicity 8
Perkins; Leroy Vinnegar (b); Lawrence Marable (d). 1955.

Leroy Vinnegar said (1983): **'Disability? I didn't hear any disability when he sat down at the piano. He had his own thing going, but he played as good as anyone around at the time and it was a crying shame he passed so young.'**

Despite a left hand crippled by polio, Perkins developed an individual style that involved a curious crabwise articulation. The disability wasn't the only problem he suffered in his short life, though his drug use might in part be explained by his physical infirmity. The

Introducing sides are mostly brief and punchy, driven along by Perkins's indefinably odd left-hand chords (which make sense once you've seen a photograph of him at the keyboard). The originals 'Carl's Blues' and 'West Side' (aka 'Mia') – there is an alternate take of the latter on the CD – are pretty generic, but there's energy in the playing and Perkins was an interesting original. Issued on Dootone, this material is also usually available on Fresh Sound.

CLIFFORD BROWN &

Born 30 October 1930, Wilmington, Delaware; died 26 October 1956, Pennsylvania Turnpike, west of Bedford
Trumpet

Alone Together
Verve 526373-2
Brown; Harold Land, Hank Mobley, Paul Quinichette, Sonny Rollins (ts); Danny Bank (bs); Herbie Mann (f); Ray Bryant, Jimmy Jones, Richie Powell (p); Barry Galbraith (g); Joe Benjamin, Milt Hinton, George Morrow (b); Roy Haynes, Osie Johnson, Max Roach (d); Helen Merrill, Sarah Vaughan (v); strings. August 1954–January 1956.

Helen Merrill said (1992): **'It's supposed to be a compliment to a singer to say she sounds like she's playing a horn. I'd say that Clifford Brown always sounded like he was singing a song. He played with real *understanding*, not just the notes, as if he felt what was happening, moment to moment.'**

All the material Brown recorded for Emarcy between 2 August 1954 and 16 February 1956 was included on a ten-CD box which sometimes turns up. Inevitably, the best of the music is in the Roach–Brown sessions. The drummer's generosity in making the younger man co-leader is instantly and awesomely repaid. The group sound on Bud Powell's 'Parisian Thoroughfare' (Richie Powell would perish with Brownie in the fatal accident) and the other August cuts is coach-built and graceful, and Brown's solo statements are crafted with such intuitive skill that they are almost beyond analysis. As an accompanist to a singer, Brown was so refined that one almost wants to hear what Miles Davis might have done in the same situation, just for comparison. Brownie was lucky with his colleagues during his short career. Merrill is exactly the kind of songful, mature singer who would highlight his voice most effectively and, in the same way, Roach's leadership and personal authority gave him a solid foundation. The wrench of Brown's departure is still felt in the music. Many jazz lives were cut short, and many of them at a moment when high promise looked ready to be delivered. The difference with Clifford Brown is that he was already nearing his peak as a performer and looked ready to make a fresh transition. Where that might have taken him is impossible to say, but it seems certain that it would have changed the shape of modern jazz.

& *See also* **Memorial Album** (1953; p. 142)

THE '50s:
1956–1960

Charlie Parker died in New York City on 12 March 1955. Despite the 'Bird lives!' graffiti that began to appear round town, it was widely understood that an era had ended, and for many conservative observers 1955 marks a distinct end-point in jazz history, after which there is nothing but muddle and hysterical noise. Some radicals share the view, though for different reasons. At Parker's post-mortem examination, a doctor mistook a 34-year-old man for 60, so heavy a toll had drugs, alcohol and overeating taken on Parker's body. Unlike Peter Pan, who was currently wowing audiences on Broadway, Parker had grown up or grown old too fast, and there was a sense that something similar had happened to jazz as well, outrunning its own technical resources and the ability or willingness of its audience to keep up.

The reality is that from the mid-'50s, and encouraged by the ability to buy exactly the kind of music one liked on long-playing records, there was no longer a jazz audience, but jazz audiences. There had always been local music scenes, often with quite distinct styles, spread right across the United States and even in redoubts of what was insultingly called 'hillbilly music' like Memphis, but increasingly New York (particularly) and Chicago exerted an enormous gravitational pull. Most of the major recording labels were based there. The downtown club scene was immeasurably larger than any other in the country. The other important media were based there.

As musicians gravitated to the city, jazz recording devolved into niches, catering for modernists, cool-school aficionados, swing loyalists, 'Dixieland' revivalists, fans of jazz singing and other smaller indulgences. The rapid spread of microgroove recordings on sleek, otter-smooth polyvinyl chloride discs, presented in handsome illustrated covers, made record albums objects of desire in themselves. Now durable enough to be carried around without risk of breakage, albums became badges of cultural positioning on campus and on the club scene: rolled newspaper, green carnation, Masonic handshake, *carte de visite* and *passe-partout*. Simply carrying the right album became a badge of status.

The image of the jazz musician was also solidifying, often ambiguously so. In 1938, Dorothy Baker had published *Young Man with a Horn*, a jazz novel loosely based on the self-destructive life of Bix Beiderbecke. It was filmed in 1950, with Harry James dubbing Kirk Douglas's horn-'playing', but became more controversial for a lesbian subplot than for its jazz content. However, the title alone became an iconic phrase, an image of the improvising musician as part angel, part devil, constantly ranged against the forces of darkness but also capable of bringing a dark vision to experience, violent and self-harming by turns, but stoutly in opposition to any given aspect of mainstream culture: black rather than white, 'entrepreneurially violent' (as Norman Mailer put it in his controversial *Dissent* essay 'The White Negro'), but a resister, differently uniformed, rejecting each and all aspects of the new commercial culture, including the new pop music. Jazz and pop would only join hands again uneasily in the '70s and '90s.

What did happen in the later '50s, though, was that jazz became the music of second resort for many music fans. Classical music listeners would soon be smuggling copies of *Sketches Of Spain* and *Kind Of Blue*, or displaying Chet Baker's cheekbones on their coffee tables. There was a loose alliance between the young, civil-rights inspired folk fans and traditional jazz players. Like it or not, this was made possible by an industry that was putting out a vast amount of musical 'product'. Even oppositional tastes put money in corporate wallets.

Novelist John Clellon Holmes had coined the 'Beat Generation' label in a November 1952 issue of the *New York Times Magazine*, published shortly after the appearance of his novel *Go*, a thinly dramatized *roman à clef* in which Holmes appears as Paul Hobbes (a significant choice of name given the Leviathan of the military-industrial complex that haunted them all) and Jack Kerouac as Gene Pasternak. The image the novel created of lives lived on the edge, socially precarious, personally abusive, but always in the interests of personal freedom and creativity, had a great impact, on which Kerouac's *On the Road*, written in 1951 but only published in 1957, built significantly. Holmes followed up the following year with *The Horn*, the story of a broken-down jazz musician's final days and the lives of the people – friends, fellow players, ex-lovers – who try to find him. It is loosely based on Charlie Parker's demise, though Parker was comfortable in a European aristocrat's apartment in his last days, not trailing the streets, spitting blood. There are ironies everywhere in the status and bearing of jazz at this period, but the new jazz warriors knew that the LP was their most potent icon, and the late '50s was a period of unparalleled musical production, hardly equalled since.

HELEN MERRILL &

Born Jelena Ana Milcetic, 21 July 1930, New York City
Voice

Helen Merrill With Clifford Brown And Gil Evans
Emarcy 838292-2
Merrill; Clifford Brown, Art Farmer, Louis Mucci (t); Jimmy Cleveland, Joe Bennett (tb); John LaPorta (cl, as); Jerome Richardson (as, ts, f); Danny Bank (f); Hank Jones, Jimmy Jones (p); Barry Galbraith (g); Oscar Pettiford, Milt Hinton (b); Joe Morello, Osie Johnson, Bobby Donaldson (d); strings, horns. December 1954–June 1956.

Helen Merrill said (1992): '**Musicians like to work with me because I built my style round the sound of instruments, not other singers. I was comfortable in just about any key and they didn't have to think about what used to be called a "girl's range".**'

Helen Merrill has never made a bad record, and while she scarcely conforms to the image of a swinging jazz singer, she's a stylist of unique poise and sensitivity. Her early work is as involving as her mature records. She worked with most of the early boppers, but also with Earl Hines, and began recording around 1954. She lived in Italy for some years, later in Japan, and returned to Chicago and New York in the '70s. A Verve contract restored her eminence in the '80s and '90s.

She sings at a consistently slow pace, unfolding melodies as if imparting a particularly difficult confidence, and she understands the harmonies of the songs as completely as she trusts her way with time. Consider what she does here on 'Falling In Love With Love'. The song comes out on the side of an agenda quite different from the usual, while 'Don't Explain' has an edge that falls between sardonic and weary. It is her unfailing sense of time, though, that gives these lingering performances a sensuality which is less of a come-hither come-on than the similarly inclined work of a singer such as Julie London. Merrill thinks about the words, but she improvises on the music too. Her treatment of 'Don't Explain' is cooler yet no less troubling than Billie Holiday's exaggerated pathos, and 'What's New' is a masterpiece. Brown's accompaniments on seven tracks make an absorbing contrast to his work with Sarah Vaughan, and Evans's arrangements on the other eight songs are some of his most lucid work in this area.

PEE WEE ERWIN

Born George Erwin, 30 May 1913, Falls City, Nebraska; died 20 June 1981, Teaneck, New Jersey
Trumpet

Complete Fifties Recordings

Lone Hill Jazz LHJ 10122
Erwin; Andy Russo (tb); Sal Pace (cl); Billy Maxted (p); Charlie Treagar (b); Tony Spargo (d). 1955–1956.

Cornetist Warren Vaché said (1982): **'He was the most generous guy in the world. I've said sometimes that he was the glue that kept me together, and that was the kind of man he was. It wouldn't have mattered who he was playing with, or teaching, he was yours for the duration.'**

Pee Wee was playing on American radio when still a boy. He worked with Benny Goodman and Ray Noble, and helped Glenn Miller create his celebrated sound. He did extensive studio work in the '40s, then gigged at Nick's through the '50s. Erwin's poise as a trumpeter is akin to Hackett's, but he was a hotter player, with more to say for himself. There's not a lot of stuff on CD; for some reason, Pee Wee doesn't seem to strike a chord nowadays. The Lone Hill jazz release brings together Erwin's two sextet albums *Accent On Dixieland* and the live *At Grandview Inn*. The players might be second-string Dixielanders, and some of the material is hoary, but the music sustains a high standard: Pace is a lusty clarinet man, Maxted is neat and tidy, and Erwin himself peels off one exemplary solo after another.

In later years, he co-owned a music store in Teaneck, New Jersey, where he befriended young mainstreamers (like Warren Vaché) and played as he pleased.

JO JONES

Known as 'Papa' and 'Chicago'; born 7 October 1911, Chicago, Illinois; died 3 September 1985, New York City
Drums

The Essential Jo Jones

Vanguard 101/2
Jones; Emmett Berry (t); Lawrence Brown, Freddie Green (tb); Lucky Thompson (ts); Rudy Powell (cl); Count Basie, Ray Bryant, Nat Pierce (p); Tommy Bryant, Walter Page (b). August 1955–April 1958.

Cornetist Ruby Braff remembered playing with Jo Jones (1983): **'He'd never say: "Let's play ... whatever." He'd just start and you'd be expected to pick it up. I'd scratch around for something that approximately fitted the beat and he'd always grin and nod as if to say: "You got it! That's *exactly* the tune I meant!" He was nuts to work with.'**

He's probably now less well known to younger fans than either Elvin Jones or Philly Joe Jones, neither of them related, though Philly Joe's name was adopted by musicians to distinguish him from Chicago. None the less, Papa was one of the most influential percussionists in the history of the music, changing the sound of the drums by switching emphasis from the bass drum to the hi-hat.

Jones was the subtle driving force of the Basie band between 1934 and 1948 and the Count repaid the compliment with a guest spot on Jo's solo disc, giving 'Shoe Shine Boy' a touch of the old magic. The other participants are familiar enough as well, with Berry, Green and Thompson all prominent. Inevitably, a lot of emphasis falls on the drums, but Jones is such a nimble, light player that he is always estimably listenable. The 1958 session with Ray and Tommy Bryant (originally an album called *Plus Two*) is mostly the pianist's work, but Jo revels in those bluesy themes and produces some of his best small-group work on record, always precise but loose-wristed and supple and capable of hair's-breadth turns in awkward spots. An essential record for anyone interested in the evolution of jazz drumming.

COLEMAN HAWKINS &

Known as 'Bean'; born 21 November 1904, St Joseph, Missouri; died 19 May 1969, New York City
Tenor saxophone

The Stanley Dance Sessions
Lone Hill Jazz LHJ 10189
Hawkins; Buck Clayton, Roy Eldridge (t); Hank Jones (p); Ray Brown, George Duvivier, Wendell Marshall (b); Mickey Sheen, Shadow Wilson (d). November 1955–February 1958.

Bassist Ray Brown said (1994): **'It was a little bit like being in the studio with Moses. You found yourself listening to Bean, as if any minute he was going to deliver something grand and mysterious. And the thing was, he was doing that all the time; it just didn't seem dramatic at the time.'**

Hawkins sailed through the bebop years like an eagle who manages to sail above the smaller falcons, now barely moving his wings, held aloft by a monumental authority. The first six tracks here constitute one of the classic Hawkins LPs, *The High And Mighty Hawk*, once issued on Felsted. Hawkins and Clayton front a swinging quintet and they open with a monumental blues performance, 'Bird Of Prey Blues', that runs for 11 gripping minutes. Lone Hill have chosen to fill up the CD with four tracks cut a few days earlier, with Eldridge (terrific on 'Honey Flower') replacing Clayton, as well as two incongruous inclusions from a 1955 New York concert where the tenorman blows a minute or so of a cappella sax before a fine 'The Man I Love'. Bits and pieces, but hard to beat as a representation of Hawk in his best latter-day form.

& *See also* **Coleman Hawkins 1929–1934** (1929–1934; p. 38), **Coleman Hawkins 1939–1940** (1939–1940; p. 74)

CURTIS COUNCE

Born 23 January 1926, Kansas City, Missouri; died 31 July 1963, Los Angeles, California
Double bass

The Complete Studio Recordings: The Master Takes
Gambit 69258 2CD
Counce; Jack Sheldon, Gerald Wilson (t); Harold Land (ts); Carl Perkins (p); Frank Butler (d). October 1956–January 1958.

Drummer Frank Butler said (1979): **'I don't know why that group wasn't noticed. Maybe it didn't fit at the time, or maybe it wasn't "West Coast" enough. Curtis swung pretty hard. He could have gone toe-to-toe with any of the New York guys.'**

Counce's late-'50s quintet was one of the more resilient bands working on the West Coast at the time. It was also one of the most influential, though seldom remarked today. This Gambit set pretty much rounds up the whole discography, though as is often the way with these exercises in out-of-copyright completism, the term turns out to be somewhat relative, for the set doesn't include any of the material on *Exploring The Future*, which was made for Dootone. Instead, it brings together three LPs, *You Get More Bounce With Curtis Counce*, *Landslide* and *Carl's Blues*, together with some other bits and pieces released later as *Sonority*. As the titles make clear, Counce liked to namecheck his solo stars, and that self-effacing quality may have contributed to his own eclipse. His own strongest moments as soloist come on 'A Night In Tunisia' and 'How Long Has This Been Going On?' from the grab-bag *Sonority*.

Landslide was a fine record, showcasing Land's beefy tenor – the title-track is a notably dark and un-Californian slice of hard bop – and Sheldon's very underrated, Dizzy-inspired playing. Perkins, remembered best for his strange, crab-wise technique, was probably on better form with this band than anywhere else on record, but the real star – acknowledged on 'The Butler Did It' from *Carl's Blues* and 'A Drum Conversation' from *Sonority* – is the percussionist, who shared Counce's instinctive swing. He is also the dedicatee of 'A Fifth For Frank' (the harmonic interval? a bottle of hooch?) on *Landslide*.

The tracks are relatively long by the standards then and there is some highly developed writing and improvising on many of the tracks, which have a decidedly modern air to them. Counce's reputation has been undergoing a small revival recently. It's worth making his acquaintance.

J. R. MONTEROSE

Born Frank Anthony Peter Vincent Monterose Jr, 19 January 1927, Detroit, Michigan; died 16 September 1993, Utica, New York
Tenor and soprano saxophones

J. R. Monterose
Blue Note 15387
Monterose; Ira Sullivan (t); Horace Silver (p); Wilbur Ware (b); Philly Joe Jones (d). October 1956.

J. R. Monterose said (1980): **'I was obsessed with having my own voice. If someone else had made a sound, I didn't want to make that sound. It led me into some strange places, and perhaps into obscurity, whatever that means. But it pleases me when anyone says I don't sound like Trane or Rollins or Dexter Gordon. That was the idea.'**

J.R. – as in 'Junior' – fell into none of the familiar tenor-playing niches and so fell out of jazz history, as he seemed to prefer. If there was a single strong influence, it was probably John Coltrane; but Monterose was anything but a slavish Trane copyist and forged his own odd but inimitable style: a slightly tight, almost strangled tone, delivered before and behind the beat, often in successive measures, thin but curiously intense and highly focused. He was also a rare exponent of electric sax, though Coltrane dabbled there, too.

Monterose's solo Blue Note record boasts an enviable personnel, and a relatively unusual one. In future years, Monterose was to work with obscure rhythm sections, mostly in out of the way places, but here the label's collegial approach delivers him a powerful rhythm section – one of Ware's best showings of the period – and a strong front-line partner in Sullivan (who admittedly isn't much associated with Alfred Lion's label). The music is mostly in a sophisticated hard-bop vein. Two versions of 'Wee-Jay' give a measure of how tightly Monterose conceived and executed his music. He doesn't sound like anyone else on this. Silver plays on insouciantly but makes it work, and Sullivan, who's perhaps no clearer what's going on some of the time, contents himself with tight, well thought-out solo statements that don't go on too long. It's an unusual set, though it isn't always easy to put a finger on why, and it stands tall with Blue Note's other progressive recordings of the day.

MEL TORMÉ

Born 13 September 1925, Chicago, Illinois; died 5 June 1999, Los Angeles, California
Voice

Sings Fred Astaire
Rhino 79847
Tormé; Pete Candoli (t); Bob Enevoldson (vtb); Vincent de Rosa (frhn); Albert Pollan (tba); Herb Geller (as); Jack Montrose (ts); Jack DuLong (bs); Marty Paich (p); Max Bennett (b); Alvin Stoller (d). November 1956.

Singer Eric Felten says: **'It's the Rosetta Stone of Tormé's singing. As agile and virtuosic a vocalist as he was, it was Astaire whose singing he most admired. Fred didn't have the facility with his voice that he did with his feet, but in introducing more standards than any other singer could ever hope to, he perfected a nonchalant, unfussy delivery that masks the precision of what he's up to. Just about every jazz singer learned something from him, but it is Tormé who distilled the essence and decanted it into the modern-jazz context of West Coast cool.'**

A child performer, Tormé graduated from radio work to touring, and his group, the Mel-Tones, were popular in the '40s, when a disc jockey gave him the nickname 'The Velvet Fog', which for some unkind reason is often given as 'The Velvet Frog'. A gifted and versatile songwriter, passable drummer and capable arranger, Tormé was enduringly popular and prolific until a stroke stopped him, surviving even the wilderness years when jazz singers were required to do pop songs; to his credit, Tormé always did his bit, even as he gave you to understand he shouldn't be lowering himself with this stuff.

We have always given high marks to an earlier Tormé date with the Dek-Tette, *Swings Shubert Alley*, but this one has steadily overtaken it and, as Eric Felten points out, it affords a better understanding of Tormé's generous, deceptively laid-back art. There is probably a thesis to be written on the respective impact of Astaire and Bing Crosby on jazz singing. What's immediately obvious here is that Marty Paich's brilliant arrangements are set up in such a way as to show off Tormé's bop virtuosity. One cannot conceive of Astaire singing 'The Way You Look Tonight' like that, but for a single-track object lesson in how Fred affected Tormé's art, one only has to go to 'They Can't Take That Away From Me', a magnificently judged and highly sophisticated performance that sounds like falling off a log. The other obvious highlights are 'Cheek To Cheek' and 'Top Hat, White Tie And Tails'. 'The Piccolino' is a curiosity and 'A Foggy Day', but for the obvious self-reference, a mistake.

TEDDY CHARLES

Born Theodore Charles Cohen, 13 April 1928, Chicopee Falls, Massachusetts
Vibraphone, marimba, piano, percussion

The Teddy Charles Tentet
Collectables COL 6161 / Fresh Sound FSRCD 2240
Charles; Art Farmer, Peter Urban (t); Gigi Gryce (as); J. R. Monterose (ts); George Barrow, Sol Schlinger (bs); Hall Overton, Mal Waldron (p); Jimmy Raney (g); Don Butterfield (tba); Teddy Kotick, Charles Mingus (b); Joe Harris, Ed Shaughnessy (d). January & November 1956.

Teddy Charles said (1991): **'It was serious stuff, this music. If you recorded with those numbers you had to have a meeting with the label, it was such a big deal. But the thing I remember was that Don Butterfield brought three tubas to the session, just so he could cover different tonalities. That serious!'**

Charles is usually respected as a harbinger of Ornette Coleman's free music; his early records aim for an independence of bebop structure which still sounds remarkably fresh. The music on *New Directions*, gathered together from rare 10-inch LPs, was an indication of Charles's ambitions but his masterpiece was the Tentet music.

It's full of pungent music from various hands. The record is a showcase for some of the sharpest arranging minds of the day: Giuffre (who posted parts from the West Coast), Brookmeyer, Waldron, Evans and especially George Russell, whose 'Lydian M-1' makes an extraordinary climax to the date. Charles's own 'The Emperor' and a transfigured 'Nature Boy' stand as tall as the rest. It all swings too hard to be dismissed as longhair music, but it was certainly out of the ordinary during the hard-bop/cool era. The playing is mostly quite restrained, but Monterose gets in some telling solos that act as a reminder of his under-appreciated talent, and Charles's own playing is bang on centre. The CD includes some material recorded later in the year with Overton, Mingus and Shaughnessy; nothing revelatory, but a nice further glimpse of Charles in a small-group setting.

CHARLES MINGUS &

Born 22 April 1922, Nogales, Arizona; died 5 January 1979, Cuernavaca, Mexico
Double bass, piano

Pithecanthropus Erectus
Atlantic 81227 5357-2
Mingus; Jackie McLean (as); J. R. Monterose (ts); Mal Waldron (p); Willie Jones (d). January 1956.

Mal Waldron said (1991): **'Mingus had this idea that you didn't need to hit the note dead centre, like a bullseye, but you could place your notes round about it, inside the concentric rings but not bang bang bang in the middle. It was liberating, though not so easy for the piano-player!'**

One of the truly great modern jazz albums. Underrated at the time, *Pithecanthropus Erectus* is now recognized as an important step in the direction of a new, freer synthesis in jazz. To some extent, the basic thematic conception (the story of humankind's struggle out of chaos, up and down the Freytag's Triangle of hubris and destruction, back to chaos) was the watered-down Spenglerism which was still fashionable at the time. Technically, though, the all-in ensemble work on the violent C section, which is really B, a modified version of the harmonically static second section, was absolutely crucial to the development of free collective improvisation in the following decade. The brief 'Profile Of Jackie' is altogether different. Fronted by McLean's menthol-sharp alto, with Monterose (a late appointee who wasn't altogether happy with the music) and Mingus working on a shadowy counter-melody, it's one of the most appealing tracks Mingus ever committed to record, and the most generous of his 'portraits'. McLean still carried a torch for orthodox bebop and soon came to (literal) blows with Mingus; the chemistry worked just long enough. 'Love Chant' is a more basic modal exploration, and 'A Foggy Day' – re-subtitled 'In San Francisco' – is an impressionistic reworking of the Gershwin standard, with Chandleresque sound-effects. Superficially jokey, it's no less significant an effort to expand the available range of jazz performance, and the fact that it's done via a standard rather than a long-form composition like 'Pithecanthropus' gives a sense of Mingus's Janus-faced approach to the music.

& *See also* **The Complete Debut Recordings** (1951–1957; p. 131), **Mingus Dynasty** (1959; p. 247), **Charles Mingus Presents Charles Mingus** (1960; p. 259), **The Black Saint And The Sinner Lady** (1963; p. 291)

TAL FARLOW

Born 7 June 1921, Greensboro, North Carolina; died 24 July 1998, New York City
Guitar

The Swinging Guitar Of Tal Farlow
Verve 559515-2
Farlow; Eddie Costa (p); Vinnie Burke (b). May 1956.

Jimmy Raney said (1984): **'Bebop demanded a different kind of picking and phrasing than had been the norm previously and Tal and I were among the first to do that. Chuck Wayne was another. That's both an advantage and a disadvantage. You're first in a field of one, or two, but there's no real awareness of what you're about, so it cancels itself. He was kind of reluctant, I think, but there were other pressures, from outside.'**

Talmadge Farlow's virtuosity and the quality of his thinking, even at top speed, inspired more than one generation of guitarists, and his neglect is mystifying. Perhaps, in the age of Bill Frisell and Pat Metheny, his plain-speaking is out of favour; unless, perversely, it stems from his early 'retirement' in 1958, when he took time away from music and worked as a sign-painter. Normally, premature absence from the scene triggers cult attention, but in Farlow's case it may simply be that fans understood his unease with the business and simply respected his privacy. Whatever the case, his reticence as a performer belied his breathtaking delivery, melodic inventiveness and pleasingly gentle touch as a bop-orientated improviser.

He got his first break in 1949 with Red Norvo – Jimmy Raney replaced him in the Red Norvo trio – who inspired him to accelerate his own technique and work as a leader in his own right. He made some marvellous records for Verve in the mid-'50s before withdrawing somewhat from the scene – actually picking his gigs with great care and often in Europe – and despite the *Finest Hour* tag perversely applied by the label to a later set of off-cuts and unreleased material, the best record is *The Swinging Guitar*. Unassumingly as he plays, one never feels intimidated by Farlow's virtuosity, even when he takes the trouble to reharmonize a sequence entirely or to blitz a melody with single-note flourishes. Burke maintains a steady pulse throughout, and Costa stays by the guitarist's side through some tough passages of bebop. 'Meteor' is Farlow's own reworking of some Parker changes; 'Yardbird Suite' is taken at a clip, and nicely varied on an alternative take; 'Taking A Chance On Love' likewise. On this showing, it's hard at first to see why such a fluent musician should take a step away, but there's a closed-off, introspective quality to him as well, almost reminiscent of an athlete or climber whose efforts are all inward-directed. The music communicates, even if the player doesn't.

CHET BAKER &

Born 23 December 1929, Yale, Oklahoma; died 13 May 1988, Amsterdam, Netherlands
Trumpet, voice

Chet Baker And Crew
Pacific Jazz 82671
Baker; Phil Urso (ts); Bobby Timmons (p); Jimmy Bond (b); Peter Littman (d). Bill Loughborough (chromatic tymp). July 1956.

Gerry Mulligan said (1990): **'I don't think you can explain a talent like Chet's or trace where it came from. It just arrived, full blown and entire.'**

The archetypal 'young man with the horn', brilliant, inward, self-destructive. He grew up in Oklahoma but was in New York to witness the birth of bebop. He developed a sound similar to Miles Davis's: quiet, restricted in range, and melodic rather than virtuosic. The famous pianoless quartet with Gerry Mulligan and a keynote performance of 'My Funny Valentine' were important in the development of cool jazz. A heroin habit destroyed the film star looks, and replaced them with a sunken and haunted image. Even so, his technique was precise and his playing and singing remained touchingly effective to the end.

Richard Bock began recording Baker as a leader when the quartet with Mulligan started to attract rave notices and even a popular audience, and the records the trumpeter made for Pacific Jazz remain among his freshest and most appealing work. For a week at the end of July 1956, the group was intensively recorded and the material is scattered over various albums, including *The Route* and *Chet Baker Sings*. This is perhaps the best single representation. It opens with a first version of 'To Mickey's Memory', one of two tracks that features Bill Loughborough on chromatic tympani, which adds an intriguing 'island' dimension. Mulligan's 'Line For Lyons' and Urso's 'Lucius Lu' are perfect for Timmons and put the lie to any suggestion that Chet didn't understand the blues. 'Worryin' The Life Out Of Me' has the two horns sparring nonchalantly, the equal of anything Chet did with the Mulligan group.

The cover image with Chet athletically bowed on a spar, his Triton's horn gleaming in the sun, is an icon of the time and makes the sharpest possible contrast with the sunken, death's head figure he became in later years.

& *See also* **Live At Nick's** (1978; p. 447), **Blues For A Reason** (1984; p. 488)

BOB BROOKMEYER &
Born 19 December 1929, Kansas City, Missouri
Valve trombone, piano

Brookmeyer
RCA Victor 74321 59152 2
Brookmeyer; Al DeRisi, Joe Ferrante, Bernie Glow, Louis Oles, Nick Travis (t); Joe Singer (frhn); Don Butterfield (tba); Gene Quill (as); Al Cohn (as, ts, cl); Al Epstein, Eddie Wasserman (ts); Sol Schlinger (bs); Hank Jones (p); Milt Hinton, Buddy Jones (b); Osie Johnson (d). September & October 1956.

Bob Brookmeyer said (1990): **'I started writing commercial compositions and arrangements for dance bands when I was 14. I was pretty much across harmony, but I still don't quite know how I got away with it. "Genius" certainly doesn't play a part. We just needed the $15.'**

Brookmeyer was the first man since Juan Tizol to favour the valve trombone over the slide instrument. He replaced Chet Baker in the Gerry Mulligan quartet, was a member of the Jimmy Giuffre Trio (a folk-jazz style he explored again with Giuffre under his own leadership on *Traditionalism Revisited*) and subsequently spent many years as a studio musician and arranger. Valve trombone has a more clipped, drier sound than the slide variety, and Brookmeyer is probably its leading exponent, though Maynard Ferguson, Stu Williamson and Bob Enevoldsen have all made effective use of it.

Brookmeyer was an attempt to showcase him in three rather different contexts, from large band down to octet. The big-band arrangements, like the opening 'Oh, Jane Snavely', are interestingly pared down, but arranged in the most intriguing way with four trumpets, three tenors, baritone and rhythm providing the background for the solitary trombone. The next session was very different, with a pair of trumpets, french horn and tuba, but just two reeds, alto doubling clarinet, and, once again supporting a roomy bottom end, Sol Schlinger's baritone. The results are no less spare and undramatic, but the subtlety and control are equally striking, and these are more compelling performances than the two later octets, 'Confusion Blues' and 'Zing Went The Strings Of My Heart'. These sessions represented quite a substantial investment in Brookmeyer's growing reputation. Even given the tastes of the time, they must have been quite difficult records to sell, but they come up to date very impressively.

& *See also* **New Works** (1997; p. 619)

CHARLIE SHAVERS

Born 3 August 1917, New York City; died 8 July 1971, New York City
Trumpet, voice

Horn O'Plenty

Lone Hill Jazz LHJR 10140
Shavers; Benny Morton, Urbie Green (tb); Buster Bailey, Sol Yaged (cl); Russell Procope (as); Sam 'The Man' Taylor (ts); Buddy Weed, Kenny Kersey, Billy Kyle (p); Barry Galbraith (g); Aaron Bell, Bob Haggart (b); Panama Francis, Specs Powell, Cozy Cole (d); Maxine Sullivan (v). October 1954–1958.

It's an old story, and not ours to repeat, but is too good to pass by. When Charlie Shavers came to Britain he was intrigued by hotel electrical sockets bearing the legend 'FOR SHAVERS ONLY'. Charlie's reaction? **'Just wait till Eldridge hears about *this*!'**

Received wisdom always had it that Shavers was little more than a showbiz show-off. He could, indeed, be flashy and vulgar, but he was also an underrated stylist, an Armstrong man who could play with discretion and lyrical beauty. He started out playing 'chamber jazz' with John Kirby and developed an interesting muted sound. His 1955 work with arranger Sy Oliver drifts perilously close to easy listening. The '50s sessions with pianist Ray Bryant aren't much more agitated, but they do deserve to be reassessed now that they're comprehensively available again. They're mostly calm and collected. Charlie tends to amble through the music, rarely extending himself to a high C and the sort of thing he was required to do at JATP shows. Instead, there is a lot of pretty playing on projects dedicated to French tunes (*Charlie Digs Paree*), warhorses (*Charlie Digs Dixie*, though he does them with good grace) and a stack of standards. Bryant fills in and the rhythm team simply mark time. Inconsequential, but they're a pleasing feature for his horn.

Horn O'Plenty is probably the disc to get for a straightforward representation of Shavers in straight jazz contexts, and given the state of the discography there's no alternative to a compilation. These choices at least put him in august Ellingtonian company. The 1954 sextet date which opens it includes a fairly outrageous 'Dark Eyes', which shows off the great man's exuberance a treat, a fine 'Moten Swing' and 'Story Of The Jazz Trumpet', where Charlie coolly goes through Armstrong, Eldridge, Cootie Williams, Ziggy Elman, Harry James and Gillespie. There are five delightful tracks with Buster Bailey and two vocals by Maxine Sullivan, and the disc ends with a session of Cole Porter tunes, with surprisingly fine work from Sam 'The Man' Taylor and Sol Yaged. He'll never be up for Gabriel's job, but Charlie was more than a journeyman and even at his sloppiest and most self-regarding he pulled off some terrific jazz.

HERBIE NICHOLS

Born 3 January 1919, New York City; died 12 April 1963, New York City
Piano

The Complete Blue Note Recordings

Blue Note 8 59355 2 3CD
Nichols; Teddy Kotick, Al McKibbon (b); Art Blakey, Max Roach (d). May 1955–April 1956.

Trombonist Roswell Rudd remembers: **'Something I've remembered about the man that also carried over into his music was/is his very natural way of getting conversations started ... you would be in it before you realized it. Herbie would get a conversation going and very gradually and gracefully prime it until the dynamic had drawn in another person at the table or in the car and it became three-way. At a certain point, Herbie would simply stop speaking and just let whatever he had started run its heated course, while he became the audience, holding back his pleasure at what he'd set in train.'**

'There is a kind of culpability in the discovery of dead artists', and in Herbie Nichols there is an almost perfect example of an artist who was largely ignored during his lifetime, only to be canonized as soon as he was gone. When Nichols died, he had been working professionally for a quarter of a century, ever since joining the Royal Baron Orchestra in 1937. Yet in all those 26 years, by A. B. Spellman's reckoning, there was not one during which he was able to earn a living making the music he loved. Nichols scuffled as a recording artist, doing R&B sides here and there, even accompanying lesbian shows, until Alfred Lion of Blue Note decided to sign him up.

Two 10-inch LPs were issued from the May 1955 sessions, both called *The Prophetic Herbie Nichols*. How forward-looking he was as a composer may be judged by his use in 'The Third World', the opening item on *The Complete*, of a chord progression that would still sound radical when John Coltrane experimented with it more than a decade later (nearer two decades from the date of composition, since it seems to have been written as early as 1947). Typically, Lion gave him generous rehearsal time, and neither McKibbon nor Blakey sounds as though he is running down unfamiliar material. The miracle of Nichols is his compositions never sound consciously 'written' but seem to emerge whole out of the nature of the piano itself. The playing is crisp and buoyant, and even alternative takes are worth hearing.

Nichols and McKibbon reconvened in August 1955 with Max Roach at the kit, and they recorded his best-known composition, 'Lady Sings The Blues', as well as the joyous 'The Gig'; but it is tunes like '23 Skiddoo' and 'Shuffle Montgomery' from the earlier sessions which have restored him to favour, largely thanks to the loyal stewardship of Roswell Rudd and a few others who recognize in him a distinguished forerunner.

This Blue Note set is perhaps his best testament, but there was also some fine material for Bethlehem, best sampled on the wonderfully titled *Love, Gloom, Cash, Love*, which just about sums it up.

CHRIS CONNOR
Born Mary Loutsenhizer, 8 November 1927, Kansas City, Missouri; died 29 August 2009, Toms River, New Jersey
Voice

Chris Connor
Atlantic 7567 80769
Connor; Nick Travis (t); Sam Marowitz, Ray Beckenstein (as); Zoot Sims (ts); Danny Bank (bs); John Lewis, Moe Wechsler (p); Barry Galbraith (g); Oscar Pettiford, Milt Hinton (b); Connie Kay, Osie Johnson (d). January–February 1956.

Chris Connor said (1985): **'I would spend hours in a record store booth listening to Peggy Lee, Anita O'Day, June Christy, Frank Sinatra. Sinatra phrased the best, and phrasing was important to me. I knew that was how you were distinctive as a singer. It was Peggy I wanted to emulate, though. She wrote the best songs, too.'**

Connor grew up in the Midwest (and double-dated with trombonist Bob Brookmeyer when a teen). She started out with Claude Thornhill, then joined Stan Kenton in 1952. After that, she worked mainly as a soloist, quietly in the '60s and '70s, more prominently again after a revival of interest in her brand of singing. The cool vocalist *par excellence*, and Connor's records for Bethlehem and Atlantic showcased the ex-Kenton singer in a way that led to some definitive interpretations: here 'Ev'ry Time', 'It's All Right With Me', 'I Wonder What Became Of Me' and several more are unlikely to be bettered. She has remained something of a cult figure, beatified by Ran Blake and other musicians, but in her prime she sold records to a wide audience and several of her Atlantics were considerable hits; this was revived as part of the label's 50th-anniversary programme. Four tracks with the quartet of Lewis, Galbraith, Pettiford and Kay (who should have been recorded on their own as well) are a marvel, as is 'When The Wind Was Green'. Her open vowel sounds have an oddly yearning quality, which is heightened by the way she can sing low notes very softly, yet make them emphatic.

BILL PERKINS &

Born 22 July 1924, San Francisco, California; died 9 August 2003, Sherman Oaks, California
Tenor, soprano and baritone saxophones, flute

Grand Encounter
Pacific 46859
Perkins; John Lewis (p); Jim Hall (g); Percy Heath (b); Chico Hamilton (d). February 1956.

Bill Perkins said (1990): **'Working in the studios meant that you did work, and work in music, which was important, obviously, but it took you further away from jazz. It's a different discipline, delivering an accurate chart by day and getting a salary cheque, playing a little jazz with a pick-up band at the weekend, and getting maybe $20. Who'd choose?'**

Perkins had an interesting life. He grew up away from the US in Chile, and after his military service he studied music and engineering in California. For a substantial period, he was in the studios and working as a sound engineer, before taking a 'day' job as part of Doc Severinson's band on the *Tonight Show*. There is, though, a surprisingly large discography, some 15 studio albums and a couple of good live dates, spread unevenly over the period from 1956, when the wonderful debut was put down, to not long before his death.

There was a carefully stoked 'rivalry' between East Coast and West Coast musicians in the mid-'50s and East-meets-West records form a tiny sub-genre in the music. Perkins's best record is probably his very first, though in later years, when the Pres influence gave way somewhat to elements of John Coltrane harmony and a harder articulation, he created some wonderfully mature music.

Grand Encounter, which is subtitled *Three Degrees East, Three Degrees West*, is a deliciously cool-toned set, on which Lewis is effectively co-leader, his more obviously intellectual approach a nice foil to Perks's Californian nonchalance. However, there are – and always were – shadow-notes in Perkins's playing at the time, a faintly melancholic tinge that comes through on 'I Can't Get Started' and the closing 'Almost Like Being In Love'. Lewis wrote the material for the long title-track, but Perkins's deceptively languorous line is the key element. A largely forgotten record, this, but one of the best 'cool' sessions of the era and long overdue a revival.

& *See also* **JOHN LEWIS**, The Golden Striker / Jazz Abstractions (1956; p. 253)

ELLA FITZGERALD &

Born 25 April 1917, Newport News, Virginia; died 15 June 1996, Beverly Hills, California
Voice

Sings The Cole Porter Songbook

Verve 537257-2 2CD

Fitzgerald; Pete Candoli, Maynard Ferguson, Conrad Gozzo (t); Milt Bernhart, Joe Howard, Lloyd Ulyate (tb); George Roberts (btb, bari tb); Bob Cooper (cl, ob, ts); Herb Geller (cl, as); Chuck Gentry (bs, bcl); Ted Nash (cl, f, ts); Bud Shank (cl, f, as); Paul Smith (p, cel); Barney Kessel (g); Corky Hale (hp); Robert LaMarchina, Edgar Lustgarten (clo); Joe Mondragon (b); Alvin Stoller (d); Buddy Bregman (arr, cond). February 1956.

Ella's manager Norman Granz said (1982): **'It's less of a challenge presenting her on record than it is managing her other public activities. Ella in the studio is money in the bank, both commercially and creatively. The other side of it is ... interesting, but not the same.'**

In January 1956, Fitzgerald began recording for Norman Granz's Verve label, and the first release, *Sings The Cole Porter Songbook*, became the commercial rock on which Verve was built. It was so successful that Granz set Ella to work on all the great American songwriters, and her series of songbook albums are an unrivalled sequence of their kind. The records work consistently well for a number of reasons. Fitzgerald herself was at a vocal peak, strong yet flexible, and her position as a lyric interpreter was perfectly in tune with records dense with lyrical detail; each disc carefully programmes familiar with lesser-known material; the arrangers all work to their strengths, Bregman and May delivering hard-hitting big-band sounds, Riddle the suavest of grown-up orchestrations; and the quality of the studio recordings was and remains outstandingly lifelike and wide-ranging on most of the discs. The Porter set is a sentimental favourite of many, in the jazz audience and beyond, and it's one of the records which typifies the first great era of the long-player and sets her most straightforwardly in the measure alongside some of the other vocal greats of the era. Granz apparently took a test pressing to Cole Porter in his suite at the Waldorf-Astoria. The composer listened intently to these interpretations of his work before commenting 'My, what marvellous diction that girl has!'

& See also **The Enchanting Ella Fitzgerald** (1950–1955; p. 125), **Ella In London** (1974; p. 410)

SERGE CHALOFF

Born 24 November 1923, Boston, Massachusetts; died 16 July 1957, Boston, Massachusetts
Baritone saxophone

Blue Serge

Capitol 94505

Chaloff; Sonny Clark (p); Leroy Vinnegar (b); Philly Joe Jones (d). March 1956.

Baritone saxophonist John Surman says: **'He was a highly underrated player, a man who brought such lyricism to the baritone horn and with an extraordinary dynamic range.'**

Hugely talented, but the career was riven by personal problems, and the end was dreadful; Chaloff contracted spinal paralysis and it killed him while still in his mid-30s. His mother was the distinguished piano teacher Marge Chaloff and his grounding in music was both thorough and broad. Nevertheless, Chaloff's approach to the baritone, which never sounded unwieldy in his hands, was restrained rather than virtuosic and concentrated on the distinctive timbre of the instrument and its under-utilized dynamics rather than outpacing all opposition. Nevertheless, he was an agile improviser who could transform a sleepy-sounding phrase with a single overblown note.

He has been significantly overlooked down the years and for long periods his few recordings have been unavailable. Fortunately, *The Fable of Mabel* and *Boston Blow-Up* (the latter with homeboy Herb Pomeroy) are now on CD, as well as the excellent *Blue Serge*. Chaloff's masterpiece is both vigorous and moving, not for the knowledge that he was so near to his own death but for the unsentimental rigour of the playing. 'Thanks For The Memory' is overpoweringly beautiful as Chaloff creates a series of melodic variations which match the improviser's ideal of fashioning an entirely new song. 'Stairway To The Stars' is almost as fine, and the thoughtful 'The Goof And I' and 'Susie's Blues' show that Chaloff still had plenty of ideas about what could be done with a bebopper's basic materials. This important session has retained all its power.

TADD DAMERON

Born Tadley Ewing Peake Dameron, 21 February 1917, Cleveland, Ohio; died 8 March 1965, New York City
Composer, piano

Fontainebleau
Original Jazz Classics OJCCD 055
Dameron; Kenny Dorham (t); Henry Coker (tb); Sahib Shihab (as); Joe Alexander (ts); Cecil Payne (bs); John Simmons (b); Shadow Wilson (d). March 1956.

Trumpeter/arranger Don Sickler of Dameronia said (1989): **'Someone called him the great romantic of jazz composition and I think that's spot on. He wrote some of the best music of the bop era, and yet he's barely known to younger musicians.'**

Dameron's remembered now for a couple of repertory compositions – 'Lady Bird', 'Hot House' – and not much else. He was an underrated performer who stands at the fulcrum of modern jazz, midway between swing and bop. He began writing arrangements in his late teens and worked with Harlan Leonard from 1939. Soon got caught up in bop and led small groups with Fats Navarro and Miles Davis. Drug and legal problems effectively ended his career. Combining the broad-brush arrangements of the big band and the new advanced harmonic language, his own recordings are difficult to date blind and a tune like 'On A Misty Night' seems to capture the evanescence that surrounds the man and the music.

The discography is spotty. Records with Fats Navarro are usually covered under the trumpeter's name and *Mating Call* is often reviewed as a John Coltrane album, though it's the pianist who's in the driving seat, subtly directing the ensemble. *Fontainebleau* dates from Dameron's last full year of freedom before the prison sentence that took him out of the jazz stream effectively for good. The title-piece is wholly written out, with no scope for improvising. It might seem similar in some respects to John Lewis's similarly inspired music, but Dameron is more thoroughly a jazz composer, with little of Lewis's classical bent. Though the title-piece is relatively formal, there is plenty of individual work elsewhere, notably from Dorham. 'The Scene Is Clean' is picked up sometimes by bop outfits, but mostly these charts are too lushly elegant for blowing purposes. Never a distinctive soloist, Dameron prefers to work within his own lush chord progressions, though he lets the group roam free on the long closing blues, 'Bula-Beige'.

STÉPHANE GRAPPELLI &

Born 26 January 1908, Paris, France; died 1 December 1997, Paris, France
Violin

Jazz In Paris: Improvisations
Emarcy 549 242 2
Grappelli; Maurice Vander (p, hpd); Pierre Michelot (b); Jean-Baptiste 'Mac Kac' Reilles (d). February & April 1956.

Guitarist Martin Taylor says: '**During the eleven years that I toured and recorded with Stéphane we rarely spoke about music, but I learned so much from just being around him. Sitting on stage with him or just chatting away in an airport lounge was a lesson in music and life. He knew the importance of communicating with the audience. People would be spellbound by him and even those who hated jazz loved him.**'

Largely self-taught, Grappelli had an approach to jazz violin that was both idiomatic and idiosyncratic, but he became the most important exponent of the instrument since Joe Venuti, and while he clung to the mainstream, even some of the avant-garde players took note. The mythology has him down as his fellow Hot Club member Django Reinhardt's temperamental opposite, but Stéphane is better regarded as a milder twin; his affability masked an iron will and sometimes torrid personality. A typical Grappelli line is fast, fleet and accurate, with a natural rhythm, but with darker overtones always lurking.

Obviously, many of the classic performances are those with the original Hot Club De France, which are covered under the first Django entry above, *Django Reinhardt 1935–1936*. It was Grappelli's pleasure and burden to carry that legend forward into one decade after another, linked by a mystical bond to a man who, by all accounts, made his life extremely difficult; Stéphane talked often about Django's 'monkey business'. Stéphane enjoyed a long, creative life after that association ended and with more modern recording methods came through ever more richly and in fuller voice.

No one belongs more securely in Emarcy's *Jazz In Paris* series than Stéphane, and this lively set, originally released on Barclay, is textbook Grappelli. Right from the opening 'The Lady Is A Tramp' you suspect he's going to stick very closely to the melody and show his stuff merely by playing it very fast. Once he's into his solo, though, it's a very different matter: daring harmonic modulations, whole countermelodies and endless grace notes – typical post-Hot Club stuff. He does the same thing on 'A Nightingale Sang In Berkeley Square'. Michelot and Vander (who doubles harpsichord on 'Someone To Watch Over Me') keep the accompaniment from becoming too obvious, and a word for the colourful Mac Kac Reilles, not the greatest drummer in the world – or even Paris – but a character and practical joker who would have put even that arch-trickster violinist Joe Venuti in the shade.

& *See also* **Django Reinhardt 1935–1936** (1935–1936; p. 51), **Pêche À La Mouche** (1947–1953; p. 111).

GEORGE RUSSELL *&*
Born 23 June 1923, Cincinnati, Ohio; died 27 July 2009, Boston, Massachusetts
Composer, bandleader, piano

Jazz Workshop
Koch 7850
Russell; Art Farmer (t); Hal McKusick (as, f); Bill Evans (p); Barry Galbraith (g); Milt Hinton (b); Teddy Kotick (b); Joe Harris, Osie Johnson, Paul Motian (d). March–December 1956.

George Russell said (1984): '**I have had a charmed life. If the army doctors hadn't found I had TB, I could be telling you now how nice the sand was at Iwo Jima, but probably not much about jazz. I had a room of my own in the hospital, with a veranda, and I had the chance to study music with a brilliant young man. He died, I didn't; that's the history.**'

After graduating in his native Cincinnati, Russell suffered a long bout of tuberculosis, during which he overturned much of what he and his teachers had thought about harmonics, and in the early '50s wrote *The Lydian Chromatic Concept of Tonal Organization*. It was the direct source of the modal or scalar experiments of John Coltrane and Miles Davis. Russell spent most of the '60s in Europe, reworking his treatise and writing little music, but in later years he enjoyed a steady resurgence and gained a hard-won recognition in his final decades.

However important Russell's theories are, they are even now not securely understood. Sometimes falsely identified with the original Greek Lydian mode, *The Lydian Chromatic Concept* is not the same at all. In diatonic terms, it represents the progression F to F on the piano's white keys; it also confronts the diabolic tritone, the *diabolus in musica*, which had haunted Western composers from Bach to Beethoven. Russell's conception assimilated modal writing to the extreme chromaticism of modern music. By converting chords into scales and overlaying one scale on another, it allowed improvisers to work in the hard-to-define area between non-tonality and polytonality. Like all great theoreticians, Russell worked analytically rather than synthetically, basing his ideas on how jazz *actually was*, not on how it could be made to conform with traditional principles of Western harmony. Working from within jazz's often tacit organizational principles, Russell's fundamental concern was the relationship between formal scoring and improvisation, giving the first the freedom of the second, freeing the second from being literally esoteric, 'outside' some supposed norm. Russell's theories also influenced his own composition. 'A Bird In Igor's Yard', a celebrated early piece, was a (rather too) self-conscious attempt to ally bebop and Stravinsky – it was also a young and slightly immature work – but it pointed the way forward.

'Ezz-thetic', which first appeared on these classic 1956 *Jazz Workshop* sessions, is one of the key pieces in an astonishing collection, including several that stand as almost unique avenues of thought in the jazz language: 'Night Sound', 'Round Johnny Rondo', 'Knights Of The Steamtable' and 'Concerto For Billy The Kid', the latter including one of Bill Evans's most remarkable solos on record.

& *See also* **Ezz-thetics** (1961; p. 274), **Live In An American Time Spiral** (1982; p. 469)

KENNY DORHAM

Born McKinley Howard Dorham (also known as 'Kinny') 30 August 1924, Fairfield, Texas; died 5 December 1972, New York City
Trumpet

'Round About Midnight At The Café Bohemia
Blue Note 33775 2CD
Dorham; J. R. Monterose (ts); Kenny Burrell (g); Bobby Timmons (p); Sam Jones (b); Arthur Edgehill (d). May 1956.

Trumpeter Jeremy Pelt says: **'There are four architects of bebop as it pertains to trumpet: Dizzy, obviously, but also Fats Navarro and Thad Jones, and Kenny Dorham belongs in there as well.'**

Somewhat like Freddie Hubbard in a later generation, Dorham had the ability to play in just about any situation that was thrown at him, which is why he turns up in so many bebop situations, Latin-tinged dates (including some south-of-the-border sessions of his own), but is also on hand on Andrew Hill's *Point of Departure*. He's self-evidently a Dizzy disciple, particularly as on *Afro-Cuban* when there are extra beats and half-beats to the measure, but Dorham had a nicely rounded tone and even attack which make him more distinctive than is usually thought.

In 1953, Dorham led a fine quintet with Jimmy Heath and Walter Bishop Jr, an outfit that romped through gulping blues passages on a minimum of harmonic oxygen. There's little apparently to keep the music moving, but Kenny always finds something inventive to say, which is one reason why he survived in the Jazz Messengers. He was modestly ambitious, though, and went off to form his own Jazz Prophets, who made some sides for Chess. It wasn't until Blue Note signed him up that he produced something close to a masterpiece. The history of live recordings for the label is slightly chequered, alternating masterworks and duds. Kenny's Café Bohemia date is one of the former, or close to it.

The hour might well have suggested a handful of minor keys. Dorham always had a predilection for a unified mood, and this session, combining the Monk tune 'Autumn In New York' with 'A Night In Tunisia' and three originals, manages to sustain a slightly brooding, intensely thoughtful atmosphere. As a foil, Monterose was an excellent recruitment. Burrell swings with the usual horn-like attack and Timmons vamps righteously, though without ever really showing his mettle. Dorham's own solos are models of grace and tact, always giving an impression of careful construction and development. Francis Wolff's subtly doctored cover shot offers an intriguing impression of the man, showing Dorham in a bright check jacket, but with a faraway look in his eyes as he clutches the microphone; above him, a ghostly image of an American townscape, vivid but also fleeting. He was what we have called elsewhere a heartland musician, not really a man for the big cities at all, but happy to ply his quiet craft in a steady narrative way.

FRIEDRICH GULDA

Born 16 May 1930, Vienna, Austria; died 27 January 2000, Weißenbach am Attersee, Austria
Piano

Friedrich Gulda At Birdland

RCA Victor PM 1355
Gulda; Idrees Sulieman (t); Jimmy Cleveland (tb); Phil Woods (as); Seldon Powell (ts); Aaron Bell (b); Nick Stabulas (d). June 1956.

Austrian-born keyboards player Joe Zawinul remembers (1992): **'Gulda? He was a crazy man, a real eccentric, but he put it over all those guys, because he was a better musician than anyone else. Better than anyone else I can think of. Any style.'**

If Gulda had had his way of it, the death date above would have been some months earlier. In 1999, he tried to hoax the media into thinking he had passed away, in order to stage his own resurrection. It was a typical gesture from a man who regarded any boundary – national, stylistic, philosophical – as something to be transgressed. Classically trained, he steered a path between straight music and jazz, but was sceptical of attempts to blend the two. He did, however, take up the cause of Joe Zawinul when the former Weather Report man was experimenting with large, 'symphonic' forms, and Gulda himself often took part in quite *outré* projects, as when he collaborated with the radical 'Krautrock' group Anima (Sound).

Gulda was exotic fruit when he arrived in the United States, somewhat as Joe Zawinul was to be. He reversed the usual jazz musician's trajectory by playing Carnegie Hall first, in 1949, and only then 'playing Birdland', though this record was actually not a live gig but a studio session. In his jazz playing, he put the lie quite definitively to the notion that classically trained musicians could not swing. Here, along with 'A Night In Tunisia' and the Leiber–Stoller 'Bernie's Tune', his band works through a set of somewhat sombre originals, including 'Dark Glow' and 'Air From Other Planets' (an indirect reference to Schoenberg). The piano sound isn't great, but Gulda's comping is absolutely spot on and there is enough solo action from the horns to make this more than a novelty record. Gulda's musicianship was of the highest order.

MELBA LISTON
Born 13 January 1926, Kansas City, Missouri; died 23 April 1999, Los Angeles, California
Trombone

And Her 'Bones
Fresh Sound FSRCD 408
Liston; Jimmy Cleveland, Bennie Green, Al Grey, Benny Powell, Frank Rehak (tb); Slide Hampton (tb, tba);
Marty Flax (bs); Ray Bryant, Walter Davis Jr (p); Kenny Burrell (g); Nelson Boyd, George Joyner (b); Frank
Dunlop, Charli Persip (d). June 1956, December 1958.

Melba Liston said (1990): **'I really think I was born to play trombone. The very first time
I saw one, I wanted it, even though I wasn't very sure what it was. And even though I
couldn't reach most of the positions, it felt like it was part of me.'**

There's something about trombone-players. More than any of the other horns, they like to
gather together *en masse*. Melba Liston is best known as an arranger, but she was a more
than decent player in her day. She doesn't have much of a showing on record, though everyone will have heard her fine sophisticated arrangements. Most of these cuts are from two
trombone-and-rhythm dates made in Christmas week 1958. She loved the sound of the horn
so much she didn't use either trumpets or woodwinds. It's not clear why the two dates have
been interwoven on this compilation. If a change of texture were called for it would have
made more sense to intersperse the 1956 cuts, with Liston paired with baritone and rhythm.
The material is mostly by Liston, Hampton, Rehak and Leonard Feather. Melba's 'You Don't
Say' and 'Insomnia' (the latter by the smaller 1956 group) are the best of the cuts, but there's
much to enjoy and it's a feast for trombone lovers.
   Slowed by a stroke in the mid-'80s, she spent her last few years confined to a wheelchair,
but still mentally active and still able to write arrangements, including some for her admirer
Randy Weston.

MARK MURPHY&
Born 14 March 1932, Fulton, New York
Voice

Crazy Rhythm: His Debut Recordings
Decca/GRP 050670-2
Murphy; orchestra including Ralph Burns (p); Don Lamond (d). June 1956–1958.

Mark Murphy said (1986): **'It took me a long time to make contact with the audience.
Listening to these things after thirty years, it sounds like I'm singing to myself. That got
easier later on, but there's something about it I still quite like.'**

Mark Murphy's been hip all his professional life. His first sessions, released as *Meet Mark
Murphy* and *Let Yourself Go*, were rarities which are welcome on CD. The sheer youthful
ebullience of these dates comes as a tonic after the self-absorbed mooning of so many of
today's would-be jazz crooners. Murphy hits the demanding tempo of 'Fascinating Rhythm'
so quickly and confidently that it makes one gasp to think this was his first outing in a
studio. Beautiful intonation, every word immaculately there, and, with helpful charts from
Ralph Burns, Murphy hardly takes a false step. On ballads he sometimes strains for a big
bel canto sound, and just occasionally he tries too hard or attempts to do too much, but that
is a young man's fancy, and it's kept the records alive.

& *See also* **Bop For Kerouac** (1981; p. 463)

ROLF ERICSON

Born 29 August 1922, Stockholm, Sweden; died 16 June 1997, Stockholm, Sweden
Trumpet

Rolf Ericson & The American Stars

Dragon DRCD 255
Ericson; Lars Gullin, Cecil Payne (bs); Duke Jordan, Freddie Redd (p); Tommy Potter, John Simmons (b); Joe
Harris, Art Taylor (d); Ernestine Anderson (v). June & July 1956.

Rolf Ericson said (1981): **'Clark Terry recommended me to Duke, but he'd taken on too
many trumpeters and Cat Anderson had just come back. But I kept hoping. I literally
missed the band bus on one occasion, and on another had to say no because I was
working with Maynard Ferguson. I eventually got the job, though.'**

Sweden was one of the few countries on earth to which a gifted jazz musician might have
chosen to return after a spell in the US, other than in abject defeat. Ericson went to America
in 1947 and played with Charlie Barnet, Woody Herman and Charles Mingus, eventually
joining Ellington in 1963. He returned home, only on tour, but his presence invigorated the
jazz scene in Scandinavia: one of their own, making it before returning home to energize
the band scene there, and, ironically, to welcome visiting American stars.

The gifted and likeable Ericson left a fine legacy on record, though comparatively little
under his own name. A totally reliable section player, he tended to hide away a gentler and
more lyrical side, though it came out at the end of his life, when he had made flugelhorn a
firm double. These 1956 recordings date from a Swedish tour when Rolf was asked to front
a band of Americans. The first tour was wrecked by the narcotic problems of two of the
visitors (all four were sent home), and only four tracks survive. The bulk of the disc has
Ericson and Gullin in the front line, with Redd, Potter and Harris in the rhythm section.
Despite the problems, the tour helped bring hard bop to Sweden, previously drawn more
to American cool. Ericson and Gullin are in brimming form, though the live recording isn't
ideal. Anderson sings on six tracks. The instrumentals tend to be better, and 'A Night In
Tunisia' is as hot as any of the great (all-)American versions. A significant talent, Ericson,
who claims more than a footnote.

DIZZY GILLESPIE&

*Born John Birks Gillespie, 21 October 1917, Cheraw, South Carolina; died 6 January 1993, Englewood,
New Jersey*
Trumpet

Birks Works: The Verve Big-Band Sessions

Verve 527900-2 2CD
Gillespie; Joe Gordon, Quincy Jones, Ermit Perry, Carl Warwick, Talib Daawud, Lee Morgan (t); Melba Liston,
Frank Rehak (tb); Rod Levitt, Ray Connor (btb); Jimmy Powell, Phil Woods, Ernie Henry (as); Billy Mitchell,
Benny Golson, Ernie Wilkins (ts); Marty Flax, Billy Root, Pee Wee Moore (bs); Walter Davis Jr, Wynton Kelly (p);
Paul West, Nelson Boyd (b); Charli Persip (d); Austin Comer (v). June 1956–July 1957.

Saxophonist Jimmy Heath said (1987): **'Dizzy never stopped teaching. Any time I saw him,
he'd have me over to the piano, show me chords, ninths alongside tenths, that kind of
thing, stuff I still use. Listen to those big bands, you can tell he's the teacher.'**

Jazz became part of America's mission to the world in the '50s and while much paranoid
ink has been spilled over CIA and State Department involvement in the presentation of jazz
as a shining example of democratic freedom (a piece of spin that casually ignored the treat-

ment of African-Americans within the US) it is. Long awaited in a comprehensive edition, these tracks cover the work of a band that Gillespie toured with as a cultural ambassador, though this is all studio work. The three original albums remain comparatively forgotten, or at least neglected, perhaps because big-band jazz wasn't quite the fashion, perhaps because the first two titles were functionally dull and the third, *World Statesman*, might not have quite sat well with the young. Nevertheless, these are essential performances, a link between bop and swing values, and with Dizzy's African-Cuban experiments subtly integrated into an ensemble sound that moved like a coherent mass.

Studded with great players, the orchestra also benefits from some of the most perceptive scoring of the day – by Liston, Wilkins, Jones, Golson and other hands – and, with Gillespie in stratospheric form as soloist, the band could hardly have failed. 'Dizzy's Business' and 'Whisper Not' are classic performances, soloist and band in absolute balance.

& *See also* **The Complete RCA Victor Recordings** (1937–1949; p. 68)

SONNY ROLLINS &
Born Theodore Walter Rollins, 7 September 1930, New York City
Tenor saxophone

Saxophone Colossus
Original Jazz Classics OJCCD 291
Rollins; Tommy Flanagan (p); Doug Watkins (b); Max Roach (d). June 1956.

Sonny Rollins said (1987): **'For some reason, people speak as if that was my first record, as if I'd appeared in the world at precisely that moment. In fact, I'd been recording since 1949 and practising 12 hours a day since I was in my teens. It was no surprise that something came of it!'**

The Master. Arguably the most compelling improviser in the entire history of the music, Rollins has never settled into a permanent style. Even in his 70s, he continues to exert severe authority over his recorded output, rejecting anything that smacks of repetition or that falls a degree below first rate. The body of recording is quite astonishing, in both amount and quality, and selecting even three or four of his records is problematic.

His older brother was taking classical music lessons and Rollins himself began on piano, switched to alto saxophone, then settled on tenor. He recorded as a teenager with Bud Powell and J. J. Johnson, later with Miles Davis and Thelonious Monk, and worked in Max Roach's group for two years. For the last half-century, he has been a leader in his own right. The approach is essentially melodic and even while Rollins is negotiating complex harmonic transitions, his improvising always sounds effortlessly logical.

The undisputed masterpiece from the mid-'50s period is *Saxophone Colossus*, and although Rollins plays with brilliant invention throughout the run of earlier records, he's at his most consistent on this disc. 'St Thomas', his irresistible calypso melody, appears here for the first time, and there is a ballad of unusual bleakness in 'You Don't Know What Love Is', as well as a rather sardonic walk through 'Moritat' (alias 'Mack The Knife'). But 'Blue Seven', as analysed in a contemporary piece by Gunther Schuller, became celebrated as a thematic masterpiece, where all the joints and moving parts of a spontaneous improvisation attain the pristine logic of a composition. If the actual performance is much less forbidding than this suggests, thanks in part to the simplicity of the theme, it surely justifies Schuller's acclaim.

& *See also* **A Night At The Village Vanguard** (1957; p. 216), **This Is What I Do** (2000; p. 653)

DUKE ELLINGTON &

Born Edward Kennedy Ellington, 29 April 1899, Washington DC; died 24 May 1974, New York City
Piano

Ellington At Newport 1956 (Complete)

Columbia C2K 64932 2CD
Ellington; Cat Anderson, Willie Cook, Ray Nance, Clark Terry (t); Quentin Jackson, John Sanders, Britt
Woodman (tb); Johnny Hodges, Russell Procope (as); Paul Gonsalves, Jimmy Hamilton (ts); Harry Carney (bs);
Jimmy Woode (b); Sam Woodyard (d). July 1956.

André Previn said (1996): **'This was the occasion when Paul Gonsalves "saved" Ellington,
or so they say, and it's part of that debunking idea that the Ellington band was "really"
about the soloists, great as they were. That's nonsense: the band was his entirely. I think
he saved them from potentially very dull careers.'**

The 1956 Newport Festival marked a significant upswing in Duke's critical and commercial
fortunes. In large part, the triumph can be laid to Paul Gonsalves's extraordinary 27 blues
choruses on 'Diminuendo And Crescendo In Blue', which CBS producer George Avakian
placed out of sequence at the end of what was to be Ellington's bestselling record. Gonsalves's unprecedented improvisation (which opened up possibilities and set standards for
later tenor saxophonists from John Coltrane to David Murray) was clearly spontaneous, yet
in a way it dogged him for the rest of his life, and Ellington continued to introduce him, years
later, as 'the star of Newport'. Gonsalves himself suggested that a particularly competitive
edge to the band that night was the real reason for his playing. Johnny Hodges had just
returned to the fold after a brief stint as an independent bandleader. His beautiful, almost
stately solo on 'Jeep's Blues' was intended to be the climax to the concert, but Hodges found
himself upstaged in the subsequent notices, and the concert firmly established Gonsalves
as one of the leading soloists in jazz. Unfortunately, much of the solo was played badly off-
mic (of which more later) and in the past it was slightly difficult to get a complete sense of its
extraordinary impact. It does, nevertheless, dominate the album, overshadowing Hodges
and, more significantly, the three-part 'Festival Suite' – which was heard in its original live
form for the first time on this release – which Ellington and Strayhorn had put together for
the occasion. The first part, 'Festival Junction', is more or less a blowing theme for a parade
of soloists, including a first excursion by Gonsalves, who gives notice of what's to come with
some blistering choruses (though not 27) on the third part, 'Newport Up'.

Columbia's new edition of the music puts an entirely fresh slant on the occasion. The
circumstances of how a 'virtual' stereo production came about are too complex to detail
here (go to Phil Schaap's notes in the booklet for that), but essentially Columbia's mono tape
was combined with a *second* mono recording of the music, made by Voice of America. It was
their microphone which Gonsalves was mistakenly playing into. That recording (rediscovered at the Library of Congress in the '90s) is on one channel and Columbia's on the other,
meticulously synchronized.The result is an astonishing advance on previous versions. The
attempted 're-creations' of the live event on the following Monday, such as the repeat of
'I Got It Bad And That Ain't Good' with two notes repaired and canned applause added,
are here, as is the studio 'Newport Jazz Festival Suite' with Norman O'Connor's remarks
from the live event spliced in. There are no fewer than ten new tracks too, mostly from the
concert itself. The overall sound is excellent and fully conveys the near-pandemonium of
the occasion!

& *See also* **Duke Ellington 1927–1929** (1927–1929; p. 28), **Duke Ellington 1937–1938** (1937–1938;
p. 64), **Never No Lament** (1940–1942; p. 81), **The Duke At Fargo** (1940; p. 81), **Black, Brown and
Beige** (1944–1946; p. 91), **The Far East Suite** (1966; p. 336)

NAT COLE&

Born Nathaniel Adams Coles, 17 March 1919, Montgomery, Alabama; died 15 February 1965, Santa Monica, California
Piano, voice

After Midnight
Capitol 520087
Cole; Harry 'Sweets' Edison (t); Juan Tizol (vtb); Willie Smith (as); Stuff Smith (vn); John Collins (g); Charlie Harris (b); Lee Young (d); Jack Costanzo (perc). August–September 1956.

Lyricist Gene Lees said (1996): **'You have to remember he was from the South. Nat's stage persona was deliberately unthreatening; even his approach to romantic material was done in a self-mocking way, as if he was saying he was no threat to dominant white men.'**

Cole's one latter-day jazz date has a huge reputation, but there are disappointing aspects to it: he didn't seem to want to stretch out and the tracks are all rather short; Tizol was a strange choice for horn soloist and Sweets tends to stroll through it all. 'Paper Moon', 'Route 66' and 'Blame It On My Youth' are outstanding tracks and the CD reissue includes material with an even larger jazz element - surprise, surprise. It's not all successful and there is an air of undue polish and a certain self-protective stance in the insistence on guest horns, but the music is still an unblemished and beautifully groomed example of small-group swing, and Cole proves that his piano-playing was undiminished by his career switchover.

& See also **Nat King Cole 1943–1944** (1943–1944; p. 92)

SONNY STITT&

Born Edward Boattner Stitt, 2 February 1924, Boston, Massachusetts; died 22 July 1982, Washington DC
Alto and tenor saxophones

New York Jazz
Verve 517050-2
Stitt; Jimmy Jones (p); Ray Brown (b); Jo Jones (d). September 1956.

Jesse Davis said (2005): **'People say he was a Charlie Parker disciple. I don't hear that at all. I think Stitt came out of something different and he took it in a direction all his own. You just have to listen to the way he phrases and the way he builds a solo.'**

It is open to dispute how much Stitt absorbed from Charlie Parker and how much he developed for himself. Album titles like *Don't Call Me Bird!* (admittedly a posthumous reissue) and *Stitt Plays Bird* point to market savvy as much as to any perceived or actual ambivalence. He played tenor in a band co-led with Gene Ammons from 1950, and thereafter drifted between that and the alto, occasionally picking up the baritone. A definitive example of the 'road musician', Stitt took every opportunity to record, often with undistinguished pick-up groups, and while his impassive professionalism meant that he seldom sounded less than strong, he diluted his reputation with an approach simultaneously dedicated and careless, and his records need careful sifting to find him genuinely at his best.

Still young and at the peak of his powers - 'lean, plunging Sonny Stitt', Nat Hentoff's note calls him - this is the Stitt that's most worth remembering and listening to again. He is helter-skelter on 'I Know That You Know', casts lyrical alto spinners on 'If I Had You' and cruises through 'Alone Together' in lightly bruised tenor mode. It's lushly melodic, yet the different astringencies he gets out of alto and tenor put an acidly personal edge on the improvising. Here and there one still gets the notion that he's just laughing at both us and the material, but this is surely the real Stitt, the 'public servant in music' who both valued his art and shrugged it off.

& *See also* **Constellation** (1972; p. 395)

CECIL TAYLOR &

Born 15 March 1929 (some sources state 25 March and 1930), Long Island, New York
Piano, voice

Jazz Advance
Blue Note 84462-2
Taylor; Steve Lacy (ss); Buell Neidlinger (b); Dennis Charles (d). September 1956.

Tony Herrington, publisher of *The Wire*, says: **'As a black, gay, intellectual, jazz piano-player in mid-'50s America, Cecil Taylor projected (or maybe harboured would be a more accurate way of putting it) a 24/7 alien identity as profound as Sun Ra's.'**

Taylor learned piano at the age of six and went on to study at the New York College and New England Conservatory. He worked in R&B and swing-styled small groups in the early '50s, then led his own band with Steve Lacy from 1956. He became the most daring of modern artists, with his music leaving tonality and jazz rhythm and structure behind. The complaint that he doesn't 'swing' is both literally accurate and beside the point. Playing on the on-beat did suggest that but his purpose was new and radical and by the '70s the work was entirely *sui generis*, incorporating poetry and a form of dance.

Taylor's first record remains one of the most extraordinary debuts in jazz, and for 1956 it's an incredible effort. The pianist's '50s music is even more radical than Ornette Coleman's, though it has seldom been recognized as such, and, while Coleman has acquired the plaudits, it is Taylor's achievement which now seems the most impressive and uncompromised. While there are still many nods to conventional post-bop form in this set, it already points to the freedoms in which the pianist would later immerse himself. The interpretation of 'Bemsha Swing' reveals an approach to time that makes Monk seem utterly straightforward; 'Charge 'Em' is a blues with an entirely fresh slant on the form; Ellington's 'Azure' is a searching tribute from one keyboard master to another. 'Sweet And Lovely' and 'You'd Be So Nice To Come Home To' are standards taken to the cleaners by the pianist, yet his elaborations on the melodies will fascinate any who respond to Monk's comparable treatment of the likes of 'There's Danger In Your Eyes, Cherie'. Lacy appears on two tracks and sounds amazingly comfortable for a musician who was playing Dixieland a few years earlier. And Neidlinger and Charles ensure that, contrary to what some may claim, Taylor's music – at this period, at least – still swings.

& *See also* **Nefertiti, The Beautiful One Has Come** (1962; p. 289), **Conquistador!** (1966; p. 339), **Celebrated Blazons** (1990; p. 541)

MAX ROACH &

Born 10 January 1924, New Land, North Carolina; died 16 August 2007, New York City
Drums

Alone Together
Verve 526373-2 2CD
Roach; Clifford Brown, Kenny Dorham, Booker Little, Tommy Turrentine (t); Julian Priester (tb); Ray Draper
(tba); George Coleman, Harold Land, Hank Mobley, Paul Quinichette, Sonny Rollins, Stanley Turrentine (ts);
Herbie Mann (f); Ray Bryant, Jimmy Jones, Richie Powell, Bill Wallace (p); Barry Galbraith (g); Joe Benjamin,
Bob Boswell, Nelson Boyd, Art Davis, Milt Hinton, George Morrow (b); Boston Percussion Ensemble; Abbey
Lincoln (v). September 1956–October 1960.

Max Roach said: **'We were learning how to work in the business and with the business.
Sometimes someone says that the music here sits oddly alongside** We Insist! [Freedom
Now Suite] **but I can't figure that out. It seems to me that with those recordings we were
making our own language and nothing is more radical than that.'**

The fierce metres of bebop, with the accent taken on the hi-hat instead of the bass drum,
were created by Kenny Clarke, Art Blakey and Max Roach, who in terms of long-term influence may be the most important of the three, and he has continued to create a radical, often
politically engaged brand of jazz in which the drum is at the centre of the action. His group
M'Boom took this to the extreme. *Alone Together* is a very valuable compilation and an excellent introduction for anyone who hasn't caught up with Roach. There are two tracks from
Max Roach + 4 and just one from *Jazz In 3/4 Time*, which was Roach's attempt to free jazz
from the constant thump of a 4/4. Most of the rest is later, some of it from less well-known
records like *The Many Sides Of Max* (1959, with Little, Priester and Coleman) and *Quiet As It's
Kept* (1960, with the Turrentines and Priester). 'Max's Variations' is based on 'Pop Goes The
Weasel' and is performed with the Boston Percussion Ensemble, a foreshadowing of later
drum orchestra projects like M'Boom.

& *See also* **We Insist! Freedom Now Suite** (1960; p. 258), **Historic Concerts** (1979; p. 454)

MAYNARD FERGUSON
Born 4 May 1928, Verdun, Quebec, Canada; died 23 August 2006, Ventura, California
Trumpet

The Birdland Dreamband
RCA Bluebird ND 86455
Ferguson; Al Derisi, Joe Ferrante, Jimmy Nottingham, Ernie Royal, Al Stewart, Nick Travis (t); Eddie Bert, Jimmy
Cleveland, Sonny Russo (tb); Herb Geller (as); Al Cohn, Budd Johnson, Frank Socolow (ts); Ernie Wilkins (bs);
Hank Jones (p); Arnold Fishkind, Milt Hinton (b); Jimmy Campbell, Osie Johnson, Don Lamond (d); collective
personnel. September–December 1956.

Trumpeter John Vallence remembers: **'Forget Dizzy's bullfrog cheeks. I stood behind
Maynard in a club once and when he hit the first high note, his whole neck seemed to
quadruple in size. The guy must have worn a horse collar.'**

There were few sights in nature more impressive than Maynard Ferguson in full flight. No
one in jazz had ever hit so many stratospheric notes with such consistent accuracy. Unfortunately, perhaps, the results often lacked grace of sophistication, but the Canadian's bands
were configured for excitement rather than profound expression. After running his own
outfit at home, in 1950 he became a key member of Kenton's notorious Innovations Orchestra. In the mid-'50s, after experience with Boyd Raeburn and others, Ferguson formed his
Birdland Dreamband and managed, against the economic current, to keep a sizeable personnel together for the better part of a decade. At a bad time for big bands, an outsize sound
and a willingness to go for the populist throat were bankable assets.
  Working to arrangements by some of the best in the business (Manny Albam, Al Cohn,

Herb Geller, Willie Maiden, Ernie Wilkins, Jimmy Giuffre, Bill Holman, Bob Brookmeyer and Marty Paich), he could hardly go wrong, but nor could the music ever be entirely unsubtle. Writing for MF's swollen trumpet sections was a challenge, but even though these were still essentially swing charts, they were imaginatively steered into polychordal sophistication on things like Brookmeyer's 'Still Water Stomp' and Giuffre's 'Say It With Trumpets'. On 'You Said It' and 'Everybody Moan', the leader's high notes reach absurd levels, but for sheer excitement, they're hard to beat. He was probably best encountered in a club, but it's still worth jacking up the volume and listening to these boisterous classics once in a while.

PHINEAS NEWBORN JR

Born 14 December 1931, Whiteville, Tennessee; died 26 May 1989, Memphis, Tennessee
Piano

Here Is Phineas

Koch International 8505
Newborn; Calvin Newborn (g); Oscar Pettiford (b); Kenny Clarke (d). May 1956.

Harold Mabern said (1991), two years after Newborn's death: **'They crucified him, you know, a man who had more music in his left hand than most piano-players have in two. He was fragile, and they broke him down.'**

A player of tremendous technical ability, often likened to Oscar Peterson, the younger Newborn was flashy, hyped-up and explosive, eating up themes like Clifford Brown's 'Daahoud' and Bud Powell's 'Celia' as if they were buttered toast. Underneath the super-confident exterior, though, there was a troubled young man who was acutely sensitive to criticism, particularly the charge that he was no more than a cold technician. Racked by negative criticism, which undermined an already frail constitution, Newborn suffered a serious nervous collapse from which he only partially recovered, and the remainder of his career was interspersed with periods of ill-health. His later recording output is spasmodic to say the least, marked by a chastened blues sound which contrasts sharply – in style and quality – with the early work. This debut record, made for Atlantic with Pettiford and Clarke, with brother Calvin in for a couple of numbers, is such a startling and vivid one that it's hard to pass over. Newborn shows his mettle at once with one of Charlie Parker's less well-known lines, 'Barbados', races through the bop changes on the Brownie and Bud themes, and seems to want to take everything at double time, even the ballad features. If that profligacy is a fault, then it's a record that will dismay some listeners. There is a brittle, hectic quality that in retrospect points to incipient problems, but for the moment at least 'the piano artistry of Phineas Newborn' is dazzling.

OSCAR PETERSON &

Born 15 August 1925, Montreal, Quebec, Canada; died 23 December 2007, Mississauga, Ontario, Canada
Piano, organ, other keyboards

At The Stratford Shakespearean Festival

Verve 513752-2
Peterson; Herb Ellis (g); Ray Brown (b). August 1956.

Norman Granz said (1982): **'In his early 20s Oscar seemed fully formed as a player. Technically, you couldn't have asked any more of him, but he was open to any situation that came along and that sometimes stretched him in unfamiliar directions.'**

According to Lalo Schifrin, Oscar Peterson is the Liszt of modern jazz, Bill Evans its Chopin; this refers back to the much-quoted assertion that the Hungarian conquered the piano, while the Pole seduced it. All through his career Peterson has seemed to have all the technical bases covered, working in styles from Tatum-derived swing to bebop, stride to near-classical ideas. What is extraordinary is how quickly and completely he matured as a stylist, barely changing thereafter. When Peterson left Canada in 1949 at Norman Granz's behest, he already had behind him a successful recording career with RCA Victor in Montreal. Peterson was known round the city as the Brown Bomber Of Boogie Woogie, and it is that style which dominates the earliest discs.

Unlike the Ahmad Jamal and Nat Cole trios, which also dispensed with drummers in favour of piano, guitar and bass, the Peterson group never sounded spacious or open-textured – the pianist's hyperactive fingers saw to that. Here, though, for once Peterson seemed able to lie back a little and let the music flow under its own weight, rather than constantly pushing it along. Peterson has described how during the daytime Brown and Ellis sat and practised all the harmonic variables that might come up during a performance. A sensible precaution, one might have thought, given a player with Peterson's hand-speed. The irony is that his vertical mobility, in and out of key, was never as rapid as all that, and there are occasions here, as on 'How High The Moon' and the closing 'Daisy's Dream', where it appears that Ellis and Brown manage to anticipate his moves and push him into configurations he hadn't apparently thought of.

& See also **Night Train** (1962; p. 290), **My Favorite Instrument** (1968; p. 351), **The Legendary Live At The Blue Note** (1990; p. 539)

SANDY BROWN
Born Izatnagar, Bareilly, India, 25 February 1929; died 15 March 1975, London
Clarinet

McJazz And Friends
Lake LACD 58
Brown; Al Fairweather (t); Jeremy French (tb); Dick Heckstall-Smith (ss); Ian Armit, Dill Jones, Dave Stephens, Harry Smith (p); Diz Disley (g, bj); Cedric West, Bill Bramwell (g); Tim Mahn, Major Holley, Brian Brocklehurst, Arthur Watts (b); Graham Burbridge, Stan Grein, Don Lawson, Eddie Taylor (d). May 1956–November 1958.

During an unforgettable 'lesson' in 1972, Sandy Brown said: **'If you want to sound better, and **** knows, you couldn't sound worse, the thing to do is to have all your teeth taken out. I could help you with that, and if you play that way again ... I will!'**

Brown enjoys legendary status among British musicians and fans of a certain age, but as memories fade there isn't much of a recorded legacy to keep him before the jazz public. He was born in India, where his father was a traffic manager with Indian Railways, but he grew up and learned to play in Edinburgh, part of the Royal High School crowd. He formed a band with Al Fairweather and went to London, moving from simple trad beginnings to a more sophisticated style, though he recorded little.

Brown's technique was dismissed by some as crude, but he had devised a way of playing clarinet that utilized freak high notes and other accidentals, and was considerably influenced by African highlife music, so he seldom fits easily into the British trad line. *McJazz And Friends* consists of the *McJazz* album, together with a selection of material from EPs and various trad compilations from the Nixa/Pye shelves. Opening on 'Go Ghana', it immediately establishes the sound and sensibility that made Sandy one of Britain's most distinctive and distinguished improvisers. There is nothing crude about 'Go Ghana' or the later 'Ognoliya', though neither of them sounds quite part of the run of things coming out of

London at the time. 'Scales' and 'The Card' are also strikingly original in tonality and delivery. There's a bonus in the material with saxophonist Dick Heckstall-Smith, a significant jazz player who was later diverted in progressive rock situations.

Any latter-day enthusiast has to be resigned to meeting Sandy Brown only in fragmentary form and minus the formidable presence. Enough of his buoyant and abrasive personality comes across on these tracks, though.

QUINCY JONES
Born 14 March 1933, Chicago, Illinois
Trumpet, composer, arranger

This Is How I Feel About Jazz
ABC Music 9569
Jones; Art Farmer, Ernie Royal, Bernie Glow, Joe Wilder (t); Jimmy Cleveland, Urbie Green, Frank Rehak (tb); Gene Quill, Phil Woods (as); Jerome Richardson (as, ts, f); Herbie Mann (ts, f); Zoot Sims, Lucky Thompson, Bunny Bardach (ts); Jack Nimitz (bs); Milt Jackson (vib); Hank Jones, Billy Taylor (p); Paul Chambers, Charles Mingus (b); Charli Persip (d); Father John Crawley (handclaps). September 1956.

Freddie Hubbard played on Jones's *Quintessence*. He said (1982): **'He hears what you can do for him and he gets it from you. With Quincy, you play things you don't necessarily want to do and don't necessarily like. But it all fits into place and it all works.'**

Jones played trumpet with Lionel Hampton, then did freelance arranging, including a stint in Europe, where he recorded with Harry Arnold. After that he toured with his own big band for a couple of years at the end of the '50s, did arrangements for Count Basie and a couple of singers, and then took an industry job at Mercury Records, the first time that an African-American had been taken on by one of the corporations at vice-president level. That, as far as most jazz fans were concerned, was that. Jones has continued to work in film music and pop (Michael Jackson!), written books and run a foundation that does substantial good in the community. But he has never quite given up on his original love. He produced a Miles Davis spectacular at Montreux shortly before the trumpeter's death and made his own kind of jazz-fusion in the '80s with *Back On The Block*, which was studded with top-drawer guest spots, including Miles.

It's hard to find anyone with a bad word to say about Quincy Delight Jones Jr, but it's equally hard to find many younger jazz fans who'll admit to a fondness for the work. That's why the release in 2008 of a Mosaic box of early big-band sessions was such an important one. Apart from the Harry Arnold material, the tracks that went to *This Is How I Feel About Jazz* were his first major jazz statement. These are classic cuts. They leap out of the speakers with a freshness and alertness that banish the intervening years. Who couldn't stir to the brasses, perfectly weighted on 'Stockholm Sweetnin'' (perhaps *the* quintessential Quincy track), or the gospelly edge of 'Sermonette'. The charts were by Jimmy Giuffre, Lennie Niehaus and Herb Geller, top-of-the-range work from the hottest talents of the moment.

RANDY WESTON
Born 6 April 1926, Brooklyn, New York
Piano

Jazz À La Bohemia
Original Jazz Classics OJC 1747
Weston; Cecil Payne (bs); Sam Gill (b); Al Dreares (d). October 1956.

Randy Weston said (1982): **'Monk was a magician. He restored magic to jazz and I guess that is a very ancient thing. I learned so much from him, but my first model was Basie: that sense of space as part of music, where you don't have to play so many notes to make a statement.'**

Strongly influenced by lessons with Monk, the impressively proportioned Weston – he is 6 feet 5 inches, hence 'Hi-Fly' – spent the late '60s and early '70s in Morocco, an experience that coloured his playing from then on. He cuts such an unignorable figure that his marginal critical standing remains an enigma. Though dozens of players every year turn to the joyous 'Hi-Fly' theme or possibly 'Little Niles', few of them probe any deeper into Weston's output. There is no doubt that his sojourn in Africa, which followed an earlier visit to Nigeria, made a strong impact but the inescapable truth is that Weston plays American music, not African music, and his studies there did little more (not to belittle their impact in any way) than to bring elements that were instinct in his writing and playing from the beginning.

His identification of Basie as a source confirms our instincts about him. The calypso 'Hold 'Em Joe' on *Jazz À La Bohemia* is a nice example of how much of that African/African-Cuban pulse inhabited Weston long before the 'epiphany' of Africa, which was only an epiphany for the critics who hitherto hadn't got a handle on his music. It isn't the case that Weston passively 'discovered' African rhythms and tonalities on one of his early-'60s study trips. As one can clearly hear from the Africanized inflexions of the Riverside sessions, Weston went in search of confirmation for what he was already doing. The set opens with a 'Solemn Meditation' that gives what follows an almost ritual significance. Gill, who wrote the intro piece, had a turn of phrase that was very different from anyone else of the time and Payne's solemn baritone here and on the other 1956 recordings suggests a Central African drone. Dreares, though not required to do anything out of the ordinary, keeps his lines long and loose, but always under control. 'You Go To My Head' has a quality quite unlike the average standards performance of the time, and Weston's own 'Chessman's Delight' stands outside the bop orthodoxy of the day.

KEN COLYER
Born 18 April 1928, Great Yarmouth, Norfolk, England; died 8 March 1988, Les Isambres, France
Cornet

Club Session With Colyer
Lake LACD 6
Colyer; Mac Duncan (tb); Ian Wheeler (cl); Johnny Bastable (bj); Ron Ward (b); Colin Bowden (d). October–November 1956.

Ken Colyer said (1981): **'Do I mind being called dogmatic or rigid? Not really. Someone has to be. And given that anything goes in music it was important that somebody stood up for what they believed was the right way to play jazz. I still think there's a right way and a wrong way.'**

Colyer has a unique place in British jazz. Nobody has ever been more revered in local circles and few were so righteously dogmatic about authenticity. As the trad boom got under way, he abjured such 'modern' style models as Armstrong and Morton and insisted on the earlier New Orleans methods of George Lewis and Bunk Johnson. Colyer's records are an intriguing muddle of stiff British orthodoxy and something that finds a genuine accord with the music that obsessed him. The purist's purist was self-taught, which is perhaps significant. He formed the Crane River Jazz Band, before joining the merchant marine and escaping to New Orleans, where he met idols like George Lewis, and famously spent some time in jail, passing as black. In 1953, he began bandleading in Britain with Chris Barber and also played guitar in skiffle situations though never relaxing his principles. His Studio 51 Club was an important traditional venue.

Club Session is the essential Colyer record and certainly his most famous single album, this live set from the Railway Hotel, West Hampstead (rather than Studio 51), catches the band at its most persuasive. The playing isn't noticeably superior to other dates – consistency was the man's long suit, after all – but in its balance of blues, gospel and standards, its driving rhythms and clipped solos, it is as close to perfect as Colyer would get at a recording. 'Creole Blues', 'The Old Rugged Cross' and 'The Thriller Rag' are perennial favourites, but there isn't a dud in the set.

BOB DOROUGH
Born 12 December 1923, Cherry Hill, Arkansas
Voice, piano

Devil May Care
JVC Victor 61464
Dorough; Warren Fitzgerald (t); Jack Hitchcock (vib); Bill Takas (b); Jerry Segal (d). October 1956.

Bob Dorough said (1991): **'I got a call from Miles Davis one day, completely out of nowhere. This would be 1962. He wanted me to write a Christmas song for him! I think he'd heard me doing "Yardbird Suite". So I wrote him "Blue Xmas" and we recorded it. It's on that record [*Jingle Bell Jazz*]. I use it to impress young people sometimes. "Yes, I remember when I was in the studio with Miles Davis ..."'**

Dorough has made only a modest number of records over his marathon career, and is mostly remembered as the author of 'Devil May Care' and other great songs. His own version is perhaps not the most exciting by today's standards, but it's brilliant singing and catches a moment in time almost perfectly. The album has been around in many different incarnations over the years, so it's likely to be available under one flag or another (Bethlehem Archives, Avenue, Charly, Rhino/WEA or the above). Whatever its port of registration, get it and enjoy Bob's 'Yardbird Suite' (two takes), 'Baltimore Oriole', 'I Had The Craziest Dream' and ten others, though at this stage only a couple of originals.

JIMMY GIUFFRE &
Born 26 April 1921, Dallas, Texas; died 24 April 2008, Pittsfield, Massachusetts
Clarinet, tenor, baritone and soprano saxophones, flute, bass flute

The Jimmy Giuffre 3
Atlantic 90981
Giuffre; Jim Hall (g); Jim Atlas, Ralph Pena (b). December 1956.

Jimmy Giuffre said (1987): **'Rhythm doesn't interest me that much, which is a heretical thing for a "jazz" musician to say. I wanted to make a personal style and rhythm is a universal, so it actually prevents you developing a personal style. Also, I react against the idea that you can only swing hard. If it means anything at all, you ought to be able to do it softly, too.'**

One of the most distinguished composer-arrangers on the '50s West Coast scene. Giuffre's long career observed a long, sometimes lonely arc that kept him apart from any bop or cool orthodoxy and along paths almost always of his own choosing. He played in an army band and then with a series of West Coast orchestras, valued for his musicianship – often baritone in those early days – as well as for his writing skills. As author of 'Four Brothers', he was a signature composer of the era. Cultivating a brown chalumeau register on his clarinet and defending the aesthetic benefits of simple quietness, Giuffre later created what he liked to call 'folk-jazz'. Later still, he went in a more abstract direction with Paul Bley and Steve Swallow.

The Jimmy Giuffre 3 contains essential early material: a fine version of 'The Train And The River', on which Giuffre moves between baritone and tenor saxophones and clarinet; and the long 'Crawdad Suite', which combines blues and folk materials. Giuffre's out-of-tempo playing recalls the great jazz singers. Jim Hall was his longest-standing and most sympathetic confrère; they were partnered either by Brookmeyer or by a bassist, most successfully Pena (Clark or Buddy, and Atlas only plays on two bonus tracks on the Atlantic CD). With Giuffre's early recordings now out of copyright, there is a confusing flurry of reissues. A Collectables option adds the 1958 *The Music Man* featuring the nonet. Quality control varies. All that matters is that you get hold of the music.

& See also **Free Fall** (1962; p. 286)

THELONIOUS MONK*&*

Born 10 October 1917, Rocky Mount, North Carolina; died 17 February 1982, Weehawken, New Jersey
Piano

Brilliant Corners
Original Jazz Classics OJCCD 026
Monk; Clark Terry (t); Ernie Henry (as); Sonny Rollins (ts); Oscar Pettiford (b); Max Roach (d). December 1956.

Saxophonist Steve Lacy said (1979): **'They're fiendish, those pieces, if you listen to them one by one. Once you start listening to them all, one after another, they start to reveal something. There isn't a key to understanding them but they're not so obscure and plain weird that they can't be understood.'**

A staggering record, imperfect and patched together after the sessions, but one of the most vivid insights into Monk's music. After two previous records for Riverside, Monk was determined to showcase himself as a composer. So bold was he in this direction that the wheels nearly came off the wagon. The title-tune was so difficult that no single perfect take was finished (after 25 tries), and what we hear is a spliced-together piece of music. Full of tensions within the band, the record somehow delivers utterly compelling accounts of 'Pannonica', with its part for celeste, 'Bemsha Swing' and a long 'Ba-Lue Bolivar Ba-Lues Are'. Miraculously, the group gets through the date pretty much intact. One hardly associates Clark Terry with music like this, but he's solid in his lines. Rollins was coming into his own and once or twice seems to buck against the leader's conception, but that only adds to the drama. Roach is quite simply amazing and his tymp additions to 'Bemsha Swing' add a faintly surreal note. After the rigours, Monk ties it up with a one-take unaccompanied reading of 'I Surrender Dear', which is as fresh as water.

& See also **Genius Of Modern Music** (1947–1948; p. 115), **Underground** (1967, 1968; p. 347)

KAI WINDING

Born 18 May 1922, Aarhus, Denmark; died 6 May 1983, New York City
Trombone

Trombone Panorama
Lone Hill Jazz LHJR CD 10315
Winding; Carl Fontana, Wayne Andre (tb, trombonium); Dick Lieb (btb, trombonium); Roy Frazee (p); Kenny O'Brien (b); Tom Montgomery (d). December 1956–August 1957.

Trombonist Mal Girvan says: **'He didn't always – this is heresy, I know – have the best tone, but the speed of his attack and the accuracy of his playing was revolutionary. Winding was what's called an "upstream" player, with the mouthpiece set down so that the air column travels up instead of down as it goes into the tubing. It maybe doesn't matter if you aren't a player, but it makes a difference you can hear.'**

J.J. brought a saxophone-like articulation to the trombone, but it was Winding who showed how it could follow the woodwind-players' fast vibrato and percussive attack and still retain its distinctive character. While with the Kenton band, Winding worked out ways of producing a very tight vibrato with the lip rather than using the slide, and this had a marked impact on a younger generation of players. A lot of the surviving Winding material is on discs also featuring J.J., Bennie Green and others, and that may have depressed him. Early on, though, the balance of innovation seemed to fall to the Dane.

The December 1956 (originally Columbia) and 1957 records are under Winding's sole leadership. His stint with Kenton had convinced him that massed trombones made the noise closest to the angels and he persisted with the choral approach. Here it works very well indeed; though some will be put off by what might be thought to be Kentonisms (an impression reinforced by the use of trombonium), they should be assured that the idiom and the arrangements are Winding's own. 'Nut Cracker' is the only track where it really cuts loose. 'Whistle While You Work' had the capacity to be a novelty track but it establishes a sober and thoughtful mood for the record, best represented on 'My Little Girl'. The pace is nicely modulated, though, and there's no mistaking this for a Third Stream experiment. 'Blue Room' romps along nicely and the muted horns are just perfectly in sync.

ANITA O'DAY
Born Anita Belle Colton, 18 October 1919, Chicago, Illinois; died 23 November 2006, Los Angeles, California
Voice

Anita Sings The Most
Verve 829577
O'Day; Oscar Peterson (p); Herb Ellis (g); Ray Brown (b); John Poole (d). January 1957.

Anita O'Day said (1985): **'If you have to get one of my old records, check if John Poole is on it. If he is, it's OK. I need to hear the drummer and what he's doing.'**

Anita O'Day lived the jazz life. She tells about it in *High Times, Hard Times* (1983). As a young woman she worked as a singing waitress and in punishing dance-marathons. She suffered abuse and violence and shot heroin until her heart began to give out in the '60s and she was forced to battle her demons cold. As is immediately obvious from her combative, sharply punctuated scatting and her line in stage patter, O'Day was nothing if not combative. As a 'chirper' with the Gene Krupa band in 1941, she refused to turn out in ballgown and gloves, and appeared instead in band jacket and short skirt, an unheard-of practice that underlined her instinctive feminism. With Stan Kenton, she gave a humane edge to a sometimes pretentiously modernist repertoire. O'Day's demanding style had few successful imitators, but

200 THE '50s: 1956-1960

she is the most immediate source for June Christy and Chris Connor, who followed her into the Kenton band.

Sings The Most is O'Day's best showing on record by a stretch. Her intonation – always suspect – was never as good again and her sparky personality comes through even on the ballads, including a strangely moving 'Bewitched, Bothered And Bewildered' right at the end of the set. 'Them There Eyes' is taken ridiculously fast and is the kind of performance that used on occasions to trip up her groups. Here, though, Peterson is equal to anything she throws at him and it's not hard to understand her attachment to the otherwise unvalued John Poole, who sets a time you could run a railway network to. In later years, O'Day became increasingly cranky and the voice went, but she retained a hypnotic authority to the very end. *Sings The Most* catches her at her sunniest.

ART PEPPER&

Born 1 September 1925, Gardenia, California; died 1 June 1982, Panorama City, California
Alto saxophone, clarinet

Meets The Rhythm Section
Original Jazz Classics OJCCD 338
Pepper; Red Garland (p); Paul Chambers (b); Philly Joe Jones (d). January 1957.

Gerry Mulligan said (1990): **'Art Pepper seems to have had the same gift as Chet [Baker], a musicality so fundamental that the external reality – or unreality – of his life hardly seemed to make any difference to his ability to play.'**

If there is a jazz musician who best represents the Hemingway ideal of grace under pressure, it is probably Art Pepper. He was a premier name among California saxophonists in the '50s, but the career was interrupted by addiction and prison sentences. His life story is told in the definitive jazz autobiography, *Straight Life*, co-written with his wife Laurie. Pepper's career began with stints in the Benny Carter and Stan Kenton big bands. Devoted compilers have found all his solo breaks from the Kenton years and the 18-year-old can be heard, already distinctive, on surveys of the early years.

Pepper's remains one of the most immediately identifiable alto sax styles in postwar jazz. If he was a Parker disciple, like every other modern saxophonist in the '40s and '50s, he tempered Bird's slashing attack with a pointed elegance that recalled something of Benny Carter and Willie Smith. He was a passionate musician, having little of the studious intensity of a Lee Konitz, and his tone – which could come out as pinched and jittery as well as softly melodious – suggested something of the duplicitous, cursed romanticism which seems to lie at the heart of his music.

After some scrappy work for Blue Note against a background of personal tribulation Pepper's records for Contemporary make up a superlative sequence. *The Way It Was, Modern Jazz Classics, Gettin' Together, Smack Up, Intensity* are titles that tell their own story. There is, however, a subtext to *Meets The Rhythm Section*. The playing of the quartet beggars belief when the circumstances are considered: Pepper wasn't even aware of the session till the morning of the date, hadn't played in two weeks, was going through difficult times with his narcotics problem and didn't know any of the material they played. Yet it emerges as a poetic, burning date, with all four men playing above themselves.

It opens with a bright, swinging 'You'd Be So Nice To Come Home To', then one of those back-of-envelope themes, 'Red Pepper Blues', scratched together by Pepper and Garland, that are one of the wonders of jazz to non-musicians. Conventional enough changes but exquisitely done. 'Imagination' is imaginatively recast. As if to disprove the hasty convention of the group, 'Waltz Me Blues' and the iconic 'Straight Life' are taken at a gallop, with

Chambers playing some of the best accompanying bass of his career. After that, it's clear that the group was relying on familiar material. Pepper's saxophone takes on a darker authority on the closing tracks, 'Birks' Works', 'Star Eyes' and 'Tin Tin Deo'. The quartet probably packed up and went their separate ways. Who knows what Art got up to and what need added to the urgency of those last cuts. Between them, they'd delivered a masterpiece.

& *See also* **Winter Moon** (1980; p. 460)

RED NORVO
Born Kenneth Norville, 31 March 1908, Beardstown, Illinois; died 6 April 1999, Santa Monica, California
Xylophone, vibraphone

Music To Listen To Red Norvo By
Original Jazz Classics OJCCD 1015
Norvo; Buddy Collette (f); Bill Smith (cl); Barney Kessel (g); Red Mitchell (b); Shelly Manne (d). January–February 1957.

Red Norvo said (1983): **'The xylophone was considered a bit of a joke instrument. When I changed to vibraharp, it was obviously louder and more like a piano, but I never wanted to lose some element of vaudeville in my work, so I sometimes missed the xylophone.'**

Norvo's early recorded work, before he made the switch from xylophone to vibes, illustrates the problem of placing so self-effacing an instrument in a conventional jazz line-up: it's sometimes difficult to separate technical limitations and compromises from conscious dynamic strategies. He'd actually started out playing marimba (and tap-dancing!) and graduated to vibes- and xylophone-playing without vibrato and with a light and almost delicate sound. Attracted by bebop, he managed to synthesize it with swing and Charles Mingus worked with him for a time. He was married to singer Mildred Bailey and his stage name arose when 'Norville' was apparently taken down wrongly in an interview.

There are large amounts of early Norvo on compilations and in poor sound. Moving into the LP era, his work was better represented. Sooner or later when dealing with so-called 'chamber-jazz', the question of its supposed pretentiousness comes into play. Norvo's 1957 sextet with Buddy Collette on flute and Barney Kessel on guitar strongly recalls Chico Hamilton's sophisticated chamber-jazz, with its soft, 'classical' textures and non-blues material. Titles like 'Divertimento In Four Movements' are apt to be seen as red rags by hard-nosed boppers. It's clear, though, from the album title if not immediately from the music itself, that there is a hefty dose of humour in Norvo's work. Structurally, the 'Divertimento' is unexceptional, with a beautiful division of parts, and is as lightweight as the genre demands. Other tracks, like 'Red Sails' and the boppish thematic puns of 'Rubricity', suggest a different side to Norvo which is actually present throughout his work, even in his 60s.

GIGI GRYCE
Also known as Basheer Qu'hsim, 28 November 1927, Pensacola, Florida; died 17 March 1983, Pensacola, Florida
Alto saxophone, flute

And The Jazz Lab Quintet
Original Jazz Classics OJCCD 1774
Gryce; Donald Byrd (t); Wade Legge (p); Wendell Marshall (b); Art Taylor (d). February–March 1957.

Gunther Schuller said (1984): **'He's completely underrated now, but a very special musician. He liked the reeds to sound very light and quick, so the effect you get is almost like water flowing over pebbles.'**

Gryce's real talent was as a leader who catalysed talent in others. He studied in Boston and Paris (went back there with Lionel Hampton, too), and saw service with many of the leading players coming out of bop. His Jazz Lab Quintet was, however, his own finest moment, though his compositions are part of the landscape now. Of the many pieces he wrote for a variety of ambitious projects – big not in numbers but in conception – the only ones which have really entered the jazz mainstream are 'Nica's Tempo' and, less so, 'Speculation' and 'Minority'. Gryce was never virtuosic, but these sessions suggest that he was more interesting than is often supposed, and was certainly not a Bird copyist. His tone was darker and with a broader vibrato, the phrasing less supple but with an emphatic, vocal quality, carried over into his flute-playing. 'Laboratory' and 'workshop' have always been weasel terms, useful camouflage for the well-founded jazz tradition of rehearsing – or experimenting – at the public's expense. Gryce, though, was a genuine experimenter, even if a relatively modest one. He never stopped trying to find new colourations and new ways of voicing chords, and this 1957 set is no exception. No great revelations, but Byrd is a responsive partner in the front line and the rhythm section is less hung-up on its own ideas, more aware, one suspects, of what Gryce himself is looking for.

ART TAYLOR

Born 6 April 1929, New York City; died 6 February 1995, New York City
Drums

Taylor's Wailers
Original Jazz Classics OJCCD 094
Taylor; Donald Byrd (t); Jackie McLean (as); John Coltrane, Charlie Rouse (ts); Ray Bryant, Red Garland (p); Wendell Marshall, Paul Chambers (b). February–March 1957.

Art Taylor said (1981): **'We had this neighbourhood group, with Sonny Rollins and Kenny Drew, and we were doing Friday evening concerts at St Charles's Church on 141st St, and that was the closest I ever got to catching the excitement of going with my dad to see Chick Webb and Big Sid [Catlett] and J. C. Heard all jamming. I think those first experiences stay with you. Everything has to match up to that standard.'**

Born to a Jamaican family, Taylor began working on the New York scene in 1950 and became one of the most prolific drummers of the hard-bop movement. One of the most scholarly of modern drummers, he moved to Europe in 1963 and collected musician interviews for his book *Notes And Tones*. He returned to New York in the '80s.

He was a prolific visitor to the studios in the '50s, drumming for Red Garland, John Coltrane, Miles Davis and many others on countless sessions, most of them for Prestige. The company gave him a few shots at a leadership date, and they're impressive in a plainly wrapped way. The album is actually compiled from two sessions, one with Coltrane, who works up his patented head of steam on 'C.T.A.', and another with Rouse, whose more circumspect passions are rather well caught in his solo on 'Batland'. 'Off Minor' and 'Well You Needn't' feature in Monk's own arrangements, and the music is delivered with fairly nonchalant authority, with Byrd his usual blandly confident self. Taylor's own playing is authoritative, although some of his mannerisms leave him a degree short of the single-minded drive of Art Blakey. Once he's in 'the crouch', though, he swings as hard as anyone.

ART BLAKEY&

Also known as Abdullah ibn Buhaina; born 11 October 1919, Pittsburgh, Pennsylvania; died 16 October 1990, New York City
Drums

Art Blakey's Jazz Messengers With Thelonious Monk
Atlantic 8122-73607
Blakey; Bill Hardman (t); Johnny Griffin (ts); Thelonious Monk (p); Spanky DeBrest (b). March 1957.

Drummer T. S. Monk, the great pianist's son, said (2002): **'The thing I notice is that there aren't the great groups any more. There's an obsession in the industry with finding star leaders, so those band relationships are neglected. You buy a record, you go see the guys play, and it's different musicians in the club, probably the leader with a bunch of college kids. Art Blakey was maybe one of the last great *bandleaders*.'**

Blakey appeared on several of Monk's seminal Blue Note sessions, and had an intuitive understanding of what the pianist wanted from a drummer. Griffin, volatile but serene in his mastery of the horn, was an almost ideal yet very different interpreter of Monk's music. The drummer was at an unequalled peak in the later '50s. Later records were doughty and mostly streets ahead of anyone else in the field, but there wasn't the same special chemistry. There are five Monk tunes and one by Griffin on this masterpiece. If Hardman wasn't on the same exalted level, he does nothing to disgrace himself and DeBrest keeps calm, unobtrusive time. The continuous dialogue between piano and drums comes out most clearly in passages such as Monk's solo on 'In Walked Bud', but almost any moment on the session illustrates their unique empathy. Both use simple materials, yet the inner complexities are astonishing and the music retains an uncanny freshness after fifty years; no passage is like any other and some of the tempos – for 'Evidence' and 'I Mean You' – are almost unique in the annals of Monk interpretation. (For those who enjoy bizarre juxtapositions, the LP is also available on Collectables, paired with the Modern Jazz Quartet at Carnegie Hall!)

& See also **A Night At Birdland** (1954; p. 150)

HERB GELLER

Born 2 November 1928, Los Angeles, California
Alto saxophone

That Geller Feller
Fresh Sound FSRCD 91
Geller; Kenny Dorham (t); Harold Land (ts); Lou Levy (p); Ray Brown (b); Lawrence Marable (d). March 1957.

Producer and friend Alastair Robertson says: **'He is virtually the last alto saxophonist who can legitimately connect to Benny Carter and Charlie Parker. Herb has a vast knowledge and love of good tunes. Even past 80 he is always well prepared and ready to play anywhere with the enthusiasm of a man half his years.'**

In 1995, Herb Geller told his own life story on a record called *Playing Jazz*, a gripping and often poignant account of nearly five decades spent in the service of jazz and swing. Remarkably, as his latter-day producer says, he is still active and very much the bright-toned player he was in 1957. Relatively untroubled by fashion, Geller set out as an orthodox, Parker-influenced bopper before turning towards a more broadly based and decidedly cooler style which incorporated elements of Desmond, Hodges and even Benny Goodman, with whom he worked in the later '50s. *That Geller Feller* is the best of the available sets. The originals – 'S'Pacific View', 'Marable Eyes', 'An Air For The Heir' and 'Melrose And Sam' – are tightly organized and demand considerable inventiveness from a group that frequently sounds much bigger than a sextet. Dorham plays a crackling solo on the opening track but is otherwise rather anonymous. Geller's own introduction to 'Jitterbug Waltz' is wonderfully delicate, with more than a hint of Benny Carter in the tone and phrasing. He also does a fine version of the Arlen–Gershwin rarity 'Here's What I'm Here For'.

Amazingly, the following year's *Stax Of Sax* was Geller's last American release before 1993 and his last as a leader for 17 years. One is used to such drop-outs in jazz careers, but this one has a poignant twist, for in October 1958 his beloved wife and pianist, the former Lorraine Walsh, died suddenly. Herb's grief drove him away from America and somewhat away from jazz for a time.

PHIL WOODS &

Born 2 November 1931, Springfield, Massachusetts
Alto saxophone

Phil & Quill

Original Jazz Classics OJCCD 215
Woods; Gene Quill (as); George Syran (p); Teddy Kotick (b); Nick Stabulas (d). March 1957.

Phil Woods says: **'That's definitely my favourite record by that group.'**

Phil Woods has never seemed like a beginner. He sprang into his recording career. Tone, speed of execution and ideas were all first-hand borrowings from bebop and, inevitably, Parker; but he sounded like a mature player from the first, and he has often suffered from a degree of neglect, both as a young musician and as a senior one. A well-educated musician, to an unusual degree for this generation, he studied with Tristano and at Juilliard, but it is his absolute, self-willed determination that sets him apart, even down to his insistence at some stages on no amplification in clubs, preferring his unadorned alto to cut through on its own. He started out touring with big bands before launching into small-group work (which may explain that easy power), but then spent a further period with the bands and in the studios before he formed his European Rhythm Machine while living in Paris. The Philology label was founded in Italy to put out Charlie Parker remnants and Woods's own material. He returned to the US in the early '70s and continues to tour tirelessly.

He formed the two-alto band with Gene Quill in 1957, though they'd recorded the previous year on *Pairing Off*. So *simpatico* was the partnership that at moments one wonders whether one is hearing some kind of studio trick, one musician doubletracked with himself. There are subtle differences, however, not least in how each of these superb players (Quill is nowadays much underrated) weighted a phrase, and the interplay between them is too obviously dynamic to be an artefact. *Phil & Quill* doesn't have an ounce of spare fat in the solos, and the spanking delivery on, say, 'A Night At St Nick's' is as compelling as anything Prestige was recording at the period. Quill's duskier tone (obvious once you register it) and more extreme intensities are barely a beat behind Woods's in terms of quality of thought. There are a couple of bonus tracks on the CD reissue, including a spanking version of Rollins's 'Airegin', which confirms that these were worthy keepers of the bebop flame.

& *See also* **Bop Stew** (1987; p. 514)

CLIFFORD JORDAN *&*
Born 2 September 1931, Chicago, Illinois; died 27 March 1993, New York City
Tenor saxophone

JOHN GILMORE
Born 28 September (other sources give 29 October) 1931, Summit, Mississippi; died 19/20 August 1995,
Philadelphia, Pennsylvania
Tenor saxophone

Blowin' In From Chicago
Blue Note 42306
Jordan, Gilmore; Horace Silver (p); Curley Russell (b); Art Blakey (d). March 1957.

John Gilmore said (1981): **'John Coltrane asked me for a lesson once. He heard me sitting
in with Willie Bobo and I couldn't make head or tail of all the percussion, so I just played
across it and Coltrane rushed up, shouting 'You got it!' That's maybe what he got from
me, the idea of playing rhythmically and melodically at the same time.'**

Is this the neglected masterpiece of Blue Note hard bop? It certainly features two figures
whose standing in the music is far lower than it ought to be. That's routinely said about
Gilmore, who devoted much of his career to Sun Ra and the Arkestra, and saying it repeatedly doesn't make it any truer. In point of fact, Gilmore probably found his creative niche
with Sun Ra. His occasional recordings suggest a powerful talent whose band-width was
narrower than most of his rival tenors of the time and certainly not the potential rival to
John Coltrane's crown that is often suggested. He had, in fact, two distinct approaches: fluent hard bop and an eldritch abstraction, the latter his required mode with Sun Ra. Jordan,
though, is simply accorded an admiring nod and passed over. He's an immensely muscular
player, but one who brings real thought and logic to his solos.
  It's worth getting *Blowin'* out of the box every now and then. It's all to easy to forget the
impact of its opening track, John Neely's driving 'Status Quo', on which Gilmore leads with
a beautifully crafted solo. The pace changes sharply on the second track, Jordan's Latinized
'Boi-Till', which gives place to Gigi Gryce's 'Blue Lights', the only tune so far that's made
it into the regular repertory. 'Billie's Bounce' is more familiar, but rarely done with the
foot pushed as far down as this. The solo exchanges are ferocious. Silver asserts himself
towards the end of the date, with a great solo on Jordan's minor blues 'Evil Eye' and then
with his own lovely composition 'Everywhere'. Even seasoned writers pass over this record
with the comment that it's 'another' of Blue Note's noisy tenor jams, and with the usual
acknowledgement of egregious neglect of Gilmore's talent. However, it's not a record that
figures often in anyone's playlist and it's time it did.

& See also **CLIFFORD JORDAN, Royal Ballads** (1986; p. 508)

RED MITCHELL
Born Keith Moore Mitchell, 20 September 1927, New York City; died 8 November 1992, Salem, Oregon
Double bass, piano

Presenting Red Mitchell
Original Jazz Classics OJCCD 158
Mitchell; James Clay (ts, f); Lorraine Geller (p); Billy Higgins (d). March 1957.

Red Mitchell said (1984): **'Putting cellists and bass-players together in the orchestra is
like putting cats and dogs in the one pen. Different tuning. A bass is "normally" tuned**

in fourths. There used to be just three strings because a gut C string would have been like a cable. My dad knew the science of all this, but I knew I was going to struggle, until I altered the tuning back to the same as a cello: C G D A, an octave down, and a bottom string that's a major third down from normal E.'

Mitchell was known for a fluent improvising style in which pulled-off (rather than plucked) notes in a typically low register (he used a retuned bass) suggest a baritone saxophone rather than a stringed instrument; Scott LaFaro was later sanctified for a broadly similar technique. Mitchell is also an accomplished pianist, with a hint of the romantic approach of his former colleague, Hampton Hawes. His brother Whitey was also a bass-player. Red did much of his early work on the West Coast, from 1954, but left for Scandinavia in the '60s and became a European star. Most of the available recordings come from the later period. They're all technically terrific, but Red's showy personality and addiction to his own voice sometimes got in the way of the music. This early stuff on OJC with the short-lived Lorraine Geller standing in for Hawes is good, boppish jazz consistently lifted by Mitchell's singing lines. His writing is nicely idiomatic for his own instrument, particularly on 'Rainy Night', but most of the set is given over to bop material: 'Scrapple From The Apple' is a joy and a delight; Sonny Rollins's 'Paul's Pal' doesn't get covered often and Clifford Brown's 'Sandu' is an ideal vehicle for Clay's rootsy-modern sound. A nice read of 'Cheek To Cheek', with the emphasis on cheek, rounds out a strong set.

CLARK TERRY&

Born 14 December 1920, St Louis, Missouri
Trumpet, flugelhorn

Serenade To A Bus Seat
Original Jazz Classics OJC 066
Terry; Johnny Griffin (ts); Wynton Kelly (p); Paul Chambers (b); Philly Joe Jones (d). April 1957.

Clark Terry says: **'St Louis is a trumpet players' town. I don't know why. We all have some traits in common. We're like cousins who don't know one another or don't meet very often, but we always recognize the kinship when we hear it. You wouldn't have heard of these guys: Charlie Creath, the king of cornet, or Levi Madison, who laughed more than he played … he could laugh for an hour at a time.'**

Known as 'Mumbles' after his famously indistinct scat style, the prodigiously hard-working Terry, who is probably the most extensively documented horn-player in all editions of the *Guide*, held down jobs in both the Basie and the Ellington bands, as well as countless other recording dates, before disappearing into the studios for more than a decade. He eventually returned in the '70s, with expressive flugelhorn added to his armoury.

Though not reducible to his 'influences', Terry hybridizes Dizzy Gillespie's hot, fluent lines and witty abandon with Rex Stewart's distinctive half-valving and Charlie Shavers's high-register lyricism; he is also a master of the mute, an aspect of his work that had a discernible impact on Miles Davis. Miles, though, remained unconvinced by Terry's pioneering development of the flugelhorn as a solo instrument; later in his career he traded four-bar phrases with himself, holding a horn in each hand. An irrepressible showman with a sly sense of humour, Terry often fared better when performing under other leaders.

The 'early' – he was 37 – *Serenade To A Bus Seat* combines a tribute to civil-rights activist Rosa Parks with pungent versions of 'Stardust' and Parker's 'Donna Lee'. Terry isn't an altogether convincing bopper, but he's working with a fine, funky band, and they carry him through some slightly unresolved moments. 'That Old Black Magic' has a nice easy swing, with a Latin twist. Griffin makes an unexpectedly natural partner and Kelly's bluesy chord shapes keep the music moving at a brisk but not hectic pace. Terry's characteristic sound, quite breathy and with a little flange to each terminal note, is immediately recognizable. Over the next 50 years, it was to become one of the signature sounds of jazz.

& See also **Color Changes** (1960; p. 260), **Memories Of Duke** (1980; p. 457)

PAUL QUINICHETTE
Born 17 May 1916, Denver, Colorado; died 25 May 1983, New York City
Tenor saxophone

On The Sunny Side
Original Jazz Classics OJC 076-2
Quinichette; Curtis Fuller (tb); John Jenkins, Sonny Red Kyner (as); Mal Waldron (p); Doug Watkins (b); Ed Thigpen (d). 1957.

Rolling Stones drummer and bebop bandleader Charlie Watts said (1990): **'He's maybe not the best-known name on my wishlist, but I'd ask Paul Quinichette to be in the band. Only I think he's dead now.'**

The Vice-Pres, but more than a slavish Lester Young copyist, who managed to convey something of the great man's tone and spirit. Very much a middle-order batsman, Quinichette was best in the loose, jam session format that Prestige favoured in the later '50s, and a complete set of sessions for Dawn sees him fairly swamped by the players around him. Nevertheless, he had a beguiling tone and a crafty way with a solo and there's a good deal to enjoy in all his work, even if it rarely raises the rafters. Mal Waldron does all the new writing on *On The Sunny Side* and his 'Cool-lypso' hands Paul a line he can do something elegant with. At this vintage, it's clear that he's no John Coltrane, but he's certainly worth more than the passing mention he now gets from aficionados.

CURTIS FULLER
Born 15 December 1934, Detroit, Michigan
Trombone

With Red Garland
Original Jazz Classics OJCCD 1862
Fuller; Sonny Red Kyner (as); Red Garland (p); Paul Chambers (b); Louis Hayes (d). May 1957.

Curtis Fuller said (1981): **'John Coltrane must have seen something in me, because he picked me for *Blue Train*, my first recording. I had a lot to learn then, about life even more than music, and I think Trane was trying to give me a message ...'**

Curtis Fuller made his mark on one of the most memorable intros in modern jazz, the opening bars of Coltrane's 'Blue Train'. For many the story stops there, ironically so, since the Blue Note session with Trane was hardly representative of what this mellifluous trombonist was about. Possessed of an excellent technique, slightly derivative of J. J. Johnson, he occasionally found it difficult to develop ideas at speed and tended to lapse, as he had on 'Blue Train', into either repetition or sequences of bitten-off phrases that sounded either diffident or aggressive. The saxophone-influenced delivery helped create a tonal ambiguity not accessible to valved or keyed horn-players.

There was some excitement about Fuller in 1957, and the early sessions for Prestige, supervised by the redoubtable Teddy Charles, promised much. Sonny Red was the working name of Sylvester Kyner; a raw player, he none the less acquits himself on both sets to come out of the sessions with enthusiasm and some ruggedly straightforward ideas. The first LP was called *New Trombone* and was designed to showcase Fuller in sympathetic company. There's a slightly different group on the second date, with Garland crucially in place of the lighter and less driving Hank Jones. Both Sonny Red and the leader are more convincing on the later date, kicking off Garland's cleaner-cut blues chords. The rhythm section is also strengthened by the addition of Chambers, who comes through powerfully, blending nicely with the trombone in unison passages. A good mix of material – including a big saxophone feature on 'Slenderella' and a gorgeous original from Fuller, 'Cashmere' – gives everyone plenty room to express themselves.

MILES DAVIS &

Born 26 May 1926, Alton, Illinois; died 28 September 1991, Santa Monica, California
Trumpet, flugelhorn, organ

Miles Ahead
Columbia CK 65121
Davis; John Carisi, Bernie Glow, Taft Jordan, Louis Mucci, Ernie Royal (t); Joe Bennett, Jimmy Cleveland, Frank Rehak (tb); Tom Mitchell (btb); Tony Miranda, Willie Ruff (frhn); Lee Konitz (as); Sid Cooper, Romeo Penque (woodwinds); Danny Bank (bcl); Paul Chambers (b); Art Taylor (d); Gil Evans (cond). May 1957.

Miles's biographer Ian Carr said (1990): **'It really did put him "miles ahead" of anyone else in the jazz world. Musicians recognized it for what it was; critics jumped on it as if the earlier small-group records had been building up to it, which ignored the fact that, marvellous as it was, it wasn't necessarily better than them, just different.'**

Having combated his personal problems with real fortitude, Miles made a comeback around 1954 and set out for Prestige a body of work that established a new standard in combo jazz. These records, with their instinctively clever titles – *Relaxin'*, *Workin'*, *Steamin'*, *Cookin'* – offer one of the first detailed documentations of Miles Davis at a key development moment. There is a tendency to think that the big live packages and the posthumous box sets of album 'sessions' were the first time this had happened. The Prestige records, in their own way, fulfil the same function and, listened to carefully, they reveal an artist who is not so much at the pinnacle of his art as anxious to break its internal barriers and move on to something larger.

Miles had worked with Gil Evans before *Miles Ahead*, but this first full-length collaboration highlighted their like-mindedness and an illuminating reciprocity of vision. Curiously, given the reputation that these records have garnered, they aren't always well played, with fluffs aplenty and shaky ensembles, though this first outing is pristine compared to the passage-work on *Porgy And Bess*, later. *Miles Ahead* was rightly identified as a concerto for Miles. Recorded over four sessions in May 1957, it has great internal consistency. It no longer makes much sense to talk about 'tracks', for the internal subdivisions here are effectively moments in a long, continuous work. Even so, certain things do stand out: 'The Maids Of Cadiz', 'My Ship', the title-track and a lovely version of Ahmad Jamal's 'New Rhumba'. Frailties of performance apart, Evans gave the music a great depth of focus, doubling up bass-lines and creating distance and tension between upper and lower lines in a way that was to affect Miles for the rest of his career. Though it is far from being expressively one-dimensional – there are moments of playful humour – the pervading tone is a melancholy lyricism. This was the first time Miles recorded with flugelhorn; every trumpeter subsequently copied him, though he himself seldom repeated the experiment. The flugelhorn's sound isn't so very different from his trumpet soloing, though palpably softer-edged. Though he plays open all the time, as he was to do again on *Milestones*, some of the burnish seems to have been replaced by a more searching sound. *Sketches Of Spain*, with its glorious interpretation of Rodrigo's *Concierto de Aranjuez* remains the favourite record of the Miles/Gil collaboration, but it is markedly inferior to this quiet masterpiece.

& See also **The Complete Birth Of The Cool** (1948–1950; p. 121), **Kind Of Blue** (1959; p. 232), **The Complete Live At The Plugged Nickel** (1965; p. 331), **In A Silent Way** (1969; p. 361), **Agharta** (1975; p. 420)

RED GARLAND
Born William M. Garland, 12 May 1923, Dallas, Texas; died 23 May 1984, Dallas, Texas
Piano

Red Garland Revisited!
Original Jazz Classics OJCCD 985
Garland; Kenny Burrell (g); Paul Chambers (b); Art Taylor (d). May 1957.

Trumpeter and Miles Davis biographer Ian Carr said (1990): **'One thinks of him as a very smooth, almost unctuous player. His chording was always very smooth. But there was a real fire there. A proud man, and with a real musical intelligence.'**

Graceful yet unaffectedly bluesy, Red Garland's manner was flexible enough to accommodate the contrasting styles of both Miles Davis and John Coltrane in the Davis quintet of the mid-'50s. His many records as a leader, beginning at about the same period, display exactly the same qualities. His confessed influences of Tatum, Powell and Nat Cole seem less obvious than his debts to Erroll Garner and Ahmad Jamal, whose hit recording of 'Billy Boy' seems to sum up everything that Garland would later go on to explore.

All of the trio sessions feature the same virtues: deftly fingered left-hand runs over bouncy rhythms, coupled with block-chord phrasing which coloured melodies in such a way that Garland saw no need to depart from them. Medium/uptempo treatments alternate with stately ballads, and Chambers and Taylor are unfailingly swinging, if often constrained. The triumvirate was well established, but rarely remarked now that piano trios are in vogue again. *Revisited!* is the first choice for anyone who wants a single Garland set from the period. His own version of 'Billy Boy' is here, there are two classic slow-burners in 'Everybody's Somebody's Fool' and 'The Masquerade Is Over', and Burrell shows up to spar on 'Four' and 'Walkin''. It's effortless music, with a gnarly edge here and there, certainly not ignorable cocktail-hour jazz.

JOHNNY GRIFFIN *&*
Born 24 April 1928, Chicago, Illinois; died 25 July 2008, Availles-Limouzine, France
Tenor saxophone

A Blowing Session
Blue Note 99009
Griffin; Lee Morgan (t); John Coltrane, Hank Mobley (ts); Wynton Kelly (p); Paul Chambers (b); Art Blakey (d). May 1957.

Johnny Griffin said (1989): **'An interviewer said to me recently: "Some of those early records ... they were just jam sessions, weren't they?"** *Just* **jam sessions?! That was how** you learned to play. **Kids now go to Berklee or some other school and they learn all there is to know and then they have to learn how to play some personality out of their instrument, except they don't think they need that any more.** *Just* **jam sessions! I don't think so.'**

The Little Giant had the reputation of being the fastest tenor-player on the block, which inevitably led sceptics to sniff that expression had been sacrificed to speed. Inevitably, the truth is somewhere round the middle. Griffin certainly had his metronome set unusually fast, but he could build an affecting solo when he chose and one rarely found him tripped up by technique.

In the mid-'50s Griffin established his fast-draw reputation with a group of records that majored on energy. One of us previously described *A Blowing Session* as 'combative, but ultimately dull'. When the authors debated that same record on a radio programme we agreed that Griffin had bested the rising star of John Coltrane and that the dullness was perhaps an artefact of having listened to too many similar but inferior sessions over the years.

Griff's first recordings, for Argo, find him more of a bebopper than was obvious later. He may have neglected ballad playing until middle age, but there are moments of surprising delicacy even this early, like 'I Cried For You' on *Johnny Griffin Tenor*, which also housed his first headlong masterpiece, 'Satin Wrap'. The first Blue Note session was made some weeks later and released as *Introducing Johnny Griffin* (Griffin had already made a few sides for OKeh three years previously), and in Wynton Kelly he had a piano-player who knew how to play the blues. Again, there's more than a sprinkle of bebop procedures and the album's clinched with a vintage 'Lover Man', a truly great reading of the song.

In the company of Coltrane and Mobley, on this the second Blue Note session, he rattles through 'The Way You Look Tonight' like some love-on-the-run hustler. Only Trane seems inclined to serenade, and it's interesting to speculate how the track might have sounded had they taken it at conventional ballad tempo. 'All The Things You Are' begins with what sounds like Reveille from Wynton Kelly and then lopes off with almost adolescent awkwardness. This was a typical Griffin strategy. For much of his most productive period he more or less bypassed ballad playing and only really adjusted his idiom to the medium and slower tempos as he aged. 'It's All Right With Me' is way over the speed limit, as if Griffin is trying to erase all memory of Sonny Rollins's magisterial reading of a deceptively difficult tune. But it's not all callow grandstanding. There are subtleties here, too, and with the hugely underrated Mobley on the strength it's a record that bears careful listening.

& *See also* **Return Of The Griffin** (1978; p. 447)

CONTE CANDOLI

Born Secondo Candoli, 12 July 1927, Mishawaka, Indiana; died 14 December 2001, Palm Desert, California
Trumpet

Conte Candoli Quartet
VSOP 43
Candoli; Vince Guaraldi (p); Monty Budwig (b); Stan Levey (d). June 1957.

Conte Candoli said (1982): **'I admired Dizzy and Clifford Brown, most of the modern fellows, in fact. Miles Davis, not so much. There are times when his intonation wasn't so good. Dizzy was always right on it ... and such a sound!'**

Elder brother and fellow trumpeter Pete Candoli was his main teacher but 'The Count' eventually trumped him. He worked with Kenton and Woody Herman before striking out on his own. For part of his career, he was in Doc Severinsen's television band and a regular on *The Tonight Show*, but the revival of interest in swing-to-modern jazz after the first cycle of pop brought him back into the limelight and he was a staple of Howard Rumsey's Lighthouse All-Stars.

Coast To Coast on Fresh Sound is the best compilation of the early '50s work, but this 1957 VSOP quartet date is a small gem on its own. They crack off with Al Cohn's delightful 'Liza', slot in a couple of good lines by the brothers and Osie Johnson's intriguing 'Meliodistic'. Guaraldi, who's never been forgiven his crossover success, comps with authority and takes some nice solos, but it's the trumpet that sits in the foreground, busy, confident and full-toned, the exact same, Dizzy-tinged voice that kept surfacing in jazz situations for the next three decades.

MARTY PAICH
Born 23 January 1925, Oakland, California; died 12 August 1995, Hidden Hills, California
Arranger

The Picasso Of Big Band Jazz
Candid CCD 79031
Paich; Buddy Childers, Jack Sheldon (t); Herbie Harper (tb); Bob Enevoldsen (tb, vtb); Vincent DeRosa (frhn); Herb Geller (as); Bob Cooper, Bill Perkins (ts); Joe Mondragon (b); Mel Lewis (d). June 1957.

Jimmy Giuffre said (1987): **'Marty was the one who had the musical education, lessons with Castelnuovo-Tedesco and all that UCLA stuff. We were always a little leery of him, because he knew more than we did.'**

It's a nice conceit, Paich as a mural painter in bright, summery colours, and it goes some way towards defining the music. Paich had worked as a piano-player before the war, in a group with Pete Rugolo, and after demob he continued to perform, acting as Peggy Lee's accompanist for a time. His interests, though, were varied and he managed – as was readily possible on the Coast – to combine jazz writing and arranging with work in the studios and in Hollywood. A couple of years before *The Picasso Of Big Band Jazz* he'd worked on the soundtrack for *The Lady and the Tramp*. Apart from 'What's New?', all the charts are Paich's and they're given a respectable span to work themselves out. The music is sophisticated rather than difficult. 'Black Rose' and 'New Soft Shoe' follow intriguingly personal lines and, though keys and pace change through the set, it has a strong coherence round major/minor ambiguities. There's perhaps just a touch of analytical cubism in the charts, a feeling that distortions to the familiar tonality are made because they can be, rather than for any obvious expressive reason. But there's no point flogging a useful metaphor or dissecting music that's cool and laid-back and thoroughly enjoyable, even after half a century.

HERB POMEROY
Born Irving Herbert Pomeroy III, 15 April 1930, Gloucester, Massachusetts; died 11 August 2007, Gloucester, Massachusetts
Trumpet

Life Is A Many-Splendored Gig
Fresh Sound FSRCD 84
Pomeroy; Augie Ferretti, Joe Gordon, Lennie Johnson, Everett Longstreth (t); Joe Ciavardone, Gene DiStachio, Bill Legan (tb); Dave Chapman, Boots Mussulli (as); Jaki Byard, Varty Haritounian, Zoot Sims (ts); Deane Haskins (bs); Ray Santisi (p); John Neves (b); Jimmy Zitano (d). June 1957.

Trombonist/bandleader Michael Gibbs remembers: **'I met him first day I arrived at Berklee – January 9th, 1959! – and he invited me to witness a studio recording session. He became my teacher, mentor, friend – a sort of father-figure from then on. He always seemed so grand, ever-wise, it wasn't till his death I realized he was only seven years my senior – so he was 28 when I met him ... and he played with Charlie Parker!!'**

Herb Pomeroy is perhaps something of an anomaly in a book devoted to recorded jazz, because he thought records were somehow beside the point, a pale representation of the real jazz experience, which relied on the physical presence of players and audience, ideally in close proximity. Consequently, far more jazz fans have heard Pomeroy praised as an influential teacher – guru, even – than heard him as a player; those few that have probably remember him from a couple of debutant recordings with Charlie Parker on the compilation *The Bird You Never Heard*, or perhaps on *The Fable Of Mabel* and *Boston Blow-Up*, made under the leadership of his associate, baritone saxophonist Serge Chaloff. A pity: Pomeroy's trumpet sound had a warm burnish and a nicely vocal authority. Once heard, it becomes addictive.

Chaloff also had a short recording career, but for more tragic reasons. Pomeroy simply redirected his energies towards teaching and developing young talent. He himself had studied at Schillinger House, which became the Berklee School, and after a period working with Stan Kenton, and with Chaloff, the equally ill-starred Richard Twardzik, Charlie Mariano and others as the Boston Jazz Workshop he started teaching at Berklee, where his distinguished students included Mariano's then wife Toshiko Akiyoshi, vibist Gary Burton (himself now a very distinguished educator) and trombonist/composer Michael Gibbs. An indefatigable supporter of young talent – Pomeroy also took over and transformed the MIT jazz band – he only began playing again when he retired from full-time teaching in the '90s.

He is far from the only fine musician whose personal creativity was sublimated in the classroom, but there is a special poignancy to Pomeroy's truncated recording career. He worked mainly in his home state, leading bands at the Stables, and among his few issued records *Jazz In A Stable, Band In Boston* and *Detour Ahead* are worth having, but still elusive on CD. *Life* was actually recorded in New York, originally for Roulette. There's a touch of sessionman gloss to the date. Zoot Sims tends to dominate as guest soloist (curiously, some question his presence at the sessions), and the charts are more concerned with straight-ahead swing than challenging ideas, but the band plays with meaty insistence and the rhythm section – all close colleagues of Pomeroy's – establish a commanding base for such as Tadd Dameron's 'Our Delight' and a version of 'It's Sand, Man' that's as good as a prime Basie workout, but with a touch of Kenton bombast, too. 'Sweet Georgia Brown' is re-imagined as 'Sprat', and scholars may note that 'Aluminum Baby' is something of an answer to Ellington's 'Satin Doll' (from Jaki Byard, who provides a rare sighting on tenor). When Pomeroy returned to active recording in 2004 with guitarist Anthony Weller and bassist David Landoni in trio format, Byard's piece was the title-cut. That there was so little in between is to be regretted, but two whole generations of Boston-educated musicians attest to Pomeroy's importance, and that makes the surviving records all the more precious.

PAUL CHAMBERS
Born 22 April 1935, Pittsburgh, Pennsylvania; died 4 January 1969, New York City
Double bass

Bass On Top
Blue Note 93182
Chambers; Hank Jones (p); Kenny Burrell (g); Art Taylor (d). July 1957.

Bassist and composer Gavin Bryars says: **'For most bass-players who emerged in the 1960s the role model was Paul Chambers, who had developed a beautiful sense of swing, immaculate intonation and an impeccable choice of notes. His clear understanding of the essence of modal jazz, whether with the Miles Davis Quintet or in Gil Evans's Porgy And Bess settings, shines through in his exquisitely lithe and supple lines, his rich and full tone, and his laid-back approach to the beat. The solos have real poise, and his assured and authoritative performance of the themes of songs produced definitive versions – "So What", "The Buzzard Song" (in unison with Bill Barber's tuba).'**

Working out of Detroit, where he grew up, 'Mr P.C.' became a prominent small-group side-man, working with Miles Davis, 1954-62, then with Wynton Kelly, Coltrane and others. Narcotics and other problems led to his early death but for a time Chambers was a star on his instrument. He led only a handful of record dates and some of these were gimcracked round a desire to feature the bass as a solo instrument, often rather artificially so. These were early days to feature the bass in a spotlight role and the 1956 *Whims Of Chambers*, with Coltrane in the line-up, awkwardly showcases the solo work. The *arco* passages may have been groundbreaking, but the tone still grates. There's more moody *arco* stuff on this 1957 record, but Chambers's best moment is the long plucked solo on 'Chasin' The Bird', exquisitely phrased and absolutely poised. 'You'd Be So Nice To Come Home To' is given near-epic proportions, but the overall feel is relaxed and laid-back, the solo spots arising with seeming spontaneity and the other group members more generously integrated. His early death was a grievous loss; Chambers would surely have embraced many of the new decade's new challenges.

BUDDY DEFRANCO

Born Boniface Ferdinando Leonardo di Franco, 17 February 1923, Camden, New Jersey
Clarinet

Wholly Cats: Complete Plays Benny Goodman And Artie Shaw Sessions, Volumes 1 & 2

Lone Hill Jazz LHJ 10282 / 10281

DeFranco; Don Fagerquist, Ray Linn (t); Georgie Auld (ts); Victor Feldman (vib); Carl Perkins (p); Barney Kessel, Howard Roberts (g); Leroy Vinnegar, Joe Mondragon (b); Stan Levey, Milt Holland (d). September 1957.

Clarinettist François Houle says: **'Buddy rejuvenated the instrument by single-handedly formulating a bebop/swing amalgam that kept the clarinet in sight throughout that era.'**

Nobody has seriously challenged DeFranco's status as the greatest post-swing clarinettist – only Eddie Daniels has any strong counterclaim – although the instrument's desertion by reed-players has tended to disenfranchise its few exponents. DeFranco's incredibly smooth phrasing and seemingly effortless command are unfailingly impressive but the challenge of translating this (some would say cold and unfeeling) virtuosity into a relevant post-bop environment hasn't been easy and he has relatively few records to show for literally decades of fine work. He worked with Charlie Barnet, Tommy Dorsey and Gene Krupa before striking out as a small-group player.

The idea behind the *Wholly Cats* sessions is obvious enough, though one might have been more interested in hearing DeFranco tackle the Parker book and a set of Dizzy tunes instead. DeFranco drew a good deal from both Benny and Artie, so the influence was obvious. These 1957 sessions, though, afforded him the opportunity to make 'Air Mail Special', say, or 'Indian Love Call' his own, giving those venerable themes and others a modernist spin. The sessions were recorded two days apart, with octet (Goodman) and sextet (Shaw) respectively, and the smaller, drier-sounding group suits its material well, while Auld and Feldman cut loose a little more on their date.

BILL HARRIS

Born Willard Palmer Harris, 28 October 1916, Philadelphia, Pennsylvania; died 21 August 1973, Hallandale, Florida
Trombone

Bill Harris And Friends
Original Jazz Classics OJCCD 083
Harris; Ben Webster (ts); Jimmy Rowles (p); Red Mitchell (b); Stan Levey (d). September 1957.

Trombonist Bob Brookmeyer said (1990): **'I revered and looked up to Bill Harris. He had this gruff, aggressive exterior, which came out in his playing. But he could do delicate things too, things you'd never expect to get from a man like that.'**

Harris had an anonymous time of it until 1944, when he joined Woody Herman, with whom he stayed on and off until 1959. He disappeared into Las Vegas bands in the '60s. Harris was always among the most distinctive and sometimes among the greatest of jazz trombonists. His style was based firmly on swing-era principles, yet he seemed to look both forward and back. His slurred notes and shouting phrases recalled a primitive jazz period, yet his knowing juxtapositions and almost macabre sense of humour were entirely modern. But he made few appearances on record away from Woody Herman's orchestra and is now a largely forgotten figure. *Bill Harris And Friends* should be known far more widely. Both Harris and Webster are in admirable form and make a surprisingly effective partnership, even kvelling good-naturedly at one point. Ben is at his ripest on 'I Surrender, Dear' and 'Where Are You', and Harris stops the show in solo after solo, whether playing short, bemused phrases or barking out high notes. An amusing reading of 'Just One More Chance' caps everything. The remastering favours the horns, but the sound is warmly effective.

WARNE MARSH &

Born 26 October 1927, Los Angeles, California; died 18 December 1987, Hollywood, California
Tenor saxophone

Music For Prancing
VSOP 8
Marsh; Ronnie Ball (p); Red Mitchell (b); Stan Levey (d). September 1957.

Warne Marsh said (1980): **'I hear myself described as a "Tristano disciple" ... and that's it! I don't have problems talking about influences, but there was more than one. I listened to Bach when I was playing piano. Bird was hugely important. So was Ben Webster. And later Lester Young. And Bartók! So without diminishing Lennie in my life, those other things need to be understood, too.'**

Warne Marsh's death onstage at Donte's club in Los Angeles, playing 'Out Of Nowhere', was oddly fitting. By far the most loyal and literal of the Tristano disciples, he sedulously avoided the 'jazz life', cleaving to an improvisatory philosophy that was almost chilling in its purity. Anthony Braxton called him the 'greatest vertical improviser' in the music, and a typical Marsh solo was discursive and rhythmically subtle, full of coded tonalities and oblique resolutions. He cultivated a glacial tone (somewhat derived from Lester Young) that splintered awkwardly in the higher register, very different to the Hodges/Bird/Rollins/Coltrane paradigms.

The early quartets are witty and smooth-toned, though Marsh sounds much closer to Stan Getz than he was to in later years. He sounds warmer, too, leavened by a rhythm section led by the remarkable Mitchell, whose unusual tunings and almost offhand ability to turn out terse countermelodies are a key element of a fine record. The association with Mitchell would prove to be one of the most successful in later years as well. 'You Are Too Beautiful' is one of those ideal blindfold test-pieces, where neither the song nor the player immediately sounds familiar. With Mitchell winding the capstan, it rolls along with an ease of swing that almost disguises how cleverly Marsh negotiates the chords. 'Everything Happens To Me' has a nicely sardonic edge. The originals are more elusive, but the group melds so well, the material seems completely familiar and under the fingers.

& See also **Ne Plus Ultra** (1969; p. 370), **Star Highs** (1982; p. 470)

JOE ALBANY
Originally Joseph Albani; born 24 January 1924, Atlantic City, New Jersey; died 12 January 1988, New York City
Piano

The Right Combination
Original Jazz Classics OJCCD 1749
Albany; Warne Marsh (ts); Bob Whitlock (b). September 1957.

Warne Marsh said (1981): **'Joe had wild horses pulling him. When he controlled them, he was capable of anything, but more often they controlled him.'**

Albany was a frustrating enigma, a pioneer of bop piano who left almost no record of his innovations. Alcohol and narcotics stalked him through what should have been his most creative and fruitful years and there were spells in jail. Albany made no studio recording of any sort until the '70s, a decade notoriously uninterested in the legacy of bop. Tragedy seemed to lie in wait for those around him, too. Albany's second wife killed herself and, when he remarried, drugs almost robbed him of another life-partner.

He had been an accomplished accordion-player in childhood but showed enough skill on piano to move to the West Coast as a member of Leo Watson's group, around 1942. There he met his first great influence, Art Tatum, but after stints with Georgie Auld and Benny Carter, Albany met Charlie Parker, who brought about a huge change in his style. The saxophonist employed him briefly but Albany was fired. He made a few recordings with Lester Young and these were the only examples of his work on record until 1957, when the music on *The Right Combination* was spliced together from an impromptu session (probably a rehearsal) at engineer Ralph Garretson's home. It caught Albany and Marsh jamming on Clifford Brown's 'Daahoud' and six Broadway standards, of which the last, 'The Nearness Of You', is only a fragment. Albany's style is a peculiar amalgam of Parker and Tatum: the complexity of his lines suggest something of the older pianist, while the horn-like right-hand figures suggest a bop soloist. Yet Albany's jumbled, idiosyncratic sense of time is almost all his own, and his solo explorations have a cliff-hanging quality.

Marsh is at his most fragmentary, his tone a foggy squeal at some points – and not helped by a very unresponsive acoustic – yet between them they create some compelling improvisations: 'Body and Soul', done at fast and slow tempos, is as personal as any version, and a dreamy 'Angel Eyes' shows off Albany's best work. Ironically, the Tatum-inspired bopper was at his most effective on ballads.

Albany didn't surface again on record until 1971, with another home recording, but he survived into the '80s and became a cult figure, more influenced latterly by Thelonious Monk but still representing an apostolic link back to the roots of bebop. One of jazz's great might-have-beens and what-ifs.

COUNT BASIE &

Born 21 August 1904, Red Bank, New Jersey; died 26 April 1984, Hollywood, Florida
Piano, bandleader

The Complete Atomic Mr Basie

Roulette 793273
Basie; Joe Newman, Thad Jones, Wendell Culley, Snooky Young (t); Benny Powell, Henry Coker, Al Grey (tb); Marshal Royal, Frank Wess (as); Eddie 'Lockjaw' Davis, Frank Foster (ts); Charlie Fowlkes (bs); Freddie Green (g); Eddie Jones (b); Sonny Payne (d). October 1957.

Saxophonist Frank Foster said (1989): **'Jaws came into that band and he was Basie's sweetheart on tenor. It made the rest of us – me, anyway – very nervous, and I was trying to make sure of my place. But Basie knew what he wanted from you, and he didn't want ballads from me. "Just swing that music, kid" was what he'd say. Swing and simplicity, that and leaving a gap for the rhythm section, who were really the key to it all.'**

In 1956, Duke Ellington had breathed new life into the big-band scene. Basie countered by throwing in his lot with the rather shady Morris Levy, who didn't have enough fingers for all the pies he had on the go. A record label was just one of the more upright of them. Basie opened his controversial contract for Roulette with a showstopper. Complete with mushroom cloud on the cover, this was a Cold War classic. It was also the last great Basie record.

He had Neal Hefti (who'd scored the hottest numbers in the band's recent book) do the whole record, and the arranger's zesty, machine-tooled scoring reached its apogee in 'The Kid From Red Bank', 'Flight Of The Foo Birds', 'Splanky' and the rest. Just as Ellington had Gonsalves, Basie had Lockjaw Davis, and his splenetic outbursts gave just the right fillip to what might otherwise have been too cut-and-dried. His playing on 'Flight Of The Foo Birds' (a variation on 'Give Me The Simple Life') is a high-point of the decade and further ammunition for those who consider Jaws critically underrated. The complete edition that appeared in 1994 revealed still more riches, but the original LP sequence still has punch, even if the original LPs, which were not well pressed, have long since been unplayable.

& See also **The Original American Decca Recordings** (1937–1939; p. 61), **The Jubilee Alternatives** (1943–1944; p. 90)

SONNY ROLLINS &

Born Theodore Walter Rollins, 7 September 1930, New York City
Tenor saxophone

A Night At The Village Vanguard

Blue Note 99795 2CD
Rollins; Donald Bailey, Wilbur Ware (b); Pete LaRoca, Elvin Jones (d). November 1957.

Sonny Rollins said (1990): **'People ask: "Are you playing in a trance?" Someone even asked if it was like a state of grace. I prefer to say it's a "stream of consciousness". I can't separate it out – you couldn't separate out the drops of water in a stream – but it is conscious! I'm not sleeping up there.'**

There are so many remarkable Rollins records from the '50s that picking one or two is impossible, if not invidious. For all its arch cleverness, *Way Out West* is a highly accomplished record, playful and deceptively light in tone. *Newk's Time* is another. *The Bridge*, from a little later, has reinforced one key element of the Rollins myth: that he once took his saxophone up onto the Williamsburg Bridge and practised there; the reality is that he did so to prevent disturbing a neighbour, but something of the lonely artist shaping his craft on high has persisted. Nothing quite captures the saxophonist at his headlong greatest than this Village Vanguard date.

The live material, originally cherrypicked for a single peerless LP, has now been stretched across two CDs, and in its latest incarnation the in-person feel is heightened by the addition of some more of Sonny's announcements. In the past we felt that the abundance of this material slightly checked the power-packed feel of the original LP, but in the new RVG edition the sound is extraordinarily deep and immediate, and the sheer impact of Rollins on top form is close to overwhelming – this is a model example of a classic record given its proper treatment. Working with only bass and drums throughout leads Rollins into areas of freedom which bop never allowed, and while his free-spiritedness is checked by his ruthless self-examination, its rigour makes his music uniquely powerful in jazz. On the two versions of 'Softly, As In A Morning Sunrise' or in the muscular exuberance of 'Old Devil Moon', traditional bop-orientated improvising reaches a peak of expressive power and imagination. Overall, these are records which demand a place in any collection.

& *See also* **Saxophone Colossus** (1956; p. 188), **This Is What I Do** (2000; p. 653)

WILBUR WARE

Born 8 September 1923, Chicago, Illinois; died 9 September 1979, Philadelphia, Pennsylvania
Double bass

The Chicago Sound

Original Jazz Classics OJCCD 1737
Ware; John Jenkins (as); Johnny Griffin (ts); Junior Mance (p); Wilbur Campbell, Frank Dunlop (d). October–November 1957.

Charlie Haden said (1983): **'At one time he played this bass that was pretty much held together by Scotch tape, but he managed to play solos on it like it was a Stradivarius violin. No one else played like him, all those thirds and fifths, very clear and distinct and with a really rhythmic quality – because Wilbur was also a drummer – that always struck me as very pure bass-playing.'**

Though much of what Ware did stemmed directly from Jimmy Blanton's 'Jack The Bear', he developed into a highly individual performer whose unmistakable sound lives on in the low-register work of contemporary bassists like Charlie Haden. Ware's technique has been questioned but seems to have been a conscious development, a way of hearing the chord rather than a way of skirting his own supposed shortcomings. He could solo at speed, shifting the time-signature from bar to bar while retaining an absolutely reliable pulse. Significantly, one of his most important employers was Thelonious Monk, who valued displacements of that sort within an essentially four-square rhythm and traditional (but not European-traditional) tonality; the bassist also contributed substantially to one of Sonny Rollins's finest recordings. He grew up in the sanctified church and there is a gospelly quality to 'Mamma-Daddy', a relatively rare original, on *The Chicago Sound*. The only other Ware composition on the record, '31st And State', might have come from Johnny Griffin's head; the saxophonist roars in over the beat and entirely swamps Jenkins, whose main contribution to the session is a composition credit on two good tracks.

Though the Ware discography is huge (with numerous credits for Riverside in the '50s), his solo technique is at its most developed on his own records. 'Lullaby Of The Leaves' is almost entirely for bass, and there are magnificent solos on 'Body And Soul' (where he sounds *huge*) and 'The Man I Love'.

TONY SCOTT

Born Anthony Joseph Sciacca, 17 June, 1921, Morristown, New Jersey; died 28 March 2007, Rome, Italy
Clarinet

A Day In New York

Fresh Sound FSRCD 160/2 2CD
Scott; Clark Terry (t); Jimmy Knepper (tb); Sahib Shihab (bs); Bill Evans (p); Henry Grimes, Milt Hinton (b); Paul Motian (d). November 1957.

Tony Scott said (1991): **'Making music is inextricable with the life you lead and the energy you put through that life. That's one of the reasons I am obsessed with the lives of the jazz greats. Know who they are and you understand their music. Know their music and you understand who they were.'**

Scott studied at Juilliard, worked as a New York sideman in the '40s and '50s, and led his own groups from 1953, playing his own version of bop on the clarinet. In 1959, he turned his back on America, wounded by the death of several friends (Hot Lips Page, Billie Holiday, Charlie Parker, Lester Young) and by what he considered the 'death' of the clarinet in jazz terms. He became a wanderer, exploring the culture and music of the East, trading in the sometimes aggressive assertions of bebop for a meditative approach to harmony that at its best is deeply moving, at its least disciplined a weak ambient decoration.

Scott enjoyed a close and fruitful relationship with Bill Evans, and perhaps his best recorded work is the session of 16 November 1957 with the Evans trio and guests, tackling a copious roster of originals and well-worn standards (including a lovely 'Lullaby Of The Leaves' with Knepper). The clarinettist's opening statements on Evans's 'Five' are almost neurotically brilliant and a perfect illustration of how loud Scott could play. 'Portrait Of Ravi' and 'The Explorer' are Scott originals, directed towards the concerns that were increasingly to occupy him. Evans's light touch and immense harmonic sophistication suited his approach ideally.

JIMMY SMITH

Born 8 December 1928, Norristown, Pennsylvania; died 8 February 2005, Scottsdale, Arizona
Organ

Groovin' At Smalls' Paradise

Blue Note 99777-2 2CD
Smith; Eddie McFadden (g); Donald Bailey (d). November 1957.

Jimmy Smith said (1983): **'I taught myself, working out the stops. I got my first organ from a loan shark and had it shipped to a warehouse. For six months, I hardly left the place, trying to work it all out.'**

Jimmy Smith got going rather late as a jazz organist. He allegedly didn't even touch the instrument until he was 28, but he quickly established and personified a jazz vocabulary for the organ: tireless walking bass in the pedals, thick chords with the left hand, quick-fire melodic lines with the right. It was a formula almost from the start, and Smith has never strayed from it, but he so completely mastered the approach that he is inimitable. At his best he creates a peerless excitement, which is seldom sustained across an entire album but which makes every record he's on something to be reckoned with.

Smith made a great stack of albums for Blue Note, and as with others in that position their quality was inconsistent, as has been their availability. On *Groovin' At Smalls' Paradise*, Smith is in his element in a club setting, and while McFadden also gets plenty of space (and doesn't do badly, in his modest way), the master's big, sprawling solos are definitive: 'After Hours' is perhaps the classic Smith blues performance, although the entire record works to a kind of bluesy slow burn. The original albums have been turned into a double-CD and, in the Rudy Van Gelder edition remastering, the years fall away. *Back At The Chicken Shack* from three years later is better known, but this is the one to get. Probably no single figure so dominated his instrument for so long as Smith did the Hammond organ – even the tenor saxophone has its alternative-division heavyweights – and everyone since has been compared to Smith, even if there is virtually no stylistic connection.

JIMMY DEUCHAR
Born 26 June 1930, Dundee, Scotland; died 9 September 1993, London
Trumpet

Pal Jimmy!
Jasmine JASCD 624
Deuchar; Ken Wray (tb); Derek Humble (as); Tubby Hayes (ts); Eddie Harvey, Harry South (p); Kenny Napper (b); Phil Seamen (d). March 1957–March 1958.

Jimmy Deuchar said (1983): **'I was in the air force and posted to Uxbridge, so I got into London from time to time and managed to meet Johnny Dankworth at Club 11. He told me to get in touch when I got out. I joined the Seven in 1950, and that was like my university. I learned everything from him, from him and from Tubby Hayes.'**

A hybrid of Bunny Berigan and Fats Navarro, Jimmy was usually recognizable within a few bars – taut, hot, but capable of bursts of great lyricism. Some of his best work is with Tubby Hayes, but these precious survivals – which exist solely through the dedication and enthusiasm of Tony Hall – are fine too. Deuchar's not well served by the recordings at this time, but the playing is of a standard that will surprise those unfamiliar with this period of British jazz, technically sound, expressively bold and utterly self-confident. If these players were in thrall to the Americans they don't sound it.
    Pal Jimmy! brings together the whole of the LP plus a stray track from a compilation. Sonny Stitt's 'Swingin' In Studio Two' gives everybody room to move around. The trumpeter's solo on the title-track blues is a classic statement. Original vinyl copies command a king's ransom, so even uncertain CD sound is very welcome indeed. Deuchar's recreational interests certainly undermined his health and he died unseasonably young having lost both legs to circulatory problems. But while he was at his peak, he was unmatched.

JIMMY CLEVELAND
Born 3 May 1926, Wartrace, Tennessee; died 23 August 2008, Lynwood, California
Trombone

Cleveland Style
Emarcy 53194
Cleveland; Art Farmer (t); Benny Golson (ts); Jay McAllister, Don Butterfield (tba); Wynton Kelly (p); Eddie Jones (b); Charli Persip (d). December 1957.

Jimmy Cleveland said (1984): **'I was happier in the orchestra and the studios. Working with small groups brings a lot of pressure. Thelonious Monk was a curious person, very brilliant, but strange, and I didn't go for that. I'm happy to play my little piece and then move back into place.'**

A terrific technician, Cleveland was one of the first significant trombonists to emerge after J. J. Johnson. Much of his career was spent in the studios, but he did manage to cut some sessions for Emarcy and Mercury – *Introducing, Cleveland Style, Map Of Jimmy Cleveland, Rhythm Crazy* – all of them gimcracked round Jimmy's dextrous slide technique and singing tone. Hard to pick out highlights, and for some the Lone Hill *Complete Recordings* might offer more generous pickings, but this 1957 record stands up fine on its own. Ernie Wilkins's arrangements are spot on for a group of this size, with tuba filling out the bottom end warmly, and Ernie brings in a couple of nice charts of his own, 'A Jazz Ballad', which highlights Jimmy's romantic side, and 'Goodbye Ebbets Field', which ends the set on a mildly elegiac note. One's always conscious of how exact a technician Cleveland is, though he lacks the fast, saxophonic delivery of a J.J., and that quality spills over into his one composition credit; 'Jimmy's Tune' is only a blowing theme, but it has structure and energy and a trajectory very like the trombonist's solo formation, which is always logical but not predictable.

BERNT ROSENGREN

Born 24 December 1937, Stockholm, Sweden
Tenor saxophone

Jazz Club 57

Dragon DRCD 326
Rosengren; Stig Söderqvist (vtb); Claes-Göran Fagerstedt (p); Torbjørn Hultcrantz (b); Sune Spångberg (d); Nannie Porres (v). 1957–1962.

Don Cherry said (1992): **'Listening to Bernt, it's possible to think that jazz maybe did come from somewhere other than America, that it had sprung up all over the world simultaneously. I'd know him in a crowd. It's like old leather that sound, you know? Like a book in a library.'**

Rosengren has been a force in Swedish jazz for some 50 years and is still undervalued on the world stage. He led Swedish hard bop as its premier young tenorman in the late '50s. He acquired some international exposure in the '60s with George Russell and others, and he plays in Krzysztof Komeda's group on the soundtrack to Polanski's *Knife in the Water*, but he has basically remained tied to his native scene as a player and bandleader. Wider availability of his earlier records would still be welcome, but the reappearance of *Jazz Club 57* was welcome. Rosengren is already in imperious form, clear-toned and logical in his development of a solo. Some profess to hear a likeness to Rollins here and there, and there is something of that logic of delivery, but he's unmistakable and nobody's obvious follower. The record also benefits from a strong and capable group. Söderqvist makes some arresting interventions on 'I'll Remember April' and 'Sputnik' but only appears on one other track.

SONNY CLARK

Born Conrad Yeatis Clark, 21 July 1931, Herminie, Pennsylvania; died 13 January 1963, New York City
Piano

Cool Struttin'

Blue Note 95327-2
Clark; Art Farmer (t); Jackie McLean (as); Paul Chambers (b); Philly Joe Jones (d). January 1958.

Clarinettist Buddy DeFranco said (2001): **'Sonny worshipped Tatum and he brought that positivity to the group. There was nothing downbeat about Sonny's work, nothing of that shut-down feeling you get from some guys. He was warm and had a great sense of humour.'**

Clark approached music with abandon. A pendulum dependence on either alcohol or narcotics never seems to have impinged on his ability to play; he worked in Buddy DeFranco's group and enjoyed a steady if short-lived tenure as Blue Note's house pianist, though being a junkie was never a disqualification in that set-up. Note-perfect, rhythmically bouncy and always ready with a quirky idea, he was an ideal group player, relatively uninterested in playing lots of solos, less convincing in a hornless group like the eponymous 1957 date. Chambers, then approaching his heyday, has a generous share of the spotlight, perhaps because Sonny's interest in soloing was limited.

His Blue Note records are consistently good: *Dial 'S' For Sonny*, *Trio*, *Sonny's Crib*; but *Cool Struttin'* is one of the key documents of hard bop. The title-piece is a long-form blues, with room for the horns to stretch out. Sonny's own finest moment is his solo on 'Blue Minor', another original. His three-note trills are almost Monkian and the percussive, spacious attack is reminiscent of the bebop giant at his most capacious. Though Clark rarely strays far from the blues, one can hear Farmer itching to break through into other dimensions. The reissue contains two extra tracks unreleased on LP: Clark's own 'Royal Flush' and a wayward interpretation of Rodgers and Hart's 'Lover'. It's buoyant music, smart, personal and confidently executed.

AHMAD JAMAL &
Born 2 July 1930, Pittsburgh, Pennsylvania
Piano

At The Pershing / Complete Live At The Pershing Lounge
Chess MCD 09108 / Gambit 69624 2CD
Jamal; Israel Crosby (b); Vernell Fournier (d). January 1958.

Ahmad Jamal remembers: **'For the historic Pershing session we used an 1890 Steinway with a cracked soundboard and it sparkled.'**

As Brian Priestley has pointed out, pianists who achieve a modicum of commercial success tend to move closer to the entertainment mainstream than any other musicians, except possibly singers, who are often thought to belong there anyway. Jamal's spare, spacious style was a reaction to the excesses of bebop, and it won him an audience. Even so, for many years, Jamal gave much of his attention to running a chi-chi club, the Alhambra, rather than to playing, but his influence on Miles Davis and the aura of his wildly successful 1958 trio kept him in prominence.

Jamal began recording at the turn of the '50s, with a drummerless trio that consisted of first Eddie Calhoun then Israel Crosby on bass and with guitarist Ray Crawford's distinctive tapped-out lines a particular feature. There were obvious affinities with Nat Cole, but Jamal seemed to be exploring other dimensions. An epic version of 'Love For Sale' and an original composition called 'New Rhumba', which caught the attention of Miles Davis and Gil Evans, suggested his originality.

From here on, though, Jamal's live records always seem better than his studio sets, as if the presence of an audience conjured something extra. The Pershing record is something of an industry phenomenon, climbing to number three on the *Billboard* 'Hot 100' on its release and staying in the chart for more than two years. Now remastered in modern sound, it demonstrates how and why Jamal was able to negotiate mainstream success. 'Poinciana' was a single, edited from the live performance, and became a jukebox and radio favourite, its celebrity extending outside jazz circles. Jamal's technique has scarcely changed over the years and remains closer to Erroll Garner than to anyone else, concentrating on fragile textures and calligraphic melodic statements (the qualities that attracted Miles) rather than the propulsive logic of bebop piano. His reinterpretations of 'Woody'n'You' and 'There Is No Greater Love' are cool and subtle, their excitements perhaps more intellectual than visceral, but Jamal does convey a very particular energy in his work.

These recordings are now out of copyright, so different versions exist. We would normally plump firmly for a favourite, but here there's a dilemma. The Gambit option has 72 minutes of music compared to Chess's 32, but in far less delightful sound: quality, width – the buyer's choice.

& *See also* **À L'Olympia** (2000; p. 656)

VICTOR FELDMAN
Born 7 April 1934, London; died 12 May 1987, Los Angeles, California
Piano, vibraphone

The Arrival Of Victor Feldman
Original Jazz Classics OJCCD 268
Feldman; Scott LaFaro (b); Stan Levey (d). January 1958.

Bassist and composer Gavin Bryars says of Scott LaFaro: **'In a tragically short working life – dead at 25, he only started playing bass at 18 – he overturned then-current concepts of the jazz bass into an instrument that could soar effortlessly in solos through all registers, with a sublimely lyrical and singing tone, as well as maintaining a rich and sustained accompaniment, whether with Bill Evans, Ornette Coleman, Stan Getz or others.**

Originally a child prodigy drummer – he played with Glenn Miller when he was ten – the Londoner switched to vibes and piano and worked with Ronnie Scott. His career took off in America and he gained his moment in jazz Valhalla when Miles Davis recorded his composition 'Seven Steps To Heaven'. To some degree, Feldman is the kind of musician's musician who is doomed to be remembered by association. He worked with Howard Rumsey at the Lighthouse, also with Woody Herman and Cannonball Adderley, and had a stint in Miles's quintet. We're guilty of the same thing by highlighting the role of his brilliant young bassist Scott LaFaro. In fact, Feldman brokered a long and varied career as a musician, making close to 30 records under his own name and surviving better than most through the fusion era with such clever sets as 1977's *The Artful Dodger*.

Arrival is a marvellous record, completed just after Victor had settled in Los Angeles. The cover wittily dramatizes the Englishman's arrival in the New World – by rowing boat and dressed as if for Ascot or the House of Lords, while LaFaro and Stan Levey help haul him ashore. Scott's role in extending the vocabulary of the piano trio is well documented in his association with Bill Evans but, given how tragically foreshortened his career was, it's surprising that these sides don't receive more attention. His playing on the opening 'Serpent's Tooth' is almost as remarkable as anything he played with Evans. As ever, the young bassist is firm-toned, melodic and endlessly inventive, and the interplay with the piano is stunning: long, highly wrought lines round a basic bop figuration. Levey's accents are quietly insistent and the whole recording seems to have been mic'ed very close, as was the practice at the time. 'Serpent's Tooth', 'Satin Doll' and 'There Is No Greater Love' are the outstanding tracks, but a word, too, for Feldman's own 'Minor Lament', a more workman-like piece, but one that shows off this subtle craft to perfection.

PEE WEE RUSSELL
Born Charles Ellsworth Russell, 27 March 1902, St Louis, Missouri; died 15 February 1969, Alexandria, Virginia,
Clarinet

Swingin' With Pee Wee
Prestige 24213-2
Russell; Buck Clayton, Ruby Braff (t); Vic Dickenson (tb); Bud Freeman (ts); Tommy Flanagan, Nat Pierce (p); Wendell Marshall, Tommy Potter (b); Osie Johnson, Karl Kiffe (d). February 1958–March 1960.

Pianist Tommy Flanagan said (1987): **'Someone said about Pee Wee that even his feet looked sad. He was a remarkable player, though, and he could have been as big as Benny Goodman, if it hadn't been for the hooch.'**

A jazz original, with a hangdog face and a lugubrious manner that disguised what was underneath, Russell came from Missouri and played in the New York school of hot music in the '20s, with Nichols, Mole and the others. From the '30s he was better known as a member of the Condon gang, but his later playing suggested his disaffection from that style of jazz, and in his final decade he played in increasingly mainstream-to-modern settings. Alcoholism, illness and depression thwarted him.

A valuable reissue of a classic Russell session, *Swingin' With Pee Wee* is one of his best latter-day records. Clayton handled the arranging duties, and the rhythm section, with Flanagan, Marshall and Johnson, was about the most modernistic Russell had had behind him at this point. The result is a stylish and triumphant assimilation of his clarinet into a vibrant mainstream setting. His dissertation on his great blues, 'Englewood', is but one example of Pee Wee at his best – and Clayton matches him in the calibre of his playing. Even more of a bonus are the tracks from the 1958 date for Counterpoint, *Portrait Of Pee Wee*, with Braff and Dickenson – not quite as good, but it only adds to the merits of an excellent reissue.

CANNONBALL ADDERLEY
Born Julian Edwin Adderley, 15 September 1928, Tampa, Florida; died 8 August 1975, Gary, Indiana
Alto and soprano saxophones

Somethin' Else
Blue Note 95392
Adderley; Miles Davis (t); Hank Jones (p); Sam Jones (b); Art Blakey (d). March 1958.

Former Adderley pianist Joe Zawinul said (1995): **'I don't think anyone gets him, man, even now. I worked with him nine, nine and a half years, and in that time he never played anything exactly the same way twice. A *real* genius, man.'**

The long critically undervalued Adderley's status as a master communicator has grown rapidly since his untimely death. The blues-soaked tone and hard, swinging alto-lines are as recognizable a sound as any in the aftermath of bebop. *Pace* Joe Zawinul, he did fall back on clichés, but just because he liked the sound of them. There's a lean, hard-won quality to his best playing and much dedication to craft.

Some of the Adderley group's best-known stuff came later, like Zawinul's 'Mercy, Mercy,

Mercy', and the group aesthetic went in the direction of soul-jazz, but in earlier days the language was heterodox hard bop. Adderley's cameo appearances on *Milestones* (five days earlier) and *Kind Of Blue* (the following year) were outclassed by the leader's returning/anticipating the favour on this classic Blue Note, which is sometimes unfairly credited to the trumpeter. It's very much Cannonball's achievement. The long, sublimely relaxed lope through 'Autumn Leaves' is the track every listener remembers, but there isn't a rote moment on the record and the rhythm section take much credit too. Take numbers steadily mount through the session and the released version of 'Dancing In The Dark' took 11 attempts to nail down. It's not clear whether fatigue or perfectionism were to blame; the results are superb and the contrast between Adderley's vitalism and Miles's narrow-eyed lyricism is a treat. No one should be without this one.

MICHEL LEGRAND
Born 24 February 1932, Paris, France
Piano

Legrand Jazz
Philips 830074-2
Legrand; Miles Davis, Ernie Royal, Art Farmer, Donald Byrd, Joe Wilder (t); Frank Rehak, Billy Byers, Jimmy Cleveland, Eddie Bert (tb); Jimmy Buffington (frhn); Gene Quill, Phil Woods (as); Ben Webster, John Coltrane, Seldon Powell (ts); Jerome Richardson (bs, bcl); Teo Macero (bs); Herbie Mann (f); Bill Evans, Hank Jones, Nat Pierce (p); Eddie Costa, Don Elliott (vib); Betty Glamann (hp); Major Holley (b, tba); Paul Chambers, George Duvivier, Milt Hinton (b); Don Lamond, Kenny Dennis, Osie Johnson (d). June 1958.

Michel Legrand said (1982): **'I didn't start writing for films because I could not make money playing jazz, or I would have given up jazz the moment I made money doing something else. The truth is that as a young man I promised myself I would play any and every kind of music that came along. Jazz is one of them.'**

Legrand's name is so widely known as a pop and movie composer that his jazz leanings are largely ignored. But his small discography is worth much more than a passing look. The sessions for the *Legrand Jazz* album are uniquely star-studded, and the quality of the writing matches up to the cast-list. Legrand chose many unexpected tunes – including ancient history such as 'Wild Man Blues', as well as the more predictable 'Nuages' and 'Django' – and recast each one in a challenging way. 'Night In Tunisia' is a controlled fiesta of trumpets, 'Round Midnight' a glittering set-piece for Davis, 'Nuages' a sensuous vehicle for Webster. The last is placed alongside a trombone section in one of the three groupings devised by the arranger; another is dominated by a four-man trumpet group. The third has the remarkable situation of having Davis, Coltrane and Evans as sidemen, playing Waller and Armstrong tunes. Many of the arrangements are tellingly compact, seven not even breaking the four-minute barrier, and it ends on a *fast* treatment of Beiderbecke's 'In A Mist'.

LOU DONALDSON
Born 1 November 1926, Badin, North Carolina
Alto saxophone

Blues Walk
Blue Note 46525-2
Donaldson; Herman Foster (p); Peck Morrison (b); Dave Bailey (d); Ray Barretto (perc). July 1958.

Lou Donaldson said (1989): **'Playing jazz without the blues is like cooking potatoes without salt. You have something, but it doesn't have any flavour. The blues are at the heart of everything I do. Even if I've added some Latin flavours – and I was the first to put in a conga player – it's still the blues.'**

Lou Donaldson has remained among the most diligent of Charlie Parker's disciples. His playing hardly altered course in 40 years of work: the fierce tone and familiar blues colourings remain constant through the '50s and '60s and, if he's as unadventurous as he is assured, at least his records guarantee a solid level of well-executed improvising. He replaces Parker's acidity with a certain sweetness which can make his work pall over extended listening. Donaldson's stack of Blue Note albums has drifted in and out of circulation.

Blues Walk, true to its title, is Donaldson at his bluesiest. The shades get lighter and darker as the context dictates, but the general effect is highly consistent throughout. It's probably at this point that Donaldson puts aside the more obvious aspects of his Parker fixation and starts to play in an earthier and more straightforward idiom. He puts Denzil Best's 'Move' in second place, right after the title-track, almost as if to show how things might be different. 'Blues Walk' itself is a great line, with a solid bounce and ample opportunity for blowing effective choruses on either the melody or the sequence (he manages both), and he brings the same attack to 'The Masquerade Is Over' and even 'Autumn Nocturne', which might be subtitled 'Nocturne Detourned' (but only by the very pretentious). Lou doesn't do crepuscular jazz; it's all neon-lit, and none the worse for that. Bailey and Barretto make a propulsive combination, and even the little-known Foster seems spot on for the date.

BUD POWELL &

Born Earl Rudolph Powell, 27 September 1924, Harlem, New York; died 31 July 1966, New York City
Piano

The Amazing Bud Powell: Volume 5 – The Scene Changes
Blue Note 46529
Powell; Paul Chambers (b); Art Taylor (d). December 1958.

Bud's friend and protector Francis Paudras said (1986): **'Even when he was *distrait* there was something grand and hopeful in Bud's playing. I never heard it express anything other than beauty and love.'**

The cover photograph is heartbreakingly symbolic: a lowering Bud looks down at sheet music on the piano in front of him, rapt, private, shut away with his thoughts, while round his left shoulder a little boy peers guardedly, like his own lost younger self. These 1958 performances for Blue Note were an attempt to rekindle the fires. All the material is original and, though most of it harks back to the bop idiom rather than forward to anything new, it contains some of his most significant statements of any period. 'Comin' Up', of which there is also an alternative take, is in the released version his longest studio performance, and one of his most exuberant and playful, almost Latinate in feel. 'Down With It' is generic bebop and not a particularly effective idea, a long melody-line over orthodox changes, and only really distinguished for Chambers's fine *arco* solo. There was an earlier tune called 'Crossin' The Channel'; this, though, is Bud's alone and is the most formally constructed piece in the set, the one item that marks him down as a significant composer. 'The Scene Changes' is the final track on the original LP. It's a curious piece in that it looks back more than forward, almost as if the next scene were fated to be like the last.

& See also **The Amazing Bud Powell: Volumes 1 & 2** (1951–1953; p. 120)

MAL WALDRON &

Born 16 August 1925 (not 1926); died 2 December 2002, Brussels, Belgium
Piano

Mal/4: Trio
Original Jazz Classics OJC 1856
Waldron; Addison Farmer (b); Kenny Dennis (d). September 1958.

Saxophonist George Haslam says: **'In 1995 when Mal celebrated his 70th birthday I asked why reference books gave 1926 as his year of birth. He explained that back in the '40s/'50s, when Americans had to serve a year's compulsory national service, the young black guys didn't count that year as part of their life – so they would always say they were a year younger than they actually were. Anyone working out their year of birth would get it a year out.'**

Waldron had two careers, divided by a nervous breakdown in 1963 and subsequent emigration to Europe. Up to that point, he had played with Ike Quebec (with whom he made his recording debut) and Big Nick Nicholas, working in a soul-jazz vein. However, he also caught the ear of Charles Mingus and was present for the recording of *Pithecanthropus Erectus* and other sessions. Between 1957 and 1959, he was Billie Holiday's accompanist, staying with her until her death, but also continuing his own recording career. After his illness he had to begin his solo career afresh, re-learning piano by listening to his own recordings and emerging from the shadows with a new sound: percussive, dark, minor-keyed and long-lined. In reality, it wasn't so much new as a chiaroscuro version of his earlier style, as heard on this, his first trio recording.

It is, on the face of it, surprising that Waldron did not make more trio records. He launched the ECM label in 1969 with a trio set, but they do not figure prominently in his discography, which majors on solo, duo (with Steve Lacy, George Haslam, Marion Brown and others) and larger group recordings. *Mal/4* is by some way the best of the Prestige discs. Its predecessors had been for quintet and sextet, but here the stripped-down sound and spacious delivery and distinctive, investigative use of repetition as a structural device are already in evidence. Waldron was in the middle of his association with Lady Day and would shortly make a first recording with Steve Lacy, who shared a devotion to the music of Thelonious Monk. Waldron's compositions of the time might be described as Monkian. There is nothing on *Mal/4* in quite the spirit of his classic 'Soul Eyes'. His originals, 'Splidium-Dow', 'J.M.'s Dream Doll' and 'Love Span' intersperse the four standards like sombre interludes. 'Like Someone I Love' and 'Get Happy' (the latter laden with allusions to Bud Powell) are good examples of how Janus-faced Waldron was, even in those days, but the real killer is his reading of 'Too Close For Comfort', a long *tour de force* that remains a career highlight.

Waldron lived on until 2002, a trickster figure whose tragic mien at the keyboard was countered by the most playful of spirits, a paradox heightened by the shock of black/white hair he carried from his moment of crisis.

& *See also* **No More Tears (For Lady Day)** (1988; p. 526)

ROY HAYNES &

Born 13 March 1925, Roxbury, Massachusetts
Drums

We Three
Original Jazz Classics OJCCD 196
Haynes; Phineas Newborn Jr (p); Paul Chambers (b). November 1958.

Roy Haynes said (2004): **'The difference between Max [Roach] and me? Well, he liked to go "ba ba BOM", and I like to go "BOM ba ba". I think that just about sums it up!'**

Nobody in modern jazz has so consistently punched beyond his weight. The little man played with Charlie Parker, Miles Davis, Bud Powell, Sarah Vaughan, Thelonious Monk, Lester Young and Eric Dolphy, and in the John Coltrane Quartet, and is still around in the 2010s leading a band he has the cheek to call his Fountain Of Youth outfit. What Haynes lacks in sheer power he gains in precision and clarity, playing long, open lines that are deceptively relaxed but full of small rhythmic tensions. He's fascinating to listen to behind a soloist, following every compression of the bar-lines, anticipating moves in an uncanny way, providing a steady rhythmic commentary.

In 1958, his work still clearly bears the mark of stints with Monk and Miles. Bar-lines shift confidently or else are dispensed with altogether, without violence to the underlying pulse. Phineas Newborn's recent association with Charles Mingus had helped pare down his slightly extravagant style, but he's still devoted to long, liquid runs. The key track is a long, long version of 'After Hours', on which pianist and drummer lock together in a remarkable tension between lyrical outburst and restraint, with Chambers sustaining the line with effortless ease. Haynes himself sounds wonderful on 'Sugar Ray' and the romping 'Our Delight', where he is almost tuneful.

& See also **Praise** (1998; p. 628)

DAVID 'FATHEAD' NEWMAN
Born 24 February 1933, Corsicano, Texas; died 20 January 2009, Kingston, New York
Tenor, alto and soprano saxophones

Fathead
Atlantic 8122-73708-2
Newman; Marcus Belgrave (t); Bennie Crawford (bs); Ray Charles (p); Edgar Willis (b); Milton Turner (d). November 1958.

David Newman said (1992): **'How'd I get my nickname? That was my music instructor in high school. I had a bad habit of memorizing the music instead of reading it. He caught me one day with my score upside down on the stand. He came up behind me, gave me a thump and called me "Fathead". It kinda stuck. Ray Charles didn't like it, though. He called me "Brains".'**

An ornery, driving saxophonist whose R&B background – including 12 years with Ray Charles – left him with a consummate knowledge in the use of riffs and licks in a soul-to-jazz context, Newman always swung and his unmistakable Texan sound is highly authoritative, but like so many musicians of a similar background he had trouble finding a fruitful context and only in his later years did he start making the kind of straight-ahead jazz records that might once have been his natural turf. Equally typically, such opportunities only really came once his chops had started to waver and it's probably best to listen to Fathead earlier in his career, when the iron-hard sound and flow of riffs was unstaunchable.

It's worth considering that when he made the *Fathead* sessions for Atlantic, under his boss's patronage and a 'Ray Charles presents' strapline, his old Texan bandmate Ornette Coleman was playing a residence with Paul Bley at the Hillcrest and just about to join the same label. Not as much as one might think separates them at this stage. Listening to individual tracks, Newman's music is pitched a little awkwardly between jazz, R&B and proto-soul sax, but taken as a whole the album delivers a raw kind of bebop, perhaps a reminder that one of Newman's teachers was Buster Smith, who also exerted an influence on Charlie Parker. 'Tin Tin Deo' is sparklingly delivered, and with a weight of sound few bop combos could muster. The band plays well – Bennie Crawford, incidentally, is Hank Crawford – and there is consistently more to *Fathead* than meets the ear. It would be foolish to present him as an innovator manqué, but Ray Charles's imprimatur may have hindered rather than helped.

RAY BRYANT

Born 24 December 1931, Philadelphia, Pennsylvania
Piano

Alone With The Blues
Original Jazz Classics OJC 249
Bryant (p solo). December 1958.

Benny Golson says: **'Ray Bryant and I grew up together in Philadelphia. He was a genius at age 14. Anything he knew he could play in any key, even then. We played together on many occasions with John Coltrane.'**

Bryant's greatness goes unquestioned by musicians, and he's adored by his fans, but he's not always on the list of blue-chip piano moderns. Bryant is not an orthodox bopper in the way Hampton Hawes once was, and his solo performances are even further from the predominant Bud Powell model of bop piano. Noted for an imaginative and influential alteration of the basic 12-bar-blues sequence on his 'Blues Changes', Bryant is a distinctive pianist who, unlike Hawes, has often been content to record solo. He had a jukebox hit with 'Little Susie' and it became the focus of his first Columbia record, along with some other tunes which didn't have quite the same impact. They all seem much of a muchness now, though listenable enough. What happened was that he seemed to get more vital and, as Tiny May suggests, youthful as the years went by. There's no division into 'early' and 'late' or 'promising' and 'mature'. Bryant came into his voice early and just got better at it. He's a feelgood performer, whatever the material and the company.

Not everyone could make a whole programme of blues – even leavened with a gospelly 'Rockin' Chair' and 'Loverman' – sound appealing, but Bryant is such a devoted exponent that these five original lines, given 'opus numbers' from his workbook, are genuine contributions to the form. Bryant isn't a radical. He doesn't dabble in 13-bar forms or 11/8 time signatures. He keeps a strong left hand chiming and works variations on the melody even as he downshifts through the changes. His coming out as a solo recording artist was a genuine classic.

GERRY MULLIGAN &

Born 6 April 1927, New York City; died 20 January 1996, Darien, Connecticut
Baritone and soprano saxophones, clarinet

What Is There To Say?
Columbia CK 52978
Mulligan; Art Farmer (t); Bill Crow (b); Dave Bailey (d). December 1958.

Gerry Mulligan said (1990): **'Anyone who came into that group was either going to be a substitute trumpet-player – like Bobby Brookmeyer, and I think he found that hard – or, worse still, a substitute Chet. Art didn't concern himself with that. He just came in, brought his own things, and played as he played. It wouldn't have worked any other way.'**

There were to be reunions with Chet Baker down the line. A fiery personality, Mulligan had had his own scrapes with narcotics – including one prison sentence – and perhaps he was inclined to be forgiving of Chet's peccadilloes. Replacing the trumpeter was not an easy task. Bob Brookmeyer became a member of the group at one stage, but Art Farmer's tenure was perhaps even happier, bringing a small-group sound that strikingly resembles some of the stacked-up brass and woodwind sound Mulligan was to develop with orchestras later.

Farmer doesn't quite have the lyrical poignancy of Chet Baker in this setting, but he has a full, deep-chested tone (soon to be transferred to flugelhorn) which combines well with Mulligan's baritone. *What Is There To Say?* was Mulligan's first recording for Columbia. It's very direct, very unfussy, very focused on the leader, but with the same skills in evidence as on the earlier *The Arranger*, which was a dry run for the label. The first album proper is a small masterpiece of controlled invention. Mulligan's solos fit into the structure of 'As Catch Can' and 'Festive Minor' as if they were machine-tooled. Farmer responds in kind, with smooth legato solos and delicate fills. There's also a live disc, *News From Blueport*, from the same group a month later that shows how well Farmer was bedded in and following his own unflurried course.

& *See also* **The Original Quartet** (1952–1953; p. 137), **The Age Of Steam** (1971; p. 383)

FRANK ROSOLINO

Born 20 August 1926, Detroit, Michigan; died 26 November 1978, Los Angeles, California
Trombone

Free For All
Original Jazz Classics OJCCD 1763
Rosolino; Harold Land (ts); Victor Feldman (p); Leroy Vinnegar (b); Stan Levey (d). December 1958.

Trombonist Eric Felten says: **'I long thought the bold declarative solo on "23 Degrees North 82 Degrees West" by the Kenton band was the definitive Rosolino moment. Then I heard "Stardust" on *Free For All*. The simple phrases of the verse are played with tense energy and clipped impatience. And then he's off: melismatic embouchure-gymnastics, intricate chromatic lines alternating with staccato arpeggios, soaring up to those trademark high Fs, played – trombonists, please note – with his slide in 3rd position, not 1st). After all the pyrotechnics he slips seamlessly into the most powerful of simple melodic statements.'**

In November 1978, suffering from depression, Frank Rosolino shot his sons, wounding them both grievously, then took his own life. It seemed an utterly untypical ending for a lively, almost hyperactive man with some reputation (unearned, in our view) as a comic vocalist. Valued for fast, responsive trombone-playing, he worked in an array of big bands, including Gene Krupa's, before joining Howard Rumsey's Lighthouse All-Stars in the later '50s. Rosolino developed a style that seemed to combine elements of bop harmony with the more durable virtues of swing. A wonderfully agile player with a tone that could be broad and humane, almost vocalized one moment, thinly abstract the next, Rosolino brings a twist of humour to almost everything he plays. The 1961 album *Turn Me Loose!* was an attempt at a comic jazz album, which mostly works, though his singing is affected and tiresome.

Though an earlier quintet album for VSOP has some enthusiastic takers, *Free For All* remains his best record. The reissue rounds out a fine session done for the Specialty label with some valuable alternative takes ('There Is No Greater Love', 'Chrisdee' and 'Don't Take Your Love From Me'; they don't add anything dramatic, but they show Rosolino's improvisational skill at work) and some great performances from the band that belie the undisciplined mood suggested by the title. 'Sneakyoso' offers a glimpse of Rosolino as a composer, a line with some comic potential, but played fairly straight here. 'Stardust' is simply inspired, a recording whose technical mastery has a superadded element of expressive magic. Land is a muscular soloist, but is none the less responsive to the mood of the session, and is capable of some extremely delicate and detailed passage-work. It's a happy, flowing session, with no storm clouds lurking. What happened 20 years later was an appalling aberration, and tragic for those involved, but it shouldn't cloud perception of his best work.

IRA SULLIVAN

Born 1 May 1931, Washington DC
Trumpet, flugelhorn, peckhorn, saxophones

Nicky's Tune

Delmark DD 422
Sullivan; Nicky Hill (sax); Jodie Christian (p); Vic Sproles (b); Wilbur Campbell (d). 1958.

Ira Sullivan said (1999): **'There were all these great horn-players round Chicago when I was there – Dexter, Stitt, Jug, Griff – and what did I do? I moved to Florida, which I'd always seen as a place people retired to. I never expected to work and didn't even take a horn, but it shaped up different to that, and I've even played at Lake Buena Vista in Disneyland.'**

A fascinating enigma, Sullivan is an important transitional figure between bop and free music, whose restless style and intriguing multi-instrumentalism may well have had an impact on the nascent AACM generation in Chicago, where he was based in his youth, a focal figure for many of the young players coming through.

Sullivan started out as a bopper, but one who assiduously avoided the basic, standards-based repertoire in favour of new material; this, it seems, was the condition he imposed when he went on the road with Red Rodney and it became his principle later, too. For a long time, Sullivan was only represented in the catalogue by two '50s albums from Delmark. There's a little more around now, but he's still not much documented. This disc, the earlier of the pair, is dedicated to the equally enigmatic Nicky Hill, one of those catalytic players who remained little known outside a small circle. Like all of Ira's output, it's a slightly puzzling and forbidding experience if you approach it expecting basic changes and contrafacts on 'I Got Rhythm', 'Cherokee' and 'How High The Moon'. Ira's harmonic sense is unimpeachable and his understanding with the excellent Christian is intuitive and sympathetic. Trumpet is the dominant voice on both records, but the saxophones and peckhorn are deployed to excellent effect. This was the period when Ira was losing patience with the formulae of bebop, even his own individual brand, and was striking out in the direction of free jazz. There are atonal and polytonal episodes on *Nicky's Tune*, fewer on the second set, *Blue Stroll*, with Johnny Griffin, who barges and blusters his way through his solos, tossing out tags and quotes as if to remind the others what else was going on in the world.

Sullivan went to Florida in the early '60s and has remained there, apparently out of the swim, but still making powerful jazz and still acting as an influence on a new generation.

SUN RA &

Born Herman Sonny Blount (also known as Sonny Bourke, Le Sony'r Ra) 22 May 1914, Birmingham, Alabama; died 30 May 1993, Birmingham, Alabama
Piano, space organ, keyboards

Jazz In Silhouette
Evidence ECD 22012

Sun Ra; Hobart Dotson (t); Julian Priester (tb); Marshall Allen, James Spaulding (as, f); John Gilmore (ts); Charles Davis (bs); Pat Patrick (bs, f); Ronnie Boykins (b); William 'Bugs' Cochran (d). 1958.

Norman Mailer said (1993): **'I remember walking down through Harlem one night in the '60s, no cabs around, freezing slush in the streets, with a bellyful of booze, a pain behind one eye, spoiling for trouble, and coming across Sun Ra and the band playing in an abandoned store. Gold costumes, masks, headdresses, lights. It was as if the Wise Ones had landed on our cold planet with a message of peace and a cure for cancer.'**

Sun Ra was either a fearsome avant-gardist or a traditionalist in the line of Fletcher Henderson, for whom he arranged early in his career. The truth about Sun Ra was that he was both those things. He grew up steeped in the blues, worked an orthodox apprenticeship with the big bands, and even when he founded his famous Arkestra, with its theatrical approach to jazz, and became a leading presence on the Chicago improvisation scene, his work was always grounded in melody and in blues changes. Sun Ra's claim to come from Saturn was one of the great metaphors of Black American music. If you are a black man from Birmingham, Alabama, how much more 'alien' does this planet need to be?

Uncertainty about Sun Ra's seriousness (and sanity) tended to divert attention from a considerable three-decade output, which included well over 100 LPs. Because much of it remained inaccessible during his lifetime, critical responses were apt to concentrate on the paraphernalia associated with his Arkestra big band, rather than on the music. Nevertheless, he was one of the most significant bandleaders of the postwar period. He drew on Ellington and Fletcher Henderson, but also on the bop-derived avant-garde, and was a pioneer of collective improvisation.

Above all, Sun Ra maintained a solitary independence from the music industry, a principled stance that certainly cost him dear in critical and commercial terms. The El Saturn discs were reissued *in toto* by Evidence, a colossal project. Sound quality is remarkably good, given the often shaky balance of the original masters and the fact that they've been subjected to uncertain storage conditions. The original titles have been preserved wherever possible, even when this has led to rather cumbersome doubling up. One of the drawbacks of Evidence's programme is the out-of-sequence pairing of sessions, rendering a strictly chronological review impossible.

The '50s were in many respects a golden age for Sun Ra and the Arkestra. The music is frankly experimental and the sci-fi apparatus was already part and parcel of American culture through the latter half of the decade. Chants like 'We Travel The Spaceways' began to sound more artful and mannered as the years went by, but for now they manage to sound almost spontaneous. There was always a suspicion that titles like 'Rocket Number Nine Take Off For The Planet Venus' were simply a diversionary addition to a fairly conventional jazz tune.

The marvellous *Jazz In Silhouette* will surely some day be recognized as one of the most important jazz records since the war. The closing 'Blues At Midnight' is sheer excitement. The baritone solo on the short 'Saturn', most probably Patrick, is an extension of Sun Ra's brilliantly individual voicings. The great surprise of this recording (though presumably no surprise to those who have taken the Saturnian aesthetic fully on board) is its *timelessness*. Listening to 'Enlightenment', given an uncharacteristically straightforward reading, it's very difficult to guess a date for the performance. As Francis Davis suggests in a useful liner-note, it is ideal 'blindfold test' material that might have been recorded at any point from the '40s to the late '80s. Only the long drum passage on 'Ancient Aiethopia' and the astonishing Dotson solo and chants that follow sound unequivocally 'modern'. Inevitably, the next track, 'Hours After', is orthodox swing.

& See also **The Magic City** (1965; p. 328), **Mayan Temples** (1990; p. 541)

BARNEY WILEN

Born 4 March 1937, Nice, France; died 25 May 1996, Paris, France
Tenor, alto and soprano saxophones

Jazz Sur Seine
Emarcy 548317-2
Wilen; Milt Jackson (p); Percy Heath (b); Kenny Clarke (d); Gana M'Bow (perc). 1958.

**Barney Wilen said (1988): '*Miles m'a dit*: "Why do you play all those awful notes?" It
sounded for a moment like my father speaking. He wanted me to practise law, but
[Blaise] Cendrars told me to follow my instincts and my dream. Same story as every jazz
guy, *hein*?'**

The poet Blaise Cendrars, a family friend, can take the credit for persuading Wilen to
become a musician. Wilen's father was American and well-to-do and the family spent the
war years away from France, not that the experience can have had any particular musical
impact on young Bernard, who was only eight when VE Day came round. Basically a tenor-
player, he made his name when Miles Davis chose him to play in a group he was fronting
in Europe in 1957 and he was part of the ensemble that made the retrospectively important
L'Ascenseur pour l'échafaud soundtrack music, which is credited with starting Miles's move
towards abstraction. But Wilen had already garnered a reputation with visiting Americans
for a considerably accomplished technique and a real mastery of hard-bop forms.
    The Universal stable has a considerable imprint devoted to reissue of classic Parisian
sessions made for Verve and it's wonderful to have some of this music back in circulation.
The rhythm section is familiar, but Milt Jackson plays piano. There's some beautiful playing by the saxophonist, his tone veiled but wonderfully singing, on the blues 'Nuages' and
'Epistrophy'.
    Wilen's subsequent visit to play at Newport in 1959 is commemorated by a Fresh Sound
CD, although there's only 20 minutes of music from that occasion. He had an interesting
later career, working in film, hopping on the punk bandwagon, pursuing music with promiscuous delight. In jazz terms, he remains of his moment, but like Bobby Jaspar a consistently underrated European.

MILES DAVIS &

Born 26 May 1926, Alton, Illinois; died 28 September 1991, Santa Monica, California
Trumpet, flugelhorn, organ

Kind Of Blue
Columbia CK 64935
Davis; Cannonball Adderley (as); John Coltrane (ts); Bill Evans, Wynton Kelly (p); Paul Chambers (b); Jimmy
Cobb (d). March–April 1959.

**Jimmy Cobb said (1986): 'We didn't think we were doing anything special on that record. It
felt like another date – a good one, but I never recognized it from some of the things that
are said about it now.'**

No other jazz record enjoys quite the same reputation as *Kind Of Blue*. Its story has been
told over and again in books and articles. The album turns up in the collections of people
who otherwise don't listen to jazz, and profess to dislike it. Its music echoes across wine
bars and jeans shops. The present authors were mischievously inclined to dismiss it as
highbrow mood music and to propose a moratorium on playing it until its marvellous freshness and intimacy could be appreciated in full again. *Kind Of Blue* came at an interesting
time in Miles's creative life. In contrast to many other of his recordings, it hadn't around it

the area of creative crisis, struggle, abnegation that usually signalled his most important transitions.

A year before, in April 1958, Miles hadn't recorded a small-group date for more than a year. A lot of thinking, woodshedding, a lot of hard conceptual work had been done in the interim. On *Milestones* he worked out ideas that had been adumbrated on the deceptively casual movie soundtrack *L'Ascenseur pour l'échafaud*, and delivered a wonderfully coherent and organic performance. There are no standards, and all the material is challenging, sometimes simply by suspending conventional harmony and by constraining complex ideas within a deceptively simple 4/4. One of the profound differences between Miles and the saxophonists is that, while they tend to play on the beat, he is almost always across it, almost always escaping the gravitational pull of the chords entirely.

Kind Of Blue marked a momentary caesura in that creative restlessness. The reason may well be the presence of another artist in the group of almost equal stature to Miles himself: not Coltrane, who always sounds like the music's special pleader, but Bill Evans. His allusive, almost impressionistic accompaniments provide the ideal platform for the spacious solos created by the horns. This was the first widely acknowledged 'modal jazz' date, and it is interesting how thoroughly it has now been absorbed into mainstream language. Tension is consistently established within the ensembles, only for Davis and Coltrane especially to resolve it in songful, declamatory solos. The steady mid-tempos and the now familiar plaintive voicings on 'So What' and 'All Blues' reinforce the weightless, haunting qualities Miles was bringing to his music. 'Flamenco Sketches' is the one track that points outward into more uncertain territory, though its 'Spanish tinge' is also an anchor point, suggesting continuity. If you will, the clinching quality of *Kind Of Blue* is that its energies are centripetal; map the harmonies and this becomes clearer. It seems – with that tiny exception – entire of itself and without the troubling restlessness of almost all Miles Davis's other records. That is not to belittle it, but to offer one clue to its almost universal appeal.

& See also **The Complete Birth Of The Cool** (1948–1950; p. 121), **Miles Ahead** (1957; p. 208), **The Complete Live At The Plugged Nickel** (1965; p. 331), **In A Silent Way** (1969; p. 361), **Agharta** (1975; p. 420)

WYNTON KELLY
Born 2 December 1931, Jamaica; died 12 April 1971, Toronto, Ontario, Canada
Piano

Kelly Blue
Original Jazz Classics OJC 033
Kelly; Nat Adderley (c); Bobby Jaspar (f); Benny Golson (ts); Paul Chambers (b); Jimmy Cobb (d). February & March 1959.

Drummer Jimmy Cobb said (1986): **'Miles always knew what he wanted from a piano-player and sometimes had two of them around. With Wynton – though he didn't use him much on *Kind Of Blue* (paid him though!) – he had two in one, he had Bill Evans and Red Garland in one man.'**

Kelly wasn't in some listeners' opinion the most obvious replacement for Bill Evans and Red Garland in the Miles Davis group, but he had a lyrical simplicity and uncomplicated touch that appealed enormously to the trumpeter, who hired him in 1959; Kelly played on only one track on the classic *Kind Of Blue*, but 'Freddie Freeloader' is enough to show what distinguished him from Evans's more earnestly romantic style. His first attempts at recording on his own account were callow and undistinguished but *Kelly Blue* is almost exactly contemporaneous with Miles's classic and the magic rubs off.

The gentle but dynamic bounce of Kelly's chording comes to the fore (which also reunites the *Kind Of Blue* rhythm section). On the title-track and 'Keep It Moving', the addition of Adderley, who also admired Kelly, and the intriguing Jaspar, always more interesting on flute than when he played Pres-and-water saxophone, makes perfect sense. Golson lends the date some much needed weight in the middle but he does sometimes overbalance the delicate strength of Kelly's arrangements. The trio cuts are far superior.

ABBEY LINCOLN

Born Anna Marie Wooldridge, 6 August 1930, Chicago, Illinois; died 14 August 2010, New York City
Voice

Abbey Is Blue

Original Jazz Classics OJCCD 069
Lincoln; Kenny Dorham, Tommy Turrentine (t); Julian Priester (tb); Stanley Turrentine (ts); Les Spann (g, f); Wynton Kelly, Cedar Walton, Les Wright (p); Bobby Boswell, Sam Jones (b); Philly Joe Jones, Max Roach (d). March 1959.

Abbey Lincoln said (1990): **'Back then [in the '50s] people in the business told you what to wear, what to sing, how to stand, what expression to use on your face and when to use it, when to laugh and speak and not speak. It was like being a prostitute. You were paid for and *owned*.'**

Lincoln's own emancipation proclamation turned her from a conventional club singer into one of the most dramatic and distinctive voices of the day, whose work touches on matters of gender and female self-determination as much as it does on matters of ethnicity and colour. As she concedes, she owes her creative emancipation to one-time husband Max Roach, with whom she worked on *We Insist! Freedom Now Suite*, but she had recorded under her own name before that. She worked in California under the name Anna Marie, Gaby Wooldridge and Gaby Lee and then began recording on her own account. She and Roach were married from 1962 to 1970, after which her career faded until a revival of interest in the '80s led to a Verve contract.

Never a conventional standards singer, Lincoln indicated her individuality and occasionally her disaffection in subtle ironies, subliminal variations and occasional hot blasts of fury. She was both respectful of her material and inclined to manipulate it without mercy or apology. 'Afro Blue', here with the Max Roach Sextet, is one of her strongest performances at any period, though slightly hectoring in tone. Her reading of Duke's 'Come Sunday' is beautiful, plaintive and proud in equal measure. 'Softly, As In A Morning Sunrise' and 'Lost In The Stars' were probably studio musts. Though she adds an edge to both, the set is stronger on the more original material and arrangements. Her own 'Let Up' is a foretaste of the strong songwriting that was to come.

TERRY GIBBS

Born Julius Gubenko, 13 October 1924, New York City
Vibraphone, xylophone, drums

One More Time

Contemporary 7658
Gibbs; Johnny Audino, Conte Candoli, Frank Huggins, Al Porcino, Ray Triscari, Stu Williamson (t); Bob Enevoldsen (vtb); Bob Burgess, Vernon Friley (tb); Joe Cadena, Med Flory, Bill Holman (ts); Joe Maini, Charlie Kennedy (as); Jack Schwartz (bs); Pete Jolly, Lou Levy (p); Max Bennett, Buddy Clark (b); Mel Lewis (d); Irene Kral (v). March–November 1959.

Terry Gibbs said (1992): **'The MCA agency didn't like my name [Julius Gubenko], so when I was with Judy Kayne, I was billed as "Terry Gibbs on drums and xylophone". I saw the flyer and thought I'd been canned. My mother was furious. How would anyone know her son was performing?'**

The wonderfully durable Gibbs was still performing in his 70s. He had a relatively uneventful time in swing bands before settling in LA in 1957 and running a part-time big band there. The Gibbs bands combined the high-energy swing of Lionel Hampton with the sophistication of the Thad Jones–Mel Lewis outfits. The arrangements, by Marty Paich, Lennie Niehaus and others, are all good, but with a sometimes uneasy emphasis on the higher horns. Gibbs's playing is closer to Hampton's percussive bounce than to any of the competing influences, and he solos with verve. It's a style that draws a great deal from bop and it's no less well-adapted to the small-group performances which he has been focusing on more recently, at least on record (he still runs editions of The Dream Band today, but says he won't record them, in order not to spoil the memory of this great outfit).

One More Time arrived as the result of Terry finding another box of tapes at home, and what a fine discovery. While it's more of a ragbag than some of his records on Contemporary, it's as loaded with atmosphere as anything in the series, and for sheer zing it sounds like the pick of the sequence to us. Irene Kral takes a couple of vocals, Conte Candoli has a couple of lovely features, and Gibbs himself has the audacity to out-Hamp the master on an 11-minute 'Flying Home'. The sound is amazingly good.

EDDIE 'LOCKJAW' DAVIS
Born 2 March 1922, New York City; died 3 November 1986, Las Vegas, Nevada
Tenor saxophone

Very Saxy
Original Jazz Classics OJCCD 458
Davis; Coleman Hawkins, Arnett Cobb, Buddy Tate (ts); Shirley Scott (org); George Duvivier (b); Arthur Edgehill (d). April 1959.

Johnny Griffin said (1989): **'Did you know he had corks under some of the keys?! I asked him about that. He said: "I don't need them, so I just cover them up"!'**

'Jaws' had a somewhat brutish power that was often best deployed in the kind of brawling, competitive jam situations the labels used to favour. He wasn't without a measure of subtlety, though, and it was obvious that he knew more than he played, with a lot of musical information lurking below the waterline. He made his name with Cootie Williams, before joining Basie in 1952, and was with him off and on till the end of the decade. After that, he was frequently paired with Shirley Scott or Johnny Griffin, before spending a further seven years with the Count and then working mainly as a solo artist. He died unexpectedly in Las Vegas, still apparently at the height of his considerable powers.

It doesn't belittle Davis's skill or presence to select a record on which he shares the billing with three other distinguished tenormen on the Prestige books, called to sit in with the Davis–Scott combo. The results are barnstorming. The programme is all simple blues, but the flat-out exuberance of the playing is exhilarating, particularly in the excellent remastered sound, and it's interesting to listen to Davis in close proximity to the others, already exploring areas of harmony and intonation perhaps more obviously associated with the younger John Coltrane. As competitive as it might appear, nobody is bested, and the clout of Davis and Cobb is matched by the suaver Tate and the grandiloquent Hawkins. Their 'Lester Leaps In' is a peerless display of saxophone sound.

CAL TJADER
Born 16 July 1925, St Louis, Missouri; died 5 May 1982, Manila, Philippines
Vibraphone

Monterey Concerts
Prestige P24026
Tjader; Paul Horn (f); Lonnie Hewitt (p); Al McKibbon (b); Willie Bobo, Mongo Santamaria (perc). April 1959.

Latin rock guitar legend Carlos Santana said (1985): **'I don't think the young people know his name now, but Cal Tjader was hugely influential in making Latin music part of the pop mainstream.'**

Though originally from the Midwest, Tjader based himself in California and, after high-profile stints with Dave Brubeck and George Shearing, led his own groups from 1954. His essentially lightweight blend of Latin, Cuban and bebop styles became popular in the late '50s and '60s, and he helped pioneer the salsa idiom, at least from a jazz perspective, a remarkable achievement for a musician with no Latin roots.

He was a great popularizer whose musical mind ran rather deeper than some have allowed. As a vibes-player, he was an able and not quite outstanding soloist, but his interest in Latin rhythms and their potential for blending with West Coast jazz was a genuine one, and his best records have a jaunty and informed atmosphere which denigrates neither side of the fusion. He made a lot of records, and many of them have been awarded reissue, which makes it difficult to choose particular winners. Tjader helped to break Willie Bobo and Mongo Santamaria to wider audiences, some time before Coltrane recorded 'Afro-Blue'.

What's immediately obvious to anyone who comes to the *Monterey Concerts* (originally released in two volumes as *Concert By The Sea*, and actually recorded in Carmel as part of the second Monterey Jazz Festival) is that the basic language is bebop. The compilation starts off with Rollins's 'Doxy', followed by 'Afro-Blue' and 'Laura', picking up again with 'A Night In Tunisia' from the second volume. This isn't necessarily what anyone expects, given his reputation as a Latin-lite musician. The timbre and tonality of his vibes are both quite gentle, but structurally Tjader was an iron-hard musical thinker, and in that he's matched by the perennially underrated Horn, who made a significant impact on West Coast jazz with Chico Hamilton before pursuing a fusion course. And, needless to say, Santamaria is a big presence.

BLOSSOM DEARIE
Born 28 April 1924 (some sources give 1926), East Durham, New York; died 7 February 2009, New York City
Voice, piano

Blossom Dearie
Verve 827743
Dearie; Herb Ellis (g); Ray Brown (b); Jo Jones (d). September 1956, April 1959.

Producer Norman Granz said (1986): **'I always thought her musicianship was poorly appreciated, the piano-playing in particular. That name really suited her, but it made her sound lightweight, which she wasn't.'**

Dearie grew up in the Catskills and made her start in New York City as a vocalist/pianist. However, it was in Paris that she made a name and it was there Norman Granz spotted and signed her up. She has ever since attracted adulation out of all proportion to her apparently quite modest approach. Newcomers who have only heard of her are taken aback by the light, sometimes paper-thin delivery. And yet, there really is something hypnotic about her playing and singing, and one can't imagine either without the other.

The debut for Granz's label isn't a splashy showcase but a subtly nuanced jazz vocal album that puts Blossom's fine piano-playing squarely in the spotlight. The voice won't appeal to everyone, but we've always questioned the 'little girl' label. It's not a big instrument, for sure, but it has unquestionable authority from "Deed I Do' onward, and the French songs she picked up while in Paris give it an intriguingly different context, 'Tout Doucement' in particular. The reissue includes three later recordings, including a bouncy 'Johnny One Note'.

FRANK STROZIER
Born 13 June 1937, Memphis, Tennessee
Alto saxophone

Fantastic Frank Strozier
Vee-Jay 12
Strozier; Booker Little (t); Wynton Kelly (p); Paul Chambers (b); Jimmy Cobb (d). December 1959, February 1960.

Jimmy Cobb recalls: **'Frank came out of Memphis with something new ... maybe a country sound.'** And Harold Mabern adds: **'He was so good John Coltrane used to follow him around, asking questions.'**

Frank Strozier's debut recording scarcely seems radical when placed alongside Ornette Coleman's first Atlantics, also recorded in 1959, or Eric Dolphy's first set as leader, which was taped some weeks after the second of the sessions included on *Fantastic*. Strozier's music has little of the alienating wallop of those two fellow altoists, both of whom were almost a decade older. At first hearing, he more obviously resembles Jackie McLean, but just as Jackie's early work always had an extra dimension that took it beyond mere Bird copyism, so Strozier doesn't sound like he's in thrall to anyone, but finding his individual way in what was still a relatively new idiom. We have long held this record in high esteem and it never fails to deliver.

Strozier made his first significant appearance on disc a year before as one of the Young Men From Memphis – the line-up included Booker Little, Louis Smith, George Coleman and Phineas Newborn Jr – who made *Down Home Reunion* for United Artists. Little was on hand again when Strozier went into Fine Sound Studios in New York on 9 December 1959 to record under his own name for the first time. With him was what was perhaps the most celebrated rhythm section of the time, who nine months earlier had taken part in Miles Davis's *Kind Of Blue* sessions.

Wynton Kelly had not yet taken over fully from Bill Evans when that iconic record was taped, but he is a key presence on Strozier's album, which was made for Vee-Jay. He makes an immediate impact on his own 'W.K. Blues', a conventional enough line, albeit with varied harmonics, but also one which allows both Little and Strozier enough leeway to shape solos that still fit the hard-bop mould while suggesting something beyond. Strozier's own 'A Starling's Theme' and 'I Don't Know' – have these strong themes ever been called for since? – add to the impression that something original is afoot, subtly angular melodies that open out onto tautly generous solos. Kelly holds the middle and his deceptive simplicity of approach in the rhythm section sometimes conspires to hide the music's sophistication.

Little's 'Waltz Of The Demons' lent its name to a further compilation of material from this and the good but sketchier February 1960 date. The tragedy of the trumpeter's early

238 THE '50s: 1956–1960

death led to this being posthumously co-credited, while the same material has also been issued by Mosaic as part of a compilation of Kelly's and Paul Chambers's Vee-Jay sessions. Thus circumstance further eclipsed Strozier's reputation. It's hard to think that anyone encountering this record will not be impressed. The saxophone tone is warm and thoughtful, but not without its jagged edges. Little is as impressive as he ever was in that short career and the rhythm section is coach-built and solidly elegant. *Fantastic* sits in very august company, but in our view more than justifies its place.

TUBBY HAYES
Born Edward Brian Hayes, 30 January 1945, London; died 8 June 1973, London
Tenor saxophone, vibraphone

The Eighth Wonder
Jasmine JASCD 611
Hayes; Terry Shannon (p); Phil Bates, Jeff Clyne (b); Bill Eyden, Phil Seamen (d). March–December 1959.

Trumpeter Jimmy Deuchar said (1983): **'Even as a teenager, he was a monstrous talent. You learned something about music, often something quite basic, every time Tubbs took a solo.'**

Hayes was a prodigy who took up saxophone at 11 and made his recording debut at 16 with Kenny Baker. He co-led the Jazz Couriers with Ronnie Scott in the '50s and visited New York in 1961. His eminence on the British scene was eclipsed by the pop boom and his final years were troubled by illness.

Tubbs has often been lionized as the greatest saxophonist Britain ever produced. He is a fascinating but problematic player. With a big, rumbustious tone and flurries of 16th notes, Hayes often left a solo full of brilliant loose ends and ingenious runs that led nowhere in particular. Most of his recordings, while highly entertaining as exhibitions of sustained energy, tend to wobble on the axis of Hayes's creative impasse. His studio records consistently fall short of the masterpiece he originally seemed destined to make. It's tempting to set forward one of the live Ronnie Scott's dates that were consigned to tape, but that seems an easy option. The studio work wasn't unfulfilled; it just seemed often to fall short of expectation.

Hayes's '50s sessions for Tony Hall's Tempo label have made their way to CD via Jasmine, though remastering is no more than fair and the designs cheap-looking. Besides Hayes himself, there are glimpses of a whole school of players whose music, especially in this period, was scarcely documented at all away from mere studio work. But it's Hayes himself that most will want to hear. He's in his pomp on *Eighth Wonder*, which is the only one of the album reissues that gets top rating. Most of it comes from the sessions for *Tubby's Groove*, perhaps Hayes's most ebullient showcase. It's true that the virtuosity of 'Tin Tin Deo' comes out of his horn all too easily, almost as if it were a routine he'd mastered without thinking, but it's hard not to enjoy the spectacle; and there is much tough-minded improvising on the date too, especially in the magnificent feast he makes out of 'Blue Hayes'. The other figure to listen to here is Terry Shannon, hardly recalled these days but one of Britain's most capable small-group pianists.

JACKIE MCLEAN &
Born 17 May 1932, New York City; died 31 May 2006, Hartford, Connecticut
Alto saxophone

New Soil

Blue Note 784013
McLean; Donald Byrd (t); Walter Davis Jr (p); Paul Chambers (b); Pete LaRoca (d). May 1959.

Jackie McLean said (1985): **'I was Bird's man. Everything Charlie Parker had done, I wanted to do, and I did. It was Charles Mingus who steered me away from that, told me I should be developing my own thing and honouring the tradition by moving it on rather than keeping it packed in ice.'**

McLean's father worked with Tiny Bradshaw, and young John grew up surrounded by music, passing on the discipline to his son René. During a spell with the Jazz Messengers, Jackie struck out on his own, recording prodigally with his quartet and patenting a sound that was compounded equally of bebop and the new, free style. His alto-playing is immediately distinctive, acidulated by a tendency to play slightly sharp; it gives his solos in particular an urgent, headlong quality, but also a curious air of innocence and freshness, as if the harmony is fresh-minted each time.

An immensely prolific player, he made a good many records in orthodox bop style, making his recording debut with Miles Davis at the turn of the '50s, later working with Charles Mingus and with Art Blakey in the Messengers. His long run of records for Blue Note started immediately after that, 17 of them in a little more than seven years. *New Soil* wasn't the first of the sessions – McLean had set down the material for *Jackie's Bag* in January of the same year, but it wasn't released till later – but it was certainly the most important and a big shift from his work for New Jazz and Prestige. Transitional and challenging, *New Soil* seems tame by later standards. McLean had passed through difficult times and was reassessing his career and direction. The extended 'Hip Strut' is perhaps the most conventional thing on the album, but the saxophonist is straining a little at the boundaries of the blues, still pushing from the inside, but definitely looking for a new synthesis. 'Minor Apprehension' has elements of freedom which are slightly startling for the period and wholly untypical of McLean's previous work. McLean would later work with Ornette Coleman on *New And Old Gospel* and it sounds from this as if he has already started paying attention to Ornette's innovations: Byrd's playing is untypical and LaRoca delivers a remarkably free drum solo.

& *See also* **Live At Montmartre** (1972; p. 397)

DONALD BYRD &

Born 9 December 1932, Detroit, Michigan
Trumpet

Byrd In Hand

Blue Note BS2 84019
Byrd; Charlie Rouse (ts); Pepper Adams (bs); Walter Davis Jr (p); Sam Jones (b); Art Taylor (d). May 1959.

Donald Byrd said (1974): **'Jazz communicates universal values. Playing together and improvising together is one way of asserting our common goal. But the audience completes that cycle and if the audience isn't there – and I mean if they don't follow the music, or appreciate it – then it's broken. So the music *has* to communicate.'**

Donaldson Toussaint L'Ouverture Byrd II was an obvious pick for the Jazz Messengers and by the end of the '50s had already recorded prolifically, as the most heavily documented of the hard-bop trumpeters. A crossover period yielded the hit album *Black Byrd*, after which he seemed to drift away from the music, studied to be a lawyer, and only made occasional forays back in the '80s and '90s. By the time he signed to Blue Note, Byrd had already recorded for Transition and Savoy, more than any of the other up-and-coming horn-players of his day. It was his easy-going proficiency that made him sought after: like Freddie Hubbard a decade later, he could sound good under any contemporary leader without entirely dominating the situation. His solos were valuable but not disconcertingly personal, dependably elegant but not strikingly memorable. His records as leader emerged in much the same way: refined and crisp hard bop which seemed to look neither forward nor backwards. Given his neutral quality, it's often the other players who'll clinch the choice of an album.

Byrd In Hand is something of an exception in that Rouse (certainly) and Adams (somewhat) fail to command much individual attention. What's impressive here is the overall sound of the record, a near-perfect balance of ensemble sound and effective if not charismatic soloing. Byrd contributes three effective lines, including the striking 'Devil Whip', that allow him to work at the edge of his comfort zone, expressive enough but never close to falling off the wire. Davis is a terrific bop accompanist and his spacious chords provide enough of a safety net for the music to cohere at every point.

& *See also* **Black Byrd** (1972; p. 394)

DAVE BRUBECK &
Born 6 December 1920, Concord, California
Piano

Time Out
Columbia CK 65122
Brubeck; Paul Desmond (as); Eugene Wright (b); Joe Morello (d). June–August 1959.

Dave Brubeck said (1991): **'I was in traction after a foolish accident at Waikiki [Brubeck was almost paralysed after diving through a wave and colliding violently with a sandbar] and I knew that when I got back to work I'd need a second voice to help lighten the load. So I wrote to Paul [Desmond] and said: "Here's the chance to form that quartet you've been talking about. [Wife] Iola said from the first time she heard us that we ought to work together."'**

This is the music everyone associates with Brubeck: cool, sophisticated and swinging, and even people with little stake in jazz are eager to show off their knowledge by pointing out that 'Take Five' itself was actually a Paul Desmond composition. So familiar is it that no one actually hears what's going on any more. As the title suggests, Brubeck wanted to explore ways of playing jazz that went a step beyond the basic 4/4 that had remained the norm long after jazz threw off the relentless predictability of B flat. The opening 'Blue Rondo A La Turk' (with its Mozart echoes) opens in an oddly distributed 9/8, with the count rearranged as 2-2-2-3. It's a relatively conventional classical *rondo* but with an almost raucous blues interior. 'Take Five' is in the most awkward of all metres, but what is remarkable about this iconic slice of modern jazz is the extent to which it constantly escapes the 5/4 count and swings effortlessly; it is possible to dance to it. Morello's drum solo is perhaps his best work on record (though his brief 'Everybody's Jumpin'' solo is also excellent) and Brubeck's heavy vamp has tremendous force. Most of the other material is in waltz and double-waltz time. Max Roach had explored the idea thoroughly on *Jazz In 3/4 Time*, but not even Roach had attempted anything as daring and sophisticated as the alternations of beat on 'Three To Get Ready' and 'Kathy's Waltz', which is perhaps the finest single thing on the album. Desmond tends to normalize the count in his solo line, and it's easy to miss what is going on in the rhythm section if one concentrates too exclusively on the saxophone. The Desmond cult may be fading slightly and as it does it may be possible to re-establish the Brubeck

Quartet's claim *as a unit* to be considered among the most innovative and adventurous of modern-jazz groups.

& See also **The Dave Brubeck Octet** (1946–1950; p. 106), **London Sharp, London Flat** (2004; p. 690)

KENNY BALL
Born 22 May 1930, Ilford, Essex, England
Trumpet

Back At The Start
Lake LACD 114
Ball; John Bennett (tb); Dave Jones (cl); Colin Bates, Ron Weatherburn (p); Dickie Bishop, Diz Disley, Paddy Lightfoot (bj); Vic Pitt (b); Tony Budd, Ron Bowden (d). June 1959–March 1962.

Kenny Ball says: **'You might think this is a bit nutty, but when I'm out there with my trumpet in one hand and mute in another, it is like holding a new baby for the first time. You think: what do I do with this to make it right? And you think that every time. It's part of me that's going on there.'**

Ball's early records will surprise anyone who just knows him as a cabaret or TV star, or who has only ever heard 'Midnight In Moscow', his banker hit. He led a tough, hard-hitting outfit which he directed with great skill. Bennett, one of the longest-serving sidemen in jazz, played urbane but gutsy trombone and the rhythm section was taut and emphatic. Ball's signing to Pye, engineered by Lonnie Donegan, was the commercial making of the band and Ball was ruthless in pursuing a style of Dixieland that was disciplined enough to attract a popular audience. This and another Lake volume bring together all of his early recordings, and they're an impressive lot.

Back At The Start opens with three obscure tracks made for the Collector label and then proceeds through the early Pyes. It's breezy, outwardly uncomplicated trad. Ball's own playing is what stands out, unfussy but surprisingly risk-taking at points. If his chops later bothered him, there's no sign of it here and he remains a model for those who want to grow up and grow old in the business: taking care of business, for a start, but pacing yourself, keeping it fresh and interesting, never losing touch with the audience. A genuine national treasure, but beyond the sentiment a genuine artist.

ALBERT NICHOLAS
Born 27 May 1900, New Orleans, Louisiana; died 3 September 1973, Basel, Switzerland
Clarinet

The New Orleans–Chicago Connection
Delmark DE 207
Nicholas; Art Hodes (p); Earl Murphy (b); Fred Kohlman (d). July 1959.

Art Hodes said (1981): **'That clarinet sound is like a fingerprint. Isn't anyone else on the planet who ever made a clarinet sound like that. It's like ripping silk.'**

Nicholas is one of the least exposed of the New Orleans clarinet masters on record, and his surviving discs are mostly delightful. For a man who played with King Oliver and Jelly Roll Morton, he seemed quite at ease in the company of musicians generations younger than himself. Art Hodes at least was a contemporary, and their Delmark album is a spirited ramble through some of the old tunes, Hodes's Chicagoan blues meshing easily with Nick's pithy solos. He has an odd way of mixing a circumspect, behind-the-hand manner with a piercing attack: a diffident statement of the melody may suddenly blossom on a sudden high note with a fast vibrato, before the line drops back into the depths of his horn. 'He could always get you with that tone,' Barney Bigard remembered, and something of the young Bechet survives in Nicholas's most sprightly playing. The original Delmark album has been fleshed out with a stack of alternative takes – 'Rose Room', 'Lover, Come Back To Me', 'Digga Digga Do' – none of them especially meaningful, but the body of the music is fine.

HAROLD LAND

Born 18 December 1928, Houston, Texas; died 27 July 2001, Los Angeles, California
Tenor saxophone, flute, oboe

The Fox
Original Jazz Classics OJC 343
Land; Dupree Bolton (t); Elmo Hope (p); Herbie Lewis (b); Frank Butler (d). August 1959.

Harold Land said (1979): **'I think it began to change for me after [*The Fox*]. I had started heeding what Coltrane was doing and I went in that direction. But that record got down what I wanted to say up to that point.'**

Land was raised in San Diego and quickly became a fixture on the West Coast scene of the late '50s and '60s. He worked with Curtis Counce and Max Roach and got round to making some records under his own name. An underrated player, hampered by a rather dour tone which masks the originality of his thinking, he made two records that belong in the top flight, this one and the slightly earlier *Harold In The Land Of Jazz*.

Any apparent resemblance at this point to Sonny Rollins (who'd also worked with Roach) is incidental. Land's delivery was less effusive, not so much spilling out notes and dealing them deftly. One senses that the compositions are always more important than their potential for soloing, and on his own lines, 'The Fox' and 'Little Chris', he seems quite content to stay close to the material. The remainder of the record was written by Hope, and there's a gnarly grace to his five compositions.

Jazz history drew a veil over Dupree Bolton's subsequent career, though he has become a somewhat cultish figure. Here, he plays with confidence and some fire, at ease with the accelerated tempo of 'The Fox' and the easier flow of 'Mirror-Mind Rose'. If Carl Perkins on the previous record recalls a crab, then Elmo Hope has to be a butterfly. His touch was as light as his ideas and colours were fleeting. One of the least dynamic of players (and singularly dependent on drummers of Butler's kidney), he was nevertheless able to keep track with a rhythm-line he wasn't actually playing, laying out astonishing melody figures on 'One Down' in what is probably his best recorded performance.

BENNY GOLSON

Born 25 January 1929, Philadelphia, Pennsylvania
Tenor saxophone

Groovin' With Golson
Original Jazz Classics OJCCD 226
Golson; Curtis Fuller (tb); Ray Bryant (p); Paul Chambers (b); Art Blakey (d). August 1959.

Benny Golson says: **'I remember it so well because Art Farmer and I were putting the Jazztet together just around that time, and Curtis Fuller was to be our trombone-player. I was so into writing material for the coming Jazztet that I had almost no time for the Prestige session. In fact, when Curtis came by my house so that we could go over to Rudy Van Gelder's together, I didn't have the last tune together, so while he sat there I quickly scratched out "The Stroller". We decided at the last minute to record "Yesterdays" because everybody knew this one. We could play this one in our sleep.'**

Golson will always be considered, primarily, as a composer and arranger, producing such standards as 'I Remember Clifford', 'Whisper Not' and 'Stablemates'. His composition book is one of the most enduring of its kind. His powers as a saxophonist have tended to be overshadowed, although his still-growing discography has reasserted the stature of his own playing. Despite contributing several hard-bop staples, his own playing style originally owed rather more to such swing masters as Hawkins, Don Byas and Lucky Thompson; a big, crusty tone and a fierce momentum sustain his solos, and they can take surprising and exciting turns, even if the unpredictability sometimes leads to a loss of focus. Golson went from jazz and R&B combos in the early '50s to arranging for Dizzy Gillespie in 1956. He had a stint in the Jazz Messengers, but then formed the Jazztet with Art Farmer in 1959. In the '60s and '70s, he worked in film and TV, but has returned to jazz since then and is still going strong.

The late-'50s groups already carried the seeds of the celebrated Jazztet. *Groovin' With Golson* hasn't always been the most admired of them but it is a record of extraordinary durability for one that was apparently put together quite casually. Roy Eldridge and Gene Krupa's 'Drum Boogie' is the first obvious throwback of the set, but Golson knows how to work the contours of a good melody and what emerges sounds like naturalized hard bop of a high order. 'Yesterdays' was also thrown in for familiarity, as was 'I Didn't Know What Time It Was', which leaves the sketchy but powerful 'The Stroller' as the only new original of the date. That might seem to put this in the second order of Golson records, but it remains true that the best versions of his compositions are by other hands and that his own records were usually best when he was there to blow, as he does here with focus and enthusiasm.

HORACE SILVER *&*

Born Horace Ward Martin Tavares Silva, 2 September 1928, Norwalk, Connecticut
Piano

Blowin' The Blues Away
Blue Note 95342-2
Silver; Blue Mitchell (t); Junior Cook (ts); Gene Taylor (b); Louis Hayes (d). August 1959.

Horace Silver said (1987): **'Blue Note in the '50s was a pretty special situation, being able to make records where the music was the important thing, not some business transaction. I was lucky in that I had pretty much a free hand. That's a blessing it's hard to imagine today.'**

Horace Silver's records present the quintessence of hard bop. He not only defined the first steps in the style but also wrote several of its most durable staples, ran bands that both embodied and transcended the idiom, and perfected a piano manner which summed up hard bop's wit and trenchancy and popular appeal. It was under Silver's name that the Jazz Messengers marquee was first used, on a 1954 Blue Note album which featured his 'The Preacher', one of the iconic hard-bop compositions.

Picking even a couple of favourites out of Silver's run of Blue Notes is an invidious task.

This one seems more than any other to exemplify all his virtues as pianist, composer and leader. The title-track goes off like a typhoon. The ten-bar ballad 'Peace' is one of his most haunting and most covered themes. 'Sister Sadie' is a soul-jazz classic which other band-leaders were quick to cover. 'The Baghdad Blues' finds him guying various kinds of jazz exoticism. And he ends the record with another version of one of his most durable pieces, 'Melancholy Mood'. It's a typical Blue Note, a characteristic Silver session, but every part of it is powerful enough to transcend what would become clichés of the idiom; and the band all play superbly. Silver's influence is hard to calculate but his immediate descendants include everyone from Chick Corea to Monty Alexander.

& *See also* **Song For My Father** (1964; p. 308)

JIMMY HEATH
Born 25 October 1926, Philadelphia, Pennsylvania
Tenor saxophone

The Thumper
Original Jazz Classics OJCCD 1828
Heath; Nat Adderley (c); Curtis Fuller (tb); Wynton Kelly (p); Paul Chambers (b); Albert 'Tootie' Heath (d).
September 1959.

Jimmy Heath said (1987): **'People have this wrong. At the beginning, I liked being called "Little Bird". I was flattered by it. But you have to start to get your own sound and your own ideas together, so I tried to set it aside. Didn't mean I stopped feeling flattered, or liking it.'**

The Heath brothers were one of jazz's first families. Bassist Percy was a stalwart of the Modern Jazz Quartet and other situations; drummer Albert ('Tootie') has made myriad recordings; the middle brother, Jimmy, has probably the solidest claim on fame but also the most uncertain reputation. Most will have heard one or more of his compositions - 'C.T.A.', 'Gingerbread Boy' - without retaining any clear idea of what Heath himself sounds like. He led big bands and small groups, but concentrated largely on writing and arranging, and became a distinguished teacher.

The records are worth reviving, though. Heath had been out of action for a time in the mid-'50s, dealing with personal problems, but was valued as a composer, and for his debut recording as leader he got together a sympathetic band which in weight and tonality already anticipates the slightly later combo and big-band work in which Heath used French horn (usually Julius Watkins) in an imaginative way. Here it's Curtis Fuller who takes an approximation of that role. The only one of the originals which has survived into the repertoire is the opening 'For Minors Only', arguably Heath's best single composition, but 'The Thumper' itself deserves a revival.

Having set aside alto saxophone - ostensibly to remove the association with Parker, more realistically because the tenor horn better suits his compositional needs - Heath makes an imperiously romantic job of the two standards 'Don't You Know I Care' and 'I Can Make You Love Me', and for anyone without a secure sense of what 'Little Bird' sounded like it'd be as well to start here. There are moments reminiscent of Sonny Stitt, and a melodic drive that anticipates some later Rollins, but, for the most, it's all Jimmy.

SHELLY MANNE
Born 11 June 1920, New York City; died 26 June 1984, Los Angeles, California
Drums

At The Black Hawk
Original Jazz Classics OJC 656–660 5CD (separately available)
Manne; Joe Gordon (t); Richie Kamuca (ts); Victor Feldman (p); Monty Budwig (b). September 1959.

Shelly Manne told this story (many times, but to us in 1979): '**I was on a date with Jimmy Bowen. They were doing "Fever", and I'd done the original with Peggy Lee [actually not; the original was Little Willie John], so I was amused to see that my part read "Play like Shelly Manne". We started and then suddenly the producer came storming out of the booth: "Can't you ****ing read? It says: 'Play it like Shelly Manne'!" "But I am Shelly Manne," I said. He turned on his heel and closed the door behind him. He sells cars now.'**

Shelly combined the classic qualities of reliability and adaptable time with an ability to play melodically, often using soft dynamics. He has something of Krupa's subtlety underneath the power, but Manne was never interested in showmanship, preferring to play for the band. It made him a first-call player and he worked with everyone from Coleman Hawkins and Charlie Parker to Ornette Coleman.

Manne made many fine sessions of his own for Contemporary, including a number of themed projects like covers of *My Fair Lady* songs and *Peter Gunn*. He also put out material recorded at his own club, the Manne-Hole, but the very best representation of him on record is the sequence of discs recorded at the Black Hawk, the dive where one of Miles Davis's most revealing live sequences was recorded during a later residency in 1961.

Manne and His Men's Black Hawk discs are among the best mainstream live dates ever released. There is almost no fat on any of them, other than the rote repetition of the band theme, 'A Gem From Tiffany'. The vinyl LPs had some murky spots, but with Feldman's piano sound lightened, Gordon and Kamuca trimmed of rough edges, and Budwig rescued from the gloom, it's near perfect. From the opening 'Our Delight' to the previously unissued material on *Volume 5*, and taking in a definitive 'Whisper Not' (plus alternate) along the way, this is club jazz at its very best. Two grand versions of Golson's 'Step Lightly' and a long read of Charlie Mariano's 'Vamp's Blues' dominate *Volume 2*; the epic Golson performances on *Volume 3* are somewhat diluted by a dull 'Black Hawk Blues' which is redeemed by a couple of good solos; and it doesn't flag from there to the end.

ORNETTE COLEMAN &
Born Randolph Denard Ornette Coleman, 9 March 1930, Fort Worth, Texas
Alto saxophone, tenor saxophone, trumpet, violin

The Shape Of Jazz To Come
Atlantic 8122 72398-2
Coleman; Don Cherry (pkt-t); Charlie Haden (b); Billy Higgins (d). October 1959, July 1960.

Pianist Paul Bley said (1992): '**Ornette changed everything completely by overturning the idea that there had to be one metre running through a piece, and replacing it with a multi-timed concept. The work he brought to us then [1958] was unbelievably rich and deep.'**

No jazz musician has so comprehensively and irremediably divided opinion. To some (early supporters included Gunther Schuller) he is a visionary genius who has changed the shape of modern music; to others – though one must say a diminishing and somewhat chastened number – he is a fraud, innocent or otherwise, whose grasp of musical theory is either shaky or so solipsistic as to be meaningless. Long before anyone had heard of 'harmolodics' it was thought that Coleman represented the third spur of the modernist revolution, a shift in approach to melody and rhythm to match Coltrane's skyscraping harmonics and Cecil Taylor's atonality.

It's almost impossible to reconstruct the impact – positive and negative – Ornette's Atlantic albums had when they first appeared. They are classic performances and scarcely bettered since. They are also something of a piece, with some of the material released out of chronological sequence, which makes discussion of 'development' or 'progress' redundant. CD transfer has brought forward the other members of the group, underlining Cherry's role and bringing Haden out of the shadows. Brash as the titles are, the music is surprisingly introspective and thoughtful. Most of the essential Coleman pieces are to be found here, though interestingly only one of them – 'Lonely Woman' – has ever come close to repertory status.

Something Else! was made shortly before Coleman's appearances with Paul Bley at the Hillcrest Club in Los Angeles and *Tomorrow Is The Question*. These are essential records, too, but *The Shape Of Jazz To Come* was released first and stands out for the sheer confidence of musical conception and group execution. From the very first phrases of 'Lonely Woman', it is clear that this is an epoch in modern jazz and that something new and essential has arrived. The set also includes 'Congeniality', 'Peace' and 'Focus On Sanity', three of his most important early compositions. The blues are not far away, but Coleman seems to have dispensed with conventional harmonic organization in favour of a highly melodic approach that allows the group to improvise intuitively round the elements of the line rather than according to the changes.

The combination of his eldritch saxophone sound – he was shown on the cover cradling an acrylic instrument, which is partly responsible for his bleached, small but dynamically supple delivery – Cherry's tinny, raw trumpet-playing and Haden's awesomely capacious bass shapes is electrifying, and Higgins's drumming suggests not so much polyrhythms in the Elvin Jones sense as a new conception of time as asynchronous and malleable.

To suggest that Coleman never surpassed these performances is unfair without some recognition of the lack of sympathetic understanding from the recording industry in future. The Atlantic years, brought together in a rich box called *Beauty Is A Rare Thing*, still seem like his peak.

& See also **At The Golden Circle, Stockholm** (1965; p. 324), **The Complete Science Fiction Sessions** (1971, 1972; p. 387), **Colors** (1996; p. 605)

JON HENDRICKS *&*
Born 16 September 1921, Newark, Ohio
Voice

A Good Git-Together
EMI 69812
Hendricks; Nat Adderley (c); Cannonball Adderley (as); Pony Poindexter (as, v); Gildo Mahones (p); Buddy Montgomery (vb); Wes Montgomery (g); Ike Isaacs, Monk Montgomery (b); Walter Bolden (d); Bill Perkins (perc). 1959.

Jon Hendricks said (1982): **'I sat in with Bird one night in Toledo. I had listened to every one of his records and I'd listened to everyone in the band. As I was going off stage, I felt him grab my coat-tail and he pulled me to a chair. Afterwards, he asked what I wanted to do. I said: a lawyer. "You ain't a lawyer. You're a jazz singer. Come to New York." I said I didn't know anyone there. "You know me."'**

Hendricks is still best known for his work with the stylish vocalese trio Lambert, Hendricks & Ross, but in all fairness he is a more accomplished artist than either of his collaborators and has retained a calm professionalism throughout his long career. He was spotted first by Charlie Parker, who advised him to stick to music. After the trio's demise he spent some time in England and working as a music critic, but continued to record.

His first album as a leader only resurfaced in 2006, reintroducing Hendricks to a generation who assumed the name belonged to Jimi. In every piece, it reflects his background as the son of an African Methodist Episcopal pastor. Right from the opening 'I'm Gonna Shout (Everything Started In The House Of The Lord)', which also closes the record, it's a set full of affirmative energy and joy. A few of the songs were co-written – with Mahones, Gigi Gryce, Randy Weston – and a couple were apparently written for Louis Jordan, whom Hendricks occasionally and remotely resembles. The backings are all good and some will be attracted to the record first for glimpses of the Adderleys and Montgomerys, but it's Jon's date and 'Minor Catastrophe', 'Social Call' and the exuberant title-track are all vintage vocal jazz.

& See also **LAMBERT, HENDRICKS & ROSS, Sing A Song Of Basie** (1955; p. 166)

CHARLES MINGUS *&*

Born 22 April 1922, Nogales, Arizona; died 5 January 1979, Cuernavaca, Mexico
Double bass, piano

Mingus Dynasty
Columbia CK 65513

Mingus; Don Ellis, Richard Williams (t); Jimmy Knepper (tb); Jerome Richardson (f, bs); John Handy (as); Booker Ervin, Benny Golson (ts); Teddy Charles (vib); Sir Roland Hanna, Nico Bunink (p); Maurice Brown, Seymour Barab (clo); Dannie Richmond (d); Honey Gordon (v). November 1959.

Sue Mingus, the composer's widow, says: '*Ah Um* is a sister record to *Mingus Dynasty*, both recorded during that banner year of jazz, 1959. There are probably more "hits" – tunes that have become familiar to a jazz audience – on *Ah Um* and there is no reason why *Dynasty* should play second fiddle, as the record company seems to have decreed. Another Mingus album, *Blues & Roots*, was released that same year on Atlantic Records and, interestingly, the tune "Jelly Roll" appears on both *Ah Um* and *Blues & Roots*, which was recorded first, except that it is "upside down" on the Columbia album, beginning from the bottom up, instead of the other way around.'

A classic period. This was the point where, rising 40 and aware of the encroachment of younger and perhaps more accommodating musicians, Mingus began to show his absolute understanding of the African-American musical tradition. *Ah Um* is an extended tribute to ancestors, cemented by the gospellish 'Better Git It In Your Soul', a mood that is also present on the slightly earlier *Blues & Roots* with the well-loved 'Wednesday Night Prayer Meeting' in its doubled-up 6/4 time. All the Mingusian components are to the fore in this period: the shouts and yells, the magnificently harmonized ostinati which fuel 'Tensions' and the almost jolly swing of 'My Jelly Roll Soul' (*Blues & Roots*), the often obvious edits and obsessive recycling of his own previous output all contribute to records which are entire unto themselves and hard to fault on any count.

Dynasty is sometimes described as if it were one of the first posthumous releases. One sees why, though the title is a pretty obvious pun. It wraps up a period of activity that seems to catch Mingus in mid-mood swing between fired up and confident and way down low. 'Strollin'' is a version of 'Nostalgia In Times Square' and the music written for the (mostly improvised) John Cassavetes film *Shadows*, in which jazz almost takes the place of orderly narrative dialogue. There is also a version of 'Gunslinging Bird', a take each of 'Song With Orange', 'Far Wells, Mill Valley', 'Slop' and, memorably, 'Mood Indigo'. As with so many other Mingus albums, this is somehow better and more coherent than it ought to be.

Though not intended to be put together in this form, it works as an entity, and one wouldn't want the original sessions to be reconstructed in any other way. As Sue Mingus has said, *Ah Um* is the canonical record out of sheer happenstance. This one takes the story on a step further and with even greater confidence and creative courage.

& *See also* **The Complete Debut Recordings** (1951–1957; p. 131), **Pithecanthropus Erectus** (1956; p. 175), **Charles Mingus Presents Charles Mingus** (1960; p. 259), **The Black Saint And The Sinner Lady** (1963; p. 291)

JOHN COLTRANE &

Born 23 September 1926, Hamlet, North Carolina; died 17 July 1967, Huntington, New York
Tenor, soprano and alto saxophones, flute

Giant Steps
Atlantic 781337
Coltrane; Tommy Flanagan, Wynton Kelly, Cedar Walton (p); Paul Chambers (b); Jimmy Cobb, Lex Humphries, Art Taylor (d). March, May & December 1959.

Pianist Tommy Flanagan said (1996): **'People chided me, and the others, for making mistakes, but Coltrane was making them too. Writers sometimes like to make all that music sound like some big spiritual journey and musicians like to say it was just a job, just a gig, and just about getting the charts down. I think I realized later that the two things were the same, that for Coltrane getting the music exactly right and making those mistakes was the spiritual journey.'**

Just ten years separate John Coltrane's first records as leader and the sombre curtain-call of *Expression*, made weeks before his death in 1967. The work he made in that period and the personal influence he exerted are still being felt in jazz today, perhaps to a degree that has stifled other, even more radical approaches to the music. One might argue that Coltrane was not a radical at all, merely a musician who pushed the existing logic of jazz harmony to its utmost, and then beyond that. By the end of his life, what had begun as subtly detoured standards performances – 'My Favorite Things' most famously – had turned into hour-long improvisations of implacably alien aspect. The political and wider cultural implications of Coltrane's subversion of American popular song haven't yet been fully worked out at a conscious level but their impact runs through the counter-culture.

Had Coltrane recorded no more than his Prestige records, his solitary Blue Note recording *Blue Train* and his appearances with Miles Davis and others, he would probably be regarded as a substantial soloist of considerable promise, but no more. It was when he began recording for Atlantic, and with what evolved into the 'classic' quartet, that he started to create a more individual and stylistically adventurous body of work.

The first album is the product of time and preparation, and it cements its status as Trane's first genuinely iconic record, with no fewer than seven original compositions, most of them now squarely established in the repertory. The big stylistic shift is the move away from chordal jazz, and a seemingly obsessive need to cross-hatch every feasible subdivision before moving on to the next in the sequence. In its place, a faster-moving, scalar approach that was to achieve its (in the event) brief apotheosis in the title-track. That this was a technically exacting theme is underlined by the false starts and alternative takes included on the expensive and atrociously titled *The Heavyweight Champion* Rhino box set, but there is a chance to sample an earlier version of the tune on this CD reissue, performed with another group a month and a half before the issued recording (which featured Flanagan, Chambers and Taylor). Cedar Walton just about goes through the motions at the 26 March session. He finds the beautiful ballad 'Naima' a more approachable proposition, though this time the released version was actually from a later session still, with Wynton Kelly and Jimmy Cobb.

It remains one of Trane's best-loved themes, a million miles away from the pitiless drive of many of his solos. Dedicated to the bassist, 'Mr P.C.' is a delightful original blues which has become part of most contemporary horn-players' repertoire. 'Syeeda's Song Flute' is a long, spun-out melody for Trane's daughter. The remaining tracks are 'Spiral', 'Countdown' and the funky, homely 'Cousin Mary'. *Giant Steps* was released on the cusp of a new decade, in January 1960. It threw down a quiet, unaggressive challenge. Once again, it is difficult to see it as anything other than a transitional record. Flanagan doesn't sound much more confident with the new idiom than Walton had been on the dry run, though he is a more intuitively lyrical player. The 'deluxe edition' includes alternates of most of the tunes; these variants have been available before, of course, but they still help to build a picture of what was going on during this remarkable session. Having them isolated in the context of the issued album is of some merit, though perhaps only newcomers to the Coltrane diaspora will be unaware of the extraordinary enterprise that had such seasoned and intelligent players wrestling with a new conception in jazz.

& *See also* **A Love Supreme** (1964; p. 314), **Ascension** (1965; p. 321)

NAT ADDERLEY
Born 25 November 1931, Tampa, Florida; died 2 January 2000, Lakeland, Florida
Cornet

Work Song
Original Jazz Classics OJC 363
Adderley; Bobby Timmons (p); Wes Montgomery (g); Keter Betts, Sam Jones (b); Louis Hayes, Percy Heath (d). January 1960.

Nat Adderley said (1985): **'Pop got Cannonball a little Sears Roebuck trumpet but Cannonball's teeth weren't right for it, and though he could *fiddle*, he didn't have much of a range on it so he put it aside and got himself an alto without pop knowing and started teaching me to play trumpet so at least one of us was playing Pop's instrument. He was a cornet-player. I guess that's where that comes from because almost everyone else was changing to trumpet back then.'**

The Adderley brothers helped keep a light burning for jazz when rock'n'roll was dominating the industry 'demographics'. Neither was ever particularly revolutionary or adventurous in style, but saxophonist Cannonball's enormous personality and untimely death, together with his participation in such legendary dates as Miles's *Kind Of Blue*, have sanctified his memory with young fans who would have found his live performances rather predictable. Younger brother Nat was often the more incisive soloist, with a bright, ringing tone that most obviously drew on the example of Dizzy Gillespie but in which could be heard a whole range of influences from Clark Terry to Henry 'Red' Allen to the pre-post-modern Miles of the '50s.

Nat came to the cornet almost by default when a school trumpet was lost or stolen and he discovered that in band music it's the cornet that gets the lead-lines. The rest, as they say, is history. By the late '50s, he was playing at his peak, with a tight, strong sound. *Work Song* is the classic, laced with a funky blues feel but marked by some unexpectedly lyrical playing (on 'Violets For Your Furs' and 'My Heart Stood Still') from the leader. Cannonball's 'Sack O' Woe' was also to become a classic, but the title-tune became something of a signature for Nat, and this version now sounds like the rhizome from which later, perhaps more inflected versions sprang. Montgomery manages to produce something more enterprising than his trademark octave-runs and hits a tense, almost threatening groove. Timmons is more predictable, but just right for this sort of set.

Unlike Cannonball, Nat enjoyed a renaissance when jazz came back into wider currency after the rock/fusion years. He'd never quite gone away and approached his final decades with the same warm enthusiasm that had suffused his work from the start.

WES MONTGOMERY

Born John Leslie Montgomery, 6 March 1925, Indianapolis, Indiana; died 15 June 1968, Indianapolis, Indiana
Guitar, bass guitar

Incredible Jazz Guitar
Original Jazz Classics OJCCD 036
Montgomery; Tommy Flanagan (p); Percy Heath (b); Albert 'Tootie' Heath (d). January 1960.

Kenny Burrell remembered (1988): **'He'd drive over to Indianapolis sometimes, to hang out and hear me play. Then he got the chance to record for Riverside, but Wes was afraid to fly and he wouldn't put his guitar on a plane, so when he came to make the record he borrowed my guitar and amplifier. He was a sweet guy, died far too young.'**

Wes had been making records for Pacific in California with brothers Monk (on vibes and piano) and Buddy (on bass) when the call came from Riverside. In fact, just four days before going into Reeves Sound in New York for the organ trio sessions with Melvin Rhyne and drummer Paul Parker, he'd recorded 'Summertime' in LA for Pacific, the flipside of the 'Finger Pickin'' single. The early Riverside material is available on an OJC called *A Dynamic New Sound*, originally *'Round Midnight* and *Trio*.

He was 24 rather than a precocious kid. In career terms, Montgomery really did seem to prefer his back porch. During the '50s, which should have been his big decade, he hung around his native Indianapolis, playing part-time. When his recording career got going again, he was still capable of great things and the huge Riverside box that documents the first New York period is packed with calm invention.

He'd been working with Nat Adderley (including the classic *Work Song*) when the *Incredible Jazz Guitar* sessions were done. It remains, perhaps, his best session and his last in New York for a year. His solo on 'West Coast Blues' is very nearly incredible, and the band subtly acknowledges it. There are already hints of banality even here, in the trademark octave runs, borrowed from Django. Flanagan may have slipped the engineer a sawbuck, for he's caught beautifully, nicely forward in the mix. His lines on Sonny Rollins's buoyant 'Airegin' are exactly complementary to the guitarist's. There's a 'D-Natural Blues' and covers of 'In Your Own Sweet Way' and 'Polka Dots And Moonbeams' which further hint at Montgomery's eventual artistic inertia, but for the moment he sounds like a master.

Nothing that followed was ever quite as good. Verve tried to balance him between a jazz and a pop audience. Only Wes could have pulled that trick off with such grace, but even then, with all the polish Norman Granz gave him, one longs for the quiet artistry of these Riverside dates.

ART FARMER &

Born 21 August 1928, Council Bluffs, Iowa; died 4 October 1999, New York City
Trumpet, flugelhorn

Meet The Jazztet
Universal 5053
Farmer; Curtis Fuller (tb); Benny Golson (ts); McCoy Tyner (p); Addison Farmer (b); Lex Humphries (d). February 1960.

Art Farmer said: **'I don't think I knew how good the Jazztet was until we got back together a few years later. The music was the same. We were pretty much the same, just a bit more experienced, but I remember thinking: "Hey, this is something special."'**

Farmer was raised in Phoenix, Arizona, and settled in LA in the late '40s, but didn't make the inevitable move to New York until the mid-'50s. Once east, he associated with Gigi Gryce, Horace Silver and Gerry Mulligan (where he effectively stood in for Chet Baker), recording a number of fine sets under his own name before the formation of the famous Jazztet. One of the great bands of hard bop, its eminence has as much to do with co-founder Benny Golson's writing as with Art's cool mastery as main soloist.

There was a knot of fine records around this period, *Portrait Of Art* and *Modern Art* in 1958, the latter with Golson and Bill Evans, and, concurrently with the Jazztet, relatively ambitious projects like *Brass Shout* and *Aztec Suite*. Though the group got back together again some years later, Farmer – or the market – seemed to favour small combos over the next half-decade; *Sing Me Softly Of The Blues* in 1965 with Steve Kuhn, Steve Swallow and Pete LaRoca was the next high-point, though it's hard to find a truly indifferent Farmer record of this vintage.

The first Jazztet record was McCoy Tyner's recording debut, and the young pianist makes an immediate impact, harmonically full, able in his few prominent solos, and solidly across Golson's charts. 'Killer Joe' put in a first appearance, along with a near definitive reading of 'I Remember Clifford'. The other well-known Golson chart is 'Blues March', but it's a more raggedy line here than elsewhere. Farmer's only composition is 'Mox Nix', but its virtues are those of his playing, ostensibly soft-edged but with a ripple of muscle just under the surface. The peerless ballad improviser of later years still isn't in evidence. He plays fast and strong, still on trumpet, and packs a lot of notes into a phrase. Yet each one has an absolutely distinct cast, and a weight of its own. One never feels that Farmer thinks too far ahead. He is as 'in the moment' as any free improviser, but with the song tracking almost subconsciously as he plays. With twin brother Addison (who died just three years later) in the line-up, there's an audibly solid axis to the group, more evident in modern sound than before, but it's Art's date as far as solos are concerned. His statement on the elegy for Brownie is exquisitely shaped. A great record, but the others of the period ought to be sampled, too.

& See also **Blame It On My Youth** (1988; p. 516)

HANK MOBLEY
Born 7 July 1930, Eastman, Georgia; died 30 May 1986, Philadelphia, Pennsylvania
Tenor saxophone

Soul Station
Blue Note 95343-2
Mobley; Wynton Kelly (p); Paul Chambers (b); Art Blakey (d). February 1960.

Saxophonist Jim Weir says: **'I never understood why Mobley was thought to be a strange or inappropriate choice for the Miles Davis group. They're so alike in so many ways: no wasted notes, no hectoring of the listener but a subtle persuasion, and above all that little regretful murmur or sigh at the end of a phrase.'**

It's not clear how much Leonard Feather knew about boxing but when he dubbed Hank Mobley the 'middleweight champion' of tenor saxophone, he surely knew that the only thing that separates a middleweight from a heavyweight is avoirdupois. Mobley was pre-eminent in his division and to imply that it was in any way inferior or less taxing is a disservice.

Hank was playing in R&B bands before joining Max Roach in 1951. He came to prominence in the Jazz Messengers three years later and then worked on numerous Blue Note record dates, many of which he led. He spent a short time with Miles Davis and then toured in other hard-bop situations, but eventually left music in the late '70s because of ill-health. There was a brief attempt at a comeback in 1986 but he died of pneumonia shortly after.

Mobley's music was documented to almost unreasonable lengths by Blue Note, with a whole array of albums granted to him as a leader, and countless sideman appearances to go with them; a collectors' favourite. His assertive and swinging delivery was undercut by a seemingly reticent tone and lightness of touch: next to his peers in the hard-bop tenor gang, he could sound almost pallid and rarely delivered a killer punch in solos But it shouldn't detract from appreciating a thinker and a solidly reliable player, who despite frequent personal problems rarely gave less than his best in front of the microphones and created some of the best music of the hard-bop period.

There is an approximate consensus that *Soul Station* is his best work. Good as the other drummers on his records are, Blakey brings a degree more finesse, and their interplay on 'This I Dig Of You' is superb. Hank seldom took ballads at a crawl, preferring a kind of lazy mid-tempo, and 'If I Should Lose You' is one of his best. 'Dig Dis' is a top example of how tough he could sound without falling into bluster; here, and on the title-track, another original, one can follow closely how much he took from the masters of the swing generation, almost as if he prefers not to phrase like a bopper at all, even as he inhabits that idiom. It's a terrific record, and a virtually perfect example of a routine date made immortal by master craftsmen.

FREDDIE REDD
Born 29 May 1928, New York City
Piano

The Music From *The Connection*
Blue Note 63836
Redd; Jackie McLean (as); Michael Mattos (b); Larry Ritchie (d). February 1960.

Novelist Norman Mailer said (1995): **'*The Connection* wasn't perfumed, drawing-room theatre. It had piss and dirt and balls, and the music was what made it immediate, an existential unfolding of desperate lives, lived in some remnant of hope.'**

Easily dismissed as a mere honest journeyman, Redd had an extraordinary gift for melody and it is strange that so little of his work survives in the melody. Who nowadays calls for 'Olé' or 'Just A Ballad For My Baby' on the stand? He made some highly effective records in the later '50s, including *San Francisco Suite*. Redd's amiable West Coast bop soundtracked an unscripted (but you've seen it) Bay Area movie: bustling streetcars, pretty girls flashing their legs, sudden fogs and alarms, an apology for a narrative. His most famous music, though, was for a real stage play, and was conceived as part of the onstage action. Jack Gelber's gritty drugs drama was one of the great successes at the Living Theater, and music and play have sustained one another intermittently down the years. Arguably, Redd's best record was *Shades Of Redd*, made right after this in the summer of 1960, but the *Connection* music isn't just a set of incidental cues; instead it's a rigorously conceived suite of tunes that mark the steps to a familiar dance of death. When 'O.D.' comes along, it strikes with tragic inevitability, but the opening 'Who Killed Cock Robin?' has a strutting *faux*-confidence and '(Theme for) Sister Salvation' is worthy of Horace Silver. For all sorts of reasons, good and bad, Jackie McLean was the only possible casting for the alto part and his bop wail carries much of the music. Redd lived on, but is only discussed by bop stalwarts. Amid so much generic hard-bop writing of the period, his work merits fuller attention.

JOHN LEWIS &

Born 3 May 1920, LaGrange, Illinois; died 29 March 2001, New York City
Piano

Golden Striker / Jazz Abstractions

Collectables 6252

Lewis; Melvyn Broiles, Bernie Glow, Alan Kiger, Joe Wilder (t); Dick Hixson, David Baker (tb); Gunther Schuller, Albert Richman, Ray Alonge, John Barrows (frhn); Eric Dolphy (as, bcl, f); Ornette Coleman (as); Bill Evans (p); Eddie Costa (vib); Joe Hall (g); Harvey Phillips, Jay McAllister (tba); George Duvivier, Scott LaFaro, Alvin Brehm (b); Sticks Evans, Connie Kay (d); Contemporary String Quartet. February–December 1960.

John Lewis said (1982): 'The exciting thing about jazz for me is the way a young music has evolved its own language in contact with so many other forms, styles and traditions, and in turn has given something of itself to them.'

Though much of his energy was poured into the Modern Jazz Quartet over its long and distinguished history, Lewis also worked extensively under his own name. He is one of the music's finest composers, and his 'Django' is one of the few instantly recognizable jazz compositions (as opposed to standards) that pops up regularly on the stand. As is well known, the MJQ evolved out of the Dizzy Gillespie band. Lewis was also around for the *Birth Of The Cool* dates, arranging a couple of pieces for those iconic sessions. He co-led an album with Bill Perkins in 1956 after the creation of the MJQ (which was originally under vibist Milt Jackson's leadership).

Lewis was fascinated by baroque music, by the *commedia dell'arte* and by modern innovations in musical language. All of these interests surfaced regularly in his work and this, coupled with his involvement in the Third Stream, persuaded some negative observers to dismiss him as a stiff, conservatory player, when in fact Lewis is one of the most melodic and rhythmic of pianists, always riding a steady, self-sustaining groove and always sticking close to blues harmony no matter what the context.

In one of Collectables' more logical juxtapositions – they can sometimes be breathtakingly perverse – two of Lewis's most interesting records are brought together. *Golden Striker* indulges his baroque leanings with a set of tunes arranged for piano and a large brass ensemble: the tone-colours are delightful, and 'Piazza Navona' and the reworked 'Odds Against Tomorrow' are gravely beautiful. It's not a much admired set, often dismissed because a good deal of the music is through-composed and therefore 'not jazz'. It's certainly a thoughtful set and a resolutely undramatic one. But the point of the Collectables disc is the reissued *Jazz Abstractions*. Lewis doesn't play on this set (he is credited as 'presenter') but it does offer Third Stream scores by Jim Hall and Gunther Schuller. Ornette Coleman is set to wail over the four minutes of 'Abstraction' for strings, and there are variations on Lewis's 'Django' and Monk's 'Criss Cross', as well as Hall's 'Piece For Guitar And Strings'. In the past the music was criticized as pretentious fusion, but any chance to hear Coleman, Dolphy and Scott LaFaro playing on the same sessions is precious. To hear Lewis the pianist, one ought to turn to the Modern Jazz Quartet and to his later work, as reviewed elsewhere here, but this was important and controversial music in its day: catalytic, pointlessly maligned as cerebral, undeniably a crucible of future talent.

& *See also* **Evolution** (1999; p. 638); **MODERN JAZZ QUARTET, Dedicated to Connie** (1960; p. 254), **The Complete Last Concert** (1974; p. 417)

MODERN JAZZ QUARTET*&*
Formed 1954
Group

Dedicated To Connie
Atlantic 82763 2CD
John Lewis (p); Milt Jackson (vib); Percy Heath (b); Connie Kay (d). May 1960.

Percy Heath said (1990): **'We'd play quiet, then we'd play really quiet, and maybe then someone in the club would realize they were being noisier than we were, and they'd shut up.'**

The MJQ – as it's universally known – was originally the rhythm section of Dizzy Gillespie's postwar band, initially with Ray Brown on bass and Kenny Clarke on drums. After 1955, Connie Kay became a permanent member, joining pianist John Lewis, vibraphonist Milt Jackson and bassist Percy Heath in one of the most enduring jazz groups of all time.

Atlantic did some strange things with the MJQ, the most egregious being the sex-doll cover for *Plastic Dreams*, but they also pushed the group strongly and brought in guest artists like Sonny Rollins to stiffen the sound and broaden the appeal on occasion. The Erteguns were market-shrewd and knew good music when they heard it and the albums kept coming.

Lewis's first exploration of characters from the *commedia dell'arte* was *Fontessa*, an appropriately chill and stately record that can seem a little enigmatic, even off-putting. The themes of *commedia* are remarkably appropriate to a group who have always presented themselves in sharply etched silhouette, playing a music that is deceptively smooth and untroubled but which harbours considerable jazz feeling.

Connie Kay had slipped into the band without a ripple; his ill-health and death were the only circumstances in the next 40 years of activity necessitating a personnel change. His cooler approach, less overwhelming than Clarke's could be, was ideal, and he sounds right from the word 'go'. His debut was on the fine *Concorde*, which sees Lewis trying to blend jazz improvisation with European counterpoint. It combines some superb fugal writing with a bright swing.

After Kay's death in December 1994, the MJQ issued a 1960 concert from Yugoslavia in his memory. As John Lewis discovered when he auditioned these old tapes, it was one of the truly great MJQ performances. Jackson's playing is almost transcendentally wonderful on 'Bags' Groove' and 'I Remember Clifford', and the conception of Lewis's opening *commedia* sequence could hardly be clearer or more satisfying. *Dedicated To Connie* is a very special record and has always been our favourite of the bunch.

& See also **The Complete Last Concert** (1974; p. 417); **JOHN LEWIS, Golden Striker / Jazz Abstractions** (1960; p. 253), **Evolution** (1999; p. 638)

JIMMY HAMILTON
Born 25 May 1917, Dillon, South Carolina; died 20 September 1994, St Croix, Virgin Islands
Clarinet

Swing Low Sweet Clarinet
Fresh Sound FSRCD 351
Hamilton; John Anderson (t); Britt Woodman, Dave Wells, Booty Wood (bhn); Paul Gonsalves (ts); Jimmy Rowles (p); Aaron Bell (b); Sam Woodyard (d). 1960.

Jimmy Hamilton said (1981): **'Being one of Duke's men was a privilege, like being in a very chi-chi club, but I think we also saw ourselves as knights of the realm, riding out to each other's defence or help. You could always get guys together for a date, no matter what.'**

The best of Jimmy Hamilton is with Ellington, of course, whom he joined in 1943, after some time around Philadelphia and with Teddy Wilson, but his own occasional sessions are always worth listening to and belong in the front rank of small-group Ellingtonia. *Can't Help Swinging* – a pair of dates for Prestige originally issued as *It's About Time* and *Can't Help Swinging* – are gently appealing, but even more so in some regards is *Swing Low Sweet Clarinet*. The players are nearly all Ellingtonians, and the interesting twist is that Woodman, Wood and incomer Wells are playing baritone horns instead of their familiar trombones (and not baritone saxophones as noted in some sources). It's a rich and capacious sound, which Hamilton exploits to the full on a set that's pretty well stocked with Duke's compositions: 'In A Sentimental Mood', 'Do Nothing Till You Hear From Me' and 'The Nearness Of You'. Jimmy contributes two ideas of his own, 'Tempo De Brazilia' and the fun 'Taj Mahal'. Gonsalves is in fine voice, though slightly restrained on a couple of his spots as if trying not to shade the leader.

FRANK WESS
Born 4 January 1922, Kansas City, Missouri
Flute, tenor saxophone

The Frank Wess Quartet
Original Jazz Classics OJCCD 11032
Wess; Tommy Flanagan (p); Eddie Jones (b); Bobby Donaldson (d). May 1960.

Frank Wess said (1990): **'My teachers at the Modern School of Music in Washington DC, pretty much laughed when I said I wanted to develop the flute in jazz. They just didn't understand it. Me, I don't understand the clarinet. I don't see the satisfactions of playing that in a jazz context.'**

One of the later stalwarts (with Frank Foster) of the Basie band, Wess is also an impressive solo star, with a tenor approach that comes from Lester Young, though with intimations of Don Byas as well. Wess's real importance, though, is in making the flute a valid solo voice. Neal Hefti found a role for flutes in the postwar Basie band, changing the character of its woodwind section entirely. He plays with a strong correct tone and is a nimble improviser. In his hands the flute is a thing of beauty, subtle and tender but without fake atmospherics. The first cut on this CD – formerly Moodsville, which suggests how it was expected to land in the market – is Alec Wilder's 'It's So Peaceful In The Country', a delightful rarity that provides the leader with a cool, sophisticated vehicle. Later, he tackles 'Stella By Starlight' (a switch to tenor), 'But Beautiful', 'Gone With The Wind', 'Star Eyes' and his own 'Rainy Afternoon'. Flanagan is at his most melodious and responsive and the bassist and drummer fit the bill perfectly.

Wess had been playing flute for some time when the record was made. His tone is already mature and steady and it influenced a growing number of players coming through, from Herbie Mann to Eric Dolphy, Hubert Laws and even Bobbi Humphrey. Though by no means a stylistic innovator, he deserves his place in the scheme of things.

ANDRÉ PREVIN
Born Andreas Ludwig Priwin, 6 April 1929, Berlin, Germany
Piano

Plays Songs By Harold Arlen
Original Jazz Classics OJCCD 1840
Previn (p solo). May 1960.

André Previn said (1982): **'One thing I notice about American jazz audiences, as opposed to Europe, is that they're inclined to seem a little defensive about liking jazz, as if it's a gesture towards something rather than a way of having fun.'**

A transplanted Berliner, Previn is still better known as a conductor than as a performer. Jazz remains his first love, though. His main contribution to jazz comes in a concentrated period of activity for Contemporary, and what a gift he must have been for the label, turning up immaculately rehearsed, straight, clean, unimpeachably professional, with a series of songbook projects (Duke, Arlen, *Pal Joey*, *Gigi*, *West Side Story*) and then laying down first-take performances one after the other. One suspects there never will be a box of André Previn out-takes and alternatives, and yet there's nothing unswinging or unspontaneous about any of these performances.

AL COHN
Born 24 November 1925, New York City; died 15 November 1988, Stroudberg, Pennsylvania
Tenor saxophone

You 'n' Me
Verve 589318-2
Cohn; Zoot Sims (ts, cl); Mose Allison (p); Major Holley (b) Osie Johnson (d). June 1960.

Al Cohn said (1980): **'We're like and unlike as people, I guess. We think the same way about a lot of things, but we play quite differently. Zoot's easy-going. I'm a bit more serious, but I enjoy working out musical problems in a way he doesn't. So we enjoy it from different perspectives.'**

The consummate jazz professional. Cohn's arrangements were four-square and unpretentious and his saxophone-playing a model of order and accuracy. One of the Four Brothers, the legendary Woody Herman saxophone section. Later, his soloing took on a philosophical authority, unexciting but deeply satisfying.

Virtually all one needs to know about Al and Zoot's long-standing association can be found on the sober-sounding 'Improvisation For Two Unaccompanied Saxophones' on *You 'n' Me*. All the virtues (elegant interplay, silk-smooth textures) and all the vices (inconsequentiality and Sims's tendency to follow his favourite patterns) are firmly in place. A and Z were apt to cover the whole expressive gamut from A to B, as Dorothy Parker once said about Miss Hepburn. The rest of this set is their all-but-patented, cheerfully swinging one-two, bodacious unisons followed by a thumping good solo out of each horn, and maybe a little cameo from Allison too. It may not dig all that deep, but you might wonder why more jazz records don't have this feel-good factor. The remastered sound has a rather fierce edge that doesn't seem quite appropriate for this music.

FREDDIE HUBBARD
Born 7 April 1938, Indianapolis, Indiana; died 29 December 2008, Los Angeles, California
Trumpet, flugelhorn

Open Sesame
Blue Note 95341-2
Hubbard; Tina Brooks (ts); McCoy Tyner (p); Sam Jones (b); Clifford Jarvis (d). June 1960.

Freddie Hubbard said (1983): **'I came to New York from Indianapolis, this little quiet car-racing town where no one went anywhere. I saw shootings, stabbings. For the first couple of months, I hardly went out. After that, I was hardly ever home.'**

Hubbard was one of the liveliest of the young hard-bop lions of the late '50s and early '60s. As a Jazz Messenger, and with his own early albums for Blue Note, he set down so many great solos that trumpeters have made studies of him to this day, the burnished tone, bravura phrasing and rhythmical subtleties still enduringly modern. He never quite had the quickfire genius of Lee Morgan, but he had a greater all-round strength, and he is an essential player in the theatre of hard bop. He first worked, back home in Indianapolis, with the Montgomery brothers and arrived in New York in 1959. He joined the Jazz Messengers in 1961 and was involved in important recordings with Ornette Coleman and Oliver Nelson, as well as leading his own dates. Uncertain of his direction in the '70s, and unable to play at all in the later '90s because of lip trouble.

His several Blue Note dates seem to come and go in the catalogue. *Open Sesame* and *Goin' Up* were his first two records for the label and their youthful ebullience is still exhilarating, the trumpeter throwing off dazzling phrases almost for the sheer fun of it. The brio of the debut is paired with the sense that this was the important coming-out of a major talent, and Hubbard's solo on the title-track is a remarkable piece of brinkmanship: in the bonus alternative take, he's a shade cooler, but that more tempered effort is less exciting, too. 'All Or Nothing At All' is taken at a pace that suggests the Indianapolis 500; power, but you feel he could play like this all night. This was an early appearance for Tyner, and a valuable glimpse of Tina Brooks, who contributes two tunes and plays with his particular mix of elegance and fractious temper. A great Blue Note set.

TEDDY EDWARDS
Born Theodore Marcus Edwards, 26 April 1924, Jackson, Mississippi; died 20 April 2003, Los Angeles, California
Tenor saxophone

Teddy's Ready
Original Jazz Classics OJCCD 1785
Edwards; Joe Castro (p); Leroy Vinnegar (b); Billy Higgins (d). August 1960.

Teddy Edwards said (1991): **'Jimmy Heath told me how he and Coltrane used to practise my solos. That really hit me, because I don't think I ever copied anyone when I was coming up. Not Lester Young, not Ben [Webster] or [Coleman] Hawkins. Good or ill, I just came by that sound my own way.'**

South-western blues and West Coast cool both inform Teddy's sound. He arrived in California working in bands originally as an altoist. In 1947, he recorded 'The Duel' with Dexter Gordon, a signature moment in West Coast bop. From then on, his progress was steady, but for a glitch or two, and he wrote the delightful 'Sunset Eyes', famously recorded by Clifford Brown. In terms of Edwards's own quite modest body of work, given his longevity, we have the greatest affection for *Together Again!*, recorded in 1961 with the recently rehabilitated Howard McGhee, but there is no question that but his masterpiece was set down the year before.

Teddy's Ready (also originally on Contemporary) has a timeless vigour that makes it end-lessly replayable. It followed a period of ill-health – not drugs-related – and one can hear the relief and delight in the over-hasty attack on 'Scrapple From The Apple' and 'Take The "A" Train'. In later years, Edwards was reliably to be found *behind* the beat. Not a great deal is known nowadays about Arizonan Castro; he tends to be thought of as a fine accompanist (Anita O'Day, June Christy) who never quite made it as a straight jazz player. On this show-ing he's more than worthy, and the support of his colleagues goes without saying: Vin-negar's legendary walk is sure-footed and firm and Higgins plays music on the kit, as ever.

MAX ROACH &

Born 10 January 1924, New Land, North Carolina; died 16 August 2007, New York City
Drums

We Insist! Freedom Now Suite

Candid CCD 79002
Roach; Booker Little (t); Julian Priester (tb); Walter Benton, Coleman Hawkins (ts); James Schenck (b); Ray Mantilla, Thomas Du Vall (perc); Abbey Lincoln (v). August–September 1960.

Abbey Lincoln said (1990): **'Those were very exciting times for us. There was a feeling that we could change anything and everything, just by altering the rhythms and the chords, not even by "protesting", just by making the kind of music we wanted.'**

Some works of art are inseparable from the social and cultural conditions which spawned them, and *We Insist!* is certainly one of these, a record that seems rooted in its moment. Within a few short years, the civil rights movement in the USA was to acquire a more obdu-rate countenance. On the threshold of the Kennedy years, though, this was as ferocious as it got. The opening 'Driva' Man' (one of Oscar Brown Jr's finest moments as a lyricist) is wry and sarcastic, enunciated over Roach's deliberately mechanical work rhythms and Coleman Hawkins's blearily proud solo, just the kind of thing you might expect from a working stiff at the end of the longest shift in history. It's followed by 'Freedom Day', which, with 'All Africa', was to be part of a large choral work targeted on the centenary of the Emancipa-tion Proclamation. 'Freedom Day' follows Roach's typically swinging address, but is dis-tinguished by a Booker Little solo of bursting, youthful emotion, and a contribution from the little-regarded Walter Benton that matches Hawkins's for sheer simplicity of diction. The central 'Triptych' – originally a dance piece – is a duo for Roach and Lincoln. 'Prayer', 'Protest' and 'Peace' was not a trajectory acceptable to a later generation of militants, but there is more than enough power in Lincoln's inchoate roars of rage in the central part, and more than enough ambiguity in the ensuing 'Peace', to allay thoughts that her or Roach's politics were blandly liberal. The closing 'Tears For Johannesburg' has more classic Little, and also good things from Priester and Benton. It follows 'All Africa', which begins in a vein reminiscent of Billie Holiday, briefly degenerates into a litany of tribal names and slogans, and hinges on a 'middle passage' of drum music embodying the three main Black drum traditions of the West: African, African-Cuban and African-American. Its influence on sub-sequent jazz percussion is incalculable, and this extraordinary record remains listenable even across four decades of outwardly far more radical experimentation.

& *See also* **Alone Together** (1956–1960; p. 191), **Historic Concerts** (1979; p. 454)

RENÉ THOMAS
Born 25 February 1927, Liège, Belgium; died 3 January 1975, Santander, Spain
Guitar

Guitar Groove
Original Jazz Classics OJCCD 1725
Thomas; J. R. Monterose (ts); Hod O'Brien (p); Teddy Kotick (b); Albert 'Tootie' Heath (d). September 1960.

Saxophonist Stan Getz said (1983): **'He had class and could swing. Someone asked me if it was like playing with Django Reinhardt. "Pretty much," I said, "but minus all the shit."'**

A fatal heart attack cut short a career that was already rather overshadowed by a more colourful and charismatic guitarist, Thomas's Belgian compatriot Django Reinhardt. Though Django must have been the unavoidable comparison when Thomas moved to North America, there really wasn't very much in common between them, and Thomas's modernist credentials allowed him to fit into the American scene more comfortably than did his illustrious predecessor. *Guitar Groove* is a fine product of his American sojourn and is one of the high-points of a poorly documented career. The original, 'Spontaneous Effort', combines firm, boppish melody with an easy swing. It's an interesting group of oddfellows. Monterose is too raw-throated for 'Milestones' but slots into 'Ruby, My Dear' with impressive ease. He sits out for 'Like Someone In Love' and O'Brien joins him on the bench for the duration of 'How Long Has This Been Going On?' The sound is better balanced on these tracks than when the horn is present, but overall it sounds very good indeed.

CHARLES MINGUS &
Born 22 April 1922, Nogales, Arizona; died 5 January 1979, Cuernavaca, Mexico
Double bass, piano

Charles Mingus Presents Charles Mingus
Candid CCD 79005
Mingus; Ted Curson (t); Eric Dolphy (as, bcl); Dannie Richmond (d). October 1960.

Dannie Richmond said (1985): **'You'd think you might be able to learn some of the lessons of being with Mingus from someone who'd gone through that experience before you. You can't. You have to go through it yourself. It's the process that matters, not the lessons you might learn.'**

Mingus's association with Candid was brief (though no briefer than the label's first existence) and highly successful. His long club residency in 1960 (interrupted only by festival appearances) gave him an unwontedly stable and played-in band to take into the studio (he recorded a fake – and uncommonly polite – night club intro for the set), and the larger-scale arrangement of 'MDM' negatively reflects the solidity of the core band. *Presents* is for pianoless quartet and centres on the extraordinary vocalized interplay between Dolphy and Mingus; on 'What Love' they carry on a long conversation in near-comprehensible dialect. 'Folk Forms' is wonderfully pared down and features a superb Mingus solo. 'All The Things You Could Be By Now If Sigmund Freud's Wife Was Your Mother' has a wry fury (Mingus once said that it had been written in the psychiatric ward at Bellevue) which is more than incidentally suggestive of 'harmolodic' and 'punk' procedures of the '80s. The 'Original Faubus Fables' was a further experiment in the use of texts, here a furious rant against what Mingus later called 'Nazi USA', and his later-'60s brothers 'Amerika'. It's powerfully felt but less well integrated in its blend of polemic and music than Max Roach's *Freedom Now Suite* on the same label.

& See also **The Complete Debut Recordings** (1951–1957; p. 131), **Pithecanthropus Erectus** (1956; p. 175), **Mingus Dynasty** (1959; p. 247), **The Black Saint And The Sinner Lady** (1963; p. 291)

CLARK TERRY&

Born 14 December 1920, St Louis, Missouri
Trumpet, flugelhorn

Color Changes
Candid CCD 79009
Terry; Jimmy Knepper (tb); Julius Watkins (frhn); Yusef Lateef (ts, f, eng hn, ob); Seldon Powell (ts, f); Tommy Flanagan, Budd Johnson (p); Joe Benjamin (b); Ed Shaughnessy (d). November 1960.

Clark Terry says: **'I was put in a lot of very casual situations, jam sessions, you know, so it was nice to record some of my own music and arrangements with a group that offered so many different colours, nice sound. Maybe it's just vanity, but there weren't too many chances to do that in 1960, not for a jazz player.'**

Terry's best record, and ample evidence that swing was still viable on the cusp of the decade that was to see its demise as anything but an exercise in nostalgia. What is immediately striking is the extraordinary, almost kaleidoscopic variation of tone-colour through the seven tracks. Given Lateef's inventive multi-instrumentalism, Powell's doubling on flute and Terry's use of flugelhorn and his mutes, the permutations on horn voicings seem almost infinite. 'Brother Terry' opens with a deep growl from Terry, a weaving oboe theme by composer Lateef and some beautiful harmony work from Watkins, who interacts imaginatively with Knepper on Terry's 'Flutin' And Fluglin''. Again arranged by Lateef, this is a straightforward exploration of the relation between their two horns; Terry has written several 'odes' to his second instrument, and this is perhaps the most inventive. 'Nahstye Blues', written by and featuring Johnson, in for the unsuitably limpid Flanagan, comes close to Horace Silver's funk. Terry is slightly disappointing, but Lateef turns in a majestic solo that turns his own cor anglais introduction completely on its head. The closing 'Chat Qui Pêche' is an all-in, solo-apiece affair that would have sounded wonderful in the Parisian *boîte* it celebrates and brings a marvellous, expertly recorded record to a powerful finish.

& See also **Serenade To A Bus Seat** (1957; p. 206), **Memories Of Duke** (1980; p. 457)

STEVE LACY&

Born Steven Lackritz, 23 July 1934, New York City; died 4 June 2004, Boston, Massachusetts
Soprano saxophone

The Straight Horn Of Steve Lacy
Candid 9007
Lacy; Charles Davis (bs); John Ore (b); Roy Haynes (d). November 1960.

Steve Lacy said (1983): **'Why the soprano? Oh, Bechet, obviously. I heard Sidney Bechet and that was it.'**

Soprano saxophone specialists are no longer the rarity they were in 1960. Steve Lacy was the inspiration behind John Coltrane's decision to double on the instrument. His own early career revolved around Dixieland playing, but he made a rapid transition to the avant-garde, working with Cecil Taylor, but obsessing about Thelonious Monk, in whose group he played briefly the same year this muted, tentative but easily underrated record was made.

Predictably, Monk and Taylor share the bulk of composition credits. Lacy sounds comfortable on 'Introspection', 'Played Twice' and 'Criss Cross' – he'd already made a full record of Monk themes called *Reflections* – his parched and particulate tone finding all sorts of unsuspected detail in the three pieces. It was an enthusiasm that Lacy never lost, forming an all-Monk group with trombonist Roswell Rudd for a time and returning to the Monastic oeuvre right to the end of his life. He rather boldly opens the set with Taylor's 'Louise', not quite the jawbreaker one might expect, given Taylor's reputation, but a theme that seems to trouble the group a little. They have a firmer purchase on 'Air' later on, but the most extended track of the set is a reading of Miles Davis's 'Donna Lee' that maybe serves to show why the soprano instrument didn't have much presence in bebop. We have been somewhat dismissive previously, but what is genuinely impressive about every one of these cuts, and the bop staple particularly, is how the group works its way not so much into a comfort zone as through any initial difficulties and ends up making a strong statement. Many of these tracks sound like first takes, even if they were not.

It's Lacy's first mature statement, but the others take a full share of credit. Davis's throaty baritone fulfils the same timbral function as Roswell Rudd's or George Lewis's trombone on later recordings, and the pianoless rhythm section generates a nicely sympathetic, if wobbly, groove for the leader.

& *See also* **Weal & Woe** (1972, 1973; p. 398), **5 x Monk 5 x Lacy** (1994; p. 580)

GIL EVANS &

Born Ian Ernest Gilmore Green, 13 May 1912, Toronto, Ontario, Canada; died 20 May 1988, Cuernavaca, Mexico
Arranger, keyboards

Out Of The Cool
Impulse! 051186-2
Evans; Johnny Coles, Phil Sunkel (t); Keg Johnson, Jimmy Knepper (tb); Tony Studd (btb); Bill Barber (tba); Ray Beckenstein, Eddie Cane (as, f, picc); Budd Johnson (ts, ss); Bob Tricarico (f, picc, bsn); Ray Crawford (g); Ron Carter (b); Elvin Jones, Charli Persip (d). December 1960.

Gil Evans said (1998): **'Some people hear the word "arranger" and they think that means you have the music down pat, organized to the very last detail. It isn't like that. I prefer to think of it as controlled chaos. Someone always jumps in if it's in danger of driving off the road, and sometimes that's me, but I prefer to wait and see what happens. Ease and predictability are the curse of the modern world, certainly a curse on the creative spirit. When everything is already known, there's nothing left to play.'**

A gentle Svengali. His association with Miles Davis was definitive of one strain of modern jazz, but Gil went on to rewrite the musical legacy of Jimi Hendrix. Born in Canada, he was leading his own group by 1933, and already arranging. He served a tough indenture in Claude Thornhill's band, extracting the modernism out of the Ellington legacy and foregrounding it in a striking new way; Evans's peerless voicings are instantly recognizable.

Out Of The Cool is Evans's masterpiece under his own name and one of the best examples of jazz orchestration since the early Ellington bands. It's the soloists – Coles on the eerie 'Sunken Treasure', a lonely-sounding Knepper on 'Where Flamingoes Fly' – that immediately catch the ear, but repeated hearings reveal the relaxed sophistication of Evans's settings, which gives a hefty band the immediacy and elasticity of a quintet. Evans's sense of time allows Coles to double the metre on George Russell's 'Stratusphunk', which ends with a clever inversion of the opening measures. 'La Nevada' is one of his best and most neglected scores, typically built up out of simple materials. The sound, already good, has been given lots more timbre by digital transfer. Be aware that *Into The Hot*, the obvious 'sequel', with Gil's picture on the cover, isn't an Evans album at all, but rightly belongs to Cecil Taylor; long story.

& *See also* **Plays The Music Of Jimi Hendrix** (1974, 1975; p. 414)

PAUL GONSALVES

Born 12 July 1920, Boston, Massachusetts; died 14 May 1974, London
Tenor saxophone

Gettin' Together

Original Jazz Classics OJCCD 203
Gonsalves; Nat Adderley (t); Wynton Kelly (p); Sam Jones (p); Jimmy Cobb (d). December 1960.

Saxophonist David Murray said (1992): **'Paul's son showed me his father's mouthpiece one time, and, you know, it was bitten almost through.'**

'Mex' – so called for his Latin looks – actually started with the Basie band but joined Duke Ellington in 1950 and stayed for the rest of his life. Addiction troubled his career, but Ellington stood by him and coaxed out countless great performances. Gonsalves's unplanned 27 blues choruses in the bridging section of 'Diminuendo In Blue' and 'Crescendo In Blue' at Newport in 1956 was his apotheosis and can be considered one of the first important extended solos in modern jazz. Gonsalves stands in a direct line with earlier masters like Chu Berry and Don Byas, and leads to Frank Lowe and David Murray. It would be absurd to compare his influence with Coltrane's, but it's now clear that he was experimenting early with tonalities remarkably similar to Trane's famous 'sheets of sound'. It's probable that more people heard Gonsalves play at the time.

His own records are less celebrated than they ought to be. Material and personnel tend to have an Ellingtonian cast, which creates the impression that these are indulgences from the day job. A date co-led with Roy Eldridge, *Mexican Bandit Meets Pittsburgh Pirate*, had some circulation, but even so rarely figures in fans' lists. *Gettin' Together* is a remarkable album, beautifully played and recorded. Morton's 'Low Gravy' is an unusual pick for players of this generation, but it fits in well and the ballads, too, have the feel of old-time work brought somewhat up to date. Kelly's work on 'Walkin'' and 'I Cover The Waterfront' is blue-chip, and Adderley's fragile, over-confident tone fits in perfectly with the leader's spinning, effortlessly logical lines. It doesn't happen here, where studio constraints keep durations down, but one always feels that Gonsalves could play on serenely on any of these themes. Even the opening 'Yesterdays' has the potential for epic.

He sojourned in London later, and passed away there, a little ahead, one suspects, of the inevitable 'rediscovery'.

BUDD JOHNSON

Born Albert J. Johnson, 4 December 1910, Dallas, Texas; died 20 October 1984, Kansas City, Missouri
Tenor saxophone

Let's Swing
Original Jazz Classics OJC 1720
Johnson; Keg Johnson (tb); Tommy Flanagan (p); George Duvivier (b); Charli Persip (d). December 1960.

Tommy Flanagan said (1987): '**Thank you for asking about Budd Johnson. No one ever asks about Budd these days. He was one of the greatest players of his instrument there ever was. He could do anything in any key, but somehow he's overlooked now and it seems a shame.**'

Budd Johnson was a jazz giant for over five decades, yet made comparatively few recordings under his own leadership. Growing up in Dallas, he started on drums but became a stylist in the Hawkins mould and worked in Kansas City as a teenager, before co-leading a group with Teddy Wilson in Chicago. He subsequently worked with Louis Armstrong and Earl Hines, for whom he arranged, staying until the early years of the war, after which he had stints with Dizzy Gillespie, Boyd Raeburn and Billy Eckstine.
  Johnson was already a veteran when he made this record: the tone settled, big, broad, soaked in blues feeling. 'Blues By Budd' is an inimitable example of Johnson at his best. There is a certain dry humour in his playing which never spills over into parody or flippancy: listen to the way he opens his solo on 'Uptown Manhattan', and hear how he intensifies his playing from that point. His brother Keg plays some cheerful solos, but it's Budd's record – try the lovely reading of 'Someone To Watch Over Me', in which the saxophonist composed a unison passage for himself and Duvivier.

DUTCH SWING COLLEGE BAND
Formed 1945
Band

Live In 1960
Philips 838765-2
Oscar Klein (c); Dick Kaart (tb); Peter Schilperoort (cl, bs); Jan Morks (cl); Arie Ligthart (g); Bob Van Oven (b); Martin Beenen (d). 1960.

Adrie Braat says: '**In 1960 the band turned professional, won innumerable prizes and still performs traditional jazz, successfully and worldwide.**'

Founded at the end of the war by Peter Schilperoort, this jazz institution is still playing with undiminished enthusiasm, though inevitably with successive new personnels. There is some classic material from the late '40s available on Lake, who preserve vast amounts of European Dixieland and trad, but the best of the DSCB comes from the year the chaps decided to turn in the day jobs and play jazz for a living. Originally an enthusiastic if uneventful trad group, the band matured into a unit which bridged the classic traditional style and a more swing-styled mainstream, although the former held sway. There were always good soloists on hand, some of the best including Morks, Klein and the very able Kaart, and the rhythm players avoided the mechanical thud of much trad. A regimen of constant touring kept their professionalism polished. The 1960 live set goes with a real punch and, with Morks and Klein in top form, is one of their liveliest records. There's not much to say about this music, other than it is endlessly enjoyable, and far from unsubtle, and has a wonderful durability; the concept survived past Schilperoort's death in 1990, more recently under the stewardship of Bob Kaper, whose battle-cry 'Have a ball!' still motivates and stirs.

CHARLIE BYRD

Born 16 September 1925, Chuckatuck, Virginia; died 2 December 1999, Annapolis, Maryland
Guitar

The Guitar Artistry of Charlie Byrd
JVC Victor 41576
Byrd; Keter Betts (b); Buddy Deppenschmidt (d). 1960.

Buddy Deppenschmidt says: **'It was me and Betts who really put together the bossa nova thing. I don't recall Charlie being that enthusiastic to begin with, but he and Getz – who did even less – got all the credit, and the money!'**

The turning point in Byrd's life was when he jammed with Django Reinhardt while still a teenager, on the great Belgian's first visit to the US. Charlie had a relatively quiet time after that, until he moved to Washington in the '50s. The release in 1962 of the evergreen *Jazz Samba* with Stan Getz, and the legal kerfuffle that followed, put Charlie Byrd firmly on the map. Like all hugely successful products, there was an element of ersatz about it, and Byrd's Latin stylings have never sounded entirely authentic.

Working here with his regular trio, he shows clearly the values that sustained him through a long career: smooth melodic invention, a natural, easy rhythm, and a sufficiently varied and interesting programme (which includes a couple of Django classics and a more unexpected reading of 'House Of The Rising Sun') to hold the attention. After *Jazz Samba* altered the demographics, Byrd was expected to play in that style for the next ten or 15 years, but one hears him revert to this classic swing somewhat later in life: undeniably in better sound, but rarely with the same freshness of invention.

ERIC DOLPHY&

Born 20 June 1928, Los Angeles, California; died 29 June 1964, Berlin, Germany
Alto saxophone, bass clarinet, flute, clarinet

Far Cry
Original Jazz Classics OJCCD 400
Dolphy; Booker Little (t); Jaki Byard (p); Ron Carter (b); Roy Haynes (d). December 1960.

Bassist Richard Davis, who recorded with Dolphy, says: **'Eric was special, like the brother you never had.'**

Like those of his friend Booker Little and of Clifford Brown, Eric Dolphy's career was strikingly and tragically foreshortened. He remains one of the music's great might-have-beens. His recording debut in 1949, with Roy Porter's bebop band in California, was something of a false start. Dolphy did not go into the studio again for nearly a decade, but in the meantime acquired an astonishing facility on alto saxophone. After joining the group of another drummer, Chico Hamilton, he began to develop a highly distinctive multi-instrumentalism, pioneering bass clarinet as a solo improvising instrument. His Parker-derived alto saxophone was strongly identified with advances in post-bop harmony, but he was also involved in the Third Stream. Much of his best work was in the company of John Coltrane and Charles Mingus, with whom he toured Europe. Unable to find sufficient challenging work in the US he tried his luck as a 'single' there in 1964 but died in Berlin of diabetes complications.

Even before his passing, Dolphy had acquired an almost saintly reputation. His generous spirit is well attested by almost everyone who worked with him, but so too is admiration of his remarkable musicianship. Dolphy's mastery of alto saxophone is uncontested, a sound and idiom that marked a definite step forward from the prevailing Charlie Parker style, but combining elements of Ornette Coleman's radicalism as well. It was to be more than a decade after his studio debut with Roy Porter before Dolphy made a record of his own. *Outward Bound* was the first in a group of records whose titles and surreal cover art emphasized his 'out' or 'outside' approach. The debut works interesting variations on bop and the blues, but Dolphy was at the same time dabbling in Third Stream and Indian-influenced projects, steadily widening his musical language and skills.

Out There, recorded in August 1960, saw him replace a piano-player with Ron Carter's cello, a decision perhaps influenced by Nathan Gershman's role in the Hamilton group. Whatever the source, it gave Dolphy the confidence to experiment more freely with large intervallic leaps, whole-tone progressions and other advanced procedures only hinted at on the earlier record. That said, the E-flat blues 'Serene' is about as conventional as anything Dolphy committed to record, and entirely lacks the alienating wallop of his most characteristic work.

The week before Christmas 1960 was packed. On Tuesday, 20 December, Dolphy took part in Gunther Schuller's *Jazz Abstractions*, taping two Third Stream pieces in the company of Ornette Coleman, Scott LaFaro, Bill Evans and Jim Hall. The following day he played in Ornette's ambitious double quartet, the sessions that were to yield one of the definitive statements of the jazz avant-garde, *Free Jazz*. The very same day, he went over the river to Hackensack, New Jersey, and recorded *Far Cry*, his one studio recording with Booker Little.

Interestingly he decided to re-record two items from *Out There*. The title-piece of the August album is repeated, tougher and boppish in style, while 'Serene' remains essentially the same, which is perhaps why it was dropped from the original release. Byard brought in two pieces which helped turn side one of the LP into an extended tribute to Dolphy's most obvious creative forerunner: 'Mrs Parker Of K.C. (Bird's Mother)' and 'Ode To Charlie Parker'.

Far Cry also marks the first recorded appearance of Dolphy's most celebrated composition, 'Miss Ann', a delightful 14-bar theme that he was to play until the end of his life; the title is black argot for a white woman of a certain type. Little drops out for 'It's Magic', one of the first times one feels Dolphy is doing something special on bass clarinet, and the whole band sits out 'Tenderly', an astonishing, unaccompanied alto solo, a piece of work that bridges Coleman Hawkins's pioneering 'Picasso' and Dolphy's own later solo bass clarinet excursions on 'God Bless The Child', except that here the tune is still very much in evidence. Some have suggested that he was influenced by Sonny Rollins's unaccompanied 'Body And Soul', recorded two years earlier.

There is a virtual consensus that *Out To Lunch!*, four years later, was Dolphy's masterpiece. It's a view that requires careful examination. Our growing conviction is that, while the later record has a profound iconic importance, coming so close to the end of Dolphy's life, and on the gilt-edge jazz label of the time, it is in no fundamental way superior to *Far Cry* and in some respects unrepresentative of Dolphy's output.

& *See also* **Out To Lunch!** (1964; p. 300)

THE '60s

Thinking in decades is a neat, but usually meaningless, journalistic habit, and the kinds of consensus it throws up are nearly always wrong, or at best misleading. One might expect, given the usual rubrics of popular culture, to turn away from the '50s with relief, confident that the new decade will deliver up a new optimism and spirit of adventure marked by bold creativity, political alertness and resistance to premature categorization. One only needs to dwell on the preceding 25 or 30 pages, or indeed the last 50, to be aware that the '50s did represent some kind of golden age in jazz history. Almost every year seems to deliver a constellation of fine recordings. Some years seem almost impossibly rich, as if the only vital things going on at the time involved men with trumpets, saxophones, pianos and drums gathered in small New York studios. And it is true that for a time jazz did seem at the cutting edge of the creative culture in a way that it had not been before and would not be again.

It is not our intention to suggest that the '60s represented a falling-away in terms of creative energy in jazz, and it is important to understand why the '50s were, or seem, richer and more 'important'. As always, there are positive and negative factors on both sides of the imaginary chronological line. The LP was still new in the '50s and the LP as an object had an impact and resonance that 78rpm records did not. They were powerfully visible, as well as audible. By the following decade, the LP was extremely well entrenched, but was also being colonized by pop culture, which took up an increasingly large share of corporate investment in music. There was also the beginning of what later became an unstoppable trend of repackaging back-catalogue material rather than issuing new recordings. The eminent Commodore – whose leading new-issue imprint was Mainstream – started doing this in the '60s, and it exerted a certain pressure both on the market and on the critical map, inviting a postwar generation of writers and fans to come to terms with music that had been made long before they reached the age of discretion. A 20-year-old fan in 1945 would have regarded most swing as *terra incognita* and while his own natural instincts might have leaned more towards tough hard bop or the new experimental music, he was still required to negotiate a music that had a clearly organized documentary history.

Arguably, the commercial presence of freshly packaged early jazz reinforced the battle lines, encouraging a young modernist to overstate his commitment to the new, but whatever the individual case the '60s saw the emergence of the first self-conscious jazz avantgarde. Its origins can be dated to somewhere between Charles Mingus's 'Newport Rebels' and Jazz Artists Guild in 1960 and trumpeter Bill Dixon's 1964 'October Revolution' in jazz. It remains an open question to what extent aesthetic radicalism was matched by a specific political agenda, and at the most cursory glance it can seem that the jazz music of the '60s was less obviously motivated by political issues than the music of the previous decade, when most of the major initiatives – civil rights, anti-militarism, student democracy and oppositionism – became active in American culture. This is not to say that the '60s were quietistic – though it's fairly obvious that of the major younger figures of that decade (Coleman, Coltrane, Davis, Dolphy, Mingus, Shepp, Taylor ...) only Mingus and Shepp seemed to have any *specific* political programme – but it seemed to represent special pleading in a way that rock, for instance, did not, and its racial agendas were complex and in some respects obstructive. Some avant-garde jazz allied itself to black nationalism (though just as much did not), and it was here that it met the most robust but usually passive resistance from the corporate economy, which simply neutralized such aims and directions by refusing to acknowledge them, or to deal with musicians who had abandoned 'slave' names in favour of new Muslim appellations: though a great many musicians of this generation changed their names, it would be a challenge to find many of those names at the top of an album sleeve.

The best and most representative work of the avant-garde may have gone undocumented, either because it was considered unmarketable, or subversive, or, as is sometimes forgotten, because its exponents held recording in some distrust.

And not just recording, for the very term 'jazz', which had always been questioned by such eminences as Duke Ellington, was also increasingly rejected by creative musicians. Miles Davis expressed disdain for it, and Charles Mingus attempted various alternatives – his classic Impulse! recording *The Black Saint and the Sinner Lady* was released under a 'folk' label, oddly – sparking an absurd attempt to cast jazz as the 'classical' music of African-Americans, a view which cannot be attributed to Mingus himself.

Nothing challenged the LP during the '60s for supremacy in the marketplace. Eight-track recordings made a brief appearance and went the way of crushed velvet bell bottoms. However, recording techniques did make significant advances during the decade. Stereophonic recording became the norm, banishing monophonic recording to the dead letter office, though there were some disastrous attempts to 'enhance' mono recordings for stereo effect. Perhaps most important to creative musicians was the steady emergence of multi-track (initially two-track) recording, which allowed for a careful balancing of musical parts and a much clearer and more faithful representation again of bass and drums, as well as the kind of tape-editing practised by Teo Macero and by Bob Thiele on Mingus's *The Black Saint*.

Almost as important was the consolidation of a group of producers and engineers who for the first time matched great technical skill with innate musicality *and* a fundamental commitment to jazz. For Blue Note, but for many other labels, too, Rudy Van Gelder established a benchmark for recorded jazz, while others, like Orrin Keepnews and Bob Thiele, later Creed Taylor, professionalized jazz recording and gave it a distinct sonority that was faithful to the music's nature rather than an adapted and compromised version of classical and pop recording. Blue Note's practice of paid rehearsal and ample studio time was also influential. No longer was a jazz record merely a recorded jam session or taped rehearsal.

However, even such masterpieces were being eclipsed in the public consciousness by *Rubber Soul, Revolver* and *Sgt Pepper's Lonely Hearts Club Band*, the Beach Boys' *Pet Sounds* and a rising tide of expensively produced and fiercely promoted pop and rock albums, which replaced jazz as the audible component of the counterculture. By the Woodstock summer, jazz – with a few notable exceptions, many of them influenced in turn by rock – had started to seem the province of older listeners, not yet elderly or entirely un-hip, but no longer where it – whatever 'it' was – was at ...

Part 1:
1961-1965

GENE AMMONS

Also known as 'Jug', born 14 April 1925, Chicago, Illinois; died 6 August 1974, Chicago, Illinois
Tenor saxophone

The Gene Ammons Story: Gentle Jug
Prestige PRCD-24155
Ammons; Richard Wyands, Patti Bown (p); George Duvivier, Doug Watkins (b); J. C. Heard, Ed Shaughnessy (d). January 1961–April 1962.

Saxophonist Henry Threadgill said (1981): **'I don't hear the younger people talking about Gene Ammons much any more. When I was coming through, he was one of the people**

you went to see, whenever he was playing. That was what the saxophone was all about, far as I was concerned.'

Son of the great boogie pianist Albert Ammons, 'Jug' worked with Billy Eckstine and Woody Herman before leading his own bands through the '50s and '60s. His career was interrupted by prison terms for drug offences and his life was cut short, but Ammons exerted a considerable influence while he was active, and his records – though less dramatic than his live appearances must have been – are still more than listenable and fascinating to set alongside those of today's more celebrated saxophonists.

Sadly, even the superior Ammons albums are spotty. Great performances follow weary ones, even on the same record, and there doesn't seem to be a particular setting that guarantees top form. One imagines he found the studio a trial. However, we wouldn't be without his music and *Gentle Jug* is a winner, bringing together *The Soulful Mood* (where he plays with Hawkins-like authority) and *Nice 'n' Cool* from the preceding year. The 1961 material is all ballad-based with a glorious version of 'Till There Was You' and the peerless 'Someone To Watch Over Me' (which figured at a key moment in the Tom Berenger film of that name). There is also a wonderful 'Willow, Weep For Me'. The only regret is that Wyands doesn't get more space to stretch out, but Patti Bown on the other set is a revelation, albeit in homeopathically small doses.

JIM ROBINSON

Also known as Big Jim; born 25 December 1892 (some sources suggest 1889 or 1890), Deer Range, Louisiana; died 4 May 1976, New Orleans, Louisiana
Trombone

Jim Robinson's New Orleans Band

Original Jazz Classics OJCCD 1844
Robinson; Ernest Cagnolotti (t); Louis Cottrell (cl); George Guesnon (g); Alcide 'Slow Drag' Pavageau (b); Alfred Williams (d). January 1961.

Trombonist Turk Murphy said (1981): **'Jim liked to get the audience up and dancing when he played. The idea of playing to a seated audience, politely clapping, just didn't make any sense to him.'**

Robinson took up the trombone while serving with the US army in France. He played in and around New Orleans for most of his long life. Much of his best work is with George Lewis or Bunk Johnson and for a time he was only a part-time player, making his living in the docks, but he did play with the Golden Leaf Band and was a significant presence on the nascent jazz scene.

The doyen of New Orleans trombonists – along with Louis Nelson – Robinson was still recording when he was past 80, despite a diffident beginning. His simple, perfectly appropriate playing wasn't too bothered by the passing of time, and he performs throughout much as he did on all the sessions he appeared on over a space of some 35 years. 'Ice Cream' was his signature piece. *New Orleans Band*, along with a second disc, *Plays Spirituals And Blues*, was originally a part of Riverside's New Orleans Living Legends series and together they were among the first occasions when Robinson had been asked to perform as a leader. Cagnolotti and Cottrell weren't much more interested than Jim in taking a lead, and as a result the front line sounds reserved here and there; but the two discs – neatly split between NO standards on this one and gospel and blues tunes on the other – are as tough and genuine as most such sessions from this period.

EDDIE HARRIS

Born 20 October 1934, Chicago, Illinois; died 5 November 1996, Los Angeles, California
Tenor saxophone, trumpet, mouthpieces, voice

Exodus To Jazz / Mighty Like A Rose

Vee-Jay VJ-019
Harris; Willie Pickens (p); Joe Diorio (g); William Yancey (b); Harold Jones (d). January–April 1961.

Eddie Harris said (1989): **'Almost nobody noticed that what I was trying to do was sound like a trumpet-player on the saxophone, up high. That's what all that experimenting with mouthpieces was about. When the electric stuff started coming in, that was no longer necessary. Until then, I could work ten days a week, playing every horn I had, but when I did my own stuff, people just said it was weird.'**

Harris learned several instruments in his youth and finally settled on saxophone as the main one; he experimented with electronic sax, a reed trumpet and other quirks. A great crowd-pleaser who didn't please the critics, he none the less remained close to the AACM people round Muhal Richard Abrams, and whatever anyone wrote about the record, he was a master technician, who came back in later years to prove his enduring toughness as an improviser. Harris had one hit that everyone still remembers, the peerless 'Freedom Jazz Dance', which apparently his bass-player Ron Carter took with him to the Miles Davis group when the trumpeter recruited him.

Harris got off to a tremendous start with his first album, *Exodus To Jazz*, with the title-theme selling a million in single form. It rather knocked his jazz credibility, but Harris was a complex talent anyway and his range of ideas was a peculiar mix of the ingenious and the bizarre. His tenor sound was high – so high that he once received votes in a 'Best Alto' poll – and his tonalities suggested a kinship with the avant-garde, only true to a degree, for Eddie actually preferred soft hard-bop or boogaloo situations that drew on the gospel and blues strains of his native Chicago.

When he moved to Atlantic, Harris continued experimenting with electric saxes, trumpets played with sax mouthpieces and other gimmicks, with varying levels of success. *The In Sound* has reappeared in a useful pair with *Mean Greens*. The key tracks are 'Freedom Jazz Dance', still a glorious experience for jazz fans of a certain age, and a lovely version of 'Theme From *The Sandpiper* (The Shadow Of Your Smile)'. Harris's eccentricities aren't too intrusive, and if one listens for the musicality of the performances rather than trying to work out what's playing, it's thoroughly satisfying music.

OLIVER NELSON

Born 4 June 1932, St Louis, Missouri; died 27 October 1975, Los Angeles, California
Alto and tenor saxophones, composer/arranger

Blues And The Abstract Truth

Impulse! 051154-2
Nelson; Freddie Hubbard (t); Eric Dolphy (as, f); George Barrow (bs); Bill Evans (p); Paul Chambers (b); Roy Haynes (d). February 1961.

Freddie Hubbard said (1983): **'I sometimes think it's the perfect record, not in the sense that there's absolutely nothing you couldn't improve a little, but that it was the sound of a man getting his concept together for the first time and finding that it worked.'**

Nelson served an unremarkable apprenticeship with Louis Jordan and the Erskine Hawkins and Quincy Jones big bands, and he probably learned most from working with Quincy, not least that ability to combine sophisticated intervals and expansive shapes with a raw blues feel. Sadly, Nelson was to spend his last few years in a similar direction, writing TV themes like *The Six Million Dollar Man*, lucrative but an unsatisfactory legacy for the man who wrote 'Stolen Moments'.

Restored to its original cover artwork (a portrait of Nelson was substituted when the stereo version appeared), this is one of the classics of the period, and if there were one Nelson track to take away to a desert island it would have to be the one that starts the album, the haunting 'Stolen Moments' with its mournful Hubbard solo and a lovely statement from Dolphy on flute. The great man left his bass clarinet behind for this session, and it isn't missed. Nelson tended to arrange for higher voices, and for this record he didn't stray outside 12-bar blues and the chords of 'I Got Rhythm'. 'Stolen Moments' is a minor blues, opening in C minor, with some fascinating internal divisions. 'Hoe Down' is a 44-bar figure based on the opening two notes. 'Teenie's Blues' is dedicated to the composer's sister, a talented singer. It rests on just three intervals, with transpositions for the two altos to maintain a level of tension and release. The rhythm section is again very fine, with Haynes relishing this setting and Chambers producing some lovely countermelodies and stop-time figures under the basic changes.

The sound is now as good as anyone could possibly want, close and sharp enough to hear Dolphy's breath across the mouthpiece of the flute.

BILL BARRON

Born 27 March 1927, Philadelphia, Pennsylvania; died 21 September 1989, Middletown, Connecticut
Tenor and soprano saxophones

Modern Windows Suite
Savoy 92878
Barron; Ted Curson (t); Jay Cameron (bs); Kenny Barron (p); Eddie Khan, Jimmy Garrison (b); Pete LaRoca, Frankie Dunlop (d). February–June 1961.

Brother Kenny Barron said (1992): **'He was a very quiet and unassuming man who didn't push himself forward or make much noise. I think that's the only reason he isn't better known.'**

Pianist Kenny Barron's elder brother was already in his 30s when he made his debut on Cecil Taylor's *Love For Sale*. He stayed around Philadelphia until then, not making a move to New York until 1958. He recorded only rather sparsely and has remained something of a musician's musician.

This Savoy disc brings together the *Suite* with *The Tenor Stylings Of Bill Barron*, although only the title-piece of the former is included. Both sessions are a striking departure from hard-bop convention. Barron's writing, involving modal forms, blues and – in the 'Suite' especially – some queer Mingus-like tonalities, sounds like little else that was going on at the time. 'Blast Off', 'Ode To An Earth Girl' and 'Nebulae' are striking modern compositions, with altered chords and an almost avant-garde approach from Barron. One can readily imagine him working with Taylor. Both he and Curson register strongly as improvisers; listen to their contrasting approaches to the ostinato section of 'Ode To An Earth Girl'. Cameron, absent on the second session, is rather less impressive. Both were poorly recorded by Savoy and Kenny's piano is very receded in the mix. But for Bill's playing alone, this is a vivid and valuable document.

BOOKER LITTLE
Born 2 April 1938, Memphis, Tennessee; died 5 October 1961, New York City
Trumpet

Out Front
Candid 9027
Little; Julian Priester (tb); Eric Dolphy (as, bcl, f); Don Friedman (p); Ron Carter, Art Davis (b); Max Roach (d, perc, vib). March & April 1961.

Trumpeter Terence Blanchard says: **'Booker Little is one of the most underrated musicians of his generation. While being one of the most creative and technically accomplished trumpet-players of all time, his bravery in forging new paths of expression is a model by which we can still be inspired.'**

Booker Little's entire recording career occupies just 38 months, from his first studio appearance with Max Roach in June 1958 to a last appearance with the drummer's octet in August 1961, just weeks before his death from uraemia. Along with his sometime collaborator Eric Dolphy, who makes a significant impact on this record, Little was one of the great might-have-beens of modern jazz, the first important trumpet stylist to emerge after the death of Clifford Brown, but similarly ill-fated.

By the beginning of 1961, having arrived in New York with the other Young Men from Memphis (Frank Strozier, Phineas Newborn, Louis Smith and George Coleman), Little was under the benign supervision of Nat Hentoff at Candid and was included in sessions fronted by Roach and Abbey Lincoln. Later in the year, he'd take part in John Coltrane's *Africa/Brass* dates, for which Dolphy had done some of the arranging. In March, though, Little had an opportunity to record under his own name and he took the opportunity with both hands.

There were probably too many 'out' titles around at this point. What's striking about *Out Front* is how logical, even inevitable, some of its most unconventional elements are. But how curious that few of these superbly wrought compositions – poised between hard bop and some fresh evolution – have been covered since. Indeed, the record remains surprisingly little known relative to any of Dolphy's, though we consider it their equal or superior, and often adduced only as an item in the saxophonist's discography.

The opening 'We Speak' is a straightforward blowing theme, but the balance of tonalities and the use of abrasive dissonance evokes Ornette's *Free Jazz*, recorded a bare four months before. Little and Roach are the axis of the music. The drummer adds timps and vibes to his armoury, and this makes up somewhat for the shortcomings in Friedman's playing, which drifts between the routine and the uncomprehending, unless we do his subtlety an injustice. The extra percussion has the effect of blurring the beat in a most enticing way. The shifting signature of 'Moods In Free Time' stretches Little's phrasing and 'Hazy Hues' explores his interest in tone-colour. 'Strength And Sanity' is a staggeringly good line, and so are 'Man Of Words' and the naggingly familiar 'Quiet Please'. The closing 'A New Day', with its hints of freedom and its fanfare-like acclamations, is an ironic title in the circumstances. *Out Front* is one of the great records of its period.

HANK CRAWFORD
Born Bennie Ross Crawford, also known as 'Splanky', 31 December 1934, Memphis, Tennessee; died 29 January 2009, Memphis, Tennessee
Alto saxophone

From The Heart
Atlantic 8122 73709
Crawford; Phillip Guilbeau (t); John Hunt (t, flhn); David Newman (ts); Leroy Cooper (bs); Sonny Forrest (g); Edgar Willis (b); Bruno Carr (d). March 1961.

Alto saxophonist David Sanborn says: **'This is some of the first music I responded to. I love the emotional directness in Hank's playing.'**

Crawford said that he tried 'to keep the melody so far in front that you can almost sing along', and that irresistibly vocal style lends his simple approach to the alto a deep-rooted conviction. His best records are swinging parties built on the blues, southern R&B and enough bebop to keep a more hardened jazz listener satisfied.

He came up with a forward-looking new generation in Memphis, with George Coleman, Booker Little and Phineas Newborn all near-contemporaries, but it was a longish tenure as member and musical director of Ray Charles's band, for whom he originally played baritone, that shaped Hank Crawford as a jazz star whose roots remained firmly in soul and R&B. It was Ray who gave him his professional first name, because of a presumed resemblance to Hank O'Day. The first Atlantic date was *More Soul.* The result is sonorous and churchy in the Brother Ray mould, with Hank and Fathead Newman taking the solo honours.

Hank and the label never saw any reason to do things differently after that. He hit stride with *From The Heart.* It centres on 'Sherri', a song written for Charles, but also includes 'The Peeper' and 'Stony Lonesome', two of Hank's best soul-jazz lines. Sonny Forrest is on hand for three tracks, filling out the harmony, but it's recorded with a piano, with what was basically the Ray Charles unit, and with the horns used as a harmonic carpet. Following his long spell at Atlantic (the Rhino compilation *Heart And Soul* offers the best of it), he renewed his career at Milestone, where he was provided with consistently sympathetic settings that ended up sounding too consistent, though they're still light years ahead of what passes for smooth jazz now.

JAKI BYARD&

Born 15 June 1922, Worcester, Massachusetts; died 11 February 1999, New York City
Piano, tenor saxophone

Out Front!
Original Jazz Classics OJCCD 1842
Byard; Richard Williams (t); Booker Ervin (ts); Ron Carter, Bob Cranshaw, Walter Perkins (b); Roy Haynes (d). March 1961.

Pianist Jason Moran, a pupil of Byard's says: **'I remember Jaki saying that he wrote the piece with Herbie Nichols' "touch" in mind. There is a certain sparkle and lightness, yet profundity, that Nichols gets, and this is what I hear on this recording. I love the way he, Roy Haynes and Ron Carter play together on this one. Jaki has a rare way of making the piano yell mid-phrase, but making one or two notes stick really far out, startling the ear, in a good way.'**

Jaki Byard's murder in 1999 remains unsolved. It was a strange and ironic end for an artist who gave so generously to others during his long working life. His enormous power and versatility are grounded on a thorough knowledge of brass, reeds – he started out on trumpet but preferred to double on tenor saxophone – drums and guitar, as well as piano, and there are definite horn influences in his soloing. Later, Byard did play more pianistically, though the distinctive left- and right-hand articulation of themes – based on a highly personal synthesis of ragtime and stride, bop and free jazz – was still strongly evident in later years. He worked with Earl Bostic, with Maynard Ferguson and, later, with Charles Mingus, with whom he regularly had a solo spot that sounded like a summation of jazz piano history up to that point. With a powerful left hand and a free approach to harmony, Jaki was able to work in almost any context, from gospelly blues to the avant-garde.

Out Front! shows off not only his own versatility as a keyboard artist, but his ability to shape a whole group sound round his own part. Where the horns are deployed – as on the unusual 'European Episode' – the voicings are quite unique and given the distinctiveness of Ervin's and Williams's sound, there is an eerie, almost alien heft to the music, which seems to flit from one idea to the next, almost as if Byard is on tour in his head. The title-piece is, like his 'Aluminum Baby', a modern classic and 'When Sunny Gets Blue' is virtually rewritten in the solo sections. A great album by a modern master.

& See also **Phantasies** (1984, 1988; p. 489)

JOE HARRIOTT
Born 15 July 1928, Jamaica; died 2 January 1973, Southampton, Hampshire, England
Alto saxophone

Abstract
Redial 538 183 2
Harriott; Shake Keane (t); Pat Smythe (p); Bobby Orr, Phil Seamen (d); Frank Holder (perc). 1961.

Pianist and bandleader Michael Garrick remembers: **'Bassist Dave Green once played Joe a Parker V-disc, borrowed from a BBC library man. "I know all dem Parker things. 'Ornithology'? I heard it many times." "But not this take, Joe" – Dave stuck to his guns – "it's never been issued." Cornered, Joe took his usual way out by pretending the last exchange hadn't taken place. "Parker, he play a few aces, yes, but there's dem over *here* can play a few aces, too. There's dem over *here* that will surprise you." These words immortalize him. They're on his grave in Bitterne churchyard. God bless him for his peerless music. He wasn't wrong.'**

Anyone who's only heard of Harriott as one of the mythical leaders of free jazz in Britain will be surprised by much of his recorded output, which doesn't immediately suggest a revolutionary. Harriott came to England with the likes of Dizzy Reece, Coleridge Goode, Shake Keane and Wilton 'Bogey' Gaynair, and shook up British jazz with new energies and priorities. His foreshortened career embraced bop, the Indo-jazz experiments of John Mayer and his own essays in freedom.

Richard Cook's reissue of *Abstract* allowed many who had only heard Harriott's name and legend to experience the music for the first time. The obvious impression is that Joe's brand of abstraction is still deeply grounded in blues, calypso and bop, but Harriott doesn't do bop from the inside; rather he dresses up his own individual conception with a boppish costume and a few Bird feathers. His harmonic grasp isn't conventional either, and it doesn't take much cynicism to suggest that this was one of the things that pushed him towards freedom. That said, it's a great record, and one that consistently belies its title. 'Shadows' might almost be a Parker line turned on its head and as with classic bebop it's the interplay of saxophone and trumpet that counts. Originals like 'Modal' are more schematic but it's Joe's revision of 'Oleo' that reveals his method most clearly, a standard bop line put to idiosyncratic and unrepeatable use.

BUCK CLAYTON
Born Wilbur Dorsey Clayton, 12 November 1911, Dorsey, Kansas; died 8 December 1991, New York City
Trumpet

Buck Clayton All Stars 1961
Storyville STCD 8231
Clayton; Emmett Berry (t); Dicky Wells (tb); Earl Warren (as); Buddy Tate (ts); Sir Charles Thompson (p); Gene Ramey (b); Oliver Jackson (d). April 1961.

Trumpeter Dizzy Reece said (1985): **'No one speaks of him this way, but I think Buck Clayton lay behind a lot of the modern movement: that very clear sound, very ringing, which was quite different from what had gone before in jazz. I think that had an effect on Miles Davis and others, but Miles especially.'**

Responsible for no particular stylistic innovation, Buck managed to synthesize much of the history of jazz trumpet up to his time with a bright, brassy tone and an apparently limitless facility for melodic improvisation, which made him ideal for the kind of open-ended jam that all too often made its way onto record. Though he was leading a big band as early as 1934, it was his time with Basie which established him as a soloist of distinction, and one who later developed a warm, brass tone and softness of delivery that were best suited to ballad playing.

Over in Europe, Buck's brand of swing didn't seem old-fashioned in 1961, and this touring octet was applauded to the rafters right across the continent, as a couple of good live sets suggest. State-of-the-art swing from a band of past masters, anxious to demonstrate that, away from America at least, they weren't past it. The Paris show finds the band in good heart and playing well, though the sound isn't as good as a TCB recording of a later date in Basel. Despite the distracting volume of the drums – Jackson is hugely loud in places – and Sir Charles is often only glimpsed peeking through the cymbals and through horns that are sometimes here, sometimes there, the music is cracking and only a hi-fi perfectionist would baulk.

GEORGE RUSSELL&

Born 23 June 1923, Cincinnati, Ohio; died 27 July 2009, Boston, Massachusetts
Composer, bandleader, piano

Ezz-thetics
Original Jazz Classics OJCCD 070
Russell; Don Ellis (t); Dave Baker (tb); Eric Dolphy (as, bcl); Steve Swallow (b); Joe Hunt (d). May 1961.

George Russell said (1984): **'It isn't for me to pronounce on the significance of the Lydian Concept, though I know it was the bible of modal jazz. The key thing about it was it gave musicians more freedom, which was what Miles Davis, for instance, was looking for. The technical aspects are important and there's a lifetime of study in them, but it's the freedom that matters.'**

As a very good start to a Russell collection there's a strong case to be made for *Ezz-thetics*, with its fine Dolphy contributions (coincidentally or not, the year of the saxophonist's death also marked the beginning of Russell's long exile in Europe and a mutual alienation from the American scene). But all the early Russells, with the exception of the slightly less achieved *The Outer View*, are indispensable.

It's often assumed that these records are entirely dominated by Russell compositions. Not so: the two main events here are Miles's 'Nardis', beautifully arranged, and with Ellis in excellent form, and Dolphy's extraordinary excursus on 'Round Midnight'. By comparison, Russell's title-piece and the cleverly named 'Lydiot' – how many 'lydiots' tried to copy him over the years – are little more than torsos, albeit played with real grace and attention by a perfectly balanced group. A great record.

& *See also* **Jazz Workshop** (1956; p. 183), **Live In An American Time Spiral** (1982; p. 469)

DEXTER GORDON &

Born 27 February 1923, Los Angeles, California; died 25 April 1990, Philadelphia, Pennsylvania
Tenor saxophone

Doin' Alright
Blue Note 784077
Gordon; Freddie Hubbard (t); Horace Parlan (p); George Tucker (b); Al Harewood (d). May 1961.

Dexter Gordon said (1979): **'I was never really "away" from jazz. Even when I wasn't putting out records, even when I didn't have a saxophone in my hand, I was running changes in my head, pretty much every waking hour.'**

Gordon's first recording after a long and painful break is one of his best. Critics divide on whether Gordon was influenced by Coltrane at this period or whether it was simply a case of the original being obscured by his followers. Gordon's phrasing on *Doin' Alright* certainly suggests a connection of some sort, but the opening statement of 'I Was Doin' Alright' is completely individual and quite distinct, and Gordon's solo development is nothing like the younger man's. For all his later attempts to downplay his absences from the music, Gordon clearly regarded this recording as something of a breakthrough. 'You've Changed' never left his basic set-list and many times in years to come he alluded to the original May 1961 solo statement, never repeating himself, but somehow conjuring up the spirit of that first occasion. In addition, when he came to play 'himself' in Tavernier's *Round Midnight*, 'Society Red' was one of the themes he chose. It's a terrific record, intriguingly unplaceable as to time or style. Hubbard does his usual buoyant job and the rhythm section is sure-footed.

& See also **Dexter Gordon On Dial** (1947; p. 113), **More Than You Know** (1975; p. 423)

HOWARD MCGHEE

Born 16 March 1918, Tulsa, Oklahoma; died 17 July 1987, New York City
Trumpet

Maggie's Back In Town!
Original Jazz Classics OJC 693
McGhee; Phineas Newborn (p); Leroy Vinnegar (b); Shelly Manne (d). June 1961.

Trumpeter Jeremy Pelt says: **'To me, Howard McGhee was the trumpeter who bridged the gap between Diz and Miles. He was the consummate stylist.'**

McGhee grew up in Detroit and won his spurs in territory bands, a background that gave him an easy facility in all forms, but may also have instilled a habit of personal neglect and abuse. He was less of an innovator than either Fats Navarro or Dizzy Gillespie, and his light, soft-edged tone and legato phrasing reflect an apprenticeship on clarinet. His recreational habits cost him dear, but he kept coming back and gigged until late in life. He was a prime mover in bebop on the West Coast, and Parker's infamous 'Loverman' sides were originally released under McGhee's name, an irony that must have resounded down the difficult years.

The late '40s saw music taking a back seat to other pursuits, but there were sessions in Paris for Vogue and Blue Star, and there was the wonderful 1948 encounter with Fats Navarro, who perhaps more than anyone shaped his style. Here, Maggie is still inclined to mimic clarinet-lines, but he moved to a crisper attack and that signature sound wasn't so much in evidence after the comeback. The '50s were pretty much a blank for McGhee, but he returned in reasonable shape. On *Maggie's Back In Town!* he sounds straightened-out and clear-headed, tackling 'Softly As In A Morning Sunrise' and 'Summertime' at a hurtling pace that sounds good in the ensembles but flags a little when he is soloing. The opening 'Demon Chase', dedicated to Teddy Edwards's son, is similarly hectic, but is good-natured enough. 'Brownie Speaks', included in homage to Clifford Brown, stretches him a little more convincingly, but by then the set is over. There is really only one ballad, and 'Willow Weep For Me' takes a slightly hysterical edge from Newborn's very tensed-up accompaniment.

The other delicious record of 1961 was the Contemporary classic with Teddy Edwards, *Together Again!*, which runs this one close, but there's a blitheness and sense of purpose to *Back In Town* that means it wins the day.

BILL EVANS&

Born 16 August 1929, Plainfield, New Jersey; died 15 September 1980, New York City
Piano

The Complete Village Vanguard Recordings 1961
Riverside 3RCD 1961-2 3CD
Evans; Scott LaFaro (b); Paul Motian (d). June 1961.

Composer and bassist Gavin Bryars says: **'There isn't a single gratuitous or fluffed note in his entire output. He is the most poetic and refined pianist in jazz, who swings prodigiously at the fastest tempo and in the slowest ballad – and no one plays a ballad better. His recordings with LaFaro and Motian represent a form of perfection in the piano trio format.'**

There may be a backlash in waiting, as once there was deep scepticism about Evans's cool, classically tinged approach to jazz, but it is unlikely to appear any time soon. For the moment, he is the most influential figure in piano jazz, his harmonically complex, lyrically intense playing a direct influence on two whole generations of piano-players, his iconic trios the model for slews of similarly configured contemporary groups. His first notable gig was with the Tony Scott group, in 1956, and his most important early liaison was with Miles Davis, with whom he recorded *Kind Of Blue*, even though he had been officially replaced in the Davis group. Thereafter he worked in a trio format for the rest of his life, although there are solo sessions, records with singers and a few with horns or orchestral arrangements. He was prolific in the studio and much taped in concert, and his records were widely disseminated and listened to by musicians, who absorbed his handling of modality and followed him out of the dead-end of bebop changes. Evans's personal difficulties were many, but may have been exaggerated to buttress the myth of isolated genius. Acute shyness did lead him to the shelter and motley of drugs, but he had wit and warmth, and one hears those qualities throughout his best recordings.

Best of the best is unquestionably the body of work recorded at the Village Vanguard in June 1961. He had been an active musician for a decade, after graduating from Southeastern Louisiana University and undergoing some sort of apprenticeship with Herbie Fields and then Tony Scott. Recordings of Evans as sideman have been reissued, showing him to be a comfortable bopper, though like his future boss Miles Davis, with his own delicate spin on what could be a brusque and even antagonistic form of jazz. When Evans began to record on his own account, with the 1956 record *New Jazz Conceptions*, it would have been hard to foresee the glories to come. By his own account, 'When I started out, I worked very simply, but I always knew what I was doing', a very typical Evans statement and a useful corrective to the romantic idea of him as a man out of control, a conduit for music rather than an active participant. There are, indeed, moments when he seems to be playing a state of grace, not least in the Village Vanguard sessions, but such epiphanies were the product of steady study and preparation. It's worth noting that 'Waltz For Debby', his single best-known composition, had been in his book for almost a decade before these definitive performances.

Evans always asked his bassists and drummers to commit to a minimum of three years with the group. Paul Motian had worked with him on the first record, but Evans had trouble finding good bassists. The recruitment of 23-year-old Scott LaFaro precipitated one of the finest piano trios ever documented. The bassist's melodic sensitivity and insinuating sound flowed between Evans and Motian like water and, while notions of group empathy have sometimes been exaggerated in discussion of this music – still very much directed by Evans himself – the playing of the three men is so sympathetic that it sets a standard which holds to this day. Both *Portrait In Jazz* and *Explorations*, also on OJC, have their small imperfections: there's an occasional brittleness in the latter, possibly a result of a quarrel between LaFaro and Evans just before the session, and the recording of both does less justice to LaFaro's tone. Yet the records culled from a day's work at the Village Vanguard are even finer. Evans's own playing is elevated by the immediacy of the occasion. His contributions seem all of a piece, lines spreading through and across the melodies and harmonies of the tune, pointing the way towards modality yet retaining the singing, rapturous qualities which the pianist heard in his material. All the Vanguard music is informed by an extra sense of discovery, as if the musicians were suddenly aware of what they were on to and were celebrating the achievement. They didn't have much time. LaFaro was killed in a car accident ten days later.

We have generally avoided completist sets and compilations in this edition, but there is nothing in this handsome box that one wouldn't wish to have. The first matinee set of 25 June 1961 begins with LaFaro's own 'Gloria's Step', briefly and simply introduced, but suddenly transfigured by the interplay between pianist and bassist over a delicate, inch-perfect snare accompaniment. LaFaro also contributes the luminous 'Jade Visions'. The original LP *Sunday At The Village Vanguard*, issued after the young genius's death, was so selected as to foreground the most prominent bass solos. Another reason for favouring the complete package is that it restores the democracy of a great group, but also the leadership and guiding spirit of its pianist. Greatest critical attention and respect has been paid to Evans's successive readings of 'Waltz For Debby' during the evening sets, but there are other high-points. The pianist's re-interpretation of Miles Davis's 'Solar' has scarcely been equalled. What one would not give to have heard the trumpeter record with this trio, as was once mooted. Evans's versions of 'My Man's Gone Now' and 'My Foolish Heart' – the latter exerted a particular influence on Gavin Bryars – are searching and profound, and packed with sly wit.

This is music which continues to provoke marvel and endless study. It is hard to imagine anyone in love with music not responding to it.

& *See also* **Conversations With Myself** (1963; p. 293)

STAN GETZ &
Born 2 February 1927, Philadelphia, Pennsylvania; died 6 June 1991, Malibu, California
Tenor saxophone

Focus
Verve 521419-2
Getz; orchestra led by Eddie Sauter. July–October 1961.

Stan Getz said (1983): **'I love that band! As it happened, my mother died, so I wasn't able to record when I was supposed to, except for one song. So I did it later, on headphones, and it worked out OK. More than OK, I think.'**

Nobody ever arranged for Getz as well as this, and Sauter's luminous and shimmering scores continue to bewitch. This isn't art-jazz scoring: Sauter had little of Gil Evans's *misterioso* power, and he was shameless about tugging at heartstrings. But within those parameters – and Getz, the most pragmatic of soloists, was only too happy to work within them – he made up the most emotive of frameworks. It doesn't make much sense as a suite, or a concerto; just as a series of episodes with the tenor gliding over and across them. In 'Her', the tune dedicated to Getz's mother, the soloist describes a pattern which is resolved in the most heartstopping of codas. This was surely Getz's finest hour. The latest version is in Verve's Master Edition series, though there's still a degree of tape hiss.

& See also **The Complete Roost Recordings** (1950–1954; p. 127), **Nobody Else But Me** (1964; p. 304)

RAHSAAN ROLAND KIRK &

Born Ronald T. Kirk, 7 August 1936, Columbus, Ohio; died 5 December 1977, Bloomington, Indiana
Tenor saxophone, manzello, stritch, flute, assorted instruments

We Free Kings
Mercury 826455
Kirk; Richard Wyands, Hank Jones (p); Art Davis, Wendell Marshall (b); Charli Persip (d). August 1961.

Saxophonist Ken Vandermark says: **'He found a way to intersect jazz with more populist and experimental forms, often simultaneously.'**

Kirk lost his sight as an infant, and learned music at a blind school. He learned to play three saxophones at once, and tinkered with hybrid instruments; he began recording under his own name at 20, and worked with Charles Mingus, but otherwise as a maverick soloist-leader, whose 'eccentricities' masked a profound musical learning and a technique that seemed to embrace every form of jazz from Dixieland to free, with few if any stops in between. Kirk's sheer musicianship remains to be rediscovered, at which point his name might start to be cited among the first rank of jazz saxophonists rather than as a side-show.

This is the first major Kirk record, and the opening 'Three For The Festival', a raucous blues, is already evidence for his greatness. Kirk's playing is all over the place. He appears out of nowhere and stops just where you least expect him to. On 'You Did It, You Did It', he creates rhythmic patterns which defeat even Persip and moves across the chords with a bizarre crabwise motion. 'My Delight' suggests that he is listening to John Coltrane's music. 'Blues For Alice' has him nail the Parker line not once, but twice, with the issue of an alternative take, quite different. The title-track is a wacky, but utterly logical version of the Christmas carol. The multi-instrumentalism is at this stage to a large degree subordinate to straightforward blowing, albeit in unfamiliar tonalities and timbres, but what one remembers about each of Kirk's solos is how logical it sounds and how complete.

& See also **The Inflated Tear** (1968; p. 351); **AL HIBBLER, A Meeting Of The Times** (1966, 1972; p. 394)

LEE KONITZ &

Born 12 October 1927, Chicago, Illinois
Alto and soprano saxophones

Motion
Verve V6 8399
Konitz; Sonny Dallas (b); Elvin Jones (d). August 1961.

Lee Konitz said (1989): **'Elvin Jones came in having worked with Coltrane the night before, in a situation with two tenors and two basses, but we just got right into it. There wasn't much discussion, just new takes when they were needed.'**

One of the great modern jazz records. Its unique chemistry is due in part to the unlikely pairing of the 'cool' Konitz with the hyperactive Jones, who was working with Coltrane at the time. The sessions were recorded pretty much straight down and some of the additional material was issued on a Verve triple set some years back; a 1990 reissue increased the track listing of the original LP to eight tunes. Nothing, though, matches the impact of the issued LP, which is now available again in digipack with original liner-notes. The trio starts off with 'Foolin' Myself', and Konitz's fleet, agile alto sound immediately gels with the surprisingly soft playing of Jones. 'You'd Be So Nice To Come Home To' is superb. Again, Konitz floats round the melody more than he disappears on the back of the chords. Dallas is firm-footed and precise. 'I'll Remember April' is another of the highlights but anyone who has the three-CD set will know that 'I Remember You' caused the trio some grief and had to be retaken. The release take is quite brilliant, flowing, seamless and harmonically subtle. The set ends with 'All Of Me', Konitz rippling through the theme and embellishing the structure from beginning to end.

& See also **Subconscious-Lee** (1949–1950; p. 118), **Star Eyes** (1983; p. 483)

YUSEF LATEEF

Born William Evans, 9 October 1920, Chattanooga, Tennessee
Tenor saxophone, flute, oboe, argol, other instruments

Eastern Sounds
Original Jazz Classics OJC 612
Lateef; Barry Harris (p); Ernie Farrow (b); Lex Humphries (d). September 1961.

Yusef Lateef said (1990): **'I dislike the word "jazz" and stopped using it many years ago. I think it debases a great art form. When you look at the associations of that word – blather, rubbish – you will understand what I mean. So I reject it.'**

Lateef adopted a Muslim name in response to his growing and eventually life-long infatuation with the musics of the Levant and Asia. One of the few convincing oboists in jazz, he has been somewhat marginalized in reputation as a 'speciality' act. Like Roland Kirk's, Lateef's music was cartooned when he came under Atlantic's wing, on albums that were enthusiastically promoted and received, but which rarely represented the best of his work. In recent years, he has concentrated somewhat on teaching, at which he charismatically excels, but he also runs his own YAL imprint and has been able to release the music that matters to him.

He worked with Dizzy Gillespie (an accelerated apprenticeship), Cannonball Adderley and Charles Mingus, but began making records of his own, for Savoy, around 1957. Like Kirk, the tenor saxophone is Lateef's natural horn, but in his best period he made jazz (or his own version of that despised term) whatever instrument he was playing. In approach, he is somewhat reminiscent of the pre-bop aspect of Sun Ra's long-time associate John Gilmore, working in a strong, extended swing idiom rather than with the more complex figurations of bebop. Just occasionally this spilled over into something schmaltzier. The *Eastern Sounds* session opens with 'The Plum Blossom', a feature for oboe and flute that immediately establishes that this will not be a conventional hard-bop date. It's built on an interesting scale and an Eastern mode but loops its way round to something like the blues, perhaps the very best one-track representation of Lateef's art. 'Blues For The Orient' confirms the direction, an extraordinary exercise in discipline for Harris, who holds the tune together at varying tempos and with minimal chordal movement. 'Don't Blame Me' is a powerful ballad that most listeners might find hard to place. Also included in the set is film music from *The Robe* and *Spartacus*, taken on flute and oboe respectively, that borders on kitsch, but the tenor-led 'Snafu' has a surging energy that leaves a very good band panting. One senses that Lateef wouldn't acknowledge this as his finest musical moment, but it remains a very good record.

BOBBY TIMMONS

Born 19 December 1935, Philadelphia, Pennsylvania; died 1 March 1974, New York City
Piano

In Person
Original Jazz Classics OJC 364
Timmons; Ron Carter (b); Albert 'Tootie' Heath (d). October 1961.

Drummer Jimmy Cobb said (1986): **'I recorded with Bobby on *This Here* [1960/1961] and I've said before, he reinvented the piano on that record, with all that high-rolling, gospel, blues stuff. He was a master of that.'**

'Dat Dere' and 'Moanin'' between them guarantee Timmons a bit of jazz immortality. He also gave Art Blakey a hit and probably helped secure the Messengers' long tenure of hard bop. Sadly, Timmons was prey to alcohol and self-doubt and his life was cut short before he was 40. His characteristic style was a rolling, gospelly funk, perhaps longer on sheer energy than on harmonic sophistication. The live *In Person* is surprisingly restrained, though Timmons takes 'Autumn Leaves' and 'Softly, As In A Morning Sunrise' at an unfamiliar tempo. Timmons's handling of more delicate material here is rather better than expected and there's a lovely countryish roll that's oddly prescient of what Keith Jarrett was doing. There are quite a number of recordings around, including *This Here* and *Moanin'*, titles which confirm what it was that made him famous and valued. He undervalued himself and there is an occasional throwaway element to his work, but he stands tall among the hard-bop pianists and composers.

BENNY CARTER &

Born 8 August 1907, New York City; died 12 July 2003, Los Angeles, California
Alto saxophone, trumpet, clarinet, voice

Further Definitions
Impulse! 051229-2
Carter; Bud Shank, Phil Woods (as); Buddy Collette, Teddy Edwards, Coleman Hawkins, Bill Perkins, Charlie Rouse (ts); Bill Hood (bs); John Collins, Barney Kessel, Mundell Lowe (g); Dick Katz (p); Ray Brown, Jimmy Garrison (b); Jo Jones, Alvin Stoller (d). November 1961–March 1966.

Saxophonist Bud Shank said (2000): **'I think Benny is just a superior-type person. You know, when [critic and pianist] Leonard Feather was dying, and already in a coma, maybe not hearing anything any more, Benny sat by his bedside every day and played his saxophone to him, right until the end. You don't get that kind of loyalty very often.'**

This is the best-known of all Carter's albums. Economics may have enjoined smaller ensembles, but Carter's feel for reed voicing is such that loss is turned to gain. The added profit is a spacious but intimate sound. Carter and Hawkins had recorded together in Paris before the war in exactly the same configuration as these sides: four saxophones, piano, bass, drums and guitar (Django Reinhardt!). Collins isn't quite up to that standard, but he has a sure and subtle touch. All the saxophones solo on 'Cotton Tail', with Benny leading off and Bean bringing things to a magisterial, slyly witty close. 'Crazy Rhythm' is an echo of the first meeting and both the senior men quote from each other's past solo. 'Blue Star' is intriguing: a complex, deceptive theme with another effective saxophone interchange. A later session (originally *Additions To Further Definitions*) came after a two-year film and TV hiatus in Carter's jazz activities. If the intention was to duplicate the sound and success of *Further Definitions*, it pretty much worked. Mundell Lowe and Barney Kessel are in a different league from Collins, and the guitar part has a prominence far beyond the earlier date. Shank and Edwards are both in strong, individual form, and Bill Perkins is splendid on a remake of 'Doozy'. Having the two dates together and in modern 20-bit sound is a huge plus; at more than 70 minutes, it's a good-value purchase.

& See also **Benny Carter 1933–1936** (1933–1936; p. 48)

MILT JACKSON &
Born 1 January 1923, Detroit, Michigan; died 9 October 1999, New York City
Vibraphone

Bags Meets Wes
Original Jazz Classics OJCCD 240
Jackson; Wynton Kelly (p); Wes Montgomery (g); Sam Jones (b); Philly Joe Jones (d). December 1961.

Percy Heath said (1990): **'Milt had this wonderful old gold-coloured Cadillac which we'd squeeze into on the way back from gigs. We called it the "Golden Dragon". It suited the man, in all sorts of ways.'**

Jackson was firmly ensconced in the Modern Jazz Quartet by this time, but occasional blowing dates were something he obviously enjoyed, and his association with Riverside led to some more challenging situations. This December 1961 date put together the two modern masters of their instruments in a setting that allowed them both free rein. That said, it's a more considered record than some of this period and nothing is allowed to go on too long. 'Stairway To The Stars' is presented as a miniature and it seems just right at that. The quintet locks into an irresistible groove on the uptempo themes and it's no surprise that the set-list is dominated by blues, with the opening 'S.K.J.' and 'Sam Sack' the most compelling of them. Bags would make plenty more records like this, including one with John Coltrane, but it stands out above the rest.

& See also **Wizard Of The Vibes** (1961; p. 118), **At The Kosei Nenkin** (1976; p. 432); **MODERN JAZZ QUARTET, Dedicated To Connie** (1960; p. 254), **The Complete Last Concert** (1974; p. 417)

IKE QUEBEC
Born 17 August 1918, Newark, New Jersey; died 16 January 1963, New York City
Tenor saxophone

It Might As Well Be Spring
Blue Note 21736
Quebec; Freddie Roach (org); Milt Hinton (b); Al Harewood (d). December 1961.

Saxophonist Johnny Griffin said (1989): **'When Ike died, they closed all the clubs for the night, and I think just about everyone who was there followed his coffin.'**

Blue Note's last recording date in Hackensack and first in its new headquarters at Engle-wood Cliffs were both by Ike Quebec. The saxophonist – it's pronounced 'queue-beck' – was a figure of considerable influence at the label, acting as musical director, A&R man and talent scout (Dexter Gordon was one of his 'finds'). He was also an important Blue Note recording artist, making some marvellous sessions just after the war and steering the label in the direction of a more contemporary repertoire. He began his career as a dancer. He developed a tenor style influenced by Basie's Herschel Evans. Before he succumbed to lung cancer at just 45 he put his creative thumbprint on many of Blue Note's most distinctive bop recordings.

It Might As Well Be Spring is pretty squarely in the tenor/organ tradition, except that Quebec has opted to record some gently expressive standards, not just the title-track but also 'Lover Man', 'Ol' Man River' and 'Willow Weep For Me', as well as his own composi-tions 'A Light Reprieve' and 'Easy – Don't Hurt'. Digital remastering has restored a bit of detail to the sound, and Roach is the one who benefits most, a surprisingly subtle player who always has plenty to say and doesn't sound as if he's merely stoking up a fairground calliope. Quebec has several times teetered on the brink of major rediscovery. He is, admit-tedly, a limited performer when set beside Gordon or any of the other younger tenor-players emerging at the time, but he has a beautiful, sinuous tone and an innate melodic sense, negotiating standards with a simplicity and lack of arrogance that are refreshing and even therapeutic.

ACKER BILK
Born Bernard Stanley Bilk, 28 January 1929, Pensford, Somerset, England
Clarinet

Stranger On The Shore / A Taste Of Honey
Redial 546458
Bilk; strings, choir, Leon Young (dir).1961–1965.

Acker Bilk says (often): **'"Stranger On The Shore"? That's my old-age pension, that is!'**

The Three Bs, Barber, Ball and Bilk, were the heirs to Ken Colyer's trad revolution. If Barber 'prettified' the Colyer style, Bilk brought an element of showmanship and humour, parading his Paramount band in Edwardian waistcoats and bowlers and scoring hits with 'Summer Set' (which also referred to his unreconstructed West Country accent) and 'Stranger On The Shore'. Denis Preston wanted Bilk to record with strings; the clarinettist reworked a theme originally written for his daughter, recorded it with the Leon Young String Chorale and saw it picked up as theme music to a television drama. It sold two million copies, a success that led to envious disdain of a musician whose early work under Colyer had been a raw-edged George Lewis style very different from the silky, evocative murmur he cultivated in later years.

Though Acker became a television favourite and a staple of Sunday morning radio request programmes, his impeccable jazz credentials kept him credible with a live audi-ence. Besides, only a musician of consummate artistry could play something like 'Stranger On The Shore' and not make it sound saccharine; the same, even more obviously, goes for 'A Taste Of Honey'.

'Serious' jazz fans sneered at the fancy vests and 'derbies' and at trumpeter Kenny Ball's moptop chirpiness in front of the cameras, but between them they kept jazz in the public eye all through the Beatles era. Anyone who saw either group in the flesh quickly recognized that the TV personas were simply a matter of rendering unto Caesar. We make no apology for the selection, or for favouring a crossover hit over some of the tougher Bilk material reis-sued by Lake. If you aren't strangely moved by these, check for a pulse.

GRANT GREEN
Born 6 June 1931, St Louis, Missouri; died 31 January 1979, New York City
Guitar

Born To Be Blue
Blue Note 84432
Green; Ike Quebec (ts); Sonny Clark (p); Sam Jones (b); Louis Hayes (d). December 1961, March 1962.

Drummer Elvin Jones said (1990): **'Someone asked me one time – some European journalist who was trying to be nice – asked if there was anyone, ever, who'd swung harder than me. I pretended to think for a moment and then I said: "Grant Green!" Guy hadn't even heard of him!'**

Green spent much of his career in the shadow of Wes Montgomery, but though he was less subtle harmonically, he had the ability to drive a melody-line and shape a solo as if telling a quietly urgent story. He also swung mightily and his long run of records for Blue Note is always approachable. We've always liked *Born To Be Blue* best of all, along with the splendid *Idle Moments* and *Street Of Dreams*. Quebec, who was Blue Note MD at the time, is still not widely admired, but he's on cracking form, and his pitch and phrasing on 'Someday My Prince Will Come' should be a lesson to all young jazz players. Green has, for us, his finest hour, rippling through 'My One And Only Love' and 'If I Should Love You' with a ruggedness of emotion that goes hand in hand with the simplicity of diction. Not a note is wasted. 'Count Every Star' actually comes from an earlier session, but it too is judged to perfection, toned down just as it threatens to get schmaltzy. Sonny Clark, another Blue Note artist still being reassessed, is also in sparkling form, with just enough light and shade to temper his colleagues' bluff romanticism. It's a hefty body of work, illuminated throughout by Green's infectiously driven beat, but along with a lot of Blue Note repertory acts, he never coasted and never repeated himself.

AL GREY
Born 6 June 1925, Aldie, Virginia; died 24 May 2000, Phoenix, Arizona
Trombone

Snap Your Fingers
Verve 0602498603079
Grey; David Burns, Donald Byrd (t); Billy Mitchell (ts); Floyd Morris, Herbie Hancock (p); Bobby Hutcherson (vib); Herman Wright (b); Eddie Williams (d). January–February 1962.

Al Grey said (1981): **'This guy was bugging me about jazz musicians being stupid and illiterate, so I puffed myself up and told him that I was the author of a book, called *Plunger Techniques*. He looked hard at me. "You're in sanitation? I thought you said you were a musician."'**

Grey will always be remembered as a Basie sideman, even though he spent more years away from the Count's band. His humorous, fierce style of improvising is more in the tradition of such colleagues as saxophonist Lockjaw Davis than in the more restrained trombone lineage, though he did rather assume Vic Dickenson's mantle as the great trombone individualist, and he was especially accomplished with the plunger mute, though perhaps too often for comfort with comic intentions.

This brings back a little-known Argo album made just after he left Basie. The first five tracks are a studio sextet date, tightly arranged around gospel and blues themes; the next three are from a live date at Birdland, where Byrd and Hancock came in for Burns and Morris, although neither is featured much. The surprise presence here is Hutcherson, in a very early appearance, who gets quite a bit of space. There's a nice atmospheric 'On Green Dolphin Street' but the CD saves the best for last with a long romp through Randy Weston's 'Hi-Fly'. Grey's solos are in a rather more modern line than his Basie work would have suggested. It's not a great record, but it's more than a satisfying time-waster, and it grows with familiarity.

JUNIOR MANCE
Born Julian Clifford Mance Jr, 10 October 1928, Evanston, Illinois
Piano, harpsichord

Junior's Blues
Original Jazz Classics OJCCD 1000
Mance; Bob Cranshaw (b); Mickey Roker (d). February 1962.

Junior Mance said (1991): **'Playing in Dizzy's group was a lot of fun, but you also learned. It was the right kind of schooling, where you don't know you're at school. You just take it in.'**

Junior Mance has been playing professionally for almost 60 years. His first lessons with Julian Mance Sr and his grounding in blues, stride and boogie woogie have stood him in good stead ever since. He did club work in Chicago, toured with Dinah Washington and with Cannonball Adderley, and spent some important time with Dizzy Gillespie. Unmistakable from a random sample of half a dozen bars as a Chicago man, Mance can sometimes be maddeningly predictable, resorting to exactly the figure one expects him to play, though that's relatively rare and stands out as a dead spot in an otherwise remarkable performance.

Recorded on Valentine's Day 1962, *Junior's Blues* is a love letter to jazz itself, as direct and uncomplicated a declaration as you'll find in the whole history of the music. Junior covers themes by Monk (with a few embellishments of his own), Ellington ('Creole Love Call') and the Jay McShann/Charlie Parker swinger 'The Jumpin' Blues'. He kicks off with his own 'Down The Line', which is as orthodox and full-hearted a 12-bar as you'll ever hear. The slightly later *Happy Time*, with Ron Carter in for Cranshaw, is almost as good.

PERRY ROBINSON
Born 17 September 1938, New York City
Clarinet

Funk Dumpling
Savoy Jazz 255
Robinson; Kenny Barron (p); Henry Grimes (b); Paul Motian (d). 1962.

Perry Robinson said (1996): **'What I tried to do back then was get a bebop sound, a saxophonic sound, on clarinet; not swing clarinet like Buddy DeFranco still did but something new, an evolution.'**

It is difficult to judge now whether the clarinet fell into disuse during the bop era because clarinettists found it difficult to play with the speed and power required for the new medium or whether the clarinet was merely so associated with swing that it seemed an anachronism, however it was played. Perry Robinson is what was once an almost absurd rarity, a modernistic – even avant-garde – jazz clarinet-player. His has been a strikingly varied career, working with Gunter Hampel and Dave Brubeck, but this first record, something of a rarity and still not much known even to modern-jazz fans, established Robinson, and with him Henry Grimes, as one of the most innovative new player/composers in New York. The pity is that the cue wasn't taken up and Robinson's subsequent discography remains just as marginal.

It looks like a supergroup, but largely in retrospect. Motian had been playing with Bill Evans, Barron was on one of his very first recordings, while Robinson and Grimes (who'd worked with Sonny Rollins) were helping each other find a way into the new music. Compositions are divided equally between the two friends, apart from the brazenly lovely opening version of 'Moon Over Moscow'. Grimes's tunes – 'Sprites Delight', 'Farmer Alfalfa' and the title-tune – seem rooted in song and dance forms, even when the armatures of those forms have been taken away. Robinson is more obviously free-form in conception, but interestingly his compositions, and particularly 'Margareta', the single best track, have a centripetal quality; they may seem harmonically chaotic, or at best unconventional, but he pulls them together in the middle, so that each one has a memorable structure; one of us could even whistle parts of 'Wahayla', not having heard it for years. A time-capsule record, to be sure, but one that fully merits inclusion here.

BABS GONZALES
Born Lee Brown, 27 October 1919, Newark, New Jersey; died 23 January 1980, Newark, New Jersey
Voice

Sunday Afternoon At Small's Paradise
Dauntless DC 6005
Gonzales; Clark Terry (t, flhn); Johnny Griffin (ts); Horace Parlan (p); Buddy Catlett (b); Ben Riley (d). 1962.

Organist Jimmy Smith said (1989): **'He'd come in with this cape round his shoulders like Batman or Superman or some shit like that. Cat went round telling everyone he had discovered me and that he was my manager. Well, no mother****er discovered me. I discovered myself, so I had to put him down. Alfred Lion [of Blue Note records] thought I'd near to killed him.'**

'Larger than life' doesn't begin to express Babs Gonzales's personality, but its outsize nature has probably eclipsed his fine musicianship. Irrepressibly hip and a fine musician, the man from Newark was among the first to give bebop a vocal dimension. His colourful autobiographies made him a cult figure.

Corny as some of his work doubtless now seems, what Babs did was colonize the rapid transitions and complex harmonies of bebop for singers. The sessions are variable in quality, but there are some delightful cuts and some intriguing experiments as well. The early work with Three Bips And A Bop is probably among the best. 'Oop-Pop-A-Da' and 'Professor Bop' are both good representations of Babs's vocalese. 'Weird Lullaby' was another of his hits and became a kind of signature tune after its Capitol release.

The material from Small's includes such delightful hokum as 'Bebop Santa Claus' and the non-PC 'Keep An Ugly Woman', but it also reunites him with Griffin, who made his debut with Babs. 'Le Moody Mood Pour Amour' is a nod to James Moody's part in the development of vocalese, but on this showing Babs is still a shade ahead of the better attested King Pleasure and Eddie Jefferson, and still pushing vocalese forward after its faddish quality had faded. The group is absolutely terrific, but it's clear that this isn't just a novelty act with accompaniment but a firmly musical band. Even 'Round About Midnight' finds something new to say.

JIMMY GIUFFRE&

Born 26 April 1921, Dallas, Texas; died 24 April 2008, Pittsfield, Massachusetts
Clarinet, tenor and soprano saxophones, flute, bass flute

Free Fall
Columbia CK 65446
Giuffre; Paul Bley (p); Steve Swallow (b). 1962.

Steve Swallow remembers: **'*Free Fall* was the last, and I think the best, of the albums this trio made until it reconvened in the '90s. It was recorded without fuss or fanfare (and, happily, without headphones as well) in the beautiful-sounding church Columbia used as its "classical" studio in those days. Jimmy clowned around a lot that day, maybe to dispel tension. His wife Juanita sat calmly in the room with us as we worked, dispensing vodka. The trio disbanded shortly after, for lack of gainful employment.'**

Giuffre's drummerless trios and cool, almost abstract tonality created nearly as much controversy as Gerry Mulligan's pianoless groups and probably with more reason. Nothing that had come along before quite prepares us for the astonishing work that Giuffre created with Paul Bley and Steve Swallow in two 1961 albums called *Fusion* (a term which hadn't yet taken on its '70s associations) and *Thesis*. Paired and remastered as *1961*, they were ECM's first-ever reissue, still sounding 'modern' after 40 years. Herb Snitzer's session photographs are in deeply shadowed black-and-white. It's arguable that Giuffre's playing is equally monochrome and its basic orientation uncomfortably abstract; but it's also often driven by an urgent swing. *Fusion* is perhaps the more daring of the two sets, balancing starkly simple ideas, as on 'Jesus Maria' and 'Scootin' About', with some complex harmonic conceptions. *Thesis* is tighter and more fully realized, and tunes like 'Ictus' and 'Carla' have been an inexhaustible element of the pianist's concert improvisations ever since. There is some live material from Stuttgart and Bremen, released on hatOLOGY as *Emphasis & Flight*.

Free Fall is a trickier and more insidious sound altogether. A mixture of Giuffre solos with duos and trios, it catches the group late on in its brief initial history. (They reconvened in the '80s.) Remarkable to think of Columbia taking on a project like this in 1962, but, whatever the exact intention of the title, it was clear that the studiousness and philosophical calm which overlaid the previous discs was no longer to be expected. What you're hearing is something that has almost run its course in practical terms but which creatively is far from exhausted. Swallow's fiery scrabbles and sharply plucked single-note runs lend the music a new momentum and the sort of energy to be found in free jazz. Bley may be the least comfortable of the three by this stage, but he has always been a restless experimenter and by 1962 his eye was probably on the next step. Giuffre often sounds as if he is in a world of his own, intensely focused, totally aware, but communicating ideas for which there was no ready-made language or critical rhetoric.

& *See also* **The Jimmy Giuffre 3** (1956; p. 197)

DIZZY REECE

Born Alphonso Son Reece, 5 January 1931, Kingston, Jamaica
Trumpet

Asia Minor
Original Jazz Classics OJC 1806
Reece; Joe Farrell (ts, f); Cecil Payne (bs); Hank Jones (p); Ron Carter (b); Charli Persip (d). March 1962.

Dizzy Reece said (1985): '**I spent a bit of time in North Africa and Asia Minor. I used to think I'd had a previous life there! Because some of those sounds were surfacing in me, even before I visited the places.**'

In 1949, Reece moved his base of operations to Europe and from 1954 to the end of the decade was established in London, where he made a number of fine but not yet distinguished recordings on which he tended to be upstaged by Tubby Hayes and Victor Feldman. Some of these have now been revived on Jasmine and are worth having. Reece started recording for Blue Note while still living in England. The best of these are his first record for the label, *Blues In Trinity*, and the subsequent *Soundin' Off.*

His most successful record of all, though, was made for New Jazz (now an OJC) and its quality is given added lustre by being his last session as leader until 1970, after which his studio appearances tailed off further. Reece was (is) a man of considerable integrity, to the point of stubbornness. Unswayed by fashion or ideology, he insisted on playing as he pleased rather than following anyone else's lead. On *Asia Minor* that was still a virtue, but it's a record that is already suffused with a certain indefinable sadness, as if autumn is coming on. Given that Reece was only 31, it was a prematurely elegiac stance but it certainly isn't the result of backward projection. It's a genuine quality of the music.

'Yamask' and 'Ackmet' reflect an interest in African and Levantine music, and while they're not particularly advanced lines they do anticipate what some more heralded Blue Note stars were doing with greater fanfare a few years later. 'The Shadow Of Khan' is similarly conceived. Payne contributes a line dedicated to Charlie Parker, and there are a couple of standards, including one of the more unusual 'Summertime' readings of that period. The marvellous band is a trump card. Farrell was just beginning to explore the kind of quartal harmony that became a calling card in an all too brief career. Payne gives the sound a lot of weight (and it often sounds like a larger outfit), but it's Dizzy's clarion delivery and simply, unaffected approach to the harmony that make it memorable, a clear case of less is more. There was a longish silence after *Asia Minor*, and we continue to wait for some fresh wisdom from a dedicated practitioner who's been unjustly neglected in recent years.

WALT DICKERSON
Born 1931, Philadelphia, Pennsylvania; died 15 May 2008, Philadelphia, Pennsylvania
Vibraphone

To My Queen
Original Jazz Classics OJCCD 1880
Dickerson; Andrew Hill (p); George Tucker (b); Andrew Cyrille (d). September 1962.

Walt Dickerson said (1995): '**To express her, my queen, and her many, many sides, I could only go through the dimension of music: her mind, her beauty, her ineffable joy and sadness. When I return to that music, I reassert our marriage.**'

A deep thinker who managed to skirt the inherent prettiness of the vibes, Dickerson has never enjoyed the kind of critical praise heaped on Bobby Hutcherson's head. Dickerson can't claim quite the same level of innovation on the instrument, but his spare, rapt style, with something of Milt Jackson's piano-based approach, is utterly distinctive and in 'To My Queen', he has one of the most beautiful of modern jazz compositions.

Written for his wife Elizabeth, it has a palpable gentleness and grace, and the group plays with exquisite control, just a few swelling rolls from Cyrille here and there, as if to express the tides of passing time. Tucker is to some extent the heart of it all, a steady, unflustered beat. He comes back again strongly on side two of the original LP with a won-derful vibes/bass duet on 'God Bless The Child'. There's also a more conventionally jazzier interpretation of 'How Deep Is The Ocean?', which sparks one of Dickerson's best extended statements, wrapping each fresh new idea round the core of the song. It is a brief record, not much more than half an hour in length, but we wouldn't change a note and even a welcome extra track or two might disturb its balance.

SHEILA JORDAN
Born Sheila Jeanette Dawson, 8 November 1928, Detroit, Michigan
Voice

Portrait Of Sheila
Blue Note 789902-2
Jordan; Barry Galbraith (g); Steve Swallow (b); Denzil Best (d). September & October 1962.

Sheila Jordan says: **'It was a great honour to record for the original Blue Note owners. George Russell had paid to have a demo tape made and Blue Note picked it up. Alfred [Lion]'s lovely wife Ruth also recommended me to Alfred. So between them I got my first record date on a respected label, and only the first or second singer they had ever recorded. Alfred and Francis [Wolff] believed in me, and I'll be forever grateful for that.'**

Jordan was turned on to modern jazz by hearing Charlie Parker – a moment she still recounts with great feeling – and began singing vocalese to Bird solos. She studied with Lennie Tristano and was married to Duke Jordan for a decade. In recent years, she has become, in no way by default, the senior female jazz singer, with a range embracing scat, ballads and art song. Arguably the Muse albums of the '80s mark the high-point of her craft but there's something wonderfully fresh and alert about *Portrait Of Sheila*, a quality heard in the strange and beautiful version of 'You Are My Sunshine' she made for George Russell.

She shows much of Duke Jordan's concentration on the melodic progress of a song. Like the truly great instrumentalists, she is content to explore the potential of the middle regis-ter, where words are more likely to remain intact, rather than over-reach her range. At the end of phrases, she deploys a superbly controlled vibrato. On *Portrait*, she ranges between the rapid 'Let's Face The Music And Dance', which anticipates the surrealism of her contri-butions to Roswell Rudd's remarkable *Flexible Flyer*, and the fragile beauty of 'I'm A Fool To Want You' and 'When The World Was Young', with its extraordinary, ambiguous ending. Bobby Timmons's 'Dat Dere' is given just to voice and bass (and Swallow is superb), and 'Who Can I Turn To?' to voice and guitar, while 'Hum Drum Blues' and 'Baltimore Oriole' are set against rhythm only, as if she were a horn.

KENNY BURRELL
Born 31 July 1931, Detroit, Michigan
Guitar

Bluesy Burrell
Original Jazz Classics OJCCD 926
Burrell; Leo Wright (as); Coleman Hawkins (ts); Tommy Flanagan, Gildo Mahones (p); Major Holley, George Tucker (b); Eddie Locke, Jimmie Smith (d); Ray Barretto (perc). September 1962–August 1963.

Kenny Burrell said (1988): **'I was playing a lot of pop sessions at that time, a *lot* of sessions. It was too artificial for me. I'd done those Prestige records, which were basically jam sessions, and recorded for Alfred Lion at Blue Note, where everything** was rehearsed carefully. That was what I liked: something in the middle, professional but not too contrived. Jazz, basically.'

An enduring light in modern jazz, Burrell has a seemingly inexhaustible supply of licks and a tone as lulling as Joe Pass's, though without Joe's rococo extravagances. The career is very much of a piece, the early dates as securely formed as the later ones, and he seems to fit seamlessly into any context. In the '50s he was popular on blowing dates and the early work for Prestige is mostly in that mould. He's apt to be cast by modern jazz fans as a spear-carrier in John Coltrane's restless drama, fronting *The Cats*, which some Trane disciples see as the saxophonist's first glimmer of greatness, but it was in the company of another, perhaps greater still horn eminence that Burrell made his best record.

Inevitably, the tracks on *Bluesy Burrell* with Hawkins have an imperious quality that nothing else on the set can quite match. But, working with his regular group of Flanagan, Holley and Locke (who sound almost as urbanely professional as a firm of lawyers), Burrell himself is at his most seductive on 'I Thought About You' and his most suavely blue on 'Montono Blues'. Playing with a very light touch and on some tracks with a nylon-strung guitar for extra delicacy of sound, he has to be recorded well, and there are no problems with that. The record was originally put out on Moodsville, a Prestige imprint that ostensibly traded in mood music; rarely of this quality, though. The record kicks off with 'Tres Palabras', a classic performance, given extra weight by Flanagan's economical solo, though it's the great tenorman who carries all before him. There's an extra track, nominally led by Gilda Mahones, which makes up the weight and offers a nice glimpse of the sturdy Leo Wright, sounding like no one but himself. It's maybe Burrell's fate to be remembered for all the people he worked with, but it's fair to say that he is still in the game, still not shouting from stage centre but always playing with impeccable grace and always for the group. There are less worthy avocations than that.

CECIL TAYLOR &

Born 15 March 1929 (some sources state 25 March and 1930), Long Island, New York
Piano, voice

Nefertiti, The Beautiful One Has Come
Revenant 202 2CD
Taylor; Jimmy Lyons (as); Sunny Murray (d). November 1962.

Cecil Taylor said (1983): 'It was singers, Ella Fitzgerald first, then Billie Holiday, who moved me first. When Billie sang, her body was always inside the rhythm of the song, the Nile queen. Rhythm starts in the body and the space it inhabits, so yes, the piano is a part of me, and the space around it, too.'

It took a long time for these recordings to appear on CD, and many newcomers to the music may wonder why they caused such fascination. The drawbacks are numerous: the original recording was never very effective; Taylor seems to be playing one of the poorest pianos Copenhagen had to offer; Murray's drums sound thin and rattly a lot of the time. Nevertheless, these sessions from the Café Montmartre should be accounted among the greatest live recordings in jazz. Taylor is still working his way out of jazz tradition and, with Murray at his heels, the playing has an irresistible momentum that creates its own kind of rocking swing, the pulse indefinable but palpable, the rhythm moving in waves from the drummer's kit. Lyons shapes his bebopper's vocabulary into gritty flurries of notes, a man caught in a squall and fighting his way through it and over it. He would become Taylor's most dedicated interpretative colleague, but here he is sharing in the discovery of a fierce new world. Melody has a part to play: the two versions of 'Lena' measure out a beleaguered lyricism, for instance. Group interaction is a matter, sometimes, of clinging tight and hanging on, but this was a trio that had already done a lot of work together, and in the multiple layers of the monumental 'D Trad, That's What' and 'Call' the musicians seem to touch on an inner calm to go with the outward intensity. The Revenant release runs to two discs and includes some previously unheard extra material (admittedly in even more terrible sound!).

& *See also* **Jazz Advance** (1956; p. 191), **Conquistador!** (1966; p. 339), **Celebrated Blazons** (1990; p. 541)

OSCAR PETERSON *&*
Born 15 August 1925, Montreal, Quebec, Canada; died 23 December 2007, Mississauga, Ontario, Canada
Piano, organ, other keyboards

Night Train
Verve 521440-2
Peterson; Ray Brown (b); Ed Thigpen (d). December 1962.

Norman Granz said (1982): **'Oscar's father was a big influence on him, as a man if not musically, and I think that record has a special place in his heart. He sat for a long time staring at the cover, quite wistfully, when he first saw it.'**

After 30 years, *Night Train* is well established as a hardy perennial and is certainly Peterson's best-known record. Dedicated to his father, who was a sleeping-car attendant on Canadian Pacific Railways, it isn't the dark and moody suite of nocturnal blues many listeners expect but a lively and varied programme of material covering 'C-Jam Blues', 'Georgia On My Mind', 'Bags' Groove', 'Honey Dripper', 'Things Ain't What They Used To Be', 'Band Call', 'Hymn To Freedom' and a couple of others. Though by no means a 'concept album', it's one of the best-constructed long-players of the period and its durability is testimony to that as much as to the quality of Peterson's playing, which is tight and uncharacteristically emotional. The beautifully remastered reissue has six extra tracks, including a fascinating rehearsal take of 'Moten Swing' and an alternative of 'Night Train', which is called 'Happy Go Lucky Local'.

& *See also* **At The Stratford Shakespearean Festival** (1956; p. 193), **My Favorite Instrument** (1968; p. 351), **The Legendary Live At The Blue Note** (1990; p. 539)

MONGO SANTAMARIA
Born Ramón Santamaria, 7 April 1922, Havana, Cuba; died 1 February 2003, Miami, Florida
Percussion

Watermelon Man
Milestone MCD 47075
Santamaria; Marty Sheller (t); Mauricio Smith (f); Bobby Capers, Pat Patrick (f, sax); Jose Chombo Silva (ts); Rodgers Grand (p); Felix Pupi Legarreta (vn); Victor Venegas (b); Frank Hernandez, Ray Lucas (d); Willie Bobo, Joseph Gorgas, Kako (perc); Rudy Calzado, La Lupe, Osvaldo 'Chihuahua' Martinez (v). December 1962, September 1963.

Mongo Santamaria said (1982): **'There was jazz in Cuba, of course, always a jazz band at the Tropicana Club in Havana, but when I went to New York in 1950, there was a lot of Cuban music there already, and Dizzy Gillespie, he was in the middle, with "Tin Tin Deo", "Manteca", "Cubana Be [Cubana] Bop", so I felt that I came to the right place.'**

Born in a poor quarter of Havana, Santamaria moved to the USA in 1950, originally to work with Cal Tjader, and became a hugely influential force in hybridizing the rhythms of Latin American music with jazz. In his own groups he adapted the *charanga* line-up to accommodate saxophones and brasses. His composition 'Afro Blue', still occasionally credited in error to John Coltrane, is a modern classic.

By the first years of the '60s, Santamaria was working in what was identifiably a jazz idiom, with strong Latin inflexions, rather than the other way round. Herbie Hancock's 'Watermelon Man', played very much in the spirit of the original but rhythmically much looser and more elaborate, delivered the percussionist his first major hit. From this point on, his reputation was firmly established. The horn voicings are very jazz-orientated and the track lengths were carefully tailored to radio and jukebox requirements. It would be good to hear longer versions of almost all of these tunes, not least the Cannonball Adderley–Joe Zawinul collaboration 'Cut That Cane'. The reissue includes six previously unissued tracks from a live Californian set recorded in 1962. These don't add much to a record that is already classic Santamaria.

CHARLES MINGUS &

Born 22 April 1922, Nogales, Arizona; died 5 January 1979, Cuernavaca, Mexico
Double bass, piano

The Black Saint And The Sinner Lady

Impulse! 051174-2
Mingus; Rolf Ericson, Richard Williams (t); Quentin Jackson, Don Butterfield (tba); Jerome Richardson (as, bs, f); Booker Ervin (ts); Dick Hafer (ts, f); Charlie Mariano (as); Jaki Byard (p); Dannie Richmond (d). January 1963.

Sue Mingus says: **'In some fashion, Charles absorbed Bob Hammer's rehearsal band for a six-week gig he had at the Village Vanguard in 1963, which provided a unique opportunity to work out, night after night, on one of his greatest compositions, *The Black Saint And The Sinner Lady*. During that six-week period, the piece grew and developed and changed and took on the colours and musical personalities of the musicians in the band as evidenced in the recording. Musicologist Andrew Homzy has noted how entirely different the original written score is compared to the actual recording, typical of Mingus's incorporation of ideas and sounds of his band members as the music developed.'**

Almost everything about *Black Saint* is distinctive: the long form, the use of dubbing, the liner-note by Mingus's psychiatrist. On its release, Impulse! altered its usual slogan, 'The new wave of jazz is on Impulse!', to read 'folk', in line with Mingus's decision to call the group the Charles Mingus New Folk Band. Ellingtonian in ambition and scope, and in the disposition of horns, the piece has a majestic, dancing presence, and Charlie Mariano's alto solos and overdubs on 'Mode D/E/F' are unbelievably intense. There is evidence that Mingus's desire to make a single continuous performance (and it should be remembered that even Ellington's large-scale compositions were relatively brief) failed to meet favour with label executives; but there is an underlying logic even to the separate tracks which makes it difficult to separate them other than for the convenience of track listing. It remains one of the most significant jazz performances of that decade and one of the greatest jazz records of all time, a splendid artefact that doesn't fail to reveal the circumstances of its creation, a kind of meta-text of modern improvisation.

& *See also* **The Complete Debut Recordings** (1951–1957; p. 131), **Pithecanthropus Erectus** (1956; p. 175), **Mingus Dynasty** (1959; p. 247), **Charles Mingus Presents Charles Mingus** (1960; p. 259)

JIMMY RUSHING

Born 26 August 1909, Oklahoma City, Oklahoma; died 8 June 1972, New York City
Voice

Five Feet Of Soul

Roulette 81830-2

Rushing; Ernie Glow, Markie Markowitz, Joe Newman, Snooky Young (t); Billy Byers, Jimmy Cleveland, Willie Dennis, Urbie Green (tb); Gene Quill, Phil Woods (as); Budd Johnson, Zoot Sims (ts); Sol Schlinger (bs); Patti Bown (p); Freddie Green (g); Milt Hinton (b); Gus Johnson (d). January 1963.

Saxophonist Buddy Tate said (1991): **'Jimmy used to say that the blues was nothing but church chords, just that two- or three-part harmony, and if you added anything, it was broke.'**

Raised in Oklahoma, Rushing started as a pianist, but began around the South-West in the mid-'20s. His greatest successes were with the Basie orchestra of the '30s and '40s, his huge physical presence partnering the great voice. A gentle and genial man, he worked right up until his death from leukaemia. Inevitably, Rushing's own-name records tend to pall a little compared to his work for Basie, and some of the later things were misconceived, but the voice never faltered.

Five Feet Of Soul was the singer's only session for Roulette (although it was actually issued on Colpix), and really isn't much more than a studio quickie – Al Cohn arrangements for a band full of session-rats, and tunes that Jimmy must have known backwards by 1963. Al copies the Count for the feel and sound, and the likes of Snooky Young and Zoot Sims throw off the righteous obbligatos. He's in hearty voice, though occasionally it gets away from him: he starts 'Trouble In Mind' mightily, but by the end the troubles seem to be getting to the tonsils. Some of them are faster than he'd like – 'Oooh! Look-A-There' is rattled off in a couple of minutes, and you start wondering how much better it might have sounded recast as a slow blues. He saves some of his best for his own lyrics, and 'Please Come Back' and 'Did You Ever' work out just fine.

SHIRLEY SCOTT

Born 14 March 1934, Philadelphia, Pennsylvania; died 10 March 2002, Philadelphia, Pennsylvania
Organ

Soul Shoutin'

Prestige PRCD 24142-2

Scott; Stanley Turrentine (ts); Major Holley, Earl May (b); Grassella Oliphant (d). January–October 1963.

Bill Cosby said (1994): **'Shirley is a soul sister, with a righteous groove and she plays with a smile on her face. Puts a smile on every other face, too.'**

Shirley Scott was used to heavy company. In 1955, in her native Philadelphia, she was working in a trio with John Coltrane. She originally studied trumpet and piano, then began working with Lockjaw Davis and switched to organ. She formed her own trio in 1960, often working with husband Stanley Turrentine. Wider recognition led to dozens of albums for Prestige, Impulse!, Atlantic and Cadet through the '70s. She remained visible in the '90s on TV with Bill Cosby, when she was still playing organ and piano.

Scott wasn't a knockabout swinger like Jimmy Smith and didn't have the bebop attack of Don Patterson, but there's an authority and an unusual sense of power in reserve which keep her music simmering somewhere near the boil. She is a strong blues player and a fine accompanist, and her right-hand lines have a percussive feel that utilizes space more than most organ-players ever did.

Of the albums made with her spouse, *Soul Shoutin'* is probably the best bet for anyone who doesn't want to get into the main run of Scott albums. It brings together the contents of the original albums *The Soul Is Willing* and *Soul Shoutin'*. The title-track off *The Soul Is Willing* is the near-perfect example of what this combination could do, a fuming Turrentine solo followed by a deftly swinging one by Scott. Though Shirley was a fine player of the bass pedals, there are bass-players on the record, which perhaps dulls one of her strengths, but it's a minor quibble.

BILL EVANS &
Born 16 August 1929, Plainfield, New Jersey; died 15 September 1980, New York City
Piano

Conversations With Myself
Verve 521409-2
Evans (p solo). January–February 1963.

Music promoter Jack Bradley used to know Evans when he lodged with his mother on tour: **'I think Bill was the loneliest man I ever met.'**

One might very reasonably ask why in a survey of the very best jazz from 1917 to the present, and given the overdetermining presence of Bill Evans in contemporary piano literature, he has only been accorded two entries when McCoy Tyner, say, has been given three. The answer is both simple and not so simple. For a start, Evans made such a substantial contribution to Miles Davis's *Kind Of Blue* that he must be considered its other begetter. More argumentatively, it is our assertion that while Evans's astonishing achievement has been widely acknowledged, Tyner's is less securely understood.

Even at this point, though, some might question why we would choose an entire album of three-way piano overdubs, something only Lennie Tristano had previously tried. *Conversations* has aroused fierce views both for and against, but in an age where overdubbing is more or less the norm in record-making, its musicality is more important. Carefully graded, each line sifted against the others, it's occasionally too studied, and the follow-up *Further Conversations With Myself* (also released together as *Art Of Duo*) is arguably more graciously realized. But it's fascinating to hear Evans meditate on Monk's structuralism here, with a fine-grained interpretation of 'Round Midnight' with extra melodic material, a superb and quite unexpected 'Blue Monk' and the bonus of 'Bemsha Swing', only the last of these in any way strained. Almost the highlight is a grandly cinematic 'Theme From Spartacus' that retains as much detail as a solo performance and on which, as throughout the set, Evans seems to gaze at his own work and find it compelling.

& *See also* **The Complete Village Vanguard Recordings 1961** (1961; p. 276)

ELLIS MARSALIS
Born 14 November 1934, New Orleans, Louisiana
Piano

The Classic Ellis Marsalis
Boplicity CDBOP 016
Marsalis; Nat Perrilliat (ts); Marshall Smith (b); James Black (d). January–March 1963.

Ellis Marsalis said (1992): **'Recording is strange because it's different to what you're usually doing as a jazz musician, making that music in the now. You make a record** and part of the deal is going back in to edit and adjust, maybe re-record, select songs. That already changes things, and with the culture so dominated by records now, it has changed the music.'

Ellis Marsalis played and taught for decades in his native New Orleans with no recognition beyond his playing circles until he sired the most famous jazz dynasty of the day. Revered as a teacher and recognized as the father of Branford, Wynton, Delfeayo and Jason, he has only belatedly been recognized as a significant performer too. Inevitably, there has been a small flurry of releases and reissues since then, but it's worth going back to something that was made (to put it in context) when Branford was a toddler.

One can hear where Wynton got his even-handed delineation of melody from and where Branford's aristocratic elegance of line is rooted. The dynastic founder isn't beyond tossing in the occasional surprise, but mostly he favours careful interpretations of standards, sparsely harmonized and delicately spelt out, with a few simple but cleverly hooked originals to lend a little extra personality. This is a rarity, a quartet dating from the early '60s originally released as *The Monkey Puzzle* on AFO Records in which the pianist leads a group featuring the Coltrane follower Perrilliat and the jittery, post-Elvin Jones drums of Black, whose unsettling beats keep the group teetering on the brink of a chaos that the others carefully navigate. Black's also the main writer at this stage, and his title-track is an offbeat winner, but it's Ellis's patient accompaniment, with all the modernist tinges one doesn't expect to hear in 'New Orleans jazz', that makes the record so fresh and successful.

SATHIMA BEA BENJAMIN
Born 17 October 1936, Cape Town, South Africa
Voice

A Morning In Paris
Ekapa S.A. 004
Benjamin; Duke Ellington, Abdullah Ibrahim, Billy Strayhorn (p); Svend Asmussen (vn); Johnny Gertze (b); Makaya Ntoshko (d). February 1963.

Sathima Bea Benjamin said (1986): **'Duke Ellington told me to be at this very grand hotel in Zurich at ten thirty the next morning. We hardly slept, Abdullah and I, but we were there the next morning. Duke sat us down in his room, told us that his accountant would give us money for fares and that we should meet him at the Barclay studios in Paris in four days' time. Which is exactly what happened ...'**

Bea Benjamin buttonholed Duke Ellington after a concert in Zurich and persuaded him to come to the Club Africana and hear her boyfriend's trio. Ever courtly, Duke insisted on hearing Bea sing as well, and was captivated. The resulting recording, *Duke Ellington Presents The Dollar Brand Trio*, established the South African pianist's career, even though Frank Sinatra of Reprise Records decided the couple weren't commercial enough for further release. That Benjamin's half of the date survives at all is due to the habit of recording engineer Gerard Lehner of keeping a private listening copy of every session he taped.

After an impromptu rehearsal – Strayhorn had never heard 'A Nightingale Sang In Berkeley Square', Benjamin did not know his 'Your Love Has Faded' – the session was recorded, with Duke accompanying on 'I Got It Bad And That Ain't Good' and 'Solitude', Strayhorn on the two rehearsed songs, the solidly Duke-influenced Brand/Ibrahim on the remainder. All are standards, but Benjamin's warm, slightly innocent delivery and sensuous (but not morbidly sensual) vibrato give familiar material like 'Lover Man', 'The Man I Love' and 'Spring Will Be A Little Late This Year' a quality that suggests, as we've noted elsewhere, that she'd never heard these songs before, or certainly never heard iconic performances of them. The trio plays well and even the curious inclusion of Asmussen on pizzicato violin adds to the record's charm. Later work had more of an African inflexion, but here Benjamin emerges as a remarkable interpreter of standards.

A tiny puzzle. This Ekapa release somewhat implies that this is the first appearance of these 'lost' tapes. Owners of our fifth (2000) edition will find it reviewed there as an Enja record. Sadly, none of Benjamin's other discs for the German label are currently available. Probably nothing since has matched that studio debut: Duke as accompanist and producer, *and* Billy Strayhorn.

BIG JOHN PATTON

Born 12 July 1935, Kansas City, Missouri; died 19 March 2002, Montclair, New Jersey
Organ

Along Came John
Blue Note 31915
Patton; Fred Jackson, Harold Vick (ts); Grant Green (g); Ben Dixon (d). April 1963.

John Patton said (1991): **'Playing a Hammond B3 is a bit like driving a truck. It doesn't handle like a sports car and it needs a bit of room. You have to watch out for other road users!'**

Patton was one of the most entertaining of the players who followed in Jimmy Smith's footsteps, and a pile of Blue Note albums became his principal legacy. Most of these have drifted out of print, though the material turns up on acid-jazz and rare groove collections. *Along Came John* is probably his great moment. After a long apprenticeship in R&B situations, he was ready to make a statement and hadn't yet become part of Blue Note's soul-jazz set-up. Green is a master of his craft and never better than on dates like this. By common consent among musicians, Vick was a giant and he proves his quality here. It all boils down to the opening 'The Silver Meter', an irresistible loping groove. Patton probably never bettered it, but then he rarely dropped below excellent.

JOE HENDERSON &

Born 24 April 1937, Lima, Ohio; died 30 June 2001, San Francisco, California
Tenor saxophone

Page One
Blue Note 98795
Henderson; Kenny Dorham (t); McCoy Tyner (p); Butch Warren (b); Pete Sims (d). June 1963.

Joe Henderson said (1992): **'I've always sounded the same way. I was playing like this before some of the people who were supposed to have "influenced" me were even on the scene. I don't get offended by it, but it's plain wrong. Besides, I learned as much about jazz from Stravinsky as I did from any saxophone-player.'**

One of the last great tenormen of the original hard-bop generation, who it's hard to imagine not in the middle of some grand, involved solo, Henderson was a thematic musician, working his way round the structure of a composition with methodical intensity, but he was also a masterful licks player, with a seemingly limitless stock of phrases that he could turn to advantage in any post-bop setting; this gave his best improvisations a balance of surprise, immediacy and coherence few other saxophonists could match. His lovely tone, which combines softness and a harsh plangency in a similar way, is another pleasing aspect of his music.

Page One was his first date as a leader, and it still stands as one of the most popular Blue Notes of the early '60s. Henderson had not long since arrived in New York after being discharged from the army, and this six-theme set is very much the work of a new star on the scene. 'Recorda-Me', whose Latinate lilt has made it a staple blowing vehicle for hard-bop bands, had its debut here, and the very fine tenor solo on Dorham's 'Blue Bossa' explains much of why Henderson was creating excitement. Everything here, even the throwaway blues 'Homestretch' is impressively handled.

& *See also* **The State Of The Tenor** (1985; p. 494)

PAUL DESMOND

Born Paul Emil Breitenfeld, 25 November 1924, San Francisco, California; died 30 May 1977, New York City
Alto saxophone

Glad To Be Unhappy
RCA Victor 7432 131311
Desmond; Jim Hall (g); Gene Cherico, Gene Wright (b); Connie Kay (d). June 1963–September 1964.

Dave Brubeck said (1991): **'He played very high up, an octave up on most players, and all these teachers would tell him he would go and ruin his tone if he persisted with it. I told him to play what he really felt because it was obvious that he nosedived if he tried to play differently.'**

Jazz history has overstated Desmond's significance in making Dave Brubeck a star. They met in the '40s and Desmond was part of the pianist's octet set-up, though their main association came later, compounded of almost telepathic understanding, some personal hurt, and a degree of professional jockeying. The saxophonist's flowing lines are unmistakable, but Brubeck gave him a winning context, almost never bettered. Desmond's glowing tone and melodic ease are almost definitive of the cool saxophone. Such was the Californian's importance to Brubeck, for whom Desmond wrote 'Take Five', that there was an agreement Desmond would never record with another piano-player. He did, however, sustain a solo career, which remains somewhat overlooked.

Desmond's recordings for RCA Victor are the pinnacle of his career, consistent and richly inflected. *Glad To Be Unhappy* is a set of torchsongs chosen to highlight Desmond's sound. They're not by any means obvious picks: 'By The River Ste Marie' and Mel Tormé's 'Stranger In Town' are superb choices for Paul, and even 'Poor Butterfly' justifies its place. Hall's in nicely supportive form and the rhythm players keep it from getting too static. Desmond's tone and quiet, lyrical delivery almost never vary from date to date. Occasionally, he will throw in a discordant interval or roughen up his timbre to add a measure of drama. It is astonishing, listening to this music in bulk, to discover how modern, even avant-garde, it is in impact. For all Anthony Braxton's insistence on Desmond as a primary influence, no one has ever quite taken the point at face value. These extraordinary sides point up how immensely thoughtful Desmond was, and how brimming with harmonic intelligence.

GRACHAN MONCUR III

Born 3 June 1937, New York City
Trombone

Evolution
Blue Note 784153
Moncur; Lee Morgan (t); Jackie McLean (as); Bobby Hutcherson (vib); Bob Cranshaw (b); Tony Williams (d).
November 1963.

Jackie McLean said (1985): **'If anyone asks me about the "state of jazz" in this year or that year, I say to them: "Easy way to tell … how many nights this month did Grachan Moncur actually work?" That way, you get a pretty good idea. Most months you might not get a very big number, and that really bugs me; guy like that can do anything.'**

Moncur's father, Grachan Moncur II, played bass with the Savoy Sultans. Our man started trombone pre-teens and became one of the first on the instrument to explore free jazz. *Evolution* wasn't the first or last attempt to convey the broader movements of humankind in a jazz setting; one thinks inevitably of Mingus's *Pithecanthropus Erectus* or George Russell's *The African Game*. Moncur's composition is less ambitious: the actual track is much shorter for a start and hovers between bop orthodoxy (strong J. J. Johnson influence) and some attempt to keep up with the free movement.

He probably had the wrong line-up to take that second route any further. Morgan's strengths were considerable but tramlined and only Hutcherson and Williams showed much interest in the avant-garde. That said, Moncur handles the players with great skill. The looseness of 'Evolution' reflects more a desire to imbue the idea with the new freedom than any lack of arranging skills. He liked to treat the rhythm section as an independent unit. That much is obvious on the opening 'Air Raid'. Moncur had debuted with Jackie McLean's band earlier the same year for One Step Beyond and that title seems even more relevant here as Jackie plays some very untypical stuff. Recorded a day before JFK was shot in Dallas (was there something in the air in America?), the whole record has a dark, *misterioso* quality that the lowering trombone sound (not prominently featured, but always there in attendance) strongly accentuates. 'The Coaster' subordinates strict metre to pulse, a device typical of Thelonious Monk, who is celebrated on the fourth track, 'Monk In Wonderland'. It's the most rigorous of the tracks, completing an invigorating and intellectually satisfying set.

BOBBY HUTCHERSON &
Born 27 January 1941, Los Angeles, California
Vibraphone, marimba

The Kicker
Blue Note 21437
Hutcherson; Joe Henderson (ts); Grant Green (g); Bob Cranshaw (b); Al Harewood (d). December 1963.

Bobby Hutcherson said (1983): **'Pee Wee Marquette used to blow cigar smoke in my face and introduce me as "Babba Hutchkins", until I gave him a $5 tip. After that, mysteriously, he remembered my name.'**

Along with Gary Burton, Hutcherson reinvented vibes-playing in the '60s. He follows, loosely, in the Hampton/Bags lineage, but throughout his career has looked for new ways to extend the range and expressive potential of an instrument whose entire history, almost uniquely, lies within jazz. In the process, Hutcherson won himself an avant-garde label, which sits a little awkwardly on his uniform, for his work is almost all concerned with deep continuities in the jazz tradition: harmony, rhythm, fresh melodic invention.

In the '60s he made a series of superb albums for Blue Note, the equal of any of the classic dates from that label, though their release history suggests a measure of canny ambivalence on the part of the label's owners, anxious to balance artistic enterprise against commercial concerns. The availability of those records has been very intermittent, although some have returned as limited editions. More surprising is the number that were never issued at the time. Hutcherson's first release for Blue Note, *Dialogue*, made in April 1965, only returned to the catalogue in early 2002. It is arguably the most adventurous thing Bobby ever did, though he had not yet found his confidence as a composer as well as soloist. Three of the group assembled – Hutcherson, Hubbard and Davis – had been involved in Dolphy's epochal *Out To Lunch!* sessions, and they carry over some of the energy and excitement of that great record.

The Kicker wasn't made available until 1999. Even if Hutcherson's standing was thought to be marginal, the presence of Joe Henderson should have been enough to see this fine, imaginative session into the light of day. The saxophonist is the main composer and Bobby is represented only by the rather slight 'For Duke P.', a tribute to Blue Note's musical director. Joe's 'Kicker' and 'Step Lightly' are cracking tunes and blistering performances from all concerned. Hutcherson's fleet, ringing lines have rarely sounded more buoyant and persuasive, and it remains a mystery that this record should have lain unreleased for 30 years. As such it stands not just as a minor modern classic but also as an emblem of the industry's aesthetic and commercial vagaries.

& *See also* **Cruisin' The 'Bird** (1988; p. 519)

LEE MORGAN &
Born 10 July 1938, Philadelphia, Pennsylvania; died 19 February 1972, New York City
Trumpet

The Sidewinder
Blue Note 95332
Morgan; Joe Henderson (ts); Barry Harris (p); Bob Cranshaw (b); Billy Higgins (d). December 1963.

Bassist Reggie Workman said (1992): **'Lee Morgan had a *giant* record collection. Seemed like he had everything and had listened to it and got it down as well. We were round the neighbourhood in Philadelphia and he was the guy who knew all the records.'**

Though he gets the month wrong, David H. Rosenthal's history of *Hard Bop* gives central symbolic place to the death of Lee Morgan, victim not of overdose or car crash like so many of his peers, but gunned down in Slugs' by a jealous girlfriend. If Morgan's passing in 1972 felt like the end of an era in jazz, it was one he had helped to define. Masaya Matsumara's painstaking website discography lists 151 sessions at which Morgan was present. We would not presume to suggest there were more, but there were certainly umpteen undocumented live dates in that same 16-year period, a prodigious outpouring of music. In 'The Sidewinder' he created what may usefully stand as the representative hard-bop tune. If he was to repeat the formula to the point of redundancy in years to come, he had the justification of having shaped the formula in the first place.

Like fellow trumpeters Fats Navarro, Booker Little and Clifford Brown before him, Lee Morgan lived fast and died young, playing with a swagger based on solid technical know-how and even when playing ballads showing a glint of steel under the velvet. Remarkably for someone who made so many records, we still tend to think of what might have been. Would a 70-year-old Lee Morgan have been one of the music's imperious balladeers?

Morgan played with the Jazz Messengers and with Hank Mobley and Donald Byrd, but was already making records under his own name. He was one of the very few top-flight players to adopt former boss Dizzy's trademark 'bent' trumpet, a homage to his biggest influence, though Morgan's punchy, out-of-kilter phrasing is all his own. He had a number of Blue Note dates in the bag before *The Sidewinder* slithered along.

Famously, the title-track was written in the heads towards the end of the session, a glorious 24-bar theme as sinuous and stinging as the beast of the title. It was both the best but also the worst thing that was ever to happen to Morgan before the awful events of 19 February 1972, and in its ambivalent way seemed to reflect something of the mood of America in the weeks after the Kennedy assassination. 'The Sidewinder' was an instant jazz hit, one of those themes, like 'So What', that insinuate themselves into the subconscious and remain there for ever. Unfortunately, it also established a more or less unbreakable pattern for future LPs, a bold, funky opener – often with a title intended to recall 'Sidewinder' – followed by half a dozen forgettable blowing themes, or, if you were lucky, another swinger to kick off the second side. The other pieces on the record have never been acknowledged to the same degree, but 'Totem Pole' and the superb 'Hocus Pocus' are the best available evidence for Morgan's gifts as a writer: vivid, often unexpectedly angled lines with every potential for extended blowing and not just off the back of a few algebraic chords. Of the other members of the group, Henderson stands out for his solo on the title-track and on 'Hocus Pocus'. Harris is rock solid from start to finish, and the bass-and-drums team can hardly be faulted.

& *See also* **Search For The New Land** (1964; p. 302)

RONNIE SCOTT

Born Ronald Schatt, 28 January 1927, London; died 23 December 1996, London
Tenor and soprano saxophones

When I Want Your Opinion, I'll Give It To You
Ronnie Scott's Jazz House JHAS 610
Scott; Stan Tracey (p); Ernest Ranglin (g); Malcolm Cecil, Rick Laird (b); Jackie Dougan, Chris Karan, Ronnie Stephenson (d). December 1963–April 1965.

Ronnie Scott said (more than once): **'Did you know that Erwin Rommel was a great jazz fan? Yes, he used to run round the Western Desert asking: "Wes Montgomery? Wes Montgomery?"'** Footnote available for American readers.

Ronnie Scott's was a virtual brand name (and later literally so), but a substantial proportion of the Japanese and American tourists who filed into the Frith Street club never heard him play. Few musician-run jazz clubs have had quite the charisma of Ronnie Scott's in London's Soho. Ronnie's career as proprietor and MC eclipsed his playing, which is a shame because he was a fine tenor-player and, in the opinion of Charles Mingus, quite the best of the 'white boys'. Some touring musicians turn out the same licks, phrases, whole solos night after night. Ronnie Scott turned out the same jokes, and even got requests for special ones. His suggestion that inert audiences 'join hands and contact the living … first time I ever saw dead people smoke' has gone down in jazz club legend. A past master of the chewish chive, he was also soaked in the blues and capable of compelling emotion in a solo, but disliked recording and did it only sparingly. There are a few bop-flavoured things from early on, and of course he was a member of the legendary Jazz Couriers with Tubby Hayes, but it peters out after that apart from a few in-house things with names like *Never Pat A Burning Dog* and this one.

 When I Want Your Opinion (a typical Scott line) brings together material from the early to mid-'60s when the club really was the crucible of modern jazz in Britain. The various groups, with either Malcolm Cecil or Rick Laird (later to join the Mahavishnu Orchestra and then to give up music for photography) were boppish in idiom, but closer in feel to the swing era. If there is a saxophonist Scott resembles on these tracks, then it must be the Janus-faced Don Byas, who also recorded at the club towards the end of his life. The presence of Ernest Ranglin brings a bouncy playfulness to 'Ronnie's Blues' from December 1963. A couple of months later, he's missing, and Chris Karan has been replaced by Jackie Dougan. Stan Tracey is the piano-player on all the tracks with keyboard (there are two trios, with just Laird and Dougan or Stephenson) and he brings his usual abrupt lyricism to 'Bye Bye Blackbird' (recorded in 1965) and a touch of deadpan humour to 'I'm Sick And Tired Of Waking Up Tired And Sick'. That last title rang hollowly when just before Christmas 1996 Ronnie Scott chose to end his own life rather than face worsening ill-health; as did his joke when he heard that that other old kvetcher Stan Getz had died: 'All the great jazzmen are leaving us ... I don't feel so good myself.'

Scott left behind an immense personal legacy, but it shouldn't be allowed to eclipse entirely Ronnie's own music.

ERIC DOLPHY&

Born 20 June 1928, Los Angeles, California; died 29 June 1964, Berlin, Germany
Alto saxophone, bass clarinet, flute, clarinet

Out To Lunch!
Blue Note 98793
Dolphy; Freddie Hubbard (t); Bobby Hutcherson (vib); Richard Davis (b); Tony Williams (d). February 1964.

Saxophonist and bass clarinettist Chris Biscoe has re-recorded many of the compositions on *Out To Lunch!*: **'The tunes are not like jazz themes, but get their power and vitality from the jazz instrumentation and interpretation. *Out To Lunch!* has come to define Eric Dolphy, but isn't typical of his output. I think what makes it outstanding and memorable isn't the individual performances, but the sense of integration and group playing.'**

By the turn of 1964, Dolphy was a seasoned presence on the new jazz scene, with experience in Charles Mingus's and John Coltrane's groups, and important recording sessions with Ornette Coleman, George Russell, Oliver Nelson and others. It seems certain, from anec-dotal evidence, that he was already suffering from the undiagnosed diabetic condition that killed him in Germany later in the year, but his productivity was undimmed for the moment and in February of his final year he cut what many would argue was his greatest record, though there are dissenters.

This was the third time Dolphy had used the word 'out' in an album title. *Out To Lunch!* now seems both more outside and more mainstream than his earlier work, which pushed bop language to the limits without breaking out into something new. It also stands in a slightly curious relation to the rest of the Dolphy discography, its reputation to some extent sentimental and to a great extent encouraged by Reid Miles's witty cover design. Dolphy's only other release for Blue Note was the posthumous *Other Aspects*, though a month later he was to have a major role in Andrew Hill's *Point Of Departure*. How high does *Out To Lunch!* stand? If it is a masterpiece, then it is not so much a flawed as a slightly tentative masterpiece.

For all his brilliant contributions to records by other leaders, Dolphy still hadn't created an entirely individual sound of his own. Since the spring 1963 sessions for Alan Douglas, Dolphy had been working towards a new compositional sophistication. The session of 25 February 1964 was engineered by Rudy Van Gelder. The sound is strong and very centred, and the new band (with Williams in for J. C. Moses and the incendiary Hubbard in for Woody Shaw) was well suited to Dolphy's increasingly dissonant and fractured conception. Hutcherson's vibraphone – again, no piano – is mixed in such a way that the most intense attacks have a very distinct, almost physical presence. Every track, as Chris Biscoe has noted, begins with a surprise device, though the initial drama isn't always sustained. The solitary flute track is inspired by the great modernist Severiano Gazelloni. It's a relatively conventional bop theme, but one distinguished by Dolphy's virtuosic articulation and bit-ing attack. In the same way, 'Straight Up And Down' and 'Out To Lunch' itself, the two alto pieces, are bordering on complete harmonic freedom, but again anchored in a strong rhythmic groove. CD transfer highlighted Davis's key harmonic role. Hutcherson's percus-sive and often polytonal lines allow Dolphy maximum freedom of invention. The radical core of *Out To Lunch!* lies in the two opening numbers. 'Hat And Beard', a tribute to Monk, and 'Something Sweet, Something Tender' are both taken on bass clarinet, and the sheer physicality and dynamism of Dolphy's entry on the first tune impart an excitement that runs through the record. It is 'angular', as the cliché runs, but also lyrical and unmistak-ably thoughtful. Throughout the record, one can hear the group messing with the metre, adding beats, then subtracting them. The later tracks are by no means a falling away, but they certainly represent a consolidation rather than an advance on what Dolphy does in those opening moments. There was to be no sequel and *Out To Lunch!*'s cachet lies as much in promise as in delivery. Its real interest lies in what a later generation has done with this beautiful, flawed template.

& *See also* **Far Cry** (1960; p. 264)

JOHNNY HODGES &

Known as 'Rabbit'; born John Cornelius Hodge, 25 July 1907, Cambridge, Massachusetts; died 11 May 1970, New York City
Alto and soprano saxophones

Everybody Knows Johnny Hodges
Impulse! A(S) 61 116
Hodges; Cat Anderson, Rolf Ericson, Herbie Jones, Ray Nance (t); Lawrence Brown, Buster Cooper, Britt Woodman (tb); Harold Ashby, Harry Carney, Paul Gonsalves, Jimmy Hamilton, Russell Procope (reeds); Jimmy Jones (p); Ernie Shepard (b); Grady Tate (d). February 1964–March 1965.

Saxophonist John Dankworth said (1993): **'After a solo, Duke would give Hodges a big ovation: "Johnny Hodges! Johnny Hodges!! Johnny Hodges!!!" Johnny would stand up, but instead of taking a bow, he'd look over at Duke and rub his fingertips together to say: "If I'm that good, pay me more money."'**

Hodges' relationship with Duke Ellington was too complex even to be described as love-hate. It went on for a very long time, for much of which Hodges was eager to be off doing his own thing. For some reason, temperamental or circumstantial, his solo projects never quite took off, and the later recordings have a slight air of the gala occasion, an indulgence rather than a definitive statement.
Impulse! was where the new thing in jazz was gathering force, but Bob Thiele and the label were also responsive to some of the older stars (Benny Carter made an admired record) and blended musicians of different generations (Duke and Trane), so Hodges seemed an obvious choice. Billy Strayhorn composed '310 Blues' specially for the occasion and takes another credit with 'A Flower Is A Lovesome Thing'. From time to time, Hodges seems upstaged by both Paul Gonsalves (then in his pomp) and Lawrence Brown. The trombonist is actually the leader on the remaining tracks on the CD – *Inspired Abandon*, included in this reissue, was his album for Impulse!, with Rabbit as featured soloist. The material here isn't as good, certainly not a patch on the small-group cuts from the February 1964 dates; the big-band tracks – 'Main Stem', 'I Let A Song Go Out Of My Heart'/'Don't Get Around Much Anymore' – are equally good, but Hodges seems slightly overpowered by the arrangements. Essential all the same.

& *See also* **Classic Solos 1928–1942** (1928–1941; p. 32)

LEE MORGAN &

Born 10 July 1938, Philadelphia, Pennsylvania; died 19 February 1972, New York City
Trumpet

Search For The New Land

Blue Note 84169
Morgan; Wayne Shorter (ts); Herbie Hancock (p); Grant Green (g); Reggie Workman (b); Billy Higgins (d).
February 1964.

Trumpeter Jeremy Pelt says: **'Back when I was getting my playing together, Lee Morgan was the player you checked out. The way he related to the audience is something that I still strive for, every day.'**

There's a conventional wisdom that after *The Sidewinder* Morgan's albums became increasingly formulaic. While there is some truth in it, it's not a generalization that stands up to extended listening. There are strong cuts on almost all the Blue Note records and Morgan's ability to engage his listeners, directly and almost viscerally, guarantees their success. However, even if one accepts that there is a generic cast to the discography, *Search For The New Land* represents something of an exception.

Search was a musical exploration as much as a programmatic one. The presence of Shorter and Hancock guaranteed a measure of lyrical unpredictability, which is immediately registered on the title-piece. 'The Joker' might be thought to be the 'Sidewinder' piece this time around, except that it's a darkly playful, rather treacherous idea built on altered chords, and certainly not a theme that encourages a relaxed or lazy approach. Workman fits into this context particularly well, and the hyperactive Higgins drills away without a pause. 'Mr Kenyatta' may point towards one possible new inspiration for Morgan's music, though the two remaining numbers, albeit more than makeweights, are more off-the-peg: 'Melancholee' is a tight, bluesy ballad and 'Morgan The Pirate' another fairly orthodox improvising tune. A fine, questing record, and a pity that – *The Gigolo* apart – there weren't to be more like it. The latest release contains some bonus tracks, though nothing that prompts a wholesale reassessment of an already surprising set.

& *See also* **The Sidewinder** (1963; p. 298)

DENNY ZEITLIN &

Born 10 April 1938, Chicago, Illinois
Piano

Cathexis

Columbia CS 8982/Mosaic Select 34
Zeitlin; Cecil McBee (b); Frederick Waits (d). February 1964.

Denny Zeitlin says: **'It was a great thrill, in my final year of medical school, to find myself in Columbia's hallowed 30th Street studio in New York recording my first trio album. With no rehearsal, I got together with Freddie Waits and Cecil McBee, and the chemistry was terrific.'**

A unique figure in modern jazz, Zeitlin trained as a psychiatrist and has practised medicine in addition to his musical career. His family background included both vocations and the youngster studied with both Alexander Tcherepnin and George Russell, giving him an understanding of both classical forms and jazz harmony which came together (with some rock music superadded) in his experimental albums of the '70s. While still a student, Zeitlin was heard by John Hammond, who signed him for Columbia.

Cathexis is one of the great modern piano trio records. The title shouldn't be confused with 'catharsis'. Cathexis is a term used for what is essentially emotional charge, the amount of psychic energy in a given situation. Its appropriateness here is obvious. The title-piece is a tense, almost incendiary theme, which seems to discharge in a series of abrupt climaxes. It's equally startling to find the work of Jewish philosopher Martin Buber cited on a jazz album, but 'I-Thou' derives its notions of personal confrontation and mutuality from Buber's once fashionable ideas. 'Little Children, Don't Go Near That House' antici-pates some of the atmospheric work of later years. It has astonishing drama, fuelled by an off-kilter metre, and its folkloric element, balancing innocence and experience, is palpable and powerful. 'Stonehenge' is reminiscent of some of McCoy Tyner's modal experiments of the period, but also something of an apocalyptic strain in '60s culture. There are a couple of repertory pieces, Gigi Gryce's 'Nica's Tempo' and the staple 'Round Midnight', which is dealt with almost skeletally, reducing the pace to its basic armature. McBee and Waits are both in exceptional form.

Zeitlin's wider reputation was only restored when he made a Maybeck Hall recital for Concord in 1992. Medical work kept him from the studios for a time, but it was his creative ambition rather than a full patient list that eclipsed the work, which was too restless and exploratory to sustain a consistent career. In retrospect, he is one of the most important stylists and composers of the time, and mercifully still playing today.

& See also **Slickrock** (2003; p. 687)

ANDREW HILL &

Born Andrew Hille, 30 June 1937, Chicago, Illinois; died 20 April 2007, Jersey City, New Jersey
Piano

Point Of Departure
Blue Note 9364
Hill; Kenny Dorham (t); Eric Dolphy (as, f, bcl); Joe Henderson (ts); Richard Davis (b); Tony Williams (d). March 1964.

Andrew Hill said (2000): **'It came together almost on its own. I'd talked to Eric about doing something. Charles Lloyd was supposed to play tenor, but he pulled out. And then Tony Williams arrived in town and was being talked about. I took the idea to Blue Note and they bought it. That was it. There was no sense of drama: just a date.'**

Born in Chicago (and not Haiti as sometimes reported), Hill drew on a Caribbean ances-try and always sounds torn between cultures – on the one hand analytical, on the other powerfully visceral. Much of the writing has a minor-key feel, even if the tonality doesn't put it that way, and there are always hints of island rhythm – sometimes one overlapping another – in the best of the compositions. After making a couple of mid-'50s trio records, Hill slipped from sight for a time, as far as the studios are concerned, but jumped quickly back into focus with the release of his first Blue Note album *Black Fire*, which immediately established him as the Toussaint l'Ouverture of modern jazz, incendiary, highly intelligent, unpredictable. He is both kin to and very unlike Thelonious Monk. Blue Note was to be his berth for the next few years and then again following his resurgence after 2000, but it's clear that as with other innovative artists (Bobby Hutcherson, say, Cecil Taylor, or Ornette Cole-man) the label didn't quite know what to do with Hill. It's significant that some of his best sessions only appeared for the first time in the '00s, as *Passing Ships* and *Dance Of Death*.

Commercial considerations invariably had to be balanced against artistic enterprise, and to some degree that is true of Hill's work itself, in which dissonant elements are forever in dialogue with a dancing, almost physical quality. It's always difficult to place, neither orthodox bop nor hard bop, nor 'avant-garde'. The pianist's aim seems to be to find new ways of speaking within an understood language. He probes restlessly, as often as not looking for new tone colours as for a new approach to chord changes.

Point Of Departure is one of the very great jazz albums of the '60s and is now available with bonus takes of three of its five compositions. Hill's writing and arranging skills matured dramatically with *Point Of Departure*. Nowhere is his determination to build on the example of Monk clearer than on the punningly titled 'New Monastery'. Hill's solo, like that on the long previous track, 'Refuge', is constructed out of literally dozens of subtle shifts in the time-signature, most of them too subliminal to be strictly counted. Typically, Hill is prepared to hold the basic beat himself and to allow Williams to range very freely. The rejected take is less secure rhythmically, and while Hill's solo is full of interesting material, the 'bonus' take adds little to the album's impact. Only the alternate take of 'Flight 19' contains much of moment. Of the issued tracks, 'Spectrum' is the one disappointment, too self-conscious an attempt to run a gamut of emotions and instrumental colours; an extraordinary 5/4 passage for the horns almost saves the day. Henderson at first glance doesn't quite fit, but his solos on 'Spectrum' and 'Refuge' are exemplary and in the first case superior to Dolphy's rather insubstantial delivery. The mood of the session switches dramatically on the final 'Dedication', a dirge with a beautiful structure that represents the sharpest contrast to the rattling progress of the previous 'Flight 19' and brings the set full circle. Rightly revered, *Point Of Departure* isn't so far ahead of Hill's other work, but it has at least been consistently available.

& *See also* **Dusk** (1999; p. 646)

STAN GETZ &

Born 2 February 1927, Philadelphia, Pennsylvania; died 6 June 1991, Malibu, California
Tenor saxophone

Nobody Else But Me
Verve 521660-2
Getz; Gary Burton (vib); Gene Cherico (b); Joe Hunt (d). March 1964.

Club owner Ronnie Scott presented Getz in London in March and April 1964, when the American appeared with the Scott house band. Then and later, it wasn't an entirely easy relationship, as Ronnie told audiences: **'I've got a bit of a slipped disc. I got it bending over backwards, trying to please Stan Getz!'**

With the umpteen-selling *Jazz Samba* and *Getz/Gilberto*, Stan became a major crossover star and to this day those smooth bossa nova stylings can be heard shimmying across wine bars and restaurants. Success had some unintended consequences, not least the withdrawal of *Nobody Else But Me*, shelved lest it interfere with the commercial success of the bossa records.

Unreleased for 30 years, it's a marvel (to adapt the name of a later album with Chick Corea). Amazingly, this – the only studio recording by a group that was a popular concert attraction – is lush and romantic, with the backbone of a master improviser's intelligence. Burton contributes '6-Nix-Pix-Flix' and opens up the harmonic base just enough to give Stan clear, lucid space for his solos. 'Summertime' is a classic, 'Waltz For A Lovely Wife' is rapture, but there's nothing less than great here and for once one doesn't feel it's just Stan-and-rhythm but a group where every member was attuned to the concept and where the leader, in his later years famously 'difficult' on tour and often brutally rebarbative in manner, seemed to respect his underlings.

& *See also* **The Complete Roost Recordings** (1950–1954; p. 127), **Focus** (1961; p. 277)

ALBERT AYLER &

Born 13 July 1936, Cleveland, Ohio; died between 5 and 25 November 1970, New York City
Tenor, alto and soprano saxophones

Spiritual Unity
Esp-Disk 1002
Ayler; Gary Peacock (b); Sunny Murray (d). July 1964.

Gary Peacock said (1984): 'I could never quite understand some of the things written about Albert's music. They seemed to miss the point, some essence. Then I listened to some of the records again and that's it: they just don't capture all of it; there was so much more to Albert than the records give you. Perhaps if he were alive today …'

Ayler's music has been the object of endless debate. It is now generally understood to be a highly personal amalgam of New Orleans brass, rhythm and blues and some of the more extreme timbral innovations of the '60s New Thing. His death in the East River in 1970 sparked a posthumous cult and some degree of paranoia about the circumstances, but the reality was that Ayler, who had been suffering from depression for some time, simply decided to end his own life. His brother Don, a significantly underrated player, also suffered from a psychiatric disorder and was hospitalized for a long period. Ayler grew up in Cleveland, played R&B on alto as a teenager, then switched to tenor during army service. He went to Sweden in 1962 and began his recording career in Scandinavia, returning to the US after a year and subsequently recording the classic records that established him as a rival to Coltrane for the tenor saxophone crown, though his approach was completely different.

The poet Ted Joans likened the impact of this trio to hearing someone scream the word 'fuck' on Easter Sunday in St Patrick's Cathedral. Subjectively, there may be some validity in this, but it makes a nonsense of what was actually going on in this group. The intensity of interaction among the three individuals, their attentiveness to what the others were doing, ruled out any such gesture. It is, in short, affirmative music. Even amid the noise, the 1964 Ayler trio was quintessentially a listening band, locked in a personal struggle which it is possible only to observe, awe-struck, from the side-lines. The discography is studded with inaccuracy, with themes misidentified on records, the same title used for different tracks and different titles for the same track: a mess, in short. Ayler, Peacock and Murray had been playing the *Spiritual Unity* material for some time, and earlier versions of a couple of these tracks, 'Ghosts' and 'The Wizard', were taped at the Cellar Café almost a month earlier on 14 June 1964. Intriguingly, only a few months before that, Ayler had recorded cover versions of traditional material ('Swing Low, Sweet Chariot', 'Ol' Man River' and others) at the Atlantic studios in New York, material released as *Swing Low, Sweet Spiritual* and *Goin' Home*. Heard in that context, it is impossible to consider *Spiritual Unity* as anything other than an extension of vernacular themes, played in an ecstatic manner typical of the African-American churches. Brief as it is, it remains a record of immitigable power and authority, but there is humour under the surface and a humanity that is rarely acknowledged.

& *See also* **Live In Greenwich Village** (1965–1967; p. 332)

TED CURSON
Born 3 June 1935, Philadelphia, Pennsylvania
Trumpet

Tears For Dolphy
DA Black Lion BLCD 8747612
Curson; Bill Barron (ts, cl); Herb Bushler (b); Dick Berk (d). August 1964.

Ted Curson said (1987): '**Miles Davis heard me play when I was a teenage kid, maybe 16. He gave me his card and said: "Come and see me." I put it in my pocket, did nothing about it. Then after I got out of school and went to New York, I called him. "Ted Curson? That little kid from Philly? I've been waiting for you for three years!"'**

Curson's big break wasn't with Miles, as it happened, but with Charles Mingus, whom he joined in 1959. He later co-led a group with saxophonist Bill Barron before moving to Europe, returning to the US in 1976. There have been a good number of records down the years, starting with *Plenty Of Horn* in 1961, but apart from 'Tears For Dolphy' (he worked with the saxophonist for some months in the Mingus band) few of his fine compositions are widely known.

The fiery bassist hadn't hired a trumpet-player – apart from Richard Williams and, equally briefly, Don Ellis – when he took on the 24-year-old, some testimony to his skill and application at the time. Curson betrays a certain Miles Davis influence, but his work is in curious ways closer to that of Thad Jones, with a strong, long-lined lyrical quality. On pocket trumpet, the most obvious lineage is Rex Stewart, and there are shades of Fats Navarro as well. But this tends to diminish Curson's individuality; he sounds like no one much but himself.

Tears For Dolphy was recorded a month or so after the death of its dedicatee, and there is a raw sorrow in the title-tune that was less evident in later versions. This reissue also includes material recorded at the same time but released as *Flip Top*, so it's a generous duration for a record of the period. Barron provides solid support and chips in with four strong charts, including the Dolphy-ish '7/4 Funny Time' and 'Desolation'. The rhythm section is very solid, but it's Curson's high, slightly old-fashioned sound on the small trumpet that commands attention. 'Kassim' and 'Searchin' For The Blues' – why has no one else put these in the band book? – are the other highlights.

ARCHIE SHEPP&

Born 24 May 1937, Fort Lauderdale, Florida
Tenor, soprano and alto saxophones, piano

Four For Trane
Impulse! 051218-2
Shepp; Alan Shorter (t); Roswell Rudd (tb); John Tchicai (as); Reggie Workman (b); Charles Moffett (d). August 1964.

Archie Shepp said (1987): '**Coltrane was a preacher on his horn. Of course his music carried a message, but the message was in the music rather than added to it. I play the blues. I tell stories that don't necessarily need words, but they are narratives of our people all the same.**'

One of the major intellectuals of modern jazz. A passionate and articulate spokesman for the music, Shepp is also a significant playwright. His early saxophone style resembled Ben Webster with a carborundum edge, but – like Pharoah Sanders – the approach has grown gentler and more lyrical down the years. Archie Shepp once declared himself something 'worse than a romantic, I'm a sentimentalist.' Shepp has tended to be a theoretician of his own work, often expressing his intentions and motivations in off-puttingly glib and aphoristic language. He has, though, consistently seen himself as an educator and communicator rather than an entertainer and is one of the few African-American artists who has effected any sort of convincing synthesis between black music and the less comfortable verbal experiments of poets like LeRoi Jones (Imamu Amiri Baraka). The dialectic between sentiment and protest in Shepp's work is matched by an interplay between music and words which, though more obvious, is also harder to assess. A playwright who also wrote a good deal of influential stage music, Shepp devised a musical style that might be called dramatic or, at worst and later in his career, histrionic.

Four For Trane is one of the classic jazz albums of the '60s, and a fascinating glimpse into how thoroughly different what was already thought of as the Coltrane revolution might sound. Shepp immediately sounds more deeply soaked in the blues than the man he is paying tribute to here; Shepp's interpretation of 'Cousin Mary' is stunningly good, and his entry on 'Syeeda's Song Flute' is one of those musical moments that stay embedded in the skin like a bee-sting, painful and pleasurable by turns. Without a harmony instrument, the group has a loose, floating quality which Coltrane himself would never have attempted. The sound is totally open and without walls. Shorter, Rudd and Tchicai (who was to play such a significant part on Trane's Ascension) are all in spanking form, and the altoist's solo on the unforgettably titled 'Rufus (Swung, His Face At Last To The Wind, Then His Neck Snapped)' has a raw urgency that recalls the very roots of this music. This is Shepp's only composition of the set and, following the love-ballad 'Naima', it makes a dramatic end to a set of powerful and committed music, as if Coltrane's dark twin had risen up and gained speech.

& See also **Attica Blues** (1972; p. 391), **Looking At Bird** (1980; p. 456)

TONY WILLIAMS &

Born Samuel Anthony Williams, 12 December 1945, Chicago, Illinois; died 23 February 1997, Daly City, California
Drums

Life Time

Blue Note 99004
Williams; Sam Rivers (ts); Herbie Hancock (p); Bobby Hutcherson (vib, mar); Ron Carter, Richard Davis, Gary Peacock (b). August 1964.

Tony Williams said (1991): **'I think there's a misunderstanding about musical "greatness". It isn't about being so good on your instrument that you never make mistakes. It's about being willing to make mistakes, all the time; make them, learn from them, accept them as part of what you are, and move on. That's what Miles Davis did.'**

Tony Williams's death following a relatively innocuous surgical procedure was doubly shocking, because it came at a time when his career was in marvellous resurgence. Williams had his baptism of fire in the Miles Davis band while still in his teens; everyone who owns it treasures the live recording from the south of France on which the MC announces: '*le jeune Tony Williams à la batterie ... il a dix-sept ans.*' Tony gave Miles a raw and unfinished sound, one that didn't know it was breaking the rules. It was clear even then that he would go places, and recordings under his own name weren't slow in coming. Williams's early Blue Notes are intense, inward-looking explorations of the rhythmic possibilities opened up by bebop. Much of what he had learned to date was concentrated into *Life Time*. Compare the crisp attacks and precise, undistorted cymbal sound with what Williams had to put up with in later years and judge how worthy the tribute is on both sides. On 'Memory', Williams turns in a remarkable trio performance with Hancock and Hutcherson (and it should be remembered that his most shining moment before this point was on Eric Dolphy's *Out To Lunch!* session, on which Hutcherson and Davis both played). Rivers's angular approach was ideally suited to the young drummer's multidirectional approach and attack.

The album title was later appropriated for Williams's crossover band Lifetime, which took him in a new and fruitful direction.

& *See also* **LIFETIME, (Turn It Over)** (1970; p. 374)

LUCKY THOMPSON

Born Eli Thompson, 16 June 1924, Columbia, South Carolina; died 30 July 2005, Seattle, Washington
Tenor and soprano saxophones

Lucky Strikes
Original Jazz Classics OJCCD 194
Thompson; Hank Jones (p); Richard Davis (b); Connie Kay (d). September 1964.

Soprano saxophonist Sam Newsome says: **'When you listen to the Lucky Thompson on** *Lucky Strikes* **you hear how the soprano sax can sound just as at ease playing bebop as the tenor sax does in the hands of Dexter Gordon. If you want to hear how to play traditional New Orleans music on the soprano, listen to Sidney Bechet. But if you want to hear how to play bebop on the soprano, listen to Lucky.'**

Thompson was a perennial outsider, whose life belied the name that had been stitched across a childhood sweatshirt. He drew on the swing era, played bebop on both the tenor and the soprano horn (of which he was an early reviver) and in retrospect seemed to prefigure much of what went on in the '60s and '70s, after his playing career was over. A highly philosophical, almost mystical man, he eventually turned his back on the music business, publically retiring in 1966, after spending some time in Europe. Though his upbringing was harsh – he had to raise siblings by himself and legend has him practising saxophone fingerings on a broom handle before he had a proper horn – the beginning of the career was garlanded with promise. He recorded with Charlie Parker just after the war (a rare example of that chimera, the bebop tenor-player), but then returned to Detroit, where he'd grown up, and became involved in R&B and publishing. Like Don Byas, whom he most resembles in tone and in his development of solos, he has a slightly oblique and uneasy stance on bop, cleaving to a kind of accelerated swing idiom with a distinctive 'snap' to his softly enunciated phrases and an advanced harmonic language that occasionally moves into areas of surprising freedom. Only uneasy longevity denied him a place with the greats.

There are some fine Thompson albums around and we have dithered in the past between *Tricotism* and *Lord, Lord, Am I Ever Going To Know?* and there are wonderful things on both records, but it is this relatively 'late' record that seems now best to sum up his artistry. Thompson moves easily between tenor and soprano. He had made significant bounds in his understanding of harmonic theory since *Accent On Tenor Sax* a decade earlier and he attempts transitions that would have been quite alien to him then. All his characteristic virtues of tone and smooth development are in place, though, and the solos are models of development, though punctuated with gentle epiphanies where Lucky seems to be rising up through the layers in real time. He subtly blurs the melodic surface of 'In A Sentimental Mood' (a curious opener) and adjusts his tone significantly for the intriguing 'Reminiscent', 'Midnite Oil' and 'Prey Loot'. A classic.

HORACE SILVER &

Born Horace Ward Martin Tavares Silva, 2 September 1928, Norwalk, Connecticut
Piano

Song For My Father

Blue Note 99002-2
Silver; Carmell Jones, Blue Mitchell (t); Junior Cook, Joe Henderson (ts); Teddy Smith, Gene Taylor (b); Roy Brooks, Roger Humphries (d). January & October 1964.

Horace Silver said (1987): **'Music passes from father to son like the shape of your head or some special skill in craft. I know I was shaped by countless generations of musicians before me, and I feel a real bond with that.'**

Silver's father – pictured on the cover in the autumn of his life – was from the Cape Verde islands and the vernacular music from there played an important part in Horace's upbring-ing. A later Blue Note – and there were to be another score and more for the label – was called *The Cape Verdean Blues*. Here, at a point where he was disbanding one group and starting a new one, Silver imports some striking elements of island rhythm. Whatever the supposed provenance of 'Calcutta Cutie', it's audible there, and it certainly plays a part on the title-track, which might seem familiar from somewhere else: it was plundered for the line of Steely Dan's 'Rikki Don't Lose That Number'. Silver always seemed to have that crossover appeal, but the interesting thing about *Song For My Father* is the unwonted level of abstraction. Henderson's awkward 'The Kicker' comes late in the set and seems to take the music off in a different direction from the gentle Latin pulse of the opening title-track. The track that follows Henderson's is 'Lonely Woman', not Ornette Coleman's famous dirge but a beautiful line by Silver, which stands among his very finest. The CD reissue brings in some other material which heightens the exotic air of the date. 'Silver Threads Among The Soul' came from the old band, and Silver had warmed up the new group on this mate-rial, recording a vast number of takes while at Pep's in Philadelphia in August, presumably with a live album in mind. By the time the recording was made in October 1964, the music fell under the fingers very easily but with real sophistication in the solo parts. A wonderful record that never fails to deliver.

& *See also* **Blowin' The Blues Away** (1959; p. 243)

HUBERT LAWS

Born 10 November 1939, Houston, Texas
Flute

The Laws Of Jazz

Rhino 71636
Laws; Jimmy Owens (t); Garnett Brown, Tom McIntosh (tb); Benny Powell (tb, btb); Chick Corea, Rodgers Grant (p); Richard Davis, Israel Cachao Lopez, Chris White (b); Jimmy Cobb, Ray Lucas, Bobby Thomas (d); Bill Fitch, Carmelo Garcia, Raymond Orchart, Victor Pantoja (perc). April 1964–February 1966.

Hubert Laws said (1997): **'I got to New York in the fall of 1960 with nothing. I was bound for Juilliard, and I was down to my last few dollars when the phone rang and I was offered something at a place called Sugar Ray's in Harlem. And I think I've been working ever since, thank goodness.'**

One recent publication referred to him as a 'floutist', which may well be a Freudian slip because the jazz mafia has always been diffident, if not openly hostile to Hubert Laws. He plays flute for a start, which isn't everyone's favourite instrument, but he also plays fusion, which is enough to damn him unheard. Laws is a formidable technician, and brother Ronnie is a pretty decent player as well. Like Herbie Mann, Hubert began his career as a pretty straight jazz player. He sounds very crisp and dynamic here on both flute and piccolo, making a surprisingly convincing solo voice of the latter instrument. His articulation is exact but the phrases still swing and there are enough blue notes and syncopated measures to justify the jazz standard waved in the title. Almost all the material is original and 'Baila Cinderella' is an idea that resurfaces later in the flautist's career. The Latin tinge is heightened by the inclusion of Corea, but it's a pity that none of the pianist's compositions are included.

Anyone who thinks of Laws as a fusion colourist should sample this reissue of his Atlantic debut, packaged with his sophomore effort, *Flute Bylaws*, which was a more ambitious but ultimately less engaging disc.

DON RENDELL

Born 4 March 1926, Plymouth, Devon, England
Tenor saxophone, flute

IAN CARR

Born 21 April 1933, Dumfries, Scotland; died 25 February 2009, London
Trumpet

Shades of Blue / Dusk Fire

BGO Records BGOCD615 2CD
Rendell; Carr; Colin Purbrook (p on **Shades Of Blue**); Michael Garrick (p on **Dusk Fire**); Dave Green (b); Trevor Tomkins (d). October 1964, March 1966.

Ian Carr said (1986): **'We were very confident with what we were doing, and while we admired the Americans, I don't think we ever felt in awe or inferior. We were making our own way in the music.'**

The Rendell–Carr Quintet are honoured presences in British jazz. These records aren't the work of fumbling journeymen, marking time professionally as Carr waited for the epiphany of jazz-rock. But nor do they have the individuality and coherence of musical vision of Stan Tracey's 1965 *Under Milk Wood*, Graham Collier's 1967 *Deep Dark Blue Centre* or even Carr's slightly later proto-jazz-rock Nucleus albums, which are also worth searching out. An insistence on original material (there isn't a single standard as a reference-point) suggests a robust self-determination, but it also makes straightforward comparison harder. Writing a whole album in blue tones doesn't mean you can play the blues. Line and swing (Green and Tomkins aside) were probably less important than colour and texture.

The front line worked to an interesting chemistry. Carr is all fire, with anger and melancholy mixed in varying proportions. But Carr is also often exact and punctilious where Rendell, seemingly the more sophisticated soloist, is approximate. The trumpet is full-voiced and ringing while Rendell's soprano pitching (particularly on 'Dusk Fire') is sometimes drab. Despite a functioning democracy, Carr only puts his name to two tracks on the first record, the formulaic 'Sailin'', and 'Big City Strut', a loose-limbed set-closer. With the second album, Mike Garrick came aboard, an immediate bonus. 'Prayer' is instantly recognizable as his, though he surely can't have imagined 'Dusk Fire' so sourly etched. It works despite that.

This is music of its time, and it is necessary to listen on its terms, without interference from the almost cultic reputation of the band. It remains an important moment in modern British jazz none the less.

CHARLES MCPHERSON
Born 24 July 1939, Joplin, Montana
Alto saxophone

Be Bop Revisited
Original Jazz Classics OJCCD710
McPherson; Carmell Jones (t); Barry Harris (p); Nelson Boyd (b); Albert 'Tootie' Heath (d). November 1964.

Charles McPherson says: **'I remember being really nervous and excited about having Carmell Jones and Barry Harris on the record. Also, the prospect of playing a "Be Bop Motif" was certainly daunting considering the level that Bird and Diz set for alto and trumpet ensemble. But I think it turned out well.'**

McPherson credits the relatively unsung Barry Harris for his schooling in bebop, but it's clear he's also a Parker disciple and he did subsequently play some of the great man's parts that couldn't be taken from records in the Clint Eastwood film *Bird*. Of the second-generation players who allegedly took up Parker's mantle – Stitt, Morgan, Jimmy Heath – McPherson is both most like the original and most characterfully himself, a paradox that isn't easy to unpack but is easily demonstrated by reference to this fine session.

McPherson had started out on the demanding Detroit scene, only coming to New York at the end of the '50s. Harris was a decade older, the perpetually underrated Carmell Jones, originally from Kansas City, just a few years older, with a reputation largely forged on the West Coast. At the time of this recording, the trumpeter was effectively in transit to Europe, where he worked for some time. McPherson himself had been working with Charles Mingus's Jazz Workshop, an experience which undoubtedly influenced his original tack on bebop.

A glance at the track-list confirms that this isn't a straightforward repertory record. McPherson's variations on a Parker blues, placed in the middle of the set, represent both homage and declaration of independence. With nicely off-centre phrasing and a pleasingly cutting tone, he emerges as a fine middle-register improviser. On the other cuts, which include another Bird line ('Si Si'), Fats Navarro's 'Nostalgia', Bud Powell's 'Wail' and Tadd Dameron's 'Hot House' (hardly obvious choices, with the possible exception of the last), he and Harris find some intriguingly original routes through the changes. To some degree, the pianist is the hero of the set, but McPherson consistently raises his game whenever the chords turn wayward under him, and his unisons with Jones always bristle with expectation. Almost a decade on from Parker's death, bop still sounds enterprisingly, even dangerously, new.

SAM RIVERS &
Born 25 September 1923 (some sources still cite 1930), Reno, Oklahoma
Tenor and soprano saxophones, flute

Fuchsia Swing Song
Blue Note 90413
Rivers; Jaki Byard (p); Ron Carter (b); Tony Williams (d). December 1964.

Sam Rivers said of Studio RivBea (1979): **'We had two floors at 24 Bond Street, a main floor and the basement. We started out with music in the basement but I brought it up to the main floor and built some little balconies and other bits, so it was a real nice space. A lot of people played there at one time or another. It was a good place to work.'**

Rivers studied composition and viola in Boston and played saxophone in local bands, backing R&B singers and show groups, though he also worked with Miles Davis (1964) and Cecil Taylor (1968–73). During the same period he was composing and leading his own bands and occasional sessions. His and wife Beatrice's Studio RivBea became a focal point for New York jazz in the '70s, and Sam has been one of the major teachers in American jazz.

Rivers's debut on Blue Note was a shrewd attempt to blend marketable hard bop with an altogether more abstract and edgy approach to composition. The title-tune here might have made it on to jukeboxes, but the others, with the possible exception of the evergreen 'Beatrice' (dedicated to his then wife), are chewier fare. 'Ellipsis' is probably the telling title. For all the formidable chording and time-keeping of a vintage band, the tracks move in quite unexpected directions, both harmonically and rhythmically, and few of the tunes are genuinely memorable, which is why they haven't turned up in other bandleaders' songbooks.

& See also **Colors** (1982; p. 471), **Portrait** (1995; p. 592)

HARRY ARNOLD

Born Harry Arnold Persson, 7 August 1920, Hälsingborg, Sweden; died 11 February 1971, Stockholm, Sweden
Arranger, bandleader

Big Band 1964/65: Volumes 1 & 2
Dragon DRCD 379 / 382
Arnold; Nat Pavone, Weine Renliden, Gösta Nilsson, Bosse Broberg, Lars Färnlöf, Bengt-Arne Wallin, Lars Samuelsson, Bertil Lövgren, Jan Allan (t); Kenny Rupp, Andreas Skjold, George Vernon, Olle Holmquist, Gunnar Medberg (tb); Arne Domnérus, Rolf Bäckman, Bertil Erixon (as); Lennart Jansson, Claes Rosendahl, Bjarne Nerem, Rolf Blomqvist, Lennart Åberg, Rune Falk (reeds); Jan Johansson (p); Rune Gustafsson (g); Georg Riedel, Roman Dylag, Sture Åkerberg (b); Egil Johansen (d). December 1964–March 1965.

Veteran Voice of America jazz presenter Willis Conover said (1984): **'If you'd played Harry Arnold's music to an American musician or jazz critic, they always assumed it was one of the big American bands. It saddens me a little – though I maybe had a hand in perpetuating it – that some of these guys always played second fiddle to Americans.'**

Harry Arnold learned a bit of clarinet, but trained himself as an arranger and seems to have come into his mature voice all at once. His Swedish big band of the late '50s and early '60s was almost good enough to pass off as an American outfit and Quincy Jones spent some time with them, reflecting that quality.

Arnold's American recordings languish in obscurity, but Lars Westin of Dragon has done his usual excellent job in bringing back these almost forgotten dates. The label's reissue programme also showcases the mark one edition of the Orchestra from 1956 to 1958, both in the studio and in concert, with arrangements mostly by Arnold but also Gösta Theselius and Bengt Hallberg. At this point the Orchestra was still basically copping American moves, but less than a decade on it had developed a more singular identity. Jan Johansson, Georg Riedel and Pete Jacques all contributed arrangements and the reed section acquired a rich and unique sonority. 'If You Could See Me Now' is a showpiece for Domnérus; Jacques offers a trim, clever reading of Ornette's 'Tomorrow Is The Question'; there is some folk material adapted by Wallin; and Johansson offers offbeat ideas. The second disc unfolds with one memorable theme after another. Astonishingly, this stuff wasn't released at the time.

WAYNE SHORTER&

Born 25 August 1933, Newark, New Jersey
Tenor and soprano saxophones

Speak No Evil
Blue Note 99001
Shorter; Freddie Hubbard (t); Herbie Hancock (p); Ron Carter (b); Elvin Jones (d). December 1964.

Soprano saxophonist Sam Newsome says: **'When I hear Wayne Shorter's music from the Blue Note period it really reinforces the idea that "less is more". His compositions are a weird juxtaposition of high art and simple folk music that's unpredictable yet very catchy.'**

Anyone who has encountered Shorter only as co-leader of Weather Report will know him primarily as a colourist, contributing short and often enigmatic brush-strokes to the group's carefully textured canvases. They may not recognize him as the formidable heir of Rollins and Coltrane (scale up and re-pitch those brief soprano saxophone statements, and the lineage becomes clear). They will emphatically not know him as a composer. As Weather Report's musical identity consolidated, Joe Zawinul largely took over as writer. However, much as Shorter's elided 'solos' (in a group that didn't really believe in solos, or believed in nothing else) still retained the imprint of a more developed idiom, so his compositions for the early records – 'Tears' and 'Eurydice' in particular – convey in essence the virtues that make him one of the most significant composers in modern jazz, whose merits have been recognized by fellow players as far apart as Art Blakey, Miles Davis ('ESP', 'Dolores', 'Pee Wee', 'Nefertiti') and Kirk Lightsey (a challenging tribute album).

Known as 'Mr Weird' in high school, Shorter cultivated an oblique and typically asymmetrical approach to the bop idiom. His five years with the Jazz Messengers are marked by an aggressive synthesis of his two main models, but with an increasingly noticeable tendency to break down his phrasing and solo construction into unfamiliar mathematical subdivisions. Working with Miles Davis between 1964 and 1970 (a period that coincides with his most productive phase as a solo recording artist), he moved towards a more meditative and melancholy style – with an increasing dependence on the soprano saxophone. Shorter's recordings at this time relate directly to his work on Miles's *In A Silent Way* and to his work with Weather Report over the following decade.

For us, *Speak No Evil* is not just Shorter's most satisfying record, but also one of the best of its period. The understanding with Hancock was total and telepathic, two harmonic adventurers on the loose at a moment when, with John Coltrane still around as a tutelary genius, the rules of jazz improvisation were susceptible to almost endless interrogation. This album created a template for a host of imitators, but so far no one has ever produced a like recording with such strength *and* internal balance. There has always been some controversy about Freddie Hubbard's role on the session, with detractors claiming that, unlike Shorter, the trumpeter was still working the hand dealt him in the Messengers and was too hot and urgent to suit Shorter's growing structural sophistication. In fact, the two blend astonishingly well, combining Hubbard's own instinctive exuberance on 'Fee-Fi-Fo-Fum' with something of the leader's own darker conception; interestingly, Shorter responds in kind, adding curious timbral effects to one of his most straight-ahead solos on the record. As with the later *Adam's Apple*, much of the interest lies in the writing. Shorter has suggested that 'Dance Cadaverous' was suggested by Sibelius's 'Valse Triste' (which he plays on *The Soothsayer*). 'Infant Eyes' is compounded of disconcerting nine-measure phrases that suggest a fractured nursery rhyme, and the title-piece pushes the soloists into degrees of harmonic and rhythmic freedom that would not normally have been tolerated in a hard-bop context. Set *Speak No Evil* alongside Eric Dolphy's more obviously 'revolutionary' *Out To Lunch!*, recorded by Blue Note earlier the same year, and it's clear that Shorter claims the same freedoms, giving his rhythm section licence to work counter to the line of the melody and freeing the melodic Hancock from merely chordal duties. It's harder to reconstruct how alien some of Shorter's procedures were because, by and large, he does remain within the bounds of post-bop harmony, but it's still clear that this is a classic.

& *See also* **Alegría** (2002; p. 676)

JOHN COLTRANE &

Born 23 September 1926, Hamlet, North Carolina; died 17 July 1967, Huntington, New York
Tenor, soprano and alto saxophones, flute

A Love Supreme
Impulse! 051155-2
Coltrane; McCoy Tyner (p); Jimmy Garrison (b); Elvin Jones (d). December 1964.

Drummer Elvin Jones said (1984): **'At the studio, John kept taking a piece of paper out of his pocket and reading it over. I couldn't make out what it had to do with the music, but it was the poem that he printed on the cover of that record, and I guess it *was* the music.'**

The first records in Coltrane's career as a leader were the work of a man who had submerged himself in heroin and alcohol and who had mortgaged his physical health as a result. In reinventing himself technically, he also seemed to take on a new – or rediscovered – spirituality which expressed itself musically when simple materials generated torrents of harmonic and expressive detail. This is quintessentially true of *A Love Supreme*. Its foundations seem almost childishly slight, and yet what one hears is a majestic outpouring of sound, a preacher's voice, ecstatic but also authoritative. It is not a piece that can be separated from the creator's intentions and programme. Coltrane explicitly stated that the final movement, 'Psalm', should be understood as an instrumental expression of the text that was printed on the sleeve. The rest has the pace of a liturgical act. 'Acknowledgement' begins with a sweeping fanfare that will return at the close. A sonorous eight-bar theme creates the background to the four simple notes – 'A love su-preme' – which have become some of the most familiar in modern jazz. Stated by Garrison, they are reworked and varied through the scale by Coltrane, whose solo defies categorization. The overdubbed vocal chant is husky, strangely moving, and seems to occupy a different space and imprint from the hectic movement of the rhythm section. If this was to be Garrison's finest hour with the group, it is probably Jones's as well. 'Resolution' stokes the emotion. Coltrane's entry has an almost violent impact, and in LP days it was difficult to find the resolve to flip the disc over and essay the other side, even though it is clear that the music is left hanging, still bereft of the other sort of resolution. 'Pursuance' takes us into the dark wood, a troubled, mid-life moment. From now until the end, the rhythms are anxious, fractured, unsure. Horn and piano stagger like pilgrims from one brief point of rest to another. The closing 'Psalm' has an almost symphonic richness, culminating in a final 'Amen', a two-note figure in which a second saxophone (said to be Archie Shepp's) joins Coltrane. A partial restatement of the opening fanfare provides a reminder of the road travelled and also of the circularity of all such journeys. The story of the making of *A Love Supreme* has been told in Ashley Kahn's fine book, which coincided with the release of a long-awaited deluxe edition of the record. This provides a further insight into what went on in the studio during the making of the studio album, including two sextet cuts with Shepp and Davis, who are thanked on the original album but aren't heard. These are alternate versions of 'Resolution' and 'Acknowledgement'. The larger group doesn't bring anything significant to light that isn't in the original piece. More interesting is the inclusion of the quartet's performance of *A Love Supreme* at the much-bootlegged Antibes Festival of July 1965. This was a relatively rare occurrence; Coltrane only rarely played the music again, which suggests either that he considered the LP version (credited to him alone, rather than the quartet) definitive or that it occupied a less central place in his thinking than usually thought. Having awaited the revelation of the deluxe edition, we find no further epiphanies in it. Even extreme familiarity fails to tarnish *A Love Supreme*. It is without precedent and parallel, and though it must also be one of the best-known jazz records of all time, it somehow remains remote from critical pigeonholing.

& *See also* **Giant Steps** (1959; p. 248), **Ascension** (1965; p. 321)

BLUE NOTES &
Formed 1962
Group

Live In South Africa, 1964
Ogun OGCD 007
Mongezi Feza (t); Dudu Pukwana (as); Nick Moyake (ts); Chris McGregor (p); Johnny Mbizo Dyani (b); Louis Moholo (d); other musicians. 1964.

Ogun co-founder Hazel Miller says: **'They came here, lived here and died here, in exile. Not even after Nelson Mandela's release were they able to return to their beloved country. Along the way, though, they supported the ANC and freedom with their music. Unforgettable, but too readily forgotten.'**

The group was founded in the year of the Sharpeville massacre, a mixed-race group (McGregor was white) playing jazz in Durban. Not long after these recordings were made, the legendary Blue Notes went to the Saint-Juan-les-Pins Jazz Festival and never returned, eventually making their way into permanent exile, mostly in England. There, one by one, they ailed and died, broken by rain and a climate of neglect and distrust, but still having produced some of the most powerful and moving music of the time. The early group was more stylistically mixed than hindsight suggested. This is essentially a swing band, playing mostly in common time and with very few bop accents. Moholo (now the only survivor) mainly keeps it straight and the solos are delivered without much of the boiling dissonance that was to be a feature of later groups like Pukwana's Spear and Zila. It's idle now to speculate how the Blue Notes might have evolved if they'd stayed in the Cape or in a more liberal climate. As the set progresses, a mixture of McGregor and Pukwana tunes (they take the bulk of the solo space, too) with 'I Cover The Waterfront' featuring a Gonsalves-like Moyake, it becomes possible to hear some intimations of the later style. Pukwana's 'B My Dear' has a tender plangency and the tune remained in everyone's repertoire for the next four decades. Feza is less assertive than one expects, nor is the sound pristine, but this still marks an important historical release and the closing 'Dorkay House' delivers raw excitement.

& *See also* **BROTHERHOOD OF BREATH, Live At Willisau** (1973; p. 403)

DON FRIEDMAN
Born 4 May 1935, San Francisco, California
Piano

Dreams And Explorations
Original Jazz Classics OJC 1907
Friedman; Attila Zoller (g); Dick Kniss (b); Dick Berk (d). 1964.

Don Friedman said (1999): '**I met Attila in 1959. We were both interested in free playing, attracted by those atonal sounds and by any possible means of breaking out of bebop.**'

For a time, Don Friedman had the distinction of being the last piano-player used by Ornette Coleman, but he has other, more relevant claims to fame. After studying classical piano, he set to work on the burgeoning West Coast scene, playing with Chet Baker, Jimmy Giuffre, Charles Lloyd, Shorty Rogers and many others, bringing aspects of the Bill Evans style, and incorporating elements of 12-tone technique and freedom. Attila Zoller proved to be a highly sympathetic collaborator, making two fine albums with Friedman in the mid-1960s and providing a welcome second lead voice. There are a couple of standards on this 1964 date, but otherwise most of the music is original, on the 'Explorations' half of the record performed spontaneously, without predetermined structures. With sympathetic rhythm sections, Friedman and Zoller create a jazz which flirts with freedom and often runs on contrapuntal – even confrontational – lines, hotter than a Tristano school date, but with something of that doctrine. After four unsparing themes on *Dreams And Explorations*, it comes almost as a relief when they tackle the melody of John Carisi's 'Israel', which isn't a tune to coast on.

GIORGIO GASLINI

Born 22 October 1929, Milan, Italy
Piano

L'Integrale; Anthologia Cronologica: Volumes 3 & 4
Soul Note 121352/3-2 2CD
Gaslini; Don Cherry, Enrico Rava (t); Dino Piana (tb); Lorenzo Nardini (sno); Steve Lacy (ss); Gianni Bedori (as, ts, bs, f, picc); Gato Barbieri (ts); Eros Ferraresi, Mario Macchio (vn); Enrico Fiorini (vla); Dino Bazzano (clo); Bruno Crovetto, Kent Carter, Jean-François Jenny-Clark (b); Franco Tonani, Gianni Cazzola (d); orchestra, choir. 1964–1968.

Giorgio Gaslini says: '**È per questo che mi sento profondamente legato da affetto, amicizia e riconoscenza al fondatore Giovanni Bonandrini e a suo figlio Flavio per tutto quanto hanno fatto nel far conoscere il mio lavoro di una vita di musica, e in particolare per questo *Integrale* – che sta proseguendo oggi a opera della nuova proprietaria, la Cam Jazz Record di Roma. Ascoltando il percorso artistico che dal 1948 ad oggi mi rappresenta è possibile vivere e comprendere i passaggi di anno in anno di una ricerca musicale sia di forme che di contenuti che mi ha accompagnato e mi accompagna sino ad oggi. Forse testimonianza del tempo in cui viviamo.**'

Only a performer and composer whose stated aim is 'total music', a grand unified synthesis of jazz, serialism, pop, classical forms and electro-acoustic procedures, could possibly relate with equal ease to Thelonious Monk, Robert Schumann and Albert Ayler, as Gaslini did on successive records for Soul Note. One of the most distinguished players in the Italian jazz lineage, he studied composition in Milan, and composed and conducted into the early '60s, before forming a jazz quartet, which performed in factories and hospitals in an effort to bring jazz to a new audience. He has also written opera and other large-scale works. The Ayler and Monk records are deeply impressive, but for the best measure of Gaslini's skills as a composer, one has to turn to the documentation of his own music undertaken by Soul Note in several volumes.

Volumes 3 and 4 perhaps stands out for the non-specialist listener for the presence of such revered international figures as Barbieri, Carter, Cherry, Jenny-Clark and Rava, but it is in no other way superior to the rest of the sequence, which is one of the most remarkable and intellectually generous documentations of a living artist we have come across.

Newcomers might be recommended to start with some of the later records, but the reference points provided by these celebrated names are a way into Gaslini's remarkable soundworld. 'Dodici Canzoni D'Amore' sets a dozen Italian love songs to a treatment by Gaslini's group and a small string ensemble. The shabby recording doesn't help, and there are a few curious touches, such as an uncredited organ which makes theremin-like sounds here and there. Gaslini says that he gave the piano the responsibility for pathos, while the others handled the atmosphere. It's a curious but beguiling piece. His score for the film *Un Amore* takes up the rest of disc 3: the quartet with orchestra and choir. If the orchestral parts sound very like vintage Morricone, that may be because they're men of like mind; either way, this is lightweight.

The fourth disc revives his most celebrated piece of the period, 'New Feelings', with Cherry, Lacy, Barbieri, Jenny-Clark and some Italian homeboys. As a clash of serialism and free playing, it has its awkward moments and, since Gaslini wrote the basic score only the night before, it's scarcely a well-prepared scenario; but all the players must have embraced the occasion, since the enthusiasm of the playing endures. Back to the quartet for 'La Stagione Incantata', a four-seasons suite: Bedori in particular sounds as if he's been liberated by his work on 'New Feelings', and in long form Gaslini makes increasing use of space, texture and astringent melodic variation.

HERBIE HANCOCK *&*
Born 12 April 1940, Chicago, Illinois
Piano, keyboards

Maiden Voyage
Blue Note 95331
Hancock; Freddie Hubbard (t); George Coleman (ts); Ron Carter (b); Tony Williams (d). March 1965.

Herbie Hancock said (1992): **'I'm not interested in virtuosity as an end in itself. What interests me is what the music projects, in terms of drama and emotion. What I have that's maybe different to other players is a certain touch, which I recognize even in musicians who've been listening to me.'**

One of the most significant composers in modern jazz, the creator of 'Watermelon Man' and 'Dolphin Dance' as well as the unforgettable 'Rockit', the Chicagoan was a child prodigy, playing Mozart as a youngster. He's understandably wary of that designation, particularly as he heads towards his 70th year, but it sticks. Following master's work at the Manhattan School of Music, Hancock made his professional debut with Coleman Hawkins. He signed up with trumpeter Donald Byrd and came to the attention of Alfred Lion at Blue Note, who agreed to allow the 22-year-old to record with a horn-led group. Made in 1962 with Freddie Hubbard and Dexter Gordon, *Takin' Off* is already mature and poised. Some fine records followed, notably the adventurous *Empyrean Isles* and some unmatched compositions, like 'Blind Man, Blind Man', but it was *Maiden Voyage* that established him as a major presence.

It has also been tussled over. Revisionists argue that it is glib and superficial, but that somehow makes accessibility and communicativeness sound like a defect. By any measure, it's a colossal achievement from a man still just 24 years old. It is a quiet record, which also may work against it, likened by Joachim Berendt to Debussy's *La Mer*. Coleman plays with delicate understatement and Hancock never puts a foot wrong. No great surprise that the chemistry was so good: with the obvious exception of Hubbard, this was Miles's group. The title-track, 'The Eye Of The Hurricane' and 'Dolphin Dance' are all securely established in the canon, but even the less well-known tracks, including 'Survival Of The Fittest', the most developed theme of the set, are of sterling quality, and Hancock's playing on them is sure-footed, timbrally inventive and wonderfully logical without yielding to predictable cadences. It belongs in the very first rank of modern jazz records.

& *See also* **Head Hunters** (1973; p. 405)

BREW MOORE
Born Milton Aubrey Moore, 26 March 1924, Indianola, Mississippi; died 19 August 1973, Copenhagen, Denmark
Tenor saxophone

I Should Care
Steeplechase SCCD 36019
Moore; Atli Bjørn (p); Benny Nielsen (b); William Schiøpffe (d). April 1965.

Zoot Sims said (1980): **'Brew was the most faithful of the Pres disciples. Hell, he even held his saxophone the same way, and he thought anyone who didn't just hadn't learned yet.'**

Moore was a terrific but star-crossed tenor-player, at his best as good as Getz and Sims but never able to get a career together as they did. He started out in New York, then spent some time on the West Coast before trying his luck in Europe. There's only a relatively small number of surviving recordings, though every now and then that distinctive 'grey' voice – Young-like, but obviously not Lester – floats up from a larger ensemble where he's in small print. This Steeplechase album is a surviving memento from a stay in Copenhagen, a sequel to *If I Had You*. There's a sub-genre of jazz like this: exiled American playing with competent, maybe star-struck European rhythm section, spinning out long, long solos that bespeak loss, defiance, an imperious superiority in technique. Those who heard him at the time say this nicely recorded set, from a radio broadcast, doesn't catch him at his best. If so, there must have been some legendary Moore nights at the Jazzhus Montmartre. The opening blues isn't much more than a blowing line, but 'Manny's Tune' and 'In A Mellotone' inspire long, beautifully crafted statements, the kind of thing that, apart from his other foibles, made Brew the toast of Copenhagen. The city turned out to be his nemesis: Moore died when he fell down some stairs there in 1973.

RAMSEY LEWIS
Born 27 May 1935, Chicago, Illinois
Piano

The In Crowd
Universal 9545
Lewis; Eldee Young (b); Redd Holt (d). May 1965.

Ramsey Lewis said (1999): **'We talked about a lot of names for the group, like The Spiders and The Bugs – I'd been in The Cleffs before that – but Daddy-O Bailey, the DJ who really pushed our music, came up with the Ramsey Lewis Trio, and that's how we went out.'**

Like George Benson's, Lewis's genuine jazz gift has been periodically overtaken by commercial success. He's a musician who genuinely thinks beyond category and seems to regard jazz as simply part of a continuum with R&B, gospel (a particular influence and interest), blues and pop. None the less, *The In Crowd*, which launched him as a chart star in 1965, is still an eminently listenable record. If its status with jazz fans is less secure than, say, Ahmad Jamal's legendary Pershing Lounge recordings from the previous decade, then the reason is probably contextual rather than intrinsic to the music. Lewis's hit came at a time when pop – and particularly the invasion of America by British bands – was at its peak, and Lewis's music reflected that.

The trio had been recording for nearly ten years when *The In Crowd* came out, mostly for Argo and latterly Chess. It was taped at the Bohemian Caverns in Washington DC, and sees Lewis appropriating not only the title-theme, but also pop material like 'You Been Talkin' 'Bout Me Baby', the themes from *Black Orpheus* and *Spartacus*, and Jobim's 'Felicidade'. Some reissues have crammed in material from earlier and later, but the original record, as is usually the case, stands up just fine on its own. Lewis's Nat Cole-like playing has its distinctive aspects and his swaying rhythmic approach is easily identified. Bassist Eldee Young rarely gets much credit, but his Slam Stewart style vocalizing was an important aspect of the album's success. Lewis went on to make many, many more records, moving into gospel territory later in life. To some degree, *The In Crowd* is a period piece, but it's a very good one and it stands up well even now.

PETE LA ROCA
Born Peter Sims, 7 April 1938, New York City
Drums

Basra
Blue Note 875259
La Roca; Joe Henderson (ts); Steve Kuhn (p); Steve Swallow (b). May 1965.

Keith Jarrett said (1990): **'Pete La Roca? You'd never mistake him for anyone else. He has a unique sense of time, very fluid and alert. You'd know who that drummer was from the first few bars.'**

Blue Note collectors will always remember him as Pete La Roca, the nickname he picked up through his expertise as a timbale player in Latin bands, 50 years ago; but he prefers plain Pete Sims. An accomplished hard-bop drummer, he came to prominence in the late-'50s Sonny Rollins group and made a couple of records of his own. The unsung hero of many a hard-bop date, he was with Coltrane right at the start of the quartet, and arguably set the bar for Elvin Jones. His early work as leader is represented by just one record. In 1968, he gave up music to practise as an attorney and has only recently returned to playing, albeit on a part-time basis. He did record *Swingtime* with erstwhile colleague David Liebman, but it isn't an easy record to find now.

The title-track is an intriguing one-chord vamp and seems to draw something from what Pete was doing in timbale bands, as does the opening *Malagueña*, though not in a conventionally 'Latin' way. It's a formidable group, the equal of the Gilmore/Corea/Booker line-up La Roca recruited for the later *Turkish Women At The Bath*, a record with a chequered release history. Kuhn is a brilliant accompanist, in all metres, and while Henderson seems a touch withdrawn on some of this material, nailing the difficult line of 'Tears Come From Heaven', he does it without much input of his own, and that's fine, for this is very much a group performance. Joe sounds easier on the standard 'Lazy Afternoon', or more willing to put his own stamp on things. As if it were needed, *Basra* provides further evidence of Swallow's gifts as an 'upright bassist'. He stands more than tall. It's the drummer's date, though, and it's always worth pausing to work out what La Roca is doing in the background. The count's often hard to pin down, flowing and idiosyncratic, but without self-conscious eccentricity. A marvellous record which benefits hugely from modern sound.

STAN TRACEY
Born 30 December 1926, London
Piano, vibraphone

Under Milk Wood
Jazzizit 9815
Tracey; Bobby Wellins (ts); Jeff Clyne (b); Jackie Dougan (d). May 1965.

Bobby Wellins remembers: **'I was watching TV one night, some detective thing, and "that solo" was playing on the stereo in someone's house. I tried to phone Stan, but it was over in a moment.'**

Stan Tracey is one of Britain's few genuinely original contributions to world jazz and now in his 80s a very senior figure indeed. The notion of him as a second-hand, Old World version of his original mentors Duke Ellington and Thelonious Monk has been as persistent as it is misleading. Tracey doesn't play 'white man's blues', but his own distinctive form, which combines insistently percussive left-hand figures, a quirky melodism and something of Duke's capacious structural understanding. His recorded work ranges from big-band projects to free-jazz duos with fellow pianist Keith Tippett (the well-named T'N'T) and saxophonist Evan Parker. Ironically, perhaps the best-known item in his entire canon of work is a saxophone solo from the 1965 *Under Milk Wood* suite, played by Scottish-born Bobby Wellins.

Though nowadays Tracey is appropriately garlanded, it is depressing to report that when we were preparing the very first edition of the *Penguin Guide to Jazz*, in 1992, not a single Stan Tracey record, not even *Under Milk Wood*, was in print, which meant according to our very strict remit that he was excluded from that book. The situation is much better now, not just in terms of new recording, much of which appears on bassist/photographer Andy Cleyndert's Trio label, but also in the steady reappearance of Tracey's substantial '60s back catalogue. Early records like *Showcase* and *Little Klunk* catch him at the very end of his period with Ted Heath and just before he became house pianist at Ronnie Scott's, a seven-year postgraduate course whose immediate benefits can be heard in the more authoritative and individual style heard on his Columbia recordings in the '60s.

Opinions vary whether *Under Milk Wood* is the best, as well as the first, of these. In terms of musical sophistication, powerful swing and pungent writing, there were equally impressive discs to come – notably *Alice In Jazzland* in 1966, the solo *In Person* and the big-band *We Love You Madly* from a couple of years later – but Tracey's meditations on Dylan Thomas's radio play are now almost as iconic as the source material, and Wellins's great solo on 'Starless And Bible Black', all aery breath, space and quiet motion, has a haunting presence that takes hold of everyone hearing it for the first time.

Wellins had been part of Tracey's New Departures Quartet the year before. He brought an easy but muscular swing as well as powerful atmosphere and it's often overlooked how many of the charts on *Under Milk Wood* are upbeat or mid-tempo pieces. Wellins's four-bar exchanges on 'Cockle Row' reflect the broad, clever humour of the original just as well as 'Starless' captures its bleak beauty. Nor are the contributions of drummer Jackie Dougan and bassist Jeff Clyne (who died suddenly in 2009) sufficiently acknowledged. Dougan's crisp, business-like percussion recalled some of the old swing drummers in small-group settings rather more than the bop orthodoxy of the time, and Clyne's ability to master the beat and still deliver a richly resonant accompaniment is well attested on 'Llareggub' (like Sonny Rollins and Horace Silver, Dylan Thomas was fond of backward spellings) and 'I Lost My Step in Nantucket'.

Later and live versions of the suite exist, some with narration, but none have surpassed the original. *Under Milk Wood* remains one of the most distinctive records of its era, a spare, unadorned setting whose purely musical virtues should be obvious to all. It remains a pioneering work and a rare instance of jazz accommodating an outside inspiration in a way that honours the qualities of both.

WOODY HERMAN &
Born 16 May 1913, Milwaukee, Wisconsin; died 29 October 1987, Los Angeles, California
Clarinet, alto and soprano saxophones, voice

Woody's Winners / Jazz Hoot
Collectables 6678
Herman; Gerry Lamy, Bill Chase, Dusko Goykovich, Bobby Shew, Don Rader, Lloyd Michaels, Linn Biviano (t); Henry Southall, Frank Tesinsky, Donald Doane, Jim Foy, Mel Wanzo, Bill Watrous (tb); Al Gibbons, Steve Marcus, Bob Pierson, Gary Klein, Sal Nistico, Andy McGhee (ts); Tom Anastas (bs); Nat Pierce, Mike Alterman (p); Charlie Byrd (g); Tony Leonard, Bob Daughery (b); Ronnie Zito (d). June 1965, March 1967.

Woody Herman said (1977): **'I dislike the term "survivor", even when it's meant kindly. It conjures up a picture of you clinging to the wreckage. I think we're still in full sail and still doing good work. That's the best you can hope for in this business.'**

Even with pop and rock firmly in the saddle, Herman had solved the problem of artistic longevity. He simply got going, evolving his sound but sticking as closely as he dared to what he was good at and what the fan base expected. *Woody's Winners* is one of the best big-band records of its time, and it still sounds terrific. For sheer excitement, none of Herman's contemporaries could have outgunned the team he had here. Live at San Francisco's Basin Street West, the band roar through the likes of '23 Red', Sal Nistico's burn-up of 'Northwest Passage', Woody's serene 'Poor Butterfly' and the climactic demolition of Horace Silver's 'Opus De Funk'. Here it's been coupled with *Jazz Hoot*, a vinyl set which was made up of out-takes from both *Woody's Winners* and the subsequent *Live East And West*. It might seem baffling that all this music is available only through the work of smaller labels licensing it from its owners, Columbia, but at least it's out there.

& *See also* **Woody Herman 1939** (1939; p. 78), **Blowin' Up A Storm** (1945–1947; p. 102)

JOHN COLTRANE &
Born 23 September 1926, Hamlet, North Carolina; died 17 July 1967, Huntington, New York
Tenor, soprano and alto saxophones, flute

Ascension
Impulse! 543413-2
Coltrane; Freddie Hubbard, Dewey Johnson (t); Marion Brown, John Tchicai (as); Pharoah Sanders, Archie Shepp (ts); Donald Garrett (bcl, b); Joe Brazil (b, perc); McCoy Tyner (p); Art Davis, Jimmy Garrison (b); Frank Butler, Elvin Jones (d); Juno Lewis (perc, v). June & October 1965.

Saxophonist John Tchicai says: **'It was a feast, incomparable. On the day of the recording, ecstasy and excitement were the prime movers. All of us did our very best to contribute and to carry out the few instructions the Master had given us. It was very African! Our Ancestors were definitely among us more than usual!'**

There is nothing else like *Ascension* in Coltrane's work; indeed, there is nothing quite like *Ascension* in the history of jazz. By the middle of 1965, Coltrane had done as much with the quartet, technically speaking, as he seemed likely to. Even so, no one could have foreseen what was to emerge from the session of 28 June. If ever Eric Dolphy was missed, it must have been on this occasion, but Dolphy had died in Berlin the previous year.

In the simplest way, *Ascension* continues what Coltrane had been doing on *A Love Supreme*. The pattern of notes which begins the piece is a clear reference to the fanfare to 'Acknowledgement', but the vast collective improvisation which follows is almost antithetical to the highly personal, almost confessional quality of the earlier piece. The group was similarly constituted to the Ornette Coleman double quartet which recorded *Free Jazz*, though much less schematic. Coltrane devised a situation in which signals – from Hubbard and Tyner, in the main – could be given to switch modes, introducing new scalar and harmonic patterns. Soloists had a measure of freedom, and distinct ideas do seem to emerge within a broken field of gestural sounds. Everything is determined by the first few bars; nothing is determined entirely. It is a work that synthesizes the rules of classic jazz with the freedoms of the New Thing. Its success is difficult to gauge; its impact is total, overwhelming. Only slowly has it been recognized, not just as an iconic record, but a great composition. Thanks to ROVA's efforts to establish it as a performable work, that aspect of it is now more clearly understood.

As ever, the original release was hopelessly confused. It seems that Coltrane had originally authorized the release of the first version recorded, and this was issued in late 1965 as Impulse! AS-95. Then the saxophonist decided that the 'wrong' master had been used, and the second take was substituted, leaving 'Ascension – Edition I' as a piece of jazz apocrypha. Hearing them on this compilation, it is difficult to argue with Marion Brown's support of Coltrane's position. The second take is more cohesive and more expressive. The involvement of players like Brown and Tchicai – and Shepp and Sanders in particular – afforded a first chance to hear the 'school of Coltrane' in action. Predictably, no one sounds anything like the master, but the overall impact of the piece does suggest that warriors were gathering round the standard.

Individual performances serve a very different purpose here from those on previous records and on other large-scale projects of the time like Coleman's. On *Free Jazz*, solos emerge out of the ensemble and impose a rather normative structure. Here, they provide an internal commentary that does not even threaten to disrupt the integrity of the piece. The main obvious difference between the two versions is the order of play. On the revised release (*Edition II*) the solos run: Coltrane, Johnson, Sanders, Hubbard, Brown, Shepp, Tchicai, Tyner and a bass duet, while on *Edition I* Shepp and Tchicai are in front of Brown, and Elvin Jones solos near the end. Coltrane must have had reasons for his preference, but there is not so very much separating the two versions qualitatively. After a time, they resemble a rock formation seen from a subtly different angle, but still unmistakably the same grand and forbidding outcrop.

& *See also* **Giant Steps** (1959; p. 248), **A Love Supreme** (1964; p. 314)

DAVE PIKE
Born 23 March 1938, Detroit, Michigan
Vibraphone, marimba

Jazz For The Jet Set
Atlantic 8122 73527-2
Pike; Clark Terry, Melvin Lastie, Martin Shellar (t); Herbie Hancock (org); Billy Butler (g); Bob Cranshaw, Jimmy Lewis (b); Bruno Carr, Grady Tate (d). October & November 1965.

Jazz DJ Detmar Roegg says: **'I was shocked to find that Dave Pike wasn't fashionable and was maybe a bit of a laughing stock with modern jazz fans. I think he was ahead of his time, harmonically and rhythmically.'**

Pike began on drums and switched later. He worked the Coast for a time in the '50s, then moved to New York and spent three years with Herbie Mann. The Dave Pike Set became popular in Germany, where he lived for several years. The Atlantic date is programmed as a jazz-meets-pop enterprise, yet there's far more to enjoy than a glance at the cover (a space age air stewardess steered the album in a bachelor pad direction) might suggest. Terry may have been hired to lead the trumpet section, but he also gets in some typically puckish solos, and Pike himself sounds hungry just to be out front and to play on a record with his name on it. He's heard on marimba throughout, and Hancock plays nothing but organ. They make a fine partnership on the keyboardist's opening 'Blind Man, Blind Man'. The pop covers are perfectly OK: strong melodies with good hooks and eventful chord sequences, so there's nothing to fear here. It's music with considerable integrity, some strong rhythmic interest (a basic Latin swing, with some freer elements) and a nicely balanced band.

BOOKER ERVIN
Born 31 October 1930, Denison, Texas; died 31 July 1970, New York City
Tenor saxophone

Lament For Booker Ervin
Enja 2054
Ervin; Kenny Drew, Horace Parlan (p); Niels-Henning Ørsted Pedersen (b); Alan Dawson (d). October 1965, 1975.

Kenny Drew said (1979): **'Booker had a big personality – which is perhaps why he got on so well with Mingus – but that time [in Berlin] he just blew. And then he blew some more. It might have been embarrassing, if it hadn't been so good. I had trouble keeping up with him, and I was playing piano!'**

Booker started out on trombone and carried over some of the brass instrument's broad portamento effects into his reed work; he's unmistakable as a result. He taught himself saxophone while in the services and instinctively veered towards the kind of blunt, blues-soaked sound of fellow Texans like Arnett Cobb and Illinois Jacquet. He had his big break with Mingus, who liked his raw, unaffected approach. The career was painfully short, but Booker packed a lot in.

He packed a lot into one evening when in Berlin in 1965 he made a stand against the limited time allocated to each musician at an all-star saxophone event by improvising for more than 27 minutes on 'Blues For You', a filibuster that equals Paul Gonsalves's Newport monologue, and more than matches it for sheer intensity. He's probably better known for the short series of 'Book' records he made in 1963 and 1964 for Bob Weinstock at Prestige. Ironically, they too now seem like an unstaunchable outpouring of musical ideas, thoughts, opinions, inchoate feelings. They're a little shapelier than that in practice and the best of them (*The Freedom Book*) is a fine modern record, but all of it pales into insignificance alongside the 1965 concert appearance which occupies most of this record, hard, Texan blues playing at its best. To make up the weight, another Mingus alumnus, Horace Parlan, recorded a lament for Booker after his premature death and it appears alongside 'Blues For You' here, a small headstone for such a large talent.

LARRY YOUNG &

Also known as Khalid Yasin Abdul Aziz; born 7 October 1940, Newark, New Jersey; died 30 March 1978,
New York City
Organ

Unity
Blue Note 56416-2
Young; Woody Shaw (t); Joe Henderson (ts); Elvin Jones (d). November 1965.

Drummer Tony Williams said (1991): **'Larry reinvented the organ. It was a different**
instrument when he played it, and had that thing where you feel the player has never
heard anyone else doing this: he's working it out for himself, in complete freedom.'

Larry Young was the first Hammond player to shake off the pervasive influence of Jimmy
Smith and begin the assimilation of John Coltrane's harmonics to the disputed border territory between jazz and nascent rock. He was to achieve almost legendary status with bands
like Tony Williams's Lifetime and Love Cry Want, and on Miles Davis's electronic masterpiece, *Bitches Brew*. On all three, and on one-off sessions like John McLaughlin's *Devotion*,
he traded on a wild, abstract expressionist approach, creating great billowing sheets of
sound. It's unfortunate that much of what survives of his work outside these groups is a
throwback to the organ/guitar/drums jazz – he'd started out working in his father's Newark
night club – he was leaving behind at the end of the '60s.
      The step forward was dramatic. *Unity* is a modern jazz masterpiece. Whipped along by
Jones's ferocious drumming and Henderson's meaty tenor, even on a soft-pedal tune like
'Softly, As In A Morning Sunrise'. Young contributes nothing as a writer, which doesn't in
any way diminish the impact of his performance. Woody Shaw's 'The Moontrane', 'Zoltan'
and 'Beyond All Limits' are a measure of *his* under-regarded significance as a composer; the
first of the three is the perfect test of Young's absorption of Coltrane's ideas, as he develops
a rather obvious (if precocious – Shaw wrote it when he was just 18) sequence of harmonics into something that represents a genuine extension of the great saxophonist, not just a
bland repetition.

& *See also* **Lifetime, (Turn It Over)** (1971; p. 374)

ORNETTE COLEMAN &

Born Randolph Denard Ornette Coleman, 9 March 1930, Fort Worth, Texas
Alto and tenor saxophones, trumpet, violin

At The Golden Circle, Stockholm: Volumes 1 & 2
Blue Note 35518 / 35519
Coleman; David Izenzon (b); Charles Moffett (d). December 1965.

Ornette Coleman said (1983): **'I don't believe there's any difference between an idea and an**
emotion. Music is language made up of notes and keys; written language is made up of
letters which are the symbols of sounds, and they change between sounds the same way
that the letters for notes can. All of this has a profound effect on us as human beings,
which is why I say I'm not playing, I'm curing, and through the medium of language
which is the only thing, apart from sex, which brings us together.'

Blue Note's purchase on the modernist movement was uncomfortably peripheral: a single
Coltrane release, a brief skirmish with Cecil Taylor's fierce atonality, a single Eric Dolphy
record, some diffidently handled work by Andrew Hill and Bobby Hutcherson, and a tentative, but in the event patiently sustained, engagement with Ornette. These sessions from

Sweden catch the trio at its peak: densely textured, dark-toned and fierce. Much has been made of Ornette's lack of reliance on pianos, but it's obvious from these sessions that Izenzon fulfils that function. The leader may not lean on chords and progressions, may even 'hear' the harmonic sequence differently, in line with his insistence that his C might not in functional terms be your C, but, as with Dewey Redman later, he needs an anchor. Coleman plays superbly throughout. Guess-the-next-note pieces like 'European Echoes' work less well than 'Morning Song' and 'The Riddle', and the obligatory fiddle-and-trumpet feature, 'Snowflakes And Sunshine', is unusually bland. 'Faces And Places' is typical of the way Ornette built a theme out of seemingly unrelated melodic cells, a honeycomb of sound without undue sweetness and without conventional symmetry. The sound is good for a club recording, faithful to the bass and to Moffett's restless overdrive. The release in 2002 of the new editions of the Gyllene Cirkeln date added five alternative versions from other sets during the residency. In reality, they're not so very different, perhaps a little flabbier; Ornette misfingers a couple of times and Izenzon has a couple of knocks on his fretboard which might easily have been ironed out. As historical documents, though, all these tracks are essential.

& *See also* **The Shape Of Jazz To Come** (1959, 1960; p. 245), **The Complete Science Fiction Sessions** (1971, 1972; p. 387), **Colors** (1996; p. 605)

DON CHERRY*&*

Born 18 November 1936, Oklahoma City, Oklahoma; died 19 October 1995, Malaga, Spain
Pocket-trumpet, wooden flutes, doussn'gouni, piano, keyboards, miscellaneous instruments, voice

Complete Communion
Blue Note 22673
Cherry; Gato Barbieri (ts); Henry Grimes (b); Ed Blackwell (d). December 1965.

French horn-player Tom Varner recorded *Second Communion* in tribute to a hero: **'Fall 1977, Boston. I'm a transfer student at New England Conservatory. My buddy, baritone-sax-player Jim Hartog, played me *Complete Communion*. It blew me away. It *swung*, and was abstract, focused, fresh, full of humour and life, joy and great beauty. It gave me direction in my life, as an improvising "weird" brass-player. Thank you, Don Cherry!'**

Born in Oklahoma, Cherry played R&B before joining the classic Ornette Coleman quartet in the mid-'50s. After that he worked with John Coltrane and with the New York Contemporary Five. He visited Europe and subsequently retained a base there. Inveterate travel and non-stop listening led to extravagantly multicultural projects. He played Coleman's music again in Old And New Dreams and with his former leader and turned up in guest situations, though hampered by various health problems.

The 'symphony for improvisers' tag was more than a metaphor for Cherry. On his first recordings after leaving the Ornette Coleman quartet, Cherry dabbled with the idea of structuring whole LP sides round two, three or more symphonic subjects which the players could reprise and vary at will, and in real time. The most explicit approach was on *Symphony For Improvisers*, recorded nine months after *Complete Communion*. Apart from the often overlooked *The Avant-Garde* with John Coltrane, the latter was his first recording as leader.

The aim – and this may be significant given how little attention, from engineers, let alone critics, the other members of the classic Ornette Coleman quartet actually received – is to give each member of the group an equal role in the improvising process, to let the simple thematic material roll round the ensemble in the freest way. It is, as yet, an experimental aesthetic, which accounts for the raw immediacy of the set and its successor. Barbieri, whom Cherry met during their respective Italian sojourns, is at his most unfettered and Ayler-like, vocalizing intensely through the horn and producing chordal effects when the horns are in unison. Grimes was poorly audible on the original LP but he comes through strongly on the reissues and one tends to listen to him now, knowing how extraordinary his future story was.

& *See also* **Brown Rice** (1975; p. 424)

KRZYSZTOF KOMEDA

Born Krzysztof Trzcinski, 8 April 1931, Poznan, Poland; died 23 April 1969, Warsaw, Poland
Piano

Astigmatic
Harkit HKRCD 8158
Komeda; Tomasz Stańko (t); Zbigniew Namysłowski (as); Günter Lenz (b); Rune Carlsson (d). December 1965.

Tomasz Stańko says: **'It was my first professional production, a year after recruitment to Komeda's band. A regal line-up, and I was only 21. I'll never forget that night at the National Philharmonic Hall in Warsaw. One could still sense the evening concert, but Komeda, with his back slightly hunched, was already embarking us on his music, and in a way known only to himself was introducing his world of sounds. That's how he created the feeling that he wanted to keep throughout the date. One night. The great "Svantetic" fresh after the evening gig, "Astigmatic", and the future worldwide hit of "Kattorna", which I keep playing until now.'**

Komeda is the Lost Leader of Polish jazz, but increasingly recognized now beyond his homeland as an important modern composer. His writing is more compelling than his playing, which was capable but not particularly distinctive in terms of attack and solo building, and for much of his short life he was better known for the film scores he wrote (latterly as Christopher Komeda) for his friend Roman Polanski, as well as for Ingmar Bergman, Henning Carlsen and others. His work on Polanski's *Rosemary's Baby* came shortly before his death. Komeda, who was an ear, nose and throat doctor who changed his name to throw off the Communist authorities, was severely injured in a car accident in California and subsequently returned to Poland, where he died within the year.

In 1956 he made his musical debut at a small, semi-official jazz festival at the coastal town of Sopot in Poland, the forerunner to the now annual Jazz Jamboree in Warsaw. There is some early work made for a ballet staged at Cracow Engineering College, and some jazz pieces that combine classical influences with an indefinably 'Polish' element, darkly romantic but quite severe. They suggest a musician with a clear but idiosyncratic understanding of American jazz, and also a composer with a wonderful gift for suggestive musical drama.

Even with this background, *Astigmatic* comes somewhat out of the blue. It is one of the finest jazz albums ever made in Europe, and we envy anyone who can come to it fresh. It is a record that never fails to repay close attention, and has an engrossing emotional charge that is almost physical. 'Kattorna' and 'Svantetic', as well as the title-track, have a dark logic, and a harmonic progression that departs in significant ways from American models. Stańko's tone is lustrous and intense and the great Namysłowski projects his complex bop-derived lines in phrases that link together like pieces of DNA into living wholes. One misses him on the live version, where again the spotlight falls on Stańko. As ever, Komeda is a presence and a unifying element rather than a commanding soloist. The studio sound favours his rather unemphatic touch, and he certainly had a better piano in Warsaw than on the road – there is a powerful live version, available on the Power Bros label – though, listening again to the concert version, we wonder if the instrument wasn't tuned a little dark. Deliberately? There is no indication that tape speed is the problem, but it raises the interesting possibility that Komeda was already experimenting with the kind of detuning and pure sound that would resurface on *Rosemary's Baby*, a film that reasserts the tragic aura that seemed to hang round Polanski and his circle.

LOWELL DAVIDSON
Born 1941, Boston, Massachusetts; died 1990, Boston, Massachusetts
Piano

Lowell Davidson Trio
ESP 1012
Davidson; Gary Peacock (b); Milford Graves (d). 1965.

Boston guitarist Joe Morris says: **'He was a unique musician and much more than his one ESP recording suggests. He was constantly expanding his range. His piano trio music grew to be more subtle, slow moving and sonic in presentation. In the 1980s when I worked with him he played drums, and aluminum acoustic bass. The music we played could only be described as early electro-acoustic/spectralism improvisation.'**

Davidson's father was a theologian. He himself studied biochemistry at Harvard, but moved to New York and played with Ornette Coleman and briefly as drummer with the New York Art Quartet. His already obscure career was foreshortened when a laboratory accident undermined his health. He died of tuberculosis, aged only 49.

Davidson is one of those obscure figures who always seems on the brink of rediscovery. Nothing hampers his rehabilitation more than the lack of adequate recordings. His only released studio recording – apparently made by ESP without a prior audition – is a technical disgrace, shoddily balanced and with almost no bass presence. The music is fascinating, immediately different from what's considered to be the dominant Cecil Taylor school. One might say Mal Waldron is closer in overall sound and spirit. Davidson nudges at small areas of sound, moving them around his keyboard until he has built up edifices of surprising complexity. 'L' is a brilliant opener, a kind of musical self-portrait that is much more open-hearted and direct than the man's reputation might lead one to expect. The resemblance to Waldron is clearest on the sombre 'Stately 1', while 'Dunce' has a nervous and subversive energy. Graves is a brilliant partner, the acme of free-jazz drumming; Peacock's solo on 'Strong Tears' would be easier to appreciate if it were properly recorded.

A fascinating might-have-been, he continued to develop through his short life, constantly stimulating a powerful imagination through hard work, sheer intuition and, as Joe Morris observes, 'extensive use of psychedelic chemicals'. But the tapes weren't rolling.

HUGH MASEKELA
Born 4 April 1939, Witbank, South Africa
Trumpet, flugelhorn

The Lasting Impressions Of Ooga Booga
Verve 531630
Masekela; Larry Willis (p); Harold Dotson (b); Henry Jenkins (d). 1965.

Hugh Masekela said (1990): **'For me, America was Louis Armstrong, and Louis Armstrong changed the world. I came to the United States [in 1960] at an exciting time. There was civil rights and talk of change, and you could walk down one street and see John Coltrane and down another and see Max Roach, or Abbey Lincoln, or Ella. And still live on what you had. That part has changed, South Africa is going to change, but music never changes.'**

Masekela is one of the key figures in South African music, a passionate voice whose sound has the throaty urgency of a street corner preacher and the delicacy of emotion associated with Miles Davis and Chet Baker. At 20, Masekela was a founder member, with Dollar Brand and Kippie Moeketsi, of the Jazz Epistles, South Africa's first significant jazz group. Masekela then married singer Miriam Makeba and left South Africa for the US, recording classic songs like 'Grazin' In The Grass' (which sold four million copies) and becoming a spokesman and icon of the anti-apartheid movement. He also went through periods of personal self-indulgence, frankly admitted in interview and in his autobiography, which is named after his biggest hit. Some felt that the addictive 'grazing' had done his art no good, but Masekela has a survivor's instinct and sufficient brilliance as a musician to paper the cracks even in the most unpromising circumstance.

The Lasting Impressions Of Ooga Booga is a compilation of two records taped live at the Village Gate. The original LP, *The Americanization Of Ooga Booga*, was not initially followed (largely because the company had no faith in the project), and it was only after the success of Masekela's blend of mbaqanga and what he himself dubbed 'township bop' that the remaining tracks were released as *The Lasting Impression Of Hugh Masekela*, one track of which has been omitted on this reissue for reasons of space. Masekela's plangent, vocalized tone is unmistakable and these tunes, written by himself, Makeba, Willis and Caiphus Semenya, are among the strongest he ever recorded. Herbie Hancock's 'Canteloupe Island' is a reminder of how different he was from American jazz musicians of the same generation; the familiar changes are utterly transformed, pushed out into new harmonic and rhythmic territory.

SUN RA &

Born Herman Sonny Blount (also known as Sonny Bourke, Le Sony'r Ra) 22 May 1914, Birmingham, Alabama; died 30 May 1993, Birmingham, Alabama
Piano, space organ, keyboards

The Magic City
Evidence ECD 22069
Sun Ra; Walter Miller (t); Chris Capers (t, perc); Ali Hassan, Teddy Nance (tb); Bernard Pettaway (btb); Danny Davis (as, f, perc); Harry Spencer (as); Marshall Allen (as, f, picc); John Gilmore (ts, perc); Pat Patrick (bs, f, tymp); Robert Cummings (bcl, perc); Ronnie Boykins (b); Roger Blank, Jimmy Johnson Jr (d); James Jackson (perc). 1965.

Novelist Ralph Ellison said (1983): **'It's no metaphor. For Sun Ra being a black man in the American South meant you might as well have been from Alpha Centauri, let alone Saturn. That music, and *The Magic City* in particular, is about a very specific and actual alienation, not science fiction.'**

Largely recorded in Babatunde Olatunji's loft, this is a key Sun Ra recording, free and abstract, but still with a weight of jazz tradition behind it. This record is about a futuristic place trapped in the present, rather than a past civilization swallowed up by history. 'The Magic City' was a promotional slogan for Birmingham, Alabama, to boost it as a commercial centre. References to slavery and race in an accompanying poem are bound up with imagery borrowed from the Bible or *Paradise Lost*, suggesting the rootedness of Sun Ra's fantastical vision in contemporary reality and in African-American tradition. The piece itself was collectively improvised, though the confident synchronization of small-group sections within the main piece strongly suggests either an element of 'conduction' or of predetermined sequences. This was the period of Ornette's *Free Jazz* and, more to the point, of Coltrane's huge *Ascension*, and *The Magic City* stands up remarkably well in that company.

The title-track opens in mystery and chaos with Boykins's bass-lines drifting unhoused in the middle distance, clavioline sounds from Sun Ra and eventually a human touch in Marshall Allen's flute. The sense of estrangement here is complete and wonderfully sustained. The shorter 'Abstract "I"' pieces are group improvisations, stinging pungent in impact but actually more diffuse than the long title-piece. Sun Ra's made many more fine records, but probably never improved on the work of this period.

& *See also* **Jazz In Silhouette** (1958; p. 230), **Mayan Temples** (1990; p. 541)

MICHAEL GARRICK

Born 30 May 1933, Enfield, Middlesex, England
Piano, harpsichord, celeste

October Woman
Vocalion CDSML 8420
Garrick; Shake Keane (t); Joe Harriott (as); Coleridge Goode (b); Colin Barnes (d); Elizabethan Singers. 1965.

Michael Garrick says: 'I wrote "October Woman" for Shake and "Little Girl" for Joe. I felt their combined sound had an authority and magic that was unique and deeply moving – and hold that opinion even stronger today. They needed minimal notation; nowadays the "jazz-trained" guys thrive on maximum detail: exact note lengths, dynamics, etc. It was an unlooked-for benison to have them with me.'

Garrick is one of those composers of a certain age whose early work is extravagantly admired whenever it is reissued, often with no more than token recognition that he is still writing and performing. We may seem guilty of the same myopia in picking out this early record, but for the recognition that Garrick did in his quiet way set a stamp on a whole style of jazz composition in Britain. He's still probably best known for his *Jazz Praises*, which took Duke Ellington's sacred music on a step, using jazz as the basis for a body of liturgical and spiritual music which swings with the gift of tongues
   Garrick's a national treasure, but it's depressing that some of the most exciting British releases of recent years have been reissues of records made 40 years ago. *October Woman* reappeared with an additional EP of 'Anthem' and 'Wedding Hymn'. The project came out of the 'Poetry And Jazz In Concert' event which is also now available on Vocalion. The Argo label wanted more of the music, but without so much of the verse. By his own admission, Garrick was new to recording and the label weren't completely *au fait* with the jazz sound so, as Garrick puts it, 'Colin Barnes's Art Blakey inspirations were relegated well to the rear.' The piano also isn't quite up to the task, but the session as a whole has a wonderful presence that has if anything grown down the years. It may be technically unsophisticated by modern standards, but it's an intensely beautiful record.

FRANK WRIGHT

Born 9 July 1935, Grenada, Mississippi; died 17 May 1990, Berlin, Germany
Tenor saxophone

The Complete ESP-Disk Recordings
ESP-Disk 4007
Wright; Jacques Coursil (t); Arthur Jones (as); Henry Grimes, Steve Tintweiss (b); Muhammad Ali, Tom Price (d). November 1965, May 1967.

Saxophonist Peter Brötzmann said (1993): **'He was a wild man, in a good sense: made music and lived life in his own way. He was one of the first black Americans we got to know really well, and we all learned a lot from that.'**

An effective but never celebrated figure of the avant-garde, Wright left a small recorded legacy but exerted a certain influence on like-minded younger players. He played bass guitar in R&B situations round Cleveland, where he met Albert Ayler and borrowed something of his fiery expressionism. Wright moved to Europe, like many others of his kind and age, but never attained any kind of stardom even there, preferring the company of musicians to the lure of an audience.

This ESP compilation at least restores some of the small but neglected Wright canon. It's padded out with some interesting but inconsequential chat with label boss Bernard Stollman, which sits oddly amid such fiery music. The debut LP, just three tracks long, wasn't as good as the sequel, *Your Prayer*, but the little-known Price and the now almost mythical Grimes do a very respectable job behind Wright, who screams and wails in the approved Ayler manner. It's a big ask, even over the scanty, half-hour duration of the first record, which is why it's a relief to turn to the quintet tracks from 1967. The set begins with Jones's 'The Lady' and culminates with Wright's own keening title-track. Coursil was no slouch and this rhythm section seems if anything better suited to Frank's torrid approach, tempering some of his excesses.

It isn't a revelatory reissue, of the kind that can reposition a reputation. There was a further ESP record in 1974, called *Unity*, and *Uhura Na Omoja* from 1970, with Noah Howard in the front line, has also been reissued, but it's a scant body of work on which to build anything other than a musicianly reputation.

PAUL BLEY&

Born 10 November 1932, Montreal, Quebec, Canada
Piano

Closer
ESP/Calibre 1021
Bley; Steve Swallow (b); Barry Altschul (d). December 1965.

Paul Bley said (1980): **'Forming a creative music label in the 1960s was like swimming against the tide with a rock tied to your feet, but can you believe it? People were even pirating ESP records. I admired what Bernard Stollman was doing, but I think he lacked a philosophy, and would put out anything that interested him.'**

No other pianist currently active has a stylistic signature as distinctively inscribed as Paul Bley's – which is ironic, for he is a restless experimenter with an inbuilt resistance to stopping long in any one place. He favours curiously ambiguous diminuendo effects, tightly pedalled chords and sparse right-hand figures, often in challengingly different metre; working solo, he creates variety and dramatic interest by gradually changing note-lengths within a steady pulse and generates considerable dramatic tension by unexpectedly augmenting chords, shifting the harmonic centre constantly. Bley was one of the first pianists of any stature to experiment with electronic synthesizers. He also established the experimental label Improvising Artists.

Bley played hard bop in New York (where he married Carla Borg, who became Carla Bley) and began recording in 1953, for Charles Mingus's Debut label. Five years later he helped introduce the music of Ornette Coleman when the saxophonist worked with him at the Hillcrest Club in Los Angeles. Bley's Canadian background – a mixture of English reticence and French *courtoisie* – lent him a certain reserve. Instead of leading the charge in terms of stylistic innovation, he has tended to work away at his own ideas, which have consequently sometimes been overlooked. He also deferred to what he considered better composers: Coleman, Carla Bley, Annette Peacock, and yet in the case of the latter two, at least, he made their music his own. Songs like Peacock's 'Blood' and Carla's 'Ida Lupino' became staples at his hand.

Bley's brief association with the forward-thinking ESP yielded one classic trio and one now largely forgotten quintet date. The earlier date saw Bley recruiting two hornmen from the Sun Ra Arkestra and much of the interest of the album, which like its successor consists entirely of Carla Bley tunes, is in hearing Johnson and Allen in a small-group context. The music is fairly hard-edged and the presence of two such confrontational players (trumpeter Dewey Johnson was on Coltrane's *Ascension*) gives the set an uncomfortably fiery complexion that tends to singe away its more subtle moments.

Closer is still a delight nearly 50 years after first release. The key track here is 'Ida Lupino', which Carla's former husband turns into a rolling, almost filmic narrative with layers of detail that belie the simple materials. Some have noted a continuing cross-fertilization of ideas with Ornette Coleman on these tracks; his 'Crossroads' was on the original side two, just ahead of Annette Peacock's 'Cartoon'. That's harder to hear if you aren't aware of the association, but the staccato rhythms and bitten-off melodic ideas do point in that direction. It's a curious record by more recent standards, with only two out of ten tracks exceeding three minutes in length and none over four. But contained within it, almost literally, is the musical language Bley was to tease out over the next four decades.

& *See also* **Axis** (1977; p. 439), **Not Two, Not One** (1998; p. 624)

MILES DAVIS &

Born 26 May 1926, Alton, Illinois; died 28 September 1991, Santa Monica, California
Trumpet, flugelhorn, organ

The Complete Live At The Plugged Nickel
Columbia CXK 66955 7CD
Davis; Wayne Shorter (ts); Herbie Hancock (p); Ron Carter (b); Tony Williams (d). December 1965.

Miles's biographer Ian Carr said (1990): **'Miles had been in hospital through the late spring and summer, having a hip joint replaced. There were rumours of other, more serious problems. He still sounds frail, but there's an indomitable quality to the playing as well.'**

The Rosetta Stone of modern jazz: a monumental document written in five subtly and sometimes starkly different dialects but within which much of the music of the post-bop period has been defined and demarcated. When future histories of the music are written – and it would be possible to write a convincing version of the story from 1945 to 1990 merely by reference to Miles's part in it – these sessions will be adduced as a turning-point. Arguably Miles's best-ever group – responsible for *E.S.P.* in January 1965, *Miles Smiles, Sorcerer, Nefertiti* subsequently – working its way out of one phase and into another in which time and harmony, melody and dynamics, were radically rethought. The improvisations here would have been inconceivable a mere couple of years earlier; they don't so much float on the chords as react against them like phosphorus. Three years later, they fed directly into Miles's electric revolution.

To set the time and place, these were recorded (officially, by Columbia engineers) at the Plugged Nickel Club in Chicago. Though the Blackhawk sessions are better than most, the registration here is superb, not much different from what one would hope for in a studio. At first glance, one might wonder whether so repetitive a documentation would be worth either the cash or the patience, particularly when there is no new material on show.

The short answer is an emphatic yes and unambiguously so, because here it is possible to observe at the closest quarters Miles and his musicians working through their ideas set by set in ways that make the named material, the songs, more or less irrelevant. Ironically, the fact that these are mostly standards and repertory pieces heightens the originality of approach. Even when it is clear he is working from 'Stella By Starlight' or 'My Funny Valentine', Miles is moving out into areas of harmonic/melodic invention and performance dynamics which were unprecedented in the music, and doing so within the concentrated span of two nights at the club.

On the two original LPs, Columbia had forgivably presumed to deliver up the 'best' of the sessions. Carr's broadcast comment came in advance of the complete box, but the real step forward came when the music was mastered for CD and it became possible to hear Carter, who'd been away from the group for a time in mid-1965, with sufficient clarity to judge his central role in this group. His role is absolutely crucial and there are times when one can almost visualize Miles flicking from one solid outcrop to another like a caddis fly. Hancock occasionally sounds diffident and detached, and he is the only one of the group who resorts to repeated licks as the sets progress. He may have been tired, but he may also, as McCoy Tyner was to do at almost exactly the same time, have realized that he was to some extent external to the real drama of this extraordinary music.

This was the second lengthy club documentation Columbia had authorized. The 1961 Blackhawk recordings have never been as much admired, but they also benefited from fuller coverage, and should anyone want to take a quick gauge of Miles's evolution through the early '60s, the respective performances of that bop staple 'Oleo' should be enough to confirm how differently he approached the music in 1965, still several years ahead of his electric dismantlement of jazz grammar.

& *See also* **The Complete Birth Of The Cool** (1948–1950; p. 121), **Miles Ahead** (1957; p. 208), **Kind Of Blue** (1951; p. 232), **In A Silent Way** (1969; p. 361), **Agharta** (1975; p. 420)

Part 2:
1966-1970

ALBERT AYLER &

Born 13 July 1936, Cleveland, Ohio; died between 5 and 25 November 1970, New York City
Tenor, alto and soprano saxophones

Live In Greenwich Village: The Complete Impulse Recordings
Impulse! IMP 12732 2 CD
Ayler; Donald Ayler (t); George Steele (tb); Michel Sampson (vn); Joel Freedman (clo); William Folwell, Henry Grimes, Alan Silva (b); Beaver Harris, Sunny Murray (d). March 1965–February 1967.

Sunny Murray said (1990): **'Albert took some of those melodies from Swedish folk music while he was over there. Even the famous things like "Ghosts"! He was a sweet guy, nice-looking in his leather suits and leather overcoat, never anything else, and a bit of a playboy. He wanted to be a soul musician, not something in the avant-garde.'**

Ayler's music did not so much evolve as steadily expose different facets of itself. Towards the end of his life, he was the object of much dismissive criticism from jazz writers for having seemingly turned away from jazz proper and towards a brand of raw R&B, as on his *New Grass* and *Music Is The Healing Force Of The Universe*. Certainly, this music had a different surface texture to that of *Spiritual Unity* or *Bells*, but it is recognizably the same musician who is involved and there is no inconsistency in the music either. In early 1965, Ayler began recording with a string-player, using Michael Sampson subsequently on violin and Joel Freedman on cello. He would later exploit another sound unfamiliar in jazz by using Call Cobbs on harpsichord. String instruments had been part of proto-jazz ensembles in the earliest days and so there was nothing unusual or alien about the practice and the distinctive tremolo of violin or cello became an important element in Ayler's work.

Live material from the new group recorded in Lörrach and Paris is available on a fine hatOLOGY issue. Whatever technical and aesthetic shortcomings these may have had (there is a nihilistic, fragmentary quality to the latter), the Village Theater and Village Vanguard sessions are hugely affirmative and satisfyingly complete without losing a jot of Ayler's angry and premonitory force. These are essential postwar jazz recordings, and they include some of Ayler's best playing on both alto ('For John Coltrane') and tenor (the apocalyptic 'Truth Is Marching In'). The second bass, in addition to either violin or cello, actually sharpens the sound considerably, producing a rock-solid foundation for Ayler's raw witness. There are distinctly 'Scotch' elements to the music, drones, snaps and quarter-tone movements, often set to a rhythm that resembles a dragged-out strathspey.

This reissue supersedes *In Greenwich Village* and *The Village Concerts* without adding very much of significance. There is a single track ('Holy Ghost') from March 1965, originally issued on the Impulse! compilation *The New Wave In Jazz*. One other track, 'Universal Thoughts', is incomplete, presumably because the tape ran out. However, having these performances together on one set is of value. John Coltrane was present, ailing and tired, when 'Truth Is Marching In' and 'Our Prayer' were recorded at the Village Vanguard. John was to die in the summer of the following year, but his spirit is everywhere here, even though Ayler was firmly in command of his own style and approach. These are Don Ayler's finest moments. Always an approximate technician, but driven by loyalty to his brother, he produces a stream of pure sound which is unique in jazz – not even Ornette Coleman on brass sounds so alien – and still hasn't been fully acknowledged. Don Ayler's personal tragedy may even have been deeper than his brother's, certainly more protracted.

& *See also* **Spiritual Unity** (1964; p. 305)

THE JAZZ CRUSADERS
Formed 1960; previously The Swingsters and Modern Jazz Sextet, subsequently The Crusaders Group

Live At The Lighthouse '66
Pacific Jazz 605435
Wayne Henderson (tb); Wilton Felder (ts); Joe Sample (ky); Leroy Vinnegar (b); Stix Hooper (d). January 1966.

Joe Sample said (2003): **'What we do together as The Crusaders is unique to that group. We never imitated anyone and what we each do on our own has nothing to do with that sound and that philosophy. I'm very clear about that. We marched to our own tune, always, and if the industry said "Everyone jump this way", we made sure to jump *that* way.'**

The familiar line-up – Henderson, Felder, Sample, Hooper – remained in place from the start, despite individual projects, falling-outs and reshuffles. The Crusaders offer a solidly funky combo music which might almost have been programmed by a computer. It hinges on Sample's bar-room piano, Felder and Henderson's uncomplicated horn-lines, and Hooper's accurate but curiously undynamic drumming. The bass position was a revolving door. The

Crusaders never delivered less and seldom any more, but it has proved to be a highly durable formula and even the early records are still listenable today.

The live date from Hermosa Beach in 1966 offers what is presumably a pretty faithful version of what the band sounded like in concert around this time: slick, capable and unshakeably jazz-centred, doing versions of 'Round Midnight', Trane's 'Some Other Blues', 'Milestones' and 'You Don't Know What Love Is', alongside the originals. These include Sample's 'Blues Up Tight', Felder's 'Miss It', Henderson's 'Scratch' and Vinnegar's rootsier 'Doin' That Thing'. Arguably, the later stuff for Motown and MCA was more original, blending soul, funk and R&B elements into a jazz mix that remains absolutely unique, but those records suffer from the over-production of the time; by contrast, even this live date has worn better.

CHARLES LLOYD &

Born 15 March 1938, Memphis, Tennessee
Tenor saxophone, flute

Dream Weaver

Collectables COL 6361
Lloyd; Keith Jarrett (b); Cecil McBee (b); Jack DeJohnette (d). March 1966.

Charles Lloyd says: 'I knew that it had been a favourite of the Grateful Dead, and they acknowledged to me that listening to it changed the way they approached performances, opening up the possibility of improvising. A few years ago, I ran into David Crosby at my favourite Mexican food restaurant, and he told me that when *Dream Weaver* came out, they used to walk around with it under their arm so they could share it with others.'

Charles Lloyd is proof that there *are* second acts in American lives. Something of a jazz champion in the rock era, he had an appeal for young white audiences who found even electric Miles too remote. It is perhaps too easy to exaggerate the differences between 'early' and 'later', the hippy crossover star who mounted the rock zenith and the Coltrane-influenced mystic of the last two decades. In reality, the Lloyd of 1965 was every bit as thoughtful and spiritually inclined as the older man, and even when his music seems most ethereal and otherworldly, Lloyd has never lost a natural melodic gift. He'd played with Gerald Wilson, Chico Hamilton and Cannonball Adderley before forming the quartet that brought him stardom.

Even without benefit of hindsight, the Lloyd quartet was pretty exceptional. In 1967, Jarrett and DeJohnette were bursting with promise. The pianist's work here is as bold and 'outside' as it was ever to be again. Lloyd's tenor sound is rich and accurate, but with a liquid quality that also emerges from his fine flute work. *Dream Weaver* is marked by some bold writing – 'Dream Weaver', 'Sombrero Sam' – and fantastic group interplay. 'Autumn Sequence', which incorporated 'Autumn Leaves', is a wonderfully open-ended suite, with some notably dark and shadowy music even in the blissful sunshine, but it's 'Dream Weaver', another open sequence, that really shows off the group's brilliant time sense and open harmonics. The record was made and released just before the group set off for Europe and it's fair to say that world touring (including the Soviet Union) and the live records that followed (*In Europe, Love-In, Forest Flower, Journey Within*) have tended to diminish its impact and quality.

& *See also* **Voice In The Night** (1998; p. 631)

ALEX WELSH

Born 9 July 1929, Leith, Edinburgh, Scotland; died 25 June 1982, London
Cornet

Strike One
Lake LACD 107
Welsh; Roy Williams (tb); John Barnes (as, bs, cl, v); Fred Hunt (p); Jim Douglas (g, bj); Ron Mathewson (b); Lennie Hastings (d). June 1966.

Welsh's friend Robert Morton said: **'If you want a perfect example of the "Caledonian anti-szyzygy" it's got to be Alex. Every note was a lament for joy unclaimed, and a celebration of the discipline of just keeping on.'**

Despite the surname, he was a Scot. A fine cornetist, influenced by Wild Bill Davison (though he emphatically denied this). When Welsh died in 1982, Humphrey Lyttelton described the Welsh band's impact as a combination of 'romanticism and rage'. A small man with a gammy leg, he played like Tam O'Shanter outrunning Cutty Sark, with a playful fear in his tone and a headlong approach that always seemed to come out just right, if ultimately tailless.

Lake have brought back most of the '50s recordings, which are often disconcertingly mixed: the *Live At The Royal Festival Hall 1954-1955* sets are crashingly enthusiastic and will rekindle some happy memories, but some of the studio sessions on the likes of *Dixieland To Duke* and *Music From The Mauve Decade* walk an awkward line between crude Dixieland, trad and a more personal, bluesy synthesis. A good best-of from the period would probably be a welcome solution, provided it included 'New Orleans Masquerade' and 'You've Been A Good Old Wagon' by the 1955-6 incarnation of the Dixielanders.

The band changed markedly in approach during the '60s, a period during which the once teetotal Welsh acquired a famous thirst for vodka (the 'Lemonade Kid' no more), moving away from the ragged, Chicagoan 'Condon style' towards a more orthodox swing approach. On *Strike One* a long 'Davenport Blues' and 'Between The Devil And The Deep Blue Sea' confirm the change and these may be the very tracks that offend Primitive Methodists most, but Welsh's musicianship was sharpened by the transition and, with fellow Scot Ron Mathewson driving the line, he is in commanding form.

DUKE PEARSON

Born Columbus Calvin Pearson Jr, 12 August 1932, Atlanta, Georgia; died 4 August 1980, Atlanta, Georgia
Piano, celeste

Prairie Dog
Collectables 6755
Pearson; Johnny Coles (t); James Spaulding (as, f); George Coleman (ts); Harold Vick (ss, ts); Gene Bertoncini (g); Bob Cranshaw (b); Mickey Roker (d). 1966.

Trumpeter Freddie Hubbard said (1983): **'Duke was a frustrated horn-player, which is why he wrote such good lines for trumpet: me, Donald Byrd, Lee Morgan - ask any trumpeter who they'd have liked to write for them and it would be Duke.'**

Pearson's stint at Blue Note has meant that his name has been scattered through every edition of our book, without his registering strongly as a leader. Pearson's natural life was uncomfortably fated. As a young man he was thwarted in his ambitions to become a trumpeter by dental problems, and his health failed while he was still in his 40s. Named after Ellington and sharing some of the great man's piano chops and big-band sound, the Atlantan had a stint as MD and producer at Blue Note, but never entirely fulfilled his potential, and succumbed to progressive multiple sclerosis.

Pearson hit his stride by the mid-'60s. Surprisingly, his best record was made for Atlantic, not Blue Note. Perhaps he felt constricted as part of Alfred Lion's operation. *Prairie Dog* opens with Spaulding's flute, promising something evanescent and exotic but erupting into a danceable swinger. The title-track has Duke running rings round the horns, lassoing everything into shape. It closes with a glorious reading of 'Angel Eyes' which is a model of restraint and sophisticated part-writing. The piano-playing is firm and true, never virtuosic but always thought-provoking, and occasional touches of celeste are judged just right. Along with 1967's *The Right Touch,* a later octet date for Blue Note, and a rare big-band date for the label from December of the same year, this is Pearson's most accomplished work and a startling reminder of his great talent.

DUKE ELLINGTON &

Born Edward Kennedy Ellington, 29 April 1899, Washington DC; died 24 May 1974, New York City
Piano

The Far East Suite
Bluebird 82876-55614-2
Ellington; Cat Anderson, Mercer Ellington, Herbie Jones, Cootie Williams (t); Lawrence Brown, Chuck Connors, Buster Cooper (tb); Harry Carney, Paul Gonsalves, Jimmy Hamilton, Johnny Hodges, Russell Procope (reeds); John Lamb (b); Rufus Jones (d). June 1966.

Saxophonist John Dankworth said (1989): **'If you were looking for just one example, for the benefit of someone who had never heard one played, of what a saxophone could do, you wouldn't go past Johnny Hodges playing "Isfahan".'**

It should really have been *The Near East Suite*. In 1963, the State Department sent the Ellington band on a tour that took in Ceylon, India and Pakistan, most of the Middle East, and Persia. The tour was eventually interrupted by the assassination of JFK, but Duke and co-writer Strayhorn slowly absorbed the sights and tone-colours of those weeks, and nearly three years later went into the studio to record the suite. Typical of Ellington's interpretation of the genre, it is really little more than a well-balanced programme of individual songs but with a greater than usual degree of overall coherence, summed up at the end by 'Amad'. 'The Tourist Point Of View' serves as an overture and a reminder of the Duke's characteristic sound, and it introduces two of the most important solo voices, Anderson and Gonsalves. 'Bluebird Of Delhi' relates to a mynah that mocked Billy Strayhorn with a beautiful song (played by Jimmy Hamilton) and then brought him down with the resounding raspberry one hears at the end of the piece.

What follows is arguably the most beautiful single item in Ellington's and Strayhorn's entire output. Hodges' solo on 'Isfahan' is like attar of roses, once smelt, impossible to forget. Critical attention has almost always focused on Hodges, but it's important to be aware of the role of the backing arrangements, a line for the saxophones that seems as monumental as the place it celebrates. The other unquestionable masterpiece of the set is 'Mount Harissa', a soft, almost spiritual opening from Ellington, building up into a sinuous Gonsalves solo over a compulsive drum-and-cymbal pattern and huge orchestral interjections. An evocation of Agra, location of the Taj Mahal, is quite properly assigned to Harry Carney, in superb voice.

Ellington's ability to communicate points of contact and conflict between cultures, assimilating the blues to Eastern modes in tracks like 'Blue Pepper (Far East Of The Blues)', never sounds unduly self-conscious. Ellington lived on for eight years, still creating, still the dominant presence in jazz, but with diminishing powers. This was his great swan song.

& *See also* **Duke Ellington 1927–1929** (1927–1929; p. 28), **Duke Ellington 1937–1938** (1937–1938; p. 64), **Never No Lament** (1940–1942; p. 81), **The Duke At Fargo** (1940; p. 81), **Black, Brown And Beige** (1944–1946; p. 91), **Ellington At Newport** (1956; p. 189)

ROSCOE MITCHELL &
Born 3 August 1940, Chicago, Illinois
Reeds

Sound
Delmark DE 408
Mitchell; Lester Bowie (t, flhn, hca); Lester Lashley (tb, clo); Maurice McIntyre (ts); Malachi Favors (b); Alvin Fielder (d). June 1966.

Trombonist and AACM historian George E. Lewis says: **'The asymmetrical compositional forms, the frequent interjections and intercutting of unusual material, the sudden and drastic shifts in texture and colour, all tended to confound expectation, placing tremendous pressure on practices of listening that demand comfortable predictability even in supposedly radical music-making.'**

Roscoe Mitchell is one of the Titans of modern jazz music, but he remains a slightly elusive figure. This is partly because he has passed a large proportion of his career wearing the mask of the Art Ensemble Of Chicago, but also because his work is of a surpassing thoughtfulness and almost forensic precision: one does not go to Mitchell for long, 'expressive' solos built on familiar themes. As the title of this important early record suggests, pure sound and the exact placement of tones are his main concerns.

The Art Ensemble began life as Mitchell's group and was only renamed and repositioned as a total-performance group after the members left the US for France. Mitchell's own recording career both predated that and continued in parallel, but as with fellow saxophonist Joseph Jarman and (until a more popular strain foreground his work) trumpeter Lester Bowie, the solo discs have never been as widely known.

What a vital, electrifying document *Sound* remains! It's perhaps the first fully documented product of AACM thinking, delivering a rich multi-instrumentalism and an approach that eschews the familiar round of themes-and-solos in favour of a genuinely collective creative entity in which 'band' and 'music' are only pointlessly distinguished. Restored to an excellent CD edition (original Delmark vinyl was seldom very clean), with an alternative version of 'Ornette' and the title-track, originally a composite of two versions, heard as two separate takes, there is a lot more music and nothing to diminish the power of the occasion. The two key pieces, 'Sound' and 'The Little Suite', are a message of freedom quite different from that being communicated by the contemporaneous recordings of Albert Ayler and Peter Brötzmann. Mitchell organizes his group around the notion of sounds entering into – and interrelating with – silence. So there are tiny gestures and startling emptinesses alongside long lines and soliloquies. Bowie, Lashley and McIntyre work in overtones and distortions more than they do in 'true' tones, and in 'The Little Suite' the sound of toys and bells and other found instruments carries as much sensitivity as the horns do elsewhere. Both a manifesto and an unrepeatable event, *Sound* remains a marvel.

& *See also* **Composition/Improvisation Nos. 1, 2 & 3** (2004; p. 697); **ART ENSEMBLE OF CHICAGO, A Jackson In Your House / Message To Our Folks** (1969; p. 369)

STANLEY TURRENTINE

Born 5 April 1934, Pittsburgh, Pennsylvania; died 12 September 2000, New York City
Tenor saxophone

The Spoiler
Blue Note 74224
Turrentine; Blue Mitchell (t); Julian Priester (tb); James Spaulding (as, f); Pepper Adams (bs); McCoy Tyner (p); Bob Cranshaw (b); Mickey Roker (d). September 1966.

Stanley Turrentine said (1990): **'You have to be an actor. Just playing a song is only the start of it. You could train a machine to do that. It only starts being jazz when you put your life experience through the horn.'**

Father Thomas played with the Savoy Sultans, and brother Tommy was a hard-bop trumpeter. 'Mr T' worked in R&B bands in the '50s before joining Max Roach and then cutting albums for Blue Note from 1960, and with Shirley Scott for Prestige. He had crossover success in the '70s but moved back to more straight-ahead playing and latterly divided his time between both situations. Turrentine's bluesy soul-jazz enjoyed considerable commercial success in the '60s and after. His forte was the mid-tempo blues, often in minor keys, played with a vibrato as broad as his grin. A long sequence of Blue Note albums started as far back as 1960 (*Look Out!*) and ended in 1969 with *Ain't No Way*, but their availability seems to confound expectation, and Stan the Man's records seem to come and go from that catalogue with bemusing rapidity.

When *The Spoiler* reappeared it immediately went back to the top of the pile. Duke Pearson's arrangements are spot on, and his opening chart on 'The Magilla' is rather special. The all-star band could be a bunch of by-the-hour pros for all the attention they get. It's all about Stanley, who's in expansive form. He breezes through 'When The Sun Comes Out' as if it just has. 'La Fiesta' is a different tune to the Chick Corea number, and it takes a solid, bouncing beat very well. 'Sunny', 'Maybe September' (from *The Oscar*) and 'You're Gonna Hear From Me' are each like a mini-movie, packed with action and intrigue. The ensemble cast could perhaps be more generously provided for, but as a spotlight on one of the great tenors of the modern era it's impossible to beat.

BUDDY RICH

Born Bernard Rich, 30 November 1917, Brooklyn, New York; died 2 April 1987, Los Angeles, California
Drums, voice

Swingin' New Big Band
Pacific Jazz 835232-2
Rich; Bobby Shew, John Sottile, Yoshito Murakami, Walter Battagello (t); Jim Trimble, John Boice (tb); Dennis Good, Mike Waverley (btb); Gene Quill (as, cl); Pete Yellin (as, f); Jay Corre, Marty Flax (ts, cl, f); Steve Perlow (bs, bcl); John Bunch (p); Barry Zweig (g); Carson Smith (b). September–October 1966.

Buddy Rich said (1976): **'You look at an orchestral percussion-player. He gets to hit his tymps once every twenty minutes or so, or maybe waits all night to crash his cymbals for the big finale. The great thing about jazz is the drummer's always busy and sometimes the star.'**

A child performer in vaudeville, Rich was a bandleader by the time he was 11. He worked in many of the big swing bands of the '30s and spent six years with Tommy Dorsey before leading his own group. When it foundered, he freelanced, sang and did some acting, and spent five years with Harry James, before re-forming a big band in 1966. Against the run of the time, it was an international success, although heart problems interrupted an otherwise tireless working schedule. A ruthless man, though with a generous side, peerless in his technique.

The late '60s were scarcely vintage times for big bands, but Rich, who was used to stopping at nothing, drove a limousine outfit through the period with concessions that didn't really bother him much. They had items like 'Uptight' and 'Ode To Billie Joe' in the book, but they still played the likes of 'In A Mellotone' and 'Sister Sadie', and among the technique-laden sections there were players who could step out and play an individualist's solo: Don Menza, Jay Corre, Bobby Shew and Art Pepper. There are a number of Pacific albums, nearly all taken from live dates, from Hollywood or Las Vegas, and since the band thrived in performance they are among Rich's most characteristic testaments. There's nothing subtle about the arranging or the musicianship: all is speed, bravado, intensity. Not to say that the band didn't have different strokes at its disposal: some of the charts on *Swingin' New Big Band* (by a variety of hands, including Oliver Nelson, Bill Holman and Phil Wilson) are as elegant as they are assertive. But Rich's rule meant that the band had to fire on all cylinders and there were no pastel shades involved.

CECIL TAYLOR &
Born 15 March 1929 (some sources state 25 March and 1930), Long Island, New York
Piano, voice

Conquistador!
Blue Note 76749
Taylor; Bill Dixon (t); Jimmy Lyons (as); Cecil Taylor (p); Henry Grimes, Alan Silva (b); Andrew Cyrille (d). October 1966.

Cecil Taylor said (1983): **'Mr Andrew Cyrille, he is part of my skin, and his rhythm is always in the dance with me. I dislike the term "jazz". It's a word that belongs in the brothelhouses. Duke Ellington called his music "Ellingtonia". This music is mine, and American in the deepest sense. And there's nothing "free" about it.'**

An all but flawless record. Dark, difficult, unique, yet operating at an artful tangent to some of the other 'difficult' Blue Note music of the period, this is Taylor at his most devious. Dixon and Lyons are deployed as a kind of 'classic' Blue Note front line, while still playing music which, say, Freddie Hubbard and even Eric Dolphy would have found close to impossible. After a break from recording, Taylor had come to Blue Note to record *Unit Structures*, arguably the most demanding record the label ever put out and one that made explicit the language-forms that Taylor was to develop steadily through the next 30 years, in which individual monads of sound, phrases, clusters, single notes, generate patterns of energy through the music. Cyrille is key to the conception here, charged not with keeping time, but with the far more difficult task of demonstrating, moment to moment, that time is, indeed, relative and constantly mobile. It is the corollary to what Taylor is doing at the keyboard. There was nothing else like this at the time and arguably nothing like it since. Unlike any of the other great modernist experiments – Coltrane's harmonics, Coleman's 'harmolodics' – Taylor does not precede a comet's tail of followers, and yet, ironically, a putative 'Cecil Taylor influence' is adduced every time a piano-player hits the keyboard robustly or plays an atonal cluster where one might expect to find a normative chord. It's nonsense, and pernicious nonsense. It hasn't done latter-day reputations any harm, but it steadily distances Taylor's own music from any approximate understanding.

& See also **Jazz Advance** (1956; p. 191), **Nefertiti, The Beautiful One Has Come** (1962; p. 289), **Celebrated Blazons** (1990; p. 541)

JOSEPH JARMAN
Born 14 September 1937, Pine Bluff, Arkansas
Alto saxophone, other instruments

Song For
Delmark DE-410
Jarman; Bill Brimfield (t); Fred Anderson (ts); Christopher Gaddy (p, mar); Charles Clark (b); Thurman Barker, Steve McCall (d). October–December 1966.

Joseph Jarman said (1988): **'When Charles [Clark] and Christopher [Gaddy] passed [in 1968 and 1969] I was down a long way, very depressed. But Roscoe, who'd been a friend at school, he asked me to come and play with him and Lester [Bowie] and Malachi [Favors]. When we went to Europe, they said: "What is the name of this band?" We looked at one another and said: "The Art Ensemble Of Chicago".'**

Jarman was neither a square peg nor a makeweight in the Art Ensemble, but he remains perhaps the least known and appreciated. He was the first to leave the Ensemble in the '90s, but his work since is scattered and often under other leaders and he has devoted much of his time since to teaching martial arts.

Song For is relatively typical of the open-eared ethos of the AACM players, marked out by a striking use of space and silence, blending vernacular forms with avant-garde procedures. Intercut with neo-Dada recitations, some of the tracks lack formal shape and seem to proceed in an almost ritual way. The supporting performers, with the exception of the drummers, are not always up to scratch, though Clark produces some wonderfully sonorous bass on 'Adam's Rib'. The long tracks – 'Non-Cognitive Aspects Of The City', 'Song For' and a second and longer unissued take of Fred Anderson's excellent 'Little Fox Run' with its skittering marimba patterns – pall slightly on repeated hearings.

Within three years, Jarman had become a permanent member of the Art Ensemble, but he continued to make occasional recordings under his own name, for Delmark again, India Navigation and Black Saint. While they all deserve reassessment, none quite comes up to the spontaneity and magic of the debut.

CHICK COREA &
Born Armando Anthony Corea, 12 June 1941, Chelsea, Massachusetts
Piano, keyboards

Tones For Joan's Bones
Atlantic 75352
Corea; Stuart Blumberg, Woody Shaw (t); Joe Farrell (ts, f); Steve Swallow (b); Joe Chambers (d). November–December 1966.

Chick Corea said (1992): **'You know, it wasn't like the business today. I didn't feel any pressure to make a record of my own and it happened when it happened. It was more important to keep working. Now it's about building up a *discography*. I'm glad I didn't have that pressure.'**

Corea is a pianist and composer of remarkable range and energy, combining a free-ish jazz idiom with a heavy Latin component and an interest in more formal structures. Massachusetts-born, he has a Latin background, which has tinged a body of music that has embraced fusion, Bartók-influenced composition and free jazz. He is a consummately expressive player with a complex intellectual stance; he is committed to Scientology, and some of his later work draws on that belief system's curious (to outsiders) mythology, but it is a mark of Corea's brilliance as a composer that even work written to an utterly hermetic narrative programme is always joyously accessible to sceptical outsiders.

Corea's stated ambition was to assimilate the 'dancing' qualities of jazz and folk musics to the more disciplined structures of classical music. He has written a half-dozen classic melodies, notably the much-covered 'La Fiesta', 'Return To Forever' and 'Tones For Joan's Bones'. Given that he had already been playing for 20 years, there is no reason to regard *Tones* as the work of a prodigy. Under no particular pressure to record as a leader, he approached the first session, produced by Herbie Mann, with a very relaxed attitude. That is evident in every track. The title-piece is a jazz classic and the opening 'Litha' deserves to be better known. Corea's classical interests are evident in the brief 'Trio For Flute, Bassoon And Piano', which is very different from the extended hard-bop idiom of the rest of the set. Chick already sounds very much his own man and in possession of every resource that he was to exploit in future years. The writing is crisp and assured, with a gutsy swing. Tunes like 'Sundance', 'Converge' and 'The Brain' are embryonic Corea, but far from undeveloped. The band is brilliantly coloured, deep blues and shouting reds, and the remainder of the rhythm section as effective as any on the scene.

Arguably, the later trios with Miroslav Vitous and Roy Haynes (*Now He Sings, Now He Sobs*) and with Circle colleagues Dave Holland and Barry Altschul (*The Song Of Singing* and *A.R.C.*) are maturer and more satisfying performances, and certainly the *Is* sessions for Blue Note in 1969 were more ambitious, but this is the early Corea record we return to most frequently: a young master, already fully formed.

& *See also* **Light As A Feather** (1972; p. 399), **Rendezvous In New York** (2001; p. 667)

SONNY SIMMONS &

Born 4 August 1933, Sicily Island, Louisiana
Alto saxophone, English horn

Music From The Spheres

Abraxa/ESP 103

Simmons; Barbara Donald (t); Bert Wilson (ts); Michael Cohn (p); Joony Booth (b); James Zitro (d). December 1966.

Clarinettist Michael Marcus later formed The Cosmosamatics with Simmons: **'I remember during one of my first gigs with Sonny in San Francisco in the '80s, while the band was in the high state of improvisation, Sonny stopped the band suddenly, turned and whispered to everyone: "Have a fit!"'**

Simmons remains one of the most underrated figures in the music, perhaps because of his devotion to his first instrument, the cor anglais, which makes him seem something of a novelty turn. In fact, he produced, almost uniquely, a very convincing form of free jazz on the double-reeded horn, even while he was pursuing a line similar to, but harmonically and timbrally different from, Dolphy's on the alto saxophone. If there were just one figure of the modern era we would hope to ease into the spotlight, it is the man from Louisiana. He went to California as a youngster, learned saxophone, and was soon playing in Prince Lasha's group.

Like everyone else who knocked on Bernard Stollman's door, Simmons was given an ESP recording date. Like most of them, it isn't in pristine sound, but in Simmons's case it was the beginning of an important association that saw him record a good deal of material for the label, and later some illuminating interviews that are included in a fine *Complete ESP-Disk Recordings* package, which is essential listening for anyone who wants to understand the modern movement. The debut record *Staying On The Watch* announced the arrival of a fine composer, working in a free-modal idiom that sometimes sounds like a liberated version of what McCoy Tyner was doing at the same time, but with an added layer of spectral ideas.

Some admirers favour *Firebirds*, made for Contemporary a year later, but *Music From The Spheres* is the best primer to Simmons the composer/improviser. Just four tracks: 'Resolutions' builds on a nicely counterpointed line for alto (no cor on this one) and Barbara Donald's sinewy trumpet. 'Zarak's Symphony' develops a structure out of tiny, dissonant fragments, a process that makes the 'let's have a fit' blow-out that follows a much less chaotic beast than might appear. 'Balladia' might almost be something of Prince Lasha's, or more remotely, Ornette Coleman's. Again, it's a finely wrought line for the horns, but with a significant intervention by Cohen, who seems to rewrite the whole thing and pass it back to the boss, like a presidential speechwriter. 'Dolphy's Days' adds Wilson's tenor and another layer of complexity, and it's only here that the sound lets the music down.

& *See also* **Transcendence** (1996; p. 602)

MARION BROWN
Born 8 September 1935, Atlanta, Georgia
Alto saxophone

Three For Shepp
Impulse! AS 9139
Brown; Grachan Moncur III (tb); Dave Burrell, Stanley Cowell (p); Norris Jones (Sirone) (b); Bobby Capp, Beaver Harris (d). December 1966.

Marion Brown says (1986): '**Recording was different in those days. You basically just went and hung out with people, got to know them, got them interested in you, and then it happened. That's how it worked with ESP and Impulse!**'

Few contemporary musicians have delved more deeply into the sources of jazz music than Marion Brown. During the '70s, he researched African instruments and black marching bands at Wesleyan University, and he has always been an important mentor and educator in the music, specializing in teaching children how to construct and play their own instruments. Inevitably, this has meant that his own voice – and a very distinctive one it is: deceptively frail and unusually pitched – has not been heard as often as his stature suggests. Ill-health over the last two decades has limited his activities greatly. But consider that Brown's first recording date on coming to New York from Atlanta in 1965 was Coltrane's titanic *Ascension*, and that he has recorded since with Bill Dixon, Leo Smith, Anthony Braxton, Chick Corea, Gunter Hampel (a long-time association) and Mal Waldron, and his importance becomes more evident.

Perhaps Brown's best-known record is *Afternoon Of A Georgia Faun*, made for ECM in 1970 with Braxton, Corea, Andrew Cyrille, Bennie Maupin, Jeanne Lee and others, but its prominence is largely due to the top-drawer label, prestigious company and a fashionable flirtation with 'little instruments'. Musically, there are better representations of Brown, early and later. The two ESP discs are among the best of that label's mid-'60s heyday and in later years made such lovely records as *November Cotton Flower* and *Recollections*, the latter an album of solo saxophone pieces. He also recorded the exquisite *Songs Of Love And Regret* in duo with Waldron.

Curiously, Brown's Impulse! records are routinely overlooked. There were two more after this one, *Geechee Recollections* and *Sweet Earth Flying*, but they came nearly a decade after *Three For Shepp*. The delay isn't unduly sinister. In the wake of this, his first successful record, Brown took to the road, playing tirelessly but curbing his studio activities. Impulse!

had already released Shepp's *Four For Trane*. This was explicitly intended as a companion project and its arresting opening – on the original only, for the reissue pointlessly reversed the order of tracks – establishes it as one of the most inventive in the label's distinguished catalogue.

'New Blue' is indeed a reworking of blues harmony. Brown isn't quite such a harmonic maverick as Ornette Coleman, but his ability to hear and make structural use of unusual intervals is insufficiently recognized. 'Fortunato' also pushes the envelope, perhaps the chewiest piece on the set. After a further Brown composition, 'The Shadow Knows', Shepp's three pieces are played, with a different rhythm section. 'Spooks' is a remarkable, incendiary line, written and played in a style that is virtually undatable, but taking in everything from early march music to bebop. 'West India' works a second, very different variant on the blues, while the closing 'Delicado' unleashes the band in a way that resembles the inspired chaos of *Ascension*, but with a more dominant underlying pulse. Brief as it is at just 35 minutes, *Three For Shepp* is so densely packed with musical information that it takes many, many listens to deconstruct: a living lesson in musical history, a passionate manifesto for the future.

MCCOY TYNER *&*

Born Alfred McCoy Tyner, 11 December 1938, Philadelphia, Pennsylvania; also briefly known as Sulaimon Saud
Piano, koto

The Real McCoy
Blue Note 97807-2
Tyner; Joe Henderson (ts); Ron Carter (b); Elvin Jones (d). April 1967.

Pianist Don Pullen said (1992): **'All the younger guys – Herbie, Chick, everyone – come out of McCoy Tyner ... if only they'd admit it.'**

Tyner is the most influential pianist-composer in modern jazz, though given the current fetishization of Bill Evans, you'd be hard pressed to know it. Where sometimes Evans's 'legacy' consists of little more than an essentially lyrical approach, Tyner is a main source for the quartal harmonies, pentatonic scales and other exotic voicings that now turn up in modern jazz, routinely and unacknowledged.

Tyner started his professional career with Benny Golson but hooked up with John Coltrane and provided the harmonic armature for the 'classic' Coltrane quartet. The group offered little outlet for Tyner's own writing, though he did make a series of records for Impulse! while working for Trane, and the relationship ended sourly when Tyner found himself out of sympathy with the work of Coltrane's late-period music; he once harshly dismissed it as 'noise'. He had a difficult period after surrendering the piano stool to Alice Coltrane, even working for Ike and Tina Turner for a period, but an arrangement with Blue Note got him back into the studio.

There had been a gap of nearly two and a half years since the final Impulse! LP, *Plays Ellington*, which again shrewdly combined the Coltrane rhythm section with the work of a jazz master, the kind of date Bob Thiele required to offset his more adventurous releases. From the very first bars of *The Real McCoy*, his strength and individuality are clearly established. A left-hander, Tyner's bass figures have a characteristic depth and weight, while his soloing has an emphatic, almost staccato quality that can, in less expressive moments, sound like a Morse dispatch of music rather than a fully achieved performance, but which usually communicates quite grandly.

At one level, this new group is simply the Coltrane quartet with Joe Henderson substituting for Coltrane, but with Tyner calling the tunes it sounds quite different: dynamics are more varied, form is more finely articulated; and while the band pushes at the limits of tonality and metre alike, it never quite breaches them.

The opening 'Passion Dance' is a definitive Tyner composition: structured round a single key but pounding through a metre which the leader noted as 'evoking ritual and trance-like states', it gathers power through the piano and saxophone statements until it sounds ready to explode; yet the concluding regrouping and subsequent variations are resolved immaculately. 'Contemplation', 'Four By Five' and 'Search For Peace' explore this brinkmanship further, through 3/4, 4/4 and 5/4 rhythms and fragments of melody which are enough to fuel all of the band's manoeuvres. Henderson is superbly resolute in avoiding cliché, Carter and Jones work with dramatic compatibility, and Tyner's own playing exults in some of his discoveries learned over the previous three years. His grand pedal-chords and fluttering right-hand lines establish the classic patterns of call and response which have dominated his manner ever since, and the sound he gets is peculiarly translucent, enabling one to hear through the clusters and follow all of his complex lines. A modern classic, now available in near-ideal sound.

& *See also* **Sahara** (1972; p. 391), **Soliloquy** (1991; p. 548)

JOHN HANDY
Born 3 February 1933, Dallas, Texas
Alto saxophone

New View!
Koch CD 7811-2
Handy; Bobby Hutcherson (vib); Pat Martino (g); Albert Stinson (b); Doug Sides (d). June 1967.

John Handy said (1982): **'There was a little thing I did with the reed, a flutter of the tongue that produced a tremolo and made the saxophone sound like a string instrument. Apart from Roland Kirk, I haven't heard anyone who can do it, and that's not being vain!'**

Not to be confused with Captain John Handy, this Handy was born in Dallas and moved to Oakland in his early teens. He recorded with Charles Mingus, briefly but including 'Goodbye, Pork Pie Hat' on *Mingus Ah Um*, and later had a hit with 'Hard Work', in an R&B vein, but has continued to experiment in new situations, including some fascinating work with Indian musicians, which has continued up until 2006's *Musical Dreamland*.

Handy's career went through various incarnations, but *New View!* is Handy's masterpiece. The opening 'Naima', performed in the last month of composer John Coltrane's life, has a particular synchronicity, and a flavour that the unusual instrumentation hammers home. The real plus, though, is the restoration to full length of 'Tears Of Ole Miss (Anatomy Of A Riot)', which now comes in at an impressive half-hour. Also on the album is 'A Little Quiet', which shows John Hammond's gifts as a producer, the live mix balanced with genuine taste. Handy's high, keening voice has rarely been heard to better advantage.

CEDAR WALTON
Born 17 January 1934, Dallas, Texas
Piano

Cedar!
Original Jazz Classics OJCCD 462
Walton; Kenny Dorham (t); Junior Cook (ts); Leroy Vinnegar (b); Billy Higgins (d). July 1967.

Cedar Walton said (1984): **'Working with the Messengers was tough, but great training. Sometimes I'd get back from something and hadn't even unpacked when Art [Blakey] called to say we were off again. It keeps you on your toes.'**

Walton has only slowly been recognized as a significant jazz composer. After a stint in the military, the Dallas-born Walton worked with Kenny Dorham and J. J. Johnson before joining (and later rejoining) the Jazz Messengers. He also served a tour as house pianist for the Prestige label. He has a confident feel for the blues but favours a kind of angular lyricism. Tunes like 'Bolivia', 'Ojos De Rojo', 'Maestro' and 'Ugetsu' rival McCoy Tyner's work for sophisticated inventiveness. Some of the material on *Cedar!* can also be found on a later compilation, *Cedar Walton Plays Cedar Walton*, but that disc misses a fine trio, 'My Ship', which is one of the highlights of the earlier years. There are only a couple of quintet selections, and for the most part Dorham and Cook are used alternately when the composition calls for a horn. 'Turquoise Twice' and 'Head And Shoulders' are by no means as well known as the Walton compositions mentioned above, but they're quality pieces and deserve wider circulation. He's a difficult fellow to pin down. The songs are expressive enough, but it's their functional elements that are impressive, full of solid harmonic thinking and nicely argued resolutions that mostly don't seem at all predictable, or even possible. Some will favour the later work, with Clifford Jordan in Magic Triangle or some of the '90s records that highlighted recent writing, but it's our view that Walton was at his best and most typical when younger, only succumbing to influences later in his career.

CLIFFORD THORNTON

Born 6 September 1936, Philadelphia, Pennsylvania; died 25 November 1989, Geneva, Switzerland
Valve trombone, trumpet

Freedom & Unity
Atavistic Unheard Music ACP/UMS 225
Thornton; New Art Ensemble, including Joe McPhee (t); Jimmy Garrison (b). July 1967.

Joe McPhee remembers: **'That recording was extraordinarily important for me. Clifford invited me to participate and in July of 1967 we began rehearsals in an apartment on Barrow St, New York, just across the hall from the apartment of Ornette Coleman, though I didn't know that at the time. There came a knock on the door and there was Ornette offering me the use of his trumpet. That's all I played at the time and he heard me practising. I almost dropped dead from shock – my god had come to earth. He was off to Fort Worth and he said just put it back in the room when you're finished. I tried a few notes, but was too overwhelmed!'**

The underrated, perhaps almost forgotten Thornton studied with Donald Byrd and worked for a time with tubist Ray Draper, but Coltrane was his real master. *Freedom & Unity* was apparently recorded the day after John Coltrane's funeral, and with Jimmy Garrison present it must have seemed like an apostolic moment. If this was the point where Albert Ayler took up the mantle and set about restoring the relationship between avant-garde jazz, R&B and older, more primitive forms, then Clifford Thornton seemed anxious to go in the other direction. The obvious later parallel might be Anthony Braxton; both taught at Wesleyan. Thompson's fleet, almost sinuous trombone style was like nothing else at the time, but the instrument wasn't fashionable and he remained a somewhat peripheral figure. John Corbett has rescued *Freedom & Unity* from obscurity, and now Thornton's other fine record, *The Panther And The Lash*, has put in an unexpected reappearance. Joe McPhee made his recording debut with Thornton's 1967 group.

Later, in France, Thornton experimented with African-traditional materials and became known as an important educator, but he was suspected of membership of the Black Panthers and deported; he died later in Switzerland. It might be thought that his political agendas are dated now, but this music stands up strongly against anything else of the time and its reissue restores his almost vanished reputation.

DON ELLIS
Born 25 July 1934, Los Angeles, California; died 17 December 1978, Hollywood, California
Trumpet

Electric Bath
Columbia CK 65522
Ellis; Bob Harmon, Glenn Stuart, Ed Warren, Alan Weight (t); Ron Meyers, David Sanchez, Terry Woodson (tb); Reuben Leon, Joe Roccisano (as, ss, f); Ira Schulman (ts, f, picc, cl); Ron Starr (ts, f, cl); John Magruder (bs, f, bcl); Mike Lang (p, ky); Ray Neapolitan (b, sitar); Frank De La Rosa (b); Dave Parlato (b); Steve Bohannon (d); Alan Estes, Mark Stevens, Chino Valdes (perc). September 1967.

Physician Bill Anderson remembers: **'I was at that Monterey concert when I was a med student and playing jazz trumpet on the side. The band were playing sevens and nines and at one point I made it nineteens. It was crazy! I heard that he had heart problems, an arrhythmia, and always wondered if there was some obscure connection.'**

'I believe in making use of as wide a range of expressive techniques as possible,' said Ellis, who never lost sight of his own challenging credo. He used a four-valve trumpet at one time and was still bent on developing a 'superbone', the ultimate brass instrument, at the time of his early death from a heart attack. Ellis had his groups playing in extreme time-signatures, the like of which hadn't been seen since Percy Grainger, who of course was something of a California personality. Ellis helpfully pops up with a breakdown of the 19-beat figure at the start of his big band's legendary 1966 Monterey appearance: '33 222 1 222 ... of course, that's just the area code!' He was serious about what he did, though. Everything about Ellis's band was distinctive. He fielded three basses and three percussionists, played his quarter-tone trumpet, and performed programmed jazz tunes with names like 'Passacaglia And Fugue' and 'Concerto For Trumpet', none of which was mere gimmickry. Monterey MC Jimmy Lyons compares the impact of the band to that of the Stan Kenton Orchestra. That to some ears might sound two-edged, but, like Kenton, Ellis manages to combine intellectual sophistication and visceral impact.

Ellis later had problems with Columbia, who issued a bastardized version of his subsequent album *Shock Treatment*, but the very fact that a commercial label – Miles Davis's label – was willing to issue material as adventurous as this was a sign of the times. With *Electric Bath*, recorded at the high-water mark of the rock revolution, Ellis showed that jazz – albeit unorthodox – could still generate the level of excitement youngsters had come to expect as of right.

By this stage Ellis had no difficulty in combining metrical complexity with hot blowing. His own solos on 'Indian Lady' and 'Turkish Bath' are endlessly fascinating. Even seasoned brass-players, perhaps forgetting that four-valve horn, still wonder how some of the phrases were articulated. The orchestra isn't quite up to speed all the time. Asking a working band to play and swing in 17/4 is asking a lot, and yet the lineaments of the music are as clear today as they must have seemed baffling 30 years ago. The most recent reissues are superbly remastered, with a ripe, fruity bass, and include the single versions of both the compositions mentioned above. It's an exhilarating experience.

GLOBE UNITY ORCHESTRA&

Formed 1966
Ensemble

Globe Unity 67 & 70
Atavistic Unheard Music Series 223
Manfred Schoof (c, t, flhn); Kenny Wheeler (t, flhn); Jürg Grau, Claude Deron, Tomasz Stańko, Bernard Vitet (t); Paul Rutherford (tb, thn); Jiggs Wigham, Albert Mangelsdorff, Malcolm Griffiths (tb); Kris Wanders (as, bcl); Gerd Dudek (ts, ss, cl, f); Evan Parker (ts, ss); Michel Pilz (ss, bcl, f); Peter Brötzmann (ts, as, bs); Heinz Sauer (bs, ts, as); Willem Breuker (bs, cl); Alexander von Schlippenbach (p, perc); Karl Berger (vib); Derek Bailey (g); Willy Lietzmann (tba); Buschi Niebergall (b, btb); Peter Kowald (b, tba); Han Bennink (d, perc, shellhorn); Jaki Liebezeit, Mani Neumeier, Sven-Åke Johansson, Paul Lovens (d). October 1967–November 1970.

Alexander von Schlippenbach said (1966): **'From the divine indifference of the spheres emerge the solos with all the impulse of revolt. The lines they trace are the images of life.'**

Though it isn't often discussed in wider contextual terms, Globe Unity was a phenom-enon very much of its times – combining postwar political radicalism with a pan-cultural, almost cosmic view informed by the example of Karlheinz Stockhausen and Sun Ra – which managed to sustain that spirit over the next four decades. Schlippenbach's most ambitious ensemble has sustained itself with rare concerts and even rarer records. Although there has been a revolving cast of players throughout the group's existence, a few hardy spirits act as points of reference. What a great find 67 & 70 was, two sets by huge editions of the Orches-tra, one from Donaueschingen, the other from Berlin, both recorded by German radio. 'Globe Unity 67', which runs for 34 minutes, is a glorious pandaemonium of sound, the 19-strong group making a magnificent racket which scarcely lets up, but which, on careful listening, revolves around a relatively harmonious structure. The 1970 performance seems tamer in comparison, yet in formal terms this is the more freewheeling and radical piece and it's interesting to follow the parallels in working philosophy observed by the London Jazz Composers' Orchestra, whose first model was American but which existed in the same orbit as Globe Unity, moving from composition to free playing and then back to something like structure.

& *See also* **ALEXANDER VON SCHLIPPENBACH, Pakistani Pomade** (1972; p. 401), **Monk's Casino** (2003–2004; p. 683); **LONDON JAZZ COMPOSERS' ORCHESTRA, Ode** (1972; p. 393)

THELONIOUS MONK&

Born 10 October 1917, Rocky Mount, North Carolina; died 17 February 1982, Weehawken, New Jersey
Piano

Underground
Columbia Legacy 513559 2
Monk; Charlie Rouse (ts); Larry Gales (b); Ben Riley (d); Jon Hendricks (v). November 1967, February 1968.

The pianist's son, T. S. Monk, said (1998): **'You have to remember that he was considered some kind of Bolshevik, a dangerous revolutionary who was out to break things down. There's a political dimension to this music no one talks about, and because Thelonious didn't talk to the press, they made up their own version of him.'**

Columbia shrewdly signed Monk just as he was making the transition from underground to mainstream, which is why there's a certain irony in the choice of *Underground* as the title of his last small-group album for the label. No one will seriously suggest that his Columbia records match up to the genius of the Blue Notes and Riversides, but they have an impressive persistence and consistency and are delivered without compromise.

The Grammy-winning cover art was pitched at the new youth culture in a year of still-born revolutions. It shows Monk at the piano in his bunker, machine pistol slung over his shoulder, grenades on the table and a Wehrmacht officer tied to a chair behind him, while a *fille de la Résistance* poses in the background. It doesn't work quite so well at CD size, but there are a few musical grenades and rapid-fire tunes to enjoy as well. And there is that cameo appearance by Jon Hendricks on 'In Walked Bud'. On his last quartet date for Columbia, Monk introduced no fewer than four new tunes, unprecedented in this period and unrepeated after as his output slowed prior to the dramatic retirement/disappearance of 1978. One of the four, 'Ugly Beauty', is Monk's only documented composition in three-quarter time, an amazing detail only if you're unused to the devoted foursquare of his subversively traditional pianism. The other new tunes are 'Raise Four', yet another brilliant reinterpretation of the blues form, and two less well-known items, 'Green Chimneys' and 'Boo Boo's Birthday'. Neither of these has found much favour with piano-players, though Kenny Drew Jr is a great exponent of 'Boo Boo'.

The real plus of the set isn't the addition of bonus tracks but that five of the seven original titles are now in unedited form. The band is as tightly disciplined and single-minded as a Resistance cell, explosive outbursts from Riley, a strict cadence from Gales, bristling wires of melody from the much maligned Rouse and strong revolutionary philosophy from Monk, still very much the master of surprise. The irony is that the most notorious Monk cover should conceal some of his least-known tunes, though it's hard to contradict producer Peter Keepnews's assertion that this would be a significant moment in the canon even if it came in plain brown wrappers.

& *See also* **Genius Of Modern Music** (1947–1948; p. 115), **Brilliant Corners** (1956; p. 198)

JAZZ COMPOSERS ORCHESTRA &
Formed 1967
Ensemble

Communications
JCOA 841124-2
Michael Mantler (dir); Don Cherry (c); Randy Brecker, Stephen Furtado, Lloyd Michaels (flhn); Bob Northern, Julius Watkins (frhn); Jimmy Knepper, Roswell Rudd (tb); Jack Jeffers (btb); Howard Johnson (tba); Al Gibbons, Steve Lacy, Steve Marcus (ss); Bob Donovan, Gene Hull, Frank Wess (as); Gato Barbieri, George Barrow, Pharoah Sanders, Lew Tabackin (ts); Charles Davis (bs); Carla Bley, Cecil Taylor (p); Larry Coryell (g); Kent Carter, Ron Carter, Bob Cunningham, Richard Davis, Eddie Gomez, Charlie Haden, Reggie Johnson, Alan Silva, Steve Swallow, Reggie Workman (b); Andrew Cyrille, Beaver Harris (d). January–June 1968.

London Jazz Composers' Orchestra founder Barry Guy says: **'My own compositional studies in the late '60s had introduced me to this "time/space" notation via Penderecki and others and whilst composing *Ode* for LJCO using this method, the arrival of Mantler's music in 1968 was an affirmation of this approach. I decided to name my own ensemble in homage to Mike Mantler (who I only met in the '90s!). I found his work invaluable and immensely satisfying, like having a wonderful Picasso painting above my work desk.'**

Formed by Michael Mantler to commission and perform new large-scale jazz compositions. JCO's best-known product is still the massive 'chronotransduction' *Escalator Over The Hill*. From the same period came the equally ambitious *Communications*. It consists of four enormous slabs of orchestrated sound and a brief 'Preview', each with a featured soloist. Or, in the case of the opening 'Communications No. 8', two soloists: Don Cherry and Gato Barbieri. Mantler's scoring is unique. Cherry's squeaky cornet is the only high-pitched brass instrument; the sections are weighted towards french horns and trombones, with flugelhorn accents generally located in the middle register and the higher-pitched parts assigned to soprano saxophones. In addition, Mantler scores for five double basses on each track, which gives each piece a complex tonal rootedness for the soloists' (mostly) unrestrained excursions.

Roswell Rudd's playing on 'No. 10' is some of his best on record; Steve Swallow's bass introduction establishes its parameters with great exactness, and again the dark scoring works superbly. The final two-part section fully justifies Cecil Taylor's top billing. His solo part is full of huge, keyboard-long runs and pounded chords and arpeggios that leave Andrew Cyrille trailing in his wake. Very much of its time, *Communications* is still an important historical document.

& *See also* **LONDON JAZZ COMPOSERS' ORCHESTRA, Ode** (1972; p. 393)

STEVE MARCUS

Also known as 'The Count'; born 18 September 1939, New York City; died 1 October 2005, New Hope, Pennsylvania
Tenor and soprano saxophones

Tomorrow Never Knows

Water Music 120
Marcus; Mike Nock (ky); Larry Coryell (g); Chris Hills (b); Bob Moses (d). April 1968.

Larry Coryell says: **'Steve Marcus is one of the greatest saxophonists who ever lived. When he promulgated "Tomorrow Never Knows", he was aiming to do his own, Coltrane-influenced improvisation on a theme that wasn't considered "jazz" at the time. Steve never thought about the labels that get applied to music; the Beatles' music turned him on, and so, in turn, he turned on his bright light of talent as a tribute to the lads from Liverpool.'**

Is this the record that launched jazz-rock? The birth of fusion? Arguably, Coryell's Free Spirits were around earlier, with a near-identical line-up to this, but Marcus's was much more of a jazz group. Though he became associated with the new jazz-rock hybrid, Marcus had played with Woody Herman, Stan Kenton and Buddy Rich and was MD of the Rich 'ghost' band. A player of enormous resource and instinctive musicality, he seemed able to turn his hand to any form and any material. His saxophone sound, pure and keening, isn't so distinctive one would instantly pick him out of a crowd, but his way of phrasing, with a kind of liquid edge to the note-groups, is all his own.

Most of the material is pop tunes, with the Lennon–McCartney title-piece (a fiery solo from Coryell in his Hendrix phase) and 'Rain', Donovan's 'Mellow Yellow', the Byrds' 'Eight Miles High' and only former Marcus employer Gary Burton from the jazz canon at all. It has a somewhat dated sound, inevitably, but only the cloth-eared and hidebound will miss the musicality behind every phrase. Marcus also released *Count's Rock Band* and *The Lord's Prayer* (Herbie Hancock was on board) around this time, and they merit a revisit as well.

HAROLD MABERN

Born 20 March 1936, Memphis, Tennessee
Piano

A Few Miles From Memphis

Prestige PRCD 7568
Mabern; Blue Mitchell (t); George Coleman, Buddy Terry (ts); Bill Lee (b); Walter Perkins, Hugh Walker (d).
March 1968.

Harold Mabern said (1991): **'I'm not saying we feel downtrodden, and I guess it's because people associate Memphis with country music, but you don't hear anyone talking about the "Memphis sound" and all the great players that come out of there. George Coleman? Booker Little? Phineas Newborn Jr and Calvin Newborn, Alberta Hunter, Frank Strozier, Dee Dee Bridgewater ... me, too!'**

There is something about Harold Mabern that just breathes Memphis. Few jazz pianists have come so close to the essence of the blues, yet there is nothing crude or revivalist about his playing, which also indicates a heavy debt to the spacious approach of Ahmad Jamal and Phineas Newborn. He took lessons with Julian Mance Sr and played later with Benny Golson and Art Farmer, as well as a stint with Hampton, often working as an accompanist. Mabern himself has pointed out the importance of regular R&B gigs, not in the sense that these overdetermine his piano style – though they influence it deeply – but more that players of his ilk were able to play continuously and professionally on that scene, constantly learning and adapting.

A Few Miles has been reissued with Rakin' And Scrapin', pretty downhome fare on both, but with Coleman's subtle harmonic awareness informing his solos. Mabern plays bop with his own inflection, using mostly original lines which reduce the complexity but open up intriguing territory for improvisation. Shrewdly, both these early discs featured one contemporary pop song each: 'There's A Kind of Hush' on A Few Miles, 'I Heard It Through The Grapevine' (electric piano) on Rakin'. Perversely, perhaps, Harold's own 'Walkin' Back' sounds more like a chart hit, another benefit of growing up in Memphis, where song is all-pervasive.

JIMMY ROWLES

Born James George Hunter, 19 August 1918, Spokane, Washington; died 28 May 1996, Los Angeles, California
Piano, voice

Our Delight

VSOP 99
Rowles; Max Bennett, Chuck Berghofer (b); Larry Bunker, Nick Martinis (d). April 1968.

Bassist Red Mitchell said (1984): **'He's a very sweet guy, but you don't take Jimmy on when there's an issue about what music's good and what isn't. He's inclined to lay down the law on that, and there is no chance of moving him. Ever.'**

Rowles had a good deal of big-band experience under his belt before settling in Los Angeles, where he did years of studio work interleaved with club gigs, occasional feature recordings, and much work as accompanist to singers, including Billie Holiday and Peggy Lee. Rowles decamped for New York in the '70s but eventually returned West. A character player in the music, but a player full of wit and sly humour and with an encyclopedic knowledge of the American songbook.

Rowles's discography is very scattered and many of his own-name records are out of print, but there are riches even in what's left out there. Only Rowles could have got away with an album called Grandpa's Vibrato, though Subtle Legend is probably a more accurate one. Our Delight is a souvenir of one of his regular club gigs of the '60s, at The Carriage

House on Burbank, and though the recording is of mediocre amateur standard the surviving pieces have a lot of definitive Rowles, including 'Moon Of Manakoora' and 'America The Beautiful'. This was taped during a period when Jimmy wasn't making records, so it's all the more valuable for that. Some will baulk at the recording quality, but the music is sublime and covers an astonishing range, including a Wayne Shorter melody.

OSCAR PETERSON&

Born 15 August 1925, Montreal, Quebec, Canada; died 23 December 2007, Mississauga, Ontario, Canada
Piano, organ, other keyboards

My Favorite Instrument
MPS 981129-6
Peterson (p solo). April 1968.

Oscar Peterson said (1991): **'It's a cliché that in this business you don't play piano, you play pianos, and when you find one you like, or one that likes you, it's like a human relationship. You allow it its idiosyncrasies. It forgives you some rough handling.'**

Between 1963 and 1968, Peterson recorded a series of six LPs for the MPS label in the Villingen home of German producer Hans Georg Brunner-Schwer. These were made in the presence of a small group of the producer's friends and the sessions are notably relaxed as a result. These sessions were available for a time as *Exclusively For My Friends*, a comprehensive four-CD set augmented with a further disc of 'lost tapes'. To mark the 40th anniversary of these recordings, MPS reissued the original discs. Frankly, and against our usual custom, we preferred the music in boxed-set form. Though the recordings spanned some five years and some changes of personnel (a number were for trio with Ray Brown, Louis Hayes and others) there was a consistency of spirit to the whole sequence that was somehow lost when divided up into separate records. Because of that, it is difficult to make clear qualitative comparisons between them, except to say that *My Favorite Instrument*, incredibly Oscar's first solo record, is far and away the best place to start with this period of his career, even if it means back-tracking. He obviously loves this piano, and it responds warmly to him. 'Perdido', 'Who Can I Turn To?' and 'Little Girl Blue' are fantastic performances by any standard. Elsewhere, there is a lovely balance of relaxation and risk in the playing.

& *See also* **At The Stratford Shakespearean Festival** (1956; p. 193), **Night Train** (1962; p. 290), **The Legendary Live At The Blue Note** (1990; p. 539)

RAHSAAN ROLAND KIRK&

Born Ronald T. Kirk, 7 August 1936, Columbus, Ohio; died 5 December 1977, Bloomington, Indiana
Tenor saxophone, manzello, stritch, flute, assorted instruments

The Inflated Tear
Warner Jazz 8211-736142
Kirk; Ron Burton (p); Steve Novosel (b); Jimmy Hopps (d). May 1968.

Ken Vandermark says: **'"The Inflated Tear" is one of the more exquisite pieces I've ever heard and, yet, how can it be defined or categorized? I believe that this erasure of boundaries is essential work for an artist, and Kirk suggested ways in which a myriad of musical aesthetics could be brought together, without sacrificing any creativity or reducing the nature of what made the styles exciting in the first place.'**

The Inflated Tear was Roland Kirk's first studio album for Atlantic and a triumphant confirmation of his improvising powers. The title-track relates to his blindness and conveys the dreamlike oddity and human passion of his music to perfection. 'The Black And Crazy Blues' is one of his most affecting performances, unexpectedly quiet and unemphatic for an opening track, but subtly constructed on many levels. 'Creole Love Call' receives a definitive reading, but it's the other Kirk originals (which mystifyingly have rarely been picked up by other musicians) that establish a faintly mournful, sometimes throat-catchingly emotional mood: 'Many Blessings', 'A Handful Of Fives', the gorgeous 'Fly By Night' and the unpronounceable 'Lovellevelliloqui'. The band isn't by any means a top-drawer outfit, but it is perfectly adapted to Kirk's needs and Burton's handling of the chords is always surprising in its oblique fittingness.

Though there were to be many more sessions for Atlantic, and some remarkable musical moments, none quite had the emotional simplicity and directness of this one. A leftfield classic.

& *See also* **We Free Kings** (1961; p. 278); **AL HIBBLER, A Meeting Of The Times** (1972; p. 394)

PETER BRÖTZMANN &
Born 6 March 1941, Remscheid, Germany
Tenor, baritone and bass saxophones, clarinet, tarogato

Machine Gun
FMP CD 24
Brötzmann; Willem Breuker, Evan Parker (ts); Fred Van Hove (p); Buschi Niebergall, Peter Kowald (b); Han Bennink, Sven Åke Johansson (d). May 1968.

Peter Brötzmann said (1990): **'It's not about self-expression. It's about reacting to the world you live in. Around 1968, we maybe thought we could change the world, which was probably f***ing stupid, but you can make small steps, just by getting someone to hear differently. It's not revolution, but it's a step.'**

Brötzmann originally studied art in Wuppertal, and still exhibits his work on occasion. He was playing traditional jazz before moving into free, but from 1968 he was in a trio with Fred Van Hove and Han Bennink, playing in the new style. From there, he has become one of the leading Europeans and is now well known – through a strong creative connection in Chicago – to American musicians and audiences as well, and he stands as example to a whole new generation of improvisers.

By the time of *For Adolphe Sax* in September 1967 – originally pressed and distributed by the saxophonist himself – Brötzmann was already an established stylist of some intensity and focus. The huge, screaming sound he makes is among the most exhilarating in the music, and while he has often been miscast as a sonic terrorist, that does insufficient justice to his mastery of the reed family. The only precedents are to be found in the ferocious three-way assault of Albert Ayler's *Spiritual Unity*, although Brötzmann arrived at his methods independently and through the later intermediacy of Frank Wright, a Cleveland veteran who based himself in Europe.

Machine Gun raised the bar. The three saxophonists fire off a ceaseless round of blasting, overblown noise, built on the continuous crescendo managed by the two drummers. As chaotic and "68' as it sounds, the music is formed by an iron purpose and control. Although the recording is crude, the grainy timbre is a fitting medium for this. The CD has two alternative takes which match the released version in their fearsome power and there's now a *Complete Machine Gun Sessions* disc which rounds out the picture further, but, as is usually the case, the release version makes the greatest impact, out of all proportion to its duration.

& *See also* **14 Love Poems Plus 10 More** (1984; p. 487)

ELVIN JONES

Born 9 September 1927, Pontiac, Michigan; died 18 May 2004, Englewood, New Jersey
Drums

Live At The Village Vanguard

Enja 2036
Jones; Hannibal Marvin Peterson (t); George Coleman (ts); Wilbur Little (b). May 1968.

Elvin Jones said (1975): **'Club owners don't like live recordings: too much stuff lying around the place, guys crawling around fixing wires getting in the way of the drinkers! But it's the purest way to record and the most honest - people are getting what you are, and what you do, not something you've worked up in the studio.'**

The kid brother of the Jones family spent five intense years with John Coltrane before being supplanted by Rashied Ali's even more radical approach. It's a period that has somewhat overdetermined our view of Elvin's career, given that he continued to work for more than 35 years *after* Trane's death, leading his own Jazz Machine and other groups and extending his polyrhythmic approach into new areas of post-bop.

Though later he would work with Ravi Coltrane and take part in various Coltrane tribute events and recordings, in the late '60s Elvin seemed content to distance himself from the legacy, turning back to a heightened hard bop with a strong African inflexion. His records tend to be drum-led, not in the sense that percussion is well forward in the mix and there are lots of drum solos, but in that the music is all driven from the kit. This 1968 date was a tough gig in terms of its abrasive, compellingly forceful soundscapes, but also because what we are hearing for most of the time is a pianoless trio, a form Jones was to experiment with for some years. Working without a harmony instrument, and leaning very heavily on big Coleman's very sophisticated and often lateral harmonic sense, Jones plays as if he's conducting an entire orchestra - but also on occasion as if he has a personal grudge against each and every member. Little is something of a passenger in this setting and spends most of his time laying down steady, patient figures with just the odd embellishment to keep himself interested. Peterson gatecrashes on 'Mr Jones', taking the shine off another perfectly good trumpet.

SONNY CRISS

Born 23 October 1927, Memphis, Tennessee; died 19 November 1977, Los Angeles, California
Alto and soprano saxophones

Sonny's Dream

Original Jazz Classics OJCCD 707-2
Criss; Conte Candoli (t); Dick Nash (tb); Ray Draper (tba); David Sherr (as); Teddy Edwards (ts); Pete Christlieb (bs); Tommy Flanagan (p); Al McKibbon (b); Everett Brown Jr (d). May 1968.

Saxophonist Teddy Edwards said (1991): **'Sonny was a sweet guy and seemed to think that music might change the world or make everyone love one another. Funnily enough, in 1968 everyone thought that and the world just passed him by.'**

Criss was perhaps a little too tightly wrapped for the destiny that seemed to await him. Though it was the altogether more robust Sonny Stitt to whom Charlie Parker promised 'the keys of the Kingdom', it was Criss out on the West Coast who inherited most of the ambiguities of Parker's legacy. He came to Los Angeles from Memphis as a teenager and struck up with Howard McGhee and others in the Californian bebop community.

Subtitled *Birth Of The New Cool*, *Sonny's Dream* features six Horace Tapscott compositions and arrangements. Though he has only recently begun to receive wider recognition, Tapscott has had an enormous influence on the West Coast, and this was a rare chance for Criss to play in front of a carefully orchestrated mid-size band. 'Sonny's Dream' is an astonishing opener, with luminous solos from both Criss and Tommy Flanagan. Criss switches to soprano for the brief 'Ballad For Samuel', dedicated to a respected teacher, but profoundly marked by Coltrane. Tapscott's inventiveness and political sensibilities are equally engaged on 'Daughter Of Cochise' (an unusually relaxed solo from Criss) and 'Black Apostles', originally dedicated to Arthur Blythe but transformed into a ferocious lament for the three martyrs of the black liberationist movement. A remarkable album that lapses only to the extent that the band is sometimes reduced to providing highly coloured backdrops for Tapscott's American history lessons and Criss's soloing.

Criss's subsequent life was chequered. He got into community work and seemed to have found some kind of balance, but took his own life in 1977 after being diagnosed with stomach cancer.

EDDIE JEFFERSON
Born 3 August 1918, Detroit, Michigan; died 9 May 1979, Detroit, Michigan
Voice

Body And Soul
Original Jazz Classics OJCCD 396
Jefferson; Dave Burns (t); James Moody (ts, f); Barry Harris (p); Steve Davis (b); Bill English (d). September 1968.

Eddie Jefferson said (1977): **'It was King Pleasure who recorded "Moody's Mood For Love" first, so people thought he wrote it, but Pleasure – my man – he told folks it was me. Otherwise, I don't imagine we'd be talking about this right now!'**

Originally a dancer, Jefferson is little known among younger jazz fans, and various attempts to revive interest in 'The Godfather Of Vocalese' in recent years have fallen flat. There is a widespread belief that King Pleasure wrote the lyrics to 'Moody's Mood For Love', a vocalized transcription of James Moody's alto saxophone solo on 'I'm In The Mood For Love'; Pleasure certainly made it a monster hit, but the song was Jefferson's, as was the lyric for Hawkins's 'Body And Soul'.

The singer's longest-standing partnership with saxophonist Moody was rekindled in the '60s when Jefferson, who had been eclipsed by smoother talents like Jon Hendricks, staged something of a comeback. He made a few good records during the decade. *Letter From Home* in 1961 has a heavyweight line-up, with Clark Terry, Johnny Griffin, Junior Mance and others, all chipping in. Joe Zawinul is the pianist and his 'Mercy, Mercy, Mercy' is one of the highlights of *Body And Soul*, alongside a lively version of Miles's 'So What'. There's still a certain resistance to vocalese – even fans who have overcome a suspicion of scat singing draw a line – but Jefferson's musicianship is palpable on every track and his buoyant delivery pushes through some slightly questionable lyrics. His end was dramatic and shocking, shot to death outside a nightclub in his home town.

GARY BURTON &

Born 23 January 1943, Anderson, Indiana
Vibraphone

Country Roads And Other Places
Koch Jazz 7854
Burton; Jerry Hahn (g); Steve Swallow (b); Roy Haynes (d). September 1968.

Gary Burton said (1983): **'You know, back in those days, if you put something as simple as a major triad in a composition, that was taken as a sign you were playing rock or country, but certainly not jazz, which was more "difficult". I was kind of intrigued by that, and by the possibility of making sophisticated jazz out of those very simple materials.'**

Burton's early recordings were driven by an ambition to synthesize jazz, rock and country music. At the same time, he was pioneering a four-mallet technique in vibes-playing which allowed him to play detailed lead-lines on top of rich but essentially simple harmonies, a major step on from Milt Jackson's two-mallet approach and blues-derived improvisations. Though not a prolific composer, Burton has specialized in definitive realization of other composers' work.

After a few relatively orthodox RCA dates, the work becomes more individual. From 1966, *Tennessee Firebird* is almost a country set. Perhaps too Nashville for some tastes, but think what Bill Frisell was doing to great critical acclaim three decades later, and most jazz purists will swallow their disdain for a record featuring Chet Atkins and Charlie McCoy. *Duster*, a year later, was one of the first jazz-rock records, and though it seems tame compared to later examples of the genre, it had impact, even if only as permission to mix rock beats and distorted guitar into a jazz performance. He recorded Carla Bley's 'dark opera without words', *A Genuine Tong Funeral*, intended for full staging with costumes and lights but known only as a recorded piece, and one which yielded the often covered 'Mother Of The Dead Man'. The CD reissue is augmented by *Lofty Fake Anagram*, which was long out of circulation, and while it lacks the energy and grace of *Country Roads*, it's a tremendous showcase for Coryell.

Country Roads is still a joy after more than 30 years. The playing is as fresh and unfettered as ever, and themes like 'Family Joy', 'And On The Third Day' and 'Country Roads' are delightfully nostalgic. The album marked the debut of Jerry Hahn – more evidence of Burton's acuity at spotting guitar-players – who keeps his occasional excesses well under control and plays smooth lines with a lot of rhythmic pace. Burton is in excellent form, dancing on the bars, and then suddenly changing pace to accommodate the gracious sweep of 'My Foolish Heart' and 'Wichita Breakdown'. There is even a small Ravel arrangement, but the main 'other place' – most citations of the album title omit its second half – is unquestionably jazz.

& *See also* **Hotel Hello** (1974; p. 411), **For Hamp, Red, Bags And Cal** (2000; p. 654)

ANTHONY BRAXTON &

Born 4 June 1945, Chicago, Illinois
Saxophones, clarinets, flutes, piano

For Alto
Delmark 420
Braxton (as solo). October 1968.

Anthony Braxton said (1993): **'The alto saxophone is my piano. At a solo concert I could play one piece on flute, one on a bass saxophone, or a clarinet, but there is a challenge to playing language type music on one instrument, and that happens to be the one I am most familiar with, right from the beginning.'**

Few modern musicians have been so extensively documented or been so controversial. Braxton joined the AACM in Chicago and emerged as a free-jazz experimenter who claims influences as far afield as the cool, white saxophone sound of Paul Desmond and Warne Marsh, the doo-wop/old town music of Frankie Lymon and the Teenagers, and the cosmic vision of Sun Ra. The Braxton discography is vast and still growing apace, perhaps the most complete documentation of any improvising artist ever. It ranges in scope from solo saxophone performances to more or less orthodox jazz combos to huge orchestral and operatic projects, the latter based on Braxton's evolving cosmology/mythography, which is admixed equally of African sources and science fiction. He is, depending on perspective, an intensely puzzling figure whose theories border on obscurantism or a sublimely direct communicator who has taken the trouble to articulate his practices in a way few 'jazz' musicians have done. His music divides to some extent into procedural periods, but essentially he deals with the same material(s) as most improvising musicians, small, cellular structures which, though numbered as individual compositions, are readily carried over from one performance to the next, creating dense palimpsests of sound.

It all comes down in the end, though, to a man standing alone playing an alto saxophone, though 40 years ago that itself seemed a radical undertaking, if it wasn't dismissed as a kind of high-end busking. Braxton had made an earlier showing on Delmark in 1968 (recorded then, at least), the year of presumptive revolutions, with *Three Compositions Of New Jazz* but it was *For Alto* that declared an epoch in modern jazz. Here Braxton virtually deconstructs his instrument. The piece dedicated to John Cage moves into areas where the saxophone is no longer played idiomatically or even identifiably but creates its own soundworld, very much in accordance with Cagean philosophy. Instrumentality of a conventional sort has been dispensed with. Bent notes, smears, trills and tongue-slaps are by no means new in jazz; indeed they have always been part of the jazz musician's dialect. What Braxton does here is to make them the basis of a new language, but one that is somehow still in contact with Charlie Parker, Paul Desmond, Johnny Hodges, familiar and reliable aspects of jazz language.

There are moments when he appears to invoke and to subvert the structure of the blues, and it is possible to hear the whole of *For Alto* as a radical gloss on that form. But it's no mere musicological exercise; nor is it polemic. Braxton creates a highly personal drama and one that was to provide the template for much of what he was to do subsequently. *For Alto* is one of the genuinely important American recordings, still powerfully listenable and endlessly fascinating.

& *See also* **New York, Fall 1974** (1974; p. 416), **Creative Orchestra Music** (1976; p. 431), **Quartet (London / ... Birmingham / ... Coventry) 1985** (1985; p. 495), **Nine Compositions (Iridium) 2006** (2006; p. 714)

ALAN SILVA
Born 22 January 1939, Bermuda
Double bass, cello, other instruments

Skillfullness
ESP 1091

Silva; Becky Friend (f, v); Mike Ephron (p, org); Dave Burrell (p); Karl Berger (vib); Barry Altschul (d); Lawrence Cooke (perc). 1968.

Alan Silva said (2007): **'I thought about ways to conduct free improvisation. I'd watched what Sun Ra did, but my model was John Coltrane's *Ascension* ... the things that Coltrane *didn't* do there. The first ten minutes of that changed everything, but if he'd gone straight on with the collective improvisation, there might have been nothing left for me to do!'**

A remarkable, complete musician, Silva took up double bass only after studying trumpet with Donald Byrd for several years, as well as violin and piano. In later years, he gave up bass playing for synthesizer, but at bottom Silva was always a composer/leader, whether working in unstructured idioms with the Free Form Improvisation Ensemble or with his own Celestrial [sic] Communication Orchestra. Some of this was, of course, inspired by Sun Ra, but that diminishes the originality of Silva's music.

It is a chaotic discography and often available only in limited editions or obscure reissues, but this early record, made just before Silva left the US for Europe and released in 1970, sums up his musical vision. The opening 'Skillfullness' has Silva playing piano, violin and cello and vocalizing rapturously. Karl Berger's vibraphone-playing is revelatory, quite outside anything else being done at the time on that instrument or any other, and Becky Friend's flute helps give the piece an otherworldly and almost weightless air. For all the hippy fantasies of rock and the space operas emerging on the fringes of jazz, nothing of the time quite captures its spirit – ethereal but grounded in sophisticated intelligence and high technical skill – quite as well.

The second piece, 'Solestrial Communications Number One', marks Silva's first documented attempt to 'conduct' an improvisation, a forerunner of the 'conductions' of Butch Morris and others, but again very much influenced by Sun Ra's gestural direction and reminiscent of Miles Davis's evolving Zen master approach to leadership, where changes in stance or expression might suggest a change of direction in the music. This is very much a *Zeitgeist* record, but much more interesting than a mere historical document. The quality of concentration and playing from the group – Silva does not perform on this track – is staggering. Burrell's instinctive polytonality and polystylistics are just right for Silva's music and Altschul's drumming compresses huge amounts of vernacular culture, from fife and drum bands to marches to Elvin Jones. It's a brief record, just those two tracks, but an essential one.

CARLA BLEY &
Born Carla Borg, 11 May 1938, Oakland, California
Piano, keyboards

Escalator Over The Hill
JCOA/ECM 839 310 2 2CD

Bley; Michael Mantler (t, vtb, p); Enrico Rava, Michael Snow (t); Don Cherry (t, f, perc, v); Sam Burtis, Jimmy Knepper, Roswell Rudd (tb); Jack Jeffers (btb); Bob Carlisle, Sharon Freeman (frhn); John Buckingham, Howard Johnson (tba); Peggy Imig, Perry Robinson (cl); Souren Baronian (cl, dumbec); Jimmy Lyons, Dewey Redman (as); Gato Barbieri (ts); Chris Woods (bs); Sam Brown, John McLaughlin (g); Karl Berger (vib); Don Preston (syn, v); Jack Bruce (b, v solo); Charlie Haden, Ron McClure, Richard Youngstein (b); Leroy Jenkins (vn); Nancy Newton (vla); Calo Scott (clo); Bill Morimando (bells); Paul Motian (d); Roger Dawson (perc); Jane Blackstone,

Paul Jones, Sheila Jordan, Jeanne Lee, Timothy Marquand, Tod Papageorge, Linda Ronstadt, Bob Stewart, Viva (v solo); Jonathan Cott, Steve Gebhardt, Tyrus Gerlach, Eileen Hale, Rosalind Hupp (v). November 1968–June 1971.

Carla Bley says: **'I used every musician I knew for the cast. I even used some people I didn't know; all they had to do was ask to be in it and I said: "Of course you can." At one point I needed some extra chorus voices quickly so I went out on the street in front of the studio and enlisted passers-by.'**

Carla Bley was, unusually, recognized first as a composer – Gary Burton performed her *Genuine Tong Funeral* to great acclaim and became with second husband Michael Mantler co-leader of the Jazz Composers Orchestra Association. The JCOA label transformed into Watt, which has put out all her recordings since, including duos with long-term partner Steve Swallow, small groups, big and very big bands. Somewhat like first husband Paul Bley, she is deeply versed in all aspects of jazz language and uses that knowledge to subvert expectations. Her compositions are typically dense, harmonically subtle or ambiguous and almost always written with key improvisers in mind.

In our cynical youth we suggested that *Escalator Over The Hill* was a terrific record to have heard but not so good for actually listening to. And yet it has remained with us for nearly 40 years, admired – and listened to – like few other new works of its period. Its faults are manifest: an impenetrable libretto by poet Paul Haines, outsize and ungainly, and yet packed with tremendous music and an aura all its own. Whatever a 'chronotransduction' is, it is more closely related to the non-linear, associative cinema of avant-garde film-makers Kenneth Anger, Stan Brakhage, Maya Deren and Jonas Mekas (at whose Cinémathèque some sessions were recorded) than to any musical parallel. The repetitious dialogue is influenced by Gertrude Stein and it's perhaps best to take Stein's Alice-in-Wonderland advice and treat everything as meaning precisely what one chooses it to mean. Musically, it's a patchwork of raucous big-band themes like the opening 'Hotel Overture', which has fine solos from Barbieri, Robinson, Haden and Rudd, heavy rock numbers like the apocalyptic 'Rawalpindi Blues' (McLaughlin, Bruce, Motian), ethnic themes from Don Cherry's Desert Band, and mysterious, ring-modulated 'dream sequences'. There is an element of recitative that, as with most opera recordings, most listeners will prefer to skip, since it doesn't advance understanding of the 'plot', and it's probably best to treat *Escalator* as a compilation of individual pieces with dispensable continuity. It was almost certainly *A Genuine Tong Funeral* rather than *Escalator* that established Bley's mature musical idiom, but as the years have rolled by this strange work has secured a unique place in the musical landscape, and one we visit surprisingly often.

& See also **Fleur Carnivore** (1988; p. 524)

HERBIE MANN
Born Herbert Jay Solomon, 16 April 1930, Brooklyn, New York; died 1 July 2003, Santa Fe, New Mexico
Flute, tenor saxophone, clarinets

Memphis Underground
Atlantic 7567 81364
Mann; Roy Ayers (vib, perc); Bobby Emmons (org); Larry Coryell, Sonny Sharrock, Reggie Young (g); Bobby Wood (p, electric p); Tommy Coghill, Mike Leach, Miroslav Vitous (b); Gene Christman (d). 1968.

Guitarist Larry Coryell remembers: **'I had just been booted out by Gary Burton because I wanted to rock! So I went over to Herbie. He said: "It's time to take some Ex-Lax." As second guitarist, I let my hair down. For his part, Herbie was a "general among generals". He had all these new, strong players and he devised a way to unify them – by covering**

R&B tunes. Herbie was the best leader for whom I ever worked – flat out. He wasn't
Hubert Laws, but he could play.'

Non-stop touring honed Mann's flute style and opened him to a huge range of influences,
from bop and bossa nova to rock and Japanese classical music. His light skipping attack is
matched by an unfailing rhythmic sureness. He slowly evolved a powerful and adaptable
technique which gave him access to virtually every mood, breathy and ethereal, smooth
and semi-vocalized (and reminiscent of his first instrument, clarinet), to a tough, metal-
lic ring ideal for funk. He started out playing bop tenor, but dabbled in more experimental
situations when he started recording as leader, playing an entire record of bass clarinet, and
another of solo flute, both rarities at the time.

He had a spell in the studios before he started exploring the Latin funk-fusion that made
his name. Almost everyone except loyal fans forgets just how good he was, and how prolific
– *Memphis Underground* was something like his 60th album, and only a quarter of the way
through his recording career. It's a hardy perennial. The recording quality would scarcely
pass muster nowadays, but the music survives unexpectedly well, as Mann and his main
soloists transform some rather lacklustre material ('Hold On, I'm Comin'', 'Chain Of Fools'
and 'Battle Hymn Of The Republic' don't promise much) into a record with real presence
and lasting power. The interplay of three guitarists, notably the Cain and Abel opposition
of Sonny Sharrock and Larry Coryell, gives it a distinctive flavour; Sharrock shreds, Coryell
coasts on the R&B/country feel of the rhythm section. The addition of Roy Ayers's vibes and
Bobby Emmons's organ gives the background a seething quality that adds depth to Mann's
slightly unemotional virtuosity. The one-time presence of Miroslav Vitous on 'Hold On ...'
is worth noting. Head and shoulders with Charles Lloyd (Lloyd apparently drew him on a
blindfold test and said 'I don't know who that is, but he's a better flautist than I am!') above
most of the crossover experimenters of the time, Mann is something of a forgotten hero of
the music at a low ebb in its public appeal.

JOHN MCLAUGHLIN &
Born 4 January 1942, Doncaster, Yorkshire, England
Guitar

Extrapolation
Polydor 841598
McLaughlin; John Surman (ss, bs); Brian Odgers (b); Tony Oxley (d). January 1969.

John Surman remembers: **'I met John Mc on a recording session for Georgie Fame. Later,
he called me for a recording. As I recall, both Oxley and I were actually playing a set with
Ronnie's nine-piece that evening, so we left the session which was in Advision near Bond
Street, walked to Ronnie's, played out a set with the band, and then came back and
finished the record.'**

Coming to London in the '60s as a young and already experienced professional drawn to
swing and the blues, McLaughlin fell into a scene where the boundaries between jazz and
rock, commercial and experimental music, were substantially blurred. Within a short time
of recording *Extrapolation* he was to travel to the US to record with Miles Davis on the
Bitches Brew sessions and to join Tony Williams's volcanic Lifetime. A little later, he would
form his own Mahavishnu Orchestra, which cast early '70s jazz-rock in a notably rarefied
and spiritual form. Later years saw McLaughlin develop a profound interest in Indian music
(with another group, Shakti) and classical forms. He remains, though, a rare virtuoso of
both electric and acoustic guitar, with a highly personal sound on each.

Extrapolation is one of the finest jazz records ever made in Europe. The circumstances of its recording are consistent with the spirit of the time, as are the forms – nearly all short with only 'Binky's Beam' significantly extended – which touch on blues, folk, swing, bebop and even some modern-classical ideas, but without settling into any specific 'genre'. The emotional range and dynamics are already typical of what became McLaughlin's familiar spectrum of gently meditative runs and furious, irregularly metred scrabbles, but with all his virtues (accuracy, power, vision) already in place. The band was state of the art for 1969. Oxley's drumming has the firmness of a rock beat, even when the count is extremely irregular, and Surman's playing is cast midway between folksy melodizing and something uniquely his own. Odgers is the least well known, but an admired player of the period. Some British jazz fans will claim 'Binky's Beam' as their favourite track of all time. The whole set has a durable, timeless feel.

& *See also* **MAHAVISHNU ORCHESTRA, The Inner Mounting Flame** (1971–1972; p. 386)

TONY OXLEY
Born 15 June 1938, Sheffield, Yorkshire, England
Drums, electronics

The Baptised Traveller
Columbia 494438 2
Oxley; Kenny Wheeler (t, flhn); Evan Parker (ts); Derek Bailey (g); Jeff Cline (b). January 1969.

Tony Oxley said (1992): **'I start out with what's like an old theatre kit, with all these bits and pieces around it, like would have been used for creating sound-effects during a performance, not at all like a big swing kit or a rock kit, and I suppose the electronics stuff emerged out of that, a whole orchestra of sounds that can be triggered from right here on the stool.'**

Tony Oxley served an apprenticeship in pub bands and then learned a more formal craft as a military conscript with the Black Watch. He was a key player in the early days of the British free scene, notably the Joseph Holbrooke trio with Derek Bailey and Gavin Bryars. Later years saw another trio, SOH, with Alan Skidmore and Ali Haurand, and the Celebration Orchestra, which reveals him to be a composer of considerable sophistication. Most of his pieces move relatively slowly, even if there is a lot of surface detail. Large acoustic masses seem to operate in three dimensions, as if rotated round some non-tonal axis.

Oxley's CBS albums have enjoyed legendary status for years, and now only *Ichnos*, an even more adventurous vehicle for Oxley's pin-sharp sound and ideas, remains un-reissued. *The Baptised Traveller* is the most representative and coherent expression of his gifts. Thirled to a quest for identity, its four themes are calmly questioning, the two horns restlessly ranging over Cline's and Oxley's unceasing shifts of direction. 'Crossing' and 'Arrival', which are segued into a single improvisation, wipe clean almost all formal expectations. Oxley's stately reading of Charlie Mariano's 'Stone Garden' is one of the masterworks of contemporary music, a slow chorale rooted in Bailey's chiming guitar chords. Their almost orchestral quality provides a starting-point for Parker's solemn quiddities and for virtuosic percussion from Oxley. The closing 'Preparation' isn't so much an anti-climax as an afterthought.

The subsequent *Four Compositions* was a title guaranteed to offend anyone who wanted to set aside any implication of predetermined structures, but it was an indication of the direction Oxley was going in, though in recent years he has more often been seen in Cecil Taylor's group or in duo situations than as an ensemble leader. Another exile without much honour in his own country.

RALPH SUTTON

Born 4 November 1922, Hamburg, Missouri; died 29 December 2001, Evergreen, Colorado
Piano

Live At Sunnie's Rendezvous 1969: Volumes 1 & 2

Storyville STCD 8286 / 8281
Sutton; Bob Wilber (ss, cl); Al Hall (b); Cliff Leeman (d). February 1969.

Just prior to the interview, Ralph Sutton said: **'Shall we just have a little taste? Get the top off this thing, and just have a little taste …?'** Several hours later, the interview began: **'Mishter Shutton …'**

Sutton was one of the premier stride and swing piano-players in jazz for 50 years, although it was only in later years that he got on record as a leader in a big way. He was playing with Jack Teagarden while still a college student, and after the war worked for many years as Eddie Condon's intermission pianist. A founder member of The World's Greatest Jazz Band in 1968, he enjoyed an Indian summer of recording and gigging in the '80s and '90s.

These Storyville sessions date from a period when he performed at a club run by his wife in Aspen. The sound is imperfect on each, and the relaxations of a club set mean that they lack the focus of his studio dates. Nevertheless this is music being made in the moment, and Sutton's occasional lapses (or more properly, the tactics he adopts to get himself out of jams) are the very stuff of this style of jazz, where error is simply a means to creativity. 'Blue Turning Grey Over You' and 'Sweet And Lovely' on the volume with Bob Wilber are perfect cases in point. It's vibrant, swinging music, and after a time there's almost a merit in the imperfect registration. Hall and Leeman aren't well known outside their circle, but they stay with it all the way.

There are several other records from Sunnie's at this period, including a nice one with Ruby Braff. You can't go wrong: heartland music, played with heart. (By the way, the interview went fine, and the hangover went on for two days …)

MILES DAVIS &

Born 26 May 1926, Alton, Illinois; died 28 September 1991, Santa Monica, California
Trumpet, flugelhorn, organ

In A Silent Way

Columbia 450982
Davis; Wayne Shorter (ts); Chick Corea (p); Joe Zawinul (p, org); John McLaughlin (g); Dave Holland (b); Tony Williams (d). February 1969.

Producer Teo Macero said (1999): **'Don't think in terms of modern editing with computer software. Those albums were made with razor blades and the bad edits were simply covered up with something. As to whose music it is, I made the albums, what you actually hear, so I am co-composer to some degree at least.'**

All through Miles Davis's career, and with increasing volume since his death, there has been controversy about creative ownership of the music that went out under his name. In what sense was the music on *The Birth Of The Cool* 'his'? Who was the main begetter of the records made with Gil Evans? Or bassist Marcus Miller, who shaped some of the last recordings? Why no musician credits, other than Miles himself for *On The Corner*? Most controversial of all is his relationship with producer Teo Macero. He himself did on occasion claim the role of co-composer, and certainly the finished artefacts that we hear are as much Macero's work as they are the musicians'.

However, it's important to put down a process of counter-mystification for what it is: sour grapes mixed with a more forgivable desire to put oneself at the forefront of this great music. Significantly, most claims of joint authorship only emerged explicitly after Miles's death. The reality is that from first to last he was the shaping force, his the vision – or its aural equivalent – that gave the music its character. The executants were simply that.

Miles had begun experimenting with electric groups as early as *Miles In The Sky*, which also saw his return to composition, after he had ceded writing duties largely to Wayne Shorter during the classic quintet period. By the end of the '60s, with rock music dominant in the marketplace, Miles was looking for new directions that carried forward his core values in a creative and relevant way. As an artefact, *In A Silent Way* is already a long way even from the increasingly abstract work of the previous couple of years.

It was in every sense a collage using 'found objects', put together with a view to the minimum detail and coloration required to make an impact. Two of the 'objects' were John McLaughlin, recruited on the nod and apparently unheard by the trumpeter, and Joe Zawinul, whose 'In A Silent Way' became a centrepiece of the album. Three electric instruments give the band a sound completely unlike the previous incarnation, though it is clear that there are very significant continuities between this record and *Miles Smiles* or *E.S.P.* In order to bring the performances up to LP length, Teo Macero stitched repeats of certain passages back into the fabric of the music, lending it a certain hypnotic circularity. Once again, a practical contingency (Miles was apparently happy with the short chunks that had been recorded) resulted in a new creative development, no less significant than Charles Mingus's overdubbing on *The Black Saint And The Sinner Lady*. Even if one had no inkling of what had gone before, *In A Silent Way* is a very beautiful album, touching and centred, its title-piece and 'Shhh/Peaceful' among the most atmospheric recordings in modern jazz.

The *Complete In A Silent Way Sessions* box was expected to yield a new vision of the work in progress. In the event, they're interesting but enigmatic. To stumble over a conclusion, hearing the raw material in its entirety makes one thankful for the genius of Miles and Teo Macero in seeing what was essential and what was of less significance. There is nothing here that improves on the released version. Some of the material, like 'Mademoiselle Mabry', 'Frelon Brun' and 'Dual Mr Anthony Tillman', was used to pad out *Filles De Kilimanjaro* and *Water Babies*; more found its way onto *Circle In The Round*. The brooding minor-key 'It's About That Time' was to become known as an anchor for important live sets by the 'lost' Davis band.

The real interest lies in the alternative takes of the title-piece and of 'Shhh/Peaceful'. These are good enough, though one cannot quibble with the decision as to issued takes. The album versions are supplemented on disc three by 'The Ghetto Walk', a genuine rarity and perhaps the only thing on the set that in any way significantly alters one's view of Miles at this period. In many ways it presages the trumpeter's return to the blues towards the end of his life. Yet this amazing track, which features sterling work from McLaughlin and Shorter as well as from the leader, is confirmation that Miles was never far from the blues. Miles carved out this masterpiece from the most obdurate of material. The albums he created and curated with Macero's help are timeless. Insights into their genesis are fascinating but ultimately unnecessary. You'll listen to *In A Silent Way* a hundred times; you might listen to these tracks thrice, and then only to wonder how the miracle was achieved.

& See also **The Complete Birth Of The Cool** (1948–1950; p. 121), **Miles Ahead** (1957; p. 208), **Kind Of Blue** (1959; p. 232), **The Complete Live At The Plugged Nickel** (1965; p. 331), **Agharta** (1975; p. 420)

PHAROAH SANDERS &

Born Farrell Sanders, 13 October 1940, Little Rock, Arkansas
Tenor saxophone

Karma

Impulse! 051153-2
Sanders; Julius Watkins (frhn); James Spaulding (f); Lonnie Liston Smith (p); Ron Carter, Richard Davis, Reggie Workman (b); William Hart, Freddie Waits (d); Nathaniel Bettis (perc); Leon Thomas (v, perc). February 1969.

Pharoah Sanders said (1982): **'Was I playing jazz music, or spirit music, or some other kind of music? I have no idea, but John Coltrane didn't worry if he was playing jazz music, or something else entirely. Maybe that's what he left me: something else entirely.'**

If the Creator does, indeed, have a master plan, then the role he has written for Pharoah Sanders – the change of name was proposed by Sun Ra, not surprising to hear – is a complex one. Like those other great saxophonists Snub Mosley and Bill Clinton, he hails from Little Rock, Arkansas, and in the '60s, while Snub was getting by and Bill was obstinately refusing to inhale, Sanders was swallowing great draughts of air to produce some of the most raucously beautiful saxophone sounds of the decade. Having worked with John Coltrane during the latter's last years, he had acquired licence to stretch harmonics to the utmost, but always, unlike Coltrane, over a hypnotically simple ground, which is why in later years Sanders was able to reinvent himself as the wicked uncle of the club and dance scene.

An ESP-Disk recording was almost *de rigueur* for anyone in the New York avant-garde. *Pharoah's First* of 1964 is better than most, though it suffers from a very anonymous band. As usual, the leader plays with enough intensity to weld metal, albeit with a softer and broader tone than Coltrane's. Like his sometime employer, he was taken up by Impulse! and given a freer hand than was strictly good for him. Unlike the admirably disciplined Trane, Pharoah never knows when an idea has run its course, and the half-hour plus of 'The Creator Has A Master Plan' (which is basically all there is of *Karma*) can tax the patience if you don't buy into the concept. Perversely, the shortness of the record, with no extra material on the CD, is another issue, but we generally prefer minding the quality to feeling the width so that isn't an issue, particularly at this juncture. 'Creator' opens with a quotation from *A Love Supreme*, but builds to an intensity that was alien even to Coltrane's conception. The saxophone part is pretty much front and centre throughout, and though Bob Thiele's production gives due weight to the other instruments and to Leon Thomas's full-on vocals there is no mistaking that it's Pharoah's gig. The short 'Colors' is a makeweight, but on reflection contains as much of promise as the main event. Sanders's other records for the label also bear investigation, with *Deaf Dumb Blind (Summum Bukmun Unyun)* and *Black Unity* getting the nod over the dismal *Tauhid*.

& *See also* **Crescent With Love** (1992; p. 568)

CHARLIE HADEN &

Born 6 August 1937, Shenandoah, Iowa
Double bass

Liberation Music Orchestra

Impulse! 051188-2
Haden; Don Cherry (c, f); Michael Mantler (t); Roswell Rudd (tb); Bob Northern (frhn, perc); Howard Johnson (tba); Perry Robinson (cl); Gato Barbieri (ts, cl); Dewey Redman (as, ts); Sam Brown (g, thumb p); Carla Bley (p, perc); Andrew Cyrille, Paul Motian (d, perc). April 1969.

Maverick composer Conlon Nancarrow, who fought with the Abraham Lincoln Brigade in the Spanish Civil War, said (1985): **'These Civil War songs are part of my bloodstream, and these versions of them quicken my blood. You rarely hear music like that now.'**

The man from Shenandoah helped redefine modern jazz with Ornette Coleman's quartet and gave a new impetus to jazz bass. Haden is the ultimate timekeeper, bending and stretching the pulse, but never losing impetus. He is also the most lyrical of soloists, and his heartbeat tone has been heard at the centre of literally hundreds of important sessions.

Haden began performing as a child in a family radio show, singing country music, but polio damaged his throat and face and he took up the bass instead. He moved to Los Angeles at the end of his teens and was soon involved in West Coast jazz and in the early experiments of Paul Bley and Ornette Coleman. Haden played on Ornette's classic Atlantic recordings, and subsequently with the Ornette repertory group Old And New Dreams, but then branched out into his own music.

Ten years after making *The Shape Of Jazz To Come*, his best performance with Coleman, Haden formed the Liberation Music Orchestra, using arrangements by Carla Bley and members of her and Michael Mantler's Jazz Composers Orchestra. The LMO was a striking blend of collectivism and radical individualism. Ensemble was everything, but solos were everything, too. The record includes a stirring version of Ornette's 'War Orphans', as well as Haden's own defiant/elegiac 'Song For Che', but the main event is a suite of anarchist and revolutionary songs from the Spanish Civil War. On the opening section, 'El Quinto Regimiento', Brown, Cherry and Haden himself are featured, followed by Rudd in the middle section and the almost caustically toned Barbieri in the conclusion, 'Viva La Quince Brigada'. The bassist dominates 'Song For Che', with Cherry and Redman in support.

A short introduction (by Bley), an interlude, an improvised 'Ending To The First Side' and a final 'We Shall Overcome' give the album a suite-like character, but, that said, there has been no attempt to prettify the music. Haden writes lyrically, but has the courage to play these pieces as if in the field. The recording is attractively rough and ready, and one can easily imagine the music being played in a shell-pocked building behind the lines.

Haden reconvened the Liberation Music Orchestra in 1982, but *Ballad Of The Fallen* lacked the bite of the original. Some put this down to a slackening of conception and conviction, citing the bassist's latter-day preference for the more melodic sound of Quartet West and the more intimate and personal setting of duo improvisation, but this misses the point: *Liberation Music Orchestra* is no less lyrical than the later work and it in turn is no less muscular than the work of the 'revolutionary' phase.

& *See also* **Quartet West** (1986; p. 509), **Beneath The Missouri Sky** (1996; p. 600)

NOAH HOWARD
Born 6 April 1943, New Orleans, Louisiana
Alto saxophone

The Black Ark
Bo'Weavil 24CD
Howard; Earl Cross (t); Arthur Doyle (ts); Leslie Waldron (p); Norris Jones (Sirone) (b); Muhammad Ali (d); Juma (perc). 1969.

Noah Howard said (1983): **'I chose the alto saxophone because it's the closest instrument to a singing voice, and that's what I tried to do on the *Black Ark* recordings, to sing myself.'**

Howard was a chorister back home in New Orleans, and that rapturous lyricism has never gone away, even if he is associated with the avant-garde. He moved to California in his late teens, but he never quite shook away his church roots. A permanent move to Brussels and reliance on his own AltSax imprint certainly affected his visibility, but for some reason his brushfire sound never caught on, even if *The Black Ark* has become an iconic modern recording. The avant-garde of the '60s was over-populated with saxophonists, and Noah seems to parade his influences somewhat like his biblical namesake, two-by-two. There was a hint of Dolphy-and-Ornette, then Trane tempered with Marion Brown's wavery pitching: all of it adding up to something different and idiosyncratic, but not always fully realized.

Originally released on the Freedom label and only briefly as a Japanese CD issue, *The Black Ark* had become a collector's item and something of a cult object among free-jazz fans. That situation sometimes leads to disappointment when a record resurfaces, the reality not quite matching up to the promise, but even with no extra material the return of Howard's best-known recording confirmed its integrity and longevity.

The playing is very much in a late-'60s free idiom, with the ostensible theme – Latin on 'Ole Negro', playful on 'Queen Anne', oriental on 'Mount Fuji' – quickly abandoned in pursuit of some fine balance between flat-out soloing and free ensemble playing. Doyle, as so often, pushes the boat out a shade too far, most irritatingly on the opening 'Domiabra', where his statement cuts across Howard's own excellent solo. The key to work of this kind often lies in the rhythm section. There is a hint of phasing on drums and percussion which gives the music a spacey aura, a not unknown device at the time, but given the title inevitably reminiscent of Sun Ra and the Arkestra. This is perhaps too scorched earth an aesthetic to align comfortably in that direction, but it's an interesting reference point.

SUNNY MURRAY

Born James Marcellus Arthur Murray, 21 September 1936, Idabel, Oklahoma
Drums

Sunshine & An Even Break (Never Give A Sucker)

Fuel 2000 061215
Murray; Lester Bowie (t); Arthur Jones, Roscoe Mitchell (as); Byard Lancaster (ss, as, bcl, f); Archie Shepp (ts); Kenneth Terroade (ts, f); Dave Burrell (p); Malachi Favors (b). 1969.

Saxophonist Tony Bevan has performed with Sunny Murray in the UK: **'The first free drummer, with Albert Ayler, and also the great listening drummer, in that great listening trio. Even when he's playing at full pelt (which he often is) within the surging power is an extraordinary level of detail that shows he's completely aware of what's going on around him, and can turn the music on a sixpence. A brilliant, hilarious, joyous man.'**

Murray played traditional jazz for a time but at 23 started working with Cecil Taylor and appeared on the celebrated 1962 Café Montmartre recordings. He also gigged with John Coltrane and was featured on Albert Ayler's *Spiritual Unity* recording. The assumption is that these masters introduced Murray to free drumming. In fact, he brought something unique to the table, a sense of rhythm influenced by Native American music, and a sense of the drumkit as an integral instrument, rather than a set of discrete sound-sources. It was Murray who sparked a particular direction in the free jazz of the '60s. Like most innovative Americans of the period, he found the United States violent and restrictive, and moved to Paris towards the end of the '60s, and remained in Europe when many of his contemporaries started to drift back 'home'. For the moment, though, as for the membership of the

Art Ensemble Of Chicago, France afforded playing and recording opportunities that were simply not available in the US.

An Even Break and *Sunshine* were both recorded for BYG and have since been reissued together. Murray had previously recorded in America for ESP. On *Sunshine* he again introduces an otherwise unknown hornman. Terroade plays one trio track ('Real') with Murray and Favors, while the rest of the set is devoted to two larger groups on 'Flower Trane' and 'Red Cross', the latter Sunny's only real repertory piece. Not much longer in duration, *An Even Break* was his finest hour of the fast disappearing '60s. 'Giblets Part 12' and the rollicking 'Invisible Rules' are the equal of anything on the first disc and the shorter, more pointed compositions are a perfect study for Murray's integrated percussion. Even on a relatively crude recording, the dynamics are quite extraordinary, everything given due weight and presence, no part of the kit dominating, an almost continuous roll of sound on every track.

ABDULLAH IBRAHIM &

Born Adolphe (Dollar) Johannes Brand, also known as Xahur, 9 October 1934, Cape Town, South Africa
Piano, flute, voice

African Sketchbook
Enja ENJ 2026
Ibrahim (p, f solo). May 1969.

Abdullah Ibrahim said (1993): **'I've studied martial arts for many years and there's a concept called** *omote***, which is about the hidden and the obvious. Most people concentrate on the obvious but accept there's a small proportion of life that remains mysterious. We reverse that, pretty much dispense with the obvious and concentrate on the mystery.'**

As Dollar Brand, he had been a member of the pioneering Jazz Epistles, but he left South Africa after Sharpeville, settling first in Europe, then the United States. It was in Europe, though, that he met up with his first influence, Duke Ellington (Monk was the other), who arranged for him to make a first recording. The Dukeish tinges have not quite disappeared but Ibrahim is utterly distinctive, percussive with rocking bass tone *ostinati* and stabbing right-hand figures.

Much of the material here, including 'The Dream', 'The Aloe And The Wildrose' and 'Hamba Khale' (the last of these reprised at the end of the session), is familiar enough from the period. The playing is notably dark and chastened, but the engineers at Radio Bern have given him a big rich sound, with a lot of resonance round the flute part. In later years, Ibrahim said that he did not listen to other music. That's already implicit here. He seems so self-determining that on those occasions when he stumbles across pianistic clichés, one senses he isn't aware of them as such, but they have simply emerged in the process of improvisation. Brand seems to be known as Xahur at this period, perhaps a transitional stage in his conversion.

& *See also* **Yarona** (1995; p. 587)

AMALGAM &
Formed 1967
Group

Prayer For Peace
FMR 109/No Business NBLP16 LP
Trevor Watts (as); Jeff Cline, Barry Guy (b); John Stevens (d). May 1969.

Trevor Watts remembers: **'I can't remember much about the recording session, except that it was the best studio I'd been in so far. What I do recall was my uncertainty at the worth of the project. I was always unsure in my younger days, something that held me back a little. This recording is constantly being asked about. A friend of mine thinks it's one of the best British jazz recordings ever. I said: "What? Only *British?*"'**

The original Amalgam created some of the most stirring improvised music ever heard in Britain. The classic *Prayer For Peace* opens on an Ornette-like dirge in C minor before opening out into total freedom. Watts's wailing alto figures sound like a Celtic folk-theme sounded across a heavy bass pedal. There's no clear metre, but a sense of underlying pulse, and Stevens at points seems to speed and slow the underlying pattern. The remaining tracks would be anti-climactic if they were not so good. The three-part 'Judy's Smile' builds into a suite of majesty and power, and doesn't in any way suggest three 'takes' of the same material. Here again, Stevens is a key element in the music, but so too is Cline, who appears on everything but the title-track, his big round sound an anchor point at the middle of things. He died in 2009 and a limited vinyl reissue of the record, projected for 2010, is dedicated to his memory. Guy is perhaps a more resonant harmonic player. The change of tone is immediately evident on 'Prayer For Peace' and Guy's ghost melodies, a feature of his own later work, are clearly in evidence, spectral figures that seem to emerge out of overtones rather than attacks.

Hereafter, Amalgam evolved into a more beat-driven outfit, in keeping with Watts's growing interest in African music. A new association with drummer Liam Genockey proved to be even longer lasting than that with Stevens, and while the music is quite different, and certainly less melancholic than *Prayer For Peace,* it is possible to hear continuities.

& See also **SPONTANEOUS MUSIC ENSEMBLE, Quintessence** (1973–1974; p. 406);
TREVOR WATTS, Trevor Watts And The Celebration Band (2001; p. 664)

MANFRED SCHOOF
Born 6 April 1936, Magdeburg, Germany
Trumpet

European Echoes
Atavistic/Unheard Music Series ALP232
Schoof; Enrico Rava, Hugh Steinmetz (t); Paul Rutherford (tb); Peter Brötzmann, Gerd Dudek, Evan Parker (ss, ts); Fred Van Hove, Alexander von Schlippenbach, Irène Schweizer (p); Derek Bailey (g); Arjen Gorter, Peter Kowald, Buschi Niebergall (b); Han Bennink, Pierre Favre (d). June 1969.

Evan Parker says: **'Manfred has his name on some of the key early documents. There was the legendary track "Eisen Perceptions" and, importantly for me, *European Echoes*, which consolidated the relationship with the Continent (as we used to call it) for Paul, Derek Bailey and me. The stories of the quintet's time in Paris at the Chat Qui Pêche, playing warming-up sets for Donald Byrd and sleeping on floors, still move me. Manfred is one of the originals.'**

A key figure on the European free scene, Schoof played with Gunter Hampel and the George Russell Orchestra, as well as less structured formations. Though it's a challenging and sometimes uncomfortable listen, the record that launched the Free Musik Produktion label is obviously a historical document as well as a remarkable performance. It's a record that struggles manfully against the recording values of the time. The larger ensembles come across as undifferentiated blocks of sound from which individual contributions are hard to separate. Given Schoof's orchestral style – a hybrid of Richard Strauss and Karlheinz Stockhausen – this may be a description rather than a criticism. There are moments of great beauty, as when Derek Bailey uses his swell pedal to mimic an entire orchestral section or when Schlippenbach, Fred Van Hove and Irène Schweizer play a seemingly scored section towards the end of what was the first LP side, a passage that anticipates some of Barry Guy's later work with Schweizer and the London Jazz Composers' Orchestra. Schoof is a major figure in German music, as an educator, administrator and interpreter of classical repertoire, including the revered Zimmermann, but it's a pity that his contribution to improvised music isn't better remembered.

MAXINE SULLIVAN

Born Marietta Williams, 13 May 1911, Homestead, Pennsylvania; died 17 April 1987, New York City
Voice, valve trombone, flugelhorn

Close As Pages In A Book
Audiophile 203
Sullivan; Bob Wilber (ss, cl); Bernie Leighton (p); George Duvivier (b); Gus Johnson Jr (d). June 1969.

Maxine Sullivan said (1980): **'I claim my little spot of fame. I sang on Broadway in** *Swinging The Dream***, which was Shakespeare put to jazz. "Darn That Dream" was my spot, and it became a standard after that. Whenever I hear it, I always call out: "That's** *my* **song!"'**

A wonderful character, with a still underrated ability to make a song her own by the subtlest variation of a line or lyric, Sullivan started a craze for jazzing folk material when Claude Thornhill did arrangements of a couple of Scottish songs for her. 'Loch Lomond' was the novelty hit which launched her career. The song (and 'Darling Nellie Gray', 'It Was A Lover And His Lass' and so forth) still works, because of Sullivan's transparent, almost ghostly singing. She didn't really swing her material so much as give it a lilting quality, floating it on phrasing that was measured and controlled without sounding excessively polite. Her version of 'St Louis Blues' sounds mousy next to a voice like Bessie Smith's, but the demure melancholy with which she invests it is surprisingly compelling. She subsequently worked with her husband John Kirby, Benny Goodman and others, then as a solo, before retiring to be a nurse during the '50s.

She came back around 1960 and kept singing (and sometimes playing valve trombone and flugelhorn) until her very last days. She had the final word on the folk song/Jacobean stuff with *Sullivan Shakespeare* in 1971, at what was a pretty good vintage for her. Her manner didn't change much, but, as recording improved, her intimate style and meticulous delivery sounded as classic as any of the great jazz singers. In her 70s there was inevitably a decline in the strength of her voice, but careful production ensured that her albums sounded very good. This record was long a collectors' favourite in its original Monmouth-Evergreen livery. The dozen songs, which inevitably include 'Loch Lomond' and 'Darn That Dream', are perfectly delivered – thoughtful, graceful, introspective without being introverted, this is peerless jazz singing, and the accompaniments by Wilber and his team are as *simpatico* as one could wish.

ART ENSEMBLE OF CHICAGO
Formed 1966
Group

A Jackson In Your House / Message To Our Folks
Charly-Snapper 509
Lester Bowie (t); Joseph Jarman (sax, perc); Roscoe Mitchell (sax, perc); Malachi Mahgostut Favors (b). June–August 1969.

Joseph Jarman said (1989): **'Lester was the doctor, the scientist in his white coat. Roscoe was the professor or businessman. Malachi and I, and Don, were the shamen, the magical figures with painted faces. It's not something you find in Western culture now and that's why it was so powerful.'**

It's a cliché, but not so far from the truth, that the Art Ensemble can't really be appreciated on record. Certainly, the visual impact of the group was a major aspect of its long appeal, but over the years we've found the discs satisfying enough. *Listening to* – as opposed to merely watching – the Art Ensemble has always helped clarify the group's subtly signified satire of both black and white culture, a process that offers due respect to both traditions. Any overemphasis on the group's self-presentation, without a due understanding of its other aesthetics, runs the risk of making the Art Ensemble seem clownish or, that cliché of African-American studies, 'tricksterish'. The group began around what developed into the AACM in Chicago, originally with Bowie, Mitchell and Favors, adding Jarman as a more or less regular member and Moye only later, in Paris, where the band apparently came up with their name when asked for one by journalists. So runs one version of the story, but the members, with Richard Abrams's encouragement, were already synthesizing aspects of post-bop jazz with European art music and other aspects of black vernacular and sanctified music, so the 'Art Ensemble' tag was far from ironic.

The choice of these very early sets might be controversial because Moye is not yet in the band, but they have seemed to us down the years the most successful representations on record of the Art Ensemble's attempted syncretism of styles. There are, to be sure, more polished sessions and certainly better recorded ones, but there is a thoughtful excitement and sense of brimming uncertainty about these early sessions that hasn't dimmed with the passing years, even as more recent records have started to sound shopworn and time-warped.

The original (French) release of both LPs was subheaded 'A.A.C.M. Great Black Music' and it documents the quartet's early effort to get away from the 'jazz' tag and create a new synthetic genre. Since all four members play additional instruments, the absence of a drummer isn't strongly felt, though at times the pulse is a little unvarying. Any sense that the Art Ensemble was a shambolic free-for-all should be quashed by 'Get In Line' on *A Jackson In Your House*. Not even James Brown and Prince ever got a group so crisply on the button.

GUNTER HAMPEL
Born 31 August 1937, Göttingen, Germany
Vibraphone, piano, reeds

The 8th Of July 1969
Birth CD 001
Hampel; Anthony Braxton (sno, ss, as, f, cbcl); Willem Breuker (ss, as, ts, bcl); Arjen Gorter (b) Steve McCall (d); Jeanne Lee (v). July 1969.

Gunter Hampel says: **'Jazz was born when the great rhythms of African pentatonic music culture met the 12-tone octave of European music. I simply repeated that process in 1969: my group, assembled with three Afro-American exponents, started a new concept of music-making in renewing the ingredients of jazz and setting new levels of group play. That process carries on to this day.'**

Göttingen was occupied by US troops during Hampel's formative years and it was through Willis Conover's Voice of America broadcasts – revered in Europe – that he came across jazz for the first time. He formed a jazz group while still a teenager, and seemed to dabble in various classic and modern styles. After military service and training as an architect, he veered towards music again and was playing professionally in his early 20s. In 1964, he formed the Heartplants group with trumpeter Manfred Schoof and pianist Alexander von Schlippenbach, but later in the decade began to associate more with visiting and exiled Americans, including vocalist Jeanne Lee, who became his wife.

A figure of extraordinary self-reliance and creative doggedness, Hampel has largely stood apart from other developments, continuing to put out his own music, often under the name Galaxie Dream Band, on his home label Birth, whose catalogue is huge but only partly transferred to CD. The first LP to be remastered was this remarkable transatlantic encounter. Hampel had recorded before, an early set with Heartplants and then the some-what unsatisfactory *Music From Europe* for ESP-Disk. The 1969 date, recorded in Baarn in the Netherlands, is strictly speaking a collaborative date, though issued under Hampel's name. As so often at this period, when so many American musicians were based in Europe, it points to essential differences in philosophy and practice, though in this case these are less obvious than in, say, Braxton's later London performances with Derek Bailey, who eschewed melody, harmony, groove with equal thoroughness.

Hampel, schooled in a classical tradition, is always the melodist and clearly well versed in the American jazz tradition. Even when the music seems chaotic, he imposes a certain order. The first piece, 'We Move', is effectively a buoyant song-setting for Jeanne Lee, and it makes for an unexpectedly accessible opening. The CD adds a couple of alternate versions of this piece, each sufficiently different to recast both the piece and the album. On 'Morning Song' Braxton is more volatile, importing altissimo screams and tearing phrases that threaten to float free of the rest of the group. The very long third piece is much more coherent in approach, with all three horn-players on bass (or contrabass) clarinets, a tonality and timbre that give 'Crepuscule' an appropriately dark and occluded cast.

A generous and open-hearted player, whose vibraphone work in particular always sounds like it's for the group rather than for individual show. That said, Hampel is often an exciting soloist on the instrument, somewhat reminiscent of Khan Jamal among the new wave of American vibists. An important catalyst on the European scene, Hampel is also widely admired by US musicians, but hasn't yet made the breakthrough to the wider audience his large body of work deserves.

WARNE MARSH &

Born 26 October 1927, Los Angeles, California; died 18 December 1987, Hollywood, California
Tenor saxophone

Ne Plus Ultra

hatOLOGY 603
Marsh; Gary Foster (as); Dave Parlato (b); John Tirabasso (d). September & October 1969.

Warne Marsh said (1980): **'I think about Bach a lot, not so much the counterpoint and harmony but the simple fact that we know so little about where thàt music came from,** what is was for. Classical people make a fetish of it but most of those things are just a skeleton; we have to put the flesh on it. Same with jazz. I don't see any distinction between a piece of Bach and a standard chord sequence.'

This was Marsh's first name recording for almost ten years and it first appeared on the Revelation label. It was taped on two separate occasions at Herrick Chapel Lounge, Occidental College, LA, with just the opening 'You Stepped Out Of A Dream' from the earlier date. Apart from Foster, who makes a convincing stand-in for Lee Konitz, the group isn't at all well-known, but Parlato and Tirabasso seem to know what they're about and when the music goes free on the long improvised 'Touch And Go', they're right there. Marsh's tenor has little of the machine-tooled quality one tends to listen for. It's as human and expressive a voice as almost any other major practitioner of comparable background and here and there a resemblance to Rollins is detectable. There's a tiny taste of Bach's 'Two-Part Invention No. 13' at the end as if to say: 'Dry and classical? Us?', but for the most part the set is devoted to Tristano themes, 'Lennie's Pennies' and '317 E. 22nd', with a nice reading of Konitz's 'Subconscious-Lee' to round it out. Marsh plays with warmth and fire.

& See also **Music For Prancing** (1957; p. 214), **Star Highs** (1982; p. 470)

MICHAEL GIBBS
Born 25 September 1937, Salisbury, Rhodesia (now Harare, Zimbabwe)
Trombone, composer

Michael Gibbs / Tanglewood '63
Vocalion CDSML 142
Gibbs; John Wilbraham (picc t); Harry Beckett, Nigel Carter, Ian Hamer, Henry Lowther, Maurice Miller, Derek Watkins, Kenny Wheeler (t, flhn); Malcolm Griffiths, Cliff Hardie, David Horler, Bobby Lambe, Chris Pyne (tb); Maurice Gee, Ken Goldy, Ray Premru (btb); Jim Buck Jr, Nicholas Busch, Alan Civil, Valerie Smith (frhn); Martin Fry, Dick Hart, Alf Reece (tba); Duncan Lamont, Mike Osborne, Tony Roberts, Alan Skidmore, Brian Smith, Stan Sulzmann, John Surman, Barbara Thompson, Ray Warleigh (reeds); Gordon Beck, Bob Cornford, Mike Pyne, John Taylor (ky); Ray Russell, Chris Spedding (g); Roy Babbington, Jack Bruce, Jeff Clyne, Brian Odgers (b); John Marshall, Tony Oxley, Clive Thacker (d); Frank Ricotti (perc, vib). September & December 1969; November & December 1970.

Michael Gibbs says: '**We recorded *Michael Gibbs* at Decca Studios in West Hampstead and I remember, whilst walking in the corridors, passing Benjamin Britten, who was also recording there!**'

Few recording careers have got off to such a glorious start as Mike Gibbs's. The opening moments of 'Family Joy, Oh Boy!' on the eponymous debut could split clouds. Gibbs had come to Britain from his native Rhodesia via Berklee, where he studied with Herb Pomeroy. A very few gigs later he was being talked about as the most vibrant new talent on the scene. Gibbs has the gift that all great leaders of big bands seem to require: that of making complex and daring ideas seem natural and inevitable. In these early records he fused advanced harmonic ideas with a groove that drew on Ellington, Gil and Miles, and rock. Having Jack Bruce and Chris Spedding both play bass guitars on one track was a stroke of genius, and the addition of piccolo trumpet and French horns gives the ensemble a unique cast.

As he demonstrated on *Tanglewood '63*, Gibbs could move from sun-kissed delight to moonstruck melancholy in a moment. Something about the voicing of the horns – Gibbs was a (reluctant) trombonist – marked him down as an individualist. He rarely asks for stratospheric playing, concentrating on the middle register. 'Sojourn', which follows 'Tanglewood '63' and the appended 'functional' fanfare, is a lonely stroll through a rich musical landscape.

The first album pays some dues – to Stan Getz, John Dankworth, Bob Moses and Gary Burton – but it is utterly individual in conception and execution. Gibbs's charts look challenging, but he has the gift of making difficult passage-work sound coherent and expressive. 'Sweet Rain', 'Throb' and 'And On The Third Day' are classics of British jazz. Surman, Warleigh and Skidmore solo on the first and last, joined on 'Third Day' by Mike Osborne and trombonist Chris Pyne for an exuberant finale that brings a wonderful album to a climax.

The end of *Tanglewood '63* is no less joyous, a long feature for guitarist Spedding over a richly textured rhythm, held together by Roy Babbington's bass guitar, a near-perfect marriage of rock and jazz that was to be Gibbs's staple for years to come, even when the idea of fusion was in retreat. A whole generation of British jazz fans cut their teeth on these records.

BARRY HARRIS
Born 15 December 1929, Detroit, Michigan
Piano

Magnificent!
Original Jazz Classics OJC 1026
Harris; Ron Carter (b); Leroy Williams (d). November 1969.

Barry Harris said: **'Jazz is my vocation, and I feel that unless you make it your vocation, you can't really quite appreciate it. I try to say that to students and look them in the eye, to see what's coming back. If there's nothing, they probably won't make it, no matter how "good" they are.'**

The career of Barry Harris suggests a self-effacing man for, although he is among the most accomplished and authentic of second-generation bebop pianists and an admired teacher, his name has rarely excited more than quiet respect. One of the Detroit school of pianists which includes Tommy Flanagan and Hank Jones, and his style suggests Bud Powell as an original mentor, yet a slowed-down, considered version of Powell's tumultuous manner. Despite the tempos, Harris gets the same dark timbres from the keyboard.

His records are unjustly little-known. There is no singleton masterpiece, just a sequence of graceful, satisfying sessions which suggest that Harris has been less interested in posterity via recordings and more in what he can give to jazz by example and study. He is himself one of the music's great teachers. It's hard to argue with the title of the 1969 album. Turning 40, Harris is musing on his uncluttered bebop roots in 'Bean And The Boys' and seeing how far he can push the envelope in the ingenious fresh voicings of 'Ah-Leu-Cha', in which Carter is a willing partner. 'Just Open Your Heart' is a Monkian original that Harris subjects to a playful twist. 'Dexterity' takes us back to first-generation bebop, but again Harris casts it in a darker, more evasive setting. A neglected classic of its day.

BETTY CARTER &
Born Lillie Mae Jones, 16 May 1930 (some sources give 1929), Flint, Michigan; died 26 September 1998, Brooklyn, New York
Voice

Finally
Roulette Jazz 53332
Carter; Norman Simmons (p); Lisle Atkinson (b); Al Harewood (d). December 1969.

Betty Carter said (1995): **'Most real jazz singing starts in church. Those are the only voices that are going to make it in jazz, to get above the racket, those big voices, full of soul.'**

The most challenging of all female jazz singers, both artistically and personally, 'Betty Bebop' sang with Lionel Hampton in the '40s, then broke off to raise a family. Returning in 1969 she became the most demanding and virtuosic of jazz singers, her touring groups little academies for young players, and until her unexpected death she maintained a ferocious appetite for performing.

She quickly transcended the 'bop vocalist' tag and created a style that combined the fluent, improvisational grace of an alto saxophone with an uncanny accuracy of diction. Even when her weighting of a lyric is almost surreal, its significance is utterly explicit and sarcastically subversive. The latter quality has allowed her to skate on the thin ice of quite banal standard material, much of which has acquired a veneer of seriousness from nowadays being heard only as instrumentals; 'Body And Soul' on *Finally* is the obvious example, medleyed with 'Heart And Soul' on this 1969 live album, taped at New York's Judson Hall.

Some of the pieces on *Finally* are left deliberately raw. 'Girl Talk' is wild, but what is she thinking about as she sings 'The Sun Died' or 'You're A Sweetheart'? With Carter the charge of emotion isn't always obvious. What these sides consistently demonstrate is a stock-in-trade ability to reshape a song so radically that it becomes something quite new which retains only a few subtle reminders of its original. A process similar, in other words, to the contrafacts on standard material made by the bebop pioneers, but with the added complication of words which overturn expectations of what female jazz singers might be expected to say.

& *See also* **The Audience With Betty Carter** (1979; p. 454)

AMM

Formed 1965
Improvising ensemble

Laminal
Matchless MRCD 31 3CD
Cornelius Cardew (p, clo); Lou Gare (ts, vn); Christopher Hobbs, Eddie Prévost (perc); Keith Rowe (g, elec); John Tilbury (p). December 1969, February 1982, May 1994.

Eddie Prévost comments: **'For me the 1982 Great Hall performance has verve and excitement unencumbered by any conscious articles of faith. Tilbury's pianism at its most uninhibited. Rowe fearless and risking more than perhaps he has done since. He probably won't agree. Me? I too am energetic and searching, more like Ed Shaughnessy or Frank Butler than I have ever been before or since! I still get members of that audience reminding me how the short-wave radio messages Keith conjured out of the ether set a menacing background to our finale.'**

In a dense and difficult book called *Noise* (*Bruits*), the French cultural theorist Jacques Attali identifies four main stages in the political economy of music, culminating in a final utopian phase which Attali calls composition. This is a music 'beyond exchange ... performed for the musician's own enjoyment, as self-communication, fundamentally outside all other communication, as self-transcendence, a solitary, egotistical, noncommercial act'. It's an argument and a model that applies well to the music of AMM, who for three and a half decades have stood outside every commercial and critical nexus and continued to make powerfully creative music. We quibble with 'egotistical', for it is almost axiomatic of 'AMMusic' (no other category exists) that ego is effectively suspended. AMM's origin lies in the British free-jazz movement – an ancestry shared with the Spontaneous Music Ensemble and one which resurfaced when the group was reduced to just saxophonist Lou Gare and drummer Eddie Prévost, the only constant member – but the political and philosophical instincts of the founding members quickly dictated its transformation into an improvising collective in which process rather than gesture was important and which redefined the growing division in new music between performers and audience. Early AMM performances were conducted in the dark and often deliberately blurred starting and finishing times.

Though 'beyond exchange' and defined entirely by the context and the collective understanding of the changing membership, the music has enjoyed a second life on record. The advent of CD meant that for the first time whole performances could be issued without breaks or editing, and Prévost has used his own Matchless imprint to document the group's early and ongoing history, starting with early classics like *The Crypt* but also including this very important historical survey, issued to celebrate AMM's 30th anniversary.

In a note to *The Crypt*, Prévost points out that *Jazz Journal* once identified the group as the 'Cornelius Cardew Quartet', a nonsensical and ironic attribution on all sorts of counts. *Laminal* usefully begins with an early performance with the problematic composer in the line-up. Cardew's later commitment to militant Albanian communism seems out of tenor with AMM's libertarian discipline, but he was an important member and catalyst. This is music which rejects instrumentalism. It matters very little after a few minutes of any performance who is playing what, particularly when conventional technique is almost entirely overthrown. In later years, as can be heard in the later performances on *Laminal*, Prévost was to return to something that demonstrated at least a kinship with jazz drumming, and Tilbury's piano-playing is more conventionally linear and expressive than Cardew's. Rowe is perhaps the key to the sound-world. He is credited as 'guitarist', but only in the most deconstructionist sense, laying the instrument flat on a table and manipulating feedback, overtones, percussive effects and accidentals, using the instrument as a sound source without a playing history.

Laminal brings together a 1969 performance from Aarhus, Denmark, with Cardew, Gare, Hobbs, Prévost and Rowe; a middle-period recording from the Great Hall at Goldsmiths' College, London in 1982 which marked the introduction of John Tilbury to the group; and a concluding tour date from the US in 1994. The juxtaposition of the intent, uneffusive music of the later period with the turbulent swirl of the late-'60s group makes for a striking contrast, but one quickly hears continuities, not least from Prévost, and an underlying narrative to one of the most remarkable musical journeys of modern times.

LIFETIME &

Also known as The Tony Williams Lifetime; formed 1969
Group

(Turn It Over)
Polygram 539118
Larry Young (org); John McLaughlin (g); Jack Bruce (b, v); Tony Williams (d, v). January 1970.

Tony Williams said (1991): **'Everyone seemed to be playing something else in that group. John was like another drummer, very rhythmic and percussive. Larry was doing all these John Coltrane things, *and* playing bass until Jack came in a bit later. I was effectively the piano-player ... in a group that didn't have a piano.'**

Arguably the greatest fusion group ever, and a forerunner to McLaughlin's Mahavishnu Orchestra and perhaps also later groups like Last Exit, Lifetime went through some variable evolutions in its history, and the early recordings are patchy. The first album, *Emergency!*, is an ugly sprawl, Williams's figure-skating drums lost in a wash of sound. *Ego* isn't a great deal better and the title was a too obvious hostage to fortune, underlining a Jimi Hendrix influence that hadn't yet been legitimized in jazz terms.

The surprise of *(Turn It Over)* was how swinging some of the music was, underneath the electronic wail. Jobim's 'Once I Loved' has a languorous, supper club quality, belied by Williams's eldritch vocal. Chick Corea's 'To Whom It May Concern' comes in two parts and like most of the album they're delivered abruptly and with little embellishment. Coltrane's 'Big Nick' is a rarity from his bag of themes. Williams contributed 'Right On' and 'Vuelta Abajo', ideas which seemed to come straight out of his experience with Miles Davis, mixing hints of modality with the new electronic abstraction. Bruce was a fourth wheel who sometimes sounded like a third wheel, recruited to relieve Young of bass-pedal duties and to contribute some of his high, slightly surreal vocals. He didn't necessarily dilute the mix, but he always sounds like an extra component. Unlike most records of its era, it passes the test of time.

& *See also* **TONY WILLIAMS, Life Time** (1964; p. 307)

THAD JONES
Born 28 March 1923, Pontiac, Michigan; died 20 August 1986, Copenhagen, Denmark
Trumpet, cornet, flugelhorn, valve trombone

Consummation
Blue Note 38226
Jones; Danny Moore, Al Porcino, Marvin Stamm, Snooky Young (t); Eddie Bert, Cliff Harser, Jimmy Knepper, Benny Powell (tb); Billy Harper, Eddie Daniels, Jerry Dodgion, Jerome Richardson (reeds); Roland Hanna (p); David Spinozza (g); Richard Davis (b); Mel Lewis (d, co-leader). January–May 1970.

Humphrey Lyttelton said (1994): **'Someone – I think it was Charles Mingus – described Thad Jones as "a Bartók who uses trumpet valves instead of a pencil": a wonderful description of a wonderful jazz composer.'**

The middle Jones brother was consistently underrated as a soloist, and was recognized mainly as a composer and arranger. Not usually considered a small-group player, or even a soloist of any unusual interest, Jones none the less had a subtle and vibrant cornet tone similar to Nat Adderley's but was able to sustain big transitions of pitch with absolute confidence. He joined Count Basie in 1954 and stayed ten years, then began arranging and composing and formed an orchestra with drummer Mel Lewis in 1965 which lasted until 1978. That experience looped back round when he ran the Basie band for a time after the leader's death.

The Jones–Lewis band kept big-band jazz to the fore at a time when it seemed not just dead but consigned to the fossil record. *Consummation* is a perfectly crafted record. Jones's arrangements are as ever spot on and there are enough fine soloists in the orchestra to guarantee a high level of interest. 'Tiptoe', the peerless 'A Child Is Born' and a long, long version of 'Fingers' are among the highlights; the last of these is a conventional enough variation on the 'I Got Rhythm' chords, but what an astonishing job Thad makes of it. He plays beautifully on 'A Child Is Born' and the first-class recording catches him, as well as the high-quality sections, to best advantage.

HOWARD RILEY&
Born 16 February 1943, Huddersfield, Yorkshire, England
Piano

The Day Will Come
Columbia 494434-2
Riley; Barry Guy (b); Alan Jackson (d). March–April 1970.

Howard Riley says: **'The thing was in those days if there was someone at one of the big labels who was interested in you, you would get a recording contract, supposedly an album a year for three years in my case. I got two records out of it, then the guy I knew left and I got a three-line thank you letter.'**

Riley played in local clubs before moving south and finding his own way to completely free playing. By the measure of some early survivals, it wasn't a tortured process, but a quite natural one, though a strong element of composed material remains in place in early days. Like a number of British musicians of the period, Riley briefly enjoyed the sunshine of a major label contract. CBS also got behind Tony Oxley at this period, which means that not only was the 'avant-garde' documented, but it is possible to hear it in superior sound.

For Riley himself, the key thing about his Columbia recordings was that they represented a working band. Other improvising musicians of the time were happy to issue what were effectively public rehearsals. By contrast, the two records by the Howard Riley Trio are terse, focused improvisations on written themes. The fully notated flute-and-piano duets, 'Three Fragments', on the earlier album, *Angle*, stand somewhat apart, but are unmistakably from the same hand. Riley is the only credited composer on that record, which perhaps accounts for its thoughtful and rather reserved character.

The introduction of Barry Guy as co-composer on the brilliant *The Day Will Come* is the key factor in our very high estimation of this record. It is worth noting that, whatever the public persona Guy has now, in 1969 Chris Wellard thought nothing of describing him in his liner-note to the first record, *Angle*, as 'rumbustious and violent'. It is he who balances the rather tender and melancholic cast of Riley's playing. His *arco* solo on 'Angle' is astonishing, and he drives the following track, 'Aftermath', into territory new in British jazz at the time. On the later album Guy tunes like 'Sad Was The Song', 'Playtime' and the title-track present genuine improvisational challenges. Of the trio members, Jackson is the one who seems to have been eclipsed by the passing years. He is a drummer of great control and precision, inch-perfect on fast numbers like 'Angle' without compromising a robustly swinging presence which recalls Phil Seamen but also has ties right back to the days of Dave Tough. This, as too the preceding *Angle*, is a key recording, now widely acknowledged as such.

& *See also* **At Lincoln Cathedral** (2001; p. 669)

KARIN KROG
Born 15 May 1937, Oslo, Norway
Voice

Some Other Spring
Meantime MR10
Krog; Dexter Gordon (ts); Kenny Drew (p, org); Niels-Henning Ørsted Pedersen (b); Epsen Rud (d). May 1970.

Karin Krog remembers: **'The Department of Justice refused Dexter permission to enter Norway because he had a criminal record. In the end, we sent Dexter, Kenny and NHØP their tickets and hoped they'd get through customs. Kenny carried the saxophone and they made it to the studio, which we only had for a day. I'd prepared most of the material but Dexter suggested the lovely ballad "Some Other Spring". I knew he had worked with Billy Eckstine and asked if he was up to singing a blues and suggested "Jelly Jelly". He grinned and said he would have a go.'**

Krog famously skipped school to see Billie Holiday sing in Oslo and that was that. One of the most astutely musical and expressive of all European jazz singers, and her substantial discography is still too little appreciated. Her recent collaborations with partner John Surman reflect the interests and backgrounds of both. The earlier work finds her working an idiosyncratic swing vein, with strong intimations of bebop.

Though still audibly a young singer, her musical confidence and awareness of history is breathtaking on *Some Other Spring*. Her own 'Blue Eyes' isn't a devastatingly complex line but it moves in an interesting way and Drew's accompaniment – on organ for this one track – has a unwontedly brooding quality that belies the tune's, and the session's, upbeat quality. Gordon plays throughout without the scowling pragmatism one sometimes heard from him at the time. He does, indeed, give 'Jelly Jelly' a go and it comes off nicely. Krog's real skill, though, lies with the ballads and the title-track belongs in any vocal collection. Pedersen and Rud are the equal of many a more celebrated American section.

Krog has shrewdly taken ownership of her own back catalogue, licensing this one from Sonet and steadily reissuing her material. Some of the same session later appeared as *Blues And Ballads* but they're amalgamated here for the CD.

HARRY BECKETT

Born 30 May 1935, St Michael Parish, Barbados; died 22 July 2010, London
Trumpet, flugelhorn

Flare Up

Jazzprint 124
Beckett; Mike Osborne (as); Alan Skidmore (ts); John Surman (ss, bs); John Taylor (p); Frank Riccotti (vib, perc); Chris Laurence (b); John Webb (d). 1970.

Harry Beckett says: 'The feel was outstanding, with an enormous amount of team work. There are two ballads I fell in love with: Graham Collier's "On The Other Side" and John Surman's "Where Fortune Smiles", but the other tunes are terrific, too. I'm probably biased, but I love beautiful music. It doesn't matter where it is coming from or who is playing it.'

Harry Beckett's trumpet and flugelhorn sound is Caribbean-warm, honeyed and mellow as ripe fruit, but it can conjure up sudden storms as well. He has been a key presence in British improvisation for four decades, ranging easily between free music and the remarkable hip-hop projects of recent years. Beckett has done time in most of the important British big bands (Westbrook, Collier, Surman, Westbrook) and his flugelhorn solos can always be picked out from the first few notes.

Unfortunately, his own discography as leader has a slightly ramshackle air, often appearing on fugitive European labels. This early disc has mercifully come back into the light, as have *Warm Smiles* and *Themes For Fega*. This one comes first, though, and it shows the British jazz of the time from a unique perspective, with compositions by Graham Collier (four of them, but the most effective is 'Go West') and John Surman ('Where Fortune Smiles') uniquely repositioned by Beckett's fiery/calm imagination. There are obvious hints of what was happening in American jazz at the time, but, as so often, British improvisers took their own tack on modalism or rhythmic freedom or the use of electricity. John Taylor's Fender Rhodes washes create a unique shimmer in the background, and the rest of the rhythm section manages to convey a springy, undogmatic beat, even when the music strays out into free air.

Beckett was maybe more daring with *Themes For Fega* two years later, but this debut recording has a character and finish all its own and the leader's playing and writing ('Flare Up' and 'Flow, Stream, Flow') are exquisite.

ATTILA ZOLLER

Born 13 June 1927, Visegrad, Hungary; died 25 January 1998, Townshend, Vermont
Guitar

Gypsy Cry
Collectables COL 6178
Zoller; Lew Tabackin (ts, f); Herbie Hancock (p); Reggie Workman, Victor Gaskin (b); Sonny Brown (d). 1970.

Pianist and collaborator Don Friedman says: **'When Peter Bernstein was a student at Attila's Vermont jazz school, Peter was practising upstairs and Attila was cooking some food in the kitchen. Attila yelled up to Peter that he was playing something wrong. Attila had a great harmonic sense and his melodic line improvisations were truly unique. I don't believe his improvising has received the recognition it deserves.'**

Zoller came of age in an occupied country. In 1948, though, he escaped Soviet-controlled Hungary and walked through mountain passes to Austria, where he took citizenship before moving to Germany in the early '50s. There he had the opportunity to meet American musicians, there to entertain another occupying force, and it was they who persuaded him to move to the US. He won a scholarship to the Lenox School of Jazz, where he shared accommodation with Ornette Coleman, an association that had some impact on his future musical development.

He had begun playing jazz in Buda-Pest jazz cellars, blending swing with elements of traditional Hungarian music. Even after he had been exposed to free jazz and formed a group with pianist Don Friedman, those influences never left him. Zoller's characteristic sound reflects his deep interest in the technology of electronic pick-ups. He favoured a very clean and direct sound, without much or any distortion but with all the string's natural overtones coming into play. Sometimes Zoller sounds similar to his compatriot Gabor Szabo, but there's a funkier element and his basic idiom is more boppish. Over the course of his career, he worked with an extraordinary range of American artists and in many different styles. A trio with Ron Carter and Joe Chambers helped consolidate his reputation in America and there were other, later groups with Lee Konitz, Albert Mangelsdorff and Franz Koglmann.

This set brings together two contrasting recordings from rather earlier, reflecting a straight jazz approach and a freer element which he developed under Ornette's influence. 'Meet In Berlin' is Zoller at his most heavyweight, with the folksy burr in his tone turned up to match Hancock's electric accompaniment. 'Gypsy Cry' itself draws on folk sources and may be a response to the Hungarian rising of 1956; there is what sounds like an ironic quote from the Soviet anthem. 'Wild Wild Wes' is a straight tribute to Montgomery and Zoller at his most open and unshaded. These are records that have appealed to acid jazz DJs, with warm, danceable grooves ('Sweet Hustler') and some unexpectedly lateral chill-out moments amid the freer tracks.

WILD BILL DAVISON

Born 5 January 1906, Defiance, Ohio; died 14 November 1989, Santa Barbara, California
Cornet

Jazz On A Saturday Afternoon: Volumes 1 & 2
Jazzology 37 / 38
Davison; Wray Thomas (tb); Herman Foretich (cl); Ernie Carson (p, c); Mike Hein (d). June 1970.

Wild Bill Davison said (1983): **'I've been told I have to give up the hooch, so these days I try to get everyone else to do my share as well. Exactly like running a jazz band!'**

The man from Defiance always sounded as if he'd slung the town sign round his neck. His cornet-playing was a delightful mixture of high, lyrical phrases and challenging growls, with a very distinctive terminal shake on specific cadences. An independently minded man and musician, he never sounded comfortable as a Condonite, and belonged instead to a fraternity of footloose jazz men happy to criss-cross the country, playing wherever there was a spot.

The title of one Jazzology disc, *Just A Gig*, may reveal more than intended, because Bill would roll up pretty much anywhere he could play and was keen to record as often as there was a tape to hand. Obviously, as age and fame mounted, that got easier, even if he didn't. The 1976 with-strings date *Sweet And Lovely* is the sound of a man spitting on an expensive, immaculately woven carpet. The Atlanta Jazz Society invited him over for a blow in the summer of 1970. Bill rolled up, found the boys could play some and let rip one of his very best dates of the period. It's not an adventurous programme, but the playing is top notch and the local fellows seem elevated by Bill's presence. Carson even gets out his own cornet and joins in on 'Royal Garden Blues'. Along with 'Big Butter And Egg Man', it's the pick of the *Volume 1* tracks, with 'Jazz Me Blues' making a strong opening to the second set. This is jazz at the pointed end of the music, raw, unglamorous, local but with the excitement of a distinguished visitor putting everyone on his mettle. It's great.

JOE ZAWINUL&

Born 7 July 1932, Vienna, Austria; died 11 September 2007, Vienna, Austria
Piano, keyboards

Zawinul
Sony 81375
Zawinul; Jimmy Owens, Woody Shaw (t); Wayne Shorter, Earl Turbinton (ss); George Davis, Hubert Laws (f); Herbie Hancock (p); Walter Booker, Miroslav Vitous (b); Joe Chambers, Billy Hart, David Lee (d); Jack DeJohnette (hca, perc). 1970.

Joe Zawinul said (1995): **'I make melodies in the bass. That's where it is with me. I have a ****ing killer left hand.'**

Perhaps the key thing about Joe Zawinul is that he started out as an accordion-player. It allowed him, when he came to piano, to swap hands and let the real melodic action happen in a place where normally one would expect to hear nothing but comping. Almost all the great Weather Report lines were great bass lines. Zawinul grew up in a working class area and retained a tough, street kid's demeanour which makes a nonsense of attempts to portray Weather Report's music as cerebral or ethereal. After working with Hans Koller he came to America and studied at Berklee. He worked with Dinah Washington, Maynard Ferguson and Cannonball Adderley; you can just glimpse him in the Clint Eastwood movie *Play Misty for Me*, already playing the electric keyboards he made his own and which brought him to the attention of Miles Davis. 'In A Silent Way' was a Zawinul composition and he was very much a component of Miles's electric evolution, bringing what the trumpeter recognized as a different rhythmic sense to the music.

One hears something of that on the earliest records Zawinul made in the US. Even generic soul jazz on *Money In The Pocket* and early 'world music'/crossover material on *The Rise And Fall Of The Third Stream* (now available as a twofer) sound different in Zawinul's hands. His attack is unlike anyone else's and this allowed him to invest electric keyboards – particularly analog instruments – with real personality and expressive power.

The eponymous Atlantic album with its haunting sepia cover – a huge close-up of Zawinul's sombre face – was made the year that Weather Report was formed and a year after Zawinul took part in the *In A Silent Way* sessions. *Zawinul* is a beautiful record. Subtitled 'Music for two electric pianos, jazz flute, trumpet, soprano saxophone, two contra-basses and percussion', it nods in the direction of his conservatory past almost as much as it anticipates the experiments in fusion music. Woody Shaw's echoplexed trumpet strongly recalls Miles (who contributes a liner-note) but, with Vitous handling one of the bass parts and Shorter replacing the little-known Turbinton on 'Double Image', the original Weather Report is already in place. *I Sing The Body Electric*, the group's second disc, was to include a live-in-Japan version of 'Doctor Honoris Causa', a piece with a complex history but here presented as a tribute to Zawinul's keyboard twin, Dr Herbie Hancock. Here it gets a much more measured reading, less frenetic and intense, more floating and indefinite, as in 'His Last Journey', where the electric piano's ability to imitate tolling bells (another Weather Report favourite) is exploited to great effect. Not just because Shorter is present, 'Double Image' is the track that most clearly points forward. The brief 'Arrival In New York' is an aural impression of the immigrant wharves; not far removed from Mingus's 'Foggy Day' on *Pithecanthropus Erectus*, it underlines an interest in pure sound, 'human sound' as Zawinul would have put it. The next decade would see him take a giant step in that direction.

& *See also* **Di-a-lects** (1986; p. 503); **WEATHER REPORT, Mysterious Traveller** (1974; p. 408)

THE '70s:

A curious decade in jazz. The music wasn't much valued by the industry, as far as new recordings and young artists were concerned, and many of them had to make a sidestep into jazz-rock, and from there onto the slippery slope that led to the dreaded 'fusion', pop-jazz and ultimately light jazz, which casts no light whatsoever. However, some of the greatest stars of jazz lived and worked on into the '70s: Louis Armstrong (just), Duke Ellington (a curtain call), Miles Davis (problematically), Count Basie, Sonny Rollins, Oscar Peterson and enough others to clinch it as the music of the long haul rather than shooting-star brevity of a pop career. A whole phalanx of mainstream giants spent the decade touring on Norman Granz's Jazz At The Philharmonic ticket. These musicians had enough momentum and sheer charisma to survive the industry's indifference, and in turn they gave work to the younger and up-and-coming.

There were other energies at work, and for the first time the centre of gravity seemed to tilt away from the United States and towards Europe. For a start, there was a substantial population of American musicians living in exile in France and Scandinavia. During the course of the decade, the impetus of jazz recording switched (it's a hefty generalization, but check the provenance of what follows) from large American labels to independent European imprints. ECM was established in 1969, the Black Saint/Soul Note axis followed in Italy, hat ART soon came along in Switzerland (originally as a means of recording multi-instrumentalist Joe McPhee), while in France Black & Blue provided much-needed recording exposure for mainstreamers, visiting Ellingtonians and blues men.

The emphasis of many of these labels was refreshingly innovative rather than conservative. In time, ECM established its own culture, a style of music that embraced European modern classicism as much as it did bebop-derived jazz. It also provided an outlet for other, regional aesthetics, and one began to find different vernacular elements creeping into the music, most notably in Scandinavia and Eastern Europe and Russia (which still laboured under Communist domination), but also in the UK, where in parallel a new improvising aesthetic was emerging.

Towards the end of the previous decade, a very specific cohort of British jazz musicians made a rapid evolution out of 'free jazz' (though some denied the term any validity) and towards 'free music' or 'free improvisation' (which conservative critics were inclined to think had nothing whatever to do with jazz, or more extremely nothing to do with music; the more articulate splutterers were apt to reach for Robert Frost's line about playing tennis with the net down). Though initially this new music was very much restricted to a small audience of London club goers (though that suggests a kind of hedonism that didn't play much part in the free-music scene), it was extensively documented by small labels and its legacy and influence have been disproportionate. Almost all the senior figures on that scene – guitarist Derek Bailey, saxophonist Evan Parker, trombonist Paul Rutherford, percussionists John Stevens and Eddie Prévost – were to be internationally recognized, which is as much as to say they worked a great deal more often abroad than at home, establishing a powerful improvising network on continental Europe and subsequently with American improvisers (particularly Chicagoans). For the moment, though, and despite the welcome anomaly of major label attention (actually the attention of individuals working at major labels) for the likes of percussionist Tony Oxley and pianist Howard Riley (see 1966–1970, above), the records made by these musicians and like-minded visitors such as saxophonist Steve Lacy remained the preserve of a small coterie of enthusiasts and writers.

Sharing many of the same personnel, but energized by a group of South African exiles in London, a new and vigorous post-bop style also prevailed in Britain, its excitements still unparalleled, though such opinions are sceptically received by those who weren't there. London is a different kind of melting-pot to New York and has a different kind of colonial history to negotiate, but its fusion of styles – 'fusion' became a bad word, but in its precise meaning, it's the only one that fits – is still not given due prominence in the histories of modern jazz.

There were some mostly unwelcome new sounds in the jazz of the '70s. The electric bass became ubiquitous for a while, though some of the finest double bassists – Ron Carter, Bob Cranshaw, Dave Holland – managed to make a convincing noise with an amplified instrument. Electric keyboards also became the norm, though here the difficulty of articulating with a recognizably individual 'touch' meant that the sound of one Fender Rhodes being played was much like the sound of any other. Drummers were more inclined than before to play a steady backbeat, even when the horn-players were improvising quite freely and there was a widening gulf between innovators like Miles Davis, Herbie Hancock and Chick Corea (in the US) or Ian Carr and Nucleus, or Soft Machine, in the UK, and the army of epigones who found 'jazz-rock' easier to play and more likely to drum up an audience than bebop.

Anyone prepared to dismiss the '70s as a lost era in jazz should be aware of how much of the jazz recording of the period has been eclipsed. The output of the Muse label – formed in 1972 by Joe Fields, later with Don Schlitten – has not been securely available since, despite various attempts at reissue. Similarly with Schlitten's Xanadu imprint, which did steady service in documenting post-bop and mainstream music, but which is, for the moment at least, locked away on ageing LP stock and known only to collectors of a certain age.

The only significant (or was it?) technical development of the time as far as music carriers were concerned turned out to be the ugliest and least resilient of all. When the *Penguin Guide* was first published, we were required to review a certain amount of music on 'cassette', a medium that robbed the music of any nuance, buried it in hiss, 'wow' and 'flutter' (how perversely nostalgic the words now seem!) and unwound in black, shining skeins if one looked askance at it. Cassettes were only useful for listening in the car, though the simultaneous availability of cheap, portable recording equipment meant that enthusiasts were soon making their own C-90s – private-use bootlegs – with hand-held equipment that could be secreted under a club table. A surreptitious expression and a dim red light through the tablecloth were the giveaways. This, though, goes somewhat ahead of the story, to an era when 'personal' listening went a step beyond 'home' listening, evolving in a generation from the Walkman to the seemingly Alexandrian iPod, on which unimaginable quantities of music can be stored. But not listened to with pleasure, given the compression.

All this, in a gallant attempt to suggest that if the '70s seem like a bleak time for jazz, there were bright patches, signs of innovative continuity and still, despite it all, some vestige of quality control in audio fidelity. It may have been a silver age, but it was not yet leaden and there are some genuinely remarkable survivals and debuts ...

Part 1:
1971–1975

DEREK BAILEY&

Born 29 January 1930, Sheffield, Yorkshire, England; died 25 December 2005, London
Guitar

Solo Guitar: Volume 1
Incus CD10
Bailey (g, syn solo). February 1971.

Derek Bailey said (1992): **'There are all these musics out there where you don't really play. You just perform a function. I'd found that even in those dance halls I was playing free, certainly freer than just playing someone's chords, so it wasn't some big new thing that came along and hit me one day.'**

It's usual, but unhelpful, to describe Derek Bailey's music by all the things it was not: not swinging, not idiomatic, not melodic or blues-based, resistant to any hint of groove or linear direction. What such characterizations routinely fail to convey is how consistent with itself a Bailey performance always was, how geometrically expressive and how completely defined by the instrument he was playing; for a 'non-idiomatic' musician, Bailey was first and foremost a guitar-player. He learned his trade in northern clubs and dance halls and retained a love of vernacular music in all its forms, even when his own work seemed to exist at a remote extreme from any populist content.

Born into a musical family, he studied guitar formally but began playing straight-ahead jazz and swing before embracing – without in his case a transition via 'free jazz', a concept he distrusted – free improvisation. He was a member of Joseph Holbrooke, a legendary improvising group which evolved out of a relatively conventional jazz trio. He was later a member of various important improvising ensembles, including Music Improvisation Company, the Spontaneous Music Ensemble and groups led by Tony Oxley, Paul Rutherford and others. He co-founded Incus records with Oxley and Evan Parker, and also curated Company, a long-standing improvisation 'congress'. In the main, though, Bailey went his own course, pioneering a line of solo improvisation which involved mostly minimal manipulation of the guitar sound, often only a swell pedal, and a huge technical resource: hard-picked single notes, fiery scrabbles on the fretboard, floating accidentals and overtone effects.

Solo Guitar now sounds curiously old-fashioned, an attractively primitive Early Church version of Bailey. There are other records from the period, including *Fairly Early* and *Domestic & Public Pieces*, which also includes cassette 'postcards' from Bailey to Emanem owner Martin Davidson. Part of the guitarist's musical life was the network of relationships that grew round the recording, cottage industry production and distribution of Incus discs, much of the work being done by partner Karen Brookman. These mostly short pieces emerge with conversational directness, but also with extraordinary discipline; none sounds a second longer than it needs to be. As well as an early glimpse of Bailey's splintery but eminently logical sound, *Solo Guitar* affords a rare glimpse of him playing the work of other composers: Willem Breuker, Misha Mengelberg and Gavin Bryars, whose 'The Squirrel And The Rickety-Rackety Bridge' is a high-point of the record. There's a rare touch of VCS3 synth on Mengelberg's 'Where Is The Police?', another piece that gives the lie to any sense that this is po-faced and abstract music. It's packed with life and humour and it feels like a setting-out: the musical journey was to last another 30 years …

& *See also* **Ballads / Standards** (2002; p. 673); **SME, Quintessence** (1973–1974; p. 406)

GERRY MULLIGAN &
Born 6 April 1927, New York City; died 20 January 1996, Darien, Connecticut
Baritone and soprano saxophones, clarinet

The Age Of Steam
A&M CDA 0804
Mulligan; Harry 'Sweets' Edison (t); Bob Brookmeyer (vtb); Jimmy Cleveland, Kenny Shroyer (tb); Bud Shank (as, f); Tom Scott (ss, ts); Ernie Watts (ts, bs); Roger Kellaway (p); Howard Roberts (g); Chuck Domanico (b); John Guerin (d); Joe Porcaro (perc). February–July 1971.

Gerry Mulligan said (1990): **'There's no sensation in the world as good as standing in front of a good band, in a warm shower of overtones … unless it's standing on the footplate of a classic locomotive!'**

Almost unrecognizably long-haired and bearded, posed in denims in front of one of the locomotives that are his other great passion, Mulligan might almost be some mythical footplateman from the great age of the frontier. In 1971, he hadn't recorded on his own account for nearly seven years. Stephan Goldman's production is recognizably modern, with Mulligan making extensive use of electric piano and guitar and both 'Country Beaver' and 'A Weed In Disneyland' include strong rock elements. That's modified with a swing rhythm on the opening 'One To Ten In Ohio', which reunites Jeru and Brookmeyer. The two finest tracks, though, are 'Over The Hill And Out Of The Woods', which Mulligan opens on piano and with a lovely Sweets solo, and the hauntingly beautiful 'Grand Tour'. The latter must be accounted among the saxophonist's most beautiful compositions, its meditative theme and misty timbre explored by the composer and Bud Shank. Even when playing solidly on the beat – 'swing' was at a discount in 1971 – Mulligan is an unmistakable voice and this was an important, possibly career-saving return to form.

& *See also* **The Original Quartet** (1952–1953; p. 137), **What Is There To Say?** (1958; p. 228)

LIONEL HAMPTON &
Born 20 April 1909, Louisville, Kentucky; died 31 August 2002, New York City
Vibraphone, drums

Salle Pleyel 1971
Laserlight 36133 2CD
Hampton; Roland Connors (t); Bob Snyder (cl); Tommy Gambino (ss, as); Illinois Jacquet, Chuck McClendon (ts); Milt Buckner, John Spruill (org, p); Billy Mackel (g); Eustis Guillemet (b); Kenny Bolds (d). March 1971.

Lionel Hampton said (1990): **'In France, they understood it was important to put on a** *show*. **Even the highbrow critics understood that.'**

In later years, Hampton became a kind of roving ambassador for jazz. In the year of Louis Armstrong's death, he seemed to pick up the mantle again. Later still, he was even close to the White House – jokes about the '*vibe*-president' abounded. There are earlier live recordings from L'Olympia in Paris, from 1961 and again halfway through the decade, when Hamp was one of the few jazz bulwarks against rock'n'roll. The 1971 concert gives plenty of space to Jacquet and Buckner, neither a shrinking violet, and something like the Sam Price blues 'Big Joe' works up a monumental head of steam. Hamp browses through a few standards that take his fancy – 'Summertime', 'Avalon', 'Who Can I Turn To' – and Jacquet gets beefy on 'Ghost Of A Chance'. Working with a smaller group, the set has more of an R&B feel (he helped invent it, after all), and although the second disc is packed with warhorses, there's lots to listen to.

& *See also* **Lionel Hampton 1937–1938** (1937–1938; p. 62)

SLAM STEWART
Born Leroy Stewart, 21 September 1914, Englewood, New Jersey; died 10 December 1987, Binghamton, New York
Double bass, voice

Slam Bam
Black & Blue 861
Stewart; Milt Buckner (p); Jo Jones (d). April 1971.

Slim Gaillard said (1989): **'My man Slam, wham! oop bop, shoo bop, paradaba, bam!'** (or as close to that as can be transcribed).

Stewart was already a star when he appeared in the movie *Stormy Weather* in 1943. During the '30s he had been a stalwart of the New York scene, playing with Art Tatum and forming an evergreen partnership (love it, hate it; it sold records) with Slim Gaillard which exploited the less serious side of Stewart's virtuosic self-harmonizing (an octave apart) on bass and vocals. However corny he now seems, few modern bass-players have taken up the technical challenge Stewart posed (though Major Holley had a stab, singing in unison with his bass), and the purely musical aspects of his work are of abiding value. The very oddity of Stewart's technique is initially off-putting, but on repeated listening its complexities begin to make an impact. It's perhaps a shame that Stewart wasn't able – or didn't choose – to record with more of the younger modern bassists. If Mingus and Pettiford are now thought to have set the instrument free, much of what they did was already implicit in Stewart's work of the '30s. By the early '70s, though, Stewart was stuck in a manner rather than a style.

CARMEN MCRAE

Born 8 April 1920, New York City; died 10 November 1994, Beverly Hills, California
Voice, piano

Sings Lover Man
Columbia CK 65115
McRae; Nat Adderley (c); Eddie 'Lockjaw' Davis (ts); Norman Simmons (p, cel); Mundell Lowe (g); Bob Cranshaw (b); Walter Perkins (d). June–July 1971.

Carmen McRae said (1983): **'Billie was my idol; always was; always will be. She scared me, she was so good. I believed when I was younger that it wasn't possible to be better than her. And I think you can hear that in my singing, that fear of anticlimax.'**

An accomplished pianist, Carmen McRae was something of a late starter as a featured vocalist, not recording a vocal session under her own name until 1954. Her fame has always lagged behind that of her close contemporaries Sarah Vaughan and Billie Holiday, but eventually she did achieve something like the honour she deserved, and her commitment to jazz singing was unflinching. The CD era has not been very kind to her. Universal's stewardship of her Decca catalogue has been insultingly negligent. It eventually took the British arm of MCA to double up *Torchy* and *Blue Moon*, although the latter has subsequently been released as a Verve Master Edition, albeit with a miserly playing time.

There's always a tigerish feel to her best vocals – no woman has ever sung in the jazz idiom with quite such beguiling surliness as McRae, and because she never had the pipes of an Ella or Sassie, she did have to rely on that sheer force of character to put a song across. She was briefly married to Kenny Clarke in the '40s and had to go the usual route of band singer (with Basie, Mercer Ellington) and intermission artist before she got a respectable break. McRae's original tribute to Billie Holiday was something she had wanted to do during her Decca period. At Columbia, where she made only one other album, she got her chance. The deft arrangements are by the often undersung Norman Simmons, and Adderley and Lockjaw Davis take on the Harry Edison and Ben Webster roles. Though she follows Holiday's manner almost to the letter on some songs, notably 'Them There Eyes' and 'Trav'lin' Light', this is all Carmen McRae. She is quite imperious on 'Yesterdays', finds a deadly, almost sardonic note in 'Strange Fruit' and is ineffably tender on 'If The Moon Turns Green'. The musicians play superbly alongside her.

KEITH JARRETT&

Born 8 May 1945, Allentown, Pennsylvania
Piano, soprano saxophone, other instruments

El Juicio (The Judgement)
Atlantic 7567 80783-3
Jarrett; Dewey Redman (ts, cl, Chinese musette); Charlie Haden (b, perc); Paul Motian (d). July 1971.

Charles Lloyd says: **'I first met Keith when we were both playing in Boston and I was blown away. I was playing downstairs with Cannonball [Adderley] and he was playing upstairs with a woman singer and he would come and check me out and I would check him out. He was amazing even then, a very spiritual, very brilliant musician who gets some strange comments behind all the adulation.'**

A child prodigy, Jarrett learned his craft in the Boston area and with the Jazz Messengers before achieving stardom with Charles Lloyd's crossover quartet. A restless experimenter who pioneered long-form solo improvisation but also, with his Standards Trio, rewrote the American songbook and then unexpectedly delved back into free music for a time.

In a series of intensive sessions in the first two weeks of July 1971, Jarrett taped enough material for *El Juicio*, *The Mourning Of A Star* and *Birth*. Haden's presence, and the fact that Atlantic had picked up Jarrett a little over a decade after the last of the classic Ornette Coleman records, inevitably conjured up comparisons: while not as radical as Ornette's music, Jarrett was no less rich in creative potential. The group sound is expanded by his own use of soprano saxophone, notably on *El Juicio* and on *Birth*'s 'Mortgage On My Soul (Wah Wah)'; Redman also deploys clarinet and musette, and there are steel pans and other percussion when called for. Though it has its detractors, for us *El Juicio* remains a high-point, and it is now available in a couple of editions from different labels, on one of them paired with the fine early trio *Life Between The Exit Signs*. The joyous countrified swing of 'Gypsy Moth' and 'Toll Road' could hardly be more infectious, or more loosely structured, at an opposite remove to the dour atmosphere of 'El Juicio' itself, a strange, brooding tone-poem which if the cover art is anything by way of confirmation conjures up first and last things, a musical eschatology. Also very different, and also confirming the Atlantic lineage, is the experimental melodism of 'Piece For Ornette'. It exists in two forms, one at nine and a quarter minutes, the other at 12 seconds! It isn't a long record and the compilation option shears out 'Pardon My Rags', but it has a freshness of approach and depth of musical intelligence that has never tarnished.

& *See also* **The Köln Concert** (1975; p. 418), **Standards: Volume 1** (1983; p. 474), **Always Let Me Go** (2001; p. 663)

MAHAVISHNU ORCHESTRA&

Formed 1971
Group

The Inner Mounting Flame
Columbia Legacy 65523
John McLaughlin (g); Jan Hammer (p, Moog); Jerry Goodman (vn); Rick Laird (b); Billy Cobham (d). August 1971.

Broadcaster and DJ Peter Easton remembers: **'They came to Glasgow once: arpeggiated gently for five minutes, then freaked out for half an hour, then played a few more arpeggios, and went home.'**

The Mahavishnu Orchestra combined sophisticated time-signatures and chord structures with drum and post-Hendrix guitar riffs of surpassing heaviness. Some elements of the Mahavishnu package – not least the leader's cheesecloth philosophy and huge doubleneck guitars – dated rather quickly, but the Orchestra's hippy reputation has given way to renewed respect among musicians, and there are at present a number of Mahavishnu repertory 'projects' in existence, the best of them curated and led by percussionist Gregg Bendian.

The formula was slightly more thoughtful than arpeggio-freakout-arpeggio. Over ambiguous harmonies and often complex time-signatures, McLaughlin produced chains of blistering high notes on both his six- and twelve-stringed guitars. He had worked in between with Miles Davis and as part of the Tony Williams Lifetime, and his sound had evolved and darkened since the making of *Extrapolation* just over two years previously. The two new additional elements were Jan Hammer's remarkably personalized and expressive Moog lines and Billy Cobham's whirlwind drumming. Rick Laird, later a distinguished photographer, maintained a steady, algebraic beat, while Jerry Goodman, despite coming from undistinguished prog-rock group Flock, showed no difficulty playing violin in 13/8.

The first Mahavishnu album was one of the essential fusion records. It's more varied than one remembers, with the soft lyricism of 'A Lotus On Irish Streams' set against the heavy blues sarcasm of 'You Know, You Know'. Ironically, just as he was pushing the electric guitar solo to new heights of amplification and creative abandon, McLaughlin was also working against the dominance of electricity and setting a new standard for acoustic performance, something he continued to develop on the second Mahavishnu record, *Birds Of Fire*. Personal and artistic differences blocked progress on a third studio album. There was conflict regarding composition credits in what was supposed to be a co-operative band. In the event, Columbia released the live Central Park recording *Between Nothingness And Eternity*. Word of bootleg copies of the studio session circulated for some time, but then studio producer Bob Belden discovered a pair of quarter-inch tapes containing the material. The 'lost' session includes Hammer's 'Sister Andrea' – also on the live record – but also two short tunes by Rick Laird ('Steppings Tones') and Jerry Goodman ('I Wonder'), though it seems that Billy Cobham held back material for his own projects.

Later incarnations of the group were on a more obviously orchestral scale. They are probably undervalued, but none ever reached the intensity and sheer beauty of the first record.

& *See also* **JOHN MCLAUGHLIN**, Extrapolation (1969; p. 359)

ORNETTE COLEMAN &
Born Randolph Denard Ornette Coleman, 9 March 1930, Fort Worth, Texas
Alto and tenor saxophones, trumpet, violin

The Complete Science Fiction Sessions
Columbia/Legacy 63569 2CD
Coleman; Bobby Bradford, Carmon Fornarotto, Gerard Schwarz (t); Don Cherry (pkt-t); Dewey Redman (ts, musette); Cedar Walton (p); Jim Hall (g); Charlie Haden (b); Ed Blackwell (d); Billy Higgins (tymp); Webster Armstrong, David Henderson, Asha Puthli (v). September–October 1971, September 1972.

Ornette Coleman said (1983): **'With the new technologies, perhaps we are ready to escape from need and pain, and all that worldly stuff. "Work" seems increasingly irrelevant, and so does the idea of a job. What am I doing? It isn't work, whatever else it is, and it isn't play-as-the-opposite-of-work either.'**

Is this Ornette's most important record since the Atlantics? The release version was muddled and patchy, but now that all the material is in the public domain, its intentions and contours are more plainly audible. It's a work of unbelievable intensity, as if Ornette were trying to reach escape velocity with his music and lift it once and for all above the quotidian standards of 'jazz'. 'Street Woman' and 'Civilization Day' mark the reunion of the classic quartet, but taken on a step. 'Rock The Clock' has Redman on musette, and Haden's bass pushed through a wah-wah pedal, stirring up an unwanted comparison with Miles Davis's electric jams; it's not an entirely absurd thought, and it may be that for a moment their philosophies unwillingly converged, but it's fleeting. 'What Reason Could I Give' and 'Science Fiction' feature vocalist Asha Puthli, world-pop of the sort one might expect if Stockhausen were the DJ. The best tracks, though, are 'Law Years' and 'The Jungle Is A Skyscraper', with Redman and Bradford added to the quartet. These are fast, intense lines, with something of the full-on disorder of *Free Jazz* reaching out towards the 'harmolodic' language of *Dancing In Your Head*, the latter a record that brought Coleman to the attention of a hip younger audience (one not much interested in jazz and attracted by the guitars) but decidedly inferior to his overlooked masterpiece. There are moments of nonsense, inevitably. David Henderson's narration doesn't make much sense in context and the originally rejected 'Good Girl Blues' is a bit daft. It may be of use to ask friends who played guitar on the *Science Fiction* session. Not many of them will jump at Jim Hall, unless they knew already. But with Ornette, the 'unlikely' partnerships – and many more were to follow – stack up so tall they start to look like normal practice for this most welcoming of musicians.

& *See also* **The Shape Of Jazz To Come** (1959, 1960; p. 245), **At The Golden Circle, Stockholm** (1965; p. 324), **Colors** (1996; p. 605)

REVOLUTIONARY ENSEMBLE &

Formed 1971
Group

Revolutionary Ensemble

ESP 3000
Leroy Jenkins (vn, vla); Sirone (b); Jerome Cooper (d, p). 1971.

Leroy Jenkins said (1991): **'Maybe we should have called ourselves the Evolutionary Trio. That might have gone down better.'**

It was Sunny Murray who introduced violinist Leroy Jenkins to bassist Sirone. They immediately discovered large areas of musical and political interest in common and formed a trio, originally with drummer Frank Clayton. Jenkins had already been dabbling in new musical systems, developing a personal language compounded of blues, jazz and classical music. Sirone had considerable experience already on the avant-garde scene and Jerome Cooper, who replaced Clayton before the first recording, was a younger Chicagoan experimenter.

The eponymous first record is a two-part improvisation called, significantly, 'Vietnam'. The music is harsh and demanding, but Jenkins's interest in developing improvisations from small cells or motives is immediately evident, as is Sirone's ability to translate such ideas into a lower register and slower delivery, and Cooper's willingness to add an abstract orchestral quality to the music as well as line and metre. It remains a powerful performance, subtler than its rather two-dimensional register suggests.

Of the trio's other records, little survives except jealously guarded collectors' copies. There is a story that a contract with A&M was cancelled when Quincy Jones played label founder Herb Alpert a selection from *The People's Republic*, sparking a violent reaction. Elsewhere, bad pressings and no distribution dented the group's visibility seriously. There was a revival in 2003, but while the fire was undimmed, the world seemed to have moved on ...

& *See also* **LEROY JENKINS, Solo** (1992; p. 567)

JOHN SURMAN &

Born 30 August 1944, Tavistock, Devon, England
Baritone and soprano saxophones, bass clarinet, keyboards

Tales Of The Algonquin

Dutton Vocalion 8410
Surman; Harry Beckett, Martin Drover, Kenny Wheeler (t, flhn); Danny Almark, Malcolm Griffiths, Ed Harvey (tb); Mike Osborne (as, cl); Alan Skidmore (ts, af); Stan Sulzmann (as, ss, f); John Warren (b, f); John Taylor (p); Harry Miller, Barre Phillips (b); Alan Jackson, Stu Martin (d). 1971.

John Surman says: **'Typically, the albums that have the most impact are recorded in a hurry and often by accident.** *Tales* **happened because I needed one album to fulfil my quota for Decca. I asked John Warren if he felt like writing something new. The Trio were in the UK to record. A studio was booked, musicians found and ... bingo.'**

John Surman first came to notice in Mike Westbrook's group, and it was a direct result of his performances on the Westbrook albums *Celebration* and *Marching Song* that persuaded producer Peter Eden to record him for Deram. The debut makes unexpected listening, being largely devoted to calypso jazz in the Sonny Rollins mode, played accurately and with some exuberance but hardly representative of Surman's great strengths.

At the same time he was developing a more individual style in a trio with Dave Holland and Alan Jackson, and the second half of the debut record was devoted to large-scale arrangements of trio material. Unfortunately that is very much the impression the album creates. The ensembles sound padded-out rather than organic, perhaps too consciously influenced by Coltrane's *Africa/Brass. How Many Clouds Can You See?* marked a step forward. It also saw a first collaboration with Canadian composer John Warren; 'Premonition' is a powerful trade-off between free jazz and more classically orientated structures and was an important pointer to what was to come later. The remainder of the record is small group-pieces, reflecting the work Surman was doing with The Trio.

Surman's time with Deram ended with his very best album to date, a full-scale collaboration with Warren. *Tales Of The Algonquin* is a masterpiece, conceived on a grand scale, meticulously executed and marked by superb soloing from Surman, Skidmore and the always wonderful Osborne. The set opens with four unrelated themes by Warren. Surman produces a boiling soprano solo on the uptempo 'With Terry's Help', which exploits double-time and displaced harmonies. 'The Dandelion' is perhaps the standout track of the album, though it is Mike Osborne's plaintive, keening solo which gives it its power. By contrast, the connected pieces which give the album its title are slightly too fey and impressionistic. 'Shingebis And The North Wind' is adventurous even by the standards of those blithely experimental days. Again Surman takes a back seat, this time to trumpeter Harry Beckett, who solos with an elemental sadness. Surman sounds most sure-footed in the immediate company of his Trio colleagues Phillips and Martin and produces his own most effective playing with them on 'The Adventures Of Manabush'. *Tales* is a record that has enjoyed almost legendary status among British jazz fans.

& *See also* **A Biography Of The Rev. Absalom Dawe** (1994; p. 585); **SOS, SOS** (1975; p. 419)

NORMA WINSTONE

Born 23 September 1941, London
Voice

Edge Of Time

Disconforme 148
Winstone; Henry Lowther, Kenny Wheeler (t, flhn); Malcolm Griffiths, Chris Pyne, Paul Rutherford (tb); Mike Osborne (as, cl); Alan Skidmore (ts); Art Themen (bs); John Taylor (p); Gary Boyle (g); Chris Laurence (b); Tony Levin (d). 1971.

Norma Winstone says: **'I made the most of it by trying to include all my friends! So, sometimes 12 musicians, sometime three (as with John Taylor and Art Themen on "Songs For A Child": the beginning of a penchant for the trio?). I had a feeling that it would be a "one-off" as they would eventually realize their mistake. I turned out to be right about this. Decca pulled out of the recording of new jazz talent pretty soon after!'**

Norma's coming out as a singer was supporting Roland Kirk at Ronnie Scott's and it was there, a short time after, that she won both the British and World section in a 1971 *Melody Maker* jazz poll. The other side-benefit was that Decca signed off for an album, perhaps cashing in on the fact that Norma had already recorded with Michael Garrick for their subsidiary Argo. Her debut as leader is still warmly admired, even if she did subsequently go on to pioneer a new kind of chamber-jazz as Azimuth with former husband John Taylor and trumpeter Kenny Wheeler, and she has continued to balance lyric singing with free-form vocalizing in a number of contexts. She has a unique voice, strong but ethereal, floating but always exact and on pitch; it sits just as well in a horn section (as on Mike Westbrook's *Metropolis*) as in front of a standards orchestra.

   Much of the drama on *Edge Of Time* comes from that crystalline voice swooping in and out of the winds. The title-track begins slow and abstractly, almost as if caught out of time itself and then the *rubato* begins to organize itself until the song runs along a big-band line that would satisfy Duke Ellington. The big piece of the album is the joyous and forthright 'Enjoy This Day', where subtle dissonance brings a hint of anxiety, almost foreboding, to an otherwise upbeat tune; Kenny Wheeler's solo is superb, a foretaste of Azimuth's sometimes uncanny empathy; Taylor's harmonic awareness is evident throughout. In contrast, 'Erebus, Son Of Chaos' ought to be dark and brooding, but comes across as rather jolly. The only weak point is the brief 'Songs For A Child', though this pure-voice balladry has influenced some surprising artists since 1971.

EARL HINES &

Known as 'Fatha'; born 28 December 1903, Duquesne, Pennsylvania; died 22 April 1983, Oakland, California
Piano

Earl Hines Plays Duke Ellington

New World NW 361/2 2CD
Hines (p solo). December 1971–April 1975.

Earl Hines said (1977): **'Duke wrote good, but I still think I'm a prettier piano player.'**

Made over a period of four years, these are much more than casual one-giant-nods-to-another records. Hines was cajoled by Stanley Dance into looking into many unfamiliar Ellington tunes and creating a memorial (Ellington died around the time of the final sessions) which is surely among the best tributes to the composer on record. Since Hines's more aristocratic touches are close in feeling to Ellington's own, there is an immediate affinity in such pieces as 'Love You Madly' and 'Black And Tan Fantasy'. But Hines finds a wealth of new incident in warhorses such as 'Mood Indigo' and 'Sophisticated Lady' and he turns 'The Shepherd' and 'Black Butterfly' into extravagant fantasies which go far beyond any of Ellington's own revisionist approaches. Even a simple piece such as 'C Jam Blues' receives a fascinating, rhythmic treatment, and the voicings conjured up for 'I'm Beginning To See The Light' upset conventional wisdom about Ellingtonian interpretation. In his variety of resource, Hines also points up all the devices he passed on to Powell, Monk and virtually every other post-swing pianist. A memorable lesson, and a fine tribute to two great piano-players, spread over two hours of music. A second volume loses pace and interest, but Hines collectors will surely want both.

& *See also* **Earl Hines Collection: Piano Solos 1928–1940** (1928–1940; p. 34)

ARCHIE SHEPP&
Born 24 May 1937, Fort Lauderdale, Florida
Tenor, soprano and alto saxophones, piano

Attica Blues
Verve 654414
Shepp; Roy Burrowes, Michael Ridley, Charles McGhee (t); Cal Massey (flhn); Clifford Thornton (c); Charles Stephens, Kiane Zawadi, Charles Greenlee (tb); Hakim Jami (euph); Marion Brown (as, fl, perc); Clarence White (as); Bill Robinson, Roland Alexander (ts); James Ware (bs); Dave Burrell, Walter Davis Jr (p); Cornell Dupree (g); Leroy Jenkins, John Blake, L. Shankar (vn); Ronald Lipscomb, Calo Scott (clo); Gerald Jemmott, Roland Wilson, Jimmy Garrison (b); Beaver Harris (d); Ollie Anderson, Jumma Santos, Nene DeFense (perc); Henry Hull (as Carl Hall), Joshie Armstead, Albertine Robinson, Joe Lee Wilson, Waheeda Massey (v); William Kunstler, Bartholomew Gray (narration). January 1972.

Archie Shepp said (1982): **'Coming from where I do, and with the background I have, there were times when I thought I should be working as a lawyer, expressing social engagement in some more direct and practical way, but you see the fallacy of that: the idea that the one is practical and useful, and the other not?'**

Shepp's other Impulse! records after *Four For Trane* have always been admired: *Mama Too Tight*, *The Way Ahead*; as has *Yasmina, A Black Woman*, which was released in France. Comparatively neglected is *Attica Blues*. Often characterized – unheard – as a Mingus-like scream of rage against the authorities who bloodily quelled America's most infamous prison riot, this is actually a much subtler record than that, and that might perversely be why it has dropped from sight for so long. Shepp alternates slow mournful ballads with funkier numbers that reflect things going on elsewhere in black music, and while this isn't *On The Corner*, it's certainly closer to that aesthetic than anything he attempted in the previous decade. 'Steam' became a regular item in his later sets; sung here by Joe Lee Wilson, it has a curiously archaic quality, a sign perhaps that Shepp was turning his back on the scorched-earth radicalism of the '60s. The more explicit agendas are articulated by civil rights attorney Kunstler but the more effective vocal elements are more oblique, like Cal Massey's daughter's touching delivery on 'Quiet Dawn'. A great album, long overlooked.

& *See also* **Four For Trane** (1964; p. 306), **Looking At Bird** (1980; p. 456)

MCCOY TYNER&
Born Alfred McCoy Tyner, 11 December 1938, Philadelphia, Pennsylvania; also briefly known as Sulaimon Saud
Piano, koto

Sahara
Original Jazz Classics OJCCD 311
Tyner; Sonny Fortune (ss, as, f); Calvin Hill (b, perc); Alphonse Mouzon (d, t, f). January 1972.

McCoy Tyner said: **'We were always talking about how jazz came out of the African experience and into the American experience. I tried to ask: "What does that actually *sound* like?"'**

After leaving Blue Note, Tyner's career floundered for a time. His first release for Milestone (now reissued as an OJC) was a poll-winning record which established his course for the '70s. Tyner had long been interested in non-Western musical traditions and in a percussive approach to the piano keyboard. On 'Valley Of Life' he deploys koto as more than a colour device, as elsewhere he was to show a facility on Appalachian dulcimer. Tyner has always chosen drummers of a particular, perhaps unexpected, type. Most recently, he has been working again with his townsman Eric Gravátt, whose early work, for Tyner and for Weather Report, can only be described as violent. Mouzon couldn't have played the way he does here but for Elvin Jones, yet his choked cymbals and relentless emphasis of the beat are very different from Jones's polyrhythmic swells. Anyone familiar with Mouzon's fusion work of the period will be astonished by his performance here. Fortune plays with uproarious power and velocity, and his solo on 'Rebirth' is electrifying; but his is essentially a decorative role, while the pianist drives and dominates the music. The group acts as the opposing face to Cecil Taylor's brand of energy music: controlled by harmonic and metrical ground-rules, nobody flies for freedom, but there is a compensating jubilation in the leader's mighty utterance. 'Sahara' and 'Ebony Queen' best express that here, although the piano solo, 'A Prayer For My Family', is a useful oasis of calm. Later Tyner records would be better engineered and realized, but this one remains excitingly fresh and a record of lasting influence.

& *See also* **The Real McCoy** (1967; p. 343), **Soliloquy** (1991; p. 548)

PAT MARTINO
Born Pat Azzara, 25 August 1944, Philadelphia, Pennsylvania
Guitar

Footprints
Savoy Jazz 17252
Martino; Bobby Rose (g); Richard Davis (b); Billy Higgins (d). March 1972.

Pat Martino said (1999): **'*Footprints* paid tribute to the influence of Wes Montgomery. I played things that made me think of him, I suppose, and thinking about what he did, rather than just copying the octaves thing, was important to the way my music came together. It's quite undefinable, but very real.'**

The title of Pat Martino's 2006 album *Remember* has to be considered ironic. Though it refers to the legacy of Wes Montgomery, it also offers a reminder that after 1980 Martino had to relearn guitar-playing after suffering an aneurysm and having life-saving surgery. He did so largely by listening to his own old recordings. He'd spent considerable time in earlier years working with organ trios and in soul-jazz, but his solo work was markedly original, indebted, but not in thrall, to Montgomery. Playing *Footprints* up against the 2006 record doesn't really help establish a clear comparison between 'early' and 'later' styles. Martino has always been quite an advanced musical thinker, with an interest in Stockhausen and in forms of fusion. His 1970 album *Desperado* found him on 12-string electric in a situation somewhat reminiscent of Tony Williams's Lifetime; by no means an aberration, for all the records flirt in some way with unconventional forms.

Of the tracks on *Footprints* only 'Road Song' is directly associated with Wes, but one can readily imagine him being attracted to the Wayne Shorter title-piece, with its aery blues aura and almost other-worldly quality. Martino rarely plays like Wes, and actually uses octaves only quite sparingly, but the older guitarist's spirit does seem to hover round tracks like 'What Are You Doing The Rest Of Your Life?', 'Insensatez' and even the opening 'The Visit', the only Martino original. The band is wonderful, of course, but it's the leader's crisp, easy playing that makes the record, which isn't just a good jazz guitar disc and not just a good Wes Montgomery tribute but an ideal example of how an artist can be creative by thinking about the example of a predecessor rather than simply copying his trademark songs and devices.

LONDON JAZZ COMPOSERS' ORCHESTRA&

Founded 1970
Ensemble

Ode

Intakt CD 041 2CD

Barry Guy (b, leader); Harry Beckett, Dave Holdsworth (t); Marc Charig (c); Mike Gibbs, Paul Nieman, Paul Rutherford (tb); Dick Hart (tba); Trevor Watts (as, ss); Mike Osborne, Bernard Living (as); Alan Wakeman, Evan Parker (ts, ss); Bob Downes (ts, b); Karl Jenkins (bs, ob); Howard Riley (p); Derek Bailey (g); Jeff Clyne, Chris Laurence (b); Tony Oxley (perc); Buxton Orr (cond). April 1972.

LJCO founder Barry Guy says: **'*Ode* was the start of a life's journey. The musicians ranged over the jazz spectrum, so the composition had to embrace individual creative spirits whilst offering a cohesive compositional strategy. Its success is testimony to the Herculean efforts of conductor Buxton Orr, who managed to convince sceptical musicians that a complex score could sit comfortably with open improvisation.'**

Barry Guy's seminal ensemble of new-music and free-improvisation figures has followed a fascinating trajectory through several quite different musical philosophies. After the recording of *Ode*, for instance, Guy tried to introduce some more composed pieces, which caused friction with the free improvisers, who regarded this as bad faith. The orchestra's subsequent history has taken in both composed and free elements, works by other hands and a variety of idioms. Modelled somewhat on American trumpeter and composer Michael Mantler's Jazz Composers Orchestra, LJCO has proved to be more durable and creatively more than just an umbrella organization for progressive players.

   It rests squarely on the vision of a leader who, in an age of hyper-specialization and stylistic antagonism, has managed to draw strength and inspiration from across a vast musical spectrum: improvisation, atonal composition, baroque music, jazz. *Ode* was Guy's attempt to integrate improvisation within the textures and dimensions of orchestral music. Conductor Buxton Orr was his composition professor. It is a grand success and remains a key text in contemporary improvisation on a large scale. *Ode* has been repeatedly referred to as a manifesto, and as a beginning to a long process of exploration. With a quarter-century's hindsight there is nothing tentative, polemical or ideological about it. Guy's conviction that the individual capacities of improvised music had been developed disproportionately better than those of ensemble playing is best reinforced here by his triumphant solution to the problem. It's not longhair or Third Stream music. The horns play with bite, the rhythm section keeps the music highly elastic and there are enough passages of roaring big-band music to keep an adventurous Kenton fan on the edge of his seat. Arguably better, arguably more ambitious and more finished works were to follow, but *Ode* has a great historical significance.

& *See also* **BARRY GUY, Study – Witch Gong Game II/10** (1994; p. 579), **Odyssey** (1999; p. 644)

AL HIBBLER *&*

Born 16 August 1915, Tyro, Mississippi; died 24 April 2001, Chicago, Illinois
Voice

A Meeting Of The Times

Warner Brothers 81227-3689-2
Hibbler; Rahsaan Roland Kirk (ts, manzello, stritch, cl, f); Hank Jones, Lonnie Liston Smith (p); Ron Carter, Major Holley (b); Oliver Jackson, Charles Crosby (d); Leon Thomas (v). March 1972, September 1966.

Television executive Chuck Dimarco says: **'I remember seeing Kirk on *Ed Sullivan*, maybe the last *Ed Sullivan* of all, and he turned into this strange circus act, and me thinking how odd it was that this man who was so insistent on the dignity of jazz should use – throw away? – such an opportunity. It was like living in the days of Dada and surrealism. An action, an *acte gratuit*. He even invited along Archie Shepp, and he *hated* Archie Shepp.'**

Born blind, Hibbler became a star with the Ellington orchestra during the war years. He modelled his early singing on Bing Crosby, but increasingly adopted a strange Cockney accent and an exaggerated melisma that is often taken to quite extraordinary lengths. A *Meeting Of The Times* – perhaps more strictly a Roland Kirk album, recorded under his contract with Atlantic but jointly credited – is a small masterpiece. It's all the better for Kirk's decision to set aside his usual multi-instrumentalism and concentrate on single horns for this deeply felt but by no means pious tribute to Ellington. By 1972, Hibbler was almost forgotten, but here his rich baritone and bizarre diction are the perfect complement. Just as nobody ever sounded quite like Kirk, nobody sang a lyric quite like Al. He slides into 'Do Nothing Till You Hear From Me' as if giving dictation, and never quite lets go the speech-song until he starts to syncopate phrases in the middle. On 'Don't Get Around Much Any More', he stretches weird triphthongs on phrases like *'moy moy-und's* never at ease'. Not since Dick Van Dyke has English been put through the mincer quite so thoroughly. Al also turns 'This Love Of Mine' into a thing of almost operatic splendour, before Kirk picks up and doubles the time on his beautifully simple solo. 'Daybreak' features Kirk on clarinet before he switches to flute for a tremulous out passage. On 'Lover, Come Back To Me', the harmonization of horns is so bizarre that it sounds as though the saxophonist is playing fiddle. Roland takes 'Carney And Bigard Place' as an instrumental, which is a welcome respite from the surrealism. The other Ellington tunes are 'Something 'Bout Believing' and 'I Didn't Know About You' and the Hammerstein–Romberg classic 'Lover, Come Back To Me' is a wonderful version, managing to sound deeply threatening underneath the romance. There's also a stray track from another session, with Leon Thomas reprising Kirk's autobiographical 'Dream', but it's very much Hibbler's moment back in the spotlight. The accompaniments are simple, funky and straightforwardly loyal to the song at hand. Perhaps because it's largely the singer's album, it's one that's rarely cited by Kirk fans, but it's a classic.

& See also **RAHSAAN ROLAND KIRK, We Free Kings** (1961; p. 278), **The Inflated Tear** (1968; p. 351)

DONALD BYRD *&*

Born 9 December 1932, Detroit, Michigan
Trumpet

Black Byrd

Blue Note 84466
Byrd; Fonce Mizell (t, v); Allan Curtis Barnes (as, f, ob); Roger Glenn (saxes, f); Joe Sample (p, ky); Fred Perren (ky, v); David T. Walker (g); Wilton Felder, Chuck Rainey (b); Harvey Mason (d); Bobbye Porter Hall, Stephanie Spruill (perc); Larry Mizell (v, arr). April & November 1972.

Donald Byrd said (1974): **'I never thought of them [hard bop and fusion] as two different kinds of music. I played pretty much the same things myself. It's just that one way I played like *this*'** – horn straight out and orthodox – **'and the other way, I played like *this*'** – bell pointing to the floor, Miles Davis-style.

Hard-bop strict-constructionists cried foul when this came out, convinced that Byrd had sold out to Mammon. The Larry Mizell arrangements, vocal parts, electric keyboards and bass all pointed in the direction of fusion, but Byrd was a savvy enough musician to keep the jazz component sufficiently high to hold on to much of his original audience, who were in any case fighting a rearguard against the post-*Bitches Brew* evolution. Byrd and Mizell assembled the musicians in the Sound Factory in LA, usually a haven for rock and soul bands, and the recording proceeded slowly, with much attention to layering a detailed sound that has more substance in it than the sometimes lumpy rhythm suggests. The presence of Sample and Felder from The Crusaders was some guarantee of quality, though the other horns rarely rise above the professional. Byrd's own competence is evident in every cut, though he sounds less polished on the make-up tracks from November, which had a different (and frankly inferior) line-up.

Does it still qualify as a jazz record? In our view, yes, though clearly it's a very different sonority from the Blue Notes of the '50s. However, it was far from a sudden change of direction. Byrd had been signalling something new from the turn of the '70s, bringing in electric instruments on a string of albums from 1969's *Fancy Free* to such underrated records as *Electric Byrd*, *Kofi* and *Ethiopian Nights*. By the time of *Black Byrd*, he had a purchase on a new, younger audience, and has been an honoured figure in acid jazz circles ever since.

& *See also* **Byrd In Hand** (1959; p. 239)

SONNY STITT &

Born Edward Boattner Stitt, 2 February 1924, Boston, Massachusetts; died 22 July 1982, Washington DC
Alto and tenor saxophones

Constellation
Gambit GCD 69269 (with *Tune Up!*)
Stitt; Barry Harris (p); Sam Jones (b); Alan Dawson, Roy Brooks (d). June 1972.

Club owner Ronnie Scott said (1989): **'He told me: "I'm like a lone wolf, but I like to fit in. I turn up to play with some guys I never met before, I don't play what I want to play. I play what they know how to play."'**

Stitt's tireless touring and drop-of-a-hat recording regimen undoubtedly diluted his recorded legacy, but 'going single' was his avocation rather than a burden and every now and then there was an opportunity to play with his peers and in more ideal circumstances. At the start of his final decade, Stitt put down a small masterpiece in *Constellation*. He'd made *Tune Up!* with essentially the same group – Alan Dawson on drums – and also for Muse a few months earlier and they are available together now as a Gambit reissue, jointly credited to Barry Harris.

It's an ideal pairing: two (almost) first-generation boppers still in love with the music's by-ways and still able to give one of Charlie Parker's less celebrated lines a fresh-minted quality. Unlike the usual club date where he would probably have to play a bag of familiar show tunes, Stitt here leans on a shared familiarity with Tadd Dameron ('Casbah'), with the deceptive line of 'Topsy' and his own 'By Accident'. Harris is in sparkling form and Brooks brings a distinctive touch; the drummer, who formed his Artistic Truth group this same year, was to drift into mental illness in succeeding years, a sorry end for one of the music's deceptive journeymen. Stitt's alto-playing is crisp and incisive, with little of the throwaway insouciance he brought to more casual sessions. It's a reminder of what a powerful presence he was for three decades, and incidentally what a vital source of strong bop the Muse label was in its heyday. It's a catalogue that has enjoyed a chequered history, but at least there is now a conservation programme.

& *See also* **New York Jazz** (1956; p. 190)

GEORGE MELLY
Born 17 August 1926, Liverpool, Lancashire, England; died 5 July 2007, London
Voice

Nuts / Son Of Nuts
Warner Jazz 8122-73747-2 2CD
Melly; John Chilton (t); Wally Fawkes (cl); Bruce Turner (as, cl); Colin Bates (p); Steve Fagg (b); Chuck Smith (d).
June 1972–September 1973.

George Melly said (1998): **'Hearing Bessie Smith, I guess that's where a lot of it came from. That's me: Bessie Smith in a tweed suit.'**

Writer, art critic, surrealist and singer, Melly was perhaps the greatest maverick in British jazz, and widely known even outside jazz circles. His cartoon strip *Flook*, illustrated by 'Trog', clarinettist Wally Fawkes, was a staple of the *Daily Mail* for many years, and Melly was a stalwart of television variety programmes, chat shows and quiz games. An habitué of Soho, he became its most vivid raconteur, telling the story of his own life in successful volumes of hysterical autobiography: *Scouse Mouse, Rum, Bum and Concertina* (about the navy from which he was allegedly canned for distributing anarchist tracts) and the superb *Owning Up*, which contains just about everything anyone needs to know about British trad.

It would be disingenuous to say that Melly's artistry was complex and subtle. He was as raucous as a costermonger, but there was a musicianship there as well, and he surrounded himself with fine players: Mick Mulligan, John Chilton, latterly Digby Fairweather. Melly belted out classic jazz and blues with leather-lunged intensity and without finessing the lyric. In a club it was impossible not to be distracted by the man. On record, it stands up remarkably well. Some of the early Pye things, made when he had hooked up with Mulligan's band, have a rootsy authenticity and he kept that going into his last few years, when he gargled a few more lines but still commanded the floor. The performances of the early '70s are as arch as Broxburn viaduct, but these ancient songs aren't prettified or turned into 'art' and Melly's renderings are far closer, surely, to the black vernacular originals and music hall descendants than most latter-day approximations. Melly was a practising Surrealist, not a dilettante. Now that he's gone, the records seem that little bit more precious.

CHARLES TOLLIVER
Born 6 March 1942, Jacksonville, Florida
Trumpet

Grand Max
Black Lion DA Music 760145
Tolliver; John Hicks (p); Reggie Workman (b); Alvin Queen (d). August 1972.

Pianist Andrew Hill said (2005): **'He has a sound that just flows out of the horn, like a molten liquid. I don't know anyone else who sounds quite like that, or who can sustain that kind of movement for so long.'**

Tolliver studied at Howard and served an apprenticeship with Gerald Wilson. He was later part of Music Inc. with Stanley Cowell and founded Strata East records with the pianist. Unfortunately, despite the enthusiasm of other musicians – including Dizzy Gillespie – Tolliver never seemed to break through to wider appreciation and was out of public circulation for quite some time, before Andrew Hill got him involved again shortly before the pianist's death. Verdicts on Tolliver's performance then varied quite sharply, but there is no mistaking the quality or daring of his earlier work.

For economic reasons, a lot of the released work on Strata East was recorded in concert. *Grand Max* was taped live at the Loosdrecht Jazz Festival and originally released under that name, before Black Lion licensed it from the ailing imprint. The title-track is a tiny prelude to a subtle and involving set that includes Tolliver's own powerful 'Our Second Father', as well as Stanley Cowell's 'Prayer For Peace' and an unexpected but effective reading of Neal Hefti's 'Repetition'. Tolliver's lead is always big and assertive, with a timbre that occasionally recalls Freddie Hubbard's, but edgier than that in delivery, and in some aspects more saxophonic in its phrasing, which perhaps reflects the influence of John Coltrane.

JACKIE MCLEAN &

Born 17 May 1932, New York City; died 31 May 2006, Hartford, Connecticut
Alto saxophone

Live At Montmartre
Steeplechase SCCD 31001
McLean; Kenny Drew (p); Bo Stief (b); Alex Riel (d). August 1972.

McLean's student, saxophonist Steve Lehman, says: **'Jackie used to tell us that we weren't playing African music and we weren't playing European music; we were playing American music.'**

A live record from Europe might seem a perverse choice, given the run of exceptional albums McLean made for Blue Note between *New Soil* and 1966, including *A Fickle Sonance, Bluesnik, Old And New Gospel, Let Freedom Ring* and *Destination ... Out!* To some degree, though, all of these simply worked out the further implications of what was adumbrated on that first release for the label. In later years, and particularly when touring, McLean seemed able to re-incorporate some of the lessons of freedom into his basic bop/blues language – later still there were elements of 'world music' and a new mythology/cosmology to take account of – and the results were exhilarating.

Listening to McLean in Europe in 1972 (and one of the authors was present at the Jazzhus Montmartre recording on 5 August) was an affirmation of American music and the freedoms it still offered at a time when America was an easy imperial bogey. For sheer *joie de vivre, Live At Montmartre* is hard to beat. Full-voiced and endlessly inventive, McLean romps through 'Smile', adding the 'shave-and-a-haircut-bay-rum' cadence to the end of his first statement with an almost arrogant flourish. 'Das Dat' follows, but already here, there is a plangent, almost chastened edge to the saxophone sound; it's a record that has its mournful, elegiac, homesick tinge as well as upbeat swing. 'Parker's Mood' is perhaps the best of his later bebop essays, shifting out of synch with Drew's excellent chording for a couple of measures.

This was by no means the end of the McLean story. He continued making records until the turn of 2000, returning to Blue Note towards the end of his life. Needless to say, all are listenable, even if none quite reaches the heights. This was one of the great jazz lives and stories and it's celebrated here with nuance and grace.

& *See also* **New Soil** (1959; p. 238)

STEVE LACY&

Born Steven Lackritz, 23 July 1934, New York City; died 4 June 2004, Boston, Massachusetts
Soprano saxophone

Weal & Woe
Emanem 4004
Lacy; Steve Potts (as, ss); Irène Aëbi (v, vla, clo); Kent Carter (b); Oliver Johnson (d). August 1972, January 1973.

Emanem curator Martin Davidson remembers: **'Lacy carried the solo tapes round Europe trying unsuccessfully to interest record labels. Their brilliant outrageousness inspired me to start one of my own. Unfortunately, Lacy's subsequent playing was rarely as adventurous. The strident anti-war message of** *The Woe* **also managed to alienate other record labels.'**

Anthony Braxton's *For Alto* opened up for saxophone-players the possibility of solo, unaccompanied performance. The earlier half of *Weal & Woe* documents Lacy's first-ever foray in the form, a solo soprano saxophone performance, made in the fine acoustic of a deconsecrated church/theatre in Avignon. Just four years after Braxton's *tour de force* it is fascinating to hear Lacy take a very different course, sinuously melodic, less antagonistic in attack than Braxton but no less percussive and definite, and no less willing to superimpose different rhythmic shapes over a basic line.

The Woe was Lacy's powerful anti-war suite. It was recorded the night before the peace treaty with Vietnam was signed, with sound-effect cassettes of aerial and ground warfare playing in the studio in real time. Interestingly, this solitary performance of the piece wasn't released for a further six years, as a Quark LP. Given that it is a studio recording, and even given the difficulty of balancing found sounds against the instruments, the sound isn't altogether friendly to Aëbi in particular and some of the quieter saxophone passages are not well registered. However, nothing detracts from the power of the music. Other musicians, notably Billy Bang, registered horror and protest at events in South-East Asia, but the violinist's Vietnam records were made long after the event. Lacy's may have come on the last night of the war, but its horror and absurdity are more robustly signified in *The Woe*: a remarkable work.

& *See also* **The Straight Horn Of Steve Lacy** (1960; p. 260), **5 x Monk 5 x Lacy** (1994; p. 580)

WOODY SHAW

Born Herman Shaw II, 24 December 1944, Laurinburg, North Carolina; died 10 May 1989, New York
City
Trumpet

Song Of Songs
Original Jazz Classics OJCCD 1893-2
Shaw; Emmanuel Boyd (ts, f); Bennie Maupin, Ramon Morris (ts); George Cables (p); Henry Franklin (b); Woodrow Theus II (d). September 1972.

Pianist Mulgrew Miller said (1999): **'You can always tell Woody. He used to combine major and minor thirds in the chord, plus other things that make him recognizable. It's too quick to say he used "pentatonic" scales, or "fourths". It's subtler than that.'**

Woody made his recording debut with Eric Dolphy at the age of 19 in what are usually thought of as the *Iron Man/Jitterbug Waltz* sessions. One reviewer was convinced that 'Woody Sho'' was a *nom de session* for Freddie Hubbard, inexplicably when you listen to his

Navarro- and Morgan-inspired attack and phrasing. It was Dolphy who taught Woody to play 'inside and outside at the same time', but it was listening to the classics that awakened a player with perfect pitch to the subtler nuances of harmony. Like all imaginative Americans, Woody was violently stretched between opposites and inexorably drawn to the things and the places that would destroy him. Europe drew him for all the usual non-musical reasons, but there is a sense, too, that Woody's foreshortened career represented a sustained fugue from the racially constrained job description of the 'jazz musician'.

Woody's best-known composition was premiered on Larry Young's Blue Note classic, *Unity*. His own version of 'The Moontrane' is on the Muse album of that name, and has been only irregularly available. Shaw was unlucky in his recording career, though he had a brief flurry in the '80s which came too late to save him. A poor manager, permanently disorganized and suffering from *retinitis pigmentosa,* to which he was losing his sight, Shaw fell under a subway train in New York, perhaps deliberately.

Song Of Songs was his second record as leader. Wonderful it is, but also undeniably timelocked, heavily dependent on George Cables's electric piano effects; yet swinging and propulsive, and replete with Shaw's characteristically shifting chromaticism. Woody's four compositions are still not fully assimilated, and not many contemporary players would attempt something as sardonic as 'The Goat And The Archer'. Redundant as it may be to make the point again, had Shaw been picked up by a sensitive label and producer at this point, afforded the players and the studio time his exacting concept demanded, then who knows what he might have achieved. As it is, this and *The Moontrane* were the best things he did until the brief starburst of the '80s.

CHICK COREA &

Born Armando Anthony Corea, 12 June 1941, Chelsea, Massachusetts
Piano, keyboards

Light As A Feather

Verve 557115-2 2CD
Corea; Joe Farrell (ss, f); Stanley Clarke (b); Airto Moreira (d, perc); Flora Purim (v, perc). October 1972.

Flora Purim said (1989): **'I met Chick at Walter Booker's apartment and next day he asked me to sing "What Game Shall We Play Today". A beautiful song.'**

Corea recorded *Return To Forever* for ECM with the same personnel eight months earlier, and would subsequently use the name for his fusion group. The language was still jazz, though, even if the electric sound that came in with *Bitches Brew* and other records of the period is increasingly evident; Corea and Moreira had been involved with Miles's electric evolution. Interestingly enough, the influence of Bud Powell (more formally acknowledged later) and, even more, Horace Silver is still obvious in these delicately swinging sessions.

Return To Forever perturbed the bebop mafia, as Flora Purim explains. The arrival of 17-year-old Stanley Clarke was similar in impact – musically positive, critically negative – to that of the teenage Michael Henderson in Miles's group. The inclusion of 'Crystal Silence' and 'What Game Shall We Play Today?' gave the LP some crossover appeal, but the jazz component was solid on 'Return To Forever' itself and the majestic climax of 'Sometime Ago/La Fiesta' with its abstract elements and flamenco tinges. *Return* wasn't released in the US for some time, so *Light As A Feather* was effectively the group debut, and the first to use the band name.

Thistledown it may be in some regards, but it's a perennial favourite. Repackaged with extra tracks from the sessions, including several versions of 'What Game Shall We Play?', it is still Chick's most engagingly approachable record. The leader bounces joyously and unselfconsciously throughout, transforming relatively simple themes like '500 Miles High', 'Captain Marvel', and the ubiquitous 'Spain' and 'Children's Song' into grand dancing processions. Purim's vocalizing is a perfect complement to Farrell's still underrated improvising, packed with quartal harmonies and unexpected note choices. Neville Potter's lyrics to 'You're Everything' would bring a tear to a glass eye, but Purim is most effective when following her own agenda on the title-track. An album almost impossible to dislike.

& *See also* **Tones For Joan's Bones** (1966; p. 340), **Rendezvous In New York** (2001; p. 667)

DAVE HOLLAND *&*
Born 1 October 1946, Wolverhampton, Staffordshire, England
Double bass, cello

Conference Of The Birds
ECM 829373-2
Holland; Anthony Braxton, Sam Rivers (reeds, f); Barry Altschul (d, perc). November 1972.

Dave Holland says: '**My first recording as a leader. The band consisted of three of the members of the Circle quartet that had recently disbanded, Anthony Braxton, Barry Altschul and myself. Barry and I had also been working with Sam Rivers. Some of the music had been written for Circle but not recorded; I added a few new compositions. We rehearsed and then performed two nights at Sam's Studio Rivbea and the next day went into the studio and recorded the music in a five-hour session.**'

In 1968, the 21-year-old Holland recorded *Karyobin* with the Spontaneous Music Ensemble and *Filles De Kilimanjaro* with Miles Davis. Even given that most bassists have a wide and varied CV, this is a pretty broad musical spectrum to pack into a few months. Holland has been spoken of in the same breath as the legendary Scott LaFaro: he shares the American's bright, exact intonation, incredible hand-speed and utter musicality. It isn't fanciful to suggest that he is the finest bassist/composer since Charles Mingus and until the as yet untested likes of Adam Lane and Ben Allison came along.

If he had never made another record as leader, *Conference Of The Birds* would still stand out as a quiet masterpiece. The title-piece, marked out by Altschul's marimba figures and the two reedmen interweaving basket-tight, was inspired by the morning chorus outside Holland's London flat, not the Persian mystical poem. But mystical much of the music is; indivisible and almost impossible to render verbally. On flutes, Rivers and Braxton are hard to separate; on saxophones, much easier. Altschul is at his very best and Holland's own part is subtly nuanced.

& *See also* **Extended Play** (2001; p. 671)

MARIAN MCPARTLAND
Born Margaret Marian Turner, 20 March 1918, Slough, Berkshire, England
Piano

Contrasts
Jazz Alliance TJA2-12044-2 2CD
McPartland; Jimmy McPartland (c, v); Vic Dickenson, Hank Berger (tb); Jack Maheu (cl); Buddy Tate (ts, bs); Michael Moore, Rusty Gilder (b); Gus Johnson, Larry Bell, Mike Berger, Joe Corsello (d). November 1972–June 1973.

Marian McPartland said (1992): **'I started playing professionally in 1938 when a man called Billy Mayerl heard me play and asked me to join his touring group, which was a kind of novelty orchestra featuring four pianos! It was a bit of a change after studying at the Guildhall!'**

Marian married trumpeter Jimmy McPartland in 1945 and moved to the US, working for a time as a soloist in Chicago but also working a long residency at New York's Hickory House in the '50s. She's now best known for her long-running *Piano Jazz* recitals on PBS.

Marian's lengthy discography begins in the early '50s but she has been unjustly neglected by reissues as far as her music from that period is concerned. So we have to start in 1973, with the two discs we have previously listed as *A Sentimental Journey* and *Music Of Alec Wilder*. The former offers a lovely memento of two engagements by bands led by Jimmy, with Marian on piano and two entertaining front lines. Jack Maheu blends a spiralling virtuosity with Pee Wee-type licks, Tate is reliable (and picks up the baritone here and there), Dickenson is absolutely himself (his 'When You Wish Upon A Star' is priceless) and Jimmy leads with typical aplomb.

The Wilder programme is one of the great single-composer recitals and it should be far better known than it is. McPartland has been intensely involved in Alec Wilder's difficult, bittersweet music for decades and she gets closer to the heart of it than any jazz player ever has. 'Jazz Waltz For A Friend', the first track, was written for her, and several of the other pieces have scarcely been touched by other improvisers. The five pieces with the lone support of Michael Moore are wonderfully lyrical and searching, and though the remaining five with Gilder and Corsello are a shade less involving, it is a memorable occasion. The only regret must be that she didn't play Wilder's unforgettable 'Where Do You Go?' at the date.

ALEXANDER VON SCHLIPPENBACH &

Born 7 April 1938, Berlin, Germany
Piano

Pakistani Pomade

Atavistic 240
Schlippenbach; Evan Parker (ss, ts); Paul Lovens (d). November 1972.

Evan Parker says: **'It started as a working title – something with a special smell. Alex insisted on using it despite my PC protestations. I guess we all three knew that we had a chemistry that was working but I doubt we thought it would still be working 40 years later. Atoms, molecules and stable compounds ... we learned to bottle the volatility.'**

The founder of the Globe Unity collective studied under Bernd Aloïs Zimmermann, a composer uniquely alert to the presence of jazz as a counterforce to other 20th-century musical movements. Interestingly enough, Schlippenbach later experimented with 12-tone jazz composition. He started out playing with trumpeter Manfred Schoof and recorded extensively with other improvisers. The Schlippenbach Trio has been making music for nearly 30 years, though Globe Unity now seems to be in abeyance. Schlippenbach is percussive and intense, but also aware of structure and responsive to traditional jazz piano as well as free music.

By 1970 Schlippenbach had to some extent turned away from total abstraction and was showing an interest not only in formal compositional principles (serialism, orthodox sonata form, aspects of *ricercare*) but also in renewing his own initial contact with early and modern jazz, blues and boogie-woogie. These interests were still obvious even underneath the radical freedoms of Globe Unity. They became much clearer in his work with the later Berlin

Contemporary Jazz Orchestra, in which he uses the conventionally swinging drummer Ed Thigpen and trumpeter Benny Bailey among the free men. Schlippenbach's conception of freedom has nearly always resulted in densely layered explorations of tonality, with a pronounced rhythmic slant. It's this that renders him surprisingly accessible as a performer.

That said, the Globe Unity records were a hard listen, particularly given the recording values of the time, and Schlippenbach is better approached – for the earlier years at least – as a solo or small-group performer. His association with Evan Parker now goes back several decades, their evolving relationship sustained by an annual winter meeting and recording. Unfortunately, even this fine body of music has been erratically available, and one of the very finest records of all, *Das höhe Lied*, disappeared along with the rest of Paul Lovens's Po Torch label. Even the magnificent *Pakistani Pomade* has not always been available and owes its survival to John Corbett. There have been times when we have considered the later *Elf Bagatellen* to be the better record, and sometimes even *Hunting The Snake*, on which bassist Peter Kowald augmented the trio. But we always come back to this one.

'A Little Yellow (And Two Seconds Monk)' lays out ideas that Schlippenbach, and Parker too, would be exploring for much of the next 30 years. It's a formidable exercise but what makes that piece and the record special is a level of playing that, here and later in their relationship, makes a word like 'interplay' or 'interaction' seem inadequate and imprecise in relation to this music. One has a sense of simultaneity, of decisions taken as if by some collective understanding in an instant. There is a moment halfway through the track when all three players fire off a new and distinct energy that accelerates the music's flow of information. This has nothing to do with the hairsbreadth changes of harmony or direction one sees from jazz musicians, though that too is an impressive skill, learnable if not easily so. This, though, marks a jump from quantity to quality, an 'event'.

& *See also* **Monk's Casino** (2003–2004; p. 683)

FRED VAN HOVE

Born 19 February 1937, Antwerp, Belgium
Piano, organ

Complete Vogel Recordings

Atavistic Unheard Music UMSCD2292 2CD
Van Hove; Cel Overberghe (ts). 1972–1974.

Fred Van Hove says: **'When it started at least, free jazz and free music were not just about music but also about the kind of society we wanted. I think that dimension is lost now and we're poorer because of that, though the ideals of freedom still mean something.'**

Van Hove's almost ancestral status in European free music isn't reflected in his available discography, or in his current critical rating, which should stand as high as anyone's in Europe. A classically trained musician, who was turned on to jazz by hearing Charlie Parker records and who became involved in the free scene with Peter Brötzmann, Van Hove has created a substantial body of music that can at first acquaintance seem quite formal, possibly scored, but whose freedoms are deep-seated and hard won. The material on these valuable recoveries provides the best possible introduction to his still undervalued work. The solo discs are better than the duo album with Overberghe, who sounds at moments like a cut-price Brötzmann on an off day. For serious collectors, the set also includes a rare 7-inch by the duo. The solo pieces are quizzical and sardonic, possibly too unshowy to capture the imagination, but definitely worth exploring.

BROTHERHOOD OF BREATH &

Formed 1969
Ensemble

Live At Willisau

Ogun OGCD 001

Harry Beckett, Marc Charig, Mongezi Feza (t); Nick Evans, Radu Malfatti (tb); Dudu Pukwana (as); Evan Parker, Gary Windo (ts); Chris McGregor (p, leader); Harry Miller (b); Louis Moholo (d). January 1973.

Harry Miller's widow, Hazel Miller, says: **'These guys took an unorthodox approach to life and music and were always at the centre of whatever was going on, which is probably why it was so full of passion, free and soulful; they played from their hearts. They were also extraordinary composers whose music is still played all round the world. Anyone who bounced up with them or had the good fortune to hear them play live never forgot.'**

The trick was to keep breathing, because Death was always nearby. Feza, Pukwana, McGregor, Miller: there was a shadow across this music, as if the life breathed into it had to be paid for with interest. McGregor formed the Brotherhood on the foundations of the legendary Blue Notes, but the larger-scale ensemble took the group in a fresh direction, somewhere between Duke Ellington's most unfettered 'jungle music' and the joyous, angry alienation of the Sun Ra Arkestra. McGregor's music combined the Presbyterian hymns of the Scottish church (his parents were missionaries), Xhosa music and the free modernism of Coltrane's *Ascension*. It's not often observed just how surreal some of the Brotherhood's music could be, a kind of hectic clowning that momentarily lightened what lay beneath. On another live recording by the group, MC Ronnie Scott explains that half the group is from Britain and half from South Africa, 'a great place to come from'! Behind all this joyous music is the pain of apartheid and exile. That fine Berlin performance (available on Cuneiform) is only just topped by the later *Live In Willisau*. From the opening moments of 'Do It', with its searing Evan Parker solo, through 'Kongi's Theme' with its strange solo by Radu Malfatti, to the relative ease of the closing 'Funky Boots', this is affirmative music of a rare sort, bringing together African *kwela*, free jazz, post-Ellington swing and even touches of classicism in a boiling mix that grips the heart.

& *See also* **BLUE NOTES, Live In South Africa** (1964; p. 315)

DEWEY REDMAN &

Born 17 May 1931, Fort Worth, Texas; died 2 September 2006, New York City
Tenor and alto saxophones, musette

Ear Of The Behearer

Impulse!/GRP 12712

Redman; Ted Daniel (t, bugle); Leroy Jenkins (vn); Jane Robertson (clo); Sirone (b); Eddie Moore (d); Danny Johnson (perc). June 1973.

Dewey Redman said (1994): **'I should go see Africa before I pass. That's the homeland, and when I say Africa I mean all of that: the Mid-East, Asia, all that space and history that is so much older than us and shaped us.'**

Redman grew up in Ornette Coleman's hometown and was the anchor member of one of Ornette's most incendiary bands between 1967 and 1974. The best advice for anyone not appreciating that music is to follow what Redman does; it makes sense. Dewey was almost

30 before he opted for a full-time musical career, and to some extent neither his recording career nor his reputation quite recovered from the slow start. He could, and should, have been one of the majors, even if one doesn't automatically associate any great stylistic innovation with him. In fact, what he brought to the music – it's audible in his work with Keith Jarrett, with Charlie Haden and with the Ornette repertory band Old And New Dreams – is a passionate interest in Middle Eastern music.

That is immediately evident on *Ear Of The Behearer*, where Redman, shortly to leave the Coleman band, plays largely on alto rather than tenor. The higher, more keening sound has an arresting Levantine quality, but what is striking about the record as a whole, particularly now that it has been paired with the material released as *Coincide* from the same session, is how varied Redman's playing is. He always stated that playing in just one style bored him and almost all of his sessions manage to touch on blues, avant-garde playing, ethnically tinged material and some tracks that come close to a modernistic swing. *Ear* has always been a favourite Redman record, with its long blowing blues on 'Boody' and the more complex 'Walls-Bridges' and 'Interconnection', but the material on *Coincide* is just as powerful; it's arguably the more coherent LP of the two and certainly the more affirmatively upbeat, with 'Joie De Vivre' and 'Funcity Dues' among the best short performances in the Redman canon. The strings work well together on their tracks and Daniel, an unsung hero of new music, has something of Don Cherry's quality, but with a crisply military attack.

& *See also* **In London** (1996; p. 608)

JULIAN PRIESTER

Born 29 June 1935, Chicago, Illinois
Trombone

Love, Love

ECM 1044
Priester; Hadley Caliman (sax, f, cl); David Johnson (sax, f); Bayete Umbra Zindiko (p, clav); Pat Gleeson (syn); Bill Connors (g); Henry Franklin, Ron McClure (b); Leon Chancler, Eric Gravátt (d). June–September 1973.

DJ Icebox said (1990): **'I never got so many questions and requests as when I played *Love, Love*. That's a cult classic, right there.'**

Priester worked in R&B and big bands before moving to New York in 1958, playing with the Max Roach group until the early '60s and subsequently freelancing. He moved to California in the '70s, and though there has been a recent flurry of activity and interest, sightings were relatively rare and Priester's cult status confirmed by the long unavailability of his ECM work.

Love, Love is a record which enjoyed almost legendary status as long as it remained unreleased on CD. Having it available again dents its glamour only temporarily, because it is one of the best albums of its period, subtly conceived and richly executed by a fascinating ensemble. Consisting of two long improvisations, somewhat in the manner of a Miles Davis record of the period, it foregrounds Priester in the kind of acoustic that shows off his rich tone and thoughtful ideas, though he's also prominently featured on synths and percussion. Much of the personnel will be relatively unfamiliar, but Connors, McClure and the soon to disappear Eric Gravátt (known from the first Weather Report albums) are all highly collectable presences. Musically, it's in a now somewhat dated jazz-rock mode (think *Mwandishi*-period Hancock or a looser version of *Bitches Brew*) and owes its cachet and collectability to its dance associations. We were quite prepared to be disappointed, but it lives up to billing surprisingly well.

HERBIE HANCOCK &
Born 12 April 1940, Chicago, Illinois
Piano, keyboards

Head Hunters
Columbia CK 65123
Hancock; Bennie Maupin (ts, ss, saxello, bcl, af); Paul Jackson (b); Harvey Mason (d); Bill Summers (perc).
September 1973.

Herbie Hancock said (1991): **'I took a chance. There was always the risk that I might make some new fans, but only at the cost of losing more established ones. This was music that I wanted to make, though, so the gamble was worth it.'**

Miles legitimized a view of black musical history that made room for Sly Stone and James Brown, as well as Charlie Parker and John Coltrane. *Head Hunters* was the direct result, an infectiously funky and thoroughly joyous record; only the closing 'Vein Melter' hints at melancholy. It was scarcely unprecedented in Hancock's career. The last albums for Warners point in this direction, as do *Mwandishi* and the joyous *Sextant*, which was recorded around the same time. Hancock includes 'Watermelon Man', not because he is short of ideas, but because he wants to demonstrate the essential continuity of his music. For the simplest demonstration, listen to Butch Warren's line on *Takin' Off* and then compare the toppling, dotted rhythm Paul Jackson brings to it on *Head Hunters*. Hancock's electric keyboards can sound one-dimensional and the Hohner Clavinet is very much an acquired taste. The latest remastering, coupled to budget release and including a new essay by Hancock, gives the biggest-selling jazz record of all time a new gloss and impetus: 'Chameleon' (on which Hancock improvises beautifully) and 'Sly' have renewed vigour. Maupin performs a role much like Wayne Shorter in Weather Report, not soloing at length or necessarily carrying the line but placing brushstrokes and punctuating moods much as Miles did. 'Vein Melter', which is perhaps his best moment on the record, is a throwback to the more introverted music of the very early '70s, but is no less effective in this context and a valuable change of mood. The album's influence was immense, and Hancock can hardly be charged with the shortcomings of his epigone. It still plays freshly and with surprising invention 30 years on.

& *See also* **Maiden Voyage** (1965; p. 317)

OREGON
Formed 1970
Group

Music Of Another Present Era
Universe 42
Ralph Towner (g, 12-string g, p, syn, c, mel, frhn); Paul McCandless (ob, eng hn, ss, bcl, tin f, musette); Glen Moore (b, cl, vla, p, f); Collin Walcott (sitar, tabla, dulc, cl, v). 1973.

Elvin Jones, who recorded *Together* with the group in 1977, said (1991): **'We spoke the same language. I didn't have any trouble with their music, and John Coltrane would have appreciated what they were doing.'**

An offshoot of the Paul Winter Consort, Oregon became a hugely successful project that makes most 'crossover' music seem bland and unthoughtful. The group was formed at a point of low commercial ebb for jazz and became a species of Modern Jazz Quartet for the '70s, drawing on 'world' and classical elements along the way. The group's longevity was unexpected and the only interruption in its stately progress was the tragic death of Collin Walcott in a road accident in 1984, though he was later replaced in the line-up by Trilok Gurtu and, more permanently, Mark Walker.

The early records were largely, but not exclusively, devoted to Towner compositions and were characterized by delicate interplay between his 12-string guitar and Paul McCandless's equally 'classical' oboe. The debut is still rather tentative, but delicately lyrical. The music on *Music Of Another Present Era* and *Distant Hills* was widely perceived as ethereal and impressionistic, and there was a tendency (perhaps encouraged by intermittent sound-balance on the original vinyl releases) to underestimate the significance of Glen Moore's firm bass-lines (see 'Spring Is Really Coming' on *Present Era*) or the forcefulness of Collin Walcott's tablas. The music combined evocative thematic writing ('Aurora' on *Present Era*, re-recorded on *North West Passage*; the classic 'Silence Of A Candle' and McCandless's 'The Swan' on *Distant Hills*) with abstract, collectively improvised pieces (like the 'Mi Chirita Suite' on *Distant Hills*; a neglected aspect of the band's career) and forcefully rhythmic tunes like 'Sail' (*Present Era*) which should have confounded a lingering belief that the band were too professorial to rock.

SPONTANEOUS MUSIC ENSEMBLE

Formed 1967
Group

Quintessence

Emanem 4217 2CD
Evan Parker, Trevor Watts (ss); Derek Bailey (g); Kent Carter (clo, b); John Stevens (perc, v). October 1973, February 1974.

Saxophonist (and future SME member) John Butcher says: **'Listening to the quintet feels like assuming five separate brains and instincts simultaneously. The music's that clear, but, like going beyond Newton's two-body problem, it's wonderfully too mysterious to solve.'**

Though both emerged out of modern jazz, SME took a different trajectory through freedom than that of AMM, which emerged around the same time on the British scene. At the heart of both groups were drummers who in their contrasting ways retained some measure of jazz rhythm in their work. Initially at least, the Spontaneous Music Ensemble, which emerged out of London's Little Theatre Club, retained a more obviously jazz-associated instrumentation. Like AMM founder Eddie Prévost, drummer John Stevens had a strong metrical sense, honed in various Royal Air Force bands, and an ability to establish a deep pulse even when there was no strict count. In addition, his close collaborator, saxophonist Trevor Watts, was a natural melodist, and in later years, following a split with Stevens, moved more in that direction.

Stevens was a volatile philosopher of improvisation who enjoined a principle of careful but intuitive listening in the group context, an aural equivalent of 'peripheral vision'. Under his tutelage, the group evolved steadily and by the time of Stevens's premature death in 1994 was entirely *sui generis*. The key collaborator, arguably, was guitarist Roger Smith, but the ability of saxophonist John Butcher to take his instrument far beyond any residual association with jazz was also an important element.

That, though, was two decades in the future. SME's first major statement had been *Karyobin* in 1968, now recognized as a classic of free music but perhaps still somewhat in the orbit of American free jazz and reflecting the divergent interests of its personnel, which included, in addition to Evan Parker and Derek Bailey, such distinctive musical imaginations as trumpeter Kenny Wheeler, trombonist Paul Rutherford and bassist Dave Holland.

Remarkable as *Karyobin* is, it now sounds – in that old critical cliché – like a 'transitional' work. In so far as any record can capture a group as protean and evolutionary as SME, *Quintessence* is the key text, triple-distilled, rarefied and raw. The group's first sustained incarnation had been as the duo of Stevens and Parker. For much of 1973, Stevens and Watts had returned to this demanding format, but following a course of intense musical austerity. The earliest recordings here are from a Little Theatre Club performance taped on 11 October 1973. Saxophone and drums inhabit a space as unassociative and stark as a Samuel Beckett staging, but with the same blunt humanity and wit the playwright brought even to the most extreme and uninflected situation. The more important piece of the pair is 'Daa-oom', ostensibly inspired by Albert Ayler and African pygmy music, and featuring Stevens's scarifying singing.

The piece is significant because it shows to what extent Stevens liked at this time, as again later, to work with a loose repertory of ideas and procedures, like 'Flower', which occupied much of their attention at this time. A week after the Little Theatre Club date, the duo was joined by bassist/cellist Kent Carter, who was touring Britain with Steve Lacy's group. 'Da-oom' is performed again, in trio format, with Carter showing a remarkable intuition for the music and for the tensely elided relationship that bore between Stevens and Watts.

He was present again in February 1974 for a quintet performance at the Institute of Contemporary Arts. With virtually no preparation, the group, which had no prior history, created a series of improvisations that have no parallel even in Martin Davidson's extensive Emanem archive. Two versions of 'Rambunctious' find the group thinking and playing at warp speed. The level of interplay borders on the uncanny. Stevens's awareness of his colleagues is instinctive rather than studied. He responds to them almost as someone might while doing something else – reading, cooking – during conversation, not rudely or detachedly, but simply because he can divide his attention. His playing is detailed but never definitive, assertive but never dogmatic, and represents a constant interrogation of the musical situation. Many recordings of SME survive, from before and after this time. All have something to recommend them, but none has quite the presence or has such an air of importance as this one, not as a 'historical document' but as a musical moment that replicates its searching energy and air of continual surprise with every fresh hearing.

JOE PASS

Born Joseph Anthony Jacobi Passalaqua, 13 January 1929, New Brunswick, New Jersey; 23 May 1994, Los Angeles, California
Guitar

Virtuoso
Pablo 2310-708
Pass (g solo). November 1973.

Joe Pass said (1986): **'It was Norman Granz who suggested I might play a solo concert. I was very nervous. Playing fast tunes without a group was very alien to me, but guitarists are used to playing alone at home and it was just a matter of taking confidence from that.'**

Already playing pro in high school, Pass toured with Charlie Barnet before naval service, then grappled with a drug problem. Cleaning up in the early '60s, he worked with George Shearing and others and became internationally known after signing with Norman Granz's Pablo operation. Revered by other players for a consummate technique, he helped restore a 'traditional' modernism, after rock nullified the open-tone electric sound.

His long series of albums for Pablo helped Pass become both a major concert attraction and a benchmark player for jazz guitar. Pass smooths away the nervousness of bop yet counters the plain talk of swing with a complexity that remains completely accessible. An improvisation on a standard may range far and wide, but there's no sense of him going into territory which he doesn't already know well. There's nothing hidden in his music, everything is absolutely on display, and he cherishes good tunes without sanctifying them. His tone isn't distinctive but it is reliably mellifluous, and he can make every note in a melody shine. Compared with Tal Farlow or Jimmy Raney, Pass took few risks and set himself fewer genuine challenges, but any guitarist will recognize a performer who has a total command over the instrument.

Pass's solo records are almost a category by themselves, and their importance in re-establishing the eminence of straight-ahead jazz guitar now seems clear. At a time when traditional jazz guitar-playing was being sidelined by the gradual onset of fusion, Joe's solo work reaffirmed the virtues of the unadorned electric guitar, and the subtleties and harmonic shrewdness of his playing are like a long drink of water after much of the overheated guitar-playing of the '70s and '80s. There was a series of *Virtuoso* albums – for once, the designation seems justified – but the first release (*Virtuoso #4* is actually an earlier recording) is definitely the best. Back to back versions of 'How High The Moon' and 'Cherokee' are breathtaking.

WEATHER REPORT&

Formed 1970; disbanded 1985
Group

Mysterious Traveller

Sony 507657-2
Joe Zawinul (ky); Wayne Shorter (ts, ss); Alphonso Johnson, Miroslav Vitous (b); Ismael Wilburn (d); Dom Um Romão (perc); additional voices. 1973, February–May 1974.

Joe Zawinul said (1995): **'Everything in Weather Report was improvised. Everything. It wasn't just themes and solos. It was all solos and the themes came out of that.'**

Weather Report is one of the great jazz groups of its time. 'Birdland' on *Heavy Weather* is one of only a tiny handful of contemporary jazz tunes that everyone seems to have heard. Though its composer, Joe Zawinul, wouldn't suffer it to be played in later years, it encapsulates perfectly the formula that made the group so successful: solid part-writing from Zawinul, Wayne Shorter's enigmatic saxophone sound, a free-floating personnel round the Zawinul–Shorter axis and great product marketing (Weather Report covers were consistently eye-catching and aesthetically pleasing).

The first two albums, the eponymous one and *I Sing The Body Electric*, had a faintly mysterious, otherworldly quality that certainly didn't reflect the group's live presence at the time, but probably did reflect the compositional influence and personality of Wayne Shorter. After *Sweetnighter* in 1972, the group was much more obviously dominated by Zawinul's very individual sense of rhythm – neither swinging, nor 'African', but something of his own – and by a funky quality which in many respects was more successfully achieved than former boss Miles Davis's explorations in the same direction. 'Boogie Woogie Waltz' was the band's most accessible track before 'Birdland' came along, and with '125th Street Congress' gave the impression of a group embarked on an endless jam. 'Will' was effectively Miroslav Vitous's farewell to the group, though he does have a brief presence on *Mysterious Traveller*, standing in for new bassist Alphonso Johnson, and as co-composer of 'American Tango'.

This is still perhaps the most sheerly beautiful of the Weather Report records, from the wild joy of 'Nubian Sundance' with its synth-enhanced crowd noises, to the cool beauty of 'Cucumber Slumber', to the quietness of 'Blackthorn Rose', a lyrical duet that may represent a point of maximum closeness between the group's founders at the very moment when Zawinul seemed set to take over; Shorter's soprano-line is still undervalued, one of his finest on record. Some of the material was recorded at Zawinul's home, with his kids romping in the background, and only later put together in the studio, and it is this balance between improvisational immediacy and brilliantly crafted overdubbing that gives the record its lasting freshness and power.

& *See also* **JOE ZAWINUL, Zawinul** (1970; p. 380), **Di-a-lects** (1986; p. 503); **Miroslav Vitous, Journey's End** (1982; p. 470)

WILLIAM PARKER&
Born 10 January 1952, New York City
Double bass

Through Acceptance Of The Mystery Peace
Eremite 12
Parker; Toshinori Kondo (t, ahn); Arthur Williams (t); Jemeel Moondoc (as); Will Connell Jr (as, f); Daniel Carter (as, ts, f, t); Charles Brackeen, John Hagen (ts); Rozanne Levine, Henry Warner (cl); Peter Kuhn (bcl); Ramsey Ameen, Billy Bang, Polly Bradfield, Jason Hwang (vn); Tristan Honsinger (clo); Dennis Charles (d); Roger Baird (perc). February 1974, January 1979.

William Parker said (1999): **'When I first played bass, I could see each string as a beam of light and the bow as a kind of prism, and each string broke up into different colour bands, different harmonics. It was very spiritual and very beautiful.'**

The most influential bassist/leader since Mingus and one of the busiest musicians of his time and place, Parker turns up in a bewildering number of contexts, though much energy in recent years has been devoted to a version of the experimental workshop which later transmuted into the Little Huey Creative Music Ensemble. His sepia-tinged bass tone was first heard in the Improvisers Collective in New York, but is now ubiquitous.

Acceptance is an important early record by the bassist, originally on Centering and now reissued with one new track. In many respects, it looks forward to the larger bands of the '90s, but here Parker develops his ideas with a series of smaller ensembles and with more emphasis than later on free blowing. Kondo is an interesting figure who has made an intermittent impact. On trumpet here, he's reminiscent of Leo Smith in declamatory form – which is much of the time – but with a roundness of tone that almost suggests cornet. He's also featured on alto horn. The smaller groups favour strings and could almost be playing classical pieces. The bigger ensembles, though, are the surest indication of what was to come. Parker delivers a recitation on the final piece, which some may find taxes the patience, but his sincerity and the completeness of his musical vision are hard to argue with, and though his bass-playing is more readily appreciated in small-group sessions, this is a fine early example of his work.

& *See also* **Mayor Of Punkville** (1999; p. 645)

BENNIE MAUPIN
Born 29 August 1940, Detroit, Michigan
Tenor saxophone, bass clarinet, others

The Jewel In The Lotus
ECM 172350
Maupin; Charles Sullivan (t); Herbie Hancock (p); Buster Williams (b); Billy Hart (d); Freddie Waits (d, mar); Bill Summers (perc). March 1974.

Bennie Maupin said (1982): **'I think in pictures, and though I don't expect you to see the same images I do, that's what I look for when I make music. One day, I'll do something with dance and theatre. For now, though, you have to enjoy the theatre in your head.'**

Always more than a spear-carrier in modern jazz, but all the same insufficiently recognized, Maupin exemplifies better than anyone the continuities between hard bop and fusion, having worked in one of trumpeter Lee Morgan's later groups, before helping to hybridize jazz and rock with Miles Davis and, crucially, with Herbie Hancock's Headhunters.

The Jewel In The Lotus was a belated reissue. The first surviving evidence of Maupin as leader is a mysterious, quite avant-garde record that refuses to conform to any labels of the time or after. It doesn't even sound particularly like Bennie's album, so much does he play for the music rather than for himself. Marked by clever percussion effects (Summers's water-filled garbage can, Waits's marimba) and Hancock's floating electric piano, it's a record that steals into the room and leaves again without introductions, but without attempting to be pointlessly enigmatic. 'Ensenada' begins the album mysteriously, emerging out of a poised silence, with Maupin's flute in syrinx territory. It's all very elemental, like a slow curtain on a mostly empty stage. How quickly, though, Maupin fills the space with business.

'Past + Present = Future' contains some intimations that Maupin might once have played jazz-funk, but it's in a remote form here and nothing on the record approaches the Head-hunters sound. Hancock seems entirely easy with his role, though it's a relatively unfamiliar one, and Williams delivers some beautiful-sounding bass in unexpected places, often pitched up quite high. A neglected record, its return to circulation confused even some of those who had barracked for it, expecting something dirtier and more downhome.

ELLA FITZGERALD &
Born 25 April 1917, Newport News, Virginia; died 15 June 1996, Beverly Hills, California
Voice

Ella In London
Pablo 2310-711
Fitzgerald; Tommy Flanagan (p); Joe Pass (g); Keter Betts (b); Bobby Durham (d). April 1974.

Tommy Flanagan said (1987): **'I played behind her on tour for a month once and I think she made one mistake in all that time, and even that no one much would have noticed; she just slipped into place and moved right along. Incredible technique.'**

Back with Norman Granz again, Ella recorded steadily through the '70s, but there was little to suggest she would either repeat or surpass the best of her earlier music. If encroaching age is supposed to impart a greater wisdom to a singer of songs, and hence to the interpretation of those songs, it's a more complex matter with Fitzgerald. While her respectful delivery of lyrics honours the wordsmithing, she brought little of the personal gravitas to the American songbook which was Sinatra's trademark. Her scatting grew less fluent and more exaggerated, if no less creative in its construction; her manipulation of time and melody became more obvious because she had to push herself harder to make it happen. There are still many good records here, but nothing that seems hallmarked with greatness. A first Montreux visit was merely OK, and much better is the London date from 1974. Probably the final chance to hear Ella in a club setting, and it's a racy and sometimes virtuosic display by the singer, a fine souvenir of a memorable visit. There was some pressure to do more recent pop repertoire, so Carole King's 'You've Got a Friend' creeps in – and out again – without tarnishing any of it. Ella could have swung an anvil, even at this point in her life, but she's more comfortable with 'Sweet Georgia Brown', 'The Man I Love' and 'It Don't Mean A Thing ...', the latter two being big chunky performances.

& *See also* **The Enchanting Ella Fitzgerald** (1950–1955; p. 125), **Sings The Cole Porter Songbook** (1956; p. 180)

GARY BURTON &
Born 23 January 1943, Anderson, Indiana
Vibraphone

Hotel Hello
ECM 835586-2
Burton; Steve Swallow (b, p). May 1974.

Gary Burton said (1993): **'Steve was introduced to me by Jim Hall and I recommended him for Stan Getz's band. When I persuaded him to come with me, he became a third hand, someone I could talk to about any aspect of the music.'**

Though not so highly regarded as Burton's other duos for ECM (*Matchbook* with Ralph Towner, and a fine *Duet* with Chick Corea), this is a quiet, musicianly masterpiece. There is scarcely a track that jumps out with any attempt at assertion, but the harmonies are oceans deep and the ability of both players to switch to keyboards (a touch of organ in Burton's case as well as some parts on marimba) gives the whole set a rich but elusive texture. Almost all the compositions are Swallow's, from the high-point of his creativity as a composer. They are all pitched around the same cycle of tones, but the variations and angles of approach are remarkable for their avoidance of familiar ground. The title-track and 'Sweeping Up' are substantial performances, each with an almost cinematic quality, as if some quietly dramatic scene had been compressed into five-minute span.

& *See also* **Country Roads And Other Places** (1968; p. 355), **For Hamp, Red, Bags And Cal** (2000; p. 654)

DAVID LIEBMAN &
Born 4 September 1946, Brooklyn, New York
Tenor and soprano saxophones

Drum Ode
ECM 159493-2
Liebman; Richie Beirach (p); John Abercrombie (g); Gene Perla (b); Bob Moses (d); Badal Roy, Collin Walcott (tabla); Steven Satten, Patato Valdes (perc); Elena Steinberg (v). May 1974.

David Liebman says: **'The feeling in the studio was exhilarating; after all, drummers know how to enjoy themselves more than any other instrumentalists in jazz. I think Manfred Eicher was a bit upset with the goings-on, but in any case this remains one of my most popular recordings.'**

Liebman studied with Lennie Tristano and Charles Lloyd and began his professional career with Ten Wheel Drive, before joining the Elvin Jones group and one version of Miles Davis's electric ensemble, where the young saxophonist's skills were almost deliberately and insultingly overlooked. He was also co-founder of two innovative groups, Lookout Farm and Quest, with pianist Richie Beirach. For a period, he abandoned tenor saxophone in favour of the soprano, and has occasionally dabbled in wood flutes and other wind instruments.

Liebman was still part of Miles Davis's band when he recorded this remarkable album, and the influence of Miles's extended percussion sections is evident in the augmented percussion and the free-form vamps and quasi-modal heads. *Drum Ode* is one of the classics of the early ECM catalogue. Where many recordings of this kind are simply loose confederations of session-players, Liebman was wise enough to recruit percussionists who were already or would be shortly stars in their own right: Moses, Walcott, Roy, Altschul would all be significant recording stars. The result is an album with an almost orchestral unity and complexity. One hears individual voices rising and falling in an impeccably choreographed mix, with his own Coltrane-influenced saxophone at the centre: an ode in an unexpectedly literal sense.

& *See also* **The Loneliness Of A Long-Distance Runner** (1985; p. 496); **QUEST, Redemption** (2005; p. 710)

TETE MONTOLIU

Born Vicenç Montoliu I Massana, 28 March 1933, Barcelona, Catalunya; died 24 August 1997, Barcelona, Catalunya
Piano

Catalonian Fire
Steeplechase SCCD 31017
Montoliu; Niels-Henning Ørsted Pedersen (b); Albert 'Tootie' Heath (d). May 1974.

Tete Montoliu said (1978): **'Learning Braille was like having a new limb. I had always been listening to music, but now I felt I had the key to it as well. The world suddenly got bigger.'**

He was born blind and started to lose his hearing, too, in later years, but Montoliu learned to play Tatum-inspired jazz piano with 'Catalonian fire'. His technique was fast, fleet and dextrous and brought in elements of other musical styles – Spanish, Catalonian, North African – that were simmered together into a distinctive voice that never sounded like generic hard bop. Discovered in Spain by Lionel Hampton and deeply influenced by having Don Byas live in the family home for a time, Montoliu played with a wide range of senior American musicians (including the blind Roland Kirk and even Anthony Braxton on *In The Tradition*), but he was best heard either solo or in small groups of his own.

Montoliu seemed to release a lot of records in the '70s, but actually he had only a few concentrated bursts of recording. There are three albums from the May 1974 date, two (*Tete!* is the other) with the trio, and the solo *Music For Perla*. All three are played with both elegance and stern commitment; Montoliu's improvisations on favourite themes have a poise and dash that make one overlook the frequent appearance of many familiar runs and manipulations of the beat. Pedersen, who loves to play with a pianist of outsize technique, holds nothing back in his own playing, while Heath's rather gruff and unfussy drumming makes him a nearly ideal timekeeper for the situation. There's an epic version of 'Falling In Love With Love', a no less impressively proportioned 'Body And Soul' (on which the three men gel almost uncannily) and a fine, incandescent 'Au Privave'. Montoliu preferred his home culture to the world stage; otherwise he would be considered one of the very greatest of modern pianists.

PAUL MOTIAN
Born 25 March 1931, Philadelphia, Pennsylvania
Drums

Tribute
ECM 519281-2
Motian; Carlos Ward (as); Sam Brown, Paul Metzke (g); Charlie Haden (b). May 1974.

Paul Motian said (1981): **'I played 4/4 for three hours a night for 1,000 nights in a row. I think I earned the right to play "free", or "abstract", whatever that means, once in a while.'**

An enormously experienced drummer, Motian had played with many of the most important moderns before the age of 40: Coleman Hawkins, Herbie Nichols, Oscar Pettiford, Paul Bley, Thelonious Monk, Bill Evans (for several years and including some of the pianist's iconic recording), Lennie Tristano, Tony Scott and even John Coltrane, who asked Motian to join his group as a second drummer.

Motian is not only a remarkable percussionist but has proved to be a very fine composer and a doggedly creative bandleader, even if his more recent work with the Electric Bebop Band has drifted in formulae. The first ECM records were startling when they first appeared, and they have retained their vigour and freshness. The single unaccompanied track on the earlier *Conception Vessel*, 'Ch'i Energy', provides a good representation of his basic sound-palette: sweeping cymbals, soft, delicately placed accents, a sense of flow and togetherness that is difficult to break down into components. Max Roach is the only other modern drummer who can sound anything like this, but Roach is a soapbox orator by comparison.

This 1974 album is a small classic. Ward is used sparingly, but the twinned guitars (destined to be a feature of Motian's groups; he started out as a guitarist, but took it no distance) are a key component and, given the prominence of Bill Frisell in later years, it's interesting to note his early use of it. The session consists of three Motian tunes, of which 'Sod House' and 'Victoria' are the best-known; also on the session, wonderful readings of Ornette's plangent 'War Orphans' and Haden's mournful but defiant 'Song For Ché'. The leader is seldom far from the centre of things, creating a pulse even when not playing strict time, but always playing with grace and composure, even when the mood is urgent.

KENNY DREW
Born 28 August 1928, New York City; died 4 August 1993, Copenhagen, Denmark
Piano

Dark And Beautiful
Steeplechase SCCD 37011/12 2CD
Drew; Niels-Henning Ørsted Pedersen (b); Albert 'Tootie' Heath (d). May 1974.

Kenny Drew said (1979): **'A good piano, good food and people, no prejudice, and a real appreciation of what we do. If anyone asks why I've been here [in Denmark] so long, all they have to do is visit.'**

Drew's first influences were Art Tatum and Fats Waller, and these were so deeply inscribed that later contact with Bud Powell and Thelonious Monk wasn't overwhelming. The gracious New Yorker spent many years in Europe, first in Paris, and later in Copenhagen in a long-lasting and well-documented residency at the Jazzhus Montmartre. He made a great many records and it may sound like damning with faint praise to say that they are consistent, low-key and rarely startling, in the sense that they continue in the same furrow he established in the '50s. The most sensitive of accompanists, Drew is sometimes understated as a solo performer and there are passages on all the records where little of moment occurs. And yet what does happen has a graciousness that is often more inspiring than showy pianism.

Essentially a group player, he benefited hugely from the presence of able – and sometimes brilliant – sidemen. He'd been in Copenhagen for a decade when *Dark And Beautiful* was recorded and the trio was an established draw at the Montmartre. This was their first recording in that format, two sessions on consecutive days, and originally released as two LPs. The playing time generous but not a whit too long. Drew's 'Dark Beauty' is a lovely line that should be better known, limpid and angular by turns. Brubeck's 'In Your Own Sweet Way' is a quiet meditation, 'A Stranger In Paradise' avoids the slushiness that tune sometimes conjures up, and the closing 'Oleo' is confirmation, if it were needed, that Drew can swing with the best of them on a bop staple. His phrasing is almost conversational, but never prosaic, and the solo development has a logic that leaves no loose ends but doesn't sound pat or contrived.

JOHN ABERCROMBIE
Born 16 December 1944, Portchester, New York
Guitar

Timeless
ECM 829114-2
Abercrombie; Jan Hammer (p, ky); Jack DeJohnette (d). June 1974.

John Abercrombie said (1999): **'It was quite a freedom to start playing things *rubato*, or more like a classical player. It isn't something you do on the blues circuit! I hadn't done it much until I started to record with Manfred Eicher at ECM. But I still – I guess – just want to play like Wes Montgomery or Jim Hall. They're my models.'**

Like several other gifted young guitarists, Abercrombie got a professional start – after four years at Berklee – with Chico Hamilton's group, before going on to record with drummer Billy Cobham. His characteristic style, which some would regard as definitive of the ECM label, is limpid and evocative and makes imaginative use of electronic sweetening and extensions. There's more filigree than flash on the early *Timeless*, and it's left to DeJohnette (the first of several tough-minded drummers Abercrombie has used as foils) and the underrated Hammer to give the set some propulsion. Abercrombie plays with a tremendous ear for dynamics, helped, no doubt, by ECM production. The two long tracks are Hammer's 'Lungs' and the closing title-track, both of which extend the improvisations. The remaining tunes, including the lovely 'Ralph's Piano Waltz', are much shorter and more songlike but Abercrombie gives each of them a weight of dramatic interest that exceeds their modest durations. There's always more to Abercrombie's playing than meets the ear and even fleeting detail is made to carry some expressive baggage, particularly on 'Timeless' itself. It's a session that continues to grow with familiarity, an altogether tougher and more resilient label debut than anyone remembers.

GIL EVANS &
Born Ian Ernest Gilmore Green, 13 May 1912, Toronto, Ontario, Canada; died 20 May 1988, Cuernavaca, Mexico
Arranger, keyboards

Plays The Music Of Jimi Hendrix
RCA Victor 09026 638722
Evans; Hannibal Marvin Peterson, Lew Soloff (t, flhn); Tom Malone (tb, btb, f, syn); Peter Gordon (frhn); Pete Levin (frhn, syn); Howard Johnson (tba, bcl, b); David Sanborn (ss, as, f); Billy Harper (ts, f); Trevor Koehler (as, ts, f); David Horovitz (p, syn); Paul Metzke (syn, b); Joe Gallivan (syn, perc); John Abercrombie, Ryo Kawasaki, Keith Loving (g); Warren Smith (vib, mar); Don Pate, Michael Moore (b); Bruce Ditmas (d); Sue Evans (perc). June 1974, March 1975.

Gil Evans said (1998): **'I don't think of his [Hendrix's] music as belonging to a particular time. He was a great composer, and would have been whenever he chose to come to earth.'**

Recognition came late for Evans. There was even a struggle to claw back royalties for his pioneering work with (or was that *for*?) Miles Davis. But the growing celebrity of Evans's regular Monday night stint at Sweet Basil established him as one of the music's elder statesmen. It didn't hurt that he was also hip to at least one composer that the young people had heard of. Arguably, Gary Burton was the one who first started to mix rock music with jazz procedures, but, in his championing of Hendrix, Evans refreshed the big-band repertoire for a second time in his career.

The great guitarist's 'Little Wing' became a signature-piece, and it's difficult to tell, while listening to these powerful tracks, whether the quality of the music is testimony to Hendrix's genius as a composer or Evans's as an arranger, or to some strange posthumous communication between the two. Some of the tunes are inevitably moved a long way from source; '1983 A Merman I Should Turn To Be' takes on a new character, as does 'Up From The Skies', two takes of which are included. 'Little Wing' remains the touchstone, though, and the recording, from spring 1975, is superb.

& *See also* **Out Of The Cool** (1960; p. 261)

PAUL RUTHERFORD &
Born 29 February 1940, London; died 5 August 2007, London
Trombone, euphonium

The Gentle Harm Of The Bourgeoisie
Emanem 4019
Rutherford (tb solo). July–December 1974.

Trombonist Gail Brand says: **'Paul Rutherford opened up the trombone and the listener to infinite possibilities of sound which many musicians, not just trombonists, found liberating, beautiful and dynamic. On "Osirac Senol" Paul plays without mutes or effects, revealing that vibrant, orthodox sound, which scotches any sense that Paul was only a master of the left-field approach.'**

The trombone is said to be the musical instrument closest to the human voice. When Paul Rutherford spoke or sang through his horn, it sounded like no instrument anyone had ever heard, a sound as lyrically potent and as expressively stressed and freighted as a whole ensemble. Rutherford played in RAF bands, then studied at the Guildhall. Notwithstanding his role as a prime mover in the Spontaneous Music Ensemble, Iskra 1903 and the London Jazz Composers' Orchestra, he remained deeply rooted in the blues and the straight-ahead jazz on which he had cut his teeth. In addition, Rutherford showed a lifelong interest in language and in political thought and action, concerns which to a degree distanced him from his contemporaries, though his own rebarbative personality and proneness to depression also had an impact. It may fairly be said that, more than most of them, Rutherford expressed himself most coherently in solo performance, using mutes and other devices, and often utilizing 'multiphonics', where he played and sang simultaneously.

The pieces that are documented on *The Gentle Harm Of The Bourgeoisie*, are as wryly subversive as the title suggests. Devotedly recorded by Martin Davidson at the Unity Theatre, it's now infinitely more listenable. Rutherford's grasp of multiphonics is already assured; additional sounds and overtones come from mutes, microphone knocks and from spittle in the horn, part and parcel of the process. On 'The Funny Side Of Discreet', the use of effects is taken to the point of comic parody, and then miraculously beyond. Rutherford never deploys technique for its own sake, but always musically. 'Osirac Senol', recorded a week before Christmas 1974, is very different, in that it scarcely steps outside orthodox brassplaying. In the process, though, it attains a kind of mournful transcendence, a warped chorale that conjures up Rutherford's solid grounding in classical technique. A mournful Grock with a strong fire of political passion, Rutherford eventually self-destructed, but not before creating a body of work unsurpassed for intellectual spontaneity and sheer sonic impact.

& *See also* **Gheim** (1983; p. 480)

ANTHONY BRAXTON &
Born 4 June 1945, Chicago, Illinois
Saxophones, clarinets, flutes, piano

New York, Fall 1974
Arista AL 4302 / Mosaic MD8 242
Braxton; Kenny Wheeler (t, flhn); Julius Hemphill (as); Oliver Lake (ts); Hamiet Bluiett (bs); Leroy Jenkins (vn); Richard Teitelbaum (syn); Dave Holland (b); Jerome Cooper (d). September & October 1974.

Saxophonist and Braxton student Steve Lehman says: '**When I first heard it I was stunned. I didn't know that you could articulate new kinds of saxophone-playing and of small-group writing while paying homage to Parker and Ornette. That you could structure a piece to compress and expand at the same time. Or that you could include electronic music, sax quartets, and blistering individual solos on the same recording. It continues to reshape our understanding of what a small-group recording can be.**'

Anthony Braxton's vast discography presents a problem. How to represent such a huge body of work without over-representing one – albeit exceptional – artist. We have chosen to pick out three relatively early works, one justifiably famous mid-period one (the 'classic' quartet on its breakthrough European tour) and one very recent and encyclopedic live documentation that saw Braxton ringing down the curtain on one phase of work and embarking on another. Such generous coverage would only be justified by work of the highest quality and a career that shows a significant evolution, and we are persuaded that this is the case, guiltily secure in the awareness that at least another dozen Braxton CDs, particularly from the '80s and '90s, might just as easily stake a claim on our attention.

The story of Braxton's time at Arista has been told – and told well – by Bill Shoemaker and others. Ironically, for all their importance, these records were out of circulation for nearly 30 years until restored by Mosaic. Three of the cuts are by the quartet with Jenkins as second lead voice. 'Composition No. 23b' finds Braxton in boppish mode, reaching back to Charlie Parker in what he describes as an 'atonal version of "Donna Lee"', while 'Nos. 23c & d' explore aspects of metre and tone duration, the former track accumulating detail like a snowball. Coming from a different composition group is a duet with Teitelbaum, which shows that Braxton, like Miles Davis, had been listening to Stockhausen; Teitelbaum would become a regular collaborator. The remaining material is played with three quarters of what would become the World Saxophone Quartet. Braxton plays everything from sopranino saxophone (with the WSQ men) to a contrabass clarinet, one of the clearest early public showings of his multi-instrumentalism. He plays with consistent fire on all of them, scorching on alto, drily effective on clarinet with the synthist and eerily out-of-body on flute, as if he were channelling Eric Dolphy.

Sometimes dismissed as Braxton lite, or performed with the requirements of a commercial label too much in mind, *NY, Fall 1974* is an excellent entry point into Braxton's music. Much as *For Alto* laid out his personal idiom (if the subjectivity is there at all), this one lays the foundations of what the composer himself would describe as his 'vibrational philosophy'. More ambitious and controversial work would follow shortly.

& *See also* **For Alto** (1968; p. 355), **Creative Orchestra Music** (1976; p. 431), **Quartet (London / ... Birmingham / ... Coventry) 1985** (1985; p. 495), **Nine Compositions (Iridium) 2006** (2006; p. 714)

MODERN JAZZ QUARTET&

Formed 1954
Group

The Complete Last Concert
Atlantic 81976 2CD
John Lewis (p); Milt Jackson (vib); Percy Heath (b); Connie Kay (d). November 1974.

British broadcaster Benny Green dismissed them as: **'four guys dressed like head-waiters, standing around, hitting things'**, while original drummer Kenny Clarke decided he no longer wanted to play, **'eighteenth-century drawing room music'**.

The MJQ's celebrity and 'crossover' appeal was so great, the group even made an appearance on the Beatles' Apple label, but it couldn't go on for ever. Given the closeness of the relationship, the prolific output and the separate ambitions of the members, it wasn't entirely surprising that the four should have decided after more than 20 years as a unit to give their individual careers a little space and air. What was billed as the last concert was very much considered to be just that, rather than a shrewd marketing ploy at the start of a short sabbatical. It would be wrong to say that the music was inspired or more intense than usual, but certainly these are all very fine performances. The short bebop section in the middle – 'Confirmation', 'Round Midnight', 'A Night In Tunisia' – gives the lie to any prejudice that the group were uneasy with those jaggy changes and rhythms; they had, after all, cut their professional teeth in such a context. But it's the other, more familiar MJQ material that is most impressive. There are several blues pieces carried over from the previous year's *Blues On Bach*, versions of 'The Golden Striker' and 'Cylinder', and a few of Lewis's more impressionistic compositions, such as 'Skating In Central Park' and 'Jasmine Tree'. One additional outstanding performance was the arrangement of Rodrigo's Miles-blessed 'Concierto De Aranjuez'.

Almost inevitably, eight years later, fans were tearing the cellophane off *Together Again* and the MJQ story picked up afresh until Connie Kay's death, and then Jackson's brought to an end the 'Beatles get back together' scenarios.

& *See also* **Dedicated To Connie** (1960; p. 254); **JOHN LEWIS, Golden Striker / Jazz Abstractions** (1960; p. 253), **Evolution** (1999; p. 638)

HARRY MILLER

Born 25 April 1941, Cape Town, South Africa; died 16 December 1983, Netherlands
Double bass

The Collection
Ogun HMCD 1/2/3 3CD
Miller; Marc Charig (c, ahn); Malcolm Griffiths, Radu Malfatti, Wolter Wierbos (tb); Mike Osborne (as); Trevor Watts (ss, as); Willem Breuker (ts, bcl); Sean Bergin (ts); Keith Tippett (p); Louis Moholo (d); Julie Tippetts (v). 1974–March 1983.

Hazel Miller remembers: **'Harry arrived in the UK before the Blue Notes, along with his childhood friend Manfred Mann. He was overjoyed when his fellow countrymen arrived and he could take his music out into shared territory with them. His partnership with Louis Moholo as the great rhythm team is legendary. He was 110 per cent musician.'**

Miller worked in R&B with Manfred Mann and gigged with trad star Alex Welsh before shipping out on cruise liners to New York, where he experienced modern jazz at first hand. Thereafter he became a key figure on the British modernist scene, working with most of the major figures and, via his and Hazel Miller's Ogun label, vigorously promoting the music of South African exiles in London and others. His early death, in a road accident while on tour, was a tragedy for British music.

Miller was an inspirational presence wherever he played, a musician who spoke entirely in his own voice, and with a quiet passion. The gentleness of his solo bass on *Children At Play* was perfectly at ease with the rhythmic intensity of his section-work on group albums like *Down South* or *Family Affair*, which he made with his group Isipingo. Most of his records as leader were released on the label he helped found, and *The Collection* has been put together with loving care by Hazel Miller and John Jack, keepers of the flame. In addition to the three albums already mentioned, the set includes *Bracknell Breakdown*, a set of duets with trombonist Radu Malfatti, and *In Conference*, with the two-saxophone front line of Trevor Watts and Willem Breuker. The box also includes a booklet of photographs and the memories of friends and fellow players.

The best measure of Harry's gifts can be had from the solo record, which has overdubbed flute and percussion parts, played over a rolling township beat that conveyed Harry's profound immersion in the musics of his native country. As with many of the South African exiles in Britain, he found the transition from settled grooves to free music perfectly congenial, and his out-of-tempo work on *Bracknell Breakdown* and *Down South* (made during the last year of his life and the only record not released on Ogun) is suggestive of a player who worked to a deeper, inner rhythm. He always had a special understanding with trombonists, perhaps drawn to that low, vocalized tonality, and some of his best work was in the company of Malfatti, Wierbos and Griffiths.

Through this set, 'Aitchy' lives.

KEITH JARRETT&

Born 8 May 1945, Allentown, Pennsylvania
Piano, soprano saxophone, other instruments

The Köln Concert
ECM 810067-2 2CD
Jarrett (p solo). January 1975.

Jarrett's biographer, Ian Carr, said (1994): **'He is no longer playing merely at a conscious level, but in something like the state of grace Bill Evans entered on some of his improvisations. Even if [*The Köln Concert*] wasn't made in the near ideal circumstances Evans enjoyed at the Village Vanguard, it's easily in that league and perhaps even beyond it. Transcendent music.'**

An epochal record in modern jazz. Made in conditions of exceptional difficulty – not least an audibly unsatisfactory piano and some of the health problems that have dogged the pianist for many years – but Jarrett not for the last time makes a virtue of adversity, carving out huge slabs of music with a rare intensity. His instrument does sound off-puttingly bad-tempered, and even an amateur piano-player could tell where the problem keys were, but his concentration on the middle register throughout the performance creates a hypnotic effect that is still entrancing listeners more than 30 years later. *The Köln Concert* is not just that rare thing, a best-selling jazz record, but that even rarer one, a record whose immense popularity isn't occasioned by a watered-down or compromised performance.

& *See also* **El Juicio (The Judgement)** (1971; p. 386), **Standards: Volume 1** (1983; p. 474), **Always Let Me Go** (2001; p. 663)

SOS
Formed 1973
Group

SOS
Ogun OGCD019
Alan Skidmore (ts, d, perc); Mike Osborne (as, perc); John Surman (ss, bs, bcl, syn). January & February 1975.

Alan Skidmore remembers: **'All three of us had been doing our own thing, but we had worked together from time to time and knew we had an affinity. Then I had a horrendous car accident and was laid up for three months. Mike Osborne also had his own health problems. John Surman was in constant touch, and it was his suggestion, while visiting me in hospital, that we should form a trio. I'll always be grateful for that.'**

There are few musical formats duller than the classical saxophone quartet, but the form has a surprisingly robust jazz history: World, 29th Street, ROVA, Position Alpha, Scotland's Hung Drawn – quartets that have made significant contributions to ideas of jazz ensemble, and without succumbing to classical formalities. SOS got round the problem of fielding only three saxophones by having John Surman programme some moody and highly effective synth patches, anticipating the kind of multitracked solo project he had sketched with *Westering Home* in 1972 and would bring to mature expression with *Upon Reflection*, recorded in 1979 for ECM. The other inspiration was to put Alan Skidmore – always a percussionist *manqué* – at the drumkit for a couple of numbers. The basic formula, though, was a set of unison *ostinati*, often with folkish themes, out of which one or other member would swoop off on a solo foray. This is evident on the opening 'Country Dance', which sounds exactly like that, while the diversified instrumentation is showcased on 'Wherever I Am'. All three players bring a different kind of intensity: Skidmore's Coltrane-tinged harmonics, Surman's already distinctive blend of traditional forms, church music and free jazz, Osborne's singing tone and highly emotional articulation. Surman's electronics were apparently recorded in February, after the main session. There's certainly no sense that the horns are following a backing track; the interplay is elastic and spontaneous. It's a great pity that there isn't some unreleased material to stretch the original session beyond the enchanting 'Calypso' but given how fondly the original LP was remembered, a whole generation of jazz fans was simply grateful to have a playable copy again. There was to be no follow-up record, which only adds to *SOS*'s enduring appeal.

MILES DAVIS &

Born 26 May 1926, Alton, Illinois; died 28 September 1991, Santa Monica, California
Trumpet, flugelhorn, organ

Agharta
Columbia 467897 2CD
Davis; Sonny Fortune (as, ss, f); Pete Cosey (g, syn, perc); Reggie Lucas (g); Michael Henderson (b); Al Foster (d); Mtume (perc). February 1975.

Miles's biographer, Ian Carr, said (1990): **'His lip is strong on those recordings, but there's a desperate quality to them as well. He sounds mournful to me, more sad than defiant or celebratory; but you marvel at the power.'**

After *Bitches Brew*, Miles Davis was a different kind of 'jazz' musician; after *Jack Johnson* and *On The Corner*, different again. But if it was hard to square the man who made those records with the Miles of *E.S.P.*, *Sorcerer* and *Nefertiti*, it was virtually impossible to reconcile the universally admired Miles Davis of *Kind Of Blue* with the chthonic monster of *Agharta* and its companion record, *Pangaea*. Here was a Miles who had left bebop pretty much behind, gone over almost completely to electric instruments and to some degree (and for whatever reason, medical or musical) 'given up' trumpet-playing. The hip problems – cue bad joke: 'Miles was so cool, even his surgery was hip' – had recurred, and with them some unfortunate psychological issues. This may seem a perverse place to take leave of Miles Davis, with 15 years of work still ahead of him and such obvious beauties as 'Time After Time' and 'Human Nature' passed over in silence. It may even seem a faddish choice, a sop to the rock, metal and noise constituency who in the '90s and '00s accepted these records as ancestral texts.

It bears repeating: Miles's trumpet-playing on these bruising, unconscionable records is of the highest and most adventurous order, not the desperate posturing of a sick and cynical man, or one who has 'given up' his main voice. The use of a wah-wah pedal is subtle, creating surges and ebbs in a harmonically static line, allowing Miles to build huge melismatic variations. The problem with these dates isn't the trumpeter but the band: Fortune gets the point, and plays some startlingly good solo material, but doesn't have to do much; Henderson tends to plod, even within his technically limited role; and the two guitarists go off on long, rock-god solos that are almost laughably tame and blustery when set alongside Miles's knife-fighter attacks. Yet, even at their most intense and freaked-out, Cosey and Lucas do little more than lay out an electric carpet, or carrier-deck, for Miles's own contributions. To the perennial question of how much creative authority he has ceded, the answer here is: very little, if any.

The music on *Agharta* and *Pangaea* was recorded at two performances at the Festival Hall in Osaka in February 1975. Unlike the studio albums with Macero, these are unmistakably unedited. A re-run 'Maishya' and a long edit from the *Jack Johnson* theme retrospectively clinch the experiments of *Live-Evil* and *Get Up With It*. The idiom incorporates Stockhausen's conception of a 'world music' that moves like creeping tectonic plates ('Pangaea' and 'Gondwana' are the names palaeo-geographers give to the primeval super-continents) to African-American popular forms, though it's clear that Sly Stone has been left as far behind as bebop. 'Gondwana' is the most coherent performance on either album. It opens on Fortune's delicate flute and proceeds trance-like, with Miles's central trumpet episode bracketed by shimmering organ outlines and sullen, percussive stabs. Key centres are only notional and deceptive; most of the rhythmic activity takes place along a single axis, but with considerable variation in the intensity and coloration of the pulse; the 'solos' are continuous and inseparable from the main thrust of the music. Although admittedly problematic and unsoftened by time, these no longer seem quite as forbidding as on first appearance. How could the man who made *Kind Of Blue* make *Agharta*? One might as well ask how the Scott Walker who had crooned 'Make It Easy On Yourself' could also have made *Tilt*, or – to push the absurdity full way – how the Louis Armstrong of 'Potato Head Blues' could have made 'Hello Dolly'. It isn't a rhetorical question and in the answer lies much of the history of recent jazz.

& See also **The Complete Birth Of The Cool** (1948–1950; p. 121), **Miles Ahead** (1957; p. 208), **Kind Of Blue** (1959; p. 232), **The Complete Live At The Plugged Nickel** (1965; p. 331), **In A Silent Way** (1969; p. 361)

GATO BARBIERI
Born Leandro Barbieri, 28 November 1932, Rosario, Argentina
Tenor saxophone, percussion, voice

Chapter 4: Alive In New York
Impulse! 4274
Barbieri; Howard Johnson (flhn, tba, bcl); Eddie Martinez (ky); Paul Metzke (g); Ron Carter (b); Portinho (d).
February 1975.

Saxophonist David Liebman said (1990): **'He's a very underrated saxophone-player. That vocalized tone and his control when playing altissimo, those are quite influential with younger players, except mostly critics assume it's coming from Albert Ayler.'**

The intense, vocalized sound and upper-register screams can easily tip over into self-parody (perhaps not helped by having his image copied as the model for the Muppet character Zoot), but Barbieri remains a greatly underrated figure whose innovations have been eclipsed by pop and film projects. He moved to Buenos Aires in his teens and began his professional career in Lalo Schifrin's orchestra. He then switched to tenor and after a period on the European avant-garde scene, working with Don Cherry, Enrico Rava and others, he began to create his own distinctive hybrid of jazz and South American folk forms.

Once with Impulse!, Barbieri embarked on a series of 'Chapter' records, beginning with what was essentially a folk-jazz album on *Chapter One: Latin America*, evolving through Brazilian jazz with avant-garde tinges to the high gloss of the Bottom Line gig documented on *Alive In New York*. Superstardom of a sort beckoned with the soundtrack music for *Last Tango In Paris*, with its unforgettable main theme, which has been a Barbieri favourite ever since, and he had also appeared in front of Oliver Nelson in big-band recordings from Switzerland put out by the Flying Dutchman label, but it's the New York record that best captures Barbieri with a small group, playing his incantatory, deceptively simple lines.

The opening 'Milonga Triste' is magnificent, a slow-burning, erotic epic that recalls the Barbieri of *Last Tango*. Johnson brilliantly elaborates the line with a countering phrase of his own, while Metzke (the most underrated guitarist of his generation) throws the saxophonist vivid cues. 'La China Leoncia Arreo La Correntinada Trajo Entre La Muchachada La Flor De La Juventud' is reprised from the previous 'Chapter' and has a darker and more brooding quality in this context. 'Lluvia Azul' provides an intense climax, its sheer energy and bravura not enough to disguise the sophistication of harmonic invention, not least from the peerless Johnson. The rhythm section is no less wonderful; Martinez understands the modal approach and is happy to work apart from conventional changes, while Carter is his usual utterly dependable self. Any feeling that the percussion sections of earlier records were more cluttered than truly effective is dispelled by Portinho's tight but expansive playing.

JACO PASTORIUS

Born John Francis Pastorius, 1 December 1951, Norristown, Pennsylvania; died 21 September 1987, Fort Lauderdale, Florida
Bass guitar

Jaco Pastorius

Epic 712761
Pastorius; Randy Brecker, Ron Tooley (t); Peter Graves (btb); Peter Gordon (frhn); Hubert Laws (picc); Wayne Shorter (ss); David Sanborn (as); Michael Brecker (ts); Howard Johnson (bs); Alex Darqui, Herbie Hancock (p, ky); Richard Davis, Homer Mensch (b); Bobby Oeconomy, Narada Michael Walden, Lenny White (d); Don Alias (perc); Othello Molineaux, Leroy Williams (steel d); Sam and Dave (v); strings. 1975.

Joe Zawinul commented (1996): **'What a musician he was, this bright, golden boy. But what an end! What a miserable, pointless end!'**

Object of a veritable cult for a brief period, and of an unhealthy martyrdom following his ugly death, Pastorius raised the bass guitar – a fretless instrument – to the level of a lead instrument, his solo features somewhat resembling Jimi Hendrix's more theatrical performances. Spectacularly gifted from childhood, Pastorius tried several instruments and played rock, soul and reggae before settling on jazz. He was a member of Weather Report – the antithesis, in all but ego, of founding member Miroslav Vitous – from 1976 to 1982, and in retrospect this was perhaps his finest hour. After departing the group, and the wise tutelage and discipline of Joe Zawinul, Pastorius continued to play and record, moving into fascinating new areas that involved elements of Caribbean music and what he called 'punk jazz', but steadily succumbing to mental problems exacerbated with drug and alcohol use. Pretty much ostracized by the music business and even old friends towards the end, he was beaten to death by a nightclub bouncer in Fort Lauderdale, where he had grown up. Pastorius picked the fight.

This Epic record – now on Sony – was made just before he joined Weather Report. Jaco makes a clear statement by starting the session with a brilliant realization on bass guitar of Miles Davis's 'Donna Lee' (one thinks of what Prince did with Charlie Parker's 'Now's The Time' a little later), but then immediately following up with a soul song, 'Come On, Come Over', which features vocals by Sam and Dave. At one level, it all sounds a little forced and more than a little like special pleading – for the fretless bass, for a certain kind of 'eclecticism' – but Jaco's musical imagination had sufficient force to hold such disparate material together and make a convincing whole of it. His collaboration with Herbie Hancock on 'Kuru/Speak Like A Child' is quite brilliantly conceived and the arrangement of 'Okonkole Y Trompa', written for bass and French horn, is among the most ambitious, but quite simple, things he ever did. 'Opus Pocus' and 'Used To Be A Cha Cha', of which two versions are included, are more free-blowing.

Pastorius is widely known outside jazz, largely because of his work with Joni Mitchell but also because he tapped into a certain rock god vein in his later work. Perversely, he remains overlooked within jazz, for precisely the same reasons: Mitchell, though, is now an honoured composer in this music, and when one gets down to it, there is no essential aesthetic difference between a 20-minute John Coltrane saxophone solo and a 20-minute Jaco Pastorius bass solo – at his height, Jaco sustained the comparison very comfortably.

DEXTER GORDON &

Born 27 February 1923, Los Angeles, California; died 25 April 1990, Philadelphia, Pennsylvania
Tenor saxophone

More Than You Know

Steeplechase SCCD 31030
Gordon; Palle Mikkelborg, Allan Botschinsky, Benny Rosenfeld, Idrees Sulieman (t, flhn); Richard Boone, Vincent Nilsson (tb); Axel Windfeld (btb); Ole Molin (g); Thomas Clausen (p, electric p); Kenneth Knudsen (syn); Niels-Henning Ørsted Pedersen (b); Alex Riel, Ed Thigpen (d); Klaus Nordsoe (perc); chamber winds and strings. February–March 1975.

Dexter Gordon said (1979): **'Some writers say that settling in Europe is bad for your music, because you don't need to try. Settling in Detroit is bad for your music if you don't keep trying, but if you do, it's pretty much like any place else, just quieter and more peaceful.'**

Between Danish radio and Steeplechase, Gordon was exhaustively documented during his sojourn in Scandinavia. Multi-disc sets of live club material were still appearing long after his death. None of it is in any way inferior, but in bulk it tests the loyalty of even the most devoted – and well-heeled – fan. Oddly, this elegant set, which casts Gordon in front of an orchestra arranged by Palle Mikkelborg, has rarely commanded the respect it conspicuously merits. Set alongside the long hours of easy-going hard bop, it's a refreshing context for the Gordon saxophone and Mikkelborg's own original of the set, 'Good Morning Sun', is a beautiful thing. That even committed Gordon fans don't know it seems passing strange. Dexter has a few nice lines of his own: 'Ernie's Tune' and 'Tivoli' aren't just blowing themes, but carefully weighted compositions, treated respectfully by the arranger. He opens the set with Coltrane's 'Naima', raising once again the old question about who influenced who, when and how much. Even after hearing this faithful but individualistic treatment, the jury won't be in a hurry to come back in with a definitive answer. It's a great set and deserves wider celebrity.

& *See also* **Dexter Gordon On Dial** (1947; p. 113), **Doin' Alright** (1961; p. 275)

ENRICO RAVA

Born 20 August 1939, Trieste, Italy
Trumpet

The Pilgrim And The Stars

ECM 847322-2
Rava; John Abercrombie (g); Palle Danielsson (b); Jon Christensen (d). June 1975.

Enrico Rava says: **'I remember I had a beautiful hat, on this recording session; also an excellent steak tartar in the restaurant near by – we were in Stuttgart. Unfortunately we were travelling in an uncomfortable Volkswagen minibus. Hard times. But Manfred Eicher was very happy about the music.'**

Rava grew up in Turin, where he met American musicians. Influenced by Miles Davis, he gravitated towards the avant-garde with Gato Barbieri, and later with Steve Lacy, and with the Globe Unity Orchestra. Much like Tomasz Stańko, whom he very superficially resembles, his interest in free jazz is tempered by an awareness of other genres and styles and over the years Rava has recorded a number of rock- and electronically tinged albums and his own brand of jazz *noir*. Some of this can be heard on the debut *Il Giro Del Mondo In 80 Giorni*, recorded for Black Saint in 1972, but when Rava went to ECM for the first of three fine albums – he returned to the label in 2003 – the label's pristine sound met the deceptively strength of the trumpet-playing perfectly and delivered a modern classic.

The Pilgrim And The Stars opens with the sky-treading title-track, a simple enough idea within which great spaces seem to open up. The central drama of the recording is the interweaving of trumpet and guitar. Abercrombie rarely pushed out quite so far and some of his lines are stretched to cracking. Even the more immediately accessible tracks like 'Bella' seem to move in the direction of total freedom, but always restore some element of precarious order. 'Parks' and 'Surprise Hotel' sound almost like soundtrack cues from some forgotten thriller, set in off-season Trieste, perhaps, with a voice-over from Claudio Magris, and they help to sew together a virtual movie for the ears. We've loved this record for half a lifetime and it never fails to deliver something new.

MIKE OSBORNE &

Born 28 September 1941, Hereford, England; died 19 September 2007, Hereford, England
Alto saxophone, clarinet

All Night Long
Ogun OGCD 700
Osborne; Harry Miller (b); Louis Moholo (d). July 1975.

Mike Osborne said (1976): **'I've never really been comfortable anywhere except when I'm playing. People talk about drugs in jazz. I think it *is* a drug, a kind of dependency.'**

Mike Osborne's voice was silenced early. Mental illness meant that after 1982 he did not play at all. For his short time on the scene, though, he blazed, appearing on countless British jazz and improvisation projects and making records of his own, all of them distinguished by that soulful, keening saxophone sound that was as distinctive as a fingerprint.

A Mike Osborne gig, with whatever line-up, was a furious dance of disparate parts: simple hymnic tunes, wild staccato runs, sweet ballad formations and raw blues, all stitched together into a continuous fabric that left most listeners exhausted, and none unmoved. *All Night Long* catches the trio at its peak, live at Willisau in 1975. The title-track is curiously reminiscent of the Ornette Coleman trio, with Miller's arco bass sawing back and forth underneath the flowing alto lines and Moholo's relaxed freebeat. 'Waltz' is the darkest dance imaginable, one of those moments when Ossie's demons seemed ready to emerge. Almost every time, though, he conjures something positive, even celebratory out of the material. 'Ken's Tune' is a long wild whirl with a substantial bebop component, while 'Round Midnight', probably his favourite jazz repertory piece, has an air of wild inevitability, as did Ossie's subsequent decline, but what he left behind was as precious as a pearl, even if not quite the 'Scotch Pearl' evoked here.

& *See also* **SOS, SOS** (1975; p. 419)

DON CHERRY &

Born 18 November 1936, Oklahoma City, Oklahoma; died 19 October 1995, Malaga, Spain
Pocket-trumpet, wooden flutes, doussn'gouni, piano, keyboards, miscellaneous instruments, voice

Brown Rice
Jazz Heritage 397001
Cherry; Frank Lowe (ts); Ricky Cherry (ky); Charlie Haden (b); Billy Higgins (d); Bunchie Fox (perc); Verna Gillis (v). 1975.

Backstage in Poland (1992), Don Cherry said: **'I feel the earth spinning under my feet, always. I like to move with it and everywhere I go, it's the same *out there* [i.e. in the auditorium]: there are friends waiting to share the vibration.'**

In later years, Cherry became a kind of planetary *griot*, much loved in Europe (where he, in turn, felt most at home), but restlessly travelling. Only familiar health problems restricted his activities. Originally released simply as *Don Cherry*, the 1975 album is a lost classic of the era and probably the best place to sample the trumpeter as both soloist – he blows some stunningly beautiful solos here – and as the shamanic creator of a unique, unearthly sound that makes dull nonsense of most 'fusion' work of the period. Miles Davis's – indeed, John Coltrane's – interest in Indian music was undoubtedly sincere, but it scarcely went below the surface when translated to his own practice. Here, though, Cherry absorbs subcontinental and African influences and instead of using them simply as colours and rhythmic variations allows them to shape the music from the inside out. It isn't 'world music', but a vivid urban melting pot of sound, as vibrant as anything his fellow trumpeter turned up after *Bitches Brew*. Lowe's saxophone squawks and yelps in ways that remove it from the familiar idiom of 'jazz sax'. Haden's wah-wah bass yaws back and forth on the title-track, which is still a club favourite, but it's the two long cuts, 'Chenrezig' and 'Malkauns', which give the album its unique character and beauty. Cherry's tone seems softer than usual, though no less emphatic, and as it drifts in and out of the foreground, one has a strong sense of going on a journey with the music. Exceptional and recommended.

& *See also* **Complete Communion** (1965; p. 325)

BILLY HARPER
Born 17 January 1943, Houston, Texas
Tenor saxophone

Black Saint
Black Saint 120001
Harper; Virgil Jones (t); Joe Bonner (p); David Friesen (b); Malcolm Pinson (d). July 1975.

Black Saint/Soul Note founder Giovanni Bonandrini says: **'It was my first recording in the studio of my very good friend Giancarlo Barigozzi. It was the LP era and we could only have about 22 minutes per side to get the best natural sound. It was also the first time I met Billy Harper. We had been in touch by mail and had planned to record in Milan while he was on tour. Billy Harper and Sun Ra are the two most deeply religious musicians I ever met. You can sense that from Billy's titles, but also from the music.'**

Initially influenced by Sonny Rollins, but increasingly by Coltrane, Harper earned his chops playing in church before going on to work with Art Blakey, Max Roach and Gil Evans, for whom he wrote 'Priestess' and 'Thoroughbred', two of the best modern-jazz compositions in the book. His gifts as a writer and his big saxophone sound should have made him a star, but the breakthrough never quite came and the majors stayed away, even when many of Harper's contemporaries were being rediscovered. Like many of his countrymen, Harper had to look to Europe for recognition, and to the Black Saint/Soul Note stable (he inaugurated both imprints) for recording opportunities.

   Black Saint is still the album people associate with Harper, a strong, eclectic blend of blues, hard-edged rock patterns and the by now familiar preaching style. Jones and Bonner are greatly admired in Europe, too, and the pianist makes his mark on the record from the very start with his tersely romantic approach and elastic chord-patterns. There is a lot of blues in Harper's sound and a gospely roll to his best pieces – it comes over in 'Priestess' – and on *Black Saint* he marries it all to a joyous, spiritual quality that's signalled at the very beginning with 'Dance, Eternal Spirits, Dance', a mysterious waltz that seems to come out of some timeless space. 'Croquet Ballet' also has a dancing quality, but the real substance of the date is the very long 'Call Of The Wild And Peaceful Heart', which occupied the original second side. Harper never surpassed it and it also contains some of Joe Bonner's most exciting work on record. A genuine classic and, given Black Saint/Soul Note's importance in documenting creative Americans over the next three decades, an epoch in modern jazz.

MARY LOU WILLIAMS &

Born Mary Elfrieda Scruggs (later Burley), 8 May 1910, Atlanta, Georgia; died 28 May 1981, Durham, North Carolina
Piano

Free Spirits
Steeplechase SCCD 31043
Williams; Buster Williams (b); Mickey Roker (d). July 1975.

Mary Lou Williams said (1975): **'Bop is the real modern jazz. Playing in smooth eighth notes was fine for the swing era and composing with 12 tones is fine for classical musicians. Bop, though, is a new language and the real means of expression for American jazz musicians.'**

In later years, Williams devoted much time to composing large-scale masses and other sacred pieces, and was much involved with charity work. She was increasingly recognized as an important composer/arranger and as a piano-player, though a planned summit with Cecil Taylor fell out disastrously, two large egos colliding. Williams did continue to enjoy small-group play and some of her best music was made in this form, even if it didn't address her larger intentions.

As a straightforward performance, *Free Spirits* is a much better record than a number of others from around the same period. Williams's health was still robust (it began to break down towards the end of the '70s) and her playing is much sharper and surer, also more relaxed and swinging. Typically, she mixes standards ('Temptation', 'Surrey With The Fringe On Top') with jazz staples (Miles's 'All Blues', Bobby Timmons's gospel-tinged 'Dat Dere') and her own work, 'Ode To Saint Cecilie', 'Gloria', 'Blues For Timme', unexpectedly adding two John Stubblefield compositions (two takes each of 'Baby Man' and 'Free Spirits') and a promising 'Pale Blue' by bassist Buster Williams, who provides a perfect complement to her light left hand.

& *See also* **The Zodiac Suite** (1945; p. 100)

HARRY 'SWEETS' EDISON

Born 10 October 1915, Columbus, Ohio; died 27 July 1999, Columbus, Ohio
Trumpet

Just Friends
Black & Blue 918
Edison; Eddie 'Lockjaw' Davis (ts); Gerry Wiggins (p); Major Holley (b); Oliver Jackson (d). July 1975.

Harry Edison said (1984): **'I don't think Jaws and I play the same way at all; never did. I think we were pretty much like opposites, but oil and vinegar that could combine into something tastier than each one on his own. That's why it worked so long.'**

A much-loved elder statesman of jazz in the two decades before his death, 'Sweets' had served his time in umpteen territory bands before joining Basie and becoming one of those jazz soloists who is identifiable from the very first note. The nickname refers to his sound, not a taste for sugar. He made surprisingly few records of his own and many of them shared the limelight with someone else – Ben Webster or Lockjaw Davis – on which occasions he was quite happy to take the rear seat. Edison's solos were always full of invention, right to the very last, and it's a pity that so many of the best of them have to be filleted out of jam situations and guest spots.

He hadn't made a record for ten years when Black & Blue, devoted sponsors of American players in France, came in with a spot for him in 1975. Davis had become a regular partner and the perfect foil to Harry's softly burnished tone. 'There Is No Greater Love' is the standout track on a fairly standard roster of material, which includes a couple of run-through originals got together for the session. Wiggins, Holley and Jackson do their business briskly and without fuss and there's a job-well-done feel to the whole proceedings. A duo record with Earl 'Fatha' Hines was made for the label at around the same time; it's also worth having.

TOSHIKO AKIYOSHI
Born 12 December 1929, Liaoyang, Manchuria
Piano

The Toshiko Akiyoshi–Lew Tabackin Big Band
Novus ND 83 106
Akiyoshi; Lew Tabackin (ts, f, picc); Stu Blumberg, Richard Cooper, Steve Huffstetter, John Madrid, Lynn Nicholson, Mike Price (t); Bobby Shew (t, flhn); Charlie Loper, Bruce Paulson, Bill Reichenbach, Jim Sawyer, Britt Woodman (tb); Bill Teele (btb); Gary Foster (ss, as, f, acl); Dick Spencer (as, f, cl); Tom Peterson (ss, as, ts, f, cl); Bill Perkins (ss, bs, f, cl, bcl); Don Baldwin, Gene Cherico (b); Peter Donald (d); Kisaku Katada (kotsuzumi); Yataki Yazaki (ohtsuzumi); Tokuku Kaga (v); collective personnel. April 1974, February & March 1975, January, February & June 1976.

Toshiko Akiyoshi said (1991): **'I came to America thinking I'd learn all there was to learn and then go home and show it to everyone there. And then you realize you haven't learned very much after all, and you just have to keep going.'**

Though considered one of the finest big-band composers and arrangers since Duke Ellington (who profoundly influenced her), Toshiko Akiyoshi is still not fully recognized and much of her best and most ambitious work has been deleted. This compilation of her mid-'70s band, co-led with second husband Lew Tabackin, is remarkable in its almost total concentration on her own compositional output: no standards or pop tunes. The middle years of the decade marked a dramatic new development in her writing, and an increased interest in her own remarkable cultural heritage.

At the end of the Second World War, Akiyoshi's immigrant parents were forced to return to Japan, settling in Beppu. The city, on the southern island of Kyūshū, was occupied by American forces, giving Toshiko her first extended exposure to Western music. Having started piano lessons at the age of seven and abandoned plans for a medical career, she began playing in a local club. She was discovered there by Oscar Peterson, who was touring Japan, and the Canadian pianist persuaded Norman Granz to record her. Two years later, in 1955, Akiyoshi applied to the Berklee School of Music and was accepted on a scholarship. While in Boston, she met alto saxophonist Charlie Mariano. They married in 1959 and formed a quartet, recorded the following years by the Candid label. She also worked with Charles Mingus.

Though she recorded with a big band in 1965, as Toshiko Mariano, Akiyoshi returned to

Japan for a period in the mid-'60s and it was only after returning to the US that she began to incorporate elements of Asian music into her work, an approach apparently inspired by Duke Ellington's naturalization of African sounds. Having married tenor saxophonist Tabackin and worked with him in a small group, Akiyoshi established a big band in California in 1972.

Though it is often said that the orchestra, rather than the piano, is her real instrument, her unaccompanied intro to 'Studio J' (originally on the 1976 LP *Insights*) suggests a formidable keyboard stylist. Her genius, though, lies in orchestration, with a highly distinctive use of multi-part harmony. The Akiyoshi/Tabackin bands used an unusually large range of instruments (including some 'ethnic' effects), but particularly various in the range of reeds and flutes. In his useful liner-note, Leonard Feather points to the combination of Bill Perkins's baritone and Tabackin's piccolo on 'Quadrille, Anyone?'

Akiyoshi's part-writing is imaginative and challenging, often stepping outside conventional tonality. 'Children In The Temple Ground', with its distinctive vocals, and 'The First Time' both come (like 'Quadrille, Anyone?') from the slightly earlier *Long Yellow Road* LP, perhaps the most self-consciously 'Eastern' of the records. Throughout her career, willingly and otherwise, Akiyoshi has been drawn to historical and political subject matter. In 1986, she recorded material written to celebrate the centenary of the Statue of Liberty. In 1999, she was pressed, over her initial reservation, to write music inspired by the Hiroshima bombing. Earlier, she had written a moving piece for the Japanese children crippled and brain-damaged by mercury poisoning at Minimata. Perhaps the most affecting of the tracks here are 'Kogun', dedicated to the Japanese soldier who didn't know the war had ended, and the skilful linking of 'Since Perry' (a reference to the American naval commodore who 'opened up' Japan to Western influence, though only at the point of naval guns) with Tabackin's exquisite 'Yet Another Tear', these from the 1976 live record *Road Time*. There is also a beautiful 'American Ballad', as reminder that Akiyoshi's cultural loyalties are complex and in a constant state of playful contention.

These are important recordings, both in the evolution of big-band jazz and in the naturalization of 'Oriental' procedures and timbres into American music. They deserve to be more widely appreciated.

TERJE RYPDAL
Born 23 August 1947, Oslo, Norway
Guitar, soprano saxophone, keyboards

Odyssey
ECM 835355
Rypdal; Torbjorn Sunde (tb); Brynjolf Blix (org); Sveinung Hovensjø (b); Svein Christiansen (d). August 1975.

Guitarist Bill Frisell said (1986): **'Long before I had any association with ECM, Terje Rypdal's music seemed like the way guitar-playing could go in jazz. I think everyone who played the instrument was affected by it.'**

Rypdal – which is pronounced 'roop-dal', incidentally – started out in rock, much influenced by Jimi Hendrix, but he came under George Russell's wing and that period of study shaped him considerably as a performer and composer, latterly of classical pieces that on closer examination are an extension of the heady, ethereal jazz impressionism of earlier days.

The cover of *Odyssey*, with a guitar-slung Rypdal sitting on the tailgate of a loaded Transit van, suggests that he might come from the Rory Gallagher end of rock and indeed some of the music is crunchingly heavy, a welcome change from the floaty *Whenever I Seem To Be Far Away*, which came out on ECM the year before. But even when the dynamics are extreme, Rypdal's sophistication is evident. There are long passages on 'Midnite', 'Adagio' and 'Farewell' which might be offcuts from a forgotten Miles Davis date. In fact, one of Rypdal's early compositions, on the eponymous first ECM album (he'd played on Garbarek's *Afric Pepperbird* previously) is named after a muttered comment of Miles's on *Bitches Brew*: 'Keep it like that. Tight.' The guitar is cranked up high and there's a Santana-like sustain to some of the single-line solo passages, but the harmonics are entirely his own and very elusive, which is why this record, and others of the time, manage to sound fresh even now.

EBERHARD WEBER
Born 22 January 1940, Stuttgart, Germany
Double bass, cello, keyboards

Yellow Fields
ECM 843205-2
Weber; Charlie Mariano (ss, shenai); Rainer Brüninghaus (ky); Jon Christensen (d). September 1975.

Eberhard Weber said (1991): **'It is a difficult instrument with which to lead. Even Charles Mingus couldn't lead with his bass, which is why his ego got so large. But electricity allows me to be heard at the front of the group, so that has made a difference. But – like Mingus, only quieter – I like to lead with ideas rather than sound.'**

Weber learned cello as a boy but switched to bass and played part-time gigs while working in film and TV. Early associations with Wolfgang Dauner and Volker Kriegel led to his own composing and bandleading, and a long tenure with ECM from 1973. He was a pioneer in using bass with electronics, playing an adapted upright model. Weber's masterpiece is essentially a period piece which nevertheless still seems modern. The sound of it seems almost absurdly opulent: bass passages and swimming keyboard textures that reverberate from the speakers, chords that seem to hum with huge overtones. The keyboard textures in particular are of a kind that will probably never be heard on record again. But there's little prolixity or meandering in this music. Weber builds keenly around riffs and rhythmical figures, and solos – Mariano sounding piercingly exotic on the shenai, heartbreakingly intense on soprano – are perfectly ensconced within the sound-field. But the key element is the inspirational series of cross-rhythms and accents which Christensen delivers, in an extraordinary crescendo towards the close of 'Sand-Glass', a sprawling performance built from simple materials. And the leader's own bass never sounded better.

PAT METHENY&
Born 12 August 1954, Lee's Summit, Montana
Guitar

Bright Size Life
ECM 827133-2
Metheny; Jaco Pastorius (b); Bob Moses (d). December 1975.

Guitarist Martin Taylor says: **'*Bright Size Life* was a turning point in jazz. Metheny took jazz into a direction that nobody else knew about. He's a true visionary and undoubtedly one of the most important figures in the music.'**

By the time he was 19 the Missourian had already been teaching at Berklee and playing with the Gary Burton group. He made a string of records for ECM and formed a hugely successful touring group, with keyboardist Lyle Mays. He has built an audience in both the jazz and the rock camps, but never settles back into a comfortable style, always testing himself against new challenges, including a recent experiment in 'Orchestrionics', using mechanically operated instruments in tribute to the player-pianos and other homespun technologies of his childhood.

When he first appeared, as a coolly melodic electric guitarist for the ECM label, Metheny seemed content to drop his playing into whatever context it might find. The first two ECM albums are a little untypical – each depends more on its respective star bassist to give it some clout – but, like the ones that follow, these are highly crafted records full of hummable tunes, rendered with such high-grade production and sometimes over-sensitive musicianship that sometimes the impression is of amiability and no more. At this time Metheny favoured a clean, open tone with just enough electronic damping to take the music out of 'classic' jazz guitar feeling, but he clearly owed a great debt to such urban pastoralists as Jim Hall and Jimmy Raney, even if he seldom moved back to bebop licks.

& *See also* **Song X** (1985; p. 497)

Part 2:
1976-1980

GEORGE BENSON
Born 22 March 1943, Pittsburgh, Pennsylvania
Guitar, voice

Breezin'
Warner Archive/Rhino 76713-2
Benson; Ronnie Foster, Jorge Dalto (ky); Phil Upchurch (g); Stanley Banks (b); Harvey Mason (d); Ralph McDonald (perc); strings. January 1976.

George Benson said (1996): **'What'd I do? I used a couple of pedals, added some keyboards and electric bass and threw in the odd vocal. And they said I was a traitor to jazz! Find me the bit of paper I signed that said I was a citizen of "jazz"!'**

Benson's pop success tended to camouflage the fact that he is a brilliant musician. His first records were made when Wes Montgomery was alive and the acknowledged master of the style which Benson developed for his own ends: a rich, liquid tone, chunky octave chording and a careful sense of construction that makes every chorus tell its own story. At his best, Benson can fire off beautiful lines and ride on a 4/4 rhythm with almost insolent ease.

Breezin' was the first jazz album to go platinum and sell a million copies, but more important was its reconciliation of Taylor's pop-jazz approach with a small-group backing in which Benson could feel genuinely at home. Claus Ogerman's arrangements are still fluffy, and the tunes are thin if not quite anodyne, but Benson and his tightly effective band get the most out of them and the blues are never far away in his playing. The new edition adds two extra tracks, one of which, 'Shark Bite', is tougher and less polite than the rest of the record. It's worth remembering that this was Benson's 20th record and it came in the middle of a decade whose musical values were not those even of the '60s. He wasn't selling out; he was keeping up.

ALBERT MANGELSDORFF

Born 5 September 1928, Frankfurt am Main, Germany; died 25 July 2005, Frankfurt am Main
Trombone

Trombonliness
Sackville SKCD 2011
Mangelsdorff (tb solo). January & March 1976.

Saxophonist Emil Mangelsdorff said (1992): **'It's maybe something that only a brother would say, but you can always tell it's Albert playing, instantly. There is no one else with that sound on the trombone. He has many followers, but he doesn't have a "school", because no one sounds quite like him.'**

Mangelsdorff came of age in the American-occupied zone of postwar Germany, and his first performances were to servicemen, who seem to have exposed him to recent developments in jazz. He acquired an enthusiasm for the music from his saxophonist brother Emil and, as a precocious teenager, had taken part in the wartime jazz underground in Frankfurt. Though he retained a big-hearted sound and some elements of classic swing, his main innovations – shared with the younger Briton Paul Rutherford – were in the area of multi-phonics, the ability to play more than one tone simultaneously. Mangelsdorff never went as far into free music as Rutherford or their fellow instrumentalist George E. Lewis and some listeners, coming to his music for the first time, are surprised by how little some of it accords with usual assumptions about the 'avant-garde'. Mangelsdorff's solo performances were striking for their logic and order as they were for their bold approach to timbre and tonality.

ANTHONY BRAXTON &

Born 4 June 1945, Chicago, Illinois
Saxophones, clarinets, flutes, piano

Creative Orchestra Music 1976
Arista AL 4080 / Mosaic MD8 242
Braxton; Kenny Wheeler, Cecil Bridgewater, Jon Faddis (t); George E. Lewis, Garrett List (tb); Earl McIntyre, Jack Jeffers (btb); Jonathan Dorn (tba); Roscoe Mitchell (ss, as, bs); Seldon Powell (as, cl, f); Ron Bridgewater (ts, cl); Bruce Johnstone (bs, bcl); Muhal Richard Abrams, Frederic Rzewski (p); Karl Berger (vib, xy, perc) Richard Teitelbaum (syn); Dave Holland (b); Warren Smith (d, b mar, perc); Barry Altschul, Philip Wilson (perc); Leo Smith (cond, t). February 1976.

George E. Lewis says: **'There was tension in the studio. Everybody knew that something special was happening that New York hadn't seen coming. In the AACM we had been doing this for years, but it scared some of the others. A new kind of musician had come, and people had to deal with it.'**

Listeners at the time wondered how 'creative orchestra music' might be different from big-band jazz and turned it down unheard with utmost prejudice. Ironically, much of the music here is turned towards Ellington, in something like the way – albeit from a different direction – that Miles Davis's music of a slightly earlier period was turned towards Ellington. In the years immediately following Duke's death, he seemed the biggest single challenge and benchmark in African-American music, and several times on this extraordinary recording one hears the orchestra, which included a number of more obviously mainstream players like Faddis, run a spectrum of Ducal sounds from the early 'jungle music' to the elegant world music of the late suites.

'Composition No. 51' is a wildly exciting chart that evokes Ellington and Fletcher Henderson, and by extension the Sun Ra Arkestra. It swings madly. 'No. 56' is in stark contrast, a slower, fogbound journey round a primeval swamp with the emphasis on clarinets and a roster of soloists that never quite breaks the sonic surface. 'No. 58' is in the realm of John Philip Sousa, an important ancestor for Braxton, while 'No. 55' goes back to something like the big-band music of the opening, but in a jagged, blocky way in which huge, awkward vamps are interspersed by solos that have only an uncertain and remote connection (by the usual standards of harmony and rhythm) to the 'head' material.

It's an exhilarating record, not at all forbidding, and still after more than 30 years one of the best things Braxton ever did on the larger scale. In time to come, finding and funding large orchestras of seasoned players capable of delivering this music became ever more difficult. As Braxton's projects grew in magnitude – and even non-jazz people knew him as the guy who wanted to put jazz orchestras on orbiting space stations – his resources, for the moment at least, shrank.

& *See also* **For Alto** (1968; p. 355), **New York, Fall 1974** (1974; p. 416), **Quartet (London / ... Birmingham / ... Coventry) 1985** (1985; p. 495), **Nine Compositions (Iridium) 2006** (2006; p. 714)

MILT JACKSON &
Born 1 January 1923, Detroit, Michigan; died 9 October 1999, New York City
Vibraphone

At The Kosei Nenkin
Pablo 26
Jackson; Teddy Edwards (ts); Cedar Walton (p); Ray Brown (b); Billy Higgins (d). March 1976.

Norman Granz said (1982): **'Vibes isn't the easiest instrument to take on the road, but Milt seemed to have an appetite for touring at that time, and I never knew him to play any less than excellently and sometimes inspirationally.'**

Jackson's signing to Pablo brought forth a flood of albums. Just as he did with Count Basie, Granz basically set Milt up in the studio and let him go, which means that all these records are solidly entertaining without ever quite going the extra distance and becoming a classic. Some of the live dates are actually much better, though the run of Pablos at the time had something of the processional about them.

This sounds like a proper group, up and ready to swing and with a basic emphasis on bop and the blues. 'Birk's Works' is a nod to old boss Dizzy Gillespie, who was also hoofing the festival boards at the time, while Miles Davis's 'All Blues' takes a more searching line on the theme than was usual at that date. 'St Thomas' is happy music, however you play it, and this was an evident crowd-pleaser. Edwards always sounds slightly huffy on dates like this and never quite gets where he's going on his solos, but the rest of the group falls into place around him and the gaps are never evident. It may not seem in the front rank of Jackson albums, but we've found it consistently excellent and with real staying power, where many records of this era sound like casual encounters or gig souvenirs.

& *See also* **Wizard Of The Vibes** (1948–1952, p. 118), **Bags Meets Wes** (1961; p. 281); **MODERN JAZZ QUARTET, Dedicated To Connie** (1960; p. 254), **The Complete Last Concert** (1974; p. 417)

BARRE PHILLIPS
Born 27 October 1934, San Francisco, California
Double bass

Mountainscapes

ECM 843167-2

Phillips; John Surman (bs, ss, bcl, syn); John Abercrombie (g); Dieter Feichtner (syn); Stu Martin (d). March 1976.

Barre Phillips said (1993): **'With John Surman, it was nearly all improvised, two voices polyphonically. I hear what he's doing from the point of view of my instrument. He hears me from the point of view of his. It's something that allows you to work instinctively with the music you can hear in your head and that's very powerful.'**

Inspired by Ornette Coleman, the San Franciscan moved east in 1962, thence to Europe. His *Journal Violone* was the first-ever solo bass record and he continued to document this hard, lonely discipline in later years as well. Phillips's first album of solo bass improvisations was originally intended as material for an electronic score, but composer Max Schubel thought the bass parts stood more than adequately on their own. Nearly 25 years later, Phillips produced an album which does make significant use of electronic processing of instrumental performance, but *Aquarian Rain* suggests that Schubel's instincts were right in the first place.

It's galling to note that Phillips's very best record is still out of the ECM catalogue. The solo *Call Me When You Get There* from 1983, with its lyrical journeyings and unfussy philosophical musings, covers similar musical territory to the much earlier but almost equally fine *Mountainscapes*, a suite of subliminally interrelated pieces which demonstrate the astonishing transformations visited on basic musical perspectives by very slight changes in the angle of vision. All three members of The Trio are present here, and the empathy is very obvious. Abercrombie doesn't sound like a spare part; his ability to play for the group is never in question, and Feichtner's synth parts – instinct with Phillips's lasting interest in electronic sound – are very much in place. It's a beautiful record, worth revisiting.

ROSWELL RUDD &

Born 17 November 1935, Sharon, Connecticut
Trombone

Blown Bone

Emanem 4131

Rudd; Enrico Rava (t); Steve Lacy (ss, perc); Kenny Davern (cl, ss); Robin Kenyatta (as); Tyrone Washington (ts); Patti Bown (p); Karl Berger (vib); Louisiana Red (g, v); Wilbur Little, Lewis Worrell, Richard Youngstein (b); Horace Arnold, Paul Motian (d); Jordan Steckel (perc); Sheila Jordan (v). September 1967 & March 1976.

Roswell Rudd says: **'It was originally released on Nippon Phonogram only, and remained virtually unknown to the rest of the planet. When the exclusivity expired, I took it around, but no takers until Martin Davidson – my hero! He liked it and ingeniously digitized what remained from quarter-inch audition tapes. Some of the folks particularly responsible for my musical development are with me here: Kenny Davern, Sheila Jordan and Steve Lacy.'**

Rudd made his professional debut with Eli's Chosen Six and, despite his adherence to the avant-garde, his approach always suggests a return to the primordial simplicities of early jazz, using slurs and growls, blustering swing and a big, sultry tone. He made frustratingly few recordings of his own since his work with the New York Art Quartet and Archie Shepp in the '60s announced a marvellously vivid and unpredictable spirit on an unfashionable horn. The trombone went pretty much out of favour with bebop; along with Julian Priester, Curtis Fuller and Albert Mangelsdorff, Rudd was one of the few significant exponents between the heyday of J. J. Johnson and the emergence of younger voices like Ray Anderson and Robin Eubanks. He did make some terrific albums, including 1974's glorious *Flexible Flyer* with Sheila Jordan, but apart from a few appearances with Steve Lacy (mostly playing Thelonious Monk music), Rudd didn't record under his own name between 1982 and 1996.

The work on *Blown Bone* is mostly from consecutive days in March 1976, with the tight quartet of the first day augmented on the following by extra horns, keyboard and others. The 11-minute 'It's Happening' is almost worth the whole set. It's a brisk, boppish theme, derived from a suite dedicated to Albert Ayler, and driven along by Little and Motian. Rudd's opening solo is no mean thing, but it's knocked for six by Rava's wryly majestic statement and then by a completely outrageous Lacy solo which seems to use the entire range of the horn, right down to tenorish growls, as well as sucked tones, perfectly controlled squeaks and pure breath sounds.

Sheila Jordan returns for the next two tracks, 'Blues For The Planet Earth' and 'You Blew It', conventional enough ecological laments redeemed by Sheila's extraordinary delivery and the free-form accompaniment. A single track from 1967 follows, with Kenyatta on alto, Karl Berger on vibraphone, two basses and percussion. The remainder of the set features a mid-size group. Rava didn't make the date, but Washington and the ever-exploring Davern are both there, with Bown on electric piano. Bata drummer Steckel is on 'Bethesda Fountain' only; on that track, Rudd tinkers with a thumb piano and assorted percussion. The oddity is 'Cement Blues', which is basically a vocal feature for Louisiana Red, but a useful reminder of how rooted Rudd was in vernacular forms. By the same token, 'Street Walking' is old-fashioned swing, with just a few modern accents thrown in and only marred by the celeste-like tinkle of the electric keyboard.

&   See also **The Unheard Herbie Nichols** (1996; p. 612)

CHARLES TYLER

Born 20 July 1941, Cadiz, Kentucky; died 27 June 1992, Toulon, France
Baritone saxophone

Saga Of The Outlaws
Nessa 16
Tyler; Earl Cross (t); John Ore, Ronnie Boykins (b); Steve Reid (d). May 1976.

Charles Tyler said (1981): **'All music is a call to arms in my view, or at least a call to rise up against the systems.'**

The key experience of Tyler's life was meeting Albert Ayler, with whom he later recorded. Tyler moved to Cleveland in 1960 and became part of the scene there. He moved restlessly around, always following the most interesting musical promises of the moment, but never quite received the recognition that he was due.

The early ESP discs are intriguing but as skimpy as anything in that catalogue. The records didn't exactly pour out after that, and *Saga Of The Outlaws* is a lucky survival, subtitled 'a polyphonic saga of the old & new West'. It was recorded live at the legendary Studio RivBea, and unfolds from a clarion in-gathering at the beginning to a pungent vernacular narrative in the middle. The set consists of one continuous performance and the energies flow back and forth between Tyler and Cross, with Reid (a significant figure today) doing much of the supportive work. The basses are muddily recorded, which makes sorting out what each man does rather difficult, but their deep rumble is always redolent of marching feet and galloping hooves and helps give the performance its sense of unstoppable impetus.

DOC CHEATHAM
Born Adolphus Anthony Cheatham, 13 June 1905, Nashville, Tennessee; died 2 June 1997, Washington DC
Trumpet

Duets And Solos
Sackville SKCD 5002 2CD
Cheatham; Sam Price (p). November 1976–November 1979.

Trumpeter (and Cheatham collaborator) Nicholas Payton said (1998): **'He was just the warmest, sweetest guy to be around, but it was also like talking to a history book. He went all the way back ...'**

Doc started out in burlesque shows, backing Bessie Smith, but also played with McKinney's Cotton Pickers and with Cab Calloway, two remarkable crucibles of new jazz talent, before striking out on his own in 1926 in emulation of Louis Armstrong. There were hiatuses along the way, and Doc found himself playing in some strange situations, but he was still working in his 80s and 90s, with a revered weekly gig in Greenwich Village.

Cheatham was one of the most enduring jazz musicians of his time – and his time seemed to span much of the history of the music. He was recording in the late '20s and his studio work of 60 years later shows little deterioration. He was rediscovered in the '70s after many years of society band work, and it's not so much that one feels sentimental attachment to such a veteran, but that Doc's sound represents an art which died out in modern jazz: the sweet, lyrically hot sound of a swing-era man.

Not until the '70s was he heard at any length as a leader. An earlier Black & Blue group date with Sam Price is rough and ready, not least because Price's piano is only approximately tuned, but *Duets And Solos* is arguably his most valuable recording, since it both recalls an earlier age – the format recalls Armstrong and Hines, with rags, stomps, blues and whiskery pop – and sits comfortably in modern sound, with a knowing sagacity as well. Price is fine, and often better than on his own recordings; 12 piano solos fill out spare space on the second disc.

ARNE DOMNÉRUS
Also known as Dompan; born 20 December 1924, Stockholm, Sweden; died 2 September 2008, Stockholm, Sweden
Alto saxophone, clarinet

Jazz At The Pawnshop
Proprius PRCD 9044 / 9058 / 7778 / 7779 4CD/LP/SACD
Domnérus; Bengt Hallberg (p); Lars Erstrand (vib); Georg Riedel (b); Egil Johansen (d). December 1976.

Pastor Kjell Brøgger says: **'I always believed that statement about jazz being the "Devil's music" until I heard Dompan playing in a little church in the north. There was praise and sorrow in it, a real link between the physical and spiritual worlds.'**

The 25-year-old's appearance at the Paris Jazz Fair wakened an interest in Swedish jazz. He honed his technique with the Swedish Radio Big Band, but 'Dompan''s small-group playing, influenced by bop and Scandinavian folk forms, established a reputation that has lasted for almost half a century. On saxophone and clarinet, he is crisp, light-toned and nimble. 'Jazz is Melody, Swing and Vitality', and Dompan's approach marks a shift away from the dominant bop influence of the early '50s in Scandinavia. Early records have him sounding closer to Benny Carter than to Parker in his phrasing, with a wan, meditative quality that frequently refers to diatonic folk themes and hymn tunes. For a time, he performed regularly in 'sacred concerts' that combined jazz and liturgical materials.

Here he is, though, in his most successful setting, a two-day club date recorded *in extenso*, and playing in the best and most sympathetic of company. Remarkably, the original *Jazz At The Pawnshop*, now available complete with the addition of later volumes from the residency, sold more than half a million copies, almost unbelievable for a record of Scandinavian bop. Sticking to the original LP, it kicks off with a rousing version of 'Limehouse Blues' that thanks to Hallberg's altered chords – the pianist is immense throughout – takes on an unexpected new direction. 'Jeep's Blues', 'Take Five', 'Oh, Lady Be Good' and 'Stuffy' suggest that this is a something-for-everyone record and the suggestion isn't unwarranted; one doesn't shift half a million units of hard and noisy abstraction. We are unprepared to criticize *Jazz At The Pawnshop* for popularity, or to imply that it's a lowest common denominator approximation of bop. It is a genuinely fine record. A later 'Mood Indigo' is perhaps the cut-out-and-keep track, but we retain an affection for the very first disc and for most tastes it will suffice.

JAN GARBAREK&

Born 4 March 1947, Mysen, Norway
Tenor and soprano saxophones, other instruments

Dis
ECM 827408-2
Garbarek; Ralph Towner (g, 12-string g); wind hp; brass sextet. December 1976.

Saxophonist Tommy Smith says: **'The wind harp that is featured on *Dis* was perched on the side of a cliff top to allow the wind to penetrate the strings. I love this eerie and haunting sound that captures the true nature of nature without any special effects.'**

Garbarek is one of the best-known, and certainly one of the most easily identified, improvising musicians in the world. His high, keening saxophone, with the familiar ECM reverb, has acquired an international resonance and has exerted as strong an influence on a generation of horn-players (Tommy Smith not least) as Michael Brecker's. If you know it is Garbarek, it will evoke Nordic landscapes; if not, it can suggest anything, desert or tundra, the wastes of Africa or northern steppes, and it's music that has turned up on more than a few wildlife and travel soundtracks. Few artists of his stature have stayed loyal to a single record label throughout their careers, to their mutual benefit. With the release of the early-music project *Officium* in the mid-'90s, Garbarek followed Keith Jarrett into immense crossover success.

Like so many Scandinavian musicians of his generation, Garbarek studied and played with George Russell, was a member of Jarrett's European quartet, and also recorded with Karin Krog. For most of his career, though, he has been a leader, moving into areas remote from jazz at some periods – Nordic vernacular music, early music – but always returning to that spring for refreshment. After a half-dozen albums for ECM, including the beautiful *Afric Pepperbird* and the unexpectedly funky *Witchi-Tai-To*, Garbarek and Ralph Towner, another of the label's stars, created an album that for some sums up the chimerical 'ECM sound'. Few modern jazz records have been as thoroughly plundered for soundtrack cameos as *Dis*. The copyright kickbacks notwithstanding, it's a beautiful album, quintessential Garbarek pitched against a wind harp (recorded at the top of a fjord, with the winds from the North Sea gusting in), guitar and a softly articulated brass ensemble. It established a style which the saxophonist was to return to many times, spells and riddles on soprano saxophone (and wood flute) and a deep, mourning tone that drifts over the rhythm. Hearing it in fragments does little justice to its consistency and thoughtfulness. Though it lacks the obvious apparatus of a jazz record – themes, solos, a 'rhythm section' – it has a powerful improvisatory presence that strikes deep with each fresh approach.

& *See also* **Twelve Moons** (1993; p. 575)

DICK WELLSTOOD
Born 25 November 1927, Greenwich, Connecticut; died 24 July 1987, Palo Alto, California
Piano

A Night In Dublin
Arbors ARCD 19241
Wellstood (p solo). February 1977.

Dick Wellstood said (1979): **'I love them all, but maybe Fats [Waller] is my idol for the way he took so much really terrible material – and in some terrible places – but made something great and grand out of it. That's the jazz musician's art.'**

A witty writer and dry humorist, and Wellstood's early death when still in great form was a loss to the music. A young upholder of swing and mainstream values, he was much prized as band player and accompanist and left a solid legacy of recordings. A jobbing musician who was content to play supper club dates, parties and tribute recordings to great predecessors like Waller, James P. Johnson and Art Tatum, Dick Wellstood is easily underestimated. Always up for a gig though he may have been, he was also a practising lawyer, and his easy, engaging stride approach masks a steel-trap understanding of every wrinkle of piano jazz, an eclecticism that allows him to play in virtually every idiom, from early ragtime to quasi-modal compositions from the shores opposite bop.

    A Night In Dublin is what it says on the box: Dick in an Irish bar, recorded by Ralph O'Callaghan on his then new reel-to-reel tape recorder, the tape sitting on his shelf for the next 23 years until Kenny Davern found it. He does 'Giant Steps' and a Paganini theme, alongside the more familiar 'Carolina Shout' and 'Maple Leaf Rag'; Trane's test-piece, 'Giant Steps', gets taken to the cleaners. Not quite as good as the 1986 *Live At The Sticky Wicket* marathon, but it's not far off, and the sound has been neatly cleaned up.

JAY MCSHANN
Born James Columbus McShann, known as 'Hootie', 12 January 1909, Muskogee, Oklahoma; died 7 December 2006, Kansas City, Missouri
Piano

Last Of The Blue Devils
Koch Jazz 8525
McShann; Joe Newman (t); Paul Quinichette, Buddy Tate (ts); John Scofield (g); Milt Hinton (b); Jack Williams (d). June 1977.

Jay McShann said (1984): **'I didn't start playing the blues because I wanted to play the blues, but because people asked me. I'd play behind Joe Turner and play some blues then, but I'd be doing my own thing at the piano and some one would come up and say "Hey, man, ain't you gonna play no blues tonight?" Wasn't healthy to say no.'**

Historically, McShann's swing band will always be remembered as the incubator for Charlie Parker's raw talent. The orchestra packed a Kansas City punch that stands squarely as second-generation Basie, but McShann as both pianist and bandleader managed to spend his entire career pretty much removed from the evolutions of jazz that were taking place on the two coasts and round the lakes. His brand of boogie-woogie and blues, inspired by James P. Johnson and still more by Pete Johnson, was best suited to solo performance and small groups. The end of the big bands was perhaps the spark for Hootie's own career; otherwise he might have continued to wander the Midwest, playing dance halls.

Last Of The Blue Devils boasts a remarkable line-up and the music more than matches up. One of the problems with the McShann discography is the relatively limited range of tunes and songs, but even familiar things like 'Hootie Blues', which he famously co-wrote with young Charlie Parker, and 'Jumpin' At The Woodside' are as fresh-minted as if they'd just been written on the piano lid. The two tenors give even the lightest of tunes a resonance and warmth and both Tate and Quinichette get off some very fine solos. The surprise in the personnel is, of course, the young Scofield, working on his formidable chops. McShann pays tribute to his greatest influence with a surprisingly gentle stride reading of Pete Johnson's 'Just For You': possibly the highlight of the record.

RON CARTER
Born 4 May 1937, Ferndale, Mississippi
Double bass, piccolo bass, cello

Third Plane
Original Jazz Classics OJCCD 754
Carter; Herbie Hancock (p); Tony Williams (d). July 1977.

Ron Carter says: **'We made this one hour after finishing a trio date for CBS, which was Herbie's label at the time. We'd just come in from Washington, having played a VSOP concert the previous evening.'**

Carter was destined to be a classical cellist, but the racist deafness of the music establishment in Detroit hadn't cleared, even postwar, and as a 17-year-old he switched to the double bass instead. In later years, he would return to his first instrument, notably with Eric Dolphy, but classical music's loss turned out to be jazz's gain. Ron Carter is possibly the most recorded instrumentalist in this book or any of its predecessors: a glance at the index in past editions will make the point. He was a member of the classic Miles Davis quintet and has played in virtually every context between Dixieland and the extreme avant-garde, always bringing the same virtues of dead-centre accuracy, strong sound and lyrical soloing, both plucked and bowed.

Inevitably, Carter hasn't made many records of his own, relative to his enormous discography, but even those who treasure his solos for Dolphy and Miles aren't aware just how many he has produced down the years. Some enthusiasts will point to the early *Where?* with Dolphy or the subsequent *Uptown Conversation* for Atlantic, but for us *Third Plane* is the outstanding document, and an interesting record to set alongside the dull corporate 'supergroup' settings some of these men drifted through in later years. As Carter suggests, these were players at the pinnacle of their careers, but very much working musicians rather than 'jazz stars' and their approach to the set is immaculately professional. There wasn't a big market for acoustic piano trio records in 1977 and some of Williams's drumming suggests a recent diet of fusion music, but the group playing on 'Stella By Starlight' and on Hancock's 'Dolphin Dance' is immaculate. Carter somewhat dominates the sound with his big, beefy fills, but there's musical substance in them all. His place in the music is assured, but it's time for renewed attention to the records he made under his own name. He's still making them.

PAUL BLEY&

Born 10 November 1932, Montreal, Quebec, Canada
Piano

Axis
Improvising Artists 123853
Bley (p solo). July 1977.

Paul Bley said (1980): **'It makes complete sense – in fact, no other situation makes complete sense – for a record company to be run by a musician. Who else would you trust with your music?'**

By the mid-'70s, Bley was documenting his performance at a remarkable rate and his work was turning up on a wide array of labels, including the nascent ECM, which was to play an important part in his working life later on. Bley had established the I.A.I. imprint as a means of controlling both production and distribution of improvised music. It was a relatively chastening experience, as he discovered just how little money rebounded to the artists in what is one of the most exploitative branches of the economy, particularly given how little money is involved in the first place. It is at this point in his career that Bley, having started out with Charles Mingus's quixotic Debut and destined to see most of his work appear on independents like Steeplechase or the very successful ECM, was at his most self-determined. The jut of his jaw on the cover, albeit with an extravagant pipe clamped there, says it all, though it is also a rather quiet and solitary image.

Axis stands somewhat apart in Bley's output. It's a meditative and in some ways rather melancholy set that draws on both familiar material – Carla's 'El Cordobes' – and the much less familiar 'Music Matador', a theme by saxophonist Prince Lasha, a schoolfriend of Ornette Coleman and associate of Eric Dolphy. The opening 'Axis' is introduced inside the piano and develops into an extended improvisation that is one of the richest timbral essays in Bley's catalogue. It's not all abstraction, though. Perhaps the best track of all is a dazzling interpretation of 'Porgy'. An intriguing blend of styles and ideas, but was the piano properly tuned, and why doesn't full personal control over the music prevent the kind of bass buzz that spoils some of Bley's romantic chorales?

& *See also* **Closer** (1965; p. 330), **Not Two, Not One** (1998; p. 624)

BUDDY TATE

Born George Holmes Tate, 22 February 1913, Sherman, Texas; died 10 February 2001, Chandler, Arizona
Tenor saxophone

The Legendary 1977 Encounter
Chiaroscuro 165
Tate; Abdullah Ibrahim (p); Cecil McBee (b); Roy Brooks (d). August 1977.

Buddy Tate said (1978): **'Everyone knew that Basie loved Herschel Evans. It was hard to fit those shoes, but I did my best and Basie always knew when you were trying to please and appreciated it.'**

Tate replaced the late Herschel Evans in the Basie band, which shows how much faith the Count placed in his high-register work. He'd worked with the Clouds Of Joy before that and was later to become a solo artist. He was one of the greatest and most durable of swing tenormen, a major performer for over half a century and a much-loved and amiable man;

but the records under his own name are perhaps a little disappointing in the light of his grand reputation, and his reticent standing as a leader may be the reason why he's never quite secured the wider fame of some of his peers. His great records were made with Basie – whom he joined following Herschel Evans's death in 1939 – and his old friend from the band, Buck Clayton; in 1947, he was still with the band but did some moonlighting in an anonymous ensemble which cut some two dozen sides that are worth listening to.

Our choice of Buddy as leader, though, comes from three decades later, when he had adopted, though not quite adapted to, that 'elder statesman' role that fell on jazz survivors from the great age. For once, Buddy rose to the occasion. The 1977 session was, of course, billed 'Meets Dollar Brand' on first release. It's not clear how much the pianist enjoyed the outing, for he seems to disappear every now and then when Tate is soloing, though instinct suggests out of admiration rather than irritation. The saxophonist seems completely at ease with Ibrahim's 'Doduka Mfundi', but equally the piano-player sounds easy enough on a standard like 'Poor Butterfly', even if the accompaniment on these is pretty skeletal; more Basie, one might say, than Ellington. Tate often seemed to thrive on that, and it's a fine and collectable set which also includes a couple of tracks for just trio, apparently recorded after Buddy had gone.

FRANK FOSTER

23 *Born September 1928, Cincinnati, Ohio*
Tenor saxophone, flute

Well Water

Piadrum 0701
Foster; Sinclair Acey, Cecil Bridgewater, Joe Gardner, Charles Sullivan (t); Bill Lowe, Charles Stevens, Kiane Zawadi (tb); Leroy Barton, C. I. Williams (as, f); Bill Saxton (ts); Doug Harris (ts, f); Bill Cody (ts, f, picc); Mickey Tucker (p); Earl May (b); Elvin Jones (d); Babafume Akunyun (perc). October 1977.

Frank Foster said (1989): **'When I got out of the service I went back to Detroit. I met a friend who I hadn't seen since Cincinnati. "Count Basie is looking for you." "How can he be looking for me? I just got here." I went to find him at the club and asked for an audition. All he said was "I'll be in touch." Then, nothing for two, three months, until one day I got a telegram from Mr Basie with a ticket to New York, one-way. The dream came true!'**

Foster turned to the tenor saxophone to free himself of the all-pervasive influence of Charlie Parker but remained profoundly influenced by bop, even as leader of the Basie band, a role he took over in 1986 after the Count's death, returning to the orchestra he had left in the mid-'60s to go freelance. He carried that torch loyally, even though his saxophone style bore a strong imprint of John Coltrane, and the loyalty probably cost him visibility as a leader and stylist in his own right. Perhaps the only arrangement most listeners associate strongly with him is 'Shiny Stockings'. Notwithstanding, he has a strong solo style, with distinctive, off-centre phrasing and an uncanny ability to lie behind the beat even as he seems to drive it along.

For a guy who worked long and hard in some of the most prestigious company in jazz, Foster didn't have much luck with his own recordings. Having been shelved by Blue Note at the end of the '60s, these 1977 recordings by the Loud Minority Big Band were not released for 30 years. Mystifying, really, since the idiom is really rather advanced (unless that is the explanation), and there are moments when one might almost be listening to a Coltrane ensemble; the unmistakable presence of Elvin Jones adds to that impression. Foster's saxophone sound is broader, less hard-edged, though, and there are distinctive flourishes on Clifford Brown's 'Joy Spring' and the original 'Cecilia Is Love' which give away the leader's identity. He switches to soprano for the closing track, 'Three Card Molly', a bonus quintet cut, but the abiding impression from the main recording date is of a tenor-player who really ought to be mentioned more often among the successful modernists.

ZOOT SIMS

Born John Haley Sims, 29 October 1925, Inglewood, California; died 23 May 1985, New York City
Tenor, alto, soprano and baritone saxophones, voice

If I'm Lucky
Original Jazz Classics OJC 683
Sims; Jimmy Rowles (p); George Mraz (b); Mousie Alexander (d). October 1977.

Zoot Sims said (1980): **'I like to have things written out, but still loose. Same way as I like playing unfamiliar things, just so long as I have them down in mind. I don't want the music to be too arranged that I can't enjoy myself. That's why I play: to enjoy myself.'**

A Californian, and one of Woody Herman's 'Four Brothers' saxophonists in the '40s, Sims continued to play in big-band situations on several tours, but from 1950 was primarily a solo artist who worked in almost countless studio and live situations. One of his most frequent collaborators was fellow tenorman Al Cohn. Instantly recognizable, and among the most consistently inventive and swinging of musicians, Sims was a paradigmatic jazzman. He died of cancer in 1985, having played for as long as he was able.

Like Jack Teagarden, Zoot Sims started out mature and hardly wavered from a plateau of excellence throughout a long and prolific career (oddly enough, Sims's singing voice sounded much like Teagarden's). As one of the 'Four Brothers', he didn't quite secure the early acclaim of Stan Getz, but by the time of these sessions he was completely himself: a rich tone emboldened by a sense of swing which didn't falter at any tempo. He sounded as if he enjoyed every solo, and if he really was much influenced by Lester Young – as was the norm for the 'light' tenors of the day – it was at a far remove in emotional terms.

When Sims signed to Norman Granz's Pablo operation, he wasn't so much at a cross-roads as contentedly strolling down an uneventful path. For a man who could fit effortlessly into any situation he chose – admittedly, he never chose a situation that might cause much trouble – Sims could have spent his final years as a nebulous figure. But his Pablo albums set the seal on his stature, sympathetically produced, thoughtfully programmed and with enough challenge to prod Zoot into his best form.

If I'm Lucky is, narrowly, the pick of the Pablos, though two more albums with the same group – *Warm Tenor* and *For Lady Day* – and an all-Gershwin set with Oscar Peterson and Joe Pass are also good. This one scores high for its ingenious choice of material, for which Rowles has to take the credit. '(I Wonder Where) Our Love Has Gone' counts as one of Sims's most affecting performances and there's uncanny communication between saxophonist and pianist. 'Legs' is a Neal Hefti line and Zoot takes it his own way, untroubled by the sequence but reinventing the melody where it suits him. Harry Warren's 'Shadow Waltz' didn't often get an outing, and it's another superb performance. In fact, the only familiar item on the list is 'You're My Everything', and Zoot glides through it like a man walking along the tideline at sunset. Glorious jazz.

HAMIET BLUIETT &

Born 16 September 1940, Lovejoy, Illinois
Baritone saxophone, alto clarinet

Birthright
India Navigation IN 1030
Bluiett (bs solo). 1977.

Hamiet Bluiett said (1991): **'I fell in love with the instrument at first sight, even before I knew what it sounded like. But I never thought its mission was to mumble in the back row. I thought it should be a lead voice. And when I eventually saw Harry Carney in the flesh, I knew I was right.'**

The baritone saxophone enjoyed a boom in the '50s. Why then? Harry Carney had turned it into a viable solo instrument; there were probably more good ensemble players around, conscious equally of the run-down on paying gigs with big bands and of the attractions of a little solo spotlight; lastly, the prevailing role-models on alto and tenor were, perhaps, a little too dominant. By contrast, no established baritone style developed; Gerry Mulligan was as different from Serge Chaloff as Chaloff was from Pepper Adams; and round the fringes there were players like Sahib Shihab and Nick Brignola doing very different things indeed.

Currently, the situation is much the same. The three most interesting baritonists all play in markedly different styles. The young Amerasian Fred Houn is very much a Carney disciple; Britain's John Surman blows baritone as if it were a scaled-up alto (which by and large it is); Hamiet Bluiett, on the other hand, gives the big horn and his 'double', alto clarinet, a dark, Mephistophelian inflexion, concentrating on their lower registers, but also capable of pushing both horns up to extraordinary heights.

Bluiett settled in with the St Louis Black Artists Group in 1969, and had begun recording on his own account before co-founding the World Saxophone Quartet, which has been his most prominent vehicle. In later years, he experimented with all-clarinet ensembles. Heard unaccompanied at The Kitchen on *Birthright*, he is dark, rootsy and at moments almost unbearably intense. 'In Tribute To Harry Carney' is a deeply personal testimonial, redolent of the blues. The saxophonist's wife Ebu is the dedicatee of a short and heartful song. Other family members, including Hamiet senior, are invoked in 'My Father's House'. Recorded without overdubbing or effects, but with multiple microphones to capture a sense of movement, the playing is hauntingly present, a vocalized sound that never becomes discursive but harks back to the most primitive of music-making and the most sophisticated gestures of the avant-garde.

& See also **WORLD SAXOPHONE QUARTET, W.S.Q.** (1980; p. 456)

AIR

Formed 1971
Group

Air Time
Black Saint 120049
Henry Threadgill (as, ts, f, bf, hubkaphone); Fred Hopkins (b); Steve McCall (d, perc). November 1977.

Henry Threadgill said (1989): **'Everything we had ever listened to went into that group. I hear elements of boogie, gospel, Mexican music, even hillbilly music, the kind of stuff you couldn't get away from on the radio. It's all there, in this "avant-garde" sound.'**

Definitive of the Chicago experimental scene of the '70s, mixing radical free improvisation with the democratic levelling of 'little instruments', Air were capable of riveting live performance, but one suspects the intimate, almost hermetic atmosphere of the studio brought out their most characteristic work. The first-ever gig was a theatre performance of Scott Joplin rags as a basis for improvisation. The group placed great emphasis on tightly co-ordinated ensemble work while exploring freedom and the sonic *terra incognita* represented by Threadgill's alien-sounding automobile accessories.

By the time the masterpiece *Air Time* came along, Air had been performing for more than a half a decade and the music had reached a level of sophistication that would not be surpassed, even after New Air emerged in the '80s. Listening in detail to *Air Time*'s five tracks – two of them very short and one haiku-like piece emerging seamlessly out of 'Subtraction' – helps illuminate the group's language, its vivid exploitation of splintered tempi, deliberately awkward and raucous phrasing, devices from other traditions (Hopkins had studied Burundi musics), and most particularly the use of voiced and pitched percussion. Threadgill's masterly control of apparently wayward lines and McCall's ability to combine forward drive with outbreaks of complete rhythmic anarchy remain the most prominent elements, but as time passes, Hopkins's role becomes ever more obvious. He is often the still centre, but he is also the trickster of the group, frequently spinning off in unpredictable directions.

LOUIE BELLSON

Born Luigi Paulino Alfredo Francisco Antonio Balasoni, 6 July 1924, Rock Falls, Illinois; died 14 February 2009, Los Angeles, California
Drums

Prime Time
Concord CCD 4064
Bellson; Blue Mitchell (t); Pete Christlieb (ts); Ross Tompkins (p); Bob Bain (g); John Williams (b); Emil Richards (perc). November 1977.

Louie Bellson said (1994): **'My father owned the music store, so I learned a little about a lot of instruments. But the only one that really excited me? That was when the parade went by – I must have been about three – and the drums found their way into my head, and stayed there.'**

Bellson was among the last survivors of a breed of tough and tirelessly energetic drummers who powered big bands and small groups alike with showmanship and sheer muscle. Young Louie won a Gene Krupa competition, which established him in line with his great hero. His work with the big-band elite, with Ellington, Goodman, Dorsey, James, gave him a nearly unrivalled experience, and his own groups are marked out by an authority which is often masked by Bellson's comparatively restrained style: virtuoso that he is, he always plays for the band.

In later years Bellson recorded extensively for Concord, though most of the work is now deleted. Later still, he became a living historian of the music, recording *Their Time Was The Greatest* as a tribute to the great jazz timekeepers, and a pair of affectionate albums with Clark Terry, who also represented a link with the past. He had, however, sustained a solid career as a working leader and some of his records from the '70s, otherwise a bleak time for jazz, have staying power. Bellson didn't always successfully resist the temptations of crossover, but did so often enough to leave a decent legacy from the period. *150 MPH* and *Dynamite!* for Concord are worth finding and are now available as a pair, but the best record for the label was *Prime Time*, a pretty much straight-ahead record that starts in great shape with a swinging version of Golson's 'Step Lightly', returns to Benny again in a fine medley that includes 'I Remember Clifford', and hits a peak with a brilliant version of Duke's 'Cotton Tail'. After that, Bain and Richards come in to fill out the band. It doesn't interrupt the flow, but the later material isn't as exciting, with the exception of Gillespie's 'And Then She Stopped'. The saxophonist's composition 'Thrash-In' sounds a warning note and there are a couple of moments of tiresome bombast. Forgivable, really, and nothing that spoils enjoyment of a first-rate modern jazz record, with fine soloing from all the principals.

LOL COXHILL
Born Lowen Coxhill, 19 September 1932, Portsmouth, Hampshire, England
Soprano, tenor and sopranino saxophones

Coxhill On Ogun
Ogun OGCD 008
Coxhill; Michael Garrick (electric p); Veryan Weston (p); Ken Shaw, Richard Wright (g); Dave Green, Paul Mitchell-Davidson (b); Colin Wood (clo); John Mitchell (perc). 1977 & 1978.

Saxophonist Raymond MacDonald remembers: **'Lol arrived in Glasgow sporting a huge orange raincoat and carrying a battered soprano case with his silver horn – repaired with an intricate arrangement of elastic bands – toothbrush and change of clothes crammed inside. Halfway through the gig the awning that was keeping us dry burst. Lol simply went inside and played 'Lover Man'. His musicianship, humble charisma and generosity of spirit drew everyone to him. After the gig, we heard stories of playing with Wilson, Betty and Keppel, Hendrix and the Stones; one night busking on Hungerford Bridge a limousine drew up and Joni Mitchell dropped a coin into his cup ...'**

Most fans are aware that Lol busked on the Thames embankment and many British fans remember him as a drily funny festival MC. His musical quality hasn't always been properly acknowledged. The CV ranges range from Canterbury whimsy to the beginnings of electronica, free jazz and elements of surreal bebop, and there is a large and scattered discography, including some wonderful free sessions on Emanem, but underlying everything is a deep love of standards jazz. Heath Robinson the Coxhill soprano may be, it is also one of the most expressive around.

Coxhill On Ogun is a slight cheat, in that it brings together two LPs, *The Joy Of Paranoia* and *Diverse*, from the later '70s, but it takes in some of his best work. *Joy* began with a live group improvisation recorded in Yorkshire; 'The Wakefield Capers' is the perfect illustration of Lol's ability to play free forms with all the sweetness of Johnny Hodges and little of fellow soprano specialist Steve Lacy's acidulous attack. Accompanied by the three guitars of 'Paws For Thought' – with Mitchell-Davidson on a wibbly bass – he weaves two long, thoughtful solos full of long, bent notes, sliding intervals and melodic ideas that rise up out of nowhere. 'The Cluck Variations' is a collaboration with pianist Weston, quite formally cast but full of anarchic invention. 'The Joy Of Paranoia Waltz' should be played at all wedding receptions just at the moment when new in-laws start to eye one another across the dance floor; it uses inventive overdubs on a simple riff. The clinching joy of the 1978 album is the pair of standards, 'Lover Man' and 'Perdido', played as duets with Michael Garrick. The Tizol tune is a revelation, reinvented wholesale. *Diverse* also appeals, a strong and inventive set consisting of one quartet and a 'solo' piece which has Lol duetting with a loose floorboard at Seven Dials in London.

SCOTT HAMILTON &

Born 12 September 1954, Providence, Rhode Island
Tenor saxophone

From The Beginning
Concord CCD 2117 2CD
Hamilton; Bill Berry (t); Nat Pierce (p); Cal Collins (g); Monty Budwig (b); Jake Hanna (d). March 1977, January 1978.

Concord founder and president Carl Jefferson remembers (1987) meeting Hamilton: **'This young kid in sneakers, with a little moustache and a pint of gin in his pocket. Looked like a character out of Scott Fitzgerald. Played like it, too.'**

He doesn't double on soprano, bass clarinet or flute. He probably doesn't know what multi-phonics are. He has never been described as 'angular', and if he was ever 'influenced by Col-trane' it certainly never extended to his saxophone-playing. And yet Scott Hamilton is the real thing, a tenor-player of the old school who was born only after most of the old school were dead or drawing bus passes. His wuffly delivery but clear tone, containing elements of Bean, Chu, Pres, Byas and Zoot, is definitive of mainstream jazz, and the affection in which Hamilton is held on both sides of the Atlantic is not hard to understand.

Hamilton's Concord debut was called *Is A Good Wind Who Is Blowing Us No Ill*, after Leonard Feather's enthusiastic imprimatur; more of a breath of fresh air in retrospect and one that refocused attention on the undischarged possibilities of pre-bebop jazz. It and the unimaginatively named *Scott Hamilton 2* are brought together on *From The Beginning*. It may seem perverse to select the very first records of an artist who went on to make so many, and still is recording at the highest level, but it's important to register the sheer surprise – shock, even – of hearing a 22-year-old playing this way in 1977. Not since the boy Jesus was found disputing with the Elders ... The opening lines of 'That's All' confirmed that a special new talent was at work. Already Hamilton had the poise and the patience of a much more experienced player. He runs ahead coltishly a couple of times, but his discipline is impressive.

The follow-up was recorded almost immediately afterwards, perhaps too soon in retro-spect. The absence of Berry was unfortunate, and the addition of guitar makes for a rather smoother and less pungent product. For the moment, Hamilton seems content to fall back on predetermined ideas. Though everything on the record is played with exemplary profes-sionalism, it never seems to get beyond that point and remains rather formulaic. After the giddy start, Hamilton took time to regroup and set out on what has been a tireless course.

& See also **Plays Ballads** (1989; p. 529)

JOHNNY MBIZO DYANI &

Born 30 November 1945, East London, South Africa; died 11 July 1986, Berlin, Germany
Double bass

Witchdoctor's Son
Steeplechase SCCD 31098
Dyani; John Tchicai (as, ss); Dudu Pukwana (as, ts); Alfredo Do Nascimento (g); Luiz Carlos De Sequeira (d); Mohamed Al-Jabry (perc). March 1978.

Trumpeter Don Cherry said (1992): **'Johnny was amongst us like a hot wind. He was fierce and strong and that blinded us to how great he was. Then suddenly he was gone, and there was a great emptiness after him.'**

Mbizo was by turns calmly visionary and volcanically angry. More than any of the South African exiles, he absorbed and assimilated a wide variety of styles and procedures. He joined Chris McGregor's Blue Notes in 1962 and came to London with them in 1965. Five years later he settled in Denmark, though he eventually died in Germany. In Scandinavia, he forged close artistic relationships with John Tchicai, Don Cherry and Abdullah Ibrahim. The music is strongly politicized but never programmatic. This and the slightly later *Song For Biko*, also with fellow exile Pukwana but with Don Cherry on cornet, come from Dyani's most consistently inventive period. A lot of the material here is traditional, arranged by Dyani with the horns and bass in mind. 'Ntyilo Ntyilo' is delightful and there are two fine takes of it, along with a couple of other bonuses from the session that suggest this music was conceived fairly tight but with opportunities for Tchicai and Pukwana to take it out and away as they chose. The bassist's own 'M'bizo' is included, and Pukwana brings in his own 'Radebe' (also two takes), which dances. The real showstopper, though, is 'Magwaza', a long improvisation over a springy bass-line that changes with every repetition but never misses its cues. Dyani never played better; less than a decade later, he was gone.

& *See also* **BLUE NOTES, Live in South Africa, 1964** (1964; p. 315)

ISHMAEL WADADA LEO SMITH &
Born 18 December 1941, Leland, Mississippi
Trumpet

Divine Love
ECM 529126-2
Smith; Lester Bowie, Kenny Wheeler (t); Dwight Andrews (af, bcl, ts, perc); Bobby Naughton (vib, mar, perc); Charlie Haden (b). September 1978.

Wadada Leo Smith says: **'*Divine Love* ... was the hardest of all my music to record. Why? Because the composition has multiple paths along which to construct each instrumental line, with the opening and closing sections being improvised.'**

One of the few practising Rastafarians in jazz music, Smith joined the AACM community as a young man and subsequently formed the Creative Construction Company, an innovative trio with Anthony Braxton and Leroy Jenkins. Neither it nor his later group New Dalta Ahkri has ever received the attention due to it but Smith has enjoyed a resurgence in recent years, playing in a variety of creative contexts and making a parallel career with guitarist Henry Kaiser as a member of the tribute/re-creation group Yo! Miles.
    Since the '70s Smith has organized his music according to the principles of 'rhythm-units', which seem to call for a mystical equivalence of sound and silence, and of 'ahkre-anvention', a method of notating improvised music. 'Tastalun' on *Divine Love* is the first of these pieces Smith had an opportunity to record, three muted trumpets weaving an extraor-dinary extended spell. So closely integrated is the playing by Smith and guests Wheeler and Bowie that it is probably pointless trying to sort out who is playing which line. The basic group, on both this record and the one below, is Smith with Naughton and Andrews. *Divine Love* opens on a long meditation for alto flute, Andrews at his atmospheric best, before Smith's tight, compressed sound comes through. The title-piece is another of his ritual works. Naughton's vibes are a key element on this record, not least because there is no conventional percussion part. He opens the last track pitched against Charlie Haden's bass, marking the pauses that constitute the work's stately rhythm unit. Andrews's bass clarinet intones ancient wisdoms while Smith sounds elevated, rapt, almost tranced.

& *See also* **Golden Quartet** (2000; p. 647)

JOHNNY GRIFFIN &

Born 24 April 1928, Chicago, Illinois; died 25 July 2008, Availles-Limouzine, France
Tenor saxophone

Return Of The Griffin
Original Jazz Classics OJCCD 1882
Griffin; Ronnie Mathews (p); Ray Drummond (b); Keith Copeland (d). October 1978.

Johnny Griffin said (1989): **'My record company told me to go to Europe to promote the music, and I was saying: "Why? What's there for me?" But when I went I realized that jazz was more appreciated by Europeans than by Americans – it's true! – and that there was already a jazz family there. It kept me working and it kept me away from the so-called avant-garde. I liked those guys, but I didn't appreciate the shit they played.'**

Griffin returned to the US without ever really having been away. The 1978 album was the product of his first visit since 1963, during which time he had become a favourite in Scandinavia, working steadily but recording virtually nothing under his own name. With the avant-garde in the ascendant and then fusion capturing the middle of the market, his style of playing had been at something of a discount for a time. To a new generation of fans, who'd come along towards the end of the '60s, if they hadn't already been programmed by rock, he might well have seemed the kind of mythological beast that graces the cover of *Return*. But the tide was turning slowly for jazz and the Galaxy recordings – this one and the subsequent *Bush Dance* – were explicitly intended to revive his fortunes, much as Dexter Gordon's had been earlier. Griff recorded *A Little New York Midtown Music* with Nat Adderley in September, played with Dexter Gordon at Carnegie Hall (*Great Encounters*) and a few weeks later was in the Fantasy studio in Berkeley to make the comeback record.

It kicks off with an 'Autumn Leaves' that has a distinct spring in its step and it's immediately obvious that Mathews is a key player, bright and responsive, and by no means put off by Griffin's hustle. The standard is deftly repositioned, with a slightly altered melody statement, which delivers a wry ambiguity. 'A Monk's Dream' is a fine original, and 'The Way It Is' suggests Griffin has been listening to some of the newer stuff and is prepared to go this far at least in the direction of jazz-funk. Copeland has never been a highly regarded player, except by other musicians, but here he's a revelation, strong, determined and always in the service of the song. 'Fifty-Six' is another nice blowing line, and it plays out on a fairly routine 'I Should Care', with the drummer in the saddle. It's not so much an anti-climax as a promise that Griffin was back and had energy in reserve.

& *See also* **A Blowing Session** (1957; p. 209)

CHET BAKER &

Born 23 December 1929, Yale, Oklahoma; died 13 May 1988, Amsterdam, Netherlands
Trumpet, voice

Live At Nick's
Criss Cross Jazz 1027
Baker; Phil Markowitz (p); Scott Lee (b); Jeff Brillinger (d). November 1978.

Gerry Mulligan said (1990): **'I never knew a musician who was so unafraid to take risks. He thought – that's the wrong word; he just did it – so quickly that mistakes just became part of the idea.'**

Demonstrating that there are second acts in American lives, Baker came through all his vicissitudes more or less intact. He had to develop a new embouchure after the loss of his teeth in a beating and he had a habit to sustain. Apparently, he owed dealers money and they exacted revenge. For the remainder of his life, Chet was a damaged vessel, someone one watched with a kind of fascinated horror, but listened to with a kind of awe. As the outer shell shrank, the inner man – the Oklahoman boy with the innate genius for music – remained true and pure.

Sceptics will tell you that Baker did nothing but sing falteringly and play 'My Funny Valentine' for the last 20 years of his life. It isn't so. His records for Criss Cross are distinguished by a notably fresh choice of material. Richie Beirach's 'Broken Wing' was written specially for Chet, but the long version of Wayne Shorter's 'Beautiful Black Eyes' is the product of an unexpected enthusiasm that fed the trumpeter with new and untried material. Markowitz is a responsive accompanist and merits his 'featured' billing on the sleeve. The Shorter track is by far the longest thing on the session, though two CD bonuses, the standards 'I Remember You' and 'Love For Sale', are both over ten minutes. Gerry Teekens is too sophisticated and demanding a producer to have settled for just another ballad album and, with the exception of the last two tracks, this is extremely well modulated, and one of the later Chet records that should be considered essential.

& See also **Chet Baker And Crew** (1956; p. 176), **Blues For A Reason** (1984; p. 488)

HORACE PARLAN
Born 13 January 1931, Pittsburgh, Pennsylvania
Piano

Blue Parlan
Steeplechase SCCD 31124
Parlan; Wilbur Little (b); Dannie Richmond (d). November 1978.

Horace Parlan said (1988): **'There were a lot of reasons for leaving America. Rock music was all that was being recorded, it seemed, and violence, especially racial violence, was on the increase. I was mugged, more than once. I won't be the first to say that in Scandinavia jazz music and jazz musicians are treated with respect and admiration. Not such a hard decision!'**

Horace overcame physical handicap – a polio-damaged right hand – to make a career. His blues-based playing, influenced by both Bud Powell and Ahmad Jamal, is solidity incarnate. He worked with Mingus and recorded for Blue Note (though these are only now available in a Mosaic box), but like other American players of the time, facing a slackening demand for jazz recording, he emigrated to Scandinavia, which he had visited on tour with Miriam Makeba. Once established there, he pursued a workmanlike and unspectacular career, documented by Steeplechase from *Arrival* onwards with almost redundant thoroughness, although the sequence ends in the '80s. The only high-spots that call for separate treatment are the very fine 1978 trio with Wilbur Little and Dannie Richmond (also, of course, a Mingus man) and the much later *Glad I Found You*, where Parlan and the late Thad Jones shrug off a rather diffident setting to produce some sparkling performances.

Blue Parlan takes a walk through some significant chapters in his earlier life, opening with 'Goodbye Pork Pie Hat' and including Jamal's 'Night Mist Blues'. There's also a Cedar Walton composition and a line from Frank Strozier, so this isn't just another run of the mill blues date but a carefully thought-out package that has a clear internal logic. Not much from the leader in writing terms, just one modestly ambitious blues outline, but some cracklingly good playing and rock-solid support from the bass and drums. Steeplechase's loyalties sometimes stretched past any obvious utility, but steady documentation did sometimes throw up sets of this quality. Thirty years on, it's still a vigorous performance.

LOUIS MOHOLO(-MOHOLO) &

Born 10 March 1940, Cape Town, South Africa
Drums

Spirits Rejoice! / Bra Louis – Bra Tebs

Ogun OGCD 017 / 018 2CD
Moholo; Claude Deppa, Kenny Wheeler (t); Nick Evans, Radu Malfatti (tb); Jason Yarde (ss, as); Toby Delius, Evan Parker (ts); Pule Pheto, Keith Tippett (p); Johnny Dyani, Roberto Bellatella, Harry Miller (b); Francine Luce (v). 1978, 1995.

Ogun founder Hazel Miller says: **'Louis is the sole (soul?) survivor of the original Blue Notes, back home at last, and still carrying the flame of this marvellous music.'**

As a young man Moholo-Moholo led a group called The Cordettes and won the drum prize at the Johannesburg Jazz Festival in 1962. On the strength of his performance he was invited by pianist Chris McGregor to join the Blue Notes, who left the Cape for Europe in 1964, eventually settling in London.

He continued to work with McGregor's Brotherhood Of Breath but also formed his own Spirits Rejoice and Viva La Black. At the end of apartheid he returned to South Africa, where he is an honoured figure and an inspirational teacher. More than most of the South African exiles active on the jazz scene in Britain Moholo was able to make the transition between time-playing and free drumming without undue strain. His own bands have always contained free or abstract elements, and Moholo has always been in demand as a more experimental improviser, where his drive and intensity are comparable to those of Americans Milford Graves, Sunny Murray and Andrew Cyrille.

Pianist Pule Pheto is an often forgotten connecting figure between Moholo's earlier and later work, a fine rhythmic player with his own idiosyncratic harmonic language. He made a fine piano/drums duet record with Moholo but also appears on the early *Bush Fire!* and returns on *Bra Louis – Bra Tebs*, which is now reissued with the earlier *Spirits Rejoice!* It's an invigorating pairing, showing how Moholo's music continued to evolve from the free interpretations of township jazz on the first disc to something much more sophisticated, but still darkly funky, on the second. There's some relatively straight-ahead stuff on 'Amaxesha Osizi' but Dyani's 'Ithi-gqi' belies its glorious sauntering line with a fearsome line from Parker. Mongezi Feza's 'You Ain't Gonna Know Me, 'Cos You Think You Know Me' is a tender reminiscence of the departed trumpeter's brilliance. It ends on a traditional 'Wedding Hymn'. On the later record, Deppa, Yarde and Delius aren't yet players with the range and subtlety of their seniors, but they play with admirable concentration. The unifying factors are Moholo's formidable metrics and elemental passion, one of the defining sounds of modern jazz.

& *See also* **BLUE NOTES, Live In South Africa, 1964** (1964; p. 315)

JACK DEJOHNETTE

Born 9 August 1942, Chicago, Illinois
Drums, percussion, piano

Special Edition

ECM 827694-2
DeJohnette; David Murray (ts, bcl); Arthur Blythe (as); Peter Warren (b, clo). March 1979.

Saxophonist and sometime duo partner John Surman says: **'Jack has boundless curiosity. Every time I meet him to play he has some new piece of percussion equipment in his** drum kit and is constantly working with drum and cymbal companies to change the sound of the instrument.'

What sets this extraordinary musician apart from the common run isn't the sheer bulk of his output but its vivid musicality. Everything he does is marked with intelligence, controlled fire and an enviable instinct for both texture and form. An early album, *The DeJohnette Complex*, was recorded a mere month after his first studio date with Miles Davis, for whom he played on *Bitches Brew*, having played with Coltrane and Jackie McLean. DeJohnette studied classical piano as a child and is still a formidable keyboard-player, as witness his *Piano Album*. However, it is as a drummer that most listeners know him, and the same values apply there; his time sense is completely instinctive, but one feels him playing melodically rather than motorically or even metrically. The pulse is everything, but DeJohnette also has something of Sunny Murray's ability to make the kit (which he varies to need) sound like a single instrument.

Remarkably, *Special Edition* was something like DeJohnette's twelfth album, but for some reason – perhaps owing to the rather functional titles: *Album, Album* or *Piano Album* – they never seemed to establish a strong market presence. The group here could hardly have been bettered at the time: Black Arthur Blythe at his most soulful, David Murray in staggeringly good form on bass clarinet for the opening 'One For Eric'. DeJohnette plays piano where needed, and on 'Zoot Suite' makes a great case for melodica as a convincing improviser's instrument; it's a delightful line and a perfect illustration of Jack's ability to make a straight-four beat sound much richer and more complex. Coltrane's 'Central Park West', on which the composer did not solo, gets a suitably quiet and almost elegiac treatment, Murray again superb on bass clarinet. 'Journey To The Twin Planet' is a freely improvised piece round a basic freebop idea, but it also points forward to DeJohnette's spiritual music of the '90s and '00s, by which time it had lost its rough exterior, but also much of its affirmative energy. Make no mistake, this is a great jazz record, not merely a Buggins' turn for the drummer.

SAL MOSCA
Born 27 April 1927, Mount Vernon, New York; died 28 July 2007, White Plains, New York
Piano

A Concert
Jazz Records JR-8
Mosca (p solo). June 1979.

Sal Mosca said (1982): **'Lennie [Tristano] was also pushing [Svatislav] Richter records at me. He dug Richter. I liked a more romantic sound, like [Vladimir] Horowitz. I heard this one Horowitz record, playing Mozart, and it sounded like Harlem stride! He used to go see Tatum – Horowitz, that is, not Mozart! – did you know that?'**

In keeping with the Tristano spirit, Mosca shunned the limelight and regarded jazz as a spiritual avocation rather than a day-job. Having studied with the master for nearly a decade, Mosca became in turn a devoted teacher, just another thing that kept him away from the clubs, though he did briefly play with Charlie Parker and other first-generation beboppers. Like Glenn Gould, he preferred the hermetic atmosphere of the recording studio, though he declined most contractual blandishments. This monastic existence denied the world a fleet, accurate, complex player, whose solos were far from without feeling.

Belatedly released in 1990, *A Concert* is a rare example of one of the leading followers of Lennie Tristano in a solo situation, and in front of an enthusiastic audience who clearly share a sense of occasion. Because Mosca has made so few recordings, his appearances always seem eventful and, despite the dour atmosphere of the CD – which settles for the grimmest monochrome packaging and presentation, a characteristic refusal to distract from the music's inner qualities – it is played electrically. Though most of the tunes are 'originals', they usually follow the standard Tristano-ite practice of an abstruse variation on a standard. Mosca's approach is formidably varied, both from piece to piece and within individual treatments. 'Co-Play', which starts as a relatively simple variation on 'Sweet And Lovely', becomes a labyrinthine investigation of the properties of the song, and 'That Time' turns 'That Old Feeling' into a fantasy on a number of kinds of jazz rhythm. Sometimes he plays it straight, but unexpectedly so: 'Prelude To A Kiss' has voicings more dense than in any authentic Ellington version. Always he is prodigiously inventive: while the music sometimes takes on a painstaking quality, Mosca's spontaneity is genuine enough to pack the programme with surprises.

JEANNE LEE

Born 29 January 1939, New York City; died 25 October 2000, Tijuana, Mexico
Voice

Freedom Of The Universe

Birth LP 030
Lee; Gunter Hampel (bcl, vib, etc). 1979.

Gunter Hampel says: **'In 1980, Jeanne and I had a duo concert in East Berlin: a huge, excited audience – encores. Our children Ruomi and Cavana played hide and seek with their favourite *Muppet Show* guest artist Dizzy Gillespie in the dressing room. When we left the stage to make room for Dizzy's band he smilingly blocked our way and said: "You are continuing *our music* beyond our *horizons*!" He then hugged us, blew a fanfare, and talked so long he almost forgot he had his own concert to do.'**

Lee was a dance student at Bard College when she met pianist Ran Blake and formed a duo partnership with him. Their 1961 record *The Newest Sound Around*, mostly recorded in slow rhythms, documents her very accurate singing and boldness with a lyric, but was perhaps more important to Blake's development as a composer fascinated by hymn tunes, movie music and the Third Stream. Lee married the German multi-instrumentalist Gunter Hampel and made many records with him, starting with a key 1969 performance that also involved Anthony Braxton.

The duo record, made in Woodstock and New York, is the high-point of their creative relationship. They did not perform songs, as such, but what might almost be esperantist messages from another civilization, little snatches of ethereal grace. Hampel's musicianship is entirely *sui generis* and as such considerably underrated, but it is Lee's unique voice, floating almost magically up and down the scale, in and out of focus as far as strict semantic logic is concerned, that makes this record and indeed any that involved her, so special. So little of her work survives in commercial form that a major reassessment is now long overdue.

RAYMOND BURKE

Born 6 June 1904, New Orleans, Louisiana; died 21 March 1986, New Orleans, Louisiana
Clarinet

Raymond Burke And Cie Frazier With Butch Thompson In New Orleans

504 CDS 27
Burke; Butch Thompson (p); Cie Frazier (d). August 1979.

Dr Sal Bridger met Raymond Burke before his death and quoted him as saying: **'Grew up in N'Orleans, had my place here, my friends and my clarinet. Never felt any need to go work in Chicago, any place like that.'**

Burke played home-made instruments as a boy, and worked in New Orleans for most of his life, through revivalism and beyond. His clarinet-playing stands squarely in the line of the New Orleans masters: he had the sweet-toned delivery of Willie Humphrey but could be as elaborate and blues-inflected as Johnny Dodds when he wished. An American Music issue of Burke's Speakeasy Boys and other personnels is really for scholars only. Most of the tracks come from 1949 acetates (they turned up in a New Orleans flea market in 1993) by a band from which Burke stands out; Wooden Joe Nicholas is weak and Joe Avery's trombone is so inept even the liner-notes describe his sound as 'ratty'. The loudest person in these terrible transfers is guitarist Johnny St Cyr! The other tracks are even more obscure: a couple of duets with pianist Woodrow Rousell, and a few things with the Hartman and Cass bands (personnels unknown).

Burke made it through the revivalist period and was still playing and playing well in his mid-70s. This 504 record is more like the way Burke should be remembered, his understated delivery the mark of a man whose unassuming approach to his art has helped it endure. The music is nothing much: a battery of tunes, played at more or less the same tempo, with Frazier marking out a steady pulse and Thompson comping and taking easy-going solos. Some are New Orleans rarities like A. J. Piron's 'I Want Somebody To Love', 'Gypsy Love Song' and 'Oh Daddy'. On a hot day, with a julep to hand, this can sound like the very heart of jazz.

STEVE SWALLOW

Born 4 October 1940, Fair Lawn, New Jersey
Bass guitar

Home

ECM 513424-2
Swallow; David Liebman (ss, ts); Steve Kuhn (p); Lyle Mays (syn); Bob Moses (d); Sheila Jordan (v). September 1979.

Steve Swallow says: **'In the mid-'70s I was struck by writer's block. To circumvent it I taped several poems by Robert Creeley to my upright piano and stared at them for hours. Inevitably, they suggested musical phrases and provoked the songs on *Home*. Recently I found myself similarly afflicted, and turned once again to Bob Creeley. For a second time, his poems worked to loosen the dreaded block's hold, resulting in the album *So There*.'**

Swallow is one of the most accomplished bassists of recent times, and a bass guitar specialist who invests that instrument with real individuality. A generous spirit, he has often sublimated his own musical vision in the service of others, not least his partner Carla Bley, and when he does record, the results are musicianly and thoughtful, but sometimes suggest he's not that bothered about them, preferring other dimensions of the business.

Swallow's earliest showings were with Paul Bley and Jimmy Giuffre, but he then worked with Stan Getz and Gary Burton for the remainder of the '60s, spending some time in California before returning east and switching from double bass to bass guitar as his sole instrument. Though he does nothing so crass as to play 'lead bass', Swallow's light intense sound is always prominent in an ensemble, favouring upscale lines and arresting melodic interventions.

Robert Creeley's poems are tiny snapshots of ordinariness that deliver their meanings precisely and without embellishment. Much the way Swallow plays. On first hearing we wondered whether there was too much going on in these arrangements, and whether it mightn't have been more effective to deliver the songs with just voice, bass and piano, but their scoring never overpowers, Liebman's playing is judged to perfection and Mays and Moses, both capable of wayward moments, help create a background for 'Nowhere One', 'In the Fall', 'Midnight' and the others which has just the right blend of sunlight and shade, ordinariness, and a sense of some existential slippage and loss. A quiet, glorious album.

ARTHUR BLYTHE

Also known as Black Arthur; born 5 July 1940, Los Angeles, California
Alto saxophone

Lenox Avenue Breakdown

Koch KOC CD 7871
Blythe; Bob Stewart (tba); James Newton (f); James Blood Ulmer (g); Cecil McBee (b); Jack DeJohnette (d); Guilherme Franco (perc). 1979.

Arthur Blythe said (1989): **'Columbia were looking for something different, but not too different, something they could sell. I insisted on making the kind of music I wanted, but with the promise that it wasn't going to be too out there. It was a relationship. It went to and fro.'**

Blythe was raised in San Diego, but moved back to his native LA at the beginning of the '60s and became involved with visionary pianist/composer Horace Tapscott. Blythe worked with Chico Hamilton, Gil Evans and others and only began his own recording career when he was nearly 40. Columbia records attempted to groom him for stardom, but Blythe's avant-gardism, which combined elements of post-bop jazz conveying the passionate immediacy of the early pioneers with elements of non-Western harmony and rhythm, was muted. Blythe has always experimented with the sound of the basic jazz group, reintroducing the tuba as a bass instrument and often using non-kit percussion. He was an erratic presence, unwilling to surrender his most radical ideas, but also desperately searching for wider recognition.

In 1979, Blythe signed with Columbia and produced what became one of the master-pieces of modern jazz. *Lenox Avenue Breakdown* is a superlative piece of imaginative instrumentation, similar in sound to a fine earlier India Navigation live set, but with the lighter and more complex sound of James Newton's flute backing the leader's extraordinary blues wail. There is scarcely a flat moment on the album, despite all four pieces being built round relatively static and repetitive ideas. Stewart's long solo on the title-piece is one of the few genuinely important tuba statements in jazz, a nimble sermon that promises storms and sunshine. McBee has his moment on 'Slidin' Through', and Blythe himself saves his main contribution for the final track, the Eastern-sounding 'Odessa', on which he cries like a *muezzin*, a *cantor* and a storefront Salvationist, all in one impeccably structured arc. DeJohnette came of age with this record, playing with fire and authority, and with the sophisticated understanding of how rhythm and melody can combine. His own *Special Edition*, which included Blythe, was recorded the same year. His work behind Blythe on that final track deserves the closest attention. The other key element to the sound is Ulmer, who in those days was also moving comfortably between 'inside' and 'outside' projects. There were more fine albums to come, but then Blythe's wind went, and he seemed lost. Much of his work in intervening years was in a pop vein, a watered-down version of the deep, urban groove he found on this great record and would rediscover in due course.

BETTY CARTER &

Born Lillie Mae Jones, 16 May 1930 (some sources give 1929), Flint, Michigan; died 26 September 1998,
Brooklyn, New York
Voice

The Audience With Betty Carter
Verve 835684 2CD
Carter; John Hicks (p); Curtis Lundy (b); Kenny Washington (d). December 1979.

Betty Carter said (1995): '"Jazz" isn't a word that opens any doors. The business people
don't hear it knock and just hope it will go away. But me, I've got my foot in the door, and
as long as I'm here, it stays open.'

Carter could sound becalmed in a studio. The title here is double-edged, because she needed
a crowd to bounce off. Over a decade on from the comeback *Inside Betty Carter*, she works
the room with consummate skill, sliding from the slightly squeaky *faux naïf* mannerisms
that prompted Hampton to call her 'Betty Bebop' (after cartoon character Betty Boop) to
soaring climbs up off the bottom that wouldn't disgrace Sarah Vaughan. It's a long album
and one that requires a bit of time spent on it. The opening piece, 'Sound (Movin' On)', is a
staggering 25 minutes in length. 'The Trolley Song' is an orthodox swinger, but who else
would have thought of handling Carlos Garnett's 'Caribbean Sun' in this way, and who else
is capable of giving 'Everything I Have Is Yours' a drench of irony? The pace changes on disc
two and one's first instinct might be that Carter has run out of steam. Emphatically not so.
'Can't We Talk It Over?' medleyed with 'Either It's Over Or It Isn't' and later 'Spring Can
Really Hang You Up The Most' are remarkable (re)inventions, subtle and deeply coded.

& *See also* **Finally** (1969; p. 372)

MAX ROACH &

Born 10 January 1924, New Land, North Carolina; died 16 August 2007, New York City
Drums

Historic Concerts
Soul Note 121100 2CD
Roach; Cecil Taylor (p). December 1979.

Cecil Taylor said (1998): 'It was a phenomenon, playing with Mr Roach in front of all those
people. Ten thousand of them listening to two of us. It was as if two angry prophets had
finally managed to get together a crowd. We maybe wondered for a moment whether it
would be more eloquent to stay quiet!'

At the end of the '70s, Roach recorded a number of duet concerts and sessions with saxophonist Anthony Braxton and with pianists Abdullah Ibrahim and Cecil Taylor. They are,
inevitably, mixed in quality. The duos with Braxton, for instance, often sound still and
combative rather than dialectical. By contrast, the summit with Taylor, recorded at the
McMillin Theater at Columbia University, is still exhilarating. Both men warm up in their
respective corners, before launching into a huge, 40-minute fantasy that sees neither surrendering a whit of individuality. As was noted at the time, it was the perfect occasion to
test the cliché about Roach the melodic percussionist and Taylor the percussive pianist
and, like all successful sound-bites, it proves to be both helpful and misleading. For much
of the opening duet, Roach fulfils a conventional drummer's role, sustaining a time-feel,
accelerating and arresting the pace of development, filling and embellishing; it is Taylor
who creates the grandly insane melodies that spring away for whole minutes at a time.

The second segment unravels more than a little, and there are symptoms of weariness in Roach's soloing. A recorded interview with the participants makes this a valuable historical document.

& See also **Alone Together** (1956–1960; p. 191), **We Insist! Freedom Now Suite** (1960; p. 258)

GEORGE E. LEWIS *&*

Born 14 July 1952, Chicago, Illinois
Trombones, sousaphone, tuba, computer

Homage To Charles Parker

Black Saint 120029
Lewis; Roscoe Mitchell (as, ss, bs, cassette recorder); Douglas Ewart (cl, bcl, sno, f, bsn, cassette recorder, perc); Muhal Richard Abrams, Anthony Davis (p); Richard Teitelbaum (syn); Leroy Jenkins (vn, vla); Abdul Wadud (clo). 1979.

George E. Lewis says: **'We were doing Afro/Euro-American experimentalism. In *Homage*, minimalism, electronics and Coltrane's *Peace On Earth* got remixed into a kind of fragility, and that Feldman-like grid for "Blues" showed that bodies and histories are what really matter. However it looked on paper, if you didn't know the blues you couldn't play it.'**

Lewis taught himself improvisation while still in his early teens by transcribing Lester Young solos for trombone. He later studied formally at Yale, but his real musical education was with the Association for the Advancement of Creative Musicians, whose ethos and aesthetics have remained with him and whose historian he has subsequently become. Growing up in a period marked by the dominance of the saxophone, he continued to take saxophone-players as his primary models; close association with Anthony Braxton, Douglas Ewart, Roscoe Mitchell and other AACM members probably reinforced that influence. His singing *legato* is still reminiscent of Pres, but also of virtually all the evolutionary stages of John Coltrane's style. Lewis habitually plays either with intense and surprisingly gentle lyricism or with a deconstructive fury. In his free improvisations, Lewis often dismantled his horn to get at new sound-colours locked away in its component parts, and this interest in sound beyond conventional instrumental sound led him to experiment with computers, and increasingly with interactive cyber-technology like his own Voyager system.

Lewis's recording career began in the mid-'70s with a *Solo Trombone Album* on the Sackville label and participation in some of Anthony Braxton's most adventurous early projects. But he was already interested in the possibilities of electronic and computer sound and these came together with impressive coherence on 'Blues' and 'Homage To Charles Parker', the two halves of Lewis's most important recording till the '90s. The music extends and synthesizes elements Lewis had been exploring for some years, combining improvisation with predetermined structures in a completely relaxed and confident way, but also reintroducing a strong programmatic element to otherwise abstract music. 'Blues' consists of four independent diatonic 'choruses' of absolute simplicity which are played in shifting configurations by the four musicians. Despite the fact that there are no conventional resolutions and no predictable coincidence of material, the piece evokes order as much as freedom. Although none of the material conforms to the blues, its 'feel' is unmistakable and authentic. If 'Blues' is a triumphant extension of the black tradition in music, 'Homage To Charles Parker' concerns itself intimately with the saxophonist's putative afterlife and musical real-presence. There is a long opening section on electronics, synthesizers and cymbals which evokes Parker's 'reality'. It gradually yields place to a series of apparently discontinuous solos on saxophone, piano and finally with no ensemble backing beyond the synthesizer sounds, which recast and project Parker's life and language. There are no explicit bebop references and, indeed, the piece seems to serve as a healing response to the fractures that separated bop from the earlier history of black American music, of which it was also the apotheosis. The music is calm and almost stately, occasionally suggesting a chorale. Lewis's concluding statements are both unbearably plangent and forcefully intelligent. In their refusal of tragedy, they also have to be seen as political statements.

& See also **Endless Shout** (1997; p. 619)

ARCHIE SHEPP&
Born 24 May 1937, Fort Lauderdale, Florida
Tenor, soprano and alto saxophones, piano

Looking At Bird
Steeplechase SCCD 31149
Shepp; Niels-Henning Ørsted Pedersen (b). February 1980.

Archie Shepp said (1982): **'As a man, Bird still belongs to the prehistory of our music. In some respects his social situation was further removed than Louis Armstrong's was, however radical his music seemed to be.'**

Shepp prefers to consider bebop as the baroque period of African-American classical music. Given the brutal accretions of his approach, it's an accurate but still slightly misleading designation. His Parker readings are irregular pearls with a raw, slightly meretricious beauty. In the past, we questioned their standing as serious examinations of the tradition but these interpretations stand up well and their prettiness doesn't in any way deaden the importance of Shepp's approach, which is always contentious, whatever the context. What's immediately clear is that Shepp – somewhat like Miles Davis – isn't a natural bopper and he sounds curiously uneasy playing the main themes of 'Ornithology' and 'Yardbird Suite', as if they really were ancient survivals of a forgotten language. However, he does explore them more thoroughly than we were previously minded to admit. There is a rather better version of 'Now's The Time' on the later *I Didn't Know About You*. The great NHØP cut his teeth on this repertoire and sounds completely at home with it, bouncing and singing through a more or less predictable roster of bebop anthems.

& See also **Four For Trane** (1964; p. 306), **Attica Blues** (1972; p. 391)

WORLD SAXOPHONE QUARTET
Formed 1977
Group

W.S.Q.
Black Saint 120046
Hamiet Bluiett (bs, f, af, acl); Julius Hemphill (f, ss, as); Oliver Lake (ss, ts, as, f); David Murray (ts, bcl). March 1980.

David Murray said (1992): **'I sometimes thought of it as a vocal group, like some street corner, old-town, doo-wop kind of thing, with myself as the lead tenor – in my dreams, anyhow.'**

No permutation of instruments can be more sheerly tedious than four saxophones together. Good saxophone quartets are rare; great ones can be counted on the fingers of one hand.

The level of musicianship rises exponentially when saxes are exposed in this way. A band section can muddle through pretty much together. In front of a supportive rhythm section, a single horn or pair of horns can cover up shortcomings that are ruthlessly exposed when four are put together with no other input. For as many years as anyone cares to remember, the World Saxophone Quartet has been the market-leader, rivalled only at the avant-garde end of the spectrum by ROVA.

Jaw-dropping in a club or concert situation, WSQ have often been slightly less compelling on record, but there are exceptions and the group's ability to follow complex changes without a harmony instrument and to swing mightily without a bass or percussion lead is highly impressive whatever the medium.

The debut album (also Black Saint) was not particularly well recorded but it helped establish the group's identity as adventurous composer/improvisers who could offer great swinging ensembles and remarkable duo and trio divisions of the basic instrumentation. The armoury of reeds was pretty modest to begin with, but increasingly after 1978 all four members began to 'double' on more exotic specimens, with Bluiett's alto clarinet and Murray's bass clarinet both lending significant variations of tonality and texture. The baritonist always likes to play towards the top end of his range and this frees the group of the whumping 'bass' that afflicts many sax quartets. 'Scared Sheetless' from the first album gives a fair impression of its not altogether serious appropriation of free-jazz devices. 'R&B' on the second album plays with genre in a friendlier and more ironic way.

The best of the earlier records, *W.S.Q.* is dominated by a long suite that blends jazz and popular elements with considerable ingenuity and real improvisational fire. 'The Key' and 'Ballad For Eddie Jefferson' are perhaps the most enjoyable elements, but Hemphill's distinctive 'Plainsong' and 'Connections' confirmed his standing as the group's main composer, the closing 'Fast Life' (a nice parallel to what Murray was doing under his own name at the time) is as fine a curtain-piece as the group has recorded.

CLARK TERRY &

Born 14 December 1920, St Louis, Missouri
Trumpet, flugelhorn

Memories Of Duke
Original Jazz Classics OJCCD 604
Terry; Joe Pass (g); Jack Wilson (p); Ray Brown (b); Frank Severino (d). March 1980.

Clark Terry says: **'Duke came to see me in my hotel in Chicago when I was still working with Basie – he'd been scouting me around for a time – and when he got out of the elevator, [Basie's guitar-player] Freddie Green opened the door to his room just opposite the elevator and just said: "Uh, oh" and closed his door. Nothing more was said, but that night on the stand, he came up to me and kind of looked off in the distance and said: "Man, you be a fool if you *don't*!" And that's how I came to work for Duke Ellington.'**

An obvious bit of curation, really, but exquisitely done, and one of Terry's best records of later years. The flugelhorn, which he picked up as a main improvising voice while working in the Ellington band, is ripe but exact, and Terry's familiarity with the material is pretty obvious, even if some of these pieces weren't associated with him at the time. Apart from the leader, the revelation of the date is Jack Wilson, a pianist who without indulging in Ducal mannerisms manages to convey some essence of the great man's small groups. There's an easy, never florid quality to his accompaniments and on every track he delivers the architecture of the song in blueprint form, unadorned but in clear perspective. It's the perfect platform for Terry. The interplay between Pass and Brown touches unsuspected areas of 'Cotton Tail' and 'Sophisticated Lady', and though Severino might have been dispensed with for at least a couple of the softer tracks, the overall sound is excellent and it's Clark's happiest latter-day (though he was still going three decades later!) recording.

& *See also* **Serenade To A Bus Seat** (1957; p. 206), **Color Changes** (1960; p. 260)

JULIUS HEMPHILL
Born ?1940, Fort Worth, Texas; died 2 April 1995
Alto saxophone

Flat-Out Jump Suite
Black Saint 120040
Hemphill; Olu Dara (t); Abdul Wadud (clo); Warren Smith (perc). June 1980.

Saxophonist and friend Tim Berne said (1997): **'People said he came out of Ornette, but that was laziness, just because he came from Texas and didn't much play the changes. He was about so much more than that – everyone from Parker to Cannonball, and with something of his own in there always.'**

Hemphill was chief composer for the World Saxophone Quartet (see p. 456), and his signature style was lean – some said 'raw' when his Texas roots were showing – and often drastically pared down. Hemphill was not only a ludicrously underrated composer, despite his influence on Tim Berne and others, but he was also fascinated by other performance dimensions in jazz, inventing a complex *alter ego* in the form of Roy Boyé/Blue Boyé, and experimenting with 'audiorama' and with costumes on stage. In part this came from his experience working the R&B circuit with the likes of Ike Turner, which he did before moving to Missouri and joining the Black Artists Guild.

Like Dolphy, his alto sound was piercing and intensely vocalized, and always locked into clear musical logics. Hemphill often favoured cello as an alternative harmony instrument, frequently working in duo or group situations with Abdul Wadud, somewhat similar to Dolphy's collaborations with Ron Carter. At first hearing, *Flat-Out Jump Suite* sounds more abstract than Hemphill's later output, but builds to a rousing funk climax on 'Body'. Hemphill intones the title to each part as it begins, starting with the soft, percussion-led figures of 'Ear', plunging into the complexities of 'Mind' (which is dominated by Wadud) and then picking up a more continuous rhythm with 'Heart', on which Hemphill begins to string together his light, slightly floating textures into a more continuous, jazz-based improvisation. On the original LP, 'Mind, Part 2' opened the second side with a brief coda to the long central piece. It makes more sense as an integral drum solo, typically understated. It is, until the very end, a remarkably quiet album that requires some concentration. Dara uses his mute a good deal and otherwise plays quite softly. Hemphill seems to play a wooden flute and gives his saxophone a soft-edged quality that is very attractive.

DAVID MURRAY&
Born 19 February 1955, Berkeley, California
Tenor saxophone, bass clarinet

Ming
Black Saint 120045
Murray; Olu Dara (t); Lawrence 'Butch' Morris (c); George E. Lewis (tb); Henry Threadgill (as); Anthony Davis (p); Wilber Morris (b); Steve McCall (d, perc). July 1980.

David Murray said (1989): **'Ornette Coleman told me that strange things happen round the tenor saxophone. Really strange things ... like raised spirits.'**

His mother was a gospel piano-player, but Murray was alerted to modern jazz by Stanley Crouch and Arthur Blythe. He moved to New York at the start of his 20s and became involved in the loft scene there. His first major exposure was as a member of the World Saxophone Quartet. His signature style is an iron-hard sound, often in the middle and lower register, and a mixture of bebop, swing and free elements, alternated with boogie and funk. Once embarked on his recording career, Murray seemed unstoppable and by the end of the '00s had appeared on more than 200 records, many of them his own. In recent years, Murray has diversified into other forms and endeavours, working with writers Amiri Baraka, Ishmael Reed and Ntozake Shange, collaborating with African musicians, following up a lifelong interest in song, even contemplating opera, while running his own imprint, but for most of his fans there is a special quality to the work of the '80s.

Some might say that the best jazz record of the decade came along before it was properly under way. *Ming* is an astonishing record, a virtual compression of three generations of improvised music into 40 minutes of entirely original jazz, played by a perfectly balanced, tensely sprung octet. The brasses are tight but so individual in tone and timbre one hears every component. As second horn, Threadgill is a Lord of Misrule. The opening 'Fast Life' has a hectic quality reminiscent of another of Murray's household gods, Charles Mingus. 'Jasvan' is a swirling 'Boston' waltz that gives most of the band, led off by the marvellous Lewis, ample solo space. 'Ming' is a sweet ballad which follows on from the troubling, almost schizophrenic 'The Hill', a piece that occupies a central place in Murray's output. The tenor sound is, as usual, closer to that of the great swing masters than the main run of post-bop players. Ironically, what is distinctive about Murray's saxophone sound is often best gauged by listening to his fleet, light-toned bass clarinet.

Home followed from the same group and perhaps touches heights *Ming* doesn't quite reach, and there are moments on *The Hill* from 1986 which suggest classic status for it, too, but over the stretch the earlier album prevails. A stainless modern masterpiece.

& *See also* **Dark Star** (1996; p. 598); **WORLD SAXOPHONE QUARTET, W.S.Q.** (1980; p. 456)

BENNY WATERS
Born 23 January 1902, Brighton, Maryland; died 11 August 1998, Columbia, Maryland
Tenor saxophone

When You're Smiling
Hep 2010
Waters; Roy Williams (tb); Joe Temperley (bs); Alex Shaw (p); Ron Mathewson (b); Martin Drew (d). August 1980.

Hep boss Alastair Robertson says: **'I decided on the date after hearing Benny and Roy playing together at the Edinburgh Jazz Festival. Ronnie Scott was in town, so I was able to grab Ron and Martin. Local piano hero Alex Shaw made up the rhythm. The night before the event I got hold of Joe Temperley. A studio was available and without the least semblance of rehearsal the band launched into a freewheeling joyous set. It shouldn't have worked but it did and that's jazz.'**

Waters was an indomitable personality, among the oldest practising jazzmen, and though his later records tended to be too accommodating for a man who doesn't like to act his age, there is much vigorous work on clarinet and alto. Like Benny Carter or Doc Cheatham, he sounds like a survivor from another age, raising his voice among us with few concessions to his surroundings. His tone, vibrato and delivery are antiquarian, but none of this suggests frailty, more an enduring style.

He studied in Boston before spending several years from 1925 with Charlie Johnson, then with Fletcher Henderson, Claude Hopkins, Jimmie Lunceford and others through the '30s and '40s. From 1955 he was mostly in Europe, touring relentlessly. A number of British recordings, made when Waters was a mere lad and only pushing 80, are likeable stuff. *When You're Smiling* is prime British mainstream, courtesy of Williams, Temperley and the rhythm section, and even without Waters there would be plenty to listen to. Benny is in grand spirits on the title-piece and Williams has three features where he makes trombone-playing seem like the easiest thing on earth.

ART PEPPER &

Born 1 September 1925, Gardenia, California; died 1 June 1982, Panorama City, California
Alto saxophone, clarinet

Winter Moon
Original Jazz Classics OJCCD 677
Pepper; Stanley Cowell (p); Howard Roberts (g); Cecil McBee (b); Carl Burnett (d); strings. September 1980.

Laurie Pepper remembered (1998): **'Art had one layer of skin less than most people. It allowed him to play like that, but off the stand everything got to him. He was very fragile, felt things far more intensely and personally than most people do.'**

Finally rehabilitated at Synano, Pepper made a comeback record in 1975 and gradually forged a new career as a surviving master of West Coast bebop alto. The later records for Galaxy are in some ways all of a piece, and it's rather appropriate that the Fantasy group chose to issue a colossal boxed set of the whole output. It's a vast and surprisingly playable archive; most such monuments seldom come off the shelf, but Pepper's resilience, febrile invention and consistency of commitment make this music endure far beyond expectations.

The best of the single albums should be in all collections. *Straight Life* appeals because of the romantic title and the return of a favourite theme. *Winter Moon* puts off those who react viscerally to the 'with strings' format. They shouldn't. It's a profoundly beautiful record which far surpasses the norm for this kind of session, and Pepper uncorks one of his greatest solos against the rhapsodic sweep of Bill Holman's arrangement on 'Our Song'. The Hoagy Carmichael title-track is also exquisitely done, with a soft bounce in the metre, and even the love theme from *The Eyes of Laura Mars* (a tune known as 'The Prisoner') has an expressive grace. Art's tone is peerless and the group do everything they can to enhance the beauty of his playing. The strings sound part of the process, rather than added on.

Art was active pretty much to the end of his life, but always under duress and only viable with the loyal support of Laurie. She stands in this book for all the women (and some men) who nursed troubled genius, sometimes literally, sometimes simply and in the modern usage by 'being there'.

& *See also* **Meets The Rhythm Section** (1957; p. 200)

GANELIN TRIO
Formed 1971
Group

Ancora Da Capo

Leo CDLR 108

Vyacheslav (Slava) Ganelin (p, g, basset, perc); Vladimir Chekasin (as, ts, cl, ob, v); Vladimir Tarasov (d, perc). October–November 1980.

Producer and label boss Leo Feigin remembers: **'This was the first ever performance of the Ganelin Trio in the West, at the Berliner Jazz Tage. Encores were prohibited at this festival. However, after a 20-minute standing ovation the artistic director of the festival, Joachim Berendt, had to throw in the towel and allow the trio to play an encore.'**

The Ganelin Trio made *fin de siècle* music, a mysterious, provocative collage of jazz, 20th-century composition, primitive technologies and ironic theatricals. The trio's first recordings had some of the allure of the clandestine, smuggled *samizdat* documents, though in fact the early *Con Anima*, originally released by the official Soviet label Melodiya, was a decent, if flawed, recording.

The group's masterpiece, *Ancora Da Capo*, brings together part one of that suite, recorded at the Autumn Rhythms Festival in Leningrad, with a recording of part two, made a few weeks earlier in Berlin. This was a breakthrough occasion. The Ganelin Trio were publicly hailed by Joachim Ernst Berendt, and their reputation in the West began. The exact history of the tapes is complicated, as with the mighty *Catalogue*, covertly recorded in East Germany in April 1979 and smuggled to the West, but suffice it to say that the work has a monolithic intensity which condenses everything the group was about: a shining expressiveness, dense, passionate playing, humour and, underlying it all, an ironclad discipline.

One of the definitive characteristics of the trio's sound is a dry, unswinging rhythm, and a seeming avoidance of the usual theme-and-variations, harmonic approach of jazz. Tarasov avoids a settled groove in favour of a light, springy metre that can move in almost any direction or in none. There is no conventional bass, though Ganelin makes distinctive use of the basset, a small keyboard instrument which mimics the sound of a string bass, but in a flat and uninflected way.

After 1980 the Ganelin Trio were able to perform on a world stage, making an important appearance in London in 1984 that divided musicians and critics, but provided overtime for the KGB abroad. Overground, if not in any sense officially sanctioned, the group seemed to make less sense and while there was fine work to come, and not least a notably sunlit American performance, the tense, subversive logic of the *samizdat* years had gone. The trio disbanded when Ganelin emigrated to Israel, and while there was to be a later reunion, the Ganelin Trio felt very much part of a history that was over. The great records endure, though.

THE '80s

If the story of each succeeding jazz decade has been one of stylistic innovation – or regression – meeting the challenge of new recording technologies, then the narrative of the '80s can be reduced quite straightforwardly to neo-traditionalism – or neo-conservatism – and the compact disc.

Jazz underwent a certain renaissance in the '80s. The scorched-earth tactics of punk had left popular music in a curiously bewildered state. At all the majors, A&R men, who had lost money and credibility during the punk spasm, were actively casting about for a new music to promote. As often in such circumstances, jazz was available as a ready-made product, and the early '80s saw what was billed as a jazz boom. In the US, it was spearheaded by a serious young trumpet-player called Wynton Marsalis, who was signed up by Miles Davis's label, Columbia, but with a musical message diametrically opposite to Miles's. With Dr Stanley Crouch at his shoulder – not since Clement Greenberg had steered Jackson Pollock's painting hand was there such a close relationship between an American artist and his ideologue – Marsalis preached a return to the purity of early jazz, rejecting all dalliances with funk, pop, rock and soul, and thus implicitly rejecting Miles's recent legacy at Columbia, which had flared darkly in the mid-'70s with two dark slabs of sound, *Agharta* and *Pangaea*, recorded in Japan and considered only releasable there. Following his return to partial health and activity, Miles decamped to Warner Bros, leaving Wynton (whom the older man famously snubbed onstage in Montreal early in the following decade) to contribute to both the label's jazz and its classical wings.

The new conservatism wasn't quite like the '40s revival, in the sense that nothing lost had been rediscovered. What happened was closer to a renewal of emphasis on the core values of jazz: melody, swing, blues tonality, individual expression within a tightly organized ensemble music. Bebop became fashionable again. In the UK, young men who would otherwise have been playing reggae, ska and soul were dressed up in suits and marketed as the 'new black British jazz', an implicit acknowledgement that jazz in the UK had been largely (though far from exclusively) a white preserve.

In Europe the Eastern frontier seemed suddenly to have rolled back. The Western discovery of the Ganelin Trio – brought out of the Soviet Union and Soviet bloc in *samizdat* form and released by Leo Feigin – was a curious dance of wild enthusiasm and considerable resistance, the group's strange theatrical approach quite alien to the determinedly unhistrionic style of most jazz at the time, but in that way almost shamingly faithful to the primitive origins of jazz as a subversive, ironic, explosive music that mimicked official culture in order to debunk it.

The documentary low fidelity of the early Ganelin Trio recordings also set them apart from the growing sophistication of jazz recording. Digital techniques and the capacity to record jazz – like commercial music – on a number of manipulable channels were mixed blessings to a form that relies to some degree on spontaneity and real-time responsiveness. While some of the signature labels of the time did continue to dabble in multi-tracking and editing (which lost its physical dimension with the introduction of digital techniques), the overwhelming preference in jazz was for 'live' or 'as live' recording, with performances recorded in real-time. For some, the introduction of digital sound robbed the music of warmth, and vinyl records persisted longer and more faithfully in jazz than elsewhere in the industry.

Compact discs offered the possibility of putting more than an hour of music on a single record. Given that many classic LP releases came in at precisely half that duration, there was briefly the possibility that major label reissue programmes would involve doubling up

LPs on a single compact disc. Unfortunately, the business chose to go in another direction, padding out classic records with 'bonus tracks', 'alternates' and sometimes even studio noise (all material which, as Rudy Van Gelder pointed out, the artist and producer had deemed substandard or unreleasable). As a means of study, having five or six 'takes' of a familiar tune – say, John Coltrane's 'Giant Steps' – was an obvious plus for the student, but once the practice was established labels found it impossible to reissue a classic LP without augmenting it with often spurious material. Ironically, in the following decade and after, as recordings of the LP era began to slip out of copyright, the practice of issuing what had once been called 'twofers' did come back into play, though usually only on budget labels.

CD duration had a (mostly negative) impact on new recording as well. Where an artist and producer might once have selected the very best 35 or 40 minutes of music from a session, now the tendency was to include everything that had been done, and if there was not sufficient good new writing, to record a couple of standards or repertory pieces as makeweights. More very definitely does not mean better. We have inveighed against the practice for years, but it is now unstoppable and the possibility of anyone – fan, critic, A&R man – keeping pace with new recording has long since gone. To repeat: the problem is not the number of new records being released, which can only be welcome, even if many do not pass through basic quality control, but their duration.

The symbolic drama of jazz in the '80s was acted out between Wynton and Miles, the polite, educated spokesman of traditionalism against the prince of darkness, air versus electricity. It was, of course, a marketing and media invention. Marsalis was capable of expressing raw violence, Miles increasingly reverted to the blues; Marsalis's deviations from 'the tradition' were often far more glaring than Miles's apparent, but not actual, rejection of it. Those who like to search for endings were presented with another *terminus ad quem* when Miles Davis died in 1991, exhausted but still ostensibly moving forward. If the history of jazz could be told in the life-stories of Louis Armstrong, Duke Ellington, Charlie Parker and Miles Davis, there was no surviving figure of comparable stature and longevity to extend that deceptively apostolic lineage. Jazz fragmented in the '80s, often creatively, sometimes confusingly, but always to someone's advantage. It became, before the term had been coined, a world music.

Part 1:
1981–1985

MARK MURPHY&

Born 14 March 1932, Fulton, New York
Voice

Bop For Kerouac
Muse MCD 5253
Murphy; Richie Cole (as); Bill Hays (ky); Bruce Forman (g, ky); Luther Hughes, Bob Magnusson (b); Jeff Hamilton, Roy McCurdy (d). March 1981.

Mark Murphy said (1986): **'Times hadn't been easy for vocal jazz, but it was coming back, partly thanks to Eddie Jefferson, and when I got a call from Richie Cole [who'd been with Jefferson when he was gunned down in 1979] it seemed like a good time to take a step back into jazz singing.'**

Murphy was away from singing for a while. He taught instead, and he was missed by those who love his scatting. That's to hint that not everyone does. There are many far more recent records than this, but *Bop For Kerouac*, with its blessed, Beat sensibility is as far down the line as most uncommitted listeners will go. The voice of later years has some burrs and roughnesses that often work to Mark's benefit, but here he comes on alongside Cole as a tough, streetwise horn-player, whipping through 'Boplicity', his own version of 'Bongo Beep' and an altogether surprising 'Goodbye, Pork Pie Hat' with a swagger. 'Down St Thomas Way' and 'Ballad Of The Sad Young Men' make for an extraordinary climax. It's as camp as a row of tents, of course, but Murphy is still able to blow almost every other male jazz singer before Kurt Elling off the map.

& *See also* **Crazy Rhythm** (1956–1958; p. 186)

BILLY BANG
Born William Vincent Walker, 20 September 1947, Mobile, Alabama
Violin

Rainbow Gladiator
Soul Note 121016-2
Bang; Charles Tyler (as, bs); Michele Rosewoman (p); Wilber Morris (b); Dennis Charles (d). June 1981.

Billy Bang said (1984): **'Some musicians don't make much of a thing of records, but for me that was my progress, right there, my life laid out. Each record was an attempt to do more and better than the last.'**

He played drums with his college friend Arlo Guthrie, then served in Vietnam (which was so gruelling he suppressed the experience for more than 20 years) and began playing seriously relatively late, drawing inspiration from Ramsay Ameen and Leroy Jenkins but also from the swing violin of Stuff Smith. His characteristic sound is combative, sometimes harsh, but always melodic. He worked for a time with Sun Ra, became a figure on the New York loft scene and was a founder member of the String Trio Of New York.

   Rainbow Gladiator is a terrific record, bright, percussive and packed with ideas. The group has a unique and immediately identifiable sound, especially when Tyler is playing baritone, and this has to count as one of Rosewoman's best early recordings. The violinist's articulation is as precise as ever and ranges from a huge, raw vibrato and a lighter, dry, almost bleached effect. The title-track opens the album on a high; almost a quarter of an hour in length, it doesn't let up for a moment. Everything else is a good deal shorter. 'Ebony Minstrel Man', 'Broken Strings' and 'Bang's Bounce' are less than five minutes each, but they show how comfortable Bang is with song forms: a dedication to Laurel Van Horn, 'Yaa – Woman Born On Thursday', is extraordinary.

   Bang eventually came to terms with his Vietnam experience in musical form, but those records are dark and difficult. For musicianship and expressive personality, *Rainbow Gladiator* is still his finest statement.

LESTER BOWIE
Born 11 October 1941, Frederick, Maryland; died 8 November 1999, New York City
Trumpet

The Great Pretender
ECM 829369
Bowie; Hamiet Bluiett (bs); Donald Smith (ky); Fred Williams (b); Phillip Wilson (d); Fontella Bass, David Peaston (v). June 1981.

Former Paris club manager Jean-Paul Allais remembers: **'One night when the Brass Fantasy were playing, a man collapsed in the foyer. Lester was going past in his white medical** coat and this guy's wife grabbed at him and screamed: "Please help us!" Lester took a look at the guy – who was basically OK – and said: "Come on, man, get up and dance!" He could see the woman looking at him strangely. "It's OK, I'm a *j-a-z-z* doctor."'

There's only an apparent paradox in Bowie's commitment to both the avant-garde and the pop-fuelled exuberance of Brass Fantasy, to the radical deconstructions of the AACM era and the buoyant sway of 'The Great Pretender'. Bowie perceived no tension between the two. He had a profound understanding of black music history, recognizing that the 'avant-garde' smears and growls of contemporary trumpet-players had their roots in the classic jazz of Bubber Miley and others, and that the line between experiment and entertainment was narrower than the usual critical ideology allowed. Lester's career began on the R&B circuit, but after his move to Chicago he became involved in the musical explorations being carried out by Muhal Richard Abrams, Jodie Christian and others, and it was here he met Roscoe Mitchell, Joseph Jarman and Malachi Favors, the core of the future Art Ensemble.

Among his records apart from the Art Ensemble (see p. 369), it is hard to choose between this and the 1978 quintet *The 5th Power* with Arthur Blythe and Amina Claudine Myers. Bowie's reinterpretation of the Buck Ram hit 'The Great Pretender' has its clownish elements, but the playing and singing are at a very high level. Just when the track seems ready to stall, Hamiet Bluiett takes the melody by the horns and charges it through into a hectic waltz. The gospel elements of *The 5th Power* are here as well, but somehow better assimilated, and when Bowie attempts a calypso – he had lived in Jamaica for a period – on 'Rios Negroes', it's stunningly effective. The elongated title-track, which comes first in the programme, actually gives a strange sense of the set's emotional dynamic, for some of the later tunes, including 'When The Doom (Moon) Comes Over The Mountain ...' and 'Oh, How The Ghost Sings', are actually quite sombre and after that downbeat ending it's worth tracking back to explore the hidden complexities of the bravura title-piece. Along with its dark twin, *The 5th Power*, this one marks his finest (solo) hour.

JAMES NEWTON
Born 1 May 1953, Los Angeles, California
Flute, alto flute, bass flute

Axum
ECM 8350192
Newton (f, af, bf solo). August 1981.

James Newton says: 'I arrived in Europe one month before the recording, and practised between eight and 16 hours each day at a friend's house on Lake Geneva in Switzerland, effort that was matched in the studio by Manfred Eicher's attention to detail and concentration. I was absorbed by Jacques Mercier's book *Ethiopian Magic Scrolls* that provided most of the inspiration for the works on the recording.'

Raised in California, Newton studied with Buddy Collette and dabbled in both funk and the avant-garde before devoting himself exclusively to flute. He characteristically projects a strong, very exact classical line, but he modifies it with various extended techniques, including multiphonics, flutter tonguing and toneless blowing. He's also a thinking musician, whose cultural purview is impressively wide. One of the first contemporary players to foster a direct Eric Dolphy influence, Newton started out as a multi-instrumentalist but gave up alto saxophone and bass clarinet towards the end of the '70s. As a virtuoso flautist, he has worked in both formal and improvised contexts and has developed a wholly original means of vocalizing while he plays. This is by no means new (Roland Kirk was exceptionally proficient at it), but Newton has taken the technique far beyond unisons and harmonies to a point where he can sing contrapuntally against his own flute line. The results are frequently dazzling, as on the African-influenced *Axum*. Newton's vocalizations allow his pieces to develop with unprecedented depth, and his tone in all registers is quite remarkable. It's not clear how or to what extent these pieces are built on predetermined structures, but they all sound logical, directed and 'finished', almost as if each piece has a specific ritual function in some lost communion.

CHICO FREEMAN
Born Earl Lavon Freeman Jr, 17 July 1949, Chicago, Illinois
Tenor saxophone

Destiny's Dance
Original Jazz Classics OJCCD 799
Freeman; Wynton Marsalis (t); Bobby Hutcherson (vib); Dennis Moorman (p); Cecil McBee (b); Ronnie Burrage (d); Paulinho Da Costa (perc). October 1981.

Producer John Koenig says: **'I remember picking Wynton up at the airport and I think the first or second thing he said to me was that he'd heard the album I'd just made with Joe Henderson. He said he was particularly excited to play with Bobby Hutcherson, whom he hadn't met before. We had a rehearsal at SIR the day before the session. It turned out it was Wynton's 20th birthday. Ronnie was excited by the quality of the sound – the album was recorded in the legendary Ocean Way studio B – and it's always nice when musicians can't complain we haven't got their sound right. Because of the rehearsal, and in spite of the complexity of the tunes, it went smoothly. Bobby, Ronnie and Cecil couldn't have been more solid and I guess that cohesiveness is evident because Chico and Wynton had a nice solid base and it showed in the playing.'**

Von Freeman's son is a Coltrane-influenced modernist – advanced harmonics, circular breathing, overblown notes – who none the less remains loyal to the basic principles of Chicago jazz. He has flirted with free jazz and with funk and fusion in his Brainstorm group but sounds at his best in front of a small group playing modern repertory, which allows him to exploit a formidable technique.

Destiny's Dance is one of the great jazz records of the '80s. The presence of Hutcherson, the premier vibraharpist of the day and a giant of an improviser, is a huge part of it, and Wynton is playing straightforwardly and with all his fire on his four tracks. Da Costa is a guest on one. Once again it seems odd to pitch Hutcherson up against a piano-player, and one of limited if perfectly serviceable talent, except that Moorman respects his space and the sound is so smoothly crafted that there is a lot of room around both, good separation and none of the muddiness that ruins such encounters. The material is all original and all strongly idiomatic, allowing Freeman to air his growing repertoire of playing techniques; again, though, technique never takes the place of musicality. The key tracks are the title-piece and 'Embracing Oneness', a moving dedication to Duke Ellington and Thelonious Monk.

BILL DIXON &
Born 25 October 1925, Nantucket, Massachusetts
Trumpet

November 1981
Soul Note 121038
Dixon; Mario Pavone, Alan Silva (b); Laurence Cook (d). November 1981.

Bill Dixon says: **'November 1981 included work that was recorded in Zurich while on tour, as well as a studio recording in Milan. The group had performed well on the road, "breaking in" some of the material and they played even better in the studio. It was a great event for me. I did what I set out to do compositionally and in terms of performance, with musicians who were all equal to the tasks at hand.'**

Dixon's first important associations were with Cecil Taylor and Archie Shepp, fellow members of the Jazz Composers' Guild and in Shepp's case a fellow member of the New York Contemporary Five. In 1964, the trumpeter organized the October Revolution In Jazz, the New Thing's equivalent of the Armory Show. He has been an important educator, largely at the Bennington College in Vermont, from which he retired in 1996. Woefully overlooked through most of his most productive years, Dixon has enjoyed some late attention for the large-scale works of the '00s, but his earlier work remains relatively little-known.

At the beginning of his career, Dixon made a number of solo trumpet recordings, largely of necessity, though they remain an important key to his slightly jagged style and thought. *November 1981* is his small-group masterpiece, patiently conceived and executed, and generously proportioned. Dixon likes to build his ideas around silence, but these statuesque themes also use rich drones provided by the bass-player; a subsequent LP deployed three contrabassists. As ever, the trumpet is used quite sparingly, with the opening 'Webern' (less than a minute and a half) there to underline his use of the *Klangfarbenmelodie* device whereby different instruments play different parts of the line and in which timbre and colour are structural principles and not just decoration. Music as concentrated as 'Penthesilea' or the 'Llaattiinnoo Suite', performed live, requires certain adjustments of musical expectation, but they are consistently satisfying and producer Giovanni Bonandrini (who provided a lifeline to creative American musicians for two otherwise sparse decades) provides a generous, albeit intimate, sound which suits Dixon very well indeed.

& See also **Vade Mecum / Vade Mecum II** (1993; p. 574)

BOB WILBER
Born 15 March 1928, New York City
Soprano saxophone, clarinet

On The Road
Jazzology JCD-214
Wilber; Glenn Zottola (t); Mark Shane (p); Mike Peters (g, bj); Len Skeat (b); Butch Miles (d); Joanne 'Pug' Horton (v). November 1981.

Bob Wilber said (1991): **'I met Sidney Bechet in 1944 at the Pied Piper club in Greenwich Village, sitting with a big Great Dane puppy. I told him I played soprano saxophone – that seemed to interest him, because there weren't too many of us around – but that my mouth and lips were sore with so much practising. "You gotta have a callous," said Sidney, and that was my first lesson!'**

Once upon a time everyone tried to play soprano sax like Sidney Bechet. Now that everyone tries to play soprano like either Coltrane or Steve Lacy, Bob Wilber seems something of a throwback. Since he actually played with Bechet and has done more than anyone to keep that master's music in circulation, there's no 'authenticity' problem here. Wilber still seeks the wide, singing tone of his mentor, but he long since became his own man, and even where there is a specific homage – as in *On The Road*, which was made by his band, Bechet Legacy – he still sounds like himself. It's a fine salute and one that uncovers some nice rarities, though inevitably 'Oh, Lady Be Good' and 'Summertime' (a couple of takes) are pushed well up-front. The delightful Pug does a couple of nice vocals, but the emphasis is very much on recapturing the spirit of Bechet's solos without pastiching them. Wilber's clarinet-playing is somewhat underrated and it's perhaps a pity that it never got more coverage. His other group, of course, was Soprano Summit, a popular double-act on the small horn with Kenny Davern, launched in otherwise dark days for straight-ahead jazz. Those records are a lot of fun, too, and probably the best of them is *Live At The Iliana Jazz Club* from 1976.

JOHN CARTER

Born 24 September 1929, Fort Worth, Texas; died 31 March 1991, Inglewood, California
Clarinet, alto and tenor saxophones, flute

Dauwhe
Black Saint 120057
Carter; Bobby Bradford (c); Charles Owens (ss, cl, ob); James Newton (f); Red Callender (tba); Roberto Miguel Miranda (b); William Jeffrey (d); Luis Peralta (perc). February & March 1982.

Clarinettist François Houle says: **'John Carter gave the clarinet a role in free jazz. His collaboration with Bobby Bradford stands as one of the most significant pairings in the history of the music, up there with Coltrane and Dolphy, Coleman and Cherry, and his later records on Gramavision put the clarinet at the forefront of the creative music scene, inspiring a new generation of players to dedicate themselves to its potentials. I'm thinking of Marty Ehrlich, Vinny Golia, Ab Baars, Michael Moore ...'**

Another of the extraordinary cohort of creative players who came out of Fort Worth, Carter played with Ornette Coleman in the '40s, then moved West in 1961 after a period of a dozen years working in the public schools system. He joined up with Bobby Bradford and together, in 1964, they founded the New Art Jazz Ensemble, one of a number of quietly influential groups that give the lie to received notions about 'West Coast jazz'. They made *Seeking*, a remarkable record and the pairing with Bradford is perhaps more easily comparable to the Coleman/Cherry axis when Carter *isn't* playing clarinet.

For the rest, there isn't as much on record as one might expect from such a richly talented musician. His dedication to teaching restricted his activities, but there was little sustained enthusiasm from the music business. It's significant that one of the most important Carter records is a shaky live tape of Carter and Bradford in concert in Worcester, Massachusetts, together with a cassette of studio work from California from three years before in 1979. Not much for such a major figure.

Fortunately, and typically, Black Saint stepped into the breach. In the decade before his death, Carter worked at a multi-part sequence of suites called *Roots And Folklore: Episodes In The Development Of American Folk Music*. Little of it remains in print, but the opening sketches are wonderful. *Dauwhe*, which represents African origins, is strongly articulate and marked by some excellent playing, from Newton in particular. It's difficult to trace a clear thematic connection between the pieces, but the progress from the long opening 'Dauwhe' to the 'Mating Ritual' that ends the record (on a definite note of suspension) is a fascinating one. Arguably it isn't as strong a record as *Castles Of Ghana* or *Fields* and *Shadows On A Wall* (the other Gramavision chapters of *Roots And Folklore*), but it has more natural sound and has stood the test of time very much better.

SARAH VAUGHAN &
Born 27 March 1924, Newark, New Jersey; died 3 April 1990, Los Angeles, California
Voice

Crazy And Mixed Up

Pablo 2312-137

Vaughan; Sir Roland Hanna (p); Joe Pass (g); Andy Simpkins (b); Harold Jones (d). March 1982.

Sarah Vaughan said (1980): **'My range is bigger than it was when I was 20. That was a very untrained voice, back then, and a nervous little girl singing with it. I guess that just opening up has done for me what years of training might do for another singer. I'm grateful for it, either way.'**

Vaughan's Pablo albums will endure as some of her most finely crafted music. *How Long Has This Been Going On?* introduced a new note of seriousness into her recording career after several years of indifferent efforts and a seemingly careless approach to the studios. The voice has never been better or more closely recorded, and the picked session players and uniformly strong material make these albums the most consistent of her career. The two *Duke Ellington* albums gave her – at last – the opportunity to stamp her identity on the greatest of jazz songbooks, and while there are a few disappointments on them, as on *How Long*, both discs stand as a worthy counterpoint to Fitzgerald's celebrated Ellington collaboration. *Copacabana* is a neglected album, with the sparest of accompaniments to support the great, glowing voice, and the bossa/samba material proving unexpectedly strong for Vaughan. *Crazy And Mixed Up* is perhaps the best of all. It's not a long set – indeed, it's disappointingly short given the standard of the material – but no one should quibble about being short-changed, for this, like most of the others of this period, is an ideally paced and delivered set of standards with the most sympathetic of accompaniments. Sassie's art was never more concentratedly presented.

& *See also* **Sarah Vaughan** (1954; p. 161)

GEORGE RUSSELL &

Born 23 June 1923, Cincinnati, Ohio; died 27 July 2009, Boston, Massachusetts
Composer, bandleader, piano

Live In An American Time Spiral

Soul Note 121049

Russell; Stanton Davis, Tom Harrell, Brian Leach, Ron Tooley (t); Ray Anderson, Earl McIntyre (tb); Marty Ehrlich (as, f); Doug Miller (ts, f); Bob Hanlon (bs); Jerome Harris (g); Jack Reilly, Mark Soskin (ky); Ron McClure (b); Victor Lewis (d). July 1982.

George Russell said (1984): **'Ornette Coleman came to New York and he freed jazz of the Broadway tune for ever, but what comes in its place? The [Lydian Chromatic] Concept offers a way of writing music that will take jazz on, but there's no one yet writing it and no single, overwhelming figure – even Ornette – who can be its figurehead.'**

The late '70s and early '80s saw a gradual wakening to Russell's importance and some important recordings, though anyone interested in his music needs to track back through things like the various versions of *Electronic Sonata For Souls Loved By Nature* and *Trip To Prillargui* (the latter even if only for early glimpses of Jan Garbarek and Terje Rypdal; yes, Russell was in European exile). At last, though, he was beginning to see his large-scale work performed.

The main piece on *Live* is a concert performance of 'Time Spiral', a work which tries to draw together many aspects of the African-American musical culture and then find a single, consistent line through them. Now that Russell is no more, it is a task for future musicologists to trace the impact of Russell's theories not just on jazz but on classical and popular music as well: Michael Jackson, Prince, Beyoncé ... Concerned again (like *The*

African Game) with the larger, almost meta-historical movements of human life, the charts have a slightly dense philosophical feel on the studio album, but they open up considerably in a live setting. The album also includes a fine reading of 'Ezz-thetic' and the faintly ironic 'D.C. Divertimento', which is also a meditation on Duke Ellington's city, given force by a (mostly) young and enthusiastic band.

& See also **Jazz Workshop** (1956; p. 183), **Ezz-thetics** (1961; p. 274)

MIROSLAV VITOUS
Born 6 December 1947, Prague, Czechoslovakia
Double bass

Journey's End
ECM 843171-2
Vitous; John Surman (ss, bcl, bs); John Taylor (p); Jon Christensen (d). July 1982.

Miroslav Vitous said (1985): **'When I came to America, it troubled me that bass-players were guys who were not able to play some other instrument. I wanted to make the bass an equal player in the group, capable of anything the other instruments were doing.'**

Vitous studied classical music in his native Prague before going to Berklee, for a brief and rather unhappy period of study. Leaving without a diploma, he worked with a variety of leaders, including Art Farmer, Miles Davis and Chick Corea, before joining Weather Report as founding bassist. A professor and sometime head of jazz at the New England Conservatory, Vitous has had a quiet career, recording sporadically in later years. He left Weather Report in 1973, having recorded three classic albums (he appears only briefly on *Mysterious Traveller*, their fourth release), and experimented with various 'lead' and 'piccolo' basses, but he doesn't seem to have acquired the confidence in their use that made Stanley Clarke and a later Weather Report member, Jaco Pastorius, such charismatic figures.

Journey's End is a rich mix of free style and deep grooves. Vitous opens with variations on a Czech folk theme, then dances into Surman's beautiful waltz 'Tess'. The next piece, 'Carry On, No. 1', is improvised by the group, with Surman providing an extraordinary effect on his saxophone keys. 'Paragraph Jay' is another theme by the Englishman, this time a roilingly intense one. 'Only One' is dedicated to the bassist's father and it's played on an electric fretless instrument, but what one notices is just how prominent the acoustic bass has been on the previous tracks, testimony to Vitous's technique and to ECM sound. It plays out on Taylor's waltz 'Windfall'. Not a showman like Jaco, the Czech none the less displays considerable musical confidence and leadership on this second and best ECM date.

WARNE MARSH *&*
Born 26 October 1927, Los Angeles, California; died 18 December 1987, Hollywood, California
Tenor saxophone

Star Highs
Criss Cross 1002
Marsh; Hank Jones (p); George Mraz (b); Mel Lewis (d). August 1982.

After hearing of Warne Marsh's death, Anthony Braxton said (1988): **'He was the most important vertical improviser in jazz, a vibrational philosopher whose harmonics had a mathematical purity but also a very direct communicative quality.'**

Gerry Teekens's label was Marsh's main berth for the last half-decade of his life and this was probably the best of the Criss Cross records. Listen to the straightened-out 'Moose The Mooche', on which Marsh does his patented elongation and simplification of the melody and accompaniment. So entire is it that theme and solos almost sound through-composed. Marsh's original lines are always intriguing. The CD includes two versions of 'Switchboard Joe', 'Star Highs' and 'Sometimes', new themes which the band obviously took some pains over. There's nothing lumpy or misconceived about the rejected takes, though one wonders why the release version of the title-track was the first take. There was to be a virtual torrent of music-making from Marsh over the next five years, and there's scarcely a substandard moment in any of it. Appropriately, he died on the stand, doing the only thing he knew how.

& *See also* **Music For Prancing** (1957; p. 214), **Ne Plus Ultra** (1969; p. 370)

ANDREW CYRILLE
Born 10 November 1939, Brooklyn, New York
Drums

The Navigator
Soul Note 121062-2
Cyrille; Ted Daniel (t, flhn); Sonelius Smith (p); Nick DiGeronimo (b). September 1982.

Andrew Cyrille said (1984): **'I'm Scorpio, a water sign. I'm not sure what all that means, but there is something with me and water. I wanted a march thing on *The Navigator*, but maybe there are other elements there, too.'**

Cyrille worked with leaders as various as Nellie Lutcher and Roland Kirk before hooking up with Cecil Taylor in the early '60s and becoming a key member of the pianist's trio at a crucial phase in his development. An intuitively musical percussionist, Cyrille is one of the few solo performers on his instrument worth listening to. That said, he's also a formidable group leader, who has an uncanny ability to shape an ensemble to his conception. On *The Navigator* each of the players in the group he calls Maono introduces a section, adding compass bearings to a collective navigation back to the source. As with many of Cyrille's records, it asserts the jazz tradition by seeming to shed it, layer by layer. These are not celebrated players, outside their own circle. Daniel has an edgy, pungent delivery and Smith seems almost elemental himself. So sure is Cyrille's awareness of time that a bassist might have seemed unnecessary in this context, as it was in the Taylor trio, but DiGeronimo is given an important structural role and he's well established in the recording. 'So That Life Can Endure: P.S. With Love' is the other key statement, superbly shaped by the drummer.

SAM RIVERS &
Born 25 September 1923 (some sources still cite 1930), Reno, Oklahoma
Tenor and soprano saxophones, flute

Colors
Black Saint 120064
Rivers; Marvin Blackman (ts, f, ss); Talib Kibwe (f, cl, ts, ss); Chris Roberts (ss, f); Steve Coleman (as, f); Bobby Watson (as, f); Nat Dixon (ts, cl, f); Eddie Alex (ts, picc); Jimmy Cozier, Patience Higgins (bs, f). September 1982.

Sam Rivers said (1996): **'Winds of Manhattan was one of those projects you kind of hope will excite promoters and record labels, but it's difficult to get anyone interested in something that isn't a basic jazz combo. Jazz people say they like new things and surprise, but they basically want it to be a familiar surprise.'**

This spectacular convocation of New York reed-playing talent went under the name Winds Of Manhattan. Playing without a rhythm section, it creates a sound that is absolutely consistent with everything Rivers had been doing over the previous 20 years, but scaled up dramatically. The usual interests in wave-forms, flux and unity, dispersement and integration, come together again in these complex charts. Rivers is unmistakably the leader, in that he determines the basic concepts, but the music as a whole is democratic and very broadly based. Those familiar with Coleman or Watson or even with the distinctive Kibwe (T. K. Blue) may well be able to pick out their voices, but this is not the point of the exercise, and *Colors* is best listened to as an orchestral piece, relatively undifferentiated and a long way removed from conventional theme-and-solos jazz.

& *See also* **Fuchsia Swing Song** (1964; p. 311), **Portrait** (1995; p. 592)

MICROSCOPIC SEPTET
Formed 1980; Phillip Johnston, born 22 January 1955, Chicago, Illinois
Group

Seven Men In Neckties: History Of The Micros
Cuneiform RUNE 236/237 2CD
Phillip Johnston (ss); Don Davis (as); John Hagen, Danny Nigro, Paul Shapiro (ts); Dave Sewelson (bs); Joel Forrester (p); David Hofstra (b, tba); Richard Dworkin (d). December 1982, January 1983, November 1984.

Phillip Johnston says: **'For a number of years I worked to rescue the Micros LPs from the scrap heap of media history along with 78s or DIY cassettes that never made the transition to CD. When I finally did, the best accidental result was that when we reunited to promote the release, we found we still liked playing together, and we've been doing it again semi-regularly ever since.'**

Favourites on the New York downtown scene of the '80s, purveying surreal modern swing; John Zorn was even a member at one point. Titles like *Take the Z Train* and *Lobster Leaps In* (they come at the beginning and the most recent point in the discographical span) pretty much sums up the Microscopic approach, tightly arranged ensemble swing built round a reeds-and-rhythm personnel, what Johnston (now based in Sydney) describes as a 'brassless little big band' or 'guitarless R&B band'. The effect is either avant-garde or retro, depending on your stance, satirical or respectful depending on your prejudices, but it's all immaculately and lovingly played with a humour rarely encountered in modern jazz. Johnston also makes reference to 'legendary bad luck' in record deals.

We've generally avoided including compilations and repackagings in this survey, but for the Micros an exception ought to be made, since much of this music might have been consigned to the dust-heap of music, or more realistically a dustily affectionate corner of folk-memory, had it not been for the estimable Cuneiform. Much of this material has been unavailable for some time, but Cuneiform have come to the rescue with a multi-volume reissue. It's a terrific documentation, with brilliant cover art by Art Spiegelman, pulling together *Z Train* and the 'live in Holland' *Let's Flip!* on this essential first volume.

The writing is tight, mostly fast and highly co-ordinated, with Johnston and Forrester sharing the credits. The pianist's titles tend to be the more enigmatic, like 'Pack The Ermines, Mary', but it's Johnston's delightfully wacky compositions that stand out on the first LP, which ends on a surreal high with 'A Strange Thought Entered My Head'. The second release is valuable not least for confirming that the Micros were by no means a studio artefact, but a formidable performance band. A Dutch audience, raised on Willem Breuker, might well be expected to appreciate the music on *Let's Flip*, which opens with 'The Lobster Parade' (Louis Jordan meets Salvador Dalí) and ends with a delightful version of Billy Strayhorn's 'Johnny Come Lately'. The Mephisto club in Rotterdam seems like the ideal setting for this strange but joyous music. A pity it was ever allowed to slip from view.

DAVID FRISHBERG

Born 23 March 1933, St Paul, Minnesota
Piano, voice

Classics
Concord CCD 4462
Frishberg; Steve Gilmore (b); Bill Goodwin (d). December 1982, March 1983.

Dave Frishberg says: **'Buy a rhyming dictionary. After that, there's really nothing to it.'**

After a supply sergeant told Dave Frishberg that 'Jazz is OK, but it ain't got no words', he has gone about supplying the lack with unparalleled wit and sophistication, delivering hip songwriting in a form that fits with his individual brand of swing piano. If he's become best known as a cabaret recitalist, Frishberg nevertheless has a strong keyboard style – heard solo on a number of later recordings – that derives from the swing masters without making him seem like a slavish copyist.

Classics gathers all his best-known songs in a reissue of two LPs made for Omnisound. Sparsely but crisply presented by the trio, here are the prototype versions of such Frishberg favourites as 'I'm Hip' (co-written with Bob Dorough), 'My Attorney Bernie', 'Slappin' The Cakes On Me', 'Old Kentucky Ham' and 'Do You Miss New York?', bittersweet odes which he is very good at investing with both warmth and wryness. Frishberg views America and Americana from a unique perspective, somewhere between Woody Allen and Edward Hopper. Only Mose Allison and, on his day, Bob Dorough have as successfully blended jazz wit with formal elegance.

BORAH BERGMAN

Born 13 December 1933, New York City
Piano

A New Frontier
Soul Note 121030
Bergman (p solo). January 1983.

Borah Bergman said (1996): **'Don't compare me to Cecil Taylor. It's not even helpful to mention his name negatively. We have quite different approaches in every way. He works at things till they come out. I don't do that. He phrases on the beat; I phrase off the beat, like a jazz musician.'**

Over the years Bergman has broken down any residual distinction between left- and right-hand functions in piano-playing. For a time, he concentrated exclusively on playing with his left hand in order to build up strength, suppleness and right-brain co-ordination. His astonishing solo performances recall the 'two pianists' illusion associated with Art Tatum, though in a more fragmentary and disorderly sound-world. Stride, ragtime, bebop and Tristano's cool/free approach are also part of Bergman's background.

On the two large-scale pieces which make up *A New Frontier* he sets up huge whirling shapes with each hand, which then engage in confrontational dialogue. There is something slightly mechanistic about the playing on 'Night Circus' that makes one think of the player-piano pieces of Conlon Nancarrow, but this is eliminated on the remarkable 'Time For Intensity', a more richly coloured pair of contrasting pieces, the second of which, 'Webs And Whirlpools', is quite astonishing.

If one can still talk in terms of 'technique' in the presence of music like this, then Bergman's technique is probably the equal of any figure in the music, on any instrument, and at just about any period. To that degree, it seems overdetermining, almost inhuman, and yet what one senses constantly from these improvisations is a rich humanity coming through the 'virtuosity'.

CRAIG HARRIS

Born 10 September 1953 (some sources give 1954), Hempstead, New York
Trombone

Black Bone
Soul Note 121055
Harris; George Adams (ts); Donald Smith (p); Fred Hopkins (b); Charli Persip (d). January 1983.

Craig Harris says: **'Being in Australia with Abdullah Ibrahim made a huge impression, hearing people play the didjeridu, an instrument that's been around for thousands of years; just a tube and breath. You can see what that might have inspired in me.'**

Prominent credits with Sun Ra, Abdullah Ibrahim, Henry Threadgill and David Murray have all been warmly acknowledged, but Harris's own work with Tailgaters' Tales and other line-ups that attempt to bridge jazz and funk have met with more resistance, perhaps because modern audiences are so hung up on saxophones, with trumpets as second best, they don't appreciate his instrument.

Harris plays in a strong, highly vocalized style which draws directly on the innovations of former Mingus sideman Jimmy Knepper, and on players like Grachan Moncur III and Roswell Rudd, who, in reaction to the trombone's recent desuetude, have gone back to the New Orleans and Dixieland traditions in an attempt to restore and revise the instrument's 'natural' idiom. This early set finds him in genial post-bop company. Adams was the perfect partner in any modern/traditional synthesis, and the rhythm section is rock-solid on such pieces as 'Conjure Man' and 'Song For Psychedelic Souls', which could almost have been by Roland Kirk. Excellent.

KEITH JARRETT&
Born 8 May 1945, Allentown, Pennsylvania
Piano, soprano saxophone, other instruments

Standards: Volume 1
ECM 1737344
Jarrett; Gary Peacock (b); Jack DeJohnette (d). January 1983.

Keith Jarrett said (1986): **'We don't plan ahead of time, so we don't know what we might play on a given night, but these songs are part of a shared language and spirit, and in some way what we pick answers the mood of the room and the group. It's both very precise and very indefinable.'**

In January 1983, at New York's Power Station studio, Jarrett, Peacock and DeJohnette set down 14 tracks, the majority of them based on show tune standards, which significantly redefined contemporary piano trio jazz and began a process of documentation that has continued to this day, to an almost unfollowable extent. The Standards Trio is one of the music's iconic groupings. Jarrett's approach to standards is nothing if not individual; for all his obvious respect and affection for the material, he consistently goes his own way. These are trio dates, though; Peacock's firmly harmonic bass and DeJohnette's imaginative drumming centre every track. It doesn't always come off. There are moments throughout the sequence which are simply flat and uninspired, but one senses that the group is working through or towards something. In the LP era, these would have been edited out. In the CD era there is room for fuller documentation. In the case of Keith Jarrett, even the least successful recordings yield up fascinating musical information and one wouldn't want this music filleted and edited for polish. 'God Bless The Child' drags its slow length along, but there's a gloriously spontaneous-sounding 'Meaning Of The Blues' and a divine 'All The Things You Are'. Many of these interpretations acquire fresh and cumulative significance as the series advances, almost as if each new convocation of the trio retrospectively alters the nuance of its predecessors.

& See also **El Juicio (The Judgement)** (1971; p. 386), **The Köln Concert** (1975; p. 418), **Always Let Me Go** (2001; p. 663)

AMINA CLAUDINE MYERS
Born 21 March 1942, Blackwell, Arkansas
Piano, organ

Salutes Bessie Smith
Leo CDLR 103
Myers; Cecil McBee (b); Jimmie Lovelace (d). February 1983.

Amina Claudine Myers said (1990): **'Where I was growing up, little black girls didn't study classical piano, but it got me noticed and when I went to Dallas, and to a vacation bible school there, it was me who could play the Baptist and Methodist hymns. That went deep.'**

Amina has forged her own hybrid of jazz, soul, gospel and blues, combined with a strong infusion of the avant-garde. Predictably, she has been largely ignored by the major labels and has recorded mainly in Europe. Even so, the discography is far skinnier than it ought to be, and natural selection has thinned the output to just the Bessie Smith homage on Leo and an exactly contemporary trio date for Black Saint called *The Circle Of Time* with Don Pate and Thurman Barker. She has, however, appeared in various situations, with Muhal Richard Abrams, Charlie Haden and others, and is a very considerable artist whose experiments with pipe organ and operatic singing in a jazz context deserve to have been more widely disseminated.

Myers had kicked off the soon to be influential Leo label with an album called *Song For Mother E*, which teamed her with percussionist Pheeroan akLaff but no bass-player. McBee is always a strong presence and, freed from the normal requirement to keep time and anchor the chords, he creates some pungent figures. Without attempting to pastiche the great blues singer, Myers gets inside Bessie Smith's music completely. Apart from the closing 'Straight To You' and 'African Blues', all the material is Smith's, handled with reverence and respect and without the vulgarisms some musicians feel it's necessary to bring to Bessie's noble art. Myers's keyboard touch is strong and mostly functional, her improvisations logical but by no means predictable. One wonders why she isn't better known: the unavoidable conclusion is a shaming one.

JAMES BLOOD ULMER
Born 2 February 1942, St Matthews, South Carolina
Guitar

Odyssey
Columbia 485101
Ulmer; Charles Burnham (vn); Warren Benbow (d). March–May 1983.

James Blood Ulmer said (1992): **'Ornette told me I was a natural harmolodic player. I guess what that means is that everything I do is musical. I don't want to see any part of life that isn't somehow set to music. That's what he does.'**

Ulmer sang gospel, played in funk groups, and then studied with Art Blakey and Ornette Coleman in turn; the former influence is often understated by commentators on his music, but it is certainly there. He's too abrasive and too uncompromising a figure to appear as a casual guest on other people's records too often (though he did do some important touring with Ornette), so Ulmer has tended to put his diverse energies into different 'name' projects: Music Revelation Ensemble, Third Rail, Blues Experience; the character of each can just about be deduced from the titles. After *Tales Of Captain Black* and the celebrated *Are You Glad To Be In America?* some of his work moved towards the black-rock of Living Color or towards straight blues, but Ulmer's jazz chops are always strongly in evidence.

Often described as a student of Ornette's 'harmolodics' – which dispenses with the normal hierarchy of 'lead' and 'rhythm' instruments, allowing free harmonic interchange at all levels of a group – Ulmer had actually started to devise similar ideas independently. In the late '60s he played with organists Hank Marr and Big John Patton, promoting a harsh modern derivative of soul-jazz. His work with drummer Rashied Ali (who rejoined one of the more abstract of Ulmer's late-'80s bands, Original Phalanx/Phalanx) brought him to the attention of Ornette Coleman. Ulmer's contract with Columbia petered out after three albums. This, the final one with the label, is a classic New York record of the period. Given a beefy, upfront sound (at last), Ulmer slimmed his group down to a bassless trio, added the almost shamanistic sound of Charles Burnham's fiddle, and set the group to rock and roll over eight rootsy chunks of American music. 'Church' and 'Little Red House' reach back to gospel, blues and country dance as transmogrified into electrical storms, the whine of the violin mingling with the bite and twang of Ulmer's chording to superb effect. 'Are You Glad To Be In America?' from the 1980 record reappears as a kind of slow lament. The essential Ulmer record.

BRANFORD MARSALIS
Born 26 August 1960, Beaux Bridge, Louisiana
Tenor and soprano saxophones

Scenes In The City
Columbia 468458-2
Marsalis; John Longo (t); Robin Eubanks (tb); Mulgrew Miller (p); Ray Drummond, Ron Carter, Charnett Moffett, Phil Bowler (b); Marvin 'Smitty' Smith, Jeff 'Tain' Watts (d). April–November 1983.

Branford Marsalis said (1992): **'I wasn't originally that drawn to jazz, but when I was 19 I went to see my brother [Wynton] with the Jazz Messengers and something just went** *click*: **the idea of being up there in a suit, playing your own thing, but playing with other members of a group where the music, not some singer, was the focus. All that seemed very powerful.'**

The eldest Marsalis brother started on alto saxophone and joined the Jazz Messengers in 1981. After a period in brother Wynton's group, he has been his own man in various jazz, pop, TV and film situations ever since, as well as teaching and doing A&R work for Columbia. Articulate, hip, funny, Branford was almost as ubiquitous a figure as his trumpeter sibling in the '80s and '90s. His tenor-playing is stonily powerful in the Rollins tradition, and he has stuck by the bigger horn on most of his solo records, with soprano a definite second.

Branford seemed to put most of what he knew and cared about into his first record. Borrowing a Charles Mingus theme for the title and one of the tracks, he stated ambitions over and beyond the usual hard-bop range. His own compositions are more workmanlike and he wisely leans on Mulgrew Miller and Kenny Kirkland for additional material. At this time, CD still wasn't a possibility for recording, but one senses that the LP is a little padded. Given what riches could be stuffed into a Blue Note album whose duration was only half an hour, and this from just two days of recording, *Scenes* does peter out before its time. At its best, though, it is imperious and a sharp reminder that the elder brother had some distance on Wynton at the start of their careers, at least. They quarrelled over Branford's dalliance with pop acts like Sting, and one suspects the saxophonist was never quite as committed to a playing career. Even so, this debut is a high-point in the decade.

MICHEL PETRUCCIANI
Born 28 December 1962, Orange, France; died 6 January 1999, New York City
Piano

100 Hearts
Blue Note 538329-2
Petrucciani (p solo). June 1983.

Michel Petrucciani said (1984): **'I like to be part of a band, and really part of a band, not just a leader with sidemen, but it's great to play solo. I like to communicate, as directly as in pop song, and it's easier to do that when it's just you and the audience.'**

Anyone who only listened to Michel Petrucciani on record would have needed to know that he was physically handicapped with a rare bone complaint called osteogenesis imperfecta, which, as it sounds, stunted his growth. Diminutive though he was, Petrucciani had a big heart and a formidable technique. He began playing with his father and brother, moved to Paris in his teens and thence to the USA in 1982, where he sought out Charles Lloyd and persuaded him to perform again. The relationship coincided with the revival of Blue Note records and the news interest in Lloyd's return and the young Frenchman's remarkable triumph over adversity stimulated both careers.

There's a freshness and quicksilver virtuosity about Michel Petrucciani's early records which is entirely captivating. He made six albums for the independent Owl Label, some of which material was gathered together for reissue after his death, as well as some Concord recording, repackaged by Blue Note as *100 Hearts*. His technique is formidable by this stage but it's all in the service of the song. The title-tune is a deliriously beautiful thing, and helped establish Petrucciani as one of the great romantic virtuosos in the jazz of his time, and more than two decades later it still sounds wonderfully fresh and alive. His own 'Three Forgotten Magic Words' was a key part of his set at the time – there's a great version on a live set from the Village Vanguard – and this one sets it down in definitive form. He opens the set with Ornette Coleman's blues-drenched 'Turnaround', and wrests it away from all the other piano-players (even the peerless Hampton Hawes) who have programmed it. Charlie Haden's 'Silence' on the same set suggests what Petrucciani had been listening to around this time. He makes a silvery thing of Sonny Rollins's 'St Thomas' and then weaves together Bill Evans's 'Very Early', 'Someday My Prince Will Come', 'All the Things You Are' and 'A Child Is Born' in one glorious medley. There were many more records, but few reached the perfection of this. Would we have admired him as much if he had been six foot two? Not a whit less.

GRAHAM COLLIER

Born James Graham Collier, 21 February 1937, Tynemouth, Northumberland, England
Double bass, composer

Hoarded Dreams

Cuneiform RUNE 252
Collier; Ted Curson (t); Henry Lowther, Manfred Schoof, Tomasz Stańko, Kenny Wheeler (t, flhn); Connie Bauer, Malcolm Griffiths, Eje Thelin (tb); Dave Powell (tba); Art Themen (ss, ts); Juhani Aaltonen (as, ts); Geoff Warren (as, af); Matthias Schubert (ts, ob); John Surman (bs, cl, bcl); Roger Dean (p, ky); John Schroder, Ed Speight (g); Paul Bridge (b); Ashley Brown (d). June 1983.

Graham Collier says: **'All those great improvisers gathered together: a composer's hoarded dream, you might say.'**

A major composer on the British scene, even if he has spent large periods of time away from the country, Collier was the first of his countrymen to study at the Berklee School of Music. His musical career began, like so many others of his generation, in an army band, originally as a trumpet-player. He later played with the Jimmy Dorsey orchestra, but after graduating he returned to the UK to form the workshop/collective/ensemble he called Graham Collier Music, which was dedicated to performing his own ambitious but deeply swinging music. Unlike many, perhaps most of his generation of British players, Collier didn't go overboard for either fusion or freedom. He incorporated elements of the former, but while many of his contemporaries dived into jazz-rock, Collier went back to examine aspects of '50s modal jazz which he considered had not been exhausted or fully exploited. He created a significant body of small-group music on record, of which *Deep Dark Blue Centre*, *Down Another Road* and *Mosaics* are perhaps the most satisfying. He also turned to large-scale composition later in life, producing such wonderful scores as the *Charles River Fragments*, *Winter Oranges* and *Bread And Circuses*.

Hoarded Dreams sits chronologically in the middle of the story. It isn't necessarily

Collier's masterwork. More fully realized work followed and some of *Hoarded Dreams*' allure undoubtedly comes from its cast-of-thousands personnel. Confidently achieved work followed in later years, but the performance of *Hoarded Dreams* (which, strictly speaking, is the name of the orchestra) at the much loved Bracknell Jazz Festival was a piquant and now nostalgic moment for British jazz fans.

In recent years, Collier has written about his desire to take improvised music off the page. One of the remarkable things about *Hoarded Dreams*, and perhaps only equalled by Charles Mingus, is the seamlessness of written material and improvisation. The international personnel each receives a solo spot and it's invidious to pick out favourites. The trumpeters steal it to some extent, with Lowther stunning in 'Part Two', Stańko in 'Part Five', and fine interventions from Schoof and Curson elsewhere. The trombones, Bauer in particular, also have a field day. The piece flows with indivisible logic. So natural are some of the transitions that they can only be scored and yet the piece as a whole is marked by spontaneity and controlled power. There are technical flaws, if one listens close enough and with a curmudgeonly spirit, but they become part of its striking humanity. Without an overt political or social programme, it still delivers an expression of togetherness and individuality in ideal balance that is hard to beat.

Collier's dream-hoard is rich, sometimes strange and entirely free of British whimsy. A lastingly satisfying experience.

KENNY BARRON
Born 9 June 1943, Philadelphia, Pennsylvania
Piano

Green Chimneys
Criss Cross 1008
Barron; Buster Williams (b); Ben Riley (d). July 1983.

Kenny Barron said (1992): **'There was music in the house constantly at home. I had two brothers and two sisters – I was the kid – and piano was compulsory! But, you know, the radio was on all the time, and that's how you pick up music. I sometimes write something down and wonder if it isn't something I heard when I was young.'**

Saxophonist Bill Barron's younger brother was a phenomenally talented youngster who developed into a graceful and gracious soloist, the perfect sideman, but also a leader of genuine presence and authority. Barron spent four years working with Dizzy Gillespie and had a stint with Yusef Lateef. One can detect the residue of both respectively in his long-term interest in Latin/African-Cuban music and in his openness to unusual tonalities, though some of that must have rubbed off from his brother. Barron also had experience accompanying singers and there is always a nice balance in his work between functional spareness and a more expressive dimension.

It is hard to pick out just one work from such a varied body of recording, but *Green Chimneys* is a perennial. Barron's extended exploration of 'There Is No Greater Love' is masterly, nearly 12 minutes of fine improvisation that keeps the song constantly in view. The two Monk tunes – 'Straight, No Chaser' is the other – are confidently despatched, with some nice variations on the melody of the title-piece. The reissue has two versions of 'Time Was', a relative rarity that might well have been the kicking-off point for another record entirely. The trio sounds tight, well-organized and thoroughly familiar with the material. It isn't an unduly dramatic record and there is nothing particularly radical about its language, but it knocks into a cocked hat most of the piano trios of today.

PAUL RUTHERFORD &

Born 29 February 1940, London; died 5 August 2007, London
Trombone, euphonium

Gheim
Emanem 4107
Rutherford; Paul Rogers (b); Nigel Morris (d). July and December 1983.

Emanem founder and producer Martin Davidson says: **'Rutherford's swings between hilarity and depression tended to alienate people; otherwise I'm sure he would have been recognized as one of the leading "first generation" improvisers. The records show that, personality aside, he was one of the all-time greats. Too bad he had to die in frustrated poverty.'**

Rutherford's later discography includes further brilliant solo performances, the astonishing overdubbed *Neuph*, where he improvises against double-speed recordings of his own trombone pushed up into cornet range, and the similarly conceived electronic programmings of 2004's *Iskra³*. Apart from his work with the London Improvisers Orchestra, a shambolic and, one suspects, ego-fraught convention of British players, of which he was usually the most interesting component, and his work with the Free Jazz Quartet, it is harder to find Rutherford in a group context under his own leadership. Though Emanem is his more familiar abode, *Gheim* actually first appeared on the Ogun imprint. The original set included the whole of a trio performance at the Bracknell Jazz Festival, caught in analogue but beautifully detailed. The opening piece weighs in at over half an hour, a long, steadily evolving idea from Rutherford that constantly hints at jazz models without a single discernible quote or allusion.

The set is arguably most important for an early glimpse of bassist Rogers, with whom Rutherford went on to make the duo *Rogues* in 1988. He's already possessed of a powerful technique, solid and percussive, full of trombone-like slides and jazzy figures but driven by an idiosyncratic logic that is still yielding impressive results. Morris is probably better known as a fusion drummer, but his unmetrical playing is equally effective and the kit has a full share in proceedings.

Bracknell MC Lol Coxhill said there would be no encores, but a few months after the summer gig the same trio was recorded in the studio: three previously unissued tracks and a valuable glimpse on 'Prindalf' of Rutherford's second-string euphonium work. It's unmistakably the same voice but with a solidity that sometimes overpowers the bassist, who cranks out a steadily unravelling ostinato in response. Rutherford's other great gift is a sense of humour. The trombone has obvious slapstick potential, but you'll come away from this smiling at the sheer joy he takes in making those beautiful, human, inhuman sounds.

& *See also* **The Gentle Harm Of The Bourgeoisie** (1974; p. 415)

DON PULLEN &

Born 25 December 1941, Roanoke, Virginia; died 22 April 1995, East Orange, New Jersey
Piano

Evidence Of Things Unseen
Black Saint 120080
Pullen (p solo). September 1983.

Saxophonist and collaborator Jane Bunnett remembers: **'People looked at Don as a tough, non-compromising musician, and he was, but he was also sensitive, generous and kind.**

When you spent time with him, he was yours completely. He had a wicked sense of humour. I remember playing him a Charles Ives recording and he responded with "He's stealing some of my shit!!"'

Don Pullen's solo records demand comparison with Cecil Taylor's, and for once the parallels are valid. Pullen's traditionalism is more obvious, but the apparent structural conservatism is more appearance than fact, a function of his interest in boogie rather than Bartók. Pullen grew up around music, but only studied in depth when he hooked up with Muhal Richard Abrams. He had a mixed apprenticeship, working with the Jazz Messengers (briefly), with multi-instrumentalist Giuseppi Logan, one of the more obscure of the New Thing musicians, but also in R&B groups (which added organ to his armoury), and it was that mixture of rawness and sophistication that brought him to the attention of Charles Mingus. Those same qualities also came out in a long-standing group co-led with saxophonist George Adams, whose own premature death – Pullen's was to follow – inspired a later album, *Ode To Life*.

An earlier *Solo Piano Album*, plainly so called and issued on Sackville, reinforces an impression of Pullen as a performer interested in large masses of sound, sometimes to the detriment of forward progress. That in turn led him back to the organ. Pullen always insisted that far from his organ-playing impacting on his pianism, it was the other way around. A duo record with Don Moye of the Art Ensemble is a dark and neglected classic, piled up with sustained chords and swirling textures.

Evidence Of Things Unseen is by far the best of his solo discs. It is a record that very deliberately observes the pendulum-swing of African-American music between rage and joy, pain and acceptance. Pullen was always capable of deep personal sympathy, and it's no coincidence that two of these rolling themes are dedications to individuals, but he was also gifted with a more generalized generosity, as in the tone-poem for an imaginary fan 'Big Alice', originally written for the Mingus group but not released until later. The trajectory of *Evidence Of Things Unseen*, from the long title-track, through 'Victory Song', 'Un Beginning' and 'Perseverance', to the tiny 'Rejoice' at the end, is absolutely typical of Pullen's work. The piano sound is sometimes thick and heavy, a device Pullen got from his sustain and damper pedals, which allowed him to generate subordinate drones underneath his line; like Taylor, he was a dancer at the keyboard. Made while the Pullen-Adams group was still active, the record has something of the R&B energy of that great outfit, but retains something, too, of the abstract. His work became ever more rhythmically active and subtle, and in his last years he devoted much time to exploring Native American and Brazilian materials. His early death from lymphoma came right on top of the premiere of his ambitious *Sacred Common Ground*.

& See also **Ode To Life** (1993; p. 570)

VIENNA ART ORCHESTRA
Formed 1977
Orchestra

The Minimalism Of Erik Satie
hatOLOGY 560
Bumi Fian, Hannes Kottek (t, flhn); Christian Radovan (tb); Harry Sokal (ss, ts, f); Wolfgang Puschnig (bcl, as, sno, f); Roman Schwaller (ts, cl); Woody Schabata (vib); John Sass (tba); Wolfgang Reisinger (perc); Lauren Newton (v); Matthias Rüegg (cond). September 1983–March 1984.

Mathias Rüegg said (1985): **'The earliest jazz musicians took material from church, from the theatre and from working songs, but they also took ideas from classical music. In putting that all back together, we're not doing anything very new.'**

The brainchild of composer and arranger Matthias Rüegg, VAO synthesize jazz and 20th-century compositional language, avant-garde and vernacular; a convocation of soloists rather than a conventional big band. The Satie project is a classic of its era – though in some ways its impact has been dispersed by subsequent work by others, it remains a benchmark recording. Most of the tracks briefly articulate a Satie theme before proceeding to work variations on it. The orchestral voicings are bright and spare, with most of the space devoted to solo material. The most remarkable sections are devoted to essays on *Vexations*, which are by a 'minimalist' VAO – only Lauren Newton, in a Berberian-derived *vocalise*, Roman Schwaller's tenor sax and Wolfgang Puschnig on bass clarinet, each duetting with vibesman Woody Schabata, who maintains a steady chordal pulse below. The closing passage with Puschnig, easily his finest hour on record, is extraordinary.

Later records have tackled everyone from Strauss to Duke Ellington, but there are more groups around now doing this kind of work. When they garner praise, it's only fair to point out that VAO were first in the field.

EMILY REMLER
Born 18 September 1957, New York City; died 4 May 1990, Sydney, Australia
Guitar

Transitions
Concord CCD 4236
Remler; John D'Earth (t); Eddie Gomez (b); Bob Moses (d). October 1983.

Guitarist Deirdre Cartwright says: **'I've no idea what she might have done had she lived, but it would have been remarkable. We all learned from Emily.'**

Emily Remler's early death was a profound shock, not just because it came suddenly or hastened by heroin use, but also because it left a very strong sense of what might have been. In truth, Remler's career might have gone any number of ways. At the time of her death, she had just released a first album of pop-jazz, ominously entitled *This Is Me*, and she continued to diversify in other ways, working with blues groups, in Broadway shows and with other artists, including David Benoit and fellow guitarist Larry Coryell. But while Remler was not in any obvious way an innovator, one had a sense listening to her that there was another dimension, another creative personality, lying in wait. Whether it would ever have emerged, or been sublimated in more conventional situations, is the teaser and it has energized a minor cult round Remler's music and personality since 1990.

Her best joke about herself presupposed that other personality: inside the nice Jewish girl from New York was a burly black man with a big calloused thumb. Remler's music was muscular hard bop, deeply influenced by Wes Montgomery, by no means tinged with obvious femininity, but always with a sense of something not yet delivered. Her final studio album for Concord was explicitly a tribute to Montgomery. The stylish *East To Wes* acquired an aura because it was her final record and because it featured such a superior group, with Hank Jones, Buster Williams and Marvin 'Smitty' Smith, but for all its glories – not least a rare latter-day reading of Claude Thornhill's lovely 'Snowfall' – it is a less creative record than the earlier pair of *Transitions* and *Catwalk*, made with a relatively unusual line-up that featured guitar and trumpet as the two lead voices.

In 1983, Remler was just a few years out of Berklee, married to pianist Monty Alexander (the union was dissolved a year later) and beginning to show signs of real originality as an artist. Of the two, and despite the fact that *Catwalk* featured nothing but original compositions, we favour the earlier disc. On *Transitions*, her instinct for fine, unexplored melody led her to Duke Ellington's rarely covered 'Searchin'' and to Keith Jarrett's 'Coral', as well as Sam Jones's 'Dal Sasser', which is almost never called for. Her own 'Nunca Mas' and the beautifully constructed title-track offer perfect vehicles for D'Earth's crisp, punchy solos and Remler's own more expansive bop lines. In the absence of a pianist – Jones again and James Williams had worked on her first Concord dates – Remler is called on to fill in the harmonic picture, but does so with a remarkably open touch, moving the title-track's already elusive tonalities ever further out of reach. Moses is a master drummer, often content to establish an underlying pulse rather than a strict metre, which suits Remler's elastic phrasing very well indeed. Gomez is only ever as good as the company he keeps and here it and he are very good indeed. All round, it's a remarkable performance and contributes to one of the very best guitar jazz records of the decade.

LEE KONITZ &

Born 12 October 1927, Chicago, Illinois
Alto and soprano saxophones

Star Eyes: Hamburg 1983

hatOLOGY 518
Konitz; Martial Solal (p). November 1983.

Lee Konitz said (1992): **'Familiarity is not a good thing when you're improvising. If I hear myself playing something I recognize, I stop and lay out for a few measures.'**

Given his level of activity it should hardly be surprising to encounter Konitz in the company of ... anyone you might mention, but this was an association that wouldn't necessarily have been high on anyone's list, for all the eminence of the partners. It's a quite remarkable record and an inexhaustible resource for anyone studying jazz harmony and the language of improvisation. In Solal's hands, even 'Cherokee', tucked away at the end of the set, seems reinvented, but it's the duo's approach to 'Star Eyes', 'It's You' and even 'Subconscious-Lee' that startles. Solal stays well inside the tune in terms of chordal patterns and basic trajectory, but his harmonies are so rich and ambiguous that Konitz is initially obliged to work his way back to the source before taking the theme out as he would normally do. There's also a reading of that old staple 'Body And Soul' which prompts an immediate return to Coleman Hawkins, who momentarily seems one-dimensional by comparison, though, of course, Hawkins's great solo is there as well, buried in the piano part.

& *See also* **Subconscious-Lee** (1949–1950; p. 118), **Motion** (1961; p. 278)

STRING TRIO OF NEW YORK

Formed 1977
Group

Rebirth Of A Feeling

Black Saint 120068
Billy Bang (vn, yokobue, f); James Emery (g, soprano g, mand); John Lindberg (b). November 1983.

James Emery says: **'At some point in the life of an ensemble, there comes a time, after the excitement of initial discovery has run its course, when the group will either continue to move forward or break up.** *Rebirth Of A Feeling* **came after just such a period; after a cooling-off cycle, we found that there was new music to be brought forth, hence the title.'**

It's different now, of course, but at the end of the '70s there weren't many string groups in modern jazz and there was a certain prejudice that any ensemble constituted on the lines of the String Trio Of New York was historically inauthentic and likely to be involved in some kind of suspect Third Stream project. Where was the saxophone? Piano? Drums? In fact, the very earliest 'jazz' or proto-jazz groups were probably string ensembles, portable and flexible units that could alternate between playing European sheet music for the residents of the big house and dance music for the workers. Any further suspicion that STNY might lean towards longhair music should have been stamped out by the presence of founder member Billy Bang, who along with fellow violinist Leroy Jenkins kept the instrument's voice alive in the American avant-garde of the '60s and '70s.

Bang's membership was relatively short and his place has been taken by a succession of others – Regina Carter, Diane Monroe, Rob Thomas – who have each brought something distinctive to STNY's brand of jazz, which has proved to be very durable and remarkably resistant to 'guest' intrusions. But so distinctive was Billy's approach, intense, folksy, muscular, but capable of real lyricism and quite different from Jenkins's more angular and dissonant style, that the trio's early Black Saints remain their most cherished discs. Some enthusiasts felt that with *Area Code 212*, recorded in November 1980, and with *Common Goal*, recorded exactly a year later, STNY had reached a peak it would never recapture. As Emery attests, there was a period of detachment, when the members concentrated on other projects, but the String Trio Of New York has always been a genuine group rather than a pragmatic alliance and after the members skipped one autumnal session it became clear that the unifying forces were greater than those keeping them apart.

Rebirth Of A Feeling claims the attention more than any of the previous or even the excellent later discs. As ever, the writing is democratically credited, with two compositions apiece by Emery and Bang, and the long and brooding 'Utility Grey' from the bassist. Bang's 'Penguins An' Other Strange Birds' is gloriously wacky and driven by some terrific interplay. His other piece, 'Karottenkopf', is an obscurely troubling piece that sounds as if it ought to be lighter-hearted than it is. Emery kicks off the session with 'Open Up' and clinches his mastery of writing for this group with the 'Ephemera Trilogy'. His guitar-playing, as ever, balances hardscrabble rhythms with musing *rubato* lines quite unlike any others in the contemporary guitar literature. He's a formidable composer and this is a remarkable record. There was one more to go before Bang moved on, and it completed a creative cycle, but we've always favoured *Rebirth* as the best place to start, where they restarted.

JIMMY KNEPPER

Born 22 November 1927, Los Angeles, California; died 14 June 2003, Triadelphia, West Virginia
Trombone

I Dream Too Much
Soul Note 121092
Knepper; John Eckert (t); John Clark (frhn); Roland Hanna (p); George Mraz (b); Billy Hart (d). February–March 1984.

Trombonist and singer Eric Felten recalls: **'If Knepper's articulation sounds muffled at times, recall that Jimmy made his name with Charles Mingus. The bass-player, in one of his psychotic rages, punched Jimmy in the mouth, knocking out his front teeth. Whenever I played with Jimmy, his pre-gig routine included gluing in his upper dentures with extra adhesive. It is a measure of his remarkable musicianship that Knepper found a way to clear that hurdle.'**

The young James Knepper made very rapid progress on his instrument and was playing professionally in his teens, working in a number of big bands. He had a stormy stint with Charles

Mingus, which caused lasting damage, and his later years were clouded by neurological illness. However, along the way Knepper created some lastingly beautiful jazz, including a
few fine records under his own name, most of them still relatively little known.

Knepper had an astonishingly agile technique (based on altered slide positions) which
allowed him to play extremely fast lines with considerable legato, more like a saxophonist than a brass-player. Eric Felten recalls that as a young man Knepper followed Charlie
Parker round the clubs, taping his solos for study. Doing so allowed him to avoid the dominant J. J. Johnson style – Felten points to Lawrence Brown as a more likely source – and to
develop the swing idiom in a direction that was thoroughly modern and contemporary, with
a bright, punchy tone. The fight with Mingus drove him out of active jazz performance for
some time, and much of the next decade was spent in relative obscurity.

He made a strong return with *Cunningbird* for Steeplechase in 1976. His active career was
largely in Europe at this time, as a member of the Jones–Lewis big band and his later recordings were also all for European labels. *I Dream Too Much* opens with a long, faintly sardonic
reading of the standard, with some delightful voicing for the three brasses. A subtle and
crafty soloist, Knepper brings those qualities to his writing as well. 'Sixpence', the first
of three originals, has an unpredictable slow bounce to the melody. 'Under The Sun' and,
particularly, 'Beholden' are more complex and the meat of the album is to be found there,
with Knepper's delightful slip-horn phrasing constantly at work in the solos. Hanna comps
beautifully throughout and is rewarded with an airing of his 'If I Say I'm Sorry', a tune that
contributes to the album's bittersweet mien. It's an understated classic.

MIKE WESTBROOK
Born 21 March 1936, High Wycombe, Buckinghamshire, England
Piano, tuba

On Duke's Birthday
Voiceprint JPVP138
Westbrook; Phil Minton (t, v); Stuart Brooks (t, flhn); Danilo Terenzi (tb); Chris Biscoe (reeds); Brian Godding
(g); Dominique Pifarély (vn); Georgie Born (clo); Steve Cook (b); Tony Marsh (d); Kate Westbrook (v, thn, picc).
May 1984.

Chris Biscoe says: **'At first run-through the music seemed relatively straightforward
but I'm surprised now how many changes of feel and sound there are. Apart from two
trumpets, every instrument stands alone: a Duke-ish sound. Favourite personal moment
– 12 minutes into "East Stratford Too-Doo", at the end of my baritone solo, Danilo tops it
off with a gorgeous phrase which has a real first take feel.'**

Britain's neglect of one of its finest postwar composers amounts to little less than a national
disgrace. Mike – and Kate – Westbrook's work covers a wide spectrum from Ellingtonian
jazz to music-theatre and reworkings of classical and pop forms. His early Concert Band was
a significant crucible of talent, and a first showcase for John Surman. The large-scale suites
Metropolis and *Citadel Room 315* introduced a new sophistication into big-band writing and
arrangement, records that combined imposing structure with considerable improvisational
freedom. With his group Solid Gold Cadillac, Westbrook delivered a refined version of jazz-
rock. Later projects based around Blake's poetry and Rossini's music were *sui generis*.

Perhaps the most satisfying single piece in the Westbrook canon to date is *On Duke's
Birthday*. As Chris Biscoe has also pointed out, it opens with a rarity, four choruses of Westbrook on piano plus rhythm section. It also ends with an ambiguous low C♯ on piano, and
one feels throughout that this is the pianist's most pianistic and most personal large-group
record. The leader's part is vital to the band in the way that Ellington was vital to his.

If it is Westbrook's finest hour that isn't because it takes its authority from Duke

Ellington, but because it does not. If this were called *New Compositions* it would still be remarkable, and might even be admired more. It's music without a hint of self-election to jazz's pantheon but yet written and executed very much in that great tradition, but with a generation of further musical thought put behind it. The opening piece, 'Checking In At Hotel La Prieure', manages to contain an extraordinary range of harmonic and melodic variation within passages of flailing swing. The writing on 'East Stratford Too-Doo' and the Gil Evans-like title-track, which form the main section of the piece, are harmonically sophisticated, rigorously arranged and played with dazzling liberty by the soloists: Westbrook imposes Ducal discipline on his 'sections' but offers commensurate liberty. A modern masterpiece.

MARTIN TAYLOR &

Born 1 January 1956, Harlow, Essex, England
Guitar

Spirit Of Django

Linn AKD 030
Taylor; Dave O'Higgins (ts, ss); John Goldie (g); Jack Emblow (acc); Alec Dankworth (b, cabassa); James Taylor (perc). June–August 1984.

Martin Taylor says: **'We never tried to imitate the Hot Club. Our instrumentation is different, and I wanted the band to acknowledge the past, but in a contemporary way. I was always fascinated with the idea of what Django might have done had he lived longer, and that's why we recorded Pat Metheny's "James". From what I learned of Django from those who knew him, he would have loved Metheny's music. And I like to think he would have approved of us, too.'**

Given the association with Grappelli, the naming of this group was no surprise, and neither was much of the repertoire; it was Grappelli who suggested the name and gave his blessing. Taylor had decided to give up unaccompanied performance for a while and concentrate on a group sound. It must have been difficult to sustain the level of highly exposed creativity he was bringing to solo concerts. What the group permits him to do is work within a much bigger harmonic and timbral framework, allowing his guitar to thread together ideas rather than sustain them all. What's clear, though, is that this isn't a pastiche band. For a start, Taylor doesn't play like Django Reinhardt but essentially in solo fingerstyle. Equally, the repertoire is kept up to date and relevant, unlike the usual run of 'gypsy jazz' groups.

In Dave O'Higgins (one of the best of the younger generation of British saxophonists) and the seasoned Jack Emblow, he has partners who are absolutely in sympathy with what he is doing. Together, they confirm from the first chorus that this is not a Hot Club imitation. In Dankworth, he has a bass-player who can sustain the tempo in a drummerless group (son James has only a bit part at this stage) but who can also lend himself to the other parameters of the music as well. On 'Night And Day' and 'Honeysuckle Rose', he is creating as much of the musical movement as anyone else. Taylor intended the record to be a tribute to his own father, as well as to the artistic parent namechecked in the title. Playing acoustically and in a setting that juxtaposes Django material ('Nuages', 'Minor Swing', 'Swing 42') against originals and Taylor's own celebrated reworking of Robert Parker's 'Johnny And Mary' theme, he sounds very different from the solo artist, less busy and layered, but instantly identifiable as himself.

& *See also* **DJANGO REINHARDT, Django Reinhardt 1935–1936** (1935–1936; p. 51), **Pêche À La Mouche** (1947–1953; p. 111)

RAY BROWN

Born 13 October 1926, Pittsburgh, Pennsylvania; died 2 July 2002, Indianapolis, Indiana
Double bass

Soular Energy
Concord CCD 4268
Brown; Red Holloway (ts); Gene Harris (p); Emily Remler (g); Gerryck King (d). August 1984.

Rehearsing his trio in the UK, prior to a BBC recording, Ray Brown was caught on-mic growling: **'My tempo!'** Then, after a pause, muttering: **'... Good enough for Charlie Parker, sure as hell good enough for you.'**

One of the most recorded jazz artists of all time, the little powerhouse witnessed the birth-pangs of bebop, acted as MD for his wife, Ella Fitzgerald, played with Charlie Parker and Dizzy Gillespie, and appears on so many records he himself must have lost count. In later years, he was a founder member of the L.A.4 and fronted a recording and touring trio for most of his last two decades, recording extensively with Concord and Telarc.

The L.A.4's festival-friendly sound and repertoire often disguised formidable musicianship, with Bud Shank, Laurindo Almeida, Jeff Hamilton or Shelly Manne. *Soular Energy* is a fine album which perhaps only needs Jeff Hamilton in his usual slot behind the drums to lift it into minor-classic status. King holds a nice, springy beat but lacks sparkle and is inclined to hurry things along. Perhaps in retaliation, Brown takes the '"A"' Train' at a pace which suggests privatization may be around the corner. Slowed to an almost terminal grind, it uncovers all manner of harmonic quirks which Brown and the attentive Harris (who came out of semi-retirement to make the date) exploit with great imagination. Holloway and Emily Remler sign up for a shortish and slightly inconsequential 'Mistreated But Undefeated Blues'. Brown's counter-melody figures on 'Cry Me A River' and, especially, the closing 'Sweet Georgia Brown' are signature devices.

PETER BRÖTZMANN &

Born 6 March 1941, Remscheid, Germany
Tenor, baritone and bass saxophones, clarinet, tarogato

14 Love Poems Plus 10 More: Dedicated To Kenneth Patchen
FMP CD 125
Brötzmann (as, ts, bs, mouthpiece, clarinets, tarogato). August 1984.

Peter Brötzmann said (1992): **'It's a very fragile, delicate thing, playing solo. You go into it with a few ideas – you can't just turn up with nothing – but maybe you forget them pretty quickly and just keep working. You learn things about who you are, playing solo, so it's important, but also quite nervous.'**

There are other, some might argue superior, solo records in Brötzmann's worklist, though interestingly not until 2009 was there a record release of a live concert. Whatever the merits of 1994's *Nothing To Say* or the later *Right As Rain*, the *Love Poems* record was a key moment in the perception of Brötzmann as a more subtly inflected player than the screamer of *Machine Gun* and *Fuck De Boere*. At first glance, the title seemed to offer as absurd a prospect as *Derek Bailey Plays Ballads*, but of course that happened, too.

Brötzmann's first unaccompanied record, *Solo* in 1976, was more than a multi-instrumentalist's show-off, but there was around it a certain feeling that these were test-pieces – 'Humpty-Dumpty' on bass saxophone, for example – whose successes remained technical first and foremost. Not so *14 Love Poems*, which is gloriously musical from the very start, even if it is no more 'expressive' (in the gushy sense) than any other Brötzmann record. The only named track is Ornette Coleman's 'Lonely Woman', played on baritone. The remainder are divided between his other instruments, tenor, clarinets (including bass clarinet), strikingly good alto on 'No. 3' and tarogato on 'No. 10', the wooden instrument delivering its usual folksy tone and offering a reminder that this saxophonist's art is also rooted in the music of his people rather than just in some imported notion of what 'free jazz' might be. It would be hard to finesse what was 'German' or 'Germanic' about the record, but there are ghostly echoes of an older vernacular music floating around it. Unusually, the 'bonus' tracks from the same session, dedicated to the anarchist poet Kenneth Patchen, really do seem like a plus.

& *See also* **Machine Gun** (1968; p. 352)

CHET BAKER &

Born 23 December 1929, Yale, Oklahoma; died 13 May 1988, Amsterdam, Netherlands
Trumpet, voice

Blues For A Reason

Criss Cross Jazz 1010
Baker; Warne Marsh (ts); Hod O'Brien (p); Cecil McBee (b); Eddie Gladden (d). September 1984.

Chico Hamilton said (1994): **'I hadn't seen or heard much of Chet in years. I was in Europe on tour, and went into a club in Amsterdam, and there was a photograph of an old man behind the bar. I asked who it was. "Chet Baker." My eyes fell out. He looked a thousand years old, and with the saddest face I ever saw.'**

Chet's final years were a strange mortal progress: sufficient gigs to feed his habit, permissions to record freely granted in return for enough to pay for a fix; a Dorian Gray story in reverse, with the man shrivelling before everyone's eyes while the music continued pure and inventive; even the voice remained compelling, whispering lyrics rather than singing them, but conveying oceans of emotion as he did so.

It's now clear that the near-abstraction and extreme chromaticism of Chet's last years were a perfectly logical outgrowth of bebop. Warne Marsh's style has been seen as equally problematic, 'cold', 'dry', 'academic', the apparent antithesis of Chet's romantic expressionism. When the two are put together, as on this remarkable session, most of the familiar generalizations and categorizations fall flat. While Baker is quite clearly no longer an orthodox changes player, having followed Miles's course out of bop, he's still able to live with Marsh's complex harmonic developments. *Blues For A Reason* stands out from much of the work of the period in including relatively unfamiliar original charts, including three by Chet himself. The best of these, 'Looking Good Tonight', is heard in two versions, demonstrating how the trumpeter doesn't so much rethink his whole strategy on a solo as allow very small textural changes to dictate a different development. Marsh, by contrast, sounds much more of a *thinking* player and, to that extent, just a little less spontaneous. The saxophonist's 'Well Spoken', with which the set begins, is perhaps the most challenging single item Baker tackled in his final decade, and he sounds as confident with it as with the well-worn 'If You Could See Me Now' and 'Imagination'.

The end was not far away, but the music of Chet Baker's last years was far from a dying fall, but a kind of triumph over mortality. In May 1988, he fell from a hotel window in Amsterdam. The circumstances have never been fully or satisfactorily explained.

& *See also* **Chet Baker And Crew** (1956; p. 176), **Live At Nick's** (1978; p. 447)

LOUIS SCLAVIS &

Born 2 February 1953, Lyons, France
Clarinet, bass clarinet, soprano saxophone

Clarinettes
IDA 004
Sclavis (cl, bcl solo); and with Christian Rollet, Christian Ville (perc). September 1984, January 1985.

Louis Sclavis said (1985): **'I find strange the dominance of the drummer in jazz, why the music has to take all its energy and direction from the one man at the drum kit. Take that away and jazz is free to move in new directions.'**

Potentially the most important French jazz musician since Django Reinhardt (who was Belgian!), Sclavis has attempted to create an 'imaginary folklore' that combines familiar jazz procedures with North African and Mediterranean music, French folk themes and *bal musette*, a form that almost certainly played a role in the shaping of jazz in New Orleans.

Unlike Sidney Bechet, who reversed the traditional order and may be an ancestral influence on the Frenchman, Sclavis's clarinet-playing is a good deal more forceful than his soprano saxophone work. His bass clarinet is particularly original, drawing little or nothing from previous models and condensing most of Sclavis's virtues: melodic invention, timbral variation, rhythmic sophistication. The most striking track of the set is 'Le Chien Aboie Et La Caravane Passe', a husky duo with percussionist Ville which puns on the gypsy saying 'the dog barks, and the caravan passes on'. But for all his interest in European folk, Sclavis considered himself unequivocally a jazz musician and a duo version of 'Black And Tan Fantasy' on the same record suggests the depth of his interest in redefining jazz language and ridding it of what he considers to be the tyranny of the drummer. In this, he may have been attempting to continue the work of the Jimmy Giuffre trio, shortly to reconvene and tour.

& *See also* **L'Imparfait Des Langues** (2005; p. 704)

JAKI BYARD &

Born 15 June 1922, Worcester, Massachusetts; died 11 February 1999, New York City
Piano, tenor saxophone

Phantasies
Soul Note 121075
Byard; Al Bryant, John Eckert, Roger Parrot, Jim White (t); Bob Norden, Carl Reinlib, Steve Swell, Steve Weinberg (tb); Stephen Calia (btb); Manny Boyd, Bob Torrence (as); Al Givens, Jed Levy (ts); Preston Trombly (bs); Ralph Hamperian (b); Richard Allen (d); The Apollo Stompers; Denyce Byard, Diane Byard (perc, v). September 1984, August 1988.

Jaki Byard said (1988): **'This is a social project, but then all jazz is supposed to be a social project. I've been lucky, playing solo and in small groups. This was an attempt to bring in a whole community of people, to make jazz that sounds like it comes from a neighbourhood.'**

In later years, Byard gave of himself selflessly as a teacher at the Hartt School (with Jackie McLean) and continued to promote his notion of jazz as an essentially social phenomenon. *Phantasies* is credited to the Apollo Stompers. There are times when the group doesn't seem to keep up with Byard's weather-changes of idiom or mood.

Working with Maynard Ferguson and then with Mingus gave Byard some insight into how to steer at high speed. Without any doubt, his excellence as a section-player fed into his solo and small-group playing as well. *Phantasies* is a brawling big-band excursion with vocals from Denyce and Diane; though it is well produced and more than adequately executed by a relatively unknown band (Swell's is perhaps the only name that jumps out), the element of pastiche may at first be difficult to take on board. Byard's historical awareness has never been more actively engaged (other than in his solo work) and never more problematically; perhaps the difficulty was writing for an ensemble that by definition did not share his purview and vision. Nevertheless, *Phantasies* grows rather than recedes in importance with the passing years and its eclecticism now seems almost fashionable. It includes some great ensemble work on the Ellington medley, and some of the modernist things – 'Lonely Woman', 'Impressions' – are excitingly done. So's a concluding read of 'Lover Man', which is unique of its kind.

A few years later *Phantasies II* was an altogether better-structured programme. On 'Concerto Grosso', Byard took a playful look at a baroque form within the context of a jazz band and brings in Vincent Lewis to do a convincing job as an Apollo crooner, a reminder that this project had a specific historical provenance, the old Apollo Theatre and its tightrope mix of high and low styes. Musically, though, the most interesting thing is 'II IV I', a title which refers to the cadence minor/dominant/major which dominates the piece. It takes Byard back to the great days of the Harlem stride pianists. As a pair they make fascinating listening, but it's the first volume that counts.

& *See also* **Out Front!** (1961; p. 272)

JIMMY LYONS
Born 1 December 1933, Jersey City, New Jersey; died 19 May 1986, New York City
Alto saxophone, flute

Give It Up
Black Saint 120087
Lyons; Enrico Rava (t, flhn); Karen Borca (bsn); Jay Oliver (b); Paul Murphy (d). March 1985.

Trumpeter Dennis González said (2005): **'I studied with Jimmy for a week in 1979. He was quiet, but he had such magical power, stillness outside, a storm within. All he ever said was "Again ... again ... again", as I tried playing my lines different ways to make them my own. At the end of that, he'd play the line on his alto and it wasn't mine any more, but his in an instant.'**

If Charlie Parker had a true heir – in the sense of someone interested in doing more than spending inheritance capital – it was Jimmy Lyons. Compared to his light-fingered onrush, most of the bop epigones sound deeply conservative. He didn't have the greatest tone in the world: 'reedy' is the only word, ironically. Lyons's delivery was always light, the lines dizzyingly extended, and in all his work he was without obvious ego. Years of playing beside Cecil Taylor, in addition to accelerating his hand-speed, probably encouraged a certain self-effacement as well.

The key text for Lyons fans is a box set of live recordings released on the Ayler label, but it's a hefty undertaking. For a single representation, one has to go to one of his Black Saint records. On *Give It Up*, Lyons seems quite content to remain within the confines of the group. Significantly pianoless and with only a secondary role for the bassist and drummer, it resolves into a series of high, intermeshed lines from the saxophone and horn, with the bassoon tracing a sombre counterpoint. Borca's role might have been clearer were she not so close in timbre to the bass, but it's worth concentrating for a moment on what she is doing; the effect is broadly similar to what Dewey Redman used to do behind Ornette and Don Cherry, and Lyons gives her plenty of solo prominence. Borca also appears to great effect on the slightly earlier *Wee Sneezawee* for the same label (the title-track is one of his best-known compositions), perhaps the most conventional of the Black Saint discs in free-bop terms but a similarly invigorating session. Only on the brief, uncharacteristic 'Ballada', with which *Give It Up* ends, does Lyons occupy the foreground. It's immediately clear that his fey, slightly detached tone doesn't entail an absence of feeling; the closing track is a sad monument to a fading career.

SLIDE HAMPTON

Born Locksley Wellington Hamilton, 21 April 1932, Jeannette, Pennsylvania
Trombone

Roots
Criss Cross 1015
Hampton; Clifford Jordan (ts); Cedar Walton (p); David Williams (b); Billy Higgins (d). April 1985.

Slide Hampton said (1985): **'Why do I play left-handed? They gave me a horn and that's the way I started to play. It's the only thing I do that way round ... it *sounds* the same.'**

Hampton's arranging has often taken precedence over his playing, but he remains a quick and skilful trombonist and the records are underrated. Projects like his World Of Trombones, which had a nine-slide front line, gave him prominence briefly, but for the most part Hampton has been a backroom man and apparently content with it. Yet every time we sample one of the records, that warm tone and deft handling of a melody stand out strongly.
   This Criss Cross session saw everything worked out just right. Hampton and Jordan are perfectly paired, the trombonist fleet yet punchy, Jordan putting a hint of dishevelment into otherwise finely tailored improvisations; and Walton has seldom played with so much vitality, yet without surrendering his customary aristocratic touch. Williams and Higgins are asked to play hard throughout the four long titles, and they oblige without flagging. Although a very fast 'Solar' is arguably the highlight, it's a fine record altogether.

FRED HO

Born Fred Wei-han Houn, 10 August 1957, Palo Alto, California
Baritone saxophone

Tomorrow Is Now!
Soul Note 121117
Ho; Sam Furnace (as, ts); Sayyd Abdul Al-Khabyyr, Al Givens (ss, ts, f); Richard Clements (p); Jon Jang (p); Kiyoto Fujiwara (b); Taru Alexander (d); Carleen Robinson (v). April 1985.

Fred Ho said (1986): **'Most forms of so-called "political" art are petty-bourgeois proscriptions, cast in one dimension. Revolutionary art is energetic and dynamic. It doesn't pacify with easy slogans and "official" forms.'**

Ho's brand of engaged and ebullient big-band jazz has obvious ties to Charles Mingus, but there are many other influences at work as well, not least a desire to synthesize modern jazz, Eastern influences and left-wing politics. Ho's Marxist thinking might be thought to run some risk of falling into that most heinous of ideological traps, *individualism*, but his emphasis on the ensemble and on the creative contention of many individualisms allows this music to vault any number of philosophical and musical traps.

We once described the music on *Tomorrow Is Now* as 'aggressively programmatic'. That remains true, in both parts, but perhaps requires a more generous qualification. Unlike much revolutionary music, the medium is often more interesting, and perhaps more likely to win hearts and minds, than the strident message. Ho has tackled so many negative aspects of contemporary society – from race and power in the 'martial arts ballet' *Once Upon A Time In Asian America*, to rape in *Yes Means Yes No Means No*, to power again in the mythological *Monkey: Parts 1 & 2* – that his musical qualities are often occluded.

Ho has a big, powerful sound reminiscent of Harry Carney, and this sets the tone for ensembles with a strongly Ellingtonian cast. The title of the first album sets up all sorts of different expectations, from Ornette Coleman's *Tomorrow Is The Question* to Max Roach's *We Insist! Freedom Now* suite. The multi-part 'Tomorrow Is Now' doesn't quite cohere, but if anything it grows with age and acquaintance. The whole configuration of the ensemble inevitably resembles Charlie Haden's Liberation Music Orchestra, but at this point Ho hadn't fully integrated political urgency and lyrical expressiveness. One senses that the 'message' comes in little discrete quanta which rest on the surrounding score rather than driving it along. On the other hand, almost every track here has great individual power: the ironic 'Pretty As A Morning Sunrise!', 'Ganbaro', 'Blues To The Freedom Fighters'. It's probably worth playing any of these alongside anything from Duke's *Far East Suite* or one of Toshiko Akiyoshi's cross-cultural projects. Ho doesn't seem out of his depth in such company.

GEORGE CABLES

Born 14 November 1944, New York City
Piano

Phantom Of The City

Contemporary C 14014
Cables; John Heard (b); Tony Williams (d). May 1985.

George Cables said (1990): 'It's vision and the concept of a band that reaches out to me, rather than individual chops. So it was Coltrane and Miles that affected me more than any single piano-player. Miles's groups always had that magic that could transport you.'

Cables is a great accompanist, an essentially modest man who likes to service the song. He's still probably best known for his duo performances with Art Pepper on a marvellous Galaxy, *Goin' Home*. Cables has a slightly sharp touch that adds an unexpected measure of tension. He gained small-group experience with Art Blakey and Max Roach in the '60s, then backed horn-players, notably Freddie Hubbard and Pepper, giving him a somewhat unfair journeyman status, which was somewhat corrected by a string of fine solo and trio albums in the '80s and '90s.

Phantom is a beautifully balanced piano trio record, and one of the very best recorded appearances by Tony Williams in the '80s. It's the drummer who gives the set much of its character, and on the Cables composition 'Dark Side, Light Side' he brings a jaw-dropping musicality, playing the melody as if working on a tuned instrument. Heard never lets the pace drop, even nudging at Williams on occasion when the drummer seems content to let the tempo ease.

Cables is completely in command, opposing long, rippling melody-lines with a firm chordal pattern and working a whole spectrum of harmonic variations on the basic tune. His touch is lighter than one would expect from a self-confident front-man, and seems less emphatic than ever after his work with electric piano on 1979's admired but dated *Cables' Vision*, but it's an individual voice and this is an unmissable record.

JOHN SCOFIELD&

Born 26 December 1951, Dayton, Ohio
Guitar

Still Warm
Gramavision GR 8508
Scofield; Don Grolnick (ky); Darryl Jones (b); Omar Hakim (d). June 1985.

John Scofield says: **'I was just leaving Miles at the time, and I still thought that electric jazz could work!'**

John Scofield was perhaps the last of Miles Davis's sidemen to break through to a major career, but his first records for Enja, made prior to his joining Davis in 1982, bespeak a substantial talent already making waves. He had studied at Berklee and played in the Boston area with a diverse group of leaders – Charles Mingus, Gerry Mulligan, Lee Konitz, Gary Burton, Billy Cobham/George Duke – before forming his own band. Scofield mustered rock power and jazz chops and made the two – at last – seem compatible. The important thing was that jazz had the upper hand.

Next came the albums for Gramavision. *Electric Outlet* was a false start: the band seems gimcracked around a dubious idea of highbrow pop-jazz, Sanborn and Anderson are there only for colour, and the attempted grooves are stiff and unyielding. But *Still Warm* solved matters at a stroke, and it's odd that even some Scofield devotees seem unpersuaded of its considerable merits. Steve Swallow's production clarified the sound without overpowering the fluidity of Scofield's arrangements, Grolnick added thoughtful keyboard textures, and Jones and Hakim (colleagues from the Miles Davis band) were tight and funky without being relentlessly so. Scofield's own playing here assumes a new authority: tones are richer, the hint of fuzz and sustain is perfectly integrated, and his solos are unflaggingly inventive: for a single sample, listen to the sharp, hotly articulated solo on 'Picks And Pans'. But why settle for a single sample? The rest of the album is richly inflected and in places (on the opening 'Techno' and on 'Protocol') almost estranged and bordering on the sinister. What was still warm? The corpse of electric jazz? Or jazz itself? Whatever the answer, Scofield was on hand with a defibrillator.

& *See also* **Quiet** (1996; p. 601)

JOE BONNER

Born 20 April 1948, Rocky Mount, North Carolina
Piano

Suite For Chocolate
Steeplechase SCCD 31215
Bonner; Khan Jamal (vib); Jesper Lundgaard (b); Leroy Lowe (d). November 1985.

Joe Bonner says: **'I shook hands with John Coltrane at the Village Vanguard ten days before he died. It was so beautiful. I could smell his aura, sense his presence. He hypnotized me.'**

Whatever happened to ...? It's a question often asked of musicians who made a flurry of recordings over a short period of time and then seemed to vanish from the catalogues. The answer in Joe Bonner's case is that he is once again self-exiled from the main jazz centres in New York City or Chicago and working with a new group called The Bonner Party in

Colorado. The pun on the tragic pioneering Donner-Reed Party isn't accidental. Bonner has often seemed to clash – or more realistically, fail to fit in – with the jazz establishment. He is a man of strong personality, which reflects in his playing. As a youngster in North Carolina, having abandoned trumpet and tuba, he took to piano lessons, but disliked Chopin as being insufficiently 'masculine'. On graduation, he made his way to New York and worked with Harold Vick (his 'Winter Blossom' appears as an extra track on *Suite For Chocolate*), fellow North Carolinian Max Roach, Roy Haynes, Pharoah Sanders and others on the fringes of the Coltrane circle. His most obvious influence on piano is McCoy Tyner, though Bonner's modalism is of a more robust and emphatic sort, his attack always forceful and forward-leaning.

After a period with the Thad Jones-Mel Lewis big band, he stayed in Europe for a while, making a number of records for Steeplechase and Theresa (some of the latter reappearing on Evidence). For the latter, he made the ambitious *Impressions Of Copenhagen*, which made use of a string trio alongside the jazz group, and this interest in larger forms, fuller orchestration and suite-like structures gives a fair sense of his compositional priorities. The very first of the Steeplechases, *Parade*, is a fresh and joyous trio with bassist Johnny Dyani and drummer Billy Higgins, but the one we return to most often is the later *Suite For Chocolate*, where the bop and modal languages are more thoroughly synthesized in the pianist's exchanges with the still underrated Jamal.

Bonner – or maybe it was Nils Winther at Steeplechase – has a particular gift for the effective shaping of an album, making it more than merely a sequence of tracks. On *Parade*, he combined some tersely modal ideas with Charlie Parker's 'Au Privave' (two fine versions on the CD), while on the later *New Beginnings* for Theresa (also his first dabble with electric piano) he reverted to Thad Jones's 'A Child Is Born', but gave it a more sombre, less rhapsodic reading than is often the case.

The set opens expansively with 'Under The Big Sky' but then immediately moves into more ambiguous tonal territory with 'Where Did You Go?'. There are African elements to some of the pieces, with Vick's piece standing as a quiet interlude in the middle of the CD. 'Chocolate' and 'Blues For Chocolate' work some interesting thematic variations and again here the empathy between Jamal and Bonner is very striking, with the vibist producing ringing passages laden with rich overtones. Bonner isn't all hustle and bustle, but his lyrical and elegiac passages all have a definite edge and urgency. He's a difficult fellow to pin down, but his pianism – often surprisingly light in attack – is highly distinctive and he deserves a renewed place among the major figures of contemporary piano jazz.

JOE HENDERSON &

Born 24 April 1937, Lima, Ohio; died 30 June 2001, San Francisco, California
Tenor saxophone

The State Of The Tenor: Volumes 1 & 2
Blue Note 828779-2 2CD
Henderson; Ron Carter (b); Al Foster (d). November 1985.

Joe Henderson said (1992): **'I dislike repetition. I even set myself the exercise of starting a phrase on a different note in the bar, changing the rhythm and the speed of the phrase. I regard it as a betrayal to play the same thing twice.'**

Although they had a mixed reception on their release, these records now sound as authoritative as their titles suggest. Henderson hadn't recorded as a leader for some time, and this was his return to the label where he commenced his career, but there is nothing hesitant or routine about the playing here. Carter and Foster provide detailed support – the dates were carefully prepared, the themes meticulously chosen and rehearsed, before the recordings were made at New York's Village Vanguard – and the bassist in particular is as inventive as the nominal leader. Henderson takes an occasional wrong turning, noted perhaps in a recourse to a favourite lick or two, which he then flurriedly rejects, but he functions mainly at the highest level. The intelligent choice of themes – from Silver, Monk, Mingus, Parker and others, none of them over-familiar – prises a rare multiplicity of phrase-shapes and rhythmical variations out of the tenorman: as a single instance, listen to his manipulations of the beat on Mingus's 'Portrait' (on *Volume 2*), with their accompanying subtleties of tone and attack. The sententious title might seem more worthy of a Congressional report, but it's amply justified: tenor-playing was never more senatorial.

& See also **Page One** (1963; p. 295)

ANTHONY BRAXTON &
Born 4 June 1945, Chicago, Illinois
Saxophones, clarinets, flutes, piano

Quartet (London / ... Birmingham / ... Coventry) 1985
Leo CD LR 200/201 / 202/203 / 204/205 (all 2CD)
Braxton; Marilyn Crispell (p); Mark Dresser (b); Gerry Hemingway (d). November 1985.

Anthony Braxton said (1985): **'If I could speak to Eric Dolphy now I know we would understand one another, though he never enjoyed a group like this who understood his philosophy and his direction. We are in the same lineage and imbued with the same spirit, though.'**

For all his compositions for amplified shovels, 100 tubas and galactically dispersed orchestras, the core of Braxton's conception at this period remains the conventional jazz quartet. The touring group of 1984–5 was of remarkable vintage and Crispell's piano-playing was one of its outstanding features. There are unauthorized recordings of this band in circulation, but the Leo sets are absolutely legitimate, and pretty nearly exhaustive; the CDs offer good-quality transfers of the original boxed set, six sides of quite remarkable music that, in conjunction with the other quartet sessions, confirm Braxton's often stated but outwardly improbable interest in the Lennie Tristano school, and in particular the superb harmonic improvisation of Warne Marsh. Those who followed the 1985 British tour may argue about the respective merits of different nights and locations, but there really isn't much to separate the London, Coventry and Birmingham sets for the non-specialist. Record sleeves – and Graham Lock's Boswellian notes – offer a breakdown of the compositions performed and their sequence, but it's worth noting how often they are collaged with 'Composition No. 96', the 'multiple-line' orchestral piece which serves as a main reference point for the Coventry date. Lock also discusses a range of subjects with Braxton: Frankie Lymon, Coltrane, Warne Marsh, chess, the blues, the nature of music itself.

Though the Birmingham set reaches a hectic climax with an encore performance of 'Kelvin 40(O)', the Coventry set benefits from the interview material, but also from the most sheerly beautiful performance in Braxton's entire recorded output, the peaceful clarinet music on 'Composition No. 40(N)' that ends the first set.

& See also **For Alto** (1968; p. 355), **New York, Fall 1974** (1974; p. 416), **Creative Orchestra Music** (1976; p. 431), **Nine Compositions (Iridium) 2006** (2006; p. 714)

DAVID LIEBMAN &

Born 4 September 1946, Brooklyn, New York
Tenor and soprano saxophones

The Loneliness Of A Long-Distance Runner

CMP CD 24
Liebman (ss solo, overdubbed). November–December 1985.

Dave Liebman says: **'This is my favourite recording for a few reasons. It is solo soprano sax so I am completely responsible for the outcome. It involved the most composition I have ever done for a recording. Personally, this was a crucial stage of my life having just turned 40, the passing of my father and getting married. It was also my first recording with a true master engineer, Walter Quintus, without whom it would never have come off.'**

The metaphor here resonates strongly with our own insistence that jazz is a long game, played out over a whole lifespan and using as its material the stuff of life itself. Liebman was to return to this material and approach many years later on the hatOLOGY set *The Distance Runner*, and it relates in form if not substance to the solo improvisation on *The Tree*, but here the music is laid out as if in representation of a marathon and all its foregoing preparation. Liebman provides detailed notes relating the music to the underlying programme and as long as one continues to think metaphorically and resists any temptation to allow the music to become pictorial or literal, it's a helpful exercise (!) to follow them. Certain themes, including a figure that might have come from one of Ornette Coleman's dirges, recur through the music, unifying the sequence and restating the loneliness theme. Some passages are multiply overdubbed to give the impression of a saxophone ensemble, but the most impressive moments are when Liebman is heard alone, the still sound of his soprano constantly redolent of Coltrane but also quite distinct from that language: more linear, more aware of the weight of each note, rather than the headlong succession of notes, and in the end more personal. This is a meditative record, but not without its strenuous aspects, and it stands as a minor classic.

& See also **Drum Ode** (1974; p. 411); **QUEST, Redemption** (2005; p. 710)

WYNTON MARSALIS &

Born 18 October 1961, New Orleans, Louisiana
Trumpet

J Mood

Columbia CK 40308
Marsalis; Marcus Roberts (p); Robert Leslie Hurst III (b); Jeff 'Tain' Watts (d). December 1985.

Wynton Marsalis said (1990): **'You know, at first I wasn't very keen on playing trumpet, and certainly not practising all I should. I was convinced that I'd get that ring round my lips from the mouthpiece and that girls wouldn't like me!'**

The most controversial figure in modern jazz: overpraised (arguably), maligned (mostly for things he has never said or done), endlessly burdened with misleading copy. What a weight of expectation and responsibility fell on Wynton Marsalis's shoulders. At 20, not quite overnight, he became the nominated leader and mouthpiece of a new traditionalism in jazz. In Stanley Crouch he had his *éminence noire*, an able polemicist and spokesman with a voice as ringingly clear as Marsalis's trumpet.

A front-line role in the Jazz Messengers obviously doesn't constitute obscurity, but there was a dramatic turn from gifted apprentice to star-in-waiting. In 1981, he parted company from Art Blakey, with the boss's blessing, went on the road with a quartet, and immediately laid claim to the then discarded mantle of Miles Davis, who later spurned the young pretender at a bizarre showdown in Canada. Marsalis took over from Miles at Columbia as the iconic trumpeter of his generation, and made it his business (with Crouch's eloquent support) to decry the electrification and commercialization of jazz which his predecessor seemed now to represent.

He was thrown into a studio with Miles's one-time rhythm section and came out unscathed. It became clear, though, that Marsalis wanted to shape his own constituency of musicians and by the time of the epochal *J Mood*, one of the finest jazz records of modern times, he had attained something like that.

This is the first time Wynton sounds completely relaxed and in possession of his own language, and though it was a record that intensified the debate about neo-traditionalism against experiment and contemporaneity, the actual music gives no sense of that. 'Much Later' seems to reference Miles Davis in some obscure way. 'Skain's Domain' and the beautiful 'Presence That Lament Brings' touch the opposite boundaries of the trumpeter's range, suggesting that his great quality is not after all virtuosic flash and fire but a deep-rooted expressiveness which maintains its integrity all the way from fiery individualism to elegiac regret. 'After' is a richly expressive slow number, and 'Melodique' is sweetly executed with the mute in place. Roberts is in exceptional form, playing in a style quite remote from his usual one of the time.

Aspects of Marsalis's technique are still open to discussion, and there are places here where the connective tissue seems absent, fine phrases but insecurely pulled together. They're few and far between, though.

& *See also* **Standard Time: Volume 6 – Mr Jelly Lord** (1999; p. 638), **Live At The House Of Tribes** (2002; p. 677)

PAT METHENY&

Born 12 August 1954, Lee's Summit, Montana
Guitar

Song X: Twentieth Anniversary Edition
Nonesuch 7559-79918-2
Metheny; Ornette Coleman (as, vn); Charlie Haden (b); Jack DeJohnette, Denardo Coleman (d). December 1985.

Pat Metheny said (2004): **'I think some of the best stuff wasn't put on the record! Ornette and I talked for about three weeks about the material and other stuff. Denardo was there sometimes, though Jack and Charlie didn't come in till later. It wasn't like I was part of a working band, but it didn't just happen spontaneously. A lot of thought went into that record.'**

Metheny's great departure still seems like a bolt from the blue, but it stands for all the other bold side-turns he has taken, and it's important to locate it in a desire to improvise with freer and more abstract forms round this time: so, not quite the aberration it was thought to be. None the less, it's the most astonishing move ever made by a middle-of-the-road jazz artist. Not only does the guitarist power his way through Coleman's itinerary with utter conviction, but he sets up opportunities for the saxophonist to resolve and creates a fusion with which Coleman's often impenetrable Prime Time bands have failed to come to terms. Melody still has a place here, which suggests that Metheny's interest in the original Coleman legacy may be carrying forward in his own work more intently than it is in the composer's. Either way, on many of the more raving episodes here both men sound exultant with the possibilities. Twenty years after its initial release, Metheny went back to the original tapes and prepared a new edition which restored six pieces left off the vinyl album. In a curious move, they appear as the first six tracks on the CD. 'Police People' and 'The Good Life' are especially interesting since they include blowing sections based around chord changes, an environment almost unthinkable for Coleman yet one which he handles with typical aplomb. 'Word From Bird', the slapstick 'Compute' and 'The Veil' put a further spin on what the group could do.

& *See also* **Bright Size Life** (1975; p. 429)

JIMMY RANEY&

Born 20 August 1927, Louisville, Kentucky; died 10 May 1995, Louisville, Kentucky
Guitar

Wisteria
Criss Cross 1019
Raney; Tommy Flanagan (p); George Mraz (b). December 1985.

Allan Holdsworth said (1986): **'Jimmy is amazing. Everything seems low-key and quiet, even when he's playing quite intricate lines, and then every now and then something goes by you, and you think: "Hang on, what *was* that? how did he *do* that?" And I'm a guitar player!'**

The early '80s saw some vintage Raney on record and the Criss Cross set-up offered him an alternative to Steeplechase as an outlet for his work, and perhaps a more receptive producer. It's hard to make an informed choice between *Raney '81, The Master* and the record above, and tempting to say that Flanagan and Mraz make the difference. At first hearing, the mix sounds slightly woolly, but this is perhaps because the three voices are arranged quite democratically. Flanagan's right hand sometimes recedes, but the material more than makes up for any purely technical quibbles. From the opening 'Hassan's Dream', with its big, dramatic gestures, to 'I Could Write A Book', the drummerless group plays at the highest level and 'Out Of The Past' is very special indeed.

& *See also* **A.** (1954–1955; p. 154)

Part 2:
1986-1990

BOBBY WATSON

Born 23 August 1953, Lawrence, Kansas
Alto and soprano saxophones

Love Remains
Red RR 123212
Watson; John Hicks (p); Curtis Lundy (b); Marvin 'Smitty' Smith (d). November 1986.

Bobby Watson says: **'This was the first Red date not recorded in Italy with Italian musicians. Sergio Veschi wired the money from Milano, allowed me to hire the** musicians, and book the studio. The MRC studio on 14th Street in Manhattan was workable with no frills. Sergio even let me do the mixing and mastering and mail the finished project to him. It was huge for me as an artist, to have that trust. I guess it came out on the recording.'

Though he has never sounded like a Bird knock-off, Watson grew up in the same Kansas City environment and has something of Parker's omnicompetence, product of many, many local gigs in tough and unforgiving company. Though these days he is a distinguished academic just over the state line at the University of Missouri, Kansas City, he has had a remarkable – and one might say old-fashioned – recording career, working with a huge range of musicians in many different styles. Watson had a formal music education, too. He was a contemporary of Jaco Pastorius and Pat Metheny at the University of Miami before trying his luck in New York City, where he worked for nearly five years as Art Blakey's musical director in the Messengers.

The distinctive components of Watson's sound are a very direct approach to phrasing, a wailing, blues-drenched tonality with seamless slides down the register and a battery of sharply percussive reed and mouthpiece sounds. The project that followed *Love Remains* was a thoroughly unexpected tribute to Johnny Hodges, *The Year Of The Rabbit*, not the kind of record young players were expected to make in the '80s, but it pointed to another important source for Watson. At his most lyrical, he is, indeed, a descendant of Ellington's most expressive soloist.

Watson has recorded with a number of groups, Horizon and the High Court Of Swing, and as an unaccompanied improviser (on another Red disc, *This Little Light Of Mine*) but for us nothing has ever topped this magnificent quartet and the record it made in November 1986. Over a late-night malt whisky in 2006, the authors of the *Guide* decided that it was probably our favourite modern jazz album of all. It is absolutely reliable, delivering musical intelligence, fantastic group interplay, high emotion and an almost unearthly beauty. From the Parker-tinged but by no means slavish 'Mystery Of Ebop' to the solemnly funky 'Dark Days' (originally an apartheid protest but retasked as a tribute to Nelson Mandela), it has a complete unity of purpose and tone. The title-piece, jointly credited to Bobby and Pamela Watson, is built round a three-note motif which means the same thing in any language. Hicks's solo is a perfect foil for Watson's plangent second entry, while Lundy and Smitty Smith sustain a dark, rolling pulse. Lundy's 'Sho Thang' is the only non-Watson composition, testimony to the closeness of their working relationship at the time. The quartet had been gigging for a period before the recording and what Watson describes as a good hook-up is evident in every track. Pam Watson's 'The Love We Had Yesterday' rounds off a wonderful set. Retrospect and repetition have never dulled this one. We've no hesitation in hailing it as a modern masterpiece.

MULGREW MILLER

Born 13 August 1955, Greenwood, Mississippi
Piano

Work!

Landmark LCD 1511
Miller; Terri Lyne Carrington (d). April 1986.

Mulgrew Miller said (1999): '**It's a huge mistake to think of the piano as this big, inflexible thing that does what it does. A piano has to be wrestled into shape, in order to get it to do the things you want from it: play like a horn, sound like drums, whatever.**'

Miller emerged as a major pianist in the '80s, following stints with Woody Shaw, the Ellington Orchestra and the Jazz Messengers. He recorded prolifically through that decade, in a style that seemed to draw loosely from McCoy Tyner, but with sufficient originality and maturity to set him apart from more slavish copyists.

The debut *Keys To The City* set him on course, and by the third album Miller was fronting a serious body of work. *Work!* is a terse, efficient album that might sound routine to inattentive ears. In fact, it's very carefully inflected and Miller's writing always seems to hearken back to bop without ever slipping into the hard-bop formulae with modernistic flourishes that passed for inventive jazz at the time. The originals 'Sublimity' and 'The Sage' are the only extended performances of the set, committed performances that find the leader typically attentive to the rhythm of the band, alert in particular to the drummer's line. The Monk title-tune gives him a chance to flex some muscle, but typically Miller highlights the song's sophistication rather than its rootsier dimensions. On 'My Man's Gone Now' he plays solo, a good test-piece for those who find him anonymous. The harmonic thinking is original and inventive, though by no means avant-garde.

After Landmark, Miller was at Novus and did some good work there, too, but the vicissitudes of jazz recording have left the discography becalmed somewhere and it wasn't until MaxJazz starting putting out live material in 2002 that he became properly prominent again.

DENNIS GONZÁLEZ
Born 1954, Abilene, Texas
Trumpet

Stefan
Silkheart SHCD 101
González; John Purcell (bcl, bf, eng hn, syn, v); Henry Franklin (b, v); W. A. Richardson (d). April 1986.

Dennis González said (1995): **'Keith Knox [of Silkheart] had written this big piece about me, in a Polish jazz magazine. Next thing I knew I had a $20,000 cheque through the mail and we were talking names, all these guys I knew and didn't think anyone else did. So I basically said yes to them all.'**

The most exciting musician to come out of Texas since Ornette Coleman, González has followed his own course doggedly and with little home support. For a time he ran his own record label, Daagnim, but became briefly prominent when taken up by the new Swedish-based Silkheart label. González speaks up for what might be called a 'new Southern' jazz which has evolved over 25 years and is now represented by Yells At Eels ('Yes, it is' in a strong Southern accent!) and various other line-ups involving the trumpeter's sons.

González's recordings for the Silkheart label were part of a determined effort to wrest creative initiative back from New York and the West Coast. The band assembled for *Debenge, Debenge* goes under the name New Dallasorleanssippi, which is more awkward than the music, wonderfully coherent and direct. González's other great achievement is to have tempted the great tenor-player Charles Brackeen out of a self-imposed semi-retirement.

Stefan is a minor masterpiece. The opening 'Enrico', dedicated to a fellow trumpeter, opens a path for magnificent flugelhorn figurations over a bass/bass clarinet accompaniment. 'Fortuity' is calm and enigmatic, like the title-track (a dedication to González's son) a simple theme on open chords, but with a dramatic interlude for voices. 'Hymn For Don Cherry' is based on 'At The Cross'. 'Boi Fuba' less successfully explores Brazilian materials, while John Purcell's closing 'Deacon John Ray' features his Dolphy-ish alto, and the trumpeter flirts with total harmonic abstraction.

González went on to make *Namesake* and *Debenge, Debenge* for the label, the former with Brackeen and Douglas Ewart, the latter with Kidd and Marlon Jordan, both with the great Malachi Favors from the Art Ensemble. It was a short-lived association but a remarkably fruitful one and Silkheart's late-'80s catalogue is still required listening for any modern jazz fan.

SAMMY RIMINGTON
Born 29 April 1942, Paddock Wood, Kent, England
Clarinet, alto saxophone

The Exciting Sax Of Sammy Rimington
Progressive PCD-7077
Rimington; David Paquette (p, v); Walter Payton (b); Placide Adams, Stanley Stephens, Ernest Elly (d). April 1986–April 1991.

Sammy Rimington said (1992): **'After working with Ken [Colyer], it was nice to break out a bit and do some different things, but you can't beat a grounding like that, that kind of discipline.'**

Rimington has had a strange career: a stalwart with Ken Colyer, a transplantation to Louisiana, where he became a bosom friend of Capt. John Handy, a flirtation with jazz-rock and now occasional sightings in sundry pick-up groups, like this one. This Progressive album – and a similarly titled sequel – features him exclusively on alto, where he sounds like Handy but phrases as if he were brother to Johnny Hodges: the result is a queer hybrid, soaked in a woozy kind of romanticism. Engagingly done, although the sound-mix (with the piano in the distance, the drums right up front) doesn't assist. They're all short, punchy tracks, with only 'Don't Blame Me' aspiring to any length, though there's also an overlong 'Reach Out To Jesus' which might well have been trimmed or dropped. It's a generous set and a nice insight into Sammy's alto-playing, which we continue to think is more interesting than his clarinet.

PALLE MIKKELBORG
Born 6 March 1941, Copenhagen, Denmark
Trumpet

Heart To Heart
Storyville SLPCD 4114
Mikkelborg; Kenneth Knudsen (ky); Niels-Henning Ørsted Pedersen (b). 1986.

Palle Mikkelborg remembers: **'The reaction we got was unusual in our world! At a huge music festival in Denmark – this was in the days when people were still allowed to smoke – the audience all took out their lighters when we played "Imagine". It became our "hit" number for the whole time the group was together.'**

Born in occupied Denmark, Mikkelborg taught himself trumpet and turned professional while still a teenager. He for a time ran the Radiojazzgruppen and worked with other big bands. His best-known small groups were Entrance, which lasted almost until the above recording was made, and a trio with Thomas Clausen and NHøP before this group was formed. Subsequently, he was best known for having written a large-scale 'concerto', Aura, for Miles Davis, and other works in classical forms. Mikkelborg's rather melancholy trumpet sound is obviously influenced by Miles, but his use of echo, live multitracking and other devices points in another direction, and when one hears him at length Chet Baker and even Howard McGhee sound like more probable sources.

Heart To Heart has been a favourite of ours for nearly 25 years. It starts with an unashamed nod to Miles, though played with a clear, brassy resonance that is all Mikkelborg's own. Fortunately, perhaps, it doesn't set a tone for the set, which is quite varied in temper, though mainly in a meditative mood. Knudsen's keyboard structures are always effective and robustly put together and NHøP is beautifully recorded for once, bringing that big, singing tone out into the foreground. This isn't just a beautiful record, but a highly effective recording that makes the most of the players' strengths.

EDWARD VESALA
Born Martti Juhani Vesala, 15 February 1945, Mäntyharju, Finland; died 4 December 1999, Helsinki,
Finland
Drums, percussion

Lumi
ECM 831517 2
Vesala; Esko Heikkinen (t, picc t); Tom Bildo (tb, tba); Pentti Lahti (as, bs, f); Jorma Tapio (as, cl, bcl, f); Tapani Rinne (ts, ss, cl, bcl); Kari Heinilä (ts, ss, f); Raoul Björkenheim (g); Taito Vainio (acc); Iro Haarla (hp); Häkä (b).
June 1986

Edward Vesala's widow, pianist/harpist Iro Haarla, remembers: '**Edward searched long for musicians who fitted his vision of music. His discipline was strict, maybe harsh, but he gave them faith and they delivered more than they knew they could. Rehearsals and recording sessions combined different emotions: severity, love, humour – the spirit of Edward's music.**'

Born in a remote, rural part of Finland – a landscape which audibly influenced his later work – Vesala trained as an orchestral percussionist at the Sibelius Academy in Helsinki but became involved in the European free-jazz scene, establishing contact with trumpeter Tomasz Stańko and saxophonist Peter Brötzmann, and making some early recordings that reflected a fascination – shared by Stańko – with slow-moving but inwardly detailed harmonics and rhythm in jazz, an interest much influenced by Miles Davis. Though he featured on the wider European scene, Vesala also established his own record label (confusingly called Leo, but nothing to do with Leo Feigin's UK-based imprint of the same name) and began to conduct workshops in improvisation to which he gave the name Sound & Fury.

This became the name of the recording and touring ensemble he sustained to the end of his life. His association with the ECM label began in 1972 on Jan Garbarek's *Tryptikon*. Six years later, he made the first of six records under his own name for Manfred Eicher, starting with *Nan Madol*. Opinions vary quite sharply as to which is the best of these. Wider media notice for the pointedly polemic title of 1991's *Ode To The Death Of Jazz* (Vesala's response to the rise of Wynton Marsalis and the neo-conservative wing in contemporary jazz) makes it a favourite contender. Others speak up for the subsequent *Invisible Storm* or *Nordic Gallery*. This one, though, remains our firm favourite.

Lumi means snow, but it is also the name of Vesala and Haarla's daughter. Everything about it is exquisitely crafted, composition, studio sound, design, but the haunting cover image of a shrouded, *golem*-like figure on a lonely road is belied to some degree by the playfulness of some of the material, particularly 'Fingo', which reflects the curious Finnish appetite for tango dancing, and 'Calypso Bulbosa'. That said, the album's most striking tracks are a new, subtly voiced version of 'The Wind', originally made with Stańko in 1974, and the wonderful static harmony of 'Frozen Melody', on which Vesala works variations on a descending repetition of four notes of the same pitch.

One might say that Iro Haarla's harp-playing stands in the same relation to the leader's conception as Alice Coltrane's did to her husband's. Unfortunately, the parallel was hammered home all too literally when Vesala died suddenly of heart failure, aged just 54. Haarla has gone on to forge a fascinating independent career as harpist and pianist, but it is her work here, at the heart of an ensemble that seems to have its own inner rhythm, dictated by Vesala's Billy Higgins-like drumming but also distinct from it, that represents her most striking contribution so far to contemporary jazz. Vesala's own project was sometimes dismissed as dry, unimpassioned and contentless, a musical equivalent of Bertolt Brecht's sour (but obliquely perceptive) impression of the bilingual Finns as a people silent in two languages. Vesala's first tongue was jazz, but there were folk and classical inputs as well, idiosyncratically mixed. His posthumous reputation outside his homeland is somewhat depressed. Even the most casual return visit to *Lumi* restores him: a record as quietly exhilarating as new-fallen snow.

JOE ZAWINUL &

Born 7 July 1932, Vienna, Austria; died 11 September 2007, Vienna, Austria
Piano, keyboards

Di-a-lects
Sony Legacy 508493
Zawinul; Bobby McFerrin, Carl Anderson, Dee Dee Bellson, Alfie Silas (v). June 1986.

Joe Zawinul said (1995): **'The way I work is I find a melody, I add a little bit on top; then another little bit, and then another, till there are all these layers. Then I want voices, for this is music for people, not *the* people, or *my* people, just people.'**

When Weather Report came to an end after *Procession* and *Sportin' Life*, and arguably some way after the group's real creative end, Zawinul tried for a time to keep the franchise going with a group called Weather Update. But it was increasingly clear that any post-Shorter project was by definition a Zawinul project, and though there was for a time a touring Zawinul syndicate, this remarkable record went out under his surname only (same as the title of the 1970 Atlantic) and with only minimal contribution from other hands; actually a vocal quartet led by Bobby McFerrin.

Zawinul's world music concerns were regarded with some suspicion by jazz purists. Interestingly the front cover of *Di-a-lects* shows every continent except the Americas, and many felt that this new initiative touched on every aspect of contemporary music except jazz. The charge is poorly drawn up, because at the root of every line here is a sense of rhythm and harmony that goes back to Zawinul's very first soul-jazz projects in the US. He had by this time devised a highly distinctive keyboard attack – only Can's Irmin Schmidt plays in a remotely similar way – and an approach to analog synthesizers that invested electronic sound with a warmth and humanity rarely achieved by other players.

That said, *Di-a-lects* has been seriously underrated by jazz critics, mostly, one suspects, because too few of them have actually listened to it. 'Waiting For The Rain' is a brilliant invention, full of harmonic drama. The following 'Zeebop' really does give bebop a 'world' twist and does so at full charge. And for sheer, dancing delight, 'Carnivilito' matches anything in the Weather Report canon. The voices speak, as Zawinul's music often does, of unknown crowds and masses, a shared complicity in making music as a social process. A home-made record that speaks of and to the world, *Di-a-lects* still exerts a powerful influence, even on those who have only heard *of* it.

& *See also* **Zawinul** (1970; p. 379); **WEATHER REPORT, Mysterious Traveller** (1973, 1974; p. 408)

COURTNEY PINE
Born 18 March 1964, London
Tenor and soprano saxophones, other instruments

Journey To The Urge Within
Island CID 9846
Pine; Kevin Robinson (t); Ray Carless (bs); Julian Joseph (p); Roy Carter (ky); Orphy Robinson (vib); Martin Taylor (g); Gary Crosby (b); Mark Mondesir (d); Ian Mussington (perc); Susaye Greene, Cleveland Watkiss (v). July–August 1986.

Courtney Pine said (1995): **'Jazz is a kind of ghetto, or it's maybe like an exclusive club where the members get away with murder because they make the rules and they have the jazz writers out there waiting to enforce the rules, like referees.'**

Pine's debut album marks something of an epoch in British jazz, the emergence of a new, young generation of black players, strenuously and somewhat crudely marketed as such. Since the appearance of the album and following the usual label shenanigans, Pine moved steadily away from straight-ahead, bop-based jazz (if he was ever securely there in the first place) to involve himself in a range of musics, from ska and reggae to hip-hop and post-rock, becoming in the process a kind of godfather figure (or maybe it's more avuncular than that) to a second generation of players. His stewardship of Jazz Warriors was an important catalyst.

His importance is inestimable, and as a result his first record, which now has to be sought out, is difficult to estimate with any accuracy. The first point to make is that Pine didn't start with jazz and drift to reggae. It was the other way around and his experiences with Clint Eastwood and General Saint are audible on *Journey*. He was and is a saxophonist of clear and outstanding capabilities and his own contribution to the record is of consistently high quality. It does, however, serve as a kind of sampler to young jazz talent and in many cases Pine is let down not so much by the lack of skill in his players (for they are all highly professional) but by their desire to be heard. 'Children Of The Ghetto' became a minor chart hit. The better stuff includes the opening 'Miss Interpret' and 'I Believe', and there are nice, thoughtful covers of Wayne Shorter's 'Dolores' and Horace Silver's 'Peace'. A couple of bonus tracks added later included Coltrane's 'Big Nick', which suggests a more abrasive side that has rarely surfaced since. There are other good moments and the sense of a group of musicians seizing their time is palpable, but inexperience and fragmentation take their toll. Keeping one's ears firmly homed onto the saxophone is the key to appreciating this one.

RAN BLAKE &
Born 20 April 1935, Springfield, Massachusetts
Piano

The Short Life Of Barbara Monk
Soul Note 121127
Blake; Ricky Ford (ts); Ed Felson (b); Jon Hazilla (d). August 1986.

Ran Blake said (2002): **'I worked as a waiter at the Jazz Gallery. I was canned for dropping a tray, right in front of Sidney Poitier and James Baldwin. I got taken back but busted down to kitchen duty, where I was taught to make fried rice for Thelonious Monk. I was [Monk's patron and companion] Nica de Koenigswarter's favourite waiter. She'd roll up at midnight in her Bentley and I'd be back out front.'**

Blake studied at Bard and Lenox, and started working in duo partnership with singer Jeanne Lee (who apparently said he reminded her of Art Tatum). He is renowned as a teacher at the New England Conservatory and exponent of the Third Stream, and his musical story is a fascinating one. His abiding interests include the ecstatic music of the evangelical churches, the great jazz singers (but particularly Chris Connor, Sarah Vaughan and Abbey Lincoln), Sephardic music and *film noir*. Indeed, he describes himself in terms that suggest less a composer/musician than a cinema *auteur*, 'storyboarding' in his improvisations.

Blake has a remarkable body of recordings, from *The Newest Sound Around* with Jeanne Lee, through the solo *Painted Rhythms* in 1985 with its Sephardic elements, to group performances and duos with an unlikely array of musicians, including saxophonists Houston Person (a tribute to Mahalia Jackson) and Anthony Braxton. The records are consistently fascinating but every now and then Blake delivers himself of a masterpiece. *The Short Life Of Barbara Monk* is a truly marvellous album, and it makes Blake's apparent unwillingness to work in ensemble settings all the more surprising. The first part ends with the title-piece, dedicated to Thelonious Monk's daughter, Barbara, who died of cancer in 1984. It's a complex and moving composition that shifts effortlessly between a bright lyricism and an edgy premonition; Blake plays beautifully, and his interplay with the young but supremely confident group is a revelation. Ford came through the jazz programme at the Conservatory and is already a singular voice.

A death also lies behind the closing track on part two. 'Pourquoi Laurent?' expresses both a hurt need to understand and a calm desire to heal, written in the face of French jazz critic Laurent Goddet's suicide. 'Impresario Of Death' is equally disturbing but so intelligently constructed as to resolve its inner contradiction perfectly. 'Vradiazi', by the Greek composer Theodorakis, is a favourite of Blake's, as is the Sephardic melody 'Una Matica De Ruda' (two eye-blink takes), which also features on *Painted Rhythms 2*. To lighten the mix a little, there are astonishing versions of Stan Kenton's theme, 'Artistry In Rhythm', and, as an unexpected opener, 'I've Got You Under My Skin'. Blake's favoured Falcone Concert Grand sounds in perfect shape.

& *See also* **All That Is Tied** (2005; p. 707)

SONNY FORTUNE
Born Cornelius Fortune, 19 May 1939, Philadelphia, Pennsylvania
Alto, tenor and soprano saxophones

Great Friends
Evidence ECD 22225
Fortune; Billy Harper (ts); Stanley Cowell (p); Reggie Workman (b); Billy Hart (d). July 1986.

Sonny Fortune says: **'It was in Paris. We were on tour. And all I can say is all of those guys are still great friends!'**

Though not perhaps a household name and not a composer of any note, Sonny Fortune has worked with Miles Davis and with both Elvin Jones and McCoy Tyner. He started out in Coltrane's home town, mostly playing R&B, but only came to New York after Trane's death, playing mostly alto, but occasionally diversifying on other horns. It was a little time before he made any impact as a leader, putting out a debut record on the musician-run Strata East, but not attracting much industry notice until Blue Note belatedly signed him a couple of decades later.

Great Friends is one of those rare supergroup, chance meeting on the road records that stands up as something other than a gig souvenir. It is, in fact, a studio recording, made at Sysmo in Paris and originally only available in Europe on Black & Blue, a label whose generosity to visiting Americans afforded many their only recording opportunities of the '70s and '80s. It's a collaborative disc, and Fortune is no more prominently featured than anyone else, and Cowell and Workman pick up most of the composition credits. But it's Sonny's pungent saxophone on 'Awakening' (his only writing credit) that brings the set to such a satisfying climax. Harper, a great hero across Europe, sets up the finish with his own 'Insight', a number that provides Hart with one of his best solos on record. Cowell, as ever, is magnificent, playing solid comps and teetering figures on the perversely titled 'Equipoise'.

A decade on, Fortune had another flurry of fine recording, with a couple more records for Blue Note, *A Better Understanding* and *From Now On*, and offered his own homage to a saxophone forebear, *In The Spirit Of John Coltrane*, which actually reflected the lineage less well than something like 'Cal Massey' on *Great Friends*. It may not strictly be Sonny's record, but it has a magic that overrides mere ownership.

EVAN PARKER &

Born 5 April 1944, Bristol, Gloucestershire, England
Tenor and soprano saxophones

The Snake Decides
psi 02.09
Parker (ss solo). 1986.

Evan Parker says: '**Michael Gerzon was a special human being. He chose the church in Oxford, set up a concert for the evening and recorded me in the afternoon for what became the record. Since he died it has become accepted that he was about 30 years ahead of all the other audio engineers in seeing the implications of the switch to digital recording. His commitment to improvised music was part of that same visionary quality.'**

If genius is the sustained application of intelligence, then Evan Parker merits the epithet. Over 30 years he has laid down a body of work which is both virtuosic in terms of saxophone technique and profoundly resistant to 'instrumentalism'; it is both abstract and rooted, deeply tinged with the English philosophical and scientific tradition. Parker has made significant contributions to improvising collectives like the Spontaneous Music Ensemble and the London Jazz Composers' Orchestra; but he is perhaps best known as a solo improviser, usually on soprano saxophone. His ability to create complex overtone series by overblowing generates music of formidable intellectual challenge, but there is also a gruff immediacy to much of his work that makes it instantly ... available is probably a safer word than accessible. It's not unusual to hear reviewers point out that behind his spectral explorations stands the ghost of John Coltrane, but it's worth saying that behind Coltrane stand two generations of saxophone improvisers (Hawkins, Young, Rollins, Gonsalves) and their impact on Parker shouldn't be ignored either.

After the fascinating solo essays *Monoceros* and *Six Of One*, recorded in the late '70s, *The Snake Decides* is a great record. Parker himself pays tribute to recording engineer Michael Gerzon, which tempts us to describe it as a *great recording*, but the inescapable truth is that Gerzon was simply the only man in Britain whose ears were as highly tuned to the highest harmonic levels as Parker's own. The record is a subtly inflected document of a moment in which Parker takes the language experiments of the previous two decades and compresses them into one flowing and involving performance. The sonority is incredibly varied, and Parker's ability to sound 32nd harmonics and above demands a reciprocal talent on the technical side. The miracle of *The Snake Decides* is that everything is registered and everything is registered cleanly and faithfully. Listened to on headphones, it can create the impression that you are actually inside an instrument, listening not just to produced sound but to all its accidentals as well. It remains an essential document of modern music, and anyone interested in its progress should hear *The Snake Decides* at least once.

& *See also* **50th Birthday Concert** (1994; p. 582), **The Moment's Energy** (2007; p. 728); **SPONTANEOUS MUSIC ENSEMBLE, Quintessence** (1973–1974; p. 406)

JOANNE BRACKEEN
Also given as Joanne; born JoAnne Grogan, 26 July 1938, Ventura, California
Piano

Fi-Fi Goes To Heaven
Concord CCD 4316
Brackeen; Terence Blanchard (t); Branford Marsalis (as); Cecil McBee (b); Al Foster (d). August 1986.

JoAnne Brackeen said (1988): **'I never really thought about being a "woman in jazz", not until they started writing about it and putting on concerts supposedly to redress the balance. I just got on with playing, though I always sort of knew that if I was to succeed, I had to be very, very good to get the spot ahead of a man.'**

Brackeen occupies an interesting footnote in jazz history as the only female Jazz Messenger, but her reputation shouldn't be consigned to the trivia box. She is a remarkable improviser whose grasp of challenging material is always sure and self-determined. Sadly, much of her extensive discography is no longer available and even a good stint on Concord is now hard to collect.

The best of the Concords is *Fi-Fi Goes To Heaven*, made around the time her ex-husband, Charles Brackeen, was coming out of retirement and making records for Silkheart. Her solo recital at Maybeck Hall might afford a better guide to her pianism, but Brackeen is a superb group player, and in Cecil McBee has found a bass-player who perfectly complements her right-biased approach to the keyboard. There's plenty of weight in her chording none the less, and even the standards here – 'Stardust', 'I Hear A Rhapsody' and Jobim's 'Zingaro' – are delivered with a weighty authority. Her playful side comes out on 'Fi-Fi Goes To Heaven', but one suspects that Brackeen likes to tease her listeners with the prospect of something lightweight and airily swinging, only to deliver a knock-out punch. The set is also distinguished by Branford Marsalis's appearance on alto, his first instrument but one that has played next to no part in his mature career. He's very convincing on it, though initially hard to place. There are some nice Brazilian touches here and there, fruits of a trip to South America with Stan Getz, but Brackeen's 'Latin stylings' are typically unorthodox, with the weight put far back in the bar, which gives the rhythm an unexpected drop in the middle.

PAUL SMOKER
Born 8 May 1941, Muncie, Indiana
Trumpet

Alone
Sound Aspects sas 018
Smoker; Ron Rohovit (b); Phil Haynes (d). August 1986.

Percussionist Harris Eisenstadt on Paul Smoker: **'At a recording session together in 2003, after a particularly arduous second take of a tricky head, I marvelled at Paul's technical precision, impassioned playing and incredible stamina. "You only live once," he answered wryly.'**

When Paul Smoker was a child, his family moved to Davenport, Iowa, the hometown of Bix Beiderbecke. Smoker's lure to the trumpet, though, was Harry James, heard on the radio. He's a highly educated musician, with a strong interest in the modern trumpet literature, and has worked for much of his life as an educator, two factors that have perhaps conspired to saddle him with an 'academic' reputation. In reality, Smoker seems to have absorbed elements of most of the trumpet greats: Armstrong's openheartedness and technical grace, Clifford Brown's clarion simplicity, Don Cherry's folkish chortle, even something of Don Ellis's complexity.

With these influences, Smoker plays free-form jazz of surpassing thoughtfulness. Though by no means averse to tackling standards, he creates a lot of his own material, cleaving to quasi-classical forms rather than blues progressions, and playing mostly with a tight, rather correct diction, though he has a ready supply of rips, wails and smeared tones at his disposal. As throughout Smoker's work, the dynamics on *Alone* are almost self-consciously varied, with one track segueing into another, giving the whole a suite-like feel. Working without a harmony instrument and with only occasional stabs at pedal notes from Smoker, the 'rhythm section' – so much more than that here – is given an unusually active function, making the set an object lesson in group improvisation. 'Mingus Amongus' may suggest one model for this, and the gesture isn't simply perfunctory and verbal; Smoker understands the roots of the Mingus aesthetic, and even manages to sound like Johnny Coles at one point. On 'Prelude', Rohovit bows long, hold-steady notes over whispering percussion (Haynes often works at the boundaries of audibility) until the trumpet enters, sounding as if its last duties were Hummel or Haydn. The standards – Armstrong's 'Cornet Chop Suey' and Ellington's 'Caravan' – are imaginatively stitched in, and the performance gives off an aura of quiet power which isn't quite achieved on the more eclectic and ironic material on *Mississippi River Rat* and *Come Rain Or Come Shine*, the former recorded in 1984, the latter from the same sessions as *Alone*. It continues to stand out as one of the forgotten records of the '80s and a major jazz statement, by no means as dry and abstract as Smoker's professorial reputation might suggest.

CLIFFORD JORDAN &

Born 2 September 1931, Chicago, Illinois; died 27 March 1993, New York City
Tenor saxophone

Royal Ballads

Criss Cross 1025
Jordan; Kevin O'Connell (p); Ed Howard (b); Vernell Fournier (d). December 1986.

Clifford Jordan said (1988): **'Every saxophone-player wants to play pretty sometimes. Even John Coltrane wanted to do that. There's nothing better than playing ballads. It's hard work, but it takes you places you didn't know about in yourself.'**

Jordan made many terrific records: *Spellbound* in 1960, *Bearcat* two years later, subsequent things like *The Glass Bead Game*, a number of live recordings with the Magic Triangle group (Cedar Walton, Sam Jones, Billy Higgins) and even a record exploring the influence of Leadbelly. No one seems to value his ballad playing, and consequently some of the later work is overlooked.

Down the years, he perfected a ballad style that was strikingly reminiscent of Wardell Gray's (an influence he shared with John Gilmore). *Royal Ballads* is a lovely record; if it steers close to easy listening on occasion, a more attentive hearing uncovers all manner of subtleties and harmonic shifts. The opening 'Lush Life' is almost lost in Fournier's constant cymbal-spray, but the drummer – who has worked to great effect with Ahmad Jamal – is a great ballad player and every bit as adept as Jordan at varying an apparently sleepy beat with odd, out-of-synch metres and quiet paradiddles. As Jordan quotes 'Goodbye, Pork Pie Hat' on the original 'Royal Blues', Fournier squeezes the tempo almost subliminally, so that the reference evades identification as the mind subconsciously readjusts to the beat. Subtle and intelligent jazz.

& See also **CLIFFORD JORDAN / JOHN GILMORE, Blowin' In From Chicago** (1957; p. 205)

CHARLIE HADEN&
Born 6 August 1937, Shenandoah, Iowa
Double bass

Quartet West
Verve 831673-2
Haden; Ernie Watts (ts); Alan Broadbent (p); Billy Higgins (d). December 1986.

Composer and bassist Gavin Bryars says: **'Those solid, resonant middle and low-register notes, with bang-in-the-middle intonation, have been with him from his earliest recordings with Ornette Coleman and have enhanced countless recordings.'**

The Liberation Music Orchestra was an ambitious ad hoc venture. Haden's diary had long been packed with dates for other leaders. The one thing seemingly not catered for was a regular, working small group. That changed with the formation of Quartet West, a lyrical ensemble featuring two unsung heroes of the mainstream, and with the recruitment of Larance Marable later a third; Higgins's credentials are, of course, unimpeachable.

The first of the Quartet West discs is still the best. Haden wanted to recapture something of the musical atmosphere he had soaked up in childhood, when he had starred in a family radio show, but this is hardly a high-concept retro record in the way of the later and more mannered *Haunted Heart*. The 1986 record is in the style of the '40s, beautifully and idiomatically played, but the inclusion of Ornette Coleman's 'The Blessing' (admittedly as a CD bonus) and the presence of Higgins in the group means it's hardly a bland exercise in nostalgia. In addition, Haden also looks forward to a later association, by programming a Pat Metheny theme first, the lovely 'Hermitage'.

Watts and Broadbent are as aware of contemporary harmonics as one would expect, but they aren't prepared to dismiss an older language either. Haden himself straddles the broad highway that runs from Jimmy Blanton to Jimmy Garrison, and some of the phrase shapes irresistibly recall Wilbur Ware. Even allowing for the crystalline quality of the record, who could with confidence have dated these performances of 'Body And Soul' or 'My Foolish Heart'? 'Taney County' is a solo feature, an evocation of the days when he played and sang on the family show; the playing is firm, sure and very expressive.

& See also **Liberation Music Orchestra** (1969; p. 363), **Beneath The Missouri Sky** (1996; p. 600)

IRÈNE SCHWEIZER
Born 2 June 1941, Schaffhausen, Switzerland
Piano, drums

Irène Schweizer/Günter Sommer
Intakt CD 007
Schweizer; Günter 'Baby' Sommer (d). February 1987.

Irène Schweizer said (1990): **'I love drummers and I love working with them. I play drums myself, too, whenever I get a chance. I suppose you could say I'm now an amateur, or a "hobby", drummer.'**

A pioneering figure in European free jazz, Schweizer founded her innovative trio in 1963 and has worked with most of the major modernists, yet her musical background – listening to dance bands in her father's restaurant – never quite deserts her. Her style is complex, dense and intellectually generous. Distrust anyone who tries to sell you the notion that Schweizer is an avant-gardist, and implicitly 'difficult'. She has a natural humanity, warmth and wit.

Fortunately, her work is well documented on the Intakt label, which she had a hand in establishing, and that mitigates the relative invisibility of her early work for FMP. Schweizer has almost inevitably been saddled with a 'female Cecil Taylor' tag, one that has been harder to shift as a result of her important sequence of duets with drummers, encounters which invite all manner of yin–yang nonsense. As a sometime percussionist herself, Schweizer makes instinctive guesses as to how her own keyboard language might meld with untuned instruments, but that is also a component of her other work in a variety of groups and as a solo pianist.

We have picked one of the duo records, not as representative or necessarily the 'best', though certainly the playing relationship with Baby Sommer has a mischievous quality that sets it apart. The other percussionists involved in the series are Louis Moholo, Andrew Cyrille, Han Bennink and Pierre Favre, and the work with the last of these is also worthy of special attention. They are quite various in approach, though it seems clear that the Europeans are much closer in basic conception to Schweizer than Moholo and Cyrille, as one might expect. Sommer and Favre are melodic players, moving round the kit much as she moves across the keyboard. Moholo creates a network of cross-rhythms that Schweizer herself likens to Elvin Jones's playing with Coltrane, but there is nothing to build on it, and one is left with an impression of two artists working at right angles, making beautiful sounds but in isolation one from the other. With Favre, the level of interaction is such that one almost seems to be hearing a meta-instrument, a source of sound which is neither one voice nor the other, but a genuine synthesis of the two. With Sommer, the connection is more dialectical, but the result is still entirely sympathetic: two voices in conjunction, mutually responsive. Andrew Cyrille was a long-standing collaborator of Cecil Taylor's and is a leader in his own right. It is difficult to gauge what is wrong on this session. One senses that Schweizer is very aware of the Taylor lineage and deliberately tries to steer away from it, though the clusters and clumped runs she falls into are immediately and inescapably redolent of the American pianist. This remarkable series was completed (for the moment) in 1990 with the Bennink session. Hearing it somewhat later suggests more consistency than difference. Schweizer never for a moment diverges from her robust, assured approach. It is her playing partners who are required to rethink their language.

TOM HARRELL

Born 16 June 1946, Urbana, Illinois
Trumpet, flugelhorn

Visions

Contemporary C 14063
Harrell; George Robert (as); Joe Lovano (ts, ss); Bob Berg, David Liebman (ss); Cheryl Pyle (f); Niels Lan Doky (p); John Abercrombie (g, g-syn); Ray Drummond, Charlie Haden, Reggie Johnson (b); Bill Goodwin, Billy Hart, Paul Motian, Adam Nussbaum (d). April 1987–April 1990.

Tom Harrell said (1990): **'Music lets me transcend my ego and get beyond the suffering and the distraction. It's true, you know: you maybe do have to suffer for art, even if it's just that suffering is a kind of excitement.'**

Hearing Tom Harrell on record is a very different experience to seeing him in a club situation. He has suffered from – or lived with – schizophrenia for many years. Off-stage, or simply when not playing, he is deeply withdrawn and uneasy, often retreating into corners for comfort. (It should be noted that the interview quoted above was conducted while Harrell stood in a gloomy corner, facing into an open cupboard, with his back to the microphone and interviewer.) However, when Harrell puts the trumpet to his lips, some psychic wire goes live and animation flows through him. The sound that flows out is strong, often romantically lyrical but equally often with a burning edge unmatched by any trumpet-player of his generation. Since it is our brief to review records, the personal context may seem irrelevant, but it simply increases the wonder of Harrell's achievement.

He is one of the finest harmonic improvisers in jazz today, often proposing resolutions which seem illogical, even impossible, but are always made both to work and to work in service of the song. The fierce tone adopted for faster numbers gives way to a round, liquid tone on ballads, but it's important not to caricature Harrel as an avatar of Chet Baker, with incremental psychic damage. His work, miraculously, gives off little air of introspection, even when it is quietest and most stilled. It communicates.

Visions gathers the tracings of a purple patch, an album of supposed 'leftovers' from the contract with Contemporary. It documents a span during which Harrell recovered some of the snap and pointed delivery people noted during his sojourn with Horace Silver. Every now and then, as on 'Visions Of Gaudi' with Liebman and Abercrombie, he delivers something that is as hard-edged and as finely detailed as mosaic. 'Autumn View' comes closer than most to self-revelation, but the central figure slips away into the mist. Harrell spends most of the album on flugelhorn, but 'Suspended View', with Berg on soprano, is a trumpet performance of magical skill, fleeting, ambiguous and endlessly replayable. It is hard to see why any of these tracks were not previously released. Even as a scattering, they have authority, indeed a fragile majesty.

KEITH TIPPETT
Born Keith Tippetts, 25 August 1947, Bristol, Gloucestershire, England
Piano

Mujician III (August Air)
FMP CD 12
Tippett (p solo). June 1987.

Keith Tippett said (1986): **'I changed my name because I got tired of seeing "Keith Tippett's group" on posters, when they couldn't get the apostrophe in the right place. Seemed simpler just to change.'**

A remarkable figure, who for much of his career has turned his back on commercial success and with his wife, Julie Tippetts (she retains the original spelling of the name), has absorbed himself in free music, diversifying into composition in later years. Perversely, he remains best known in some quarters for recordings he made with prog-rock band King Crimson, and, if not for that, then for his ultra-big band Centipede (50 pairs of legs) and its one recording, *Septober Energy*, which continues to enjoy a cult following.

While Tippett's small-group work and occasional large ensemble projects (like Ark) are always compelling and his collaborations with wife Julie are among the most beautiful recorded works of recent time, he's still best heard as a solo performer. It may turn out that the three *Mujician* albums made for FMP during the '80s (the word was his daughter's childish version of her father's vocation and became the name of his collaborative improvising group with Paul Dunmall, Paul Rogers and Tony Levin) will be regarded as among the most self-consistent and beautiful solo improvisations of the decade and a significant reprogramming of the language of piano. Tippett has always insisted that listeners should not concern themselves with how particular sounds are made in his performances, but absorb themselves in what he clearly sees as a spontaneous expressive process in which 'technique' is not separable from the more instinctual aspects of the music. In addition to now relatively conventional practices like playing 'inside', he makes use of distinctive sound-altering devices, such as laying soft wood blocks on the strings, producing zither and koto effects. Though there are similarities, this is very different from John Cage's use of 'prepared piano'. Cage's effects, once installed, are immutable; Tippett's are spontaneous and flexible.

The long 'August Air' is one of the essential performances of the decade. It seems to complete a cycle whose development can only be experienced and intuited, not rationalized. The transfer of the two first Mujician discs to CD allows the sequence to be heard as a whole and, though a goodly span of time separates the three records, they make sense heard as a continuous sequence, an extended dialogue with the piano and with Tippett's musical sources.

MARILYN CRISPELL
Born Marilyn Braune, 30 March 1947, Philadelphia, Pennsylvania
Piano

For Coltrane
Leo CDLR 195
Crispell (p solo). July 1987.

Marilyn Crispell remembers: **'I was living alone. I didn't have much at all. And then someone played me *A Love Supreme*. And that just seemed to change everything, right from that moment.'**

There are few critical shorthands more dead-eared than the assumption that any piano-player who favours heavy, knotted clusters and passages of extreme dissonance must be labouring under a 'Cecil Taylor influence'. Borah Bergman has been so labelled, quite ludicrously, and so, too, has Marilyn Crispell, despite strong protestations by both. Apparently wiser voices have pointed out that John Coltrane is actually Crispell's main influence – very few of them note that she grew up in Trane's home town – but she does, indeed, admire Taylor and has learned much from him, as her tribute piece 'Au Chanteur Qui Danse' (to be found on the nearly contemporary Victo CD *Labyrinths*) warmly acknowledges. What exactly she takes from each, and thence what makes her such a powerful and interesting keyboard improviser, is best judged by this remarkable concert set from London in the summer of 1987, when Crispell supported Alice Coltrane and her sons with a solo set dedicated to Alices's late husband.

Crispell learned piano as a child at the Peabody in Baltimore and later studied at the New England School of Music. She married and for a time gave up playing to concentrate on a medical career, but following a divorce and the epiphany of *A Love Supreme* she resumed her musical activities and came to prominence as a member of Anthony Braxton's most celebrated quartet. *For Coltrane* came two years after the Braxton tour. Crispell already had a couple of solo and duo recitals in catalogue, notably *Rhythms Hung In Undrawn Sky* and *And Your Ivory Voice Sings* for Leo.

Solo performances by Crispell are dramatic, harmonically tense and wholly absorbing. In London, Crispell opens with a torrid 'Dear Lord' that has never been as generously admired as the more obviously romantic and billowing 'After The Rain' that closes the show. Crispell clearly responds to Coltrane as a melodist as well as a harmonic improviser, but what's really important about this recital is the piece called 'Coltrane Time', derived from rhythmic cells on which the saxophonist had been experimenting before his death and which had apparently been given to Crispell by Andrew Cyrille. She also improvises a series of 'collages' in memory of the great saxophonist. Only the title is at fault, for these do not sound like pasted-together forms but organic upgrowths from a deep place in her musical imagination. Crispell made many subsequent records, but even if this one can be categorized as 'early' it is the work of a mature artist already at the height of her powers, engaged with a profound modern tradition.

SIR ROLAND HANNA

Born 10 February 1932, Detroit, Michigan; died 13 November 2002, Hackensack, New Jersey
Piano

Persia My Dear
DIW 8015
Hanna; Richard Davis (b); Freddie Waits (d). August 1987.

Sir Roland Hanna said (1985): **'I played concerts for high school kids in Liberia, as part of their education. The president, Mr William Tubman, gave me a knighthood. I like "Sir Roland". You don't get that kind of recognition in the US.'**

Bud Powell was the single most important influence, but the Detroit man also took careful note of Teddy Wilson and of his fellow townsman Tommy Flanagan. He is, in fact, another in the run of great Detroit piano-players. He worked with Mingus, with the Jones–Lewis orchestra and others, and had a hand in starting the New York Jazz Quartet. His own recordings are not widely celebrated, and are scattered over an array of labels.

This DIW date is the best by some distance, done in good sound with a cracking bass and drums combination in Davis and Waits. He's still recognizably the piano-player who recorded the *Destry Rides Again* music at the end of the '50s, exact but not buttoned up, harmonically fluid over a solid architecture, and interested in melody. The trio functions very comfortably as a unit, and these late DIW recordings are a fine reminder once again of what a loss Freddie Waits was.

CHARLES BRACKEEN

Born 1940, White's Chapel, Oklahoma
Tenor and soprano saxophones

Worshippers Come Nigh
Silkheart SHCD 111
Brackeen; Olu Dara (c); Fred Hopkins (b); Andrew Cyrille (d, perc); Dennis Gonzalez (perc). November 1987.

Trumpeter Dennis González said (1992): **'He's had more obituaries than anyone I know, 25 years of them. I found him mowing lawns in Los Angeles. He said that was the only way he could earn a living.'**

Though initially strongly influenced by Ornette Coleman, Brackeen created his own intense sound and a style that, in parallel to Coleman's, combined primitivism with profound sophistication. Much admired by fellow musicians, he remains little known to the jazz public. He was married for a time to the pianist JoAnne Grogan (Brackeen) and raised four children.

Apart from a 1968 disc, *Rhythm X*, for Strata East with three quarters of the Ornette Coleman group, Brackeen was a stranger to the studios until in 1986 the managing director of the Swedish label Silkheart persuaded the reclusive saxophonist to record again. In contrast to most reed-players active at the time, Coltrane wasn't the main influence. The stop-start melodic stutter of 'Three Monks Suite' on *Bannar*, the first Silkheart disc, is immediately reminiscent of Ornette, while 'Allah' on the same album recalls Ayler. Brackeen favours a high, slightly pinched tone; his soprano frequently resembles a clarinet, and his tenor work often disappears into the altissimo range. Interestingly, 'Three Monks Suite' is wholly composed and Brackeen only really lets rip as a soloist on 'Story', a limping melody with enough tightly packed musical information to fuel two superb solos from the horns.

González is a fine, emotive trumpeter, but he lacks the blowtorch urgency of Dara's more hotly pitched cornet on the third Silkheart; *Attainment* was recorded at the same time. 'Worshippers Come Nigh' is an exciting jazz piece. 'Bannar' confusingly finds its way onto this session rather than the one named after it. 'Ible' and 'Cing Kong' are also free-jazz classics and both lean heavily on Hopkins and Cyrille to steer them out of potential chaos. The ride is exhilarating and Brackeen's lead is a consistent revelation. Casual listeners might hazard a remote guess at Dewey Redman, but he lacks Dewey's normalizing approach to the harmony and tends to plunge straight for the spots where the material looks weakest, always managing to create a convincing statement out of the scantest materials.

PHIL WOODS &

Born 2 November 1931, Springfield, Massachusetts
Alto saxophone

Bop Stew
Concord CCD 4345
Woods; Tom Harrell (t); Hal Galper (p); Steve Gilmore (b); Bill Goodwin (d). November 1987.

Phil Woods says: **'I think *Bop Stew* is the classic of the Concord period.'**

It's rare that a festival record receives such high praise – Woods himself seems to single it out – and an even tougher call given the unstinting high quality of his work down the years. This is, though, a special date. Recorded live at the 1987 Fujitsu-Concord festival in Japan, where Woods is something of a hero, it features a seasoned band working at the highest level, and there's an additional treat in Woods's clarinet feature on 'Poor Butterfly'.

Galper and Harrell, in their different ways, are both generally regarded as lyrical, reflective players, but it's clear from this that their more introspective and troublous material is built on solid bop foundations. The pianist contributes the title-tune, and shows his deftness with the changes. 'Dreamsville' is pitched just right, with terrific energy coming off the group, and while it falls away in precision a bit after 'Poor Butterfly' – a studio producer would probably have asked for 'Yes, There Is A C.O.T.A.' – the playing has such brio only a philistine would have stopped it. They play out on Phil's theme 'How's Your Mama?' It isn't a long record, by present-day standards, but by our estimate there's more vivid bop per minute here than you'll find anywhere else in the catalogue.

& See also **Phil & Quill** (1957; p. 204)

FRANK MORGAN &

Born 23 December 1933, Minneapolis, Minnesota; died 14 December 2007, Minneapolis, Minnesota
Alto saxophone

Reflections

Original Jazz Classics OJC 1046
Morgan; Joe Henderson (ts); Bobby Hutcherson (vib); Mulgrew Miller (p); Ron Carter (b); Al Foster (d). January 1988.

Frank Morgan said (1989): **'It was music that allowed me to survive jail, and specifically my saxophone. If I got to despairing, I could take it out and it seemed to stand for hope of some sort, though whether that was hope for me or just hope for the world, I don't know.'**

After 30 years off the scene, Morgan came back, seemingly untarnished and sounding very much as he had in earlier days. San Quentin is a tough woodshed, but he prevailed and the latter-day albums have a calm authority and likeable warmth. *Easy Living* was a remarkably poised album for a man who had been away from the world for so long, but the best of the Indian summer records was *Reflections*.

Billed as an All-Stars date, it does lean heavily on the other principals, Henderson, Hutcherson and Miller, but not to Frank's detriment. The decision to go with mostly new material was a good one. Miller's 'Old Bowl, New Grits' is a line made for Morgan's homely voice and he delivers a wry statement. Monk's 'Reflections' engages his blues tone while 'Sonnymoon For Two', the only other repertory piece in the release version, is a good bop workout. The meat of the record is in Hutcherson's 'Starting Over' and Henderson's glorious 'Black Narcissus', on which the horns mesh beautifully. A bonus performance of 'Caravan' on the CD reissue almost steals the show. Though it might by then have seemed an almost routine date for Morgan, it's an exceptional performance from all concerned and there's evidence that the band found him a moving and inspirational presence.

& See also **Gene Norman Presents Frank Morgan** (1955; p. 167)

HERB ROBERTSON

Born 21 February 1951, Plainfield, New Jersey
Trumpet, flugelhorn, other instruments

Shades of Bud Powell

Winter & Winter 919019
Robertson; Brian Lynch (t); Robin Eubanks (tb); Vincent Chancey (frhn); Bob Stewart (tba); Joey Baron (d). January 1988.

Herb Robertson says: **'I remember bringing in the hand-copied scores and parts to the session and finishing up the written music just before we started recording. The main comment from all involved was ... "Where's the Bud Powell?!" I responded: "It's in there; mixed up and discombobulated backwards and forwards. You'll hear it, guys." And they did ...'**

A maverick presence on a whole range of downtown projects, Robertson often gives the impression that he only took up the trumpet that afternoon and discovered he had an aptitude for it. His tone is raw, breathy and of a sort to make orthodox brass-teachers throw themselves out of upper-storey windows. However, he's never less than wholly musical and his tight, often pinched sound, which often sounds as if it's coming from a pocket- or piccolo-trumpet, is instantly attractive. He studied at Berklee, played in rock and jazz bands as a young professional but became closely associated with saxophonist Tim Berne at the beginning of the '80s and that seemed to demarcate his musical contacts for a time. Robertson, though, can turn his hand to almost anything and his own records are strikingly individual.

Arranging Bud Powell for a brass ensemble was a genius idea that works brilliantly and yields one of Robertson's own best recorded performances. His level of playing here is almost uncanny as he makes the horn sing on 'Un Poco Loco', 'Hallucinations' and others. As he suggests, the original themes are inverted and cleverly concealed in the arrangements, often only emerging in *Klangfarben* style, played fragmentarily by different instruments. As always, he gets strong support from the other members of the Brass Ensemble and Baron's drumming is a joy. The set ends with Robertson's own meditation on Bud. It might conceivably have gone first in the running order, since it acts almost as an overture, with mosaic elements of Powell's language beaded together into a fine, and extended, whole.

CASSANDRA WILSON
Born 4 December 1955, Jackson, Mississippi
Voice

Blue Skies
Winter & Winter 919018-2
Wilson; Mulgrew Miller (p); Lonnie Plaxico (b); Terri Lyne Carrington (d). February 1988.

Cassandra Wilson said (1993): **'You have to know a song before you can sing it, and I mean *really* know it: what the words mean, what the chords do, who has sung it before and what they've done with it. Only when you get all that together are you ready to sing even the simplest one.'**

Wilson emerged in the '80s as a peripheral member of the so-called M-Base group of New York musicians. Following a number of records for JMT, she signed to Blue Note and scored major successes with her first releases for the label, making a name that threatened to stretch beyond the jazz community.

Wilson's early records contain all the seeds of the success she has enjoyed at Blue Note, but with one exception they rarely cohere as albums of any particularity or sustained success. *Blue Skies* was the least typical but easily the best of her JMT records, since reissued on Winter & Winter: though made up entirely of standards (something she didn't attempt again until 2007's *Loverly*) with a conventional rhythm section, the recital finds Wilson investing the likes of 'Shall We Dance?' with a wholly unfamiliar range of inflexions and melodic extensions which is captivating. Her third-person version of 'Sweet Lorraine' is peculiarly dark and compelling and, while some of the songs drift a little too far off base, it's a remarkable record.

ART FARMER&
Born 21 August 1928, Council Bluffs, Iowa; died 4 October 1999, New York City
Trumpet, flugelhorn

Blame It On My Youth
Contemporary CCD 14042
Farmer; Clifford Jordan (ss, ts); James Williams (p); Rufus Reid (b); Victor Lewis (d). February 1988.

Art Farmer said (1991): **'I'm not interested in just getting to the next note as quickly as possible. If the note you're playing isn't exactly the right one, played just right, then there's nowhere to go until you do get it right.'**

Unlike many of his contemporaries, Farmer continued to record right through the '70s. Firmly based in Europe, he continued a majestic output, mostly on non-American labels but also through Creed Taylor's CTI. Many of his countrymen started to enjoy a renaissance in the following decade, but Art was there already, an elder statesman almost before his time and thanks to regular work with the Clarke–Boland band and others never obliged to scuffle.

As he entered his 60s, he was playing better than ever, now focused entirely on the flugelhorn – he later experimented with a hybrid 'flumpet' – and with a delivery that, for all its burnish, could also present a fast, intricate line without fluff or fudge. The albums he made for Contemporary between January 1987 and April 1989 marked a career high, speaking as eloquently as any record on behalf of the generation of players who followed the first boppers yet can still make modern music with a contemporary rhythm section. Marvin 'Smitty' Smith was the favoured drummer, but Victor Lewis on the middle record was subtler and gave higher polish.

Something To Live For, dedicated to Billy Strayhorn's music, was a little doleful on the ballads but is otherwise perfectly pitched. The later *Ph.D* benefited from a guest appearance by Kenny Burrell (and shared with the others the exquisite production touch of Helen Keane) but it doesn't come up to quite the same standard.

The middle record, *Blame It On My Youth*, is a discreet masterpiece. The tunes are mostly obscurities, which is part of its radiant charm, and the only reasonably well-known themes are the title-track and Benny Carter's 'Summer Serenade'. Art's reading of 'Blame It On My Youth' is a definitive ballad statement, good even by his high standard. Otherwise, it's mostly middle-pace. Clifford Jordan is on hand for these tracks and plays with outstanding subtlety and guarded power, taking a memorable feature on the other slow ballad, the closing 'I'll Be Around'. Williams leads the rhythm section with consummate craft and decisiveness, steering the band through Pauer's 'Fairy Tale Countryside' (how many of them had played it before?), but it's Lewis, showing unsuspected versatility, who really makes the music fall together, finding an extra ounce of power and crispness in every rhythm he has to mark out.

& *See also* **Meet The Jazztet** (1960; p. 250)

STEVE TURRE
Born 12 September 1948, Omaha, Nebraska
Trombone, shells

Fire & Ice
Stash STCD 7
Turre; Cedar Walton (p); Buster Williams (b); Billy Higgins (d); Quartette Indigo/John Blake (strings). February 1988.

Steve Turre said (1989): **'Things changed for the trombone with bebop, which was hard and challenging. The only man who could stand up with Bird and Diz was J. J. Johnson, and that sort of underlined the idea that the trombone wasn't such a central instrument in new jazz. But that's a short-term thing. As long as there has been jazz, there has been a trombone at the heart of it.'**

Turre was an in-demand brassman throughout the '70s, '80s and '90s, and his occasional albums as leader have investigated a series of increasingly fanciful fusions of idiom, with his shell-playing often taking a strong role. They introduce a pleasantly alien tonality and timbre to the records, but they aren't a novelty element. Turre played with Roland Kirk, briefly with the Messengers and in the Jones–Lewis orchestra, but struck off boldly on his own. He's perhaps a difficult musician to sell (or plays an instrument that doesn't at once appeal to modern audiences) for his recording history has been slightly chequered.

No recent thing stands up to the sheer aural delight of *Fire & Ice*. Turre's use of a string quartet was a clever idea, and they're left to their own devices on one number. Turre has crafted a sequence of original compositions that foreground the trombone in a way that is both idiomatic and challenging, and standards that allow him to establish a foothold in tradition. The discipline of working in sections and for other leaders has given him an emphatic but never abrasive delivery. Every note seems to come out like a brazed sphere, but shimmering with heat, but he can also play with chilly reserve when the situation calls for it. Fire and ice, indeed.

MICHAEL JEFRY STEVENS
Born 13 March 1951, New York City
Piano

Mosaic Sextet
GM Recordings GM3045
Stevens; Dave Douglas (t); Michael Rabinowitz (bsn); Mark Feldman (vn); Joe Fonda (b); Harvey Sorgen (d). January 1988–March 1990.

Michael Jefry Stevens says: **'When Joe Fonda and I created the band we wanted to explore different timbres. Mark and Dave met in my living room in Brooklyn and with Michael Rabinowitz on bassoon the sound of the sextet was immediately original and distinct. We rehearsed every week from 1988 through 2000. It was a very special project.'**

A New Yorker of Italian and Russian-Jewish descent, Stevens is a remarkable musician and composer who, for reasons too embarrassingly trivial to reveal, has not featured much in previous volumes of the *Guide*, other than as a member of the long-standing Fonda–Stevens group, co-led with the bassist of the Mosaic Sextet.

The group title is worth glancing at twice, because Mosaic isn't just a form of decorative tiling, but also the adjective from Moses, and a word that carries an unmistakable overtone of law. The music on this record pulls together a German release on Konnex called *Today, This Moment* after the impressive main track, together with other unreleased tracks. It is a special set in including not just the familiar, rock-solid but attentive and contentious partnership of Stevens and Joe Fonda, but also such distinguished contemporary improvisers as Dave Douglas, who contributes a good deal of the composed material and is already a powerful writer, and Mark Feldman.

Stevens spent – as opposed to mis-spent – some of his youth playing rock, much of it on organ, and a pulsing energy underlies many of these tracks, and notably 'Anthem', which one can readily imagine rescored for guitars and electric basses. That here it involves an ensemble one might just as easily find in a new-music context is a measure of Stevens's range and adaptability as a composer. This is a very special record, one that seems to mark a cusp in the career of not just its principal, who lays down the law but has a magical touch of Aaron about him, too, but almost everyone involved, and it has real durability.

YANK LAWSON
Born John Rhea Lawson, 3 May 1911, Trenton, Missouri; died 18 February 1995, Indianapolis, Indiana
Trumpet

Something Old, Something New, Something Borrowed, Something Blue
Audiophile APCD-240
Lawson; George Masso (tb); Johnny Mince (cl); Lou Stein (p); Bucky Pizzarelli (g); Bob Haggart (b); Nick Fatool (d). March 1988.

Yank Lawson said (1985): **'Sure, I enjoy myself now, and why not? It's not like doing brain surgery, this music, and besides, I had my hungry times. There was a spell in the South when we were so broke we were setting mouse-traps with seed and catching sparrows to eat!'**

After playing in local orchestras in Missouri, Lawson joined Ben Pollack's band in 1933, then spent a period (interrupted by an argument) with Bob Crosby. In the '50s and '60s he often worked with Bob Haggart, and they formed the World's Greatest Jazz Band together in 1968. A big man – at 6 feet 4 inches a giant for his generation – he was an imposing but genial presence and that was reflected too in his musicianship. Tommy Dorsey highlighted his skills in the Clambake Seven, and he had spells with Benny Goodman and (after making up) Bob Crosby before forging the alliance with bassist Bob Haggart that defined the rest of his career.

Yank Lawson and Bob Haggart (who died in 1998) played together for almost 60 years and the records for Audiophile and Jazzology maintained a formidable standard: Yank's tough, growling solos have a bite and pungency which he retained, even into his 80s, and Haggart's steady propulsion never faltered at all. They are a splendid group of discs and only the relatively tame repertoire on the later ones keep them out of the top bracket. The mostly recent material on *Something Old* is so fresh and is played so enjoyably that one wishes the group had stuck to originals over warhorses. A lovely 'Blues For Louise', a Spanish-sounding 'Bumps', played by a trio of Lawson, Stein and Fatool, and a swaggering 'Come Back, Sweet Papa' are the three highlights, but Yank's own 'Atlanta' is a nice line and there's a vigorous play-out in 'Big Crash From China', co-written by Haggart and Ray Bauduc. The blues is never far away, even when the structures point in another direction.

BOBBY HUTCHERSON *&*

Born 27 January 1941, Los Angeles, California
Vibraphone, marimba

Cruisin' The 'Bird
Landmark LCD 1517
Hutcherson; Ralph Moore (ss, ts); Buddy Montgomery (p); Rufus Reid (b); Victor Lewis (d). April 1988.

Vibist Joe Locke says: **'Bobby Hutcherson's default setting is "search". At this point in such an illustrious career, other artists would have rested on their laurels. Bobby still pushes the envelope.'**

Hutcherson is the archetypal exponent of jazz as a long game, expecting no dramatic break-through, but not content to rest on a single style and play it out as a safe career position. *Cruisin'* is anything but a relaxed, straight-ahead session and not, as one American reviewer of the time assumed (did he *listen* to it?), a tribute to Charlie Parker. The second apostrophe gives it away. Hutcherson's 'Bird is a 1964 convertible the size of a swimming pool and a fair image of the classic aerodynamics and effortless acceleration that had reappeared in the vibist's playing two decades later. It might also stand for a certain nostalgia. It was harder to promulgate Bobby's kind of adventure in the '80s.

It's nice to see him return to 'All Or Nothing At All' in the familiar headlong mood, but with a more reasoned argument running underneath. The originals are also cast in such a way that he has to work on several levels at once. Hometown associate Buddy Montgomery (himself normally a vibist) fulfils a solidly supportive role in what's a footsure platform for the leader. English-born Moore plays some distinctive soprano on the ballad 'Sierra', and Hutcherson switches to marimba for the same track and in a curious way it's the wooden instrument that now more often reflects his familiar, firmly struck but skatingly mobile style. It's a deceptively demanding record, whose immediate excitements give way to something deeper and more satisfying: there's so much detail, incident, evidence of *thinking*, that it has remained a steady favourite of ours for more than 20 years.

& See also **The Kicker** (1963; p. 297)

TOOTS THIELEMANS

Born Jean-Baptiste Thielemans, 29 April 1922, Brussels, Belgium
Harmonica, guitar, whistling

Only Trust Your Heart

Concord CCD 4355
Thielemans; Fred Hersch (p); Marc Johnson, Harvie Swartz (b); Joey Baron (d). April–May 1988.

Fred Hersch says: **'When I was playing with Toots in the mid-'80s, the last "real" jazz album he'd done was with Bill Evans. We'd worked a lot with Marc Johnson and Joey Baron and I thought he was really on top of his game. I had a recording studio and a relationship with Concord Records, who were keen on recording him. I chose a fair amount of new material along with what was unrecorded in the band book. I think it is one of his very strongest pure jazz recordings, played with great energy, imagination and swing.'**

If you were a young Belgian jazz fanatic in the early '40s, you took up guitar in emulation of Django. Thielemans recorded 'Bluesette' in 1961, after working with George Shearing; his first hit had him playing guitar and whistling, but he subsequently became the pre-eminent harmonica-player in jazz. He quickly found himself in the awkward and unsatisfactory position of coming first in a category of one or consigned to 'miscellaneous instruments'. Though ubiquitous in the blues, the harmonica has made remarkably little impact in jazz, and there are no recognized critical standards for his extraordinary facility as a whistler. Thielemans's pop and movie work has tended further to downgrade his very considerable jazz credentials. Surprisingly, to those who know him primarily as a performer of moodily atmospheric soundtrack pieces (*Midnight Cowboy* above all) or as composer of 'Bluesette', his roots are in bebop and in the kind of harmonically liberated improvisation associated with John Coltrane. That's perhaps most obvious in the dark, Chicago-influenced sound of *Man Bites Harmonica* from 1957.

More recent years saw the romantic side win out. *Only Trust Your Heart* is his masterpiece. The harmonica-playing is superb. The choice of material and Fred Hersch's arrangements are impeccable and the production first-rate, with Thielemans front and centre and the band spread out very evenly behind him. The set kicks off with a marvellous reading of Wayne Shorter's 'Speak No Evil', and includes 'Sophisticated Lady', Monk's 'Little Rootie Tootie' and Thad Jones's 'Three And One', transposed unfamiliarly high to bring it within the range of Thielemans's instrument, which takes on the slightly yodelling timbre of soprano saxophone. Throughout, Thielemans's solo development merits the closest attention, particularly on the original 'Sarabande', the better of two duets with Hersch. The pianist's other composition, 'Rain Waltz', deserves wider distribution. Apparently nearly all first takes, each of the dozen tracks represents Thielemans's undervalued art at its finest.

UMO JAZZ ORCHESTRA

Formed 1975
Ensemble

UMO Plays The Music Of Muhal Richard Abrams
UMO CD 101
Anders Bergcrantz, Chuck Findley, Heiki Haimila, Esko Heikkinen, Simo Salminen (t); Juhani Aaltonen, Mikael Långbacka, Mircea Stan, Markku Veijonsuo (tb); Kari Heinilä, Eero Koivistoinen, Pentti Lahti, Pertti Päivinen, Teemu Salminen (sax); Seppo Kantonen (p); Kirmo Lintinen (syn); Lars Danielsson (b); Klaus Suonsaari (d); Mongo Aaltonen (perc). May 1988.

Trombonist George E. Lewis said (2007): **'What UMO does is hugely impressive. It's a tribute to what a little money, creatively and sensitively spent, can do for improvised music and jazz.'**

To the envy of all, UMO receives state support in Finland, but does not fritter it away on makeweight projects. The orchestra is widely recognized for ambitious repertoire, inch-perfect section-work, some genuinely individual solo voices, and an intriguing leaven of guest musicians. The Muhal Richard Abrams disc is at the chewier and more adventurous side of UMO's remit; they've 'done' Miles and Ellington since, much less successfully in our view. Since the composer himself supervised the sessions, we have to assume that he was relatively pleased with the results, but they are rather flat and mechanical and without the fire that a Chicago outfit might have brought to the proceedings. But then, the Windy City hasn't been in any rush to offer Abrams recording opportunities of this sort. Among the pieces included are 'Ritob', 'Fotex', 'Melancholia' and 'Symtre' and there is a fine Abrams arrangement of Duke's 'Melancholy' for contrast. As ever, the section-work is impeccable and there are some good solo spots from the likes of Lahti and Bergcrantz.

J. J. JOHNSON &
Born James Louis Johnson, 22 January 1924, Indianapolis, Indiana; died 4 February 2001, Indianapolis, Indiana
Trombone

Quintergy: Live At The Village Vanguard
Emarcy 842814 / 510059
Johnson; Ralph Moore (ts); Stanley Cowell (p); Rufus Reid (b); Victor Lewis (d). July 1988.

J. J. Johnson said (1985): **'People still talk as if I only cared about playing as fast as possible, "virtuosically" or as if I was playing a valve instrument. Others said the only thing I ever cared about was expressiveness. It's not so! I only ever wanted to play with clarity, maximum clarity. If it turned out fast, that was OK. If there was a little expression there, that was good. But it was clarity and ... logic that I wanted.'**

Johnson was never an overwhelming performer. One rarely gasps at his technique and rarely feels that he has plumbed some inner agony to produce the sounds. He represents an unfashionable kind of musicianship, unconcerned with style or inscape, but instead with purely musical values. Dapper and shy, he was not an obvious contender for headlining tour artist, but the JATP/Pablo style of concert presentation perhaps suited him much better than the club circuit and Johnson thrived over this next period as a performer again, after a longish sojourn in the studios making blaxploitation soundtracks. A live recording from Yokohama with Nat Adderley co-leading broke his duck and, after that, Johnson was pretty much back on the circuit.

Even nearing retirement age, Johnson sounded as full of controlled energy as ever and the Village Vanguard dates find him in vintage form. There is a wonderful opening arrange-ment of 'When The Saints Go Marching In' and a brief but beautiful unaccompanied ver-sion of 'It's All Right With Me'. J.J.'s tone and phrasing are faultless on the faster numbers,

Kenny Dorham's 'Blue Bossa', Wayne Shorter's exacting 'Nefertiti' and his own title-track. Johnson's tone and line are faultless, and if clarity was his bellwether he has followed it all the way home. There was a second, standards set from the same engagement, probably good economics for the label, but it makes for a duller listen and not even J.J.'s immaculate playing saves some tunes that really ought to be out in a field somewhere, grazing quietly.

& See also **The Eminent Jay Jay Johnson** (1953–1955; p. 144)

DANIEL HUMAIR
Born 23 May 1938, Geneva, Switzerland
Drums

9–11 p.m. Town Hall
Label Bleu LBLC 6517
Humair; Michel Portal (sax, bcl, bandoneon); Joachim Kühn, Martial Solal (p); Marc Ducret (g); Jean-François Jenny-Clark (b). June 1988.

Daniel Humair said (1989): **'Jazz thrives in France, and France has produced some great musicians because everyone has good technique, or if they don't, you don't see them again. Jazz is about expressing yourself, but in order to do that, you have to know how to play, and I think the French system guarantees that.'**

Humair moved to Paris at 20 and established himself as the most able percussionist on the French scene, forming an important association with Martial Solal, and becoming a respected accompanist for visiting Americans. He was also regular drummer with the George Gruntz band and sustains a parallel career as a painter.

It might be a cheat to include a collaborative record as an example of Humair's leadership, but he was the straw boss on this one and it is his vibrant drumming that makes the music work. Inevitably, the writing is all credited to Kühn, Portal and Solal (with three such writers in the group, it would be hard to stake a rival claim), and it is Kühn's harmonically loaded 'From Time To Time, Free' which starts the set and establishes it as an essential document in European jazz of the time. The pianist's 'Easy To Read' is a more romantic conception and a nice contrast at this point. Solal plays one of his finger-busting medleys, putting in more swing and bop material than seems possible given the duration. Then Portal claims the stage with 'Pastor', a piece that conjures the best out of the rhythm section, Humair sticking close to the bass clarinet but commenting quirkily on the line whenever he can. The saxophonist's 'Alto Blues' is more of a blowing piece, again powered from the back. There's another piece of Kühn's at the end, but it's hardly necessary. Admirers of Humair's work should also listen to his work with organist Eddy Louiss and violinist Jean-Luc Ponty, and with his regular trio of François Jeanneau and Henri Texier, but for those who simply want a snapshot of jazz in Europe at this time, the Town Hall date is hard to beat.

BUDDY COLLETTE
Born William Marcel Collette, 6 August 1921, Los Angeles, California
Saxophones, clarinets, flutes

Flute Talk
Soul Note 121165
Collette; James Newton (f); Geri Allen (p); Jaribu Shahid (b); Giampiero Prina (d). July 1988.

Buddy Collette said (1987): **'This is my home town and I'm committed to it, but it's hard to be heard in Los Angeles. Eric [Dolphy], he went to New York and at once was calling** back, saying: *"This* is the place." But I stayed, and I teach and I work at making jazz understandable to young people. I don't expect awards for it, or money.'

A revered figure on his local scene, but still too little recognized elsewhere, Buddy Collete was the man who brought on Charles Mingus – as recounted in the bassist's memoir *Beneath the Underdog* – and played with Chico Hamilton ahead of another of his pupils, Eric Dolphy. A genuine multi-instrumentalist, Collette perhaps also suffers critically because of the diversity of his skills. He spent considerable time buried away in the studio and band sections or organizing big bands for Monterey. However, there are superb Collette records out there if only anyone went in search of them.

One or two, like the obviously titled *Man Of Many Parts* are gimcracked round Buddy's multi-instrumentalism. To get the best of him, one perversely has to pick one of the discs where he pretty much narrows his focus, like *Nice Day*, where the main horn is woodsy clarinet, or the much later *Flute Talk*, which finds the 67-year-old in the studio with the leading flautist of the next generation, James Newton.

Pupil and master meet on respectful rather than combative terms, but Allen is her usual unpredictable self, alert in places, apparently asleep in others, but helped out by a terrific bass/drum alliance. It's Buddy's first record for two decades, possibly the best group he's ever had in the studio, and probably his strongest instrument. The recording isn't spot on for the flutes, but overall is pretty good. The title-tune is an improvised collaboration, but over the years Buddy had built up a book of pretty decent themes, and 'Roshanda', 'Crystal' and the mildly unusual 'Blues In Torrance' make for an interesting set and a nice reintroduction to an old master, who's still to the fore.

DOUG RANEY

Born 29 August 1956, New York City
Guitar

The Doug Raney Quintet

Steeplechase SCCD 31249
Raney; Tomas Franck (as); Bernt Rosengren (ts); Jesper Lundgaard (b); Jukkis Uotila (d). August 1988.

Doug Raney said (1988): **'Do I sound like my father? I think yes and no. My musical roots are different. I've come up in a different world to him and one that puts a different value on jazz, but it would be strange, wouldn't it, if there were no resemblance at all? So I guess you could say there's a kinship there.'**

Jimmy Raney's son was raised to the family craft, but quickly established his own identity and a more contemporary idiom that also seemed to draw on swing guitar (missing out, that is, much of the bebop influence his father has sustained). Less robust rhythmically than his father, Raney slots more conventionally into a horn-and-rhythm set-up. His technique is scratchier than Jimmy's and lacks that creamy, Jim Hall-like legato, but perhaps there was a semi-conscious intent to distinguish himself from the parental style. Ironically, father and son were paired on some recordings of the period, which underlined the kinship even as it demonstrated the individuality of their respective approaches.

Taken out of family context, Doug is the more old-fashioned player. He doesn't have Jimmy's speed of thought, even if his articulation easily matches his father's, but he brings a gamier sensibility to blues-based material in particular and avoids the residual folksiness that sometimes creeps into Jimmy's ballads. The neutrally titled 1988 album, like the earlier *Guitar Guitar Guitar*, may be intended to give the signal that here is a working band, under the command of its leader, playing full on and undistractable. There's a bold version of Wayne Shorter's 'Fee Fi Fo Fum' (a very interesting read of that strange tune) and long clips through Franck's 'Fata' and 'The Parting Of The Ways'. The original Raney material doesn't jump out quite so prominently, but then neither of the originals is given quite such a thorough workout. The two horns/no piano format is quite challenging and Raney leans a little on Lundgaard to hold it all together, but there are few problems navigating such estimably organized music.

JOHN HICKS

Born 12 December 1941, Atlanta, Georgia; died 10 May 2006, New York City
Piano

Naima's Love Song
DIW 823
Hicks; Bobby Watson (as); Curtis Lundy (b); Victor Lewis (d). August 1988.

John Hicks said (1991): **'So many of the young musicians today learn much of their music from listening to records. I think that makes them very good at making records, but what they don't have is that sense of person-to-person, instrument-to-instrument interaction that you only learn from playing with others.'**

This most urbane of modern pianists grew up in California and was given piano lessons at home by his mother before studying formally at Lincoln University in Missouri and at Berklee. The son of a minister – Hicks performed at his father's former charge in Harlem just three days before his own death – he brought not so much a holy, holy gospel roll to his playing as a quieter, hymnic quality. It comes out in his best-known composition, 'Naima's Love Song' (which is dedicated to his daughter and has nothing to do with the Coltrane melody). The most responsive of musicians, he had a background in accompanying singers (Della Reese originally) and was always a selfless group player. Some would argue that this made his solo performances rather less than exciting, but Hicks was a more abrasive performer in these contexts than usually thought and while some of his later collaborations with flautist wife Elise Wood are gentle and unforceful, they are also deeply thoughtful and musicianly.

One of Hicks's finest moments on record was his role in Bobby Watson's luminous *Love Remains*. The saxophonist returned the favour two years later on *Naima's Love Song*. Hicks defies any stereotype by turning in a set that swings, fiercely on Rollins's 'Pent-Up House' and with an athlete's ease on Lundy's opening 'Elementary, My Dear Watson'. Bobby contributes one of his own almost gospelly lines on 'Someday Soon', one of three extended pieces that stretch the band and allow everyone generous solo space. Waldron's 'Soul Eyes' is arguably untypical of the composer, though his most recognized tune; Hicks takes it in a new direction, seeming to quote from a Methodist hymn in his solo and giving it a more ... soulful aspect than usual. The peerless title-track is saved for the end, straight after the white-hot Rollins tune, and everyone stretches out on it.

Hicks made many records, including a particularly fine Maybeck Hall recital for Concord, one of the best of that inconsistent series, but this brings together all his qualities: lyricism, restrained power, harmonic sophistication and that indefinable ability to respond in real time to the men around him; it's a polished studio record that has the urgency and immediacy of a live date.

CARLA BLEY *&*

Born Carla Borg, 11 May 1938, Oakland, California
Piano, keyboards

Fleur Carnivore
Watt/21 839 662

Bley; Lew Soloff, Jens Winther (t); Frank Lacy (frhn, flhn); Gary Valente (tb); Bob Stewart (tba); Daniel Beaussier (ob, f); Wolfgang Puschnig (as, f); Andy Sheppard (ts, cl); Christof Lauer (ts, ss); Roberto Ottini (bs, ss); Karen Mantler (hca, org, vib, chimes); Steve Swallow (b); Buddy Williams (d); Don Alias (perc). November 1988.

Carla Bley says: **'I looked in my seed catalogues to find the name of a flower to title this piece. I decided on "Venus Fly Trap", but discovered that Stevie Wonder had already used it. So I used the French translation, which is "Fleur Carnivore". Aside from the American musicians I brought from New York, I tried to fill out the band with one musician from each European country: Italy, France, England, Germany, Austria, Denmark were represented. Have I forgotten a country?'**

This is something like a masterpiece. In the '80s, Bley returned wholeheartedly to large-scale scoring and arranging, touring with a Big Band and a Very Big Band. The title-track here is worthy of Gil Evans, a majestically decadent ballad with superb solos by Soloff and Puschnig. The three-part 'Girl Who Cried Champagne' is a cracked bossa line with the kind of solo from Sheppard that Gato Barbieri used to deliver; Karen Mantler does a Stevie Wonder thing on harmonica. 'Song Of The Eternal Waiting Of Canute' also pairs the soloists, with a strong feature from the leather-lunged Valente and a terrific statement from Lauer.

The relation of parts to whole is far more confident than in times gone by and the solos are good largely because the writing is so acute. The concert recording – taped at the Montmartre in Copenhagen – manages to balance 'live' energy with studio precision and fullness of sound.

& *See also* **Escalator Over The Hill** (1968–1971; p. 357)

ART HODES &
Born 14 November 1904, Nikoliev, Ukraine, Russia; died 4 March 1993, Harvey, Illinois
Piano

Keepin' Out Of Mischief Now
Candid CCD 79717

Hodes (p solo). November 1988.

Art Hodes said (1981): **'Bebop? Avant-garde? Yeah, I heard of them. I also heard of these kids called the Bright Brothers – Wright Brothers? – who claim they can make you fly. It'll never catch on, none of it.'**

Hodes survived by *not* bending to the winds of fashion. Though over-represented as a solo performer in comparison with his group work, Hodes conjures some interesting variations on Jelly Roll Morton, his greatest single influence, on the November 1988 *Pagin' Mr Jelly* and *Mischief* (we marginally favour the latter) and this is perhaps the place for fans of either to start. Hodes's only originals, the title-tune and the related 'Mr Jelly Blues', are virtually impossible to pick out from a session that sticks to only the most sanctified of early jazz tunes: the march 'High Society', 'Wolverine Blues', 'Mr Jelly Lord', 'Winin' Boy Blues', 'Buddy Bolden's Blues' and 'The Pearls'. What's wonderful about Hodes's approach to this material, the Morton stuff in particular, is how *natural* he sounds. There's no pressure or effort, no hint of pastiche, just straightforward playing of magnificent music on a decent piano.

& *See also* **The Jazz Record Story** (1943–1944; p. 90)

MAL WALDRON &

Born 16 August 1925 (not 1926), New York City; died 2 December 2002, Brussels, Belgium
Piano

No More Tears (For Lady Day)
Timeless TTD 328
Waldron; Paulo Cardoso (b); John Betsch (d). November 1988.

Saxophonist and duo collaborator George Haslam remembers: **'He told me he found it trying that every interviewer started off with: "So, tell me about Billie Holiday." Shortly afterwards I was within earshot when a journalist began: "So, Mal, what was it like with Billie Holiday?" Mal smiled and proceeded to describe how special she was. Typical Mal.'**

Waldron spent the last almost 40 years of his life living and working in Europe. During that period he produced a vast number of recordings, often on very small labels, but with a bewildering array of collaborators and personnels. Late in life, he worked increasingly again with singers, including Abbey Lincoln and Jeanne Lee, Judi Silvano and others. He had actually contributed to a Billie Holiday tribute instrumental record as early as June 1957, around the beginning of his association with the singer, when he played on trumpeter Webster Young's *For Lady*.

In later years, there was growing pressure, sometimes unwelcome, sometimes unavoidable, to return to some aspect of his relationship with Holiday. To his credit, Waldron usually approached such projects obliquely rather than as 'songbook' situations. His earlier Black Lion record *For Lady Day* combines songs she sang with tributes written by Waldron specifically to celebrate her, but for the most part they are Waldron records with only an incidental relationship to their ostensible subject.

That's both the case and not with *No More Tears*. Almost 30 years after her death, one senses him trying – on the self-written title-track in particular, but also the subsequent 'Melancholy Waltz' – to come to terms with his own emotional involvement with a charismatic, indeed iconic, singer. His delivery is consistently thoughtful, the attack almost suspended in places, and it's drummer John Betsch, an undersung star in modern jazz, who gives the set much of its backbone. Even when Waldron flirts with cliché on 'Yesterdays', 'Smoke Gets In Your Eyes' and 'Alone Together', his angle on the melody and chords is always unexpected, and sometimes, as on the last track, quite subversive.

Selecting just one record from his later years is virtually impossible. The duos with Lacy, Haslam, Brown and others all command attention, as do group records like *The Git-Go* and *The Seagulls Of Kristiansund*. This one, though, holds us in thrall. It's by no means a throwaway performance, done with an eye to the market, but one of his most profound statements.

& *See also* **Mal/4** (1958; p. 226)

HENRY THREADGILL &

Born 15 February 1944, Chicago, Illinois
Alto and tenor saxophones, clarinet, flute

Rag, Bush And All
Novus 3502
Threadgill; Ted Daniels (t, flhn); Bill Lowe (btb); Dierdre Murray (clo); Fred Hopkins (b); Newman Baker, Reggie Nicholson (d). December 1988.

Henry Threadgill said (1989): **'Where AACM was strong and gave strength was that it wasn't possible to be interested in just jazz, or just jazz since Coltrane, or since bebop.**

You were allowed to, and thus expected to, listen to just about everything, including Stockhausen and Varèse, blues, field music, singers, opera ...'

The free-for-all theatricality of the Art Ensemble Of Chicago was out of favour in the more hidebound '80s, subordinated to a revival of interest in form. Classically trained and an inventive composer, Threadgill did sterling service with Air, another of the legendary groups to grow out of the AACM proving ground, and one distinguished by an interest in early jazz and its procedures. He is not an effusive soloist, putting more emphasis on unusual ensemble arrangements that have effectively eroded the old hierarchy of lead, harmony and rhythm instruments. Threadgill habitually used low brasses (sometimes instead of string bass, as in the early jazz groups), twinned drummers, and sometimes electric guitarists as well, somewhat in the manner of Ornette Coleman's Prime Time; Dierdre Murray's cello was another key ingredient.

The first records for RCA, *You Know The Number* and *Easily Slip Into Another World*, sound matted and slightly chaotic, though the production is at fault here, for Threadgill's arrangements seem admirably open-textured. *Rag, Bush And All* stands out as one of the finest achievements of the later '80s. Uncategorizable, it shifts the emphasis away from smaller-scale blowing tunes to generously proportioned themes which gradually reveal, as on the opening 'Off The Rag' and the long 'Sweet Holy Rag', a firm structural logic. 'Gift' sings solemn praises and 'Dancin' With A Monkey' is pure African-surrealism, soundtrack music for an Amos Tutuola novel.

Threadgill's later groups, Very Very Circus and Make Your Move, continued in this adventurous direction and delivered out-there music that resists 'avant-garde' classification without ever getting seriously danceable. He's a one-off.

& *See also* **Everybody's Mouth's A Book** (2001; p. 662)

TOMMY FLANAGAN
Born 16 March 1930, Detroit, Michigan; died 16 November 2001, New York City
Piano

Jazz Poet
Timeless TTD 301
Flanagan; George Mraz (b); Kenny Washington (d). January 1989.

Tommy Flanagan said (1987): **'Poetry, pictures, people, places ... especially people and places, I guess ... music can't just be about music ... it has to be about all those other things as well.'**

Tommy Flanagan is, if you will, the link between John Coltrane and Ella Fitzgerald. He stumbled on 'Giant Steps' – though no more than the man who wrote it – and he shaped some of Ella's most beautiful ballads. The combination of harmonic sophistication and an ability to set moods like no other pianist of his generation. Flanagan came up in the tough Detroit school before coming to New York after his military service. He quickly became a dependable presence in the studios, to the extent that his own creativity was somewhat restricted. Some good albums appeared on Prestige, including *Overseas* and *The Cats*, a label all-star date that yielded some of Coltrane's first significant solos. After his skirmish with 'Giant Steps', Flanagan began working for Ella, and stayed with her with one three-year break for 15 years.

His own career blossomed somewhat after that, and for the rest of his life Flanagan was a busy performer, playing a fortnight residency every year at the Village Vanguard, picking up the prestigious Jazzpar prize in Europe and becoming revered in Japan. It's hard to pick out one representative Flanagan record, and tempting to suggest (an old critical cop-out) that his best work was for other people. *Jazz Poet* is the most convincing candidate. Made just over a decade after leaving Ella, and with a trio perfectly attuned to his artistry, its title is a fair description of the man; a beautifully judged and perfectly performed record that repays frequent listening. A few years before, Flanagan had recorded a tribute to Coltrane, playing several of the tunes from *Giant Steps*. Here, that harmonic language is still present but not so overt, and fed back into things like Billy Strayhorn's 'Raincheck', 'Caravan', 'Willow Weep For Me' and a quite unexpected reading of 'St Louis Blues'. Mraz's countermelodies and fills are flawless and Washington plays musically and declines to muscle in. Up-and-coming piano trios – and there are plenty of them, God knows – would do worse than to devote a rehearsal afternoon to listening to this.

DON GROLNICK
Born 23 September 1947, Brooklyn, New York; died 1 July 2006, New York City
Piano, keyboards

The Complete Blue Note Recordings
Blue Note 57197
Grolnick; Randy Brecker (t); Barry Rogers, Steve Turre (tb); Michael Brecker, Joe Lovano (ts); Bob Mintzer, Marty Ehrlich (bcl); Dave Holland (b); Peter Erskine, Bill Stewart (d); collective personnel. February 1989, September 1992.

Don Grolnick's widow, Jeanne O'Connor, says: **'Don used to talk about how he liked the simultaneous horn-playing in traditional Dixieland music, and he tried to bring that feel to the modern jazz idiom. "One thing I love about Mingus's parts for horns," he once said, "is the way they sound improvised, even though they're written." At these sessions, he encouraged the players to "mess around" with the parts – how they got from one note to the other was up to them.'**

In the late '80s, after a successful career working with pop stars like Steely Dan, Linda Ronstadt and James Taylor, Don Grolnick decided to return to his first love and make an acoustic jazz record. He'd already put out an album of sophisticated fusion – *Hearts And Numbers* on Hip Pocket – which utilized some of the personnel he would deploy for his second coming as a jazz musician, but there was a huge jump in quality between that shiny first record and *Weaver Of Dreams*, the first of two Blue Note albums made before his very untimely death.

In this edition of the *Guide*, we've mostly tried to avoid including compilation albums and box sets, but Grolnick's Blue Note oeuvre is so much of a piece and so consistent in quality that it merits inclusion as a single work. On both records, Grolnick directed a starry personnel with exemplary finesse, letting each man test the weight of the music in his own way. *Weaver Of Dreams* reworked 'I Want To Be Happy' from the ground up in a way that recalls the analytical revisionism of George Russell's '50s small groups, but the cutting neo-bop of 'Nothing Personal' and clear-eyed balladry of 'Persimmons' are wholly contemporary. And there's always an added extra. 'Or Come Fog' works some spooky variations on 'Come Rain Or Come Shine', with just a minimum of studio manipulation, and apparently one musician told a delighted Grolnick that 'Taglioni' could be the national anthem of a yet to be discovered planet. There was, indeed, an unearthly or otherworldly tinge to some of this music.

Nighttown was, if anything, even better. The title-track, with its stunningly beautiful muted trumpet solo, is revered by young jazz composers as a yardstick against which to measure their own efforts and 'Heart of Darkness' absolutely blazes by. As before, the best music is often where Grolnick references the tradition. His brilliant update on 'What Is This Thing Called Love?' is a recurring surprise. Randy Brecker (who with Holland is the only player common to both dates), Turre and Lovano play to their best, but it's Ehrlich's bass clarinet which provides the key voice. Grolnick never sets out to be a virtuoso leader; his input is the writing and arranging, but the piano plays a wise and effective role, more than merely composer's comping.

SCOTT HAMILTON &
Born 12 September 1954, Providence, Rhode Island
Tenor saxophone

Plays Ballads
Concord CCD 4386
Hamilton; John Bunch (p); Chris Flory (g); Phil Flanigan (b); Chuck Riggs (d). March 1989.

Concord founder and president Carl Jefferson said (1987): **'He's hailed as a terrific up-tempo and mid-tempo player, but for me Scott is *the* balladeer of this generation ... maybe of any generation!'**

It might seem perverse to devote another entry to an artist who at first blush didn't develop or evolve in any essential way since his first recordings. The fact is, he may not have changed much as a technician, and certainly hasn't embraced harmolodics or any other avant-garde philosophy, but Hamilton has grown in both stature and depth and the late Carl Jefferson's verdict on him, which anticipated this recording, is well taken.

For many fans, this is Hamilton's best record, not because the ballad programme offers paths of least resistance, but simply because this is the sort of material which allows him to show off his strengths: harmonic subtlety at the kind of tempo where any hint of fudge would show, almost seamless transitions between ideas, and an ability to invest a familiar melody with maximum expression. 'Round Midnight' and 'In A Sentimental Mood' are read with an intriguing slant which freshens up the Monk tune considerably. 'Two Eighteen', dedicated to Hamilton's wife (and we suspect it may refer to the number of a honeymoon suite), is surprisingly his first recorded composition; it doesn't suggest a writing talent commensurate with his playing skills, but it's a fine piece nevertheless. The Don Byas-associated 'Laura' and an oblique 'Body And Soul' (also considerably freshened) were added only when *Ballads* was transferred to CD. This seems odd, because these are the outstanding performances on the record and, we hear, are much enjoyed by Don and Bean up in heaven.

& *See also* **From The Beginning** (1977, 1978; p. 445)

TIM BERNE
Born 1954, Syracuse, New York
Alto and baritone saxophones

Fractured Fairy Tales
Winter & Winter 919030
Berne; Herb Robertson (t, laryngeal crowbar); Hank Roberts (clo, elec); Mark Dresser (b, giffus, bungy); Joey Baron (d, elec). June 1989.

Tim Berne said (2001): **'That record was a turn-around for me. After that the writing got much denser, everything got longer, with ideas branching out of each other, rather than just themes and solos.'**

Berne has never been considered one of the great instrumentalists of modern jazz, but his ability to shape a dense, hyperactive ensemble sound is second to none and his dogged self-determination and application to a starkly challenging idiom commend him as an experimenter. Berne has long been devoted to the compositions of Julius Hemphill, a stern master for any musician. While most players of his generation were turned on by *A Love Supreme* or *Ascension,* for Berne it was Hemphill's *Dogon A.D.* For a number of years at the turn of the '80s, he released records as an unsigned independent and has returned to that more recently with the formation of his Screwgun label, which has put out a steady stream of unapologetically ugly and uncompromising music. He made some records for Soul Note, a regular resort for creative Americans, before signing up with JMT, a short-lived but always fascinating imprint. Much of its catalogue has been brought back to life by Winter & Winter.

With *Fractured Fairy Tales* Berne began to create the kind of work he would be associated with in the '90s with almost every piece of any length seeming like a miniature suite of wild dances, free passages and strange sounds (note the array of unusual 'instruments' in the personnel listing above). 'Evolution Of A Pearl' is a two-part epic that over 19 minutes manages to find a way from *musique concrète* to funk. 'The Telex Blues' uses processed speech (laryngeal crowbar?) to create a strangely alienating world of non-communication that comes close to summing up Berne's aesthetic of the time. 'Hong Kong Sad Song'/'More Coffee' is a crazed medley on which Robertson does some kind of Miles Davis thing with a wah-wah. Berne's solo is as far from Johnny Hodges as it is possible to get on an alto saxophone. Few artists divided the authors more completely. Both were and are admirers, but we tended to admire quite different records and as our minds and opinions changed, as change they must, we tended to go to opposite poles. This one, though, was one of the few where a consensus prevailed: an important modern record, tough-going and almost perverse, but packed with innate musicianship and an increasingly distinctive vision.

PUTTE WICKMAN
Born Hans-Olof Wickman, 10 September 1924, Falun, Sweden; died 14 February 2006, Stockholm
Clarinet

Some O' This And Some O' That
Dragon DRCD 187
Wickman; Roger Kellaway (p); Red Mitchell (b). June 1989.

Saxophonist Mats Gustaffson says: **'A true virtuoso, also known for his love of large American cars, touring around in a variety of Mercurys, Dodges and Chryslers in the '50s. He also introduced one of the greatest Swedish musicians ever! Wickman's 1960 EP *Blue Room* has the young Eje Thelin playing trombone and making arrangements.'**

One of the godfathers of postwar Swedish jazz, Wickman styled himself a swing player at first but – despite the unfashionable nature of his instrument – he increasingly adopted a personal take on the cooler side of bebop language. He spent time away from jazz – even leading a gospel group at one stage – but to the end of his long career he seemed fully aware of every kind of development in the music. There was a resurgence in later years, some recognition in America and the kind of respect shown to a touring jazzman who would turn up immaculately groomed whatever the venue and play with absolute conviction and impeccable chops.

Not nearly enough of an extensive discography survives in circulation, but the later Dragons find him in excellent fettle. A duo set with Red Mitchell is momentarily troubled by the bassist's capricious streak: his fascination with the lowest register sometimes strays into indulgence, and the huffing momentum won't be to all tastes. When Kellaway joins in, the music spreads itself out (eight pieces take 72 minutes here, whereas there are 13 in 68 minutes on the duo record), and Kellaway's extravagant imagination is perfectly checked by Wickman's insidious, wily lines. The recording is sometimes a little flat, since both discs were made in Red Mitchell's apartment rather than a studio, but it suits the intimacy of the music.

RICHARD DAVIS
Born 15 April 1930, Chicago, Illinois
Double bass

One For Frederick
Hep CD 2047
Davis; Cecil Bridgewater (t); Ricky Ford (ts); Sir Roland Hanna (p); Frederick Waits (d). July 1989.

Richard Davis said (1999): **'Ahmad Jamal was my first big job, something that went beyond local. He once said to me: "You want to know my favourite bass-player? ... You are, because you're working with me." That was a lesson right there, the idea that you have to confront and work with the people you have around you; no one else matters.'**

Also Stravinsky's favourite bass-player, Davis draws somewhat on the example of fellow Chicagoan Wilbur Ware, bringing considerable rhythmic virtuosity and a tremendous range of pitches and timbre, both *arco* and plucked. He remains best known to modern jazz fans for his role on Eric Dolphy's *Out To Lunch!* session and on other key recordings of that period, but in addition to a distinguished career as an educator Davis has sustained a modest recording career under his own name, all the way back to the unsatisfactory *Heavy Sounds* with Elvin Jones on Impulse! in 1967. As with many American musicians of his generation, Davis had to look to European and Japanese labels for support. This Hep recording and the slightly earlier *Persia My Dear* are perhaps his best showing, in this case abetted rather than hindered by the live recording at the Sweet Basil.
     The date features a regular group of the time, one that was very underrated, and is dedicated to the drummer, who died some four months later. Waits's introduction to 'City Bound' (and to the album) is very strong, and he turns in a fine accelerated solo on 'Brownie Speaks'. There are some unusual items in the programme: 'Every Time We Say Goodbye' is followed by the unusual 'Sunrise'. Bridgewater contributes a typically strong line (one can imagine it popping up in one of his solos) on 'As I Live And Breathe'. The chord sequence isn't unfamiliar but the distribution is. At the heart of all this, Davis himself is all calm and assurance, playing with a big, sure tone and putting himself in the forefront only when there is something positive to say. His solos are savvy and well-crafted, but they have a tinge of humour, too, as if to say: I know this is only the *bass* solo, but did you know we could do *this*, and sing pretty as well?

STANLEY COWELL
Born 5 May 1941, Toledo, Ohio
Piano

Sienna
Steeplechase SCCD 31253
Cowell; Ron McClure (b); Keith Copeland (d). July 1989.

Stanley Cowell said (1999): **'I'm often asked about teaching, as if it's somehow taking something away from the playing. Quite the opposite. When I'm teaching, I feel I'm learning, so much of the benefit flows back to me.'**

One of jazz's genuine thinking musicians, Cowell had a background in classical perform-ance as well as a jazz apprenticeship. At six, he saw Art Tatum and was hooked; it was his first and main influence, but it isn't one that necessarily stands out in the mature work, which is sombre-toned and makes use of wide intervals and unusual overlapping steps in the sequence. Bud Powell is also discernible in the DNA. He was a member of Music Inc. and with Charles Tolliver founded the influential musician-led label Strata East. He has taught at the City University of New York and the New England Conservatory and is valued as a teacher whose musical range goes well beyond jazz, into modern composition, elec-tronics and music history.

For too long, Cowell's recorded output was restricted to work as a jobbing sideman on the Galaxy label. Even now, a substantial proportion of his work as leader is out of print. *Sienna* is his finest moment on record (though the Maybeck Hall recital has him in an ideal acoustic on a superb piano). The Steeplechase date, which ushered in a period of intense activity in the studio, is a tightly marshalled and endlessly inventive session. The two opening tracks, 'Cal Massey' and the gentle ballad 'I Think It's Time To Say Goodbye', take the measure of Cowell's broad expressive range. Copeland deserves to be better known. He seems a little out of place on the slower tracks, a couple of which might better have been done as duos with McClure, but his abrupt unison accents on 'Evidence' are startlingly effective: quite the best version of Monk's tune since the master's own. A long 'I Concentrate On You' adds nothing much to the hundreds that have gone before, waffling round the chords almost distractedly, but with the title-track, one of a cycle of 'Sienna'-related compositions, and the closing 'Dis Place' Cowell lets loose his remarkable harmonic and rhythmic intelligence.

HANK JONES
Born 31 July 1918, Vicksburg, Mississippi; died 16 May 2010, New York City
Piano

Lazy Afternoon
Concord CCD 4391
Jones; Ken Peplowski (as, cl); Dave Holland (b); Keith Copeland (d). July 1989.

Hank Jones said (1990): **'Tatum was always number one, but I listened to Teddy Wilson and admired that very elegant approach. When bebop – and I don't like the word – came along, some of that elegance was thrown away, and that was a pity.'**

The oldest, and last surviving, of the Jones brothers is as quiet and unassuming as Elvin was extrovert, but he shares something of Thad's sophistication. Hank served his time in territory bands before joining the remarkable cohort of Detroit pianists who emerged after the war.

A bopper with an elegant touch and a nice sense of space and timing, he was a valued group player and accompanist, but never quite made the solo statement one might have expected of him. The piano recitals all tend to the polite. Hank had been recording for 40 years when he made this one. *Lazy Afternoon* is a peach: warm, vibrant jazz with the modulation and pace of a good club date. Jones is generous with solo space for his side-men, though his unusual approach to Kurt Weill's 'Speak Low' is marred by an intrusive solo from the otherwise excellent Copeland. Holland and the drummer had acted as the pianist's performing trio, with an evident empathy; quite properly, the bassist is featured strongly, with particularly fine excursions on J. J. Johnson's 'Lament', and the succeeding

'Comin' Home Baby'. Jones's fine touch as a colourist is evident on the title-track, where a hint of celeste under Ken Peplowski's smooth clarinet spices what might have been a bland idea. *Lazy Afternoon* and the 1977 *Rockin' In Rhythm* are also available as a two-header called *The Touch*.

CARLO ACTIS DATO
Born 21 March 1952, Torino, Italy
Tenor and baritone saxophones, bass clarinet

Ankara Twist
Splasc(h) H 302
Dato; Piero Ponzo (cl, bcl, as, bs, f); Enrico Fazio (b); Fiorenzo Sordini (d). October 1989.

Carlo Actis Dato says: **'Con il quartetto abbiamo vinto una scommessa: riuscire a rendere divertente una musica "difficile". Ritmo e melodie ispirati a musiche al di fuori del "jazz", molto prima che la "world music" diventasse di moda, perlomeno in Europa.'**

He started out with Art Studio, a catalytic presence on the Italian new-music scene, and has also been a member of Italian Instabile Orchestra. However, Actis Dato's most original contributions have been as a small-group leader with his Actis Band, Brasserie Trio and Atipico Trio, a figure unusually happy to submerge his own creative leadership to the needs of the group.
 He's most at home on baritone and bass clarinet, a volatile and unpredictable player with a compensating instinct for timing and the structure of a solo. He writes themes that suggest some bridging-point between jazz, Balkan and other folk musics. *Ankara Twist* features a long-standing quartet: no harmony player, so the understanding between Dato and Ponzo has to be complete and confident. These are mostly short pieces and there are a lot of them. At first one might wish to hear some developed in a more conventional way, but Dato is closer to Albert Ayler than he is to John Coltrane: extended harmonic improvisation isn't his thing. Once that's understood, it's clear that even tracks as condensed as 'Scottix' and 'Brutti Anatroccoli' are full of coiled invention. That isn't to say this imagination doesn't function over a longer span. His improvisations on 'Zambesi' and 'Caronte' are graceful and pungent by turns. *Ankara Twist* offers a rapid tour round Italy's cultural penumbra; if one needs fresh ears to appreciate it, it's never wasted effort to dispense with presuppositions, even for a moment or two.

ANDY SHEPPARD
Born 20 January 1957, Warminster, Wiltshire, England
Tenor and soprano saxophones, flute

Soft On The Inside
Antilles ANCD 8751
Sheppard; Claude Deppa (t); Kevin Robinson (t, flhn); Gary Valente (tb); Chris Biscoe (ss, as, ts); Pete Hurt (ts, bcl); Steve Lodder, Dave Buxton (ky); Mano Ventura (g); Ernst Reijseger (clo); Pete Maxfield (b); Han Bennink, Simon Gore (d). November 1989.

Andy Sheppard said (1990): **'There's a fear of big-band music around, even Carla Bley's, as if somehow it's necessarily more conservative than small-group music. I find it very strange and very limiting, though money's the real issue.'**

Sheppard came to some prominence in the '70s bands Sphere and Spirit Level, before spending time in Paris, returning in time to catch star status in the '80s jazz boom. His reputation settled down in the '90s, with film and TV projects and small-group work with Steve Lodder, and since then he has been most often seen as a member of Carla Bley's touring small groups and big bands.

Sheppard was much more fully formed as a player than most of the other new stars when the '80s boom put jazz in the spotlight and so, consequently and perversely, he has been less appreciated since. A short period with Blue Note – is there any other kind for British artists? – in the '90s allowed him to put out the intriguing *Rhythm Method* and *Delivery Suite*, but it was clear that some of his best work was already in the past and rendered doubly distant by the disappearance of the Antilles catalogue. At time of writing, he has been taken up at last by ECM, but despite a promising start it remains to be seen where that will go.

Sheppard's best album is boldly arranged, with many of the instruments paired with an opposite, bringing the univocal immediacy and rhythmic suppleness of his basic sextet to his first venture in big-band scoring. Sheppard had worked with both Carla Bley and George Russell's European band and draws elements of his scoring and a new melodic obliqueness from the experience. 'Carla Carla Carla Carla' makes one debt clear, calling on Lodder for a wry accordion-like synth solo. 'Rebecca's Silk Stockings' turns a Morse message from the brass into another freewheeling blow that is topped only by the percussive batter of 'Adventures In The Rave Trade', a finely conceived whole-side two-parter that marks a real step in Sheppard's compositional progress. Outstanding among the soloists are Robinson ('Carla' and 'Rave Trade'), Reijseger ('Soft On The Inside'), Deppa ('Silk Stockings') and Valente, another Bley man, on the opening of 'Rave Trade'. The sound is big but rather compressed towards the middle. A video version used to be available, but we lost ours years ago.

FRANZ KOGLMANN

Born 1947, Mödling, Austria
Trumpet, flugelhorn

A White Line

hat ART 6048
Koglmann; Jean-Christoph Mastnak (frhn); Raoul Herget (tba); Mario Arcadi (ob); Tony Coe (cl, ts); Paul Bley (p); Burkhard Stangl (g); Helmut Federle (acc); Klaus Koch (b); Gerry Hemingway (d); Gustav Bauer (cond). November 1989.

Franz Koglmann says: **'A *White Line* was the attempt to explore whether there was something like a white line of jazz history. Unsurprisingly, the endeavour was accused of being racist. But the world being what it is: scandal is only detrimental to those who do not have it. And, much to my surprise, "white line" was used as a technical term in literature not long thereafter.'**

For a short time, Franz Koglmann looked set to be as violently controversial in jazz circles as another, earlier Austrian was in European politics. Bizarrely, and absurdly, the trumpeter was accused of the musical equivalent of white supremacism, bleaching jazz of its African-American origins. One might say it travels from Bix Beiderbecke to Chet Baker, taking in Shorty Rogers on the way. Most heinous, Koglmann was suspected of trying to strip jazz of its defining 'swing' and substituting a pedestrian metre redolent of 20th-century classical modernism (Anton von Webern would be the bogey-figure here).

Koglmann's ideas were unquestionably controversial, asserting that at the end of the 20th century jazz had entered an academic late phase, exhausting most harmonic possibilities – from 'seventh chords to atonality' – and had passed through what Koglmann calls the 'afterglow' of expression. This was, of course, widely read as another funeral address over the corpse of jazz, but, as Koglmann pointed out, by the time J. S. Bach came along the baroque was effectively 'dead' as a style. Just as Bach created some of the highlights of the music, so, Koglmann suggested, there was no reason to think that jazz might not yet yield some revelatory music on its own terms, but more significantly had infused the general musical culture with specific new values, like individual sound and phrasing (not hitherto a characteristic of classical performance) and a free-floating groove. These, according to Koglmann, lived on as 'particulate matter in international pop and serious music'.

His personal response, articulated in a fine series of records for hat ART and subsequently his own Between the Lines label, was to create a body of music that takes its parchment-like tone and dry sound-world as much from classical forms as from cool jazz. The presence of Ran Blake on an earlier Koglmann record, *Orte Der Geometrie*, might suggest some Third Stream situation, but for all his referencing of classicism, and the literary and plastic arts, Koglmann is actually much closer to jazz than that. In exploring 'the tradition' – and in this regard unlike Anthony Braxton – Koglmann has generally gone for the work of jazz outsiders. The manifesto-like *About Yesterday's Ezzthetics* from 1987 is a homage to George Russell. The obscure pianist Richard Twardzik's 'The Fable Of Mabel' appears on *A White Line*, as does the Original Dixieland Jazz Band's 'At The Jazz Band Ball', a tune rarely called for, other than by trad and revivalist players, and almost never by 'progressive' musicians.

At some level, *A White Line*'s nonet personnel is a nod to *The Birth Of The Cool*, but with that quiet formalism grafted onto Paul Bley's brand of musical freedom. Koglmann had included John Carisi's 'Israel' on *Orte Der Geometrie* and programmes Gil Evans's 'Jambangle' and Gerry Mulligan's 'Festive Minor' here, but alongside two free-form ideas of the pianist's. Gerry Hemingway, who began himself to explore formal composition around this time, is the ideal percussionist for the date, but he is used only sparingly, and not at all like a conventional jazz drummer. Koglmann's own sound can best be described as bleakly sentimental, but scaled up one can imagine a Kenton brass section playing some of these lines. Coe's romanticism is more overt, but his clarinet-playing in particular has strong roots in chamber music. The additional brasses, foundation sound of the group Koglmann called his Pipetet on the following year's *The Art Of Memory*, are generally asked to play with a solemn exactness.

The mood is that of Claudio Magris's writing about Trieste, a place somehow outside of familiar history and outside of conventional time. Vienna might seem a more obvious location, and while the Viennese schools, first and second, both play a part here, those dominant traditions seem to have been circumvented. There is nothing decadent, effete or even elegiac about Koglmann's music. For all his apparent resistance to swing, there is a strong and very witty pulse to these tracks. Though a brief sound sample of the title-track, which opens the album, might persuade a casual listener that he is hearing a piece of modernist art-music, no one will retain that impression for long. *A White Line* conveys its message with sly and insidious sophistication. Its original themes are ear-worms, hard to banish. Even its standard performances, such as a limpid 'Out Of Nowhere', stand alongside more canonical versions. Coming at decade's end, it is one of the key records of the '80s and one of the most satisfying of the period to return to. As Koglmann concedes, a carefully stoked furore over the 'white line' gave way rather quickly to guilty emulation. *A White Line* points forward to many of the ideas and procedures that became commonplace, though rarely so well executed, during the following decade's flowering of creative music.

GARY THOMAS
Born 10 June 1961, Baltimore, Maryland
Tenor saxophone, flute

While The Gate Is Open
Winter & Winter 919037
Thomas; Greg Osby (as); Kevin Eubanks (g); Anthony Cox, Dave Holland (b); Dennis Chambers (d). November 1989.

Jack DeJohnette said (1990): **'Gary is a highly intelligent musician, but also a highly intelligent man. The two things don't always go together, but when they do, you always get a certain added value, more depth in the music.'**

Thomas was one of the most assertive and acerbic of the M-Base musicians, with a punchy, insistent tone that is most forceful on his own records but which has also contributed materially to records by other leaders, including Uri Caine, Peter Herborn and John McLaughlin. He was exceptionally good with Jack DeJohnette's Special Edition group. Thomas's first record for the newly founded W&W label wisely attempted to do no more than consolidate the sound he had been trading in for years at JMT. As if to prove it, the early JMTs have been reissued and the first of them, *By Any Means Necessary*, is the archetypal M-Base record, rhythmically rugged, harmonically subtler than it sounds at first, ultimately less alienated from the post-bop mainstream than you might think. The surprise on *While The Gate Is Open* was that Thomas, seemingly so resistant to anything not as fresh as today's papers, was still willing to work with standards. His readings of 'Epistrophy' and 'Star Eyes' are wonderfully engaging and this work was streets ahead of the polystylistic shambles of his somewhat later and much-praised *The Kold Kage*.

JIM SNIDERO
Born 29 May 1958, Redwood City, California
Alto saxophone

Blue Afternoon
Criss Cross 1072
Snidero; Brian Lynch (t); Benny Green (p); Peter Washington (b); Marvin 'Smitty' Smith (d). December 1989.

Jim Snidero says of *Blue Afternoon*: **'It kind of capsulized a period in the '80s when I often collaborated with Brian Lynch, Benny Green and others. We all appreciated the tradition but tried to infuse it with what was happening at that moment. Though it's probably not as polished as my later work, it has plenty of youthful exuberance.'**

Snidero kept busy after making the *de rigueur* transition to New York when he had completed his studies in Texas. He comes out of a bop idiom, and has a substantial CV of band associations, including a stint in the Sinatra orchestra, as well as a tough facility at all levels and speeds. We were told the title of the debut Criss Cross *Mixed Bag* wasn't to be taken too literally, or not in the negative sense at least, but it was just that: a terrific band, same as this one with the exception of Tain Watts for Smith, and it tried to do too much at once. A couple of further recordings on the Italian Red label gave a better account of Snidero as a working musician and then this one came along.

Youthful exuberance it still has, and while the leader hadn't yet shaved off the tango-dancer moustache, he had put a maturer check on some of his showier moves. The two opening cuts, 'Enforcement' and 'Forethought', were more than just conventional blowing lines, and set the group some interesting harmonic terrain to cross. Lynch contributed 'The Trifle', which isn't, but somehow manages to divert the session a little. After that, though, Snidero absolutely nails Waldron's peerless 'Soul Eyes' and Shorter's 'Infant Eyes' and pushes an energetic record to a very satisfying conclusion. Arguably there were better discs later, on Milestone and Savant, but it's the balance of ambition and energy that makes *Blue Afternoon* so attractive.

HORACE TAPSCOTT

Born 6 April 1934, Houston, Texas; died 27 or 29 February 1999, Los Angeles, California
Piano

The Dark Tree
hatOLOGY 2-2053 2CD
Tapscott; John Carter (cl); Cecil McBee (b); Andrew Cyrille (d). December 1989.

Arthur Blythe said (1989): **'I met him at a friend's house, where he was rehearsing with his trio and asked me to sit in. Making contact with Horace Tapscott was like discovering your own people after wandering in the desert. He had that quality about him, to make you belong.'**

Tapscott's music and his views on integration and racial equality cannot be separated, and yet he rarely composed anything resembling programme or agit-prop music, preferring to let the free flow of creativity do the job of discourse for him. Inevitably, given his views, he was held apart from the critical mainstream and, despite a substantial body of recording from the time of his comeback in 1978 onwards, most of it was for his own Nimbus label. He remains, perversely, best known for the compositions and arrangements on Sonny Criss's 1968 album *Sonny's Dream*. In 1961, Tapscott helped establish the Union Of God's Musicians And Artists' Ascension, out of which grew the Pan-Afrikan People's Arkestra, both attempts to find uncompromised work for talented, young black musicians. Their work is fiercely disciplined, built up out of deceptively simple elements, but with subtle polychordal shadings that reflect Tapscott's solo work and his intriguing duos and trios with members of the PAPA. Much of this work was issued on his own Nimbus label.

The Dark Tree is special in having two neglected giants of modern jazz working with instinctive sympathy, intelligence and bottomless expression. Both pianist and clarinettist are entirely at ease with brusque, angular melodies and more sweepingly lyrical passages. Huge ostinato passages provide a base for fiery improvisation, and while the music is 'avant-garde' in sensibility, it is also accessible, in the way of saxophonist Arthur Blythe's music. Tunes like 'Lino's Pad' exploit unusual and often difficult time-signatures, combinations of metre which present no problems to players as deft as McBee and Cyrille. Alternative versions of 'The Dark Tree' can be found elsewhere, on the trio disc *Live At Lobero: Volume 1* and on a valuable Novus/BMG compilation called *West Coast Hot* which pops up every now and then and is well worth the search. The two versions here, though, are the key statements, along with the wonderful, almost Dolphy-like 'Sketches Of Drunken Mary'; one can't say 'definitive' of pieces that are defined by their fugitive, experimental quality, but the interplay between Carter and Tapscott is astonishing and one's only regret is that they didn't choose to make some duo versions as well.

LOUIS HAYES

Born 31 May 1937, Detroit, Michigan
Drums

Una Max
Steeplechase SCCD 31263
Hayes; Charles Tolliver (t); Gerald Hayes (as); John Stubblefield (ts); Kenny Barron (p); Clint Houston (b). December 1989.

Louis Hayes said (1999): **'I think maybe playing drums is a hereditary thing, like it might be in an African village. I was first taught by my father, Louis Hayes Sr. There was a piano at home as well, and that helps shape your voice, whatever the instrument you choose.'**

Louis Hayes remains one of the master hard-bop drummers, a key figure in the Detroit community and a player whose undemonstrative virtue of playing for the band has told against his wider reputation. Whether working with Cannonball Adderley or Oscar Peterson, he's often the most interesting thing about the music, but without pushing himself into the foreground.

A fine sequence of records for Steeplechase found him making a serious mark as leader for the first time. Besides Hayes's own playing the first point of interest is the return of Tolliver to active duty after a number of years away. He sounds rusty on *Light And Lively*, but the two later records are better showcases for him. Watson is a shade too slick for the company on the first record, but *Una Max* – it's a nice pun – is a record that grows in stature on repeated hearings: Stubblefield is in the mood for some grand oratory, Tolliver's spacious solos accumulate strength, and the rougher, unpredictable alto of the younger Hayes is an interesting wild card. 'Geri' and 'Saudade' see the leader working in an approximate samba rhythm and sounding completely across it. The title-track is presumably dedicated to Max Roach and, if so, it's as generous and as challenging a tribute as can be imagined, lots of subtle play on three-against-four, lots of room for improvisation even in a quite modest span.

KENNY WHEELER
Born 14 January 1930, Toronto, Ontario, Canada
Trumpet, flugelhorn

Music For Large And Small Ensembles
ECM 843152-2 2CD
Wheeler; Alan Downey, Ian Hamer, Henry Lowther, Derek Watkins (t); Hugh Fraser, Dave Horler, Chris Pyne, Paul Rutherford (tb); Julian Argüelles, Duncan Lamont, Evan Parker, Ray Warleigh (sax); Stan Sulzmann (ts, f); John Taylor (p); John Abercrombie (g); Dave Holland (b); Peter Erskine (d); Norma Winstone (v). January 1990.

Norma Winstone said (1999): **'Kenny just isn't interested in recognition. I've never known anyone so wholly concentrated on the music. Nothing else seems to matter to him.'**

The brilliant Canadian moved to London in the '50s and after some trad work very quickly became associated with the avant-garde, playing in some of the most advanced groups of the day. It was clear, though, that his limpid, very pure tone was also amenable to other styles and that his interests veered to composition every bit as much as to free improvisation. Wheeler's body of work for the ECM label is definitive of its devotion to advanced musical language, great purity of sound and a constant trade-off between experimentalism and accessibility. The early ECM records – *Gnu Nigh* and *Deer Wan* – have a rare beauty that remains consistent through the following years, but for sheer sophistication of thought and elegance of execution they pall in comparison to the more ambitious later work.

Music For Large And Small Ensembles contains some of Wheeler's most distinctive scores and is perhaps the best place to gain an understanding of how Wheeler's particular grasp of tonality and instrumental colour works in a mixture of scored and improvised settings. As in Azimuth, he uses Norma Winstone's voice to increase the chromaticism of his arrangements and further humanize unwontedly personal and self-revealing pieces, full of folk echoes and deeply embedded North American themes (the 'Opening' to 'Sweet Time Suite' sounds like a variant on a cowboy tune, and there's a wide-open quality to the voicings that can be heard in fellow Canadian Leonard Cohen's eclectic jazz-buckskin-*musette*-rock syntheses). The trios that conclude disc two (there are also three duets which do not involve Wheeler as a player) are closer to his free-abstract work than to the thematic improvisations on his best-known ECM records.

OSCAR PETERSON &

Born 15 August 1925, Montreal, Quebec, Canada; died 23 December 2007, Mississauga, Ontario, Canada
Piano, organ, other keyboards

The Legendary Live At The Blue Note
Telarc 8617 4CD
Peterson; Herb Ellis (g); Ray Brown (b); Bobby Durham (d). March 1990.

Ray Brown said (1994): **'For Oscar, ageing just meant letting younger pianists catch up. He has had his problems over the years, but nothing seems to dent his confidence or slow him down.'**

Whatever stiffness crept into Peterson's fingers in later years – even before the stroke that interrupted his activities for a time – has served only to increase the feeling he injects into his playing. It's hard to relate 'Peace For South Africa' on the first volume of this set to the torrents of sound he conjured up in his big-hall Pablo days. This is quieter, more intimate and more thoughtful, and the ballad medley at its centre shows genuine melodic inventiveness. A must for Peterson fans, and 'Honeysuckle Rose' offers a good – albeit second-gear – impression of the Tatum-derived technique which overlaid his earlier commitment to Nat Cole.

The second volume was recorded the following night. It's a more varied, less familiar programme, but the playing is pretty much by the numbers. The 'final' visit and the almost inevitable *Encore* volume are even more subdued and formal. The elegance of Peterson's segues begins to pall long before the end. Fans will value 'It Never Entered My Mind' on the last but one, but more casual purchasers might want to plump for the first volume, simply *Live At The Blue Note*, and leave it at that, even if it means missing the *Encore* performance of 'I Wished On The Moon', which, though brief, is exquisite.

& *See also* **At The Stratford Shakespearean Festival** (1956; p. 193), **Night Train** (1962; p. 290), **My Favorite Instrument** (1968; p. 351)

ODEAN POPE

Born 24 October 1938, Ninety Six, South Carolina
Tenor saxophone

The Ponderer
Soul Note 121229
Pope; Byard Lancaster, Julian Pressley, Sam Reed (as); Glenn Guidone, Bob Howell, Middy Middleton, John Simon (ts); Joe Sudler (bs); Eddie Green (p); Tyrone Brown, Gerald Veasley (b); Cornell Rochester (d). March 1990.

Odean Pope says: **'I remember going to the studio to record in Brooklyn very early on a bright sunny day and feeling inspired by the musicians' upbeat expressions. There was a great spirit in the recording studio because the producer from Milan was preparing to put our music out to the world. We had rehearsed for weeks, on a high. However, I have to tell you that *The Ponderer* may be the least favourite of my CDs! I am much more excited by my current work.'**

'I tried to imagine what it would sound like if I played at the bottom range of my instrument like Coltrane played at the top.' This is pretty much what Odean Pope has done. If he sounds less like his fellow Philadelphian (and native North Carolinian) and more like Sam Rivers or even Jimmy Heath, Pope is nevertheless profoundly influenced by some less exposed aspects of Coltrane's approach: its concern with ensembles rather than its torrential out-pouring of personal feelings, its rootedness rather than its God-bothering excursions. Pope is a profoundly modest individual who aligns himself with the pianist Ibn Hassan Ali's belief that Coltrane's music is a not quite conscious expression of some higher state. Behind Pope's Saxophone Choir – it succeeded Catalyst, an adventurous group with some crossover potential – is the fiery, inchoate music of *Ascension*, but also something of the voicing of the later Ellington orchestras, as they negotiated with 'world music'.

Pope rehearses the Choir meticulously and then records live in the studio with no over-dubs. The charts are intricate and demanding, a broad orchestral sound punctuated with episodes from a roster of players who, like the leader himself, are not well-known outside this context. Byard Lancaster, also a Philadelphian, has an earthy wail redolent of Jackie McLean and Ornette Coleman, and he blends perfectly with Pope's multiphonics on 'The Ponderer', title-piece on the best of the Choir albums. Like the others, it has a strong inter-nal consistency and is almost written like a continuous symphonic work, from 'Overture' to the Spanish-tinged 'Phrygian Love Theme'. Eddie Brown's 'One For Bubba' serves as an encore piece and a chance for the rhythm section to do its stuff. There are even hints of Ornette's 'harmolodic' approach in some of Pope's layering of rhythmic figures and melo-dies. He has such generous gifts as a composer and such a distinctive sound and solo style that it is extraordinary he is not more widely known outside his circle. This record, and even the ambitious but flawed *Epitome* from 1993, documents a bold and rewarding experiment in modern jazz.

EITHER/ORCHESTRA

Formed December 1985 by Russ Gershon, born 11 August 1959, New York City
Group

The Calculus Of Pleasure

Accurate ACC-3252
Tom Halter, John Carlson (t, flhn); Russell Jewell, Curtis Hasselbring (tb); Rob Rawlings (as); Douglas Yates (as, bs); Russ Gershon (ss, ts); Charlie Kohlhase (bs); John Medeski (ky); Mark Sandman (g); Bob Nieske (b); Matt Wilson (d). April–June 1990.

Russ Gershon looks back: **'Even after 20 years, it's no surprise what a broad and deep record it remains. It would be quite impossible now to get that talent into a couple of vans for six weeks, but that's how we got so comfortable with those complicated charts that we could play them like falling out of bed. We were lucky that everybody was at a place in their lives to be able to be so devoted to this music – and each other.'**

A modest-sized big band full of outsize talents, Either/Orchestra has for 25 years bucked the almost impossible restrictions that modern budgets set for a band of this kind. It's a heroic accomplishment that the group is as swinging, exciting and cheerfully cutting-edge as it is, and its importance is underlined by the number of future stars who have passed through its ranks (invidious to choose only three, but Andrew D'Angelo, John Medeski and Matt Wilson immediately spring to mind). Gershon has shrewdly maintained Accurate Records as an outlet for the group. It isn't that other imprints wouldn't have taken them on, but they would certainly have vetoed some of E/O's more venturesome projects: how many majors would have signed off on *More Beautiful Than Death*, the group's 1999 treatment of Ethiopian pop?

The first three records were a joyous ragbag of cover versions, bristling originals and complexities. *Dial E* delivered Sonny Rollins's 'Doxy' as an outlandish shuffle. Gershon has the chutzpah to take apart 'Brilliant Corners'; and the extravagantly extended '17 December' is a pungent E/O manifesto. *Radium* ran a live gamut from a tragedian's version of 'Wil-low Weep For Me' to a madcap distillation of 'Nutty' and 'Ode To Billie Joe', with Roscoe

Mitchell's 'Odwallah' as a bonus. *The Half-Life Of Desire* expanded the palette with Medeski's arrival; this brilliant keyboardist has a sure grasp of which electronics will and which won't work in a neo-trad context. Rock and 'world' musics get only a modest look-in in this group's work; its material comes largely from within jazz language itself. Yet it still manages to cover the King Crimson metal blow-out 'Red' and tamper with Miles Davis's 'Circle In The Round' on the same record.

The Calculus Of Pleasure, part live and part studio, and with a brand new rhythm section, is a contemporary masterwork, brilliant and perverse (as the Caravaggio cover possibly signals). There is an astonishing arrangement of Horace Silver's 'Ecaroh', previously a piano trio tune, and a sour, lavish update of Benny Golson's 'Whisper Not' which is an object lesson in renewing stale jazz repertory. Julius Hemphill's 'The Hard Blues' also comes in for a grandly decadent interpretation, with brass and reeds fattening up the harmonies. This leaves five originals from within the band's own ranks.

CECIL TAYLOR &

Born 15 March 1929 (some sources state 25 March and 1930), Long Island, New York
Piano, voice

Celebrated Blazons
FMP CD 58
Taylor; William Parker (b); Tony Oxley (d). June 1990.

Tony Herrington, publisher of *The Wire*, says: **'His music is partly an art of quotation and recontextualization. His improvisations draw from a vast library of fragments – established phrases, motifs, licks and riffs; favourite intervals, inversions and voicings – which he summons into the here and now each time he solos, reconfiguring and recombining them, impacting them at great speed and with immense force. This is why listening to a solo can bring forth sensations of déjà vu and alienation simultaneously. The familiar is made strange by being rendered in shockingly new conjunctions.'**

Tony Oxley is probably the best time drummer on the planet at the moment, which was true even before the death of Elvin Jones. It raises the old litmus question of swing *vis-à-vis* Taylor's music, since his ever-widening horizons sound more in touch with and touched by jazz tradition than ever, even at a time when he might as likely recite verse – a strange Mayan variant on Charles Olson's 'composition by field' prosody – or dance around the space created by the piano as attack the keyboard immediately. Oxley's drumming is a more European flavour than anything Taylor's other regular drummers have created, yet it only serves to emphasize the huge rhythmic resources of the leader's own playing. Where Cyrille's magnificent breakers would sometimes obscure the keyboard, Oxley's playing – a unique blend of lumpen momentum and detailed percussive colour – reveals more of it. Parker, too, is coming into his own, deflecting off what the others do while speaking his own piece. Nearly an hour of music, and, as long as one abandons any narrow construction of the term, it swings.

& *See also* **Jazz Advance** (1956; p. 191), **Nefertiti, The Beautiful One Has Come** (1962; p. 289), **Conquistador!** (1966; p. 339)

SUN RA &

Born Herman Sonny Blount (also known as Sonny Bourke, Le Sony'r Ra), 22 May 1914, Birmingham, Alabama; died 30 May 1993, Birmingham, Alabama
Piano, space organ, keyboards

Mayan Temples
Black Saint 120121
Sun Ra; Ahmed Abdullah, Michael Ray (t, v); Tyrone Hill (tb); Noel Scott (as); Marshall Allen (as, f); John Gilmore (ts, perc); James Jackson (bsn, perc); Jothan Callins (b); Clifford Barbaro, Earl 'Buster' Smith (d); Ron McBee, Elson Nascimento Santos, Jorge Silva (perc); June Tyson (v). July 1990.

Bassist Richard Davis said (1987): **'This happened way back earlier but it tells you something about Sun Ra, several things maybe. We were playing in this club and there was a guy drunk in a booth, head rolling about all over the place, drooling, just about conscious. Sun Ra nodded at me and then nodded toward him and started playing these really weird sounds on his keyboard. I was staring at his hands, but he nodded again toward the drunk guy and he was up, alert and looking hard toward us, apparently sober. The power of Sun Ra music!'**

In later years, the Sun Ra discography increasingly became a kind of touring record, with concerts recorded on the fly, and often with no more audio fidelity than those early El Saturn recordings. There was a degree of repetitiveness in the material as well, familiar chants, familiar/unfamiliar oddity of instrumentation, and mixed in with the Henderson-like big-band swing occasional inspired moments of surprise, like the sets devoted to Walt Disney themes.

As Francis Davis points out in his liner-note, this studio session restores the emphasis to Sun Ra's piano-playing. Illness would shortly curtail his ability to play acoustic keyboards this crisply. His introductions and leads are absolutely in the line of Ellington, and the voicings are supple, open-ended and often quietly ambiguous, leaving considerable emphasis on the soloists. As always, Gilmore is a giant and Marshall Allen's searing solo on 'Prelude To Stargazers' is a model of controlled fury. Ra re-records 'El Is A Sound Of Joy' (from *Supersonic Jazz*), a late-'50s theme that sounds completely contemporary and brings a freshness and simplicity to 'Alone Together' that is quite breathtaking. 'Discipline No. 1' is a lovely ballad, illustrating Sun Ra's ability to give simple material an unexpected rhythmic profile (Davis rightly points to the example of Mingus in this case) and the closing 'Sunset On The Night On The River Nile' is one of his very best space anthems. Few Sun Ra albums give a better sense of his extraordinary versatility.

& *See also* **Jazz In Silhouette** (1958; p. 230), **The Magic City** (1965; p. 328)

MUHAL RICHARD ABRAMS
Born 19 September 1930, Chicago, Illinois
Piano

Blu Blu Blu
Black Saint 120117
Abrams; Joel Brandon (whistle); Jack Walrath (t); Alfred Patterson (tb); Mark Taylor (frhn); Joe Daley (tba); John Purcell (as, f, bcl); Bob DeBellis (as, cl, bcl); David Fiuczynski (g); Lindsey Horne, Brad Jones (b); Warren Smith (vib, tim); Thurman Barker (d). November 1990.

Bassist Brad Jones says: **'On the first day of rehearsal. I kept hearing a mysterious sound playing the intricate lead melody. At first, I thought it was a synthesizer-player out of my sight-line. Then I noticed a gentleman sitting in front of the saxophones with a microphone directly in front of his puckered lips, whistling one of Muhal's difficult melodies with perfect intonation. It was Joel Brandon, who just recently passed away. I can't remember what I said to him after the rehearsal – I guess a lot of dumbfounded marvelling – but what really threw me was talking to Muhal after Joel had left and learning that he didn't whistle by blowing outward. He blew inward!'**

There is no reliable means of measuring 'influence'. If there were, Abrams would sit very high indeed in the canon. Like any catalyst, he seems remarkably unchanged by the forces he has set in motion. He has no 'style' of his own – that is his great strength – but remains a free agent in a current of Black and European idioms, from stride to serialism. Trombonist George Lewis credits him with giving a generation of black musicians – Chicagoans most obviously – permission to attempt anything in music.

A local legend, he founded the Experimental Band in 1960 and co-founded the legendary Association For The Advancement Of Creative Musicians, of which he became first president. Perhaps inevitably, Abrams's own work has been significantly undervalued. His piano-playing comes out of bebop – Bud Powell rather than Monk – but is rarely foregrounded. There are solo performances but they are little remarked and it's Abrams's ensemble writing and leading that seem to define him.

Blu Blu Blu was his tenth recording for Italian label Black Saint, an association that kept the American avant-garde in view. Given the quality of his output, it is hard to select just one album, but this one remains essential. It continues Abrams's effort to integrate avant-garde procedures with the most nourishing aspects of Black vernacular, particularly the blues. The title-piece is a dedication to Muddy Waters, played without much development. The whole set, though, is almost hijacked by the remarkable Brandon (who also worked with David Murray); his high, bird-like tones are surreally beautiful and 'One For The Whistler' is a *tour de force*. Abrams really gets going as a pianist only on the final 'Stretch Time', leaving most of the foreground to a tonally varied and adventurous band. Fiuczynski's guitar initially sounds out of place, but he is an extraordinary technician. Of the brasses, Walrath is the unchallenged star: punchy, accurate and full of drollery. Barker takes control of the engine room. Abrams is an important figure in the history of the music. One wouldn't want to stop with this record. He needs to be explored in depth.

GARY BARTZ

Born 26 September 1940, Baltimore, Maryland
Alto, soprano and sopranino saxophones, clarinet, flute, wood flute, percussion

There Goes The Neighborhood!
Candid CCD 79506
Bartz; Kenny Barron (p); Ray Drummond (b); Ben Riley (d). November 1990.

Gary Bartz said (1991): **'The thing for my generation was to find your own voice. If someone wanted Cannonball Adderley that was who they called. They didn't call me and ask me to sound like Cannonball. That's where the work lies, but once you find that voice, that is who you are. Literally who you are.'**

Bartz modified the usual tendency for instrumentalists to be influenced by the dominant saxophone sound of the day. As well as hitching his star to Charlie Parker's wagon, as he did in early days, he was later equally affected by brass-players, mainly Lee Morgan and Grachan Moncur III, with whom he studied. He came to notice with Max Roach's group and his precocious talents won him a place in the Jazz Messengers, though by this time Bartz had already formed his Ntu Troop, a group which changed rapidly in style over succeeding years. At the start of the '70s he was recruited to Miles Davis's electric band, a prominent gig which did much to harden up what was already a strong interest in Afro-funk.

On alto, Bartz still has traces of Charlie Parker bebop, but his sound is nothing like Jackie McLean's or Sonny Criss's or any other contender for the keys of the kingdom. There's an anguished wail in it, but also a defiant weight of delivery, with distinct, emphatic phrasing. Bartz's own early records were admired, and some still crop up in acid-jazz contexts, but it wasn't until the end of the '80s that he appeared to come through as a distinctive leader, a moment in jazz history when bebop language became more prominently viable and a basic idiom.

There Goes The Neighbourhood! is Gary's finest hour. The opening 'Racism' is a boiling blues, an original played with an increasingly noticeable Coltrane inflexion. The first of two Tadd Dameron compositions, 'On A Misty Night' was originally recorded in the mid-'50s in a band that included Coltrane; the mid-point of the set is a severe interpretation of 'Impressions'. Bartz's homage isn't limited to a growing repertoire of anguished cries and dissonant transpositions. He has also paid attention to how the younger Coltrane framed a solo; working against the trajectory of Dameron's theme, but sitting comfortably inside the beat, he constructs an ascending line that culminates each time in a beautifully placed false note. The result is as lovely as it is unsettling.

Johnny Mercer's 'Laura' receives a serene and stately reading, with Drummond featured. Bartz's coda restatement is masterful. He tackles 'Impressions' in the most boiled-down way, with only minimal rhythmic support, concentrating on the basics. Barron returns to the foreground for 'I've Never Been In Love' and the closing 'Flight Path', his own composition. Throughout, his touch is light but definite, freeing his accompaniments of any excess baggage.

Though Charles McPherson and Bobby Watson have previously laid claim to Parker's alto crown, Bartz appears to have come into his kingdom at last. A superb album; recorded live at Birdland, it's well balanced and free from extraneous noise.

CHICO HAMILTON &

Born Foreststorn Hamilton, 21 September 1921, Los Angeles, California
Drums

Arroyo
Soul Note 121241
Hamilton; Eric Person (as, ss); Cary DeNigris (g); Reggie Washington (b). December 1990.

Chico Hamilton said (1993): **'I never really knew whether Eric [Dolphy] was taken too soon or whether he had done all he came here to do. From my own point of view, I value each new day as offering something else. It would have been a waste if I had not been allowed to carry on all these years. I feel blessed by life,** *euphoric.***'**

This is the latter-day group that Hamilton calls Euphoria. By the time he recorded *Arroyo*, he had been in the business four decades, worked as Lena Horne's drummer and tasted a bit of commercial success (*The Sweet Smell of Success*) in movie music. Much later press copy emphasized his relationship with Dolphy over his own music, and two years later the same group – almost – made *My Panamanian Friend* in homage to the departed, whose family were originally from Panama.

Though it's as far in style as it is in years from the '50s quintet, there are clear lines of continuity. Hamilton's preference for a guitarist over a piano-player helps free up the drums, allowing Hamilton to experiment with melodic improvisation. Typically, DeNigris is given considerable prominence – much as Jim Hall, Larry Coryell and John Abercrombie were at different times – with Person assigned a colourist's role.

The long opening 'Alone Together' is a vibrantly inventive version of a chestnut. Hamilton's polyrhythms open the tune to half a dozen new directions and Washington produces some of his best work of the set. The other standard, Lester Young's and Jon Hendricks's 'Tickle Toe', has the drummer scatting with the same relaxed abandon he applies to his kit. His writing on 'Sorta New', 'Cosa Succede?' and the intriguingly titled 'Taunts Of An Indian

Maiden' is still full of ideas, exploiting band textures to the full. DeNigris and Person both claim at least one writing credit, and the guitarist's 'Stop' is ambitious and unsettling. A strong statement by one of the music's most creative presences.

& *See also* **Live At The Strollers** (1955; p. 163)

MEREDITH D'AMBROSIO
Born 1941, Boston, Massachusetts
Voice, piano

Love Is Not A Game
Sunnyside SSCD 1051
d'Ambrosio; Eddie Higgins (p); Rufus Reid (b); Keith Copeland (d). December 1990.

Meredith d'Ambrosio said (1992): **'I think I was drawn to Bill [Evans] because both of us were deeply, deeply shy, not natural performers at all. But I hang on everything he did, every sound he made, as if they were messages from somewhere else! I felt something similar meeting John Coltrane. I didn't find him difficult or awkward, probably because he sensed similar things in me, but I just didn't feel ready to go on that tour.'**

D'Ambrosio's is a remarkable story, and she tells it with engaging frankness. Being star-crossed in her younger years has allowed her to sing romantic songs with a convincing plainness. She studied at Schillinger House for a time and was taken up by Roger Kellaway and Maynard Ferguson. She even turned down an opportunity to tour Japan with John Coltrane on his final tour to the Far East. Subsequently married to the late pianist Eddie Higgins, she has turned out a steady sequence of fine vocal albums, though she has had a parallel career in art, creating pictures in eggshell mosaic and dabbling in other forms. Her piano-playing isn't negligible, but it took second place as long as Higgins was around.

We are convinced that her masterpiece may be 2004's *Wishing On The Moon*, but the earlier record draws us back inexorably. Tomorrow, it might be *Lost In His Arms*, *Little Jazz Bird* or *South To A Warmer Place*, or any one of the other dozen records she has put out between the late '70s and now: subtly beautiful records, all. She was influenced by Bill Evans and is often thought to represent in vocal form what he did at the keyboard. However, much of her thinking about music was shaped by the British pianist Pat Smythe, who exerted a little-discussed influence on Evans; d'Ambrosio met him at the New York home of Richard Rodney Bennett.

An exceptional series of records for Sunnyside – how many artists are so consistently favoured by one label? – went to a new level in 1985 with *It's Your Dance*, arguably her most fully realized record. The voice is too small for jazz virtuosity, but she achieves a different authenticity through economies of scale. *South To A Warmer Place* continues the run and is always a good place to start with d'Ambrosio, not least for Lou Colombo's Bobby Hackett-like brass. *Love Is Not A Game* is packed with memorable treatments: J. J. Johnson's 'Lament', Denny Zeitlin's 'Quiet Now', as well as 'Young and Foolish', which is almost unbearably personal, and 'Autumn Serenade'. On 'Oh Look At Me Now', she starts a new practice by extending the song into a coda which has her composing new lyrics for a variation on the tune. It's an approach she carried over, with somewhat mixed success, on *Shadowland*, where five of the 12 tunes have improvised tailpieces. She always sounds best on more introspective material, but it communicates at a very direct level. One doesn't feel the need to go in search of her.

BUD SHANK&

Born Clifford Everett Shank Jr, 27 May 1926, Dayton, Ohio; died 2 April 2009, Tucson, Arizona
Alto saxophone

Lost In The Stars
Fresh Sound FSRCD 18
Shank; Lou Levy (p). December 1990.

Bud Shank said (1985): **'Great jazz only comes from knowing your instrument inside out and knowing the material better than the man who wrote it. You read these editorial pieces saying "new this!" and "new that!" and then you listen to the music and it's old stuff badly understood and worse played. I don't want to seem like a total conservative but there are no revolutions in jazz, just steady progress into the past!'**

Later in life, a little like Lee Konitz, Shank showed more of an interest in bebop. It remains present as harmonic colour in much of the later work, even if it doesn't seem to affect his intonation or phrasing. It's part of what gives *Lost In The Stars* its unique edge. The album's a Sinatra songbook, marked by the quirky brilliance of Levy and by Shank's attractive alto sound, which sounds as if it's been in and out of retirement as often as the man himself. 'This Love Of Mine', a much overlooked standard, is played with just the right balance of sentiment and cynicism. Levy delivers something majestically solitary on 'Spring Is Here', hope and loss in perfect balance, while Shank saves one of his best ever solos for the title-track. There isn't much else to say about the record, other than that it is the most lyrically beautiful performance we've heard in what is often a lazy format; saxophone and piano can often get sloppy, but this one is a model of long preparation and intimate knowledge.

& *See also* **Jazz in Hollywood** (1954; p. 154)

THE '90s

In the winter 1973 issue of *Tri Quarterly* magazine, the literarary critic Philip Stevick published an influential essay called 'Sheherazade runs out of plots, keeps on talking – the king, intrigued, listens' which suggested that realistic fiction had come to an end, to be replaced by a form of fabulation in which word-spinning took the place of conventional narrative. Around the same time, the novelist Ronald Sukenick published a collection called (and you have to wait for the full title) *The Death of the Novel and Other Stories*. The implication in both was clear: that even if the 19th-century novel was 'dead', there was still a lot of imaginative work to be done, either on the corpse or on its tomb-slab. Sighs of relief all round.

Roughly the same thing happened to jazz around the turn of the '90s. The death in 1991 of Miles Davis, who had appeared to abolish jazz – the term and most of the identifying features – from his work two decades before, in fact, around the time Stevick was writing, seemed epochal. The impression was reinforced when two influential European musicians, trumpeter Franz Koglmann and percussionist Edward Vesala, suggested that jazz, too, might be 'dead'. Vesala put out an *Ode On The Death Of Jazz*. Koglmann brought forward an interesting parallel with the baroque in classical music, suggesting that the style was 'dead', in the sense of having no new technical permutations to explore, by the time J. S. Bach came along, and yet there would be a clear consensus that Bach was the pinnacle of what we call 'the baroque'. Why not the same scenario with jazz?

John Coltrane had pushed harmony to the limits. Free jazz and free music had broken down the familiar components into sometimes unrecognizable parts. The music no longer seemed geographically, culturally or ethnically specific. Creative jazz flourished – albeit on a small and usually uncommercial scale – everywhere and everywhere drew something from the fostering culture. A Rastafarian trumpeter migrated to Iceland. Sami *joiks* appeared in a jazz context, where Broadway tunes might once have done. The familiar shape of the jazz group – a horn or two, a piano, a bass violin and a drum kit – had started to break down. Improvisers toted a bewildering array of instruments. Anthony Braxton singlehandedly brought the poor cousins of the saxophone family out of retirement and some of the obscurer clarinets, too.

The word everyone was reaching for, and to their credit rejecting, was 'post-modern'. Jazz seemed to have stumbled into the condition of post-modernism without intending to. Styles were collapsed and conflated. It was no longer possible to tell whether something was 'avant-garde' or 'traditional'. We once were submitted a record review in which a new American recording was described as 'avant-traditional'. Seriousness and self-expression of the kind that had been mandatory during the bop and hard-bop era gave way to a new kind of playfulness, wry, sardonic, self-conscious, technically astute but insouciantly so. After Coltrane in particular, virtuosity was at a discount, though Braxton, Evan Parker, others, maintained its market value in improvised music.

Nobody quite knew what jazz was and what it was for as the '90s gathered. But what became clear was that – much like the cartoon character whose legs start to spin ever more wildly when he realizes there is no ground under his feet – jazz musicians were not going to let jitters of self-definition keep them from making and recording music. New CDs flew out of the studios, workshops and factories, an exponential proliferation that meant for the first time in the music's history it was not possible to hear jazz entire and whole, a situation that was unsettling not just for jazz critics, but for that hard to pin down and notionally embattled constituency, the jazz audience, as well. The best of times? the worst of times? Both, perhaps ...

Part 1:
1991-1995

BOBBY PREVITE
Born 16 July 1957: 'I was born in Niagara Falls, New York, in one of the summers between 1951 and 1961'
Drums

Weather Clear, Track Fast
Enja ENJ 6082
Previte; Graham Haynes (c); Robin Eubanks (tb); Don Byron (cl, bcl); Marty Ehrlich (as, f, cl, bcl); Anthony
Davis, Steve Gaboury (p); Anthony Cox (b). January 1991.

Bobby Previte says: **'We were supposed to start in the morning, and we were setting
up when Cox, coming from Kingston, called to say that 87 was a total parking lot, and
he had no idea when he would arrive. Instead of having everyone wait and the energy
slowly dissipate, I sent everyone home, went out to a movie (Brian DePalma I think), and
reconvened at night. Rough start, but it all worked out.'**

Previte's drumming has an engagingly loose, unfettered quality that effectively camou-
flages just how accurate a timekeeper he is. In the nearly 25 years since he began recording
under his own name – enthusiasts may remember the splendid *Bump The Renaissance* from
1985 with Tom Varner and Lenny Pickett – he has shown an ability to function in all sorts of
contexts, drawing on musics outside jazz, stamping everything with wry personality.

The records often sound like soundtracks to an imaginary movie, with a multiplicity
of characters, an enigmatic storyline and no particular axe to grind. *Claude's Late Morning* and *Empty Suits* from 1988 and 1990 were very much in that vein. *Weather Clear, Track
Fast* – which became Previte's band name – was more obviously a jazz album. The tunes are
more stretched out and developed, leaving ample space for improvised passages. There's a
racetrack theme going on, and the seven tracks feel somewhat like a unified suite, with the
speciality 'Quinella' (Gaboury from the drummer's Empty Suits band in for Davis) tacked
on at the beginning like an overture. Previte works the same pungent magic with the metre
on the title-track and the closing 'Weather Cloudy, Track Slow', but the real rhythmic *tour
de force* is the long 'Traffic Along The Rail', one of the best pieces Bobby has committed to
record.

Byron plays an expansive role, but he's overshadowed by the always resourceful Ehrlich,
who has a bewildering array of voices at his disposal, always managing to sound like a
40-a-day man, whether playing raw bop saxophone, bronchial bass clarinet or winded flute.
Cox more than makes up for his initial tardiness with a rock-solid performance. Haynes and
Eubanks complete a terrific line-up and contribute substantially to what was one of the first
great jazz records of the '90s.

MCCOY TYNER &
*Born Alfred McCoy Tyner, 11 December 1938, Philadelphia, Pennsylvania; also briefly known as Sulaimon
Saud*
Piano, koto

Soliloquy
Blue Note 796429-2
Tyner (p solo). February 1991.

McCoy Tyner said (1994): **'Music is an expression of love for others and of communication with them. And that sometimes comes out most strongly when you are playing alone.'**

It staggers even purported fans of McCoy Tyner that he has made more than 70 records to date. How many could the average enthusiast actually name? There isn't just a quantitative element to the often stinting and half-hearted appreciation he has attracted down the years. Tyner's contribution to jazz pianism is as large as his harmonic innovation, an assessment perhaps best sampled in the context of a solo recording.

Tyner's second, very happy spell at Blue Note opened with a triptych of solo works that sums up his art: rushing, open-hearted, grand of gesture, ineffably romantic, muscular, florid. He still takes every chance to overplay his hand, but that is his way: 'Willow Weep For Me', for instance, is about as aggressive a version of this tune as has ever been recorded. Yet his best melodies – either written or improvised out of tunes by Powell, Coltrane and, surprisingly, Dexter Gordon – are as communicative as they are powerful. He has written for long enough to make his own choices of tune a reflection on his own dynasty: 'Effendi' dates back to his earliest Impulse! sessions, 'Española' – a haunting use of the Spanish tinge – is brand new, and both are performed with fine evocative skill. Together with *Things Ain't What They Used To Be* (which included some duets with George Adams and John Scofield) and *Revelations*, both of them recorded in near ideal sound at New York's Merkin Hall, this ushers in the grand late period work of a modern master.

& *See also* **The Real McCoy** (1967; p. 343), **Sahara** (1972; p. 391)

JOEY BARON
Born 26 June 1955, Richmond, Virginia
Drums

Tongue In Groove
Winter & Winter 919056
Baron; Steve Swell (tb); Ellery Eskelin (ts). May 1991.

Joey Baron said (1993): **'With me, less really is more. I never wanted to work with some gigantic kit and I wouldn't get any more music out of one. Just a four-piece kit, with a ride, sizzle, crash, hi-hat. It all comes from that.'**

Baron plays with a smile on his face, delivering a skittering, melodic line that is always more solid and substantial than on first hearing. He has a background in rock and has worked in virtually every conceivable contemporary form, but seems at his best in a challenging modern jazz setting. Unfortunately, his discography as leader is quite small and some of the records have not been granted a long life in the marketplace. The live *Tongue In Groove*, formerly on Polygram, features a bold instrumentation under the group name Barondown; Joey has enjoyed working without harmony or other rhythm instruments and this early venture is the best of them, a rollicking set that doesn't lack for high thought and sophistication. Apart from the traditional 'Terra Bina Kia Jeena', most of the tracks are very short, the majority under two minutes, but they deliver a solid impact every time and they aren't all tongue in cheek. 'The Shadow Of Your Smile' is genuinely romantic, in its perky way.

DONALD HARRISON
Born 23 June 1960, New Orleans, Louisiana
Alto saxophone

Indian Blues
Candid CCD 79514
Harrison; Cyrus Chestnut, Mac Rebennack (Dr John) (p, v); Phil Bowler (b, v); Carl Allen (d, v); Bruce Cox, Howard Smiley Ricks (perc, v); Donald Harrison Sr (v). May 1991.

Donald Harrison said (1995): **'The Mardi Gras Indians have their roots in Africa. That's where those rhythms come from. And those rhythms have become a kind of universal language. You find them in R&B and soul music; they turn up in hip-hop, which is a very traditional music, and you find them in jazz'.**

Before Katrina struck, New Orleans had regained its centrality in American jazz. Much of the credit goes to Ellis Marsalis, who was one of Harrison's teachers at NOCA. Like many of the younger generation, Harrison has tried to fuse traditional idiom – he has a hereditary role in one of the leading New Orleans 'tribes', the marching bands of Mardi Gras – with a thoroughly contemporary style honed during his stint with the Jazz Messengers. For a time, Harrison played the Eric Dolphy role in a latter-day version of the Dolphy–Booker Little Quintet.

Hard bop is still the basic language here, but Harrison has also tried to combine the Blakey sound with that of his real father. Donald Harrison Sr has been leader of the Guardians Of The Flame, who also feature on the album. 'Hiko Hiko' and 'Two-Way-Pocky-Way' are traditional (the former is credited to the legendary Black Johnny); 'Ja-Ki-Mo-Fi-Na-Hay' and the opening 'Hu-Tan-nay' are credited to the Harrisons. Dr John sings and plays piano on the two originals, sings on Professor Longhair's 'Big Chief' and plays piano on 'Walkin' Home' and Big Chief Jolly's 'Shave 'Em Dry'.

There's no sense of a break between the densely rhythmic New Orleans numbers with their chattering percussion and the more orthodox jazz tracks. Harrison plays 'Indian Red' pretty much as a straight alto feature, but then adds a rhythmic line to the prototypical standard 'Cherokee' that gives it an entirely new dimension. His own 'Indian Blues' and 'Uptown Ruler' reflect a decision in 1989 to 'mask Indian' again and join the feathered throngs that march on Mardi Gras. In touching his roots, he's brought them right up to date.

SERGEY KURYOKHIN
Born 16 June 1954, Murmansk, Russia; died 9 July 1996, St Petersburg, Russia
Piano

Some Combinations Of Fingers And Passion
Leo CDLR 179
Kuryokhin (p, perc solo). June 1991.

Producer and label boss Leo Feigin remembers: **'It was recorded in the basement of the World Service of the BBC on an unused and out-of-tune piano. Halfway through the session two keys got stuck and Kuryokhin had to play avoiding those two keys and choosing some unusual combinations of fingers. Hence the title …'**

There was something of the *yurodivy* – or Holy Fool – about Sergey Kuryokhin. Many of his public pronouncements were baffling, as was his later commitment to the extremely doctrinaire National Bolshevik Party, and his most famous group, Pop Mechanics, hovered uneasily between avant-gardism, rock populism and elements of the put-on or happening; his mixed-media pieces ape Western forms in a deliberately exaggerated, 'Martian' fashion that is not so much satirical as clownishly respectful. As with the Ganelin Trio, it is perhaps impossible to understand Kuryokhin's music without some understanding of the cultural politics of his country, which is perhaps impossible for an outsider. Musically, he was a genius, trained in classical piano after arriving in Leningrad in 1971, but his progress was erratic and his output uneven. Since his untimely death, aged just 42, the major source for Kuryokhin enthusiasts is *Divine Madness*, a multiple-CD set of mostly unreleased material which covers his solo piano work and his pop mechanics projects in some detail. This, though, will be too much for the uncommitted, and it is, in addition, a rare and expensive item. The surviving single discs are a better bet.

The early *Ways Of Freedom*, originally on the state music label Melodiya, now on Leo's Golden Years of New Jazz imprint, presents a musician of preternatural facility, comparable only to Tatum or Paderewski in terms of speed and accuracy of articulation; but it also finds Kuryokhin treating the whole soundbox of the piano as an instrument, tapping out percussive lines, working directly on the strings in a spirit closer to the non-canonical one of Pop-Mekhanika, which was born four years later in 1985, by which time the West had enjoyed the first few confusing glimpses of the new Russian music, thanks to Leo Feigin.

The tragedy is that Kuryokhin rarely had an opportunity – unless he spurned them – to play in ideal circumstances and on first-rate equipment. The first record is either a technical mess or an expression of some subversive spirit. With *Some Combination*, recorded on the fly in London, it becomes clearer that Kuryokhin was resigned to ill-fortune. And yet, the curious sound and obvious no-go areas of these recordings do somehow heighten his distinctive technique.

Kuryokhin was more likely to reference Rachmaninov than Tatum in his solo performances; indeed, he seems to make it a point of principle to avoid direct reference from the jazz tradition, except, arguably, the 'bar-room piano' sound. 'Blue Rondo A La Russ – A Tribute To Dave Brubeck', combining 'power and passion', is an apparent exception, but Kuryokhin's tribute is typically oblique. His technique is interesting largely for its avoidance of the usual jazz piano dichotomy between the left hand, with its rhythmic chording, and the right, which carries the melody and the subsequent improvisation. In addition, Kuryokhin was a virtuosic user of the pedals ('hands and feet' in another of the variations here), creating some quite remarkable two-piano illusions. Rapidly pedalling also creates an occasional sense, as on the long 'Passion And Feelings' section of the later session, that tiny segments of music are being edited together at high speed, creating the studied artificiality of tone one hears throughout his earlier work. Kuryokhin's is difficult music to characterize, because it consistently undermines its own premises.

ITALIAN INSTABILE ORCHESTRA
Formed 1990
Group

Live In Noci And Rive De Gier
Leo CDLR 182
Pino Minafra (t, flhn, didjeridu); Guido Mazzon (t, flhn); Alberto Mandarini (t); Giancarlo Schiaffini (tb, tba); Sebi Tramontana (tb, v); Lauro Rossi (tb); Martin Mayes (frhn); Mario Schiano (as, v); Eugenio Colombo (as, ss, f); Carlo Actis Dato (ts, bs, bcl); Daniele Cavallanti (ts, bs); Gianluigi Trovesi (as, cl in A, bcl); Renato Geremia (vn); Paolo Damiani (clo, b, v); Bruno Tommaso (b); Giorgio Gaslini (p); Vincenzo Mazzone, Tiziano Tononi (d, perc). June 1991, January 1992.

Saxophonist Carlo Actis Dato says: **'IIO è un collettivo che riunisce musicisti provenienti da tutta Italia e di diverse generazioni, ognuno leader di propri gruppi. A turno si suonano e dirigono proprie composizioni, rendendo lo stile dell'Orchestra molto vario e inimitabile.'**

Founded in 1990 by trumpeter Pino Minafra and the poet Vittorino Curci, the orchestra was originally intended as an ad hoc project to play at a festival in Noci. It immediately became clear that it should continue on co-operative lines, and it became one of those rare large-scale groups who manage to buck the economics through sheer dedication, consistently inventive music and a modest but intensely loyal fanbase. IIO subsequently benefited from the attentions of ECM and producer Steve Lake, who delivered a richly inflected sound on the 1994 recording *Skies Of Europe*. We've continued to enjoy the first record as well as any in the orchestra's discography.

The aesthetic is uncategorizable. Like ARFI in France, the Orchestra seeks to articulate an 'imaginary folklore', an improbable common ground between popular forms, formal composition and free improvisation. All but one of the pieces were recorded at Radio France's international jazz festival at Rive-de-Gier. The exception is Giorgio Gaslini's 'Pierrot Solaire', which proposes a sunshine cure for the moonstruck icon of musical modernism. Relaxed, funny, joyous and a long way from Schoenberg, except, of course, he's in there too. The set opens with Damiani's 'Detriti', a Noah's ark of musical and textual specimens rescued from the latter-day flood of genres and styles. The only disappointment is Eugenio Colombo's 'Ippopotami', which merely provides an excuse for a free-jazz free-for-all. Minafra's 'Noci ... Strani Frutti ... No. 1' is a surreal modern classic. There's a more convincing free-jazz workout – reminiscent of Globe Unity on a sunny day – right at the end, with 'I Virtuosi De Noci', which must have been a gas to watch as well as listen to.

DON BYRON

Born 8 November 1958, New York City
Clarinet, bass clarinet

Tuskegee Experiments

Elektra Nonesuch 79280
Byron; Bill Frisell (g); Joe Berkowitz, Edsel Gomez (p); Kenny Davis, Lonnie Plaxico, Reggie Workman (b); Richie Schwarz (mar); Pheeroan akLaff, Ralph Peterson Jr (d); Sadiq (v). November 1990, July 1991.

Don Byron says: **'I thought of it as a sampler of the stylistic range of my later CDs: the quartets with Frisell, *Music For Six Musicians*, the *Arias* and *Lieder* record, the Mickey Katz, and the *Blaxploitation* record are foreshadowed by the two core bands. It was made in two halves, the poetry, Schumann and Diego Rivera pieces in the latter session. It was all very exciting and new.'**

The sight of a young, dreadlocked black man playing klezmer with the same facility as music by Robert Schumann and post-bop jazz was perhaps the most vivid anticipation of the pan-stylism of the 1990s. One of the first young players to emerge with a bang at the start of the decade, Byron also gave jazz clarinet a fresh visibility. He worked with a range of creative people – Frisell, Gerry Hemingway, Bobby Previte and as part of Hamiet Bluiett's Clarinet Family – often producing some of the most exciting music in those groups, but made a substantial critical splash on his own account with a first record for Elektra.

It has become something of a critical cliché – and we are guilty of it – to criticize a debut record for packing in too much, showcasing too many styles and compositional strategies. Byron seems to concede that this was exactly the purpose of *Tuskegee Experiments* and increasingly it seems a strength rather than a failing. Ending a jazz record with a straight reading of Schumann's 'Auf Einer Burg' might seem unduly self-conscious. Nor did many jazz records of the period namecheck Diego Rivera, the Mexican muralist who influenced many American artists in the '30s and '40s, but this is a period which seems to fascinate Byron. The title-piece relates to a bizarre and shocking 'medical' programme conducted in Alabama from 1932, by which black syphilitics were neither treated for nor even informed about their condition, in order to document prognosis. The second experiment involved subjecting intelligent black men of military age to systematic humiliation in order to prove that they were not suitable to fly military aircraft.

Byron's anger is impressively contained, though a vocal by the Detroit poet Sadiq comes close to violating the dignity of his response. 'Tuskegee Experiment' is scored for quintet, with piano, marimba, electric bass and drums generating a threatening, percussive sound. On the opening 'Tuskegee Strutter's Ball', 'Next Love' and the beautiful 'Tears', Byron establishes his theme in unison with Frisell, favouring a bright coloratura and spiky stop-start phrasing. On 'Diego Rivera' and 'In Memoriam: Uncle Dan' (the latter a duet with Workman), he doubles on bass clarinet and switches to the longer line and romantic phrasing first heard on the unaccompanied 'Waltz For Ellen' that starts the record.

A klezmer-inspired record followed, then work for Blue Note intended to showcase Byron as a distinctive post-bop composer. So far, though, nothing has surpassed the debut.

SONNY SHARROCK

Born Warren Harding Sharrock, 27 August 1940, Ossining, New York; died 25 May 1994, Ossining, New York
Guitar

Ask The Ages
Axiom 422 848957 2
Sharrock; Pharoah Sanders (ts); Charnett Moffett (b); Elvin Jones (d). 1991.

Guitarist Larry Coryell says: **'Sonny really committed to the pure avant-garde approach – you know, with a comb in his left hand like a slide, really abstract, influences coming from Albert Ayler and Pharoah Sanders. Before he died he made the best record for that genre ever made, the one with Pharoah and Elvin Jones. He reached the "completion point" of his concept there.'**

Sharrock's first musical experiences were in doo-wop, until he was turned on to jazz by hearing *Kind Of Blue*. An asthmatic condition meant he had to abandon saxophone. He later played with Miles Davis on 'Willie Nelson' on *A Tribute To Jack Johnson*, but turned down an invitation to join the group. One wonders whether he would have lasted long or whether his avant-garde approach would have been too much for the trumpeter. Ironically, Sharrock made a splash with Herbie Mann on *Memphis Underground*, even if he does sometimes sound as if he's on the wrong date. Catch him on 'Philly Dog', from the 1968 Mann record *Live At The Whisky A Go Go*. Phew.

Sharrock began recording under his own name, making a number of records with his wife Linda's vocalizing as a second front-line instrument. But he seemed to have been overlooked by the music business and it wasn't until he emerged with Bill Laswell, Peter Brötzmann and Ronald Shannon Jackson as Last Exit that Sharrock became a *bona fide* jazz star. Ironically, he made his one *bona fide* masterpiece almost at the end of his life.

Ask The Ages reunited him with Pharoah Sanders, who used Sharrock on a couple of early records, and teamed him with Elvin Jones and Charles Moffett's son, Charnett. The writing ranged from dense and dark on 'Many Mansions', the one track that came close to a Last Exit aesthetic, to almost wistfully romantic on 'Who Does She Hope To Be?', which melts the heart, but the record is best summed up by the fire music of the opening 'Promises Kept', as exciting a start to an album as any from that decade. Sanders is in great form, avoiding self-indulgence and playing open, direct lines that mostly sit in behind the leader's. Anyone who knows Sharrock from *Monkey Pockie Boo* or *Space Ghost Coast To Coast* might not at first recognize some of this, but its quality is unmissable and it's tragic that Sonny didn't stick around long enough to build on it.

DAVE BURRELL
Born 10 September 1940, Middletown, Ohio
Piano

The Jelly Roll Joys
Gazell 4003
Burrell (p solo). 1991.

Dave Burrell says: '**Sam Charters of Gazell called out of the blue some 20 years ago. He'd heard some Jelly Roll in my playing and asked if I'd be interested in recording some of Morton's compositions. At the time I didn't have any of them under my fingers, so when I first saw James Dapogny's 500-page *Ferdinand "Jelly Roll" Morton: The Collected Piano Music* I knew I had my work cut out. The book contains every piece he ever published, some 40 compositions. I searched for the ones with strains that would lend themselves to modern improvisation. There is something unique in each of them, but the rhythms in "Freakish" and "The Crave" are unpredictably amazing.'**

It will seem perverse to represent one of the finest contemporary composers in the music by a record of Jelly Roll Morton themes, but Burrell stands squarely in that distinguished tradition and, importantly, his own work is represented here by two selections, 'Popolo Paniolo' from his jazz opera *Windward Passages* and the 24-bar stride piece 'A.M. Rag' (aka 'Margy Pargy'), and these in turn are placed alongside John Coltrane's 'Giant Steps' and 'Moment's Notice', and Charlie Parker's 'Billie's Bounce', all played in stride.

Gazell's Sam Charters is, like Burrell himself, a devoted historian of the music. The pianist grew up in Hawaii; both parents sang. He went to Berklee and established a career while still a student. The avant-garde beckoned but even the band name Untraditional Jazz Improvisation Team suggested that the tradition was always there for Burrell to work with/against and that approach can be heard clearly in his Morton interpretations, which are both strikingly faithful to the original conception of each song and also invested with a freedom of gesture within the hard – rather than strict – rhythms that makes them sound at once familiar and attractively alien. Burrell understands instinctively what Morton meant by the 'Spanish tinge' and it's evident here in the rich arpeggiations and rhythmic snaps that shape some of the pieces. A triumphant performance of key jazz repertoire.

HOUSTON PERSON
Born 10 November 1934, Florence, South Carolina
Tenor saxophone

The Lion And His Pride
Muse 5480
Person; Philip Harper (t); Benny Green (p); Christian McBride (b); Winard Harper (d). September 1991.

Houston Person says: '**I believe music is a force for good. It brings people together, irrespective of colour or creed. It's a common language. It has nothing to do with politics. It lifts people up. An education without music isn't any kind of education at all.'**

A relatively late starter in music, Person has become a godfather to a younger generation of musicians, and to fans, who have adopted him as one of the heroes of acid jazz. A fine ballad player with a low, urgent tone in the lineage of Coleman Hawkins, but probably more like Gene Ammons or Arnett Cobb, he is a respected figure in the business, producing records at both High Note and Savant. Thanks to those associations, his most recent work, much of it with or celebrating the life of his long-time partner, Etta Jones, is readily available. The vagaries of jazz recording and distribution, though, have meant that his substantial body of work for Muse now has to be hunted for.

Which is as good a cue as any for *The Lion And His Pride*, which explicitly casts Houston as Mufasa to a group of up-and-comers who are as ready to be cuffed down by one of his quietly magisterial solos as they are to pipe up on their own account. It's a not unchallenging programme, with the love theme from *Black Orpheus*, 'I Remember Clifford', Miles's 'Dig', a couple of romantic standards and 'Captain Hook', all done in a style that might be located at the soul-jazz end of hard bop. There are the buoyant comping of Benny Green, crisp, Lee Morgan-like lines from Philip Harper and a confident rhythm from Chris McBride, who learned more than he maybe imagined from this date, and the other Harper sibling. Person is one of the good guys of the business, and so is too often overlooked. Time this one made a reappearance.

JANE BUNNETT
Born 22 October 1956, Toronto, Ontario, Canada
Soprano saxophone, flute

Spirits Of Havana
Denon CAN 9011
Bunnett; Larry Cramer (t, flhn); Frank Emilio, Flynn Rodrigues, Gonzalo Rubalcaba, Hilario Durán Torres (p); Ahmed Barroso (g); Kieran Overs (b); Eduardo Diaz Anaya, Justo M. Garcia Arango, Orlando Lage Bozva, Guillermo Barreto Brown, Ignacio Ubicio Castillo, Jacinto Soull Castillo, Ernestoi Rodriguez Guzman, Francisco Hernández Mora, Roberto García Valdes (perc); Merceditas Váldes, Grupo Yoruba Andabo (v). September–October 1991.

Jane Bunnett says: **'When I went to Cuba it was like getting hit by lightning. It changed everything. Cuban music was my missing link. I used to wonder: "What if Coltrane had come here?"'**

Given that her introduction to modern jazz was hearing the Mingus group and a subsequent period of study with Steve Lacy, one might have expected Bunnett to go down a very different route, something perhaps close to fellow soprano specialist Jane Ira Bloom's individualistic modernism. Bunnett, though, has embraced Cuban music, and with an application that takes her work far beyond 'Latin' dabbling and towards a historically inflected view of an important tradition marginalized by politics.

She originally studied piano, but injury put paid to that. Switching to saxophone and flute she has developed a dry, unembellished sound that relies on a sophisticated rhythmic sense to bring drama to the line. Bunnett has been shrewd in associating herself with senior practitioners – Dewey Redman and Don Pullen played on early records – and in basing herself and trumpeter husband Larry Cramer for quite long periods in the Cuban capital and countryside.

She is therefore entitled to be adamant that *Spirits Of Havana* isn't just another Latin jazz date, but a genuine attempt to inhabit a Cuban perspective. Bunnett was already listening to and playing salsa before her first DNA-changing visit to Havana, but as a musician who always seems to play for the group she was immediately and instinctively drawn to an idiom which puts ensemble playing at a premium. The opening 'Hymn' is a flute tribute to the spirit of Miles Davis, who had just died: what if Miles had ever gone to Havana? There is a searing 'Epistrophy' with Cuban percussion not so much added as incorporated into the composition. For the rest, the material is nearly all traditional African-Caribbean or specially written in collaboration with Guillermo Barreto Brown, who masterminded the project.

Bunnett's soprano and flute are haunting on 'La Luna Arriba' by husband Larry Kramer, who is superb on the Monk tune. Frank Emilio's 'G.M.S.' opens with pan-American flute but gets lost in a thicket of percussion, the only time the mix gets uncomfortably busy. Mercedi-tas Váldes's vocals will not be to everyone's taste, but they're integral to this music. Argu-ably, there were better and more highly finished projects to come, not least the CD *Ritmo + Soul* (attributed to Bunnett and the Spirits Of Havana) or the Cuban Piano Masters project, but this record stands out as the footprint of a musical discovery, with all the excitement and sense of adventure that implies.

JOE WILDER

Born 22 February 1922, Colwyn, Pennsylvania
Trumpet

Alone With Just My Dreams

Evening Star ES-101
Wilder; James Williams (p); Remo Palmieri (g); Jay Leonhart (b); Sherman Ferguson (d). August 1991.

Trumpeter Pete Smith says: **'Joe told me that one time he was playing in a club in Kansas and a white woman came up and said: "You remind me of a young man my husband used to play with." Joe asked what his name had been and she said: "Bix Beiderbecke." Turned out it was Frankie Trumbauer's wife.'**

Wilder is something of a forgotten man, who came up through the ranks of the bands – Les Hite – and then disappeared into the studios again. He made a few early records of his own, mostly professional smoothies for the bachelor pad market, but all of them marked by a rugged professionalism and never a fudged note. Like many who could duplicate the story, he re-emerged in later life, freshly admired but perhaps lacking the natural command of previous years. That's certainly true in Wilder's case. His articulation isn't that of a young man, but his choice of notes and august delivery are still wonderful to hear. He made a nice group of records for Evening Star over a two-year period. Though there are better-known names on the later ones, the first is the best: on 'Struttin' With Some Barbecue' he evokes memories of a lost generation of hot trumpetmen, but the ballads are special and the clos-ing 'What A Wonderful World' will melt hearts of stone.

PER HENRIK WALLIN

Born 17 July 1946, Stockholm, Sweden; died 15 June 2005
Piano

Dolphins, Dolphins, Dolphins

Dragon DRCD 215
Wallin; Mats Gustafsson (ss, ts, bs); Kjell Nordeson (d). August 1991.

Saxophonist Mats Gustafsson remembers: **'Per Henrik was the greatest teacher, just by being himself! To have witnessed him and Erik Dahlbäck playing a free duo one night in Stockholm at a social club for dancing (!) was just … hilarious. They played for an hour, some bars straight-ahead, but then at lightning speed into free territory. It caused the dancers a few problems. Quite surreal.'**

A major figure at home and generously recorded by Dragon as a leader, Wallin is little known anywhere else, though musicians who have encountered him or his work invariably enthuse. He is far from being in the normal run of 'musicians' musicians', though, but a player who combines real sophistication of form with a heady excitement when he improvises. Wallin's activities were truncated by a crippling accident in 1988, after which he recorded much less.

He was a fascinating pianist, taking whatever he wanted from free- and post-bop piano language. A bravura delivery, involving tumultuous climaxes and moment-by-moment contrast, makes him hard to follow or even like at times, but he was surely a European original. In the '80s, he recorded with a series of power trios, using bassist Johnny Dyani before his premature death, drummer Erik Dahlbäck and bassist Torbjörn Hultcrantz, and turning out such varied records as *Coyote*, with its massive 'Strange Adventures Of Jesper Klint', or *Deep In A Dream*, with its offbeat standards playing.

He came back from the accident with seemingly little of his power depleted. The shade most closely evoked here is Thelonious Monk, since 'Nu Nu Och Då Nu Går Då Och Nu' sounds like a perversion of 'Round Midnight', and other Monkish melodies drift through the remaining tunes. But the level of interplay here – confrontational and conspiratorial in equal proportion – goes against the impression given by much of his earlier work that Wallin is best by himself, although his long solo 'J.W.' is a wonderfully expressive tribute to a painter friend.

The permutation of solos, duos and full trio tracks is intelligently balanced and it's only just to point out that this is a collaborative record rather than Wallin's own. Gustafsson is gothically powerful and jagged, Nordeson works with military intensity, nobody misses the bass and it's all splendidly recorded. Almost as an afterthought, Wallin concludes with 'I Should Care', underlining that what he cared about wasn't necessarily orthodox, but was always stimulating.

CHARLES GAYLE
Born 28 February 1939, Buffalo, New York
Tenor saxophone, piano

Touchin' On Trane
FMP CD 48
Gayle; William Parker (b); Rashied Ali (d). October–November 1991.

Charles Gayle said (1996): **'When you live on the street, it isn't like you can play at a street corner and then pack up and go home. There's something else involved, and I need that. I miss that. I might follow a sound, but not to play with it: because it was there and part of that situation. It's a different thing entirely.'**

Like a latter-day Moondog, Gayle played as a street musician, apparently homeless and without possessions, until his late-'80s lionization as an heir to Ayler and folkloric savant. Gayle's music has become more accessible, in the sense of being more melodic, in recent years, and he has added piano to his armoury, but his saxophone-playing still has a raw urgency and, without sentimental projection, a survivalist's urgency which makes the usual critical considerations seem like mere aesthetics.

Gayle's records of the '90s still astonish, even in the aftermath of so many kinds of free-jazz outrage, largely because of his starkness and simplicity. He has clearly developed the iron chops that go with playing in the open for hours on end, but the conception and realization of these records is monumental. His holy, holy delivery makes one think of both Coltrane and Ayler at their most consciously spiritual, but there is also Gayle's own superbly harsh lyricism. He is unusually adept at both the highest register of the tenor and control of the most outlandish overblowing. Solos are not so much fashioned as drawn straight from the moment; nothing seems to be created in advance, and a performance might run on seemingly without end. This is the outright masterpiece; and it seems likely to be a central document in the free music of the decade. The three men touch on Coltrane from moment to moment (Ali renews his old relationship in triumph), but this is new, brilliant, eloquent free playing.

BENNY GREEN
Born 4 April 1963, New York City
Piano

Testifyin': Live At The Village Vanguard
Blue Note 98171
Green; Christian McBride (b); Carl Allen (d). November 1991.

Benny Green said (1993): **'Jazz isn't really about numbers. It's about communicating your self, and your humanity, to as many people as turn out to hear you. In a concert hall, with the lights in your face, you might as well be alone in some ways. In a club, the audience is always there, close to you and therefore part of what you do.'**

Green came to prominence as pianist with Betty Carter's group, and his mastery of bebop piano – particularly the chunky rhythms of Horace Silver – was leavened by an apparent interest in swing styles as well. His main influence is Oscar Peterson, but it isn't slavish. Green hits the keyboard hard on uptempo tunes, and has a preference for beefy chords and straight-ahead swing. The albums for Criss Cross feature a lot of piano, but there's nothing particularly outstanding about them. The deletion scythe has been through his Blue Note work as well, but *Testifyin'* stands upright and remains as listenable as ever.

It's a top-notch club date from a sanctified venue, and has some of the pluses and few of the minuses of a live recording. The tracks don't go on for ever, though Green solos so punchily one can't imagine him plugging away at it for more than a few minutes at a time, plus his ballad playing is of a briskly unsentimental sort, which doesn't require long balcony scenes.

A lot of artists fall back on very familiar material for live dates, but Green has confidence in his sidemen and can stretch out with new material to some degree. His own compositions are bouncy enough and harmonically subtle; they're intelligent pieces rather than roof-lifters. 'Bu's March' (for Art Blakey) and the title-track are the best of them, but 'Sheik Of Araby' and the gospelly 'Down By The River Side' are the surprise items. Time to bring back the other Blue Notes, but you can't go wrong with *Testifyin'*.

JOE LOVANO
Born 29 December 1952, Cleveland, Ohio
Tenor and alto saxophones, other saxophones, clarinets, percussion

From The Soul
Blue Note 798363
Lovano; Michel Petrucciani (p); Dave Holland (b); Ed Blackwell (d). December 1991.

Joe Lovano says: **'We had never played together as a unit until the downbeat of the first tune "Evolution" and the spontaneous collective free-flowing music that follows is alive and full of magic to this day. *From The Soul* tells a story not only about who we are as musicians but what jazz music is all about. On the eve of my 39th birthday this session was a springboard to the future in the blessed world of music.'**

Joe Lovano stands at the heart of contemporary jazz, a figure who, solo by solo, album by album, demonstrates the continuing fertility of the genre. He worked with Woody Herman in the late '70s, and in trio with Bill Frisell and Paul Motian the following decade, but made his mark with an impressive run of Blue Note recordings. His stance on the jazz tradition – whether it is Coleman Hawkins or John Coltrane – is always respectful but creatively rather than slavishly so.

Lovano's 'Body And Soul' wins him lifetime membership of the tenor club. Interestingly, though, he takes John Coltrane's rarely covered 'Central Park West' on alto, as if doing it on the bigger horn were unpardonable arrogance. What's wonderful about the record is how beautifully modulated the tracks are. There's not a cliché in sight. Lovano's own writing – 'Evolution', 'Lines & Spaces', 'Modern Man', 'Fort Worth' and the closing waltz, 'His Dreams' – has a clean muscular edge, and from the opening fanfare of 'Evolution' onwards it's clear that the album is going to be something special.

Petrucciani established such a presence as a recording artist in his own right that it's easy to forget how superb an accompanist he could be. The Frenchman's responses on 'Left Behind', unfamiliar territory for him, are startling. He sits out 'Fort Worth', leaving Holland and Blackwell to steer a markedly abrasive theme. Though ailing and by no means as dynamic as in former years, the drummer still sounds completely masterful. His delicate mallet figures on 'Portrait Of Jenny' are one of the instrumental high-points of a thoroughly compelling record.

LARRY CORYELL

Born 2 April 1943, Galveston, Texas
Guitar

Twelve Frets To One Octave
Shanachie 97015
Coryell (g solo). 1991.

Larry Coryell says: **'This was the first time I took a budget from a record company and used it to my discretion. I chose the studio, borrowed some vintage guitars from friends that I felt would give more variety to the tracks, and some microphones from my old friend, the late and great recording engineer David Baker. So it was very hands-on, the first time I self-produced. I used my sons on one track each and took the opportunity to write something about my daughter, Allegra; that was a good memory.'**

Coryell started out in Mike Mandel's group before joining Chico Hamilton and Gary Burton, where his Hendrix-influenced rock-tinged sound came to wide notice. He played with Sonny Sharrock on Herbie Mann's *Memphis Underground* and showed that the excitements of rock could be married with the subtleties and intellectual sophistication of jazz. In the '70s, he played jazz-rock, first with Mandel in Foreplay and later with his own Eleventh House, one of the few groups that managed to avoid the blandness of 'fusion'. More recently, he has moved between pure-bop, fusion and Latin styles, limpidly delivered but with real power and with a trademark sensitivity to dynamics.

Coryell's return to straight jazz playing has been fascinating. He credits Ellis Marsalis with the revelation that 'Giant Steps' could be done as a solo guitar piece, recast in waltz time and slowed down. It's one of the high-points of an earlier Shanachie record, *Dragon Gate*, along with a fine interpretation of Wes Montgomery's 'West Coast Blues'. On *Twelve Frets To One Octave*, he relies even more on pure technique and simplifies the programme dramatically. From raw, rootsy blues to the sober, classical shapes of 'Bartók Eleven' to the lovely lilt of 'Transparence', Coryell has it all taped. His single-note runs are fleet and dexterous, his chording has harmonic mass, and his rhythms and counter-rhythms frequently create the impression that more than one musician must be involved. A beautifully shaped album, it starts out nakedly personal with 'Allegra's Ballerina Song', changes pace and direction with 'Blue Monk' and builds to the climax of 'Alfonsina Del Mar' (he called the flautist Nestor Torres to check that he was playing the line correctly), which ranks with Coryell's very best recorded solos.

JOHN TCHICAI
Born 28 April 1936, Copenhagen, Denmark
Alto, tenor and soprano saxophones, other reeds

Grandpa's Spells
Storyville STCD 4182
Tchicai; Misha Mengelberg (p); Margriet Nabrier (syn); Peter Danstrup (b); Gilbert Matthews (d). March 1992.

John Tchicai says: '**Matthews, Danstrup and Mengelberg were the perfect choice for the very varied repertoire I chose for this concert series and recording. Few could skip through the genres with such grace and inventiveness as they did it then. Since those days Mengelberg has been ill so I'm glad we were able to do this when he was still in fine form.**'

The saxophonist is half Danish, half Congolese. He started out on violin and, after switching to saxophone, was noticed by Archie Shepp and others on the European festival circuit. Tchicai moved to the United States in the early '60s and joined Archie Shepp and Bill Dixon in the New York Contemporary Five; but he went on to lead a more significant, if less well-known, group, known as the New York Art Quartet, with percussionist Milford Graves and trombonist Roswell Rudd. In the following year he played alongside fellow altoist Marion Brown (whom he somewhat resembles in approach) on John Coltrane's epic *Ascension*, before returning to Europe to work on a number of individual projects.

Originally rather dry and papery in tone, Tchicai has become more emotionally nuanced over the years. The '80s saw him shift away from alto saxophone. His tenor and soprano work was initially competent but rather anonymous, and it really came into its own only during the following decade, as on the excellent *Grandpa's Spells*. The Jelly Roll Morton title-piece is a perfect vehicle for both the leader's rowdy neo-traditionalism and Mengelberg's surreal approach to melody – they also tackle 'Cannonball Blues' – but the outstanding cuts are the collectively improvised tracks, Mengelberg's strange, Monk-referencing 'Elevator No. 2' and an entirely unexpected and very beautiful version of a Carl Nielsen melody, which underlines a slow recognition that, even when Tchicai was playing hard-edged free music, he was still a romantic at heart.

TOM VARNER
Born 17 June 1957, New York City
French horn

The Mystery Of Compassion
Soul Note 121217-2
Varner; Steve Swell (tb); Dave Taylor (btb); Matt Darriau, Ed Jackson (as); Rich Rothenberg, Ellery Eskelin (ts); Jim Hartog (bs); Mark Feldman (vn); Mike Richmond (b); Tom Rainey (d). March 1992.

Tom Varner remembers: '**I went for broke: Mingusy swing, free bop morphing into funky blues, 12-tone mini-concerto for violin, thrash punk quickies, odes to *Ascension*, and a sombre prayer. My friend Bobby Previte produced. We fought a bit – I'd never had a** producer before – but our tensions helped to make the recording the best I had ever done. Our friendship survived, too!'

Varner's decision to apply french horn as a weapon in the New York avant-garde might once have seemed improbable, but with every kind of instrument pressed into service in that milieu, no longer. Nor was he the first. David Amram and Julius Watkins had tried to make the horn a jazz voice, and it was Gunther Schuller's instrument, too. There is an unavoidable first impression that it's a trombonist we're listening to, but Varner has taken pains to develop his own vocabulary, and breaks down the horn's intractability.

Varner made a series of good records for Soul Note without as yet shaking the foundations, playing uneventful freebop and depending on satisfying solos to make a modest impact. *The Mystery Of Compassion*, though, was in a class by itself. Everything Varner loved went into the date, which was also 'my first multi-tracked fat two-inch analog tape project'. Varner's alarming juxtapositions make coherent sense without losing their capacity to surprise, and the other players respond with a passionate intensity which is rare even among these driven musicians. The central group is a quintet made up of Varner, Jackson, Rothenberg, Richmond and Rainey. On all-out barnstormers like 'How Does Power Work?' and '$1000 Hat' they play with unstinting panache. 'The Well' is a concerto-like piece for Feldman, and 'Death At The Right Time' uses a tentet to create a bemusing recall of Coltrane's *Ascension*. Varner's own improvising has never been better – he actually makes the instrument assert its personal qualities – and he closes the record on a sombre antiphonal piece for low brass called 'Prayer' which makes a moving coda to the rest.

There were great things to come. Some days, 1996's *Martian Heartache* seems better still, and Varner continued the run after leaving Soul Note, with superb records on New World (*The Window Up Above*) and on Omnitone (*Swimming* and *Second Communion*, the latter a remarkable meditation on Don Cherry's masterpiece), but for us this one remains his masterpiece, a record we've returned to constantly.

HILTON RUIZ
Born 29 May 1952, New York City; died 6 June 2006, New Orleans, Louisiana
Piano

Manhattan Mambo
Telarc CD 83322
Ruiz; Charlie Sepulveda (t); Papo Vasquez (tb); David Sanchez (ts, perc); Andy Gonzalez (b, bell); Ignacio Berroa (d, perc); Joe Gonzalez, Giovanni Hidalgo (perc). April 1992.

Hilton Ruiz said (2001): **'Jazz and classical music? Yes, they are different things and you can't just pretend they're the same. But that doesn't mean you can't master both of them. It just needs a different discipline.'**

The title is an apposite one, because no one better illustrated the cultural melting pot of New York City, and in particular its naturalization of Latin music, than Hilton Ruiz. Ironically and tragically, he died after being found unconscious in the street in New Orleans where he had been working on a Hurrican Katrina benefit project; he had apparently been the victim of a fall rather than foul play.

Ruiz was a child prodigy of Puerto Rican descent who at one time seemed bent on a classical career, playing at Carnegie Hall when only eight years old. He worked with Freddie Hubbard for a time, and studied with Mary Lou Williams, but came to prominence with Rahsaan Roland Kirk, with whom he worked between 1974 and 1977. Ruiz's desire to give jazz a Latin accent runs a little deeper than the usual south-of-the-border trimmings. Ruiz has a deep understanding of popular forms – samba, *soca*, *clave* – and makes them an integral element in his writing and reworking of standards and classics. The early Steeplechase

Piano Man, made when he was just 23, is a terrific album, performed by a top-flight trio, with Buster Williams's singing bass and Billy Higgins's tuneful drums complementing his own two-handed style.

Manhattan Mambo lines up three incandescent horn-players, all steeped in the idiom, to duck and dive over the rhythms and the thump of the piano. The basic language here is bop, though a luminously delivered version of John Coltrane's 'Impressions' suggests he was also well-versed in later evolutions, and what one gets isn't so much 'Latin jazz' in the usual Tex-Mex fusion way, but modern jazz heard and played through a very particular cultural filter. This isn't simply a matter of super-added rhythm. The voicings are distinct and different, too, and there's a sharp mind behind the arrangement of Perez Prado's 'Mambo Numero Cinco' which opens the record. The definitive album by a prematurely lost master.

LEW TABACKIN &
Born 26 May 1940, Philadelphia, Pennsylvania
Tenor saxophone, flute

I'll Be Seeing You
Concord CCD 4548
Tabackin; Benny Green (p); Peter Washington (b); Lewis Nash (d). April 1992.

Lew Tabackin said (1991): **'When I was starting out, everyone sounded like Coltrane, and what I didn't want to be was a white man playing bad Coltrane, so I listened to everyone else and tried to find my own route. I didn't want to be a good tenor saxophonist who played bad flute – plenty of them around – so I worked at that, too.'**

Still an outrageously underrated saxophonist, Tabackin actually derives more from the great swing masters – especially Ben Webster and Don Byas, though he says Coleman Hawkins proved to be beyond him – than he does to the modern movement. However, the strong infusion of Asian ideas that has developed in parallel with his wife Toshiko Akiyoshi and in the big band they have co-led has bled through from his highly distinctive flute work into his saxophone-playing as well.

Tabackin's own discography – aside, that is, from the co-led big band – is surprisingly large and of consistently high quality. There is a Rollins-like exposition of melody, but the harmonic approach is all his own, sometimes reminiscent of Joe Farrell's thwarted experiments but without the emphasis on quartal harmony. Tabackin tackles a couple of obvious saxophone icons, Coltrane's rarely covered 'Wise One' and the glorious Johnny Hodges feature 'Isfahan', which allows him to explore a measure of the Eastern modality he brings to his work on both flute and tenor. The group is behind him all the way and Green's chord colours are especially effective on the slower numbers. Why is Tabackin not better known or more widely appreciated? Well, he's an understated player, and resolutely undramatic. It takes time, even for this masterly album, to get to the heart of what he does.

& *See also* **TOSHIKO AKIYOSHI, Toshiko Akiyoshi–Lew Tabackin Big Band** (1974–1976; p. 427)

TOMMY SMITH
Born 27 April 1967, Edinburgh, Scotland
Tenor saxophone

Paris
Blue Note CDP 780612
Smith; Guy Barker (t); Julian Argüelles (ss, as); Jason Rebello (p); Mick Hutton (b); Jeremy Stacy (d). May 1992.

Tommy Smith says: **'I hated my first Blue Note record, *Step By Step*. It was terrible, especially the sound. The company was unhappy that I used unknown British colleagues on the next two records; they wanted superstars. But I thought *Paris* was strong and diverse and still do. We had a ball in the studio, playing Coltrane's "Transition" really loud to stoke the fire within. Blue Note never released the record in the USA, which I found strange. A few months after its European release I was canned.'**

Saddled with quite unreasonable expectations when he emerged as a 15-year-old, Smith has done the most difficult thing of all in surviving the 'prodigy' label and continuing to develop as a mature artist. He is now a major force in British jazz and in jazz education, heading a much respected youth jazz orchestra which has proved to be a crucible for talent similar to his own. But Smith's importance as a figurehead has tended to blur two important recognitions: that he is now a saxophone soloist of magisterial presence and emotional depth, but also that this intensity was always present, albeit initially buried under a sometimes over-eager and self-absorbed virtuosity.

Though its circumstances were somewhat damaging for Smith, as he explains above, *Paris* was a record of the very highest quality. Smith had been living in Paris for two years, with 'too much time on my hands', and the music on the record reflects a period spent studying and writing, but also inspired by the city. It was, however, recorded in London with ECM engineer Jan Erik Kongshaug, who gives Smith and his colleagues a big, expansive sound with a lot of atmosphere and detail.

The perversity of Blue Note's decision to drop Smith's contract after four records was that he grew in stature with each one. The debut *Step By Step*, with Mitchel Forman, John Scofield, Eddie Gomez and Jack DeJohnette was a cruel mismatch, but its poor quality has nothing to do with any lack of authority on Smith's part. Musically and sonically, it simply sounds like a dialogue of the deaf. *Standards*, which followed, was an attempt to mainstream the young signing, still only 24. It's a more than listenable record, as is *Peeping Tom*. But *Paris* is in a different class altogether. The music is blunt, immediate and subtly modulated. Only on the long 'Phraseology' and the closing 'Occidentalism' does Smith lapse into showy technical rhetoric. The other long track, 'Day Light', is as fresh a theme as Smith has ever written, topped by a solo that reaches a new plane of maturity.

Having a second saxophonist in the ensemble seems to help Smith along; his voicings on the opening 'Dischord' are subtle and wry. Argüelles is a wonderfully poised player, but doesn't carry his baritone for this date, which is a pity. The only other quibble is that Rebello is sometimes a touch florid when what is called for is something of the thump of a Stan Tracey, another Briton who enjoyed mixed fortunes with Blue Note at this time.

Smith returned to Scotland following the demise of his American contract, signed up with local label Linn and began again the process of building a strong recording relationship, which he did on 2000's excellent *Blue Smith*. After that, he founded his own Spartacus imprint. No one missed the barb in the title.

GIANLUIGI TROVESI
Born 1944, Nembro, Italy
Alto and soprano saxophones, clarinets, other winds

From G To G
Soul Note 121231-2
Trovesi; Pino Minafra (t, flhn, didjeridu, v); Rodolfo Migliardi (tb, tba); Marco Remondini (clo); Roberto Bonati, Marco Micheli (b); Vittorio Marinoni (d); Fulvio Maras (perc). May 1992.

Gianluigi Trovesi says: **'*From G To G* può essere inteso anche come un giro intorno al ricco microcosmo dell'intervallo di ottava, come un *ricercare* e un *toccare*, secondo le dizioni antiche, emozioni e regioni del sapere musicale, con la rapidità e la rapacità** che è propria del tempo in cui vivo e faccio musica. L'incontro tra tensioni armoniche estreme e la caricatura affettuosa del jazz d'antan; il dialogo tra Bartok e Stravinskij e un mediterraneo onirico e immaginario; le affinità imprevedibili tra asimmetrici ritmi balcanici e gli effetti d'eco della polifonia rinascimentale: sono questi alcuni dei vocaboli di un dialogo che mette in conto anche lo scontro, il contrasto, l'imprevisto.'

Trovesi is a key figure in Italy's new jazz, as performer, composer and organizer. He became known as a member of Giorgio Gaslini's small group and as a key fixer with the Italian Instabile Orchestra. His work is a deeply personal exploration of the frontiers of jazz, classical music and Italian vernacular music. An adaptable instrumentalist, he is less distinctive in terms of sound than in the quality of his ideas. Even on an unfamiliar instrument, one is often able to pick him out from the sheer daring and beauty of the idea.

From G To G is a small classic. Without sacrificing any of his intensities, Trovesi has created a colourful, unpredictable, brilliant marshalling of devices drawn from jazz and far beyond. While there are hints of Italian folk music and remote echoes of ancient masters of Italian composition, the synthesis leads inexorably to a real Italian jazz. 'Herbop' uses two themes which are split and reshaped continuously through 18 minutes of music, soloists and ensemble set in perfect balance. 'Now I Can' and 'Hercab' are satirical without being heavy-handed and without losing an underlying severity which Trovesi uses to pare off any fat in the music. But the finest piece is probably 'From G To G' itself, a long, serenely effective dirge in memory of a friend, with a memorable solo from Minafra. The brass-player turns in some of his most lucid work here, Migliardi is rumbustious on tuba and urgently expressive on trombone, but it's Trovesi himself who leads from the front, his alto solos elegantly moving forward from Dolphy and Coleman into a sonority that again suggests the tradition of Italian song.

JOSHUA REDMAN
Born 1 February 1969, Berkeley, California
Tenor saxophone

Joshua Redman
Warner Bros 945242-2
Redman; Kevin Hays, Mike LeDonne (p); Christian McBride, Paul LaDuca (b); Gregory Hutchinson, Clarence Penn, Kenny Washington (d). May & September 1992.

Joshua Redman says: **'This session kind of caught me by surprise. The thought of recording an album as a leader had never really occurred to me, so I was woefully unprepared. Before this, I had only written one song in my entire life. I had no original material. I cobbled together five tunes in the month leading up to the date.'**

He could easily be a tenor-player of an older generation, but for the sharp, knowing delivery and occasional latter-day references in the solos. Winner of the 1991 Thelonious Monk competition, Dewey Redman's son – who didn't grow up with his father, so there is no early influence there – became a figurehead for the young American jazz movement of the '90s, largely preferring straight-ahead settings and a purist approach to recording.

Redman's first albums caused a sensation: few discs from this period have communicated such sheer joy in playing as these. Academically gifted, it looked for a time as though music might be a part-time avocation for him. Although he had already made some interesting sideman appearances, the saxophonist's eponymous set was a stunning debut: a canny blend of bop, originals that don't sound so much cobbled together as natural and unforced, standards (a very sober and straight 'Body And Soul'), the odd tricky choice (Monk's 'Trinkle Tinkle') and young man's fancy (James Brown's 'I Got You (I Feel Good)'), all of it buoyed up on the kind of playing that suggests an instant maturity. His lean tone turned out to be as limber or as weighty as he wished, his phrasing had plenty of spaces but could cruise at any bebop height, and his invention sounded unquenchable. The euphoric but controlled feeling extends to his sidemen, Hays, McBride and Hutchinson (two odd tracks were drafted in from other sessions). And it's beautifully recorded, which is how you know it's a modern record.

JOHN LINDBERG &

Born 16 March 1959, Royal Oak, Michigan
Double bass

Dodging Bullets
Black Saint 120108
Lindberg; Albert Mangelsdorff (tb); Eric Watson (p). June 1992.

John Lindberg says: **'These were the first performances by this assemblage of three diverse yet kindred spirits. Seemingly effortless, magical and joyful moments unfolded one after another ... and the session was swiftly done. Not much talking. Smiles all around.'**

A member of the Human Arts Ensemble at just 19 and of Anthony Braxton's quartet shortly after, Lindberg was also a founding member of the String Trio Of New York, one of the most distinctive and innovative standing groups in modern jazz. His solo output has been steady and impressive, perhaps less showy and innovative than his fellow bassist Mark Dresser (also a sometime Braxton sideman) but with more sustained compositional muscle. Dresser uses a number of imaginative add-ons that significantly expand the language of the double bass; Lindberg on the other hand sustains the instrument's core values and strengths, producing a big, stringy sound that first came to wider notice on an early solo recording, *Comin' And Goin'*, for the Leo label.

He made his Black Saint debut with *Dimenson 5* in 1981 and followed up with the fine *Give And Take* and the ambitious *Trilogy Of Works For Eleven Instruments*. A decade into his association with Giovanni Bonandrini's imprint, he delivered an early masterwork with *Dodging Bullets*. With the addition of Ed Thigpen, this group made two more records for Black Saint, but neither of them – no blame attaches to the drummer – comes up to the joyous spontaneity and almost magical understanding of the first one. All three members take a recording credit, and Watson plays a closing solo version of Lindberg's 'Ceilings', an unexpected but very effective end to the set. There are a couple of improvised numbers in the middle, gaspingly short but not a note too long. Mangelsdorff's 'The Horn Is A Lady' and 'Fersengeld' are subtly done and what one takes from the very first track is an impression of three players comfortably bridging the avant-garde and jazz tradition. Lindberg went on to make an album that meditated on the legacy of Ives and Gottschalk. Those concerns aren't far away here. In fact, Ives is a very good composer to keep in mind while listening to John Lindberg, the same couthy wit, the same structural daring, the same sense that everything is possible, but only within understood bounds. Exhilarating.

& *See also* **String Trio Of New York, Rebirth Of A Feeling** (1983; p. 483)

DAVE MCKENNA

Born 30 May 1930, Moonsocket, Rhode Island; died 18 October 2008, Moonsocket, Rhode Island
Piano

A Handful Of Stars
Concord CCD 4580
McKenna (p solo). June 1992.

Dave McKenna said (1986): **'Someone praised my "technique", but all I was doing was playing the song, and it needed all those things. I don't think I have much technique, not like some of the great players and the new, good players. I just try to deliver the song I think I know.'**

McKenna hulked over the keyboard, a big man with an imposing presence. One of the most dominant mainstream players on the scene, and his immense reach and two-handed style distributed theme statements across the width of the keyboard. He possibly quite rightly demurred at comments about his apparent virtuosity because often what he did was quite physical, flat-thumbing three notes at once in the middle of an otherwise open-plan passage, or playing a locked-hand accent that seems to interrupt a flowing passage of arpeggios. McKenna never sounded inept or amateurish, though. His improvisations proceeded with impressive logic.

He worked with Charlie Ventura, Boots Mussulli, Woody Herman and Gene Krupa, all situations that required a firm hand, and he was nearly 30 before he began recording on his own account. Concord took him up in a big way and Carl Jefferson allowed him to develop his favourite programmes of thematically related songs. These only look contrived on paper, like a 'Knowledge Medley' which takes in 'Apple For The Teacher', 'I Didn't Know What Time It Was', 'I Wish I Knew', 'You'll Never Know', and so on but work superbly in performance, where titles don't really matter. McKenna's attitude seemed to be that with so many great songs out there, one principle of organization was as good as any other. He gave Concord a set of Hoagy Carmichael tunes in 1983, an Arthur Schwartz tribute a little later. He did a Maybeck recital in that beautiful Berkeley hall, and then it began.

Our favourite of the medley-records is *A Handful Of Stars*, not because it's meltingly romantic, but on the contrary because McKenna takes 'Star Eyes' at a clip and squeezes the mush out of others. His touch always seems appropriate to the moment, and the choice of material, which stretches to the Brazilian pop song 'Estrela Estrela' is always imaginative. The Concord catalogue is much reduced, and though the new owners have brought back some classic items, here's one that cries out for reissue.

STEVE GROSSMAN
Born 18 January 1951, New York City
Tenor and soprano saxophones

I'm Confessin'
Dreyfus FDM 36902
Grossman; Harold Land (ts); Fred Henke (p); Reggie Johnson (b); Jimmy Cobb (d). June–July 1992.

Steve Grossman said (1993): **'I got going on Charlie Parker when I was about eight years old. Then I started checking out John Coltrane, and that has continued pretty much ever since.'**

Grossman was working with Miles Davis in his teens, making appearances on the Fillmore live records and the *Jack Johnson* sessions and it's tempting to suggest that his career peaked too early. He has been out of the American loop for much of the time since, making his way in France and Italy, but rarely appearing in the US since the time of the French recording selected here. Though Miles edited out all his tenor solos, he has a prodigious command of the bigger horn and a fearless energy, which puts him in the same class as Michael Brecker and Bill Evans, but a sometimes faceless facility can also make him appear as just another hired-gun Coltrane/Rollins disciple.

Persistence made Grossman into an impressive character. For consistency, he's hard to beat, but if the sheer strength of his playing usually transcends banality, he seldom goes for broke either and the impression is of a very centred, very uncompetitive player, content to say what he says without bluster. It's a rare quality. The difference here is in the calibre of his accompanists. This meeting with Land, which seems to have been reissued in 2007, is a relaxed affair. The older man settles Grossman into an easy groove, and there's palpable enjoyment in his playing.

THOMAS CHAPIN

Born 9 March 1957, Manchester, Connecticut; died 13 February 1998, Providence, Rhode Island
Alto saxophone, flute, other saxophones

Night Bird Song
Knitting Factory KFRCD 240
Chapin; Mario Pavone (b); Michael Sarin (d). August–September 1992.

Mario Pavone remembers: 'One chorus from Thomas contained as much info and soul as most players put out in a whole set. I recall an electrifying midnight performance in Portugal in 1994. After an hour and a half onstage the audience was going crazy. The promoter asks: "Can you calm them down?" Two concise ballad choruses from Thomas on his "Aeolus". Complete satisfaction. We feasted until dawn with the entire village.'

Chapin's first influences were R&B saxophone and the timbrally and tonally adventurous Rahsaan Roland Kirk. Through his short career, he experimented with saxophones outside the normal range, including a mezzo-soprano instrument in F. He was, though, primarily an alto player, with a wonderful 'cry' in his tone and, for all his musical and actual wanderings, a deep grounding in jazz and the blues.

Many of the early recordings drifted out of circulation even before Chapin succumbed to leukaemia, but there was a flurry of issues around his death and many of his earlier discs were reissued. Towards the end of his life, Chapin turned to a more meditative style, but there is energy aplenty on *Night Bird Song*. It was only released posthumously, having been recorded, mastered and even designed during Tom's lifetime. The album is as tightly woven as the Panamanian *mola* cloth on the cover art. Three of the tunes – the title-track, 'Alphaville' and 'Changes Two Tires' – also appeared on a companion piece from 1996 called *Sky Piece*, which suggests how assiduously Chapin rethought and reworked his compositions. The former pair are welded together with a dark, almost chordal tonality on saxophone, supported by Pavone's bass. 'Cliff Island' is played on sopranino, as is the cartoonish 'Tweety's Last Adventure'. Ever searching for new sounds, he blows a reedless alto on 'The Roaring S', but most moving of all is the flute track 'Aeolus', a soaring, anchored, paradoxical duet with Pavone, which half a decade later was to be the last piece he played in public.

LEROY JENKINS *&*

Born 11 March 1932, Chicago, Illinois; died 24 February 2007, New York City
Violin, viola

Solo

Lovely Music 134
Jenkins (vn solo). October 1992.

Leroy Jenkins said (1991): '**Someone described us [Revolutionary Ensemble] as "ahead of our time". I don't think so, and, you know, we got work back then. It's now, with Wynton Marsalis' music defining what people think of as jazz, that things are difficult and hostile.**'

Jenkins's percussive, rasping delivery rarely departed from an identifiable tonal centre or melodic logic and had an almost classical sense of form, deriving from his early love of Jascha Heifetz. His preference is for looping statements, punctuated by abrupt rhythmic snaps. In jazz terms, the most obvious influence is Stuff Smith, but much of his language was made fresh in keeping with the self-determined spirit of AACM. He joined the organization on returning to Chicago after a period spent teaching in the South. He was later a founding member of two influential but short-lived groups, the Revolutionary Ensemble and Sting, the former a collaborative trio, the latter a vehicle for his own work.

It isn't clear whether the solo record was a long-cherished plan or simply a reflection of how difficult it was to form lasting ensembles. There is a grizzled majesty to *Solo*, a confident conflation of traditions. Tackling 'Giant Steps' and Dizzy's 'Wouldn't You' on fiddle and viola bespeaks some courage, but Jenkins skates across those familiar harmonics with breathtaking ease. The recording is in close-up, an intimate glimpse of a master at work but, sadly, on his last surviving record.

& *See also* **REVOLUTIONARY ENSEMBLE, Revolutionary Ensemble** (1971; p. 388)

PHAROAH SANDERS &

Born Farrell Sanders, 13 October 1940, Little Rock, Arkansas
Tenor saxophone

Crescent With Love

Evidence ECD 22099 2CD
Sanders; William Henderson (p); Charles Fambrough (b); Sherman Ferguson (d). October 1992.

Pharoah Sanders said (1985): '**John [Coltrane] never said much to me. We didn't talk much about music, but sometimes he'd give me some little thing to work on, maybe a little bit of rhythm. And these things are turning up in my work now, unannounced, nearly 25 years after he passed.**'

The 25th anniversary of Coltrane's death spawned a rash of tribute albums, few of them as apostolically convincing as this. A perfectly balanced band, with Henderson steadily growing in stature and Fambrough showing once again what a responsive and intelligent player he can be in the right company. Five Coltrane tunes, opening with 'Lonnie's Lament', then 'Wise One', 'Naima' and 'Crescent' and closing disc two with 'After The Rain', these interspersed with 'Misty', 'Too Young To Go Steady', 'Feeling Good', Pietro Piccioni's 'Light At The Edge Of The World' and one original, Henderson's 'Softly For Shyla'. Sanders sounds thoughtful and even a little wistful, as befits a tribute to his friend, but he never lets his playing drift into sentiment. A strong, creative record, and one of the few of its type that doesn't merely doff a cap to Coltrane but takes his music on a ways.

& *See also* **Karma** (1969; p. 363)

MASSIMO URBANI

Born 8 May 1957, Rome, Italy; died 24 June 1993, Rome, Italy
Alto saxophone

The Blessing

Red RR 123257-2
Urbani; Maurizio Urbani (ts); Danilo Rea (p); Giovanni Tommaso (b); Roberto Gatto (d). February 1993.

Saxophonist Carlo Actis Dato says: **'E' stato il primo in Italia tra i giovani jazzisti degli anni '70 a suonare il sax con quella "furia vitale" tipica dei sassofonisti neri americani. E' passato poi dal free al be-bop con una padronanza tecnica strabiliante!'**

Urbani's senseless death robbed Europe of a player whose records are a flawed testament to a bopper of enormous guts and facility. Marcello Piras described him as a 'wastrel genius'. He emerged as a 17-year-old prodigy in Giorgio Gaslini's group, but was prodigal with his own health and succumbed to a heroin overdose aged only 36. Urbani's earlier records sometimes fail to live up to the *Wunderkind* reputation, and the surviving discography is spotty, with a good many releases of dubious provenance, sure sign of a morbid posthumous cult.

The opening of the first Red album, *360 Degrees Aeutopia*, consists of an astonishing outburst of alto on 'Cherokee', at a suitably hectic tempo, a good measure of Urbani's bop mastery. He later tackled Coltrane and Ayler too, but less persuasively, though there's a lustrous, acerbic 'Naima' on *Dedications* as well as one of his fighting bebop miniatures in 'Scrapple From The Apple'. *Easy To Love* saw him not so much tamed as under rein, playing a relatively straightforward programme of standards and one original, 'A Trane From The East'.

It might seem perverse or morbid to favour the last record of all over any of these, particularly when it comes so close to Urbani's death (at around the same age as Parker, it turned out). It does, however, sum up his art. For all the glances in the direction of Coltrane, Urbani was a diehard bopper to the end as his race through 'My Little Suede Shoes' confirms. Interestingly, his tenor-playing brother's two appearances offer a tart contrast in styles on a pair of originals by Tommaso; Maurizio seems to be looking in a different stylistic direction. But Urbani's coruscating tone and energy command all the attention, and the two contrasting takes of 'The Way You Look Tonight' are curtain calls of genius. He ends, as he began, with a solo tribute to the master: 'Blues For Bird' takes the story back round to the 22-year-old's arc-welded 'Cherokee'. Had he lived, Urbani would not yet be 60. What might he have achieved?

BILL FRISELL

Born 18 March 1951, Baltimore, Maryland
Guitar

Have A Little Faith

Elektra Nonesuch 79301
Frisell; Don Byron (cl, bcl); Guy Klucevesek (acc); Kermit Driscoll (b); Joey Baron (d). March 1993.

Bill Frisell says: **'My first few albums were made up mostly of original compositions. It was important for me to establish what my own musical world might sound like. (I haven't gotten there yet, but am still trying.) Recording *Have A Little Faith* gave me the opportunity to play music that had inspired me. Hopefully it also gives the listener a hint as to where I come from and a context into which they can place my compositions.'**

Once the first-call guitar man of the '80s scene, a countrified Hendrix with robust jazz chops, Frisell has developed in his own unique direction, mixing up avant-garde noise and lyricism, clean-plucked lines and heavy processing, musical adventure with something of Charlie Haden's elegiac conservatism.

Frisell was raised in Denver and studied for a time at Berklee, where Pat Metheny was a contemporary. His first jazz influence was Wes Montgomery, but without displacing jazz as his main language other American vernaculars, the music of the hinterland, began to play an increasing role in his work. While recording for ECM, he made a number of albums, notably 1987's *Lookout For Hope*, that seemed to synthesize jazz with folk and country forms. This was picked up again when he moved to the more pop-savvy Elektra and released *Before We Were Born*. By the early '90s, Frisell was moving in a direction quite different to Jimmy Giuffre's folk-jazz, but with strong similarities.

On 1992's *This Land*, Frisell restores much of the *Lookout For Hope* line-up and experiments further with stylistic hybrids, tuneful miniatures that have the resonant familiarity of Aaron Copland's *Appalachian Spring* and *Billy The Kid*. Sonically, it's a fascinating combination, with Fowlkes and Byron often combining to provide elegant dissonances (as on 'Jimmy Carter, Part 1'). On the marvellous *Have A Little Faith* those duties, and those of cellist Hank Roberts on *Lookout*, are taken on by master accordionist Guy Klucevesek. Frisell's affectionate examination of Americana takes in Stephen Foster, Sousa, Ives, Copland, Sonny Rollins, Bob Dylan and, most controversially, Madonna. There's no attempt to debunk or satirize, and even Madonna's 'Live To Tell', despite a heavily distorted cadenza with all Frisell's switches and pedals on, sticks pretty close to the original. Byron's role is relatively marginal, perhaps even decorative, but by this stage he was exploring his own eclectic directions, and it's Klucevesek and Baron who rise to the leader's gentle challenge. It's a pretty record, with rattlesnake bite and some heavy hitting behind the familiar material.

DON PULLEN &

Born 25 December 1941, Roanoke, Virginia; died 22 April 1995, East Orange, New Jersey
Piano

Ode To Life
Blue Note B2-89233
Pullen; Carlos Ward (as, f); Nilson Matta (b); Guilherme Franco, Mor Thiam (perc). February 1993.

Trumpeter Larry Kramer says: **'His music had it all: power, swing, warmth, freedom. He came from gospel and R&B, then through the avant-garde and pulled in the rest of the world: Brazil, Cuba, Native American.'**

Saxophonist and co-leader George Adams died in November 1992 and left a large hole in Pullen's spirit. A couple of years earlier, the pianist had begun recording with a new group called African Brazilian Connection. The debut recording was a bright and propulsive project called *Kele Mou Bana*. Pullen had been signed by Blue Note, but there was only a diffident response to his new direction and the more sombre, half-resigned, half-defiant tone one hears on the sequel, *Ode To Life*, is not just an expression of grief but also of dissatisfaction with how his work was treated and received in the US.

Ode To Life is dedicated to Adams, and at its heart is the warm but pained 'Ah, George, We Hardly Knew Ya', in which Pullen stitches together a series of aural memories of the great saxophonist. Ward is more than up to the task, sounding like a rarefied version of Adams, but with that typical, almost folksy wail in his tone. It's preceded by 'El Matador', a relatively generic 'Spanish tinge' piece, and followed by Mor Thiam's extravagantly rhythmic 'Aseeko! (Get Up And Dance)', an invitation that sounds more bittersweet with each hearing. There is a decidedly autumnal feel to this record. It begins with something like a swagger on 'The Third House On The Right' and once again it confidently chops styles and traditions into a very personal stew. But there is no mistaking the record's shadowy sub-texts and when Pullen settles into the aching melody of the title-track, strictly 'Variation On Ode Io Life', it is clear that all paths on this emotionally effortful record lead to the grave, and that the triumphs of song are hard-won.

& *See also* **Evidence Of Things Unseen** (1983; p. 480)

SHIRLEY HORN
Born 1 May 1934, Washington DC; died 20 October 2005, Cheverly, Maryland
Voice, piano

Light Out Of Darkness
Verve 519703-2
Horn; Gary Bartz (as); Charles Ables (g, b); Tyler Mitchell (b); Steve Williams (d). April–May 1993.

Singer Claire Martin recorded a tribute to Shirley Horn: **'There are so many things about her singing that enthral me, but that very short audible intake of breath she does at the end of a perfect phrase, almost as if she is gasping at the very thought of what she has just said, is my absolute favourite quirk. That and insisting that she be paid in dollars even when in the UK because "I don't want notes with some broad's picture on it."'**

Horn studied piano at college and was an underrated keyboard exponent. She started leading groups as early as 1954, but remained a DC secret until she started touring Europe in the '80s, when the Steeplechase label picked her up for a belated 'debut' – there was a scattering of early stuff – that yielded a spare, reflective trio music quite different from what most new-comers to Horn's music profess to expect. At the end of the decade, Verve cottoned on to the possibility of a new diva. What amounted to Horn's second comeback was distinguished by a perfect touch and luxury-class production values. Actually, in terms of her own perfor-mances or those of another supportive trio there's no special advance on the Steeplechases. The first two Verves continue to work at favourite standards, but *You Won't Forget Me* is a step forward in its pristine attention to detail, awesome array of guest star soloists – Miles Davis was a great Horn admirer, but is well below his best – and the faithfulness with which Horn's voice is recorded. There was a later tribute to Miles, which was the culmina-tion of the Verve period, but *Light Out Of Darkness* is a superior record. It's pitched as a tribute to Ray Charles, another singer-pianist, and they found her some interesting guests to appear with the trio. The doughty Ables usefully switches to guitar here and there, with Tyler Mitchell stepping in on bass. After the heavyweight emoting of the preceding *Here's To Life*, Horn sounds almost carefree on the likes of 'Hit The Road Jack' and 'I Got A Man'. Bartz lends a few swinging obbligatos, but the emphasis here is on Horn's understanding of the beat, her dry, almost elemental phrasing and the intuitive touch of her regular group.

DON BRADEN
Born 20 November 1963, Cincinnati, Ohio
Tenor saxophone

After Dark
Criss Cross 1081
Braden; Scott Wendholt (t, flhn); Noah Bless (tb); Steve Wilson (as); Darrell Grant (p); Christian McBride (b); Carl Allen (d). May 1993.

Don Braden said (1995): **'I got pushed along at summer camp, a Jamey Aebersold thing, but a lot of my practising was done to the radio, and I can recommend that: you play along to *everything*, and you find yourself working in some pretty difficult keys, especially when the music's rock or funk.'**

Braden's Criss Cross debut was widely praised but it wasn't a patch on the sequel, an elegant set of standards and refreshingly straightforward originals. Instead of overloading themes with harmonic changes, Braden builds in bridge sections which shift the tempo from fours to threes. He's an intelligent arranger, too. The third album for Gerry Teekens marked a sudden and dramatic maturing of his style. Not only is Braden playing with grace and beauty as before, but his writing and arranging skills seem to have made a huge step forward and the septet tracks are so confidently and naturally written that the music has the open texture of a smaller group, but with all the weight and substance of a mid-size ensemble. There is a nocturnal programme to the record which gives it a sombre, though by no means downbeat, emphasis. Originals like the uneasy 'R.E.M.' and the gently upbeat 'Dawn' are interspersed with 'You And The Night And The Music', 'Monk's Dream' and Stevie Wonder's 'Creepin'', which may well represent a throwback to those days practising in front of the wireless. An essential contemporary record and the kind of thing Blue Note might have been putting out three decades earlier.

ORPHY ROBINSON

Born 30 October 1960, London
Vibraphone, marimba, soprano saxophone

The Vibes Describes

Blue Note 829223
Robinson; Joe Bashorun (p, ky); Rowland Sutherland (f, af, picc); Tunde Jegede (clo, kora); Nik Cohen, Dudley Phillips (b); Andy Gangadeen (d); Winston Clifford (d, perc); Nana Vasconcelos (perc); Leroy Osbourne (v, g); Mae McKenna (v). May 1993.

Bassist Hugh Hopper said (2001): **'I always get irritable when anyone describes him as "Orphy Robinson, vibist". Orphy is what we all aspire to be, a complete musician. The vibes just happens to be the instrument he plays.'**

Orphy Robinson has followed a fascinating course in music, starting with a highly original and personal concept, as represented by his two Blue Note records, and then moving into free music, a challenging but certainly not lucrative end of the jazz 'market'. Robinson's debut record, *When Tomorrow Comes*, was a surprise. No one expected a straight-ahead jazz album, but equally no one was quite prepared for anything quite as original. As always on his own projects, he took a modest share of solo space, preferring to concentrate on a subtly inflected group sound. Technically, the sequel lacked some of the gloss, perhaps because Robinson decided to produce himself. But his own playing has leapt forward and Annavas (as he called the band) now sounds like a solid unit, its roots and influences teasingly difficult to pin down. Compositions like 'Fore To The Power Of M' and 'The Loneliest Monk' – a reference to Mao Zedong, we believe – balance imagination and taste with impeccable arranging skills, and he has the self-confidence to include an arrangement of the Stranglers' 'Golden Brown'. He's as interesting a musician as any to emerge in the '80s in Britain and the influence of these records is still being felt, even if Blue Note did its usual U-turn and failed to get behind him for longer.

CECIL PAYNE
Born 14 December 1922, Brooklyn, New York; died 27 November 2007, Camden, New Jersey
Baritone saxophone, flute

Cerupa
Delmark DE 478
Payne; Freddie Hubbard, Dr Odies Williams III (t); Eric Alexander (ts); Harold Mabern (p); John Ore (b); Joe Farnsworth (d). June 1993.

Cecil Payne said (2000): **'Once I'd heard Lester Young that was it, I wanted to be a saxophone-player. My father wanted me to be a dentist, but can you really imagine getting your teeth fixed by "Dr Payne"?'**

Payne switched from alto to baritone in 1946 while working with J. J. Johnson, but developed a light, limber approach with a Pres-like tone. Along with Leo Parker, Payne did much to adapt the hefty baritone to the rapid transitions and tonal extremities of bebop.

Payne's work for Delmark was something of an Indian summer. The formula is pretty much the same on all three records: a weighty, two-saxophone front line (Lin Halliday is pacemaker on *Scotch And Milk*, with Marcus Belgrave on trumpet), and parts for Freddie Hubbard and the little-known Odies Williams on *Cerupa*, trombonist Steve Davis on *Payne's Window*. The rhythm section is anchored by Mabern, who is one of the great post-bop pianists. Eric Alexander is a Mabern pupil and has absorbed much of the pianist's vast knowledge of the idiom, creating solos that bespeak historical awareness as well as formidable technique.

Cerupa is C. Ruth Payne, the saxophonist's wife. He gets out his flute for the title-track and demonstrates an unusually individual touch on it. There are unexpected Latin elements here and there, though not on 'Cuba'. After a free-blowing opening, 'Bolambo' shows some acquaintance with the free movement, but moves into a stately dance theme. 'I Should Care' is the only standard and is played with insouciant ease. Payne's reputation isn't large and he's virtually unacknowledged as a flautist. This one redresses the balance more than a little.

PAGO LIBRE
Formed 1990
Group

Shooting Stars And Traffic Lights
Leo CD LR 345
John Wolf Brennan (p, mca); John Voirol (syn, ss, ts); Tscho Theissing (vn); Daniele Patumi (b); Alex Cline (d, perc). 1993.

John Wolf Brennan says: **'The title appeared as a metaphor to point at the "ultrafast" and "stop-in-this-very-fraction-of-a-second" method we used as a group in various of the pieces.'**

There have been all sorts of efforts to explain the band name, some of them quite plausible for music of such freedom and abandon, but very simply it derives from the initial letters of group members, which at first included violinist Steve GOodman and trumpeter Lars LIndvall, though that rationale has vanished with changes in personnel. The most recent incarnation is a drummerless quartet with Arkady Shilkloper on French horn and flugelhorn.

A unique line-up and instrumentation, the music takes much of its energy from

Brennan's playful but thoughtful aesthetic, which combines an almost classical order with a strong measure of aural surrealism. There have been many recordings over the years, but *Shooting Stars And Traffic Lights* is the group at its most luminously free. Theissing plays a quite formal melody on the title-track and one might almost be bound for an episode of chamber-jazz, but for the cheerful anarchy of what overtakes the lead-line. 'Toccattacca', in several parts, is a typical Brennan conception, using classical form (and some Messiaen chords) against the drive of a jazz group. 'Ognatango' works similarly, but it's misleading to imply that this is satirical music. Cline's 'A.L.P.traum' combines the 'Anna Livia Plurabelle' chapter in *Finnegans Wake*, where the washerwomen of Dublin try to guess the personalities of the wearers from tell-tale signs in their underwear, with the German word for a nightmare, *Alptraum*. Such references are all integral to the performance and not just a way of leading the listener astray.

Almost any of the records are worth investigating, but this little masterpiece was so long out of circulation that it is worthy of special attention.

BILL DIXON &

Born 25 October 1925, Nantucket, Massachusetts
Trumpet

Vade Mecum / Vade Mecum II
Soul Note 121208 / 121211
Dixon; Barry Guy, William Parker (b); Tony Oxley (d). August 1993.

Bill Dixon says: **'It might seem there were too many imponderables – the group had never worked together before – and the faint-hearted might have wondered what we might be able to achieve. But things worked out well; in fact they worked out marvellously; all of the players indicated that they wanted to play the music we were confronting that day, which, incidentally, was a beautiful and sunny Italian day totally fit for the recording that we made.'**

Dixon not only relied on a European label. He also found European – in this case, British – musicians to be responsive to his music. Inside almost all of Dixon's small-group recordings there is a dark pressure, like the imprint of a much larger composition that has been denied full expression. That is profoundly evident on *Vade Mecum*, which begins Dixon's association with British percussionist Tony Oxley; it later resulted in a pair of Soul Note CDs called *Papyrus*. It might be argued that both Oxley and compatriot Guy are too 'strong' to conform to Dixon's exceptionally disciplined approach, and there is a hint that this may have resulted in conflict when one finds Oxley's role dismissed as 'background' on the later duo records. The two bassists take very different parts: Parker is sonorous and inward, while Guy flitters rapidly on what may be a chamber bass. 'Anamorphosis' on the first record is one of Dixon's most thoughtful conceptions, and it is clear that the group responded very positively to the forms he proposed. For a time we considered the second volume, recorded at the same session, the stronger of the two – 'Ebonite' and 'Reflections' are both immensely powerful ideas, anchored in the bass and coloured with Oxley's unique spectrum of sounds – but really this is just a single superlative record that might easily have been released as a double disc. Too much to absorb in one sitting, perhaps, but richness for the ages in the music.

& *See also* **November 1981** (1981; p. 466)

JAN GARBAREK&

Born 4 March 1947, Mysen, Norway
Tenor and soprano saxophones, other instruments

Twelve Moons

ECM 519500-2
Garbarek; Rainer Brüninghaus (ky); Eberhard Weber (b); Manu Katché (d); Marilyn Mazur (perc); Mari Boine, Agnes Buen Garnås (v). September 1993.

Saxophonist Tommy Smith says: **'Garbarek's sound possesses the call from the wild and the planet's soundscapes. The sonic experience, whether it's live or from the studio, is extremely important to Jan. The wonderful trait that he shares with Arild Andersen is the desire for their audiences to hear their live concerts as if they were studio recordings.'**

The end of the '70s established a pattern whereby Garbarek went into the studio at each year's end to consolidate and capture what had been learned in performance and to send out new feelers for the year ahead. It is what a village bard might have done in winter quarters, spin tales about the year past and boast about what would come when the sun returned, and the folkloric strain became more evident as Garbarek's music moved in the direction of improvisational folk music.

Star in 1991 was widely hailed as the saxophonist's return to straighter jazz playing, but it was a curiously woolly album – the contributions of Miroslav Vitous and Peter Erskine notwithstanding – that never quite delivered on its promise, and it was *Twelve Moons* that restored something of the atmospheric beauty and deep pulse of *Dis*. Appropriately, it was Garbarek who was chosen to front ECM's 500th release. It finds him at an interesting point of development, still exploring folklore but again espousing a jazz-orientated programme. There's an emphasis on soprano saxophone, perhaps to blend better with the voices, but even here the tone is stronger and heavier than of yore. Katché is essentially a rock drummer, with a crude but immensely vibrant delivery. One thinks occasionally of Ginger Baker, but among previous associates he is closer to Edward Vesala than to Jon Christensen. This time around, in addition to Sami *joiks*, Garbarek includes an arrangement of national composer Edvard Grieg's gentle 'Arietta', and a new version of the late Jim Pepper's 'Witchi-Tai-To'.

& *See also* **Dis** (1976; p. 436)

MICHAEL MOORE

Born 1 January 1954, Eureka, California
Clarinet, alto saxophone

Chicoutimi

Ramboy 06
Moore; Fred Hersch (p); Mark Helias (b). September 1993.

Michael Moore says: **'Having been active with ICP, Clusone trio, Guus Janssen and Maarten Altena for a few years this was a date I needed to do to balance my musical life. I had been going in this direction before I realized that Jimmy Giuffre had done it all 30 years before me. My biggest regret is spelling his name wrong on the cover! Everything was easy working with Fred and Mark and there is clearly a Dutch influence in the music.'**

After training at the New England Conservatory, Moore moved to Europe and has been based in Amsterdam ever since. His associations there have included Han Bennink, Misha Mengelberg and the Instant Composers Pool, and he has also been at various times a member of Available Jelly, Clusone 3 and drummer Gerry Hemingway's small group. Much of his work has been issued on his own Ramboy label. Moore's multi-reed approach always bristles with pawky intelligence. He has a firm, almost vocal tone on his main horns and his solos resemble quirky monologues.

Chicoutimi – and the subsequently released *Bering* from the same group date – is a beautiful record, exquisitely executed and thoughtfully expressed, poised between modernist and mainstream, edgy and sentimental by turns. The opening 'Anomalous Soul' is absolutely in the spirit of Giuffre, its lopsided line seemingly detached from Hersch's chords and Helias's muscly but contained accompaniment; its logic only becomes entirely clear when it's over, by which time the group has moved into the more abstract territory of 'Bruce', one of a number of tracks that sound collectively improvised. The bassist's *arco* work doesn't get quite enough of an outing here for us, but it's devastating when it does appear and the closing sequence is as satisfying as anything of the period, with an Astor Piazzolla tango playing out a programme that has a strong internal logic. Coming around mid-way, 'In The Company of Angels' is Moore's show-stopper. Listen to it, and you might understand what he means by a 'Dutch influence' on the music.

ERNIE WATTS
Born 23 October 1945, Norfolk, Virginia
Tenor and soprano saxophones

Reaching Up
Samson Music 29932
Watts; Arturo Sandoval (t); Mulgrew Miller (p); Charles Fambrough (b); Jack DeJohnette (d). October 1993.

Ernie Watts says: **'This was the first session I played on a brand-new saxophone, my Julius Keilwerth SX 90R, which I got just two weeks before – and have now used continuously for 16 years. So I had to get to know my saxophone at the same time I was making the recording, which made it even more of an adventure.'**

Ernie Watts describes himself as an analog man in a digital world; he even used that designation for a recent album. One might add that he is something of an invisible man as far as the recording world is concerned. Few of his records have stuck in catalogue, despite their obvious merits, and apart from his membership of Charlie Haden's Quartet West and a few other high-profile situations, he remains largely unknown to a wider jazz public or else dismissed as a world music and fusion dabbler.

His chief influence is Coltrane, but the Coltrane of the earlier, sheets-of-sound period. Watts is essentially a romantic player, but he's far from undaring and the failure of his work to remain in catalogue is more a reflection of its uncategorizability than of its quality, which is consistently high. In 1991, he recorded *Afoxé* – say it 'aff-oshay' – a set of tautly dancing world grooves that would have intrigued Miles Davis had he lived to hear it.

Reaching Up, from two years later, is more obviously a jazz record, and a pretty headlong one, too. If Watts was trying out a new saxophone, he wasn't breaking it in gently. The solos are driving and intense. Some profess to hear a resemblance to Michael Brecker, and there is a brittle edge here and there that points in that direction, but it's unmistakably Watts in his own voice. Jack DeJohnette, who had contributed drums and keyboard kalimba to *Afoxé*, provides the fuel, but credit also goes to that underrated composer and bassist Charles Fambrough, who brings 'The High Road', 'Sweet Lucy' and a good deal of invention and class to the set. Sandoval is featured on just two cuts, which is just about right; any more and he might have overheated things. Miller's comping is exact but attractively loose. Watts includes a Coltrane tune ('Mr Syms') and a standard ('I Hear A Rhapsody'), but his own material dominates, particularly the concluding pair of 'Angel's Flight' and 'Sweet Rhapsody'. Some might find the multi-noted approach a little excessive, but there's structural iron in every solo.

KEITH NICHOLS

Born 13 February 1945, Woodford, Essex, England
Piano

Henderson Stomp

Stomp Off CD 1275

Nichols; René Hagmann (c, tb); Bent Persson, Guy Barker, Mike Henry, Rolf Koschorrok (t); Alistair Allan (tb); Claus Jacobi (ss, as, bsx, cl); Nicholas Payton (as, cl); Michel Bard (ts, cl); Martin Wheatley (bj); Graham Read (sou); Richard Pite (d). November 1993.

Keith Nichols says: **'We took great pains to match the sound of the original instruments. Trombonist René Hagmann managed to find a pre-war instrument – the same model Jimmy Harrison played in 1927. The pieces were taken from 1924-31, ranging from the Louis Armstrong period to early swing. Playing and arranging styles in hot dance music evolved out of all recognition during that time, demanding great versatility from the musicians on this CD. It was an education for us all and we're very proud of it.'**

Nichols is a British specialist in American repertory: ragtime, hot dance music, New York jazz of the '20s, Blake, Morton, Berlin, whatever. He has a versatile background in acting and entertaining, but is primarily a practising scholar of ragtime and early jazz repertory. His piano-playing and Hoagy Carmichael-like singing are less important than the mastery of old form that he successfully displays on his records.

Henderson Stomp is surely his finest hour to this point and one of the most convincing pieces of authentic-performance jazz ever set down. Stomp Off producer Bob Erdos has always been keen on authenticity, with the accent on lesser-known pieces. Transcriptions were done by Nichols, Claus Jacobi and Bent Persson. Twenty-two of Fletcher Henderson's most effective pieces – from several hands, though many of Don Redman's somewhat familiar charts are bypassed in favour of other arrangements – are re-created by a picked team of some of the most talented repertory players and revivalists in Europe: the brass team alone is gold-plated, with the amazingly versatile Persson and Barker set alongside the brilliant Hagmann. The reed section seems totally schooled in the appropriate section sound of the period – Guy Barker sits almost unnoticed in the section, but is just as good as Marsalis, or Payton, at this kind of thing – and each of the tunes emerges with the kind of rocking swing that is properly flavoursome of the era. With such a strong team of soloists, the various breaks and carefully fashioned improvisations have the nous needed to transcend any scripted mustiness.

GLENN SPEARMAN

Born 14 February 1947, New York City; died 8 October 1998, San Francisco, California
Tenor saxophone

Smokehouse

Black Saint 120157

Spearman; Larry Ochs (ts, sno); Chris Brown (p, DX7); Ben Lindgren (b); Donald Robinson, William Winant (d). November 1993.

Glenn Spearman said (1992): **'I got saddled with the reputation of being this crazy/John Coltrane/screamer/out-there type and that never left me. I don't think it's done any real harm, but it maybe didn't do that much good either.'**

Spearman's death from liver cancer left a sense of things undone and of a major talent not yet properly recognized. His blues-soaked sound bears comparison with anyone from Illinois Jacquet to Archie Shepp. He'd got involved in creative music-making in Oakland in the '60s, but was a relative latecomer to recording. Spearman was over 40 before he made *Utterance* for Cadence, so not surprisingly he already sounded settled into a strong and individual voice. He started out as a Coltrane-influenced screamer but quickly recognized that a more thoughtful delivery might well bear dividends.

Spearman made a couple of fascinating records for Black Saint in the early '90s with a group that included ROVA's Larry Ochs, percussionist William Winant and others on that Californian free scene. Dedicated to Ornette Coleman (and to the structured freedom on Ornette's *Free Jazz*), *Mystery Project* consists of a large three-part suite, in which the direction of the music is dictated not so much by notated passages as by the distribution of the personnel. As in ROVA man Larry Ochs's 'Double Image', the basic group is a palette from which various colours and shadings can be drawn. Spearman's personal colour-code would seem to be black and red. He's a fierce player, overblowing in the upper register and virtually incapable of anything less than full throttle. He never sacrifices subtlety to power, though. This is intelligent music that never palls or sounds dated.

The follow-up record has the same line-up and makes similarly effective use of doubled instruments. It's a long – 75-minute – suite with an intermission built in, not because an LP version required a break, but because the music is so unremittingly present that one couldn't absorb any more without some surcease. Spearman's time in Europe opened up many interesting compositional ideas to him, but these performances are squarely in the tradition of the '60s avant-garde, and their strength comes from Spearman's profound conviction that the ideas adumbrated at that time are far from exhausted but still constitute a *lingua franca* for improvisation. The 'in-take' and 'out-take' of 'Axe, Beautiful Acts' exude a fierce poetry that is worthy of Cecil Taylor.

REGGIE WORKMAN
Born 26 June 1937, Philadelphia, Pennsylvania
Double bass

Summit Conference
Postcards POST1003
Workman; Julian Priester (tb); Sam Rivers (ts, ss); Andrew Hill (p); Pheeroan akLaff (d). December 1993.

Reggie Workman said (1995): **'I spent a lot of time supporting other artists in their projects, and I realized that it wouldn't be easy to jump back in and assert myself with my concept, which might not be something the industry wanted at that time. But I know that those who have followed my evolution will understand.'**

As befits his name, Workman has clocked up a formidable number of credits: with Coltrane (*Olé*, the 1961 European tour, the *Africa/Brass* sessions) and with Wayne Shorter, Mal Waldron, Art Blakey, Archie Shepp and David Murray. It has often been asked what might have happened had he remained with Coltrane, but it's academic: impending personal loss and other responsibilities meant he had to move on and it seems both patronizing and potentially hurtful to dwell on it as if his life stalled at that point. He played R&B as a teenager, then worked in New York hard-bop groups in the '60s before moving towards the freer styles of Coltrane and Archie Shepp. Far from being a closeted avant-gardist, Workman is a communicator and a selfless teacher. But he is also a forceful composer and leader who has moved on to explore areas of musical freedom influenced by African idioms and frequently resembling the trance music of the *griots*.

There are Latin tinges, too, in the music, African-Cuban rather than ersatz south-of-the-border stuff. It energizes *Summit Conference* and the equally superb *Cerebral Caverns*, which followed from a similar high-octane group. It's a wish-list line-up. Rivers and Priester are in boilingly good form; akLaff keeps the pace up. Hill isn't a delicate player and it worried us at first that he didn't seem to be coming through the mix, but he's there, under it all. The bulk of the session is uptempo, often in subtly fractured metres that still get their information across straightforwardly. The Sonelius Smith tune 'Conversation' shows how much Workman stays close to his roots, but there's still room for a heart-on-sleeve ballad, Rivers's 'Solace', introduced by trombone, piano and sax before the composer goes up a gear and delivers his most magisterial solo for years. Priester's 'Breath' is pitched in a distant, sharp-ridden key, and the set closes with Rivers on flute, duetting with Hill on the pianist's 'Gone'. Workman is self-effacing on his own date, but he marshals the energy and one is always conscious of him at the centre of the music. On another day, we might pick *Cerebral Caverns* ahead of this one, if only for Geri Allen's unpredictable presence, but ...

BARRY GUY&

Born 22 April 1947, London
Double bass, chamber bass

Study – Witch Gong Game II/10
Maya 9402
Guy; John Korsrud (t); Ralph Eppel (tb); Bruce Freedman (ss); Graham Ord (ss, ts, picc); Saul Berson (as); Coat Cooke (ts, bs, f); Paul Plimley (p); Ron Samworth (g); Peggy Lee (clo); Clyde Reed, Paul Blaney (b); Dylan van der Schyff (d). February 1994.

Barry Guys says: **'The score, one large-format sheet, is graphic in nature and is designed to take into account the mixed abilities of this co-operative ensemble. Various "modules" of musical material hover over a dark void which can be brought into play via flash cards. This void is graphically indicative of the fragility of co-operative groups where the passing of time may implode or explode the artistic intentions of its members.'**

Guy is relatively unusual in the field of improvised music in having kept up a parallel career in composition and in performance of the baroque. What impact this has on his improvisations is a matter for discussion, but one senses the presence of other musical influences, as a kind of 'back story'. Guy has been at the hub of British free music and organized improvisation since the end of the '60s, when he was a member of the Spontaneous Music Ensemble, Iskra 1903 and Amalgam, who along with AMM staked out British free music's field of enquiry. He is also the founder and motive force of the London Jazz Composers' Orchestra, whose long history provides a barometric reading of current musical philosophies. In addition, Guy has performed in trio with Evan Parker and Paul Lytton.

Apart from some of the LJCO works, Guy's large-scale compositions and improvisation structures are still not as widely regarded as, say, Braxton's, which is surprising and somewhat unjust. Few figures in the field so confidently blend intellectual sophistication with the flexibility one associates with improvising ensembles. *Study – Witch Gong Game II/10* was commissioned by the New Orchestral Workshop in Vancouver and is performed by that group here. It is an important work, inspired by the Scottish painter and saxophonist Alan Davie's series of paintings of the same name and it has continued to be part of Guy's working repertoire.

The Canadian group take to the discipline vigorously, but one senses that discipline is the operative word and that Guy controls the procedures quite strictly. That shouldn't imply a work of conservatory dryness, for *Study – Witch Gong Game II/10* has a dark and scarifying cast, a musical *Walpurgisnacht* that makes for very unsettling, but also very satisfactory, listening. The other piece on the record, 'Study', is a briefer, drone-based work that uses minimal material to push the ensemble steadily towards a breakout point for improvisation. Its lighter presence complements the main recording's uncanny sound-world rather well.

& *See also* **Odyssey** (1999; p. 644); **LONDON JAZZ COMPOSERS' ORCHESTRA, Ode** (1972; p. 393)

HAROLD DANKO
Born 13 June 1947, Youngstown, Ohio
Piano

After The Rain
Steeplechase SCCD 31356
Danko (p solo). 1994.

Harold Danko says: **'Staying in Italy with my friends Enzo and Claudio Verdelli, right before coming to Denmark for the recording, I was slightly overwhelmed by the prospect of making a permanent pianistic document of the great music of John Coltrane. Turning from practice, I scanned one of the only English books in the house, dealing with the Japanese tea ceremony. (I drink coffee, particularly in Italy, so this was nicely off-topic.) I found one of those wonderful words for which there is no English counterpart: *wabi*, which translates roughly as "appreciation of the imperfections in art over time". Pragmatist rather than philosopher I immediately sought to apply this to my situation, and it came in very handy. During playbacks, instead of being overly critical I simply acknowledged the many instances of future *wabi* I may have created.'**

Steeplechase producer Nils Winther has an instinct for piano-players and gives Danko, who's not a showy or histrionic player but someone who shapes his music with warmth and intelligence, a nicely expansive sound that helps it all communicate. Where Tommy Flanagan treated a similar date as an occasion for richly abstract meditations on Coltrane material, Danko approaches it both more modestly and more radically. He tackles no fewer than 14 Coltrane compositions, ranging from 'After The Rain', 'Lonnie's Lament' and a brilliantly re-conceived 'Syeeda's Song Flute' to less obvious material like 'Dahomey Dance', 'Mr Day' and 'Straight Street'. What is remarkable is that Danko makes these tunes sound both naturally pianistic and utterly his own. To be sure, he doesn't take on anything from *Interstellar Space* and treats each theme in an essentially song-like way, but that isn't to suggest that this is Coltrane-lite. Even his reading of 'After The Rain', which has become something of a piano cliché, with all those tumbling chords and lavish voicings, has solid structural muscle. Though clearly intended as a homage, there is no obstacle to wholesale reinvention, and Danko recasts 'Mr Sims' and 'Wise One' with a free hand.

Danko's a modest fellow, but among contemporary piano-players he is one of the wise ones, a musical thinker who's worth the outlay of time whatever the context, but never more revealing than when he plays solo.

STEVE LACY&
Born Steven Lackritz, 23 July 1934, New York City; died 4 June 2004, Boston, Massachusetts
Soprano saxophone

5 x Monk 5 x Lacy
Silkheart SHCD 144
Lacy (ss solo). March 1994.

Steve Lacy said: **'When I was a young man, I guess I used to haunt Monk. I'd go along to a club and stand right next to the piano. He'd ignore me for the longest time and then at the end look up and say in a tired voice: "Oh, it's you again, Steven."'**

Emanem curator Martin Davidson's point that the daring Lacy showed in his very first solo saxophone performances in the early '70s was rarely seen again is well taken, but also somewhat misleading. In 1994, Lacy turned 60. At least some of the fire and Eugene Gant hunger for musical experience was stilled. In the early '90s, he had seemed content to be part of a band, to showcase his own compositions and arguably to take fewer improvisational chances than in the past.

But having spent a good deal of time over the previous few years working with the group and with larger-scale arrangements, Lacy showed every sign of wanting to return to unaccompanied performance. The gesture in itself suggests that his appetite for raw self-exposure hadn't gone, though of course there are also strong economic reasons for unaccompanied touring. This recording was made during an improvisation festival in Stockholm.

It is pretty much exactly as described, five tunes by the master and five originals, including the familiar 'The Crust' and 'Deadline', both of them well-established Lacy repertory tunes. His approach to both 'Pannonica' and 'Evidence' is notable for subtle shifts in the geometry of the tune, changing internal relationships without changing the components, rather like one of those relativity diagrams in which time-space is presumed to be gridded on a sheet of rubber which can then be stretched and folded but not cut or torn. The fabric of Monk's composition remains intact, but dramatically changed.

& *See also* **The Straight Horn Of Steve Lacy** (1960; p. 260), **Weal & Woe** (1972, 1973; p. 398)

PETER KOWALD
Born 21 April 1944, Meiningen, Germany; died 21 September 2002, New York City
Double bass

Was Da Ist
FMP CD 62
Kowald (b solo). 1994.

Peter Kowald said (1991): **'I don't play jazz and I don't play any instrument other than the bass, which was intended for European art music and then found itself playing different things, in New Orleans and Chicago and anywhere one floated up. I take sounds from all over, and I pause with respect in front of them, but I only pause: I don't hesitate to take from any music I hear, and use it.'**

One of the most individual of the European free players, Kowald is more often advanced as an influence on other players than for his own work. The catalogue is thin enough, but what is available is of consistently excellent quality, concentrated and intense, with an independence of spirit audible in the voice which recalls Pettiford and Mingus. In the late '80s, Kowald curated and participated in an epic sequence of improvising duos with European, American and Japanese players that opened up fresh contacts and associations in free music.

It may seem difficult, if not impossibly perverse, to justify our selecting a record of solo contrabass improvisations. We are unrepentant. This is music of the very highest order, technically adroit, emotionally and intellectually concentrated, and beautifully recorded. Only Derek Bailey and Evan Parker have shown themselves capable of sustained solo performance at this level; what distinguishes Kowald is the light, dry humour he brings to these pieces, philosophical quiddities that seem perfectly content not to be answered. Without other instruments in attendance, Kowald goes for a stronger and more than usually resonant attack which mitigates a slightly dry sound. A record to savour and ponder; a record to return to, as often as time allows.

EVAN PARKER &

Born 5 April 1944, Bristol, Gloucestershire, England
Tenor and soprano saxophones

50th Birthday Concert
Leo CD LR 212/213 2CD
Parker; Alexander von Schlippenbach (p); Barry Guy (b); Paul Lovens, Paul Lytton (d). April 1994.

Evan Parker says: **'It came in the period after I had left Incus and before psi was up and running, so I was reliant on other independents to record. Leo Feigin called and said: "But Evan, it muuuust be recorded. Leave it to me." He used all his old BBC connections to make sure it was done well. He got two good sets. Those two trios are still working, and people are still buying the CD. It was a great night.'**

'The echoing border zones ...' Robert Graves's poetry seems the ideal source for titles for these performances, which again combine Parker's gritty involvement in ideas and history, though this time the history is his own. The two trios represented his most important long-term associations. Despite the essential Englishness of much of his aesthetic (not the Englishness of the pastoralists or the Georgians, but of those who built an empire on empiricism and craft), Parker has always gravitated to the European scene. As he describes in an unwontedly personal liner-note, bassist Peter Kowald, promoter and label boss Jost Gebers and pianist Alex von Schlippenbach were largely responsible for widening his musical horizons, in terms of playing partnerships. The Schlippenbach trio with Lovens is the perfect counterbalance to the more familiarly documented work with Guy and Lytton. This is probably the only small group with two separate entries in this editon of the *Guide*: see under Schlippenbach (p. 401). The textures are more open and more concerned with radical harmonics. Lovens and Lytton are occasionally confused – verbally – even by people who know the scene well. They couldn't be mixed up even on the briefest hearing. Lovens is immensely detailed, a microsurgeon of the pulse, while Lytton tends to favour broader and more extended areas of sound, opening and unfolding like an anatomist. The long opening piece with Schlippenbach, 'Hero Of Nine Fingers', is supremely well argued, with Parker and the pianist trading ideas at a dazzling pace. This isn't energy playing, but it generates its own energies moment to moment. The only quibble is that disc one is just 45 minutes in length (and disc two a mere 40); but that does not alter the sheer brilliance of conception and execution.

The remaining pieces with Guy and Lytton seem particularly focused on this celebratory occasion. Rising 50 himself, Guy has regularly rethought his musical parameters, and one can almost hear him refining his language as he plays. Lytton is flawless on the long 'In Exultation', though he's the one musician on the set who probably isn't well served by the sound. The occasion, recorded in Dingwalls Club in north London, was very special. These documents are no less so. It would be hard to imagine music less ephemeral.

& *See also* **The Snake Decides** (1986; p. 506), **The Moment's Energy** (2007; p. 728); **SPONTANEOUS MUSIC ENSEMBLE, Quintessence** (1973–1974; p. 406)

CLAUDIO RODITI

Born 28 May 1946, Rio de Janeiro, Brazil
Trumpet

Free Wheelin'

Reservoir RSRCD 136
Roditi; Andres Boiarsky (ss, ts); Nick Brignola (ss, bs); Mark Soskin (p); Buster Williams (b); Chip White (d). July 1994.

Claudio Roditi said (1999): **'My mother's sister married an American man and it was spending a holiday with them in Bahia that opened up jazz to me. My uncle was interested and he told me about Charlie Parker and Dizzy Gillespie, Miles, modern things. There was a great Frank Rosolino album, too, with Sam Noto on trumpet on the *Stan Kenton Presents* series.'**

An eclectic musician who never sounds like he's butterflying from one style to the next, Roditi came up from Rio to study at Berklee and then settled in New York, though these days he turns up almost anywhere, doing a mix of things from Latin to relatively orthodox hard bop. Roditi doing a tribute to Lee Morgan sounds like a recipe for overcooking it. Yet *Free Wheelin'* comes close to being exactly the classic album the trumpeter might have in him. This is the best band he's had in the studio: Boiarsky is a heavyweight, and the rhythm section, especially the inimitable Williams, are right there with the horns. But it's Roditi's concentration of his own powers that impresses here. Without trading in any of his fire, he keeps all his solos tight and impeccable, which makes flare-ups like those on 'Trapped' and 'The Joker' all the more exciting. 'The Sidewinder' follows the original arrangement – in his notes Roditi confesses that he couldn't see any point in messing around with the original charts – and still sounds entirely different from Morgan's original. Nine of the ten tunes are from Morgan's own pen, but the new twist on 'A Night In Tunisia' – with trumpet overdubs and a two-soprano section – is a startling departure. Brignola guests on three and is a welcome visitor.

JOHN ZORN

Born 2 September 1953, New York City
Alto saxophone

Bar Kokhba

Tzadik TZ 7108
Zorn; Dave Douglas (t); David Krakauer, Chris Speed (cl); John Medeski (org, p); Anthony Coleman (p); Marc Ribot (g); Mark Feldman (vn); Erik Friedlander (clo); Greg Cohen, Mark Dresser (b); Kenny Wolleson (d). August 1994–March 1996.

Publisher of *The Wire*, Tony Herrington, says: **'The man is quite remarkable. He is up at 5 a.m. and he spends half the day on the phone to this huge constituency of people who know him as musical collaborator, teacher and guru, label boss, producer, landlord and friend. He has a whole culture shaped around him.'**

A good deal of Zorn's music falls outside the remit of this book, and this book is too small to deal adequately with the range of Zorn's music, which has covered free improvisation governed by game theory, quasi-bop projects, interpretations of Jewish traditional music, large-ensemble scores for movies and pretty much everything else in between.

A single sample does no justice to the man or his work, but we console ourselves with the thought that this applies to pretty much everyone else in the book and that choosing 50 Zorn projects wouldn't get much closer to exhausting his diversity.

A lifelong New Yorker, Zorn studied briefly in St Louis but made his mark with the circle of improvisers based in New York in the mid-'70s. He steadily came to wider attention through relentless work, composing, performing and eventually gaining major-label recognition, though this was soon sidelined in favour of his own label, Tzadik, which releases most of his work. Groups down the years include Naked City, Painkiller and Masada. Outspoken, furiously prolific but ruthless about quality control, Zorn has fashioned his own multiple-idiom music, of which jazz remains a buried but tangible part.

Zorn's major creative enterprise of the last 15 years has been a steady and passionate (re-)discovery of his own Jewish musical heritage. On Tzadik he has curated a sequence of records called 'Radical Jewish culture', but his own most direct input has been the improvising quartet he calls Masada, which has produced a very substantial body of work based on small, folkish-sounding themes that stand in the same relation to Zorn's work as Anthony Braxton's 'Ghost Trance' and 'language music' compositions do to his, with all the obvious differences accounted for. Masada has also incorporated other instrumental elements over time and *Bar Kokhba* is a fine example of how confidently Zorn expands the concept. These are exquisitely voiced folkloric essays, executed without strain. Zorn's own part in these ensembles is more distant than in the quartet, where he is inevitably the lead voice. The quartet is also more obviously a 'jazz' ensemble, where here the music sounds as if it arises out of the culture intact and without mediation, which is considerable testimony to his powers of synthesis and persuasion. It is exquisitely beautiful and often very moving. Douglas and Speed are the most effective solo performers, though Dresser's rich bass-playing is a huge asset. And yet, it is Zorn, as always, who dominates as composer/ historian if not this time as instrumentalist. That, though, is worth a footnote, for it is often forgotten just how fine an alto saxophonist Zorn is, fleet and boppish and with an unmistakable tonality that predates his active interest in Jewish musical culture; even then, its 'blue notes' always seemed to come from another place.

RICH PERRY

Born 25 July 1955, Cleveland, Ohio
Tenor saxophone

Beautiful Love

Steeplechase SCCD 31360
Perry; Jay Anderson (b); Victor Lewis (d). October 1994.

Rich Perry says: **'I listened to it yesterday, and as I thought, I've improved so much since that recording. I should record those tunes again; maybe I will because I've no other ideas at the moment! I must say I liked "But Not For Me" best. I remember Nils Winther also recorded me with Paul Bley that same week with Jay and Victor, kind of a package deal. Wish I could do that one over again, too! I came late to small-group recording, but the experience I got on those early Steeplechases really paid off down the road.'**

Previously hidden in big-band sections and sideman roles for some 20 years, the tenorman's absolute command goes with a soft-edged tone and an undemonstrative delivery that creates a paradox at the centre of his style. Other commentators have cited Getz, Marsh and Rollins among his models, yet Perry doesn't sound much like anyone else and his individuality takes some time to tease out; once it's evident, though, he suddenly becomes quite distinctive, even when he pops up on someone else's date. Perry manages to be consistent without being boring and there's little to choose between the early dates for Steeplechase. Instead, more depends on the context. *Beautiful Love* is the pick of the three, since without a piano the skill and judicious intensity of the sax-playing come through more clearly. There are truly marvellous improvisations on 'Prisoner Of Love', 'All The Things You Are' and 'I Fall In Love Too Easily' at the heart of the record, and for once eight quite lengthy tracks don't seem a moment too long. 'But Not For Me' has an almost philosophical calm at the heart, and at a stroke raises Perry to the first rank of young contemporaries. Anderson and the superb Lewis are also in good order.

JOHN SURMAN &

Born 30 August 1944, Tavistock, Devon, England
Baritone and soprano saxophones, bass clarinet, keyboards

A Biography Of The Rev. Absalom Dawe
ECM 523749-2
Surman (reeds, ky solo) October 1994.

John Surman says: **'It was inspired by my great-great-grandfather, who lived in Portesham, Dorset. I never met him, but I heard many, many stories as a youngster. How many were true I'll never know – but I found inspiration in the legend at any rate.'**

As long ago as 1972, the year after *Tales Of The Algonquin*, Surman had been experimenting with solo performance and with the possibilities of overdubbing. *Westering Home* is a spare, sometimes raw but very intense record. To some degree this was a necessary fix for a musician whose label contact had been severed, but it was also an aspect of music-making that fascinated him, particularly now that The Trio, his main improvising small group, was no more. New groups followed, including the all-saxophone trio SOS, but with the recording in 1975 of *Morning Glory*, and contact with the eponymous group's Scandinavian member, Terje Rypdal, Surman was in every way embarked on a course that would lead him to ECM.

He first recorded for Manfred Eicher in 1979. *Upon Reflection* was the first in a series of multi-tracked solo projects on which he improvised horn-lines over his own synthesizer tracks. It was similar to what he had been doing with SOS, but it also saw a strong return for his baritone-playing, which had been somewhat set aside in favour of the soprano. Now, Surman was required to play right through the 'section'. As Surman's facility with this kind of project grew, he placed steadily less emphasis on synthesized *ostinati* and more on the detailed interplay of horn-lines. Adding alto clarinet to his armoury delivered an important new timbre and tonality, and many of these pieces seem to be lighter and more plain-spoken than the earlier ECMs. It is the same mix of jazz, folk and church themes, however, the only difference lying in the more relaxed, less stressed opposition of tension and release, and in the significance accorded to individual lead-lines. Right at the heart of the album, ''Twas But Piety' marks almost a summing up of Surman's musical explorations up to that point, an impassioned saxophone piece, but with 'organ' accompaniment at beginning and end and with a loose and limber approach to counterpoint.

We are admirers of all Surman's solo ventures, but this one has a special quality that sets it apart.

& *See also* **Tales Of The Algonquin** (1971; p. 389); **SOS, SOS** (1975; p. 419)

RICHARD GALLIANO
Born 12 December 1950, Le Cannet, France
Accordion, piano, trombone

Laurita

Dreyfus FDM 36572
Galliano; Michel Portal (bcl); Didier Lockwood (vn); Toots Thielemans (hca); Palle Danielsson (b); Joey Baron (d). November 1994.

Richard Galliano said (1999): **'The accordion is a travelling instrument. It's not like a piano or an organ. You have it here, strapped to your front, on the train or in the street. That is why it is everywhere in world music.'**

Ubiquitous the accordion may be, but it has surprisingly little presence in jazz, and at present Galliano is its most distinguished practitioner. His background is that of French *musette*, which he has carried forward and modernized somewhat in the way his great mentor Astor Piazzolla modernized Argentinian tango.

Piazzolla is the presiding genius of modern accordion. Galliano is by no means in thrall to him, but like any accordion-player he draws heavily on Piazzolla themes, notably 'Libertango' and 'Milonga del Angel' on the wonderful *Laurita*. The core trio has a close understanding. Baron, that most musical of drummers, plays with real grace and delicacy and Danielsson is always lyrical. The guest players deliver exactly what you would expect of them, and no more. Their presence is welcome, but not necessary. Delightfully, this isn't just a record of swooning romanticism. A tribute to zydeco king Clifton Chenier is the penultimate track, giving the tail of the set a vibrant, upbeat, dancing quality that transforms its occasional Debussy-meets-Bill-Evans airs into something more robust and earthy. It's an almost perfectly balanced record.

JOHN GILL

Born 28 January 1954, New York City
Banjo, trombone, voice

Looking For A Little Bluebird

Stomp Off CD 1295
Gill; Chris Tyle, Duke Heitger (t); Frank Powers (cl, v); Steve Pistorius (p); Eddy Davis (bj, v); Vince Giordano (tba); Hal Smith (d). December 1994.

Stomp Off boss Bob Erdos said (1998): **'The label had a hand in putting this band together and what it gives you is a flavour of how Dixieland jazz might have sounded with modern audio fidelity.'**

Part of the Californian revival, Gill has multi-threaded credentials in a series of groups, including the alarmingly named Novelty Orchestra Of New Orleans, but driven by a sincere passion for New Orleans music. Shading between revivalism and a straight and strict re-creation of hot dance, Gill's outfit sometimes errs on the side of the latter, which will tend to switch off all but the more dedicated archivists. Gill plays trombone rather than banjo on the later sets, calls the group – which achieved considerable festival success in the later '90s – The Dixieland Serenaders, and has them play the stuffing out of a repertoire brimful of Oliver, Morton, Dodds – and Lu Watters-Turk Murphy revivalism. Except that this group actually sounds better than the oldtimers of San Franciscan jazz usually did. The two-trumpet front line blows over the rest of the band like a particularly cussed zephyr, and Giordano and Smith give the group a terrific lift even when they're playing a simple two-beat. The result is a shakedown of a lot of mothballed tunes that puts a new lease on almost all of them. We like *Looking For A Little Bluebird* for its maniacal 'Alligator Hop' and the beautiful extended treatment of 'Farewell To Storyville', and for Richard Bird's sound, which shoves the band right in your face while still giving them a full and clear balance. The sequel, *Take Me To the Midnight Cakewalk Ball*, is almost as good.

ABDULLAH IBRAHIM &

Born Adolphe (Dollar) Johannes Brand, also known as Xahur, 9 October 1934, Cape Town, South Africa
Piano, flute, voice

Yarona
Tiptoe 888820
Ibrahim; Marcus McLaurine (b); George Johnson (d). January 1995.

Abdullah Ibrahim said (1993): **'We were in Seattle when [Nelson Mandela] was set free. We knew from ANC that something was going on, that something large was going to be resolved, and by peaceful means. We watched all night on television, a very emotional time.'**

Ibrahim's career has obviously reflected to a large degree the situation in his native South Africa, which changed on 11 February 1990 when 'Madiba' (Nelson Mandela) was freed from jail. One does not hear an immediate loosening in Ibrahim's music, but certain buried currents do begin to rise to the surface. He had for so long sublimated his anger into expression that there was no question of that energy abating.

Yarona is a truly magisterial performance by the 60-year-old, bringing the house down at Sweet Basil in New York City. He still hits the piano very hard, using the bass almost as a drone, alternating narrow intervals and often allowing the drummer considerable licence to range outside the metre. The left hand is relentless and, in the other sense, timeless, the melody-lines stripped down and ritualized. 'Duke 88' once again acknowledges a personal debt. 'Nisa' is an exclamatory hymn to another, the womenfolk of South Africa. There is a reworking of 'African Marketplace' and a concert outing for 'Stardance', one of the lovelier themes from the *Chocolat* soundtrack. The love song 'Cherry' (not, as one critic assumed, a tribute to the trumpeter) shows his more lyrical side.

& *See also* **African Sketchbook** (1969; p. 366)

JIM HALL

Born 4 December 1930, Buffalo, New York
Guitar

Dialogues
Telarc CD 83369
Hall; Tom Harrell (flhn); Joe Lovano (ts); Bill Frisell, Mike Stern (g); Gil Goldstein (acc); Scott Colley (b); Andy Watson (d). February 1995.

Jim Hall said (1992): **'When I was a young teenager, about 13 years old, I heard a Charlie Christian record: "Grand Slam". That was it. That was my life's calling, right there.'**

Hall's smooth, gentlemanly approach got seriously interesting only once he had passed his 60th birthday and started to work with larger groups. Totally professional, Hall delivers reliably every time, with no apparent difference in approach between live and studio sessions. The former don't lack for polish but nor do they ramble on any longer than they need to. Hall can never be accused of redundancy, for his solos are always unimpeachably controlled. Nor can he be described without qualification as a mainstream swinger, for he has impeccable credentials with some of the key modernists, appearing on records with Jimmy Giuffre, Sonny Rollins, Art Farmer, even with John Lewis, Gunther Schuller and Ornette Coleman in a Third Stream context, and in more recent times with fellow guitarists Pat Metheny and Bill Frisell as well. He studied classical music and later took an interest in Argentinian music too, and both of those surface – often subliminally – in his mature work.

We wouldn't suggest that Hall isn't worth listening to before 1990, but there is a curious shortfall in the surviving discography that might suggest such a thing. Concord, Music-masters and Creed Taylor's CTI all recorded him, but not much survives from that time, and it wasn't until the (almost) solo *Dedications & Inspirations*, made for Telarc in 1993 with an experimental new playback system which allowed him to duet with himself, that Hall started to sound like a major recording artist. The solo concept was to take a step further on *Dialogues*, though there are only two duet tracks, both with Goldstein on his regular and bass accordion. The rest are small-group performances designed to highlight horns and guitar, and with Colley and Watson taking pretty much a back seat. With the exception of the closing 'Skylark', which features Harrell in exquisite form, all the tunes are Hall originals, written with a playing partner in mind – 'Frisell Frazzle', 'Calypso Joe', and 'Stern Stuff' – and it is Mike Stern who delivers the surprise of the session with an offbeat blues sound on 'Uncle Ed'. Frisell is in typically playful form on the opening dedication, reappearing on 'Simple Things', which has more of a country feel. The saxophonist has had more convincing days, but he manages to give his two appearances a reasonably personal slant. Telarc recordings are famously good, but on this occasion John Snyder and Jane Hall have outdone themselves. Holding back a notch on the rhythm section was a risky stratagem, but what they have produced has near-perfect balance and no loss of definition.

BRIAN LEMON
Born 11 February 1937, Nottingham, England
Piano

But Beautiful
Zephyr ZE CD 1
Lemon; Dave Cliff (g); Dave Green (b); Allan Ganley (d). January & March 1995.

Bassist Dave Green said (1996): **'He's solid, he's forgotten more songs than most piano-players will ever learn, but, above all, he's never boring.'**

'Is that a nickname?' an American fan asked on being told who the piano-player was. 'If so, it's not just cruel, it's irrelevant. He's terrific.' He is, indeed, and has been for five decades, though it was John Bune's lemon-liveried Zephyr imprint that put the pianist on the recording map. The label debut throws up three bars from the first. It's a quality record. The title-track is a model of its kind, and the medley of 'Exactly Like You' and 'I Thought About You' works at all sorts of levels. A version of Sonny Rollins's 'St Thomas' doesn't sit quite as obviously for Lemon's technique but, following as it does the one original, 'Blues For Suzanna', it underlines his other gift, the pacing and direction of a set. The most common criticism of the records that followed is that they tend to be polite, perhaps a little chummy, but jazz isn't all sparring and intrigue. Sometimes it's possible to let the songs speak for themselves, and Lemon does this with sure-footed intuition.

DAVE DOUGLAS &
Born 24 March 1963, Montclair, New Jersey
Trumpet

Constellations
hatOLOGY CD 673
Douglas; Brad Schoeppach (g); Jim Black (d, perc). February 1995.

Label boss Werner Uehlinger reports Dave Douglas's reaction to the record: **'Yes, that was a good day!'**

Fifteen years ago, the authors of the *Guide* were calling – together and severally – for a moratorium on the cult of Miles Davis and due attention to a rising generation of trumpet masters, and most particularly Dave Douglas. He wasn't the least obvious horse to back, a player of staggering technique and laconic but capacious musical vision, who seemed effortlessly to take in early jazz, the avant-vernacular of Lester Bowie, Balkan music and much else in between. He began improvising while an exchange student in Spain and had an extended musical education; not just the requisite Berklee sojourn, but the New England Conservatory and New York University as well. The alumnus is an individualist whose grasp of history is apparent mainly in elision and omission rather than homage. Here was a contemporary jazz artist confident enough to include Webern in one early set-list and with a purview that went beyond music to world affairs: no closeted aesthete or style-policeman.

Douglas has led a number of different groups, more recently Charms Of The Night Sky, which is named after a fine Winter & Winter record. The Tiny Bell Trio with Brad Schoeppach (now Shepik) and Jim Black was perhaps his first important ensemble, a lean, flexible group with an intriguing Balkan-improv remit.

The best of the Tiny Bell records, *Constellations* was recorded off-road but mid-tour. One hears immediately that this is a working unit. Douglas's Balkan interests – both musical and political – come through strongly. 'Taking Sides' is inspired by the brutal civil war in the former Yugoslavia, a raw, powerful expression of anger and mourning. In an entirely different vein, 'Maquiladoras' takes up cudgels for low-paid migrant workers. 'Scriabin' is a thoughtful essay in extreme chromaticism, almost serial in quality, and 'Hope Ring True' sounds like '60s agit-prop jazz. To underline his eclecticism and sense of history, Douglas hands the pianoless group a forgotten Herbie Nichols theme, 'The Gig', and makes it sound utterly contemporary as well. Douglas seems confident in his partners, allowing Black in particular to stretch out and express himself. Schoeppach throws deliciously complex harmonic shapes, a crushed-velvet foil to the trumpeter's bright lines.

& *See also* **Convergence** (1998; p. 623)

TONY COE
Born 29 November 1934, Canterbury, Kent, England
Clarinet, tenor saxophone

Captain Coe's Famous Racearound
Storyville STCD 4206
Coe; Danish Radio Jazz Orchestra. March 1995.

Saxophonist John Dankworth said (1998): **'French players and fans ask you about *Tonee Coe*, the Danes have given him this big jazz prize, an American lady asked me if I knew Tony Co-ay ... the only place he doesn't seem to be appreciated is England.'**

Possessed of a glorious clarinet sound and an approach on tenor saxophone that often resembles Paul Gonsalves (who spent his last period in the UK, so there may be a connection), Coe is at home in almost any style from Dixieland to free, and has even – like his mentor, Alan Hacker – experimented in more formal settings. He took over the Plas Johnson saxophone role in later *Pink Panther* films and it is rumoured he played on a Beatles recording, though Coe himself has forgotten the occasion.

His albums are dotted about all over the place, on labels as improbably matched as Nato, hat ART, Storyville, between the line, Hep and Zephyr, and despite the warm admiration of fans he has always seemed to work just under the radar. Fortunately, there are exceptions. In 1995, Coe was deservedly awarded the Jazzpar Prize, which brings a big-band performance as part of the award. The title-piece makes a strong and lyrical climax to an album that combines large-scale charts with a small combo that included Bob Brookmeyer, David Hazeltine, Henrik Bolberg Pedersen, Thomas Ovesen and Steve Argüelles. In addition to Coe, there are compositions by Brookmeyer, Argüelles and Maria Schneider. Unusual for a Jazzpar winner to be so retiring about his own work, but Coe won his award primarily as a player, one suspects, and so 'Fools Rush In' and 'How Long Has This Been Going On?' (the latter for full orchestra) are both superb. Coe's tone is as pure as spring water, with none of the quavering 'oboe' sound he so much dislikes in the post-Coltrane players.

JOE MORRIS &

Born 13 September 1955, New Haven, Connecticut
Guitar, double bass

No Vertigo
Leo CD LR 226
Morris (g, mand, banjouke solo). April 1995.

Joe Morris says: **'This is the manifestation of 20 years of figuring out that my interest in music was going to present itself in more than one approach. One producer I knew found fault with my plan to separate the different tracks by instrument. He thought I should mix up the sequence. But it really has to be the way it is because they are all so different.'**

The Boston-based guitarist has a highly distinctive playing style, almost always in fast, single-note lines, with distinctive mid-phrase trills and a notable use of space. A charter member of the Boston Improvisers Group, Morris was an actively eclectic sideman and local star before he made it big as a recording artist. He has a facility for straight blues and fusion playing, but works in a pumped-up free style that works in quite stark, abstract ways. His self-determination extended to putting out records on his own Riti label, which has undergone a renaissance.

It may seem excessive to include two Morris records from within essentially the same time period, but it is our conviction that the guitarist – who also plays double bass when occasion demands – is one of the most important musicians of recent times and it is testimony to his prodigal talent that no artist in this book provoked more changes of mind as to which records to highlight. If there were a new edition tomorrow, there might be two different choices.

No Vertigo is a solo *tour de force*. Morris has obviously been influenced by British improviser Derek Bailey. His acoustic work is very reminiscent of Bailey's '70s work but with a hint of a jazz groove always hovering in the background, which Bailey seldom permits. He also includes tracks on an electric instrument (the long, very detailed 'For Adolphus Mica'), banjouke ('Long Carry') and even mandolin (a sequence called 'The Edges'). There is nothing slipshod about this music and neither do the individual instruments fall back into stereotypical 'voices' – 'banjo means folk, electric means rock' – something that even Bill Frisell has been guilty of. Even without playing partners Morris is a stern disciplinarian and the defining characteristic of all his music is a kind of responsiveness to context and a willingness to let the music exist spatially, as an object of attention, rather than as simply a passing phenomenon, each moment eaten up by the one that follows.

& *See also* **A Cloud Of Black Birds** (1998; p. 631)

ROY HARGROVE
Born 16 October 1969, Waco, Texas
Trumpet, flugelhorn

Parker's Mood
Verve 527907-2
Hargrove; Stephen Scott (p); Christian McBride (b). April 1995.

Roy Hargrove said (1996): **'Bop, rap: it doesn't seem to me so far apart. Parker's tunes were like parts of solos, with everything going round to the beginning again. You listen to that and you listen to … LL Cool J or KRS-One, and it's not so very different.'**

Spotted by Wynton Marsalis – who probably doesn't share his insistence on the continuity of black vernacular music from hot jazz to rap – Hargrove was one of the first post-Miles trumpeters to show an equal facility in post-bop and other forms. He went on to record eclectically, but with jazz always in the foreground. Interestingly, Hargrove only spent a year at Berklee. He's a raw, self-determined talent, who doesn't appreciate academic solutions. Recorded in Parker's 75th anniversary year, *Parker's Mood* is a delightful meeting of three young masters, improvising on 16 themes from Bird's repertoire. Hargrove's luminous treatment of 'Laura' again suggests he may be turning into one of the music's pre-eminent ballad players, but it's the inventive interplay between the three men that takes the session to its high level. One clever aspect of the record is that it isn't always three guys. 'Chasin' the Bird' is done as a trumpet/bass duet and other tracks are taken as solos. Scott, sometimes burdened on his own records, plays as freely as he ever has, and McBride is simply terrific. No musician of his time provokes more curiosity in us, even if at times the signs of greatness refuse to break through.

DJANGO BATES
Born Leon Bates, 2 October 1960, Beckenham, Kent, England
Piano, keyboards, peckhorn, tenor horn

Summer Fruits (And Unrest)
Winter & Winter 919065
Bates; Sid Gauld, Chris Batchelor (t); Roland Bates (tb); Richard Henry (btb); Eddie Parker (f, bf); Sarah Homer (cl, bcl); Iain Ballamy (ss, as); Steve Buckley (ss, as, bcl); Mark Lockheart (ts); Barak Schmool (ts, picc, bsx); Julian Argüelles (bs); Stuart Hall (g, vn, bj); Steve Watts, Michael Mondesir (b); Martin France (d); Thebe Lipere (perc). 1995.

Django Bates said (2003): **'I'm not really interested in jamming, that side of jazz. I need every piece to have its own character and shape and that comes from knowing the musicians you work with and writing things that you know they can play – not just in terms of technique but that they might do something interesting with.'**

After stints with London bands Borderline and Zila, Bates worked with his own small group Human Chain and was a central player in the big band Loose Tubes, whose sophomoric humour sometimes camouflaged Bates's brilliance as a composer. He remains committed to a view of jazz that allows play and playfulness full rein, but inevitably Britain took revenge on his creativity by starving him of commissions. Bates wisely decamped to Denmark and his occasional home visits are paid for in *kroner*.

Summer Fruits is the first part of a loose, seasonal cycle of records that also includes *Winters Fires (And Homes Ablaze)*, the solo piano album *Autumn Fire (And Green Shoots)* and, belatedly, *Spring is Here (Shall We Dance?)*. The first record, originally on JMT, where everything was subject to a cold seasonal wind, alternates big-band arrangements with tracks from Bates's Human Chain. It's not an entirely happy combination and, for once, one feels a need for two discs to reflect what sound like rather different aspects of his musical personality. The vices of Loose Tubes are still in evidence: over-writing, a blokey exuberance and a callow suspicion of straightforward expression. Bates's dense scores and the pieces for Delightful Precipice (the big band) are thickly notated. They're undeniably lively, but the circus pieces, inspired by an earlier collaboration, are glibly ironic, and some of the most virtuosic scoring is lost in 'off-the-cuff' gestures. The Human Chain tracks, notably 'Food For Plankton (In Detail)' and 'Little Petherick' (which provides the best Bates solo of the disc) are much more coherent.

SAM RIVERS &

Born 25 September 1923 (some sources still cite 1930), Reno, Oklahoma
Tenor and soprano saxophones, flute

Portrait
FMP CD 82
Rivers (ts, ss, f, p, v solo). June 1995.

Sam Rivers said (1996): **'It's important to make contact with yourself from time to time, see who's in there, what he's doing, whether there's anything you can take from it and apply to your work.'**

A self-portrait presumably and of the artist at over 70, espousing what he describes in a notably effusive liner-note as an 'uninhibited emotion-driven free-flowing river of vibrant, bold, melodic inventions'. It's a piece of text that runs dangerously close to self-review: 'dazzling', 'musical perfection', 'eloquently phrased' and so on. What saves it is that there is hardly a word with which one might disagree. These unaccompanied essays, with their characteristic one-word titles – 'Image', 'Reflection', 'Shadow' and the overlong 'Cameo' – are magnificently crafted and thoroughly imbued with the creator's personality. Full attributions are given for all the instruments used, Keilwerth saxophones, a Bösendorfer Imperial and a Gemeinhardt flute, while under 'voice' it says laconically 'Sam Rivers', which is a version of 'model's own' on the fashion pages. Again, it makes complete sense, for this is the most thoroughly individual thing he has done for many years, a magnificent testament to his creative range, his generosity of spirit and his great, great intelligence.

& *See also* **Fuchsia Swing Song** (1964; p. 311), **Colors** (1982; p. 471)

JANE IRA BLOOM

Born 1955, Boston, Massachusetts
Soprano saxophone, electronics

The Nearness
Arabesque AJ0120
Bloom; Kenny Wheeler (t, flhn); Julian Priester (tb); Fred Hersch (p); Bobby Previte (d). July 1995.

Jane Ira Bloom remembers: **'We recorded *The Nearness* in one of the worst summer heat waves in NYC. First the studio air conditioning went out. Then the independent mix controls went on the fritz, so we would end up recording the entire album with a single headphone mix. At one point, we canned the headphones altogether and recorded on radar ears alone!'**

It's an instrument that claims a very particular loyalty from its exponents, but there are still very few soprano specialists around. Bloom went to Yale and Berklee, before moving to New York and settling on the straight horn. She ran her own Outline label for a while, and seems to have revived it recently. Some of her work in the '80s – including a couple of quickly deleted Columbias – suggest that she may have become disenchanted with straight-ahead jazz, but her spare, considered delivery, eschewing vibrato and sentimentality alike, resembles nothing else in contemporary jazz.

Bloom made an impressive return to form in the early '90s with a new Arabesque contract. *Art And Aviation* was intended to suggest a concept of flying through dark skies and the music does indeed soar and glide. It introduced a partnership with Kenny Wheeler, who's in terrific form, the two horns so confident in formation that there are unintended gasps at every turn. It's quite frosty music, and the touches of live electronics suggest some high-atmosphere event, but this is all to the good on an otherwise overheated and earth-bound scene.

The surprise card on *Nearness* is Priester and, with no electronics and several standards in the programme, this might have been an orthodox blowing record. Instead, Bloom recasts every melody and form in refreshing ways. The originals are typically thoughtful: 'Flat6 Bop' puts a complex harmonic idea inside a rawly exciting *ostinato* form, and 'The All-Diesel Kitchen Of Tomorrow' has a Zappa-like quality that goes beyond the title. Incredibly, she finds something new to do with 'Round Midnight', here done as a sober dance for the horns. The ballads 'The Nearness Of You' and 'In The Wee Small Hours' are almost spoken, with cadences of melody soft enough to suggest music drifting down from the stars. Wheeler is irresistible, the rhythm section marvellous, and the original 'It's A Corrugated World' keeps navel-gazing at bay. Why's she not better known?

NED ROTHENBERG
Born 15 September 1956, Boston, Massachusetts
Reeds

Power Lines
New World NW 80476
Rothenberg; Dave Douglas (t); Josh Roseman (tb); Kenny Berger (bs, bcl); Mark Feldman (vn); Ruth Siegler (vla); Erik Friedlander (clo); Mark Dresser (b); Michael Sarin (d); Glen Velez (frame d). August 1995.

Ned Rothenberg says: 'I'm tremendously proud of *Power Lines*, but sorry that I couldn't make more music with this aggregation. It took a number of factors falling into place, a generous commission for the composition, the availability of a superb group of players, and a golden age at New World, with serious budgets for projects like this. The engineer, James Farber, did a superb job of giving transparency to this multi-layered music.'

A charter member of the New Winds ensemble, Rothenberg has embraced many branches of the music, from Dolphy-influenced post-bop to formal composition and solo improvisation. He is one of the few Westerners to sound convincing on shakuhachi. Rothenberg refers to solo improvisation – of which he has released some particularly interesting examples on the Tzadik *Lumina Recordings* and the Leo *The Crux* – but here he is with a much larger group that allows him to continue those experiments in a responsive and beautifully modulated musical environment.

If this is 'avant-garde jazz', bring it on! Rothenberg plays hard *ostinati* runs so long and complex you suspect he must be fitted with gills. Five beautifully extended tracks conclude with the 20-minute-plus 'In The Rotation', which builds to a whooping climax that brings everyone in. The start's every bit as good, with 'Hidalgo' calling the band in like a trumpeter at a corrida. Berger gives it all a solid bottom end, allowing Dresser to improvise more freely than he might otherwise. As he would time and again in future years, Rothenberg gets the strings fully involved and insists that they swing and stomp, too, rather than simply adding colour-washes in the background. Sarin's a great drummer for this kind of project, but Velez adds a special dimension on his two tracks. For some listeners and critics, unaccompanied playing provides a quick listening fix (not so true for the performer!), with no need to consider overlapping lines, textures and tonalities. *The Crux* is a tremendous record, but *Power Lines* is on a different order of scale.

JACK WALRATH
Born 5 May 1946, Stuart, Florida
Trumpet

Solidarity
ACT 9241
Walrath; Ralph Reichert (sax); Buggy Braune (p); Christian Havel (g, v); Andreas Henze (b); Joris Dudli (d).
August 1995.

Jack Walrath said (1987): **'Mingus taught me that there's no point knowing the music if you can't also hear it, and you'll notice I didn't say "play it" or "give it some expression". You have to hear it, and good hearing is a kind of energy you can detect in a band, an active presence.'**

Walrath is a brassy, upfront kind of trumpet man and has been a stalwart in some strong repertory bands. He has terrific technique, strong ideas and great humour (with a particular obsession for horror films) but has been so busy over the years that he's made surprisingly little impact as a leader. He has tended to bury himself away in collective groups – Revival and Change being two early examples, the Masters of Suspense a more recent one – or in the hard-school of the Mingus band, where he served for five demanding years in the mid- to late '70s. In addition, he popped up in Europe, playing with the likes of Spirit Level and the majority of his records are on European labels: Steeplechase, TCB and ACT.

Solidarity is a blues-soaked and – as Jack points out – very American-sounding recording that could again almost be a Mingus offshoot. Reichert's father owns the Hamburg club where the recording was made; it's an atmospheric place and a strong, smouldering set. The two-part 'Hamburg Concerto' and the title-track bespeak anew Walrath's ability to give long forms the immediacy and the visceral punch of a simple blues, while 'Hot-Dog For Lunch', 'Political Suicide' and 'Psychotic Indifference' underline his more capricious and satirical side. Reichert claims joint honours, and his father's production yields up a sound which favours the horns over the rest of the group – not overwhelmingly so, but with a definite edge. America's loss; Europe's gain.

KENNY GARRETT
Born 10 October 1960, Detroit, Michigan
Alto saxophone

Triology
Warner Bros 9 45731
Garrett; Kiyoshi Kitagawa, Charnett Moffett (b); Brian Blade (d). 1995.

To be spoken in a hoarse, papery whisper: **'Kid, you sound like you're wearing Sonny Stitt's dirty drawers.'**

Miles Davis's pungent summing-up is typically accurate. Garrett's characteristic sound does not simply follow the familiar 'Charlie Parker line' but proposes other ways out of bebop, and in particular Stitt's more elongated phrasing and more literal take on the blues. Garrett's father was an amateur musician and though he has a solid music education, young Kenny gained his skills working on the local scene, including an R&B stint with organist Lymon Woodward. His major break, of course, was the stint with Miles, during which Garrett seemed to be treated with more respect and consideration than most of Miles's latter-day saxophone-players.

Garrett made a strong debut with a record on Criss Cross, but then made a promising switch to Atlantic, who were again promoting creative jazz. His first major-label recordings *Prisoner Of Love* and *African Exchange Student* made an impact but were scarcely around long enough for the majority of hard-bop fans to catch up. Garrett moved again, to Warners, and after a promising start (*Black Hope*) and a disappointing sequel (*Threshold*) delivered the record everyone knew he was capable of.

Triology is a very special record, made with Garrett's working trio (Moffett's on a couple of tracks). Garrett is still content to play standards and repertoire pieces, and he brings fresh angles to Brubeck's 'In Your Own Sweet Way' and the old warhorse 'Giant Steps', which he plays with a respectful insouciance; his major encounter with Coltrane was still to come, in the following year's *Pursuance*. He also includes dedications to Joe Henderson and Sonny Rollins, suggesting a more discursive and linear approach to his line. The saxophone tone is not quite as hard and forthright as on some of the early records, but what one notices more than anything is a newly mature reticence. Garrett never overpacks his line. There's refreshingly little ego on show, and *Triology* suggests the work of a young master musician who knows his place in the tradition.

JOE MANERI

Born 9 February 1927, Brooklyn, New York; died 24 August 2009, Boston, Massachusetts
Alto saxophone, clarinet

Three Men Walking
ECM 531023-2
Maneri; Joe Morris (g); Mat Maneri (vn). October–November 1995.

Joe Maneri said (1996): **'I didn't do so well at school. I had disabilities with regular schooling, but my refuge – or revenge – was to make up my own languages. In *there*, I knew everything and could do anything.'**

Maneri was 'discovered' only rather late in his career. He learned clarinet as a youngster and played with a succession of dance and other bands, often incorporating elements of Greek *syrto*, Turkish and klezmer music. After the war, he began studying 12-tone music and experimenting with microtones. He made some recordings at the start of the '60s, which have been reissued, but pretty much dropped from sight after that. In 1970, he was appointed to the faculty of the New England Conservatory of Music and published *Preliminary Studies in the Virtual Pitch Continuum*, still the essential book on microtonality.

Maneri's coming-out as a *bona fide* star was at the 1992 Montreal Jazz Festival, where he appeared alongside Paul Bley, an old associate from New York days. The buzz was immediate, and comparisons were made – somewhat misleadingly – to Ornette Coleman's controversial emergence 35 years before. There are parallels, but the differences are obvious and more important.

As with Hal Russell, Maneri's belated apotheosis was confirmed by a call from ECM. It was apparently Bley, that tireless and selfless talent scout, who put the label in touch. The acoustic is all wrong, but Maneri sounds wonderful in this context. He had been working extensively with his violinist son Mat, but also in a quartet with Randy Peterson and John Lockwood. The *Three Men Walking* line-up has a different dimension. The album title comes from a Giacometti sculpture of three attenuated figures, insecurely attached to the ground and heading off in different directions, yet for the moment bound to the same patch of earth. It's a lovely visual echo of music that is both airy and earthy, solid and insubstantial, jazz and something else. As with other ECM sessions of this vintage, the group breaks down into its constituents. Joe opens on unaccompanied clarinet, a sound harder and darker than Giuffre's, though superficially similar. The group improvisations, 'Bird's [*sic*] In The Belfry', 'Three Men Walking' and 'Arc And Point', are exceptional, but the features for Mat and Joe are equally impressive, underlining the different idioms and responses at work in this material. While Mat seems resolutely committed to his father's idiom, often using the lower end of his six-string electric violin as the bass and percussion voice, Morris often sounds detached and even remote – but companionably so, the most errant of those three bronze men. The one standard in the book at this point, 'What's New', was a revelation in performance and is again here, richly rethought and brightly played. 'For Josef Schmid' is a little bouquet to the man who taught Joe the 'Schoenberg method'.

Maneri went on to introduce his private poetic language on a later ECM date, *Tales Of Rohnlief*, on which he and Mat worked with bassist Barre Phillips, but one can hear that sensibility at work here. Listening to *Three Men Walking* is like wakening suddenly in a foreign country, with strange voices and musical sounds: exhilarating and frightening by turns.

FRANK LOWE
Born 24 June 1943, Memphis, Tennessee; died 19 September 2003, New York City
Tenor saxophone

Bodies & Soul
CIMP 104
Lowe; Tim Flood (b); Charles Moffett (d). November 1995.

Frank Lowe said (1984): **'Soon as that mic is switched on, then I get real nervous. It's not that I think I'm going to make a *mistake*, or that some cat ain't going to *like* what I do. It's not that. It's because I think: that's my life going down on that little strip of stuff. That's my *life*, man!'**

Like fellow Tennessean George Coleman, Lowe had little truck with the scorched-earth radicalism of his generation, constantly asserting an unfashionable interest in classic swing players like Chu Berry and proto-boppers like Don Byas. His career was cut short, so there's less of Lowe on record than one might wish, which makes the survivors that bit more precious. There's a good early ESP-Disk release and a superb Black Saint called *The Flam*. After that, it thins out. The dearth of albums also, to be fair, reflects the saxophonist's diffidence and suspicion of the studio process. As often with CIMP discs, there's a good deal of information on *Bodies & Soul* about the recording session. It seems Lowe was dissatisfied with many of the early takes on this date, re-recording pieces by Coltrane ('Impressions') and Don Cherry ('Art Deco') several times, seven times in one case, until he was satisfied.

The group's as spare and stern as the great Ornette Coleman Trio of the '60s, which Moffett also graced, though it's the previously unrecorded Flood who's the revelation. It's a terrific recording, ideally caught in CIMP's signature veritism. There is a lot of music here, with material by Pharoah Sanders and Ornette ('Happy House') in addition to the Coltrane and Cherry material and two original Lowe compositions dedicated to the trumpeter, who had died the previous month. Listening again to 'Impressions' in full awareness of the pains Lowe took over it, and thinking why it opens the set, one has to conclude that the saxophonist wanted to demonstrate both respect for and distance from Coltrane's and, later, Coleman's language. By placing 'Body And Soul' last, he shows more clearly than ever before how much he sees himself standing on the shoulders of earlier giants. It's a delicate performance, unaccompanied, lighter-toned and more intimate than Lowe often is.

Part 2:
1996–2000

MAKANDA KEN MCINTYRE

Born 7 September 1931, Boston, Massachusetts; died 13 June 2001, New York City
Alto saxophone, flute, oboe, bassoon, others

In The Wind: The Woodwind Quartets
Passin Thru 41220
McIntyre (overdubbed ss, as, ts, bs; f, af, bf; cl, acl, bcl; ob, ehn, bsn). October 1995, April 1996.

Ken McIntyre said (1985): **'I feel like I'm outside. Even friends would say they didn't understand what I was doing, and that pushes you inside yourself. I know I hear things differently to some, very high up. If you understand that and want that, I'm your man. If not, I'll do my own thing.'**

It remains McIntyre's misfortune to be remembered chiefly for his brief association with Eric Dolphy. Early appearances suggest a musician deeply influenced by Parker, but sounding like his own man in the search for a language beyond the orthodoxies of bebop. With the like-minded Dolphy in tow, McIntyre made a more promising excursion on the well-named *Looking Ahead*, which in 1960 was one of the most progressive recordings of its time. With Dolphy's rise, though, McIntyre seemed to recede from view and after *Year Of The Iron Sheep* for United Artists there wasn't any continuity of recording. He made some interesting albums down the years, but only a Dolphy tribute project kept him in view at the start of the '90s, a period when he also adopted his new first name.

Towards the end of his life, with fresh interest in the music of his early period, McIntyre enjoyed a resurgence. *In The Wind* is a quite astonishing curtain-call, posthumously released. The title is oddly moving, for however much artifice there necessarily is in over-dubbing multiple horn parts, these 11 performances have an entirely natural and evanescent quality that suggests they happened spontaneously. In terms of instrumentation, the most familiar sounds here are those of the two saxophone quartets. 'Puunti' is a gentle calypso, initially stated by the soprano, but featuring the other horns in turn, with the baritone kicking in last with a weighty but still limber solo. 'Black Sugar Cane' is even more remarkable; hard to believe that Makanda had to co-ordinate the different solo parts in the studio. He opens with an old favourite, 'Peas'N'Rice', another Caribbean-flavoured line which has appeared throughout his career, but played here on clarinets. There's another calypso – this time for flutes – in 'Amy'. On this, the final cut of the set, McIntyre again varies the timbres and textures wonderfully, vocalizing and overblowing like Roland Kirk. The other flute pieces are more obviously lyrical, but their accessibility doesn't in any way compromise the astonishing harmonic sophistication of 'Blanche' or 'Charsee'. The double-reed cuts are the furthest from conventional jazz instrumentation, but they're arguably the most swingingly integrated things on the album. 'Chitlins And Cavyah' is raw and funky, while 'Chasing The Sun' sits among McIntyre's neglected classics, with a harmonic freight that will take even quick-eared listeners some time to unravel.

All in all, a record to savour over time, and a fitting memorial to a genuine original who diverted his talent to helping others.

DAVID MURRAY&

Born 19 February 1955, Berkeley, California
Tenor saxophone, bass clarinet

Dark Star

Astor Place TCD 4002
Murray; Omar Kabir, Hugh Ragin, James Zollar (t); Craig Harris (tb); Robert Irving III (p, org, syn); Bob Weir (g); Fred Hopkins (b); Renzell Merritt (d). January 1996.

David Murray said (1997): **'Listen, I'm an American – a Californian – born 1955. How could I *not* respond to the Grateful Dead. What does it have to do with *jazz*? What did George Gershwin have to do – really – with jazz? There's no difference.'**

It was David Crosby who described the Grateful Dead's music as 'Electronic Dixieland' and there were few jazz musicians more attuned to the idea of a continuum of American music, into and out of African-American strains, than David Murray. It is on the face of it odd that the Dead's long, free-form jams on what were essentially country and blues themes should ever have seemed different from, let alone antithetical to, modern jazz. Jazz coverage of Jimi Hendrix's music – by Gil Evans and others – opened the doors.

Listening to this tribute, recorded not long after Jerry Garcia's death, it's not hard to see what Crosby means, and the only surprise is that no one had thought of turning to the Dead's long, floating lines and open-ended aesthetic before. The material is far from predictable. It includes things like the traditional 'Samson And Delilah' and Bob Weir's 'One More Saturday Night' but saves the real joys for what was the vocal entry on 'Dark Star'. In keeping with the Dead's own philosophy, there is more emphasis on group interplay than on soloing as such, though Murray does tend to dominate the foreground, sounding ever more like one of the swing-era masters, effortlessly melodic but increasingly spare and unhurried. It might be argued that a record where he pays homage to other composers does disservice to his own writing, but Murray was at a point of transition here, having set down some of the best jazz themes of recent times in his '80s work and not yet embarked on the new cross-cultural journey that took him through the start of the new millennium. The group is tight and loose in all the right places. Sometimes the brasses don't seem quite right, but that has more to do with their position in the mix than anything else. Bob Weir is on hand for 'Shoulda Had Been Me' to add a seal of approval.

& *See also* **Ming** (1980; p. 458); **WORLD SAXOPHONE QUARTET, W.S.Q.** (1980; p. 456)

TOMASZ STAŃKO&

Born 11 July 1942, Rzeszów, Poland
Trumpet

Leosia

ECM 531693-2
Stańko; Bobo Stenson (p); Anders Jormin (b); Tony Oxley (d). January 1996.

Tomasz Stańko says: **'Leosia is one of my most beloved albums. I recorded it just after the passing of my mother, who friends nicknamed "Leosia", and there is something about passing on it, a reverie on existence and love. I grieved her death very profoundly and I think it shows in the music – in the bleak "Morning Heavy Song", the redefined "Hungry Howl" that we first played with Edward Vesala, and a symbol of my personal philosophy "Die Weisheit Von Le Comte Lautréamont". A bleak production, and very typical for me.'**

Stańko's imagination is fired as much by words and by visual images as by music. He is certainly not confined to jazz formulae, and at first hearing his music might seem to have more kinship with the abstract experimentalism of the Polish avant-garde than with orthodox or even free jazz. This is deceptive, for the trumpeter is deeply versed in the defining elements of jazz. His first big influence was Chet Baker, he says, though subsequently Miles Davis would become almost as important.

Totally free playing has never played a large part on the Polish scene and even when the setting is abstract there is still an underlying jazz 'feel', expressible both as a pulse and as dimly familiar harmonies and structures. Though some important records for long-time collaborator Edward Vesala's Leo Records in Finland have not appeared on CD, the even earlier *Music For K* is still around, a forceful, sometimes inchoate session, but one which reconnects the trumpeter to his first gigs with Krzysztof Komeda's group in 1965.

After a period in the wilderness, Stańko was taken up by ECM records and given the kind of studio sound his fragile trumpet and quietly inflected music deserve. To date, there hasn't been a disappointing session for the imprint, but *Leosia* is one of the finest jazz records of recent times, a work of immense creative concentration made by a band at the peak of its powers. Stańko has probably played better, and the later *Litania* is the critics' favourite, but never with such instinctive support from his colleagues. As was the norm with ECM sessions at this time, considerable emphasis is put on the component members of the ensemble and on subdivisions of the basic group. Oxley, Jormin and Stenson are the begetters of 'Trinity' and bassist and drummer collaborate on the similarly constructed 'Brace'. 'No Bass Trio' is self-explanatory, and very fine, but the real action comes around these tracks, on the numbers drawn from an earlier Power Bros album, *Bossanossa*, and on the long title-piece, which ends the album on a creative high, a long, perfectly weighted theme that seems to have no beginning or end.

& *See also* **KRZYSZTOF KOMEDA, Astigmatic** (1965; p. 326)

PHIL MINTON
Born 2 November 1940, Torquay, Devon, England
Voice, trumpet

A Doughnut In One Hand
FMP CD 91
Minton (v solo). January 1996.

Phil Minton says: **'The Friends Meeting House in Welwyn Garden City was the most friendly, generous and responsive of spaces. Each part of the room I sang in seemed to have a different personality, and I felt it enjoyed the vibrations as much as I did.'**

Minton worked with Mike Westbrook, initially as a trumpeter and still within a recognizable jazz idiom, but gradually his unique vocal skills came to the fore. He is a stunning vocal improviser, with a tonal and timbral range that seems quite uncanny, moving between choirboy falsetto and feral growls in an instant. His partnership with Maggie Nicols and Julie Tippetts (as Voice) was an indication of how vital free-vocal music was in Britain; other associations – with percussionist Roger Turner – were no less creative.

Minton has an impressive body of recordings, some in unaccompanied situations. *A Doughnut In Both Hands* gathers together work inspired by the literature of the First World War and other pieces, including a tiny dedication to revolutionist Emma Goldman. 'Cenotaph' and 'Wreath' are only three quarters of a minute apiece, but overflowing with pain and pride, anger and redemption, and painfully up to date. The 'doughnut' title was to crop up again in 1996. This category-stretching return to solo singing has no intrinsic relation to the earlier disc. Now one doughnut short, Minton also has a spare hand free to conduct himself through a disciplined and rigorous sequence of miniatures, 30 tracks in an hour of spectacular vocal acrobatics.

Relations between groups of pieces – 'Dough Songs', 'Para Songs', songs about 'drainage' and a Mr Wilkins, and 'Tip Head' – are never made entirely explicit, but by sequencing the CD differently one gets a strong impression of areas of concern approached and developed organically and then reordered to create a fractured narrative. The voice has seldom been better and Minton's use of space and microphone distance (the only kind of processing on the record) adds dimensions that are entirely unexpected. It isn't easy listening, but once one grasps the relationship between Minton's highly refined art and the cracked, artless singing of pub amateurs, workmen and tramps, it has a Beckettian purity and warmth. Whatever its lineage, it is unmissable.

RUBY BRAFF&

Born 16 March 1927, Boston, Massachusetts; died 9 February 2003, Chatham, Massachusetts
Cornet

Being With You: Ruby Braff Remembers Louis Armstrong
Arbors ARCD 19163
Braff; Joe Wilder (flhn); Jon-Erik Kellso (c); Dan Barrett (tb); Scott Robinson (bs, cl); Jerry Jerome (ts); Bucky Pizzarelli (g); Johnny Varro (p); Bob Haggart (b); Jim Gwin (d). April 1996.

Writer Mick Carlon remembers: **'Ruby Braff was once pulled out of a coma by a Louis Armstrong recording. "That's the second time Pops saved my life," he said. When was the first? "The first time I heard his music."'**

After a long period of neglect, coinciding with the rise of rock and the jazz avant-garde, Braff began to be recognized again as the real thing and the last four decades of his life were a blur of activity, slowed only somewhat towards the end by pulmonary problems.

Armstrong was always the single greatest influence on Braff's playing, and this nicely crafted tribute shows some of the ways. The group is a mixture of the great-and-good and relative unknowns, but the playing is of the highest quality. Though Joe Wilder is around for only a single track, the long 'Royal Garden Blues', he brings such colour and vibrancy to it as to colour the whole album. The opening take on 'I Never Knew (Where Roses Grew)' sets the tone for a richly varied session that ends on the theme tune ('When It's Sleepy Time Down South') and on a point of rest. At a stroke, Armstrong's music is before us again, not as a museum piece but as the permanent revolution of modern music, a volatile source that few tapped as courageously and as feelingly as Braff.

& *See also* **2 x 2** (1955; p. 165)

CHARLIE HADEN&

Born 6 August 1937, Shenandoah, Iowa
Double bass

Beneath The Missouri Sky (Short Stories)
Verve 537130-2
Haden; Pat Metheny (g, sitar). 1996.

Composer and bassist Gavin Bryars says: **'Charlie Haden's bass is the most instantly recognizable in all jazz. His many duo collaborations represent his best work.'**

This sold like SnoCones in the desert, prompting the inevitable canard that it wasn't 'really' a jazz record at all. The truth is, as Gavin Bryars has stated, that much of Haden's most distinctive work has been in duo situations, where he is an equal voice in the musical partnership. His partners have included Chris Anderson, Kenny Barron, Ornette Coleman, Alice Coltrane, Egberto Gismonti, Hampton Hawes, Keith Jarrett, John Taylor ... which hardly sounds as though he coasts through these situations.

Metheny has proved to be an adventurous collaborator down the years and this session with an old friend never lapses into the merely conversational. The original intention was to record a set of acoustic duets, but these have been embellished with guitar overdubs and with Metheny's previously unveiled acoustic guitar/sitar. At the heart of the set, two tunes dedicated to Haden's late parents: Roy Acuff's country classic 'The Precious Jewel' (which strikingly resembles one of Bill Frisell's Americana projects, dense with overdubbing) and the traditional 'He's Gone Away'. Also in the line-up, Jim Webb's 'The Moon Is A Harsh Mistress' and two themes from the movie *Cinema Paradiso*. It's easy enough to dismiss this music as undemanding, pastelly and soft-focus, but in fact the alien element is the bop idiom that keeps surfacing. As ever, it's formidably disciplined, and there's a hint of rock only just under the surface.

& *See also* **Liberation Music Orchestra** (1969; p. 363), **Quartet West** (1986; p. 509)

JOHN SCOFIELD &
Born 26 December 1951, Dayton, Ohio
Guitar

Quiet
Verve 533185-2
Scofield; Randy Brecker (t, flhn); Wayne Shorter (ts); Charles Pillow (f, cor, ts); Lawrence Feldman (f, ts); John Clark, Fred Griffin (frhn); Roger Rosenberg (bcl); Howard Johnson (bs, tba); Steve Swallow (b); Bill Stewart, Duduka Fonseca (d). April 1996.

John Scofield says: **'This was the only time I used acoustic guitar. What I really wanted to do was write for horns ... and I was lucky to get Wayne Shorter on board!'**

Scofield's transfer to Blue Note moved his career and his music substantially forward, but nobody was staying at that great old imprint for long any more and Sco moved on again, but only after making the excellent *Hand Jive* and *Groove Elation*, which confirmed the label's apparent conviction that the best sex comes when the relationship is almost over. These were funky records, so what happened when the guitarist threw in his lot with Verve was a bit of a surprise.

Having already tried numerous settings for Blue Note, Scofield's Verve debut was different again. Playing acoustic guitar exclusively is one departure; setting it against the mournful sound of low brass and woodsy reeds is another. The horn charts are just witty enough to inject a certain wryness and just eerie enough to lend a sometimes other-worldly air to the likes of 'After The Fact'. The addition of Shorter, playing his now unaccustomed tenor on three tracks, seems like an unlikely bonus, but he fits in uncannily well. Scofield's own playing is made to seem less conspicuous by his playing acoustic, yet it lends a certain piquancy to his improvising. And then there is Swallow, co-producing and seeming to direct much of the playing with high, light bass-lines of the utmost ingenuity and relevance. The result comes close to Scofield's finest hour.

& *See also* **Still Warm** (1985; p. 493)

SONNY SIMMONS &
Born 4 August 1933, Sicily Island, Louisiana
Alto saxophone, English horn

Transcendence
CIMP 113
Simmons; Michael Marcus (stritch, manzello); Charles Moffett (d). April 1996.

Producer Robert Rusch says: **'During one of the takes, I passed a note to engineer Marc Rusch saying: "Is this as good as I think it is?" He just nodded. The next day we all went to the listening room to revisit the previous night's work. Mr Simmons turned to me and said: "Caesar" (which is what he called me), "I don't know where we go from here. How can we do better?" It was a transcendent moment.'**

The only record issued under Sonny Simmons's name between 1970 and 1990 is a 1982 West Wind session called *Backwoods Suite*, with Michael Marcus and Billy Higgins, though there are a couple of on-the-fly live dates as well. How could a musician and composer so original and remarkable simply slip through the net? Part of the answer is that Simmons has always favoured working with community musicians and out of range of the 'industry', but the neglect is still inexplicable. There were a couple of small-label things at the start of the next decade, recorded with local musicians, before the estimable Bob Rusch fixed up a session at CIMP, an imprint that puts a premium on faithful audio documentation of improvised music.

Transcendence is a challenging listen. Marcus's adoption of manzello and stritch (instruments associated with Roland Kirk) and the lack of a harmony instrument mean that these solos, duos and trios are played out on the edge, and with no recognized paths back. The sleeve-notes say something about the saxophonist's resolve and intensity, revealing the strained circumstances of both sessions, and the bloody virulence of the playing can at times seem as exhausting to listen to as it was to perform. Moffett's swing- and jazz-time are one leavening agent; the lovely sound of Marcus's horns intertwining with Simmons is another. Sonny plays unaccompanied alto on 'Geraldine's Dream', but his 'Nuclear Fission' is more typical of the session, which also introduces 'Cosmosomatics', later adapted as a group name.

A second disc, *Judgement Day*, was issued from a subsequent session, with Sonny on tenor and Marcus doubling on the thin-voiced C-melody saxophone, but the addition of a bass-player contributes less than one might expect. Of the two, it's *Transcendence* that earns its title.

& *See also* **Music From The Spheres** (1966; p. 341)

JOE MCPHEE
Born 3 November 1939, Miami, Florida
Trumpet, tenor saxophone, valve trombone, other instruments

As Serious As Your Life
hatOLOGY 514
McPhee (ts, t, p solo). May 1996.

Joe McPhee says: **'As Serious As Your Life is, of course, a tribute to Valerie Wilmer's marvellous book and the musicians she championed, but more personally it is a tribute to my father. It was he who gave me the gift of music and he had recently passed away.'**

A deep thinker as well as a passionate musician, McPhee is a rare exponent of both brass and woodwind instruments, doubling on trumpet and saxophone on many of his records, using other horns as circumstance dictates. He developed his musical learning in the military, exposed to the traditional jazz which has always profoundly affected his work. He emerged as a significant player with the 1969 album *Underground Railroad* on the CjR label he co-founded. Other rarities from that period have re-emerged in recent years. Perhaps the two great intellectual wakenings of his life were his reading of Edward De Bono's heterodox psychological theories, which led to McPhee's 'Po' aesthetic, and his meeting with radical composer Pauline Oliveros, whose philosophy of Deep Listening chimed strongly with his own ideas.

McPhee has many recordings, featuring many permutations of instruments, but it seems only appropriate to include one of his great hat ART dates, not just because it is a remarkable record, but because the label was established (in 1975) by Swiss businessman Werner X. Uehlinger specifically to put out McPhee's music, some 14 records between 1970's *Black Magic Man* and this.

McPhee has identified 1996 as an important transitional year, a point at which he looks back and forwards, with the oneiric logic that dominates the 'Project Dream Keeper' sequence. Working alone and with ambient sound welcomed rather than edited out, he creates a body of work which is as evocative and expressive as anything he has ever made. 'Tok' is a Coltrane-influenced tenor piece which harks back to the earlier solo performance. 'Conlon In The Land Of Ra' documents an imaginary meeting between Sun Ra and the radical composer Conlon Nancarrow. Dedicated to Marilyn Crispell, Coltrane's 'After The Rain' is a piano solo played on the house piano of the Village Gate jazz club and played with the sustain pedal depressed throughout, giving it a floating, fugitive quality. On 'The Man I Love', McPhee brings a highly personal focus to the Gershwin standard, a similar tonality and language to the two parts of 'As Serious As Your Life', named after an important book by British jazz writer and photographer Val Wilmer. As well as these, there is the opening 'Death Of Miles Davis', a heartfelt tribute, and 'Haiku Study #1', a sketch for work developed later in duets with violinist David Prentice.

JAMES CARTER
Born 3 January 1969, Detroit, Michigan
Soprano, alto, tenor, baritone and f-mezzo saxophones, bass and contrabass clarinets, flute

Conversin' With The Elders
Atlantic 7567 82908
Carter; Lester Bowie, Harry 'Sweets' Edison (t); Larry Smith (as); Buddy Tate (ts, cl); Hamiet Bluiett (bs); Craig Taborn (p); Jaribu Shahid (b); Tani Tabbal (d). June 1996.

Cecil Taylor said (2002): **'That music is alive! I almost cried. He plays one sound, aah! and walks off; another sound, eeh! and walks off again. But when he confronts that sound, that new sound out of rhythm and blues, there is such passion. His life is there.'**

From those initials much was expected; not miracles perhaps, but certainly something special. Carter's coming out was rapturously received and almost everything since has been
fascinating. He arrived in the unlikely packaging of the Tough Young Tenors. It was an
inspired idea to throw Carter up against those ancestral voices and with a programme that
takes in swing to bop and beyond to the contemporary avant-garde. Both guests and material come from out of a past not always so very distant, but certainly very different from the
scene the young man inherited. Carter's loyalty to Shahid, Tabal and Taborn is exemplary,
and they form a unified background for the guest spots.

The most venerable, chronologically speaking, are Edison and Tate, and 'Lester Leaps
In' and 'Centrepiece' with Sweets and 'Moten Swing' and 'Blue Creek', the latter with Buddy
on clarinet, are convincingly, supremely authentic. The paired altos on 'Parker's Mood'
almost cancel each other out, so rigorously do they observe the master's cadence, and Smith
– heard, as all the guests are, through the left channel – doesn't seem to want to bust loose.
A hometown legend, the Detroiter has very few recording credits to his name. The set kicks
off, wonderfully but rather deceptively, with Bowie's 'Freereggaehibop', on which his entire
armoury of rips, snorts, smears and impossibly low-register vocalizations are used. Appropriately, he comes back to round off the album with 'Atitled Valse', but by then the honours
have already been secured by Bluiett and by two fantastic baritone duets, on Coltrane's
'Naima' and, more boldly, on Anthony Braxton's march-metred 'Composition 40Q', one of
the more approachable themes in the Braxton canon, but still a startling piece to cover.

Carter is playing with dazzling confidence and restrained power. His early tendency
to over-emphasize the attack has given way to a breathily intimate sound which can be
scaled up or down in keeping with the material. His multi-instrumentalism is so much in
service to the song that one scarcely notices the switch while understanding instinctively
that such-and-such a tune could only be played that way on that horn. That's the sign of a
master.

KENNY DAVERN

Born 7 January 1935, Huntington, New York; died 12 December 2006, Sandia, New Mexico
Clarinet, soprano saxophone

Breezin' Along

Arbors ARCD 19170
Davern; Bucky Pizzarelli, Howard Alden (g); Greg Cohen (b); Tony DeNicola (d). June 1996.

Kenny Davern said: **'All my teachers did was give me a lot of things I didn't need to know.
I learned music – and everyone should learn music – by listening. Otherwise, you're
standing there in the middle of the band, knowing everything, but not able to play.'**

Davern had claims to being the major clarinettist in jazz, having forsaken the soprano saxophone ('I play soprano once a year and it takes only a few moments to confirm that I made
the right decision'). It did, however, provide him with a good platform during otherwise
dark days for jazz when he co-fronted Soprano Summit with Bob Wilber in the '70s. Though
associated at various times with avant-garde projects, Davern remained true to older loyalties and waved the flag for New Orleans jazz at a time when modernism reigned. As obituaries pointed out, Davern might have been working with Steve Lacy in the '80s but he made
his recording debut in 1954 with Jack Teagarden.

It's a relatively extensive discography, but the Arbors records gave Davern the bright,
uncluttered sound his light, nimble delivery required and the late discs are generally terrific. *Breezin' Along* is a peach, though. Pizzarelli and Alden make a great team, driving the
fast numbers and softly suggesting the harmonic detail in the slower ones. Davern measures the material with an almost insouciant virtuosity: two Beiderbecke chestnuts, 'Since
My Best Girl Turned Me Down' and 'Jazz Me Blues', are super, but 'Baby, Won't You Please

Come Home' is Kenny at his peak. Sometimes his note choices are unexpected, but only the unwary would assume this was any sign of the avant-garde peeping through. Kenny was playing with Red Allen at 16 and most of his language still dates back to players of that generation, including the 'out of tune' snaps, altissimo endings and almost toneless phrases, many of them most effectively deployed in the stripped-down situations Davern liked as rhythmic devices. A lyrical player, though, and always a joy to hear.

KURT ROSENWINKEL
Born 28 October 1970, Philadelphia, Pennsylvania
Guitar

East Coast Love Affair
Fresh Sound New Talent FSNT 016
Rosenwinkel; Avishai Cohen (b); Jorge Rossy (d). July 1996.

Pat Metheny said (2004): **'He's one of the younger guitarists I most admire, not just for his technique. His whole approach is just right.'**

A ubiquitous presence on the New York club scene of the late '90s, Rosenwinkel is one of those rare musicians whose rise from sideman to leader status has been earned rather than merely taken as a matter of routine course. He got a break working with his teacher, Gary Burton, and has been building on that. His busy diary probably gets in the way of developing projects of his own, but he has ideas to burn and will certainly prevail, even if the move up to Verve did him no obvious favours.

There's already a substantial body of recorded work, but we still return to the first album, the first of two live sets he has put up; a later one, on ArtistShare, was recorded at the Village Vanguard. The debut has a beautiful feel – the three men were recorded in Small's Club, where Rosenwinkel has had a regular gig, and the sound of the record is close, almost humid. The interplay lifts the material to a high level of invention – when they fade 'All Or Nothing At All', it sounds as though they could have gone on in that groove for hours yet. Rosenwinkel plays with a clean, almost classical sound and his melody-lines are spacious and paced to suit whatever tempo they've chosen – he never seems to feel he has to rush through his phrases. The title-piece suggests a composer who's not working outside his comfort zone yet, but time will tell. Cohen and Rossy are just as generous of spirit on a very enjoyable set. It's certainly more successful than the subsequent Criss Cross *Intuit*, which is all right but basically uneventful bebop, as that provenance would suggest. Rosenwinkel, though, could make Dixieland sound modern and remains a man to watch.

ORNETTE COLEMAN &
Born Randolph Denard Ornette Coleman, 9 March 1930, Fort Worth, Texas
Alto and tenor saxophones, trumpet, violin

Colors
Verve/Harmolodic 537789
Coleman; Joachim Kühn (p). August 1996.

Ornette Coleman said (1983): **'A piano gets in the way.'**

Coleman's contract with Verve, albeit under his own Harmolodics imprint, didn't set off a tide of later recordings. In fact, the flow of material has been slower than ever. It was initially a surprise when the duo album with Joachim Kühn was announced, initially because he was a piano-player, and Coleman had shown little enthusiasm for keyboards since he worked with Walter Norris and Don Friedman years before. The same year as *Colors*, though, he did also work with Geri Allen, so yet again the mould was broken, or had never been that entire in the first place. In addition, by any standard, Kühn seemed an ideal duo partner. There are few more sophisticated and few more heterodox harmonic thinkers around and, whatever else, the encounter promised to spark off some interesting conflicts of style, the German's ethereal classicism (if you hear it that way) against Ornette's 'jazz' roots.

It's interesting to compare their encounter with another, almost contemporary Verve release, the *1 + 1* duo by Herbie Hancock and Wayne Shorter, which is pipe-and-slippers compared to this restless, searching set, recorded live in Germany, at the Leipzig Opera. Kühn had recorded in a duo context before, with CMP in-house genius Walter Quintus, and with guitarist Jan Akkerman. Both times he demonstrated a responsive intelligence that thrives on harmonic ambiguity and on a suspension of conventional harmonic resolutions. The record opens in relatively straight-ahead fashion with 'Faxing', which is more unexpected for the pianist's part than Ornette's. He's in more familiar territory on 'Three Ways To One', which might almost be a through-composed chamber piece. All the tracks, relatively short by live-performance standards, were written specially for the date. 'Refills', 'Story Writing' and 'Night Plans' are the most substantial pieces, though most of the detail comes from Kühn rather than Ornette. A wholly unexpected meeting of minds.

& See also **The Shape Of Jazz To Come** (1959, 1960; p. 245), **At The Golden Circle, Stockholm** (1965; p. 324), **The Complete Science Fiction Sessions** (1971, 1972; p. 387)

ELLERY ESKELIN
Born 16 August 1959, Wichita, Kansas
Tenor saxophone

One Great Day
hatOLOGY 502
Eskelin; Andrea Parkins (acc, sampler); Jim Black (d). September 1996.

Ellery Eskelin says: **'What should rightly have been a disaster – a location recording made in a room with strange acoustics using questionable equipment run by an engineer with peculiar attitudes about the whole affair – miraculously turned out to be one of our best-sounding recordings!'**

Eskelin stands apart from the throng. He has a querulous tone and likes to stretch phrases into elongated shapes that follow a logic all their own. He was raised in Baltimore from an early age and studied at Kenton Orchestra summer schools, but despite the fact that his father was the cultish songwriter Rodd Keith the main early musical influence was his mother, Bobbie Lee, who played organ and led her own groups.

After a bunch of earlier records, some of which have disappeared into the void, Eskelin convened this unusual trio for a 1994 record called *Jazz Trash*. Its roots in sax-and-organ soul-jazz aren't difficult to excavate, but typically Eskelin grafted new ideas and procedures onto the basic stock. On that first meeting, he created a record which is undeniably interesting, but doesn't quite make the next step. He appeared again with Parkins on *Green Bermudas*, his most out-there and uncategorizable disc, on which the saxophonist decorates her oddball array of sampled sounds (singalong pop, varispeed drums, chunks of Eskelin himself from *Premonition*) with some of his sparsest playing. A lot of it feels like experimental bits and bites, at least until the two long tracks which close the record, each a testing dialogue.

One Great Day restores the *Jazz Trash* situation; Black's compendium of jazz, rock and free rhythms is spontaneously exciting; Parkins conjures unpredictable shapes out of her instrument; Eskelin plays with real physicality, seeming to grab and twist the sound as it emerges from his horn. 'Vertical Hold' is an astonishing piece that like the title-track seems to weave together a freebop sensibility with a warped version of television music (presumably what the title means) and does so with a kind of playful seriousness. The inclusion of Roland Kirk's 'The Inflated Tear' is a useful pointer to the kind of aesthetic this trio pursues. Black is a percussion giant who frequently gives his skins a rest and finds other ways of making sounds. On 'Fallen Angel', our pick of the tracks, he sounds as if he might be picking out the swaying rhythm on a suitcase, while Eskelin emotes elegiacally and Parkins toys with dance measures: *sardana*? Or something closer to home?

Eskelin takes enormous pains with sound, treating the studio like a fourth member of the group. However difficult the circumstances of the recording, it's a near-flawless disc by one of the undersung leaders and underexposed groups of the last 20 years.

ROVA *&*

Formed 1977
Group

Bingo
Victo CD 056
Bruce Ackley, Steve Adams, Larry Ochs, Jon Raskin (sax). September 1996.

Larry Ochs says: **'*Bingo* sums up our plan of attack in the '90s. We admired the British improvised music scene and with grant support from Meet The Composer we were able to get Barry Guy to write his first version of *Witch Gong Game* for us; the beautiful score hangs in both Raskin's and my homes. I always loved playing the opening sopranino solo in Lindsay Cooper's "Face In The Crowd", even though the tuning was always an issue!'**

An American all-saxophone group, its name derived from the surname initials of the players, although Andrew Voigt has been replaced by Steve Adams (ROAA would be harder to pronounce). Though their music seeks an exact balance between composition and improvisation, and they have over 30 years created an extensive body of remarkable music for saxophone quartet, they have lately been written for extensively by many different composers. As Larry Ochs points out, *Bingo* is not representative of the major works composed by himself and bandmates Adams and Raskin, but together with the preceding *Ptow!* and *Resistance* on Victo it offers a spectrum of ROVA music ranging from free improvisation and structured improvisation to composition for improvisers. That said, Ochs's piece 'Initials' is one of the strongest in the group's collective history, and it sits beautifully alongside two pieces by Lindsay Cooper, two versions of Barry Guy's 'Witch Gong Game' and Fred Frith's 'Water Under The Bridge', their presence here a striking tribute to ROVA's interest in British improvisation/composition.

The album opens with Cooper's intricate 'Face In The Crowd', which is delivered with perfect dynamics by the quartet. If it stands as a kind of symphonic tone-poem for quartet, then the first, short version of the Barry Guy piece is almost a concerto for baritone, with Raskin backed by written saxophone parts from the others. Frith's standing as a fine contemporary composer still doesn't go unquestioned, but the piece here – dedicated to Jimmy Giuffre – should dispel any doubt. It's audibly part of some larger design, but it stands impressively on its own, breezily present and evanescent by turns. It also sets up the long – 25-minute – version of 'Witch Gong Game', which is the set's climax.

As the culmination of a trilogy, *Bingo* completes the card, but ROVA is a group best heard in bulk and anyone intrigued by this should scroll back to the early records and on to the collaborations of recent years, of which more below …

& *See also* **Electric Ascension** (2003; p. 686)

JESSICA WILLIAMS
Born 17 March 1948, Baltimore, Maryland
Piano

Jessica's Blues
Jazz Focus JFCD 014 / 018
Williams; Jay Thomas (t, ts, f); Jeff Johnson (b); Mel Brown (d). October 1996.

Jessica Williams says: **'That session was hard. Jay was incredible, but the bass-player and drummer were fighting. Remembering what Duke said about dealing with hostile machinations in the band, I put his theory to work, getting them so riled they wanted blood. I said to Jeff: "The drummer says you're dragging" and then to Mel: "The bass-player says you're slowing the time down." After that, each tried to outplay the other, scowling and grunting and glaring. They're good friends now but they sure were mad at that session, and that's why it *burns* – that time is *aggressive*! Just like I wanted it.'**

Williams performed for a time as Jessica Jennifer Williams using electronic keyboards, and didn't make much of a splash in the jazz mainstream till she started releasing acoustic jazz records in the '80s, when her distinctive style – compounded of Tatum, Monk, Evans, Brubeck – became immediately evident. She has been prolific ever since, despite living off the beaten track in north California and one suspects that for Williams CDs are more than calling cards or gig souvenirs, but an important aspect of her art.

She has most often been heard either solo (including a Maybeck Hall date) or in a trio context, so it was surprising and at first unsettling to hear her work with horns. A slightly earlier disc with Thomas and Hadley Caliman was called *Joy*. It certainly emoted but there was a distracting busyness to some numbers which is all but eliminated here. Straightforward melody statement is the priority, leaving ample room for soloing. Williams contributes a catchy whistle to the opening 'Smoking Section', an excellent original dedicated to Roland Kirk. Most of the first half is devoted to Williams compositions, all of them testy and potentially lethal, though one now understands why the mood was so abrasive. There's a change of pace and tone with 'See See Rider', and later on Thomas plays his trumpet on 'St Louis Blues', getting a ripe old sound out of it: a rare musician who seems as easy on brass as on a saxophone where his solos are funky and to the point. 'Raise Four' allows Williams to exercise her Monk obsession again, but to dramatic effect. It's a cracking performance and this is perhaps her best record. The other players challenge her and mitigate the somewhat florid intellectualism of some of the solo recitals.

DEWEY REDMAN *&*
Born 17 May 1931, Fort Worth, Texas; died 2 September 2006, New York City
Tenor and alto saxophones, musette

In London
Palmetto PM 2030
Redman; Rita Marcotulli (p); Cameron Brown (b); Matt Wilson (d). October 1996.

Dewey Redman said (1999): **'That's one of my best records. I like to play in Europe. I think they appreciate jazz music there, more than in America, except perhaps New York. And you sense that and you try things, knowing that no one minds if you fall on your ass.'**

In his last years, Redman's reputation was almost eclipsed by that of his son Joshua, with whom he sustained an arm's-length but affectionate and respectful relationship. Of course, Joshua's success also introduced the father to a generation who hadn't been buying records when *Ear Of The Behearer* was made. Like Pharoah Sanders, who had worked with Redman in one of his earliest bands, Dewey got mellower as the years went by. The more eldritch qualities of his attack were almost gone by the beginning of his last decade. Instead, there was a philosophical calm beneath which roiled the remnants of his avant-garde persona.

Recorded live at Ronnie Scott's club, Redman sounds rejuvenated and adventuresome with a band that splits down naturally into two pairs, himself and long-standing collaborator Brown up against the Italian Marcotulli and Wilson. The band actually work from a different axis on 'Tu-Inns', the most adventurous tune on the set. Piano and bass take off darkly, building up a steady, brooding *ostinato* against which saxophone and drums enter with an explosion of sound. As ever, Redman mixes outside and relatively mainstream styles, giving 'The Very Thought Of You', his tribute to Dexter Gordon, a loose, swinging energy and Sammy Cahn's 'I Should Care' an easy, melodic interpretation. 'Portrait In Black And White' is an unexpectedly straightforward Jobim cover, but what's interesting about all of these middle-of-the-road numbers is how carefully they're juxtaposed with the more adventurous material. Tunes like 'I-Pimp', 'Kleerwine' and 'Elevens' are a reminder that Redman hadn't entirely abandoned his avant-gardism and commitment to the new. An old lion, still dangerous, and nowhere close to falling on his ass.

& *See also* **Ear Of The Behearer** (1973; p. 403)

CLAIRE MARTIN
Born 6 September 1967, London
Voice

Make This City Ours
Linn AKD 066
Martin; Gerard Presencer (t, flhn); Antonio Hart (as); Gareth Williams (p, v); Peter Washington (b); Gregory Hutchinson (d). October 1996.

Claire Martin says: **'Apart from Peter Washington nailing "Estate" in 5/4 in one take, the highlight was a photo shoot with the late, great William Claxton. Afterwards, I was alone in the back of a limo – the driver's next job was to pick up Clint Eastwood! – thinking: "I've really made it ... check me out!" when a *huge* truck slammed into us and the dream came to a swearing, honking, sticky end. I had to go back on the subway, but for just a moment ... queen of the world.'**

Martin was the most exciting female jazz singer to emerge in the '90s and an inspired signing for Scottish-based label Linn. Though her British groups have done her consistently proud, American success and a fruitful association with Richard Rodney Bennett have propelled her onto a new stage; for once, the label that shaped her career has been able to come along and enjoy the fruits. Influenced by some of the great cool jazz singers, Chris Connor most obviously, but with a hint of Julie London's laid-back sense of drama, too, Martin never over-dramatizes a lyric, but shows a clear understanding of what she is singing. Much of her early work for Linn has been parcelled up in compilation boxes. These are a good way to make her acquaintance, but for a quick fix of Martin in mature form, it's best to go straight to *Make This City Ours*.

Martin approached her 30th birthday with a solid reputation, but not yet with a statement on record that matched up to her live presence. She also had, so far, no real reputation in the US. If one album deserves to establish her as a singer with real star potential, then it's this one. Even the title sounds like a confident declaration of intent. Recorded in New York, with Washington, Hart and Hutchinson guesting, it has a more cosmopolitan feel than any of its predecessors. Presencer's trumpet-playing conveys innocence and weary maturity, and Hart always sounds good around singers. A new Martin composition, 'Empty Bed', bodes well. We were divided on her arrangement of Bruno Martino's 'Estate', with words by Joel Siegel, but it stands up strongly on repeated hearings and only 'Another Night' sounds remotely formulaic. Arguably, there were even better records to come, notably a tribute to Shirley Horn called *He Never Mentioned Love* and *A Modern Art*, but it's always great to hear an artist coming into her own, and that's what happened one autumn in New York.

TERELL STAFFORD
Born 26 November 1966, Miami, Florida
Trumpet

Centripetal Force
Candid CACD 79718
Stafford; John Clark (frhn); Ron Blake, Tim Warfield (ts); Russell Malone (g); Stefon Harris (vib); Stephen Scott (p); Ed Howard (b); Victor Lewis (d); Daniel Moreno (perc). October 1996.

Nat Adderley said (1985): '**... and Terell Stafford, there's another young trumpet-player out of Florida. There's definitely something in the water, except all these guys sound different and distinctive, and I like Terell's sound.**'

Stafford was a regular member of Bobby Watson's group Horizon, which also numbered Simon and Lewis, and he came to his own debut recording with a sensibility very much marked by Watson's small-group/big-sound idea. Stafford isn't just another latter-day run-of-the-mill bopper. Though he draws on a range of influences running from Fats Navarro (a fellow Floridan) and Clifford Brown to mid-period Miles and Lee Morgan, he already has a distinctive inflexion and a very personal phraseology.

Centripetal Force is exactly what's at work here, a group which is working very closely and sympathetically. Again Tim Warfield brings his clean, youthful sound, but on just one track this time. A version of 'Daahoud' is a special dedication, but it also points up the Brown influence again. Though the whole band is never heard together, the richer palette suits the trumpeter admirably and he produces some magnificent statements on 'I'll Wait' and 'Skylark', a back-to-back pair that are as sheerly refreshing as anything from the last few years. Thad Jones's 'A Child Is Born' is for trumpet and guitar, and 'My Romance' is an elegant trumpet solo.

ALAN BROADBENT
Born 23 April 1947, Auckland, New Zealand
Piano

Personal Standards
Concord CCD 4757
Broadbent; Putter Smith (b); Joe LaBarbera (d). October 1996.

Alan Broadbent said (1997): '**Maybe jazz really isn't for everyone. If you don't have that subtlety and that responsiveness to changes in time, maybe it just doesn't work for you, and you're always going to be just OK with fusion, or whatever. I look for things like that in a song before I can do anything with it; the beauty of time, if you like.**'

Broadbent went to Berklee in 1966 and from there joined Woody Herman as pianist-arranger. His career has divided along those lines ever since. He worked with Chet Baker and has more recently worked with Diana Krall, but his most prominent playing roles have been as a member of Charlie Haden's Quartet West and as a solo and duo recitalist in Concord's

Maybeck Hall series. He deserves to be better known. There's great clarity of thought to Broadbent's playing, the interpretations entire and well-formed rather than merely busked, and if that suggests a lack of spontaneity, he always manages to make the music sound fresh. Broadbent takes his cues first from Parker and Powell, yet one seldom thinks about bop while listening to his two-handed approach.

Personal Standards is superlative. Here he tackles eight originals, plus one he wishes he had written himself, Smith's 'North'. It's something of a shock to come across such a rich vein of writing and not be able to identify by name any of these beautiful melodies. 'Song Of Home' and 'The Long Goodbye' are familiar from Quartet West performances, but who has picked up that remarkably original blues 'Uncertain Terms' or 'Idyll'? The playing is so impeccable, the responsiveness of the group so refined (LaBarbera has never played better), that one is left at a loss for words. Broadbent deserves the highest acclaim.

ARILD ANDERSEN
Born 27 October 1945, Lilleström, Norway
Double bass

Hyperborean
ECM 537342-2
Andersen; Bendik Hofseth (ts); Tore Brunborg (ts, ss); Kenneth Knudsen (ky); Paolo Vinaccia (d, perc); Cikada String Quartet. December 1996.

Saxophonist Tommy Smith has played with Arild Andersen: **'It's not only the note or space that's crucial; it's the when and the how. Arild's personality is as big as his bass sound. A man who is the centre of every party and a man who is at the centre of all his music.'**

Like many players of his generation in Scandinavia, Andersen was much influenced by exiled guru George Russell's Lydian Chromatic approach to harmony. The bassist has worked in a wide range of contexts and was leader of Masqualero, a latter-day simulacrum of the Miles Davis quintet. His characteristic manner is resonant and fleet, with much of the harmonic complexity Russell's influence imbued.

He probably isn't immediately thought of as one of ECM's main stars – in the way that Garbarek, Jarrett, Rypdal, Weber, even Surman are – but he has been a constant and steady presence at the label and on the European scene, his big but not insistent sound at the centre of many fine recordings. The earlier ECMs, *Molde Concert, If You Look Far Enough*, the folksier *Sagn*, are varied enough to suggest that Andersen doesn't have a single compositional style, but writes very much for specific contexts. The only surprise is that ECM have never seen fit to record him unaccompanied, as they have with other bass-players on the roster. Andersen would easily command such a space.

Hyperborean is a reference to the cool, ageless land the Greeks believed lay beyond the north wind. The music is disciplined, unromantic and timeless. Andersen dispenses with effects pedals, combining his increasingly elaborate improvisations in real time with keyboards and string quartet, lending the whole – ironically enough – a jazzier feel than anything he has done since Masqualero. Hofseth and Brunborg are reduced to supporting cast and it's the Cikada Quartet that dominates the first half. Things loosen up later, albeit leaving an uneasy sense that Andersen has delivered his main ideas upfront and is then struggling to fill the slot. Though structurally less elaborate than *Sagn*, which is organized as a three-part suite, *Hyperborean* has a unity of tone and an overall sense of direction lacking on the earlier discs. Andersen dominates completely. His sound is immense and his soloing involved and compelling. Every time one hears Andersen at work, one wonders why he isn't automatically on every list of influential contemporaries.

GERRY HEMINGWAY
Born 23 March 1955, New Haven, Connecticut
Drums, percussion

Waltzes, Two-Steps And Other Matters Of The Heart
GM Recordings Inc GM 3043
Hemingway; Walter Wierbos (tb); Michael Moore (as, cl, bcl); Ernst Reijseger (clo); Mark Dresser (b). November 1996.

Gerry Hemingway says: **'The swan song of my wonderful quintet of the '90s, cobbled together from mostly radio recordings made on the most ambitious tour I ever put together, 27 gigs in 28 days all over Europe. Despite a very high level of stress, including a heated feud between Ernst and Michael, I think an elegant view of this versatile ensemble shone through. One favourite piece, "Gitar", is still in the repertoire.'**

Hemingway is a (somewhat distant) kinsman of the great novelist, and a dogged exponent of the principle of grace under pressure. He won his spurs with Anthony Braxton's group, where he held the percussion job for more than a decade. The Hemingway Quintet toured tirelessly during 1996. Two of those dates are represented here. Hemingway had recently taken charge of his own management and distribution, an overload which might have been disastrous had happenstance not lightened his load. The electronic samples which were to have accompanied the tour were lost when a computer crashed. The mishap threw Hemingway back on the band's internal resources, and *Waltzes* is a superb representation of its improvisational versatility. There are duos and trios, solo spots and areas of near silence as all five ponder decays in the markedly different acoustics of the Berlin Jazz Festival and Fasching in Sweden.

Hemingway had been writing a lot of material in waltz-time, though in practice the count is often 7/4 or 9/4 rather than a strict three-quarter. That is acknowledged on the opening 'Waltz In Seven', with its mournful *rubato* opening. The first of the long tracks is the slow, stately 'Gitar', which opens with Hemingway on harmonica, albeit an instrument so oddly pitched that he sounds like a consort of Tibetan Buddhists playing shawms. The main melody could almost be Aaron Copland in a melancholic mood, with Wierbos playing in the lower reaches of his register. By contrast to the open-form pieces, 'Gospel Waltz' is a relatively straight-ahead blowing piece, though each of the group approaches its changes and melodic form in a quite different way. 'XI' is an arrangement of a madrigal by Gesualdo, further evidence of how tirelessly Hemingway ranges for new inspiration. 'Ari' is a traditional German waltz and an ideal curtain-piece.

ROSWELL RUDD &
Born 17 November 1935, Sharon, Connecticut
Trombone

The Unheard Herbie Nichols: Volumes 1 & 2
CIMP 133/146
Rudd; Greg Millar (g, perc); John Bacon (d, vib). November 1996.

Roswell Rudd says: **'This project was on my mind since 1960, when I first spent time with Herbie. He was using these compositions to teach me form and improvisation. I realized then that what we were doing needed to be recorded. No takers ... until, fast forward to two exhausting, uplifting, back-to-back days at CIMP in Redwood, New York. It was a modest budget but we had free rein and were able to lay down respectful outlines of 15 of the folio of 27 songs. It was a long, long hope come true.'**

Rudd worked with Herbie Nichols for nearly two years between 1960 and 1962. The pianist died a year later and since then Rudd has been the most dogged keeper of the spirit, campaigning with Steve Lacy to reverse the great pianist and composer's marginalization. In 1982, on a record that punctuated what was to be a long studio silence, he joined Steve Lacy on a record of Nichols and Monk tunes called *Regeneration*, a satisfying tribute to both.

The CIMP session was an opportunity to concentrate on Nichols entirely and to dig out some of the most obscure themes. Rudd contacted CIMP boss Robert Rusch, who has a deserved reputation for putting out adventurous music by artists who otherwise might lack recording opportunities. There are some surprises in instrumentation. On 'Some Wandering Bushmen', Rudd played trumpet on the first take, before reprising the theme on his usual horn. On the long 'Jamaica' (*Volume 1*) he plays percussion, and elsewhere on the same disc gets out the little-used mellophone. He's always been an enthusiastic rather than polished singer and gives his all to 'Vacation Blues' at the end of *Volume 2*.

Much of this material is genuinely unknown and unheard, even by those who do know 'Shuffle Montgomery' and 'Lady Sings The Blues'. It seems extraordinary that tunes like 'Freudian Frolics', the far from lightweight 'Tee Dum Tee Dee', 'Prancin' Pretty Woman' and 'Karna Kanji' are not in the wider repertoire. The trio is well-balanced and responsive, with Millar taking much of the accompanist's role. He and Bacon duet on 'Dream Time', leaving Rudd to play 'One Twilight' and 'Passing Thoughts' unaccompanied; the latter is quite remarkable. A valuable insight into two great – and sadly under-documented – artists.

& *See also* **Blown Bone** (1967, 1976; p. 433)

MINGUS BIG BAND
Formed 1991
Ensemble

Live In Time
Dreyfus FDM 36583 2 2CD
Randy Brecker, Ryan Kisor, Earl Gardner, Alex Sipiagin (t); Frank Lacy, Robin Eubanks, Conrad Herwig, Britt Woodman, Dave Taylor (tb); Steve Slagle, Gary Bartz (as); John Stubblefield, Seamus Blake, Mark Shim (ts); Gary Smulyan, Ronnie Cuber (bs); Kenny Drew Jr, John Hicks (p); Andy McKee (b); Adam Cruz, Tommy Campbell (d). 1996.

Sue Mingus says: '**This was an ambitious recording, done live over three days at the Time Café. What I most remember is that because the energy was beginning to flag on the second day, I called up Ku-umba Frank Lacy, whom I had fired the summer before, and begged him to come back. The band caught fire on that third day. Sy Johnson, who arranged nine of the pieces, calls it his favourite MBB recording because of the "thorny, challenging material", like "Number 29" and "Children's Hour Of Dream". The band rose to the occasion, bringing the fire and spirit one expects of Mingus music. (In addition, Kenny Drew [Jr] came in and sight read the piano part on "Children's Hour", something few other players on the planet could have achieved!)'**

Of the projects dedicated to the great man's memory and legacy, this is perhaps the most important, and now the most durable as well, enjoying the active blessing of the composer's widow and access to tapes and manuscripts from the huge Mingus archive. The band began round a regular Thursday session at Fez under the Time Café in New York City. Mingus had shrewdly recognized that a band could rehearse at the public's expense if an event was labelled a 'workshop' rather than a concert, and so the Mingus Jazz Workshops were born. These days the task is perhaps less urgent, and less driven by constraint; the Big Band provides an opportunity to work through the scrolls, providing exegesis and commentary on a vast body of work.

Live In Time of course refers to the venue, but it also underscores the vital, ongoing nature of the project and the fact that all of this music is being worked out in real time. A huge slab of music spread over two discs, it comes the closest of the group's recordings to recapturing the spirit of Mingus himself. The opening is stunning; 'Number 29' was written by Mingus as a challenge to all the gunslinging trumpet-players in town – and, as written, it was impossible. Arranger Sy Johnson has spread the part through the trumpet section and given it a hard, bi-tonal quality that is pure Mingus. Two early pieces, 'Baby, Take A Chance With Me' and 'This Subdues My Passion', are recorded here for only the second time since they were written in the '40s. Conrad Herwig solos on the second, Frank Lacy and Gary Bartz on the first. 'So Long Eric' is a *tour de force*, a solo feature for the entire horn section; sheer excitement.

The second disc is not quite as powerful as the first, though Johnson's long arrangement on 'The Shoes Of The Fisherman's Wife Are Some Jive-Ass Slippers' and the superb 'E's Flat, Ah's Flat Too' are impeccably conceived and performed. The night ends a day late with 'Wednesday Night Prayer Meeting', a stunning solo from Randy Brecker, ably supported by Shim and Eubanks.

MICHAEL MARCUS
Born 25 August 1952, San Francisco, California
Clarinet, other reeds

This Happening
Justin Time JUST 98
Marcus; Jaki Byard (p). December 1996.

Michael Marcus says: **'Being with Jaki in the studio was so relaxed. When we recorded the slow blues in A ("The Continuum"), Jaki turned to me with his beautiful face and smiled. Every tune on the recording was one take!'**

Marcus didn't get the idea of manzello and stritch directly from Roland Kirk, but from George Braith, a Rahsaan follower who recorded briefly for Blue Note and Prestige in the '60s. Michael's microtonal approach is a near equal hybrid of R&B and modernist poly-tonality, reflecting an apprenticeship on the chitlin' circuit with the likes of Bobby 'Blue' Bland. Interestingly, in recent times, Marcus has set aside his odd-shaped horns – including saxello and Conn-O-Sax, a saxophonic variant of the cor anglais, in F – and his bass clarinet in favour of the B-flat clarinet, on which he gets a wonderful tone, concentrated but not effortful.

The records are as varied as the instrumentation used to be. There are recent duos with trumpeter Ted Daniel and various outings with the Cosmosamatics group he co-leads with Sonny Simmons. For that reason, it's hard to pick just one. Justin Time has acquired an impressive knack of putting together intriguing duos – Paul Bley and Kenny Wheeler being a more obviously homegrown promotion for the Montreal label – and on this one it has excelled itself. Byard's weird barrelhouse-meets-free-jazz style suits Marcus perfectly. On *This Happening* he sticks largely to the stritch (a straightened-out alto, also in E-flat) but also plays a saxello. On just one track he reverts to bass clarinet, a medley of 'Giant Steps' and 'Naima' in the spirit of Eric Dolphy. The only other familiar tune is 'Darn That Dream', an eccentrically romantic end to a wonderful, offbeat record. Jaki's death in 1999 robbed Marcus of his most responsive playing partner to date, a musician who instinctively understood his balance of traditionalism and experiment. A second record, recorded a year later, is less sure-footed, but together they offer a valuable glimpse of a brief association.

BRAD MEHLDAU
Born 23 August 1970, Jacksonville, Florida
Piano

The Art Of The Trio: Volume 2 – Live At The Village Vanguard
Warners 46848-2
Mehldau; Larry Grenadier (b); Jorge Rossy (d). 1997.

Brad Mehldau says: **'The *Art Of The Trio* series nicely captured the development of that group of three musicians over the course of a few years.'**

Without any question, the dominant piano influence in contemporary jazz is Bill Evans, an overdetermining presence similar to that of Coltrane for saxophone-players. Mehldau is certainly the most accomplished, because also the most individual, and is now among the most keenly followed pianists in the music. His Warners records are a formidable lot, but the early Fresh Sound releases which signalled his arrival and which he probably looks back on as mere student-work are already exceptional. Under his Warners contract, Mehldau set out to create a sequence of albums under the *Art Of The Trio* heading. There are five of them, but they stand as comfortably apart as they do in order and there's no reason not to pick a later one as a starting-point.

This is the first of two recorded at the legendary New York club, and it has all the virtues of a modern live recording, with extended performances, heightened by place and moment, taken down in high-quality sound. At the Vanguard, Mehldau played a new version of Coltrane's 'Countdown', which has acted as a marker for his progress since the debut album on Warners. Where the earlier version was created out of disparate lines, this one is detailed and dense – he gets a long, long way into the piece, which his unaccompanied passage seems suddenly to illuminate, as if abruptly finding answers to a lot of questions. This is perhaps a more ambitious record, sparked by the live situation, and it's like a detailed addendum to the finished elegance of the first volume. 'Moon River' is exquisite, but also full of unexpected detail. 'Monk's Dream' seems outside Mehldau's usual realm, but he nails it with a faint swagger. 'Young And Foolish' is a fine version of that often overlooked staple. Rossy and Grenadier follow Mehldau without a stumble. In the presence of a player as omnicompetent as this, their role is inevitably more subdued, and there is no hint of Scott LaFaro's relationship with Grenadier, excellent as he is, but at the best moments this is unmistakably a trio playing, not just a pianist and rhythm.

T. S. MONK
Born Thelonious Sphere Monk Jr, 27 December 1949, New York City
Drums

Monk On Monk
N2K Encoded Music N2KW 10017
Monk; Laurie Frink, Virgil Jones, Wallace Roney, Arturo Sandoval, Don Sickler, Clark Terry (t); Roy Hargrove (flhn); Eddie Bert (tb); David Amram, John Clark (frhn); Bobby Porcelli, Bobby Watson (as); Wayne Shorter (ts, ss); Jimmy Heath, Roger Rosenberg, Grover Washington, Willie Williams (ts); Howard Johnson (bs, tba); Geri Allen, Herbie Hancock, Ronnie Mathews, Danilo Perez (p); Ron Carter, Dave Holland, Christian McBride, Dave Wang (b); Nnenna Freelon, Kevin Mahogany, Dianne Reeves (v). February 1997.

T. S. Monk said (1999): **'My task is to clarify, to put this music in a form that will be reachable by anyone who wants to experience it. That isn't diluting it, but clarifying it.'**

Thelonious Jr made his public debut with his dad at the age of just ten and, after some time away from jazz working in R&B, has devoted himself to the old man's memory and to a sound that is intended to recapture the melodic energy of '50s Blue Note hard bop, influenced by Art Blakey, Max Roach and Tony Williams.

By the time *Monk On Monk* appeared, one might have expected the rising-50-year-old to have pushed out into territory he could legitimately call his own, rather than continue playing dad's work. The dedication and obvious affection are hard to fault and some of the playing is very fine indeed. On this occasion, T.S. has assembled a superband which must have been the envy of the block. All the songs are by Monk, though 'Ruby My Dear' and 'In Walked Bud' have been transformed into vocal vehicles for Kevin Mahogany and Nnenna Freelon respectively. Herbie Hancock and Ron Carter solo on 'Two Timer', but the best double act of the evening bouquet goes to Bobby Watson and Wallace Roney for their spirited and lyrical attack on 'Jackie-ing'.

MARILYN MAZUR
Born 18 January 1955, New York City
Drums, percussion

Small Labyrinths
ECM 533679-2
Mazur; Nils Petter Molvaer (t); Hans Ulrik (reeds); Elvira Planar (ky); Eivind Aarset (g); Klaus Hovman (b); Audun Kleive (d); Aina Kemanis (v). 1997.

Marilyn Mazur says: **'The music on *Small Labyrinths* with my group Future Song consists of four of my compositions for the group, the other eight tracks are actually collective improvs in the studio, inspired by conceptual titles, the used titles on the CD are in return inspired by the music we made.'**

Mazur was born in New York but grew up in Denmark, where she led her own Primi Band in the '80s before high-profile stints with Miles Davis, Wayne Shorter and Jan Garbarek. She was the 2001 winner of the Jazzpar prize. Dance has also been an important component of her work.

In addition to Primi, Mazur has run three groups: Pulse Unit, Percussion Paradise and, more recently, Future Song. Future Song evolved while Mazur was touring with Miles and has remained pretty much intact since 1989. An earlier Stunt record is very good, but nothing matches the exquisite sound on her first ECM disc, where the added presence of Molvaer and Aarset gives more colour and texture to the ensemble. Most of the pieces are very short, like pinhole-camera captures of fleeting scenes, but 'See There', 'Back To Dreamfog Mountain' and 'The Holey' are all substantial cuts that document the evolution of a group language.

VALERY PONOMAREV
Born 20 January 1943, Moscow, USSR
Trumpet

A Star For You
Reservoir RSR CD 150
Ponomarev; Bob Berg (ts); Sid Simmons (p); Ken Walker (b); Billy Hart (d). April 1997.

Valery Ponomarev says: '**Listening to it right after the recording session I couldn't help thinking that everyone played beautifully. Everyone except me. I was the only one who failed. I could have done much better. For a long time I didn't want to listen to it. Much later, I needed to check out the title-track and ended up going through the whole CD. Bob, Sid, Kenny and Billy sounded just as great. And me? I couldn't believe how much I liked it this time. "It's me playing," I kept thinking. "Not bad, Ponomarev."'**

A Muscovite under Clifford Brown's spell, he defected in 1973 and joined the Jazz Messengers in 1977, before leading his own group, Universal Language. That's a rather wonderful band name for a man who left Russia during the deep freeze of the Brezhnev years in order to play jazz in the West. If anyone confirms that hard bop had become not just a musical *lingua franca* but also a confident assertion of human freedom, it is Ponomarev. He has an immediately attractive tone, round, ringing and accurate, and he has always had an instinctive swing with just a few subtle indicators of a non-American background.

Though he has made many fine records, *A Star For You* remains the vintage Universal Language date. Ponomarev makes it clear that this is a set very much dedicated to the spirit and memory of Art Blakey, perhaps because the 25th anniversary of his arrival in America wasn't so far away. The opening 'Commandments From A Higher Authority' is absolutely in the spirit of the Messengers' great days, a wheeling, driving theme which never quite comes to rest but exudes authority in every measure. Bob Berg is the key addition to this group, superb on 'Dance Intoxicant' and the long standard 'We'll Be Together Again', adding a warm-toned confidence to every track. Simmons and Walker get to show why they got the call, playing with intelligence and taste, never over-fussy, but subtle when the tune calls for another dimension.

FONDA/STEVENS GROUP
Formed c.1995
Group

Evolution
Leo CD LR 260
Joe Fonda (b); Herb Robertson (t, flhn); Mark Whitecage (as, ss); Michael Jefry Stevens (p); Harvey Sorgen (d). April–October 1997.

Michael Jefry Stevens says: '**This was the last recording with the original group. When we listened to the Eindhoven recording of my composition "Birdtalk", I realized that I had "laid out" for virtually the entire song, without realizing it. Funny what happens when you give yourself over to the power of music.'**

Long-standing groups are relatively rare in jazz, where there is a premium on flexible personnels and fleeting encounters. Fonda/Stevens underlines the enormous benefit of settled relationships, even if individual careers go on in parallel. This is a group of relatively unfashionable – if not exactly 'outsider' – improvisers, who for the last decade and a half have produced music of consistent high intelligence and often great loveliness. Selecting their first release is a decision taken *faute de mieux*, since there is scarcely a weak or slack set in the entire output, and because we have a special affection for this line-up. Robertson and Whitecage are both conservative radicals whose most splenetic moments wouldn't cause an earthquake. It's their solos and dialogues with different members of the rhythm section that tend to direct the music, even though the writing is all by the leaders. The compositions are either open-ended sketches or Coleman-like melodies counterpointed between the instruments, and if the latter carry less conviction it's because the playing is ragged when it should be pointed.

Evolution, recorded live in Europe, sees the group move back and forth in musical time. 'Birdtalk' is a clear reference to the bop roots of most of the players. So absorbing is the music that after countless listens we hadn't quite noticed that Stevens was largely absent, until he pointed it out. Robertson's solo is superb, somewhere between Dizzy Gillespie and Booker Little, while 'Song For My Mother' breathes poetry. 'Second Time Around' was an intriguing rhythmic exercise, with just a few indications written out by Fonda for the players: no set harmonic or melodic material. Stevens's 'Strayhorn' is a tender portrait of a great composer.

By the time of *Live At The Bunker* (recorded at a favourite and supportive venue in Bielefeld; as a Jew of German extraction, Stevens isn't blind to the irony of playing in a Second World War bunker!), Robertson had been replaced by Smoker, and Whitecage had moved on, too. It's a new balance of sound and the group has continued to evolve, integrating new personnel here and there. For us, though, this remains the Fonda/Stevens record the others have to match up to.

MICHEL PORTAL

Born 27 November 1935, Bayonne, France
Saxophones, clarinets, bandoneon

Dockings
Label Bleu LBLC 6604
Portal; Markus Stockhausen (t); Bojan Zulfikarpašić (p); Bruno Chevillon, Steve Swallow (b); Joey Baron (d). June 1997.

Michel Portal said (1998): **'I would play compositions by Mozart or Debussy and think: "I can play this now, but what do I do next?" It became very mechanical. But I was also listening to American music on the radio and hearing Charlie Parker, or Jimmie Noone, or Duke Ellington, and I was ...** *bouleversé***. Excited, but I knew that I was not an American and did not think like an American. How was I to be a musician, and express** *myself*?**'

Portal is one of the few musicians in our book who has had a parallel performing career in modern composition. He was in earlier days an important interpreter of Pierre Boulez's complex music, which some might regard as the antithesis of jazz. Portal, however, feels no strain between the two languages and has managed to carry over elements of each to the other. The only comparable figures on the recent scene have been trombonist Vinko Globokar and bassist Barry Guy.

Portal developed a style which absorbed the formal rigours of classical playing with an improvisatory freedom that sounds complex, but proceeds from quite basic premises. *Dockings* is a quiet masterpiece from an all-star band. Portal's daring in using such strong musical personalities so delicately and sparingly more than pays dividends, and it would be hard to imagine a record of such poise and grace. Baron and Swallow happily move between insistent *ostinato* figures and more or less free time, leaving Chevillon to anchor the basic metre. Bojan Z is as usual tasteful and responsive, and the two horns are deployed with great subtlety. Though there isn't a vibraphone, the most obvious model for the sound is the Dolphy group of *Out To Lunch!* (Eric is the dedicatee of the second track), but rendered ever more abstractly lyrical. Stockhausen, who needs to be added to the roster of bi-partisan players above, has the penetrating intensity of a Freddie Hubbard, but with a softer and more plangent quality. The mourning dove timbre of Portal's clarinet on 'Dolphy', building in intensity over Baron's pattering accompaniment, is matched only by their interaction on 'Ida Lupino', this time with Portal on bandoneon.

BOB BROOKMEYER &
Born 19 December 1929, Kansas City, Missouri
Valve trombone, piano

New Works: Celebration
Challenge CHR 70066
Brookmeyer; Thorsten Beckenstein, Jorg Engels, Ralf Hesse, Torsten Maass, Sebastian Strempel (t); Christian Jakso, Ludwig Nuss, Ansgar Striepens (tb); Edward Partyka (btb); Marko Lackner, Stefan Pfeifer (as); Nils Van Haften, Paul Heller (ts); Marcus Bartelt, Scott Robinson (bs); Kris Goessens (p); Jurgen Grimm (ky); Ingmar Heller (b); John Hollenbeck (d); Christopher Dell (perc). July 1997.

Bob Brookmeyer said (1999): **'My life fell into two parts, you know: the drinking part and the sober part. Though, to be honest, I don't really think of it as "sober". I think I'm a free spirit – or nuttier – when I don't drink!'**

Having weathered difficult professional situations – acting as intermediary between Jim Hall and Jimmy Giuffre in the Giuffre trio, struggling with Gerry Mulligan's combative spirit (and terrible piano-playing) – Brookmeyer eventually succumbed to his own personal demons and there were long, blank spells in his career. Defying once again the stale dictum that there are no second acts in American lives, he came back in his '60s and '70s with a body of exceptionally fine new music. Warmly recognized as a composer in Europe, he often had to rely on non-American orchestras and labels to allow it to be heard.

The earlier things on this delightful set were written for a festival in Lübeck in 1994, with Gerry Mulligan as guest soloist. Posthumously documented on record, it features the multi-talented Scott Robinson in the solo role, turning the folk- and dance-based material into something at once familiar and strange. Robinson is a formidable soloist and he brings a genuine individuality to the part. Of the other tracks, 'Cameo' is essentially a solo spot for Brookmeyer, while 'Duets', built on one of Bob's minimalist themes, is a great basis for improvisation and includes some inventive drumming from John Hollenbeck. The closing item, 'Boom Boom', is derived from the earlier 'Danish Suite' and provides a light-toned and joyous closer. Brookmeyer has rarely written or played better.

& *See also* **Brookmeyer** (1956; p. 177)

GEORGE E. LEWIS &
Born 14 July 1952, Chicago, Illinois
Trombones, sousaphone, tuba, computer

Endless Shout
Tzadik TZ 7054
Lewis; John Korsrud, Bill Clark (t); Ralph Eppel, Rod Murray (tb); Brad Muirhead (btb, tba); Mark Nodwell (ss); Saul Berson, Coat Cooke (as, f); Paul Cram, Graham Ord (ts); Vinny Golia (bs, picc); Paul Plimley, Sarah Cahill (p); Ron Samworth (g); Peggy Lee (clo); Paul Blaney, Clyde Reed (b); Dylan van der Schyff (d); Steven Schick (perc); Quincy Troupe, Kate Hammett-Vaughan (v). September 1995–November 1997.

George Lewis says: **'In *Voyager*, where the computer and I improvise together, and the grid-structured "Shadowgraph 4", you could say that orchestras became self-aware sonic bodies.'**

As the years have gone by, Lewis has emerged as a benign philosopher of new music, confidently communicating across the human–machine 'divide', discoursing generously on the non-problem of the compo/impro dichotomy. The '90s saw a rich new vein of work emerge. *Voyager* in 1993 was a collaboration with Roscoe Mitchell, a trombone and saxophone duo in the presence of interactive computer technology, yielding a multi-layered work quite unlike anything else around.

Endless Shout is more diverse, almost a sampler of Lewis's range of interests and achievements, from trombone–computer interactivity to a full-scale performance of one of the 'Shadowgraph' pieces.The title-piece is a four-part piano work, dedicated to Richard Abrams, and a homage to the stride and boogie masters – seeking to 'reinterpret blues utterance in the light of my own experience'. Sarah Cahill gives an eloquent performance. 'North Star Boogaloo' fragments and reshapes a Quincy Troupe poem around a notated percussion part – deft, humorous, vibrant. But the most imposing pieces are a 1997 revision of 'Shadowgraph 4', where Lewis conducts the NOW Orchestra and enables them to pack a tremendous amount into an 11-minute rendition, and a new version of 'Voyager', where the composer-trombonist and his technology explore 'one potential outcome between the improviser and the computer'. A memorable collection and a work that may in future seem historically important, too.

& *See also* **Homage To Charles Parker** (1979; p. 455)

GUY BARKER
Born 26 December 1957, Chiswick, London
Trumpet

What Love Is
Emarcy 558381
Barker; Jamie Talbot (cl, f, af); Perico Sambeat (as); Andy Panayi (f, af); David Hartley (p); Geoff Gascoyne (b); Gene Calderazzo (d); Sting (v); strings. November 1997.

Guy Barker remembers: '**Richard [Cook] knew the label would want standards, but we talked about doing more unusual material, jazz ballads by Monk, Strayhorn and Jimmy Rowles, even an Ornette Coleman medley. "Crazy She Calls Me" wasn't going right. Richard wanted to cut a section out, but [arranger] Colin Towns and I didn't think there was anything wrong. The next day we did the piece the way Richard wanted it and immediately it felt different. Something just happened. Even the introduction felt different. It felt fantastic. I went back into the recording booth and Richard was sitting there with tears in his eyes. He bent his head and said: "That's my favourite track."'**

Barker's standing as the doyen of Britain's younger trumpeters has scarcely resulted in a flood of recordings under his own name. However, he has remained busy and has prevailed in recent years with some fine recording for the Provocateur label and with a self-produced Mozart-inspired project that won considerable critical acclaim. Barker's early recordings appeared on Spotlite and Miles Music before he was picked up by Polygram, where his records were produced by the late Richard Cook. This one bespeaks growing confidence in both men, and in the working relationship. It's an elegant record and all the more striking for blending in adventurous material among the standards. Opening with Rowles's 'The Peacocks' immediately suggests its originality, but it is with 'Monk's Mood' and the Ornette medley that it really takes shape. Barker is in inspired form and the strings play with understanding.

Barker would go on to even more adventurous work but this one stands apart and remains one of his finest moments.

ELTON DEAN

Born 28 October 1945, Nottingham, England; died 8 February 2006, London
Alto saxophone, saxello

Newsense

Slam CD 229

Dean; Jim Dvorak (t); Roswell Rudd, Paul Rutherford, Annie Whitehead (tb); Alex Maguire (p); Marcio Mattos (clo); Roberto Bellatalla (b); Mark Sanders (d). November 1997.

Elton Dean said (1997): **'Ninesense was wonderful, like an old-fashioned touring band. We'd find ourselves driving round Norfolk, lost in the fog, looking for some little venue or college. There aren't places like that to play any more. I loved it.'**

He gifted part of his name to early blues associate Elton John, when they were both working for Long John Baldry (who supplied the other half), and took his inspiration from the saxophone heavyweights like Trane and Joe Henderson. Along the way, assisted by a vintage King saxello, a sort of curvy soprano, Dean created a sound all his own, tight-toned and highly expressive, that was always identifiable whether working in a neo-rock context or even when buried away in the free regiment of the London Improvisers Orchestra. His debut album, since revived by the splendid Cuneiform, was recorded while Dean was still with Soft Machine, made largely with fellow Softs. It was mainly improvised, though 'Neo Caliban Grides' was a band number. The washes of electric piano are reminiscent of Miles's electric experiments, with Marc Charig's plaintive cornet clinching the connection.

After leaving Soft Machine, Dean seemed to be everywhere, leading his own post-bop groups (and eventually Soft Heap), playing with Keith Tippett and Howard Riley, and turning up in almost every conceivable setting the UK offered. Recognition in America awaited the rediscovery of the old stuff by Cuneiform. One of the happiest periods was with the almost-big-band Ninesense, three pairs of horns plus rhythm and a book of strong anthemic tunes influenced by Tippett and the Brotherhood Of Breath. The group made one record for Ogun and some BBC tapes turned up a few years ago, still with the ill-fated Mongezi Feza in the line-up.

Not surprisingly, Dean tried to re-create the experience twenty years later. The new outfit was further fruit of Dean's association with Roswell Rudd. The brass are excellent, with American-born Dvorak more than holding his own against the trombones, a tight, high sound that always sounds as if it might tear but never does. The paired bass and cello are very effective with Mattos's wailing, mystical sound pushed well to the fore. He and Dean are the two most provocative and moving voices in the ensemble. Dean has rarely sounded as exuberant and joyous, and the improvised 'Snap, Crackle And Pop' with Rudd and Whitehead is a delight from start to finish.

KEN PEPLOWSKI

Born 23 May 1959, Cleveland, Ohio
Clarinet, tenor saxophone

Grenadilla

Concord CCD 4809

Peplowski; Kenny Davern (cl); Marty Ehrlich (cl, bcl); J. D. Parran (cbcl); Scott Robinson (acl); Ben Aronov (p); Howard Alden (g); Greg Cohen (b); Chuck Redd (d). December 1997.

Ken Peplowski says (2005): **'I have a love affair with the clarinet. It isn't just a saxophonist's "double". It's a quite different instrument and it deserves to be treated that way. I don't just practise; I *really* practise, and in a pretty structured way.'**

Peplowski is already a veteran of the swing-repertory school which has kept that stream of American jazz robust through some very lean times, but he is also a player who, like his fellow clarinettist Kenny Davern, isn't afraid to venture into free territory when called upon. Peplowski grew up in Cleveland and started his career young, playing in polka groups, before working with the posthumous Tommy Dorsey band, and with Benny Goodman, before his idol's death in 1986.

Like a number of the catalogue's stars, he has a very big discography on Concord, but much of it fell foul of corporate 'rationalization', a situation Peplowski openly regrets. They're all worth looking for, but *Grenadilla* stands out on a number of counts. It might seem perverse to choose a record that reflects a less familiar side of his playing personality, but it is a powerful and ambitious record, too little recognized as such on first release.

Grenadilla is the wood from which the majority of quality clarinets are made. Like any other rainforest tree, it is endangered, and Peplowski dedicates this remarkable album to its preservation. Perhaps even more importantly, though, he makes the record an expression of his own desire to preserve jazz tradition even as he pushes it forward creatively. Here, the guests represent wildly different aspects of contemporary clarinet-playing.

Working together for the first time, Peplowski and the veteran Kenny Davern combine on the New Orleans Rhythm Kings' 'Farewell Blues', a tune first recorded in 1922. Davern's calm delivery complements Peplowski's own characteristically fervid statement; he has seldom sounded more like Benny Goodman's modernist descendant. At the opposite end of the spectrum are Marty Ehrlich's 'The Reconsidered Blues' and 'The Soul In The Wood' and Greg Cohen's brief, powerful 'Variations', on which Parran, Robinson and Ehrlich again guest. At first blush, Ehrlich might seem the arch-modernist, but his moody clarinet and bass clarinet, and Parran's subterranean contrabass instrument, are put to quite traditional ends. Peplowski has a nice way of making musicians reveal their roots.

The rest of the original writing is credited to Ben Aronov, who continues to surprise. He is the composer of the two quartet tracks and the opening 'Benny's Pennies' (no real relation to the Tristano number), on which Alden makes the first of several strong contributions. At the end of the album, 'Farewell Blues' is sandwiched between two classics which show the guitarist and the leader at their intuitive best: Victor Herbert's 'Indian Summer' and, done as a drummerless, pianoless trio, 'Cry Me A River'. An exquisite end to a remarkable album.

KENNY DREW JR
Born 14 June 1958, New York City
Piano

Passionata
Arkadia 70561
Drew; Peter Washington (b); Lewis Nash (d); strings. January 1998.

Kenny Drew Jr said (1991): **'My first gig was courtesy of [pianist] John Hicks who heard me play, liked what he heard and asked me to sub for him at a date where he could only play the first half. When I got there, I realized the piano was missing keys and had busted strings. I got through it and, as well as surviving, was given a cheque for $35 ... which bounced. Welcome to the jazz life!'**

The fruit rarely falls far from the tree, but Drew Jr is a very different fellow to his father. He's a tough-minded and clearly spoken proponent of creative values in jazz and, one dares say, a more adventurous stylist than Kenny Sr. Inevitably, the discographical record is patchy, with a lot of early material out of circulation and only to be found on Japanese and European imprints and in specialist stores. But it's worth seeking out. Kenny's pianism is brisk, effective and unmistakably modern.

He bears his father's name, but was raised by relatives, so any direct influence can only have been through records, or by conscious effort a little later. It wasn't until the end of the '90s that Kenny Jr began to programme his father's work prominently. *Passionata* is a full-scale tribute, titled after an unfinished song, played here for the first time. The set also includes Drew Sr material like 'Dark Beauty', one of the old man's finest compositions, and standards that he must have played a thousand times. There's even a delightful reading of 'Hush-a-Bye', a European lullaby that Kenny Sr apparently enjoyed and which seems to ghost into a couple of his improvisations in the Steeplechase years. These are fresh interpretations, though; 'Summertime' is given a classical spin and other tracks veer from the expected line. This is certainly the most accommodating and inventive trio Kenny has worked with. Washington has an enormous range and a capacity for free, full melody alongside a strong, sure beat, leaving Nash to embellish and elaborate. The strings are arranged by Bob Belden, unobtrusive, idiomatic and cleanly registered.

DAVE DOUGLAS *&*
Born 24 March 1963, Montclair, New Jersey
Trumpet

Convergence
Soul Note 121316-2
Douglas; Mark Feldman (vn); Erik Friedlander (clo); Drew Gress (b); Michael Sarin (d). January 1998.

Pianist Michael Jefry Stevens, with Douglas the main composer for the Mosaic Sextet, says:
'I met Dave around 1985. He was probably 19 and walked into a jam session I led every Sunday afternoon at the now defunct Seventh Avenue South jazz club in the West Village, owned by the Brecker Brothers. This innocent-looking kid proceeded to walk up onto the stage (uninvited) and played his ass off. The rest, as they say, is history ...'

... and that history has taken Douglas into some remarkable musical situations. The whole course of his career has been about assuming permission to tackle whatever music appeals to him, whether it is standards jazz, classical modernism or southern European folk music, and to use music as a vehicle for social and political ideas. Douglas's youthful confidence had more to do with vision than innocence.

It might seem perverse to select another Douglas record from the '90s when in the following decade he continued to make remarkable albums, and launched his own Greenleaf label. However, *Convergence* is in every way exceptional. This is the same band that made *Parallel Worlds* and *Five*, with the single change of Drew Gress for Mark Dresser. No surprise by this stage in the game to find Douglas programming 'Desseins Éternels' from Olivier Messiaen's organ work *La Nativité du seigneur*, and following it with Weill's 'Bilbao Song'. The trumpeter claims he first heard the Messiaen piece in a blindfold test set by a friend, and thought it was 'Joe Zawinul, early Weather Report', which attests to a sharp ear, for the French composer's strong bass pedals are very similar to Zawinul's signature procedure. The two key tracks here are a farewell to drummer Tony Williams, a perfect illustration of Douglas's ability to invest long form with real significance, and 'Meeting At Infinity', which indirectly gives the album its title and underlines how Douglas likes to have separate musical lines converge only virtually, leaving them to their own instrumental logic. *Convergence* is an important work, a strong synthesis of past approaches, with a tantalizing hint of new directions.

& *See also* **Constellations** (1995; p. 588)

GREG OSBY
Born 3 August 1960, St Louis, Missouri
Alto saxophone

Banned In New York
Blue Note 496860 2
Osby; Jason Moran (p, org); Atsushi Ozada (b); Rodney Green (d). January 1998.

Greg Osby says: **'*Banned In New York* was my attempt to capture the true and more realistic essence of my touring band without the polish that a "staged" live recording offers. It was documented with a single minidisc recorder and no announcement to the audience (or to the band) was made. A pure, no-frills, untampered, anti-production.'**

Osby studied in Washington DC, and at Berklee before moving to New York and becoming a prime mover in M-Base. That period and the early records that came after it now seem distractions from his mature work. Dabbling in rap and hip-hop was *de rigueur* at the period and he already had a background in R&B and funk, but it isn't work that stands the test of time. There were strong statements along the way, like *Zero* and *New Directions*, but occasionally Osby looked like a man hampered rather than encouraged by major-label attention.

It is perhaps significant that his best record by a country mile and one that features essentially the same studio group was made for next to nothing and issued mid-price as an official bootleg. *Banned In New York* documents a single gig by the quartet, set down on a DAT player and rush-released as a report on work in progress. Osby's own '13th Floor' starts things off, but from there he brings in Rollins, Ellington, Parker and Monk tunes and uses the material to fashion an utterly compelling treatise on the tradition and how it can fuel the playing of contemporary spirits on the bandstand, here and now. Each of the musicians makes his individual mark, but it's the way the quartet develops and processes ideas, caught on the hoof, that makes the record so powerful and immediate. Osby has said that he wishes he could release several records a year, in the manner of the old Blue Note performers, and, if the results are like this, it's a sentiment we echo.

PAUL BLEY&
Born 10 November 1932, Montreal, Quebec, Canada
Piano

Not Two, Not One
EDM 559447
Bley; Gary Peacock (b); Paul Motian (d). January 1998.

Paul Bley said (1999): **'The philosophy was that it wasn't necessary to respond to one another when we played, that we could have three independent voices in parallel, playing in counterpoint and actually competing for attention at times.'**

We were prematurely dismissive of *Not Two, Not One* in previous editions, though admittedly baffled rather than hostile. The dynamic of the group, right from the opening 'Not Zero: In Three Parts', doesn't accord with the usual language assumptions of an improvising trio. There doesn't seem to be communication between the elements and the music has at points an oddly randomized quality. However, once one accepts this as description rather than criticism, the music begins to make more sense and a new kind of empathy becomes evident, one that is readily modelled in the natural world when entities of quite different types and species are required to occupy a limited space. It is equivalent to the logic of a dance rather than an aural experience and the spatial metaphor works well for almost every track on the record, which, *pace* our previous doubts, now seems one of Bley's most important and compelling.

& *See also* **Closer** (1965; p. 330), **Axis** (1977; p. 439)

EDDIE HENDERSON
Born 26 October 1940, New York City
Trumpet, flugelhorn

Reemergence
Sharp Nine Records CD 1012-2
Henderson; Kevin Hays (p); Joe Locke (vib); Ed Howard (b); Billy Drummond (d). March 1998.

Eddie Henderson said (1999): **'The main thing I learned from Miles had nothing to do with trumpet-playing. It was about how to put people together, how to shape a group that will deliver the music as you hear it.'**

Miles Davis was a Henderson house-guest during a residency at the Blackhawk and, while obviously impressed by the youngster's ability to play through *Sketches Of Spain* without a fluff, pointed out that Eddie was going to have to work out his own approach and voice. He was also apparently forgiving of the youngster's criticism of *his* trumpet-playing, which didn't match what young Eddie had been taught.

Henderson has certainly created an individual voice, but despite gigs with Miles, Herbie Hancock (during the electric/pre-Head Hunters period), Joe Henderson and his own group, he has remained essentially a part-time player, and has continued practising psychiatric medicine. For that reason, the discography has a slightly spotty aspect. There were a couple of good electric/fusion records early on, after leaving Hancock, but only in more recent times has the trumpeter established a significant list.

Dominated by the long and graceful 'Gershwin Suite', *Reemergence* is a triumphant record, a near-perfect articulation of Henderson's skills as a leader. One of his gifts is to allow his players to complete the process of creation by leaving themes, notably his own composition 'Dreams', open-ended and only loosely arranged, so that performance actually completes the process of composition and arrangement. This time around, there are only a couple of Henderson originals in the set, which ends with the brief 'Natsuko-san', played straight and without solos, a simple message of love to his wife. Joe Locke is a key element and he brings the epic sweep of 'Saturn's Child' to the date.

The Gershwin material is pitched just right: clever, warm, life-aware and sardonic without a hint of cynicism. 'Summertime' needs something a bit special these days, and the trumpeter gives it a soaring presence that blows the clichés away. 'Embraceable You' is equally good at the end of the sequence, expressive but disciplined. Everything on the album, from Wayne Shorter's 'This Is For Albert' to the close, seems perfectly placed.

MARTIAL SOLAL &
Born 23 August 1927, Algiers, Algeria
Piano

Balade Du 10 Mars
Soul Note 121340 2
Solal; Marc Johnson (b); Paul Motian (d). March 1998.

Martial Solal said (1985): **'Jazz enjoyed some very good times and there was some very good music using popular songs, songs from Broadway shows. But the time now is for jazz to concentrate on building its own repertoire of compositions, and not just a few chords and a small melody, proper compositions that will set free and challenge all musicians.'**

Solal moved to France from his native Algeria in his early 20s, worked with Django Reinhardt and accompanied visiting or exiled Americans. He is a remarkable composer, creating complex themes out of simple intervals and brief melodic cells. At times, Solal has headed big bands and has written for film, but his main contribution is as a small-group and solo performer.

When Solal made his American debut at Newport 1963, Paul Motian was in the group. The association was revived 25 years later and produced some of the best music of the pianist's career. Martial celebrated his 70th birthday with Paul and Gary Peacock on *Just Friends* (Dreyfus) and has rarely sounded more blues-based and swinging, eliding at least some of his subtler, 'European' configurations to produce what is arguably his most straight-ahead album ever. This is not to say that it lacks individuality. No one who has listened to him with any attention will mistake who the soloist is on 'Willow Weep For Me' or 'You Stepped Out Of A Dream', though it is not until halfway through the record, and a markedly original 'Hommage À Frédéric Chopin', that something of a more familiar Solal comes through.

Balade Du 10 Mars is even better. The free-form improvisation on Motian's 'Gang Of Five' is the most outside playing Solal has done on record for many years. 'Round Midnight' is a duet for piano and drums, recalling the same piece on the Newport record, which RCA should think hard about reissuing. Johnson stands in for Gary Peacock on this occasion and, as might be expected, the rhythm is looser and less rugged. As before, echoes of the classic Bill Evans trio are everywhere and it would be wonderful to hear either version of this group tackle 'Gloria's Step' or 'Waltz For Debby'. Martial's touch is as deft and lyrical as ever, but there is a new and welcome hint of wildness to the playing, as if finally he feels relaxed enough in his own technique to cut loose and challenge the harmonic rules. Unusual to hear Solal concentrate so absolutely on standards and jazz repertory. 'Night And Day', 'Softly, As In A Morning Sunrise', 'Almost Like Being In Love', 'The Lady Is A Tramp' and 'My Old Flame' round out the programme, with a fine, unhackneyed interpretation of 'Round Midnight' and just one other original, 'The Newest Old Waltz', coming in right at the end.

& See also **Solitude** (2005; p. 702)

CHRIS SPEED
Born 1967, Seattle, Washington
Tenor saxophone, clarinet

Deviantics
Songlines SGL 1547-2
Speed; Cuong Vu (t); Skuli Sverrisson (b); Jim Black (d). October 1998.

Chris Speed said (1999): **'I actually started on alto saxophone, but my teacher persuaded me to switch to clarinet. In the school band, I got switched to tenor because someone couldn't make rehearsals and it just clicked. As to who influenced me, I honestly think that aside from the obvious people – Coltrane, Rollins, etc. – it's been friends and associates who've made the biggest impact.'**

One of the busiest players on the scene, Speed turns up in almost any kind of context, bringing with him a stern technique and a generous supply of kindred ideas. His background in classical music is occasionally evident, but, like other equally busy players, the work under his own name sometimes lacks focus and finish.

This group, named after the first album *Yeah No* (Pachora has an overlapping personnel), has produced some fascinating work, however. On *Yeah No*, the frantic 'Scribble Bliss', the ghostly 'The Dream And Memory Store', the intense and purposeful 'Merge' each use the resources of the quartet to good ends without quite suggesting a particular vision. On its own terms, this is a sharp, funny exploration of some of the musics that Speed's come across – jazz and everything else. In many ways the key player is Black, whose nutty rhythms are what really brings the group to life, as boisterous as the horns are.

Deviantics pushes the ideas a little harder into a more coherent shape. This has elements of post-bop in it, but Vu is a strange player, as likely to play against the grain of whatever's going on as to follow it, and the stew of influences is getting thicker and richer. Sverrisson's odd 'Tulip' is a very curious mélange, and the following 'Wheatstone' is a storming modal blow. 'Valya' has an East European feel.

CHARLIE MARIANO

Born 12 November 1923, Boston, Massachusetts; died 16 June 2009, Cologne, Germany
Alto, tenor and soprano saxophones, flute, nagaswaram

Savannah Samurai
Jazzline JL 1153 2
Mariano; Vic Juris (g); Dieter Ilg (b); Jeff Hirshfield (d). 1998.

Charlie Mariano said (1999): **'Interviewers put on this very serious face and say: "But of course you live in Europe now", as if I had lost a leg! I say to them: "Yes, and I work with Indian musicians ... does that mean I don't play jazz any more?" Music is music. Where it comes from doesn't matter very much.'**

Critics were hasty in placing Mariano in the gaggle of post-Bird alto-players. He was born only three years after Parker, but his first and greatest influence remains Johnny Hodges. His studies in Indian music, and on the wooden, oboe-like nagaswaram, have helped emphasize the exotic overtones he absorbed from Hodges and which are already evident in the early, bop-inspired sessions. Mariano grew up in the Boston area and began his career with Shorty Sherock and with Stan Kenton, before co-leading a group with his then wife Toshiko Akiyoshi. He also worked with Mingus and for a time in the later '60s dabbled in fusion music with an outfit called Osmosis. However, Mariano's interests always lay further afield and he began to take an active interest in Indian music. *Bangalore* from 1998 was a fascinating multi-cultural montage, but it was another record from that year that brought together Mariano's various interests in one convincing package.

No tablas, mridangam, veena, ghatam or konnakol here, and the title points to cultural traditions well away from the subcontinent, but it's clear from just a few moments that underneath the whipsmart post-bop of *Savannah Samurai* there's a solid but unconventional foundation of harmonic and rhythmic ideas that point away from the usual European-African sources. 'Children's Steps' is a delightful opener, funky but with folkish qualities and a basic walking rhythm underpinning it. The guitarist's 'Luna Doone' is taken on soprano, which became increasingly important to Mariano over the years and emphasizes his Hodges lineage. 'Dark Alley' is another Juris composition, with a hint of Bobby Watson in the line. There is a reprise at the end of the record, interestingly comparable to the Ornette Coleman–Pat Metheny *Song X*. Ilg, always an interesting writer, contributes the title-tune and the delightful 'Waltz For Dani', which tips its hat in the direction of Bill Evans. Charlie's high, plaintive tone is so pure one might almost be listening to an oboe or cor, perhaps the pay-off from his own dabbling with double-reeded horns. The final four tracks constitute a 'Climate Suite' – a 'Four Seasons' to you and me – and are collectively composed. Here again, Mariano combines an elemental straightforwardness of outline with maximum expression.

GEORGE COLEMAN
Born 8 March 1935, Memphis, Tennessee
Tenor saxophone

I Could Write A Book: The Music Of Richard Rodgers
Telarc 83439
Coleman; Harold Mabern (p); Jamil Nasser (b); Billy Higgins (d). May 1998.

Saxophonist Gordon Cruickshank said (1996): **'His appearances in London in the '80s were a revelation. I guarantee that if you did before-and-after comparisons on half a dozen British saxophonists after those Ronnie Scott's appearances – and they were all there – you'd hear George Coleman's influence. He maybe isn't Coltrane, but I think he might have a longer-lasting impact on jazz harmony.'**

Greatly admired by other players, including Miles Davis, the Memphis-born saxophonist came through in a richly talented cohort of hometown players – Frank Strozier, Charles Lloyd, Phineas Newborn, Harold Mabern – and developed into a deceptively complex harmonist and challenging improviser. He was only briefly in Miles's great quintet, following Coltrane, and his achievement there is still undervalued, as are his own recordings. He is a deceptively complex harmonist and challenging improviser.

Coleman made some interesting records for Theresa (now on Evidence), including the richly textured *Manhattan Panorama*, but he seemed the most neglected of the major-league tenor men at the end of the '90s until Telarc threw him a line, and the promise of top-quality sound. The material is hardly unexpected, but George finds new things to do with 'Lover' and 'My Funny Valentine', roughening up the changes and investing 'Valentine' with a dark sobriety that banishes winsomeness. The band includes two old friends from Memphis, Mabern and Nasser, and the presence of Higgins at the kit guarantees a pungent swing. 'Thou Swell' is a duet for saxophone and drums, and 'People Will Say We're In Love' is just by the rhythm section. Nothing definitive in these interpretations, just standards playing of the very highest rank.

ROY HAYNES *&*
Born 13 March 1925, Roxbury, Massachusetts
Drums

Praise
Dreyfus 36598
Haynes; Graham Haynes (c, flhn); Kenny Garrett (ss, as); David Sanchez (ts); David Kikoski (p); Dwayne Burno (b). May 1998.

Roy Haynes said (2004): **'I heard "Morning Has Broken", Cat Stevens, played on the radio and really liked it. When it was over, the DJ just said: "Praise!" and I thought that was a pretty good name for a record.'**

Blessed with a terrific physique and natural good health, Haynes seemed to go from strength to strength as he entered his 70s, his exuberance undimmed, his musicianship subtler with each passing year. Unlike Elvin Jones, he doesn't dominate the bands he leads, but steers them generously from behind. As so often for players of this generation, Europe was often more responsive and it was the French Dreyfus label which took him up at this period. Haynes plays one of his most persuasive recorded solos on the closing 'Shades Of Senegal', a performance that is as expressive as it is rhythmically astute. The album covers every possible permutation, from solo percussion to septet, and at every level it is Roy who leads musically. Son Graham and the two saxophone-players each have interesting things to say, but it is the rhythm section, with Kikoski very much in the foreground, that makes things happen. Some of the selections, like John Carisi's 'Israel', are less than ideally suited to this personnel, but 'My Little Suede Shoes', the Charlie Parker classic, and the traditional 'Morning Has Broken' are both sterling performances, and Roy has rarely sounded more gleefully in charge.

& See also **We Three** (1958; p. 226)

SATOKO FUJII
Born 9 October 1958, Tokyo, Japan
Piano

Kitsune-Bi
Tzadik TZ 7220
Fujii; Sachi Hayasaki (ss); Mark Dresser (b); Jim Black (d). May & November 1998.

Saxophonist Raymond MacDonald says: **'Anybody who is lucky enough to play in Tokyo with Satoko not only experiences her endless generosity with time and energy but also realizes very quickly the huge affection and trust she has from the musicians around her.'**

Classically trained Fujii and trumpeter/partner Natsuki Tamura have forged a powerful body of work which combines romantic abandon with free-jazz daring. They divide their time between Japan and New York, but record so frequently that it is hard to imagine them actually in transit. The influence of Paul Bley on Fujii's work is unmistakable, though so, too, is the example of classical pianist Koji Taku, who gave up academic work at the age of 60 to play jazz. Stylistically, though, it's Bley who determines much of the language and a 1994/1995 four-handed album is a fascinating study in creative influence.

Kitsune-Bi was something of a breakthrough record for Fujii. Divided into two sessions, one of duets with the little-known but impressive Hayasaki (think Jane Ira Bloom on a scholarship to Nagoya), the other a brilliant trio with Dresser and Black. There is also a stunning solo piano piece, 'Sound Of Stone', which in itself is enough to establish Fujii's remarkable pedigree. 'Past Of Life' with the trio follows her usual practice of mixing freedom with some very infectious grooves, leading to a hypnotic, almost trance-like effect that sustains interest all the way through. The trio-only record is, if anything, better still, a thoughtful but by no means pastel record very different from her large-scale pieces. The long title-piece comes first and dominates the rest, to its detriment, but reprogrammed it makes for a compelling, even compulsive listening experience. The only things against it as a representative Fujii work are that Namura isn't involved on this occasion, and secondly the very idea that such an astonishing body of work could yield up one 'typical' record. She's worth investigating, and rapidly becomes an addiction.

URI CAINE
Born 8 June 1956, Philadelphia, Pennsylvania
Piano

Gustav Mahler In Töblach: I Went Out This Morning Over The Countryside
Winter & Winter 910 046 2
Caine; Ralph Alessi (t); David Binney (as); Mark Feldman (vn); Aaron Bensoussan (oud, v); Michael Formanek (b); Jim Black (d); DJ Olive (elec, turntables). July 1998.

Uri Caine says: **'In 1997, my first CD of Mahler arrangements received the Gustav Mahler International record award in Töblach amid some controversy. Many of the judges were upset that a jazz-influenced recording was even considered and made their displeasure known. When we were invited to play the following summer at the festival, many diehard Mahler fans protested and staged a walk-out while others greeted our music with enthusiasm. The CD is a live Italian radio recording of the concert; perhaps the controversy infused our playing with a special intensity.'**

The son of academics (his mother is also a poet), he studied with Bernard Peiffer and later with George Rochberg and acquired an eclectic approach to composition and arrangement. Though there is a Herbie Hancock influence, much of his recorded work consists of bold reworkings of classical material. His first record, *Sphere Music*, was a typical debut, with just about everything thrown in: the Monk tributes hinted at in the title, avant-garde procedures, elements of klezmer and other Jewish musics (an enthusiasm shared with Don Byron, who was an important collaborator). Nothing much about the record or its successor, *Toys*, prepared Caine's growing audience for the astonishing use of Mahler themes as 'standards'.

Chosen to kick off Winter & Winter's 'New Edition' imprint, *Urlicht* was an extraordinary feat of imaginative projection. The basic concept for the label is clearly modelled on ECM's swing towards new music, though perhaps Stefan Winter is more interested in fusion and crossover experimentation than is Manfred Eicher. The notion that Mahler's music, for much of the last two decades (and certainly before the popular advent of Górecki, Pärt, *et al.*) the only classical composer to appeal to a rock generation, might be adaptable to a jazz aesthetic is a pretty startling one. For the most part, the studio album works very well, not least because Caine refuses to 'jazz up' the source material. He takes themes from the first and second symphonies (including the 'primal light' theme from the 'Resurrection' Symphony), as well as songs from *Kindertotenlieder* and *Des Knaben Wunderhorn*, and turns them into open-ended, loose-woven melodic shapes that invite not so much harmonic improvisation as retexturing.

The live recording from Töblach (the composer's summer retreat) of the same material is a revelation. From the tightly reined-in piano introduction to the funeral march from the Fifth Symphony, with its wry Beethoven reference and high harmonics from Feldman and the DJ, to the sweeping romanticism of 'The Farewell' from *Das Lied von der Erde*, the audience is taken on a journey that has little to do with musicological orthodoxy, but everything to do with thoughtful deconstruction. Caine intuits how much of Mahler's music comes from folk sources and he hands over these famously sonorous themes to a wailing village band. The strange swoops of live electronics are a convincingly alien presence, hinting at birdcalls, spirit-possession, or merely creaking wheels and axles.

The two selections from *Kindertotenlieder* are exquisitely done. 'Oft denk' ich, sie sind nur ausgegangen' is recast as a mournful duet for violin and trumpet, ever more distant and desolated; children call in the background. There are fresh interpretations of 'Urlicht', the Adagietto from the Fifth Symphony and songs from *Des Knaben Wunderhorn* and *Lieder eines fahrenden Gesellen*. A remarkable conception.

CHARLES LLOYD &

Born 15 March 1938, Memphis, Tennessee
Tenor saxophone, flute

Voice In The Night

ECM 559445-2
Lloyd; John Abercrombie (g); Dave Holland (b); Billy Higgins (d). May 1998.

Charles Lloyd says: **'This was my first ECM recording with Master Billy Higgins. The first day, we got caught in traffic two blocks from the studio. I got very agitated about the delay. Higgins suggested I cross my toes and say: "Yes, Charles; yes, Charles; yes, Charles." I did and then jumped out of the car and walked the rest of the way. All of my recordings with Billy are precious testimony to our deep friendship.'**

Lloyd gradually turned his back on jazz after the end of the '60s. By the end of the following decade, the sabbatical was assumed to be permanent. His return to performance has been much discussed. Whether his return was instigated by Michel Petrucciani is now a matter of question. The fact is that he came back, first at a Blue Note event and then as an unexpected ECM signing, though Jarrett surely had a hand in that. The early albums for Manfred Eicher were fine, but they all now sound like way-stations, pilgrim moments.

As he passed his 60th birthday, Lloyd seemed to pause and take stock. Here, having seemed for many years to have turned his back on much of his past work, Lloyd revisits 'Voice In The Night' and the glorious 'Forest Flower', as well as covering Strayhorn's 'A Flower Is A Lovesome Thing' and Elvis Costello's and Burt Bacharach's 'God Give Me Strength', which stays close to the original. Also, much as he once did with 'Memphis Green' and similar downhome numbers, he gives himself the space to blow righteously on 'Island Blues Suite'.

This was also Lloyd's first comeback recording with an all-American group (expat Holland notwithstanding) for almost three decades. And what a band it is! Higgins does very much the kind of job that DeJohnette did, a driving, innately musical beat, and he was to become Lloyd's closest musical partner until his death in May 2001, making *The Water Is Wide*, *Hyperion With Higgins* and a very moving film by Dorothy Darr, which also yielded the duos on *Which Way Is East?*, two men wrapped up and embarked on quite different journeys towards God, but on the same road. Abercrombie and Holland bring their own insights, compounded of rock, free music and the latter-day atmospherics associated with the label's core roster. 'Forest Flower' is a delightful re-creation, unfolding the song's rich colours in a series of time-lapse shifts that don't so much spark nostalgia for the original and its setting in a happier age as instil a sense of the timelessness and universality of this music.

& *See also* **Dream Weaver** (1966; p. 334)

JOE MORRIS &

Born 13 September 1955, New Haven, Connecticut
Guitar, double bass

A Cloud Of Black Birds

AUM Fidelity AUM 009
Morris; Mat Maneri (vn); Chris Lightcap (b); Jerome Dupree (d). June 1998.

Joe Morris says: **'A friend in the business thought that my liner-notes were too personal. I explained that the music and the title were about the point of realization I had when I decided that I needed to be an artist. I reminded him about Coltrane and *A Love Supreme*** and how personal that was. Personal is rare in the jazz world. It's usually about the technique or the tradition or something.'

While Morris was attending a special school in the Boston area, as he movingly relates, he spent a lot of time alone watching starlings flock and fly outside his bedroom window. Their movement – patterned, complex, only seemingly chaotic – made a great impression on Joe, and some of that experience comes out in the densely packed music on 'A Cloud Of Black Birds'. One senses that here Morris does something similar to the Black Mountain poets' 'composition by field', where line and immediate detail is less important than constellations of sound, or on the analogy of the title, flock-movements. Reunion with Maneri sparks off a lot of shared experience, and their interaction, notably on the duo, 'Renascent', is close, intelligent and thoroughly sympathetic. The group tracks are inevitably denser in conception but no less powerful. The same language applies in the trio setting, except Morris is more obviously out front as a soloist. Here, Morris acknowledges a debt to the pianist and composer Lowell Davidson, whose advanced notational ideas involved colour imaging, use of light and extremes of concentration.

A Cloud Of Black Birds isn't a grand spiritual statement in the usual sense. It has no totalizing philosophy and offers no promise of redemption. But as a creative statement, it has immense and immediate presence.

& See also **No Vertigo** (1995; p. 590)

VON FREEMAN

Born Earl Lavon Freeman Sr, 3 October 1922, Chicago, Illinois
Tenor saxophone

75th Birthday Celebration
Half Note Records 4903 2
Freeman; Chico Freeman (ts); Willie Pickens (p); Brian Sandstrom (b); Robert Shy (d); Dianne Reeves (v). July 1998.

Von Freeman said (1997): **'What's the Chicago saxophone sound? Tough ... tough and very windy!'**

For a long time he seemed very much in the shadow of his son, Chico – guitarist George Freeman is Von's brother – and he spent a lot of time away from jazz altogether. In his 50s, though, he returned to the fold and since then has created a body of eccentrically clustered but virile Chicago swing. While Chico has explored sometimes baffling extremes of free jazz and neo-funk, Von Freeman has stuck with a curious downhome style that occasionally makes his saxophone sound as if it is held together with rubber bands and sealing wax. Von was 50 before he made his debut as leader. Roland Kirk produced it for Atlantic. There wasn't exactly a rush of records after that, and Von is now one of those older stars who has been in the studios more often since he reached pension age than he was before. A little like Ellis Marsalis, he also found himself making records with his better-known son and not infrequently cutting him in the process.

The 75th birthday album came a year late, but the idea was sparked by an appearance by Von and Chico, alongside George, at the Chicago Jazz Festival the year before; drummer Bruz Freeman, another brother, stayed home in Hawaii, but remarkably Von's mother, almost 100, was there in spirit, listening to the show go out on radio.

Having honoured the old man back home, Chico's idea was to give him a further party in New York at the Blue Note, and the record is a document of two summer nights with Chico's group there. The material is pretty much out of the book – 'Softly, As In A Morning

Sunrise', 'There Is No Greater Love' and 'Lover Man' – but they also do Chico's delightful 'To Hear A Teardrop In The Rain'. It's great to hear the Freemans playing together, as it always is, the lad all fabulous technique and gleaming speed, the dad content with pedal power and guile, but still getting there ahead as often as not. Dianne Reeves does a pretty guest spot on 'Comes Love', but since it's placed early in the set, it doesn't really change its character, which is thoughtful, driving saxophone improvisation, culminating in Newk's 'Tenor Madness'.

IAIN BALLAMY
Born 20 February 1964, Guildford, Surrey, England
Tenor saxophone

Food
Feral Records ASFA 101
Ballamy; Arve Henriksen (t, v, elec); Mats Eilertsen (b); Thomas Strønen (d, perc). July 1998.

Iain Ballamy recalls: **'Food is the only band I have ever been in that could either clear the room or transport people en masse to another place. This recording was from our first ever concerts, at the Molde Jazz Festival in Norway. Two girls who were clearly struggling with the music got up to leave. At that precise moment the band suddenly stopped dead for no particular reason and I cried: "Come back – I think I love you ..." then BANG! we carried on playing!'**

Loose Tubes was the talent pool for white British jazz in the '80s, but it became something of a jail for those of its members who weren't prepared to sit their finals and move on. Ballamy always sounded like a man who wanted to learn as well as blow. Unfortunately, early solo albums came and went, including the excellent debut, *Balloon Man*, and the strikingly chastened *All Men Amen*. Band commitments, including a stint with guitarist Billy Jenkins's Voice Of God Collective, coupled with some personal misfortune, and the usual shabby treatment of creative musicians by 'the industry' meant that his own career seemed to go on the back-burner for periods of time.

Food was a complete surprise, and a very delightful one. It was the first release on the Feral imprint which Ballamy set up with Dave McKean, and it also documents what was a very close and creative musical association, one that didn't necessarily, or at all, tick all the current 'industry' boxes. Ballamy's Norwegian colleagues create an entirely new environment for him: rich, tense, not necessarily comfortable. Strønen and Henriksen in particular have proved to be provocative collaborators, allowing Ballamy to place his notes not with more care but perhaps with a more anarchic and daring philosophy of improvisation. At moments, particularly on a track like 'Strange Burn', the music harks back to the British free jazz of the late '60s, which is another of Ballamy's sources. Recorded live to two-track, the sound is very raw and immediate, with Eilertsen's bass foregrounded and plenty of roomy ambience. The tracks are attractively spare, with a stark quality to the horns (Henriksen occasionally plays more than one trumpet simultaneously) that implies a much bigger sound-world than is actually present. A decade after its first release, *Food* sounds bigger and better with every listen.

VINNY GOLIA
Born 3 January 1946 (not 1956, as in many sources), New York City
Reeds

Sfumato
Clean Feed CF036
Golia; Bobby Bradford (t); Ken Filiano (b); Alex Cline (d). August 1998.

Vinny Golia says: **'We were in the studio very late at night and I was amazed at how Bobby, a bit older than the rest, was constantly coming up with these great solos during the improvisation sections. How did he do that! Also Ken Filiano, constantly upbeat and remarkably present in his ideas and focus. Although late, about three or four in the morning, these guys all gave it their all on every take. Later I found out that the original masters were lost and the CD was made from rough mixes. Amazing!'**

It is some testament to Vinny Golia's enormous energy and willingness to work with young adventurous musicians (the Cline twins, Wayne Peet, John Rapson) that his age is often given at a decade less than the actual chronology. Formerly a painter, he switched to full-time music in 1971 and since then has been the Boswell of the West Coast improvising underground, creating a body of work not much remarked in the orthodox histories but every bit as interesting as anything coming out of New York.

A genuine multi-instrumentalist, Golia has in recent years spent some time recording sets of *Music For Like Instruments* (the E-flat saxophones, the flutes, and so on), issuing these remarkable documents, as he does with much of the work he is involved with, on the influential Nine Winds label. He also gives employment to some of the more challenging members of the wind family, most recently the mighty tubax, which indeed sounds remarkably like Chewbacca on a grouchy day.

Some of Golia's most interesting record releases have been with his Large Ensemble – *Pilgrimage To Obscurity, Decennium Dans Axlan, Commemoration* – but these tend to minimize his impact as a solo reed voice. *Sfumato* – and the exactly contemporary *Lineage* with the same group – remains our favourite incarnation. Along with some astonishing group improvisations – listen to Golia's flute tussling with Bradford on a tribute to Albert Ayler – the Clean Feed, recorded in Portugal, where the group was playing at a festival, also features some terrific pre-composed material, with 'All Together Now' an especially good outing for Vinny's bass clarinet. As ever, when Bradford is involved, or when one hears this kind of line-up, the classic Ornette Coleman quartet is conjured up. These guys have taken the language on a generation, though.

Lineage confirms that. It's a release on the home label and, as with the Portuguese CD, it documents a generous conversation among old friends. The cadences of the playing on both have a well-worn and settled quality: it's a music not of surprise but of supportive empathy. The pleasures come in the skill and grace which these experts use as they go into free space.

REBECCA KILGORE
Born 24 September 1948, Waltham, Massachusetts
Voice

Rebecca Kilgore
Jump JCD 12-22
Kilgore; Dan Barrett (c, tb); Bob Reitmeier (cl, ts); Keith Ingham (p). October 1998.

Rebecca Kilgore says: **'Regarding that first 1998 recording on Jump, I remember wondering if the group would suffer for not having a bass, but not so. Keith covered it all, and the impromptu horn-lines that Bob and Dan came up with were superb, and it all worked.'**

Becky Kilgore isn't a profound singer, at least not in the way we understand Billie Holiday and Sarah Vaughan to be, but she has enormous charm and a sweet control over her material. Previously a computer programmer, she took up singing part-time in 1980 and worked in and around Portland, Oregon. She now sings full-time and specializes in vintage repertory. Her first records find her matched with one of Dan Barrett's swing groups, and they sparkle on his canny arrangements of standards and obscurities. If it all sounds a fraction precise and calculated, it must be because this kind of repertory date has become a commonplace in its craft and sunny expertise.

Appropriate that this Jump CD was recorded at the Manchester Craftsmen's Guild. The music is sheer unpretentious class, as close to perfect as a repertory CD can be. Barrett and Ingham confect little arrangements for 18 songs, of which only 'Just You, Just Me' could be called even close to hackneyed, and Becky's clear, melodious voice sings through the lyrics without any trace of routine. She finds a poignancy in 'Very Good Advice' which makes one wonder why this song is so obscure, and even the cutesy 'Ain't We Got Fun' has a dignity about it. And the instrumentalists are in superb fettle.

SPIKE ROBINSON

Born Henry Berthold Robinson, 16 January 1930, Kenosha, Wisconsin; died 29 October 2001, Writtle, Essex, England
Tenor saxophone

The CTS Session

Hep CD 2098
Robinson; John Williams (p); Louis Stewart (g); Bill Crow (b); Pete Cater (d). October 1998.

Hep producer Alastair Robertson says: **'The night before, his precious vintage Elkhart saxophone was stolen from his car. Most other players would have justifiably called off but Spike borrowed a horn and mouthpiece and played the date as the consummate artiste and professional he was.'**

An American who came to Britain on a navy posting in 1951, Robinson liked the place and became a frequent visitor. He passed away in Britain in 2001. Although he played tenor subsequently, Robinson was an altoman entirely under Parker's spell when he made some early tracks in London in 1951. His switch to tenor may have deprived us of a fine Bird-man, but his command of the bigger horn is scarcely less impressive on what were comeback recordings. His models were Getz, Sims and – at the insistence of some – Brew Moore, but Robinson was deft enough to make the comparisons sound fully absorbed. Working as an engineer, Spike didn't become a full-time musician till he was past 50.

There are two fine live CDs from Chester's in Southend, recorded during a 1984 visit, and Hep built up a strong relationship with the saxophonist, putting out another half-dozen excellent records, more than matching in quality the albums Spike made for Capri. The best of the Heps came when Spike was nearing 70. The idea was a Stan Getz tribute date with a version of Stan's old rhythm section, but drummer Frank Isola took ill and was replaced (successfully) by Pete Cater. In addition, Robinson's tenor was stolen on tour in Britain. There's no edge and no sense of problems afoot in the playing. Spike's light, by now seemingly effortless approach lets him glide over 'Smoke Gets In Your Eyes' as if it were no more substantial than smoke. Stewart makes a few well-judged appearances on acoustic guitar, a nice variation of sound. Robinson played as he was: generously, humorously and with understated intelligence.

ESBJÖRN SVENSSON
Born 14 April 1964, Västerås, Sweden; died 14 June 2008, Ingarö, Sweden
Piano

From Gagarin's Point Of View
ACT 9005-2
Svensson; Dan Berglund (b); Magnus Öström (d). May–November 1998.

Esbjörn Svensson said (1999): **'I think sometimes "improvisation" becomes a bit of a fetish. It's what the music is all about, but it's not the only thing it's about and if you don't have strong compositions, it's just exercises. So that's what I work at: melodies you'll remember tomorrow after the gig.'**

Svensson was working the local Stockholm scene by the mid-'80s, but his trio, originally named for him but ultimately given collective status as E.S.T., was to become one of the leading jazz groups of the '90s and '00s. His early records are comparatively modest, but he was already telling an attractive story at the piano. The music on them was lightly impressionistic post-bop, nodding at Keith Jarrett's Standards Trio but scaling down the grand gestures to a more manageable size. The trio play together in a loose but cleanly focused way that gives a degree of relaxation to themes which might sound merely uptight.

By the end of the decade, working in comparative isolation in Stockholm, he was producing piano trio records ready to take on the best of whatever the rest of the jazz world could retaliate with. Recorded in 1997, *Winter In Venice* sustains the Jarrett comparison but takes the music on to a new level. *From Gagarin's Point Of View* – the title is taken from a performance marking in a piano piece by the Brythonic composer Ronald Stevenson – continues in the same vein, perhaps even more inventively. If jazz musicians are going to effect any kind of rapprochement with rock or dance music, then one way might be via the kind of fusion which the trio suggests in 'Dodge The Dodo', where Öström plays a sort of hip-hop beat at the kit and Svensson still lets the melodious theme determine the end result. It's just one of 11 diverse, ingenious compositions. The shaping of these episodes into a sequence may strike some as a bit too artful, but it's the act of musicians who are of a generation that knows about their vast range of options and still want to play acoustic jazz. At any rate, Svensson does more than enough here to show why, along with such performers as Jason Moran, Guus Janssen, Yosuke Yamashita and Brad Mehldau, he helped to keep the piano trio situation full of new music.

The zenith no sooner reached, Svensson was drowned in a scuba accident off the coast near Stockholm. He was just 44. Posthumously released material suggests he was only hitting his stride as a composer and performer.

TRYGVE SEIM
Born 25 April 1971, Oslo, Norway
Tenor and soprano saxophones

Different Rivers
ECM 159521-2
Seim; Arve Henriksen (t, v, trumpophone); Øyvind Braekke (tb); Hild Sofie Tafjord (frhn); Nils Jansen (sno, bsx, cbcl); Håvard Lund (cl, bcl); Stian Carstensen (acc); Bernt Simen Lund, Morten Hannisdal (clo); David Gald (tba); Per Oddvar Johansen, Paal Nilssen-Love (d); Sidsel Endresen (v). 1998–1999.

Trygve Seim says: **'The interesting thing is to reach a place where the music under the solos is quite carefully written but the solos are quite free, but to leave no sign of the join between those two.'**

Seim's debut is little short of amazing and heralds the arrival of a new star. Not since Edward Vesala's *Lumi* has there been such a riveting opening to an ECM session as 'Sorrows'. Seim's music seems to follow a direct route from the great early discs by Garbarek, Arild Andersen and Vesala. There are no guitars and no keyboards; Seim is interested in human breath, the sound in wind instruments. In the magnificent 'Ulrika Dans', he leads nine musicians through a carefully shaded score that's a small masterpiece of writing for horns, hoisted aloft by Johansen's brilliant drum part and illuminated by the leader's own tenor solo. He seems to have a knack for making a band sound conversational and ritualistic at the same moment. 'Different Rivers' itself is a splicing of two versions of the same piece, with the musicians doubling on different instruments, a seamless montage which seems different on every hearing. In the stately procession of 'Breathe', over Sidsel Endresen's recitation, everything is sublimated into long cathedral chords that suggest a never-ending echo.

DAVID S. WARE
Born 7 November 1949, Plainfield, New Jersey
Tenor saxophone

Live In The World
Thirsty Ear THI 57153.2 3CD
Ware; Matthew Shipp (p); William Parker (b); Susie Ibarra, Hamid Drake, Guillermo E. Brown (d). 1998-2003.

David S. Ware said (2006): **'That's the advice my mother gave me: "Go see the world." I've tried to do that, and I think about those words all the time, and do good by them and by her.'**

Ware grew up in New Jersey, attended Berklee for a couple of years at the end of the '60s and then formed his own group, Apogee, before moving to New York City. He has worked extensively with drummer Andrew Cyrille and with Cyrille's mentor, Cecil Taylor. He drove taxis for a while before moving back into music and recording a good number of albums under his own name, all of them in a fierce, modernist style that makes much use of over-blowing and multiphonics. The Ayler influence is evident but Ware's 'fire music' is often more thoughtful and considered than first appears. He pointed to another, less obvious influence when in 2002 he revisited Sonny Rollins's barely pioneered 1958 masterpiece *The Freedom Suite*.

Live In The World was more than a touring compilation, but a major statement. The title can be read two ways, as a straightforward description of these live dates from Switzerland and Italy, but also as an injunction not to overlook the near-at-hand. For all his mysticism Ware is profoundly committed to the basic mechanics of the music. There's some older material here – 'Elder's Path' from the Silkheart *Passage To Music*, 'Co Co Cana' from the mid-'90s – but the approach has changed almost as much as the titles. 'Freedom Suite' is a later, more universalized attempt on the same ground as the 1995 *Dao*. 'The Way We Were' has been a Ware staple since his Columbia debut, *Go See The World*. Much of the rest calls on a shared pool of ideas and structures that have been worked on many times by the group. Shipp fulfils his usual function, bending and splitting the harmonics in exactly the same way the percussionists multiply the rhythms. Parker stands his ground, and both pianist and bassist are richly featured on the second and third parts of 'Freedom Suite'.

Ware himself ventures less often into the altissimo range than he used to. One of the more obvious differences between the 1998 material and the Italian tapes five years later is how even and contained his articulation has become. There's no less fury, but his lines have become much less abstract. It was cynically assumed, and we were guilty of it, that the more 'inside' approach on Ware's disappointing final Columbia record, *Surrendered*, was at the behest of the label. It may well be that he was moving in that direction entirely on his own account. By the same token, Guillermo Brown's unemphatic performance – compared to Edwards's tymps and bells, Ibarra's delightful exuberance – was probably just what was ordered. He fulfils that impression here, and the clincher is when the third CD plays out with a bonus track from the earlier line-up, at Chiasso in 1998.

It was David's mother who gave him the title *Go See The World*. That was her blessing and mission for him when he was a baby. He said farewell to her on 2001's *Corridors & Parallels* with 'Mother, May You Rest In Bliss', and here he takes that promise on one more step.

JOHN LEWIS &

Born 3 May 1920, LaGrange, Illinois; died 29 March 2001, New York City
Piano

Evolution

Atlantic 7567-83211-2
Lewis (p solo). January 1999.

John Lewis said (1999): **'The Modern Jazz Quartet fed my interest in group playing. When that ended I played more on my own, partly because I hadn't done as much of that as I might have wanted, partly because that close relationship wasn't there any more. But they're different things. One isn't a reaction to the other.'**

Lewis was one of the last senior survivors of the bebop era, and this marvellous solo album underscores what an extraordinary figure he was in jazz for over 50 years. As a composer, he is mysteriously neglected when it comes to source material for other players, but perhaps only Lewis's Lewis really hits the mark. He revisits five of his own favourites, and each is an affectionate new look at an old friend: 'Django', for instance, is elegantly recast around a left-hand bass that sounds almost like a tango. 'Sweet Georgia Brown' and 'Cherokee' are sketches that suggest a summing-up of both swing and bebop. 'Afternoon In Paris' muses on his lifelong affinity with the old world. Moving yet wonderfully fresh and unaffected, this is a consummate recital by the master.

Hardly any less masterful, generous or absorbing, the second part of what sadly proved to be Lewis's farewell sessions is as fine as the first. Though he has support from other hands on *Evolution II* , mostly it's all about what's going on at the piano – and that includes 'One! Of Parker's Moods', his final thoughts on the blues; 'That! Afternoon In Paris', a delightful revision of an old favourite; and another look at 'Django', the tango feel of the previous encounter here cleverly evolved into something else.

& See also **Golden Striker / Jazz Abstractions** (1960; p. 253); **MODERN JAZZ QUARTET, Dedicated To Connie** (1960; p. 254), **The Complete Last Concert** (1974; p. 417)

WYNTON MARSALIS &

Born 18 October 1961, New Orleans, Louisiana
Trumpet

Standard Time: Volume 6 – Mr Jelly Lord

Columbia CK 69872
Marsalis; Lucien Barbarin (tb); Wycliffe Gordon (tb, tba, t); Wessell Anderson (as); Victor Goines (ss, ts, cl); Michael White (cl); Harry Connick Jr, Eric Lewis, Danilo Perez, Eric Reed (p); Donald Vappie (bj, g); Reginald Veal (b); Herlin Riley (d). January 1999 (December 1993).

Wynton Marsalis said (1990): 'I don't think what I propose is conservative. I think it's democratic and that is what America is supposed to be. The New Orleans jazz was about community and mutual help. You had the right to express yourself, but you had the obligation to help someone else do that, too, and sound good doing it.'

Marsalis started to make regular forays back into the tradition in 1986 with the first of the *Standard Time* records. Over the next dozen years, he kept returning to the idea, even diverting enough from his apparent comfort zone to cover a set of Thelonious Monk material. *Mr Jelly Lord* was one of the more elaborate set-ups. It's a flawed record in some respects, with too much packed in, but it's a perfect snapshot of Marsalis's musical thinking in action and aside from all the media buzz.

Sometimes even Wynton must wish Stanley Crouch would keep his mouth shut. Likening these modern – but unmodernized – versions of Jelly Roll Morton tunes to actor/director Kenneth Branagh's Shakespearean films isn't necessarily the most helpful imprimatur. As it turns out, Wynton's performance needs no Mortonesque hyperbole. There is no attempt to lend these astonishing compositions any false grandeur; they have quite enough as it is.

Wynton's playing has rarely sounded so relaxed and so raw. Even his cover-picture, looking tired, slumped astride a packing crate and resting an elbow on his instrument, suggests a measure of artisanly relaxation, like a man just coming off shift rather than a man waiting backstage at Carnegie Hall. 'The Pearls' and 'Dead Man Blues' see him reach levels of expression that will astonish even admirers.

Perez and Connick have cameo parts only, but the basic line-up is by now a familiar one. We have never been persuaded by the clarinet-playing of Dr Michael White, which sounds a quarter-note sharp, but the two trombone-players are majestically idiomatic and the saxophonists never sound as if they are on day-release from Bebop Academy. Our only faint quibble would be the drumming of Herlin Riley, which occasionally seems anachronistic.

A must for blindfold tests of the future is track 15. On 6 December 1993, Wynton and pianist Eric Reed went to the Edison National Historic Site at West Orange, New Jersey, and recorded 'Tom Cat Blues' direct to a wax cylinder. The result is still unmistakably Marsalis, but the old technology helps provide a ghostly coda to a remarkable record.

& *See also* **J Mood** (1985; p. 496), **Live At The House Of Tribes** (2002; p. 677)

STEFON HARRIS
Born 23 March 1973, Albany, New York
Vibraphone, marimba

BlackActionFigure
Blue Note 99546 2
Harris; Steve Turre (tb); Greg Osby (as); Gary Thomas (ts, af); Jason Moran (p); Tarus Mateen (b); Eric Harland (d). February 1999.

Stefon Harris said (2000): 'I actually prefer the sound of the marimba on uptempo tunes, though I wouldn't forsake the vibes for a ballad. I like to move across the instrument, rather than play linear solos, and the marimba gives me something there.'

Harris quickly showed a highly developed musical personality. His original intention was to be an orchestral player and there is substantial ambition in his work as the recent *Grand Unification Theory* might suggest. The debut album, *A Cloud Of Red Dust*, is interestingly structured. Rather than a sequence of discrete tracks, Harris has woven them together with short interludes to create an almost continuous suite. It grips the attention from the very start and flags only very briefly, with a June Gardner vocal feature. Some of the shorter pieces are quirky and playful, but Harris's most characteristic sound is a flowing lyricism, grafted onto a swinging shuffle beat, a combination of metres that is always threatening to fall apart but never quite does.

BlackActionFigure builds on the strengths of its predecessor. As before, the writing is strong and archetypal, vindicating Harris's idealist belief that all music pre-exists and is merely transcribed. 'The Alchemist' and the stately 'Chorale' which follows are perfect illustrations of this: timeless-sounding compositions with a strange mnemonic quality. It isn't often you come away from a contemporary jazz album humming the tunes; perhaps this is why Harris got a Grammy nomination. This has the odd effect of making the album's two standards, 'There Is No Greater Love' and 'You Stepped Out Of A Dream', sound brand-new by comparison, particularly when the soloing takes them so far from the starting-point. The only other repertory piece is a version of Onaje Allan Gumbs's 'Collage'.

SILVER LEAF JAZZ BAND
Formed c.1993
Group

New Orleans Wiggle
GHB BCD-347
Chris Tyle (c, v); Orange Kellin (cl); Steve Pistorius (p); John Gill (d). 1999.

George Melly said (1998): '"Authentic" is the most dangerous word in this business because it implies comparison with a standard we cannot know anything about. We know how some of the New Orleans groups sounded when they were cleaned up, given new clothes and teeth and stuck into a studio, but that's hardly the same. "Honest" recording of New Orleans music is better. I'd even settle for "sincere". But not "authentic".'

Chris Tyle leads this group of New Orleans wannabes. Even though the group is based in the city, few of them are authentic NO musicians, and followers of this axis of tradi-tional players will recognize many of the names. They got off to a somewhat ordinary start with *Streets And Scenes Of Old New Orleans*: the best numbers are the more obscure pieces, including several by Johnny Wiggs. The subsequent Jelly Roll Morton set, *Jelly's Best Jam*, is much more like the right thing: a shrewd blend of familiar and less hackneyed Morton titles is arranged with enough élan to sidestep mere copycat tactics, and the inclusion of four of Morton's 1938 piano solos offers a ghostly echo of the master's presence.

Two Stomp Off discs follow a similar line of homage without artifice. *Sugar Blues* is a tribute to King Oliver that walks a very difficult line. Tyle's aim was to fashion the sound of the Oliver Creole Jazz Band and put it to use not only on Oliver's repertoire but also on contemporary tunes that he might have played. Tyle is a shrewd judge of tempos and he gets amazingly close to a hi-fi treatment of Oliver's band sound. Even tougher to pull off is the Freddie Keppard homage, *Here Comes The Hot Tamale Man*. With so little surviving evidence to go on, Tyle has still managed to weave together 19 tracks and a sound that seems like a plausible echo of Keppard's terse, often relentless music.

On *New Orleans Wiggle*, the style isn't really Dixieland, revivalism or even 'New Orleans': it's a modern methodology applied to classic principles, and the results are entirely of their own time. The material goes as near in as 'St Louis Blues' and as far out as Lovie Austin's 'Stepping On The Blues' – a mix of populism and connoisseurship which ought to appeal to anybody. Tyle and Kellin play with stinging spirit and not *too* much finesse, Pistorius finds all the right feeds and stomps with superb élan, but if one player stands out it's Gill, whose tumbling bravado and dazzling sticksmanship make the quartet into an orchestra. Essential.

MATT WILSON
Born 27 September 1964, Galesburg, Illinois
Drums

Smile
Palmetto 2049
Wilson; Joel Frahm (ss, ts, bcl); Andrew D'Angelo (as, bcl); Yosuke Inoue (b). March 1999.

The irrepressible Mr Wilson says: *'Smile* **was an easy album to name. Why? Because the music reflects a team effort that is possible only through doing a whole bunch of gigs. You hear the joy of us being together and how a band is a living and breathing life form. Woo! Hoo!'**

Wilson moved to Boston in the late '80s and immediately won a reputation as an intelligent, subtle, and often very playful percussionist who could adapt his approach to any situation. Unusually for a drummer, he has been able to record regularly as leader. The debut album, *As Wave Follows Wave*, was pretty much stolen by fellow Palmetto star Dewey Redman, whose own recording opportunities have been dismayingly few over the years. The subsequent *Going Once, Going Twice* featured an auctioneer (Ned Sublette), which is a first for this book. It's a very funny, very cleverly conceived track, also featuring banjoist Pete McCann in a role that might have suited Bill Frisell. It's a set that combines intelligent jazz themes with Pete Seeger's version of Ecclesiastes, 'Turn! Turn! Turn!' So, no ordinary kind of jazz drummer/leader.

    Smile – no obvious connection to the Beach Boys epic, but we wouldn't put it past him – was a big jump forward, a set that mixes in the humour ever more comfortably. 'Take Me Out To The Ball Game' is hilarious, as is 'Go, Team, Go!', though what's interesting is how seamlessly Wilson and his men weave their larking into some fairly robust outside jazz. Frahm's bass clarinet work was likened to Eric Dolphy on this record's first appearance, and while it's an absurd comparison at face value, you can hear what was meant. 'A Dusting Of Snow' shows what a fine impressionistic drummer Wilson can be in a more thoughtful mood, while 'Daymaker' is just great small-group arranging. Of the brought-in material, Monk's still rarely played 'Boo Boo's Birthday' is outstanding and there is a fine reading of 'Strangers In The Night', which is virtually unrecognizable as such until it's almost over.

BUCKY PIZZARELLI
Born John Paul Pizzarelli, 9 January 1926, Paterson, New Jersey
Guitar

April Kisses
Arbors ARCD 19227
Pizzarelli (g solo). March 1999.

Bucky Pizzarelli said (1991): **'I took things from just about everyone I ever heard, like a sponge. It was George Van Eps who developed the seven-string guitar, for Epiphone. It gives you extra weight, a little muscle.'**

He was hidden away in NBC studio orchestras for many years but began an association with Benny Goodman in 1966 and since then has become a regular contributor to mainstream-modern small groups on record and on the road. His son John is a chip off the old block.

    Pizzarelli's more vigorous ensemble playing can be found all over the place, but this charming solo disc shows off his more gentle and sweet-toned style on the seven-string acoustic guitar. The first disc is mostly music from the books of his first influences: Eddie Lang, Carl Kress, George Van Eps. Kress's 'Helena' is a superb choice of opening cut. It has a decided Spanish or Catalan tinge, and though Bucky's articulation rarely suggests the fire and show-off virtuosity of flamenco, it has something of those. He says one of the finest moments of his life was playing Django tunes with Stéphane Grappelli and 'Tears' here is a nice tribute to that repertoire. There are nods as well to Slam Stewart (the dance-like original 'Slamerino') and to Duke ('Come Sunday'), but it's the Kress stuff that dominates the list, eclipsing even Van Eps's 'Squattin' In The Grotto'. Not the kind of record that will have the neighbours banging on your walls, but an hour of quiet delight, and the follow-ups discs – further chapters of musical autobiography – are good, too.

BOBO STENSON
Born 4 August 1944, Västerås, Sweden
Piano

Serenity
ECM 543611 2CD
Stenson; Anders Jormin (b); Jon Christensen (d). April 1999.

Bobo Stenson said (2005): **'I come from a small city, though perhaps quite a big one by Swedish standards, and one with a surprising number of musicians. Maybe we had something like critical mass, because I feel we had to do things and think about things for ourselves. That means you don't get too influenced by others, except the people you meet every week.'**

Stenson has been a major figure on the Stockholm post-bop scene since 1966. As co-founder of Rena Rama in 1971, he seemed embarked on an effort to hybridize jazz with Balkan and Indian folk music, a somewhat quixotic enterprise which coloured his work for many years. Stenson's career began with Börje Fredriksson, and after a brief apprenticeship under the Swedish tenor saxophonist he branched out with high-profile gigs for Stan Getz (in Africa, of all places) and Red Mitchell. Increasingly in the last ten years he has been associated with ECM's efforts to reshape and redefine modal jazz, in addition to making records with Jan Garbarek, Charles Lloyd and Thomas Stańko, among others. At times, he has seemed the label's *de facto* house pianist.

This is a towering achievement. The integration of free jazz, serialism and atonality, elements of bebop and a folkish lyricism yield a double-set of great power and almost inexhaustible invention. The pianist and his two associates both contribute originals, and there is a wonderful version of Wayne Shorter's 'Swee' Pea', but it is the reworking of themes by Charles Ives, Alban Berg and Hanns Eisler that impresses most thoroughly. In Berg's 'Die Nachtigall', Stenson takes the basic row and transforms it into a softly lyrical jazz theme that sounds like nothing else in the canon. He does something similar with Eisler's 'Die Pflaumenbaum', though here the music already seems more susceptible to such treatment. It is interesting how French some of the leader's keyboard strategies are; the sources notwithstanding, his harmony seems to draw on Debussy and Ravel more than anyone and his melodic touch owes little to the Austro-German school. Jormin and Christensen, both of whom are represented early on by strong compositions – 'T.' and 'North Print', and 'East Print', respectively – add their idiosyncratic touches to a sequence of pieces that demands patient and attentive listening.

RYAN KISOR
Born 12 April 1973, Sioux City, Iowa
Trumpet

Power Source
Criss Cross 1196
Kisor; Chris Potter (ts); James Genus (b); Gene Jackson (d). June 1999.

Freddie Hubbard said, during a 'blindfold test' (2001): **'He's listened to a lot of the older guys: Kenny Dorham, Lee Morgan, me? Dizzy. But he's got his own voice, and he doesn't play the horn as if it's a saxophone, like a lot of the younger men do. Who is it? He's good.'**

Kisor has some of the ebullience of the young trumpet masters of hard-bop yore. He doesn't have that measure of originality or capacity to surprise, but there's a kindred energy in his playing, and he has quite a personal, immediate sound. His two deleted Columbia albums put him in heavyweight company, as major labels like to do, but his more recent work has seen him at the head of *simpatico* groups who work well behind him and don't crowd him out.

With no keyboard on *Power Source*, Kisor takes a risk which he is fully up to facing and, with the invincible Potter standing at his shoulder, the music has a feel of synthesis which takes in all manner of post-bop jazz directions. As he gets older, the tone's losing some of its brassy snap, taking on a faintly cloudier edge, and with the saxophonist if anything moving in the other tonal direction, it makes for an attractive contrast. The covers are a superb lot, with Jimmy Heath's 'New Picture' outstanding. We're not so keen on 'Boogie Stop Shuffle', which doesn't really scale down, but the closing 'Bird Food' was an audacious choice that the players peck off in the hungriest manner.

TERENCE BLANCHARD
Born 13 March 1962, New Orleans, Louisiana
Trumpet

Wandering Moon
Sony Classics SK 89111
Blanchard; Aaron Fletcher (as); Branford Marsalis, Brice Winston (ts); Edward Simon (p); Dave Holland (b); Eric Harland (d). June 1999.

Terence Blanchard says: **'It came from my experiences on the road. There were times when I missed my family dearly and would really rather be home. During those times, I would look at the moon and realize that that same moon would be over my family's head in just a few hours. That would make me feel much closer to them.'**

When Terence Blanchard replaced Wynton Marsalis in the Jazz Messengers, the term 'post-Wynton' was heard for the first time. In fact, the two trumpeters had come up together – Marsalis is the older by six months – and the young Blanchard had taken lessons from Ellis Marsalis among others. For a time, he seemed to align himself with a modernist strain in jazz, taking the Booker Little role opposite Donald Harrison in a latter-day version of the Dolphy–Little quintet, but as the years have gone by Blanchard and Harrison have largely returned to their Louisianan roots. Where the saxophonist has been involved with the 'tribal' band scene, with its distinctive traditions, Blanchard has evolved a kind of grand neo-traditionalism, related to Wynton's but in a less doctrinaire way. He has also become a highly successful film composer, soundtracking most of Spike Lee's work and contributing a passionate score for the Hurricane Katrina documentary *A Tale of God's Will*. In fact, so thoroughly overdetermined by film work is Blanchard's CV now that his other recordings have tended to be overlooked.

Sadly, most of Blanchard's fine run for Columbia, including the wonderful *Romantic Defiance*, is now not consistently available. Under benign exile to Sony Classics, Blanchard goes for a long (over 75 minutes), ballad-orientated record which seems full of near dark-ness. Originals such as 'Luna Viajera' and 'If I Could, I Would' distil a sense of melancholy which is mitigated by the serenity of the playing. Holland's intro to 'My Only Thought Of You' is sublime, even by his high standard, and what follows from Blanchard and Marsalis is the equal of it. Blanchard's line on 'Sweet's Dream' gives an ironic twist to the 'post-Wynton' tag. Even though there are one or two tear-ups, from Marsalis in particular, what one remembers about the record is its poise, its cool dedication to instrumental mastery. None is more masterful than the leader himself. The closing version of 'I Thought About You', taken at the slowest of tempos, is a definitive treatment which silences criticism and in its final moments leaves the listener dumbfounded.

BARRY GUY&

Born 22 April 1947, London
Double bass, chamber bass

Odyssey
Intakt CD070
Guy; Marilyn Crispell (p); Paul Lytton (perc). 1999.

Barry Guy says: **'The piano trio has played a significant role in my musical life, representing a "classical" formation in terms of instrumental demarcation and sonic compatibility. This "classical" notion is, however, open to creative impulses that welcome a degree of alternative strategies devised with very special musicians in mind.'**

Guy has been so much associated with large-scale projects over the years – the London Jazz Composers' Orchestra and his *Witch Gong Game* ensembles, ECM recordings with his partner Maya Homburger – that one tends to forget what a formidable small-group player he is. His bass-playing in trio situations has all the authority and presence of his early work in these forms. In addition to this remarkable trio, there are also recordings with Evan Parker and Paul Lytton.

A number of the pieces on *Odyssey* – 'Harmos', 'Double Trouble', 'Odyssey' – are Guy compositions, more or less familiar from other projects, and only four tracks are collectively improvised. The tonality is mostly quite sombre, though 'Rags' is a loud and skittish idea, and after the bass/percussion introduction 'Harmos' turns into a brooding processional that brings out the very darkest colours in Crispell's palette. The level of interaction is very high and there is constant empathy between the players. How much of this is down to Guy's scores and direction is difficult to gauge from the outside. These don't sound like dot-driven pieces; the emphasis is still very much on improvisation, but within very definite structures and trajectories. It's not without humour: 'Heavy Metal' gives Lytton a chance to explore his expanded kit and for the others to lean back a bit as well. Hearing Guy's bass at the centre of the mix offers insight into his compositional procedures, an approach that often implies excluded areas, abysses or moments of silence that punctuate and impel the music as black holes punctuate and drive the universe. It's quite dizzying listening to him at some points. What is said is much less important than what is left out.

& *See also* **Study – Witch Gong Game II/10** (1994; p. 579); **LONDON JAZZ COMPOSERS' ORCHESTRA, Ode** (1972; p. 393)

MUNDELL LOWE
Born 21 April 1922, Laurel, Mississippi
Guitar

When Lights Are Lowe
Acoustic Music 3191190
Lowe; Hendrik Meurkens (vib); Chris Berger (b); Mark Taylor (d). 1999.

Mundell Lowe says: **'Mr Benny Carter was a long-time friend of mine. I always wanted to record "When Lights Are Low" to put to truth Miles Davis's mistake that he never fixed. Miles recorded the wrong bridge. When I recorded the song, Mr Carter called to thank me for using the right one.'**

Lowe started out playing both Dixieland and country music, but worked in swing for a time, including a postwar stint with Mary Lou Williams, before becoming a staff arranger at NBC. Studio and TV work dominated much of his career, but he always kept a jazz side going and made a number of fine records that highlight his cool, restrained tone and delivery.

Given that Lowe was rising 80, *When Lights Are Lowe* was never likely to be a great stylistic revelation or a sudden swerve into electronic noise. What it delivers in every track is crisply executed jazz, oscillating between bop and swing and always providing some new insight into a mostly standards programme: 'Lady Be Good' brings out the best in the partnership with regular collaborator Meurkens, who's an undervalued exponent of his instrument, and the opening 'Star Eyes' sums up a whole history of approaches to that lovely song. The title-track does indeed get the bridge right, but more importantly it creates a delightful gloaming atmosphere that is still full of laughter and warmth. An exceptional album by a talent whose reputation has been turned down too low for too many years. Time to cast a stronger light on Mundell Lowe.

WILLIAM PARKER&
Born 10 January 1952, New York City
Double bass

Mayor Of Punkville
Aum Fidelity 15 2CD
Parker; Roy Campbell (t, flhn); Lewis 'Flip' Barnes, Richard Rodriguez (t); Masahiko Kono, Alex Lodico, Steve Swell (tb); Chris Jonas (ss); Ori Kaplan (as); Charles Waters (as, cl); David Sewelson (bs); Cooper-Moore (p); Dave Hofstra (b, tba); Andrew Baker (d); Aleta Hayes (v). July–November 1999.

William Parker said (1999): **'You know why jazz and improvised music are marginalized? Why great musicians are playing to a handful of people in a cellar still? Because we lost the support of the community. We lost any sense that this music belongs to a community. We can't blame anyone else for that. We just have to try to get it back.'**

The bassist's work with the Improvisers Collective led directly to the foundation of the Little Huey Creative Music Orchestra, which has become one of the most compelling large units on the scene and this remarkable performance clinches Parker as a composer of large-scale dramatic works. The title-piece and the equally long 'I Can't Believe I Am Here' are structured around deceptively simple ideas, melodic cells and simple *ostinati* which open up improvising possibilities for the soloists. Parker includes two curious 'interludes' which sound like rehearsal material, but with 'Three Steps To Noh Mountain' he demonstrates a capacity for jewel-like perfection and a pristine logic, even in a small span. There is so much to admire here that it's virtually impossible to single out tracks, but, along with those already mentioned, 'Oglala Eclipse' and the closing 'Anthem' are outstanding.

& *See also* **Through Acceptance Of The Mystery Peace** (1974, 1979; p. 409)

ANDREW HILL&

Born Andrew Hille, 30 June 1937, Chicago, Illinois; died 20 April 2007, Jersey City, New Jersey
Piano

Dusk
Palmetto 2057
Hill; Ron Horton (t); Marty Ehrlich, Gregory Tardy (reeds); Scott Colley (b); Billy Drummond (d). October 1999.

Pianist Jason Moran says: **'I became a student of Andrew's during the rehearsal for *Dusk*. I went to Baldwin piano studios, and Andrew was there with his band rehearsing the song "15/8". Andrew dances and stumbles around that intoxicating bass-line for the first three and a half minutes of the piece. This is his signature. He is free with his inner rhythm. It's as if what he's playing is more of a comment about the rhythm of the bass and drums, and not just a solo that sits on top of the bass and drums. It's his dialect, and it takes a while to translate.'**

Dusk was warmly, even rapturously received on its release, less for its content than because a major African-American composer seemed at last able to come out of the shadows. It's a record that requires time to assimilate and it's worth bearing in mind that here was an artist who had recorded very little, relative to his stature and to the density of Blue Note documentation, for two decades.

Hill had presented some of the material already, and it can be found on a quite obscure solo record called *Les Trinitaires*. There are solo tracks on *Dusk* as well. 'Tough Love' and 'Formulaic' feature the pianist on his own; both are quirky and idiosyncratic, but curiously remote. 'Sept' and '15/8' are inward-leaning exercises in metre, the debate conducted within the band, so not as communicative as we normally expect such a thing to be. There's not much that is emotionally involving in either of them, but perhaps that's intended; in later life, Hill adopted a curiously detached stance, as if to indicate that he was equally unimpressed by the canonization of past work and the overdue recognition that greeted his 'comeback'. The long opening 'Dusk' is about the best thing on the record, built over a long, looping bass-line, knotted harmony from the horns and urgent little excursions like bat-flight. 'ML' is a typical Hill waltz. There is also a heartfelt tribute to the late Thomas Chapin, 'T.C.', which features Ehrlich and Tardy on what sound like bass clarinets, though none are listed on the sleeve.

The apparent programme to the record is Jean Toomer's Harlem Renaissance classic *Cane*, but its enigmatic lyricism is replaced by something drier and more abstract. Hill's health broke down not long after *Dusk* was recorded, and though there were other albums to come, they never quite captured him at his best. Here at least, there is clear confirmation that he was one of the leading composers in the music.

& *See also* **Point Of Departure** (1964; p. 303)

STEVE KUHN

Born 24 March 1938, Brooklyn, New York
Piano

The Best Things
Reservoir 162
Kuhn; David Finck (b); Billy Drummond (d); Luciana Souza (v). December 1999.

Steve Kuhn said (2001): **'Bill Evans turned me around, in a different way to Coltrane. Coltrane showed me a life where music was first and last. Bill Evans showed me that technique was nothing if there wasn't something of yourself behind it.'**

A piano pupil of the celebrated Margaret Chaloff, then a student at Harvard and the Lenox School, Kuhn worked the New York scene from the late '50s and was John Coltrane's first pianist in what became the classic quartet. He lived in Stockholm in the late '60s, accompanying Sheila Jordan and leading his own groups. His recording career started with a curious country-and-western-meets-jazz album co-led with Toshiko Akiyoshi and has more recently returned to the Coltrane repertoire.

Kuhn struck a rich seam with Reservoir, and his trio records for the label find him playing some of the best jazz of his career and are modern jazz pianism at its best. The earliest of the three of them is the most easily overlooked, but it is a more than competent and often very thoughtful session that paves the way for the achievement of *Countdown*. Opening with a Coltrane composition (the title-track) was a stroke of genius and the inclusion of Steve Swallow's 'Wrong Together' – the two Steves seem like creative soulmates and apparently it was Swallow who persuaded Kuhn to do more writing – is the clincher.

Steve kicks off *The Best Things*, the most recent of the group, with a chestnut, 'The Best Things In Life Are Free', but manages to transform it, as he does Parker's 'Confirmation', which reduces the outline to fragments and reassembles them, and the following 'Poem For #15', which takes every second of its ten-plus minutes to unravel. 'Two By Two' is an interesting contemporary blues, not Kuhn's usual style, its threatened resolutions always second-guessed by the composer. The vocalist is used to add some wordless tone-colours to 'Adagio', but by then the set has been firmly clinched. An artist in his pomp, overdue some serious attention.

ISHMAEL WADADA LEO SMITH &
Born 18 December 1941, Leland, Mississippi
Trumpet

Golden Quartet
Tzadik TZ 7604
Smith; Anthony Davis (p); Malachi Favors (b); Jack DeJohnette (d). January 2000.

Wadada Leo Smith says: **'I wanted to create an ensemble of master composers/ performers who would perform my music in the quartet form, which has all the condition of an orchestra, and is the purest, most complete unit in all music.'**

In the spring of 1995 Smith unveiled a large-scale, multi-ensemble piece called *Odwira*. It was the clearest sign of how far he had moved from small-group improvisation to a new conception of himself as a composer, albeit a heterodox one. Recent years have seen him personally and musically involved with Oriental culture, which bears on the work in philosophical rather than strictly sonic or timbral ways. In other words, Smith is still playing jazz music, but within sight of two powerful camps, and receiving emissaries from both.

The association with Tzadik both reflects and extends this situation and the recorded work of recent years has seen him issue some of his most vibrant work for two decades. On 'Celestial Sky And All The Magic', Smith demonstrates again how much he owes to

Miles Davis (mute very much in place), but also how far he has travelled beyond. His muted introduction is as delicately moving as his rapid-fire exposition on 'America's Third Century Spiritual Awakening' is rousing. The opening 'DeJohnette' is a Milesian tribute to a band member and affords the drummer lots of space to spread out and show his wares. Jack is an utterly compelling soloist and his ability to understand where Smith is coming from generates the key relationship of the set. Davis is sympathetic enough, but he doesn't quite have the chops to equal Smith. 'America's Third Century Spiritual Awakening' is brimming with urgency and excitement: an anthem for the Obama years?

& See also **Divine Love** (1978; p. 446)

RANDY SANDKE
Born 23 May 1949, Chicago, Illinois
Trumpet

Inside Out
Nagel Heyer 2025
Sandke; Ray Anderson, Wycliffe Gordon (tb); Ken Peplowski (cl, ts); Marty Ehrlich (ss, cl, bcl, af); Scott Robinson (ss, bs, cbsx, bcl, f, theremin); Uri Caine (p); Greg Cohen (b); Dennis Mackrel (d). January 2000.

Randy Sandke says: **'The Inside Out Band was a coming together of musicians associated with two different musical camps: mainstream and the New York downtown new music scene. In reality, our mutual respect and desire to create fresh and exciting music erased any supposed barriers that critics are fond of imposing.'**

Born in Chicago, Sandke followed the music of idols such as Bix and Louis and seemed bound for a trumpet career on his own account, when he developed throat problems that required surgery. Sandke worked for ASCAP and played guitar for a time but began playing jazz again and found himself in demand in swing/mainstream circles. In the '90s he took on an ambassadorial role for the styles he loved, but also recorded more *outré* material on his own records.

Had *Inside Out* been released by a major American label it would most likely have been greeted with all kinds of ballyhoo. Instead, Sandke's audacious project, aligning himself and Peplowski alongside the likes of Ehrlich, Anderson and Caine, thereby lining up the new mainstream and New York's downtown side by side, barely got a mention in most parts of the jazz press. Sandke put in three of his own tunes and scored 'Creole Love Call', but he also got everyone else to contribute a tune and the compatibility of the playing, even when the music's kicking at doors which some of these players don't care to open, is wonderful. As an ensemble they get a gorgeous sound, the reeds making up a voluptuously rich range and the rarity of two trombones in a nine-piece band also makes its mark. One or two of the pieces are more jokey than good-humoured – Gordon's 'Sam Bone' is just a bit of nonsense for himself and Anderson – but Ehrlich's 'Like I Said', Sandke's 'Inside Out' and Cohen's 'Trapianti Di Scimmia' alone make the record special.

MATS GUSTAFSSON
Born 29 October 1964, Umeå, Sweden
Baritone saxophone, other saxophones, fluteophone

The Thing
Crazy Wisdom 001/159073
Gustafsson; Ingebrigt Håker Flaten (b); Paal Nilssen-Love (d). February 2000.

Mats Gustafsson says: **'It was recorded for the newly started Crazy Wisdom with me and two younger Norwegians. I thought Ingebrigt would be this great *female* bass-player, since my late grandmother's name was Ingabritt. It turned into a ferocious session of first takes, a very, very late bar-hang and no sleep, which is obvious from the photo session for the album. Three pale-faced Scandinavians as *one* entity. A good start for the group!'**

Somewhat like Ken Vandermark in the US, Gustafsson turns up in a bewildering array of musical situations, all of them enriched by his big, turbulent presence. Or perhaps he's more like a Peter Brötzmann, a catalytic figure who makes things happen around him. Certainly, Gustafsson is the most prominent and now senior figure on the Swedish free scene and has been responsible for bringing its best players to wider notice, as a member of Gush (with Sten Sandell and Raymond Strid) and The Thing. He has also worked with such varied luminaries as Barry Guy, Thurston Moore and Jim O'Rourke, and in situations that range from post-bop to post-rock. We suspect there is a collection of cool jazz at home as well.

Like the great Lars Gullin before him, Gustafsson is basically a baritone specialist, but he also plays other members of the family, is the only known exponent of the fluteophone (a concert flute with a sax mouthpiece stuck in the end), and he disguises any passing resemblance to Gerry Mulligan, Serge Chaloff or Gullin by stuffing a crushed beer can into the bell of his big horn. Blessed with a seemingly effortless technique, a wittily deconstructive approach to his instrument(s) and a generous intelligence, he never produces work that is less than thoughtful or other than exuberant. There is now so much of it on record that any single choice is invidious, but this is the one we return to most often and most enthusiastically

Though he isn't a player who thinks that altissimo screaming is sufficient, this trio find him in power mode. Aside from two brief items, it consists of extended rampages through four Don Cherry pieces, with Gustafsson sticking for once to alto and tenor. The group makes a joyful noise out of 'Cherryco', a black squall out of 'Awake Nu' and a grand showpiece out of 'Trans-Love Airways' that runs from stately bass intro to all-out attack. A great modern free-jazz record, complemented by superb work from both Flaten and the amazingly energetic Nilssen-Love. It's the man out front who claims both ears, though, one of the new giants of European improvisation.

BILL CHARLAP

Born 15 October 1966, New York City
Piano

Written In The Stars

Blue Note 27291
Charlap; Peter Washington (b); Kenny Washington (d). March 2000.

Bill Charlap said (2001): **'No one's in this business for stardom, or no one with any sense, at least. My mother was pretty famous in the '60s, but no one much remembers her now, and I don't feel resentful of that. It's how it goes. In the same way, I don't think of myself as playing one style or concept or "school" of music. I just play the best I can.'**

Bill is the son of songwriter Moose Charlap (who wrote the musical numbers for *Peter Pan*) and singer Sandy Stewart, so grew up with a clear sense of the American songbook and its by-ways. The early records all showed skill and confidence, sweetly done but perhaps lacking a certain measure of excitement. As time went by, Charlap's background began to seem more and more like an enormous assist. He did not come to the standard repertoire as someone who grew up on pop and rock; rather, this kind of material is very much the family business, and on *Written In The Stars* he reads melodies like 'In The Still Of The Night' and 'The Nearness Of You' with intuitive understanding. The Blue Note debut is close to perfection in this idiom, and Charlap plays with the confidence of a man who knows where he wants to go with each song. If it's not the sound of surprise, it's expert craftsmanship, and left to his own devices, he's the big mainstream piano star of the moment.

PAUL DUNMALL
Born 6 May 1953, Welling, Kent, England
Saxophones, other reeds, bagpipes

The Great Divide
Cuneiform RUNE 142
Dunmall; Gethin Liddington (t); Paul Rutherford, Hilary Jeffries (tb); Elton Dean (as); Simon Picard (ts); Evan Parker (ss, ts); Keith Tippett (p); John Adams (g); Paul Rogers (b); Tony Levin, Mark Sanders (d). March 2000.

Paul Dunmall says: **'Those who believe in spirit consider parting as temporary; atheists believe it's final; either way, there's the "great divide". I believe in continuing consciousness after death so I reflected that here, with the octet being this life and the double octet the continuation of consciousness (even more poignant now with Elton and Rutherford no longer with us). I had other things in mind, too, like the great divide between countries, religions, the sexes and so on.'**

The obvious points of reference are John Surman and Evan Parker, though Dunmall's influence from folk is obviously closer to the former. He was for a time best known as a member of long-standing improvising group Mujician, but he has steadily built up a huge catalogue of work, ranging from solo performances to – more rarely, of course – large-scale compositions for substantial ensembles.

As Dunmall has suggested, *The Great Divide* is subject to a whole multiplicity of interpretations. The first and most obvious is that it is a work which straddles and penetrates the line between composition and improvisation, one that non-believers in both camps consider absolute, while others regard it as non-existent. Dunmall doesn't break through without effort. His climax, which doubles the basic octet to what is essentially a big band, is far from certain at the outset, but achieved by effort and application; each of the first five sections is more expressive and more capacious than the last. When the extra instruments appear, it is as if a new storyteller has stepped into the firelight. The effect is curiously reminiscent in mood of John Surman's/John Warren's *Tales Of The Algonquin* (see p. 389), but with a deeper and darker philosophical understanding. It is, as Dunmall concedes, doubly poignant that two of the strongest voices in the large ensemble – Elton Dean and Paul Rutherford – have since passed on to uncertain rest. There is a live recorded version of *The Great Divide*, which underlines its durability and adaptability as a potential repertory piece, but there are few opportunities for regular work on this scale, and Dunmall isn't the kind of musician who dwells on his past successes; he prefers to document and move on.

WALLACE RONEY
Born 25 May 1960, Philadelphia, Pennsylvania
Trumpet

No Room For Argument
Stretch 9033
Roney; Antoine Roney (ss, ts); Geri Allen (p, ky); Adam Holzman (p, org, ky); Buster Williams (b); Lenny White (d). April 2000.

Wallace Roney says: **'The project started without a label. After a fight with Warners and a long struggle during which record companies showed interest then reneged, I was asked by Herbie Hancock to take part in a Miles and Coltrane tribute with Ravi Coltrane, Dave Holland and Jack DeJohnette. I wrote "Homage And Acknowledgement", which utilized Miles's "Filles De Kilimanjaro" against the "Love Supreme" bass-line, with an African highlight beat in 7/4 metre. Verve squashed the idea and agreed to support the tour if I and Ravi – the only direct links to Miles and Coltrane – were replaced by Roy Hargrove and Michael Brecker. I was angry and hurt and decided to finish the project on my own terms expressing how I felt about life and music, using quotes from Marcus Garvey, Malcolm X, Martin Luther King, the Honorable Elijah Muhammad, Deepak Chopra, Yogananda and Buster Williams, and interspersed their relevant messages that united music and humanity as dependent on each other as one, honouring the highest living/ spiritual force.'**

While Wynton Marsalis and Terence Blanchard parcelled out the mainstream tradition, Roney established himself as the eclectic heir of Miles Davis. He is married to, and has regularly recorded with, pianist Geri Allen. A fluent and graceful trumpeter, Roney – whose brother Antoine is also a gifted saxophone-player – has had poor fortune with the recording business. A substantial amount of his work is locked up in the Muse catalogue and he has rubbed up against corporate issues ever since. Here, though, is a recording that does seem to reflect his vision, which is both traditional, in the sense of absolutely jazz-based, but also alert to modern sounds. Roney was one of the very first jazz musicians to use turntablists and electronica in his work.

Whatever its unhappy background (though it should be said that Roney was reconciled with Hancock later and worked happily with him), *No Room For Argument* is a most impressive tapestry of styles and sounds, incorporating free-form passages, straight(ish) bop and some intriguing spoken-word samples from African-American heroes. Wallace pays homage to John Coltrane in a version of the 'Acknowledgement' section from *A Love Supreme*; Buster Williams takes that famous bass-line and makes it triumphantly his own. 'Straight No Nothing' and 'Midnight Blue' are both originals but are clearly intended to make direct reference to the modern jazz canon. In terms of trumpet-playing, Wallace refers quite explicitly to Miles, Dizzy, Booker Little and Freddie Hubbard, but the voice is now most distinctively his own and the impact of the album as a whole is considerable. Chick Corea produces and Glen Kolotkin engineers with a delicate touch.

WILLIAM HOOKER
Born 18 June 1946, New Britain, Connecticut
Drums, piano, voice

Black Mask
Knitting Factory KFCD 305
Hooker; Roy Nathanson (sax); Jason Hwang (vn); Andrea Parkins (acc, etc). April 2000.

William Hooker said (2000): **'New York? You can do anything you want in New York, musically. It's all there, even if you can't afford some of it.'**

Hooker is an eternal outsider. Considered suspect by the jazz establishment, he owes much of his visibility in New York to Thurston Moore of Sonic Youth (whose work the drummer has covered from time to time) and to the Knitting Factory, where he found a niche for his often aggressively out-there work. Hooker maintains a doughty stance, living in Hell's Kitchen, teaching out in Flatbush, carrying on his career outside the usual networks and continuing to bring a spoken-word element to his records and performances. Reactions to his work vary and many of his more recent recording fall outside the jazz orbit and into something like post-rock, but along the way Hooker has developed an interesting line of collaboration with string-players, first Billy Bang on the fine 1994 Silkheart *Joy (Within)!* and then Jason Hwang, with whom he has made a number of recordings.

Their exchanges provide some of the best moments on this set of torrid duos. Hwang has the power of an electric guitarist (someone of Moore's sensibility perhaps) and Hooker is not afraid to unleash polyrhythmic waves at his collaborators. The duos with Nathanson (and particularly the long 'An Unknown Feeling') are very reminiscent of Rashied Ali's work with Louie Belogenis; some may find these crude by comparison, but Hooker's energy is unmistakable. His association with Parkins is more inflected, largely because she is such an elusive presence. They fence and circle on 'Orange' and 'Volatility', with Hooker's vocalizations adding a surreal dimension to the music. He will never be an A-list musician, but anyone who wants to understand the riptides and undertows of New York music has to deal with him.

BEN ALLISON
Born 27 November 1966, New Haven, Connecticut
Double bass

Riding The Nuclear Tiger
Palmetto PM 2067
Allison; Ron Horton (t); Michael Blake (ss, ts); Ted Nash (ss, as, ts, bcl); Frank Kimbrough (p, prepared p); Tomas Ulrich (clo); Jeff Ballard (d). May 2000.

Ben Allison remembers: **'Sorcerer Sound [studio] was an ominous basement box, with a green room filled with taxidermy and old microphone power supplies that threw out random sparks. Two-inch analog tape was so expensive I had to record over my *Medicine Wheel* date. Engineer David Baker was in rare and brilliant form, turning dials, yelling at assistants, all the while draped in strips of edited tape and brandishing razor blades.'**

Allison is the talented and tireless artistic director of the Jazz Composers Collective in New York City and a leading light in the research, performance and recording group the Herbie Nicols Project. Among a generation of Mingus-inspired bassists, he is one of the few whose compositional language approaches the same turbulent power and camouflaged subtlety. His group Medicine Wheel takes its name from the second album in what was from the start an impressively focused recording career. Allison's sophistication was immediately evident on the debut *Seven Arrows* with compositions as buoyantly various as 'Dragzilla', 'King Of A One Man Planet' and the Monkish 'Delirioso'. Medicine Wheel's stock-in-trade was a settled understanding among the players and many, many hours spent developing and patiently working out ideas. There is not a slackly run-down line or ad hoc structure on any of the records. Allison's is seldom the dominant voice, though the pairing of bass and cello offers an intriguing counterbalance to the horns and piano.

The gentleness of the debut evaporated on *Medicine Wheel*, a more assertively downtown album with a Knitting Factory aspect and marked by some notably pungent conceptions. A third record, *Third Eye*, consolidated the picture and paved the way for the bold sweep of *Riding The Nuclear Tiger*. The title-track has a vigorously contemporary feel, with unexpected elements of Techno thrown in. In sharp contrast is the Mingus-referencing 'Love Chant Remix', which shows how thoroughly Allison has brought his main influence up to date. The group now has a thoroughly seasoned feel and a desire to explore yet more new textures. The addition of an oud hadn't made much impact on *Third Eye* but here pianist Kimbrough plays direct on open strings and prepares his piano with coins and fishing line for 'Swiss Cheese D' (it's a basketball reference!), while on the 3/4 'Weazy' saxophonist

Blake plays two horns simultaneously (but without sounding like Roland Kirk!). Horton has more than one bag to dip into: some of his statements are smokingly pungent, reminiscent of Booker Little, but he can also play with a melting simplicity. Blake is featured as a composer on 'Harlem River Line' and even gets the boss to drop out towards the end, which is some kind of grateful. Kimbrough, a seasoned leader in his own right, is always worth tracking on any of these discs. His parts, like Allison's structures, are brilliant collages, which according to the leader only made sense when the layers were assembled. Perhaps the single cut along with the title-track that sums up everything is the one that follows it, 'Jazz Scene Voyeur': sounds like it might be one of John Zorn's Naked City thrashes, but in fact it's a wry and quite delicate thing that depends on careful call and response in a form Miles Davis would have understood and approved. Allison never shows off his understanding of jazz history. It's always just there, among the contemporary references and artful boho stylings. Whatever the genre, this is strong new music.

SONNY ROLLINS &

Born Theodore Walter Rollins, 7 September 1930, New York City
Tenor saxophone

This Is What I Do
Milestone MCD-9310-2
Rollins; Clifton Anderson (tb); Stephen Scott (p); Bob Cranshaw (b); Perry Wilson, Jack DeJohnette (d). May–June 2000.

Sonny Rollins said (1990): **'I consider it a privilege to have been part of this music and to have been able to play it so long. When I was away from jazz [1962 and 1968] I did wonder whether that was the end of the story. I used to think I had done *something* but not all I wanted. Here I am, still, and part of something that began with Louis Armstrong and Tatum and Waller. That's a privilege. I hope I earned it.'**

It's a commonplace that jazz has for the most part lost its small legion of charismatic figures who have shouldered its great innovations, embodied its major advances. Who are the surviving giants? Cecil Taylor, Ornette Coleman ... Sonny Rollins. If Taylor's massive advances exemplify the jazz of a once and future era, Rollins belongs to a bygone golden age, an almost classical figure. He is, perhaps, jazz's Sinatra, absolutely 'traditional', even conservative now, yet so enormously individual that he dictates his own space in his culture. He may have tried modish flavours from time to time, but if they didn't fit with him he simply discarded them. Each new session is nothing more than a set's worth of Rollins, blowing as lustily as he felt at that point. His bandsmen have included distinguished players – Stephen Scott is the best pianist he's had for years, and DeJohnette, who plays on four of the six tracks, is hardly a mere sideman – but they are little more than framing devices for the saxophone.

More than ever, this set dismisses ornamentation. The studio sound is unsparing on the players, with a new immediacy in the mix: Rollins's records of recent times have seldom sounded so close and alive. The material is *sui generis*: a new calypso, 'Salvador'; a more-or-less blues, 'Charles M'; a surprising memento of a nearly forgotten tenorman, 'Did You Hear Harold Vick?'; and three improbable standards, two of them all but unknown to jazz repertory. He makes 'Sweet Leilani' into something approaching a gospel piece, and 'The Moon Of Manakoora', a choice to gladden the hearts of Dorothy Lamour fans, is fractious and regal. Here and throughout, the tenor tone has an almost crusty grandeur, the old supreme-steel sound mottled and scarred, but superbly resilient. His solos no longer sweep through numberless choruses, instead focusing around fragments of the material. The rhythmic chops have been hurt by the passage of time, perhaps, but there's a compensating sense that he's phrasing everything to his own particular clock. If anything, he has gone back to the performer whose sets he always tried to catch after his own night's work, Billie Holiday. 'A Nightingale Sang In Berkeley Square', with the leader lagging imperiously behind the beat, might almost be a late-period Holiday interpretation. The others do their duty, and often handsomely. Scott gets off some shapely and even ingenious solos. Anderson is the patient colourist, and he has some nice muted work on 'Charles M'. But nothing they do is anything other than an intermission, while we impatiently await the saxophonist's return. *This Is What I Do* is unmistakable, and great Sonny Rollins.

& *See also* **Saxophone Colossus** (1956; p. 188), **A Night At The Village Vanguard** (1957; p. 216)

GARY BURTON &
Born 23 January 1943, Anderson, Indiana
Vibraphone

For Hamp, Red, Bags And Cal
Concord CCD 4941
Burton; Mulgrew Miller, Makoto Ozone, Danilo Perez (p); Russell Malone (g); Christian McBride, John Patitucci (b); Lewis Nash (d); Luis Quintero (perc). May–June 2000.

Gary Burton said (1993): **'I like to give all the instruments an equal role. My first model for a group was a classical string quartet, with an equality among the voices. I'm always thinking in terms of a band, rather than just three or four guys who can accompany me. And that affects my choices very significantly.'**

This is Gary's most explicit tribute to his great ancestors on the vibraphone. At a time when such homages were ten-a-penny, an easy A&R option for labels still querulous about the possibility of 'selling' jazz, this one stands out. Each of the great names is represented by two or three tunes, and while no special effort is made to reproduce their style, the spirit of the ancestors imbues the record. 'Flying Home' is maybe the best example, a breezy, swinging performance that recalls Hamp's classic years. 'Django' and 'Bags' Groove' are for Jackson, of course, and are wonderfully adept, but it is the sheer strangeness of Red Norvo's 'Dance Of The Octopus' at the end of the record that is likely to send even uncommitted listeners back to the start. Gary can rarely have been recorded so well, and the different groups are bedded in round him intimately but with enough space to keep the voices individual and strong.

& *See also* **Country Roads And Other Places** (1968; p. 355), **Hotel Hello** (1974; p. 411)

CHRIS POTTER
Born 1 January 1971, Chicago, Illinois
Tenor, alto and soprano saxophones, bass clarinet, flutes

Gratitude
Verve 549433-2
Potter; Kevin Hays (p); Scott Colley (b); Brian Blade (d). September 2000.

Chris Potter said (2001): **'I heard musicians say: "I was influenced by the Coltrane of this or that period, but I've moved beyond that now ...", and I realized that I couldn't divide up what Coltrane meant to me into periods, and certainly couldn't say that I was done with any of it!'**

Potter has grown into one of the major saxophonists of today. His astonishingly confident and full-blooded debut on Criss Cross in 1992 showed his prowess with any one of his chosen horns, and there's amazingly little to choose between his alto- (which he's subsequently all but given up) and tenor-playing. Both of them are muscular in the post-bop manner but full of surprising stylistic twists that make one think of both Parker's generation and the elegant elaborations of Benny Carter and Hodges.

Potter made some good records for Gerry Teekens at Criss Cross, but he sounded as if the hard-bop ethos – never doctrinaire enough to be an ideology, but certainly the house style – was holding him back a little. If Potter's major-label move held any fears for him, you wouldn't know from this confident sprint through the history of jazz saxophone, conceived as a salute to a string of masters old and new. Some of the jumping around from horn to horn – he gets through six of them here, including a debut on Chinese wood flute – underlines that this would be a record pitched as a coming-out, even after all those listed above. It's still rather coolly conceived, too. The opening dedication to Coltrane, 'The Source', avoids the master's grandest gestures and scales him down to a pocket-sized blues that is both cheekily reductive and completely respectful, and 'Sun King' is Rollins refracted through 'an odd-meter context' that needs all four men to keep their eye unswervingly on the pulse. There are tributes, too, to Wayne Shorter ('Eurydice') and Lester Young ('The Visitor'). Here, and in the best of the session (at a few key points Potter's concept gets away from him; he brings little of interest to the Parker piece, 'Star Eyes', and the flute tune 'Vox Humana' sits oddly with the rest), one gets the exultant feel of players at the top of their game, working within a mutually understood language that isn't yet closed to surprise. Hays, who's been somewhat in shadow since his Blue Note albums, performs well, and Colley and Blade are top-notch.

JOHN ELLIS
Born 13 April 1974, Raleigh, North Carolina
Tenor saxophone

Roots, Branches & Leaves
Fresh Sound New Talent FSNTCD124
Ellis; Nicholas Payton (t); Aaron Goldberg (p); Roland Guerin (b); Jason Marsalis (d); Bilal Oliver (v). October 2000.

John Ellis says: '**It was recorded to ADAT at Word Of Mouth in New Orleans, by Tim Stambaugh, who had to leave during the second day for a rehearsal, leaving his assistant to handle things. ADAT requires two VHS tapes to be synchronized – which is why this was a transitional technology. The machine froze while Tim was gone, and that's when we realized his assistant didn't know how to work the machine, and couldn't help us fix it. That was the only day we had Bilal with us, and as the clock ticked, we panicked. Somehow we got things cranked up again, but most of Bilal's stuff ended up as a first take, a race against the clock.**'

A deft composer, Ellis has worked with guitarist Charlie Hunter but seems destined to make his own way. The debut is a strange and magical record. It begins with a recording of Ellis's grandmother singing 'John Brown's Gun', from which the opening track emerges. Vocalist Oliver is involved here, and later on 'Nowny Dreams' and 'The Lonely Jesus'. We've not heard anything quite like this music, and with Goldberg switching to Fender Rhodes here and there and Payton making a couple of guest appearances (on 'Ed' and 'Who', the two jazziest cuts) the music is rich and varied. Ellis himself isn't earth-shaking as a saxophone-player; his role here is mainly as composer/auteur of a fascinating aural experience that's equivalent to looking at an exhibition of photos, old and new, coloured and sepia, familiar things and unknown portraits. Lovely.

AHMAD JAMAL*&*
Born 2 July 1930, Pittsburgh, Pennsylvania
Piano

À L'Olympia
Dreyfus FDM 36629 2
Jamal; George Coleman (ts); James Cammack (b); Idris Muhammad (d). November 2000.

Former nightclub owner Jean-Paul Allais says: **'I grew up listening to At The Pershing and could sing every solo on it. I didn't get to see Ahmad Jamal for real till that night, and the sound was exactly the same, but even stronger. It felt like being on Olympus, not just at L'Olympia.'**

Jamal was an honoured figure in Europe through the '90s, playing a sophisticated jazz that went down particularly well in France. Marking his 70th birthday with another concert in Paris, Jamal doesn't lie back and enjoy the occasion but seems bent on delivering a performance to rival the celebrated *At The Pershing*. That he does so – and royally – is partly down to the magisterial presence of big George Coleman, whose solo on 'How Deep Is The Ocean' is one of the finest of his distinguished career, solidly engineered and delicately crafted. Jamal responds with one of several toughly lyrical solos.

Jamal's style hasn't changed much over the years, but any appearance of a new toughness shouldn't be confused with the crudity that comes with declining technique. Jamal has acquired muscle. Where once he made solos out of spiderweb and spun sugar, now they're of fine, tensile steel. The set gives early notice of intent with a long, pungent performance of 'The Night Has A Thousand Eyes' and Jamal astonishes with a brilliantly inventive uptempo introduction to 'Autumn Leaves'; a classic reinvented. Coleman creeps in slyly from off-mic and together they no more than tag the familiar melody before taking it off in new directions. Muhammad's drumming, which elsewhere is businesslike and orderly, makes a substantial contribution. 'My Foolish Heart' is more straightforwardly melodic, but Coleman brings a gentle stridency to his solo, popping his pads softly here and there, which gives the tune a new poignancy.

'Appreciation' and the encore, 'Aftermath', are showpieces for piano and rhythm. The latter, unusually, is the only Jamal composition on the set, though recent years have seen him concentrate ever more fixedly on reinvented standards and less on original fare. It would have been good to get George back on for one last hurrah, but it was Jamal's night and it would be hard to better *À L'Olympia*.

& *See also* **At The Pershing / Complete Live At The Pershing Lounge** (1958; p. 221)

ERNST REIJSEGER
Born 13 November 1934, Naarden, Netherlands
Cello

I Love You So Much It Hurts
Winter & Winter 910 077 2
Reijseger; Franco D'Andrea (p). 2000.

Percussionist Gerry Hemingway says: **'Ernst is something we don't have too many positive examples of any more, a musician with huge ears who is also a natural showman, conjuring up the wonderful virtuosity of the vaudeville era through his humour, incisive rhythmic command and sophisticated use of extended techniques.'**

Unlike fellow cellist Tristan Honsinger, Reijseger has never committed himself absolutely to abstract music and has always retained a measure of melody and euphony in his cello-playing. He has been associated with projects as various as Clusone 3 and the Gerry Hemingway group and always brings a combination of solid technique and a kind of playful libertinism to whatever music is on the agenda.

His diversity is almost a philosophical position, as if he meets the world through the medium of music: one might find him collaborating one minute with a Senegalese poet (Mola Sylla) and the next working with film director Werner Herzog. Given that range, the duets with D'Andrea are more conventional in form, at first hearing at least. They sit somewhat in the line of horn/piano duets, which can be one of the laziest situations in improvised music. There is nothing conventional or lazy about the playing, though. 'In A Sentimental Mood' and 'Night And Day' start proceedings on relatively familiar ground, though the rest of the album ranges more freely and eclectically. Reijseger seems to concentrate on keeping his cello within the range of a tenor singing voice, which heightens the songbook feel of the record. D'Andrea solos sparingly and often with affecting reticence, but no mistaking the emotion.

AVISHAI COHEN
Born 22 April 1971, Kibbutz Kabri, Israel
Double bass, bass guitar, piano

Colors
Stretch 9031
Cohen; Steve Davis, Avi Lebovich (tb); Jimmy Greene (ss, f); Jason Lindner (p); Amos Hoffman (g, oud); Jeff Ballard (d, perc); Yagil Baras (b); Antonio Sanchez (d); Claudia Acuña (v); string quartet. December 2000.

Avishai Cohen says: **'Colors was a very natural recording: once we started recording, it was like playing a good live show.'**

Confusingly, there is another Avishai Cohen, who plays trumpet. For the moment, this one is the star. There's an understandable assumption that Cohen did service in the Chick Corea group and was given a chance to record on Stretch by way of thanks. In reality, the recording came first and the chance to play with Chick after that, which is more remarkable.

Cohen returned to the double bass after doing different service, in the Israeli military. He'd begun as a bass guitarist and studied music in Jerusalem before moving to the US. The debut record, *Adama*, showed great confidence; bright compositional ideas, sometimes in intriguingly stripped-down settings and with label boss Corea, Brad Mehldau and Danilo Perez on hand to provide a touch of class.

Colors took Cohen's career into a new dimension. The writing is bright and thoughtful, the arrangements (with trombones, soprano saxophone and string quartet on the title-track) full-voiced and the improvisation impressively difficult to separate from written passages. Some of the melodies might well be from one of John Zorn's 'radical Jewish culture' projects for Tzadik, though there is nothing ideological about Cohen's work and no special pleading in his playing, which sounds light and free and very much in the line of American bass-playing defined by Paul Chambers. Yagil Baras takes over bass-playing duties when Cohen is otherwise engaged. All 13 songs are originals, though 'IB4U' is co-credited to Avi Levobich, and there isn't a weak or formulaic moment on the set.

WARREN VACHÉ
Born 21 February 1951, Rahway, New Jersey
Cornet, flugelhorn

2gether
Nagel Heyer 2011
Vaché; Bill Charlap (p). December 2000.

Warren Vaché says: '**Bill and I recorded it in a day at a studio in Connecticut. Recording a duet is challenging work. I think I sprained my brain concentrating. Charlap as usual tossed off some brilliant playing. Aside from a couple of heated disagreements of what the melody does where, it was a joy to do. After a couple of years, the result of those disagreements is the most valuable part of the recording for me.**'

The son of bassist Warren Sr and elder brother of clarinettist Allan, Vaché came to prominence re-creating the solos of Bix Beiderbecke and ever since has been addicted to the backward glance. He is one of the leading swing players of the last couple of decades and is arguably the first cornetist since Ruby Braff (with whom he has shared a couple of labels over the years) to try to build on the example of Pops. But whereas Ruby is always incisive, pugnacious and sometimes downright filthy, Vaché has a curiously mild approach to swing which takes time to work its undoubted magic. He has the facility to play extremes of pitch very quietly and with estimable control, but for the longest time seemed to us an excellent technician who had little of moment to say.

All this changed when in 1981 he recorded *Iridescence*, a gorgeous jazz record whose mellow exterior, with Vaché's creamy tone, disguised some powerful jazz playing. And from there it just got better, with excellent sets for the British Zephyr label and a nice outing with brother Allan called *Mrs Vaché's Boys*.

2gether is an unqualified delight. 'We wanted to play some nice old tunes, and at tempos you don't hear any more. Guys I admire did it – maybe it's because nobody dances.' Vaché's remarks recall an era in jazz now gone, as does the music – except, then or now, it was rarely played with as much finesse, joyous invention and unassuming charm as this. Many of these pieces are as close to perfection as you can imagine a duet could ever be. Warren's tone, whether tightly muted or luxuriously open, speaks directly to the listener, and his playing has taken on a mantle which goes back past Braff and Hackett, maybe to Armstrong himself. Yet it's modern music – there's no whiff of mustiness, or stale old repertory here. Charlap, who can seem like a merely fail-safe executant on some records, is equally inspired, turning in swinging accompaniments at every tempo, every line logical but never falling in quite the place you expect. Few contemporary mainstream records have given us such pleasure.

THE RECENT SCENE
2001–2010

By the close of our survey, jazz has passed its hypothetical centenary. It is clear that the music had been around and had evolved in significant ways before anyone thought to put it down. As we've seen, many of the earliest recordings may distort the picture by presenting the music in a misleadingly polite or formal way. Some romantics still nurse the hope that the legendary cylinder recording said to have been made by Buddy Bolden, the *Ur*-hero of jazz and the source of many of its most problematic mythologies (Bolden spent the last years of his life in an insane asylum, living on unheard until 1931, by which time jazz was poised for its next evolutionary step), will be uncovered in some abandoned cellar. When Hurricane Katrina devastated New Orleans in 2005, there were those who predicted that the music of some previously lost, antediluvian period might float up in the floodwaters. As things turned out, the reconstruction did help refocus attention on New Orleans's vivid musical culture, though at a human cost few would consider worth the gain.

Even 90 years into its *recorded* history, it is music that presents a double face at every step. No one has quite determined – and nor should they – whether jazz is an art or a branch of entertainment (as if the two were incompatible), whether it is essentially radical or conservative in spirit, a music of freedom and individualism or a music that celebrates the collective above all. For much of the last 15 to 20 years, there has been an ongoing argument as to whether jazz is any longer an exclusively American let alone an African-American music. For our part, we consider such discussions perilous at best, absurd at worst. Anyone who argues that the centre of gravity in jazz has switched from the United States to Europe is either *parti pris* or else deluded. America, and particularly the great metropolitan centres – New York, Chicago, Los Angeles – remain the crucible of much that is vital and innovative in the music. European, Asian, African and Australasian contributions are important and welcomed, but they are still essentially footnotes to the main drama and will remain so for the conceivable future. There is probably more creative jazz in New York City on a given night than in most European countries in many, many weeks and months, and it serves no wider purpose to argue any other position.

We have, however, loyally documented some of the best jazz coming out of the UK and the other European countries, and we have dipped a toe into other waters as well, though scarcely enough to satisfy an Australian fan, say, or a Hungarian. The internet has brought these burgeoning 'scenes' closer to hand than they could possibly have been before, but it remains difficult to get a sense of an overall scene without spending time with it or ideally in it. The sense of connectedness that the World Wide Web has brought is largely illusory. One can very easily order up a CD by a Finnish musician, one working quietly in Akron or Cleveland, and one whose beat is the Tokyo club scene, but these, like ethnic food, are often little more than exotic flavours that vary the diet.

It is our unfashionable contention that jazz remains an American music with valuable manifestations in other countries and cultures. It is also still very much a minority music. Our efforts to see it accorded more media attention have, we hope, never gone as far as to suggest that jazz is somehow superior to or more important than other musical cultures. This is plain nonsense and a kind of aggressive special pleading that has done the music no service. That said, we do not consider it a badge of honour that jazz is enjoyed by the few. It is simply in the nature of the music. It is, as Richard Cook has elsewhere put it, a long game, five-day cricket rather than the brightly coloured 20-over variety Richard disliked. Its practice involves dedication, small reward and a certain cosmic stoicism and humour. Which is why in this final section of the *Guide* you will find as many senior figures approaching the end of their lives as you will bright young talents starting out on their playing careers. It is not always the case that older musicians produce the best work and we have tired of hearing that this or that visiting American is 'at the peak of his powers', when clearly he was at the peak of his powers in 1959, when he was neglected or derided by the mainstream media. However, unlike pop culture, where novelty and youth are part of both medium and message, lack of years does not always connote freshness and energy.

It is our settled opinion that the jazz of the first decade of the 21st century is in no way inferior to that of the great past. It is in many respects a very different music, but not because it has made peace with other parts of the musical culture – classical, pop, 'world' music – but because it has become more itself. Younger artists have insisted on performing their own music rather than 'standards' or repertory, or they have established a new canon of standards – Radiohead, Joni Mitchell and Nick Drake instead of George Gershwin, Vernon Duke and Richard Rodgers – and no musician of an earlier decade would be surprised to learn that this was the case. Jazz has always responded to the surrounding culture as well as to its own internal dictates. Indeed, the periods where it has not have often been those when the music seemed to mark time, though such has been the speed of its evolution that jazz has never ossified.

It would be tempting to suggest that in 2010 jazz is on the verge of a new technological shift, with downloaded music taking the place of the long-dominant CD. So far, this has not been the case. The CD is an ideal vehicle for jazz, though the emphasis on packed durations remains questionable. Jazz's greatest single problem at the moment isn't the lack of an audience – there is always a sufficient audience – but the sheer weight of the back catalogue, which in the early years of the decade proliferated at an alarming rate. Having gone through periods of extinction, jazz culture is now Alexandrian, with almost everything in the music's history (exceptions noted in earlier chapters) commercially available, not always well-mastered, often poorly annotated, sometimes of questionable provenance but challengingly in the public domain.

What follows is our sense of what has been most exciting and consistently enjoyable over the last ten years. By definition we have heard this music much less often and carried it with us through fewer of life's changes than the music of previous decades, but after so many years listening to jazz with close attention and unflagging passion, we like to think we know good from average, and that we might be able to flag up the great among the good.

Needless to say, some of the records reviewed below were only made and released after Richard Cook's premature passing. They were and are listened to as if he were still around, two pairs of ears being a better sytem of quality control than monaural listening. For us, the most poignant aspect of his passing is that he is not here to share that moment when track one engages and the counter starts to tick off the seconds on what might be music for the ages...

DICK HYMAN
Born 8 March 1927, New York City
Piano, organ

Forgotten Dreams
Arbors ARCD 19248
Hyman; John Sheridan (p). January 2001.

Dick Hyman says: '**John Sheridan and I find great value in this forgotten repertoire. It is often venturesome and at its best ingenious and touching, and reflects an era when the piano was uniquely revered.**'

Dick Hyman has had a pretty paradoxical career. He studied with Teddy Wilson and in the '40s was playing with both Charlie Parker and Benny Goodman. Working as a studio musician through much of the next two decades, he also recorded novelty tunes, under various pseudonyms, as well as Scott Joplin's complete works. He loves early jazz, is an expert on the jazz piano tradition, can re-create pit-band orchestrations or ragtime arrangements to order – yet was also one of the first to record an album of tunes played on prototype synthesizers and has undertaken such quixotic projects as playing 'A Child Is Born' in the style of Cecil Taylor and Scott Joplin, and everyone in between.

The discography is as large, as eclectic and as full of surprises as this might suggest, but having dedicated himself to the legacy of most of the great piano improvisers, he has also stood up for the preterite, the neglected and mostly anonymous mass. Here Hyman and John Sheridan tackle the buried legacy of novelty piano, one of the last undiscovered corners of the jazz tradition. Now that everyone from Reginald Robinson to Morten Gunnar Larsen has worked over the ragtime tradition, where next but the vast and almost untapped resources of the likes of Zez Confrey, Rube Bloom, Billy Mayerl and Willie Eckstein? Those last two don't figure here, but this record cried out for a sequel even before it was in the shops. Instead, they focus on Willie 'The Lion' Smith, Confrey, Bloom and Bob Zurke, with Bix's 'In A Mist' and W. C. Polla's 'Dancing Tambourine' to fill the gaps. This set works better than Hyman's other two-piano dates because it's less about improvising (which scarcely plays a role here) and more about the graceful juxtaposition of complementary parts. These are, rhythmically, carefully honed essays on very early swing and syncopation; harmonically, they're dense with detail; but the melodies are so direct and wholesome, naïve in a pre-modern way, that some ideal balance is created which makes the results neither too knowing nor too gauche. Handsomely recorded, these forgotten dreams are, in their way, a daring revival.

ALEX CLINE

Born 4 January 1956, Los Angeles, California
Drums

The Constant Flame
Cryptogramophone 110
Cline; Vinny Golia (ss); Wayne Peet (ky); Nels Cline, G. E. Stinson (g); Jeff Gauthier (vn); Michael Elizondo (b); Peter Erskine (d); Brad Dutz (perc); Aina Kemanis (v); additional voices. January 2001.

Alex Cline says: **'Conceived as a companion piece to *Sparks Fly Upward* and designed to feature guest artists, *The Constant Flame* was both deeply satisfying and bittersweet, as I knew it was to be our last recording together: Aina told me months earlier that she was retiring from music altogether. Despite recording material the group had never played before (and just two rehearsals), the experience was memorably smooth. However, having all the right people play the music in all the right ways and to have it captured, guided and made manifest by all the right people in the best ways imaginable couldn't completely soothe my underlying sadness. It marked the end of an era for me.'**

Alex is the twin brother of Nels Cline, who has experienced stardom as a member of Wilco. The brothers worked together initially, forming a group called Quartet Music with the brilliant bassist and composer Eric von Essen, but their musical courses have diverged somewhat since then. While Nels seeks out rockier terrain, Alex has pursued a music based around lush textures and thick, harmonic swirls – an unusual course for a percussionist, perhaps, although his vast kit of drums, cymbals, bells and percussive devices is as appropriate to melodic needs as much as to rhythmical ones.

Nevertheless, the Clines have continued to work together on a project-by-project basis. Alex struck a purple patch at the end of the '90s with a sequence of three very powerful records. Made in 1998, *Sparks Fly Upward* is packed with ethereal beauty. *The Other Shore* is a trio with Jeff Gauthier and G. E. Stinson, a set of music that pretty much dispenses with any vestige of conventional swing in favour of a music that seems to hover, substantially but ungraspably, in front of the listener. With violin and heavily processed guitar dominating, Cline's percussion devices, which include kantele, autoharp and other exotica, have very little to do with establishing metre and more to do with sustaining an overall mood. The ending is extraordinary, slowing almost to stasis and delivered in a hushed and almost reverential tone: 'Nothing To Teach'.

The addition of saxophone, bass and keyboards, extra percussion and the reintroduction of vocalist Aina Kemanis and other voices lends *The Constant Flame* a more familiar profile but also a ritual quality of farewell. Producer Peter Erskine creates a rich and varied sonic landscape. The title-piece is dedicated to a former boss, clarinettist John Carter, and shows how thoroughly Cline has learned how to combine organized structure with improvisatory freedom. Other tracks are also personal dedications: 'Bridge' is for the adventurous pop vocalist David Sylvian; 'Evening Bell' is for Toru Takemitsu and marked by a Zen-like spareness. Cline is at his most urgent on the opening 'Paramita', written for Don Cherry; heavyweight drumming gives way to kantele and synthesized backgrounds. Kemanis is used to great and economical effect, ending the set with a delightful 'Benediction', which is spiritual but resolutely unsolemn. The music has a gently climactic quality, marking the end of something, but without sentimentality.

HENRY THREADGILL &

Born 15 February 1944, Chicago, Illinois
Alto and tenor saxophones, clarinet, flute

Everybody's Mouth's A Book
Pi 1
Threadgill; Brandon Ross (g); Bryan Carrott (vib, mar); Stomu Takeishi (b); Dafnis Prieto (d). February 2001.

Henry Threadgill said (1989): **'Ornette Coleman reinvented melody, by taking it back to the values of traditional jazz. It's the way the bass-line moves, and moulds itself to the other voices. That was an important idea for me.'**

Threadgill's most inventive album for ten years was released simultaneously with *Up Popped The Two Lips*, which featured a different group, called Zoo-Id. This one goes out as Make Your Move. The latter is an amplified unit, hinged on Brandon Ross's and Stomu Takeishi's electric guitars and sounding not unlike a freaked-out version of Ornette's Prime Time, if such a thing is imaginable. The writing is as quirky and cranky as ever, with some delirious playing from the leader on alto and flute. 'Don't Turn Around' is amazing, a headlong flurry of sound from start to finish but governed as ever by Henry's unquantifiable musical vision. There's a lot of wild funk here, on 'Don't Turn Around' and 'Shake It Off', tracks that sound as if they might have gone through Funkadelic hands on a particularly weird day. Carrott's vibes-playing is delightfully eccentric, and it's Takeishi again who provides the specific gravity, delivering a deceptively crude line that constantly floats free. Threadgill's own playing has become simpler over the years, with much less emphasis on multi-instrumentalism. The group has become his main expressive vehicle.

& *See also* **Rag, Bush And All** (1988; p. 526)

JASON MORAN
Born 21 January 1975, Houston, Texas
Piano

Black Stars
Blue Note 32922-2
Moran; Sam Rivers (ts); Tarus Mateen (b); Nasheet Waits (d). March 2001.

Jason Moran says: **'I wanted to open my music by having a guest, and could think of no one better than Sam Rivers. My teachers, Andrew Hill and Jaki Byard, worked with him extensively. I loved his ability to exist as a free improviser *and* as a member of Dizzy's '80s group. He immediately entered our landscape with confidence, and gave us the energy to plough behind him. I think his work on "Foot Under Foot" and on "Sound It Out" are my favourites for sheer intensity and precision.'**

The title of Moran's Blue Note debut was *Soundtrack To Human Motion*, which despite various media attempts to correct to 'emotion' give a strong clue to this brilliant young musician. What he's about – as with many of the most interesting young players in this precinct – is the momentum and the dynamic of his music as much as its body-weight of 'feeling'. Some of the pieces on the first record are self-consciously hip and trickily built, as if Moran was concerned that he might be seen not to present strong enough meat for a top dog like Greg Osby to work on. And then there's 'Le Tombeau de Couperin' and a piece called 'Retrograde', inspired by playing an Andrew Hill LP backwards. But there's nothing much wrong with showing off when you are this talented. The follow-up record was almost as good, and so was *Black Stars*, and so was the one after that, *Modernistic*, and the next again. It was only with 2006's disappointing *Artist In Residence* that Moran seemed willing to show any human frailty, and even it was better than most pianists' crowning achievement.

By 2000, Moran had shaped a trio of quite breathtaking empathy and intensity, in which his sometimes mystifying complexities seemed to fit and function. *Black Stars* brings off the coup of enlisting paterfamilias Sam Rivers. His presence is almost a bonus in what's otherwise a hard, detailed, highly achieved trio record, but there are moments, especially on the strong opening 'Foot Under Foot', when it sounds a little like a Rivers disc and it's a tribute to the pianist's compositional strength and character that he keeps the project focused on his contemporary agenda. Moran goes back to an ancient piece of Ellington, 'Kinda Dukish', and mingles it with the here-and-now, 'Draw The Light Out' and 'Gangsterism On A River'. Where some pianists impose themselves on their material by spinning out ever more fanciful embroidery, Moran already seems to be seeking essences and irreducible core matter. Nothing here goes on for very long; every piece is brilliantly finished.

KEITH JARRETT&
Born 8 May 1945, Allentown, Pennsylvania
Piano, soprano saxophone, other instruments

Always Let Me Go
ECM 1800/01 2CD
Jarrett; Gary Peacock (b); Jack DeJohnette (d). April 2001.

Keith Jarrett said (2002): **'When I think about this period in our music, I – funnily enough – think about bebop. That's what it makes me think of. It's not the notes, or the harmony, or anything in the rhythm. It's a sense that we are playing energy, not playing with it, or using it to play the "material", but *playing energy*.'**

In 1990, the Standards Trio took a new direction. *Changeless* contained original material which is deeply subversive of jazz as a system of improvisation on 'the changes'. Typically, Jarrett invests the term with quite new aesthetic and philosophical considerations. On *Changeless*, there are no chord progressions at all; the trio improvises each section in a single key, somewhat in the manner of an Indian raga. The results are impressive and thought-provoking. With *Inside Out* in 2000, Jarrett's interest in free playing, always evident, evolved again. Here, instead of simply abandoning changes, Jarrett and the trio abandoned all thought of predetermined structure. To some degree, this was instinct with the spontaneous approach of the group, but it was applied with even more rigour.

Always Let Me Go was recorded live in Japan, where Jarrett has played to rapt attention throughout his career. The philosophy is the same as on *Inside Out*, a free programme without standards or structures decided beforehand. Jarrett has described the music as a 'volcanic eruption', but that suggests something messier and more haphazard than this. Or it works if one accepts that the trio delivers pure magma, without the dust, smoke and noise. Jarrett is in exceptionally fiery form and Peacock rages quietly during some of the more intense passages. As so often, though, it's DeJohnette who gives shape and form to the music, constantly revealing himself as the complete musician rather than merely a timekeeper. It's an exceptional recording as well, vivid, detailed and with a sense of real presence. Jarrett sounds intimate, almost confidential, in quieter passages, while the trio delivers a massive sound when playing full out. The opening 'Hearts In Space' is a full half-hour of intense trio improvisation, ranging from taut blues and boogie passages to more abstract shapes. 'Waves' is longer still and eclectic in terms of stylistic reference. Jarrett even seems to impersonate Bud Powell at one point. Interspersed are much shorter tracks, like the roistering 'Paradox', which touches on similar areas, and the tiny 'The River', which Jarrett plays solo. The last three tracks might not seem to be first-choice inclusions but none the less, as a document of Jarrett's almost 150th performance in Japan, this is impeccable.

& *See also* **El Juicio (The Judgement)** (1971; p. 386), **The Köln Concert** (1975; p. 418), **Standards: Volume 1** (1983; p. 474)

TREVOR WATTS &
Born 26 February 1939, York, England
Alto and soprano saxophones

Trevor Watts And The Celebration Band
Arc CD 010
Watts; Rob Leake (ss, ts); Marcus Cummins (ss, as); Amy Metcalf (ts); Geoff Sapsford (g); Roger Carey (b); Giampaolo Scatozza (perc); Jamie Harris (djembe, djarabouka, perc). April 2001.

Trevor Watts says: **'I mentored this group for four years and got them to a very good standard. They were inexperienced, but I know how to shape my own music. We got together three times a week for months, because in my work there's an underlying rhythmic concept that the players need to know in order to get to that moment of "lift" without which it sounds flat.'**

A stalwart of the British free-jazz scene, Watts came through like many others in RAF bands and pitched up in London just as free jazz was posing a new creative challenge. He was a founder member of both Amalgam and the Spontaneous Music Ensemble, but has subsequently turned his back very largely on abstract music in order to explore the strongly rhythmic, non-European language of his two main groups of the '80s, the Drum Orchestra and Moiré Music. The word 'moiré' refers to the shimmering patterns one sees in watered silk, and what Watts was trying to do was to create such patterns musically by overlaying rhythmic patterns and textures in live performance.

With the Celebration Band, the Moiré concept transferred to something much closer to the multi-horn lines of earlier groups but with an emphasis on repeated and overlaid patterns, close integration of contrapuntal material and steady rhythmic variation. This sounds very unlike orthodox British free bop but the basic idiom is still audible. Guitar and bass guitar thicken up the harmonies and there are genuinely individual voices in the ensemble, aside from Watts himself, who continues to play in the same rhapsodic manner of his Amalgam days; Sapsford in particular is a real find. '8 In 7' kicks off proceedings in the most arresting way; at 13 minutes it could hardly be more ambitious, and yet it passes as vividly as a jewelled miniature, for all its complex time-signature. 'Spring Sunrise' is more reflective, but 'Out Of The Street' restores the energy, bringing an outstanding album to a climax.

& *See also* **AMALGAM, Prayer For Peace** (1969; p. 366); **SPONTANEOUS MUSIC ENSEMBLE, Quintessence** (1973–1974; p. 406)

ENRICO PIERANUNZI
Born 5 December 1949, Rome, Italy
Piano

Live In Paris
Challenge 70126 2CD
Pieranunzi; Hein Van de Geyn (b); André Ceccarelli (d). April 2001.

Enrico Pieranunzi said (2002): **'The separation of "jazz" and "classical" is based on false assumptions about both. Much jazz is very formal; some classical music, and some of the best, has a very raw, physical, maybe pagan quality. In my work, I like to bring those two closer together.'**

Pieranunzi is not an extravagant virtuoso: his self-effacing manner recalls something of Hancock, but he uses all the ground-breaking modern discoveries in modality, rhythm and the broadening of pianistic devices to his own ends. As with the Space Jazz trio (perhaps familiar from some late recordings of Chet Baker's), which he apparently leads with the bassist Enzo Pietropaoli, he is an exponent of post-modern jazz, sounding perfectly self-aware yet concerned to introduce elements of abstraction and emotional flow alike. His most recent work has included a recital of Scarlatti pieces which well illustrates his desire to reconcile jazz-based improvisation and baroque or classical formalism.

Perhaps the best measure of his piano-playing, though, is the live date from 2001. It's an almost flawless performance, packed with imagination and spiced with surprise. 'Body And Soul' is given a vivid intro that opens onto caverns of unexpected harmonic invention. The original 'Hindsight' is an epic that should be transcribed and studied. Shorter's 'Footprints' runs new variations on those familiar modes (and returns very positively to Shorter after a so-so record devoted to the saxophonist's work) and 'Some Day My Prince Will Come' is rendered almost unrecognizable, to anyone, one suspects, except Miles Davis, who would surely have understood where Pieranunzi was going. Van de Geyn is masterly, adding areas of harmonic detail and filling out the bottom with complete authority. Ceccarelli is one of the best around in this field, too. But it's the pianist who really catches the attention with this minor classic.

DAVID SÁNCHEZ
Born 1968, Guaynabo, Puerto Rico
Tenor saxophone

Travesía
Columbia 85948
Sánchez; Miguel Zenón (as); Edsel Gomez (p); Hans Glawischnig (b); Antonio Sánchez (d); Pernell Saturnino, Adam Cruz (perc). May–June 2001.

David Sánchez said (2003): **'I switched from percussion to saxophone in order to play jazz. That was the motivation, and coming to New York was about that as well. It was fortunate that there were already a lot of guys here from Puerto Rico. I worked with Eddie Palmieri and Charlie Sepulveda and word sort of got round from there.'**

When he made his first record, *Departure*, Sánchez was already in his mid-20s, still young but not a raw and untamed stripling, and there was a callowness in it which is only briefly engaging. Sánchez has a big, broad, old-fashioned sound that some have likened to Johnny Griffin but which in approach borrows much from Rollins and very little from Coltrane, though he claims him as an early hero. He also learned a bit working with Dizzy Gillespie.

Sánchez seems to have had a relatively happy time with Columbia. The debut *Sketches Of Dreams* was a terrific album and the label seemed content to let him grow artistically at his own pace. Around the turn of the decade, the work seemed to take on a more overtly political tone. *Melaza*, from 2000, refers to one of the island's greatest exports, the molasses that comes from sugar cane, a sweetness that comes not out of strength but out of exploitation and cruelty. Sánchez is a wiser artist than to lard his music with editoria, but he does make it clear what passion and anger lie behind these themes. The working band is now a more than competent vehicle for his ideas and Branford Marsalis's hand at the production desk is a guarantee of quality as well. There are guest percussionists and Adam Cruz sits in for a couple of tunes, but the basic line-up is the key. The sound is rich and detailed, and the writing strong enough to support the ideas being communicated.

Travesía shares a vivid sound and some brilliant compositional ideas. It doesn't have the same ideological baggage as the previous disc and in some respects is the better for it, since it delivers a more various and pleasurable product. For the first time quite this explicitly, Sánchez explores aspects of Puerto Rican folk music, casting three pieces in *bomba* and *plena* forms and melding them beautifully with the jazz idiom. He also throws in 'River Tales', a brooding melody in double waltz-time. A more than confident consolidation on the strengths of its predecessor.

STEVE COLEMAN
Born 20 September 1956, Chicago, Illinois
Alto saxophone

Resistance Is Futile
Label Bleu LBLC 6643/4 2CD
Coleman; Jonathan Finlayson, Ambrose Campbell-Akinmusire (t); Geoffroy DeMasure (tb); Andy Milne (ky); Anthony Tidd (b); Sean Rickman (d); Jesús Diaz (perc, v). July 2001.

Steve Coleman said (2002): **'Five Elements was originally concerned with developing a new rhythmic base from which to redefine some of the concepts of older African-American music, particularly Duke Ellington and Charlie Parker. That procedure has evolved via the expansion of voice-leading and an organic approach to sound which gives the players more potential material for improvisation.'**

Coleman's debut marked the first broad acceptance of what became known as the M-Base school of music. The immediate impression is of a looser and more harmonically conventional version of his namesake Ornette's earlier years. Steve's alto has a keening insistence that carries a lot of weight and information. He won his spurs with the Thad Jones-Mel Lewis band, Sam Rivers and Cecil Taylor, but then took a more independent course and helped found M-Base as a setting for music that draws on all aspects of African-American music, not just the 'jazz' ghetto. Coleman takes a mystical line on his music, believing that it is a symbolic language expressing both the order and the chaos of the universe. He runs groups with such names as Metric, The Secret Doctrine, Five Elements, Renegade Way and The Mystic Rhythm Society. Because of this, it is difficult to pick a representative work that offers a rounded sense of his direction over 25 years. It's tempting to pick the recent solo record *Invisible Paths: First Scattering*, which is intended as a 'sonic commentary' on his practice, and is, predictably, both more accessible and more obscure than any of its predecessors.

The early records on JWT (now Winter & Winter) have their strengths, but the marriage of funk and obscurity sounds like just that, and they haven't worn well. Coleman entered the new decade/century/millennium with what we regard as his strongest statement yet, though the subsequent *Weaving Symbolics* on the same European label is also a strong contender for attention. Coleman's progress is such that he can now review some of his own history, hence the presence on this live-in-Montpellier double-CD of old Five Elements favourites such as 'Wheel Of Nature' and 'Change The Guard', which go all the way back to 1986's *On The Edge Of Tomorrow*. There are new spirits in his fold – scarcely a familiar name in the personnel – and every one of them is quick, precise, unblinkingly assured and able to solo on cryptic materials without a stumble. On long pieces such as 'Wheel Of Nature' and '9 To 5', Coleman is overseeing ensemble performances that personify the sculpted astringency of his own saxophone-playing.

Here and there he touches on 'the tradition'. Parker's 'Ah-Leu-Cha' is barely recognizable, and entirely unbopped. A ballad treatment of 'Easy Living' isn't so much cool as neutral, the saxophonist working it out almost mathematically. Yet Mal Waldron's 'Straight Ahead' emerges as an oddly poignant performance. When they tag 'Straight No Chaser' onto the end of 'Hits', it's like a bizarre echo of another time and place.

CHICK COREA &
Born Armando Anthony Corea, 12 June 1941, Chelsea, Massachusetts
Piano, keyboards

Rendezvous In New York
Stretch 038 023 2 2CD

Corea; Terence Blanchard (t); Steve Davis (tb); Steve Wilson (ss, as); Michael Brecker, Tim Garland, Joshua Redman (ts); Gonzalo Rubalcaba (p); Avishai Cohen, Eddie Gomez, Christian McBride, John Patitucci, Miroslav Vitous (b); Jeff Ballard, Steve Gadd, Roy Haynes, Dave Weckl (d); Bobby McFerrin (v). September 2001.

Bassist Avishai Cohen remembers: **'I was there as a member of two different bands of Chick's, Origin and the new trio, and I remember how much music there was to juggle, an enormous amount. It was fascinating, but challenging.'**

There are interesting parallels and contrasts between Corea's later career and that of fellow Miles alumnus Keith Jarrett. Both were by the '90s elder statesmen of jazz, able to release records at will and not just single albums but chunky documentations of club residencies, like Miles's Blackhawk and Plugged Nickel sets.

Chick celebrated 60 years young with a special event at the Blue Note in New York, where he had in 1998 recorded a week of vivid playing with his current group, released as a fascinating multi-volume set. *Rendezvous* reunited him with some of the musicians who have played a role in his extraordinary career. There are nine different bands and pairings represented here, and thus nine different aspects of his playing personality. It all begins joyously enough with three duets with Bobby McFerrin, who kicks straight into 'Armando's Blues', followed by a fine version of 'Blue Monk' and an astonishing medley of 'Concierto De Aranjuez' and Chick's own 'Spain'. Even if it was rehearsed, it sounds totally spontaneous and utterly wonderful.

What follows is more sombre – 'Matrix' from the *Now He Sings, Now He Sobs* trio of Miroslav Vitous and Roy Haynes, ten minutes of restlessly exploratory piano trio. The *Remembering Bud Powell* band does its stuff on 'Glass Enclosure' and 'Tempus Fugit' before Chick and Gary Burton renew their acquaintance on 'Crystal Silence'. The Akoustic Band and Origin are both strongly featured on disc two, as is the New Trio with Avishai Cohen and Jeff Ballard and the *Three Quartets* band with Mike Brecker, Eddie Gomez and Steve Gadd. The real highpoint of the second disc, though, is a wonderful second read of 'Concierto De Aranjuez' with fellow pianist Gonzalo Rubalcaba; breathtaking and a fitting celebration of a master musician.

& *See also* **Tones For Joan's Bones** (1966; p. 340), **Light As A Feather** (1972; p. 399)

IAN SHAW
Born 2 June 1962, St Asaph, Flintshire, Wales
Voice

A World Still Turning
441 Records 20
Shaw; Eric Alexander (ts); Paul Bollenback (g); Billy Childs (p); Peter Washington (b); Mark Fletcher (d); Mark Murphy (v). September 2001.

Ian Shaw says: **'When the album was being mixed (at the studio where Bowie did "Let's Dance") the towers fell and producer Todd Barkan's dear mum passed away. The world suddenly became a very grown-up place; loss and love shaped the record. We added Horace Silver's "Peace" as a last-moment thing and Todd, over his morning bagel, muttered something about a world still turning. That same day, Mark Murphy turned up with some lilies and I asked if he'd sing a Bobby Bland tune with me. We did it in one take and gave him $300 in cash.'**

Shaw is a grown-up singer with a big voice, a musicianly understanding, and a good deal of what psychologists now call 'emotional intelligence'. He feels every word he sings, which means that he doesn't emote spuriously, but simply lets the meaning of a lyric dictate its own appropriate weight.

Like Linn label-mate Claire Martin, he's had to wait in line to break through in America, but soon showed that he had stuff to spare. With the release in 1998 of *A New York Minute*, with Cedar Walton and bassist David Williams providing a background that would make any singer sound good and Britain's Iain Ballamy offering a second voice up front, Shaw came close to greatness. Though he's flirted with soul, pop and supper club styles in the past, he folds all his expertise into a bullseye delivery in these songs. He doesn't really swing in the manner of a Tormé descendant and tends to fashion his own tightrope relationship with the beat, which in the past has often seemed jerky. And he carried that wisdom over into *A World Still Turning*.

It's difficult for a non-musician to grasp why a singer like Shaw might want to keep putting out seemingly routine standards sets while nurturing the ambition to make an album as engaged, passionate and musically rewarding as this one. The outstanding performance here is 'Rockabye', no relation to the Samuel Beckett play, though possibly inspired by it, which deals with the grief of a bereaved Gulf War mother. A stunning performance. He does a batch of songs that obviously meant something to him in earlier years: by Bowie, Elton John, even Gilbert O'Sullivan. He saves the now obligatory Radiohead cover for the end; 'The Tourist' is one of their better songs and this version adds a nice dimension to it. Alexander, Childs (with whom he duos on 'I'm Glad There Is You') and Bollenback are all in great form. Inviting in Mark Murphy for a guest spot was a high-risk strategy. Just as Shaw has stolen albums he has guested on in the past, so the master might well have pinched this one. All it does, though, is confirm that the Welshman – and his country's stored vocal tradition – are now very much up there.

HOWARD RILEY&

Born 16 February 1943, Huddersfield, Yorkshire, England
Piano

At Lincoln Cathedral
Heliopause HPVP105 + enhanced CD
Riley (p solo). September 2001.

Howard Riley says: **'I'd had one previous experience of playing in a cathedral, at Le Mans, and I was a bit worried about the reverb, so I spent only ten minutes with the piano before we recorded, and then slowed down my playing to take account of it. Everything was done in one take.'**

On the face of it, this sounds like an ideal context for Riley: a fine Steinway piano and the magnificent acoustic of one of England's most impressive church buildings. The reality is well up to expectation, a concentrated and very thoughtful solo recital which shows up even better on the Binaural Surround Sound Stereo tracks on CD2; the final cut, with video, requires a DTS decoder/surround amplifier or all you will hear is white noise.

Riley uses the cathedral acoustics as part of his performance, allowing slow decays and echo to generate another level of harmonic activity. He also exploits the extremes of his instrument, notably on the very beautiful 'Timeless', knowing that their effect will be considerably heightened in this environment. A single standard, 'Round Midnight', is played with unexpected plainness, allowing the richness of a much performed and therefore under-appreciated theme to shine through without extravagant variation of deconstruction. A marvellous set, for which promoter Rob Ayling, engineers Chris Thorpe and Dallas Simpson, and film-maker Steve Lee deserve a full share of credit.

& *See also* **The Day Will Come** (1970; p. 375)

CHARLIE HUNTER

Born 23 May 1967, Rhode Island
Eight-string guitar

Songs From The Analog Playground
Blue Note 33550 2
Hunter; John Ellis (sax); Stephen Chopek (d); Chris Lovejoy (perc); Mos Def, Theryl de Clouet, Kurt Elling, Norah Jones (v). September 2001.

Charlie Hunter said (2001): **'I'm trying to create a new language out of aspects of two different instruments, and build a harmony, counterpoint thing out of that. Lots of guitarists have tried the instrument, for a minute or two, but it's specialized and it's different, a new technique.'**

Part of a community of jamming musicians who emerged from the Bay Area in the early '90s, Hunter is a virtuoso guitarist playing an eight-string model, with bass- and lead-lines combined. His virtuosity is remarkable, and while he skirts close to pop and rock models (having made a Bob Marley cover album) and an improvising aesthetic closer to the Grateful Dead than to most post-bop situations, Hunter is an astonishing improviser, as a recent collaboration with Bobby Previte as Groundtruther has underlined. This developed out of a duo album with drummer Leon Parker, as part of Hunter's Blue Note contract.

His ability to make his instrument sound like – and occasionally *remarkably* like – a Hammond B-3 ties him into the label's history and the early records – *Bing ... Bing ... Bing* and *Ready ... Set ... Shango!* – seemed part of an attempt to shape a latter-day version of Blue Note's commercially successful soul-jazz, with rock overtones.

Hunter isn't just a Stanley Jordan-like novelty act. His improvising credentials are formidable and on *Songs From The Analog Playground* they are perfectly integrated into a whole performance. This is the moment we learned to love Norah Jones! There are some sublime moments here. The band sounds seasoned and strong, and has the flexibility to push these songs – stray memories from Charlie's youth – out into new territory. That's nowhere more evident than on things like 'Mighty Mighty', the old Earth, Wind & Fire tune, reworked by de Clouet, who also does a chillingly beautiful version of Willie Dixon's 'Spoonful'. Elling is more obviously a jazz singer. His vocal line on 'Desert Way' and 'Close Your Eyes' is exemplary. Mos Def is streetier but less convincing, and the real heartbreaker is Norah's delightful alto on the Roxy Music swoon 'More Than This', which becomes quite majestic, with Charlie strumming like a string section underneath. She tops that with Nick Drake's 'Day Is Done', which is near perfect. A gorgeous record.

JAMES EMERY
Born 21 December 1951, Youngstown, Ohio
Guitar

Transformations
Between The Lines btl 027
Emery; Franz Koglmann (flhn); Tony Coe (ts, cl); Peter Herbert (b); Klangforum Wien, Emilio Pomárico (cond). September 2001.

James Emery remembers: **'Everything related to it remains in a kind of dream-state, from the writing and orchestration – eight months of nine-hour days – to the performance and recording in Vienna. Knowing that I had musicians who could play anything I wrote was liberating, and even though the project was completed in the gloom of 9/11, a most luminous recording was produced.'**

An early James Emery record was called, delightfully, *Standing On A Whale Fishing For Minnows*. He always sounds as if he's after bigger game than that; certainly, his musical imagination has foundations that are more solid. Emery's big, splintery lines and driving chordal runs have been a key element of the String Trio Of New York since its inception, but he's had a parallel career as a solo artist, almost always for European labels, and the results have been consistently impressive. In 2003, having already made one fine disc for Franz

Koglmann's Between The Lines imprint, Emery delivered *Transformations*, a record on a scale very few musicians might conceive, let alone have the opportunity to document.

It opens with the titular eight-part suite, punctuated by short, meditative interludes by the three soloists. Any sense that this is the work of a jazz musician dangerously outside his comfort zone should be set aside. There is nothing blandly 'symphonic' about Emery's writing. The forms make reference to a number of procedures familiar in modern composition – serialization, atonality, uncommon rhythms – but there is no mistaking that it is the work of a jazz musician, its movements limber and springy even when the orchestra is fully engaged, its destinations difficult to predict.

The remaining tracks are for the three soloists plus bassist Peter Herbert, material much closer to the cool, 'white line' jazz associated with Koglmann and his label, but with four such distinctive voices at play the improvisations are not just structurally intriguing but timbrally gorgeous.

DAVE HOLLAND &

Born 1 October 1946, Wolverhampton, Staffordshire, England
Double bass, cello

Extended Play
ECM 038505-2 2CD
Holland; Robin Eubanks (tb); Chris Potter (ss, ts); Steve Nelson (vib); Billy Kilson (d). November 2001.

Dave Holland says: **'This quintet had been together for several years and had made three studio recordings. I really wanted to document a live performance so we taped a four-day engagement at Birdland. Live, we often play longer versions of songs that allow more time for development and these versions of mostly previously recorded things gave me a chance to show how those songs had changed and developed.'**

Holland's first recording for ECM was *Music From Two Basses*, made in 1971 with Barre Phillips, something of a rarity now. Between then and the turn of the millennium he made a further 13 recordings, which together represent one of the finest bodies of modern jazz composition. Holland's '80s bands were the antithesis of what he had been doing 15 years before, whether with the SME or with Miles. Tightly arranged, with much of the drama enacted between bass and brass, they manage to steer a path between freedom and fixity of detail. Freedom seemed an element in composition rather than a goal in itself. *Prime Directive* and *Not For Nothin'* are majestic performances from a quintet which managed to accommodate occasional changes of personnel without strain while maintaining a highly consistent sound.

Extended Play was the first live Holland disc on ECM: a pity, perhaps, because these groups almost always found an extra yard in performance, and they do so here at Birdland. Eubanks always sounds more unfettered and Nelson and Kilson vie with each other to keep up the pace. Some of the tracks are very long indeed: the opener lasts more than 20 minutes, though so rich in ideas is this performance of 'The Balance' that it could have been stretched to half as much again. 'Free For All' is the only makeweight, but 'Claressence' and the long closing 'Metamorphos' offer ample testimony to Dave's continuing creativity and strong instincts as a leader. Potter was a valuable addition. Most double CDs could easily be edited down to just one, but it's hard to see what could have been dropped from this. Even 'Free For All' stands the test of time.

& *See also* **Conference Of The Birds** (1972; p. 400)

TORD GUSTAVSEN
Born 5 October 1970, Oslo, Norway
Piano

Changing Places
ECM 016397
Gustavsen; Harald Johnsen (b); Jarle Vespestad (d). November 2001–June 2002.

Tord Gustavsen said (2003): **'Ideas are sketched and written down, but the music really emerges by being played, and before we recorded *Changing Places* a lot of that stuff had been played enough to open up the possibilities and not so much that they were exhausted.'**

Gustavsen is one of the second – or is it third? – generation of ECM masters. His style is all simplicity – aphoristic melodies, gently syncopating rhythms (he's played a good share of traditional jazz), blues figures, rocking sequences. Somehow he puts this together into a style which is utterly captivating, and somewhat like Esbjörn Svensson has the capacity and vision to put his own personal language to the service of a settled group, which very quickly took on its own character. On *Changing Places* it helps that one of the modern masters of kit-drumming, Jarle Vespestad, is in the group, although he is obliged to play very differently from his normal power-packed style. The group work through 13 pieces that feel all alike yet are without any suspicion of routine or preset pattern-playing. A star of tomorrow.

CONRAD BAUER
Born 3 July 1943, Halle, Germany
Trombone

Between Heaven And Earth
Intakt CD 079
Bauer; Peter Kowald (b); Günter Sommer (d). December 2001.

Conrad Bauer said (2002): **'Peter Kowald always says: if you want to break the rules, you have to know the rules. And because we were in the East, I felt that even more, like I wouldn't be taken seriously as a "free" musician if I didn't also know how to play like an American musician.'**

Bauer's brother Johannes is also a trombone-player and they have worked together, in duo and in larger improvising ensembles. Conrad actually began well away from jazz, as an R&B and soul guitarist, then bassist, and singer, coming to the trombone through trumpet lessons. On his main instrument, he became a key player in the small group of East German improvisers at work from the end of the '60s.

Bauer is a remarkable solo performer, tailoring his improvisations to the shape and resonance of a room or studio. The unaccompanied *Hummelsummen* and the later, magnificent *Der Gelbe Klang* are remarkable records, but it would be misleading to play down Bauer's ensemble work. *Between Heaven And Earth* is an improvised set of such concentration it is difficult to believe that there are no predetermined structures. Recorded just a few months before Peter Kowald's premature death, this captures the bassist with two of his most sympathetic collaborators, perhaps united by years spent on the 'wrong' side of the Iron Curtain. The 11 improvisations are so titled and organized as to suggest a progress through life from birth to rebirth. Bauer is the dominant voice, but both Kowald and Sommer are so attuned to this idiom that one hears a group rather than individuals. Right in the middle of the set, 'Travelling' and 'Loving' represent its emotional core, intense and quietly fiery improvisations that would be hard to improve upon.

ADAM LANE
Born 22 September 1968, Brooklyn, New York
Double bass

New Magical Kingdom
Clean Feed CF 052
Lane; Darren Johnston (t); Jeff Chan (ts); Aaron Bennett (sax); John Finkbeiner (g); Lynn Johnston (b); Vijay Anderson (d). 2001-2004.

Adam Lane says: **'I remember that I wore my Mötörhead T-shirt to both sessions and many of the gigs leading up to the recordings to remind the fellas and myself that we weren't just a one-dimensional jazz ensemble.'**

Lane may yet have to slug it out with Ben Allison for the title of most interesting bassist-leader since Mingus. He divides his time between East and West coasts and between an unforgiving improv approach, heard on a number of Cadence/CIMP discs, and a more considered and structured language.

It may be the kiss of death to describe a contemporary record as 'important', but Lane's septet is working towards a new ensemble sound that picks up the challenge of Mingus's Jazz Workshops and propels it in a new direction. There are tinges of rock here and there, sometimes not all that well judged, but for the most part this is subtle, sophisticated jazz, shaped with impressive authority by the bassist and unlike the usual sense of good, fair and average tracks, shaped into a coherent whole.

Lane has some roots in bop, as 'Avenue X' suggests, but he also throws some Caribbean shapes on 'The Schnube' and some more free-form elements elsewhere. The opening 'In The Centre Of The Earth, Looking For Mike' has an epic cast, presumably designed to showcase his Full Throttle Orchestra to best advantage. To some degree, the album feels like a cushioned box and wrapping for 'Sienna', easily the most beautiful 'ballad' by a contemporary jazz composer and a piece that combines beauty with a certain real-life toughness that makes it doubly compelling. This isn't an accidental 'hit' but the culmination of an impressive phase of work. Lane seems a patient fellow and while those CIMP discs have a rough-and-ready exterior, they too are a privileged glimpse of a composer and leader who's bound to make a serious mark.

DEREK BAILEY&
Born 29 January 1930, Sheffield, Yorkshire, England; died 25 December 2005, London
Guitar

Ballads / Standards
Tzadik TZ 7007 / 7620
Bailey (g solo). January & March 2002.

Saxophonist Tony Bevan says: **'The thing most people would find surprising about Derek – given a reputation for iconoclasm – was *how much he loved music*. More than anybody I've ever met. Just not the sort of music he was supposed to like. He was always telling me about some small band that he'd caught in some tiny bar. He even went to check out the village brass band at my local. I suppose that love of his art is the only way to explain his extraordinary achievements, and his great integrity.'**

The idea of Derek Bailey playing standards only seemed absurd to those who didn't understand his background. Vernacular music was in his bloodstream. Bailey's language never came off a blank page but existed in the presence of a vast reservoir of blues, swing, bop, free and, yes, ballads. These projects were suggested by Tzadik executive producer John

Zorn, and they're quite wonderful. Bailey approaches a dozen themes (two versions each of 'Gone With The Wind' and 'Rockin' Chair') with an awkward tenderness, hinting at the melody rather than stating it and certainly not troubling himself over-much with the changes, though it's clear from 'Body And Soul' that he knows them inside out. Hearing these performances offers a salutary lesson when listening to other musicians who move from relatively free situations to fusion or pop: it isn't necessarily easier or less creative to play in this way. On the *Standards* set, he does things like 'When Your Liver Has Gone' and keeps even further away from familiar melody than with the ballads, but the skeleton of the song is there. The delicacy of his playing is astonishing, and there is something profoundly moving about the whole set, almost like hearing Samuel Beckett sit down in a bar snug to sing old Irish songs.

& *See also* **Solo Guitar: Volume 1** (1971; p. 382); **SPONTANEOUS MUSIC ENSEMBLE, Quintessence** (1973–1974; p. 406)

GERALD WILSON
Born 4 September 1918, Shelby, Mississippi
Trumpet, bandleader

New York, New Sound
Mack Avenue MAC 1009

Clark Terry (t, flhn); Jimmy Owens, Eddie Henderson, Jon Faddis, Frank Greene, Sean Jones (t); Benny Powell, Luis Bonilla, Dennis Wilson (tb); Douglas Purviance (tb, btb); Jesse Davis (as); Jerry Dodgion (f, as); Jimmy Heath (ts); Frank Wess (f, ts); Jay Brandford (bs); Kenny Barron, Renee Rosnes (p); Anthony Wilson, Oscar Castro-Neves (g); Bob Cranshaw, Trey Henry, Larry Ridley (b); Lewis Nash, Stix Hooper (d); Lenny Castro (perc). 2002.

Gerald Wilson said (2002): **'With the Lunceford band, Edwin Wilcox used to say: "You have 12 notes to play around with. Make sure you use them all." I've pretty much followed that advice. I like harmony and I like it to be full of notes.'**

One of Eric Dolphy's first compositions was a swaggering thing called 'G.W.', a tribute to one of the liveliest and most creative spirits on the West Coast. Gerald Wilson joined the Jimmie Lunceford Orchestra just around the time America joined the Second World War. After a stint in the navy, the talented young trumpeter and composer decided to form his own band. It was a progressive outfit, whose faintly experimental air has long since been eclipsed by Stan Kenton's more abrasive approach, but the early recordings are full of interest.

A brilliant and charismatic bandleader, Wilson has enjoyed great longevity and in the '90s and '00s started to come into his own as a composer. In his 80s, Wilson was writing the best music of his career, still visiting new places to have his work played, and it was a marvellous initiative by Stix Hooper's Mack Avenue label to record this all-star collective swinging through some of his material. The big piece is a comprehensive revision of his 1997 'Theme For Monterey' (which had been done for the 40th anniversary Monterey Jazz Festival), but there are other Wilson favourites such as 'Blues For Yna Yna', and the orchestra bristle through these vintage charts in a mercurial high gear. How much longer anyone will be able to assemble a band which has the likes of Jimmy Heath, Clark Terry and Frank Wess sitting alongside Jesse Davis and Renee Rosnes is impossible to say, but this is a meeting of generations working together on some of the masterpieces of modern big-band writing and creating a record any jazz lover should be delighted to hear.

KALAPARUSH(A) MAURICE MCINTYRE
Born 24 March 1936, Clarksville, Arkansas
Tenor saxophone, bass clarinet, percussion

Morning Song
Delmark 553
McIntyre; Jesse Dulman (tba); Ravish Momin (d). September 2002.

Ravish Momin says: **'Kalaparush's playing can be virtuosically fierce or intensely lyrical. Having a heartfelt romanticism at his musical centre-of-gravity, he's able to spin endlessly creative variations on the melody, often making daringly angular rhythmic shifts and intervallic leaps.'**

At first blush, McIntyre is a fairly orthodox New Thing modernist, exploiting Coltrane's extended harmony and the hands-on, little-instrument approach which was the AACM aesthetic. He also prefers open-textured, spacious music to the multi-note approach of some of his saxophone peers. His early albums for Delmark, *Humility In The Light Of The Creator* and *Forces And Blessings*, find him in Aylerish mode, with elements of Coltrane's harmonic approach and a Chicagoan rough-and-readiness in the group aesthetic. There wasn't much of note to report after that – other than a good Black Saint record from 1979 – until he started recording with a fascinating pianoless trio called The Light. They made a fine session for CIMP, and another for Entropy Stereo, and then Kalaparush went back to Delmark for the 2002 record.

Despite the silliness of titles like 'Symphony No. 1', this is a set in which blues, bebop, raw field shouts and more abstract classical forms all seem to have contributed to an extraordinary musical alloy. There is a further and better version of 'I Don't Have An Answer ...', which suggests how much the group has evolved. 'In My Morning Song' and 'Morning' contain some hints that he has been studying Indian raga (not improbable with Momin in the group) and these pieces, while still approximately located in the blues, have a transcultural feel that is most beguiling. At nearly 70, the saxophonist seems to be coming into a new phase of creativity, warm and personal but with a preacher's fire.

JOHN TAYLOR
Born 25 September 1942, Manchester, Lancashire, England
Piano

Rosslyn
ECM 1599
Taylor; Marc Johnson (b); Joey Baron (d). April 2002.

Pianist Mal Waldron said (1990): **'His harmonic sense is very refined and he knows the classics, but he has a voice all of his own. I'd say it was an English pastoral sound, but it has a lot more going for it than that.'**

John Taylor arrived in London in 1964 and began leading his own groups as well as recording with others on the modern scene. Never an entirely comfortable free player, he evolved towards an impressionistic style reminiscent in part of Bill Evans but with its own distinctive, almost folkish cadence. In 1977, he co-formed Azimuth with ex-wife Norma Winstone and trumpeter Kenny Wheeler. They recorded on ECM, but while Wheeler became a regular on that label, putting out a good deal of small- and large-group material, Taylor and Winstone were for the moment passed over as far as individual projects were concerned. That was put right in 2002 with Taylor's magnificent *Rosslyn*.

One rather hoped that, having a former Bill Evans bassman in the trio, Taylor might consider programming some Evans material, particularly given that he has been compared to the American many times. In fact, what one gets is a set that is Evans-like in temperament rather than content. Taylor doesn't pack this first solo set for ECM with original material, but brings in compositions by Ralph Towner (the lovely 'Tramonto') and Kenny Wheeler ('Ma Bel') as well as a standard, 'How Deep Is The Ocean', to which he gives a slyly Jarrett-like spin. His original themes, each of them with a folkish tinge, are swung much harder by this group than one imagines would be the case with British sidemen, and Taylor seems to be lighter in spirit and faster in response here than on previous records. However, all *Rosslyn* really does is clinch his pedigree as one of the finest pianists in Europe (and he spends much of his time in Europe rather than England).

THE BAD PLUS
Formed 1990
Group

Give
Columbia 510666
Ethan Iverson (p); Reid Anderson (b); David King (d). October 2002.

Ethan Iverson said (2003): **'There's a certain rulebook in jazz and from time to time I like to quote from those rules, just to show I know them, but for the most part I keep well away from anything that sounds like "jazz". And if that upsets some listeners, hey, I think that's a good thing.'**

You don't expect the stately trinity of piano/bass/drums to qualify as a power trio but that's what happened with The Bad Plus, who came along at exactly the right moment, riding on the bow-wave of a plethora of polite, Bill Evans-inspired piano trios, and basically blew them all away with a riot of self-determined sounds and styles. On the Fresh Sound debut, Iverson, Anderson and 'certifiable Midwestern drum star' King got at a group of originals, one standard ('Blue Moon') and two pop tunes. Abba's 'Knowing Me, Knowing You' is a textbook example of the jazz transformation of an uneventful melody, and Nirvana's 'Smells Like Teen Spirit' (which the others forced Iverson to learn!) is a glorious, helter-skelter set-piece, the tune stirred and thickened by the pianist's voicings while King swings them off the stand.

   Although they do an apocalyptic 'Iron Man' (Black Sabbath, not Eric Dolphy) to close *Give*, the originals are getting more prominence and are played with fierce conviction. Who could resist a track called 'Cheney Piñata', which is Iverson's, though it's the other two who score highest on writing credits with whipsmart themes that manage to skirt mere satire and deliver solid musical thump, as exciting and fresh as Nirvana were in rock when they came through. The persistent suggestion that BP purvey jazz for Neanderthals is absurdly wide of the mark. These are required listening.

WAYNE SHORTER&
Born 25 August 1933, Newark, New Jersey
Tenor and soprano saxophones

Alegría
Verve 543558
Shorter; Chris Gekker, Jeremy Pelt, Lew Soloff (t); Bruce Eidem, Jim Pugh, Steve Davis, Papo Vasquez, Michael Boschen (tb); Marcus Roja (tba); Chris Potter (bcl, ts); Brad Mehldau, Danilo Perez (p); John Patitucci (b); Brian Blade, Terri Lyne Carrington (d); Alex Acuña (perc); woodwinds, strings. 2002.

Wayne Shorter said (2002): **'I don't think in terms of "expressing myself" in jazz. I think that's a misunderstanding. You make this thing, and you make it the best you can, and if it isn't "jazz" and it doesn't say anything about you, or me, that's OK. Expression is what other people put on you.'**

Shorter's post-Blue Note career has a funny shape. For a decade and a half, he devoted his talents to Weather Report, but listening to that discography in sequence creates a curious impression that Wayne is detaching himself from Joe Zawinul and the group, but with infinite slowness. There were good things in some of his own records, but as of the '90s a generation who had grown up hearing word of his eminence was not hearing anything new to match the reputation. Shorter experimented with grown-up fusion, and other formats, but looked to be heading for a technical knockout when *Footprints Live!* with a strong new group revisited some of his great compositions and signalled a return to the terse, phlegmatic post-bop of earlier years. All that remained then was the follow-up punch, and the saxophonist's critical comeback would look secure. *Alegría* is it. With some reservations.

The obvious problem is that Shorter's first all-acoustic studio album for 35 years (!) doesn't present a consistent line-up throughout. There is such a difference between Perez's swinging but one-dimensional playing and Mehldau's more harmonically ambitious approach. The two pianists' differences could have been brokered into an interesting contrast, but instead one feels the album shifting in tone and intention from track to track, which is less satisfactory. That said, the individual components are very good indeed.

The opening could hardly be more promising, with Shorter on soprano kicking into 'Sacajawea' with more power and commitment than has been heard from him in some time. There are older pieces in the set, and the now expected classical essay in the shape this time of Leroy Anderson's 'Serenata' and Villa-Lobos's 'Bachianas Brasileiras No. 5', a theme that lends itself perfectly to Shorter's playing. 'Angola' and 'Orbits' are both familiar ideas given unfamiliar readings, the latter slowed down to the point where the line seems to break down into its components. 'She Moves Through The Fair' seems an odd choice, but it works well and serves as the best possible contrast to the stone groove of the opening track. It isn't *Speak No Evil* and probably doesn't come up to *Adam's Apple* either, but it's a terrific record by a modern master.

& See also **Speak No Evil** (1964; p. 313)

WYNTON MARSALIS *&*
Born 18 October 1961, New Orleans, Louisiana
Trumpet

Live At The House Of Tribes
Blue Note 77132
Marsalis; Wessell Anderson (as); Eric Lewis (p); Kengo Nakamura (b); Joe Farnsworth (d); Orlando Q. Rodriguez, Robert Rucker (perc). December 2002.

Wynton Marsalis said (1990): **'I've grown up feeling not connected with my generation of young people, which makes me sad sometimes, but I think a lot of the differences and a lot of the criticisms that have come to me are based on ignorance and misunderstanding. Yes, I have a different background in music but it's not so utterly different. We come out of the same people and culture, just different aspects of the tradition.'**

In the first years of the new decade, Marsalis moved from Columbia to Blue Note, a partnership that guaranteed renewed media interest in his work. After a period in which he had grown ever more ambitious in form, creating large-scale works like *Blood On The Fields* and issuing an eight-CD live set from the Village Vanguard, it was difficult to keep Marsalis in perspective. The tired old question about whether he was 'really' a classical performer who'd been positioned in jazz like a clubbable candidate in a rapidly ageing ward came back again.

At first, the new contract with Blue Note was a disappointment. On the first record Marsalis sounded as if he'd gone back several years in developmental terms, or perhaps he's pitching his thing to what he thinks is a less sophisticated audience. Either way, it's a mistake and *The Magic Hour* doesn't even sit with the middle order of his Columbia albums. *House Of Tribes*, though, is a near-perfect live record, packed with atmosphere and marked by some powerful, wise playing from Wynton and a strong new band. It stands absolutely in line with the classic live recordings of Blue Note's golden age, by Art Blakey, Kenny Dorham and others. Marsalis immediately and subtly repositions himself in a post-bop idiom by starting with 'Green Chimneys'. It's still recognizably himself, but the material points another way. 'You Don't Know What Love Is', 'Donna Lee' and 'What Is This Thing Called Love?' are all bop-inspired and Marsalis sharpens his attack to suit. The audience is much in evidence, but almost as participants rather than as a distraction, and there's a spontaneity to the whole thing, as when Robert Rucker gets up to bash a tambourine in the second-line finale.

Here's a man anxious to *belong*, to reinscribe himself on the history page of modern jazz. The anxiety is misplaced. Without Wynton Marsalis, modern jazz would have a very different shape and status.

& See also **J Mood** (1985; p. 496), **Standard Time: Volume 6 – Mr Jelly Lord** (1999; p. 638)

PETER KING

Born 11 August 1940, Kingston upon Thames, Surrey, England
Alto and soprano saxophones, clarinet

Footprints
Miles Music CD087
King; Steve Melling (p); Jeremy Brown, Arnie Somogyi (b); Stephen Keogh (d). 2002.

Saxophone collector Hartmut Geiss says: **'At the start of the decade, Peter King changed from his Selmer Mark VI alto to a Yanagisawa A9932Z, made of solid silver and phosphor bronze. It's a magnificent horn. I think the sound is maybe a little brighter, but I believe he is now playing with a new custom-made mouthpiece.'**

King remains Britain's most eminent keeper of the bebop alto flame. He was still a teenager when he opened at Ronnie Scott's Club in 1959, though he shouldn't be confused with the late Pete King who was Ronnie's business partner in the club. Though King has continued to be associated with Charlie Parker's style of bebop (he was even caught on YouTube playing Bird's Grafton acrylic saxophone), he has steadily absorbed other, more recent influences, including elements of Coltrane's harmonic thinking.

All of King's records are worthwhile, even if it's only for the peerless sound of his alto, but *Footprints* is a phenomenal live set, recorded at Pizza Express. There are very strong versions of the Wayne Shorter title-piece and McCoy Tyner's 'Search For Peace', a fantastic final version of Victor Feldman's 'Joshua' and strong originals from Melling, who's a dark horse on the British scene. The real *tour de force*, though, is an emotive rendition of Waldron's 'Soul Eyes' on which King plays one of his best recorded solos. The disc was recorded at different sessions, which explains the two bassists. Another great one from King.

GORDON BECK
Born 16 September 1936, London
Piano

Not The Last Waltz
Art Of Life 1008
Beck; Bruno Rousselet (b); Philippe Soirat (d). January & July 2003.

Singer Helen Merrill, recording with Beck at BBC's Maida Vale studios (1992): **'Do you people realize what you have here? Gordon Beck is the best improvising accompanist on the planet!'**

A veteran British modernist, Beck drew attention in the Tubby Hayes group of the '60s, as Ronnie Scott's house pianist and as the anchor and motor force of Phil Woods's European Rhythm Machine around the turn of the decade. Since then he has freelanced, worked as an educator and helmed occasional albums, but has hardly been garlanded with work or praise in his native country.

Beck's early work has been belatedly rediscovered. Made in 1967, *Experiments With Pops* introduced the nascent talent of 'Johnny' McLaughlin, apparently a late inclusion on what otherwise was meant to be a trio date. Given the pop provenance of the material, it was a brilliant wheeze bringing him aboard. The guitarist transformed the set, adding a gear and providing the kind of forceful attack he would later demonstrate on *Extrapolation* and with the Mahavishnu Orchestra. After that came the fine *Gyroscope*, also the name of Beck's group, but for a disturbing number of even British fans the story ends there.

Working largely abroad, like many of his most creative countrymen, Beck has continued to work in trio formats, treading a course influenced but not overdetermined by Bill Evans's classic trios, and working as an accompanist, notably for Helen Merrill. In admiring the early discs, it's vital not to overlook the more recent ones. Here is Beck, live and working with a French trio, and playing some of the best music of his career. The cover has a delightful monochrome of youthful waltzers at a ballroom dance display, and there is an appropriate freshness to the playing and choice of material. Beck has always valued strong jazz composition and the two Ron Carter pieces he has included here, the opening 'Einbahnstrasse' and the closing 'First Trip', are among the best things on the record, the latter a long and thoughtful exploration of Carter's idea. 'Miss Day' is a Beck composition, couched in a sombre bebop idiom. 'Not The Last Waltz' is in three-quarter time, but taken at a furious pace that challenges the two rhythm men. They are generously featured throughout and amply repay Gordon's confidence. 'This Heart Of Mine' starts some way in, presumably because of tape problems, but for the most part this is a beautifully recorded set that should strike shame into the hearts of British concert promoters and warm the hearts of those who have yet to make Gordon Beck's acquaintance.

OLIVER LAKE &
Born 14 September 1942, Marianna, Arkansas
Alto and soprano saxophones, flute

Dat Love
Passin Thru 41219
Lake; Reggie Washington (b); Damon Duewhite (d); Lyndon Achee (steel d). February 2003.

Oliver Lake said (2003): **'You get wonderful overtones when you put sax and steel pans together. They seem to surround you and carry you along.'**

One of the most prominent Dolphy disciples around, Lake was exploring that area of enquiry long before anyone else, and consequently has gone deeper into it. His saxophone sound is immediately arresting, blues-tinged and original, with an urgency that stands out in almost any context. Much as, say, Roscoe Mitchell seemed to cede some personal prominence to membership of a collective, so Lake is still mainly known as a member, and often the lead voice, of the World Saxophone Quartet. His importance goes back before this to membership of the influential Black Artists Group (BAG), where he experimented alongside future WSQ member Julius Hemphill. After a period in Paris, Lake returned to the US and the quartet was launched.

In more recent years, he has experimented with various groups and forms, including a solo record, and has acknowledged his debt to Dolphy in a tribute album, but perhaps his most creative outfit is the Steel Quartet. Its first appearance on *Kinda Up* could have been more auspicious, but the basic concept was in place and Lyndon Achee is a remarkable musician. It is surprising, given the island influence in American jazz that steel pans haven't played a more significant part in the music. Lake finds something in the sound. It frees up his harmonic thinking and creates an accompaniment so open-ended he can negotiate long chromatic drifts with ease. *Dat Love* is a consistently fascinating and absorbing record, and the concept is clinched. Opening with an arrangement of 'Stolen Moments' by Oliver Nelson was a masterstroke, as is the reading of Horace Silver's 'Senor Blues', but he isn't afraid to include the Stevie Wonder/Mary J. Blige song 'Time' as well. AkLaff gives way to the impressive Duewhite here, a less seasoned voice and a less mannered percussionist, but spot on for this material. Not easy to record this music, but they've got it just right: uncluttered, crisp and shimmering.

& See also **WORLD SAXOPHONE QUARTET, W.S.Q.** (1980; p. 456)

BRIAN LYNCH
Born 12 September 1956, Milwaukee, Wisconsin
Trumpet

Fuchsia/Red
Cellar Live CL020201
Lynch; Brad Turner (p); André Lachance (b); Bernie Arai (d). February 2003.

Brian Lynch said (2001): **'I'm not very concerned about questions of genre, because jazz plays a defining role in lots of musical styles, and particularly the Latin styles. It's a way of thinking about music, a procedure rather than something fixed and absolute.'**

Lynch's eclectic approach is a refreshing alternative to the elbows-out approach of many hard-bop dogmatists. He has worked with Art Blakey and with Prince, and his projects include a Latin jazz strand as well as a more eclectic – and electric – approach. Lynch first made an appearance on Criss Cross and his debut, *Peer Pressure*, was a reminder that hard bop, however inflected with modern concerns, was still alive and well. After that, Lynch made records for Sharp Nine, including a more than usually interesting *Tribute To The Trumpet Masters*, which made room on its roster for Charles Tolliver, who's not often cited with the Lee Morgans, Blue Mitchells and Booker Littles.

That same capacious understanding of the tradition plays a strong part on this live album as well, recorded at the Vancouver club and released on the house imprint. What other contemporary horn-player can so confidently pick up Booker Little and Charles Tolliver licks, take new bearings on Lee Morgan's 'Search For The New Land' and cap a fine solo on the Björk tune ('Aurora') with a quote from 'It Don't Mean A Thing, If It Ain't Got That Swing'?

This is the trumpeter's 'electro-mechanical' mode with Turner on Fender Rhodes, which he never tries to play as if it were a Bechstein but lets the shimmer work for him. Arai complements him with a lot of cymbal work on the title-track and Lynch falls in line with a long reverb. There are moments as tough and tender as Prewett playing taps in *From Here To Eternity* and passages of almost free abstraction, before the beats kick in and bassist Lachance finally gets to show his Ron Carterish mettle. If it's a 'fusion' record, so be it: it's a damned good fusion record. 'Red' and 'Mysteries Of Travel' find Turner squarely in a Chick-and-Keith idiom, with some nice displacement of the trumpet sound which makes it sound as if Brian might actually be out walking round the tables; good live sound from the Cellar.

MALACHI THOMPSON

Born 21 August 1941, Princeton, Kentucky; died 16 July 2006, Chicago, Illinois
Trumpet

Blue Jazz
Delmark DE 548
Thompson; Kenny Anderson, Elmer Brown, David Spencer (t); Steve Berry, Bill McFarland, Kirk Tracy (tb); Gary Bartz (ss, as); Ari Brown (ts, cl); Gene Barge, Billy Harper (ts); Kirk Brown (p, org); Harrison Bankhead (b); Leon Joyce (d); Dee Alexander, the Big DooWopper (v). February 2003.

Malachi Thompson said (2002): 'Jazz is about time, and whatever some of the scientists tell you, time only moves in one direction and that's forward into the future. Other music might deal with the past, but not this one and not this trumpet-player.'

Mixing hard bop with free playing in about equal measure, Thompson is of the generation which fuelled the new music of Chicago in the '60s, although he took a fundamentally more conservative line. With 20 years of recording behind him and no real recognition on a world stage, Thompson quietly built up a catalogue of records for Delmark in his home base of Chicago. Despite a serious illness diagnosed as lymphoma in 1989, he has come back with a personal take on new Chicagoan developments which bespeaks a courageous outlook. If he is not an especially outstanding technician or any kind of innovator, his music is a skilled synthesis of several threads from the Chicagoan repertory. None of the early records really stands out as a classic. All have strengths, and some disappointments.

Blue Jazz was effectively his curtain call but it's a terrific record on every level. The writing is great, with everything but Wayne Shorter's 'Footprints' a Thompson original and that exception a brilliant big-band arrangement; the sections are packed with fine players and soloists; the charts are mobile and inventive without being avant-garde; and the sound delivered by Delmark engineers is true and accurate. This is Africa Brass, but it's the saxophonists who probably catch the ear first – Bartz and Harper, Brown and local legend 'Dr G' Barge. 'Black Metropolis', 'Blues For A Saint Called Louis' and 'Genesis/Rebirth' are all powerful ideas, and even the smaller, rootsier tracks like 'Po' Little Louie' and 'Get On The Train' bespeak a great composing talent who died relatively unrecognized and still not finished with his work.

VIJAY IYER

Born 26 October 1971, Albany, New York
Piano

In What Language?

PI 109

Iyer; Ambrose Akinmusire (t); Rudresh Mahanthappa (as); Dana Leong (clo, tb); Liberty Ellman (g); Stephan Crump (b); Trevor Holder (d), Mike Ladd, Latasha N. Nevada Diggs (v, elec); Allison Easter, Ajay Naidu (v). May 2003.

Vijay Iyer says: '**We never set out to make a "jazz" or "hip-hop" album. It was about honouring the people we tried to portray. What I like most is that the music is always in service to the storytelling. When Latasha's character on "Security" fantasizes of escaping her dreary circumstance, Rudresh's alto immediately takes flight, bringing the thought to life. And haunting everything, Mike's vintage analog synth swoops – the sound of surveillance! He was a crucial foil, never afraid to say when I wrote something that sucked.**'

Iyer is a first-generation New Yorker who has himself transplanted to the West Coast. Some aspects of his Indian heritage surfaced on the debut *Memorophilia*, but since then, through a number of regular groupings (Fieldwork, Poisonous Prophets, Spirit Complex) and associations with other leaders such as Steve Coleman, and like-minded musicians, including Rudresh Mahanthappa, hip-hopper Mike Ladd and Tyshawn Sorey, he has attempted to create a vital new jazz soundtrack to an America that having witnessed the melting-pot work was now witnessing the separation of some of its ores and amalgams. Iyer has very wisely pointed out that some of the 'Indian' elements in his music were learned from Bud Powell. There has been an unfortunate tendency to look at the personnels of his records and make guesses at the content, rather than listening to it. One might suggest that Andrew Hill is a major source, certainly on the early *Architextures*, less obviously on the fine *Blood Sutra*, which appeared nearly seven years later, released at around the same time as Iyer's remarkable post-9/11 meditation, *In What Language?*

Political art doesn't come much more direct or shattering. The title is drawn from the complaint of Iranian film-maker Jafer Panahi, detained for hours at JFK airport while passing through New York – 'I am just an Iranian, a film-maker. But how could I tell this, in what language?' The deeper irony is that this incident took place prior to 9/11. The shorter pieces have a disproportionate authority: 'Plastic Bag' squeezed immensities into small measure, and 'Density Of The 19th Century' flirts with post-First World War futurism as much as post-9/11 paranoia. Speech and rap are integrated into music which sounds much closer to the M-Base system than Iyer's other music. But this is clearly a different situation. It is uncomfortable listening, but as a piece of sonic collage it's been created with formidable skill and clarity.

JEREMY PELT

Born 4 November 1976, Newport Beach, California
Trumpet

Close To My Heart

Max Jazz 403

Pelt; Mulgrew Miller (p); David O'Rourke (g); Peter Washington (b); Lewis Nash (d). June 2003.

Jeremy Pelt says: '**My favourite part was actually *before* we recorded it, when I would go over the string parts with the arranger, David O'Rourke. He wrote everything so that they could be played on his computer and I could play along. That's when I knew that there was something special afoot. Recording the session was probably one of the easiest things I've done. We pretty much nailed every song within two takes.**'

Pelt plays with an unashamed nostalgia for the great days of Blue Note but still manages to produce records which are fresh and contemporary. He may favour a retro sound, but he doesn't lack the confidence to inscribe the idiom in his own terms. Most of the material on his first forays as leader is original, and promisingly individual. The debut album, *Profile* on Fresh Sound, is full of strong, committed writing and he had the wisdom to anchor the group – and its successor – on Ralph Peterson's motivational drumming; no one plays badly in front of RP.

A different, but even tighter, line-up for *Close To My Heart* and it marks a process of change in Pelt's music, on record at least. There aren't many young trumpeters around who can move from Charles Mingus to Jimmy Rowles with aplomb. Pelt kicks off his new contract with a version of 'Weird Nightmare' and only then returns to the hard-bop idiom which made his name. One's tempted to say that his faster stuff – like an unexpected reading of 'Take Me In Your Arms' – puts him close to Hubbard or Morgan copyism, but listen a little longer and it's clear that here's a guy who grew up in a rock and hip-hop era. The phrasing is subtly different, more pungently on the beat and yet still with a strong sense of swing. Pelt's flugelhorn solo on '52 Blues (Drinkin' And Drivin')' remains a career high. As exposed as this, without another horn, and even with subtle backing from O'Rourke, he can't afford to coast and there isn't a lazy or poorly thought-out track on the album.

ALEXANDER VON SCHLIPPENBACH &
Born 7 April 1938, Berlin, Germany
Piano

Monk's Casino
Intakt CD 100 3CD
Schlippenbach; Axel Dörner (t); Rudi Mahall (bcl); Aki Takase (toy p); Jan Roder (b); Uli Jennessen (d). June 2003, February 2004.

Alexander von Schlippenbach says: **'I think Monk is probably the greatest composer in jazz. In this, Steve Lacy was my teacher. We met in Paris in the '60s, and he later played with Globe Unity. He showed me so much he had learned from and through Monk. I copied everything.'**

Schlippenbach's clean, atonal lines are far more reminiscent of Thelonious Monk than of Cecil Taylor, the figure who is usually adduced as ancestor for this kind of free music, almost always incorrectly. An extraordinary project, *Monk's Casino* is executed with vision, humour and considerable intelligence. Schlippenbach had long been fascinated by these pieces: he featured 'Trinkle Tinkle' on *Smoke* with Sunny Murray, who joined him again on tour in 1996 for some all-Monk programmes. First conceived in that same year, *Monk's Casino* was an attempt to go further still and arrange the great pianist and composer's work for a single, whole-evening performance. The idea came to fruition two years later, when Norddeutsche Rundfunk broadcast the work entire. Festival and club appearances followed, including a rendition at A-Trane in Berlin, from which these recordings are taken.

In his liner-note, John Corbett makes a wise distinction between a songbook and an oeuvre. Monk's tunes (or at least the better-known ones) have been a resource for jazz improvisers for 50 years and more. This, though, represents a different take: Monk's music as a highly flexible singularity, articulate in the original sense, and with its own internal motions and logic. How freely Schlippenbach has interpreted the music can be heard in a long, abstract introduction to 'Bemsha Swing' on the first CD, three and a half minutes dominated by Dörner's microscopic trumpet. Just a couple of tracks earlier, 'Stuffy Turkey' had been despatched in just 44 seconds. This is very much the pattern for the set. Some pieces are explored at some length – 'Misterioso'/'Sixteen'/'Skippy' the longest at just over ten minutes – while others ('Raise Four', 'Light Blue', 'Ruby, My Dear' and 'Bye-Ya') get less than 60 seconds.

The instrumentation is pared down to the minimum necessary to get the music across, much as on Monk's own records. The only exceptions are the medley of 'Japanese Folk Song', 'Children's Song' and 'Blue Monk', on which Schlippenbach plays trumpet and Dörner the piano; that and 'A Merrier Christmas', on which Aki Takase plays toy piano. Jennessen's lightly swinging drums are the key element, often left to sound out a cadence while the other instruments lay out for a bar or two. Stylistically, the arrangements range from near-pastiche to the outside treatment of 'Evidence'.

A modern masterpiece, nothing more or less, and not merely of interest to Monk fans. This is a project that asks deep questions about the nature of jazz composition, the identity and persistence of an artist's entire body of work, and what makes a 'standard'. *Monk's Casino* is essential listening.

& See also **Pakistani Pomade** (1972; p. 401)

KEN VANDERMARK
Born 22 September 1964, Warwick, Rhode Island
Reeds

Elements Of Style / Color Of Memory
Atavistic ALP 150 / 166
Vandermark; Jeb Bishop (tb); Dave Rempis (sax); Kent Kessler (b); Tim Daisy (d). July 2003, July 2004.

Ken Vandermark says: **'Coinciding with *Elements* was my last work on the Free Jazz Classics project, the music of Roland Kirk. I decided to abandon the exploration and documentation of other composers' material, because I felt that certain listeners and critics found it easier to consider my arrangements of celebrated composers than to look at my own work ... *Color* was the final recording made with Jeb Bishop, one of the original members of the Vandermark 5. It was difficult to see him leave the band after so many years, but we decided to continue by asking Fred Lonberg-Holm to join the ensemble, effectively re-energizing the music and the group.'**

As we have said elsewhere, Vandermark is the Kevin Bacon of contemporary jazz and improvisation. This isn't just cracking wise: not only does he appear on a bewildering array of albums (how does he find the time?), but he seems adaptable to almost any performing situation. Being a confident multi-instrumentalist is, of course, an advantage.

Proposing a two-for-one Vandermark deal is a bit of a cheat, particularly when it means no representation of his other groups – the DKV Trio in particular (or Steelwool, or the AALY Trio ...) – but the reedman, whose career kicked away from New York, in Boston and Montreal, has charged straight to the front of free music in America. One could call him an archetypal post-modernist, working in rock, R&B and jazz alike, except with Vandermark there's nothing cool or once-removed about his expressiveness. He's a full-on energy player a lot of the time, a canny organizer of groups and musical forms, a man perhaps destined to make things happen. While he's primarily a tenor saxophonist, he often picks up both bass and B-flat clarinets, and he espouses European models as readily as American ones – Evan Parker arabesques might invade a solo as plausibly as Dolphyesque skirlings and Lockjaw Davis-like pugilistics. Vandermark likes structure – most of these records start off from compositions, sometimes of considerable complexity – but his music can take off into the most provocative and open-ended byways. He also knows a lot of great players, most of them stalwarts of a scene which Vandermark himself has been crucial in documenting and bringing to wider attention.

Names are often dropped all over his early records, but when someone like George Clinton or Witold Lutoslawski is cited it never means that Vandermark is about to get either funky or neo-classical. What he loves is jazz language in the raw, and this is how the earlier discs sound.

Their qualities notwithstanding, the Vandermark 5 is the keynote group. We aren't in the business of who-is-the-greatest; we evaluate records. But it's difficult to think of another jazz combo currently active that is working to this incredible standard. Both of these annual reports from the V5 are utterly compelling from first to last. The compositions explore new terrain even as they value their various toeholds on the tradition. The supportive nature of the group is democracy in profitable action, even as the band is driven by Vandermark's vision. It's rarely solos that you remember, fine as they individually are, it's the music of a living organism that relishes detail and enjoys throwing its weight around. If you aren't tuning in, right now, why on earth not?

KURT ELLING

Born 2 November 1967, Chicago, Illinois
Voice

Man In The Air

Blue Note 80834
Elling; Jim Gailloreto (ss); Laurence Hobgood (p); Stefon Harris (vib); Rob Amster (b); Frank Parker Jr (d). 2003.

Kurt Elling said (2003): **'The male jazz voice is devalued because there's no church singing any more, not as a norm, and no school singing, and the popular culture has gone in a different direction, right away from swing. But that doesn't trouble me and nor does the suggestion that I'm first in a field of one. I want to communicate, and not just to five people in a club with a bad piano. This music deserves more than that.'**

Almost unbelievably, Elling sent a demo tape to Blue Note and got a contract that over two or three albums confirmed him as the leading male jazz vocalist of recent times. It's easy to see him as a contemporary version of Mark Murphy, but Frank Sinatra was a powerful influence as well. The early Blue Note records *Close Your Eyes* and *The Messenger* were marvellous, literary and quietly daring, but nothing quite prepared for the masterpieces that followed, one for Blue Note and another after he had moved on to Concord.

Nightmoves for the latter label is an astonishing record, but perhaps it has already become a little formulaic, albeit in a most unusual way. *Man In The Air* is *the* jazz vocal album of the last decade. Almost ten years on from his debut, Elling delivers a bold and accomplished performance, marked by a highly original choice of material and some devastating playing from his regular band. Elling's scat and his delivery of a ballad are now so confident that he is able to take on material like John Coltrane's 'Resolution' and bring to it a genuine philosophical understanding as well as a musically coherent performance. He also includes Joe Zawinul's lovely ballad 'Time To Say Goodbye' and Herbie Hancock's 'A Secret I', both of them thoroughly original and intelligent interpretations. Hobgood is the key, a master of subtle harmonic shifts and rhythmic changes. Harris's contribution is more dramatic, but less thoughtful, and Gailloreto is more a foil to Elling's voice than a completely successful soloist. It's so good, it's almost sinful.

ROVA *&*

Formed 1977
Group

Electric Ascension

Atavistic ALP 159
Bruce Ackley, Steve Adams, Larry Ochs, Jon Raskin (sax); with Nels Cline (g); Clara Kihlstedt (vn, effects);
Jenny Scheinman (vn); Fred Frith (b); Ikue Mori (d machine, sampler); Don Robinson (d); Otomo Yoshihide
(turntables, elec); Chris Brown (elec). July 2003.

Larry Ochs says: '**I remember staring at this single piece of paper with only four chords on it, with just five melodic strands spread there, and thinking: where's the music coming from? Certainly the most underrated piece of music in jazz history.**'

In 1995, and in what seemed like an act of hubris, ROVA attempted a fresh realization of John Coltrane's *Ascension*, a work whose revolutionary compositional elements have always been subordinated to the collective free-for-all of the solos. The sheer audacity of the project was entirely justified by the result. Trane and his men were taking early steps in a new world; ROVA has existed in that world since a decade after the great saxophonist's death. The result is a realization which makes up in assured power what it might lack in 'pure' freedom. The music was released on a Black Saint record and that seemed to be that. The story was far from over, though, and ROVA have continued to give occasional realizations of the piece ever since, where funds and logistics permit.

It may seem perverse to admirers to have picked two records by the group which involve other composers and additional members, as *John Coltrane's Ascension* and the record under consideration here both did, but it is our belief that while ROVA's body of work for saxophone quartet represents one of the real compositional challenges and achievements of contemporary jazz, their most distinguished achievements have always been those that have drawn other voices into their sometimes hermetic world.

ROVA first performed the piece in concert at the Bolzano Jazz Festival in 1997. Music, group spirit and like-minded collaborators – Dave Douglas, Raphe Malik, Glenn Spearman – allowed them to rise above an unsatisfactory sound set-up and produce a memorable performance, but for sheer musical majesty it would (surely?) be impossible to surpass the performance released as *Electric Ascension*. Remarkably, the second recorded ascent – taken on the fly from a KFJC radio recording in Los Altos, California, and only cleared for release later – is even braver, bringing in a huge battery of electronics to fill out what sounds like a vast, seething orchestra. The opening and closing theme is, once again, immediately recognizable, but in between ROVA and friends have taken Coltrane's 'structured improvisation' (as Larry Ochs prefers) and put it through conceptual grids based on nearly 40 years of new freedoms, as well as new technologies undreamt of when Coltrane was alive. The result is still chaotic, still desperately trying to break free of its bounds, but the sense of liberation and transcendence is unmistakable. The two violinists play a vital role, similar in some respects to that undertaken by string-players in the later groups of Albert Ayler, Trane's most original disciple. Cline on electric guitar and the trio of Brown, Mori and Yoshihide (who are credited with the other guests as Rhythm & Noise) stretch the framing theme further still. Fred Frith makes a rare appearance on electric bass.

We have no hesitation in hailing *Electric Ascension* as one of the key recordings of recent times. It is a unique, but endlessly repeatable, experience, and – who knows? – ROVA may yet reach even higher.

& See also **Bingo** (1996; p. 607)

AKI TAKASE
Born 26 January 1948, Osaka, Japan
Piano

The Dessert
Leo CD LR 370
Takase; Rudi Mahall (bcl, cbcl). 2003.

Pianist Beat Witten says: **'Her style is only "free" in the sense that it doesn't sit in any one category for long. I hear a lot of bop, a lot of stride and boogie-woogie, even at times passages that sound like Oscar Peterson playing a left-handed piano. It's not "eclectic". It's just a very personal voice with a distinctive sense of jazz piano history.'**

Once a student of Yosuke Yamashita, Takase rises out of jazz piano history with unique intensity and panache. Her earlier music suggested a pianist who was involving herself in earlier methods only reluctantly – most of the music leapt into the darkness of free playing at the earliest opportunity. She has proved to be a particularly interesting duo player, working with her husband, pianist Alexander von Schlippenbach, more recently with clarinettist/ saxophonist Louis Sclavis (the brilliant *Yokohama*), with David Murray and with Mahall.

Mahall is by no means intimidated by the knowledge that Murray has already played this duettist role on a Takase record. He's a mercurial player, making light of the lumbering reputation of the bass clarinet, with a slightly pinched tone and a quacking approach to a line. Ten Dolphy tunes – a big chunk of his œuvre, in fact – are whistled through on *Duet With Dolphy* (1997), along with three originals and a peg-leg treatment of 'I'm Confessin''. Miniaturized into briefly explosive or bittersweet episodes, it's an inventive, droll record.

Five years on their merrymaking remains infectious. Most of the tracks are named for something likely to be served at table and the playing is suitably flavoursome and impeccably cooked. Thirteen compositions all have their own special detail and quality, and some of the performances, such as 'Panna Cotta', are so beautifully modulated that one can't imagine them being bettered. As a kind of encore, they uncork four brief improvisations, whose scattershot qualities underscore how fastidiously the preceding tunes were performed. The duo picked up again in 2008 with *Evergreen*, attesting to a lastingly creative relationship.

DENNY ZEITLIN &
Born 10 April 1938, Chicago, Illinois
Piano

Slickrock
MaxJazz #209
Zeitlin; Buster Williams (b); Matt Wilson (d). August 2003.

Denny Zeitlin says: **'My composition "Slickrock" evokes a dangerous mountain bike adventure with my wife, and the spirit of exploration carries through this whole album. The recording felt more like a live performance than a studio date, and I couldn't have asked for better trio soulmates than Buster and Matt.'**

Almost four decades after his debut on Columbia, Zeitlin is still creating formidable new music, here with another sterling trio. Apart from a Maybeck Hall recital, which sparked renewed interest in his work, he remains surprisingly little-known to a wider audience.

As ever when he tackles a standard, 'You And The Night And The Music' avoids any hint of predictability, but it's immediately clear that the creative energy in this group is shared with Williams, the most melodic of bassists, and the astonishing Wilson. Zeitlin programmes more standards than usual here, perhaps, but his treatment of 'Body And Soul' (which is completely reharmonized) and 'Put Your Little Foot Right Out' is dazzlingly original. He has recorded his own 'Every Which Way' before, but not with a trio, and it's an illuminating version of a theme that ought to be in every pianist's book.

The 'Slickrock' sequence that ends the set starts with high adventure, with a tense juxtaposition of keys and some whippy turns in the piano solo of 'On The Trail'. The suite begins in almost free mode, an impressionistic 'Dawn' and setting-out. 'Recovery' marks some downtime on the journey, while 'On The Trail Again' (does it reference Ferde Grofé?) restores a spirit of fun and adventure, for which Wilson is the perfect partner. Tonally subtle, rhythmically daring, emotionally satisfying, Zeitlin's music is terrain waiting to be (re) discovered.

& *See also* **Cathexis** (1964; p. 302)

LINCOLN CENTER JAZZ ORCHESTRA
Formed 1988
Big band

A Love Supreme
Palmetto 2106
Wynton Marsalis, Ryan Kisor, Marcus Printup, Lew Soloff (t); Vincent Gardner, Andre Hayward, Ronald Westray (tb); Walter Blanding, Victor Goines, Joe Temperley, Wessell Anderson (sax); Eric Lewis (p); Carlos Henriquez (b); Herlin Riley (d). August 2003.

Wynton Marsalis said (1999): **'You can't preserve a musical tradition by putting it in a jar with some alcohol and a label. Or at least, you can preserve it that way, but only dead and cold. Jazz only lives when it's moving forward and the orchestra will keep moving forward.'**

Lincoln Center is the hub of uptown arts in New York City and, alongside opera and dance, jazz has at last been properly recognized by the mainstream culture. The powerhouse of the Lincoln Center Jazz Orchestra is Wynton Marsalis, a controversial but powerful figure in the music, whose advocacy counts for much. Inevitably, much of the band's recorded output has been devoted to the great composers, Ellington, Mingus (who mightn't seem to sit naturally in Marsalis's familiar purview) and, here, Coltrane.

If Marsalis feels that Coltrane's legacy has been warped to inauthentic ends, there's no sign of it in this moving re-creation of the composer's most personal statement. Of all the current reworkings of Coltrane's great spiritual statement, this one is the most unexpected and the grandest. If the work has a symphonic, continuous structure, divided into movements, the jazz equivalent of the New York Phil seems the ideal messenger. The sections are packed with extraordinary players, the production (Delfeayo Marsalis) is crisp and detailed and the familiar themes are given weight but allowed to fly upwards, particularly in the climactic final movement. There are dull bits, like the 'Love Supreme' motto itself, and Riley's bridge into 'Pursuance' is sketchy. But it's a worthy response to a masterwork and a strong indication of what Lincoln Center contributes to the music.

GERI ALLEN
Born 12 June 1957, Pontiac, Michigan
Piano

The Life Of A Song
Telarc CD 83598
Allen; Marcus Belgrave (flhn); Clifton Anderson (tb); Dwight Andrews (as); Dave Holland (b); Jack DeJohnette (d). January 2004.

Geri Allen said (2004): **'There were enough powerful and charismatic women in jazz – Alice Coltrane, the great singers, Mary Lou Williams, maybe less well-known women like [pianist] Terry Pollard – that I don't think there was ever any resistance. Women have made their mark on the tradition, maybe more than in other fields.'**

It took some time for Allen to establish herself as a leader, and for a time she seemed to perform better on other people's records than on her own. In a curious way, she came up the old-fashioned way but at a time when artists – and particularly female artists – were being pushed through the recording system prematurely and hastily, with more of an eye to presentation and possible press copy than to the music. She is a formidable technician, drawing elements from all over the modern piano tradition – Bud Powell, Monk, tinges of Cecil Taylor, less celebrated figures like Herbie Nichols and Mary Lou Williams – and from non-pianists like Eric Dolphy, whose spiky, restless ideas are also reflected in her writing.

Allen studied piano as a child and began playing in Detroit, where Marcus Belgrave was her teacher. She taught herself for a time in Washington DC, before moving to New York City and becoming involved in the M-Base collective. Her earliest works, including *The Printmakers* and some fine trio work with Charlie Haden and Paul Motian, are good but somewhat enigmatic, as if she were withholding something. In more recent years, after making something of a round of the labels, Allen has found a sympathetic berth at Telarc, where they value piano-players. This is essentially a trio date, with the horns reserved for a delicious closing version of Mal Waldron's 'Soul Eyes'. If Geri found sympathetic partners in Charlie Haden and Paul Motian in earlier years, the association with Holland and DeJohnette (heard to wonderful effect in their work with Betty Carter) has attained an organic wholeness and empathy that makes this one of the most effective piano trios around.

In her liner-note, Allen suggests the possibility – almost the reverse of what Eric Dolphy said – that when music is over it continues to reverberate outwards. By extension, are our attempts to make music the product of will or are we just caught up in a time-line of past music? These are heavyweight philosophical questions, but Allen, Holland and DeJohnette answer them by creating a graceful mixture of originals and standards which not only reference past performances but create a shimmering unity of sound that one can very readily imagine hovering in the ether long after the record is over. Allen's readings of 'Lush Life' and of Bud Powell's 'Dance Of The Infidels' are both historically rooted, but also aware of present-day harmonic imperatives. DeJohnette's sudden change of metre halfway through the second chorus is typical of the way this trio manages to invest familiar, even hackneyed material with new emphases. Holland's soloing is impeccable throughout, notably on 'Lush Life' and 'Mount And Mountains', where he phrases like a saxophonist, though without losing touch with a string bass idiom.

More conventional in attitude than some previous records, this is none the less an album that repays repeated listens.

ALAN BARNES
Born 23 July 1959, Altrincham, Cheshire, England
Clarinet, alto and baritone saxophones

Songs For Unsung Heroes
Woodville WVCD 106
Barnes; Bruce Adams (t, flhn); Mark Nightingale (tb); Stan Sulzmann (as, ts, f); Robert Fowler (ts, cl); Brian Dee (p); Simon Thorpe (g, b); Clark Tracey (d); Liz Fletcher (v). January 2004.

Alan Barnes says: **'Alan Plater suggested writing these songs, I agreed and the emailed lyrics started arriving: songs about Lester Young, slobs, British A roads, Miles Davis fans and a defiant declaration of a chicken refusing to be eaten by Slim Gaillard! I've never asked Alan to change a lyric and he's never asked me to change the music. Apart from that we get on very well.'**

Barnes has been a stalwart saxophonist in all kinds of British jazz situations since the early '80s, and he keeps coming up trumps in fans' polls, which is a welcome indication that musical quality and popularity do go together. A phenomenal technician, he is all over his instruments, and as time has gone by has applied much of that virtuosity (for once the word is justified) to writing as well, with a fondness for suites: Sherlock Holmes and Marbella both figure in the subject box, and on this record a shared but highly personal pantheon/ Room 101 of heroes and others.
    Lyricist Alan Plater, who has forgotten more about jazz than most fans learn in a lifetime, but hides his affection under a sardonic mask, gets a co-credit here, and apologies from us for calling him Alan Parker in the last edition though they come too late: Alan passed away in the summer of 2010. The band, tight as a nut, is packed with the best of British talent, including regular oppo Bruce Adams and the big voiced Mark Nightingale. There's even a number about Joe Harriott, which suggests again how awkwardly Barnes fits into the 'mainstream' bag that has all the longhair 'progressives' dismiss him as a lightweight. Woodville is the 'home' imprint, steadily taking over from Zephyr as the home of some of the best British jazz of the last two decades.

DAVE BRUBECK&
Born 6 December 1920, Concord, California
Piano

London Sharp, London Flat
Telarc 83625
Brubeck; Bobby Militello (as); Michael Moore (b); Randy Jones (d). January 2004.

Iola Brubeck said (2001): **'The extraordinary thing is that you can see him getting stronger as he plays. Even when he's tired or unwell, there is something about sitting down at the piano that lights the fires and stokes the boiler!'**

The first reaction is admiring disbelief: that at nearly 84 Brubeck should turn in a composition as daring as the title-track – opposite runs in sharps and flats for each hand – and secondly that the band should take it on so confidently. Moore is right behind him, as he always is in such contexts, and Militello plays one of his best solos on a Brubeck disc. It's almost like the 'classic' quartet reconvened, except that everyone sounds different and the music is unmistakably more modern. The remainder of the record isn't quite up to that standard of inventiveness, but he digs into some fascinating material, old and new. 'To Sit And Dream' survives from a Langston Hughes-based commission; 'Yes, We All Have Our Cross To Bear' is co-written with his daughter-in-law for a sacred concert and 'Steps To Peace' was written by the father of one of the 9/11 hijack victims, and both seem to belong in a different world to the opening cut. But there is also 'Mr Fats' and a revival of a song written while Brubeck was in uniform, 'Ballad Of The Rhine'. At the same time, Dave recorded a fascinating musical memoir *Private Brubeck Remembers*, which brings his early years back to vivid life. A jazz institution, and part of its evolving history.

& See also **The Dave Brubeck Octet** (1946–1950; p. 106), **Time Out** (1959; p. 240)

SAMO ŠALOMON
Born 9 October 1978, Maribor, Slovenia
Guitar

Ornethology
Samo SSCD 03
Šalomon; Achille Succi (as, bcl); Salvatore Maiore (b); Zlatko Kaucic (d, perc). 2004.

Samo Šalomon says: **'At this period I was virtually obsessed with Ornette Coleman; I really liked his openness and melodic approach to soloing, so I transcribed almost all of his solos with the legendary quartet! That changed my playing for ever! Of course, at this time I was also totally into Scofield as well: nice mix ...'**

Much admired by his friend and fellow guitarist John Scofield, Šalomon has enterprisingly released much of his music so far on his own imprint, and it has paid off with recent attention for more established imprints. The first albums pay respectful debt – 'Blues For Sco' and 'For Susan And John' – to an influential supporter, but more importantly they confirm a strong writing talent, which emerges ever more fully formed on subsequent releases.

Even if the home releases are hard to find, *Ornethology* is worth searching for. The brief, improvised pieces show a brilliant instinct for texture as well as strong lines and unusual chords. 'Does Your Girlfriend Know You Play Free Jazz?' is as wry as it sounds, but the major statements are 'Something Ology', which may be taking a sideswipe at efforts to pigeonhole this music as Adriatic Ornette, the powerful 'Tribeca' and 'Humpty Dumpty'. The relative absence of blues cadences distinguishes the sound from '80s Scofield, but there is no mistaking Šalomon's modern jazz sensibility or his staying power.

MARK DRESSER
Born 26 September 1952, Los Angeles, California
Double bass

Unveil
Clean Feed CF043
Dresser (b solo). January 2003, February 2004.

Mark Dresser says: **'In 2002 luthier Kent McLagan designed me a set of custom-made pick-ups embedded behind the fingerboard which facilitated ideas I have worked on since 1983 regarding multi-voiced solo potentials. With subdub performer, producer and composer Raz Mesinai in the basement of his mother's apartment in Manhattan I recorded a series of edited improvisations. With the exception of the title-cut, there was no overdubbing.'**

Often assumed to be a lifelong New Yorker, Dresser cut his musical teeth in his native LA, where he studied with the great Bertram Turetzky. He later worked with David Murray and Arthur Blythe, and was a member of the celebrated Anthony Braxton quartet of the mid-'80s.

His own discography is impressively substantial for such a busy player, and early records like *Force Green* and *Banquet* (his threnody for the victims of TWA 800) bespeak not just a fine compositional talent, but an artist interested in exploring new sonic possibilities.

Solo bass performance is a tough discipline and the unconverted might be resistant, but there are few more thoroughly musical records around than *Unveil*. Dresser's use of the Giffus, a system of pick-ups suspended from the scroll of the bass, has evolved steadily over the years. He now employs a system developed for him by luthier and electronics expert Kent McLagan which affords much more control and consistency. In addition to this, he continues to experiment with notes played above rather than below the stop, creating a fascinating range of harmonics and bitones. Apart from the acoustic 'Bacachaonne' (loosely based on a Bach partita), everything here is electronically manipulated, but strictly in real time. The results are easier to enjoy than to describe, but the combination of pick-ups and subtly altered finger pressure creates a buzzing effect which gives these pieces a richness of sound that seems impossible from a single instrument and player.

STEVE HARRIS / ZAUM
Born 16 August 1948, Mansfield, Nottinghamshire, England; died 11 January 2008, Dorchester, Dorset, England; Zaum formed 2001
Drums / group

Above Our Heads The Sky Splits Splits Open
Slam CD258
Harris; Geoff Hearn (ss, ts); Karen Wimhurst (cl, bcl); Udo Dzierzanowski, Matthew Olczaki (g); Cathy Stevens (vla, violectra); Adrian Newton (live, found samples); Chrome Strings. March 2004.

Steve Harris said (2006): **'I steer clear of the "jazz" label. My favourite-ever song is Bobby Darin singing "Beyond The Sea", though I'd have mixed the drums up just a little bit in the bridge.'**

After a background in pop and punk – he even auditioned for T Rex – Harris drummed in saxophonist Jan Kopinski's Pinski Zoo, but left to work in music education, before forming Europe's most exciting improvising ensemble. If the Spontaneous Music Ensemble, ISKRA 1903, AMM and the various aggregations round Derek Bailey's Company established a basic discourse for British improvisation from the '60s onward, Steve Harris's Zaum took up the torch and moved that language on a step further. The ensemble takes its name from the Futurist notion of a new guttural language that might approximate the hard discontinuities of (post)modern life. The group's music does not follow a hard-line 'non-idiomatic' course but explores new sonorities within and against a recognizable instrumental discourse. A Zaum performance is always in flux, always trading warmly 'organic' sounds against tonalities that are not so much dissonant or alien as uncanny, in the strict and original sense. It is a profoundly humane music that communicates at a very deep level.

In 2004, *Above Our Heads* seemed a remarkable disc. With hindsight, and remastering, it has repositioned our listening to British improvised music. Even with an augmented ensemble, the group's main energy comes from Harris himself. He is constantly in motion, stoking insistent cross-rhythms and building the deep, slow pulses that give each of these remarkable records their shape. His rock background is shared to some degree with long-term associate Hearn and with Dzierzanowski, but that is tempered by Stevens's and Wimhurst's background in classical music, though both have also worked in other genres. It was meeting the Ganelin Trio that redirected Harris's career, and while *Zaum, As Slow As Flowers* and *Above Our Heads* were all recorded at home in Poole in a gallery space normally associated with fine arts (painters were literally at work around them when the first record was made), there is a sense of quiet, intimate theatre to a Zaum performance.

Zaum saw the group finding its feet, having only come together immediately before the performance. *As Slow As Flowers* is a masterpiece. *Above Our Heads* utilizes many instrumental permutations to create a vivid soundtrack whose abstractions are none the less rooted in palpable human dramas. The fourth date, from which Wimhurst was absent on family duties and on which she is only audible among Newton's samples, is a confident consolidation by what has been the most exciting group in Europe. The most recent inevitably lacks the sheer surprise and freshness of its predecessors, but it does find Harris confidently assimilating another new voice into the group. Parkins sounds as if she might have been a founder member; Harris plays more gently, as perhaps befits the title, but there are moments of real edge and danger to the playing throughout and the climactic 'Juarez' and 'Watt's Curve' are high-points in contemporary improvised music. Harris's premature death from liver cancer was a tragedy and a posthumous release of live material has only underlined how much extraordinary music was cut suddenly short.

ROSARIO GIULIANI
Born 1967, Terracina, Italy
Alto saxophone

More Than Ever
Dreyfus FDM 36669
Giuliani; Jean-Michael Pilc (p); Richard Galliano (acc); Rémi Vignolo (b); Benjamin Henocq (d). April 2004.

Rosario Giuliani said (2004): **'After I studied, I worked with Giovani Talenti Del Jazz Europea, and working with a bigger band was great study, but I had so many ideas for writing for a small group. I could hear it in my head from the very beginning.'**

Though he had made a couple of earlier records in Italy, Giuliani exploded on the scene with *Luggage*, but without carrying any undue baggage from his influences. One of them is hinted at in Wayne Shorter's 'Oriental Folk Song', but while the angular attack and severe minimalism of line might come from Shorter, the rest of the sound emphatically does not. This young man has listened deeply in the jazz literature rather than merely follow current trends. The second album prompted yet more head-scratching about Giuliani's models on the alto with everyone from Eric Dolphy to Charles MacPherson getting a mention. Fact is, he emerged pretty fully formed and has already devised his own idiom, which is eclectic, slightly mysterious in tonality, and inherently dramatic, but not yet fully formed.
   A new band oozes with confidence on *More Than Ever*. The first quarter of an hour zings with energy – and a good deal of carefully marshalled abstraction – before Giuliani wheels on Galliano for two lovely compositions by the accordionist, a tribute to Astor Piazzolla and the equally effective 'J.F.'. Thus softened up, we're prepared for 'Suite Et Poursuite', a three-part idea that suggests the saxophonist's ambitions may take him in ever newer directions.

KEVIN NORTON *&*
Born 21 January 1956, Brooklyn, New York
Drums, vibraphone

Time-Space Modulator
Barking Hoop BKH-008
Norton; Dave Ballou (t, c); Tony Malaby (ts); John Lindberg (b). August 2003, April 2004.

Kevin Norton says: '**The basis of the sound and approach of** *Time-Space Modulator* **is built on my CD** *Knots*, **after years of both free improvisation and composition; the interaction of my drumming with Lindberg's bass and the sound of my vibraphone influencing the horn writing ... the space between ringing notes over the intense density of bass and drums.'**

A period of work with Anthony Braxton, a record dedicated to the founder of Situationism, a work-list that includes composition for new-music ensembles, theatre and dance: one can hear the Jazz Police rattling their batons in the distance. But Norton is the real thing, a jazz drummer who, like Jack DeJohnette or fellow Braxton alumnus Gerry Hemingway, is also a complete musician. His recordings of the '90s and after are essential listening for anyone interested in the direction of contemporary music, and he's worth searching out, too, as an ensemble member (Braxton again) or duo player (with Joëlle Léandre and others).

Before *Time-Space Modulator*, Norton's most important records were *For Guy Debord* (the above-mentioned Situationist) and *Knots*, which in 1999 immediately marked him out as a significant presence. *Time-Space Modulator* is credited to Norton's Bauhaus Quartet, which implies yet another political agenda but more fundamentally a commitment to old-fashioned – or rather new-fashioned – craft. The title is an adaptation of Moholy-Nagy's 'light-space modulator', a synaesthetic receiver for as yet undeveloped media. The analogy answers nicely here, because Norton and his men seem to be moving in umpteen dimensions at once: fiery Braxton-like grooves, long abstract episodes and deceptively simple material that harks back to the drummer's early work with bass master Milt Hinton. The opening 'Mother Tongue' is a blast, with the two horns playing in relatively unfamiliar guise, though Ballou is an avid shape-shifter. 'Seoul Soul' is collectively improvised and perhaps the least successful item on the set. The other long tracks, 'Didkovsky' and 'Moonstruck', are vintage Norton, subtle, thoughtful, packed with cheerful guile.

& *See also* **JOËLLE LÉANDRE/KEVIN NORTON, Winter In New York** (2006; p. 721)

POLAR BEAR
Formed 1999
Group

Dim Lit
Babel BDV 2446
Mark Lockheart, Pete Wareham (ts); Tom Herbert (b); Sebastian Rochford (d); Julia Biel (v). 2004.

Sebastian Rochford says: '**It was recorded in the 93 Feet East studio in Brick Lane. A friend of producer Paul Epworth believed in our music and offered to do the album for free. We recorded for three days in this tiny little hot room, fuelled by fruit and curry.'**

Few British groups of recent times have been so extravagantly hyped and yet Polar Bear do, on closer inspection, really match up to the publicity and press raves. Rochford is a formidable musician and in Lockheart and Wareham he has seasoned players who know their way around a range of idioms. They weave in and out of Rochford's deceptively quiet playing; this, perhaps, is the point of the name – polar bears are attractive, cuddly creatures but among the fiercest beasts on the planet – and there is a dark energy to these tracks reminiscent of Radiohead at their most extended. Rochford's rock and avant-rock tastes are evident here and there on both this record and the later *Held On The Tips Of The Fingers*, but there is no hint that his ambitions run to either prog-rock or Nu Jazz. A formidable improviser, he keeps jazz playing in focus at all times.

'Eve's Apple' (one of the great contemporary jazz songs) and 'Wild Horses' were apparently done in the hope that Björk (elderly jazz fans scratch their heads) might do a guest vocal. As it is, Julia Biel does just fine on her spots, more than fine when the voice relaxes out of 'projecting' mode, but this is the first album's only besetting fault, an air of eagerness and self-consciousness that sometimes blunts the music. 'New Dark Park' is an anthem for the new age, for good or ill.

RUDRESH MAHANTHAPPA

Born 4 May 1971, Trieste, Italy
Alto saxophone

Codebook
Pi 21
Mahanthappa; Vijay Iyer (p); François Moutin (b); Dan Weiss (d). June 2004.

Rudresh Mahanthappa says: '**This was an attempt to humanize and even beautify the perceived coldness of cryptography, data encryption and the mathematic concepts behind both. Engaging such methodology in music composition is nothing new but my goal was to be blunt with it while putting forth something emotionally varied and aesthetically complete that is worthy of multiple listens.**'

An Indian-American based in NY since 1997, Mahanthappa addresses questions of identity and culture within his own jazz idiom. Tired of being asked: 'Do you speak Indian?', he gave a powerfully direct answer in *Mother Tongue*, a sequence of compositions that are 'directly based on melodic transcriptions of Indian-Americans responding to such questions in their native Indian tongues'. It was a high-concept project compared to the usual jazz date, but he delivered a convincing statement, somewhat reminiscent of some of Greg Osby's small-group music, punctuated with bittersweet episodes and steep contrapuntal inclines. A couple of limited-circulation CDs, *Yatra* and *Black Water*, preceded *Mother Tongue*, but it was what came after that consolidated his reputation as one of the most interesting younger players on the New York scene. He arrived in the Big Apple in 1997.

Mahanthappa can be terse and inward in his delivery, but he has a fine, wounding sound on the alto and on *Codebook* he seems to have got past all vestiges of polemic and into an idiom that bids for nothing less than a rich new musical metalanguage. One sees immediately how these concerns arise out of those of *Mother Tongue*, but the music, peppery and sometimes confrontational, is rich and inclusive, with every note there for a purpose, and no fat. It might sound belittling to liken this to logic and algorithms, but there's something of that cleanness. 'The Decider' and 'Refresh' make for a fine opening, but the set ends on 'My Sweetest', and if 'ballad' playing is the ultimate test of a saxophonist's skill and vision, Mahanthappa passes here too: it's a subtle but by no means cloying statement, worthy of Stan Getz.

BEN GOLDBERG

Born 8 August 1959, Sycamore, Illinois
Clarinet

The Door, The Hat, The Chair, The Fact
Cryptogramophone 126
Goldberg; Devin Hoff (b); Carla Kihlstedt (vn); Rob Sudduth (ts); Ches Smith (d). June 2004.

Ben Goldberg says: '**This music is for my hero, Steve Lacy, written after I learned he had cancer. I idolized Steve and used to listen four times a day to *Evidence*, made in 1961 with Don Cherry. I memorized his solos. What was he doing? The note that lifts all other notes** up into the world. Punctuation. The line that's backwards and forwards and the pop of logic more logical than logic. He gave me a lesson once. Steve said you had to know the difference between materials and material. He talked matter of factly about the invisible. I worked on his exercises for ten years. I had booked the studio for June 7th; Steve passed away June 4th. We had a rehearsal and then made the record. It was a sad time.'

Goldberg is an experienced voice in and out of jazz. He's an adept of klezmer as well and savvy about modern composition. At heart, he's an improviser, despite the 'correct' tonality and very accurate pitching. Few players in this realm dare to let the note-choices do the work, without 'expressive' contortions, and he's to be commended for it. The trio record *Almost Never* is reminiscent of a latter-day Jimmy Giuffre project, albeit the reed tone is different, but Goldberg has an even more ambitious game to follow.

After 2000, Goldberg seemed to look around and take stock. There seemed to be a break of almost five years in recording under his own name. His return came freighted with emotion following the death of his inspiration, Steve Lacy. The great man's personality is woven through these mournfully effervescent tracks. The title comes from Lacy's favourite poet, Robert Creeley. The most explicit tribute is Lacy's own 'Blinks', which then informs writing of a markedly numinous sort. The playing is outwardly chaotic, with the three leads vying for space, but there's a stern inner logic, even if it doesn't present in logical forms. This seems to be the album's subtext. There is 'Cortège', but there is also 'Song And Dance', though not in the expected order. It's a record full of complex messages and stunning play. Hoff and Smith create an intricate web of rhythm patterns, leaving the front three, with Kihlstedt doubling on vocals, to create a rich, ambiguous drama.

MARIA SCHNEIDER
Born 27 November 1960, Windom, Minnesota
Composer, arranger

Concert In The Garden
ArtistShare 5734
Schneider; Laurie Frink, Tony Kadleck, Greg Gisbert, Ingrid Jensen (t, flhn); Keith O'Quinn, Rocky Ciccarone, Larry Farrell, Pete McGuinness (tb); George Flynn (btb, cbtb); Rich Perry, Scott Robinson, Tim Ries, Charles Pillow, Donny McCaslin, Andy Middleton (reeds); Frank Kimbrough (p); Ben Monder (g); Gary Versace (acc); Jay Anderson (b); Clarence Penn (d); Jeff Ballard, Gonzalo Grau (perc); Luciana Souza (v). July 2004.

Maria Schneider says: **'That recording will always be close to my heart. It was my first record that felt like one cohesive musical statement. I got exactly the sound I wanted on it (our engineer, David Baker, died shortly after it was mixed, and it was the last record found in his CD player), it was my first record on ArtistShare that was completely funded by listeners, it brought us our first Grammy.'**

After lessons from Bob Brookmeyer and a stint as assistant to Gil Evans, she had the best possible grounding in big-band jazz, and yet setting out on her own, as she did in 1989, was brave in the extreme; but a Monday night residency at Visiones in New York gave her a platform. Schneider's characteristic voice is closer to Brookmeyer's than to the more obvious Svengali, a rich fabric of sound that is alert to nuance but still capable of great power. Her use of a relatively straightforward rhythm section belies the sophistication of the metre, and often the horns are playing improbable counts over a basic 4/4. Schneider was blessed from the very start by a team of time-served craftsmen with enough musical individuality to temper the slightly too accurate placing of the charts.

Concert In The Garden is the great achievement of her career so far, a flowing, sometimes enigmatic, more often uplifting set that finally brings together all of Schneider's strengths. A Grammy win helped put the seal on things. The closing 'Buleria, Sole Y Rumba' is the most obvious acknowledgement of all she learned from Gil Evans, but the 'Three Romances' which make up the middle of the record, with wonderful wordless vocalizing from Luciana Souza, are remarkable too. The only slight disappointment is the long opening title-track, which meanders, though Monder, Kimbrough and Versace trace a lovely path through it. Jensen's 'Pas De Deux' with Pillow is another highlight, while McCaslin (who got a Grammy nomination, too) and Gisbert star on that amazing final track. A contemporary master-piece.

ROSCOE MITCHELL &
Born 3 August 1940, Chicago, Illinois
Reeds

Composition/Improvisation Nos. 1, 2 & 3
ECM 1716989
Mitchell; Corey Wilkes (t, flhn); Evan Parker (ss, ts); Anders Svanoe (as, bs); John Rangecroft (cl); Neil Metcalfe (f); Craig Taborn (p); Philipp Wachsmann (vn); Nils Bultmann (vla); Marcio Mattos (clo); Barry Guy, Jaribu Shahid (b); Paul Lytton, Tani Tabbal (d, perc). September 2004.

Evan Parker says: 'We played together for the first time in Chicago, at a club called The Hot House – it was summer and the landlord had switched the air conditioning off in a battle with Marguerite Horberg, the tenant and owner of the club, so it was *hot*. We decided to try to work together after that, but it took the Transatlantic Art Ensemble project in Munich to galvanize things. The connection between London and Chicago is strong.'

In the autumn of 2004, Mitchell and Evan Parker came together in a Munich concert hall to record a grouping that involves members both of the Englishman's ensemble and of the Note Factory, as well as others, under the ad hoc title The Transatlantic Art Ensemble. The immediate feel is very much of a classical group, with strings, tymps and piano generating a sound-world reminiscent of European art music. Indeed, there is little obviously impro-vised about the longish opening track. Mitchell plays soprano saxophone throughout, while Parker also deploys his tenor, but what defines this music most clearly as the American's is not the sound of his horn *per se*, but something about the way the music organizes itself, periods of intense activity bracketed by silence, duos (beginning with Lytton and Tabbal in the second section) breaking out of the ensemble.

The sequence of 'movements', nine in all, and the title reference to three parts don't quite seem to square unless one checks the sleeve frequently, but that is why the title is not given as *Composition & Improvisation* (as if a set of themes and variations) but with a slash that more or less suspends any fundamental distinction between the two. As with much of Mitchell's work, the delivery is mostly rather quiet and unemphatic, with a tendency to dwell not just on exact pitchings but also on the precise tone-colour of particular sounds. Taborn's role is fascinating. At moments, he seems to be articulating some approximate tonal centre for the music, some gravitational point of reference that never quite manages to resist the centrifugal energy of the strings and horns; at others, he is the archetypal pia-nist-as-percussionist, banging out sharp attacks that are more reminiscent of Cecil Taylor's famous '88 tuned drums' definition than most of the work lazily and misleadingly attrib-uted to Taylor's influence. The long 'Movement III' moves into something like 'free jazz', but while there is considerable exhilaration in the playing, this is arguably the least typical and least successful aspect of the performance. After some more short sequences, there are two extended movements – 'VII/VIII' – in which the integration of elements seems more complete though not subject to any discernible logic or determination. The coda is deliciously ambiguous. Far from reaching a climax, the sequence dissolves into a shimmer, as if some tiny subset of the whole cosmological process has gone into reverse, solids turning to gas, orbits no longer regular or fixed, location and velocity uncertain. Nothing in the canon of 20th-century Western art music conveys so much satisfying mystery.

& See also **Sound** (1966; p. 337); **ART ENSEMBLE OF CHICAGO, A Jackson In Your House / A Message For Our Folks** (1969; p. 369)

MARTY EHRLICH
Born 31 March 1955, St Paul, Minnesota
Reeds

News On The Rail
Palmetto 2113
Ehrlich; James Zollar (t); Howard Johnson (tba); James Weidman (mca); Greg Cohen (b); Allison Miller (d).
November 2004.

Marty Ehrlich says: **'The title comes from a phrase Jerome Harris heard in North Carolina. "I'm wondering what's waiting on the rail for the lizard." Howard Johnson thought the emphasis should be on the second syllable of "lizard". Every player on this recording has their own vernacular dialect, with rich blues roots. A lot of flavours to write for, luxuriate in, and give context to.'**

Ehrlich studied with Ran Blake and others at the New England Conservatory and after establishing himself in New York at the end of the '70s became an indispensable figure on the scene there, his multi-instrumentalism a huge asset to any group. He'd begun his professional career with Human Arts Ensemble before starting to develop a line of work of his own that seems to us to pick up where Eric Dolphy laid off.

Some of Ehrlich's previous records were marred by inconsequential writing. An earlier Palmetto session, *Line On Love*, fails on this account. What's immediately striking right from the opening of *News On The Rail* is how confidently this sextet crackles along on the vivid charts for 'Enough Is Enough'. A relatively unusual instrumentation comes into its own on 'Hear You Say', with the redoubtable Johnson setting down a righteous groove for Ehrlich's stunning alto solo. Elsewhere the leader favours his clarinet, interweaving with more unique ensemble effects; melodica's not often strongly featured in jazz, but it has its place and Weidman makes the strongest possible case for it. Miller keeps everything tight but not regimented and Cohen, who plays a sweeping intro to the title-track, is in excellent supportive form.

BERNARDO SASSETTI
Born 24 June 1970, Lisbon, Portugal
Piano, percussion

Unreal: Sidewalk Cartoon
Clean Feed CF070
Sassetti; Sérgio Carolino (tba); Perico Sambeat (ss, as, f, fluteophone); José Lopes, José Massarão (as); Mário Marques (ts); Alberto Roque (bs); Rui Rosa (cl, bcl); Nuno Inácio (f); Angelina Rodrigues (f, picc); Jean-Michel Garetti (ob); António Augusto Aguiar (b); José Salgueiro (d); Miquel Bernat, Nuno Aroso, Pedro Oliveira, Rui Rodrigues, Francesco Aparisi, António Sérgio, João Cunha, João Tiago (perc). December 2005–October 2006.

Bernardo Sassetti says: '**I've met a lot of people in my life and a lot of musical instruments, but I never thought there were so many until I first went into Drumming's percussion room. It changed my life. It was almost shocking to see hundreds of small instruments, dozens of huge ones. It was then I decided to go ahead with** *Unreal: Sidewalk Cartoon*.'

Sassetti spent some time in London in the '90s and became familar to British audiences from his work in the Guy Barker group. You may have seen him as a member of the Napoli Jazz Sextet in the Anthony Minghella movie *The Talented Mr Ripley*. He's now back in Lisbon and thriving in the burgeoning live and recording situation there.

An early recording is out of circulation but Sassetti has found a niche with Clean Feed and his previous records, *Nocturno* (an astonishingly mature self-assessment) and *Indigo*, should be checked out for a glimpse of his elegant pianism and compositional vision. A hugely ambitious project that unites Sassetti's jazz-based work with his cinematic projects. It's a collaboration with percussion ensemble Drumming (GP), and on some tracks the Quarteto Saxofinia and Cromeleque Quinteto; the basic group is a fine but unorthodox sextet comprising reeds, flute, tuba, double bass and drums. Sassetti himself works at the keyboard and inside his Kawai concert grand and also plays marimba, glockenspiel, steel drums and gongs. The sound is rich, delicate, flowing and constantly inflected in new ways, all laid over a pattering, softly ringing accompaniment.

If jazz is largely concerned with line, trajectory and movement, this is much more like that contemporary cliché, an 'immersive' experience. Nothing clichéd about Sassetti's approach, though, and in the final analysis it is still essentially a jazz record. Sambeat's exquisite line on 'Conjuntivo Plural Do Iniciativo', which follows the abstract prologue, is reminiscent of some of Carlos Ward's spacious, folk-tinged solos. There's even a reading of Monk's 'Evidence', a stop/start interpretation that opens up the original metre and finds acres of new territory to explore. The closing 'Sidewalk Cartoons', which is listed separately to the main course of tracks and begins with what sounds like studio chatter, is almost a new-music piece, and testimony to the precision and careful integration of the ensemble. It's possible to fake an entry on a woodwind instrument, sliding in behind the beat, but quite impossible on percussion – either it's there or it's not.

The pianist's own finest moment comes on the lyrical 'I Left My Heart In Algandros De Baixo', a graceful ballad. Quite the finest work from Sassetti to date, this is music beyond category and, for us, pretty much beyond criticism. The pianist is also responsible for the booklet artwork, a mysterious collage which reflects the aesthetic of the music perfectly. A moving, involving experience.

JOHN BUTCHER
Born 25 October 1954, Brighton, East Sussex, UK
Soprano and tenor saxophones

The Geometry Of Sentiment
Emanem 4142
Butcher (ss, ts, feedback solo). November 2004, May, September, October & November 2006.

John Butcher says: '**Live situations can stimulate playing intentions as varied as thinking about Derek Bailey, making sense of multiple reverberations and taming feedback into song. The CD is a virtual solo concert from different mental and geographical states.**'

Often hailed as a successor to Evan Parker, Butcher has moved on a parallel path, exploring solo saxophone improvisation, joining a latter-day configuration of the Spontaneous Music Ensemble, and diversifying into electronic manipulations. He is, however, a distinct and highly independent musical thinker who began his career as a theoretical physicist, researching quarks and their mysterious property of 'charm'. His first forays into music were with pianist Chris Burn's group and playing Stockhausen's 'intuitive' scores. Since then, he has worked in a wide variety of contexts, extending contemporary saxophone language in free music, scored composition and electronic context, but with a growing interest in the properties of feedback and site-specific resonances.

Now a prolific recording artist, under his own name and with ensembles as various as Polwechsel and the London Improvisers Orchestra, Butcher first came to wider notice with the 1991 solo record *Thirteen Friendly Numbers*. One of the most remarkable developments of his music since that time has been his ability to blur the distinction between 'acoustic' and electronic sounds, and those produced in conjunction with the playing environment. The first two and the last of these quite extraordinary performances were made respectively in the Ova Stone Museum at Utsunonimaya in Japan, and in a rebuilt gasometer at Oberhausen, Germany. The latter deal with elements of delay and decay in a way that other instrumentalists have also examined, but the Japanese recordings make use of the location's strange, square-cut space in a quite unique fashion, yielding a sound radically divorced from any conventional – or 'extended' – saxophone language. On 'A Short Time To Sing', the use of amplification/feedback yields a curious percussive effect. The other piece which uses this approach is 'Soft Logic', from the same London performance. Perhaps the most straightforward saxophonic playing on the set comes on 'But More So', recorded in Paris in November 2006 in tribute to Derek Bailey.

DAVID HAZELTINE
Born 27 October 1958, Milwaukee, Wisconsin
Piano

Modern Standards
Sharp Nine 1032-2
Hazeltine; David Williams (b); Joe Farnsworth (d). December 2004.

David Hazeltine says: **'I was worried how some of the tunes/arrangements such as "How Deep Is Your Love" would actually work and then go over with jazz fans. I remember listening to it months later and thinking: "Mission accomplished", mostly because of how David and Joe brought things to life!'**

Hazeltine's list of influences includes Oscar Peterson, Barry Harris, Buddy Montgomery, Cedar Walton. He's a communicator in the Peterson manner, voicing melodies in a recognizable yet inventive way, adding just enough rhythmic nuance to take an interpretation out of the ordinary and placing absolute trust in his musicians, and he himself always works for the band. Though he says he prefers to work with more modern material ('Betcha By Golly Wow' is on the debut Criss Cross), he still does very well out of more familiar standards when the need arises, an unerring sense of tempo helping to swing the melodies and set the pace for constructions that are intricate without seeming fussy or deliberately complex.

There's an easeful consistency to Hazeltine's music that might threaten to consign it to the background if he weren't shrewd enough to keep the material fresh. The move away from Criss Cross – though Teekens had done him proud – was positive and well-timed. *Modern Standards* is, if anything, better even than the earlier *Classic Trio*, and merits every enthusiasm. Impeccably produced by Marc Edelman, the trio gets a full, rounded sound which maximizes its virtues. The tunes are familiar but not hackneyed, and Hazeltine bites the bullet on pop material: 'Yesterday', 'How Deep Is Your Love' and 'For The Love Of You' are all shaped with logic and finesse.

KAHIL EL'ZABAR

Born Clifton Blackburn, 11 November 1953, Chicago, Illinois
Drums, percussion, other instruments

Live At River East Art Center

Delmark DE566 CD/DVD
El'Zabar; Ari Brown (ts); Billy Bang (vn); Yosef Ben Israel (b). December 2004.

Kahil El'Zabar says: **'A very emotional recording for me: the music acknowledges the spirit of my friend and mentor Malachi Favors, who taught me the importance of perseverance. I believe Malachi would have been proud of us, for the music represents something he was fond of repeating: "Ancient to the Future, a Power stronger than itself." I felt very much in the moment and very much alive. The spirit expressed in our Oneness amplifies the baptismal ritual in living for the arts!'**

A leading light among the spirits who emerged from AACM, the Chicagoan's small groups, the Ethnic Heritage Ensemble and the Ritual Trio, seek big-scale results in terms of creating new African-American fusions. He once designed dresses for Nina Simone, played with rock groups and has more recently done the musical arrangements for the stage version of *The Lion King*. Above all, he upholds the communitarian values that framed and sustained AACM.

Somewhat like the Art Ensemble Of Chicago, El'Zabar's groups are almost always best experienced live, something that Delmark's DVD imprints are making possible. However, none of his records are anything less than exciting and intensely colourful, with a smack of spiritual uplift. Earlier records like *Renaissance Of The Resistance* and *Big Cliff* had involved Favors and Bang, and after the bassist's death Bang rejoined for this tribute. There is, incidentally, a second tribute disc on Delmark, called *Big M*, but we find it strangely lacklustre.

The River East recording begins with a long, long El'Zabar intro on 'Big M', brilliant on kalimba, with Brown and Bang only coming in well through the track. The sound isn't pristine, but the sense of occasion is palpable. The man with the hardest job on the night, new bassist Israel, has an opportunity to stake his claim at the start of 'Return Of The Lost Tribe', a deceptively easy-going jazz piece originally on the *Bright Moments* CD with Joseph Jarman and Kalaparush Maurice McIntyre, pushed along by El'Zabar's solid kit-playing. 'Where Do You Want To Go?' has a curious mixture of poignancy and anger, also reflected in Kahil's vocal contributions. He testifies exuberantly on 'Be Exciting', a memorial testimony to Favors but also a jeremiad on the post-9/11 world. El'Zabar always holds the centre, with Israel as his anchor, but it's Bang and the outrageously underrated Brown who make this fine record. The crowd buzz merely adds to the party atmosphere and we're not persuaded you really need the DVD to catch the mood of the event.

STEVE LEHMAN

Born 1 September 1978, New York City
Alto and sopranino saxophones

Demian As Posthuman

Pi 17
Lehman; Vijay Iyer (p); Me'shell Ndegeocello (b); Eric McPherson, Tyshawn Sorey (d); Jahi Lake (turntables). March & June 2005.

Steve Lehman says: **'I had Craig Taborn's *Junk Magic* and Braxton's *Fall 1974* knocking around my subconscious. I remember being able to write dense and challenging pieces** like "Demian" knowing that they would be executed with precision by a combination of sequenced instruments and Tyshawn's remarkable drumming. It was good to sneak in a chamber work for saxophone quartet, percussionist and live electronics, and to present compositions from multiple vantages (Cognition, Damage Mobility, Logic).'

A pupil of both Jackie McLean and Anthony Braxton, the impressive New Yorker works in an advanced post-bop vein. He first came to notice in Braxton's ensemble, but has made rapid progress on his own account and as a member of Fieldwork.

Lehman's breakthrough record was *Interface* in 2003, a spare, exposed trio with bassist Mark Dresser and percussionist Pheeroan akLaff (also a teacher at Wesleyan, where Lehman studied). As the sole horn, he sometimes over-elaborates ideas, notably on the long 'Motion', but a new emphasis on sopranino saxophone sets some stern harmonic hurdles which he clears without seeming effort and with some aplomb. The writing is hugely impressive.

Demian As Posthuman (the name is a Hesse reference) took him on a somewhat different course. Basically a set of duets with the brilliant Sorey, some pieces are reworked with almost a hip-hop sensibility. There was to have been a hip-hop track on the disc but copyright problems meant it was withdrawn. Lehman treats ideas like 'Damage Mobility' in a neo-Cubist way, using multiple saxophone perspectives and tough harmonizations in the overdubbing. Some tracks are played over strong bass vamps from Ndegeocello, but the drama always returns to Lehman's work with the drummer. Everything he has done since confirms his standing as a star of some magnitude. This one, though, stands out strongly.

MARTIAL SOLAL &

Born 23 August 1927, Algiers, Algeria
Piano

Solitude
CamJazz 7794-2
Solal (p solo). April 2005.

Trumpeter Dave Douglas says: '**He has a unique writing style, with very long lines and very intricate in rhythm, to an extent that you can't believe it was written down like that, but it was. He has the ability to make very complex things swing, in a way that is quite unique.**'

Solal has just got better, steadily developing his compositional approach in ever more subtle ways. A duo album with Dave Douglas made around the same time as *Solitude* and for the same label is testimony to his continuing interest in new directions in jazz. But this CamJazz record is a near-perfect solo piano recital that combines favourite standards with a central section of originals. 'Darn That Dream' is broodingly romantic, but the romanticism is grounded in complex harmonic development and a deceptively loose metre that gradually pulls together towards the end. The alternate that bookends the record doesn't have quite the same architecture, but it's bolder still in terms of repositioning the original song and chords.

Any sense that this is an old man – he was nearly 80 – musing quietly on well-trodden themes and declining to exert himself is quickly dispelled by the next three tracks. 'Caravan' is breathtaking, spilled out with dash and a kind of dangerous glamour. The fulcrum of 'Our Love Is Here To Stay' is a descending chordal pattern that is all the more dramatic for being so utterly right in context. Then, cleverly, he programmes three originals. 'Chi Va Piano ...' is all angles and determined purpose. 'Medium' might almost be Monk in places, but with hammered chords and sharp left-hand chimes that could be boxing bells. And then 'Bluesine', which remains perhaps the one Solal composition that everyone knows. On that score, he'd be entitled to indulge himself a little, but he takes the pace right down and lets it merely ... happen, brisk triplets, tightly pedalled chords and low, low bottom-end accents. You realize that much as he loves trio playing he can do bass and drums parts pretty much on his own. Superb.

& See also **Balade Du 10 Mars** (1998; p. 625)

PETER EVANS
Born 1981, New York City
Trumpet

More Is More
psi 06.08
Evans (t, picc t solo). 2005.

More Is More appeared on saxophonist Evan Parker's label: **'I asked Peter what was the longest period he'd taken off from practice since he started at the age of seven, and he told me: "Five days."'**

A new star. Evans studied at Oberlin and has since turned up in some of the most exciting projects around, including the warped (non-)repertory group Mostly Other People Do The Killing, Histrionics, Carnival, and the Sparks duo with Tom Blancarte, who also plays in Evans's quartet. However, he first made a wider impact in that most difficult of all forms, a solo trumpet recital.

More Is More is jaw-droppingly good, a calmly studied deconstruction of jazz trumpet that makes for one of the most exciting records of recent years and one that at a stroke proposes new directions for the instrument. It is not so much that Evans dives deep into 'extended technique', more that he harnesses the instrument's untapped potential for ideas and procedures that immediately affect how a 'lead horn' might sound in a group situation. Evans made those implications clear in his first quartet record a year or so later, where the usual hierarchies of horn and rhythm and the familiar parameters of melody, harmonic architecture, pulse are not so much subverted as cheerfully circumvented: a brand-new jazz sound, equalled for freshness and invention only by someone like guitarist Mary Halvorson.

Though it is far more than a set of exercises, the technique on *More Is More* is extraordinary, whether on piccolo trumpet (his apparent preference) or a concert instrument: notes are bent, stretched, pulled through timbral spectra and sometimes stabbed into the air with an almost physical intensity. It might not grab someone whose expectations are based on Lee Morgan or Miles Davis, but consider how close to the early jazz masters he sometimes sounds. This is music in a powerful lineage, not on a blank page.

INGRID JENSEN
Born 12 January 1966, North Vancouver, British Columbia, Canada
Trumpet, flugelhorn

At Sea
ArtistShare AS0039
Jensen; Geoff Keezer (p, ky); Lage Lund (g); Matt Clohesy (b); Jon Wikan (d, perc); Hugo Alcazar (perc). April 2005.

Ingrid Jensen says: **'A magical and mystical adventure into many of my past and present life influences. Through the music we made, I still hear and feel things that I never thought I could translate into sound: the ocean I grew up near, the open trail that I spend hundred of hours horseback riding on, all of the many powerful voices of song and groove I've heard and responded to – we just channelled it all.'**

At 25, Jensen became the youngest faculty member at the Bruckner Conservatory in Linz. Early recognition came in Europe partly because she had chosen to study there, initially with Austrian pianist Hal Galper. In terms of trumpet sound, she is a cross between Woody Shaw (an acknowledged hero) and Art Farmer, with whom she also took classes; the latter debt is predictably most evident when she switches to flugelhorn, a warm, ringing sound but with a solid-metal core.

Jensen's early recordings on Enja were consistently impressive, and *Here On Earth* in particular is worth tracking down. However, her work matured rapidly during the early years of the new decade, not so much in terms of playing skill as in maturity of conception. *At Sea*, released on the estimable, fan-supported ArtistShare, is an altogether more impressionistic record than its predecessors, but in the most positive sense. The opening is a moody soundscape with the trumpet heavily reverbed over piano, keys and cymbals. Keezer's 'Captain Jon' and 'Tea And Watercolours' are driven along more familiar grooves. 'There Is No Greater Love' has a mournful, elegiac quality. Then the tracks become longer and more exploratory, with 'Everything I Love' coming in over nine minutes, the original 'Swotterings' and 'KD Lang' (with wah-wah Rhodes from Keezer (!) and Ingrid double-tracked) at ten and 12 respectively. It's a powerful final section.

Jon Wikan's production and Eric Troyer's deft engineering lend the trumpet immense presence, accurately pitched but with delightful little burrs of overtone round the edges. A simply beautiful record.

LOUIS SCLAVIS &

Born 2 February 1953, Lyons, France
Clarinet, bass clarinet, soprano saxophone

L'Imparfait Des Langues
ECM 1954
Sclavis; Marc Baron (as); Paul Brousseau (ky, g); Maxime Delpierre (g); François Merville (d). April 2005.

Louis Sclavis said (2004): **'Words and language come to me and then recede. I write things down in a notebook and then lose the notebook, but by being lost the words acquire some importance in the music that follows, I think.'**

Having set out his vision of an 'imaginary folklore' in music in the '80s, Sclavis in the next decade established a core ensemble of players around violinist Dominique Pifarély, bassist Bruno Chevillon and drummer François Merville, though not a regular group, and signed up with the ECM label to produce a string of highly original and successful albums that were like nothing else of the time. *Les Violences De Rameau*, *Napoli's Walls* and *L'Affrontement Des Prétendants* are all marvellous records, but in 2005 and with a new group, Sclavis created something exceptional.

Enjoying a new-found openness in his approach, Sclavis decided to take on a new commission from the Spring Arts Festival in Monte Carlo with an almost entirely new band. Merville is the only one here who has served much time with Sclavis. Baron is a ferociously talented 23-year-old, while Delpierre has a buzz-saw guitar style very different to anything else in the previous Sclavis canon. It would have seemed perverse to give a group convened in this way very formal charts, so Sclavis set about writing basic themes and ideas that would challenge his improvisational imagination in new ways. Ironically, the death of Prince Rainier led to the cancellation of the Monaco festival, so Sclavis took his group and new charts into the studio instead. It's a powerful, very spontaneous performance, some of it deliberately sketchy, but featuring some fascinating ideas that might be blues, might be folk tunes, might also be classical tone rows, all transformed by a mint-fresh ensemble. Many of the tracks are quite short and some have noted a resemblance – perfectly convincing – to early Soft Machine in the rhythms and song-like forms. It's a near-perfect record, whatever its provenance, and testimony to Sclavis's importance to jazz composition in the new decade. 'Le Verbe' is a classic.

& See also **Clarinettes** (1984, 1985; p. 489)

STEFANO BATTAGLIA
Born 1965, Milan, Italy
Piano

Re: Pasolini
ECM 1998-99 2CD
Battaglia; Michael Gassman (t); Mirco Mariottini (cl); Dominique Pifarély (vn); Vincent Courtois, Aya Shimura (clo); Bruno Chevillon, Salvatore Maiore (b); Roberto Dani, Michele Rabbia (d). April–July 2005.

Stefano Battaglia says: **'Pasolini was the complete artist, because he brought opposites together and united them without losing their separate character: the sacred and profane, different art forms, images and words, academic culture and popular culture. He is the model for this music, not just its dedication.'**

Classically trained, and also active in that realm, Battaglia moves between free and post-bop structures with a rare elegance. His joining the ECM label put a deeper focus on his music. *The Book Of Jazz* was an encyclopedic survey of the major composers, neither deconstructions, nor reinventions, but rather interpretations of such elegant understanding that they seem to reposition the originals and remove all the spurious authority of authorship.

Which brings us neatly round to Pasolini, whose sense of personal identity always hovered on the edge of extinction. Pasolini's terrible murder remains an unanswered question in Italian culture, largely in that it snuffed out a writer, film-maker, political activist, poet and thinker who seemed to embody much of the Italianness of contemporary Italian culture in its most contradictory forms. Over two discs, Battaglia tries to give the life and work some kind of musical correlative. He opens with a wonderful song dedicated to Pasolini's muse, Laura Betti, continues with evocations of the Italian countryside as viewed through the prism of Pasolini's verse, and using a sextet with strongly canonical connotations establishes a dialogue between the formal and improvised, (neo-)classical and romantic elements of Pasolini's art.

The second disc, featuring players most closely associated with Louis Sclavis (Pifarély, again), has a more agitated and improvisational quality, culminating in the bleak sonics of 'Ostia', where Pasolini was gruesomely murdered on the beach. Following that, there is only a brief musical headstone and then silence. A demanding listen over two long discs, but absolutely essential modern music; whether all of it jazz or not hardly seems the issue.

ROBERT GLASPER
Born 1978, Houston, Texas
Piano

Canvas

Blue Note 77130
Glasper; Mark Turner (ts); Vincente Archer (b); Damion Reid (d); Bilal (v). May 2005.

Robert Glasper says: '**I did my first record for Fresh Sound, and basically the feeling was "It's Fresh Sound; no one's going to hear that." I treated it as a gig. You can't do that on Blue Note, so that record was very much about the compositions, and thinking about them.**'

It's encouraging to find Blue Note still signing artists like Robert Glasper. *Canvas* is a fine record, basically an orthodox, but by no means dull, piano trio with some guest spots, and it sounds very much as if he's conceived it as a white space on which to inscribe some of his strongest thoughts. His mother was the distinguished gospel and blues singer Kim Yvette Glasper, and Glasper studied at the High School for the Performing Arts in his home town, so there's a lot of heredity and training pushing from behind.

On the Blue Note debut, he has a close, at moments almost uncanny, understanding with Archer and Reid that allows the group to move efficiently, sometimes startlingly, as on the well-named 'Rise And Shine', but above all as a unit. Archer often takes a strong initiative and pulls the line away from the piano; Reed responds in kind, giving the whole a centrifugal – or just plain fugal – character that is highly appealing. The title-track has a rich palette as well but the surprises come later, in the tiny 'Centelude' and on 'Chant', where Bilal's wordless vocalizing serves as a horn part. Turner also thickens up the mix, but while the variety is welcome, there's nothing wrong with what Glasper and his two stalwarts are doing. The only non-original is Herbie Hancock's 'Riot'.

MARIO PAVONE

Born 11 November 1940, Waterbury, Connecticut
Double bass

Deez To Blues

Playscape 050505
Pavone; Steven Bernstein (t, slide t); Howard Johnson (tba, bcl, bs); Peter Madsen (p); Charles Burnham (vn); Michael Sarin (d). May 2005.

Mario Pavone remembers: '**It was recorded on the Mexican celebration of "Cinquo de Mayo" and early in George W. Bush's disastrous second term. Bernstein and Burnham cracked us up all day with jokes, quips and asides, where to order the upside-down cakes, a reference to my description of the compositional intent. Later, the humour and the vibrant colours of the music knocked me out.**'

It was going to John Coltrane's funeral that persuaded Pavone to make music his career. He had trained as an engineer and taken contrabass lessons with Bertram Turetzky, and was already gigging quite extensively when he had his epiphany. Pavone has a big, ringing sound and a seemingly bottomless supply of ideas. A regular in the late Thomas Chapin's trio (he recorded a moving tribute after the saxophonist's early death), he has also worked with Bill Dixon, Anthony Braxton and Paul Bley. One distinctive feature of his own albums has been the prominence given to trombone or other low brass. Unlike so many of the dashed-off themes that pass for contemporary jazz 'compositions', Pavone's are built from the ground up, with solid foundations and durable architecture. The engineering background hasn't been thrown away.

Even after a dozen fine records, he still wouldn't have been on many non-New Yorkers' list of most important contemporary composer-leaders, but it's hard to think who else has delivered so much consistently high-quality new jazz since the turn of the decade. This is his masterpiece to date, not so much a return to the 'old' sound of the septet *Song For* or the fiercely engaged *Sharpeville* but an affirmation of its continuing potential. The richness of the voicings on 'Xapo' and 'Zines' is immediately intoxicating, though it takes a couple of hearings to pick up on Pavone's compositional subtleties. It's an exquisitely voiced ensemble, with trumpet, Johnson's horns and violin all given distinct roles, but combining with the bass to produce a thick, rich ensemble stew. Through it all, Pavone throbs, sings, keeps time, marches and dances. An essential contemporary record.

MARK FELDMAN
Born 17 July 1955, Chicago, Illinois
Violin

What Exit
ECM 9876537
Feldman; John Taylor (p); Anders Jormin (b); Tom Rainey (d). June 2005.

Mark Feldman says: **'*What Exit* was my first "jazz" recording leading my own group, playing my own music. I was 50 years old when I recorded it. In the next 25 years or so I have decided to procrastinate less and be more ambitious.'**

Feldman might seem like a late starter in jazz terms. He certainly wasn't a late starter as a musician, already playing bars as a teenager, having picked up the violin in childhood. He moved to Nashville and worked on scores of country sessions there before removing to New York, where he became a significant downtowner. He was a member of the Arcado string trio, the only significant rival to the String Trio Of New York.

As he implies, there's precious little under his own name, and certainly nothing that sat easily in a 'jazz' bag. *Music For Violin Alone* was a solo set for John Zorn's Tzadik in 1994, a programme with a strong new-music tinge. There was also a 1997 record called *Chromatic Persuaders*, which featured a superb interpretation of Scott LaFaro's 'Gloria's Step', but Feldman, who's since recorded brilliant work in a jazz context with guitarist Michael Musillami and others, doesn't seem to regard this as a jazz date, or his date, or worth mentioning; it did initially appear on a very small label.

What Exit was worth the wait. Feldman doesn't so much bathe in the wonderful sound Manfred Eicher and engineer James Farber lay out for him as rise to the challenge of it. Feldman's violin has become a compelling improvisational voice and the huge opening 'Arcade' is a virtuoso exploration of musical space. Nothing else on the record quite matches up to it, either in scale or in beauty, though the small title-piece is the perfect finish and the double-stopped dirge of 'Elegy' is pretty unforgettable. Taylor sounds more unguarded than usual and Jormin and Rainey find a real empathy, with the drummer particularly responsive to his leader's moves.

RAN BLAKE *&*
Born 20 April 1935, Springfield, Massachusetts
Piano

All That Is Tied
Tompkins Square TSO1965
Blake (p solo). 2005.

Ran Blake said (2005): **'Am I in the film or am I directing the film? All I know is that when I'm at the piano and improvising, what I'm really doing is storyboarding, and doing it in real time. I don't write film music because I don't write well, but I can turn down the light and let the images flicker.'**

Blake was 70 when this was made. He had released some 35 albums, but this was his first proper solo disc for some time. It is a quiet masterpiece, marked by the same almost mystical approach to harmony and melody that has marked recent projects. It is wrong to call Blake an eclectic. He assimilates his influences and passions too thoroughly for that. The opening track here, actually written by producer Jonah Kraut, opens quietly, almost musingly, before breaking off a huge, complex discord. Like the remainder of the album, the track remains quiet, contemplative and patient, gradually working through the ramifications of Blake's astonishing grasp of harmony. 'Thursday' seems to quote 'Lover Man' towards the end, leaving the listener with the thought that perhaps the whole thing had been a meditation on those changes from the start; probably not, but Blake's mind works in widening circles of association. 'Impresario Of Death' is magnificently moody and intense, but with a Messiaen-like delicacy. The only moment where the pace picks up significantly is on 'Church Of Latter Rain Christian Fellowship', whose gospelly roll is deeply infectious. A magnificent record from an American master.

& *See also* **The Short Life Of Barbara Monk** (1986; p. 504)

MATTHEW SHIPP
Born 7 December 1960, Wilmington, Delaware
Piano, keyboards

One
Thirsty Ear THE 57166
Shipp (p solo). August 2005.

Matthew Shipp says: **'This was a return to recording acoustic jazz after my electro improv CDs. It was cool to rediscover the joy of acoustic jazz. The session had a freshness for that reason. The only problem I remember is before the session the piano tuner sat playing a bunch of Chick Corea tunes as if trying to impress me with it and it took a little time in the session to get those out of my head.'**

A musician whose sense of adventure is impressively balanced by a steady thoughtfulness, Shipp didn't begin recording until the '90s, after periods of study at Berklee and the New England Conservatory. There is probably no more intelligent and well-versed player on the contemporary scene. He was a member of David S. Ware's group but began appearing in challenging contexts with a wide range of others, including William Parker, whom he met after coming to New York in the mid-'80s. In recent years, Shipp has been curator of the Thirsty Ear label's highly eclectic Blues Series, which reflects his own explorations beyond post-bop jazz.

He acknowledged this most explicitly on *Nu Bop*, one of a number of fine records made for Thirsty Ear since the turn of the decade. It was a record which combined solo piano with group material and electronic processing. There is no implication that either Shipp or his admirers considered this line of enquiry to be exhausted, but there was a stir of excitement when in 2005 he returned to solo piano recording (a 2002 disc was released in Italy). However senior he might now be, Shipp isn't above revisiting his influences and on this extraordinary solo set, his first since *Songs*, he delves into the worlds of Cecil Taylor, Bud Powell and Thelonious Monk, but without ever once referencing any of these ancestral presences directly. It is as if the terms of the cult forbid those great names from being spoken. In keeping with his instinct for form, these relatively short pieces all seem to have an internal logic and structure, palpable but resistant to analysis. 'Arc' works slowly and by increment, each chord taking on new harmonic colours with each return. 'Patmos' is a delirious, almost evangelical thing, an agglutination of single-line testimonies that leads towards a moment of revelation. The longer cuts, 'The Encounter', 'Gamma Ray' and 'Module', are the most successful, and the middle one of the group has a flayed excitement that both invites and dismisses comparison with Cecil Taylor. A major contemporary presence, Shipp is one of the select group of current players and composers one would have to tag 'essential'.

RALPH TOWNER &

Born 1 March 1940, Chehalis, Washington
Guitar, piano

Time Line
ECM 987 5911
Towner (g solo). September 2005.

Ralph Towner said (1999): **'Don't ask me too many questions about the music. I just write it. It's intuitive, and I get completely lost in the process, much as I do in playing, but probably more so. But don't ask me to articulate about it.'**

'Only tenuously connected with jazz', it says in *Grove*, so what's he doing here? For our money, there has never been any question about Towner's importance as a contemporary improviser. He was, admittedly, a gift to the ECM label or to what has sometimes been parodied as 'the ECM sound' – cool, acoustic, European, very spacious and classical in intent. On the 1972 *Trios/Solos* he marshalled three quarters of Oregon for a lovely record of unaccompanied and group pieces, including Bill Evans's 'Re: Person I Knew'; he once told Joachim Berendt that his aim was to play his guitar 'pianistically' as if it was a piano trio, like Evans's. His ability to work simultaneous lines, sustain rich harmonics and drones (especially on the 12-string), and even get a percussive counterpoint out of the snap of the strings and the thud of the sound-box is what makes his solo playing so rich and multi-dimensional.

Diary (1973) was a genuine solo performance that found him trying to cut a trail between the two great 'twelves' of modern music: the blues and Viennese dodecaphony, which he studied in Europe in 1963 and 1967; the addition of 12-string guitar gives the mix an almost mystical quality. *Diary* is for some fans *the* Ralph Towner record. But it palls somewhat when set alongside the stunning solo records of more recent years. *Time Line* is a supremely professional record, mostly done in miniatures which couldn't be improved by so much as a note. An opening sequence of brief songs and sketches has the exact trajectory and weight of an old LP side, a definite chapter-end. Titles like 'Oleander Etude' may curl the toes, but it's a far more substantial thing as played than it looks on paper. Similarly the 'Five Glimpses', only the first of which breaks a minute, and even then only 61 seconds. These are almost sublimely good and the koto-like final one is the most unexpected thing Towner has ever put on a record.

After that the album changes direction again. 'The Lizards Of Eraclea' is something of a technical exercise, but this final section includes two standards, a still relatively unusual practice for Towner. 'Come Rain Or Come Shine' is deeply influenced by Bill Evans's versions. It emerges over a softly rocking rhythm and subtle harmonics, both greatly enhanced by the acoustic at Propstei St Gerold, now a favourite ECM location. The real clincher, though, is 'My Man's Gone Now', which is soaked in the blues but surrounded by chords of orchestral richness that bears comparison with Miles Davis's and Gil Evans's *Porgy & Bess*.

& *See also* **OREGON, Music Of Another Present Era** (1973; p. 405)

QUEST&
Formed 1981
Group

Redemption: Quest Live In Europe
hatOLOGY 642
David Liebman (ss); Richie Beirach (p); Ron McClure (b); Billy Hart (d). November 2005.

Dave Liebman says: **'Quest was and is for me a gift because that rhythm section can literally do anything. The emotional range from awesome power to tranquillity is quite dramatic.'**

Dave Liebman and Richie Beirach share a rich vein of musical understanding that, put together, always seems to create a fresh entity, a kind of collective spirit. That is reflected in the music of Quest. Though Liebman was the driving force in organizational terms, it was a group of equals and all four members contributed compositions. There were some early changes of personnel, with original bassist George Mraz subsequently replaced by Ron McClure, a formidable stylist and composer. His presence somewhat heightens a resemblance – more than fancied, more than passing – with the classic '60s Charles Lloyd Quartet and Quest often delivers something of that rich eclecticism – part post-Coltrane modal harmony, part rock excitement – that made the Lloyd group such a powerful draw and such an influential component of modern jazz.

The early Quest records are hard to find now, but the group reconvened after a 15-year break and the live tapes were impressive enough to merit a second life on disc. We are usually sceptical about such reunions, usually undertaken at the behest of promoters and with nostalgia as a subtext. There's no hint of that here. Playing together again after so long was clearly a happy experience for all involved. Liebman's work, like Beirach's, has gone through some considerable changes. That said, surprisingly for a group invested with so many fine composers, much of the material played is from the modern repertory, opening with 'Round Midnight', a perfect vehicle for the pianist, and continuing with Coltrane's all too rarely covered 'Ogunde', a telling sign of Liebman's searching interrogation of that legacy. There is also a fine short version of Ornette's 'Lonely Woman'. Liebman's tribute to the destroyed World Trade Center, medleyed with Beirach's similarly inspired and equally powerful 'Steel Prayers', touches on some notably raw emotion, an instant standard that one hopes to hear approached by other musicians. So, too, with Hart's title-track, which rounds out a superb disc. Again, the recording quality is easily equal to a group of such subtlety, with every inflection of all the instruments precisely registered. Strongly recommended, and if you missed them first time round, Quest hasn't lost its exploratory edge.

& *See also* **DAVID LIEBMAN**, Drum Ode (1974; p. 411), **Loneliness Of A Long-Distance Runner** (1988; p. 496); **RON MCCLURE, Soft Hands** (2006; p. 712)

WAYNE HORVITZ
Born 1 September 1955, New York City
Piano, keyboards

Way Out East
Songlines 1558
Horvitz; Ron Miles (t); Sarah Schoenbeck (bsn); Peggy Lee (clo). August 2005.

Wayne Horvitz says: **'Creating this band was the culmination of something I'd been looking for my entire career. I finally felt that I had a concept, an ensemble, and the right** players and instrumentation to create a music that didn't go beyond the categories of classical versus jazz but simply avoided them altogether.'

Horvitz was one of the leading personalities of the New York downtown circle but has now based himself in Seattle. A strong, even idiosyncratic, player and composer, he roves back and forth between situationist improvisation and more generic grooves. He got off to a brisk start as a recording leader with *Some Order, Long Understood* and *Miracle Mile*, the first a trio with Butch Morris and William Parker, the latter by his savvy electro-acoustic band The President; other discs seemed to drift out of circulation rather quickly, a sure sign that an artist isn't running in commercial tram-lines. Other records followed in short order but it was only with 2005's *Way Out East* that Horvitz delivered a record – this time determinedly acoustic – that seemed to offer a generous pay-off for his efforts.

Exquisitely conceived and executed, this is by no means the 'chamber-jazz' date the instrumentation might lead you to believe. Horvitz is still in swinging form, especially when he takes to Hammond organ and when he throws elements of boogie and ragtime into the mix. The sequence that contains 'Between Here And Heaven', built around rich drone shapes, and the long 'Berlin 1914' around the middle of the album is classic contemporary music, lyrical, uncategorizable, but with a tough improvisatory edge. 'World Peace And Quiet' closes the set, and it wouldn't be surprising to find it taken up by an enterprising lyricist.

FRANÇOIS HOULE
Born 11 August 1961, Montréal, Québec, Canada
Clarinet

La Lumière De Pierres
psi 07.02
Houle; Evan Parker (ts); Benoît Delbecq (prepared p). October 2005.

François Houle says: **'It was recorded all in one take. The only editing done was to create the three separate tracks on the CD. We played for less than an hour, looked up and knew we were done! No edits, no alternate takes, no doubts about the music. Just a strong feeling of joy in playing together.'**

Based in Vancouver, Houle is a classically trained clarinet specialist who was turned on to improvised music by Evan Parker and Steve Lacy. This is, of course, a trio record and very much the work of equal partners. Houle has a highly distinctive approach, often working with the components of his clarinet to create a sound that is not just original but also remarkably self-consistent. It's unusual to hear Parker as something like a third wheel, but the relationship between Houle and Delbecq – a real empathy – is so close that there are times here when he continues musing as if to himself. It's strikingly effective, though: the idea of improvised music as a 'conversation' or 'dialogue' is so redundant as to be pernicious and should be avoided in all but a few special circumstances. Parker's role doesn't necessarily resonate with risk and danger, but his relative reticence here provides the fulcrum for the music and much of the interest of the date comes in the interaction between clarinets and (minimally) prepared piano.

STEVE DAVIS
Born 14 April 1967, Worcester, Massachusetts
Trombone

Update
Criss Cross 1282
Davis; Roy Hargrove (t); Anthony Wonsey (p); Peter Bernstein (g); Joe Farnsworth, Nat Reeves (d). December 2005.

Steve Davis says: **'When I found out Roy Hargrove was available for the date, I wrote him "Grove's Groove". Benny Golson heard _Update_ and called me one day, out of the blue. He loved that tune so much he asked me to join the New Jazztet. We recorded the tune and opened every performance with it! So I thank Roy, Peter, Anthony, Nat and Joe for swinging so hard that snowy day in 2005. They got me a gig with Benny Golson!'**

The last-ever recruit to the Jazz Messengers in 1989, he'd previously studied with Jackie McLean and now represents the purest lineage of hard bop, with a string of fine CDs on Criss Cross, the Blue Note of its day. Davis is an adept, articulate musician who doesn't overplay but is always generous with his lines and even when at his most intense always plays for the band. There's nothing revolutionary in his technique and his evolution has been so steady that there are no obvious epochal moments along the way, just the steady maturation of a strong talent. The albums are relatively conventional but full and satisfying.

In 2004, Davis made _Alone Together_ for Mapleshade, working as sole horn and showing surprisingly often how important Miles Davis – Steve actually started out as a trumpet-player – was to his conception; the Miles, that is, of the modal period rather than _On The Corner_. Something seemed to open up in the sound around this time. While not exactly a huge leap, _Update_ sounds like aspects of the technique have been subtly tweaked. Right from the off, Shorter's 'Marie Antoinette', Davis seems to be adding harmonics, embellishing the basic line, taking chances with his trajectory through the song. When he plays with Hargrove, as on Jackie McLean's 'Bird Lives', and the edgy 'Grove's Groove', there's an itchy excitement. The set includes a second Shorter line in 'Wildflower' and ends with a version of Ray Drummond's seldom-covered 'Leanin' and Preenin'' that could be off a late-'50s Prestige date.

RON MCCLURE &
Born 22 November 1941, New Haven, Connecticut
Double bass

Soft Hands
Steeplechase SCCD 31615
McClure; Rich Perry (ts); George Colligan (p). January 2006.

Ron McClure says: **'One reviewer suggested that he missed the drums, but with players the calibre of Rich and George, I don't. On _New Moon_, our 2009 Steeplechase CD, Billy Drummond joined us for a last date at Masuo's studio, with his great Steinway "B" and the sound in general was much better. _Soft Hands_ featured an "attack piano" used by rock'n'rollers, but George made it work. I hope he comes back from Manitoba, where he's teaching. Rich makes everyone smile, and Billy can make anyone sound good. I'm a happy camper!'**

A follower of Paul Chambers, whom he replaced in Wynton Kelly's group, McClure worked in big bands for a time, before joining Blood, Sweat & Tears and then Charles Lloyd's highly successful crossover jazz group. McClure himself experimented with a fusion group called Fourth Way, but since the '80s has been established as a regular mainstream leader and composer. A superb soloist, with a highly developed _arco_ sound, he is also an exceptional composer who draws on non-jazz tonalities. One of his characteristic devices is a percussive, almost marimba-like thrum achieved by striking the strings against the fingerboard.

McClure has been a fixture in the Steeplechase catalogue for two decades, since the release of *McJolt* in 1989, and the records simply get better and better. Ron marked his 65th year with a quiet masterpiece, his best record since *Closer To Your Tears* a decade earlier. These eight tunes are the work of a mature and assured composer and the drummerless format keeps the tempos open enough to allow at least some of the songs to change direction internally, as the last track, 'Marble Room', does to devastating effect. It's by some way the longest cut of the set, but the rest all seem designed to give all three members a chance to address the material at reasonable length. The title-tune and 'Gates Of Saffron' are the other two pieces in a closing stretch that must be heard.

& *See also* **QUEST, Redemption** (2005; p. 710)

DAVE BALLOU
Born 22 April 1963, Peace Dale, Rhode Island
Trumpet

Insistence
Steeplechase SCCD 31611
Ballou; Michael Formanek (b); Randy Peterson (d). January 2006.

Dave Ballou says: **'We improvised all the tracks in the order that they appear. There was no plan or discussion prior to the performance of each piece. Michael, Randy and I share an approach to improvisation that combines search for structure and sonic expression.'**

Ballou is one of those 'inside-outside' players whose versatility might almost be thought a handicap. His clear tone and deftness are a clear plus for any other leader, but he hasn't always found the right formula on his solo projects. Few jazz artists nowadays enjoy the kind of commitment from a label Ballou has had from Steeplechase, with eight records in catalogue at time of writing. The debut *Amongst Ourselves* was a bit lumpy, but repeated returns to these discs suggest not an artist struggling to find things to say on his own account, but one searching for adequate forms in which to express them. Some of the earlier records feature a piano-player – George Colligan on *The Floating World* and *Rothko*, Frank Kimbrough on *Regards* – but Ballou has stoutly refused the safety net and persisted with the tough discipline of trio playing. On *Insistence*, he pulls it off, and handsomely repays the label's investment. Ballou himself has suggested he considers the record a culmination of his time with Steeplechase.

On it, he returns to the skeletal format of *Volition* and *Dancing Foot*, but what a difference! These are confident, muscular improvisations, most of them so well-constructed as to suggest a predetermined form but one that stands up to fresh interrogation. It's hard to believe that these are spontaneous performances. 'MF' is a nicely ambiguous title: might refer to another iron-lunged trumpeter; might suggest that Dave is trying to throw off any artsy-fartsy reputation (Rothko, indeed!) and blow open and straight. The overall trumpet tone is, paradoxically, more hooded and insinuating than before, but Formanek holds the centre beautifully, allowing Ballou to take some interesting chances without falling flat. Peterson is so utterly musical that he works best in the sparest situations. On 'Once Round' and 'Silly Dance And Coda' Ballou demonstrates real authority and a graceful wit. Other people's gigs are obviously part of the deal, but here's an artist who has things to say and a voice individual enough to carry them. A more selfish tack might be in order.

BRAD GOODE
Born 10 October 1963, Chicago, Illinois
Trumpet

Nature Boy
Delmark DE 578
Goode; Jeff Jenkins (p); Johannes Weidenmüller (b); Todd Reid (d). February 2006.

Brad Goode says: **'I hope to capture the spirit of live performance on my straight-ahead recordings. This session was done quickly; one or two takes of each tune, no pausing to listen to playbacks. My philosophy is, just live with the truth about your playing.'**

A Chicagoan who studied in Kentucky and made his base in Colorado, Goode has doughtily resisted New York's gravitational pull and still created a lively, self-determined career for himself. He made some good records for Steeplechase before returning to the Chicago fold on Delmark and upping his game as he did so. There's nothing unusual any more about a player who can work both 'outside' and 'inside', but few manage to maintain a high level of creativity in both.

On *Nature Boy*, Goode's still a quietly daring fellow. Compare the plangent lyricism of 'Nature Boy', the notes delicately strained with emotion, with the stop-time bugling effects of 'Nightmare Of The Mechanized World'. Then 'Sealed With A Kiss' receives a poppy treatment over a back-beat, Brad playing with his mute in. The set goes on in something like this vein, though none of the other juxtapositions are quite so stark. Eddie Harris's 'Infrapolations' is an interesting inclusion, again muted, and the closing 'All Through The Night' bustles along unexpectedly. Intriguing and enigmatic.

ANTHONY BRAXTON &
Born 4 June 1945, Chicago, Illinois
Saxophones, clarinets, flutes, piano

Nine Compositions (Iridium) 2006
Firehouse 12 04-03-001 9CD/DVD
Braxton; Taylor Ho Bynum (c, picc t, bt, flhn, trumpbone, shell); Reut Regev (tb, flugelbone); Jay Rozen (tba, euph); Andrew Raffo Dewar (ss, Cmel, cl); James Fei, Stephen H. Lehman (as, sno); Nicole Mitchell (picc, f, af, bf, v); Sara Schoenbeck (bsn, suona); Mary Halvorson (g); Jessica Pavone (vn, vla); Carl Testa (b, bcl); Aaron Siegel (perc, vib). March 2006.

Anthony Braxton said (2003): **'The concept of Ghost Trance Musics is that of streams of consciousness, streams of notated material that are continuously present in the music, and which become established as a mutable logic construct, on top of which improvisation happens.'**

If the unfolding Yoshi's material from 1997 were Braxton's *Friday/Saturday At The Blackhawk*, then this is his Plugged Nickel set, a comprehensive documentation of a working group developing a challenging repertoire over the course of a club residency, though of course in Braxton's case this doesn't involve varying a list of four or five favourite standards but working through the sequence of Ghost Trance Musics which still occupied him at the time, even as he was moving on into new phases of composition.

Braxton on Times Square. It seems improbable, but these four nights at Iridium represent what he himself regards as the most important summation of his work so far, and the culmination of the Ghost Trance Music series, a body of work whose rationale is not so very different, in the final analysis, from conventional jazz procedures. Though Miles

Davis, Chick Corea and to a degree Keith Jarrett preceded him in terms of comprehensive documentation of a working residency, whether in a 'club' or concert setting, examples of an 'avant-garde' musician being documented in this detail and with such a lavish production are vanishingly rare. The set, complete with commentaries and other texts, is presented in an impressive box with booklet. The music is rich, strange and as vividly textured as the instrumentation would suggest. Bynum's role is crucial, but Lehman, Fei, Halvorson and Rozen are now as securely embedded in Braxton's musical philosophy (and perhaps with fewer residual preconceptions) as were the 'classic quartet' of Crispell, Dresser or Lindberg, and Hemingway, whose time with Braxton was, after all, two decades ago.

The worklist is now showing opus numbers that go beyond 350. In essence, though, these are mainly heads and themes that can be worked and reworked much as a conventional standards-and-changes player would work a basic jazz set. Braxton's music requires – and deserves – demystification, and while this sumptuous box is only likely to appeal to established fans, it would do very well as a means of induction to Braxton's misleadingly forbidding aesthetic. Here he is, doing what bandleaders have done for decades: leading a working band, making mistakes, having off-nights (the second disc is shaky in places) and some great moments (it gets ever stronger towards the end), and for the most part enjoying being in out of the cold and in the company of sympathetic fellow-travellers. What a long, strange trip it has been and it shows no sign of being over. A survey of Braxton's work is more notable in the omission than the inclusion. Nothing from the '90s, for instance, when he became increasingly prominent and no longer a coterie enthusiasm; no example of his controversial standards playing, which is fascinating, but at best problematic; no more of his large-scale operatic/orchestral productions; and no more of his solo alto recitals: the number of Braxton records currently available defies belief and two more arrived on the day of writing, albeit cut on the fly during overseas tours. He is a quintessential modern artist and a quintessential modern American, intriguingly held suspended between several strong gravitational fields, immense and unignorable.

& See also **For Alto** (1968; p. 355), **New York, Fall 1974** (1974; p. 416), **Creative Orchestra Music 1976** (1976; p. 431), **Quartet (London / … Birmingham / … Coventry) 1985** (1985; p. 495)

ADAM ROGERS
Born 19 August 1965, New York City
Guitar

Time And The Infinite
Criss Cross 1286
Rogers; Scott Colley (b); Bill Stewart (d). March 2006.

Adam Rogers said (2007): 'I always liked the idea of working in a trio. It gives you a lot to do, being the only melody instrument, but gives a lot of space as well.'

Rogers was a well-respected sideman long before he made a move to record under his own name, but as so often in such cases, it was worth the wait, and a string of good Criss Crosses have issued, all illustrating Rogers's bubbling, restless sound. He keeps his hand in for other styles as a charter member of fusion group Lost Tribe, but never sounds like a rock player *manqué*.

The debut *Art Of The Invisible* suffered from trying to do too much, but the guitarist's coming out was more than welcome, since his considerable light has been under a bushel for some years. Wisely, Rogers stayed with the same line-up for *Allegory*, which in every way is a more coherent and polished effort. Perhaps it lacks the runaway energy and unfettered emotion of its predecessor, but it's a more successful album for that. *Apparitions* was a barnstormer. The sleeve-notes aver that 'the sound is anything but impenetrable and dense', but density is actually the key to the music's power: Rogers likes to pile up sonic bulk, and with the addition of Chris Potter, declaiming with tremendous intensity, he's got a band of worldbeaters. It's a classic modern record and so's *Time And The Infinite*, which gets our vote by a whisker: state-of-the-art modern guitar jazz and trio playing of the very highest order. Rogers's liking for abstract album titles – even notionally pretentious titles – might put off some potential listeners. It shouldn't. He's a wonderfully grounded player and his blend of standards ('Night And Day', 'I Loves You, Porgy') with originals like the title-track and 'Elegy' is pitch-perfect. The latter are sufficiently familiar in form to be comfortably assimilated; the former sufficiently rethought to make them interesting. Colley and Stewart complete an ideal line-up, both of them masters of what they do. Rogers may do better yet, which is a sobering thought on this form.

LOREN STILLMAN
Born 14 June 1980, London
Alto saxophone

Blind Date
Pirouet PIT 3024
Stillman; Gary Versace (p); Drew Gress (b); Joey Baron (d). June 2006.

Loren Stillman says: **'It really was a "blind date". We'd never played together before, which meant it had the potential to be a complete disaster, but having known the playing personalities of each musician ahead of time allowed me freedom to write for individuals. This lent itself very naturally to our way of playing together. I hope it's a much fun to listen to as it was to make.'**

Stillman was only 15 when he made *Cosmos*, which guaranteed his debut a certain level of attention. His light, agile tone was immediately sometimes likened to Lee Konitz's and like the older man he was happy to dabble in free playing, as on the title-piece. Through no fault of his own, he got more attention for the date on his birth certificate than for the music, and it was some time before anyone recognized that here was a genuine writing talent and a musician who was in for the long haul rather than just a few column inches of 'prodigy' copy.

   Inevitably, it took a little time to deliver a master statement. *Blind Date* featured a band to die for, elegant sound engineered by Jason Seizer and Stephan V. Wylick, and a batch of fine new compositions from Loren. It all adds up to a cracking contemporary jazz record. His alto sound has the kind of edge at the extremes of register that makes you wonder why he doesn't double (notably) on 'Shape Shifter' and 'Theme For A New Regime', but at the same time glad that he sticks to his guns. Gress and Baron make a great partnership, tight and springy, and Versace keeps the ideas buoyant and alert. Hard to beat on the contemporary scene.

SAM NEWSOME
Born 28 April 1965, Salisbury, Maryland
Soprano saxophone

Monk Abstractions
Sam Newsome 6589
Newsome (ss solo). June 2006.

Sam Newsome says: **'Making the record was a transforming experience. With no band to hide behind, I truly felt what it's like to be exposed – the vulnerability of letting people hear the real me. When it was all over and done with, it wasn't as bad as I had anticipated. It many ways, it made me even more fearless.'**

Newsome settled on music after trying out for a time as a comedian, though frankly going from stand-up to solo saxophone performance is a little like jumping out of the frying pan into the fire. A scattering of early records – mostly on tenor – suggested a highly inventive player who was a little constrained by the exigencies of hard bop. He courted trouble by framing tributes to both Coltrane and Rollins on the debut, but 'In The Vein Of Trane', basically a simple F-minor vamp, manages to reflect on its subject without slavishly copying him, and 'Pent-Up House' settles for the brazen confidence rather than the delivery of the young Sonny. Actually, Newsome takes his time in his improvising, building solos methodically, savouring his best phrases and going for tonal extremes only when he sees their logical point.

Recent years have seen Newsome work in more interesting areas and with the courage to work out on his own, not just as an unaccompanied performer but without a commercial label to back him up. *Monk Abstractions* is a fascinating project: ten Monk themes, interspersed with some very short 'abstractions' of Newsome's, which obviously attempt to extract some common essence from the work. The obvious – too obvious – comparison is Steve Lacy, but Newsome plays as if Steve's meditations simply didn't exist, and he doesn't really 'do' the obvious, this man. Starting out with an improv and then 'Boo Boo's Birthday' keeps it from seeming in any way predictable. He keeps the bluesy quality of the originals intact but tinkers with the form, which is an interesting alternative approach. Some quibbles with the sound, but mostly it's good and certainly sustains attention.

MICHAEL BRECKER

Born 29 March 1949, Philadelphia, Pennsylvania; died 13 January 2007, New York City
Tenor saxophone

Pilgrimage
Emarcy 1726531 SACD
Brecker; Herbie Hancock, Brad Mehldau (p); Pat Metheny (g); John Patitucci (b); Jack DeJohnette (d). August 2006.

Michael Brecker said (2001): **'What would I like to be remembered for? ... Doing a good job; playing great music; being part of it, I guess. Posterity and influence: those aren't things that interest me much.'**

Michael Brecker appeared on more than 500 record dates, but made few discs as solo leader. His steely brilliance and sense of structure inform almost every solo he played; whether it was matched with emotional resonance may depend on the listener. He exerted an influence on contemporary saxophone-players like no one since John Coltrane (who had influenced him) and Wayne Shorter, and while he made no innovations commensurate with theirs, his cumulative impact on contemporary jazz is immense.

Brecker and trumpet-playing older brother Randy made a name as the Brecker Brothers, playing a savvy jazz-fusion that allowed them to move almost at will into bop-based situations or rock and pop, whichever way the phone call went. It's perhaps unfortunate that Michael didn't make more records of his own, and he surely would have if illness hadn't foreshortened his career, but he was the type of a working jazzman and his diary must have been a sight to see. To compound the perspective, the early GRP albums have been out of circulation for some time. However, the later Verve records are around, and they pretty much sum him up in high-quality surroundings.

Time Is Of The Essence was a tag-team effort with three different quartets; Michael cruised along imperiously. He was outwardly less convincing on the ballad album *Nearness Of You*, but his discomfort with more expressive agenda was perhaps a self-fulfilling prophecy. There were other problems, common with these big-money dates and this was perhaps the most expensive band ever put together: it sounded like a supergroup idling in the departure lounge.

Pilgrimage was posthumously released, which guaranteed it even better press. It may seem harsh to say it, but Brecker's enormous reputation and influence are rarely suggested by his own records and his great talent often best expressed itself on other leaders' work. That said, a line-up like this could hardly have produced a bad record and Brecker's late-developing interest in composition yielded some fascinating lines here, notably the two long tracks, 'Anagram' (which may be too much like the old closed-off Michael) and the moving finale, 'Pilgrimage'. Whether ill-health made a physical difference ('When Can I Kiss You Again?' is a direct reference to his chemotherapy, something his son apparently said) or whether he had simply found a new philosophical calm in the face of mortality, there is a calm authority here which avoids the parade ground playing of previous years. The pianists seem to treat him very respectfully, and as a memorial it's pretty good. We suggested in our previous edition that our rating might have been less generous if Michael were still around. This was somewhat misread. So impressive, so meticulously crafted were his solos, and so many of them in circulation, that it was always easy to think there would be another one along any minute. Until 13 January 2007, that was the case. The ensuing silence has changed the value of what went before.

RAVISH MOMIN
Born 9 July 1973, Hyderabad, India
Percussion, voice

Miren (A Longing)
Clean Feed CF087
Momin; Sam Bardfeld (vn); Tanya Kalmanovitch (vla); Brandon Terzic (oud, effects). September & October 2006, March 2007.

Ravish Momin says: **'While we all carry "miren" (sadness from lack of closure to past events) with us, this recording allowed me to come to terms with my own. We painstakingly recorded the entire album in a lovely studio, but scrapped most of it in favour of live cuts from a tour that immediately followed. They captured the raw emotional energy I'd been looking for. The second take of "Fiza", with the added violist, is my favourite track, a step closer to my dream of adding a mixed "east/west" string section to the band sound.'**

It was hard to keep track of the different ethnic traditions feeding into Momin's first two Trio Tarana CDs. He spent his childhood in Bombay and Bahrain and has also studied Japanese and Afghan music. While some musicians might turn all this into an undifferentiated 'world music' mélange, Momin has clear lines of direction and a strong sense of how they should be communicated.

The debut CD, *Climbing The Banyan Tree*, teamed him with violinist Jason Kao Hwang and bassist/oudist Shamir Ezra Blumenkranz, who between them shaped a record that visited Chinese opera one moment and archaic Levantine ritual the next. Momin's percussion is always melodic in nature, weaving a collage of musical philosophies. Few recent records have opened up such a strong sense of new rhythmic possibilities available to 'jazz' or post-jazz.

A second CD, released on the Polish Not Two label, consolidated the group's language.

With a new personnel, though, *Miren* is both sensational and more obviously a jazz project. Bardfeld has more in common than Hwang with contemporary jazz violin-players like Mark Feldman, and Terzic maintains a steady drone behind the others, even when he isn't featured. Kalmanovitch is only present on a second version of 'Fiza', which suggests the potential for all these pieces to be recast in larger, possibly even orchestral, forms. 'Ragalaya' is based on a traditional theme and finds Momin at his most physical, using hands and body to accentuate the linear progress of the piece as well as its visceral impact. 'What Reward?' is the most interesting hybrid, coming over like a cross between a gutbucket blues and some pan-Asian thing of complex provenance. 'Fiza' in both its forms is the best of the set, especially when Momin uses Paul Motian-influenced cymbals as a backdrop to the violin. Impressive, and lovely.

STEVE NOBLE
Born 16 March 1960, Streatley, Berkshire, England
Drums

Obliquity
Bo'Weavil 23CD
Noble; Alan Wilkinson (as, bs, v); John Edwards (b). October 2006.

Steve Noble says: **'*Obliquity* was recorded in the rehearsal room I shared with Wilkinson – a dingy, damp room in an old hospital in Dalston, London. This was only the fourth time the trio had played together! An 11 a.m. start, a four-hour session; do or die! London calling – free jazz style, innit?'**

Though consistently underrated, Noble has been a key figure on the British improvisation scene for more than two decades. He studied with Nigerian master drummer Elkan Ogunde and all his work has an alertness of context that suggests he considers music a social rather than a merely individualistic activity. He has worked in partnership with Alex Maguire, Derek Bailey and countless others, but typically, he's not well-represented on record as a 'leader'. Noble's listed first on the superb *Obliquity*, though it obviously has to be considered the work of a collaborative trio. Wilkinson's fiery, often humorous tack on improvisation suits Noble's approach to perfection. The level of interplay between the two is extraordinary, often curiously reminiscent of Coltrane and Rashied Ali. In Edwards, there's a third contemporary master in the group, a stunning technician who seems to play with bottomless enjoyment. Much of it is headlong and fierce, but Noble's sense of time and its elasticity means that the music isn't just a blow-heater but has pace, dynamics and considerable subtlety.

MYRA MELFORD
Born 5 January 1957, Evanston, Illinois
Piano

Big Picture
Cryptogramophone 134
Melford; Mark Dresser (b); Matt Wilson (d). 2006.

Myra Melford says: **'Playing with Mark and Matt is always a great pleasure, whether performing for an audience or recording. There's a sense of trust that the music can go anywhere and everyone will be right there enjoying the ride.'**

Melford's piano training, which began with boogie and blues and moved on to lessons with Art Lande and Don Pullen, is hardly orthodox, even for a latter-day avant-gardist. What is consistently delightful about her work is the ability to sound like a musician in touch with all the jazz traditions, even when she is spinning a free line, and to sound edgy and oblique even when she is playing within an orthodox form. Some of her comfort in developing an amalgam of vernacular and advanced procedures has to be put down to an apprenticeship in the groups of Leroy Jenkins and Henry Threadgill, both leaders who command a blurring of forms.

Melford moved to New York in the mid-'80s, but didn't begin recording under her own name until almost a decade later. Her early discography has sadly disappeared into the deleted zone, but recognition came from hat ART, Arabesque and then Cryptogramophone and, together with recordings for other leaders, there has been pretty much an album a year since the mid-'90s, the titles often taken from Rumi's mystical poetry, the music ever more confident.

Big Picture comes from Melford's Trio M and jumps straight into the 'essential' category. It might seem strange that a record in what has become the most conventional of all jazz instrumentations should seem such an imperative, but even allowing that this is very much a collaborative trio, she's never played with such command and authority. 'BrainFire And BugLight' is a wild surreal thing, 'For Bradford' revisits Ornette Coleman on the least Ornettish of instruments, 'Freekonomics' suggests a world turned upside down, while 'Secrets To Tell You' is a small-scale emotional epic that must be stunning in live performance, with prominent roles for all three. A definitive modern jazz record.

GARY SMULYAN
Born 4 April 1956, Bethpage, New York
Baritone saxophone

More Treasures
Reservoir RSR 190
Smulyan; Mike LeDonne (p); Dennis Irwin (b); Steve Johns (d). November 2006.

Gary Smulyan says: **'At the end of the day, this session felt less focused and cohesive than its precursor, *Hidden Treasures*, but there were moments of excellence. We completed the session in five hours and most tunes in one or two takes. It had the spontaneous feel of a blowing session from the 1950s and '60s.'**

We beg to differ somewhat, about the first point if not the rest. Or, perhaps it's because this one sounds so uncluttered and immediate that we like it so much. Smulyan is easily the most interesting mainstream baritonist of the moment, a follower of Pepper Adams, though by no means a slavish copyist. His tone is indeed peppery and with none of the unctuous quality that sometimes overtook even the great Gerry Mulligan. Smulyan's also a fascinating student of the repertory, favouring rarities over more familiar themes. His most recent disc was a jazz interpretation of Frankie Laine songs! *Hidden Treasures* (2005) stuck closer to the jazz canon, but kicked off with Art Farmer's 'Stretch In F' and ended with a Coltrane rarity, 'Fifth House', taking in little-known material by Harold Vick, Donald Byrd ('Omicron') and Tadd Dameron ('Jahbero') along the way. The set's one standard, 'A Woman Always Understands', is associated with Nat Cole, but few younger listeners would know that. To make things tougher still, Smulyan chose to work without piano, in a spare trio setting.

He brings in Mike LeDonne for about half the tracks, and has the late, great Dennis Irwin and the estimably tight Steve Johns in the rhythm section. LeDonne delivers an exquisitely shaped accompaniment and solo on 'Chick's Tune', but tops it with his spot on the baritone ballad 'Beautiful You', dragging the chords romantically without losing touch with the basic pulse. Smulyan seems to be making bigger stretches on his horn now, modulating his expressive sweeps up and down the scale with impressive ease.

It's a bold mix of themes. Apart from the Chick Corea tune and the solitary Smulyan ballad original, there's Gigi Gryce's 'Sans Souci', Horace Silver's 'Quick Silver', Sal Nistico's rarely covered 'For You', Monk's 'Suburban Eyes' and Sonny Rollins's 'Evans', a programme that would guarantee intrigue even if it weren't so beautifully played. The leader's reservations notwithstanding, we have no hesitation in pulling this one out of the bag; anyone who samples it will doubtless want to hear the others, and make a personal judgement.

JOËLLE LÉANDRE
Born 12 September 1951, Aix-en-Provence, France
Double bass, voice

Winter In New York
Leo CDLR499
Léandre; Kevin Norton (vib, perc). December 2006.

Joëlle Léandre says: '**Les nombreuses rencontres en duo que je fais, que j'ai fait et que je ferai encore sont simplement un plaisir intense et une réflexion toujours chez moi, de la musique, de l'écoute, de la mise en forme, l'improvisation au fond ne s'improvise pas, c'est un sujet de structure/forme/mémoire et l'écoute, surtout l'écoute, et un travail immense ... C'est une musique "risquée", mais la vie ne l'est elle pas? Le duo avec Kevin contient tout cela. Les sons "claquent", les mélodies et rythmes sont justes, les interactions vivent; j'aime tout l'aspect aussi des timbres et couleurs avec le vibra! Et puis toujours ces questions: est-ce du jazz ou pas? Arrêterons-nous un jour de nous la poser? La musique est bien plus importante que les "bacs à disques" ... Créons! Inventons! Le duo avec Kevin est d'une fragilité et richesse d'écoute absolue. Au fond il faudrait beaucoup aimer et être "à fleur de sons" (jeu de mots pour "à fleur de peau") ... l'aventure de la musique est toute notre vie! Un son peut contenir toutes les musiques du monde!**'

Raised in the South of France, Léandre studied double bass in Paris and Buffalo, where she met the musics of Feldman, Cage and Scelsi, who remain powerful influences. Her work has straddled improvisation and modern composition. She was drawn to free playing by Derek Bailey but has worked in so many contexts and with such an individual voice (in the instrumental sense; she also vocalizes) that it is impossible to pigeonhole her. There is now a substantial discography, in solo and group situations, and Léandre has been on a remarkable creative streak since the turn of the '00s, performing at a higher and higher level.

Since no single work is 'representative' and all of it is undertaken with the same high passion and commitment suggested above, it's only possible to pick out one outstanding disc among many. Like Léandre's text, it sums up many of the issues that confront the improvising community. It is also a formidably fine and disciplined performance. The clichés have run out: metal and wood, earth and air, yin and yang, cold without, heat within. The New York encounter with Norton was a remarkable thing, caught live at the Stone club. Léandre has rarely, if ever, sounded better, strongly centred and so technically assured that merely technical issues are set aside from the start. Norton is one of North America's genuine innovators, a man destined for lasting greatness on his instrument(s). The tone colours of the vibraphone resonate with the persistent overtones of the bass. It's clever music, in the sense that high-order musical concepts are invoked, but it also has a visceral intensity that lasts and lasts.

TONY MALABY
Born 12 January 1964, Tucson, Arizona
Tenor saxophone

Tamarindo
Clean Feed CF 099
Malaby; William Parker (b); Nasheet Waits (d). 2006.

Tony Malaby says: **'Originally the trio was called Exploding Heart. I had to change it because a punk band from the Pacific Northwest threatened to sue if we went with their name. As a boy growing up in Tucson I often ate tamarind pulp with chili. In Spanish it's called Tamarindo. It was the first thing that came to mind when renaming the band: earthy, spicy, stringy pulp.'**

Malaby is a remarkable fellow, not least in his modest refusal to conform to the notion of the improvising saxophonist as an inspired and ecstatic voice. His music is thoughtful, not stripped of emotion but not given over to it either, and, as the cliché runs, Tony plays very much for the band. For that reason, he turns up in a good many contemporary situations, but mostly unsung, other than by fellow players, who admire him greatly.

On *Cosas* for Nine Winds, he shared composition credits with trombonist Joey Sellers and that looked to be a terrific partnership; sample 'Mesopotamian Love God', which seems to be a reworking of the 'Girl Talk' line, unlikely as that sounds. However, Malaby has been striking out in his own directions and *Tamarindo* is an essential contemporary record, all the more persuasive for its modesty of purpose and refusal of rhetoric. On 'Buried Head', 'Mariposa' and 'Mother's Love' (the last of these notably unsentimental), Malaby weaves lines that have the clarity and directness of prose. Parker's tendency to the sententious is reined in and Waits plays free time with great discipline. It's an almost impossible record to fault.

ANDREW RATHBUN
Born 29 September 1970, Toronto, Ontario, Canada
Saxophones, clarinet, keyboards

Affairs Of State
Steeplechase SCCD 31630
Rathbun; Taylor Haskins (t); Gary Versace (p); John Herbert (b); Mike Sarin (d). January 2007.

Andrew Rathbun says: **'*Affairs Of State* was conceived during a difficult period in American politics; the country was engaged in an unjust war based on misdirection and fear, and only the privileged were represented in Washington. More damage was done to the future of this nation than at any other time in US history. This CD was my commentary.'**

Politically engaged jazz artists have not been particularly thick on the ground in recent times, which makes Rathbun all the more intriguing. The Canadian – and perhaps it's because he *is* Canadian – wears his heart on his sleeve. He makes an impressive showing as a sideman, but his own projects are quite ambitious in form, drawing on an interest in the relation between music and verse. The whole of his first record, *Jade*, came out of seeing something written in the subway; the second, *True Stories*, takes the work of Margaret Atwood as its starting-point. The third, *Sculptures*, recorded in the month of the WTC attacks in New York, also implies an extra-musical programme, but has no vocal part. He's a deft composer and already a sophisticated soloist. He has a nicely rasping touch when it's called for, though for the most part the early records look for a lyrical/expressive vein.

They were all made for Fresh Sound New Talent, but in 2006 Rathbun switched to Stee-plechase and made a firm start with *Shadow Forms*. Its sequel sees him hit stride and reach a new maturity. It was already clear that his reaction to 9/11 (which happened in his adopted home city) was neither *pro forma* nor sentimental. On *Affairs Of State*, with a fine band at his back, he delivers a heated verdict on post-9/11 America. No poetry, no soapboxing, just tersely written modern jazz which lets form and harmony tell its own story. 'Break The Chains' and 'Folly (Of The Future Fallen)' are both devastating statements and Rathbun's own voice rises to meet the challenge.

TINA MAY
Born 30 March 1961, Gloucester, England
Voice

The Ray Bryant Songbook
33 Records 33JAZZ156
May; Don Sickler (t, flhn); Bobby Porcelli (as, f, af, cl); Jay Brandford (bs, cl, bcl); Patience Higgins (ts, bcl); Ray Bryant (p); Tim Givens (b); Vince Cherico (d, perc); Len Bryant (perc). 2007.

Tina May says: **'The Van Gelder Studio is a sight to behold – church-like and all wood inside; it sounds beautiful. We had a "team" photo taken on the "John Coltrane steps". During a take of "Little Lullaby" – a gentle piece with Patience Higgins and Jay Brandford playing bass clarinet – we suddenly heard the great New Jersey voice of Rudy himself saying: "Patience, you moved!" Mr Higgins had drifted off the legendary Neumann microphone. Great ears, Rudy ... a true artist, with a dry sense of humour, too.'**

Trained as an actress as well as a singer, May has one of the best and boldest jazz voices in the United Kingdom, with an unmissable onstage presence and an ability to sparkle one moment and communicate deep melancholy the next. She has some of the lean, light quality of the bop singers of Buddy Stewart's generation, yet her deep, English voice is strik-ingly apart from American influences; and she has a worldly, been-around-the-block qual-ity which doesn't prevent her from investing even familiar lyrics with wonder.

Her run of albums for 33 Records has been of consistently high quality. *Jazz Piquant* from 1998 shows off her complete mastery of the French language in a set of the native songs, and with Coe on top form this is an irresistible confection. But it has to bow to the quite superb *One Fine Day*, recorded the following year, a repertory set so finely achieved it should make most singers nod in appreciation.

The streak continued into the new decade, throwing May together with some of the most expressive reed-players around – Scott Hamilton on *I'll Take Romance*, Tony Coe on *More Than You Know*, Stan Sulzmann on *A Wing And A Prayer* – partners who helped under-line just how elegant an improvising instrument the May voice is as well as being a finely dramatic vehicle for song. The next in the sequence, though, was quite, quite dazzling, in both conception and execution. While other singers rag-pick the Great American Song-book, May goes straight for the song at the heart of jazz's bluesiest contemporary master. Sickler's arrangements are spare and sassy; Rudy Van Gelder gives the studio a plain, inti-mate sound, with Tina sounding as if she's sitting on a barstool in a half-circle of players. 'Dreaming My Life Away' is a throwback to the great bop singers, but with a fresh-minted quality that keeps it miles from pastiche. The Bryant duets conjure up a lost era in jazz, with 'Little Susie' deliciously transformed. A faultless vocal album.

PETE MALINVERNI
Born 16 April 1957, Niagara Falls, New York
Piano

Invisible Cities
Reservoir RSRCD192
Malinverni; Tim Hagans (t); Rich Perry (ss, ts); Ugonna Okegwo (b); Tom Melito (d). 2007.

Pete Malinverni says: '**Italo Calvino's fantastic imagination harnessed by impeccable craft is a good metaphor for the jazz musician. Places have many meanings, corporeal and super-earthly: every time I've visited Venice I've found it to be a city of many disorientating layers of memory. The recording also gave me a chance to comment on the sad fate of New Orleans after Katrina. And I thought: "Lonely Town" would stand for any city when one is alone, at least in the heart.**'

Malinverni already had a fine body of recording when this fine quintet date came along. He's among the most thoughtful of contemporary composers and is also inspired by a strong religious faith, which has fed into a number of recent gospel-inspired projects like *Joyful!* and the *Good Shepherd Suite*. *Invisible Cities* has a strongly philosophical cast, inspired by Calvino's narratological games and speculations in the book of that name. In it, Marco Polo tells the Khan about the ever more improbable places he has been in the realm and in doing so sparks a meditation of desire, time and place. Malinverni has been very subtle in translating the spirit and mood of the book into music, though Malinverni's cities are real locations, only revealing what he describes as their 'super-earthly levels' as each composition progresses. In addition to learning Italian in order to read *Invisible Cities* in the original, Malinverni gave a copy to each of his colleagues in the band and it became a kind of meta-score for the session.

The disc begins conventionally enough with a version of 'I Love Paris', but even here the City of Light is revealed to have another side, not necessarily dark but certainly mysterious. 'Lonely Town' is the other standard, though one somehow aches to hear how he might have handled 'A Foggy Day' with this personnel. Hagan's hooded tone and Perry's subtle harmonics contribute to the mystery and the other rhythm section players keep the music alert and shifting. Among the other locations visited are Istanbul, Chicago, Venice and the Salem of Nathaniel Hawthorne's *A Scarlet Letter*. Hagans leads the mourning song for hurricane-wracked New Orleans with a trumpet solo that proposes an alternative to Wynton Marsalis or Terence Blanchard. Unsurprisingly, given Malinverni's beliefs, the set ends in 'The City Of Heaven', reinforcing the impression that each of these corporeal visits has been leading towards some moment of transcendence. The leader's piano-playing has never been more vivid and rich, but he plays for the group, or rather for the music, which grows in stature with each appearance.

MIKE REED
Born 26 May 1974, Bielefeld, Germany
Drums

Last Year's Ghost
482 Music 1055
Reed; Greg Ward (as); Jason Adasiewicz (vib); Tomeka Reid (clo); Josh Abrams (b). 2007.

Mike Reed says: '**The recordings started in 2005 and completed in 2006. The original sessions were lost and also included tracks with Jeff Parker and Jim Baker. The actual** record was my best attempt to salvage what would have been the record. The title, which has many meanings, also alludes to the lost, or "ghost", recordings of the year before.'

Reed's a fascinating figure in that he deploys large elements of freedom within what's essentially a contemporary post-modal jazz idiom, or perhaps vice versa. He is the kind of musician who makes things happen around him, a member of groups led by fellow Chicagoans Josh Berman and Rob Mazurek, leader of his own Loose Assembly (as in *Last Year's Ghost*) and People, Places & Things, but also the founder of Emerging Improvisers Organization, a body which supports creative music in the Chicago area.

Reed put out *In The Context Of* with 482 Music in 2005, using a group that included such local luminaries as flautist Nicole Mitchell and guitarist Jeff Parker. It was a record full of intrigue and intricacy, but still reaching, and our first reaction to the shorter improvised pieces on *Last Year's Ghost* was that they were primers to the group's language rather than fully achieved tracks. Listening again in the knowledge that the whole record is a re-creation of something earlier and lost repositions listening and makes these pieces sound more integral with the rest. The band has a new, alert sound: Reid's cello provides a fascinating new improvising voice, Ward is terse and arresting, while Adasiewicz has proved to be among the most interesting young players on his instrument in years. 'The Entire State Of Florida' shows how much the group is embedded in old Chicago blues-jazz. The folk melody of 'Temporary States' leads directly into the double waltz-time of 'Ghost Writer', the best single track, while 'Day Of The Dead' conjures up a strange dreamy space. Reed closes in that same displaced vein: 'Dreaming With Jill' is an avant-garde ballad, none the less lovely for its disturbing undercurrents. If ever a contemporary record grows with familiarity, this is it.

MICHAEL MUSILLAMI

Born 28 July 1953, Sacramento, California
Guitar

The Treatment
Playscape PSR#050607 CD/DVD
Musillami; Mark Feldman (vn); Joe Fonda (b); George Schuller (d). May 2007.

Michael Musillami says: **'This was a landmark release for two reasons. It was only the first time we had added a fourth member to the complete programme. It was also a way to give a gentle nod to my old departed friend, Thomas Chapin. Thomas brought Mark Feldman to my attention on his "and strings" release** *Haywire* **and I promised myself then that Mark and I would work together in future.'**

Originally inspired by rock, Musillami took lessons with the charismatic Joe Diorio and started out playing a mixture of R&B and more straight-ahead jazz before, having moved east, he hooked up with Thomas Chapin, Mario Pavone and others round the Hillside Club in Waterbury, Connecticut. One interesting influence that the guitarist claims is Bill Barron, and his themes certainly manage to revise conventional forms in the way that Barron's compositions often would. That, along with the company of Chapin's cohort of savvy young innovators, gave Musillami a sound that is in some superficial way conventional enough but always brimming with unexpected harmonic possibilities and unclichéd melodic ideas.

The Playscape label took its name from a band Musillami was going out with around 1999, when he established his imprint. It's an elegant operation, with a solid contemporary list, and it has given the guitarist an outlet for his own work. After the excellent *Perception*,

Those Times and *Dachau* came *The Treatment*, easily the best of the bunch. The live DVD performance of three of the pieces was recorded in Connecticut three days before the studio recording. There are, we suppose, a few rough edges, but it's a delight to have so much more of this remarkable music. Musillami's in great form, but it's Feldman who steals the show. His quotation from 'Surrey With The Fringe On Top' in the middle of 'Brooms' is a sign of how quickly he's thinking and his articulation is needle-sharp all the way. 'Human Conditions' has him playing mostly pizzicato, an extraordinary effect when combined with guitar and bass. 'Stark Beauty' is exactly what it says it is. Musillami has come on in bounds even since the last record, not least in his ability to integrate a new voice into the trio. This one is a minor modern classic.

GONZALO RUBALCABA
Born 27 May 1963, Havana, Cuba
Piano, keyboards

Avatar
Blue Note 8418
Rubalcaba; Mike Rodriguez (t, flhn); Yosvany Terry (ss, as, ts); Matt Brewer (b); Marcus Gilmore (d). May & June 2007.

Saxophonist and Cuban music specialist Jane Bunnett says: **'During the powerful changes that took place in jazz from 1959 to the 1970s (African influence and powerful polyrhythms) the American embargo left Cuba out of the party. But that influence is always there and it could yet have a seismic effect on American jazz.'**

A Cuban émigré pianist, Rubalcaba created a minor sensation with his early appearances and was quickly signed up by Blue Note, for whom he recorded through the '90s. He's perhaps the most singular of those Cuban musicians who have made an impact on the American jazz scene of late. While he plays with as much grandstanding power as any of his countrymen, there is a compensating lightness of touch which one sometimes misses in the perpetually ebullient tone of most Cuban jazz.

After a run of excellent records for the label, brilliant but sometimes lacking in emotion, it sounds like Rubalcaba has taken a deep breath before this one and let the feeling come through. It's still a technically dazzling performance but 'This Is It' and 'Hip Side' (both written by the brilliant Terry) lift the music onto a new level, astute but liberated from merely technical concerns. The long, long 'Aspiring To Normalcy', by Brewer, is another clever line. Horace Silver's 'Peace' implies another line of descent for Rubalcaba, whose own 'Infantil' sounds like a gloss on Silver's work. The rising star of the band is Rodriguez, who has touches of everyone from Booker Little to Woody Shaw and sounds as if he could walk into a Messengers date tomorrow and blow everyone away.

NICOLE MITCHELL
Born 17 February 1967, Syracuse, New York
Flute

Xenogenesis Suite
Firehouse 12 FH12-04-01-006
Mitchell; David Young (t); David Boykin (ts); Tomeka Reid (clo); Justin Dillard (p); Josh Abrams (b); Marcus Evans (d); Avreeayl Ra (perc); Mankwe Ndosi (v). June 2007.

Nicole Mitchell says: '*Xenogenesis Suite* is a science fiction-inspired composition. My goal was to explore the emotional process of fear, which Octavia Butler's book *Dawn* developed through her character Lillith, who was plucked from the earth and brought into an alien environment. Facing fear head on is a human experience that we all may feel in the moments before real transformation.'

Currently co-president of AACM and 2006's Chicagoan of the Year, Mitchell has made a considerable splash with her Black Earth Ensemble, whose music is not so much a throwback to 40 years ago as a strong reminder of how much has moved forward in cultural politics. Some of the creative ethos is still the same though, and there is no mistaking the power and ambition of Mitchell's writing. Her flute-playing has an instantly compelling quality, as distinctive and arresting as a speaking voice, and on 'Wonder', the opening track of this remarkable sequence, she establishes a musical environment in which almost anything seems possible. Science fiction has often in the past provided a stimulus to creative jazz but those narrative energies have not been prominently engaged in recent years and Mitchell's use of Octavia Butler is bold and self-determined.

The ensemble is tightly disciplined but still free to explore the dimensions of Mitchell's big idea on their own individual terms. Mankwe Ndosi has a more specialized role than the others, but the combination of flute, voice and cello is what gives this incarnation of BEE its special character, those and the terrific combination of Evans's drums and Avreeayl Ra's percussion. One suspects that Mitchell, who already has a substantial discography and one breakthrough record, *Black Unstoppable*, is an important voice for the future and an unstoppable force in Chicago and beyond.

CUONG VU
Born 19 September 1969, Saigon, Vietnam
Trumpet, voice

Vu-Tet
ArtistShare 0073
Vu; Chris Speed (ts, cl); Stomu Takeishi (b); Ted Poor (d). July 2007.

Cuong Vu says: '**Recording in Mexico City was an excuse for Stomu, Ted and I to gorge ourselves on some seriously kick-ass Mexican food with our new buddies. Chris Speed refused to take advice about what *not* to eat (street vendor food and raw lettuce) and got food poisoning that started to "cripple" him right as he played the last notes of "Never, Ever, Ever", the last take of the record.'**

The son of a Vietnamese pop singer mother and multi-instrumentalist father, Vu moved to Seattle when he was six. He swapped saxophone for trumpet and developed a remarkably powerful voice. In style, his recorded work ranges freely between Miles-influenced impressionism and a species of advanced rock, with a few more abstract soundscapes interspersed. He was always going to have to go some to improve on the debut record, *Bound*, which was one of our favourite contemporary records till *Vu-Tet* hove into view.

The quartet immediately sounds like a working group, evidenced by the improvised intro to the disc. That gives place to 'Accelerated Thoughts', a post-bop, post-jazz rush that re-establishes the close empathy between Vu and Speed. 'Solitary Confinement' dispels its own initial melancholia with some finely affirmative playing. 'Never, Ever, Ever' has a twitchy quality (and now we know why) but maintains a fine group discipline. The only oddity is the neo-traditionalist groove of 'I Promise' right at the end, but if this is Vu pointing to a possible future direction, bring it on.

EVAN PARKER &

Born 5 April 1944, Bristol, Gloucestershire, England
Tenor and soprano saxophones

The Moment's Energy

ECM 1774798
Parker; Peter Evans (t); Ned Rothenberg (cl, bcl, shakuhachi); Agusti Fernández (p, prepared p); Kô Ishikawa
(sho); Philipp Wachsmann (vn, elec); Barry Guy (b); Paul Lytton (perc); Richard Barrett, Lawrence Casserley,
Walter Prati, Joel Ryan, Marco Vecchi (elec). November 2007.

Evan Parker says: '**This is the closest I've come to how it must be to make a film.**'

In the mid-'90s, to no one's great surprise, Evan Parker began to work with electronics,
using the vastly underrated Philipp Wachsmann and soundmen Walter Prati and Marco
Vecchi to create a sonic environment in which the levels of harmonic information the saxophonist attained on his solo saxophone recitals were suddenly and exponentially increased.
More surprising was how quickly the Electro-Acoustic Ensemble became a permanent part
of Parker's language-group, bringing in the brilliant Lawrence Casserley and, as occasion
dictated, musicians from electronics ensemble Furt and from other musical traditions.

The culminating achievement of the Ensemble was a commission from the Huddersfield Contemporary Music Festival in England, a composed piece for improvising ensemble
that delivered a work of unparalleled sophistication and presence. Parker acknowledges the
role played by the commissioning body, engineer Steve Lowe, producer Steve Lake and the
ECM label, and clearly the sound-world of the piece is determined to a broad extent by the
individual performers, but it is Parker's imagination – capacious, responsive, but in no way
totalizing – that makes the piece so successful.

Given the size of the ensemble and the technical resources on hand, it is a surprisingly
restrained and even in places almost reticent work. It harnesses energy rather than dis-
sipating it. There are extremely forceful passages – 'Part IV' is an immense free chorale
and the closing 'Part VII' borders on the apocalyptic – but the overall tone is outstandingly
calm and centred. British 'free improvisation', if the term still deserves currency and the
nationalist attribution makes any sense of what is an international project, has travelled a
great distance since its emergence in the late '60s. Though some might cite the Ensemble's
transatlantic collaboration with Roscoe Mitchell as a greater achievement, this remarkable
collaborative work is its masterpiece.

& *See also* **The Snake Decides** (1986; p. 506), **50th Birthday Concert** (1994; p. 582);
SPONTANEOUS MUSIC ENSEMBLE, Quintessence (1973–1974; p. 406)

LARRY OCHS

Born 3 May 1949, New York City
Reeds

Stone Shift

Rogueart ROG0025
Ochs; Natsuki Tamura (t); Satoko Fujii (p, syn); Scott Amendola, Donald Robinson (d). November 2007.

Larry Ochs says: '**When I called Satoko to ask if she and Natsuki would join the Drumming
Core, I already had "Stone Shift" composed in my head, and told her I only wanted
synthesizer. She said: "Synthesizer!? I cannot play it." I replied: "But I heard you play it
on Tamura's electric quartet CD." She said: "I have no experience. I just turned it on and
reacted to the others." I said: "Great, that's exactly what I am looking for!"**'

One might assume that membership of a long-standing ensemble like the ROVA saxophone quartet might have convinced Larry Ochs that the best music is always to be had from situations where the participants are all alert to their companions' every likely move. In fact, Ochs has proved to be a most welcoming musician, constantly making space on his own projects for new faces and voices. Hence the introduction into Sax & Drumming Core of new music's most energetic couple, Satoko Fujii and Natsuki Tamura.

Though he has commented privately that subsequent encounters profoundly enhanced the empathy between group and guests, no one approaching *Stone Shift* without preconception could possibly imagine that this was not already a settled partnership. Ochs's long welcoming speech on 'Across From Over' is one of the best available representations on record of his remarkable post-post-Coltrane style, an ironclad line that ripples with harmonic potential. Tamura's trumpeting takes some time to make its presence felt and Fujii's initial movements on the synthesizer are tentative at best. By the time 'Abstraction Rising' is complete, though, each member of the ensemble has staked out a distinct territory within the sound space. Fujii does move to her piano for this one – Ochs commented that otherwise it would have been like asking Trane to play, but only on soprano! – and her utterly distinctive pianism, compounded of folk-like shapes, attractively ragged clusters and calligraphic splashes of pure tone, fits into the mix without strain.

'Stone Shift' was a well-attested trio piece when this recording was made, but Ochs allows the guest couple to inhabit it as they will. The dedication to Kurosawa makes complete sense. If this is 'Oriental music', it's Eastern in a way that Shakespeare is Eastern, which is to say, universal. Saxophone and drums return to the heart of things on the closing 'Finn Veers For Venus', with trumpet, piano and tatters of synth taking a more decorative role than elsewhere.

It seems likely that the relationship documented will continue and grow, but for the moment this is a near-perfect hour of contemporary creative music.

JOE LOCKE
Born 18 March 1959, Palo Alto, California
Vibraphone

For The Love Of You
Koch 2046
Locke; Geoff Keezer (p); George Mraz (b); Kenny Washington (v). May 2009.

Joe Locke says: '**It celebrates the art of songwriting: stories of love, loss and elation given a new twist, while maintaining their integrity. Very different from previous projects, which focused on developing and performing new original music with atypical forms, this is a return to tradition.**'

While Joe Locke can easily assert the kind of virtuosity associated with Gary Burton, it's Bobby Hutcherson's asymmetrical lines and dark, eruptive solos to which he sounds most in debt. He gets an idiosyncratic sound from the notoriously faceless instrument – he keeps the sparkle of the vibes but loses their glassiness. As an improviser, he weaves very long lines out of open harmonic situations, maintaining a momentum over short or long distances – he can send up resonant clouds of notes or pare a trail back to its sparsest origins. He can also make the most of slow tempos.

The son of a classical music teacher, Locke studied privately after moving to New York in childhood and quickly established himself as a thoughtful and expressive player, working a line parallel to Hutcherson's boldly lyrical approach. Locke is an intensely emotional player. Every phrase seems packed with meaning. His early Steeplechase records have this quality in abundance, but it has grown deeper now that Locke has managed to avoid the risk he once ran of becoming a full-time guest star and is concentrating on his own luminous records.

For The Love Of You is a lyrical masterpiece. The material ranges from delicious originals ('Verrazano Moon', 'I Miss New York (When I Been Gone Too Long)'), Morricone's 'Cinema Paradiso' theme, the Isley Brothers title-track, Neil Young's 'Birds', and standards as unashamedly romantic as 'The Shadow Of Your Smile' and 'Two For The Road'. The Morricone is outstanding, with a plangently bowed solo from Mraz (one of the few bassists who delivers as much *arco* as he does when plucking) and one of Keezer's most finely achieved solos on record.

It's a romantic's record, for romantics, but it would be unwise to overlook the steely musicianship that goes into even the apparently lightweight opener. There's real authority here, and Locke finally lays secure claim to Milt Jackson's crown.

INDEX OF PERFORMERS